CONTENTS

Crime in the United States

CRIME IN THE UNITED STATES

2010

FOURTH EDITION

Bernan Press

Lanham, MD

Published by Bernan Press
A wholly owned subsidiary of The Rowman & Littlefield Publishing Group, Inc.
4501 Forbes Boulevard, Suite 200, Lanham, Maryland 20706
http://www.bernan.com
800-865-3457; info@bernan.com

ISBN: 978-1-59888-411-1 (paperback)
ISBN: 978-1-59888-412-8 (electronic)

∞™ The paper used in this publication meets the minimum requirements of American National Standard for Information Sciences—Permanence of Paper for Printed Library Materials, ANSI/NISO Z39.48-1992.

Printed in the United States of America

SECTION I:

SUMMARY OF THE UNIFORM CRIME REPORTING (UCR) PROGRAM

SUMMARY OF THE UNIFORM CRIME REPORTING (UCR) PROGRAM

Bernan Press is proud to present its fourth edition of *Crime in the United States*. This title was formerly published by the Federal Bureau of Investigation (FBI), but is no longer available in printed form from the government. This edition contains final data from 2008, the latest data that are currently available.

This section examines the best way of using the publication's data and discusses the history of the UCR Program, which collects the data used in *Crime in the United States*.

About the UCR Program

The UCR Program is a nationwide, cooperative statistical effort of nearly 17,800 city, university and college, county, state, tribal, and federal law enforcement agencies who voluntarily report data on crimes brought to their attention. Since 1930, the FBI has administered the UCR Program and continued to assess and monitor the nature and type of crime in the nation. The program's primary objective is to generate reliable information for use in law enforcement administration, operation, and management; however, its data have over the years become one of the country's leading social indicators. Criminologists, sociologists, legislators, municipal planners, the media, and other students of criminal justice use the data for varied research and planning purposes. In 2008, law enforcement agencies active in the UCR Program represented more than 288 million United States inhabitants—94.9 percent of the total population. The coverage amounted to 96.0 percent of the population in metropolitan statistical areas, 87.6 percent of the population in cities outside metropolitan areas, and 90.0 percent of the population in nonmetropolitan counties.

Note for Users

It is important for UCR data users to remember that the FBI's primary objective is to generate a reliable set of crime statistics for use in law enforcement administration, operation, and management. The FBI does not provide a ranking of agencies; instead, it provides alphabetical tabulations of states, metropolitan statistical areas, cities with over 10,000 inhabitants, suburban and rural counties, and colleges and universities. Since crime is a sociological phenomenon influenced by a variety of factors, the FBI discourages data users from ranking agencies and using the data as a measurement of the effectiveness of law enforcement.

To ensure that data are uniformly reported, the FBI provides contributing law enforcement agencies with a handbook that explains how to classify and score offenses and provides uniform crime offense definitions. Acknowledging that offense definitions may vary from state to state, the FBI cautions agencies to report offenses according to the guidelines provided in the handbook, rather than by local or state statutes. Most agencies make a good faith effort to comply with established guidelines.

The UCR Program publishes the statistics most commonly requested by data users. More information regarding the availability of UCR Program data is available by telephone at (304) 625-4995, by fax at (304) 625-5394, or by e-mail at <cjis_comm@leo.gov>. E-mail data requests cannot be processed without the requester's full name, mailing address, and contact telephone number.

Variables Affecting Crime

Until data users examine all the variables that affect crime in a town, city, county, state, region, or college or university, they can make no meaningful comparisons.

Caution Against Ranking

In each edition of *Crime in the United States*, many entities—including news media, tourism agencies, and other organizations with an interest in crime in the nation—use reported figures to compile rankings of cities and counties. However, these rankings are merely a quick choice made by that data user; they provide no insight into the many variables that mold the crime in a particular town, city, county, state, or region. Consequently, these rankings may lead to simplistic and/or incomplete analyses, which can create misleading perceptions and thus adversely affect cities and counties, along with their residents.

Considering Other Characteristics of a Jurisdiction

To assess criminality and law enforcement's response from jurisdiction to jurisdiction, data users must consider many variables, some of which (despite having significant impact on crime) are not readily measurable or applicable among all locales. Geographic and demographic factors specific to each jurisdiction must be considered and applied in order to make an accurate and complete assessment of crime in that jurisdiction. Several sources of information are available to help the researcher explore the variables that affect crime in a particular locale. U.S. Census Bureau data, for example, can help the user better understand the makeup of a locale's population. The transience of the population, its racial and ethnic makeup, and its composition by age and sex, educational levels, and prevalent family structures are all key factors in assessing and understanding crime.

Local chambers of commerce, planning offices, and similar entities provide information regarding the economic and cultural makeup of cities and counties. Understanding a jurisdiction's industrial/economic base, its dependence upon neighboring jurisdictions, its transportation system, its economic dependence on nonresidents (such as tourists and convention attendees), and its proximity to military installations, correctional institutions, and other types of facilities all contribute to accurately gauging and interpreting the crime known to and reported by law enforcement.

The strength (including personnel and other resources) and aggressiveness of a jurisdiction's law enforcement agency are also key factors in understanding the nature and extent of crime occurring in that area. Although information pertaining to the number of sworn and civilian employees can be found in this publication, it cannot be used alone as an assessment of the emphasis that a community places on enforcing the law. For example, one city may report more crime than another comparable city because its law enforcement agency identifies more offenses. Attitudes of citizens toward crime and their crime reporting practices—especially for minor offenses—also have an impact on the volume of crimes known to police.

Make Valid Assessments of Crime

It is essential for all data users to become as well educated as possible about understanding and quantifying the nature and extent of crime in the United States and in the more than 17,000 jurisdictions represented by law enforcement contributors to the UCR Program. Valid assessments are possible only with careful study and analysis of the various unique conditions that affect each local law enforcement jurisdiction.

Some factors that are known to affect the volume and type of crime occurring from place to place are:

- Population density and degree of urbanization
- Variations in composition of population, particularly in the concentration of youth
- Stability of the population with respect to residents' mobility, commuting patterns, and transient factors
- Modes of transportation and highway systems
- Economic conditions, including median income, poverty level, and job availability
- Cultural factors and educational, recreational, and religious characteristics
- Family conditions, with respect to divorce and family cohesiveness
- Climate
- Effective strength of law enforcement agencies
- Administrative and investigative emphases of law enforcement
- Policies of other components of the criminal justice system (i.e., prosecutorial, judicial, correctional, and probational policies)
- Residents' attitudes toward crime
- Crime reporting practices of residents

Although many of the listed factors equally affect the crime of a particular area, the UCR Program makes no attempt to relate them to the data presented. **The data user is therefore cautioned against comparing statistical data of individual reporting units from cities, counties, metropolitan areas, states, or colleges or universities solely on the basis on their population coverage or student enrollment.** Until data users examine all the variables that affect crime in a town, city, county, state, region, or college or university, they can make no meaningful comparisons.

Historical Background

Since 1930, the FBI has administered the UCR Program; the agency continues to assess and monitor the nature and type of crime in the nation. Data users look to the UCR Program for various research and planning purposes.

Recognizing a need for national crime statistics, the International Association of Chiefs of Police (IACP) formed the Committee on Uniform Crime Records in the 1920s to develop a system of uniform crime statistics. After studying state criminal codes and making an evaluation of the recordkeeping practices in use, the committee completed a plan for crime reporting that became the foundation of the UCR Program in 1929. The plan included standardized offense definitions for seven main offense classifications known as Part I crimes to gauge fluctuations in the overall volume and rate of crime. Developers also instituted the Hierarchy Rule as the main reporting procedure for what is now known as the Summary Reporting System of the UCR Program.

The seven main offense classifications, known as Part I crimes, included the violent crimes of murder and nonnegligent manslaughter, forcible rape, robbery, and aggravated assault; also included were the property crimes of burglary, larceny-theft, and motor vehicle theft. By congressional mandate, arson was added as the eighth Part I offense category. Data collection for arson began in 1979. Agencies classify and score offenses according to a Hierarchy Rule (with the exception of justifiable homicide, motor vehicle theft, and arson) and report their data to the FBI. More information about the Hierarchy Rule is presented in Section II.

During the early planning of the program, it was recognized that the differences among criminal codes precluded a mere aggregation of state statistics to arrive at a national total. Also, because of the variances in punishment for the same offenses in different states, no distinction between felony and misdemeanor crimes was possible. To avoid these problems and provide nationwide uniformity in crime reporting, standardized offense definitions were developed. Law enforcement agencies use these to submit data without regard for local statutes. The definitions used by the program can be found in Appendix II.

In January 1930, 400 cities (representing 20 million inhabitants in 43 states) began participating in the UCR Program. Congress enacted Title 28, Section 534, of the United States Code that same year, which authorized the attorney general to gather crime information. The attorney general, in turn, designated the FBI to serve as the national clearinghouse for the collected crime data. Since then, data based on uniform classifications and procedures for reporting have been obtained annually from the nation's law enforcement agencies.

Advisory Groups

Providing vital links between local law enforcement and the FBI for the UCR Program are the Criminal Justice Information Systems Committees of the IACP and the National Sheriffs' Association (NSA). The IACP represents the thousands of police departments nationwide, as it has since the program began. The NSA encourages sheriffs throughout the country to participate fully in the program. Both committees serve the program in advisory capacities.

In 1988, a Data Providers' Advisory Policy Board was established. This board operated until 1993, when it combined with the National Crime Information Center Advisory Policy Board to form a single Advisory Policy Board (APB) to address all FBI criminal justice information services. The current APB works to ensure continuing emphasis on UCR-related issues. The Association of State Uniform Crime Reporting Programs (ASUCRP) focuses on UCR issues within individual state law enforcement associations and also promotes interest in the UCR Program. These organizations foster widespread and responsible use of uniform crime statistics and lend assistance to data contributors.

Redesign of UCR

Although UCR data collection was originally conceived as a tool for law enforcement administration, the data were widely used by other entities involved in various forms of social planning by the 1980s. Recognizing the need for more detailed crime statistics, law enforcement called for a thorough evaluative study to modernize the UCR Program. The FBI formulated a comprehensive three-phase redesign effort. The Bureau of Justice Statistics (BJS) agency in the Department of Justice responsible for funding criminal justice information projects, agreed to underwrite the first two phases. These phases were conducted by an independent contractor and structured to determine what, if any, changes should be made to the current program. The third phase would involve implementation of the changes identified.

During the first phase, which began in 1982, the historical evolution of the UCR Program was examined. All aspects of the program, including its objectives and intended user audience, data items, reporting mechanisms, quality control issues, publications and user services, and relationships with other criminal justice data systems, were studied.

Early in 1984, a conference on the future of UCR Program launched the second phase of the study that examined the program's potential and concluded with a set of recommended changes. Phase two ended in early 1985 with the production of a report, *Blueprint for the Future of the Uniform Crime Reporting Program.* The study's Steering Committee reviewed the draft report at a March 1985 meeting and made various recommendations for revision. The committee members, however, endorsed the report's concepts.

In April 1985, the phase two recommendations were presented at the eighth National UCR Conference. Various considerations for the final report were set forth, and the overall concept for the revised UCR Program was unanimously approved. The joint IACP/NSA Committee on UCR also issued a resolution endorsing the *Blueprint.*

The final report, the *Blueprint for the Future of the Uniform Crime Reporting Program,* was released in the summer of 1985. It specifically outlined recommendations for an expanded, improved UCR Program to meet future informational needs. There were three recommended areas of enhancement to the UCR Program:

- Offenses and arrests would be reported using an incident-based system.
- Data would be collected on two levels. Agencies in level one would report important details about those offenses comprising the Part I crimes, their victims, and arrestees. Level two would consist of law enforcement agencies covering populations of more than 100,000 and a sampling of smaller agencies that would collect expanded detail on all significant offenses.
- A quality assurance program would be introduced.

To begin implementation, the FBI awarded a contract to develop new offense definitions and data elements for the redesigned system. The work involved (a) revising the definitions of certain Part I offenses, (b) identifying additional significant offenses to be reported, (c) refining definitions for both, and (d) developing data elements (incident details) for all UCR Program offenses in order to fulfill the requirements of incident-based reporting versus the current summary system.

Concurrent with the preparation of the data elements, the FBI studied the various state systems to select an experimental site for implementing the redesigned program. In view of its long-standing incident-based program and well-established staff dedicated solely to UCR, the South Carolina Law Enforcement Division (SLED) was chosen. The SLED agreed to adapt its existing system to meet the requirements of the redesigned program and to collect data on both offenses and arrests relating to the newly defined offenses.

Following the completion of the pilot project conducted by the SLED, the FBI produced a draft of guidelines for an enhanced UCR Program. Law enforcement executives from around the country were then invited to a conference where the guidelines were presented for final review.

During the conference, three overall recommendations were passed without dissent: the establishment of a new, incident-based national crime reporting system; the FBI as the managing agency for the program; and the creation of an Advisory Policy Board composed of law enforcement executives to assist in directing and implementing the new program.

Information about the redesigned UCR Program, call the National Incident-Based Reporting System, or NIBRS, is contained in several documents. The *Data Collection Guidelines* publication (August 2000) contains a system overview and descriptions of the offense codes, reports, data elements, and data values used in the system. The *Error Message Manual* (December 1999) contains designations of mandatory and optional data elements, data element edits, and error messages. The *Data Submission Specifications* publication is for the use of local and state systems personnel who are responsible for preparing magnetic media for submission to the FBI. The document is available on the FBI's Web site at <www.fbi.gov/ucr/ucr.htm>. Another publication, *Handbook for Acquiring a Records Management System (RMS) that is Compatible with NIBRS,* is also available on that site.

A NIBRS edition of the *UCR Handbook* was published in 1992 to assist law enforcement agency data contributors implementing the NIBRS within their departments. This document is geared toward familiarizing local and state law enforcement personnel with the definitions, policies, and procedures of the NIBRS. It does not contain the technical coding and data transmission requirements presented in the other NIBRS publications.

The NIBRS collects data on each single incident and arrest within 22 crime categories. For each offense known to police within these categories, incident, victim, property, offender, and arrestee information are gathered when available. The goal of the redesign is to modernize crime information by collecting data currently maintained law enforcement records, making the enhanced UCR Program a by-product of current records systems while maintaining the integrity of the program's long-running statistical series.

The FBI began accepting NIBRS data from a handful of agencies in January 1989. As more contributing law enforcement agencies become educated about the rich data available through incident-based reporting and as resources permit, more agencies are implementing the NIBRS. Based on 2008 data submissions, approximately 39 percent of reporting agencies are certified for NIBRS participation. These agencies include one individual agency each in Alabama, Georgia, Illinois, and the District of Columbia, as well as the state UCR Programs of the following 31 states: Arizona, Arkansas, Colorado, Connecticut, Delaware, Idaho, Iowa, Kansas, Kentucky, Louisiana, Maine, Massachusetts, Michigan, Missouri, Montana, Nebraska, New Hampshire, North Dakota, Ohio, Oregon, Rhode Island, South Carolina, South Dakota, Tennessee, Texas, Utah, Vermont, Virginia, Washington, West Virginia, and Wisconsin. Among those that submit NIBRS data, 13 states (Delaware, Idaho, Iowa, Michigan, Montana, New Hampshire, Rhode Island, South Carolina, South Dakota, Tennessee, Vermont, Virginia, and West Virginia) submit all their data via the NIBRS. Nine state UCR Programs are in various stages of testing the NIBRS. Six other state agencies are planning and developing the NIBRS.

Suspension of the Crime Index and Modified Crime Index

In June 2004, the CJIS APB approved discontinuing the use of the Crime Index in the UCR Program and its publications and directed the FBI to publish a violent crime total and a property crime total. The Crime Index, first published in *Crime in the United States* in 1960, was the title used for a simple aggregation of the seven main offense classifications (Part I offenses) in the Summary Reporting System. The Modified Crime Index was the number of Crime Index offenses plus arson.

For several years the CJIS Division studied the appropriateness and usefulness of these indices and brought the matter before many advisory groups including the UCR Subcommittee of the CJIS APB, the ASUCRP, and a meeting of leading criminologists and sociologists hosted by the BJS. In short, the Crime Index and the Modified Crime Index were not true indicators of the degrees of criminality because they were always driven upward by the offense with the highest number, typically larceny-theft. The sheer volume of those offenses overshadowed more serious but less frequently committed offenses, creating a bias against a jurisdiction with a high number of larceny-thefts but a low number of other serious crimes such as murder and forcible rape.

Expanded Offense Tables

The FBI collects the number of offenses for the crimes of murder, forcible rape, robbery, aggravated assault, burglary, larceny-theft, motor vehicle theft, and arson through the Uniform Crime Reporting Program. In addition to the number of offenses known to the police, the FBI also collects additional data about these offenses, such as the locations of robberies, time of day of burglaries, and other analyses about the offenses. These expanded data also include trends (2-, 5-, and 10-year comparisons) in both crime volume and crime rate per 100,000 inhabitants. Expanded homicide data, (supplemental details about murders such as the age, sex, and race of both the victim and the offender, the weapon used in the homicide, the circumstances surrounding the offense, and the relationship of the victim to the offender) are also available.

Expanded offense data, including expanded homicide data, are information collected beyond the reports of the number of crimes known. As a result, law enforcement agencies can report an offense without providing the supplemental data about that offense. These additional tables are not included in this publication, but can be found at <http://www.fbi.gov/ucr/cius2008/offenses/expanded_information/index.html>.

SECTION II:
OFFENSES KNOWN TO POLICE

VIOLENT CRIME OFFENSES

- Murder
- Forcible Rape
- Robbery
- Aggravated Assault

PROPERTY CRIME OFFENSES

- Burglary
- Larceny-Theft
- Motor Vehicle Theft
- Arson

VIOLENT CRIME

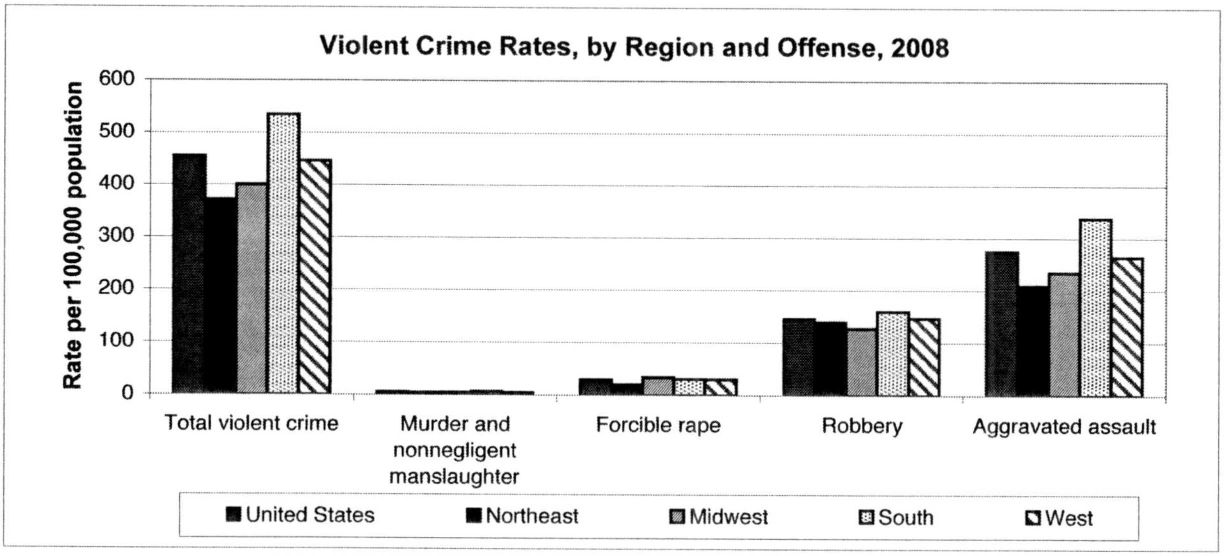

Definition

Violent crime consists of four offenses: murder and nonnegligent manslaughter, forcible rape, robbery, and aggravated assault. According to the Uniform Crime Reporting (UCR) Program, run by the Federal Bureau of Investigation (FBI), violent crimes involve either the use of force or the threat of force.

Data Collection

The data presented in *Crime in the United States* reflect the Hierarchy Rule, which counts only the most serious offense in a multiple-offense criminal incident. In descending order of severity, the violent crimes are murder and nonnegligent manslaughter, forcible rape, robbery, and aggravated assault; these are followed by the property crimes of burglary, larceny-theft, and motor vehicle theft. More information on the expanded violent crime tables (which are available online but not included in this publication) can be found in Section I.

National Volume, Trends, and Rate

In 2008, an estimated 1,382,012 violent crimes occurred in the United States, showing a decrease of 1.9 percent from the 2007 estimate. There were an estimated 454.5 violent crimes per 100,000 inhabitants in 2008. Aggravated assaults accounted for 60.4 percent of violent crimes, the highest number of violent crimes reported to law enforcement. Robbery made up 32.0 percent of violent crimes, forcible rape accounted for 6.4 percent, and murder accounted for 1.2 percent of estimated violent crimes in 2008. (Table 1)

All violent crimes decreased in 2008 compared to the 2007 estimates. Murder decreased by 3.9 percent; aggravated assault fell 2.5 percent; forcible rape declined 1.6 percent; and robbery decreased 0.7 percent. The 2008 murder rate, 5.4 offenses per 100,000 inhabitants, was a 4.7 percent decrease when compared with the rate for 2007. (Tables 1 and 1A)

The UCR Program reports data in 2-year, 5-year, and 10-year increments to formulate trend information. The 2008 estimated violent crime total was 1.6 percent above the 2004 level, but 3.1 percent below the 1999 level. The 5-year and 10-year trend data showed that the violent crime rate decreased 1.9 percent between 2004 and 2008 and decreased 13.1 percent between 1999 and 2008. The rate of violent crime declined in 2008 to 454.5 per 100,000, a decrease of 2.7 percent when compared with 2007 data. (Tables 1 and 1A)

In 2008, offenders used firearms in 66.9 percent of the nation's murders, 43.5 percent of robberies, and 21.4 percent of aggravated assaults. (Weapon data are not collected for forcible rape offenses.) (Expanded Homicide Table 7, Robbery Table 3, and Aggravated Assault Table)

Regional Offense Trends and Rate

The UCR Program divides the United States into four regions: the Northeast, the South, the Midwest, and the West. (More details concerning geographic regions are provided in Appendix III.) The population distribution of the regions can be found in Table 3, and the estimated volume and rate of violent crime by region are provided in Table 4.

The Northeast

The Northeast accounted for an estimated 18.1 percent of the nation's population in 2008 and an estimated 14.7 percent of its violent crimes. (Table 3) The estimated number of violent crimes remained relatively unchanged in 2008 when compared with the estimate from 2007. Murder increased 1.4 percent in the Northeast and estimated forcible rapes increased 1.5 percent. Estimated aggravated assaults dropped 0.8 percent from 2007. The only region to show an increase, 1.0 percent, in robberies was the Northeast. In 2008, there were an estimated 370.8 violent crimes per 100,000 inhabitants. (Table 4)

The Midwest

With an estimated 21.9 percent of the total population of the United States, the Midwest accounted for 19.3 percent of the nation's estimated number of violent crimes in 2008. (Table 3) The region had a 2.4 percent decrease in violent crime from 2007 to 2008. While all four regions experienced declines in the estimated number of aggravated assaults, the greatest decrease, 3.8 percent, was in the Midwest. The estimated number of robberies decreased 0.3 percent, the number of murders declined 0.8 percent, and the estimated number of forcible rapes fell 1.0 percent from 2007 to 2008. The rate of violent crime per 100,000 inhabitants in the Midwest declined 2.5 percent from 2007 to 2008. (Table 4)

The South

The South, the nation's most populous region, accounted for a 36.7 percent of the nation's population in 2008. Over 43 percent (43.2) of violent crimes in 2008 occurred in the South. (Table 3) Violent crime in the South decreased 1.7 percent from 2007 to 2008, with declines in all four types of violent crime offenses. The estimated number of forcible rapes declined by 3.1 percent in the South, the largest decrease of the four regions. Murders had the largest decline (5.3 percent) of the four offenses, followed by aggravated assaults (1.7 percent) and robberies (1.1 percent). The estimated rate of violent crime in the South was 533.9 incidents per 100,000 inhabitants in 2008. (Table 4)

The West

With 23.3 percent of the nation's population in 2008, the West accounted for an estimated 22.8 percent of the nation's violent crime. (Table 3) While the estimated number of violent crimes decreased in three of the four regions, the largest decrease (2.9 percent) occurred in the West. All four violent offense categories decreased in number from 2007 to 2008: murder declined 6.8 percent, aggravated assault fell 3.7 percent, robbery decreased by 1.6 percent, and forcible rape dropped 1.1 percent. The region's violent crime rate in 2008 was 445.4 per 100,000 population, a 2.9 percent decrease from the 2007 rate. (Table 4)

Community Types

The UCR Program aggregates crime data into three community types: metropolitan statistical areas (MSAs), cities outside MSAs, and nonmetropolitan counties outside MSAs. Appendix III provides additional information regarding community types. In 2008, 83.5 percent of the nation's population lived in MSAs. Residents of cities outside MSAs accounted for 6.6 percent of the country's population, while 9.9 percent of the population lived in nonmetropolitan counties. (Table 2)

Nearly 90 percent of the estimated number of violent crimes in the United States occurred in MSAs, 5.7 percent occurred in cities outside MSAs, and 4.5 percent occurred in nonmetropolitan counties. By community type, the violent crime rates were estimated at 489.0 incidents per 100,000 inhabitants in MSAs, 392.0 incidents per 100,000 inhabitants in cities outside MSAs, and 205.1 incidents per 100,000 inhabitants in nonmetropolitan counties. (Table 2)

Population Groups: Trends and Rates

In the UCR Program, data are also aggregated into population groups; these groups are described in more detail in Appendix III. The nation's cities had an overall decrease of 2.5 percent in the estimated number of violent crimes from 2007 to 2008. By city population group, cities with 250,000 to 499,000 inhabitants had the largest percentage decline in the estimated number of violent crimes (4.2 percent). (Table 12)

The law enforcement agencies in the nation's cities collectively reported a rate of 552.8 violent crimes per 100,000 inhabitants in 2008. Law enforcement agencies in cities subset of 500,000 to 999,999 inhabitants reported the highest violent crime rate, with 956.4 violent crimes per 100,000 inhabitants; the violent crime rate for all cities with 250,000 or more inhabitants was 866.5 per 100,000 inhabitants. Agencies in cities with 10,000 to 24,999 inhabitants reported the lowest violent crime rate (313.7 incidents per 100,000 inhabitants). Law enforcement agencies in the nation's metropolitan counties reported a collective violent crime rate of 324.5 per 100,000 inhabitants, while agencies in nonmetropolitan counties reported a collective rate of 215.3 violent crimes per 100,000 inhabitants. (Table 16)

MURDER

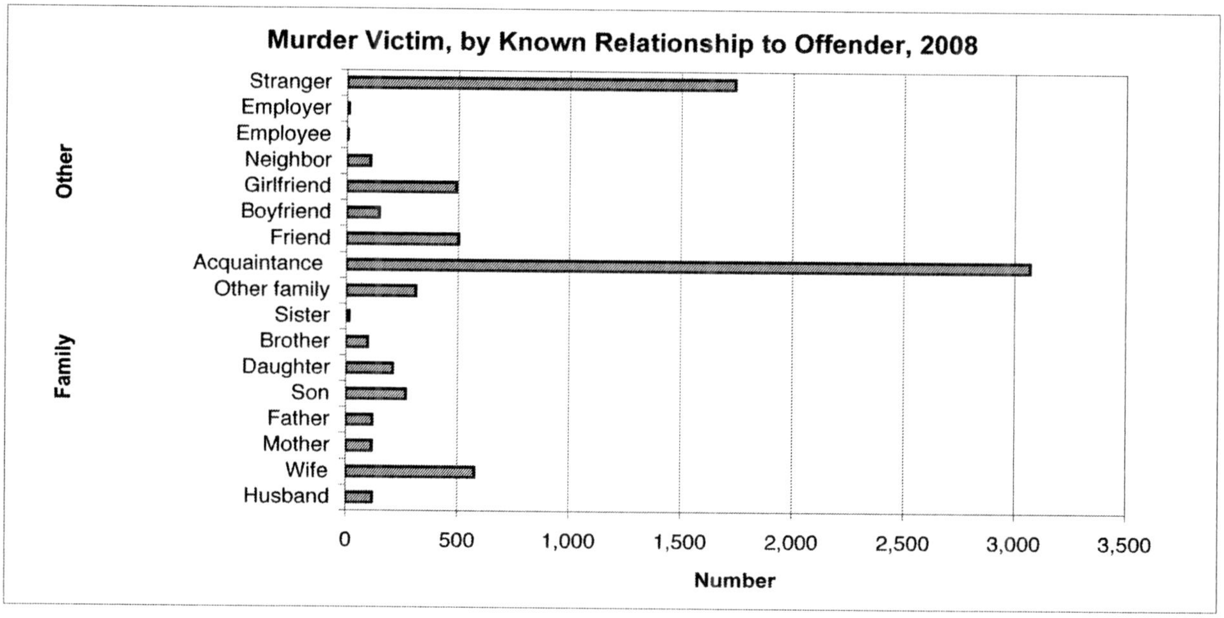

Definition

The UCR Program defines murder and nonnegligent manslaughter as the willful (nonnegligent) killing of one human being by another. The classification of this offense is based solely on police investigation, rather than on the determination of a court, medical examiner, coroner, jury, or other judicial body. The UCR Program does not include the following situations under this offense classification: deaths caused by negligence, suicide, or accident; justifiable homicides; and attempts to murder or assaults to murder, which are considered aggravated assaults.

Data Collection/Supplementary Homicide Reports (SHR)

The UCR Program's *Supplementary Homicide Report* (SHR) provides information about murder victims and offenders by age, sex, and race; the types of weapons used in the murders; the relationships of the victims to the offenders; and the circumstances surrounding the incident. Law enforcement agencies are asked to complete an SHR for each murder reported to the UCR Program. Data from SHRs can be viewed in the Expanded Homicide Data section, found on the FBI Web site: <http://www.fbi.gov/ucr/cius2008/offenses/expanded_information/homicide.html>. Of the estimated 16,272 murders that were committed in the United States in 2008, law enforcement agencies contributed data to the UCR Program through SHRs for 14,180 murders. More information on these reports and the expanded homicide tables can be found in Section I. Highlights from these tables have been included in this overview.

National Volume, Trends, and Rates

An estimated 16,272 persons were murdered nationwide in 2008. This number was a 3.9 percent decrease from the 2007 estimate, a 0.8 percent increase from the 2004 figure, and a 4.8 percent increase from the 1999 estimate. The 2008 murder rate, 5.4 offenses per 100,000 inhabitants, was a 4.7 percent decrease when compared with the rate for 2007. Murder accounted for 1.2 percent of the overall estimated number of violent crimes in 2008. (Table 1)

Regional Offense Trends and Rates

The UCR Program divides the United States into four regions: the Northeast, the South, the Midwest, and the West. (More details concerning geographic regions are provided in Appendix III.) In 2008, the estimated number of murders decreased in three of the four regions, with the largest decrease, 6.8 percent, occurring in the West. Murder increased 1.4 percent in the Northeast.

The Northeast

In 2008, the Northeast accounted for an estimated 18.1 percent of the nation's population and 14.1 percent of its estimated number of murders. With an estimated 2,293 murders, the Northeast saw a 1.4 percent increase compared with the 2007 figure. The offense rate for the Northeast was 4.2 murders per 100,000 inhabitants, up from 4.1 murders per 100,000 inhabitants in 2007. (Tables 3 and 4)

The Midwest

The Midwest accounted for an estimated 21.9 percent of the nation's total population and 19.7 percent of the country's estimated number of murders in 2008. There were an estimated 3,198 murders in the Midwest in 2008, a 0.8 percent decrease from the estimated figure for 2007. The Midwest experienced a rate of 4.8 murders per 100,000 inhabitants in 2008, slightly lower than in 2007. (Tables 3 and 4)

The South

The South, the nation's most populous region, experienced a 1.1 percent growth in population from 2007 to 2008. The region accounted for an estimated 36.7 percent of the nation's population in 2008 and 45.2 percent of the nation's murders, the highest proportion among the four regions. The estimated 7,348 murders represented a 5.3 percent decrease in the estimated number of murders from 2007 to 2008. The region's estimated rate of 6.6 murders per 100,000 inhabitants represented a decrease of 6.4 percent from the estimated rate for 2007. (Tables 3 and 4)

The West

The West accounted for an estimated 23.3 percent of the nation's population and 21.1 percent of the estimated number of murders in 2008. The region's population grew 1.1 percent from 2007 to 2008. The West experienced an estimated 3,433 murders, a 6.8 percent decrease from the 2007 estimate. The region's murder rate was 4.8 per 100,000 inhabitants, a 7.8 percent decrease from the 2007 rate. (Tables 3 and 4)

Community Types

The UCR Program aggregates data for three community types: metropolitan statistical areas (MSAs), cities outside MSAs, and nonmetropolitan counties outside MSAs. (See Appendix III for definitions.) In 2008, MSAs accounted for 83.5 percent of the nation's population and 89.4 percent of the estimated total number of murders. With 14,550 estimated homicides, MSAs experienced a rate of 5.7 murders per 100,000 inhabitants in 2008. Cities outside MSAs accounted for 6.6 percent of the U.S. population and (with an estimated 693 murders) accounted for 4.3 percent of the estimated murders in the nation. The murder rate for cities outside MSAs was 3.5 per 100,000 inhabitants. In 2008, 9.9 percent of the nation's population lived in nonmetropolitan counties outside MSAs. An estimated 1,029 murders took place in these counties, accounting for 6.3 percent of the nation's estimated total. (Table 2)

Population Groups: Trends and Rates

The UCR Program uses the following population group designations in its data presentations: cities (grouped according to population size) and counties (classified as either metropolitan or nonmetropolitan). A breakdown of these classifications is provided in Appendix III.

From 2007 to 2008, the nation's cities experienced a 5.6 percent decrease in homicides. The only city group to experience an increase (4.5 percent) was those with populations below 10,000. The city group with the largest decrease (9.4 percent) was those with 100,000 to 249,999 inhabitants. Metropolitan counties experienced a decrease in homicides of 1.8 percent from 2007 to 2008, while nonmetropolitan counties experienced an increase of 9.1 percent. (Table 12)

In 2008, cities collectively had a rate of 6.4 murders per 100,000 inhabitants. Cities with 500,000 to 999,999 inhabitants had the highest murder rate (12.7 murders per 100,000 inhabitants). Cities with 10,000 to 24,999 inhabitants and those with fewer than 10,000 inhabitants had the lowest murder rates, both at 2.6 murders per 100,000 inhabitants. The homicide rates for metropolitan and nonmetropolitan counties were 4.0 and 3.6 per 100,000 inhabitants, respectively. Suburban areas had a homicide rate of 3.3 per 100,000 inhabitants. (Table 16)

Supplementary Homicide Reports Data

Victims/Offenders

Based on 2008 supplemental homicide data (where the ages, sexes, or races of the murder victims were *known*), 87.8 percent of victims were over 18 years of age, 24.4 percent were under age 22, 10.5 percent were under 18 years of age, and the age of 1.6 percent of the victims was unknown. Of the 14,137 murder victims of 2008 for whom gender was known, 78.2 percent were male. Concerning murder victims for whom race was known, 49.0 percent were White, 48.6 percent were Black, and 2.3 percent were from other races. Race was unknown for 239 victims. (Expanded Homicide Tables 1 and 2) For murders where the gender of the offender was known, 90.0 percent were males. Of the offenders for whom race was known, 51.5 percent were Black, 46.2 percent were White, and 2.4 percent were from other races. (Based on Expanded Homicide Data Table 3)

Victim-Offender Relationships

For incidents in which the victim-offender relationship was known, 23.3 percent of victims were slain by family members, 22.0 percent were murdered by strangers, and 54.7 percent were killed by acquaintances (neighbor, friend, boyfriend, etc.). Among female victims for whom relationships with their offenders were known, 34.7 percent were murdered by their husbands or boyfriends. (Based on Expanded Homicide Data Tables 2 and 10)

Circumstances/Weapons

Concerning the known circumstances surrounding murders, 42.0 percent of victims were murdered during arguments (including romantic triangles) in 2008. Felony circumstances (rape, robbery, burglary, etc.) accounted for 22.9 percent of murders. Circumstances were unknown for 35.3 percent of reported homicides. (Based on Expanded Homicide Data Table 12) Of the homicides for which the type of weapon was specified, 71.9 percent involved the use of firearms. Of the identified firearms used, handguns made up 88.3 percent. (Based on Expanded Homicide Data Table 8)

Justifiable Homicide

Certain willful killings must be reported as justifiable, or excusable, homicide. In the UCR Program, justifiable homicide is defined as, and is limited to, the following:

- The killing of a felon by a peace officer in the line of duty.
- The killing of a felon, during the commission of a felony, by a private citizen.

Because these killings are determined by law enforcement investigation to be justifiable, they are tabulated separately from murder and nonnegligent manslaughter. Law enforcement reported 616 justifiable homicides in 2008. Of those, law enforcement officers justifiably killed 371 individuals, and private citizens justifiably killed 245 individuals.

FORCIBLE RAPE

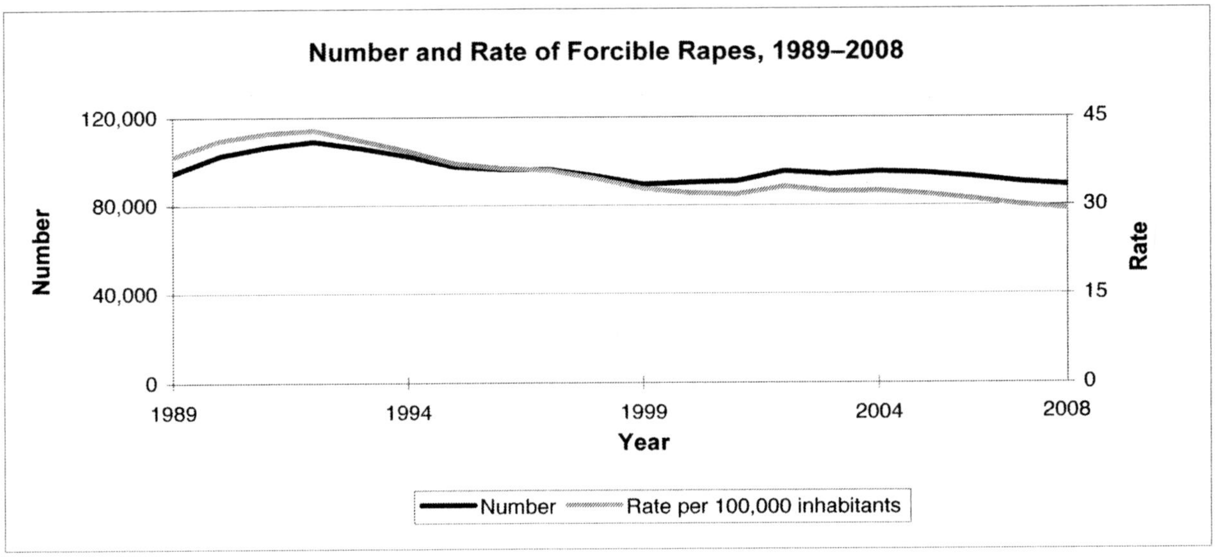

Definition

Forcible rape is the carnal knowledge of a female forcibly and against her will. Assaults and attempts to commit rape by force or threat of force are included; however, statutory rape (without force) and other sex offenses are excluded.

Data Collection

The UCR Program counts one offense for each female victim of a forcible rape, attempted forcible rape, or assault with intent to rape, regardless of the victim's age. A rape by force involving a female victim and a familial offender is counted as a forcible rape not an act of incest. The Program collects only arrest statistics concerning all other crimes of a sexual nature. The offense of statutory rape, in which no force is used but the female victim is under the age of consent, is included in the arrest total for the sex offenses category. Sexual attacks on males are counted as aggravated assaults or sex offenses, depending on the circumstances and the extent of any injuries.

For this overview only, the FBI deviated from standard procedure and manually calculated the 2007 and 2008 rates of females raped based on the national female population provided by the U.S. Census Bureau.

National Volume, Trends, and Rates

In 2008, the estimated number of forcible rapes (89,000)—the lowest figure in the last 20 years—decreased 1.6 percent from the 2007 estimate. The estimated volume of rapes in 2008 was 6.4 percent lower than in 2004 and was 0.5 percent below the 1999 level. (Tables 1 and 1A)

In preparing rate tables, the UCR Program's computer system automatically calculates offense rates per 100,000 inhabitants for all Part I crimes, which include murder and nonnegligent manslaughter, forcible rape, robbery, aggravated assault, burglary, larceny-theft, motor vehicle theft, and arson. (See Appendix II for more information.) Thus, the rate data are based upon the total U.S. population. However, for this overview, the 2008 rate of female rapes has been recalculated based upon the national female population provided by the Census Bureau. The recalculation resulted in a rate of 57.7 offenses per 100,000 females, a 2.4 percent decrease when compared with the 2007 estimated rate of 59.2.

Of the forcible rapes known to law enforcement agencies in 2008, rapes by force made up 92.5 percent of reported rape offenses, and assaults to rape attempts accounted for 7.5 percent of reported rape offenses. (Tables 1 and 19)

Regional Offense Trends and Rates

The UCR Program divides the United States into four regions: the Northeast, the South, the Midwest, and the West. (More details concerning geographic regions are provided in Appendix III.) Regional analysis offers estimates of the volume of female rapes, the percentage change from the previous year's estimate, and the rate of rape per 100,000 female inhabitants in each region. (Tables 3 and 4)

The Northeast

The Northeast made up 18.1 percent of the U.S. population in 2008 and experienced a 0.4 percent increase in population from 2007 to 2008. In 2008, an estimated 10,981 forcible rapes of females—12.3 percent of the national total—

occurred in the Northeast. This was an increase of 1.5 percent from the 2007 estimated figure. (Tables 3 and 4)

The Midwest

The Midwest, which accounted for 21.9 percent of the U.S. population in 2008, experienced a 0.3 percent increase in population from 2007 to 2008. Over one-quarter (25.4 percent) of all forcible rapes in the nation occurred in the Midwest in 2008. The 2008 estimate (22,624 forcible rapes) represented a decline of 1.0 percent from the 2007 estimate. (Tables 3 and 4)

The South

The South, the nation's most populous region, accounted for an estimated 36.7 percent of the nation's population in 2008 (and experienced a population growth of 1.1 percent from 2007 to 2008); the region also accounted for an estimated 38.2 percent of the nation's estimated number of forcible rapes. There were an estimated 33,972 female victims of forcible rape in the South in 2008, down 3.1 percent from 35,073 in 2007. (Tables 3 and 4)

The West

The West, which experienced a population growth of 1.1 percent from 2007 to 2008, accounted for 23.3 percent of the nation's population in 2008. The region also accounted for 24.1 percent of the nation's total number of estimated forcible rapes with an estimated 21,423 offenses. The West saw a 1.1 percent decline in forcible rapes from 2007 to 2008. (Tables 3 and 4)

Community Types

Using the U.S. Office of Management and Budget's designations, the UCR Program aggregates crime data by type of community in which the offenses occur: metropolitan statistical areas (MSAs), cities outside MSAs, and nonmetropolitan counties outside MSAs. (Appendix III provides more detailed information about community types.)

MSAs

In 2008, MSAs accounted for 83.5 percent of the nation's population and 83.5 percent of the nation's estimated number of forcible rapes. An estimated 74,339 females were forcibly raped in metropolitan areas. (Table 2)

Cities Outside MSAs

Cities outside MSAs are mostly incorporated areas served by city law enforcement agencies. Though accounting for only 6.6 percent of the U.S. population in 2008, cities outside MSAs accounted for 8.6 percent of the nation's estimated forcible rapes (7,620 offenses). (Table 2)

Nonmetropolitan Counties

In 2008, approximately 9.9 percent of the nation's population lived in nonmetropolitan counties outside MSAs (counties made up of mostly nonincorporated areas served by noncity law enforcement agencies). Collectively, these areas had an estimated 7,041 forcible rapes, representing 7.9 percent of the nation's estimated total. (Table 2)

ROBBERY

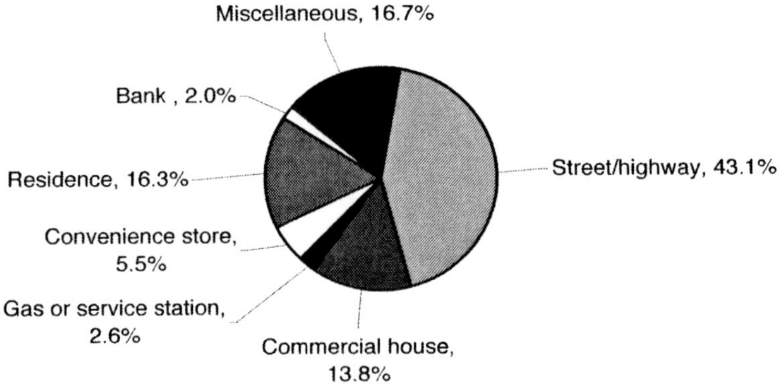

Definition

The UCR Program defines robbery as the taking or attempting to take anything of value from the care, custody, or control of a person or persons by force or threat of force or violence and/or by putting the victim in fear.

National Volume, Trends, and Rates

In 2008, the estimated robbery total (441,855) decreased 0.7 percent from the 2007 estimate. However, the 5-year robbery trend (2004 data compared with 2008 data) showed an increase of 10.1 percent. The 2008 estimated robbery rate (145.3 per 100,000 inhabitants) showed a decrease of 1.5 percent when compared with the 2007 rate. (Tables 1 and 1A)

Regional Offense Trends and Rates

The UCR Program divides the United States into four regions: the Northeast, the South, the Midwest, and the West. (More details concerning geographic regions are provided in Appendix III.)

The Northeast

The Northeast, with an estimated 18.1 percent of the nation's population in 2008, accounted for 17.2 percent of its estimated number of robberies. (Table 3) The estimated number of robberies increased 1.0 percent from 2007. The Northeast was the only region that experienced an increase in robberies from 2007 to 2008. The rate for this region was 138.5 robberies per 100,000 inhabitants up slightly from 137.8 robberies per 100,000 inhabitants in 2007. (Table 4)

The Midwest

The Midwest accounted for 21.9 percent of the total population of the United States, and 19.1 percent of its estimated number of robberies, in 2008. The region experienced a 0.3 percent growth in population from 2007 to 2008. (Table 3) There were an estimated 84,385 robberies in the Midwest in 2008, a 0.3 percent decrease from the estimated figure from 2007. The region's robbery rate was 126.8 robberies per 100,000 inhabitants in 2008, the lowest rate among the four regions. (Table 4)

The South

The South, the nation's most highly populated region, experienced a 1.1 percent growth in population from 2007 to 2008; in 2008, it accounted for an estimated 36.7 percent of the nation's population and 40.2 percent of the nation's estimated number of robberies. (Table 3) There were an estimated 177,691 robberies in 2008, representing a 1.1 percent decrease from the 2007 figure. The region experienced the highest rate of robberies per 100,000 inhabitants (159.1), a 2.3 percent drop from the 2007 rate. (Table 4)

The West

The West, having experienced a population growth of 1.1 percent from 2007 to 2008, was home to an estimated 23.3 percent of the nation's population and accounted for 23.5 percent of the nation's estimated number of robberies in 2008. (Table 3) The estimated number of robberies in the region in 2008 represented a 2.6 percent decrease from the 2007 figure. The rate of robberies per 100,000 inhabitants in the West was 146.4, a 2.3 percent decrease from the 2007 rate. This was the second highest rate among the four regions. (Table 4)

Community Types

The UCR Program aggregates data for three community types: metropolitan statistical areas (MSAs), cities outside MSAs, and nonmetropolitan counties outside MSAs. MSAs include a central city or urbanized area with at least 50,000 inhabitants, as well as the county that contains the principal city and other adjacent counties that have, as defined by the U.S. Office of Management and Budget, a high degree of social and economic integration as measured through commuting. Cities outside MSAs are mostly incorporated areas, and nonmetropolitan counties are made up of mostly unincorporated areas served by noncity law enforcement.

In 2008, MSAs were home to an estimated 83.5 percent of the nation's population, and 95.8 percent of the nation's estimated number of robberies took place in these areas. Robberies in MSAs occurred at a rate of 166.7 per 100,000 inhabitants. Cities outside MSAs accounted for 6.6 percent of the U.S. population and accounted for 3.0 percent of the estimated number of robberies in the nation. The robbery rate for cities outside MSAs was 67.1 per 100,000 inhabitants. Nonmetropolitan counties made up 9.9 percent of the nation's estimated population and 1.2 percent of the nation's estimated robberies, at a rate of 17.1 robberies per 100,000 inhabitants. (Table 2)

Population Groups: Trends and Rates

The national UCR Program aggregates data by various population groups, which include cities, metropolitan counties, and nonmetropolitan counties. A definition of these groups can be found in Appendix III. The number of robberies in cities as a whole decreased 1.3 percent. Among the population groups labeled *city*, those cities with fewer than 10,000 inhabitants had the greatest increase in the number of robberies (3.7 percent), while cities with 50,000 to 99,999 inhabitants had the largest decline in the number of robberies (2.4 percent). Nonmetropolitan counties had a 2.5 percent increase in the estimated number of robberies, and metropolitan counties showed a 0.7 percent decrease. The number of robberies in suburban areas fell 0.8 percent. (Table 12)

Among the population groups, the nation's cities collectively had a rate of 197.3 robberies per 100,000 inhabitants. Of the population groups and subsets designated *city*, those with 500,000 to 999,999 inhabitants had the highest rate (373.3 per 100,000 inhabitants), while those with fewer than 10,000 inhabitants had the lowest rate (57.8 per 100,000 inhabitants) of robberies. Of the two county groups, metropolitan counties had a rate of 77.9 robberies per 100,000 inhabitants, while nonmetropolitan counties had a rate of 17.6 robberies per 100,000 inhabitants. Suburban areas had a robbery rate of 781. (Table 16)

Offense Analysis

The UCR Program collects supplemental data about robberies to document the use of weapons, the dollar loss associated with the offense, and the location types.

Robbery by Weapon

Firearms were used in 43.5 percent of robberies in 2008. Strong-arm robberies accounted for 40.2 percent of the total. Offenders used knives or cutting instruments in 8.7 percent of these crimes. In the remainder of the robberies, the offenders used other types of weapons. (Table 19)

Loss by Dollar Value

Based on the supplemental reports from law enforcement agencies, robberies cost victims, collectively, an estimated $581 million in 2008. (Tables 1 and 23) The average loss per robbery was $1,315. Average dollar losses were the highest for banks, which suffered an average loss of $4,854 per offense. Gas and service stations lost an average $1,007 per offense. Commercial houses, which include supermarkets, department stores, and restaurants, had average losses of $1,651. An average of $1,589 was taken from residences. An average of $712 was lost in each offense against convenience stores. (Table 23)

Robbery Trends by Location

Among the location types, convenience store robberies had the greatest percentage decrease from 2007 to 2008, declining 5.5 percent. Robberies that occurred at residences increased 2.5 percent. The number of robberies on streets and highways decreased 0.5 percent, and robberies at banks decreased 5.3 percent. (Table 23)

By location type, the greatest proportion of robberies in 2008 occurred on streets and highways (43.1 percent). Robbers targeted commercial houses in 13.8 percent of offenses and residences in 16.3 percent of offenses. Convenience stores accounted for 5.5 percent of robberies, followed by gas and service stations (2.6 percent) and banks (2.0 percent). (Table 23)

AGGRAVATED ASSAULT

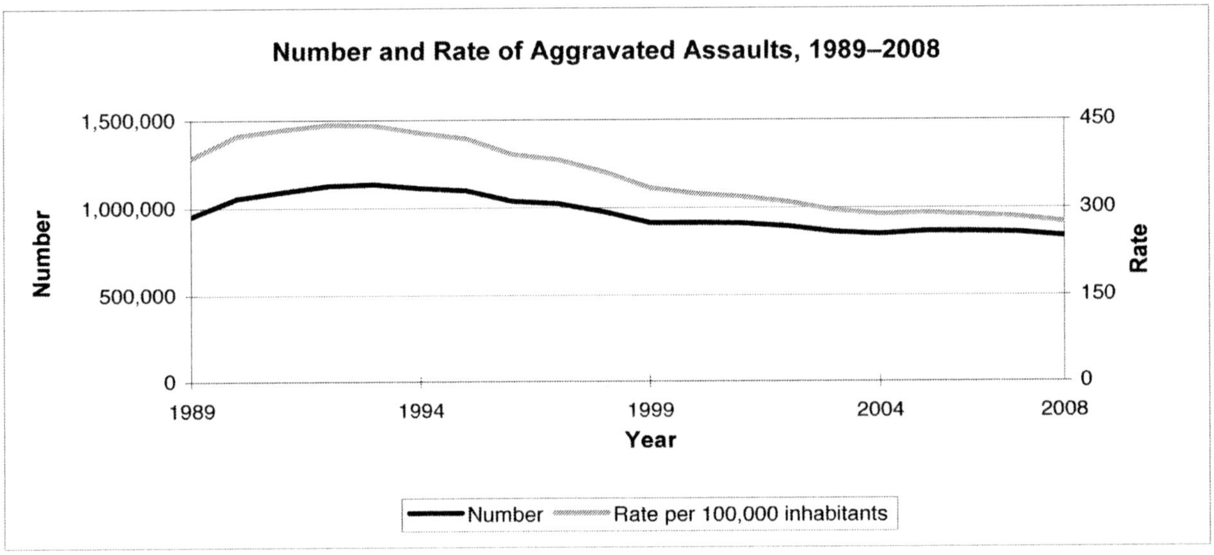

Definition

The UCR Program defines aggravated assault as an unlawful attack by one person upon another for the purpose of inflicting severe or aggravated bodily injury. This type of assault is usually accompanied by the use of a weapon or by other means likely to produce death or great bodily harm. Attempted aggravated assaults that involve the display or threat of a gun, knife, or other weapon are included in this crime category because serious personal injury would likely result if these assaults were completed. When aggravated assault and larceny-theft occur together, the offense falls under the category of robbery.

National Volume, Trends, and Rates

In 2008, estimated occurrences of aggravated assaults totaled 834,885, a 2.5 percent decrease from the 2007 figure. According to 2- and 10-year trend data, the estimated number of aggravated assaults in 2008 declined 2.5 percent and 8.4 percent, respectively, when compared with the estimates for 2007 and 1999. The 2008 data also show a decrease for the third consecutive year in the rate of aggravated assault per 100,000 U.S. inhabitants. This rate, estimated at 274.6, represents a 3.2 percent decrease from the 2006 rate. It also represents a 4.8 percent decrease from the 2004 (5-year trend) rate and a 17.9 percent decrease from the 1999 (10-year trend) rate. (Tables 1 and 1A)

Among the four types of violent crime offenses (murder, forcible rape, robbery, and aggravated assault), aggravated assault typically has the highest rate of occurrence. This trend continued in 2008 with aggravated assault accounting for 60.4 percent of all violent crime. (Table 1)

Regional Offense Trends and Rates

The UCR Program divides the United States into four regions: the Northeast, the South, the Midwest, and the West. (More details concerning geographic regions are provided in Appendix III.) All four regions experienced decreases in the number of aggravated assaults from 2007 to 2008. (Table 4)

The Northeast

The region with the smallest proportion of the nation's population (an estimated 18.1 percent in 2008) also accounted for the smallest proportion of the nation's estimated number of aggravated assaults (13.7 percent). (Table 3) Occurrences of aggravated assault decreased 0.8 percent from 2007 to 2008, down to an estimated 114,332. The region also had the lowest aggravated assault rate in the nation, at 208.2 incidents per 100,000 inhabitants, a 1.2 percent decline from the 2007 rate. (Table 4)

The Midwest

With 21.9 percent of the nation's total population in 2008—and with a 0.3 percent growth in population from 2007 to 2008—the Midwest accounted for approximately 18.7 percent of the nation's estimated number of aggravated assaults. (Table 3) Occurrences of this offense decreased 3.8 percent from the estimated total for 2007, declining to an estimated 156,105 incidents. The region's aggravated assault rate, at 234.5 incidents per 100,000 inhabitants, represented a 4.0 percent decrease from the 2007 rate. (Table 4)

The South

The South, the nation's most populated region, accounted for an estimated 36.7 percent of the nation's population in 2008. (Table 3) From 2007 to 2008, the estimated number of aggravated assaults decreased 1.7 percent, falling to a total of 377,414 incidents. The rate of aggravated assaults declined to 337.8 per 100,000 inhabitants. (Table 4)

The West

In 2008, the West was home to an estimated 21.9 percent of the nation's population and experienced a 1.1 percent growth in population from 2007 to 2008. The region accounted for 22.4 percent of the nation's estimated number of aggravated assaults. (Table 3) From 2007 to 2008, the estimated number of offenses decreased 3.7 percent to 187,034 incidents. The rate, estimated at 264.0 offenses per 100,000 inhabitants, fell 4.8 percent from 2007. (Table 4)

Community Types

The UCR Program aggregates data for three community types: metropolitan statistical areas (MSAs), cities outside MSAs, and nonmetropolitan counties outside MSAs. MSAs include a central city or urbanized area with at least 50,000 inhabitants, as well as the county that contains the principal city and other adjacent counties that have a high degree of social and economic integration as measured through commuting. Cities outside MSAs are mostly incorporated areas, and nonmetropolitan counties are made up of mostly unincorporated areas. (For additional information about community types, see Appendix III.)

In 2008, 83.5 percent of the nation's population lived in MSAs, where the rate of aggravated assault was an estimated 287.3 per 100,000 inhabitants. Cities outside MSAs (with 6.6 percent of the U.S. population) had the next-highest rate of aggravated assault at 283.3 offenses per 100,000 inhabitants. Nonmetropolitan counties accounted for 9.9 percent of the U.S. population and had an offense rate of 161.1 aggravated assaults per 100,000 inhabitants. (Table 2)

From 2007 to 2008, the number of aggravated assaults fell for all cities. Cities with 250,000 to 499,999 inhabitants experienced the greatest decrease (6.0 percent), followed by cities with fewer than 10,000 residents and cities with populations of 100,000 to 249,999—both fell 4.9 percent. In metropolitan counties, the number of aggravated assaults declined 3.5 percent; in nonmetropolitan counties, this number increased 1.9 percent. Aggravated assaults in suburban areas declined 3.0 percent from 2007 to 2008. (Table 12)

Based on reports from agencies submitting 12 months of complete data for 2008, aggravated assault occurred at an estimated rate of 281.6 offenses per 100,000 inhabitants nationwide. The collective rate for cities was 317.1 aggravated assaults per 100,000 inhabitants. Among city population groups, rates ranged from a high of 530.8 offenses per 100,000 inhabitants (in cities with 500,000 to 999,999 inhabitants) to a low of 203.9 offenses per 100,000 inhabitants (in cities with 10,000 to 24,999 inhabitants). The aggravated assault rate was 219.1 in metropolitan counties and 201.7 in nonmetropolitan counties. (Table 16)

Offense Analysis

Aggravated Assault by Weapon

Of the aggravated assault offenses for which law enforcement agencies provided expanded data in 2008, 33.5 percent were committed with blunt objects or other dangerous weapons; 26.2 percent involved personal weapons such as hands, fists, and feet; 21.4 percent were committed with firearms; and 18.9 percent involved knives or other cutting instruments. (Table 19)

PROPERTY CRIME

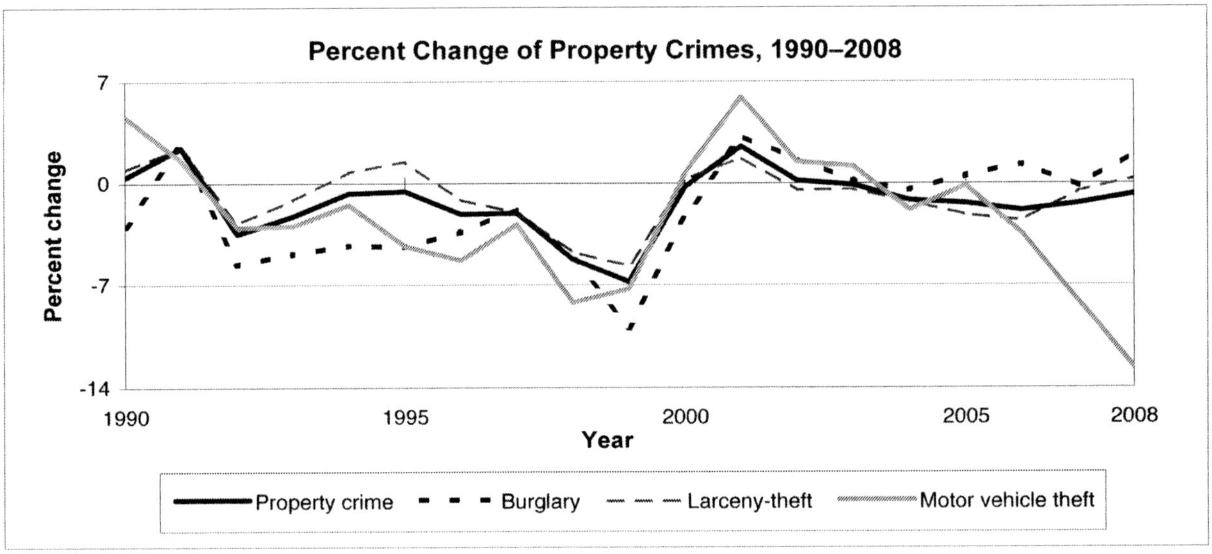

Definition

The Uniform Crime Reporting (UCR) Program's definition of property crime includes the offenses of burglary, larceny-theft, motor vehicle theft, and arson. The object of theft-type offenses is the taking of money or property without the use of force or threat of force against the victims. Property crime includes arson because the offense involves the destruction of property; however, arson victims may be subjected to force. Because of limited participation and the varying collection procedures conducted by local law enforcement agencies, only limited data are available for arson. Arson statistics are included in the trend, clearance, and arrest tables in *Crime in the United States*, but they are not included in any estimated volume data. More information on the expanded arson tables (which are available online but not included in this publication) can be found in Section I.

Data Collection

The data presented in *Crime in the United States* reflect the Hierarchy Rule, which counts only the most serious offense in a multiple-offense criminal incident. In descending order of severity, the violent crimes are murder and nonnegligent manslaughter, forcible rape, robbery, aggravated assault; these are followed by the property crimes of burglary, larceny-theft, and motor vehicle theft. The Hierarchy Rule does not apply to the offense of arson.

National Volume, Trends, and Rates

An estimated 9,767,915 property crimes were committed in the United States in 2008, representing a 0.8 percent decrease from the 2007 (2-year trend) estimate, a 5.3 percent decrease from the 2004 (5-year trend) estimate, and a 4.3 percent decrease from the 1999 (10-year trend) estimate. (Tables 1 and 1A)

From 2007 to 2008, motor vehicle theft fell by 12.7 percent. While larceny-theft (0.3 percent) and burglary (2.0 percent) both showed increases from their 2007 estimates. However, larceny-theft estimates are down from both the 2004 and 2008 estimates. (Tables 1 and 1A)

The estimated property crime rate per 100,000 inhabitants in 2008 was 3,212.5, a 1.6 percent decrease from the 2007 rate, an 8.6 percent decrease from the 2004 rate, and a 14.2 percent decrease from the 1999 rate. The number of burglaries grew 5.8 percent from 1999 to 2008, but the burglary rate per 100,000 population fell 5.1 percent. The motor vehicle theft rates per 100,000 residents fell from 422.5 in 1999 to 314.7 in 2008. (Tables 1 and 1A)

Regional Offense Trends and Rates

The UCR Program separates the United States into four regions: the Northeast, the Midwest, the South, and the West. (Geographic breakdowns can be found in Appendix III.) Property crime data collected by the UCR Program and aggregated by region reflected the following results.

The Northeast

The Northeast region accounted for 18.1 percent of the nation's population and experienced a 0.4 percent increase in population from 2007 to 2008. The region also accounted for 12.6 percent of the nation's estimated number of property crimes in 2008. (Table 3) Law enforcement in the Northeast saw a 2.5 percent increase in the estimated number of property crimes from 2007 to 2008. The property crime rate for the Northeast, estimated at 2,248.8 incidents per 100,000 inhabitants, was 2.0 percent higher than the 2007 rate. (Table 4)

The Midwest

The Midwest, with 21.9 percent of the U.S. population in 2008 and a 0.3 percent growth in population from 2007 to 2008, accounted for 20.9 percent of the nation's estimated number of property crimes. (Table 3) Law enforcement in the Midwest saw a 2.6 percent decrease in the estimated number of property crimes in the Midwest from 2007 to 2008. The rate of property crime in the Midwest in 2008, estimated at 3,066.5 incidents per 100,000 inhabitants, represented a 2.9 percent decrease from the 2007 rate. (Table 4)

The South

The South, the nation's most populous region, accounted for 36.7 percent of the U.S. population in 2008 and experienced a 1.1 percent growth in population from 2007 to 2008. The region also accounted for an estimated 43.2 percent of the nation's property crimes. (Table 3) The South experienced a 0.6 percent increase in its estimated number of property crimes from 2007 to 2008. The 2008 property crime rate, an estimated 3780.8 incidents per 100,000 inhabitants, was 0.6 percent lower than the 2007 rate. (Table 4)

The West

In 2008, the West accounted for 23.3 percent of the nation's population; the region experienced a 1.1 percent growth in population from 2006 to 2007. The West also accounted for 23.2 percent of the nation's estimated number of property crimes. (Table 3) From 2007 to 2008, the estimated number of property crimes in this region decreased 3.2 percent. The estimated property crime rate in the West in 2008, 3,200.7 incidents per 100,000 inhabitants, was 4.2 percent lower than the 2007 rate. (Table 4)

Community Types

The UCR Program aggregates data by three community types: metropolitan statistical areas (MSAs), cities outside metropolitan areas, and nonmetropolitan counties. (Additional in-depth information regarding community types can be found in Appendix III.) In 2008, 83.5 percent of the U.S. population lived in MSAs. The property crime rate for MSAs was 3,212.5 per 100,000 inhabitants. Cities outside metropolitan areas, which accounted for 6.6 percent of the total population in 2008, had a property crime rate of 3,352.0 per 100,000 inhabitants. Nonmetropolitan counties, with 9.9 percent of the nation's population in 2008, had a property crime rate of 1,681.1 per 100,000 inhabitants. (Table 2)

Population Groups: Trends and Rates

The UCR Program organizes the agencies that contribute data into population groups, which include cities, metropolitan counties, and nonmetropolitan counties. (Appendix III provides further details about these groups.) From 2007 to 2008, law enforcement in the nation's cities collectively reported a 1.7 percent decrease in the number of property crimes. All city groups experienced decreased in the number of property crimes; cities with 250,000 to 499,999 inhabitants or more had the largest declines at 5.1 percent. While metropolitan counties experienced a increase of 0.5 percent from 2007 to 2008; property crime increased in nonmetropolitran counties by 0.2 percent. (Table 12)

The nation's cities collectively had a property crime rate of 3,759.1 incidents per 100,000 inhabitants in 2008. Nonmetropolitan counties had a rate of 1,716.3 incidents per 100,000 inhabitants, and metropolitan counties had a rate of 2,432.6 incidents per 100,000 inhabitants. (Table 16)

Offense Analysis

The estimated dollar loss attributing to property crimes, not including arson, in 2008 was $17.2 billion. Among the individual property crime categories, the dollar losses were an estimated $4.6 billion for burglary, $6.1 billion for larceny-theft, and $ 6.4 billion for motor vehicle theft. (Tables 1 and 23) Arson had an average dollar loss of $16,015. Arsons of industrial/manufacturing structures resulted in the highest average dollar losses with an average loss of $212,388. (Expanded Arson Table 2) In 2008, the average dollar value per motor vehicle stolen in the United States was $6,751. The average dollar value of property taken during burglaries was $2,079; during robberies, $1,315; and during larceny-thefts, $925. The average dollar loss per arson offense was $16,015.

BURGLARY

Burglary, by Location and Time, 2008

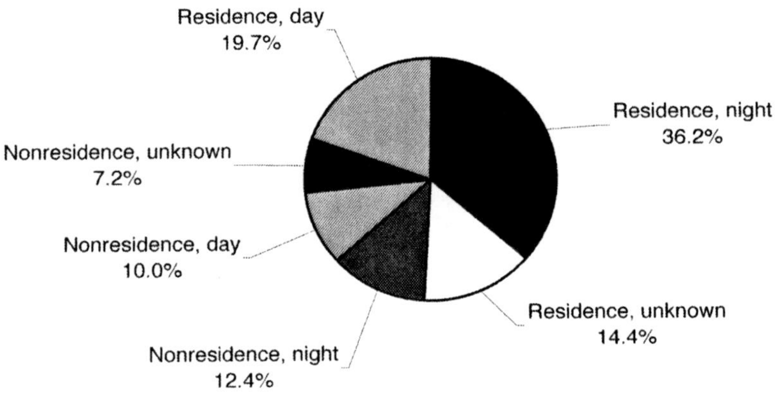

Definition

The UCR Program defines burglary as the unlawful entry of a structure to commit a felony or theft. To classify an offense as a burglary, the use of force to gain entry need not have occurred. The program has three subclassifications for burglary: forcible entry, unlawful entry where no force is used, and attempted forcible entry. The UCR definition of "structure" includes, but is not limited to, apartments, barns, house trailers or houseboats (when used as permanent dwellings), offices, railroad cars (but not automobiles), stables, and vessels (i.e., ships).

National Volume, Trends, and Rate

In 2008, there were an estimated 2,222,196 burglaries—an increase of 2.0 percent when compared with 2007 data. There was an increase of 3.6 percent in the number of burglaries in 2008 when compared with the 2004 estimate and an increase of 5.8 percent when compared with the 1999 estimate. Burglary accounted for 22.7 percent of the estimated number of property crimes committed in 2008. The burglary rate for the United States in 2008 was 730.8 incidents per 100,000 inhabitants, a 1.1 percent decrease from the 2007 rate. (Tables 1 and 1A)

Regional Offense Trends and Rates

The UCR Program divides the United States into four regions: the Northeast, the Midwest, the South, and the West. (Details regarding these regions can be found in Appendix III.) An analysis of burglary data by region showed the following details.

The Northeast

In 2008, 18.1 percent of the nation's population lived in the Northeast, which experienced a 0.4 percent increase in population from 2007 to 2008. This region accounted for 10.6 percent of the estimated total number of burglary offenses in the nation in 2008. The region's burglary rate, an estimated 429.5 offenses per 100,000 inhabitants, represented an increase of 2.5 percent from the 2007 rate. The Northeast had the lowest burglary rate of the four regions. (Tables 3 and 4)

The Midwest

The Midwest accounted for 21.9 percent of the nation's population in 2008 and experienced a 0.3 percent growth in population from 2007 to 2008. This region accounted for 20.4 percent of the nation's estimated number of burglaries. The estimated number of burglaries in this region increased 1.2 percent from 2007 to 2008. The Midwest had a burglary rate of 681.1 offenses per 100,000 inhabitants, a 0.9 percent increase from the 2007 rate. (Tables 3 and 4)

The South

The South, the nation's most highly populated region, had the most burglaries in 2008 (an estimated 1,051,616). With 36.7 percent of the nation's population (and having experienced a 1.1 percent growth in population from 2007 to 2008), this region accounted for 47.3 percent of all burglaries in the United States. The estimated rate of burglary in the South was 941.3 incidents per 100,000 inhabitants, a 2.1 percent increase from the 2007 rate. (Tables 3 and 4)

The West

The West accounted for 23.3 percent of the nation's population in 2008 and experienced a 1.1 percent growth in population from 2007 to 2008. In 2008, this region accounted for an estimated 21.7 percent of the nation's burglaries. The region's burglary rate was 679.3, a 1.5 percent decrease from the 2007 rate. The total number of burglaries (481,316) represented a 0.5 percent decrease from the 2007 figure. The West was the only one of the four regions with a decrease in the number of burglaries. (Tables 3 and 4)

Community Types

The UCR Program aggregates data by three community types: metropolitan statistical areas (MSAs), cities outside MSAs, and nonmetropolitan counties. (See Appendix III for more information regarding community types.) In 2008, 83.5 percent of the U.S. population lived in MSAs, and an estimated 85.3 percent of all burglaries occurred in this type of community. Inhabitants of cities outside MSAs accounted for 6.6 percent of the total population in 2008 and 7.3 percent of the estimated number of burglaries; nonmetropolitan counties, with 9.9 percent of the U.S. population, accounted for 7.4 percent of all burglaries. The burglary rates per 100,000 inhabitants were 745.8 in MSAs, 813.9 in cities outside MSAs, and 549.2 in nonmetropolitan counties. (Table 2)

Population Groups: Trends and Rates

In addition to analyzing data by region and community type, the UCR Program aggregates crime statistics by population groups. Cities are categorized into six groups based on the number of inhabitants; counties are categorized into two groups, metropolitan and nonmetropolitan. (Appendix III offers further details regarding these population groups.)

An examination of data from law enforcement agencies that provided statistics for at least six common months in 2007 and 2008 showed that the nation's cities experienced a collective 1.2 percent increase in burglaries from 2007 to 2008. Burglaries decreased the most in cities with a population between 250,000 to 499,999. While cities with 500,000 to 999,999 inhabitants had the highest increase (2.4 percent). The volume of burglaries increased 2.8 percent in metropolitan counties, 1.9 percent in nonmetropolitan counties, and 2.5 percent in suburban areas. (Table 12)

The UCR Program calculates burglary rates for population groups from the information provided by participating agencies that submitted all 12 months of offense data for the year. In 2008, the nation's cities had 805.2 offenses per 100,000 inhabitants. Cities with 500,000 to 999,999 population had the highest burglary rate at 1,197.5 incidents per 100,000 inhabitants. Cities with 10,000 to 24,999 inhabitants had the lowest burglary rate—638.3 incidents per 100,000 inhabitants. Metropolitan counties had a rate of 630.4 per 100,000 inhabitants, and nonmetropolitan counties had a rate of 561.3 per 100,000 inhabitants. (Table 16)

Offense Analysis

The UCR Program requests that participating law enforcement agencies provide details regarding the nature of burglaries in their jurisdictions, such as type of entry, type of structure, time of day, and dollar loss associated with each offense.

Of all burglaries, 61.2 percent involved forcible entry, 32.3 percent were unlawful entries (without force), and the remainder (6.4 percent) were forcible entry attempts. (Table 19)

Victims of burglary offenses suffered an estimated $4.6 billion in lost property in 2008; overall, the average dollar loss per burglary offense was $2,079.

As in the past, burglars targeted residences more often than nonresidential structures. In 2008, burglaries of residential properties accounted for 70.3 percent of all burglary offenses. Law enforcement agencies were unable to determine the time of day for 21.6 percent of all reported burglaries. However, of the burglaries for which time of day could be established, most burglaries of residences (64.8 percent) occurred during the day, while most burglaries of nonresidential structures (55.3 percent) occurred at night. (Table 23)

LARCENY-THEFT

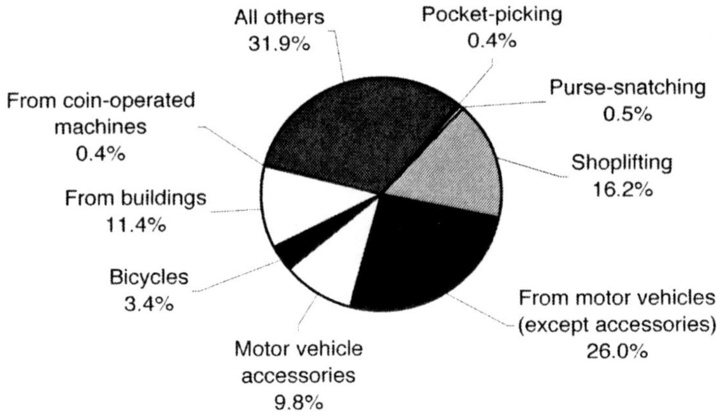

Definition

The UCR Program defines larceny-theft as the unlawful taking, carrying, leading, or riding away of property from the possession or constructive possession of another. Examples are thefts of bicycles, motor vehicle parts and accessories, shoplifting, pocket picking, or the stealing of any property or article not taken by force and violence or by fraud. Attempted larcenies are included. Embezzlement, confidence games, forgery, check fraud, etc., are excluded from this category.

National Volume, Trends, and Rates

There were an estimated 6.6 million (6,588,873) larceny-thefts nationwide in 2008. Larceny-thefts accounted for an estimated 67.5 percent of property crimes in 2008. There was a 0.3 percent increase in the estimated number of larceny-thefts in 2008 compared with the 2007 estimate. The 2008 figure showed a 5.3 percent decline compared with the 1999 estimate. The trend data also showed decreases in the larceny-theft rates per 100,000 inhabitants during these periods. The rate of larceny-thefts declined 0.5 percent from 2007 to 2008, and the rate declined 15.0 percent from 1999 to 2008. (Table 1)

Regional Offense Trends and Rates

The UCR Program defines four regions within the United States: the Northeast, the Midwest, the South, and the West. (See Appendix III for a geographical description of each region.) Larceny-theft decreased in the Midwest and the West, 2.5 percent and 0.5 percent, respectively, while such offenses increased 4.0 percent in the Northeast and 1.0 percent in the South. (Tables 3 and 4) The following paragraphs provide a region overview of larceny-theft.

The Northeast

The Northeast was the region with the smallest proportion (18.1 percent) of the U.S. population in 2008. The region's population grew by 0.4 percent from 2007 to 2008. The region also experienced the fewest larceny-thefts in the country, accounting for only 13.7 percent of all larceny-thefts. (Table 3) The estimated number of offenses in 2008—903,474—represented a 4.0 percent decline from 2007, and the estimated rate—1,644.9 incidents per 100,000 inhabitants—represented a 3.5 percent decline. (Table 4)

The Midwest

With 21.9 percent of the U.S. population in 2008, and a 0.3 percent growth in population from 2007 to 2008, the Midwest accounted for an estimated 214 percent of the nation's larceny-thefts. (Table 3) The estimated number of offenses (1,412,944) declined 2.5 percent compared with the 2007 data, and the estimated rate of occurrences (2,122.8 incidents per 100,000 inhabitants) declined 2.7 percent. (Table 4)

The South

With more than one-third of the U.S. population in 2008 (36.7 percent), the South experienced a 1.1 percent growth in population from 2007 to 2008. The region had the nation's highest proportion of larceny-theft offenses: an estimated 42.7 percent. (Table 3) Estimated offenses in this region totaled 2,810,699, a 1.0 percent increase from the

2007 estimate. The South's larceny-theft rate—estimated at 2,515.9 offenses per 100,000 inhabitants—decreased 0.1 percent from the 2007 estimate. (Table 4)

The West

In 2008, an estimated 23.3 percent of the U.S. population lived in the West, which experienced a 1.1 percent growth in population from 2007 to 2008. This region was also where 22.2 percent of the nation's estimated number of larceny-thefts took place. (Table 3) Occurrences of larceny-theft declined 0.5 percent from 2007 to 2008, dropping to an estimated total of 1,461,756 offenses. The region's larceny-theft rate, estimated at 2,063.0 offenses per 100,000 inhabitants, declined 1.5 percent from the 2007 rate. (Table 4)

Community Types

The UCR Program aggregates data for three community types: metropolitan statistical areas (MSAs), cities outside MSAs, and nonmetropolitan counties outside MSAs. MSAs include a central city or urbanized area with at least 50,000 inhabitants, as well as the county that contains the principal city and other adjacent counties that share a high degree of social and economic integration as measured through commuting. Cities outside MSAs are mostly incorporated areas, and nonmetropolitan counties are composed of unincorporated areas. (See Appendix III for more information regarding community types.)

In 2008, MSAs were home to an estimated 83.5 percent of the nation's population and experienced 87.0 percent of the nation's larceny-theft incidents. Cities outside MSAs accounted for 6.6 percent of the U.S. population and 8.4 percent of larceny-theft offenses. Nonmetropolitan counties, which were home to 10.1 percent of the nation's population, accounted for 4.6 percent of the estimated number of larceny-theft offenses. (Table 2)

Population Groups: Trends and Rates

In cities, collectively, occurrences of larceny-theft declined 0.5 percent between 2007 and 2008. Cities with 1,000,000 ore more inhabitants, experienced an increase of 0.5 percent. Among the city groups, cities with 250,000 to 499,999 inhabitants experienced the greatest decrease (3.7 percent) followed by cities with fewer than 10,000 inhabitants (1.3 percent). In both metropolitan and nonmetropolitan counties larceny-theft increased, by 1.6 and 0.1 percent, respectively. (Table 12)

Based on reports of larceny-theft offenses from U.S. law enforcement agencies that submitted 12 months of complete data for 2008, this offense occurred at a rate of 2,200.1 offenses per 100,000 inhabitants. The collective rate for cities was 2,568.3 offenses per 100,000 inhabitants. Among city population groups, cities with 500,000 to 999,000 inhabitants had the highest larceny-theft rate, 3,269.3 incidents per 100,000 inhabitants. Cities with over 1,000,000 inhabitants had the lowest rate, at 2,278.5. In metropolitan counties, the rate was 1,557.8 incidents per 100,000 inhabitants; in nonmetropolitan counties, the rate was 1,027.0 incidents per 100,000 inhabitants. (Table 16)

Offense Analysis

Distribution

Thefts from motor vehicles accounted for the majority of larceny-theft offenses in 2008 (35.8 percent). Table 23 provides a further breakdown of larceny-theft offenses, including shoplifting, thefts from buildings, thefts of motor vehicle accessories, thefts of bicycles, thefts from coin-operated machines, purse snatching, and pocket picking. The "all other" category, which includes the less-defined types of larceny-theft, accounted for 31.9 percent of all offenses.

Loss by Dollar Value

Larceny-theft offenses cost victims an estimated $6.1 billion dollars in 2008, up from $5.8 billion in 2007. (Tables 1 and 23) The average value of property stolen was $925 per offense. Larceny-theft from buildings had the highest average dollar loss per offense at $1,540. Thefts from motor vehicles had an average dollar loss of $724 per offense; thefts of motor vehicle accessories, $532; purse snatching, $427; pocket picking, $563; thefts from coin-operated machines, $354; thefts of bicycles, $289; and shoplifting, $196. (Table 23)

Offenses in which the stolen property was valued at more than $200 accounted for 45.0 percent of all larceny-thefts. Table 23 provides further analysis, including the average dollar value per offense, of all offenses in the overall category of property crime.

MOTOR VEHICLE THEFT

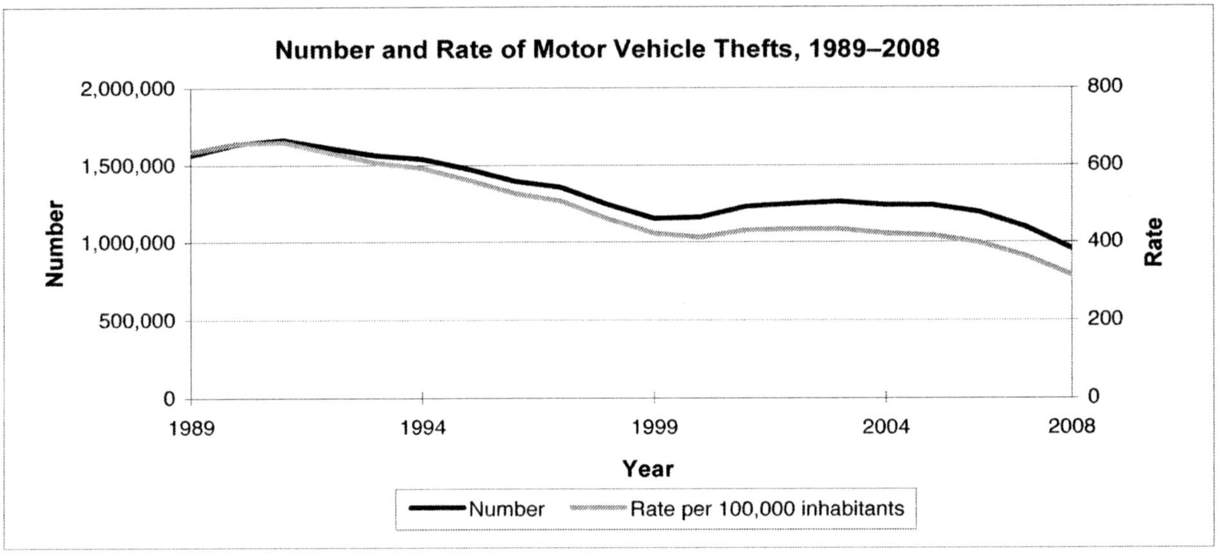

Definition

The UCR Program defines motor vehicle theft as the theft or attempted theft of a motor vehicle. The offense includes the stealing of automobiles, trucks, buses, motorcycles, snowmobiles, etc. The taking of a motor vehicle for temporary use by a person or persons with lawful access is excluded.

National Volume, Trends, and Rates

In 2008, an estimated 956,846 motor vehicle thefts took place in the United States. The estimated number of motor vehicle thefts declined 12.7 percent when compared with data from 2007, 22.7 percent when compared with 2004 figures, and 16.9 percent when compared with 1999 figures. (Table 1)

The estimated rate of motor vehicle theft in 2008 was 314.7 incidents per 100,000 inhabitants. In the 2-year, 5-year, and 10-year trend data, this rate showed decline: the 2008 rate was 13.4 percent lower than the 2007 rate, 25.3 percent lower than the 2004 rate, and 25.5 percent lower than the 1999 rate. (Table 1)

Regional Offense Trends and Rates

In order to analyze crime by geographic area, the UCR Program divides the United States into four regions: the Northeast, the Midwest, the South, and the West. (Appendix III provides a map delineating the regions.) This section provides a regional overview of motor vehicle theft.

The Northeast

The Northeast accounted for an estimated 18.1 percent of the nation's population in 2008 and experienced a 0.4 percent decline in population from 2007 to 2008. The region also accounted for an estimated 10.0 percent of its motor vehicle thefts. (Table 3) An estimated 95,813 motor vehicle thefts occurred in the Northeast in 2008, representing a 10.5 percent decrease from the 2007 estimate. This was the largest decline among the regions. The estimated rate of 174.4 motor vehicle thefts per 100,000 inhabitants in the Northeast in 2008 represented a 10.9 percent decline from the 2007 rate. (Table 4)

The Midwest

An estimated 21.9 percent of the country's population resided in the Midwest in 2008, and the region experienced a 0.3 growth in population from 2007 to 2008. The region accounted for 18.3 percent of the nation's motor vehicle thefts. (Table 3) The Midwest had an estimated 174,760 motor vehicle thefts in 2008, a 9.3 percent decrease from the previous year's total. The motor vehicle theft rate was estimated at 262.6 motor vehicles stolen per 100,000 inhabitants, a 12.6 percent decrease from the 2007 rate. (Table 4)

The South

The South, the nation's most populous region, was home to an estimated 36.7 percent of the U.S. population in 2008 and experienced a 1.1 percent growth in population from

2007 to 2008. This region accounted for 37.8 percent of the nation's motor vehicle thefts. (Table 3) The estimated 361,520 motor vehicle thefts in the South decreased 9.3 percent from the 2007 estimate. Motor vehicles in the South were stolen at an estimated rate of 323.6 per 100,000 inhabitants in 2008, a rate that was 10.3 percent lower than the 2007 rate. (Table 4)

The West

With approximately 23.3 percent of the U.S. population in 2008, the West experienced a 1.1 percent growth in population from 2007 to 2008. This region accounted for 33.9 percent of all motor vehicle thefts in the nation in 2008. (Table 3) An estimated 324,753 motor vehicle thefts occurred in this region. This number represented a 16.9 percent decrease from the previous year's estimate. The motor vehicle theft rate for the West was also lower in 2008 than in 2007; the 2008 rate of 458.3 motor vehicles stolen per 100,000 inhabitants was 17.8 percent lower than the 2007 rate. (Table 4)

Community Types

The UCR Program aggregates data by three community types: metropolitan statistical areas (MSAs), cities outside MSAs, and nonmetropolitan counties. MSAs are areas that include a principal city or urbanized area with at least 50,000 inhabitants and the county that contains the principal city and other adjacent counties that have, as defined by the U.S. Office of Management and Budget, a high degree of economic and social integration.

In 2008, the vast majority (83.5 percent) of the U.S. population resided in MSAs, where approximately 92.8 percent of motor vehicle thefts occurred. For 2008, the UCR Program estimated an overall rate of 349.5 motor vehicles stolen per 100,000 MSA inhabitants. Cities outside MSAs accounted for 3.3 percent of motor vehicle thefts, and nonmetropolitan counties accounted for 3.9 percent of motor vehicle thefts. The UCR Program estimated a 2008 rate of 159.9 motor vehicles stolen for every 100,000 inhabitants in cities outside MSAs and a rate of 124.0 motor vehicles stolen per 100,000 inhabitants in nonmetropolitan counties. (Table 2)

Population Groups: Trends and Rates

The UCR Program aggregates data by various population groups, which include cities, metropolitan counties, and nonmetropolitan counties. (A definition of these groups can be found in Appendix III.)

In cities, collectively, the number of motor vehicle thefts decreased 13.5 percent from 2007 to 2008. The number of motor vehicle thefts decreased for all city groups. Cities with 250,000 to 499,999 inhabitants experienced the greatest decline—15.6 percent. Both metropolitan and nonmetropolitan counties experienced decreases, at 11.0 percent and 5.4 percent, respectively. (Table 12)

In 2008, cities had a collective motor vehicle theft rate of 385.6 per 100,000 inhabitants. Among the population groups, cities with 500,000 to 999,999 inhabitants experienced the highest rate of motor vehicle thefts with 724.6 motor vehicle thefts per 100,000 inhabitants. Conversely, the nation's smallest cities, those with populations under 10,000, had the lowest rate of motor vehicle theft with 162.0 incidents per 100,000 in population. Within the county groups, metropolitan counties had a rate of 244.4 motor vehicles stolen per 100,000 inhabitants, while nonmetropolitan counties had a rate of 128.0 incidents per 100,000 inhabitants. (Table 16)

Offense Analysis

Based on the reports of law enforcement agencies, the UCR Program estimated the combined value of motor vehicles stolen nationwide in 2008 at approximately $6.4 billion. (Tables 1 and 23) In 2008, the average dollar value per motor vehicle stolen in the United States was $6,751. Automobiles were, by far, the most frequently stolen vehicle, accounting for 72.4 percent of all vehicles stolen. Trucks and buses accounted for 17.9 percent of stolen vehicles, and other vehicles accounted for 9.6 percent of stolen vehicles. (Expanded Motor Vehicle Theft Table)

By type of vehicle, automobiles were stolen at a rate of 239.9 cars per 100,000 inhabitants in 2008. Trucks and buses were stolen at a rate of 59.4 vehicles per 100,000 in population, and other types of vehicles were stolen at a rate of 31.9 vehicles per 100,000 inhabitants. (Table 19)

ARSON

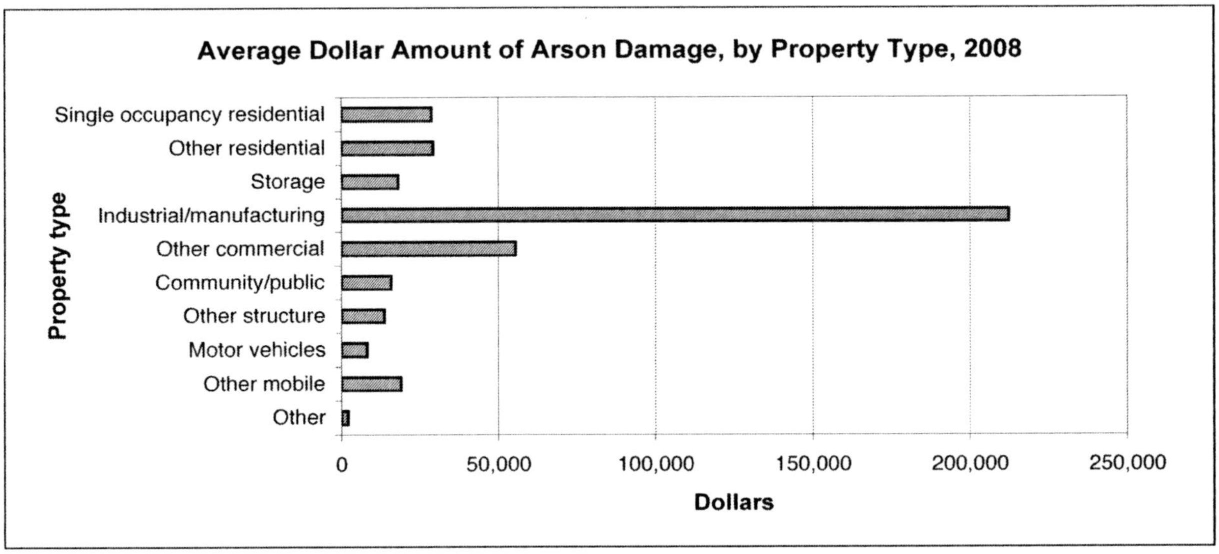

Definition

The UCR Program defines arson as any willful or malicious burning or attempt to burn (with or without intent to defraud) a dwelling house, public building, motor vehicle, aircraft, personal property of another, etc.

Data Collection

Only fires that investigators determined were willfully set (not fires labeled as "suspicious" or "of unknown origin") are included in this arson data collection. Points to consider regarding arson statistics include:

National offense rates per 100,000 inhabitants (found in Tables 1, 2, and 4) do not include arson data; the FBI presents rates for arson separately. Arson rates are calculated based upon data received from all law enforcement agencies that provide the UCR Program with data for 12 complete months.

Arson data collection does not include estimates for arson, because the degree of reporting arson offenses varies from agency to agency. Because of this unevenness of reporting, arson offenses are excluded from Tables 1 through 7, all of which contain offense estimations.

The number of arsons reported by individual law enforcement agencies is available in Tables 8 through 11. Arson trend data (which indicate year-to-year changes) can be found in Tables 12 through 15, and arson clearance data (crimes solved) can be found in Tables 25 through 28.

National Coverage

In 2008, 14,011 agencies (providing 1 to 12 months of data) reported 62,807 arson offenses. Of those agencies, 13,980 provided expanded offense data about 56,972 arsons. (Unpublished Expanded Arson Table 1; see Section I for more information)

Population Groups: Trends and Rates

The number of arsons reported in 2008 decreased 3.6 percent from the 2007 figure. Law enforcement agencies in the nation's cities collectively reported a 3.7 percent decline in the number of arsons from the 2007 figure. The number of arsons declined for all population groups. Among the population groups labeled *city,* the subset with 500,000 to 999,999 inhabitants had the largest year-to-year decrease in reported arsons, 8.2 percent. Agencies in the nation's metropolitan counties reported a 2.9 percent decrease in the number of arsons, and those in nonmetropolitan counties reported a 5.6 percent decline. (Table 12)

Arson rates were based on information received from 11,729 agencies that provided 12 months of complete arson data to the UCR Program. An examination of data indicated that in 2008, the highest rate among city groups—39.2 arsons per 100,000 inhabitants—was reported in cities with 250,000 or more inhabitants. Among cities with 250,000 or more inhabitants, those with a population of 250,000 to 499,999 had the highest rate at 45.0 per 100,000 inhabitants. Cities with 10,000 to 24,999 inhabitants had the lowest rate of arson at 17.9 per 100,000 inhabitants. Metropolitan counties had 20.1 arsons per 100,000 inhabitants, and nonmetropolitan counties had 15.4 arsons per 100,000 inhabitants, the lowest of all the population groups. (Expanded Arson Table 1)

Offense Analysis

The UCR Program breaks down arson offenses into three property categories: structural, mobile, and other. In addition, the structural property type is broken down into seven types of structures, and the mobile property type consists of two subgroupings. The program also collects information on the estimated dollar value of the damaged property.

Property Type

The total number of arsons decreased in 2008. Arsons for the structural property type decreased 1.5 percent and other arsons fell 8.2 percent. Arsons for the mobile property type increased 0.3 percent from 2007 to 2008. (Table 15)

Distribution by Property Type

Arsons involving structures (residential, storage, public, etc.) accounted for 43.4 percent of the total number of arson offenses; arsons involving mobile property accounted for 28.9 percent; and other types of property (such as crops, timber, fences, etc.) accounted for 27.7 percent of reported arsons. Of the arsons involving structures, 62.6 percent involved residential properties. Of the residential arsons, nearly three-fourths were single-occupancy residences. Nineteen percent of structures were not in use when the arson occurred. Mobile arsons accounted for 28.9 percent of all arsons. Within this category, nearly 95 percent of offenses involved the burning of motor vehicles. Other types of property, such as crops, timber, fences, etc., accounted for 27.7 percent of reported arson offenses. (Expanded Arson Table 2)

Dollar Loss

In monetary terms, the average dollar loss in 2008 for arson was $16,015. The average dollar loss for a structural arson was $29,701. Within the structural arson category, the industrial/manufacturing subcategory had the highest average dollar loss at $212,388. Within that same category, single-occupancy dwellings had an average dollar loss of $28,788. Mobile property had an average dollar loss of $8,766. Other property types had an average dollar loss of $2,099. (Expanded Arson Table 2)

Table 1. Crime in the United States, by Volume and Rate per 100,000 Inhabitants, 1989–2008

(Number, rate per 100,000 population, percent.)

Year	Population[1]	Violent crime		Murder and nonnegligent manslaughter		Forcible rape		Robbery		Aggravated assault	
		Number	Rate	Number	Rate	Number	Rate	Number	Rate	Number	Rate
1989	246,819,230	1,646,037	666.9	21,500	8.7	94,504	38.3	578,326	234.3	951,707	385.6
1990	249,464,396	1,820,127	729.6	23,438	9.4	102,555	41.1	639,271	256.3	1,054,863	422.9
1991	252,153,092	1,911,767	758.2	24,703	9.8	106,593	42.3	687,732	272.7	1,092,739	433.4
1992	255,029,699	1,932,274	757.7	23,760	9.3	109,062	42.8	672,478	263.7	1,126,974	441.9
1993	257,782,608	1,926,017	747.1	24,526	9.5	106,014	41.1	659,870	256.0	1,135,607	440.5
1994	260,327,021	1,857,670	713.6	23,326	9.0	102,216	39.3	618,949	237.8	1,113,179	427.6
1995	262,803,276	1,798,792	684.5	21,606	8.2	97,470	37.1	580,509	220.9	1,099,207	418.3
1996	265,228,572	1,688,540	636.6	19,645	7.4	96,252	36.3	535,594	201.9	1,037,049	391.0
1997	267,783,607	1,636,096	611.0	18,208	6.8	96,153	35.9	498,534	186.2	1,023,201	382.1
1998	270,248,003	1,533,887	567.6	16,974	6.3	93,144	34.5	447,186	165.5	976,583	361.4
1999	272,690,813	1,426,044	523.0	15,522	5.7	89,411	32.8	409,371	150.1	911,740	334.3
2000	281,421,906	1,425,486	506.5	15,586	5.5	90,178	32.0	408,016	145.0	911,706	324.0
2001[2]	285,317,559	1,439,480	504.5	16,037	5.6	90,863	31.8	423,557	148.5	909,023	318.6
2002	287,973,924	1,423,677	494.4	16,229	5.6	95,235	33.1	420,806	146.1	891,407	309.5
2003	290,788,976	1,383,676	475.8	16,528	5.7	93,883	32.3	414,235	142.5	859,030	295.4
2004	293,656,842	1,360,088	463.2	16,148	5.5	95,089	32.4	401,470	136.7	847,381	288.6
2005	296,507,061	1,390,745	469.0	16,740	5.6	94,347	31.8	417,438	140.8	862,220	290.8
2006	299,398,484	1,418,043	473.6	17,030	5.7	92,757	31.0	447,403	149.4	860,853	287.5
2007	301,621,157	1,408,337	466.9	16,929	5.6	90,427	30.0	445,125	147.6	855,856	283.8
2008	304,059,724	1,382,012	454.5	16,272	5.4	89,000	29.3	441,855	145.3	834,885	274.6

Year	Property crime		Burglary		Larceny-theft		Motor vehicle theft	
	Number	Rate	Number	Rate	Number	Rate	Number	Rate
1989	12,605,412	5,107.1	3,168,170	1,283.6	7,872,442	3,189.6	1,564,800	634.0
1990	12,655,486	5,073.1	3,073,909	1,232.2	7,945,670	3,185.1	1,635,907	655.8
1991	12,961,116	5,140.2	3,157,150	1,252.1	8,142,228	3,229.1	1,661,738	659.0
1992	12,505,917	4,903.7	2,979,884	1,168.4	7,915,199	3,103.6	1,610,834	631.6
1993	12,218,777	4,740.0	2,834,808	1,099.7	7,820,909	3,033.9	1,563,060	606.3
1994	12,131,873	4,660.2	2,712,774	1,042.1	7,879,812	3,026.9	1,539,287	591.3
1995	12,063,935	4,590.5	2,593,784	987.0	7,997,710	3,043.2	1,472,441	560.3
1996	11,805,323	4,451.0	2,506,400	945.0	7,904,685	2,980.3	1,394,238	525.7
1997	11,558,475	4,316.3	2,460,526	918.8	7,743,760	2,891.8	1,354,189	505.7
1998	10,951,827	4,052.5	2,332,735	863.2	7,376,311	2,729.5	1,242,781	459.9
1999	10,208,334	3,743.6	2,100,739	770.4	6,955,520	2,550.7	1,152,075	422.5
2000	10,182,584	3,618.3	2,050,992	728.8	6,971,590	2,477.3	1,160,002	412.2
2001[2]	10,437,189	3,658.1	2,116,531	741.8	7,092,267	2,485.7	1,228,391	430.5
2002	10,455,277	3,630.6	2,151,252	747.0	7,057,379	2,450.7	1,246,646	432.9
2003	10,442,862	3,591.2	2,154,834	741.0	7,026,802	2,416.5	1,261,226	433.7
2004	10,319,386	3,514.1	2,144,446	730.3	6,937,089	2,362.3	1,237,851	421.5
2005	10,174,754	3,431.5	2,155,448	726.9	6,783,447	2,287.8	1,235,859	416.8
2006	9,983,568	3,334.5	2,183,746	729.4	6,607,013	2,206.8	1,192,809	398.4
2007	9,843,481	3,263.5	2,179,140	722.5	6,568,572	2,177.8	1,095,769	363.3
2008	9,767,915	3,212.5	2,222,196	730.8	6,588,873	2,167.0	956,846	314.7

[1] Populations are U.S. Census Bureau provisional estimates as of July 1 for each year except 1990 and 2000, which are decennial census counts.
[2] The murder and nonnegligent homicides that occurred as a result of the events of September 11, 2001, are not included in this table.

Table 1A. Crime in the United States, Percent Change in Volume and Rate per 100,000 Inhabitants for 2 Years, 5 Years, and 10 Years

(Percent change.)

Year	Violent crime		Murder and nonnegligent manslaughter		Forcible rape		Robbery		Aggravated assault	
	Number	Rate	Number	Rate	Number	Rate	Number	Rate	Number	Rate
2007–2008	-1.9	-2.7	-3.9	-4.7	-1.6	-2.4	-0.7	-1.5	-2.5	-3.2
2004–2008	+1.6	-1.9	+0.8	-2.7	-6.4	-9.6	+10.1	+6.3	-1.5	-4.8
1999–2008	-3.1	-13.1	+4.8	-6.0	-0.5	-10.7	+7.9	-3.2	-8.4	-17.9

Year	Property crime		Burglary		Larceny-theft		Motor vehicle theft	
	Number	Rate	Number	Rate	Number	Rate	Number	Rate
2007–2008	-0.8	-1.6	+2.0	+1.2	+0.3	-0.5	-12.7	-13.4
2004–2008	-5.3	-8.6	+3.6	+0.1	-5.0	-8.3	-22.7	-25.3
1999–2008	-4.3	-14.2	+5.8	-5.1	-5.3	-15.0	-16.9	-25.5

Table 2. Crime in the United States, by Community Type, 2008

(Number, percent, rate per 100,000 population.)

Area	Population[1]	Violent crime	Murder and non-negligent manslaughter	Forcible rape	Robbery	Aggravated assault	Property crime	Burglary	Larceny-theft	Motor vehicle theft
United States Total	304,059,724	1,382,012	16,272	89,000	441,855	834,885	9,767,915	2,222,196	6,588,873	956,846
Rate per 100,000 inhabitants		454.5	5.4	29.3	145.3	274.6	3,212.5	730.8	2,167.0	314.7
Metropolitan Statistical Areas										
Area actually reporting[2]	254,002,827	1,168,181	13,723	68,494	397,696	688,268	8,083,781	1,804,719	5,428,750	850,312
Estimated total	96.0%	1,242,047	14,550	74,339	423,309	729,849	8,514,199	1,894,453	5,732,128	887,618
Rate per 100,000 inhabitants	100.0%	489.0	5.7	29.3	166.7	287.3	3,352.0	745.8	2,256.7	349.5
Cities Outside Metropolitan Areas	19,957,718									
Area actually reporting[2]	87.6%	69,858	605	6,568	11,787	50,898	657,892	142,752	486,482	28,658
Estimated total	100.0%	78,232	693	7,620	13,387	56,532	747,713	162,443	553,355	31,915
Rate per 100,000 inhabitants		392.0	3.5	38.2	67.1	283.3	3,746.5	813.9	2,772.6	159.9
Nonmetropolitan Counties	30,099,179									
Area actually reporting[2]	90.0%	57,121	945	6,118	4,743	45,315	464,029	151,350	277,937	34,742
Estimated total	100.0%	61,733	1,029	7,041	5,159	48,504	506,003	165,300	303,390	37,313
Rate per 100,000 inhabitants		205.1	3.4	23.4	17.1	161.1	1,681.1	549.2	1,008.0	124.0

[1] Population figures are U.S. Census Bureau provisional estimates as of July 1, 2008.
[2] The percentage reported under "Area actually reporting" is based on the population covered by agencies providing 3 months or more of crime reports to the FBI.

Table 3. Crime in the United States, Population and Offense Distribution, by Region, 2008

(Percent distribution.)

Region	Population	Violent crime	Murder and non-negligent manslaughter	Forcible rape	Robbery	Aggravated assault	Property crime	Burglary	Larceny-theft	Motor vehicle theft
United States Total[1]	100.0	100.0	100.0	100.0	100.0	100.0	100.0	100.0	100.0	100.0
Northeast	18.1	14.7	14.1	12.3	17.2	13.7	12.6	10.6	13.7	10.0
Midwest	21.9	19.3	19.7	25.4	19.1	18.7	20.9	20.4	21.4	18.3
South	36.7	43.2	45.2	38.2	40.2	45.2	43.2	47.3	42.7	37.8
West	23.3	22.8	21.1	24.1	23.5	22.4	23.2	21.7	22.2	33.9

[1] Because of rounding, the percentages may not add to 100.0.

Table 4. Crime, by Region, Geographic Division, and State, 2007–2008

(Number, rate per 100,000 population, percent.)

Area	Population[1]	Violent crime		Murder and nonnegligent manslaughter		Forcible rape		Robbery		Aggravated assault	
		Number	Rate	Number	Rate	Number	Rate	Number	Rate	Number	Rate
UNITED STATES TOTAL[2,3,4]											
2007	301,621,157	1,408,337	466.9	16,929	5.6	90,427	30.0	445,125	147.6	855,856	283.8
2008	304,059,724	1,382,012	454.5	16,272	5.4	89,000	29.3	441,855	145.3	834,885	274.6
Percent change		-1.9	-2.7	-3.9	-4.7	-1.6	-2.4	-0.7	-1.5	-2.5	-3.2
Northeast											
2007	54,680,626	203,632	372.4	2,261	4.1	10,821	19.8	75,326	137.8	115,224	210.7
2008	54,924,779	203,654	370.8	2,293	4.2	10,981	20.0	76,048	138.5	114,332	208.2
Percent change		*	-0.4	+1.4	+1.0	+1.5	+1.0	+1.0	+0.5	-0.8	-1.2
New England											
2007	14,264,185	43,334	303.8	357	2.5	3,395	23.8	12,225	85.7	27,357	191.8
2008	14,303,542	46,682	326.4	380	2.7	3,580	25.0	12,696	88.8	30,026	209.9
Percent change		+7.7	+7.4	+6.4	+6.1	+5.4	+5.2	+3.9	+3.6	+9.8	+9.5
Connecticut											
2007	3,502,309	8,965	256.0	106	3.0	658	18.8	3,607	103.0	4,594	131.2
2008	3,501,252	10,427	297.8	123	3.5	674	19.3	3,907	111.6	5,723	163.5
Percent change		+16.3	+16.3	+16.0	+16.1	+2.4	+2.5	+8.3	+8.3	+24.6	+24.6
Maine											
2007	1,317,207	1,554	118.0	21	1.6	391	29.7	349	26.5	793	60.2
2008	1,316,456	1,547	117.5	31	2.4	375	28.5	333	25.3	808	61.4
Percent change		-0.5	-0.4	+47.6	+47.7	-4.1	-4.0	-4.6	-4.5	+1.9	+1.9
Massachusetts											
2007	6,449,755	27,832	431.5	184	2.9	1,634	25.3	7,006	108.6	19,008	294.7
2008	6,497,967	29,174	449.0	167	2.6	1,736	26.7	7,069	108.8	20,202	310.9
Percent change		+4.8	+4.0	-9.2	-9.9	+6.2	+5.5	+0.9	+0.2	+6.3	+5.5
New Hampshire											
2007	1,315,828	1,807	137.3	15	1.1	333	25.3	432	32.8	1,027	78.0
2008	1,315,809	2,069	157.2	13	1.0	391	29.7	419	31.8	1,246	94.7
Percent change		+14.5	+14.5	-13.3	-13.3	+17.4	+17.4	-3.0	-3.0	+21.3	+21.3
Rhode Island											
2007	1,057,832	2,404	227.3	19	1.8	256	24.2	751	71.0	1,378	130.3
2008	1,050,788	2,621	249.4	29	2.8	277	26.4	879	83.7	1,436	136.7
Percent change		+9.0	+9.8	+52.6	+53.7	+8.2	+8.9	+17.0	+17.8	+4.2	+4.9
Vermont											
2007	621,254	772	124.3	12	1.9	123	19.8	80	12.9	557	89.7
2008	621,270	844	135.9	17	2.7	127	20.4	89	14.3	611	98.3
Percent change		+9.3	+9.3	+41.7	+41.7	+3.3	+3.2	+11.3	+11.2	+9.7	+9.7
Middle Atlantic											
2007	40,416,441	160,298	396.6	1,904	4.7	7,426	18.4	63,101	156.1	87,867	217.4
2008	40,621,237	156,972	386.4	1,913	4.7	7,401	18.2	63,352	156.0	84,306	207.5
Percent change		-2.1	-2.6	+0.5	*	-0.3	-0.8	+0.4	-0.1	-4.1	-4.5
New Jersey											
2007	8,685,920	28,601	329.3	380	4.4	1,050	12.1	12,549	144.5	14,622	168.3
2008	8,682,661	28,351	326.5	376	4.3	1,122	12.9	12,701	146.3	14,152	163.0
Percent change		-0.9	-0.8	-1.1	-1.0	+6.9	+6.9	+1.2	+1.2	-3.2	-3.2
New York											
2007	19,297,729	79,915	414.1	801	4.2	2,926	15.2	31,094	161.1	45,094	233.7
2008	19,490,297	77,585	398.1	836	4.3	2,801	14.4	31,778	163.0	42,170	216.4
Percent change		-2.9	-3.9	+4.4	+3.3	-4.3	-5.2	+2.2	+1.2	-6.5	-7.4
Pennsylvania											
2007	12,432,792	51,782	416.5	723	5.8	3,450	27.7	19,458	156.5	28,151	226.4
2008	12,448,279	51,036	410.0	701	5.6	3,478	27.9	18,873	151.6	27,984	224.8
Percent change		-1.4	-1.6	-3.0	-3.2	+0.8	+0.7	-3.0	-3.1	-0.6	-0.7
Midwest[2,3]											
2007	66,388,795	273,018	411.2	3,225	4.9	22,863	34.4	84,674	127.5	162,256	244.4
2008	66,561,448	266,312	400.1	3,198	4.8	22,624	34.0	84,385	126.8	156,105	234.5
Percent change		-2.5	-2.7	-0.8	-1.1	-1.0	-1.3	-0.3	-0.6	-3.8	-4.0
East North Central[2,3]											
2007	46,338,216	199,337	430.2	2,483	5.4	16,099	34.7	68,120	147.0	112,635	243.1
2008	46,395,654	194,647	419.5	2,348	5.1	15,879	34.2	68,395	147.4	108,025	232.8
Percent change		-2.4	-2.5	-5.4	-5.6	-1.4	-1.5	+0.4	+0.3	-4.1	-4.2
Illinois[2,3]											
2007	12,852,548	68,528	533.2	752	5.9	4,103	31.9	23,100	179.7	40,573	315.7
2008	12,901,563	67,780	525.4	790	6.1	4,118	31.9	24,054	186.4	38,818	300.9
Percent change		-1.1	-1.5	+5.1	+4.7	+0.4	*	+4.1	+3.7	-4.3	-4.7

[1] Populations are U.S. Census Bureau provisional estimates as of July 1, 2008, and July 1, 2007.
[2] Limited data for 2007 and 2008 were available for Illinois.
[3] The data collection methodology for the offense of forcible rape used by the Illinois and the Minnesota state UCR Programs (with the exception of Rockford, IL, and Minneapolis and St. Paul, MN) does not comply with national UCR guidelines. Consequently, their state figures for forcible rape (with the exception of Rockford, IL, and Minneapolis and St. Paul, MN) have been estimated for inclusion in this table.
* Less than one-tenth of 1 percent.

Table 4. Crime, by Region, Geographic Division, and State, 2007–2008—*Continued*

(Number, rate per 100,000 population, percent.)

Area	Property crime		Burglary		Larceny-theft		Motor vehicle theft	
	Number	Rate	Number	Rate	Number	Rate	Number	Rate
UNITED STATES TOTAL[2,3,4]								
2007	9,843,481	3,263.5	2,179,140	722.5	6,568,572	2,177.8	1,095,769	363.3
2008	9,767,915	3,212.5	2,222,196	730.8	6,588,873	2,167.0	956,846	314.7
Percent change	-0.8	-1.6	+2.0	+1.2	+0.3	-0.5	-12.7	-13.4
Northeast								
2007	1,204,978	2,203.7	229,187	419.1	868,763	1,588.8	107,028	195.7
2008	1,235,168	2,248.8	235,881	429.5	903,474	1,644.9	95,813	174.4
Percent change	+2.5	+2.0	+2.9	+2.5	+4.0	+3.5	-10.5	-10.9
New England								
2007	337,359	2,365.1	70,828	496.5	235,947	1,654.1	30,584	214.4
2008	347,477	2,429.3	71,125	497.3	248,304	1,736.0	28,048	196.1
Percent change	+3.0	+2.7	+0.4	+0.1	+5.2	+4.9	-8.3	-8.5
Connecticut								
2007	84,052	2,399.9	15,162	432.9	59,723	1,705.2	9,167	261.7
2008	86,087	2,458.7	15,011	428.7	62,113	1,774.0	8,963	256.0
Percent change	+2.4	+2.5	-1.0	-1.0	+4.0	+4.0	-2.2	-2.2
Maine								
2007	31,992	2,428.8	6,676	506.8	24,057	1,826.4	1,259	95.6
2008	32,285	2,452.4	6,522	495.4	24,587	1,867.7	1,176	89.3
Percent change	+0.9	+1.0	-2.3	-2.3	+2.2	+2.3	-6.6	-6.5
Massachusetts								
2007	154,246	2,391.5	35,662	552.9	103,592	1,606.1	14,992	232.4
2008	155,959	2,400.1	36,094	555.5	107,128	1,648.6	12,737	196.0
Percent change	+1.1	+0.4	+1.2	+0.5	+3.4	+2.6	-15.0	-15.7
New Hampshire								
2007	24,896	1,892.0	4,986	378.9	18,611	1,414.4	1,299	98.7
2008	27,526	2,091.9	4,286	325.7	21,853	1,660.8	1,387	105.4
Percent change	+10.6	+10.6	-14.0	-14.0	+17.4	+17.4	+6.8	+6.8
Rhode Island								
2007	27,743	2,622.6	5,236	495.0	19,281	1,822.7	3,226	305.0
2008	29,849	2,840.6	5,750	547.2	20,899	1,988.9	3,200	304.5
Percent change	+7.6	+8.3	+9.8	+10.6	+8.4	+9.1	-0.8	-0.1
Vermont								
2007	14,430	2,322.7	3,106	500.0	10,683	1,719.6	641	103.2
2008	15,771	2,538.5	3,462	557.2	11,724	1,887.1	585	94.2
Percent change	+9.3	+9.3	+11.5	+11.5	+9.7	+9.7	-8.7	-8.7
Middle Atlantic								
2007	867,619	2,146.7	158,359	391.8	632,816	1,565.7	76,444	189.1
2008	887,691	2,185.3	164,756	405.6	655,170	1,612.9	67,765	166.8
Percent change	+2.3	+1.8	+4.0	+3.5	+3.5	+3.0	-11.4	-11.8
New Jersey								
2007	192,226	2,213.1	37,482	431.5	132,791	1,528.8	21,953	252.7
2008	199,126	2,293.4	40,401	465.3	138,545	1,595.7	20,180	232.4
Percent change	+3.6	+3.6	+7.8	+7.8	+4.3	+4.4	-8.1	-8.0
New York								
2007	381,816	1,978.6	64,857	336.1	288,929	1,497.2	28,030	145.3
2008	388,533	1,993.5	65,735	337.3	297,684	1,527.3	25,114	128.9
Percent change	+1.8	+0.8	+1.4	+0.4	+3.0	+2.0	-10.4	-11.3
Pennsylvania								
2007	293,577	2,361.3	56,020	450.6	211,096	1,697.9	26,461	212.8
2008	300,032	2,410.2	58,620	470.9	218,941	1,758.8	22,471	180.5
Percent change	+2.2	+2.1	+4.6	+4.5	+3.7	+3.6	-15.1	-15.2
Midwest[2,3]								
2007	2,095,999	3,157.2	448,126	675.0	1,448,457	2,181.8	199,416	300.4
2008	2,041,087	3,066.5	453,383	681.1	1,412,944	2,122.8	174,760	262.6
Percent change	-2.6	-2.9	+1.2	+0.9	-2.5	-2.7	-12.4	-12.6
East North Central[2,3]								
2007	1,456,791	3,143.8	324,218	699.7	989,766	2,136.0	142,807	308.2
2008	1,431,644	3,085.7	331,812	715.2	973,512	2,098.3	126,320	272.3
Percent change	-1.7	-1.8	+2.3	+2.2	-1.6	-1.8	-11.5	-11.7
Illinois[2,3]								
2007	377,322	2,935.8	75,524	587.6	267,911	2,084.5	33,887	263.7
2008	378,355	2,932.6	78,968	612.1	266,815	2,068.1	32,572	252.5
Percent change	+0.3	-0.1	+4.6	+4.2	-0.4	-0.8	-3.9	-4.2

[2] Limited data for 2007 and 2008 were available for Illinois.

[3] The data collection methodology for the offense of forcible rape used by the Illinois and the Minnesota state UCR Programs (with the exception of Rockford, IL, and Minneapolis and St. Paul, MN) does not comply with national UCR guidelines. Consequently, their state figures for forcible rape (with the exception of Rockford, IL, and Minneapolis and St. Paul, MN) have been estimated for inclusion in this table.

Table 4. Crime, by Region, Geographic Division, and State, 2007–2008—*Continued*

(Number, rate per 100,000 population, percent.)

Area	Population[1]	Violent crime		Murder and nonnegligent manslaughter		Forcible rape		Robbery		Aggravated assault	
		Number	Rate	Number	Rate	Number	Rate	Number	Rate	Number	Rate
Indiana											
2007	6,345,289	21,165	333.6	356	5.6	1,742	27.5	7,872	124.1	11,195	176.4
2008	6,376,792	21,283	333.8	327	5.1	1,720	27.0	7,532	118.1	11,704	183.5
Percent change		+0.6	+0.1	-8.1	-8.6	-1.3	-1.8	-4.3	-4.8	+4.5	+4.0
Michigan											
2007	10,071,822	53,988	536.0	676	6.7	4,579	45.5	13,414	133.2	35,319	350.7
2008	10,003,422	50,166	501.5	542	5.4	4,502	45.0	12,964	129.6	32,158	321.5
Percent change		-7.1	-6.4	-19.8	-19.3	-1.7	-1.0	-3.4	-2.7	-8.9	-8.3
Ohio											
2007	11,466,917	39,360	343.2	516	4.5	4,452	38.8	18,260	159.2	16,132	140.7
2008	11,485,910	39,997	348.2	543	4.7	4,419	38.5	18,719	163.0	16,316	142.1
Percent change		+1.6	+1.5	+5.2	+5.1	-0.7	-0.9	+2.5	+2.3	+1.1	+1.0
Wisconsin											
2007	5,601,640	16,296	290.9	183	3.3	1,223	21.8	5,474	97.7	9,416	168.1
2008	5,627,967	15,421	274.0	146	2.6	1,120	19.9	5,126	91.1	9,029	160.4
Percent change		-5.4	-5.8	-20.2	-20.6	-8.4	-8.9	-6.4	-6.8	-4.1	-4.6
West North Central[3]											
2007	20,050,579	73,681	367.5	742	3.7	6,764	33.7	16,554	82.6	49,621	247.5
2008	20,165,794	71,665	355.4	850	4.2	6,745	33.4	15,990	79.3	48,080	238.4
Percent change		-2.7	-3.3	+14.6	+13.9	-0.3	-0.9	-3.4	-4.0	-3.1	-3.7
Iowa											
2007	2,988,046	8,805	294.7	37	1.2	904	30.3	1,313	43.9	6,551	219.2
2008	3,002,555	8,520	283.8	76	2.5	888	29.6	1,248	41.6	6,308	210.1
Percent change		-3.2	-3.7	+105.4	+104.4	-1.8	-2.2	-5.0	-5.4	-3.7	-4.2
Kansas											
2007	2,775,997	12,566	452.7	107	3.9	1,231	44.3	2,016	72.6	9,212	331.8
2008	2,802,134	11,505	410.6	113	4.0	1,190	42.5	1,684	60.1	8,518	304.0
Percent change		-8.4	-9.3	+5.6	+4.6	-3.3	-4.2	-16.5	-17.2	-7.5	-8.4
Minnesota[3]											
2007	5,197,621	15,003	288.7	116	2.2	1,873	36.0	4,770	91.8	8,244	158.6
2008	5,220,393	13,717	262.8	109	2.1	1,805	34.6	4,177	80.0	7,626	146.1
Percent change		-8.6	-9.0	-6.0	-6.4	-3.6	-4.1	-12.4	-12.8	-7.5	-7.9
Missouri											
2007	5,878,415	29,682	504.9	385	6.5	1,714	29.2	7,165	121.9	20,418	347.3
2008	5,911,605	29,819	504.4	455	7.7	1,615	27.3	7,390	125.0	20,359	344.4
Percent change		+0.5	-0.1	+18.2	+17.5	-5.8	-6.3	+3.1	+2.6	-0.3	-0.8
Nebraska											
2007	1,774,571	5,367	302.4	68	3.8	527	29.7	1,108	62.4	3,664	206.5
2008	1,783,432	5,416	303.7	68	3.8	583	32.7	1,299	72.8	3,466	194.3
Percent change		+0.9	+0.4	0.0	-0.5	+10.6	+10.1	+17.2	+16.7	-5.4	-5.9
North Dakota											
2007	639,715	911	142.4	12	1.9	207	32.4	70	10.9	622	97.2
2008	641,481	1,068	166.5	3	0.5	232	36.2	72	11.2	761	118.6
Percent change		+17.2	+16.9	-75.0	-75.1	+12.1	+11.8	+2.9	+2.6	+22.3	+22.0
South Dakota											
2007	796,214	1,347	169.2	17	2.1	308	38.7	112	14.1	910	114.3
2008	804,194	1,620	201.4	26	3.2	432	53.7	120	14.9	1,042	129.6
Percent change		+20.3	+19.1	+52.9	+51.4	+40.3	+38.9	+7.1	+6.1	+14.5	+13.4
South[4]											
2007	110,454,786	606,667	549.2	7,759	7.0	35,073	31.8	179,728	162.7	384,107	347.8
2008	111,718,549	596,425	533.9	7,348	6.6	33,972	30.4	177,691	159.1	377,414	337.8
Percent change		-1.7	-2.8	-5.3	-6.4	-3.1	-4.2	-1.1	-2.3	-1.7	-2.9
South Atlantic[4]											
2007	57,860,260	332,090	574.0	4,097	7.1	16,274	28.1	103,124	178.2	208,595	360.5
2008	58,398,377	323,332	553.7	3,877	6.6	15,888	27.2	102,360	175.3	201,207	344.5
Percent change		-2.6	-3.5	-5.4	-6.2	-2.4	-3.3	-0.7	-1.7	-3.5	-4.4
Delaware											
2007	864,764	5,960	689.2	37	4.3	336	38.9	1,706	197.3	3,881	448.8
2008	873,092	6,141	703.4	57	6.5	366	41.9	1,838	210.5	3,880	444.4
Percent change		+3.0	+2.1	+54.1	+52.6	+8.9	+7.9	+7.7	+6.7	*	-1.0
District of Columbia[4]											
2007	588,292	8,320	1,414.3	181	30.8	192	32.6	4,261	724.3	3,686	626.6
2008	591,833	8,509	1,437.7	186	31.4	186	31.4	4,430	748.5	3,707	626.4
Percent change		+2.3	+1.7	+2.8	+2.1	-3.1	-3.7	+4.0	+3.3	+0.6	*
Florida											
2007	18,251,243	131,880	722.6	1,201	6.6	6,151	33.7	38,162	209.1	86,366	473.2
2008	18,328,340	126,265	688.9	1,168	6.4	5,972	32.6	36,273	197.9	82,852	452.0
Percent change		-4.3	-4.7	-2.7	-3.2	-2.9	-3.3	-4.9	-5.3	-4.1	-4.5

[3] The data collection methodology for the offense of forcible rape used by the Illinois and the Minnesota state UCR Programs (with the exception of Rockford, IL, and Minneapolis and St. Paul, MN) does not comply with national UCR guidelines. Consequently, their state figures for forcible rape (with the exception of Rockford, IL, and Minneapolis and St. Paul, MN) have been estimated for inclusion in this table.

[4] Includes offenses reported by the Zoological Police and the Metro Transit Police.

* Less than one-tenth of 1 percent.

Table 4. Crime, by Region, Geographic Division, and State, 2007–2008—*Continued*

(Number, rate per 100,000 population, percent.)

Area	Property crime		Burglary		Larceny-theft		Motor vehicle theft	
	Number	Rate	Number	Rate	Number	Rate	Number	Rate
Indiana								
2007	215,526	3,396.6	46,919	739.4	149,050	2,349.0	19,557	308.2
2008	212,715	3,335.8	48,645	762.8	146,615	2,299.2	17,455	273.7
Percent change	-1.3	-1.8	+3.7	+3.2	-1.6	-2.1	-10.7	-11.2
Michigan								
2007	308,775	3,065.7	75,428	748.9	191,196	1,898.3	42,151	418.5
2008	293,585	2,934.8	74,176	741.5	183,168	1,831.1	36,241	362.3
Percent change	-4.9	-4.3	-1.7	-1.0	-4.2	-3.5	-14.0	-13.4
Ohio								
2007	396,209	3,455.2	98,508	859.1	263,922	2,301.6	33,779	294.6
2008	391,862	3,411.7	102,544	892.8	260,786	2,270.5	28,532	248.4
Percent change	-1.1	-1.3	+4.1	+3.9	-1.2	-1.4	-15.5	-15.7
Wisconsin								
2007	158,959	2,837.7	27,839	497.0	117,687	2,100.9	13,433	239.8
2008	155,127	2,756.4	27,479	488.3	116,128	2,063.4	11,520	204.7
Percent change	-2.4	-2.9	-1.3	-1.8	-1.3	-1.8	-14.2	-14.6
West North Central[3]								
2007	639,208	3,188.0	123,908	618.0	458,691	2,287.7	56,609	282.3
2008	609,443	3,022.2	121,571	602.9	439,432	2,179.1	48,440	240.2
Percent change	-4.7	-5.2	-1.9	-2.4	-4.2	-4.7	-14.4	-14.9
Iowa								
2007	78,154	2,615.6	16,941	567.0	56,328	1,885.1	4,885	163.5
2008	72,689	2,420.9	16,450	547.9	51,907	1,728.8	4,332	144.3
Percent change	-7.0	-7.4	-2.9	-3.4	-7.8	-8.3	-11.3	-11.7
Kansas								
2007	102,120	3,678.7	20,263	729.9	73,293	2,640.2	8,564	308.5
2008	94,635	3,377.2	19,612	699.9	67,628	2,413.4	7,395	263.9
Percent change	-7.3	-8.2	-3.2	-4.1	-7.7	-8.6	-13.7	-14.5
Minnesota[3]								
2007	157,829	3,036.6	29,670	570.8	115,633	2,224.7	12,526	241.0
2008	148,810	2,850.6	26,410	505.9	112,322	2,151.6	10,078	193.1
Percent change	-5.7	-6.1	-11.0	-11.4	-2.9	-3.3	-19.5	-19.9
Missouri								
2007	219,759	3,738.4	43,446	739.1	152,529	2,594.7	23,784	404.6
2008	216,585	3,663.7	45,788	774.5	150,032	2,537.9	20,765	351.3
Percent change	-1.4	-2.0	+5.4	+4.8	-1.6	-2.2	-12.7	-13.2
Nebraska								
2007	56,102	3,161.4	9,046	509.8	41,855	2,358.6	5,201	293.1
2008	51,338	2,878.6	8,775	492.0	38,375	2,151.8	4,188	234.8
Percent change	-8.5	-8.9	-3.0	-3.5	-8.3	-8.8	-19.5	-19.9
North Dakota								
2007	12,088	1,889.6	2,164	338.3	9,010	1,408.4	914	142.9
2008	12,152	1,894.4	2,106	328.3	9,164	1,428.6	882	137.5
Percent change	+0.5	+0.3	-2.7	-2.9	+1.7	+1.4	-3.5	-3.8
South Dakota								
2007	13,156	1,652.3	2,378	298.7	10,043	1,261.3	735	92.3
2008	13,234	1,645.6	2,430	302.2	10,004	1,244.0	800	99.5
Percent change	+0.6	-0.4	+2.2	+1.2	-0.4	-1.4	+8.8	+7.8
South[4]								
2007	4,199,649	3,802.1	1,018,197	921.8	2,782,863	2,519.5	398,589	360.9
2008	4,223,835	3,780.8	1,051,616	941.3	2,810,699	2,515.9	361,520	323.6
Percent change	+0.6	-0.6	+3.3	+2.1	+1.0	-0.1	-9.3	-10.3
South Atlantic[4]								
2007	2,164,134	3,740.3	516,401	892.5	1,430,636	2,472.6	217,097	375.2
2008	2,212,433	3,788.5	539,121	923.2	1,474,978	2,525.7	198,334	339.6
Percent change	+2.2	+1.3	+4.4	+3.4	+3.1	+2.1	-8.6	-9.5
Delaware								
2007	29,143	3,370.1	6,341	733.3	20,486	2,369.0	2,316	267.8
2008	31,303	3,585.3	6,760	774.3	22,002	2,520.0	2,541	291.0
Percent change	+7.4	+6.4	+6.6	+5.6	+7.4	+6.4	+9.7	+8.7
District of Columbia[4]								
2007	28,908	4,913.9	3,926	667.4	17,382	2,954.7	7,600	1,291.9
2008	30,211	5,104.6	3,788	640.0	19,958	3,372.2	6,465	1,092.4
Percent change	+4.5	+3.9	-3.5	-4.1	+14.8	+14.1	-14.9	-15.4
Florida								
2007	746,347	4,089.3	181,833	996.3	490,858	2,689.4	73,656	403.6
2008	758,934	4,140.8	188,467	1,028.3	506,958	2,766.0	63,509	346.5
Percent change	+1.7	+1.3	+3.6	+3.2	+3.3	+2.8	-13.8	-14.1

[3] The data collection methodology for the offense of forcible rape used by the Illinois and the Minnesota state UCR Programs (with the exception of Rockford, IL, and Minneapolis and St. Paul, MN) does not comply with national UCR guidelines. Consequently, their state figures for forcible rape (with the exception of Rockford, IL, and Minneapolis and St. Paul, MN) have been estimated for inclusion in this table.

[4] Includes offenses reported by the Zoological Police and the Metro Transit Police.

Table 4. Crime, by Region, Geographic Division, and State, 2007–2008—*Continued*

(Number, rate per 100,000 population, percent.)

Area	Population[1]	Violent crime		Murder and nonnegligent manslaughter		Forcible rape		Robbery		Aggravated assault	
		Number	Rate	Number	Rate	Number	Rate	Number	Rate	Number	Rate
Georgia											
2007	9,544,750	47,075	493.2	718	7.5	2,178	22.8	17,340	181.7	26,839	281.2
2008	9,685,744	46,384	478.9	636	6.6	2,195	22.7	17,357	179.2	26,196	270.5
Percent change		-1.5	-2.9	-11.4	-12.7	+0.8	-0.7	+0.1	-1.4	-2.4	-3.8
Maryland											
2007	5,618,344	36,062	641.9	553	9.8	1,179	21.0	13,258	236.0	21,072	375.1
2008	5,633,597	35,393	628.2	493	8.8	1,127	20.0	13,203	234.4	20,570	365.1
Percent change		-1.9	-2.1	-10.8	-11.1	-4.4	-4.7	-0.4	-0.7	-2.4	-2.6
North Carolina											
2007	9,061,032	42,262	466.4	585	6.5	2,385	26.3	13,548	149.5	25,744	284.1
2008	9,222,414	43,099	467.3	604	6.5	2,284	24.8	14,334	155.4	25,877	280.6
Percent change		+2.0	+0.2	+3.2	+1.4	-4.2	-5.9	+5.8	+4.0	+0.5	-1.2
South Carolina											
2007	4,407,709	34,746	788.3	352	8.0	1,739	39.5	6,346	144.0	26,309	596.9
2008	4,479,800	32,691	729.7	305	6.8	1,638	36.6	6,599	147.3	24,149	539.1
Percent change		-5.9	-7.4	-13.4	-14.7	-5.8	-7.3	+4.0	+2.3	-8.2	-9.7
Virginia											
2007	7,712,091	20,798	269.7	406	5.3	1,745	22.6	7,651	99.2	10,996	142.6
2008	7,769,089	19,882	255.9	368	4.7	1,758	22.6	7,437	95.7	10,319	132.8
Percent change		-4.4	-5.1	-9.4	-10.0	+0.7	*	-2.8	-3.5	-6.2	-6.8
West Virginia											
2007	1,812,035	4,987	275.2	64	3.5	369	20.4	852	47.0	3,702	204.3
2008	1,814,468	4,968	273.8	60	3.3	362	20.0	889	49.0	3,657	201.5
Percent change		-0.4	-0.5	-6.3	-6.4	-1.9	-2.0	+4.3	+4.2	-1.2	-1.3
East South Central											
2007	17,944,829	88,127	491.1	1,221	6.8	6,140	34.2	25,355	141.3	55,411	308.8
2008	18,084,651	87,027	481.2	1,196	6.6	5,977	33.1	25,166	139.2	54,688	302.4
Percent change		-1.2	-2.0	-2.0	-2.8	-2.7	-3.4	-0.7	-1.5	-1.3	-2.1
Alabama											
2007	4,627,851	20,732	448.0	412	8.9	1,545	33.4	7,398	159.9	11,377	245.8
2008	4,661,900	21,111	452.8	353	7.6	1,617	34.7	7,346	157.6	11,795	253.0
Percent change		+1.8	+1.1	-14.3	-14.9	+4.7	+3.9	-0.7	-1.4	+3.7	+2.9
Kentucky											
2007	4,241,474	12,513	295.0	204	4.8	1,381	32.6	4,069	95.9	6,859	161.7
2008	4,269,245	12,646	296.2	198	4.6	1,408	33.0	4,004	93.8	7,036	164.8
Percent change		+1.1	+0.4	-2.9	-3.6	+2.0	+1.3	-1.6	-2.2	+2.6	+1.9
Mississippi											
2007	2,918,785	8,502	291.3	208	7.1	1,040	35.6	2,866	98.2	4,388	150.3
2008	2,938,618	8,373	284.9	237	8.1	890	30.3	3,016	102.6	4,230	143.9
Percent change		-1.5	-2.2	+13.9	+13.2	-14.4	-15.0	+5.2	+4.5	-3.6	-4.3
Tennessee											
2007	6,156,719	46,380	753.3	397	6.4	2,174	35.3	11,022	179.0	32,787	532.5
2008	6,214,888	44,897	722.4	408	6.6	2,062	33.2	10,800	173.8	31,627	508.9
Percent change		-3.2	-4.1	+2.8	+1.8	-5.2	-6.0	-2.0	-2.9	-3.5	-4.4
West South Central											
2007	34,649,697	186,450	538.1	2,441	7.0	12,659	36.5	51,249	147.9	120,101	346.6
2008	35,235,521	186,066	528.1	2,275	6.5	12,107	34.4	50,165	142.4	121,519	344.9
Percent change		-0.2	-1.9	-6.8	-8.4	-4.4	-6.0	-2.1	-3.7	+1.2	-0.5
Arkansas											
2007	2,834,797	15,007	529.4	191	6.7	1,268	44.7	3,024	106.7	10,524	371.2
2008	2,855,390	14,374	503.4	162	5.7	1,395	48.9	2,735	95.8	10,082	353.1
Percent change		-4.2	-4.9	-15.2	-15.8	+10.0	+9.2	-9.6	-10.2	-4.2	-4.9
Louisiana											
2007	4,293,204	31,317	729.5	608	14.2	1,393	32.4	6,083	141.7	23,233	541.2
2008	4,410,796	28,944	656.2	527	11.9	1,232	27.9	5,994	135.9	21,191	480.4
Percent change		-7.6	-10.0	-13.3	-15.6	-11.6	-13.9	-1.5	-4.1	-8.8	-11.2
Oklahoma											
2007	3,617,316	18,072	499.6	222	6.1	1,559	43.1	3,373	93.2	12,918	357.1
2008	3,642,361	19,184	526.7	212	5.8	1,466	40.2	3,683	101.1	13,823	379.5
Percent change		+6.2	+5.4	-4.5	-5.2	-6.0	-6.6	+9.2	+8.4	+7.0	+6.3
Texas											
2007	23,904,380	122,054	510.6	1,420	5.9	8,439	35.3	38,769	162.2	73,426	307.2
2008	24,326,974	123,564	507.9	1,374	5.6	8,014	32.9	37,753	155.2	76,423	314.1
Percent change		+1.2	-0.5	-3.2	-4.9	-5.0	-6.7	-2.6	-4.3	+4.1	+2.3

* Less than one-tenth of 1 percent.

Table 4. Crime, by Region, Geographic Division, and State, 2007–2008—*Continued*

(Number, rate per 100,000 population, percent.)

Area	Property crime		Burglary		Larceny-theft		Motor vehicle theft	
	Number	Rate	Number	Rate	Number	Rate	Number	Rate
Georgia								
2007	372,342	3,901.0	90,690	950.2	239,058	2,504.6	42,594	446.3
2008	388,935	4,015.5	100,629	1,038.9	248,678	2,567.5	39,628	409.1
Percent change	+4.5	+2.9	+11.0	+9.3	+4.0	+2.5	-7.0	-8.3
Maryland								
2007	192,796	3,431.5	37,095	660.2	127,308	2,265.9	28,393	505.4
2008	198,165	3,517.6	38,849	689.6	133,983	2,378.3	25,333	449.7
Percent change	+2.8	+2.5	+4.7	+4.4	+5.2	+5.0	-10.8	-11.0
North Carolina								
2007	370,354	4,087.3	108,800	1,200.7	233,588	2,577.9	27,966	308.6
2008	372,961	4,044.1	111,602	1,210.1	234,616	2,544.0	26,743	290.0
Percent change	+0.7	-1.1	+2.6	+0.8	+0.4	-1.3	-4.4	-6.0
South Carolina								
2007	188,282	4,271.7	45,214	1,025.8	126,042	2,859.6	17,026	386.3
2008	189,683	4,234.2	45,967	1,026.1	126,064	2,814.1	17,652	394.0
Percent change	+0.7	-0.9	+1.7	*	*	-1.6	+3.7	+2.0
Virginia								
2007	190,209	2,466.4	31,688	410.9	144,467	1,873.3	14,054	182.2
2008	195,634	2,518.1	31,993	411.8	150,382	1,935.6	13,259	170.7
Percent change	+2.9	+2.1	+1.0	+0.2	+4.1	+3.3	-5.7	-6.3
West Virginia								
2007	45,753	2,525.0	10,814	596.8	31,447	1,735.5	3,492	192.7
2008	46,607	2,568.6	11,066	609.9	32,337	1,782.2	3,204	176.6
Percent change	+1.9	+1.7	+2.3	+2.2	+2.8	+2.7	-8.2	-8.4
East South Central								
2007	635,759	3,542.9	162,688	906.6	421,127	2,346.8	51,944	289.5
2008	638,310	3,529.6	170,277	941.6	421,332	2,329.8	46,701	258.2
Percent change	+0.4	-0.4	+4.7	+3.9	*	-0.7	-10.1	-10.8
Alabama								
2007	183,798	3,971.6	45,331	979.5	124,237	2,684.6	14,230	307.5
2008	190,343	4,082.9	50,408	1,081.3	126,477	2,713.0	13,458	288.7
Percent change	+3.6	+2.8	+11.2	+10.4	+1.8	+1.1	-5.4	-6.1
Kentucky								
2007	106,813	2,518.3	27,683	652.7	70,455	1,661.1	8,675	204.5
2008	110,314	2,583.9	28,839	675.5	73,808	1,728.8	7,667	179.6
Percent change	+3.3	+2.6	+4.2	+3.5	+4.8	+4.1	-11.6	-12.2
Mississippi								
2007	93,424	3,200.8	27,959	957.9	58,084	1,990.0	7,381	252.9
2008	86,408	2,940.4	26,024	885.6	54,032	1,838.7	6,352	216.2
Percent change	-7.5	-8.1	-6.9	-7.5	-7.0	-7.6	-13.9	-14.5
Tennessee								
2007	251,724	4,088.6	61,715	1,002.4	168,351	2,734.4	21,658	351.8
2008	251,245	4,042.6	65,006	1,046.0	167,015	2,687.3	19,224	309.3
Percent change	-0.2	-1.1	+5.3	+4.3	-0.8	-1.7	-11.2	-12.1
West South Central								
2007	1,399,756	4,039.7	339,108	978.7	931,100	2,687.2	129,548	373.9
2008	1,373,092	3,896.9	342,218	971.2	914,389	2,595.1	116,485	330.6
Percent change	-1.9	-3.5	+0.9	-0.8	-1.8	-3.4	-10.1	-11.6
Arkansas								
2007	112,061	3,953.1	32,072	1,131.4	72,979	2,574.4	7,010	247.3
2008	109,508	3,835.1	33,694	1,180.0	69,303	2,427.1	6,511	228.0
Percent change	-2.3	-3.0	+5.1	+4.3	-5.0	-5.7	-7.1	-7.8
Louisiana								
2007	174,991	4,076.0	44,602	1,038.9	115,209	2,683.5	15,180	353.6
2008	168,630	3,823.1	43,320	982.1	111,567	2,529.4	13,743	311.6
Percent change	-3.6	-6.2	-2.9	-5.5	-3.2	-5.7	-9.5	-11.9
Oklahoma								
2007	127,562	3,526.4	34,121	943.3	79,982	2,211.1	13,459	372.1
2008	125,384	3,442.4	35,081	963.1	79,422	2,180.5	10,881	298.7
Percent change	-1.7	-2.4	+2.8	+2.1	-0.7	-1.4	-19.2	-19.7
Texas								
2007	985,142	4,121.2	228,313	955.1	662,930	2,773.3	93,899	392.8
2008	969,570	3,985.6	230,123	946.0	654,097	2,688.8	85,350	350.8
Percent change	-1.6	-3.3	+0.8	-1.0	-1.3	-3.0	-9.1	-10.7

* Less than one-tenth of 1 percent.

Table 4. Crime, by Region, Geographic Division, and State, 2007–2008—*Continued*

(Number, rate per 100,000 population, percent.)

Area	Population[1]	Violent crime		Murder and nonnegligent manslaughter		Forcible rape		Robbery		Aggravated assault	
		Number	Rate	Number	Rate	Number	Rate	Number	Rate	Number	Rate
West											
2007	70,096,950	325,020	463.7	3,684	5.3	21,670	30.9	105,397	150.4	194,269	277.1
2008	70,854,948	315,621	445.4	3,433	4.8	21,423	30.2	103,731	146.4	187,034	264.0
Percent change		-2.9	-3.9	-6.8	-7.8	-1.1	-2.2	-1.6	-2.6	-3.7	-4.8
Mountain											
2007	21,360,990	93,652	438.4	1,112	5.2	7,918	37.1	24,252	113.5	60,370	282.6
2008	21,784,507	91,024	417.8	964	4.4	7,930	36.4	23,627	108.5	58,503	268.6
Percent change		-2.8	-4.7	-13.3	-15.0	+0.2	-1.8	-2.6	-4.5	-3.1	-5.0
Arizona											
2007	6,338,755	30,600	482.7	468	7.4	1,856	29.3	9,618	151.7	18,658	294.3
2008	6,500,180	29,059	447.0	407	6.3	1,673	25.7	9,697	149.2	17,282	265.9
Percent change		-5.0	-7.4	-13.0	-15.2	-9.9	-12.1	+0.8	-1.7	-7.4	-9.7
Colorado											
2007	4,861,515	16,906	347.8	153	3.1	1,998	41.1	3,453	71.0	11,302	232.5
2008	4,939,456	16,946	343.1	157	3.2	2,098	42.5	3,365	68.1	11,326	229.3
Percent change		+0.2	-1.3	+2.6	+1.0	+5.0	+3.3	-2.5	-4.1	+0.2	-1.4
Idaho											
2007	1,499,402	3,589	239.4	49	3.3	578	38.5	233	15.5	2,729	182.0
2008	1,523,816	3,483	228.6	23	1.5	551	36.2	241	15.8	2,668	175.1
Percent change		-3.0	-4.5	-53.1	-53.8	-4.7	-6.2	+3.4	+1.8	-2.2	-3.8
Montana											
2007	957,861	2,754	287.5	14	1.5	290	30.3	191	19.9	2,259	235.8
2008	967,440	2,497	258.1	23	2.4	294	30.4	172	17.8	2,008	207.6
Percent change		-9.3	-10.2	+64.3	+62.7	+1.4	+0.4	-9.9	-10.8	-11.1	-12.0
Nevada											
2007	2,565,382	19,257	750.6	192	7.5	1,096	42.7	6,932	270.2	11,037	430.2
2008	2,600,167	18,837	724.5	163	6.3	1,102	42.4	6,473	248.9	11,099	426.9
Percent change		-2.2	-3.5	-15.1	-16.2	+0.5	-0.8	-6.6	-7.9	+0.6	-0.8
New Mexico											
2007	1,969,915	13,085	664.2	162	8.2	1,032	52.4	2,321	117.8	9,570	485.8
2008	1,984,356	12,896	649.9	142	7.2	1,139	57.4	2,172	109.5	9,443	475.9
Percent change		-1.4	-2.2	-12.3	-13.0	+10.4	+9.6	-6.4	-7.1	-1.3	-2.0
Utah											
2007	2,645,330	6,210	234.8	58	2.2	908	34.3	1,420	53.7	3,824	144.6
2008	2,736,424	6,070	221.8	39	1.4	893	32.6	1,421	51.9	3,717	135.8
Percent change		-2.3	-5.5	-32.8	-35.0	-1.7	-4.9	+0.1	-3.3	-2.8	-6.0
Wyoming											
2007	522,830	1,251	239.3	16	3.1	160	30.6	84	16.1	991	189.5
2008	532,668	1,236	232.0	10	1.9	180	33.8	86	16.1	960	180.2
Percent change		-1.2	-3.0	-37.5	-38.7	+12.5	+10.4	+2.4	+0.5	-3.1	-4.9
Pacific											
2007	48,735,960	231,368	474.7	2,572	5.3	13,752	28.2	81,145	166.5	133,899	274.7
2008	49,070,441	224,597	457.7	2,469	5.0	13,493	27.5	80,104	163.2	128,531	261.9
Percent change		-2.9	-3.6	-4.0	-4.7	-1.9	-2.6	-1.3	-2.0	-4.0	-4.7
Alaska											
2007	683,478	4,519	661.2	44	6.4	529	77.4	583	85.3	3,363	492.0
2008	686,293	4,474	651.9	28	4.1	441	64.3	645	94.0	3,360	489.6
Percent change		-1.0	-1.4	-36.4	-36.6	-16.6	-17.0	+10.6	+10.2	-0.1	-0.5
California											
2007	36,553,215	191,025	522.6	2,260	6.2	9,013	24.7	70,542	193.0	109,210	298.8
2008	36,756,666	185,173	503.8	2,142	5.8	8,903	24.2	69,385	188.8	104,743	285.0
Percent change		-3.1	-3.6	-5.2	-5.7	-1.2	-1.8	-1.6	-2.2	-4.1	-4.6
Hawaii											
2007	1,283,388	3,501	272.8	22	1.7	326	25.4	1,105	86.1	2,048	159.6
2008	1,288,198	3,512	272.6	25	1.9	365	28.3	1,086	84.3	2,036	158.1
Percent change		+0.3	-0.1	+13.6	+13.2	+12.0	+11.5	-1.7	-2.1	-0.6	-1.0
Oregon											
2007	3,747,455	10,777	287.6	73	1.9	1,255	33.5	2,862	76.4	6,587	175.8
2008	3,790,060	9,747	257.2	82	2.2	1,156	30.5	2,641	69.7	5,868	154.8
Percent change		-9.6	-10.6	+12.3	+11.1	-7.9	-8.9	-7.7	-8.8	-10.9	-11.9
Washington											
2007	6,468,424	21,546	333.1	173	2.7	2,629	40.6	6,053	93.6	12,691	196.2
2008	6,549,224	21,691	331.2	192	2.9	2,628	40.1	6,347	96.9	12,524	191.2
Percent change		+0.7	-0.6	+11.0	+9.6	*	-1.3	+4.9	+3.6	-1.3	-2.5
Puerto Rico											
2007	3,941,459	8,942	226.9	728	18.5	97	2.5	5,134	130.3	2,983	75.7
2008	3,954,037	9,484	239.9	807	20.4	95	2.4	5,467	138.3	3,115	78.8
Percent change		+6.1	+5.7	+10.9	+10.5	-2.1	-2.4	+6.5	+6.1	+4.4	+4.1

* Less than one-tenth of 1 percent.

Table 4. Crime, by Region, Geographic Division, and State, 2007–2008—*Continued*

(Number, rate per 100,000 population, percent.)

Area	Property crime		Burglary		Larceny-theft		Motor vehicle theft	
	Number	Rate	Number	Rate	Number	Rate	Number	Rate
West								
2007	2,342,855	3,342.3	483,630	689.9	1,468,489	2,094.9	390,736	557.4
2008	2,267,825	3,200.7	481,316	679.3	1,461,756	2,063.0	324,753	458.3
Percent change	-3.2	-4.2	-0.5	-1.5	-0.5	-1.5	-16.9	-17.8
Mountain								
2007	763,997	3,576.6	158,301	741.1	495,656	2,320.4	110,040	515.1
2008	750,405	3,444.7	157,505	723.0	507,107	2,327.8	85,793	393.8
Percent change	-1.8	-3.7	-0.5	-2.4	+2.3	+0.3	-22.0	-23.6
Arizona								
2007	279,794	4,414.0	57,825	912.2	173,580	2,738.4	48,389	763.4
2008	278,920	4,291.0	56,481	868.9	185,221	2,849.5	37,218	572.6
Percent change	-0.3	-2.8	-2.3	-4.7	+6.7	+4.1	-23.1	-25.0
Colorado								
2007	146,141	3,006.1	28,751	591.4	100,598	2,069.3	16,792	345.4
2008	140,725	2,849.0	28,256	572.0	98,950	2,003.3	13,519	273.7
Percent change	-3.7	-5.2	-1.7	-3.3	-1.6	-3.2	-19.5	-20.8
Idaho								
2007	33,685	2,246.6	6,977	465.3	24,482	1,632.8	2,226	148.5
2008	32,019	2,101.2	6,701	439.8	23,650	1,552.0	1,668	109.5
Percent change	-4.9	-6.5	-4.0	-5.5	-3.4	-4.9	-25.1	-26.3
Montana								
2007	26,489	2,765.4	3,027	316.0	21,707	2,266.2	1,755	183.2
2008	25,182	2,603.0	3,332	344.4	20,277	2,095.9	1,573	162.6
Percent change	-4.9	-5.9	+10.1	+9.0	-6.6	-7.5	-10.4	-11.3
Nevada								
2007	96,916	3,777.8	24,840	968.3	49,745	1,939.1	22,331	870.5
2008	89,640	3,447.5	24,156	929.0	49,581	1,906.8	15,903	611.6
Percent change	-7.5	-8.7	-2.8	-4.1	-0.3	-1.7	-28.8	-29.7
New Mexico								
2007	73,394	3,725.7	18,992	964.1	45,463	2,307.9	8,939	453.8
2008	77,572	3,909.2	21,713	1,094.2	47,855	2,411.6	8,004	403.4
Percent change	+5.7	+4.9	+14.3	+13.5	+5.3	+4.5	-10.5	-11.1
Utah								
2007	92,594	3,500.3	15,541	587.5	68,241	2,579.7	8,812	333.1
2008	91,873	3,357.4	14,682	536.5	69,996	2,557.9	7,195	262.9
Percent change	-0.8	-4.1	-5.5	-8.7	+2.6	-0.8	-18.3	-21.1
Wyoming								
2007	14,984	2,865.9	2,348	449.1	11,840	2,264.6	796	152.2
2008	14,474	2,717.3	2,184	410.0	11,577	2,173.4	713	133.9
Percent change	-3.4	-5.2	-7.0	-8.7	-2.2	-4.0	-10.4	-12.1
Pacific								
2007	1,578,858	3,239.6	325,329	667.5	972,833	1,996.1	280,696	576.0
2008	1,517,420	3,092.3	323,811	659.9	954,649	1,945.5	238,960	487.0
Percent change	-3.9	-4.5	-0.5	-1.1	-1.9	-2.5	-14.9	-15.4
Alaska								
2007	23,098	3,379.5	3,682	538.7	16,998	2,487.0	2,418	353.8
2008	20,124	2,932.3	3,240	472.1	15,246	2,221.5	1,638	238.7
Percent change	-12.9	-13.2	-12.0	-12.4	-10.3	-10.7	-32.3	-32.5
California								
2007	1,108,660	3,033.0	237,025	648.4	652,243	1,784.4	219,392	600.2
2008	1,080,747	2,940.3	237,835	647.1	650,385	1,769.4	192,527	523.8
Percent change	-2.5	-3.1	+0.3	-0.2	-0.3	-0.8	-12.2	-12.7
Hawaii								
2007	54,228	4,225.4	9,097	708.8	38,416	2,993.3	6,715	523.2
2008	46,004	3,571.2	9,379	728.1	31,492	2,444.7	5,133	398.5
Percent change	-15.2	-15.5	+3.1	+2.7	-18.0	-18.3	-23.6	-23.8
Oregon								
2007	132,143	3,526.2	22,821	609.0	94,773	2,529.0	14,549	388.2
2008	124,397	3,282.2	20,879	550.9	92,187	2,432.3	11,331	299.0
Percent change	-5.9	-6.9	-8.5	-9.5	-2.7	-3.8	-22.1	-23.0
Washington								
2007	260,729	4,030.8	52,704	814.8	170,403	2,634.4	37,622	581.6
2008	246,148	3,758.4	52,478	801.3	165,339	2,524.6	28,331	432.6
Percent change	-5.6	-6.8	-0.4	-1.7	-3.0	-4.2	-24.7	-25.6
Puerto Rico								
2007	53,937	1,368.5	17,160	435.4	28,955	734.6	7,822	198.5
2008	59,254	1,498.6	19,138	484.0	33,113	837.4	7,003	177.1
Percent change	+9.9	+9.5	+11.5	+11.2	+14.4	+14.0	-10.5	-10.8

Table 5. Crime, by State and Area, 2008

(Number, percent, rate per 100,000 population.)

Area	Population	Violent crime	Murder and non-negligent man-slaughter	Forcible rape	Robbery	Aggravated assault	Property crime	Burglary	Larceny-theft	Motor vehicle theft
ALABAMA										
Metropolitan Statistical Area	3,328,232									
Area actually reporting	95.8%	15,781	285	1,119	6,323	8,054	145,200	38,552	95,811	10,837
Estimated total	100.0%	16,207	289	1,157	6,439	8,322	149,171	39,764	98,264	11,143
Cities outside metropolitan areas	599,012									
Area actually reporting	81.6%	2,972	37	246	654	2,035	24,945	5,801	17,881	1,263
Estimated total	100.0%	3,619	45	299	790	2,485	30,320	7,068	21,714	1,538
Nonmetropolitan counties	734,656									
Area actually reporting	91.8%	1,179	17	148	107	907	9,960	3,282	5,965	713
Estimated total	100.0%	1,285	19	161	117	988	10,852	3,576	6,499	777
State Total	4,661,900	21,111	353	1,617	7,346	11,795	190,343	50,408	126,477	13,458
Rate per 100,000 inhabitants		452.8	7.6	34.7	157.6	253.0	4,082.9	1,081.3	2,713.0	288.7
ALASKA										
Metropolitan Statistical Area	338,417									
Area actually reporting	100.0%	3,068	13	310	582	2,163	11,609	1,439	9,217	953
Cities outside metropolitan areas	121,702									
Area actually reporting	89.7%	570	5	71	27	467	3,894	556	3,078	260
Estimated total	100.0%	635	6	79	30	520	4,341	620	3,431	290
Nonmetropolitan counties	226,174									
Area actually reporting	100.0%	771	9	52	33	677	4,174	1,181	2,598	395
State Total	686,293	4,474	28	441	645	3,360	20,124	3,240	15,246	1,638
Rate per 100,000 inhabitants		651.9	4.1	64.3	94.0	489.6	2,932.3	472.1	2,221.5	238.7
ARIZONA										
Metropolitan Statistical Area	6,032,461									
Area actually reporting	99.5%	27,035	398	1,583	9,549	15,505	266,499	53,086	177,436	35,977
Estimated total	100.0%	27,133	399	1,590	9,579	15,565	267,708	53,361	178,233	36,114
Cities outside metropolitan areas	202,505									
Area actually reporting	83.7%	801	3	41	80	677	6,546	1,511	4,471	564
Estimated total	100.0%	958	4	49	96	809	7,820	1,805	5,341	674
Nonmetropolitan counties	265,214									
Area actually reporting	100.0%	968	4	34	22	908	3,392	1,315	1,647	430
State Total	6,500,180	29,059	407	1,673	9,697	17,282	278,920	56,481	185,221	37,218
Rate per 100,000 inhabitants		447.0	6.3	25.7	149.2	265.9	4,291.0	868.9	2,849.5	572.6
ARKANSAS										
Metropolitan Statistical Area	1,709,152									
Area actually reporting	98.1%	10,254	111	950	2,223	6,970	74,982	21,710	48,575	4,697
Estimated total	100.0%	10,382	111	964	2,240	7,067	76,003	22,062	49,187	4,754
Cities outside metropolitan areas	500,029									
Area actually reporting	96.5%	2,651	20	257	410	1,964	22,084	7,549	13,608	927
Estimated total	100.0%	2,747	21	266	425	2,035	22,884	7,822	14,101	961
Nonmetropolitan counties	646,209									
Area actually reporting	86.8%	1,081	26	143	61	851	9,222	3,308	5,223	691
Estimated total	100.0%	1,245	30	165	70	980	10,621	3,810	6,015	796
State Total	2,855,390	14,374	162	1,395	2,735	10,082	109,508	33,694	69,303	6,511
Rate per 100,000 inhabitants		503.4	5.7	48.9	95.8	353.1	3,835.1	1,180.0	2,427.1	228.0
CALIFORNIA										
Metropolitan Statistical Area	35,922,181									
Area actually reporting	100.0%	181,952	2,114	8,621	69,012	102,205	1,062,787	232,054	639,889	190,844
Cities outside metropolitan areas	269,326									
Area actually reporting	100.0%	1,389	11	128	218	1,032	9,323	2,589	6,028	706
Nonmetropolitan counties	565,159									
Area actually reporting	100.0%	1,832	17	154	155	1,506	8,637	3,192	4,468	977
State Total	36,756,666	185,173	2,142	8,903	69,385	104,743	1,080,747	237,835	650,385	192,527
Rate per 100,000 inhabitants		503.8	5.8	24.2	188.8	285.0	2,940.3	647.1	1,769.4	523.8
COLORADO										
Metropolitan Statistical Area	4,260,351									
Area actually reporting	97.2%	14,830	139	1,834	3,200	9,657	121,651	24,930	84,261	12,460
Estimated total	100.0%	15,134	140	1,877	3,258	9,859	125,052	25,495	86,776	12,781
Cities outside metropolitan areas	308,538									
Area actually reporting	92.9%	1,089	10	140	86	853	10,815	1,729	8,635	451
Estimated total	100.0%	1,173	11	151	93	918	11,646	1,862	9,298	486
Nonmetropolitan counties	370,567									
Area actually reporting	88.2%	563	5	62	12	484	3,551	793	2,536	222
Estimated total	100.0%	639	6	70	14	549	4,027	899	2,876	252
State Total	4,939,456	16,946	157	2,098	3,365	11,326	140,725	28,256	98,950	13,519
Rate per 100,000 inhabitants		343.1	3.2	42.5	68.1	229.3	2,849.0	572.0	2,003.3	273.7

Table 5. Crime, by State and Area, 2008—*Continued*

(Number, percent, rate per 100,000 population.)

Area	Population	Violent crime	Murder and non-negligent man-slaughter	Forcible rape	Robbery	Aggravated assault	Property crime	Burglary	Larceny-theft	Motor vehicle theft
CONNECTICUT										
Metropolitan Statistical Area	2,821,572									
Area actually reporting	100.0%	9,789	113	573	3,792	5,311	77,807	12,874	56,550	8,383
Cities outside metropolitan areas	158,076									
Area actually reporting	100.0%	242	1	38	62	141	2,992	607	2,211	174
Nonmetropolitan counties	521,604									
Area actually reporting	100.0%	396	9	63	53	271	5,288	1,530	3,352	406
State Total	3,501,252	10,427	123	674	3,907	5,723	86,087	15,011	62,113	8,963
Rate per 100,000 inhabitants		297.8	3.5	19.3	111.6	163.5	2,458.7	428.7	1,774.0	256.0
DELAWARE										
Metropolitan Statistical Area	685,609									
Area actually reporting	100.0%	5,058	51	268	1,620	3,119	25,098	5,026	17,864	2,208
Cities outside metropolitan areas	41,305									
Area actually reporting	100.0%	352	0	24	125	203	2,402	541	1,799	62
Nonmetropolitan counties	146,178									
Area actually reporting	100.0%	731	6	74	93	558	3,803	1,193	2,339	271
State Total	873,092	6,141	57	366	1,838	3,880	31,303	6,760	22,002	2,541
Rate per 100,000 inhabitants		703.4	6.5	41.9	210.5	444.4	3,585.3	774.3	2,520.0	291.0
DISTRICT OF COLUMBIA[1]										
Metropolitan Statistical Area	591,833									
Area actually reporting	100.0%	8,509	186	186	4,430	3,707	30,211	3,788	19,958	6,465
Cities outside metropolitan areas	None									
Nonmetropolitan counties	None									
Total	591,833	8,509	186	186	4,430	3,707	30,211	3,788	19,958	6,465
Rate per 100,000 inhabitants		1,437.7	31.4	31.4	748.5	626.4	5,104.6	640.0	3,372.2	1,092.4
FLORIDA										
Metropolitan Statistical Area	17,257,234									
Area actually reporting	99.9%	120,225	1,116	5,620	35,474	78,015	726,217	177,962	486,917	61,338
Estimated total	100.0%	120,266	1,116	5,622	35,488	78,040	726,521	178,030	487,128	61,363
Cities outside metropolitan areas	189,567									
Area actually reporting	94.6%	1,798	6	102	355	1,335	9,428	2,578	6,308	542
Estimated total	100.0%	1,901	6	108	375	1,412	9,970	2,726	6,671	573
Nonmetropolitan counties	881,539									
Area actually reporting	99.1%	4,062	46	240	406	3,370	22,243	7,642	13,042	1,559
Estimated total	100.0%	4,098	46	242	410	3,400	22,443	7,711	13,159	1,573
State Total	18,328,340	126,265	1,168	5,972	36,273	82,852	758,934	188,467	506,958	63,509
Rate per 100,000 inhabitants		688.9	6.4	32.6	197.9	452.0	4,140.8	1,028.3	2,766.0	346.5
GEORGIA										
Metropolitan Statistical Area	7,893,647									
Area actually reporting	99.2%	38,296	560	1,765	15,846	20,125	325,509	85,208	204,109	36,192
Estimated total	100.0%	38,572	563	1,779	15,950	20,280	328,043	85,833	205,766	36,444
Cities outside metropolitan areas	671,634									
Area actually reporting	84.9%	4,223	35	204	985	2,999	30,042	6,438	22,449	1,155
Estimated total	100.0%	4,971	41	240	1,159	3,531	35,367	7,579	26,428	1,360
Nonmetropolitan counties	1,120,463									
Area actually reporting	84.7%	2,405	27	149	210	2,019	21,607	6,109	13,954	1,544
Estimated total	100.0%	2,841	32	176	248	2,385	25,525	7,217	16,484	1,824
State Total	9,685,744	46,384	636	2,195	17,357	26,196	388,935	100,629	248,678	39,628
Rate per 100,000 inhabitants		478.9	6.6	22.7	179.2	270.5	4,015.5	1,038.9	2,567.5	409.1
HAWAII										
Metropolitan Statistical Area	906,349									
Area actually reporting	100.0%	2,575	18	203	928	1,426	31,781	6,370	21,473	3,938
Cities outside metropolitan areas	None									
Nonmetropolitan counties	381,849									
Area actually reporting	100.0%	937	7	162	158	610	14,223	3,009	10,019	1,195
State Total	1,288,198	3,512	25	365	1,086	2,036	46,004	9,379	31,492	5,133
Rate per 100,000 inhabitants		272.6	1.9	28.3	84.3	158.1	3,571.2	728.1	2,444.7	398.5
IDAHO										
Metropolitan Statistical Area	1,001,505									
Area actually reporting	99.7%	2,563	12	405	194	1,952	23,232	4,843	17,247	1,142
Estimated total	100.0%	2,571	12	406	195	1,958	23,307	4,857	17,304	1,146
Cities outside metropolitan areas	236,594									
Area actually reporting	99.3%	523	3	86	33	401	5,581	1,023	4,298	260
Estimated total	100.0%	527	3	87	33	404	5,619	1,030	4,327	262
Nonmetropolitan counties	285,717									
Area actually reporting	100.0%	385	8	58	13	306	3,093	814	2,019	260
State Total	1,523,816	3,483	23	551	241	2,668	32,019	6,701	23,650	1,668
Rate per 100,000 inhabitants		228.6	1.5	36.2	15.8	175.1	2,101.2	439.8	1,552.0	109.5

[1] Includes offenses reported by the Zoological Police and the Metro Transit Police.

Table 5. Crime, by State and Area, 2008—*Continued*

(Number, percent, rate per 100,000 population.)

Area	Population	Violent crime	Murder and non-negligent man-slaughter	Forcible rape	Robbery	Aggravated assault	Property crime	Burglary	Larceny-theft	Motor vehicle theft
ILLINOIS[2,3]										
State Total	12,901,563	67,780	790	4,118	24,054	38,818	378,355	78,968	266,815	32,572
Rate per 100,000 inhabitants		525.4	6.1	31.9	186.4	300.9	2,932.6	612.1	2,068.1	252.5
INDIANA										
Metropolitan Statistical Area	4,989,614									
Area actually reporting	86.5%	18,709	297	1,345	7,011	10,056	165,176	38,380	112,205	14,591
Estimated total	100.0%	19,610	310	1,437	7,217	10,646	179,230	41,263	122,442	15,525
Cities outside metropolitan areas	500,292									
Area actually reporting	79.2%	760	3	111	190	456	17,498	3,210	13,444	844
Estimated total	100.0%	960	4	140	240	576	22,106	4,055	16,985	1,066
Nonmetropolitan counties	886,886									
Area actually reporting	61.5%	438	8	88	46	296	6,994	2,045	4,418	531
Estimated total	100.0%	713	13	143	75	482	11,379	3,327	7,188	864
State Total	6,376,792	21,283	327	1,720	7,532	11,704	212,715	48,645	146,615	17,455
Rate per 100,000 inhabitants		333.8	5.1	27.0	118.1	183.5	3,335.8	762.8	2,299.2	273.7
IOWA										
Metropolitan Statistical Area	1,689,224									
Area actually reporting	99.0%	5,921	54	656	1,080	4,131	50,751	10,938	36,716	3,097
Estimated total	100.0%	5,948	54	660	1,082	4,152	51,097	11,003	36,983	3,111
Cities outside metropolitan areas	585,345									
Area actually reporting	93.1%	1,825	7	150	143	1,525	15,751	3,607	11,353	791
Estimated total	100.0%	1,961	8	161	154	1,638	16,918	3,874	12,194	850
Nonmetropolitan counties	727,986									
Area actually reporting	96.2%	587	13	64	12	498	4,495	1,513	2,625	357
Estimated total	100.0%	611	14	67	12	518	4,674	1,573	2,730	371
State Total	3,002,555	8,520	76	888	1,248	6,308	72,689	16,450	51,907	4,332
Rate per 100,000 inhabitants		283.8	2.5	29.6	41.6	210.1	2,420.9	547.9	1,728.8	144.3
KANSAS										
Metropolitan Statistical Area	1,907,099									
Area actually reporting	99.5%	8,436	88	808	1,476	6,064	68,880	13,862	48,871	6,147
Estimated total	100.0%	8,471	88	812	1,480	6,091	69,147	13,907	49,077	6,163
Cities outside metropolitan areas	569,367									
Area actually reporting	95.9%	2,219	18	276	172	1,753	19,647	3,984	14,808	855
Estimated total	100.0%	2,314	19	288	179	1,828	20,487	4,154	15,441	892
Nonmetropolitan counties	325,668									
Area actually reporting	95.9%	691	6	86	24	575	4,797	1,488	2,983	326
Estimated total	100.0%	720	6	90	25	599	5,001	1,551	3,110	340
State Total	2,802,134	11,505	113	1,190	1,684	8,518	94,635	19,612	67,628	7,395
Rate per 100,000 inhabitants		410.6	4.0	42.5	60.1	304.0	3,377.2	699.9	2,413.4	263.9
KENTUCKY										
Metropolitan Statistical Area	2,451,356									
Area actually reporting	92.0%	9,417	103	702	3,354	5,258	72,904	17,166	50,479	5,259
Estimated total	100.0%	9,708	105	736	3,443	5,424	76,232	18,018	52,749	5,465
Cities outside metropolitan areas	523,235									
Area actually reporting	80.8%	904	7	129	275	493	12,837	3,010	9,312	515
Estimated total	100.0%	1,119	9	160	340	610	15,893	3,726	11,529	638
Nonmetropolitan counties	1,294,654									
Area actually reporting	91.4%	1,663	77	468	202	916	16,626	6,485	8,711	1,430
Estimated total	100.0%	1,819	84	512	221	1,002	18,189	7,095	9,530	1,564
State Total	4,269,245	12,646	198	1,408	4,004	7,036	110,314	28,839	73,808	7,667
Rate per 100,000 inhabitants		296.2	4.6	33.0	93.8	164.8	2,583.9	675.5	1,728.8	179.6
LOUISIANA										
Metropolitan Statistical Area	3,269,753									
Area actually reporting	97.0%	21,071	439	882	5,196	14,554	127,741	31,736	84,385	11,620
Estimated total	100.0%	21,584	445	907	5,279	14,953	131,822	32,590	87,399	11,833
Cities outside metropolitan areas	384,508									
Area actually reporting	57.5%	1,987	26	94	281	1,586	11,375	3,208	7,657	510
Estimated total	100.0%	3,456	45	163	489	2,759	19,789	5,581	13,321	887
Nonmetropolitan counties	756,535									
Area actually reporting	85.7%	3,347	32	139	194	2,982	14,589	4,414	9,298	877
Estimated total	100.0%	3,904	37	162	226	3,479	17,019	5,149	10,847	1,023
State Total	4,410,796	28,944	527	1,232	5,994	21,191	168,630	43,320	111,567	13,743
Rate per 100,000 inhabitants		656.2	11.9	27.9	135.9	480.4	3,823.1	982.1	2,529.4	311.6

[2] Limited data for 2008 were available for Illinois.

[3] The data collection methodology for the offense of forcible rape used by the Illinois and the Minnesota state UCR Programs (with the exception of Rockford, IL, and Minneapolis and St. Paul, MN) does not comply with national UCR guidelines. Consequently, their state figures for forcible rape (with the exception of Rockford, IL, and Minneapolis and St. Paul, MN) have been estimated for inclusion in this table. "Table 8. Offenses Known to Law Enforcement, by State and City" provides the reported female forcible rape crime figure.

Table 5. Crime, by State and Area, 2008—*Continued*

(Number, percent, rate per 100,000 population.)

Area	Population	Violent crime	Murder and non-negligent man-slaughter	Forcible rape	Robbery	Aggravated assault	Property crime	Burglary	Larceny-theft	Motor vehicle theft
MAINE										
Metropolitan Statistical Area	769,193									
Area actually reporting	100.0%	965	15	220	288	442	19,755	3,719	15,301	735
Cities outside metropolitan areas	276,344									
Area actually reporting	100.0%	389	8	106	39	236	8,374	1,389	6,772	213
Nonmetropolitan counties	270,919									
Area actually reporting	100.0%	193	8	49	6	130	4,156	1,414	2,514	228
State Total	1,316,456	1,547	31	375	333	808	32,285	6,522	24,587	1,176
Rate per 100,000 inhabitants		117.5	2.4	28.5	25.3	61.4	2,452.4	495.4	1,867.7	89.3
MARYLAND										
Metropolitan Statistical Area	5,332,290									
Area actually reporting	100.0%	34,203	479	1,064	12,970	19,690	189,212	36,639	127,673	24,900
Cities outside metropolitan areas	79,007									
Area actually reporting	100.0%	547	4	25	148	370	4,315	873	3,295	147
Nonmetropolitan counties	222,300									
Area actually reporting	100.0%	643	10	38	85	510	4,638	1,337	3,015	286
State Total	5,633,597	35,393	493	1,127	13,203	20,570	198,165	38,849	133,983	25,333
Rate per 100,000 inhabitants		628.2	8.8	20.0	234.4	365.1	3,517.6	689.6	2,378.3	449.7
MASSACHUSETTS										
Metropolitan Statistical Area	6,471,015									
Area actually reporting	98.3%	28,785	165	1,708	6,998	19,914	152,910	35,388	105,004	12,518
Estimated total	100.0%	29,116	166	1,733	7,059	20,158	155,227	35,957	106,585	12,685
Cities outside metropolitan areas	26,781									
Area actually reporting	100.0%	58	1	3	10	44	732	137	543	52
Nonmetropolitan counties	171									
Area actually reporting	100.0%	0	0	0	0	0	0	0	0	0
State Total	6,497,967	29,174	167	1,736	7,069	20,202	155,959	36,094	107,128	12,737
Rate per 100,000 inhabitants		449.0	2.6	26.7	108.8	310.9	2,400.1	555.5	1,648.6	196.0
MICHIGAN										
Metropolitan Statistical Area	8,160,670									
Area actually reporting	97.8%	46,028	509	3,365	12,679	29,475	251,966	64,634	152,960	34,372
Estimated total	100.0%	46,519	511	3,434	12,776	29,798	256,464	65,604	156,112	34,748
Cities outside metropolitan areas	638,021									
Area actually reporting	90.4%	1,267	5	308	116	838	16,273	2,504	13,311	458
Estimated total	100.0%	1,370	6	334	122	908	17,711	2,725	14,487	499
Nonmetropolitan counties	1,204,731									
Area actually reporting	93.0%	2,118	23	683	61	1,351	18,061	5,441	11,695	925
Estimated total	100.0%	2,277	25	734	66	1,452	19,410	5,847	12,569	994
State Total	10,003,422	50,166	542	4,502	12,964	32,158	293,585	74,176	183,168	36,241
Rate per 100,000 inhabitants		501.5	5.4	45.0	129.6	321.5	2,934.8	741.5	1,831.1	362.3
MINNESOTA[3]										
Metropolitan Statistical Area	3,905,117									
Area actually reporting	98.5%		96		4,037	6,335	122,577	21,286	92,599	8,692
Estimated total	100.0%		97		4,065	6,384	124,415	21,534	94,095	8,786
Cities outside metropolitan areas	499,297									
Area actually reporting	98.1%		5		84	678	14,131	1,952	11,632	547
Estimated total	100.0%		5		86	691	14,398	1,989	11,852	557
Nonmetropolitan counties	815,979									
Area actually reporting	98.2%		7		26	541	9,815	2,834	6,259	722
Estimated total	100.0%		7		26	551	9,997	2,887	6,375	735
State Total	5,220,393	13,717	109	1,805	4,177	7,626	148,810	26,410	112,322	10,078
Rate per 100,000 inhabitants		262.8	2.1	34.6	80.0	146.1	2,850.6	505.9	2,151.6	193.1
MISSISSIPPI										
Metropolitan Statistical Area	1,295,027									
Area actually reporting	88.6%	3,727	116	391	1,657	1,563	42,458	11,182	27,438	3,838
Estimated total	100.0%	3,956	123	425	1,708	1,700	45,684	11,992	29,572	4,120
Cities outside metropolitan areas	590,822									
Area actually reporting	71.9%	1,790	45	166	686	893	18,529	5,742	11,936	851
Estimated total	100.0%	2,490	63	231	954	1,242	25,767	7,985	16,599	1,183
Nonmetropolitan counties	1,052,769									
Area actually reporting	51.4%	990	26	120	182	662	7,685	3,107	4,039	539
Estimated total	100.0%	1,927	51	234	354	1,288	14,957	6,047	7,861	1,049
State Total	2,938,618	8,373	237	890	3,016	4,230	86,408	26,024	54,032	6,352
Rate per 100,000 inhabitants		284.9	8.1	30.3	102.6	143.9	2,940.4	885.6	1,838.7	216.2

[3] The data collection methodology for the offense of forcible rape used by the Illinois and the Minnesota state UCR Programs (with the exception of Rockford, IL, and Minneapolis and St. Paul, MN) does not comply with national UCR guidelines. Consequently, their state figures for forcible rape (with the exception of Rockford, IL, and Minneapolis and St. Paul, MN) have been estimated for inclusion in this table. "Table 8. Offenses Known to Law Enforcement, by State and City" provides the reported female forcible rape crime figure.

Table 5. Crime, by State and Area, 2008—*Continued*

(Number, percent, rate per 100,000 population.)

Area	Population	Violent crime	Murder and non-negligent man-slaughter	Forcible rape	Robbery	Aggravated assault	Property crime	Burglary	Larceny-theft	Motor vehicle theft
MISSOURI										
Metropolitan Statistical Area	4,431,679									
Area actually reporting	99.9%	25,412	400	1,326	7,068	16,618	179,730	37,464	123,314	18,952
Estimated total	100.0%	25,413	400	1,326	7,068	16,619	179,751	37,468	123,329	18,954
Cities outside metropolitan areas	640,561									
Area actually reporting	99.5%	2,493	18	181	273	2,021	24,801	4,409	19,557	835
Estimated total	100.0%	2,506	18	182	274	2,032	24,931	4,432	19,660	839
Nonmetropolitan counties	839,365									
Area actually reporting	99.4%	1,889	37	106	48	1,698	11,835	3,866	7,003	966
Estimated total	100.0%	1,900	37	107	48	1,708	11,903	3,888	7,043	972
State Total	5,911,605	29,819	455	1,615	7,390	20,359	216,585	45,788	150,032	20,765
Rate per 100,000 inhabitants		504.4	7.7	27.3	125.0	344.4	3,663.7	774.5	2,537.9	351.3
MONTANA										
Metropolitan Statistical Area	340,604									
Area actually reporting	100.0%	869	7	96	110	656	11,429	1,474	9,306	649
Cities outside metropolitan areas	210,221									
Area actually reporting	97.3%	637	5	89	41	502	7,240	804	6,063	373
Estimated total	100.0%	655	5	92	42	516	7,445	827	6,234	384
Nonmetropolitan counties	416,615									
Area actually reporting	97.4%	947	11	103	19	814	6,143	1,004	4,613	526
Estimated total	100.0%	973	11	106	20	836	6,308	1,031	4,737	540
State Total	967,440	2,497	23	294	172	2,008	25,182	3,332	20,277	1,573
Rate per 100,000 inhabitants		258.1	2.4	30.4	17.8	207.6	2,603.0	344.4	2,095.9	162.6
NEBRASKA										
Metropolitan Statistical Area	1,039,893									
Area actually reporting	99.9%	4,327	52	347	1,195	2,733	35,124	5,832	25,862	3,430
Estimated total	100.0%	4,328	52	347	1,195	2,734	35,144	5,835	25,878	3,431
Cities outside metropolitan areas	392,104									
Area actually reporting	87.9%	740	10	176	76	478	11,007	1,825	8,744	438
Estimated total	100.0%	842	11	200	87	544	12,529	2,077	9,953	499
Nonmetropolitan counties	351,435									
Area actually reporting	86.0%	212	4	31	15	162	3,152	742	2,188	222
Estimated total	100.0%	246	5	36	17	188	3,665	863	2,544	258
State Total	1,783,432	5,416	68	583	1,299	3,466	51,338	8,775	38,375	4,188
Rate per 100,000 inhabitants		303.7	3.8	32.7	72.8	194.3	2,878.6	492.0	2,151.8	234.8
NEVADA										
Metropolitan Statistical Area	2,335,456									
Area actually reporting	100.0%	18,155	151	1,022	6,406	10,576	85,038	22,774	46,753	15,511
Cities outside metropolitan areas	47,239									
Area actually reporting	100.0%	178	3	21	26	128	1,376	345	943	88
Nonmetropolitan counties	217,472									
Area actually reporting	100.0%	504	9	59	41	395	3,226	1,037	1,885	304
State Total	2,600,167	18,837	163	1,102	6,473	11,099	89,640	24,156	49,581	15,903
Rate per 100,000 inhabitants		724.5	6.3	42.4	248.9	426.9	3,447.5	929.0	1,906.8	611.6
NEW HAMPSHIRE										
Metropolitan Statistical Area	820,353									
Area actually reporting	90.6%	1,301	8	215	301	777	15,727	2,419	12,425	883
Estimated total	100.0%	1,368	8	230	312	818	16,863	2,590	13,336	937
Cities outside metropolitan areas	447,139									
Area actually reporting	87.8%	570	3	130	91	346	9,121	1,365	7,375	381
Estimated total	100.0%	649	3	148	104	394	10,385	1,554	8,397	434
Nonmetropolitan counties	48,317									
Area actually reporting	100.0%	52	2	13	3	34	278	142	120	16
State Total	1,315,809	2,069	13	391	419	1,246	27,526	4,286	21,853	1,387
Rate per 100,000 inhabitants		157.2	1.0	29.7	31.8	94.7	2,091.9	325.7	1,660.8	105.4
NEW JERSEY										
Metropolitan Statistical Area	8,682,661									
Area actually reporting	99.9%	28,341	376	1,122	12,696	14,147	199,047	40,385	138,488	20,174
Estimated total	100.0%	28,351	376	1,122	12,701	14,152	199,126	40,401	138,545	20,180
Cities outside metropolitan areas	None									
Nonmetropolitan counties	None									
State Total	8,682,661	28,351	376	1,122	12,701	14,152	199,126	40,401	138,545	20,180
Rate per 100,000 inhabitants		326.5	4.3	12.9	146.3	163.0	2,293.4	465.3	1,595.7	232.4

Table 5. Crime, by State and Area, 2008—*Continued*

(Number, percent, rate per 100,000 population.)

Area	Population	Violent crime	Murder and non-negligent man-slaughter	Forcible rape	Robbery	Aggravated assault	Property crime	Burglary	Larceny-theft	Motor vehicle theft
NEW MEXICO										
Metropolitan Statistical Area	1,315,538									
Area actually reporting	99.8%	9,101	94	796	1,831	6,380	55,477	14,555	34,167	6,755
Estimated total	100.0%	9,114	94	797	1,832	6,391	55,551	14,571	34,217	6,763
Cities outside metropolitan areas	397,834									
Area actually reporting	93.1%	2,676	28	222	265	2,161	16,366	4,758	10,822	786
Estimated total	100.0%	2,873	30	238	285	2,320	17,573	5,109	11,620	844
Nonmetropolitan counties	270,984									
Area actually reporting	83.5%	759	15	87	46	611	3,712	1,697	1,684	331
Estimated total	100.0%	909	18	104	55	732	4,448	2,033	2,018	397
State Total	1,984,356	12,896	142	1,139	2,172	9,443	77,572	21,713	47,855	8,004
Rate per 100,000 inhabitants		649.9	7.2	57.4	109.5	475.9	3,909.2	1,094.2	2,411.6	403.4
NEW YORK										
Metropolitan Statistical Area	17,944,434									
Area actually reporting	99.9%	74,456	812	2,419	31,509	39,716	357,697	58,693	274,704	24,300
Estimated total	100.0%	74,489	812	2,420	31,521	39,736	358,070	58,751	275,005	24,314
Cities outside metropolitan areas	564,768									
Area actually reporting	97.6%	1,530	8	154	181	1,187	15,681	2,889	12,455	337
Estimated total	100.0%	1,567	8	158	185	1,216	16,059	2,959	12,755	345
Nonmetropolitan counties	981,095									
Area actually reporting	91.8%	1,404	15	205	66	1,118	13,223	3,695	9,110	418
Estimated total	100.0%	1,529	16	223	72	1,218	14,404	4,025	9,924	455
State Total	19,490,297	77,585	836	2,801	31,778	42,170	388,533	65,735	297,684	25,114
Rate per 100,000 inhabitants		398.1	4.3	14.4	163.0	216.4	1,993.5	337.3	1,527.3	128.9
NORTH CAROLINA										
Metropolitan Statistical Area	6,483,533									
Area actually reporting	99.0%	32,013	430	1,661	11,652	18,270	268,633	76,639	171,808	20,186
Estimated total	100.0%	32,291	432	1,681	11,733	18,445	271,886	77,393	174,151	20,342
Cities outside metropolitan areas	849,069									
Area actually reporting	94.1%	5,521	54	256	1,764	3,447	49,722	13,564	33,748	2,410
Estimated total	100.0%	5,855	57	272	1,869	3,657	52,746	14,384	35,807	2,555
Nonmetropolitan counties	1,889,812									
Area actually reporting	98.6%	4,883	113	326	722	3,722	47,652	19,547	24,313	3,792
Estimated total	100.0%	4,953	115	331	732	3,775	48,329	19,825	24,658	3,846
State Total	9,222,414	43,099	604	2,284	14,334	25,877	372,961	111,602	234,616	26,743
Rate per 100,000 inhabitants		467.3	6.5	24.8	155.4	280.6	4,044.1	1,210.1	2,544.0	290.0
NORTH DAKOTA										
Metropolitan Statistical Area	311,685									
Area actually reporting	99.6%	690	2	137	58	493	8,044	1,259	6,247	538
Estimated total	100.0%	692	2	138	58	494	8,078	1,264	6,274	540
Cities outside metropolitan areas	137,224									
Area actually reporting	92.1%	247	1	65	12	169	2,495	412	1,909	174
Estimated total	100.0%	269	1	71	13	184	2,711	448	2,074	189
Nonmetropolitan counties	192,572									
Area actually reporting	91.1%	98	0	21	1	76	1,241	359	743	139
Estimated total	100.0%	107	0	23	1	83	1,363	394	816	153
State Total	641,481	1,068	3	232	72	761	12,152	2,106	9,164	882
Rate per 100,000 inhabitants		166.5	0.5	36.2	11.2	118.6	1,894.4	328.3	1,428.6	137.5
OHIO										
Metropolitan Statistical Area	9,267,288									
Area actually reporting	88.2%	35,481	488	3,494	17,404	14,095	304,742	82,532	197,203	25,007
Estimated total	100.0%	37,200	503	3,786	18,054	14,857	333,494	88,535	218,518	26,441
Cities outside metropolitan areas	921,678									
Area actually reporting	77.4%	1,336	15	299	427	595	28,148	5,432	21,971	745
Estimated total	100.0%	1,726	19	386	552	769	36,379	7,020	28,396	963
Nonmetropolitan counties	1,296,944									
Area actually reporting	84.7%	908	18	209	96	585	18,632	5,922	11,754	956
Estimated total	100.0%	1,071	21	247	113	690	21,989	6,989	13,872	1,128
State Total	11,485,910	39,997	543	4,419	18,719	16,316	391,862	102,544	260,786	28,532
Rate per 100,000 inhabitants		348.2	4.7	38.5	163.0	142.1	3,411.7	892.8	2,270.5	248.4
OKLAHOMA										
Metropolitan Statistical Area	2,324,166									
Area actually reporting	100.0%	14,711	159	1,034	3,302	10,216	90,973	25,562	56,669	8,742
Cities outside metropolitan areas	706,342									
Area actually reporting	99.7%	3,126	24	312	349	2,441	26,222	6,531	18,372	1,319
Estimated total	100.0%	3,134	24	313	350	2,447	26,287	6,547	18,418	1,322
Nonmetropolitan counties	611,853									
Area actually reporting	99.5%	1,332	29	118	31	1,154	8,083	2,957	4,313	813
Estimated total	100.0%	1,339	29	119	31	1,160	8,124	2,972	4,335	817
State Total	3,642,361	19,184	212	1,466	3,683	13,823	125,384	35,081	79,422	10,881
Rate per 100,000 inhabitants		526.7	5.8	40.2	101.1	379.5	3,442.4	963.1	2,180.5	298.7

Table 5. Crime, by State and Area, 2008—*Continued*

(Number, percent, rate per 100,000 population.)

Area	Population	Violent crime	Murder and non-negligent man-slaughter	Forcible rape	Robbery	Aggravated assault	Property crime	Burglary	Larceny-theft	Motor vehicle theft
OREGON										
Metropolitan Statistical Area	2,949,725									
Area actually reporting	99.2%	8,392	70	959	2,392	4,971	101,369	16,280	75,151	9,938
Estimated total	100.0%	8,430	70	966	2,400	4,994	101,894	16,387	75,521	9,986
Cities outside metropolitan areas	395,284									
Area actually reporting	97.6%	905	7	123	201	574	15,360	2,514	12,050	796
Estimated total	100.0%	927	7	126	206	588	15,738	2,576	12,346	816
Nonmetropolitan counties	445,051									
Area actually reporting	82.9%	323	4	53	29	237	5,610	1,589	3,582	439
Estimated total	100.0%	390	5	64	35	286	6,765	1,916	4,320	529
State Total	3,790,060	9,747	82	1,156	2,641	5,868	124,397	20,879	92,187	11,331
Rate per 100,000 inhabitants		257.2	2.2	30.5	69.7	154.8	3,282.2	550.9	2,432.3	299.0
PENNSYLVANIA										
Metropolitan Statistical Area	10,465,127									
Area actually reporting	98.9%	46,765	654	2,847	18,285	24,979	260,739	49,561	190,350	20,828
Estimated total	100.0%	47,031	655	2,864	18,355	25,157	263,087	49,913	192,227	20,947
Cities outside metropolitan areas	923,487									
Area actually reporting	94.3%	2,307	18	245	327	1,717	19,557	3,333	15,622	602
Estimated total	100.0%	2,447	19	260	347	1,821	20,746	3,536	16,571	639
Nonmetropolitan counties	1,059,665									
Area actually reporting	100.0%	1,558	27	354	171	1,006	16,199	5,171	10,143	885
State Total	12,448,279	51,036	701	3,478	18,873	27,984	300,032	58,620	218,941	22,471
Rate per 100,000 inhabitants		410.0	5.6	27.9	151.6	224.8	2,410.2	470.9	1,758.8	180.5
PUERTO RICO										
Metropolitan Statistical Area	3,758,119									
Area actually reporting	100.0%	9,167	776	91	5,345	2,955	56,900	18,086	31,927	6,887
Cities outside metropolitan areas	195,918									
Area actually reporting	100.0%	317	31	4	122	160	2,354	1,052	1,186	116
Total	3,954,037	9,484	807	95	5,467	3,115	59,254	19,138	33,113	7,003
Rate per 100,000 inhabitants		239.9	20.4	2.4	138.3	78.8	1,498.6	484.0	837.4	177.1
RHODE ISLAND										
Metropolitan Statistical Area	1,050,788									
Area actually reporting	100.0%	2,606	27	272	879	1,428	29,774	5,750	20,867	3,157
Cities outside metropolitan areas	None									
Nonmetropolitan counties	None									
Area actually reporting	100.0%	15	2	5	0	8	75	0	32	43
State Total	1,050,788	2,621	29	277	879	1,436	29,849	5,750	20,899	3,200
Rate per 100,000 inhabitants		249.4	2.8	26.4	83.7	136.7	2,840.6	547.2	1,988.9	304.5
SOUTH CAROLINA										
Metropolitan Statistical Area	3,416,295									
Area actually reporting	99.9%	24,609	229	1,292	5,360	17,728	144,756	33,736	96,771	14,249
Estimated total	100.0%	24,611	229	1,292	5,360	17,730	144,772	33,739	96,783	14,250
Cities outside metropolitan areas	269,123									
Area actually reporting	99.6%	3,203	24	113	624	2,442	17,014	3,884	12,313	817
Estimated total	100.0%	3,216	24	113	627	2,452	17,087	3,901	12,366	820
Nonmetropolitan counties	794,382									
Area actually reporting	100.0%	4,864	52	233	612	3,967	27,824	8,327	16,915	2,582
State Total	4,479,800	32,691	305	1,638	6,599	24,149	189,683	45,967	126,064	17,652
Rate per 100,000 inhabitants		729.7	6.8	36.6	147.3	539.1	4,234.2	1,026.1	2,814.1	394.0
SOUTH DAKOTA										
Metropolitan Statistical Area	369,048									
Area actually reporting	92.5%	1,058	10	279	100	669	7,763	1,348	5,949	466
Estimated total	100.0%	1,100	11	294	101	694	8,061	1,412	6,167	482
Cities outside metropolitan areas	207,818									
Area actually reporting	87.6%	267	3	84	10	170	3,589	563	2,807	219
Estimated total	100.0%	304	3	96	11	194	4,098	643	3,205	250
Nonmetropolitan counties	227,328									
Area actually reporting	78.4%	169	9	33	6	121	842	294	495	53
Estimated total	100.0%	216	12	42	8	154	1,075	375	632	68
State Total	804,194	1,620	26	432	120	1,042	13,234	2,430	10,004	800
Rate per 100,000 inhabitants		201.4	3.2	53.7	14.9	129.6	1,645.6	302.2	1,244.0	99.5
TENNESSEE										
Metropolitan Statistical Area	4,558,480									
Area actually reporting	100.0%	37,577	349	1,655	10,111	25,462	197,562	49,789	132,090	15,683
Cities outside metropolitan areas	605,092									
Area actually reporting	100.0%	4,102	27	227	546	3,302	30,695	6,968	22,204	1,523
Nonmetropolitan counties	1,051,316									
Area actually reporting	100.0%	3,218	32	180	143	2,863	22,988	8,249	12,721	2,018
State Total	6,214,888	44,897	408	2,062	10,800	31,627	251,245	65,006	167,015	19,224
Rate per 100,000 inhabitants		722.4	6.6	33.2	173.8	508.9	4,042.6	1,046.0	2,687.3	309.3

Table 5. Crime, by State and Area, 2008—*Continued*

(Number, percent, rate per 100,000 population.)

Area	Population	Violent crime	Murder and non-negligent man-slaughter	Forcible rape	Robbery	Aggravated assault	Property crime	Burglary	Larceny-theft	Motor vehicle theft
TEXAS										
Metropolitan Statistical Area	21,339,780									
Area actually reporting	99.9%	113,882	1,252	7,087	36,748	68,795	896,963	208,760	606,888	81,315
Estimated total	100.0%	113,903	1,252	7,088	36,754	68,809	897,227	208,815	607,078	81,334
Cities outside metropolitan areas	1,376,122									
Area actually reporting	99.0%	6,415	53	602	822	4,938	48,597	12,499	33,922	2,176
Estimated total	100.0%	6,459	54	607	825	4,973	48,949	12,595	34,166	2,188
Nonmetropolitan counties	1,611,072									
Area actually reporting	100.0%	3,202	68	319	174	2,641	23,394	8,713	12,853	1,828
State Total	24,326,974	123,564	1,374	8,014	37,753	76,423	969,570	230,123	654,097	85,350
Rate per 100,000 inhabitants		507.9	5.6	32.9	155.2	314.1	3,985.6	946.0	2,688.8	350.8
UTAH										
Metropolitan Statistical Area	2,437,372									
Area actually reporting	99.9%	5,609	38	805	1,384	3,382	85,111	13,323	64,931	6,857
Estimated total	100.0%	5,613	38	806	1,385	3,384	85,175	13,333	64,980	6,862
Cities outside metropolitan areas	146,125									
Area actually reporting	87.3%	230	0	41	23	166	3,797	642	2,983	172
Estimated total	100.0%	263	0	47	26	190	4,349	735	3,417	197
Nonmetropolitan counties	152,927									
Area actually reporting	88.3%	171	1	35	9	126	2,074	542	1,412	120
Estimated total	100.0%	194	1	40	10	143	2,349	614	1,599	136
State Total	2,736,424	6,070	39	893	1,421	3,717	91,873	14,682	69,996	7,195
Rate per 100,000 inhabitants		221.8	1.4	32.6	51.9	135.8	3,357.4	536.5	2,557.9	262.9
VERMONT										
Metropolitan Statistical Area	207,874									
Area actually reporting	100.0%	398	1	58	57	282	7,476	1,444	5,781	251
Cities outside metropolitan areas	205,381									
Area actually reporting	100.0%	277	1	37	22	217	5,166	878	4,125	163
Nonmetropolitan counties	208,015									
Area actually reporting	98.0%	166	15	31	10	110	3,068	1,118	1,782	168
Estimated total	100.0%	169	15	32	10	112	3,129	1,140	1,818	171
State Total	621,270	844	17	127	89	611	15,771	3,462	11,724	585
Rate per 100,000 inhabitants		135.9	2.7	20.4	14.3	98.3	2,538.5	557.2	1,887.1	94.2
VIRGINIA										
Metropolitan Statistical Area	6,664,217									
Area actually reporting	100.0%	17,875	298	1,519	7,080	8,978	175,420	27,532	135,850	12,038
Cities outside metropolitan areas	268,624									
Area actually reporting	99.6%	770	19	77	180	494	8,164	1,266	6,608	290
Estimated total	100.0%	773	19	77	181	496	8,194	1,271	6,632	291
Nonmetropolitan counties	836,248									
Area actually reporting	100.0%	1,234	51	162	176	845	12,020	3,190	7,900	930
State Total	7,769,089	19,882	368	1,758	7,437	10,319	195,634	31,993	150,382	13,259
Rate per 100,000 inhabitants		255.9	4.7	22.6	95.7	132.8	2,518.1	411.8	1,935.6	170.7
WASHINGTON										
Metropolitan Statistical Area	5,742,340									
Area actually reporting	99.9%	19,960	176	2,275	6,124	11,385	219,008	45,450	146,886	26,672
Estimated total	100.0%	19,979	176	2,278	6,130	11,395	219,273	45,498	147,072	26,703
Cities outside metropolitan areas	338,434									
Area actually reporting	94.6%	1,017	5	200	153	659	15,529	3,118	11,604	807
Estimated total	100.0%	1,075	5	211	162	697	16,412	3,295	12,264	853
Nonmetropolitan counties	468,450									
Area actually reporting	100.0%	637	11	139	55	432	10,463	3,685	6,003	775
State Total	6,549,224	21,691	192	2,628	6,347	12,524	246,148	52,478	165,339	28,331
Rate per 100,000 inhabitants		331.2	2.9	40.1	96.9	191.2	3,758.4	801.3	2,524.6	432.6
WEST VIRGINIA										
Metropolitan Statistical Area	1,007,935									
Area actually reporting	91.4%	2,858	36	237	640	1,945	27,658	6,591	19,162	1,905
Estimated total	100.0%	3,055	38	252	675	2,090	29,975	7,089	20,824	2,062
Cities outside metropolitan areas	221,426									
Area actually reporting	78.9%	543	5	23	100	415	5,442	971	4,239	232
Estimated total	100.0%	688	6	29	127	526	6,901	1,231	5,376	294
Nonmetropolitan counties	585,107									
Area actually reporting	89.4%	1,095	14	72	78	931	8,699	2,455	5,486	758
Estimated total	100.0%	1,225	16	81	87	1,041	9,731	2,746	6,137	848
State Total	1,814,468	4,968	60	362	889	3,657	46,607	11,066	32,337	3,204
Rate per 100,000 inhabitants		273.8	3.3	20.0	49.0	201.5	2,568.6	609.9	1,782.2	176.6

Table 5. Crime, by State and Area, 2008—*Continued*

(Number, percent, rate per 100,000 population.)

Area	Population	Violent crime	Murder and non-negligent man-slaughter	Forcible rape	Robbery	Aggravated assault	Property crime	Burglary	Larceny-theft	Motor vehicle theft
WISCONSIN										
Metropolitan Statistical Area	4,099,798									
Area actually reporting	100.0%	13,691	123	897	5,034	7,637	125,692	21,883	93,482	10,327
Cities outside metropolitan areas	624,257									
Area actually reporting	99.9%	1,010	10	101	63	836	18,548	2,337	15,668	543
Estimated total	100.0%	1,011	10	101	63	837	18,558	2,338	15,677	543
Nonmetropolitan counties	903,912									
Area actually reporting	100.0%	719	13	122	29	555	10,877	3,258	6,969	650
State Total	5,627,967	15,421	146	1,120	5,126	9,029	155,127	27,479	116,128	11,520
Rate per 100,000 inhabitants		274.0	2.6	19.9	91.1	160.4	2,756.4	488.3	2,063.4	204.7
WYOMING										
Metropolitan Statistical Area	161,180									
Area actually reporting	100.0%	379	4	65	51	259	5,916	912	4,708	296
Cities outside metropolitan areas	217,657									
Area actually reporting	97.9%	635	4	85	32	514	6,741	907	5,549	285
Estimated total	100.0%	649	4	87	33	525	6,888	927	5,670	291
Nonmetropolitan counties	153,831									
Area actually reporting	100.0%	208	2	28	2	176	1,670	345	1,199	126
State Total	532,668	1,236	10	180	86	960	14,474	2,184	11,577	713
Rate per 100,000 inhabitants		232.0	1.9	33.8	16.1	180.2	2,717.3	410.0	2,173.4	133.9

Table 6. Crime, by Metropolitan Statistical Area, 2008

(Number, percent, rate per 100,000 population.)

Area	Population	Violent crime	Murder and non-negligent man-slaughter	Forcible rape	Robbery	Aggravated assault	Property crime	Burglary	Larceny-theft	Motor vehicle theft
Abilene, TX M.S.A.	159,257									
Includes Callahan, Jones, and Taylor Counties										
City of Abilene	116,267	648	7	88	180	373	4,500	1,206	3,061	233
Total area actually reporting	100.0%	716	7	95	188	426	5,124	1,417	3,443	264
Rate per 100,000 inhabitants		449.6	4.4	59.7	118.0	267.5	3,217.4	889.8	2,161.9	165.8
Akron, OH M.S.A.	699,914									
Includes Portage and Summit Counties										
City of Akron	206,845	1,897	17	167	801	912	10,721	3,770	6,001	950
Total area actually reporting	92.0%	2,331	23	265	948	1,095	21,555	5,865	14,254	1,436
Estimated total	100.0%	2,430	24	282	987	1137	23,183	6,178	15,489	1,516
Rate per 100,000 inhabitants		347.2	3.4	40.3	141.0	162.4	3,312.3	882.7	2,213.0	216.6
Albany-Schenectady-Troy, NY M.S.A.	856,504									
Includes Albany, Rensselaer, Saratoga, Schenectady, and Schoharie Counties										
City of Albany	94,152	1,033	9	48	361	615	4,405	1,027	3,153	225
City of Schenectady	61,506	654	9	35	288	322	3,054	925	1,905	224
City of Troy	47,567	392	5	19	152	216	2,363	600	1,650	113
Total area actually reporting	100.0%	2,808	23	180	956	1,649	22,040	4,374	16,788	878
Rate per 100,000 inhabitants		327.8	2.7	21.0	111.6	192.5	2,573.3	510.7	1,960.1	102.5
Albuquerque, NM M.S.A.	846,731									
Includes Bernalillo, Sandoval, Torrance, and Valencia Counties										
City of Albuquerque	527,464	4,718	38	370	1,350	2,960	31,994	6,224	21,098	4,672
Total area actually reporting	100.0%	6,763	64	521	1,594	4,584	41,539	9,589	26,125	5,825
Rate per 100,000 inhabitants		798.7	7.6	61.5	188.3	541.4	4,905.8	1,132.5	3,085.4	687.9
Allentown-Bethlehem-Easton, PA-NJ M.S.A.	811,166									
Includes Warren County, NJ and Carbon, Lehigh, and Northampton Counties, PA										
City of Allentown, PA	107,335	805	16	33	497	259	5,653	1,423	3,738	492
City of Bethlehem, PA	72,537	225	0	12	107	106	2,422	399	1,885	138
Total area actually reporting	97.3%	1,960	23	123	824	990	20,611	3,655	15,801	1,155
Estimated total	100.0%	2,011	23	126	838	1,024	21,064	3,723	16,163	1,178
Rate per 100,000 inhabitants		247.9	2.8	15.5	103.3	126.2	2,596.8	459.0	1,992.6	145.2
Altoona, PA M.S.A.	125,036									
Includes Blair County										
City of Altoona	46,236	183	2	13	67	101	1,218	369	793	56
Total area actually reporting	95.8%	359	4	29	88	238	2,549	632	1,811	106
Estimated total	100.0%	371	4	30	91	246	2,656	648	1,897	111
Rate per 100,000 inhabitants		296.7	3.2	24.0	72.8	196.7	2,124.2	518.3	1,517.2	88.8
Amarillo, TX M.S.A.	244,209									
Includes Armstrong, Carson, Potter, and Randall Counties										
City of Amarillo	187,674	1,474	13	122	324	1,015	10,310	2,419	7,150	741
Total area actually reporting	100.0%	1,558	15	134	329	1,080	11,125	2,626	7,694	805
Rate per 100,000 inhabitants		638.0	6.1	54.9	134.7	442.2	4,555.5	1,075.3	3,150.6	329.6
Ames, IA M.S.A.	85,516									
Includes Story County										
City of Ames	55,249	173	4	26	10	133	1,636	346	1,228	62
Total area actually reporting	100.0%	245	5	38	10	192	2,297	499	1,697	101
Rate per 100,000 inhabitants		286.5	5.8	44.4	11.7	224.5	2,686.0	583.5	1,984.4	118.1
Anchorage, AK M.S.A.	301,010									
Includes Anchorage Municipality and Matanuska-Susitna Borough										
City of Anchorage	280,068	2,647	10	263	544	1,830	9,211	1,191	7,254	766
Total area actually reporting	100.0%	2,778	10	265	551	1,952	10,172	1,276	8,088	808
Rate per 100,000 inhabitants		922.9	3.3	88.0	183.1	648.5	3,379.3	423.9	2,687.0	268.4
Anderson, SC M.S.A.[1]	182,566									
Includes Anderson County[1]										
City of Anderson	26,498	195	4	14	62	115	1,837	341	1,344	152
Total area actually reporting	100.0%	1,198	18	55	204	921			5,810	994
Rate per 100,000 inhabitants		656.2	9.9	30.1	111.7	504.5			3,182.4	544.5

[1] The FBI determined that the agency's data were overreported. Consequently, affected data are not included in this table.

Table 6. Crime, by Metropolitan Statistical Area, 2008—*Continued*

(Number, percent, rate per 100,000 population.)

Area	Population	Violent crime	Murder and non-negligent man-slaughter	Forcible rape	Robbery	Aggravated assault	Property crime	Burglary	Larceny-theft	Motor vehicle theft
Ann Arbor, MI M.S.A.	350,369									
Includes Washtenaw County										
City of Ann Arbor	115,148	295	0	32	66	197	3,121	622	2,353	146
Total area actually reporting	100.0%	1,320	11	128	296	885	9,527	2,301	6,611	615
Rate per 100,000 inhabitants		376.7	3.1	36.5	84.5	252.6	2,719.1	656.7	1,886.9	175.5
Appleton, WI M.S.A.	219,912									
Includes Calumet and Outagamie Counties										
City of Appleton	69,975	155	0	20	19	116	2,217	324	1,837	56
Total area actually reporting	100.0%	254	2	41	24	187	5,551	664	4,728	159
Rate per 100,000 inhabitants		115.5	0.9	18.6	10.9	85.0	2,524.2	301.9	2,150.0	72.3
Asheville, NC M.S.A.	409,862									
Includes Buncombe, Haywood, Henderson, and Madison Counties										
City of Asheville	74,215	535	2	33	251	249	4,268	907	2,951	410
Total area actually reporting	99.5%	1,154	9	94	357	694	11,648	3,342	7,364	942
Estimated total	100.0%	1,164	9	95	360	700	11,756	3,367	7,442	947
Rate per 100,000 inhabitants		284.0	2.2	23.2	87.8	170.8	2,868.3	821.5	1,815.7	231.1
Athens-Clarke County, GA M.S.A.	189,226									
Includes Clarke, Madison, Oconee, and Oglethorpe Counties										
City of Athens-Clarke County	113,950	535	2	54	204	275	6,445	1,706	4,374	365
Total area actually reporting	84.7%	676	3	58	210	405	8,020	2,015	5,560	445
Estimated total	100.0%	775	5	64	251	455	8,970	2,290	6,121	559
Rate per 100,000 inhabitants		409.6	2.6	33.8	132.6	240.5	4,740.4	1,210.2	3,234.8	295.4
Atlanta-Sandy Springs-Marietta, GA M.S.A.[2]	5,396,819									
Includes Barrow, Bartow, Butts, Carroll, Cherokee, Clayton, Cobb, Coweta, Dawson, DeKalb, Douglas, Fayette, Forsyth, Fulton, Gwinnett,[2] Haralson, Heard, Henry, Jasper, Lamar, Meriwether, Newton, Paulding, Pickens, Pike, Rockdale, Spalding, and Walton Counties										
City of Atlanta	533,016	7,403	105	126	3,308	3,864	38,978	9,989	22,499	6,490
City of Sandy Springs	82,953	223	0	17	161	45	3,118	885	1,953	280
City of Marietta	67,492	399	3	15	248	133	2,522	616	1,606	300
Total area actually reporting	99.9%	27,006	397	1,070	11,775	13,764	215,348	58,084	130,313	26,951
Estimated total	100.0%	27,034	397	1,071	11,785	13,781	215,601	58,136	130,494	26,971
Rate per 100,000 inhabitants		500.9	7.4	19.8	218.4	255.4	3,995.0	1,077.2	2,418.0	499.8
Atlantic City-Hammonton, NJ M.S.A.[3]	271,795									
Includes Atlantic County										
City of Atlantic City[3]	39,425	654	12	37	288	317			1,748	160
City of Hammonton	13,558	22	0	0	1	21	211	48	148	15
Total area actually reporting	100.0%	1,321	21	67	527	706			7,056	454
Rate per 100,000 inhabitants		486.0	7.7	24.7	193.9	259.8			2,596.1	167.0
Auburn-Opelika, AL M.S.A.	132,798									
Includes Lee County										
City of Auburn	55,649	181	2	17	56	106	2,894	1,022	1,818	54
City of Opelika	26,015	326	1	28	100	197	1,582	456	1,098	28
Total area actually reporting	100.0%	617	6	65	183	363	6,422	2,149	4,064	209
Rate per 100,000 inhabitants		464.6	4.5	48.9	137.8	273.3	4,835.9	1,618.2	3,060.3	157.4
Augusta-Richmond County, GA-SC M.S.A.[4]	531,442									
Includes Burke,[4] Columbia, McDuffie, and Richmond Counties, GA and Aiken and Edgefield Counties, SC										
Total area actually reporting	99.3%		41	252	1,009		25,543	6,222	16,770	2,551
Estimated total	100.0%		41	253	1,015		25,705	6,255	16,886	2,564
Rate per 100,000 inhabitants			7.7	47.6	191.0		4,836.8	1,177.0	3,177.4	482.5
Austin-Round Rock, TX M.S.A.	1,646,660									
Includes Bastrop, Caldwell, Hays, Travis, and Williamson Counties										
City of Austin	753,535	3,935	23	273	1,333	2,306	44,801	8,586	33,582	2,633
City of Round Rock	102,411	128	0	19	30	79	2,689	396	2,213	80
Total area actually reporting	100.0%	5,690	33	474	1,547	3,636	64,292	12,988	47,828	3,476
Rate per 100,000 inhabitants		345.5	2.0	28.8	93.9	220.8	3,904.4	788.7	2,904.5	211.1

[2] Because of changes in the state/local agency's reporting practices, figures are not comparable to previous years' data.
[3] The FBI determined that the agency's data were underreported. Consequently, affected data are not included in this table.
[4] It was determined that the agency did not follow national Uniform Crime Reporting (UCR) Program guidelines for reporting an offense. Consequently, this figure is not included in this table.

Table 6. Crime, by Metropolitan Statistical Area, 2008—*Continued*

(Number, percent, rate per 100,000 population.)

Area	Population	Violent crime	Murder and non-negligent man-slaughter	Forcible rape	Robbery	Aggravated assault	Property crime	Burglary	Larceny-theft	Motor vehicle theft
Bakersfield, CA M.S.A.	804,287									
Includes Kern County										
City of Bakersfield	326,046	2,077	25	48	708	1,296	16,160	4,168	9,476	2,516
Total area actually reporting	100.0%	4,631	57	233	1,289	3,052	31,907	9,252	17,422	5,233
Rate per 100,000 inhabitants		575.8	7.1	29.0	160.3	379.5	3,967.1	1,150.3	2,166.1	650.6
Baltimore-Towson, MD M.S.A.	2,666,452									
Includes Anne Arundel, Baltimore, Carroll, Harford, Howard, and Queen Anne's Counties and Baltimore City										
City of Baltimore	634,549	10,080	234	137	4,026	5,683	30,570	7,832	17,230	5,508
Total area actually reporting	100.0%	20,292	300	536	7,158	12,298	95,254	19,121	64,944	11,189
Rate per 100,000 inhabitants		761.0	11.3	20.1	268.4	461.2	3,572.3	717.1	2,435.6	419.6
Bangor, ME M.S.A.	148,610									
Includes Penobscot County										
City of Bangor	31,902	51	1	4	21	25	2,018	255	1,715	48
Total area actually reporting	100.0%	113	2	14	38	59	4,830	818	3,857	155
Rate per 100,000 inhabitants		76.0	1.3	9.4	25.6	39.7	3,250.1	550.4	2,595.4	104.3
Barnstable Town, MA M.S.A.	223,304									
Includes Barnstable County										
City of Barnstable	47,828	372	1	39	41	291	1,638	450	1,105	83
Total area actually reporting	100.0%	971	2	80	95	794	6,651	2,177	4,247	227
Rate per 100,000 inhabitants		434.8	0.9	35.8	42.5	355.6	2,978.5	974.9	1,901.9	101.7
Baton Rouge, LA M.S.A.[4]	783,283									
Includes Ascension, East Baton Rouge, East Feliciana, Iberville, Livingston, Pointe Coupee,[4] St. Helena, West Baton Rouge, and West Feliciana Parishes										
City of Baton Rouge	226,920	2,690	67	65	1,032	1,526	12,468	3,783	7,711	974
Total area actually reporting	94.9%	4,685	102	153	1,395	3,035		8,290	19,972	
Estimated total	100.0%	4,876	105	163	1,427	3,181		8,611	20,988	
Rate per 100,000 inhabitants		622.5	13.4	20.8	182.2	406.1		1,099.3	2,679.5	
Battle Creek, MI M.S.A.	135,300									
Includes Calhoun County										
City of Battle Creek	61,405	702	4	62	118	518	3,449	1,056	2,245	148
Total area actually reporting	100.0%	987	5	106	159	717	5,737	1,543	3,976	218
Rate per 100,000 inhabitants		729.5	3.7	78.3	117.5	529.9	4,240.2	1,140.4	2,938.7	161.1
Bay City, MI M.S.A.	106,303									
Includes Bay County										
City of Bay City	33,703	198	3	30	35	130	1,120	328	725	67
Total area actually reporting	100.0%	342	3	67	56	216	2,782	629	2,014	139
Rate per 100,000 inhabitants		321.7	2.8	63.0	52.7	203.2	2,617.0	591.7	1,894.6	130.8
Beaumont-Port Arthur, TX M.S.A.	375,242									
Includes Hardin, Jefferson, and Orange Counties										
City of Beaumont	109,103	1,015	7	75	331	602	6,404	1,925	4,170	309
City of Port Arthur	55,032	403	9	35	126	233	2,410	957	1,265	188
Total area actually reporting	100.0%	2,033	18	168	599	1,248	14,501	4,537	8,988	976
Rate per 100,000 inhabitants		541.8	4.8	44.8	159.6	332.6	3,864.4	1,209.1	2,395.3	260.1
Bellingham, WA M.S.A.	196,614									
Includes Whatcom County										
City of Bellingham	78,804	181	2	23	59	97	4,358	641	3,515	202
Total area actually reporting	100.0%	444	2	70	87	285	7,193	1,458	5,361	374
Rate per 100,000 inhabitants		225.8	1.0	35.6	44.2	145.0	3,658.4	741.6	2,726.7	190.2
Bend, OR M.S.A.	159,500									
Includes Deschutes County										
City of Bend	77,898	139	0	25	35	79	2,513	471	1,914	128
Total area actually reporting	100.0%	289	0	53	48	188	4,723	902	3,573	248
Rate per 100,000 inhabitants		181.2	0.0	33.2	30.1	117.9	2,961.1	565.5	2,240.1	155.5
Billings, MT M.S.A.[2]	151,343									
Includes Carbon and Yellowstone Counties										
City of Billings[2]	103,196	272	2	40	54	176	4,261	618	3,367	276
Total area actually reporting	100.0%	364	3	54	55	252	5,189	784	4,070	335
Rate per 100,000 inhabitants		240.5	2.0	35.7	36.3	166.5	3,428.6	518.0	2,689.3	221.4

[2] Because of changes in the state/local agency's reporting practices, figures are not comparable to previous years' data.

[4] It was determined that the agency did not follow national Uniform Crime Reporting (UCR) Program guidelines for reporting an offense. Consequently, this figure is not included in this table.

Table 6. Crime, by Metropolitan Statistical Area, 2008—*Continued*

(Number, percent, rate per 100,000 population.)

Area	Population	Violent crime	Murder and nonnegligent manslaughter	Forcible rape	Robbery	Aggravated assault	Property crime	Burglary	Larceny-theft	Motor vehicle theft
Binghamton, NY M.S.A.	245,658									
Includes Broome and Tioga Counties										
City of Binghamton	44,746	276	1	11	84	180	2,389	342	2,000	47
Total area actually reporting	100.0%	582	2	85	131	364	6,860	1,079	5,636	145
Rate per 100,000 inhabitants		236.9	0.8	34.6	53.3	148.2	2,792.5	439.2	2,294.2	59.0
Birmingham-Hoover, AL M.S.A.	1,118,275									
Includes Bibb, Blount, Chilton, Jefferson, St. Clair, Shelby, and Walker Counties										
City of Birmingham	228,314	3,249	82	212	1,499	1,456	20,054	5,153	12,761	2,140
City of Hoover	70,731	111	2	13	62	34	2,315	436	1,761	118
Total area actually reporting	94.8%	6,470	113	455	2,672	3,230	51,376	13,523	33,608	4,245
Estimated total	100.0%	6,644	115	470	2,719	3,340	52,986	14,019	34,597	4,370
Rate per 100,000 inhabitants		594.1	10.3	42.0	243.1	298.7	4,738.2	1,253.6	3,093.8	390.8
Bismarck, ND M.S.A.	104,611									
Includes Burleigh and Morton Counties										
City of Bismarck	59,988	155	2	16	10	127	1,629	211	1,324	94
Total area actually reporting	100.0%	222	2	46	14	160	2,270	319	1,811	140
Rate per 100,000 inhabitants		212.2	1.9	44.0	13.4	152.9	2,169.9	304.9	1,731.2	133.8
Blacksburg-Christiansburg-Radford, VA M.S.A.	157,811									
Includes Giles, Montgomery, and Pulaski Counties and Radford City										
City of Blacksburg	41,509	55	0	8	11	36	656	127	503	26
City of Christiansburg	19,466	50	2	14	9	25	789	126	632	31
City of Radford	16,109	79	1	4	8	66	537	166	356	15
Total area actually reporting	100.0%	359	6	58	42	253	4,299	928	3,177	194
Rate per 100,000 inhabitants		227.5	3.8	36.8	26.6	160.3	2,724.1	588.0	2,013.2	122.9
Bloomington, IN M.S.A.	184,646									
Includes Greene, Monroe, and Owen Counties										
City of Bloomington	72,337	268	3	31	43	191	2,782	635	1,997	150
Total area actually reporting	83.5%	339	4	42	57	236	4,203	1,011	2,956	236
Estimated total	100.0%	379	4	47	66	262	4,834	1,142	3,414	278
Rate per 100,000 inhabitants		205.3	2.2	25.5	35.7	141.9	2,618.0	618.5	1,848.9	150.6
Boise City-Nampa, ID M.S.A.	603,185									
Includes Ada, Boise, Canyon, Gem, and Owyhee Counties										
City of Boise	203,770	551	1	81	64	405	5,896	1,105	4,576	215
City of Nampa	83,007	274	0	64	20	190	2,378	502	1,714	162
Total area actually reporting	99.5%	1,427	5	231	127	1,064	13,556	2,928	9,949	679
Estimated total	100.0%	1,435	5	232	128	1,070	13,631	2,942	10,006	683
Rate per 100,000 inhabitants		237.9	0.8	38.5	21.2	177.4	2,259.8	487.7	1,658.9	113.2
Boston-Cambridge-Quincy, MA-NH M.S.A.	4,513,046									
Includes the Metropolitan Divisions of Boston-Quincy, MA; Cambridge-Newton-Framingham, MA; and Peabody, MA and Rockingham County-Strafford County, NH										
City of Boston, MA	604,465	6,676	62	237	2,398	3,979	22,429	3,493	16,531	2,405
City of Cambridge, MA	101,362	414	2	14	155	243	3,138	396	2,500	242
City of Quincy, MA	95,061	347	2	15	105	225	1,872	598	1,139	135
City of Newton, MA	83,191	117	0	8	19	90	1,111	186	896	29
City of Framingham, MA	64,519	196	1	11	40	144	1,600	268	1,166	166
City of Waltham, MA	60,459	89	0	9	15	65	848	108	696	44
City of Peabody, MA	51,846	144	1	9	22	112	1,318	171	1,024	123
Total area actually reporting	96.9%	17,505	116	995	4,912	11,482	99,308	19,903	71,116	8,289
Estimated total	100.0%	17,811	117	1,026	4,967	11,701	101,998	20,475	73,063	8,460
Rate per 100,000 inhabitants		394.7	2.6	22.7	110.1	259.3	2,260.1	453.7	1,618.9	187.5
Boston-Quincy, MA M.D.	1,874,072									
Includes Norfolk, Plymouth, and Suffolk Counties										
Total area actually reporting	95.8%	10,438	83	507	3,454	6,394	46,138	8,662	33,278	4,198
Estimated total	100.0%	10,669	84	524	3,496	6,565	47,760	9,060	34,385	4,315
Rate per 100,000 inhabitants		569.3	4.5	28.0	186.5	350.3	2,548.5	483.4	1,834.8	230.2
Cambridge-Newton-Framingham, MA M.D.	1,482,271									
Includes Middlesex County										
Total area actually reporting	99.8%	3,991	15	248	915	2,813	30,361	6,208	21,969	2,184
Estimated total	100.0%	4,001	15	249	917	2,820	30,430	6,225	22,016	2,189
Rate per 100,000 inhabitants		269.9	1.0	16.8	61.9	190.2	2,052.9	420.0	1,485.3	147.7

Table 6. Crime, by Metropolitan Statistical Area, 2008—*Continued*

(Number, percent, rate per 100,000 population.)

Area	Population	Violent crime	Murder and non-negligent man-slaughter	Forcible rape	Robbery	Aggravated assault	Property crime	Burglary	Larceny-theft	Motor vehicle theft
Peabody, MA M.D.	738,226									
Includes Essex County										
Total area actually reporting	99.5%	2,589	15	142	474	1,958	15,983	3,997	10,403	1,583
Estimated total	100.0%	2,599	15	143	476	1,965	16,052	4,014	10,450	1,588
Rate per 100,000 inhabitants		352.1	2.0	19.4	64.5	266.2	2,174.4	543.7	1,415.6	215.1
Rockingham County-Strafford County, NH M.D.	418,477									
Includes Rockingham and Strafford Counties										
Total area actually reporting	86.6%	487	3	98	69	317	6,826	1,036	5,466	324
Estimated total	100.0%	542	3	110	78	351	7,756	1,176	6,212	368
Rate per 100,000 inhabitants		129.5	0.7	26.3	18.6	83.9	1,853.4	281.0	1,484.4	87.9
Bowling Green, KY M.S.A.	117,583									
Includes Edmonson and Warren Counties										
City of Bowling Green	54,865	336	0	47	90	199	2,998	569	2,313	116
Total area actually reporting	99.1%	361	0	53	94	214	3,729	755	2,820	154
Estimated total	100.0%	364	0	53	95	216	3,767	763	2,848	156
Rate per 100,000 inhabitants		309.6	0.0	45.1	80.8	183.7	3,203.7	648.9	2,422.1	132.7
Bradenton-Sarasota-Venice, FL M.S.A.	691,365									
Includes Manatee and Sarasota Counties										
City of Bradenton	53,244	483	2	12	160	309	2,371	553	1,652	166
City of Sarasota	51,818	582	8	22	196	356	3,666	815	2,662	189
City of Venice	21,086	48	0	1	5	42	679	109	545	25
Total area actually reporting	100.0%	4,399	28	192	1,154	3,025	29,428	7,297	20,619	1,512
Rate per 100,000 inhabitants		636.3	4.0	27.8	166.9	437.5	4,256.5	1,055.4	2,982.4	218.7
Bremerton-Silverdale, WA M.S.A.	237,527									
Includes Kitsap County										
City of Bremerton	33,735	308	1	52	53	202	1,564	383	1,076	105
Total area actually reporting	100.0%	1,103	5	195	112	791	6,405	1,676	4,416	313
Rate per 100,000 inhabitants		464.4	2.1	82.1	47.2	333.0	2,696.5	705.6	1,859.2	131.8
Bridgeport-Stamford-Norwalk, CT M.S.A.	878,111									
Includes Fairfield County										
City of Bridgeport	136,327	1,638	20	58	737	823	6,174	1,269	3,768	1,137
City of Stamford	118,597	390	5	27	172	186	2,131	325	1,590	216
City of Norwalk	83,503	415	2	12	125	276	1,915	284	1,426	205
City of Danbury	79,753	109	1	15	41	52	1,626	275	1,237	114
City of Stratford	48,891	144	2	4	59	79	1,548	208	1,159	181
Total area actually reporting	100.0%	2,871	34	135	1,198	1,504	18,285	3,124	13,072	2,089
Rate per 100,000 inhabitants		327.0	3.9	15.4	136.4	171.3	2,082.3	355.8	1,488.7	237.9
Brownsville-Harlingen, TX M.S.A.	394,064									
Includes Cameron County										
City of Brownsville	176,893	634	4	26	173	431	10,139	1,590	8,205	344
City of Harlingen	64,922	455	4	33	88	330	4,387	1,016	3,181	190
Total area actually reporting	100.0%	1,666	13	133	321	1,199	19,168	4,081	14,323	764
Rate per 100,000 inhabitants		422.8	3.3	33.8	81.5	304.3	4,864.2	1,035.6	3,634.7	193.9
Buffalo-Niagara Falls, NY M.S.A.	1,122,844									
Includes Erie and Niagara Counties										
City of Buffalo	270,289	3,716	37	174	1,539	1,966	15,474	4,112	9,503	1,859
City of Cheektowaga Town	78,303	208	0	18	73	117	2,596	408	2,048	140
City of Tonawanda	14,792	19	0	1	6	12	396	41	333	22
City of Niagara Falls	51,192	562	3	24	171	364	2,747	827	1,759	161
Total area actually reporting	100.0%	5,493	44	286	2,001	3,162	34,924	7,858	24,405	2,661
Rate per 100,000 inhabitants		489.2	3.9	25.5	178.2	281.6	3,110.3	699.8	2,173.5	237.0
Burlington, NC M.S.A.	147,580									
Includes Alamance County										
City of Burlington	50,058	378	3	15	117	243	3,300	924	2,231	145
Total area actually reporting	98.6%	689	4	32	167	486	5,861	1,752	3,842	267
Estimated total	100.0%	697	4	33	169	491	5,961	1,775	3,914	272
Rate per 100,000 inhabitants		472.3	2.7	22.4	114.5	332.7	4,039.2	1,202.7	2,652.1	184.3
Burlington-South Burlington, VT M.S.A.	207,874									
Includes Chittenden, Franklin, and Grand Isle Counties										
City of Burlington	38,370	152	0	19	23	110	1,654	253	1,358	43
City of South Burlington	17,785	16	0	7	2	7	687	78	590	19
Total area actually reporting	100.0%	398	1	58	57	282	7,476	1,444	5,781	251
Rate per 100,000 inhabitants		191.5	0.5	27.9	27.4	135.7	3,596.4	694.7	2,781.0	120.7

Table 6. Crime, by Metropolitan Statistical Area, 2008—*Continued*

(Number, percent, rate per 100,000 population.)

Area	Population	Violent crime	Murder and non-negligent man-slaughter	Forcible rape	Robbery	Aggravated assault	Property crime	Burglary	Larceny-theft	Motor vehicle theft
Cape Coral-Fort Myers, FL M.S.A.	604,488									
Includes Lee County										
City of Cape Coral	163,403	363	7	31	93	232	5,061	1,353	3,485	223
City of Fort Myers	65,107	797	11	35	231	520	3,342	642	2,346	354
Total area actually reporting	100.0%	2,834	46	157	775	1,856	21,212	6,199	13,520	1,493
Rate per 100,000 inhabitants		468.8	7.6	26.0	128.2	307.0	3,509.1	1,025.5	2,236.6	247.0
Cape Girardeau-Jackson, MO-IL M.S.A.	93,556									
Includes Alexander County, IL and Bollinger and Cape Girardeau Counties, MO										
City of Cape Girardeau, MO	37,374	177	3	18	56	100	2,234	338	1,868	28
City of Jackson, MO	13,715	19	0	0	1	18	424	74	334	16
Total area actually reporting	91.1%	330	4	24	63	239	3,117	577	2,480	60
Estimated total	100.0%	343	4	24	66	249	3,194	593	2,537	64
Rate per 100,000 inhabitants		366.6	4.3	25.7	70.5	266.2	3,414.0	633.8	2,711.7	68.4
Carson City, NV M.S.A.	54,316									
Includes Carson City										
Total area actually reporting	100.0%	231	0	0	24	207	1,265	291	874	100
Rate per 100,000 inhabitants		425.3	0.0	0.0	44.2	381.1	2,329.0	535.8	1,609.1	184.1
Casper, WY M.S.A.	73,249									
Includes Natrona County										
City of Casper	53,430	159	1	30	19	109	2,289	368	1,805	116
Total area actually reporting	100.0%	194	1	36	21	136	2,773	500	2,121	152
Rate per 100,000 inhabitants		264.9	1.4	49.1	28.7	185.7	3,785.7	682.6	2,895.6	207.5
Cedar Rapids, IA M.S.A.	255,214									
Includes Benton, Jones, and Linn Counties										
City of Cedar Rapids	126,984	448	3	34	136	275	5,949	1,252	4,353	344
Total area actually reporting	96.3%	514	5	47	141	321	7,370	1,647	5,283	440
Estimated total	100.0%	529	5	49	142	333	7,567	1,684	5,435	448
Rate per 100,000 inhabitants		207.3	2.0	19.2	55.6	130.5	2,965.0	659.8	2,129.6	175.5
Charleston, WV M.S.A.	303,474									
Includes Boone, Clay, Kanawha, Lincoln, and Putnam Counties										
City of Charleston	50,132	592	3	21	125	443	2,997	608	2,177	212
Total area actually reporting	85.8%	1,179	13	71	209	886	9,101	2,001	6,352	748
Estimated total	100.0%	1,276	14	79	225	958	10,199	2,248	7,126	825
Rate per 100,000 inhabitants		420.5	4.6	26.0	74.1	315.7	3,360.7	740.8	2,348.1	271.9
Charleston-North Charleston-Summerville, SC M.S.A.	643,759									
Includes Berkeley, Charleston, and Dorchester Counties										
City of Charleston	111,645	800	14	60	288	438	4,535	724	3,399	412
City of North Charleston	92,749	1,375	14	69	570	722	6,705	1,202	4,721	782
City of Summerville	46,405	163	1	8	57	97	1,511	164	1,204	143
Total area actually reporting	99.9%	4,639	48	261	1,344	2,986	25,760	5,453	17,570	2,737
Estimated total	100.0%	4,641	48	261	1,344	2,988	25,776	5,456	17,582	2,738
Rate per 100,000 inhabitants		720.9	7.5	40.5	208.8	464.1	4,004.0	847.5	2,731.1	425.3
Charlotte-Gastonia-Concord, NC-SC M.S.A.	1,701,049									
Includes Anson, Cabarrus, Gaston, Mecklenburg, and Union Counties, NC and York County, SC										
City of Charlotte-Mecklenburg, NC	758,769	7,070	83	272	2,984	3,731	46,934	11,933	29,735	5,266
City of Gastonia, NC	71,486	646	7	21	237	381	5,326	1,210	3,678	438
City of Concord, NC	65,725	183	9	19	82	73	3,105	527	2,340	238
City of Rock Hill, SC	66,906	749	4	43	102	600	2,970	596	2,137	237
Total area actually reporting	98.8%	11,160	136	515	3,847	6,662	78,314	20,082	50,674	7,558
Estimated total	100.0%	11,244	137	521	3,871	6,715	79,293	20,309	51,379	7,605
Rate per 100,000 inhabitants		661.0	8.1	30.6	227.6	394.8	4,661.4	1,193.9	3,020.4	447.1
Charlottesville, VA M.S.A.	194,483									
Includes Albemarle, Fluvanna, Greene, and Nelson Counties and Charlottesville City										
City of Charlottesville	41,216	219	5	23	79	112	1,950	186	1,616	148
Total area actually reporting	100.0%	414	9	59	124	222	4,961	678	3,973	310
Rate per 100,000 inhabitants		212.9	4.6	30.3	63.8	114.1	2,550.9	348.6	2,042.9	159.4
Chattanooga, TN-GA M.S.A.[1]	518,576									
Includes Catoosa, Dade,[1] and Walker Counties, GA and Hamilton, Marion, and Sequatchie Counties, TN										
City of Chattanooga, TN	171,611	1,875	20	63	511	1,281	12,864	2,843	8,937	1,084
Total area actually reporting	100.0%		29	130	617		22,841	5,302	15,711	1,828
Rate per 100,000 inhabitants			5.6	25.1	119.0		4,404.6	1,022.4	3,029.6	352.5

[1] The FBI determined that the agency's data were overreported. Consequently, affected data are not included in this table.

Table 6. Crime, by Metropolitan Statistical Area, 2008—*Continued*

(Number, percent, rate per 100,000 population.)

Area	Population	Violent crime	Murder and non-negligent man-slaughter	Forcible rape	Robbery	Aggravated assault	Property crime	Burglary	Larceny-theft	Motor vehicle theft
Cheyenne, WY M.S.A.	87,931									
Includes Laramie County										
City of Cheyenne	55,931	122	2	24	25	71	2,565	284	2,171	110
Total area actually reporting	100.0%	185	3	29	30	123	3,143	412	2,587	144
Rate per 100,000 inhabitants		210.4	3.4	33.0	34.1	139.9	3,574.4	468.5	2,942.1	163.8
Chico, CA M.S.A.	219,628									
Includes Butte County										
City of Chico	84,086	304	2	31	101	170	2,700	874	1,540	286
Total area actually reporting	100.0%	836	7	92	169	568	6,663	1,860	4,016	787
Rate per 100,000 inhabitants		380.6	3.2	41.9	76.9	258.6	3,033.8	846.9	1,828.5	358.3
Cincinnati-Middletown, OH-KY-IN M.S.A.	2,150,520									
Includes Dearborn, Franklin, and Ohio Counties, IN; Boone, Bracken, Campbell, Gallatin, Grant, Kenton, and Pendleton Counties, KY; and Brown, Butler, Clermont, Hamilton, and Warren Counties, OH										
City of Cincinnati, OH	332,608	4,204	73	269	2,419	1,443	20,264	6,330	12,328	1,606
City of Middletown, OH	51,266	320	2	52	115	151	3,820	894	2,737	189
Total area actually reporting	85.8%	7,716	104	770	3,666	3,176	63,555	15,046	44,971	3,538
Estimated total	100.0%	8,106	107	833	3,799	3,367	69,829	16,425	49,527	3,877
Rate per 100,000 inhabitants		376.9	5.0	38.7	176.7	156.6	3,247.1	763.8	2,303.0	180.3
Clarksville, TN-KY M.S.A.	265,686									
Includes Christian and Trigg Counties, KY and Montgomery and Stewart Counties, TN										
City of Clarksville, TN	121,386	953	6	59	209	679	4,693	1,386	3,045	262
Total area actually reporting	99.6%	1,427	7	98	303	1,019	8,537	2,566	5,447	524
Estimated total	100.0%	1,430	7	98	304	1,021	8,574	2,574	5,474	526
Rate per 100,000 inhabitants		538.2	2.6	36.9	114.4	384.3	3,227.1	968.8	2,060.3	198.0
Cleveland, TN M.S.A.	111,956									
Includes Bradley and Polk Counties										
City of Cleveland	39,420	453	1	17	44	391	2,306	432	1,783	91
Total area actually reporting	100.0%	788	3	36	54	695	3,716	858	2,650	208
Rate per 100,000 inhabitants		703.8	2.7	32.2	48.2	620.8	3,319.2	766.4	2,367.0	185.8
College Station-Bryan, TX M.S.A.	205,756									
Includes Brazos, Burleson, and Robertson Counties										
City of College Station	81,925	245	1	42	55	147	3,012	628	2,283	101
City of Bryan	72,815	573	4	41	100	428	3,665	1,029	2,441	195
Total area actually reporting	100.0%	1,018	10	113	171	724	8,220	2,061	5,778	381
Rate per 100,000 inhabitants		494.8	4.9	54.9	83.1	351.9	3,995.0	1,001.7	2,808.2	185.2
Colorado Springs, CO M.S.A.	618,723									
Includes El Paso and Teller Counties										
City of Colorado Springs	378,403	1,999	24	335	518	1,122	16,067	3,402	11,541	1,124
Total area actually reporting	99.9%	2,910	31	415	549	1,915	19,052	4,286	13,385	1,381
Estimated total	100.0%	2,911	31	415	549	1,916	19,079	4,290	13,405	1,384
Rate per 100,000 inhabitants		470.5	5.0	67.1	88.7	309.7	3,083.6	693.4	2,166.6	223.7
Columbia, MO M.S.A.	164,226									
Includes Boone and Howard Counties										
City of Columbia	101,033	392	5	19	138	230	3,951	836	2,968	147
Total area actually reporting	100.0%	542	7	27	152	356	5,364	1,150	4,005	209
Rate per 100,000 inhabitants		330.0	4.3	16.4	92.6	216.8	3,266.2	700.3	2,438.7	127.3
Columbia, SC M.S.A.	728,119									
Includes Calhoun, Fairfield, Kershaw, Lexington, Richland, and Saluda Counties										
City of Columbia	125,485	1,079	13	56	334	676	6,825	1,182	4,998	645
Total area actually reporting	100.0%	5,443	40	244	1,165	3,994	29,083	6,369	19,618	3,096
Rate per 100,000 inhabitants		747.5	5.5	33.5	160.0	548.5	3,994.3	874.7	2,694.3	425.2
Columbus, GA-AL M.S.A.	282,227									
Includes Russell County, AL and Chattahoochee, Harris, Marion, and Muscogee Counties, GA										
City of Columbus, GA	186,217	1,274	30	72	635	537	14,537	3,271	9,656	1,610
Total area actually reporting	96.6%	1,523	34	88	692	709	16,555	3,856	10,856	1,843
Estimated total	100.0%	1,558	35	90	706	727	16,877	3,947	11,050	1,880
Rate per 100,000 inhabitants		552.0	12.4	31.9	250.2	257.6	5,979.9	1,398.5	3,915.3	666.1

Table 6. Crime, by Metropolitan Statistical Area, 2008—*Continued*

(Number, percent, rate per 100,000 population.)

Area	Population	Violent crime	Murder and non-negligent man-slaughter	Forcible rape	Robbery	Aggravated assault	Property crime	Burglary	Larceny-theft	Motor vehicle theft
Columbus, IN M.S.A.	75,091									
Includes Bartholomew County										
City of Columbus	39,889	46	1	5	13	27	1,978	177	1,695	106
Total area actually reporting	99.5%	70	2	5	14	49	2,377	217	2,032	128
Estimated total	100.0%	71	2	5	14	50	2,390	219	2,042	129
Rate per 100,000 inhabitants		94.6	2.7	6.7	18.6	66.6	3,182.8	291.6	2,719.4	171.8
Columbus, OH M.S.A.	1,773,358									
Includes Delaware, Fairfield, Franklin, Licking, Madison, Morrow, Pickaway, and Union Counties										
City of Columbus	751,887	5,821	109	615	3,590	1,507	48,282	14,708	28,263	5,311
Total area actually reporting	88.2%	6,985	120	865	4,103	1,897	72,440	19,770	46,377	6,293
Estimated total	100.0%	7,230	123	908	4,183	2,016	76,682	20,864	49,304	6,514
Rate per 100,000 inhabitants		407.7	6.9	51.2	235.9	113.7	4,324.1	1,176.5	2,780.3	367.3
Corpus Christi, TX M.S.A.	415,807									
Includes Aransas, Nueces, and San Patricio Counties										
City of Corpus Christi	286,348	2,224	19	192	490	1,523	17,634	3,461	13,489	684
Total area actually reporting	100.0%	2,628	21	243	539	1,825	22,566	4,881	16,824	861
Rate per 100,000 inhabitants		632.0	5.1	58.4	129.6	438.9	5,427.0	1,173.9	4,046.1	207.1
Corvallis, OR M.S.A.	81,844									
Includes Benton County										
City of Corvallis	51,343	60	0	11	15	34	1,341	200	1,073	68
Total area actually reporting	100.0%	110	1	20	20	69	1,942	329	1,506	107
Rate per 100,000 inhabitants		134.4	1.2	24.4	24.4	84.3	2,372.8	402.0	1,840.1	130.7
Cumberland, MD-WV M.S.A.	98,503									
Includes Allegany County, MD and Mineral County, WV										
City of Cumberland, MD	20,558	170	1	13	27	129	1,217	298	899	20
Total area actually reporting	99.3%	447	5	25	41	376	2,652	641	1,938	73
Estimated total	100.0%	448	5	25	41	377	2,676	645	1,957	74
Rate per 100,000 inhabitants		454.8	5.1	25.4	41.6	382.7	2,716.7	654.8	1,986.7	75.1
Dallas-Fort Worth-Arlington, TX M.S.A.	6,286,760									
Includes the Metropolitan Divisions of Dallas-Plano-Irving and Fort Worth-Arlington										
City of Dallas	1,276,214	11,420	170	499	6,466	4,285	75,759	21,149	42,402	12,208
City of Fort Worth	701,345	4,601	49	350	1,706	2,496	35,325	9,018	23,562	2,745
City of Arlington	375,836	2,262	23	141	694	1,404	20,149	4,461	14,140	1,548
City of Plano	265,739	602	7	48	144	403	8,132	1,549	6,171	412
City of Irving	200,470	722	7	31	238	446	8,560	1,819	5,867	874
City of Carrollton	125,607	293	4	17	134	138	3,935	1,017	2,556	362
City of Denton	120,295	357	0	70	93	194	3,333	667	2,507	159
City of McKinney	126,659	267	3	51	42	171	2,744	503	2,136	105
City of Richardson	100,597	269	4	23	112	130	3,379	850	2,282	247
Total area actually reporting	99.9%	28,759	348	1,951	11,667	14,793	255,483	62,753	166,296	26,434
Estimated total	100.0%	28,760	348	1,951	11,667	14,794	255,501	62,757	166,309	26,435
Rate per 100,000 inhabitants		457.5	5.5	31.0	185.6	235.3	4,064.1	998.2	2,645.4	420.5
Dallas-Plano-Irving, TX M.D.	4,210,336									
Includes Collin, Dallas, Delta, Denton, Ellis, Hunt, Kaufman, and Rockwall Counties										
Total area actually reporting	99.9%	19,095	257	1,180	8,739	8,919	169,747	42,894	106,885	19,968
Estimated total	100.0%	19,096	257	1,180	8,739	8,920	169,765	42,898	106,898	19,969
Rate per 100,000 inhabitants		453.6	6.1	28.0	207.6	211.9	4,032.1	1,018.9	2,538.9	474.3
Fort Worth-Arlington, TX M.D.	2,076,424									
Includes Johnson, Parker, Tarrant, and Wise Counties										
Total area actually reporting	100.0%	9,664	91	771	2,928	5,874	85,736	19,859	59,411	6,466
Rate per 100,000 inhabitants		465.4	4.4	37.1	141.0	282.9	4,129.0	956.4	2,861.2	311.4
Dalton, GA M.S.A.	135,123									
Includes Murray and Whitfield Counties										
City of Dalton	34,095	127	0	10	32	85	1,214	206	953	55
Total area actually reporting	98.4%	441	1	25	50	365	3,833	789	2,844	200
Estimated total	100.0%	453	1	26	54	372	3,934	810	2,916	208
Rate per 100,000 inhabitants		335.3	0.7	19.2	40.0	275.3	2,911.4	599.5	2,158.0	153.9
Danville, VA M.S.A.	104,868									
Includes Pittsylvania County and Danville City										
City of Danville	44,383	262	11	7	110	134	2,704	510	2,097	97
Total area actually reporting	100.0%	337	13	19	128	177	3,352	751	2,453	148
Rate per 100,000 inhabitants		321.4	12.4	18.1	122.1	168.8	3,196.4	716.1	2,339.1	141.1

Table 6. Crime, by Metropolitan Statistical Area, 2008—*Continued*

(Number, percent, rate per 100,000 population.)

Area	Population	Violent crime	Murder and non-negligent man-slaughter	Forcible rape	Robbery	Aggravated assault	Property crime	Burglary	Larceny-theft	Motor vehicle theft
Dayton, OH M.S.A.	834,203									
Includes Greene, Miami, Montgomery, and Preble Counties										
City of Dayton	154,218	1,672	37	105	808	722	9,466	3,237	5,061	1,168
Total area actually reporting	95.6%	2,929	42	324	1,306	1,257	28,219	7,117	18,825	2,277
Estimated total	100.0%	2,995	43	335	1,332	1,285	29,303	7,326	19,647	2,330
Rate per 100,000 inhabitants		359.0	5.2	40.2	159.7	154.0	3,512.7	878.2	2,355.2	279.3
Decatur, AL M.S.A.	150,005									
Includes Lawrence and Morgan Counties										
City of Decatur	55,941	291	3	29	123	136	3,996	976	2,889	131
Total area actually reporting	100.0%	392	6	40	134	212	5,690	1,537	3,968	185
Rate per 100,000 inhabitants		261.3	4.0	26.7	89.3	141.3	3,793.2	1,024.6	2,645.2	123.3
Deltona-Daytona Beach-Ormond Beach, FL M.S.A.	501,508									
Includes Volusia County										
City of Daytona Beach	63,642	995	8	30	362	595	4,644	1,051	3,131	462
City of Ormond Beach	38,173	125	0	16	27	82	1,255	274	921	60
Total area actually reporting	99.4%	2,954	15	161	722	2,056	19,149	5,068	12,647	1,434
Estimated total	100.0%	2,971	15	162	728	2,066	19,274	5,096	12,734	1,444
Rate per 100,000 inhabitants		592.4	3.0	32.3	145.2	412.0	3,843.2	1,016.1	2,539.1	287.9
Denver-Aurora-Broomfield, CO M.S.A.	2,505,132									
Includes Adams, Arapahoe, Broomfield, Clear Creek, Denver, Douglas, Elbert, Gilpin, Jefferson, and Park Counties										
City of Denver	592,881	3,361	40	282	951	2,088	19,316	5,173	10,547	3,596
City of Aurora	316,323	1,622	18	188	555	861	10,660	2,216	7,146	1,298
City of Broomfield	55,820	37	0	10	7	20	1,247	98	1,083	66
Total area actually reporting	99.1%	8,933	81	1,062	2,247	5,543	71,736	14,424	48,222	9,090
Estimated total	100.0%	8,984	81	1,070	2,251	5,582	72,100	14,512	48,465	9,123
Rate per 100,000 inhabitants		358.6	3.2	42.7	89.9	222.8	2,878.1	579.3	1,934.6	364.2
Des Moines-West Des Moines, IA M.S.A.	556,378									
Includes Dallas, Guthrie, Madison, Polk, and Warren Counties										
City of Des Moines	196,680	1,330	12	171	319	828	10,016	1,999	7,253	764
City of West Des Moines	55,765	131	1	18	28	84	1,746	217	1,482	47
Total area actually reporting	100.0%	1,853	16	250	380	1,207	16,699	3,217	12,438	1,044
Rate per 100,000 inhabitants		333.0	2.9	44.9	68.3	216.9	3,001.4	578.2	2,235.5	187.6
Dothan, AL M.S.A.	140,899									
Includes Geneva, Henry, and Houston Counties										
City of Dothan	65,416	394	3	30	186	175	3,485	846	2,493	146
Total area actually reporting	96.9%	548	4	53	210	281	4,961	1,241	3,447	273
Estimated total	100.0%	567	4	54	217	292	5,160	1,288	3,586	286
Rate per 100,000 inhabitants		402.4	2.8	38.3	154.0	207.2	3,662.2	914.1	2,545.1	203.0
Dover, DE M.S.A.	155,344									
Includes Kent County										
City of Dover	36,291	298	4	19	81	194	2,016	186	1,705	125
Total area actually reporting	100.0%	1,039	8	98	194	739	5,375	1,146	3,877	352
Rate per 100,000 inhabitants		668.8	5.1	63.1	124.9	475.7	3,460.1	737.7	2,495.8	226.6
Dubuque, IA M.S.A.	92,937									
Includes Dubuque County										
City of Dubuque	57,262	356	0	21	25	310	1,915	487	1,357	71
Total area actually reporting	100.0%	417	0	26	25	366	2,210	576	1,538	96
Rate per 100,000 inhabitants		448.7	0.0	28.0	26.9	393.8	2,378.0	619.8	1,654.9	103.3
Duluth, MN-WI M.S.A.[5]	273,527									
Includes Carlton and St. Louis Counties, MN[5] and Douglas County, WI										
City of Duluth, MN[5]	84,171		2		128	195	4,211	520	3,524	167
Total area actually reporting	98.9%		4		171	367	9,402	1,509	7,441	452
Estimated total	100.0%		4		172	369	9,494	1,521	7,516	457
Rate per 100,000 inhabitants			1.5		62.9	134.9	3,471.0	556.1	2,747.8	167.1
Durham-Chapel Hill, NC M.S.A.	488,133									
Includes Chatham, Durham, Orange, and Person Counties										
City of Durham	221,785	1,815	24	75	886	830	11,958	3,490	7,584	884
City of Chapel Hill	52,034	152	2	9	74	67	1,882	531	1,261	90
Total area actually reporting	100.0%	2,509	38	112	1,130	1,229	20,759	6,077	13,326	1,356
Rate per 100,000 inhabitants		514.0	7.8	22.9	231.5	251.8	4,252.7	1,244.9	2,730.0	277.8

[5] The data collection methodology for the offense of forcible rape used by the Minnesota state UCR Program (with the exception of Minneapolis and St. Paul, MN) does not comply with national UCR Program guidelines. Consequently, their figures for forcible rape and violent crime (of which forcible rape is a part) are not published in this table.

Table 6. Crime, by Metropolitan Statistical Area, 2008—*Continued*

(Number, percent, rate per 100,000 population.)

Area	Population	Violent crime	Murder and non-negligent man-slaughter	Forcible rape	Robbery	Aggravated assault	Property crime	Burglary	Larceny-theft	Motor vehicle theft
Eau Claire, WI M.S.A.	158,895									
Includes Chippewa and Eau Claire Counties										
City of Eau Claire	65,344	84	1	13	14	56	1,827	362	1,406	59
Total area actually reporting	100.0%	160	2	30	23	105	3,443	661	2,672	110
Rate per 100,000 inhabitants		100.7	1.3	18.9	14.5	66.1	2,166.8	416.0	1,681.6	69.2
El Centro, CA M.S.A.	163,673									
Includes Imperial County										
City of El Centro	39,865	169	0	10	52	107	2,230	509	1,412	309
Total area actually reporting	100.0%	474	8	22	127	317	6,228	1,948	3,193	1,087
Rate per 100,000 inhabitants		289.6	4.9	13.4	77.6	193.7	3,805.1	1,190.2	1,950.8	664.1
Elizabethtown, KY M.S.A.	112,156									
Includes Hardin and Larue Counties										
City of Elizabethtown	23,926	80	1	9	25	45	1,091	192	863	36
Total area actually reporting	100.0%	368	1	42	47	278	2,029	432	1,516	81
Rate per 100,000 inhabitants		328.1	0.9	37.4	41.9	247.9	1,809.1	385.2	1,351.7	72.2
Elkhart-Goshen, IN M.S.A.	199,699									
Includes Elkhart County										
City of Elkhart	52,654	210	7	33	161	9	3,567	906	2,464	197
City of Goshen	32,152	45	0	13	21	11	1,282	196	1,048	38
Total area actually reporting	100.0%	314	8	69	204	33	7,157	1,768	4,917	472
Rate per 100,000 inhabitants		157.2	4.0	34.6	102.2	16.5	3,583.9	885.3	2,462.2	236.4
Elmira, NY M.S.A.	87,619									
Includes Chemung County										
City of Elmira	29,255	108	3	4	34	67	1,168	276	872	20
Total area actually reporting	100.0%	204	4	18	37	145	2,132	441	1,652	39
Rate per 100,000 inhabitants		232.8	4.6	20.5	42.2	165.5	2,433.3	503.3	1,885.4	44.5
El Paso, TX M.S.A.	741,662									
Includes El Paso County										
City of El Paso	612,374	2,825	17	181	456	2,171	19,702	2,079	14,870	2,753
Total area actually reporting	100.0%	3,242	19	212	517	2,494	23,064	2,734	17,225	3,105
Rate per 100,000 inhabitants		437.1	2.6	28.6	69.7	336.3	3,109.8	368.6	2,322.5	418.7
Erie, PA M.S.A.	278,759									
Includes Erie County										
City of Erie	103,881	646	7	88	317	234	3,554	1,111	2,280	163
Total area actually reporting	100.0%	852	9	126	360	357	6,884	1,742	4,872	270
Rate per 100,000 inhabitants		305.6	3.2	45.2	129.1	128.1	2,469.5	624.9	1,747.7	96.9
Eugene-Springfield, OR M.S.A.	346,191									
Includes Lane County										
City of Eugene	150,297	496	2	60	223	211	9,821	1,704	6,814	1,303
City of Springfield	57,081	245	1	14	41	189	3,858	506	2,843	509
Total area actually reporting	100.0%	1,133	8	110	302	713	16,504	3,048	11,326	2,130
Rate per 100,000 inhabitants		327.3	2.3	31.8	87.2	206.0	4,767.3	880.4	3,271.6	615.3
Evansville, IN-KY M.S.A.	350,434									
Includes Gibson, Posey, Vanderburgh, and Warrick Counties, IN and Henderson and Webster Counties, KY										
City of Evansville, IN	115,639	462	5	65	124	268	5,433	1,104	4,083	246
Total area actually reporting	79.2%	691	8	83	134	466	8,147	1,524	6,280	343
Estimated total	100.0%	873	10	100	191	572	10,182	1,939	7,771	472
Rate per 100,000 inhabitants		249.1	2.9	28.5	54.5	163.2	2,905.5	553.3	2,217.5	134.7
Fairbanks, AK M.S.A.	37,407									
Includes Fairbanks North Star Borough										
City of Fairbanks	35,131	272	3	41	28	200	1,189	141	921	127
Total area actually reporting	100.0%	290	3	45	31	211	1,437	163	1,129	145
Rate per 100,000 inhabitants		775.3	8.0	120.3	82.9	564.1	3,841.5	435.7	3,018.2	387.6
Fargo, ND-MN M.S.A.1, [5]	194,942									
Includes Clay County, MN[1, 5] and Cass County, ND										
City of Fargo, ND	92,883	273	0	52	27	194	2,906	442	2,252	212
Total area actually reporting	100.0%		0		36	258			3,708	319
Rate per 100,000 inhabitants			0.0		18.5	132.3			1,902.1	163.6
Farmington, NM M.S.A.[1]	123,156									
Includes San Juan County										
City of Farmington[1]	42,956		3	91	38		1,689	781	772	136
Total area actually reporting	100.0%		8	150	49		2,968	1,159	1,545	264
Rate per 100,000 inhabitants			6.5	121.8	39.8		2,410.0	941.1	1,254.5	214.4

[1] The FBI determined that the agency's data were overreported. Consequently, affected data are not included in this table.

[5] The data collection methodology for the offense of forcible rape used by the Minnesota state UCR Program (with the exception of Minneapolis and St. Paul, MN) does not comply with national UCR Program guidelines. Consequently, their figures for forcible rape and violent crime (of which forcible rape is a part) are not published in this table.

Table 6. Crime, by Metropolitan Statistical Area, 2008—*Continued*

(Number, percent, rate per 100,000 population.)

Area	Population	Violent crime	Murder and non-negligent man-slaughter	Forcible rape	Robbery	Aggravated assault	Property crime	Burglary	Larceny-theft	Motor vehicle theft
Fayetteville, NC M.S.A.	351,539									
Includes Cumberland and Hoke Counties										
City of Fayetteville	171,457	1,621	23	72	653	873	13,499	3,920	8,684	895
Total area actually reporting	100.0%	2,567	40	111	900	1,516	21,170	6,280	13,523	1,367
Rate per 100,000 inhabitants		730.2	11.4	31.6	256.0	431.2	6,022.1	1,786.4	3,846.8	388.9
Fayetteville-Springdale-Rogers, AR-MO M.S.A.[2]	447,732									
Includes Benton, Madison, and Washington Counties, AR and McDonald County, MO										
City of Fayetteville, AR	73,999	334	1	38	44	251	2,757	568	2,072	117
City of Springdale, AR	69,759	295	1	65	21	208	2,527	587	1,790	150
City of Rogers, AR[2]	57,205	142	2	39	15	86	1,939	399	1,494	46
City of Bentonville, AR[2]	35,972	53	0	3	5	45	616	88	508	20
Total area actually reporting	99.3%	1,383	8	244	95	1,036	10,889	2,660	7,690	539
Estimated total	100.0%	1,398	8	246	97	1,047	11,008	2,698	7,766	544
Rate per 100,000 inhabitants		312.2	1.8	54.9	21.7	233.8	2,458.6	602.6	1,734.5	121.5
Flagstaff, AZ M.S.A.	128,071									
Includes Coconino County										
City of Flagstaff	60,400	262	3	43	61	155	3,364	409	2,867	88
Total area actually reporting	97.4%	467	3	79	69	316	4,783	685	3,975	123
Estimated total	100.0%	477	3	80	72	322	4,914	715	4,061	138
Rate per 100,000 inhabitants		372.4	2.3	62.5	56.2	251.4	3,836.9	558.3	3,170.9	107.8
Flint, MI M.S.A.	430,816									
Includes Genesee County										
City of Flint	113,462	2,297	32	103	686	1,476	6,889	3,273	2,707	909
Total area actually reporting	99.7%	3,205	37	239	934	1,995	15,893	5,601	8,629	1,663
Estimated total	100.0%	3,208	37	239	935	1,997	15,927	5,608	8,653	1,666
Rate per 100,000 inhabitants		744.6	8.6	55.5	217.0	463.5	3,696.9	1,301.7	2,008.5	386.7
Florence, SC M.S.A.	200,297									
Includes Darlington and Florence Counties										
City of Florence	31,508	533	8	27	111	387	3,088	526	2,374	188
Total area actually reporting	100.0%	2,008	22	90	339	1,557	10,784	2,633	7,293	858
Rate per 100,000 inhabitants		1,002.5	11.0	44.9	169.2	777.3	5,384.0	1,314.5	3,641.1	428.4
Florence-Muscle Shoals, AL M.S.A.	143,463									
Includes Colbert and Lauderdale Counties										
City of Florence	37,594	155	3	16	65	71	1,877	485	1,335	57
City of Muscle Shoals	12,925	78	0	3	19	56	635	128	487	20
Total area actually reporting	100.0%	572	6	48	127	391	5,232	1,375	3,663	194
Rate per 100,000 inhabitants		398.7	4.2	33.5	88.5	272.5	3,646.9	958.4	2,553.3	135.2
Fond du Lac, WI M.S.A.	99,281									
Includes Fond du Lac County										
City of Fond du Lac	42,037	144	0	27	7	110	1,232	120	1,069	43
Total area actually reporting	100.0%	213	1	38	10	164	1,855	234	1,549	72
Rate per 100,000 inhabitants		214.5	1.0	38.3	10.1	165.2	1,868.4	235.7	1,560.2	72.5
Fort Collins-Loveland, CO M.S.A.	292,381									
Includes Larimer County										
City of Fort Collins	135,785	549	2	75	39	433	4,607	784	3,582	241
City of Loveland	66,204	109	1	23	20	65	1,797	291	1,431	75
Total area actually reporting	100.0%	791	5	130	68	588	8,138	1,428	6,302	408
Rate per 100,000 inhabitants		270.5	1.7	44.5	23.3	201.1	2,783.4	488.4	2,155.4	139.5
Fort Smith, AR-OK M.S.A.	291,712									
Includes Crawford, Franklin, and Sebastian Counties, AR and Le Flore and Sequoyah Counties, OK										
City of Fort Smith, AR	84,847	660	2	90	107	461	4,711	1,068	3,386	257
Total area actually reporting	98.0%	1,290	7	157	134	992	8,042	2,106	5,417	519
Estimated total	100.0%	1,317	7	160	138	1,012	8,267	2,178	5,560	529
Rate per 100,000 inhabitants		451.5	2.4	54.8	47.3	346.9	2,834.0	746.6	1,906.0	181.3
Fort Walton Beach-Crestview-Destin, FL M.S.A.	180,599									
Includes Okaloosa County										
City of Fort Walton Beach	18,831	93	0	9	21	63	792	178	574	40
City of Crestview	19,865	102	0	16	22	64	683	43	600	40
Total area actually reporting	100.0%	689	3	56	139	491	5,539	1,047	4,198	294
Rate per 100,000 inhabitants		381.5	1.7	31.0	77.0	271.9	3,067.0	579.7	2,324.5	162.8

[2] Because of changes in the state/local agency's reporting practices, figures are not comparable to previous years' data.

Table 6. Crime, by Metropolitan Statistical Area, 2008—*Continued*

(Number, percent, rate per 100,000 population.)

Area	Population	Violent crime	Murder and non-negligent man-slaughter	Forcible rape	Robbery	Aggravated assault	Property crime	Burglary	Larceny-theft	Motor vehicle theft
Fort Wayne, IN M.S.A.	412,265									
Includes Allen, Wells, and Whitley Counties										
City of Fort Wayne	251,194	816	25	96	479	216	10,314	2,410	7,238	666
Total area actually reporting	94.5%	904	25	123	500	256	12,434	2,835	8,785	814
Estimated total	100.0%	922	25	126	503	268	12,771	2,921	9,014	836
Rate per 100,000 inhabitants		223.6	6.1	30.6	122.0	65.0	3,097.8	708.5	2,186.5	202.8
Fresno, CA M.S.A.	907,820									
Includes Fresno County										
City of Fresno	475,723	2,782	40	80	984	1,678	22,056	4,173	14,106	3,777
Total area actually reporting	100.0%	4,287	65	172	1,284	2,766	37,249	7,688	23,536	6,025
Rate per 100,000 inhabitants		472.2	7.2	18.9	141.4	304.7	4,103.1	846.9	2,592.6	663.7
Gadsden, AL M.S.A.	103,419									
Includes Etowah County										
City of Gadsden	36,700	288	2	36	135	115	2,452	575	1,716	161
Total area actually reporting	94.8%	378	5	47	148	178	3,548	758	2,583	207
Estimated total	100.0%	401	5	48	157	191	3,791	815	2753	223
Rate per 100,000 inhabitants		387.7	4.8	46.4	151.8	184.7	3,665.7	788.1	2,662.0	215.6
Gainesville, FL M.S.A.	257,041									
Includes Alachua and Gilchrist Counties										
City of Gainesville	113,286	1,046	3	87	235	721	5,961	1,382	4,165	414
Total area actually reporting	99.7%	2,048	6	134	358	1,550	10,863	2,858	7,331	674
Estimated total	100.0%	2,053	6	134	360	1553	10,899	2866	7356	677
Rate per 100,000 inhabitants		798.7	2.3	52.1	140.1	604.2	4,240.2	1,115.0	2,861.8	263.4
Glens Falls, NY M.S.A.	129,422									
Includes Warren and Washington Counties										
City of Glens Falls	13,923	16	0	0	1	15	520	46	468	6
Total area actually reporting	100.0%	227	2	40	13	172	2,288	351	1,896	41
Rate per 100,000 inhabitants		175.4	1.5	30.9	10.0	132.9	1,767.9	271.2	1,465.0	31.7
Goldsboro, NC M.S.A.	113,923									
Includes Wayne County										
City of Goldsboro	37,445	330	5	4	117	204	2,869	746	1,929	194
Total area actually reporting	97.4%	541	11	5	155	370	5,343	1,659	3,255	429
Estimated total	100.0%	554	11	6	159	378	5,491	1,693	3,362	436
Rate per 100,000 inhabitants		486.3	9.7	5.3	139.6	331.8	4,819.9	1,486.1	2,951.1	382.7
Grand Forks, ND-MN M.S.A.[5]	97,825									
Includes Polk County, MN[5] and Grand Forks County, ND										
City of Grand Forks, ND	52,064	142	0	25	14	103	1,769	273	1,391	105
Total area actually reporting	98.7%		1		16	151	2,477	399	1,934	144
Estimated total	100.0%		1		16	152	2,511	404	1,961	146
Rate per 100,000 inhabitants			1.0		16.4	155.4	2,566.8	413.0	2,004.6	149.2
Grand Junction, CO M.S.A.	142,140									
Includes Mesa County										
City of Grand Junction	48,870	288	5	46	29	208	2,501	365	1,960	176
Total area actually reporting	97.7%	471	7	82	44	338	4,154	821	3,029	304
Estimated total	100.0%	479	7	83	46	343	4,256	837	3,105	314
Rate per 100,000 inhabitants		337.0	4.9	58.4	32.4	241.3	2,994.2	588.9	2,184.5	220.9
Grand Rapids-Wyoming, MI M.S.A.[2]	774,538									
Includes Barry, Ionia,[2] Kent, and Newaygo Counties										
City of Grand Rapids	193,096	1,981	15	81	767	1,118	9,209	2,286	6,470	453
City of Wyoming	70,552	269	0	45	82	142	1,784	486	1,122	176
Total area actually reporting	99.1%	3,390	18	349	986	2,037	22,601	5,177	16,301	1,123
Estimated total	100.0%	3,410	18	351	991	2,050	22,793	5,215	16,437	1,141
Rate per 100,000 inhabitants		440.3	2.3	45.3	127.9	264.7	2,942.8	673.3	2,122.2	147.3
Great Falls, MT M.S.A.	82,142									
Includes Cascade County										
City of Great Falls	59,093	162	1	8	30	123	2,791	281	2,381	129
Total area actually reporting	100.0%	210	2	11	31	166	3,118	329	2,635	154
Rate per 100,000 inhabitants		255.7	2.4	13.4	37.7	202.1	3,795.9	400.5	3,207.9	187.5
Greeley, CO M.S.A.	252,815									
Includes Weld County										
City of Greeley	91,900	518	4	46	69	399	3,415	748	2,461	206
Total area actually reporting	97.9%	771	6	73	93	599	6,292	1,451	4,420	421
Estimated total	100.0%	785	6	75	96	608	6,460	1,477	4,546	437
Rate per 100,000 inhabitants		310.5	2.4	29.7	38.0	240.5	2,555.2	584.2	1,798.2	172.9

[2] Because of changes in the state/local agency's reporting practices, figures are not comparable to previous years' data.

[5] The data collection methodology for the offense of forcible rape used by the Minnesota state UCR Program (with the exception of Minneapolis and St. Paul, MN) does not comply with national UCR Program guidelines. Consequently, their figures for forcible rape and violent crime (of which forcible rape is a part) are not published in this table.

Table 6. Crime, by Metropolitan Statistical Area, 2008—*Continued*

(Number, percent, rate per 100,000 population.)

Area	Population	Violent crime	Murder and non-negligent man-slaughter	Forcible rape	Robbery	Aggravated assault	Property crime	Burglary	Larceny-theft	Motor vehicle theft
Green Bay, WI M.S.A.	303,250									
Includes Brown, Kewaunee, and Oconto Counties										
City of Green Bay	100,531	502	2	76	104	320	3,107	651	2,303	153
Total area actually reporting	100.0%	605	2	106	112	385	7,116	1,250	5,556	310
Rate per 100,000 inhabitants		199.5	0.7	35.0	36.9	127.0	2,346.6	412.2	1,832.2	102.2
Greensboro-High Point, NC M.S.A.	707,329									
Includes Guilford, Randolph, and Rockingham Counties										
City of Greensboro	249,561	2,157	24	109	998	1,026	15,809	4,942	9,759	1,108
City of High Point	100,631	707	11	30	305	361	6,011	1,922	3,695	394
Total area actually reporting	99.8%	3,666	45	196	1,493	1,932	32,833	10,178	20,504	2,151
Estimated total	100.0%	3,671	45	196	1,495	1,935	32,894	10,192	20,548	2,154
Rate per 100,000 inhabitants		519.0	6.4	27.7	211.4	273.6	4,650.5	1,440.9	2,905.0	304.5
Greenville, NC M.S.A.	175,515									
Includes Greene and Pitt Counties										
City of Greenville	77,960	632	6	13	243	370	5,105	1,538	3,304	263
Total area actually reporting	100.0%	1,038	8	28	310	692	8,826	2,852	5,513	461
Rate per 100,000 inhabitants		591.4	4.6	16.0	176.6	394.3	5,028.6	1,624.9	3,141.0	262.7
Hagerstown-Martinsburg, MD-WV M.S.A.	265,492									
Includes Washington County, MD and Berkeley and Morgan Counties, WV										
City of Hagerstown, MD	40,002	206	3	1	83	119	1,482	294	1,058	130
City of Martinsburg, WV	16,649	109	0	5	34	70	1,130	109	974	47
Total area actually reporting	99.6%	717	6	33	178	500	6,431	1,445	4,539	447
Estimated total	100.0%	720	6	33	179	502	6,472	1,452	4,571	449
Rate per 100,000 inhabitants		271.2	2.3	12.4	67.4	189.1	2,437.7	546.9	1,721.7	169.1
Hanford-Corcoran, CA M.S.A.	150,711									
Includes Kings County										
City of Hanford	50,602	227	2	12	66	147	1,899	371	1,316	212
City of Corcoran	25,235	69	0	1	6	62	209	86	99	24
Total area actually reporting	100.0%	614	7	27	110	470	3,636	873	2,266	497
Rate per 100,000 inhabitants		407.4	4.6	17.9	73.0	311.9	2,412.6	579.3	1,503.5	329.8
Harrisburg-Carlisle, PA M.S.A.	531,150									
Includes Cumberland, Dauphin, and Perry Counties										
City of Harrisburg	47,118	780	9	46	483	242	2,615	743	1,637	235
City of Carlisle	18,427	75	0	7	49	19	647	82	548	17
Total area actually reporting	99.5%	1,697	19	163	726	789	11,750	2,195	9,031	524
Estimated total	100.0%	1,703	19	163	728	793	11,804	2,203	9,074	527
Rate per 100,000 inhabitants		320.6	3.6	30.7	137.1	149.3	2,222.3	414.8	1,708.4	99.2
Harrisonburg, VA M.S.A.	118,335									
Includes Rockingham County and Harrisonburg City										
City of Harrisonburg	44,346	142	1	12	25	104	1,224	246	903	75
Total area actually reporting	100.0%	172	2	21	28	121	1,828	378	1,337	113
Rate per 100,000 inhabitants		145.4	1.7	17.7	23.7	102.3	1,544.8	319.4	1,129.8	95.5
Hartford-West Hartford-East Hartford, CT M.S.A.	1,006,641									
Includes Hartford, Middlesex, and Tolland Counties										
City of Hartford	124,610	1,503	31	61	629	782	6,374	1,000	4,048	1,326
City of West Hartford	60,411	104	0	4	62	38	1,640	254	1,211	175
City of East Hartford	48,586	222	1	22	88	111	1,611	361	1,069	181
City of Middletown	48,048	78	1	4	52	21	1,644	220	1,329	95
Total area actually reporting	100.0%	2,995	42	209	1,226	1,518	28,858	4,799	20,852	3,207
Rate per 100,000 inhabitants		297.5	4.2	20.8	121.8	150.8	2,866.8	476.7	2,071.4	318.6
Hickory-Lenoir-Morganton, NC M.S.A.	363,694									
Includes Alexander, Burke, Caldwell, and Catawba Counties										
City of Hickory	41,414	331	3	22	116	190	3,180	615	2,361	204
City of Lenoir	17,843	64	4	1	21	38	971	198	708	65
City of Morganton	17,069	60	0	3	14	43	668	209	428	31
Total area actually reporting	99.3%	1,003	29	65	264	645	12,553	3,565	8,172	816
Estimated total	100.0%	1,014	29	66	267	652	12,675	3,593	8,260	822
Rate per 100,000 inhabitants		278.8	8.0	18.1	73.4	179.3	3,485.1	987.9	2,271.1	226.0
Hinesville-Fort Stewart, GA M.S.A.	71,471									
Includes Liberty and Long Counties										
City of Hinesville	30,523	188	1	6	53	128	1,802	539	1,202	61
Total area actually reporting	100.0%	316	5	20	72	219	2,787	921	1,750	116
Rate per 100,000 inhabitants		442.1	7.0	28.0	100.7	306.4	3,899.5	1,288.6	2,448.5	162.3

Table 6. Crime, by Metropolitan Statistical Area, 2008—*Continued*

(Number, percent, rate per 100,000 population.)

Area	Population	Violent crime	Murder and non-negligent man-slaughter	Forcible rape	Robbery	Aggravated assault	Property crime	Burglary	Larceny-theft	Motor vehicle theft
Holland-Grand Haven, MI M.S.A.	259,600									
Includes Ottawa County										
City of Holland	26,591	107	1	24	18	64	947	146	776	25
City of Grand Haven	10,486	47	0	10	6	31	314	37	274	3
Total area actually reporting	97.3%	438	4	128	53	253	4,568	904	3,535	129
Estimated total	100.0%	459	4	130	58	267	4,771	944	3,679	148
Rate per 100,000 inhabitants		176.8	1.5	50.1	22.3	102.9	1,837.8	363.6	1,417.2	57.0
Honolulu, HI M.S.A.	906,349									
Includes Honolulu County										
City of Honolulu	906,349	2,575	18	203	928	1,426	31,781	6,370	21,473	3,938
Total area actually reporting	100.0%	2,575	18	203	928	1,426	31,781	6,370	21,473	3,938
Rate per 100,000 inhabitants		284.1	2.0	22.4	102.4	157.3	3,506.5	702.8	2,369.2	434.5
Hot Springs, AR M.S.A.	97,366									
Includes Garland County										
City of Hot Springs	39,451	513	1	19	104	389	3,922	737	2,996	189
Total area actually reporting	100.0%	642	4	44	118	476	6,426	1,889	4,166	371
Rate per 100,000 inhabitants		659.4	4.1	45.2	121.2	488.9	6,599.8	1,940.1	4,278.7	381.0
Houma-Bayou Cane-Thibodaux, LA M.S.A.	203,144									
Includes Lafourche and Terrebonne Parishes										
City of Houma	32,592	286	0	11	80	195	1,458	302	1,082	74
City of Thibodaux	14,126	98	2	3	19	74	595	107	476	12
Total area actually reporting	100.0%	922	11	52	173	686	6,449	1,063	4,954	432
Rate per 100,000 inhabitants		453.9	5.4	25.6	85.2	337.7	3,174.6	523.3	2,438.7	212.7
Houston-Sugar Land-Baytown, TX M.S.A.	5,752,684									
Includes Austin, Brazoria, Chambers, Fort Bend, Galveston, Harris, Liberty, Montgomery, San Jacinto, and Waller Counties										
City of Houston	2,238,895	24,779	294	750	10,603	13,132	110,759	26,947	68,598	15,214
City of Sugar Land	81,763	138	0	5	46	87	1,729	253	1,381	95
City of Baytown	70,596	324	6	41	100	177	3,457	741	2,371	345
City of Galveston	56,870	443	4	78	145	216	3,085	748	2,079	258
Total area actually reporting	99.9%	39,597	447	1,772	14,693	22,685	219,190	54,853	138,826	25,511
Estimated total	100.0%	39,598	447	1,772	14,693	22,686	219,208	54,857	138,839	25,512
Rate per 100,000 inhabitants		688.3	7.8	30.8	255.4	394.4	3,810.5	953.6	2,413.5	443.5
Huntsville, AL M.S.A.	393,173									
Includes Limestone and Madison Counties										
City of Huntsville	172,794	1,222	18	93	412	699	10,647	2,369	7,196	1,082
Total area actually reporting	100.0%	1,657	19	131	516	991	15,701	3,744	10,518	1,439
Rate per 100,000 inhabitants		421.4	4.8	33.3	131.2	252.1	3,993.4	952.3	2,675.2	366.0
Idaho Falls, ID M.S.A.	121,458									
Includes Bonneville and Jefferson Counties										
City of Idaho Falls	53,566	219	1	30	12	176	1,669	306	1,282	81
Total area actually reporting	100.0%	344	2	51	15	276	2,826	582	2,094	150
Rate per 100,000 inhabitants		283.2	1.6	42.0	12.3	227.2	2,326.7	479.2	1,724.1	123.5
Indianapolis-Carmel, IN M.S.A.	1,717,530									
Includes Boone, Brown, Hamilton, Hancock, Hendricks, Johnson, Marion, Morgan, Putnam, and Shelby Counties										
City of Indianapolis	808,329	9,735	114	475	4,023	5,123	49,177	14,267	28,466	6,444
City of Carmel	65,982	23	0	3	5	15	970	134	788	48
Total area actually reporting	83.5%	10,552	120	560	4,196	5,676	63,010	16,191	39,621	7,198
Estimated total	100.0%	10,963	127	600	4,293	5,943	69,271	17,439	44,217	7,615
Rate per 100,000 inhabitants		638.3	7.4	34.9	250.0	346.0	4,033.2	1,015.4	2,574.5	443.4
Iowa City, IA M.S.A.	149,310									
Includes Johnson and Washington Counties										
City of Iowa City	67,600	257	7	24	55	171	1,692	388	1,232	72
Total area actually reporting	95.1%	419	8	51	75	285	2,980	710	2,136	134
Estimated total	100.0%	431	8	53	76	294	3,129	738	2,251	140
Rate per 100,000 inhabitants		288.7	5.4	35.5	50.9	196.9	2,095.6	494.3	1,507.6	93.8
Ithaca, NY M.S.A.	101,591									
Includes Tompkins County										
City of Ithaca	30,114	58	0	1	28	29	1,094	207	861	26
Total area actually reporting	100.0%	137	2	14	35	86	2,329	424	1,850	55
Rate per 100,000 inhabitants		134.9	2.0	13.8	34.5	84.7	2,292.5	417.4	1,821.0	54.1

Table 6. Crime, by Metropolitan Statistical Area, 2008—*Continued*

(Number, percent, rate per 100,000 population.)

Area	Population	Violent crime	Murder and non-negligent man-slaughter	Forcible rape	Robbery	Aggravated assault	Property crime	Burglary	Larceny-theft	Motor vehicle theft
Jackson, MI M.S.A.	162,183									
Includes Jackson County										
City of Jackson	33,755	323	2	62	57	202	1,893	408	1,392	93
Total area actually reporting	98.0%	616	4	118	84	410	4,376	991	3,148	237
Estimated total	100.0%	626	4	119	86	417	4,472	1,010	3,216	246
Rate per 100,000 inhabitants		386.0	2.5	73.4	53.0	257.1	2,757.4	622.8	1,982.9	151.7
Jackson, MS M.S.A.	540,558									
Includes Copiah, Hinds, Madison, Rankin, and Simpson Counties										
City of Jackson	174,734	1,652	63	136	942	511	13,035	4,334	6,990	1,711
Total area actually reporting	83.2%	2,058	72	196	1,033	757	18,402	5,747	10,603	2,052
Estimated total	100.0%	2,206	76	218	1,069	843	20,525	6,268	12,030	2,227
Rate per 100,000 inhabitants		408.1	14.1	40.3	197.8	155.9	3,797.0	1,159.5	2,225.5	412.0
Jackson, TN M.S.A.	113,254									
Includes Chester and Madison Counties										
City of Jackson	63,620	707	7	28	244	428	4,630	1,093	3,124	413
Total area actually reporting	100.0%	924	10	42	259	613	5,939	1,486	3,921	532
Rate per 100,000 inhabitants		815.9	8.8	37.1	228.7	541.3	5,244.0	1,312.1	3,462.1	469.7
Jacksonville, FL M.S.A.	1,308,904									
Includes Baker, Clay, Duval, Nassau, and St. Johns Counties										
City of Jacksonville	806,080	8,032	115	262	2,938	4,717	46,198	12,012	30,157	4,029
Total area actually reporting	100.0%	10,745	127	378	3,286	6,954	62,582	15,607	42,060	4,915
Rate per 100,000 inhabitants		820.9	9.7	28.9	251.0	531.3	4,781.3	1,192.4	3,213.4	375.5
Jacksonville, NC M.S.A.	164,774									
Includes Onslow County										
City of Jacksonville	75,770	286	5	29	89	163	2,545	505	1,921	119
Total area actually reporting	100.0%	600	11	60	143	386	5,916	1,684	3,888	344
Rate per 100,000 inhabitants		364.1	6.7	36.4	86.8	234.3	3,590.4	1,022.0	2,359.6	208.8
Janesville, WI M.S.A.	160,438									
Includes Rock County										
City of Janesville	63,353	172	1	23	53	95	2,796	507	2,215	74
Total area actually reporting	100.0%	397	4	56	114	223	5,457	988	4,196	273
Rate per 100,000 inhabitants		247.4	2.5	34.9	71.1	139.0	3,401.3	615.8	2,615.3	170.2
Johnson City, TN M.S.A.	194,959									
Includes Carter, Unicoi, and Washington Counties										
City of Johnson City	61,690	309	0	20	51	238	2,849	535	2,203	111
Total area actually reporting	100.0%	713	3	44	74	592	5,583	1,287	4,019	277
Rate per 100,000 inhabitants		365.7	1.5	22.6	38.0	303.7	2,863.7	660.1	2,061.5	142.1
Johnstown, PA M.S.A.	144,050									
Includes Cambria County										
City of Johnstown	23,172	114	2	3	42	67	756	212	501	43
Total area actually reporting	96.2%	272	6	20	55	191	2,704	542	2,059	103
Estimated total	100.0%	285	6	21	58	200	2,817	559	2,149	109
Rate per 100,000 inhabitants		197.8	4.2	14.6	40.3	138.8	1,955.6	388.1	1,491.8	75.7
Jonesboro, AR M.S.A.	117,434									
Includes Craighead and Poinsett Counties										
City of Jonesboro	64,187	278	5	32	89	152	3,227	1,269	1,853	105
Total area actually reporting	97.5%	444	7	55	95	287	4,596	1,802	2,636	158
Estimated total	100.0%	457	7	56	97	297	4,712	1,839	2,710	163
Rate per 100,000 inhabitants		389.2	6.0	47.7	82.6	252.9	4,012.5	1,566.0	2,307.7	138.8
Joplin, MO M.S.A.	172,779									
Includes Jasper and Newton Counties										
City of Joplin	49,551	356	3	42	55	256	4,312	692	3,308	312
Total area actually reporting	100.0%	674	7	75	71	521	7,643	1,449	5,680	514
Rate per 100,000 inhabitants		390.1	4.1	43.4	41.1	301.5	4,423.6	838.6	3,287.4	297.5
Kalamazoo-Portage, MI M.S.A.	321,552									
Includes Kalamazoo and Van Buren Counties										
City of Kalamazoo	72,110	742	1	60	221	460	4,244	1,170	2,806	268
City of Portage	46,210	85	0	16	22	47	1,934	277	1,594	63
Total area actually reporting	98.4%	1,408	6	187	334	881	11,787	2,925	8,214	648
Estimated total	100.0%	1,424	6	189	338	891	11,934	2,954	8,318	662
Rate per 100,000 inhabitants		442.9	1.9	58.8	105.1	277.1	3,711.4	918.7	2,586.8	205.9

Table 6. Crime, by Metropolitan Statistical Area, 2008—*Continued*

(Number, percent, rate per 100,000 population.)

Area	Population	Violent crime	Murder and non-negligent man-slaughter	Forcible rape	Robbery	Aggravated assault	Property crime	Burglary	Larceny-theft	Motor vehicle theft
Kennewick-Pasco-Richland, WA M.S.A.	234,413									
Includes Benton and Franklin Counties										
City of Kennewick	62,930	235	1	38	40	156	2,382	409	1,810	163
City of Pasco	55,612	166	1	19	46	100	1,664	468	1,030	166
City of Richland	45,522	101	0	25	14	62	1,048	206	788	54
Total area actually reporting	100.0%	596	2	95	107	392	6,183	1,423	4,302	458
Rate per 100,000 inhabitants		254.3	0.9	40.5	45.6	167.2	2,637.7	607.0	1,835.2	195.4
Killeen-Temple-Fort Hood, TX M.S.A.	375,230									
Includes Bell, Coryell, and Lampasas Counties										
City of Killeen	115,906	885	10	66	216	593	4,757	1,711	2,877	169
City of Temple	58,812	243	3	27	107	106	2,794	557	2,082	155
Total area actually reporting	99.7%	1,511	16	148	382	965	11,862	3,427	7,915	520
Estimated total	100.0%	1,514	16	148	383	967	11,901	3,435	7,943	523
Rate per 100,000 inhabitants		403.5	4.3	39.4	102.1	257.7	3,171.7	915.4	2,116.8	139.4
Kingsport-Bristol-Bristol, TN-VA M.S.A.	303,904									
Includes Hawkins and Sullivan Counties, TN and Scott and Washington Counties and Bristol City, VA										
City of Kingsport, TN	44,350	374	2	18	53	301	2,764	542	2,083	139
City of Bristol, TN	25,485	124	7	11	7	99	1,328	176	1,053	99
City of Bristol, VA	17,563	72	0	14	15	43	709	129	541	39
Total area actually reporting	100.0%	1,092	16	118	120	838	10,452	2,500	7,301	651
Rate per 100,000 inhabitants		359.3	5.3	38.8	39.5	275.7	3,439.2	822.6	2,402.4	214.2
Kingston, NY M.S.A.	182,305									
Includes Ulster County										
City of Kingston	22,520	69	0	5	48	16	645	115	510	20
Total area actually reporting	100.0%	462	6	51	71	334	3,210	814	2,298	98
Rate per 100,000 inhabitants		253.4	3.3	28.0	38.9	183.2	1,760.8	446.5	1,260.5	53.8
Knoxville, TN M.S.A.	689,656									
Includes Anderson, Blount, Knox, Loudon, and Union Counties										
City of Knoxville	184,559	1,992	28	140	668	1,156	12,186	2,661	8,383	1,142
Total area actually reporting	100.0%	3,498	40	234	895	2,329	25,670	6,741	16,828	2,101
Rate per 100,000 inhabitants		507.2	5.8	33.9	129.8	337.7	3,722.1	977.4	2,440.1	304.6
Kokomo, IN M.S.A.	99,575									
Includes Howard and Tipton Counties										
City of Kokomo	45,779	217	3	19	59	136	2,684	519	2,078	87
Total area actually reporting	100.0%	279	3	24	68	184	3,645	857	2,662	126
Rate per 100,000 inhabitants		280.2	3.0	24.1	68.3	184.8	3,660.6	860.7	2,673.4	126.5
La Crosse, WI-MN M.S.A.[5]	131,303									
Includes Houston County, MN[5] and La Crosse County, WI										
City of La Crosse, WI	50,569	206	1	16	32	157	1,891	308	1,495	88
Total area actually reporting	95.2%		1		36	204	3,238	508	2,602	128
Estimated total	100.0%		1		39	209	3,436	535	2,763	138
Rate per 100,000 inhabitants			0.8		29.7	159.2	2,616.8	407.5	2,104.3	105.1
Lafayette, IN M.S.A.	193,802									
Includes Benton, Carroll, and Tippecanoe Counties										
City of Lafayette	63,990	325	3	24	53	245	3,000	610	2,191	199
Total area actually reporting	95.5%	447	4	40	65	338	5,299	1,131	3,859	309
Estimated total	100.0%	459	4	41	68	346	5,475	1,168	3,987	320
Rate per 100,000 inhabitants		236.8	2.1	21.2	35.1	178.5	2,825.0	602.7	2,057.3	165.1
Lafayette, LA M.S.A.	260,236									
Includes Lafayette and St. Martin Parishes										
City of Lafayette	113,770	1,276	10	73	307	886	6,766	1,421	4,839	506
Total area actually reporting	91.3%	1,819	14	111	400	1,294	9,274	2,068	6,494	712
Estimated total	100.0%	1,946	15	117	420	1,394	10,319	2,278	7,282	759
Rate per 100,000 inhabitants		747.8	5.8	45.0	161.4	535.7	3,965.2	875.4	2,798.2	291.7
Lake Havasu City-Kingman, AZ M.S.A.	199,207									
Includes Mohave County										
City of Lake Havasu City	57,616	100	1	18	10	71	1,385	244	1,056	85
City of Kingman	28,725	95	0	15	17	63	1,587	301	1,186	100
Total area actually reporting	100.0%	450	8	51	65	326	7,093	1,894	4,675	524
Rate per 100,000 inhabitants		225.9	4.0	25.6	32.6	163.6	3,560.6	950.8	2,346.8	263.0

[5] The data collection methodology for the offense of forcible rape used by the Minnesota state UCR Program (with the exception of Minneapolis and St. Paul, MN) does not comply with national UCR Program guidelines. Consequently, their figures for forcible rape and violent crime (of which forcible rape is a part) are not published in this table.

Table 6. Crime, by Metropolitan Statistical Area, 2008—*Continued*

(Number, percent, rate per 100,000 population.)

Area	Population	Violent crime	Murder and non-negligent man-slaughter	Forcible rape	Robbery	Aggravated assault	Property crime	Burglary	Larceny-theft	Motor vehicle theft
Lakeland-Winter Haven, FL M.S.A.	579,765									
Includes Polk County										
City of Lakeland	92,669	528	10	36	199	283	5,249	1,029	3,879	341
City of Winter Haven	32,886	287	5	20	78	184	2,273	472	1,598	203
Total area actually reporting	99.5%	2,831	44	164	702	1,921	23,533	6,635	15,264	1,634
Estimated total	100.0%	2,850	44	165	708	1,933	23,676	6,667	15,363	1,646
Rate per 100,000 inhabitants		491.6	7.6	28.5	122.1	333.4	4,083.7	1,149.9	2,649.9	283.9
Lancaster, PA M.S.A.	501,669									
Includes Lancaster County										
City of Lancaster	54,595	534	3	36	240	255	3,075	609	2,284	182
Total area actually reporting	97.7%	932	7	118	348	459	10,306	1,856	7,933	517
Estimated total	100.0%	959	7	120	355	477	10,547	1,892	8,126	529
Rate per 100,000 inhabitants		191.2	1.4	23.9	70.8	95.1	2,102.4	377.1	1,619.8	105.4
Lansing-East Lansing, MI M.S.A.[2]	453,640									
Includes Clinton, Eaton, and Ingham Counties										
City of Lansing	114,415	1,181	11	95	269	806	4,261	1,462	2,484	315
City of East Lansing[2]	46,215	188	0	17	27	144	1,038	270	718	50
Total area actually reporting	80.0%	1,773	12	193	351	1,217	10,585	2,668	7,378	539
Estimated total	100.0%	1,977	13	231	380	1,353	12,392	3,105	8,624	663
Rate per 100,000 inhabitants		435.8	2.9	50.9	83.8	298.3	2,731.7	684.5	1,901.1	146.2
Laredo, TX M.S.A.	238,490									
Includes Webb County										
City of Laredo	222,870	1,357	10	78	311	958	14,340	2,091	10,522	1,727
Total area actually reporting	100.0%	1,436	11	82	322	1,021	14,750	2,238	10,745	1,767
Rate per 100,000 inhabitants		602.1	4.6	34.4	135.0	428.1	6,184.7	938.4	4,505.4	740.9
Las Cruces, NM M.S.A.	201,390									
Includes Dona Ana County										
City of Las Cruces	91,982	491	4	37	78	372	4,419	869	3,312	238
Total area actually reporting	98.9%	858	9	68	93	688	6,353	1,397	4,513	443
Estimated total	100.0%	871	9	69	94	699	6,427	1,413	4,563	451
Rate per 100,000 inhabitants		432.5	4.5	34.3	46.7	347.1	3,191.3	701.6	2,265.8	223.9
Las Vegas-Paradise, NV M.S.A.	1,868,909									
Includes Clark County										
City of Las Vegas Metropolitan Police Department	1,353,175	13,324	120	729	4,932	7,543	53,160	14,902	26,856	11,402
Total area actually reporting	100.0%	15,706	136	881	5,749	8,940	68,546	18,983	35,610	13,953
Rate per 100,000 inhabitants		840.4	7.3	47.1	307.6	478.4	3,667.7	1,015.7	1,905.4	746.6
Lawrence, KS M.S.A.	115,531									
Includes Douglas County										
City of Lawrence	91,089	412	4	40	78	290	4,656	801	3,656	199
Total area actually reporting	100.0%	458	4	49	79	326	5,371	967	4,179	225
Rate per 100,000 inhabitants		396.4	3.5	42.4	68.4	282.2	4,649.0	837.0	3,617.2	194.8
Lawton, OK M.S.A.	113,817									
Includes Comanche County										
City of Lawton	91,459	1,001	6	78	201	716	4,248	1,445	2,574	229
Total area actually reporting	100.0%	1,014	6	80	203	725	4,425	1,528	2,659	238
Rate per 100,000 inhabitants		890.9	5.3	70.3	178.4	637.0	3,887.8	1,342.5	2,336.2	209.1
Lebanon, PA M.S.A.	128,795									
Includes Lebanon County										
City of Lebanon	24,212	114	1	8	38	67	810	162	604	44
Total area actually reporting	100.0%	307	2	21	59	225	2,268	396	1,779	93
Rate per 100,000 inhabitants		238.4	1.6	16.3	45.8	174.7	1,760.9	307.5	1,381.3	72.2
Lewiston, ID-WA M.S.A.	60,233									
Includes Nez Perce County, ID and Asotin County, WA										
City of Lewiston, ID	31,911	45	1	9	7	28	1,059	237	774	48
Total area actually reporting	100.0%	89	3	12	11	63	1,693	337	1,296	60
Rate per 100,000 inhabitants		147.8	5.0	19.9	18.3	104.6	2,810.8	559.5	2,151.6	99.6
Lewiston-Auburn, ME M.S.A.	106,715									
Includes Androscoggin County										
City of Lewiston	35,183	94	1	22	34	37	1,065	204	830	31
City of Auburn	23,205	44	1	8	14	21	743	120	595	28
Total area actually reporting	100.0%	160	2	36	48	74	2,466	492	1,872	102
Rate per 100,000 inhabitants		149.9	1.9	33.7	45.0	69.3	2,310.8	461.0	1,754.2	95.6

[2] Because of changes in the state/local agency's reporting practices, figures are not comparable to previous years' data.

Table 6. Crime, by Metropolitan Statistical Area, 2008—*Continued*

(Number, percent, rate per 100,000 population.)

Area	Population	Violent crime	Murder and non-negligent man-slaughter	Forcible rape	Robbery	Aggravated assault	Property crime	Burglary	Larceny-theft	Motor vehicle theft
Lexington-Fayette, KY M.S.A.	452,390									
Includes Bourbon, Clark, Fayette, Jessamine, Scott, and Woodford Counties										
City of Lexington	281,473	1,780	12	137	529	1,102	9,724	2,259	6,878	587
Total area actually reporting	94.6%	2,057	15	174	608	1,260	14,685	3,264	10,597	824
Estimated total	100.0%	2,097	15	179	620	1,283	15,129	3,375	10,903	851
Rate per 100,000 inhabitants		463.5	3.3	39.6	137.0	283.6	3,344.2	746.0	2,410.1	188.1
Lima, OH M.S.A.	104,842									
Includes Allen County										
City of Lima	37,507	498	2	67	157	272	2,959	953	1,812	194
Total area actually reporting	91.3%	563	2	81	183	297	4,576	1,306	3,031	239
Estimated total	100.0%	579	2	84	189	304	4,842	1,357	3,233	252
Rate per 100,000 inhabitants		552.3	1.9	80.1	180.3	290.0	4,618.4	1,294.3	3,083.7	240.4
Lincoln, NE M.S.A.	295,470									
Includes Lancaster and Seward Counties										
City of Lincoln	251,550	1,282	4	113	213	952	10,168	1,569	8,251	348
Total area actually reporting	100.0%	1,315	6	119	217	973	11,011	1,718	8,928	365
Rate per 100,000 inhabitants		445.1	2.0	40.3	73.4	329.3	3,726.6	581.4	3,021.6	123.5
Little Rock-North Little Rock-Conway, AR M.S.A.[2]	673,330									
Includes Faulkner, Grant, Lonoke, Perry, Pulaski,[2] and Saline Counties										
City of Little Rock	187,978	2,356	40	132	819	1,365	15,003	3,576	10,272	1,155
City of North Little Rock	59,369	810	11	36	274	489	6,107	1,527	4,137	443
City of Conway[2]	58,945	230	0	32	62	136	2,778	906	1,743	129
Total area actually reporting	99.3%	4,814	64	360	1,319	3,071	35,913	9,826	23,610	2,477
Estimated total	100.0%	4,837	64	362	1,323	3,088	36,107	9,888	23,733	2,486
Rate per 100,000 inhabitants		718.4	9.5	53.8	196.5	458.6	5,362.5	1,468.5	3,524.7	369.2
Logan, UT-ID M.S.A.	124,922									
Includes Franklin County, ID and Cache County, UT										
City of Logan, UT	48,670	44	1	13	2	28	943	218	694	31
Total area actually reporting	100.0%	91	2	36	2	51	2,050	399	1,598	53
Rate per 100,000 inhabitants		72.8	1.6	28.8	1.6	40.8	1,641.0	319.4	1,279.2	42.4
Longview, TX M.S.A.	204,851									
Includes Gregg, Rusk, and Upshur Counties										
City of Longview	75,524	788	9	44	214	521	4,984	1,117	3,481	386
Total area actually reporting	99.4%	1,297	15	97	284	901	9,306	2,227	6,282	797
Estimated total	100.0%	1,300	15	97	285	903	9,348	2,236	6,312	800
Rate per 100,000 inhabitants		634.6	7.3	47.4	139.1	440.8	4,563.3	1,091.5	3,081.3	390.5
Longview, WA M.S.A.	101,545									
Includes Cowlitz County										
City of Longview	36,887	150	1	34	43	72	1,925	310	1,453	162
Total area actually reporting	100.0%	297	2	94	62	139	3,805	735	2,738	332
Rate per 100,000 inhabitants		292.5	2.0	92.6	61.1	136.9	3,747.1	723.8	2,696.3	326.9
Los Angeles-Long Beach-Santa Ana, CA M.S.A.	12,872,427									
Includes the Metropolitan Divisions of Los Angeles-Long Beach-Glendale and Santa Ana-Anaheim-Irvine										
City of Los Angeles	3,850,920	26,553	384	949	13,422	11,798	100,821	19,726	58,472	22,623
City of Long Beach	467,055	3,158	40	120	1,487	1,511	12,991	3,080	7,039	2,872
City of Santa Ana	339,674	1,726	30	66	842	788	6,980	1,097	4,348	1,535
City of Anaheim	333,746	1,312	11	83	573	645	8,331	1,604	5,633	1,094
City of Glendale	197,182	351	3	21	151	176	4,105	708	2,891	506
City of Irvine	209,278	129	1	18	54	56	3,211	452	2,556	203
City of Pomona	153,201	1,158	20	37	463	638	4,939	1,101	2,663	1,175
City of Pasadena	144,545	621	3	21	260	337	4,182	858	2,957	367
City of Torrance	141,819	306	2	21	175	108	3,071	509	2,109	453
City of Orange	134,852	220	1	8	100	111	3,022	426	2,207	389
City of Fullerton	132,776	410	2	36	145	227	4,143	816	2,935	392
City of Costa Mesa	108,898	350	1	39	120	190	3,367	516	2,547	304
City of Burbank	103,640	235	2	17	86	130	2,941	589	1,834	518
City of Compton	94,519	1,738	28	48	595	1,067	3,333	896	1,409	1,028
City of Carson	93,170	565	8	19	215	323	2,528	445	1,433	650
City of Santa Monica	87,572	536	4	21	218	293	2,904	557	2,104	243
City of Newport Beach	79,821	151	0	5	44	102	2,197	454	1,629	114
City of Tustin	71,272	109	1	11	52	45	1,555	210	1,193	152
City of Montebello	62,318	213	5	10	110	88	1,896	527	837	532
City of Monterey Park	61,664	114	2	1	78	33	1,242	309	698	235
City of Gardena	58,814	369	3	11	229	126	1,567	306	879	382
City of Paramount	55,636	396	5	14	189	188	1,956	379	848	729
City of Arcadia	56,605	128	2	4	62	60	1,550	343	1,084	123
City of Fountain Valley	55,524	104	0	2	36	66	1,376	276	1,006	94
City of Cerritos	51,655	140	1	6	90	43	1,893	306	1,317	270
Total area actually reporting	100.0%	67,425	878	2,603	29,765	34,179	323,387	66,115	193,337	63,935
Rate per 100,000 inhabitants		523.8	6.8	20.2	231.2	265.5	2,512.2	513.6	1,501.9	496.7

[2] Because of changes in the state/local agency's reporting practices, figures are not comparable to previous years' data.

Table 6. Crime, by Metropolitan Statistical Area, 2008—*Continued*

(Number, percent, rate per 100,000 population.)

Area	Population	Violent crime	Murder and non-negligent man-slaughter	Forcible rape	Robbery	Aggravated assault	Property crime	Burglary	Larceny-theft	Motor vehicle theft
Los Angeles-Long Beach-Glendale, CA M.D.	9,872,263									
Includes Los Angeles County										
Total area actually reporting	100.0%	59,788	806	2,173	26,731	30,078	259,682	54,532	148,579	56,571
Rate per 100,000 inhabitants		605.6	8.2	22.0	270.8	304.7	2,630.4	552.4	1,505.0	573.0
Santa Ana-Anaheim-Irvine, CA M.D.	3,000,164									
Includes Orange County										
Total area actually reporting	100.0%	7,637	72	430	3,034	4,101	63,705	11,583	44,758	7,364
Rate per 100,000 inhabitants		254.6	2.4	14.3	101.1	136.7	2,123.4	386.1	1,491.9	245.5
Louisville/Jefferson County, KY-IN M.S.A.	1,243,209									
Includes Clark, Floyd, Harrison, and Washington Counties, IN and Bullitt, Henry, Jefferson, Meade, Nelson, Oldham, Shelby, Spencer, and Trimble Counties, KY										
City of Louisville Metro, KY	629,679	4,306	71	220	1,762	2,253	29,420	7,278	19,523	2,619
Total area actually reporting	95.2%	5,152	77	312	2,106	2,657	42,816	10,237	29,028	3,551
Estimated total	100.0%	5,280	79	322	2,141	2,738	44,556	10,542	30,347	3,667
Rate per 100,000 inhabitants		424.7	6.4	25.9	172.2	220.2	3,584.0	848.0	2,441.0	295.0
Lubbock, TX M.S.A.	269,446									
Includes Crosby and Lubbock Counties										
City of Lubbock	219,594	2,098	8	82	298	1,710	12,271	3,109	8,564	598
Total area actually reporting	100.0%	2,266	9	108	312	1,837	13,685	3,596	9,405	684
Rate per 100,000 inhabitants		841.0	3.3	40.1	115.8	681.8	5,078.9	1,334.6	3,490.5	253.9
Lynchburg, VA M.S.A.	244,588									
Includes Amherst, Appomattox, Bedford, and Campbell Counties and Bedford and Lynchburg Cities										
City of Lynchburg	71,805	347	4	30	101	212	2,739	425	2,160	154
Total area actually reporting	100.0%	554	8	80	128	338	5,411	858	4,220	333
Rate per 100,000 inhabitants		226.5	3.3	32.7	52.3	138.2	2,212.3	350.8	1,725.4	136.1
Macon, GA M.S.A.	229,719									
Includes Bibb, Crawford, Jones, Monroe, and Twiggs Counties										
City of Macon	92,576	884	19	41	370	454	7,758	1,963	4,972	823
Total area actually reporting	99.4%	1,241	23	66	461	691	12,304	3,034	8,037	1,233
Estimated total	100.0%	1,247	23	66	463	695	12,364	3,046	8,080	1,238
Rate per 100,000 inhabitants		542.8	10.0	28.7	201.6	302.5	5,382.2	1,326.0	3,517.3	538.9
Madera-Chowchilla, CA M.S.A.	148,935									
Includes Madera County										
City of Madera	57,636	464	7	24	153	280	1,199	330	669	200
City of Chowchilla	19,268	28	1	1	5	21	350	193	143	14
Total area actually reporting	100.0%	744	10	37	185	512	3,257	1,043	1,706	508
Rate per 100,000 inhabitants		499.5	6.7	24.8	124.2	343.8	2,186.9	700.3	1,145.5	341.1
Madison, WI M.S.A.	562,105									
Includes Columbia, Dane, and Iowa Counties										
City of Madison	231,231	891	10	50	368	463	8,256	2,038	5,720	498
Total area actually reporting	100.0%	1,357	14	112	455	776	15,751	3,272	11,714	765
Rate per 100,000 inhabitants		241.4	2.5	19.9	80.9	138.1	2,802.1	582.1	2,084.0	136.1
Manhattan, KS M.S.A.	119,523									
Includes Geary, Pottawatomie, and Riley Counties										
Total area actually reporting	100.0%	450	4	65	53	328	3,217	651	2,423	143
Rate per 100,000 inhabitants		376.5	3.3	54.4	44.3	274.4	2,691.5	544.7	2,027.2	119.6
Mankato-North Mankato, MN M.S.A.[5]	91,966									
Includes Blue Earth and Nicollet Counties[5]										
City of Mankato[5]	36,316		0		13	53	1,785	255	1,472	58
City of North Mankato[5]	12,467		0		0	2	197	4	177	16
Total area actually reporting	100.0%		0		14	83	2,661	393	2,157	111
Rate per 100,000 inhabitants			0.0		15.2	90.3	2,893.5	427.3	2,345.4	120.7
Mansfield, OH M.S.A.	125,317									
Includes Richland County										
City of Mansfield	49,428	183	3	30	83	67	2,639	799	1,774	66
Total area actually reporting	100.0%	245	3	49	96	97	5,131	1,411	3,579	141
Rate per 100,000 inhabitants		195.5	2.4	39.1	76.6	77.4	4,094.4	1,125.9	2,856.0	112.5

[5] The data collection methodology for the offense of forcible rape used by the Minnesota state UCR Program (with the exception of Minneapolis and St. Paul, MN) does not comply with national UCR Program guidelines. Consequently, their figures for forcible rape and violent crime (of which forcible rape is a part) are not published in this table.

Table 6. Crime, by Metropolitan Statistical Area, 2008—*Continued*

(Number, percent, rate per 100,000 population.)

Area	Population	Violent crime	Murder and non-negligent man-slaughter	Forcible rape	Robbery	Aggravated assault	Property crime	Burglary	Larceny-theft	Motor vehicle theft
McAllen-Edinburg-Mission, TX M.S.A.	729,820									
Includes Hidalgo County										
City of McAllen	130,039	371	9	18	135	209	7,875	818	6,599	458
City of Edinburg	71,734	285	3	21	69	192	4,306	846	3,082	378
City of Mission	68,236	118	5	2	53	58	2,846	438	2,042	366
City of Pharr	66,084	260	3	20	80	157	3,731	868	2,503	360
Total area actually reporting	99.8%	2,624	51	176	667	1,730	33,640	7,427	23,352	2,861
Estimated total	100.0%	2,628	51	176	668	1,733	33,690	7,437	23,388	2,865
Rate per 100,000 inhabitants		360.1	7.0	24.1	91.5	237.5	4,616.2	1,019.0	3,204.6	392.6
Medford, OR M.S.A.	201,601									
Includes Jackson County										
City of Medford	73,019	282	0	44	41	197	2,882	300	2,453	129
Total area actually reporting	100.0%	461	2	74	68	317	5,352	714	4,401	237
Rate per 100,000 inhabitants		228.7	1.0	36.7	33.7	157.2	2,654.7	354.2	2,183.0	117.6
Memphis, TN-MS-AR M.S.A.	1,290,901									
Includes Crittenden County, AR; DeSoto, Marshall, Tate; and Tunica Counties, MS, and Fayette, Shelby, and Tipton Counties, TN										
City of Memphis	672,046	12,937	138	366	4,787	7,646	53,839	15,874	32,548	5,417
Total area actually reporting	99.9%	15,582	163	522	5,272	9,625	74,154	21,314	46,046	6,794
Estimated total	100.0%	15,585	163	522	5,273	9,627	74,208	21,326	46,085	6,797
Rate per 100,000 inhabitants		1,207.3	12.6	40.4	408.5	745.8	5,748.5	1,652.0	3,570.0	526.5
Merced, CA M.S.A.	248,898									
Includes Merced County										
City of Merced	78,598	612	11	30	153	418	3,453	720	2,382	351
Total area actually reporting	100.0%	1,541	21	70	267	1,183	9,023	2,267	5,658	1,098
Rate per 100,000 inhabitants		619.1	8.4	28.1	107.3	475.3	3,625.2	910.8	2,273.2	441.1
Miami-Fort Lauderdale-Pompano Beach, FL M.S.A.	5,395,910									
Includes the Metropolitan Divisions of Fort Lauderdale-Pompano Beach-Deerfield Beach, Miami-Miami Beach-Kendall, and West Palm Beach-Boca Raton-Boynton Beach										
City of Miami	427,740	5,709	63	42	2,415	3,189	22,198	4,941	13,591	3,666
City of Fort Lauderdale	182,932	1,628	22	73	848	685	10,419	2,633	6,939	847
City of Pompano Beach	101,769	1,208	9	58	422	719	5,690	1,232	3,906	552
City of West Palm Beach	100,434	967	18	47	446	456	5,845	1,445	3,887	513
City of Miami Beach	83,609	990	6	50	405	529	8,215	1,279	6,144	792
City of Boca Raton	84,630	210	1	15	74	120	3,254	564	2,505	185
City of Deerfield Beach	73,665	524	0	14	139	371	2,691	576	1,899	216
City of Boynton Beach	68,033	709	2	6	205	496	3,667	869	2,526	272
City of Delray Beach	63,795	676	2	23	208	443	3,527	763	2,541	223
City of Homestead	60,184	850	1	25	279	545	3,014	1,017	1,734	263
Total area actually reporting	100.0%	41,301	409	1,593	14,939	24,360	257,000	54,960	175,095	26,945
Rate per 100,000 inhabitants		765.4	7.6	29.5	276.9	451.5	4,762.9	1,018.5	3,245.0	499.4
Fort Lauderdale-Pompano Beach-Deerfield Beach, FL M.D.	1,754,213									
Includes Broward County										
Total area actually reporting	100.0%	10,637	85	515	4,045	5,992	71,758	15,684	49,866	6,208
Rate per 100,000 inhabitants		606.4	4.8	29.4	230.6	341.6	4,090.6	894.1	2,842.6	353.9
Miami-Miami Beach-Kendall, FL M.D.	2,373,744									
Includes Miami-Dade County										
Total area actually reporting	100.0%	22,005	228	685	8,047	13,045	131,060	26,030	88,930	16,100
Rate per 100,000 inhabitants		927.0	9.6	28.9	339.0	549.6	5,521.2	1,096.6	3,746.4	678.3
West Palm Beach-Boca Raton-Boynton Beach, FL M.D.	1,267,953									
Includes Palm Beach County										
Total area actually reporting	100.0%	8,659	96	393	2,847	5,323	54,182	13,246	36,299	4,637
Rate per 100,000 inhabitants		682.9	7.6	31.0	224.5	419.8	4,273.2	1,044.7	2,862.8	365.7
Michigan City-La Porte, IN M.S.A.	109,674									
Includes La Porte County										
City of Michigan City	31,726	123	5	8	64	46	1,770	315	1,315	140
City of La Porte	21,031	47	0	10	17	20	1,476	226	1,192	58
Total area actually reporting	96.8%	204	5	27	93	79	4,307	865	3,193	249
Estimated total	100.0%	214	5	28	96	85	4,437	885	3,294	258
Rate per 100,000 inhabitants		195.1	4.6	25.5	87.5	77.5	4,045.6	806.9	3,003.4	235.2

Table 6. Crime, by Metropolitan Statistical Area, 2008—*Continued*

(Number, percent, rate per 100,000 population.)

Area	Population	Violent crime	Murder and non-negligent man-slaughter	Forcible rape	Robbery	Aggravated assault	Property crime	Burglary	Larceny-theft	Motor vehicle theft
Midland, TX M.S.A.	127,849									
Includes Midland County										
City of Midland	104,742	419	4	66	94	255	3,476	833	2,485	158
Total area actually reporting	100.0%	518	4	71	100	343	4,161	1,066	2,910	185
Rate per 100,000 inhabitants		405.2	3.1	55.5	78.2	268.3	3,254.6	833.8	2,276.1	144.7
Milwaukee-Waukesha-West Allis, WI M.S.A.	1,548,830									
Includes Milwaukee, Ozaukee, Washington, and Waukesha Counties										
City of Milwaukee	602,131	7,339	71	208	3,207	3,853	36,562	6,409	23,615	6,538
City of Waukesha	66,984	84	0	23	24	37	1,443	320	1,050	73
City of West Allis	59,602	220	2	6	108	104	3,154	569	2,382	203
Total area actually reporting	100.0%	8,436	76	314	3,644	4,402	59,309	9,417	42,433	7,459
Rate per 100,000 inhabitants		544.7	4.9	20.3	235.3	284.2	3,829.3	608.0	2,739.7	481.6
Minneapolis-St. Paul-Bloomington, MN-WI M.S.A.[5]	3,231,521									
Includes Anoka, Carver, Chisago, Dakota, Hennepin, Isanti, Ramsey, Scott, Sherburne, Washington, and Wright Counties, MN[5] and Pierce and St. Croix Counties, WI										
City of Minneapolis, MN	376,753	4,779	37	367	2,005	2,370	20,777	5,591	12,776	2,410
City of St. Paul, MN	276,083	2,199	18	147	765	1,269	11,524	2,936	6,770	1,818
City of Bloomington, MN[5]	80,996		1		51	60	3,213	255	2,798	160
City of Plymouth, MN[5]	71,713		0		16	33	1,664	299	1,309	56
City of Eagan, MN[5]	63,754		0		21	27	1,627	190	1,398	39
City of Eden Prairie, MN[5]	62,516		0		10	33	1,333	138	1,166	29
City of Minnetonka, MN[5]	50,231		1		5	14	1,084	222	830	32
Total area actually reporting	98.6%		86		3,756	5,494	104,309	18,432	78,088	7,789
Estimated total	100.0%		87		3,778	5,533	105,755	18,627	79,265	7,863
Rate per 100,000 inhabitants			2.7		116.9	171.2	3,272.6	576.4	2,452.9	243.3
Missoula, MT M.S.A.	107,119									
Includes Missoula County										
City of Missoula	68,445	181	1	17	22	141	2,463	225	2,131	107
Total area actually reporting	100.0%	295	2	31	24	238	3,122	361	2,601	160
Rate per 100,000 inhabitants		275.4	1.9	28.9	22.4	222.2	2,914.5	337.0	2,428.1	149.4
Mobile, AL M.S.A.[6]	405,797									
Includes Mobile County										
City of Mobile[6]	251,041	1,204	42	27	875	260	13,846	3,305	9,470	1,071
Total area actually reporting	98.6%	1,912	65	63	1,178	606	19,570	5,089	12,717	1,764
Estimated total	100.0%	1,938	65	65	1,188	620	19,833	5,151	12,901	1,781
Rate per 100,000 inhabitants		477.6	16.0	16.0	292.8	152.8	4,887.4	1,269.4	3,179.2	438.9
Modesto, CA M.S.A.	516,995									
Includes Stanislaus County										
City of Modesto	205,750	1,439	18	65	429	927	10,874	2,393	7,014	1,467
Total area actually reporting	100.0%	2,829	31	141	810	1,847	23,178	5,646	13,583	3,949
Rate per 100,000 inhabitants		547.2	6.0	27.3	156.7	357.3	4,483.2	1,092.1	2,627.3	763.8
Monroe, LA M.S.A.	173,540									
Includes Ouachita and Union Parishes										
City of Monroe	50,988	493	11	21	141	320	4,360	1,219	3,010	131
Total area actually reporting	98.8%	845	11	28	192	614	8,812	2,439	6,033	340
Estimated total	100.0%	857	11	29	194	623	8,908	2,458	6,106	344
Rate per 100,000 inhabitants		493.8	6.3	16.7	111.8	359.0	5,133.1	1,416.4	3,518.5	198.2
Monroe, MI M.S.A.[2]	153,241									
Includes Monroe County[2]										
City of Monroe	21,461	88	0	15	19	54	723	181	512	30
Total area actually reporting	100.0%	378	2	87	62	227	3,798	936	2,656	206
Rate per 100,000 inhabitants		246.7	1.3	56.8	40.5	148.1	2,478.4	610.8	1,733.2	134.4
Montgomery, AL M.S.A.	369,292									
Includes Autauga, Elmore, Lowndes, and Montgomery Counties										
City of Montgomery	204,398	883	23	49	463	348	12,545	3,513	8,117	915
Total area actually reporting	97.2%	1,226	28	96	547	555	17,234	4,670	11,368	1,196
Estimated total	100.0%	1,253	28	99	553	573	17,474	4,753	11,505	1,216
Rate per 100,000 inhabitants		339.3	7.6	26.8	149.7	155.2	4,731.8	1,287.1	3,115.4	329.3

[2] Because of changes in the state/local agency's reporting practices, figures are not comparable to previous years' data.
[5] The data collection methodology for the offense of forcible rape used by the Minnesota state UCR Program (with the exception of Minneapolis and St. Paul, MN) does not comply with national UCR Program guidelines. Consequently, their figures for forcible rape and violent crime (of which forcible rape is a part) are not published in this table.
[6] The population for the city of Mobile, Alabama, includes 61,856 inhabitants from the jurisdiction of the Mobile County Sheriff's Department.

Table 6. Crime, by Metropolitan Statistical Area, 2008—*Continued*

(Number, percent, rate per 100,000 population.)

Area	Population	Violent crime	Murder and non-negligent man-slaughter	Forcible rape	Robbery	Aggravated assault	Property crime	Burglary	Larceny-theft	Motor vehicle theft
Morristown, TN M.S.A.	135,979									
Includes Grainger, Hamblen, and Jefferson Counties										
City of Morristown	27,579	237	0	19	52	166	2,087	202	1,766	119
Total area actually reporting	100.0%	526	3	42	77	404	4,902	1,100	3,451	351
Rate per 100,000 inhabitants		386.8	2.2	30.9	56.6	297.1	3,605.0	808.9	2,537.9	258.1
Mount Vernon-Anacortes, WA M.S.A.	118,241									
Includes Skagit County										
City of Mount Vernon	31,237	91	0	19	26	46	1,732	275	1,374	83
City of Anacortes	17,020	27	0	3	5	19	504	109	364	31
Total area actually reporting	100.0%	243	9	50	55	129	5,350	1,069	3,939	342
Rate per 100,000 inhabitants		205.5	7.6	42.3	46.5	109.1	4,524.7	904.1	3,331.3	289.2
Muncie, IN M.S.A.	114,943									
Includes Delaware County										
City of Muncie	65,084	349	0	30	78	241	2,627	494	2,003	130
Total area actually reporting	100.0%	389	1	39	85	264	3,505	684	2,629	192
Rate per 100,000 inhabitants		338.4	0.9	33.9	73.9	229.7	3,049.3	595.1	2,287.2	167.0
Muskegon-Norton Shores, MI M.S.A.[2]	173,418									
Includes Muskegon County										
City of Muskegon[2]	39,319	384	1	36	101	246	2,367	566	1,658	143
City of Norton Shores	23,408	39	0	8	6	25	794	94	677	23
Total area actually reporting	100.0%	805	4	111	175	515	7,323	1,317	5,652	354
Rate per 100,000 inhabitants		464.2	2.3	64.0	100.9	297.0	4,222.7	759.4	3,259.2	204.1
Napa, CA M.S.A.	132,946									
Includes Napa County										
City of Napa	74,420	249	1	25	46	177	1,907	368	1,360	179
Total area actually reporting	100.0%	832	1	39	70	722	3,253	768	2,178	307
Rate per 100,000 inhabitants		625.8	0.8	29.3	52.7	543.1	2,446.9	577.7	1,638.3	230.9
Naples-Marco Island, FL M.S.A.	320,551									
Includes Collier County										
City of Naples	21,460	51	2	1	8	40	825	83	730	12
City of Marco Island	15,703	13	0	2	2	9	204	19	182	3
Total area actually reporting	100.0%	1,174	8	56	234	876	6,183	1,360	4,502	321
Rate per 100,000 inhabitants		366.2	2.5	17.5	73.0	273.3	1,928.9	424.3	1,404.5	100.1
Nashville-Davidson–Murfreesboro–Franklin, TN M.S.A.	1,548,974									
Includes Cannon, Cheatham, Davidson, Dickson, Hickman, Macon, Robertson, Rutherford, Smith, Sumner, Trousdale, Williamson, and Wilson Counties										
City of Nashville	602,181	8,404	76	301	2,384	5,643	32,347	6,326	23,764	2,257
City of Murfreesboro	102,536	646	6	31	162	447	4,439	1,029	3,217	193
City of Franklin	58,997	116	1	13	18	84	908	142	739	27
Total area actually reporting	100.0%	12,101	100	552	2,889	8,560	56,041	11,910	40,354	3,777
Rate per 100,000 inhabitants		781.2	6.5	35.6	186.5	552.6	3,617.9	768.9	2,605.2	243.8
New Orleans-Metairie-Kenner, LA M.S.A.	1,114,055									
Includes Jefferson, Orleans, Plaquemines, St. Bernard, St. Charles, St. John the Baptist, and St. Tammany Parishes										
City of New Orleans	281,440	2,869	179	65	1,085	1,540	14,880	4,591	7,081	3,208
City of Kenner	64,597	376	7	20	129	220	2,623	528	1,848	247
Total area actually reporting	99.9%	6,929	250	259	2,060	4,360	44,539	11,571	27,093	5,875
Estimated total	100.0%	6,933	250	259	2,061	4,363	44,570	11,577	27,117	5,876
Rate per 100,000 inhabitants		622.3	22.4	23.2	185.0	391.6	4,000.7	1,039.2	2,434.1	527.4
New York-Northern New Jersey-Long Island, NY-NJ-PA M.S.A.	19,004,225									
Includes the Metropolitan Divisions of Edison-New Brunswick, NJ; Nassau-Suffolk, NY; Newark-Union, NJ-PA; and New York-Wayne-White Plains, NY-NJ										
City of New York, NY	8,345,075	48,430	523	890	22,186	24,831	149,989	19,867	117,682	12,440
City of Newark, NJ	279,788	2,660	67	51	1,387	1,155	9,750	2,000	3,996	3,754
City of Edison Township, NJ	99,562	234	1	6	80	147	2,179	447	1,563	169
City of White Plains, NY	57,932	86	0	1	20	65	1,167	40	1,103	24
City of Union Township, NJ	53,777	127	1	8	64	54	1,383	239	1,008	136
City of Wayne Township, NJ	53,956	48	0	2	16	30	1,415	143	1,214	58
City of New Brunswick, NJ	50,605	319	5	18	122	174	2,242	667	1,375	200
Total area actually reporting	99.9%	75,769	855	1,845	34,693	38,376	354,037	57,125	264,350	32,562
Estimated total	100.0%	75,772	855	1,845	34,694	38,378	354,067	57,130	264,374	32,563
Rate per 100,000 inhabitants		398.7	4.5	9.7	182.6	201.9	1,863.1	300.6	1,391.1	171.3

[2] Because of changes in the state/local agency's reporting practices, figures are not comparable to previous years' data.

Table 6. Crime, by Metropolitan Statistical Area, 2008—*Continued*

(Number, percent, rate per 100,000 population.)

Area	Population	Violent crime	Murder and non-negligent man-slaughter	Forcible rape	Robbery	Aggravated assault	Property crime	Burglary	Larceny-theft	Motor vehicle theft
Edison-New Brunswick, NJ M.D.	2,327,779									
Includes Middlesex, Monmouth, Ocean, and Somerset Counties										
Total area actually reporting	100.0%	3,951	29	208	1,491	2,223	45,987	8,741	34,995	2,251
Rate per 100,000 inhabitants		169.7	1.2	8.9	64.1	95.5	1,975.6	375.5	1,503.4	96.7
Nassau-Suffolk, NY M.D.	2,877,560									
Includes Nassau and Suffolk Counties										
Total area actually reporting	99.9%	4,864	71	185	2,096	2,512	49,730	7,357	38,831	3,542
Estimated total	100.0%	4,867	71	185	2,097	2,514	49,760	7,362	38,855	3,543
Rate per 100,000 inhabitants		169.1	2.5	6.4	72.9	87.4	1,729.2	255.8	1,350.3	123.1
Newark-Union, NJ-PA M.D.	2,123,803									
Includes Essex, Hunterdon, Morris, Sussex, and Union Counties, NJ and Pike County, PA										
Total area actually reporting	100.0%	8,367	135	289	4,181	3,762	47,618	9,839	29,066	8,713
Rate per 100,000 inhabitants		394.0	6.4	13.6	196.9	177.1	2,242.1	463.3	1,368.6	410.3
New York-White Plains-Wayne, NY-NJ M.D.	11,675,083									
Includes Bergen, Hudson, and Passaic Counties, NJ and Bronx, Kings, New York, Putnam, Queens, Richmond, Rockland, and Westchester Counties, NY										
Total area actually reporting	100.0%	58,587	620	1,163	26,925	29,879	210,702	31,188	161,458	18,056
Rate per 100,000 inhabitants		501.8	5.3	10.0	230.6	255.9	1,804.7	267.1	1,382.9	154.7
Niles-Benton Harbor, MI M.S.A.	157,892									
Includes Berrien County										
City of Niles	11,229	65	0	16	18	31	482	90	367	25
City of Benton Harbor	10,677	120	0	9	20	91	250	84	140	26
Total area actually reporting	98.3%	615	2	108	103	402	4,942	1,026	3,699	217
Estimated total	100.0%	623	2	109	105	407	5,019	1,041	3,754	224
Rate per 100,000 inhabitants		394.6	1.3	69.0	66.5	257.8	3,178.8	659.3	2,377.6	141.9
Norwich-New London, CT M.S.A.	142,186									
Includes New London County										
City of Norwich	36,471	178	1	28	49	100	944	272	610	62
City of New London	25,891	199	1	15	22	161	952	165	712	75
Total area actually reporting	100.0%	493	6	56	90	341	3,511	700	2,634	177
Rate per 100,000 inhabitants		346.7	4.2	39.4	63.3	239.8	2,469.3	492.3	1,852.5	124.5
Ocala, FL M.S.A.	329,862									
Includes Marion County										
City of Ocala	53,799	600	7	53	187	353	3,049	690	2,234	125
Total area actually reporting	100.0%	2,076	22	165	312	1,577	8,338	2,365	5,469	504
Rate per 100,000 inhabitants		629.4	6.7	50.0	94.6	478.1	2,527.7	717.0	1,658.0	152.8
Ocean City, NJ M.S.A.	95,311									
Includes Cape May County										
City of Ocean City	14,802	31	0	8	6	17	892	138	747	7
Total area actually reporting	97.4%	304	0	31	72	201	4,567	953	3,515	99
Estimated total	100.0%	310	0	31	75	204	4,618	963	3552	103
Rate per 100,000 inhabitants		325.3	0.0	32.5	78.7	214.0	4,845.2	1,010.4	3,726.7	108.1
Odessa, TX M.S.A.	130,731									
Includes Ector County										
City of Odessa	97,644	675	7	2	73	593	3,970	893	2,809	268
Total area actually reporting	100.0%	776	10	4	88	674	5,234	1,194	3,664	376
Rate per 100,000 inhabitants		593.6	7.6	3.1	67.3	515.6	4,003.6	913.3	2,802.7	287.6
Ogden-Clearfield, UT M.S.A.	535,090									
Includes Davis, Morgan, and Weber Counties										
City of Ogden	83,353	386	4	42	127	213	4,200	699	3,154	347
City of Clearfield	27,649	46	0	6	10	30	856	122	709	25
Total area actually reporting	100.0%	847	9	160	241	437	14,547	2,392	11,402	753
Rate per 100,000 inhabitants		158.3	1.7	29.9	45.0	81.7	2,718.6	447.0	2,130.9	140.7
Oklahoma City, OK M.S.A.	1,206,660									
Includes Canadian, Cleveland, Grady, Lincoln, Logan, McClain, and Oklahoma Counties										
City of Oklahoma City	552,452	5,400	57	318	1,524	3,501	32,563	9,225	19,439	3,899
Total area actually reporting	100.0%	7,017	76	523	1,851	4,567	51,824	13,980	32,648	5,196
Rate per 100,000 inhabitants		581.5	6.3	43.3	153.4	378.5	4,294.8	1,158.6	2,705.7	430.6

Table 6. Crime, by Metropolitan Statistical Area, 2008—*Continued*

(Number, percent, rate per 100,000 population.)

Area	Population	Violent crime	Murder and non-negligent man-slaughter	Forcible rape	Robbery	Aggravated assault	Property crime	Burglary	Larceny-theft	Motor vehicle theft
Olympia, WA M.S.A.	242,881									
Includes Thurston County										
City of Olympia	45,189	149	3	24	42	80	2,192	366	1,676	150
Total area actually reporting	100.0%	630	4	88	112	426	8,269	1,711	6,087	471
Rate per 100,000 inhabitants		259.4	1.6	36.2	46.1	175.4	3,404.5	704.5	2,506.2	193.9
Omaha-Council Bluffs, NE-IA M.S.A.	838,325									
Includes Harrison, Mills, and Pottawattamie Counties, IA and Cass, Douglas, Sarpy, Saunders, and Washington Counties, NE										
City of Omaha, NE	437,238	2,648	44	180	949	1,475	18,792	3,175	12,892	2,725
City of Council Bluffs, IA	60,108	415	3	68	66	278	4,237	866	2,957	414
Total area actually reporting	99.9%	3,497	50	311	1,046	2,090	29,172	5,199	20,404	3,569
Estimated total	100.0%	3,498	50	311	1,046	2,091	29,192	5,202	20,420	3,570
Rate per 100,000 inhabitants		417.3	6.0	37.1	124.8	249.4	3,482.2	620.5	2,435.8	425.8
Orlando-Kissimmee, FL M.S.A.	2,060,706									
Includes Lake, Orange, Osceola, and Seminole Counties										
City of Orlando	229,808	3,829	43	131	1,320	2,335	19,703	4,279	13,693	1,731
City of Kissimmee	62,815	581	1	16	154	410	2,777	746	1,817	214
Total area actually reporting	100.0%	16,910	163	799	4,934	11,014	92,080	24,987	58,805	8,288
Rate per 100,000 inhabitants		820.6	7.9	38.8	239.4	534.5	4,468.4	1,212.5	2,853.6	402.2
Oshkosh-Neenah, WI M.S.A.	162,698									
Includes Winnebago County										
City of Oshkosh	64,747	186	0	13	29	144	2,294	460	1,767	67
City of Neenah	25,005	34	2	4	5	23	413	76	326	11
Total area actually reporting	100.0%	319	3	28	42	246	3,963	816	3,003	144
Rate per 100,000 inhabitants		196.1	1.8	17.2	25.8	151.2	2,435.8	501.5	1,845.8	88.5
Oxnard-Thousand Oaks-Ventura, CA M.S.A.	799,817									
Includes Ventura County										
City of Oxnard	186,434	817	14	21	452	330	4,299	895	2,876	528
City of Thousand Oaks	124,106	148	2	16	37	93	1,769	308	1,367	94
City of Ventura	103,483	397	2	23	156	216	3,288	669	2,387	232
City of Camarillo	63,843	77	2	9	25	41	1,038	220	756	62
Total area actually reporting	100.0%	2,137	31	124	867	1,115	16,099	3,279	11,459	1,361
Rate per 100,000 inhabitants		267.2	3.9	15.5	108.4	139.4	2,012.8	410.0	1,432.7	170.2
Palm Bay-Melbourne-Titusville, FL M.S.A.	537,212									
Includes Brevard County										
City of Palm Bay	101,759	539	4	24	74	437	2,424	757	1,515	152
City of Melbourne	77,286	969	8	31	222	708	4,202	977	2,991	234
City of Titusville	43,769	344	3	39	86	216	1,983	569	1,099	315
Total area actually reporting	100.0%	3,690	22	179	663	2,826	18,648	4,935	12,445	1,268
Rate per 100,000 inhabitants		686.9	4.1	33.3	123.4	526.0	3,471.3	918.6	2,316.6	236.0
Palm Coast, FL M.S.A.	93,654									
Includes Flagler County										
Total area actually reporting	100.0%	273	0	14	56	203	2,182	539	1,508	135
Rate per 100,000 inhabitants		291.5	0.0	14.9	59.8	216.8	2,329.9	575.5	1,610.2	144.1
Panama City-Lynn Haven-Panama City Beach, FL M.S.A.	164,007									
Includes Bay County										
City of Panama City	36,339	426	3	10	86	327	2,197	453	1,609	135
City of Lynn Haven	15,369	49	2	3	2	42	475	112	342	21
City of Panama City Beach	15,453	81	0	16	17	48	993	198	795	0
Total area actually reporting	100.0%	1,076	11	94	172	799	6,725	1,615	4,747	363
Rate per 100,000 inhabitants		656.1	6.7	57.3	104.9	487.2	4,100.4	984.7	2,894.4	221.3
Pascagoula, MS M.S.A.	152,652									
Includes George and Jackson Counties										
City of Pascagoula	23,139	96	0	13	61	22	1,417	301	990	126
Total area actually reporting	87.4%	349	4	57	125	163	4,827	1,213	3,142	472
Estimated total	100.0%	376	5	61	130	180	5,191	1,309	3,374	508
Rate per 100,000 inhabitants		246.3	3.3	40.0	85.2	117.9	3,400.5	857.5	2,210.3	332.8
Pensacola-Ferry Pass-Brent, FL M.S.A.	453,297									
Includes Escambia and Santa Rosa Counties										
City of Pensacola	53,385	502	4	34	136	328	2,696	528	2,024	144
Total area actually reporting	100.0%	3,007	24	178	718	2,087	14,480	3,511	10,009	960
Rate per 100,000 inhabitants		663.4	5.3	39.3	158.4	460.4	3,194.4	774.5	2,208.0	211.8

Table 6. Crime, by Metropolitan Statistical Area, 2008—*Continued*

(Number, percent, rate per 100,000 population.)

Area	Population	Violent crime	Murder and non-negligent man-slaughter	Forcible rape	Robbery	Aggravated assault	Property crime	Burglary	Larceny-theft	Motor vehicle theft
Philadelphia-Camden-Wilmington, PA-NJ-DE-MD M.S.A.	5,836,682									
Includes the Metropolitan Divisions of Camden, NJ; Philadelphia, PA; and Wilmington, DE-MD-NJ										
City of Philadelphia, PA	1,441,117	20,771	331	1,038	9,618	9,784	62,584	12,845	40,681	9,058
City of Camden, NJ	76,182	1,777	54	70	815	838	4,912	1,221	2,693	998
City of Wilmington, DE	72,888	1,410	26	27	573	784	3,806	834	2,333	639
Total area actually reporting	99.7%	36,662	530	1,899	14,919	19,314	173,779	33,245	123,428	17,106
Estimated total	100.0%	36,697	530	1,901	14,929	19,337	174,082	33,292	123,668	17,122
Rate per 100,000 inhabitants		628.7	9.1	32.6	255.8	331.3	2,982.6	570.4	2,118.8	293.4
Camden, NJ M.D.	1,248,666									
Includes Burlington, Camden, and Gloucester Counties										
Total area actually reporting	99.9%	4,546	79	293	1,788	2,386	34,369	7,184	24,402	2,783
Estimated total	100.0%	4,550	79	293	1,790	2,388	34,397	7,190	24,422	2,785
Rate per 100,000 inhabitants		364.4	6.3	23.5	143.4	191.2	2,754.7	575.8	1,955.8	223.0
Philadelphia, PA M.D.	3,891,020									
Includes Bucks, Chester, Delaware, Montgomery, and Philadelphia Counties										
Total area actually reporting	99.7%	27,363	396	1,417	11,531	14,019	114,232	20,552	81,626	12,054
Estimated total	100.0%	27,394	396	1,419	11,539	14,040	114,507	20,593	81,846	12,068
Rate per 100,000 inhabitants		704.0	10.2	36.5	296.6	360.8	2,942.9	529.2	2,103.5	310.2
Wilmington, DE-MD-NJ M.D.	696,996									
Includes New Castle County, DE; Cecil County, MD; and Salem County, NJ										
Total area actually reporting	100.0%	4,753	55	189	1,600	2,909	25,178	5,509	17,400	2,269
Rate per 100,000 inhabitants		681.9	7.9	27.1	229.6	417.4	3,612.4	790.4	2,496.4	325.5
Phoenix-Mesa-Scottsdale, AZ M.S.A.	4,283,537									
Includes Maricopa and Pinal Counties										
City of Phoenix	1,585,838	10,465	167	481	4,825	4,992	82,689	18,783	48,685	15,221
City of Mesa	456,821	2,289	16	161	656	1,456	17,516	2,866	12,603	2,047
City of Scottsdale	238,905	423	5	28	130	260	7,903	1,488	5,897	518
City of Tempe	176,388	856	6	34	323	493	10,242	1,545	7,584	1,113
Total area actually reporting	99.9%	19,487	281	1,041	7,503	10,662	182,198	39,699	115,550	26,949
Estimated total	100.0%	19,497	281	1,042	7,506	10,668	182,316	39,726	115,628	26,962
Rate per 100,000 inhabitants		455.2	6.6	24.3	175.2	249.0	4,256.2	927.4	2,699.4	629.4
Pine Bluff, AR M.S.A.	100,732									
Includes Cleveland, Jefferson, and Lincoln Counties										
City of Pine Bluff	50,144	819	16	71	248	484	4,674	1,596	2,648	430
Total area actually reporting	97.8%	945	21	85	260	579	5,760	2,036	3,194	530
Estimated total	100.0%	956	21	86	262	587	5,848	2,064	3,250	534
Rate per 100,000 inhabitants		949.1	20.8	85.4	260.1	582.7	5,805.5	2,049.0	3,226.4	530.1
Pittsburgh, PA M.S.A.	2,345,727									
Includes Allegheny, Armstrong, Beaver, Butler, Fayette, Washington, and Westmoreland Counties										
City of Pittsburgh	309,757	3,358	72	136	1,541	1,609	12,625	3,108	8,258	1,259
Total area actually reporting	98.3%	8,603	122	474	2,806	5,201	49,793	10,212	36,228	3,353
Estimated total	100.0%	8,698	123	480	2,831	5,264	50,624	10,337	36,892	3,395
Rate per 100,000 inhabitants		370.8	5.2	20.5	120.7	224.4	2,158.1	440.7	1,572.7	144.7
Pittsfield, MA M.S.A.	129,918									
Includes Berkshire County										
City of Pittsfield	42,597	298	0	53	16	229	1,105	374	672	59
Total area actually reporting	96.2%	505	2	76	24	403	2,880	998	1,758	124
Estimated total	100.0%	520	2	77	27	414	2,981	1,023	1,827	131
Rate per 100,000 inhabitants		400.3	1.5	59.3	20.8	318.7	2,294.5	787.4	1,406.3	100.8
Pocatello, ID M.S.A.	87,959									
Includes Bannock and Power Counties										
City of Pocatello	54,946	185	1	37	11	136	1,654	260	1,328	66
Total area actually reporting	100.0%	250	1	45	16	188	2,488	339	2,061	88
Rate per 100,000 inhabitants		284.2	1.1	51.2	18.2	213.7	2,828.6	385.4	2,343.1	100.0
Portland-South Portland-Biddeford, ME M.S.A.	513,868									
Includes Cumberland, Sagadahoc, and York Counties										
City of Portland	62,656	254	4	42	107	101	2,769	483	2,157	129
City of South Portland	23,796	54	0	4	19	31	1,116	125	969	22
City of Biddeford	21,663	66	0	20	28	18	1,050	180	847	23
Total area actually reporting	100.0%	692	11	170	202	309	12,459	2,409	9,572	478
Rate per 100,000 inhabitants		134.7	2.1	33.1	39.3	60.1	2,424.6	468.8	1,862.7	93.0

Table 6. Crime, by Metropolitan Statistical Area, 2008—*Continued*

(Number, percent, rate per 100,000 population.)

Area	Population	Violent crime	Murder and non-negligent man-slaughter	Forcible rape	Robbery	Aggravated assault	Property crime	Burglary	Larceny-theft	Motor vehicle theft
Portland-Vancouver-Beaverton, OR-WA M.S.A.	2,207,851									
Includes Clackamas, Columbia, Multnomah, Washington, and Yamhill Counties, OR and Clark and Skamania Counties, WA										
City of Portland, OR	553,023	3,445	26	250	1,132	2,037	29,243	4,307	21,597	3,339
City of Vancouver, WA	163,574	605	0	105	176	324	6,298	842	4,248	1,208
City of Beaverton, OR	92,198	200	0	24	41	135	2,072	296	1,566	210
City of Hillsboro, OR	94,373	162	0	36	62	64	2,536	293	2,079	164
Estimated total	98.9%	6,434	45	809	1,976	3,604	71,509	10,841	52,704	7,964
Total area actually reporting	100.0%	6,472	45	816	1,984	3,627	72,034	10,948	53,074	8,012
Rate per 100,000 inhabitants		293.1	2.0	37.0	89.9	164.3	3,262.6	495.9	2,403.9	362.9
Port St. Lucie, FL M.S.A.	406,587									
Includes Martin and St. Lucie Counties										
City of Port St. Lucie	159,735	387	3	38	44	302	3,970	1,114	2,760	96
Total area actually reporting	100.0%	1,994	13	115	512	1,354	12,689	3,446	8,676	567
Rate per 100,000 inhabitants		490.4	3.2	28.3	125.9	333.0	3,120.9	847.5	2,133.9	139.5
Poughkeepsie-Newburgh-Middletown, NY M.S.A.	675,735									
Includes Dutchess and Orange Counties										
City of Poughkeepsie	29,606	394	5	23	162	204	1,122	261	784	77
City of Newburgh	28,180	476	7	13	162	294	1,063	333	640	90
City of Middletown	25,928	177	5	14	75	83	1,016	216	755	45
Total area actually reporting	99.5%	1,932	18	114	575	1,225	13,780	2,288	10,955	537
Estimated total	100.0%	1,937	18	114	577	1,228	13,843	2,298	11,006	539
Rate per 100,000 inhabitants		286.7	2.7	16.9	85.4	181.7	2,048.6	340.1	1,628.7	79.8
Prescott, AZ M.S.A.	217,520									
Includes Yavapai County										
City of Prescott	43,190	119	1	2	22	94	1,230	244	946	40
Total area actually reporting	100.0%	753	4	42	46	661	5,005	1,239	3,476	290
Rate per 100,000 inhabitants		346.2	1.8	19.3	21.1	303.9	2,300.9	569.6	1,598.0	133.3
Providence-New Bedford-Fall River, RI-MA M.S.A.	1,597,765									
Includes Bristol County, MA and Bristol, Kent, Newport, Providence, and Washington Counties, RI										
City of Providence, RI	170,965	1,162	12	44	498	608	9,063	1,875	5,701	1,487
City of New Bedford, MA	91,473	1,191	4	59	301	827	3,353	1,056	1,978	319
City of Fall River, MA	90,760	1,088	3	65	240	780	3,528	842	2,337	349
City of Warwick, RI	84,326	83	0	19	21	43	2,737	300	2,291	146
City of Cranston, RI	79,987	136	1	16	55	64	2,184	331	1,605	248
Total area actually reporting	100.0%	5,904	42	453	1,570	3,839	44,475	9,648	30,548	4,279
Rate per 100,000 inhabitants		369.5	2.6	28.4	98.3	240.3	2,783.6	603.8	1,911.9	267.8
Provo-Orem, UT M.S.A.	516,198									
Includes Juab and Utah Counties										
City of Provo	119,189	184	0	40	21	123	2,994	451	2,401	142
City of Orem	94,228	66	2	22	9	33	2,584	246	2,222	116
Total area actually reporting	100.0%	472	3	131	68	270	12,056	1,806	9,715	535
Rate per 100,000 inhabitants		91.4	0.6	25.4	13.2	52.3	2,335.5	349.9	1,882.0	103.6
Punta Gorda, FL M.S.A.	152,292									
Includes Charlotte County										
City of Punta Gorda	16,699	28	0	0	4	24	471	191	272	8
Total area actually reporting	100.0%	530	3	15	72	440	5,007	1,274	3,506	227
Rate per 100,000 inhabitants		348.0	2.0	9.8	47.3	288.9	3,287.8	836.6	2,302.2	149.1
Racine, WI M.S.A.	195,756									
Includes Racine County										
City of Racine	82,226	542	10	19	293	220	3,930	1,299	2,431	200
Total area actually reporting	100.0%	642	10	25	331	276	6,135	1,644	4,181	310
Rate per 100,000 inhabitants		328.0	5.1	12.8	169.1	141.0	3,134.0	839.8	2,135.8	158.4
Raleigh-Cary, NC M.S.A.[1]	1,085,760									
Includes Franklin,[1] Johnston, and Wake Counties										
City of Raleigh	388,661	2,245	34	95	1,025	1,091	13,220	3,095	9,178	947
City of Cary	125,277	107	3	12	47	45	2,342	503	1,761	78
Total area actually reporting	97.7%		50	213	1,408		28,607	7,230	19,439	1,938
Estimated total	100.0%		51	220	1,439		29,843	7,517	20,329	1,997
Rate per 100,000 inhabitants			4.7	20.3	132.5		2,748.6	692.3	1,872.3	183.9
Rapid City, SD M.S.A.	121,526									
Includes Meade and Pennington Counties										
City of Rapid City	64,556	346	2	73	50	221	2,572	392	2,035	145
Total area actually reporting	85.8%	468	3	132	53	280	3,160	530	2,464	166
Estimated total	100.0%	498	4	145	54	295	3,324	577	2,570	177
Rate per 100,000 inhabitants		409.8	3.3	119.3	44.4	242.7	2,735.2	474.8	2,114.8	145.6

[1] The FBI determined that the agency's data were overreported. Consequently, affected data are not included in this table.

Table 6. Crime, by Metropolitan Statistical Area, 2008—*Continued*

(Number, percent, rate per 100,000 population.)

Area	Population	Violent crime	Murder and non-negligent man-slaughter	Forcible rape	Robbery	Aggravated assault	Property crime	Burglary	Larceny-theft	Motor vehicle theft
Rapid City, SD M.S.A.	121,526									
Includes Meade and Pennington Counties										
City of Rapid City	64,556	346	2	73	50	221	2,572	392	2,035	145
Total area actually reporting	85.8%	468	3	132	53	280	3,160	530	2,464	166
Estimated total	100.0%	498	4	145	54	295	3,324	577	2,570	177
Rate per 100,000 inhabitants		409.8	3.3	119.3	44.4	242.7	2,735.2	474.8	2,114.8	145.6
Reading, PA M.S.A.	405,335									
Includes Berks County										
City of Reading	80,860	868	10	33	452	373	4,208	1,268	2,150	790
Total area actually reporting	100.0%	1,340	16	65	560	699	10,292	2,142	6,959	1,191
Rate per 100,000 inhabitants		330.6	3.9	16.0	138.2	172.4	2,539.1	528.5	1,716.9	293.8
Redding, CA M.S.A.	180,598									
Includes Shasta County										
City of Redding	90,881	635	3	86	75	471	3,168	742	2,175	251
Total area actually reporting	100.0%	1,174	4	133	104	933	5,013	1,433	3,134	446
Rate per 100,000 inhabitants		650.1	2.2	73.6	57.6	516.6	2,775.8	793.5	1,735.3	247.0
Reno-Sparks, NV M.S.A.	412,231									
Includes Storey and Washoe Counties										
City of Reno	218,556	1,532	15	83	488	946	9,714	1,975	6,757	982
City of Sparks	88,913	410	0	51	128	231	3,486	903	2,279	304
Total area actually reporting	100.0%	2,218	15	141	633	1,429	15,227	3,500	10,269	1,458
Rate per 100,000 inhabitants		538.0	3.6	34.2	153.6	346.7	3,693.8	849.0	2,491.1	353.7
Richmond, VA M.S.A.	1,223,648									
Includes Amelia, Caroline, Charles City, Chesterfield, Cumberland, Dinwiddie, Goochland, Hanover, Henrico, King and Queen, King William, Louisa, New Kent, Powhatan, Prince George, and Sussex Counties, and Colonial Heights, Hopewell, Petersburg, and Richmond Cities										
City of Richmond	199,674	1,588	31	53	779	725	8,148	1,787	5,331	1,030
Total area actually reporting	100.0%	4,289	76	272	1,876	2,065	34,558	6,957	24,674	2,927
Rate per 100,000 inhabitants		350.5	6.2	22.2	153.3	168.8	2,824.2	568.5	2,016.4	239.2
Riverside-San Bernardino-Ontario, CA M.S.A.	4,175,614									
Includes Riverside and San Bernardino Counties										
City of Riverside	299,384	1,922	19	109	726	1,068	11,059	2,208	7,230	1,621
City of San Bernardino	200,617	2,074	32	65	779	1,198	9,438	2,215	5,073	2,150
City of Ontario	172,543	882	5	63	379	435	5,466	1,000	3,279	1,187
City of Victorville	114,305	683	4	33	254	392	4,188	1,384	2,290	514
City of Temecula	98,663	151	3	15	54	79	2,432	704	1,482	246
City of Chino	84,595	199	2	14	90	93	2,317	532	1,497	288
City of Redlands	70,730	253	1	19	111	122	2,771	540	1,868	363
City of Hemet	71,789	427	2	28	136	261	3,356	786	2,106	464
City of Colton	51,177	269	3	6	121	139	1,825	417	1,029	379
Total area actually reporting	100.0%	18,756	209	992	6,311	11,244	128,171	33,573	73,461	21,137
Rate per 100,000 inhabitants		449.2	5.0	23.8	151.1	269.3	3,069.5	804.0	1,759.3	506.2
Roanoke, VA M.S.A.	296,477									
Includes Botetourt, Craig, Franklin, and Roanoke Counties and Roanoke and Salem Cities										
City of Roanoke	91,983	745	11	48	213	473	5,090	983	3,811	296
Total area actually reporting	100.0%	1,005	18	86	254	647	8,477	1,550	6,459	468
Rate per 100,000 inhabitants		339.0	6.1	29.0	85.7	218.2	2,859.2	522.8	2,178.6	157.9
Rochester, MN M.S.A.[1, 5]	182,815									
Includes Dodge,[1] Olmsted, and Wabasha Counties[5]										
City of Rochester[5]	100,589		4		65	133	2,853	534	2,133	186
Total area actually reporting	98.2%		5		67		3,756	712	2,792	252
Estimated total	100.0%		5		69		3,858	726	2,875	257
Rate per 100,000 inhabitants			2.7		37.7		2,110.3	397.1	1,572.6	140.6
Rochester, NY M.S.A.	1,029,201									
Includes Livingston, Monroe, Ontario, Orleans, and Wayne Counties										
City of Rochester	205,341	2,302	42	98	1,059	1,103	11,130	2,808	7,060	1,262
Total area actually reporting	99.7%	3,355	49	218	1,336	1,752	27,535	5,479	20,213	1,843
Estimated total	100.0%	3,360	49	218	1,338	1,755	27,601	5,489	20,266	1,846
Rate per 100,000 inhabitants		326.5	4.8	21.2	130.0	170.5	2,681.8	533.3	1,969.1	179.4

[1] The FBI determined that the agency's data were overreported. Consequently, affected data are not included in this table.
[5] The data collection methodology for the offense of forcible rape used by the Minnesota state UCR Program (with the exception of Minneapolis and St. Paul, MN) does not comply with national UCR Program guidelines. Consequently, their figures for forcible rape and violent crime (of which forcible rape is a part) are not published in this table.

Table 6. Crime, by Metropolitan Statistical Area, 2008—*Continued*

(Number, percent, rate per 100,000 population.)

Area	Population	Violent crime	Murder and non-negligent man-slaughter	Forcible rape	Robbery	Aggravated assault	Property crime	Burglary	Larceny-theft	Motor vehicle theft
Sacramento–Arden-Arcade–Roseville, CA M.S.A.	2,119,553									
Includes El Dorado, Placer, Sacramento, and Yolo Counties										
City of Sacramento	467,065	4,660	49	168	1,761	2,682	22,499	5,216	12,373	4,910
City of Roseville	112,817	325	0	25	70	230	4,099	629	3,089	381
City of Folsom	69,523	96	0	13	29	54	1,546	244	1,219	83
City of Woodland	54,210	183	0	18	63	102	1,955	487	1,250	218
Total area actually reporting	100.0%	11,060	112	589	3,770	6,589	70,648	16,262	43,329	11,057
Rate per 100,000 inhabitants		521.8	5.3	27.8	177.9	310.9	3,333.2	767.2	2,044.3	521.7
Saginaw-Saginaw Township North, MI M.S.A.	199,649									
Includes Saginaw County										
City of Saginaw	55,634	1,833	21	50	309	1,453	2,644	1,508	915	221
Total area actually reporting	98.9%	2,374	24	108	392	1,850	6,636	2,513	3,724	399
Estimated total	100.0%	2,381	24	109	394	1,854	6,700	2,526	3,769	405
Rate per 100,000 inhabitants		1,192.6	12.0	54.6	197.3	928.6	3,355.9	1,265.2	1,887.8	202.9
Salem, OR M.S.A.	391,860									
Includes Marion and Polk Counties										
City of Salem	153,831	572	9	58	136	369	7,173	1,094	5,428	651
Total area actually reporting	100.0%	958	16	101	215	626	13,504	2,372	9,915	1,217
Rate per 100,000 inhabitants		244.5	4.1	25.8	54.9	159.8	3,446.1	605.3	2,530.2	310.6
Salinas, CA M.S.A.	406,198									
Includes Monterey County										
City of Salinas	143,520	1,050	25	38	337	650	5,299	1,415	2,646	1,238
Total area actually reporting	100.0%	1,973	36	99	587	1,251	11,491	3,056	6,541	1,894
Rate per 100,000 inhabitants		485.7	8.9	24.4	144.5	308.0	2,828.9	752.3	1,610.3	466.3
Salisbury, MD M.S.A.	120,076									
Includes Somerset and Wicomico Counties										
City of Salisbury	28,455	661	4	18	155	484	2,244	534	1,618	92
Total area actually reporting	100.0%	1,104	8	39	231	826	4,695	1,217	3,226	252
Rate per 100,000 inhabitants		919.4	6.7	32.5	192.4	687.9	3,910.0	1,013.5	2,686.6	209.9
Salt Lake City, UT M.S.A.	1,131,292									
Includes Salt Lake, Summit, and Tooele Counties										
City of Salt Lake City	180,514	1,420	12	75	486	847	16,169	2,044	12,282	1,843
Total area actually reporting	99.8%	3,937	22	448	1,041	2,426	53,388	8,059	39,989	5,340
Estimated total	100.0%	3,941	22	449	1,042	2,428	53,452	8,069	40,038	5,345
Rate per 100,000 inhabitants		348.4	1.9	39.7	92.1	214.6	4,724.9	713.3	3,539.1	472.5
San Angelo, TX M.S.A.	108,373									
Includes Irion and Tom Green Counties										
City of San Angelo	90,739	369	6	63	66	234	4,476	1,046	3,198	232
Total area actually reporting	100.0%	398	6	69	66	257	4,821	1,129	3,443	249
Rate per 100,000 inhabitants		367.3	5.5	63.7	60.9	237.1	4,448.5	1,041.8	3,177.0	229.8
San Antonio, TX M.S.A.	2,027,812									
Includes Atascosa, Bandera, Bexar, Comal, Guadalupe, Kendall, Medina, and Wilson Counties										
City of San Antonio	1,351,244	9,699	116	424	2,743	6,416	97,564	18,908	70,651	8,005
Total area actually reporting	100.0%	11,568	156	643	3,089	7,680	120,122	24,290	86,617	9,215
Rate per 100,000 inhabitants		570.5	7.7	31.7	152.3	378.7	5,923.7	1,197.8	4,271.5	454.4
San Diego-Carlsbad-San Marcos, CA M.S.A.	2,979,368									
Includes San Diego County										
City of San Diego	1,271,655	6,047	55	376	2,019	3,597	40,365	7,743	21,945	10,677
City of Carlsbad	97,670	227	2	24	51	150	2,358	507	1,662	189
City of San Marcos	81,683	213	1	8	55	149	1,609	401	934	274
City of National City	59,390	486	0	25	183	278	2,182	365	1,024	793
Total area actually reporting	100.0%	12,874	90	845	4,018	7,921	84,294	16,931	47,389	19,974
Rate per 100,000 inhabitants		432.1	3.0	28.4	134.9	265.9	2,829.3	568.3	1,590.6	670.4
Sandusky, OH M.S.A.	77,057									
Includes Erie County										
City of Sandusky	25,625	193	1	8	51	133	1,480	393	1,049	38
Total area actually reporting	98.7%	242	2	13	58	169	2,652	617	1,952	83
Estimated total	100.0%	244	2	13	59	170	2,682	623	1,975	84
Rate per 100,000 inhabitants		316.6	2.6	16.9	76.6	220.6	3,480.5	808.5	2,563.0	109.0

Table 6. Crime, by Metropolitan Statistical Area, 2008—*Continued*

(Number, percent, rate per 100,000 population.)

Area	Population	Violent crime	Murder and non-negligent man-slaughter	Forcible rape	Robbery	Aggravated assault	Property crime	Burglary	Larceny-theft	Motor vehicle theft
San Francisco-Oakland-Fremont, CA M.S.A.	4,230,321									
Includes the Metropolitan Divisions of Oakland-Fremont-Hayward and San Francisco-San Mateo-Redwood City										
City of San Francisco	798,144	6,744	98	166	4,108	2,372	36,301	5,401	25,142	5,758
City of Oakland	401,587	7,905	115	338	3,323	4,129	21,488	4,488	8,915	8,085
City of Fremont	200,964	575	2	37	232	304	4,893	1,097	3,099	697
City of Hayward	140,984	868	7	57	517	287	4,537	1,080	2,114	1,343
City of Berkeley	101,170	652	8	25	496	123	6,837	1,095	4,790	952
City of San Mateo	91,650	360	1	28	118	213	2,288	234	1,766	288
City of San Leandro	77,474	513	1	17	356	139	3,894	652	2,231	1,011
City of Redwood City	73,369	250	1	22	75	152	2,122	343	1,447	332
City of Pleasanton	66,829	75	0	6	22	47	1,488	186	1,188	114
City of Walnut Creek	63,122	144	1	3	57	83	2,707	568	1,952	187
City of South San Francisco	62,027	152	2	11	61	78	1,639	392	996	251
City of San Rafael	55,589	202	2	13	78	109	1,573	297	1,002	274
Total area actually reporting	100.0%	26,897	344	1,116	13,070	12,367	153,391	28,719	93,621	31,051
Rate per 100,000 inhabitants		635.8	8.1	26.4	309.0	292.3	3,626.0	678.9	2,213.1	734.0
Oakland-Fremont-Hayward, CA M.D.	2,481,921									
Includes Alameda and Contra Costa Counties										
Total area actually reporting	100.0%	17,375	223	766	8,041	8,345	94,194	19,166	52,809	22,219
Rate per 100,000 inhabitants		700.1	9.0	30.9	324.0	336.2	3,795.2	772.2	2,127.7	895.2
San Francisco-San Mateo-Redwood City, CA M.D.	1,748,400									
Includes Marin, San Francisco, and San Mateo Counties										
Total area actually reporting	100.0%	9,522	121	350	5,029	4,022	59,197	9,553	40,812	8,832
Rate per 100,000 inhabitants		544.6	6.9	20.0	287.6	230.0	3,385.8	546.4	2,334.2	505.1
San Jose-Sunnyvale-Santa Clara, CA M.S.A.	1,802,847									
Includes San Benito and Santa Clara Counties										
City of San Jose	945,197	3,643	31	220	1,124	2,268	22,298	3,457	13,612	5,229
City of Sunnyvale	131,052	184	2	17	65	100	2,590	350	1,894	346
City of Santa Clara	110,712	231	4	20	83	124	3,024	450	2,172	402
City of Mountain View	70,401	289	6	7	55	221	1,820	233	1,444	143
City of Milpitas	67,282	149	0	10	66	73	2,072	228	1,592	252
City of Palo Alto	58,203	83	2	5	42	34	1,744	366	1,307	71
City of Cupertino	53,385	52	0	2	19	31	1,065	169	851	45
Total area actually reporting	100.0%	5,695	53	372	1,727	3,543	43,671	7,323	28,930	7,418
Rate per 100,000 inhabitants		315.9	2.9	20.6	95.8	196.5	2,422.3	406.2	1,604.7	411.5
San Luis Obispo-Paso Robles, CA M.S.A.	263,017									
Includes San Luis Obispo County										
City of San Luis Obispo	43,421	136	0	32	38	66	1,717	334	1,328	55
City of Paso Robles	29,183	121	0	19	22	80	835	216	559	60
Total area actually reporting	100.0%	780	4	106	112	558	6,170	1,517	4,308	345
Rate per 100,000 inhabitants		296.6	1.5	40.3	42.6	212.2	2,345.9	576.8	1,637.9	131.2
Santa Barbara-Santa Maria-Goleta, CA M.S.A.	402,753									
Includes Santa Barbara County										
City of Santa Barbara	85,791	492	2	26	117	347	2,512	488	1,911	113
City of Santa Maria	86,744	622	9	57	100	456	2,591	528	1,573	490
City of Goleta	29,551	24	0	2	6	16	386	103	263	20
Total area actually reporting	100.0%	1,653	14	136	292	1,211	9,408	2,035	6,561	812
Rate per 100,000 inhabitants		410.4	3.5	33.8	72.5	300.7	2,335.9	505.3	1,629.0	201.6
Santa Cruz-Watsonville, CA M.S.A.	250,002									
Includes Santa Cruz County										
City of Santa Cruz	55,255	446	2	19	112	313	2,091	412	1,534	145
City of Watsonville	50,211	353	3	14	81	255	1,872	290	1,358	224
Total area actually reporting	100.0%	1,247	8	77	276	886	7,882	1,585	5,601	696
Rate per 100,000 inhabitants		498.8	3.2	30.8	110.4	354.4	3,152.8	634.0	2,240.4	278.4
Santa Fe, NM M.S.A.	144,261									
Includes Santa Fe County										
City of Santa Fe	74,496	331	10	29	76	216	3,647	1,778	1,675	194
Total area actually reporting	100.0%	575	13	57	95	410	4,617	2,410	1,984	223
Rate per 100,000 inhabitants		398.6	9.0	39.5	65.9	284.2	3,200.4	1,670.6	1,375.3	154.6
Santa Rosa-Petaluma, CA M.S.A.	462,650									
Includes Sonoma County										
City of Santa Rosa	154,874	751	8	49	149	545	3,681	791	2,520	370
City of Petaluma	54,454	213	0	20	29	164	902	149	698	55
Total area actually reporting	100.0%	2,031	12	145	274	1,600	8,699	2,060	5,824	815
Rate per 100,000 inhabitants		439.0	2.6	31.3	59.2	345.8	1,880.3	445.3	1,258.8	176.2

Table 6. Crime, by Metropolitan Statistical Area, 2008—*Continued*

(Number, percent, rate per 100,000 population.)

Area	Population	Violent crime	Murder and non-negligent man-slaughter	Forcible rape	Robbery	Aggravated assault	Property crime	Burglary	Larceny-theft	Motor vehicle theft
Savannah, GA M.S.A.	332,641									
Includes Bryan, Chatham, and Effingham Counties										
City of Savannah-Chatham Metropolitan	211,475	1,285	26	37	804	418	11,250	2,974	7,064	1,212
Total area actually reporting	100.0%	1,655	27	58	896	674	14,573	3,643	9,440	1,490
Rate per 100,000 inhabitants		497.5	8.1	17.4	269.4	202.6	4,381.0	1,095.2	2,837.9	447.9
Scranton–Wilkes-Barre, PA M.S.A.	547,925									
Includes Lackawanna, Luzerne, and Wyoming Counties										
City of Scranton	72,247	238	5	30	97	106	2,629	639	1,851	139
City of Wilkes-Barre	40,976	180	2	17	104	57	1,521	250	1,170	101
Total area actually reporting	98.1%	1,411	24	114	301	972	12,479	2,398	9,395	686
Estimated total	100.0%	1,435	24	116	307	988	12,693	2,430	9,566	697
Rate per 100,000 inhabitants		261.9	4.4	21.2	56.0	180.3	2,316.6	443.5	1,745.9	127.2
Sebastian-Vero Beach, FL M.S.A.	132,682									
Includes Indian River County										
City of Sebastian	20,667	47	0	5	3	39	556	148	399	9
City of Vero Beach	16,689	86	0	4	29	53	689	147	526	16
Total area actually reporting	100.0%	474	4	39	102	329	4,285	1,088	3,045	152
Rate per 100,000 inhabitants		357.2	3.0	29.4	76.9	248.0	3,229.5	820.0	2,295.0	114.6
Sheboygan, WI M.S.A.	114,653									
Includes Sheboygan County										
City of Sheboygan	47,813	80	0	10	27	43	2,188	349	1,772	67
Total area actually reporting	100.0%	118	0	16	29	73	3,162	467	2,606	89
Rate per 100,000 inhabitants		102.9	0.0	14.0	25.3	63.7	2,757.9	407.3	2,272.9	77.6
Sherman-Denison, TX M.S.A.	119,673									
Includes Grayson County										
City of Sherman	38,039	153	0	3	18	132	1,560	366	1,141	53
City of Denison	24,276	112	2	1	24	85	951	221	687	43
Total area actually reporting	100.0%	335	3	15	47	270	3,484	898	2,433	153
Rate per 100,000 inhabitants		279.9	2.5	12.5	39.3	225.6	2,911.3	750.4	2,033.0	127.8
Shreveport-Bossier City, LA M.S.A.	391,302									
Includes Bossier, Caddo, and De Soto Parishes										
City of Shreveport	199,434	1,897	27	105	474	1,291	10,553	2,512	7,182	859
City of Bossier City	62,500	1,173	6	24	104	1,039	2,704	431	2,095	178
Total area actually reporting	99.0%	4,081	37	147	615	3,282	15,537	3,384	10,908	1,245
Estimated total	100.0%	4,102	37	148	618	3,299	15,714	3,420	11,041	1,253
Rate per 100,000 inhabitants		1,048.3	9.5	37.8	157.9	843.1	4,015.8	874.0	2,821.6	320.2
Sioux City, IA-NE-SD M.S.A.	143,016									
Includes Woodbury County, IA; Dakota and Dixon Counties, NE; and Union County, SD										
City of Sioux City, IA	82,404	327	5	38	55	229	2,699	522	2,024	153
Total area actually reporting	96.9%	391	6	45	57	283	3,306	658	2,458	190
Estimated total	100.0%	396	6	46	57	287	3,362	665	2,505	192
Rate per 100,000 inhabitants		276.9	4.2	32.2	39.9	200.7	2,350.8	465.0	1,751.6	134.3
Sioux Falls, SD M.S.A.	233,355									
Includes Lincoln, McCook, Minnehaha, and Turner Counties										
City of Sioux Falls	155,110	522	5	130	46	341	3,937	659	3,030	248
Total area actually reporting	97.4%	584	7	146	47	384	4,515	805	3,410	300
Estimated total	100.0%	591	7	147	47	390	4,593	815	3,475	303
Rate per 100,000 inhabitants		253.3	3.0	63.0	20.1	167.1	1,968.2	349.3	1,489.1	129.8
South Bend-Mishawaka, IN-MI M.S.A.	316,014									
Includes St. Joseph County, IN and Cass County, MI										
City of South Bend, IN	103,561	819	15	73	409	322	6,965	2,284	4,179	502
City of Mishawaka, IN	49,756	189	0	16	75	98	3,482	500	2,776	206
Total area actually reporting	100.0%	1,266	18	136	514	598	14,008	3,791	9,283	934
Rate per 100,000 inhabitants		400.6	5.7	43.0	162.7	189.2	4,432.7	1,199.6	2,937.5	295.6
Spartanburg, SC M.S.A.	279,521									
Includes Spartanburg County										
City of Spartanburg	38,726	802	6	23	203	570	3,572	953	2,352	267
Total area actually reporting	100.0%	1,871	19	124	425	1,303	11,969	3,060	7,850	1,059
Rate per 100,000 inhabitants		669.4	6.8	44.4	152.0	466.2	4,282.0	1,094.7	2,808.4	378.9
Spokane, WA M.S.A.	461,536									
Includes Spokane County										
City of Spokane	201,491	1,352	13	94	460	785	11,025	2,269	7,218	1,538
Total area actually reporting	100.0%	1,917	19	136	559	1,203	17,592	3,654	11,707	2,231
Rate per 100,000 inhabitants		415.4	4.1	29.5	121.1	260.7	3,811.6	791.7	2,536.5	483.4

Table 6. Crime, by Metropolitan Statistical Area, 2008—*Continued*

(Number, percent, rate per 100,000 population.)

Area	Population	Violent crime	Murder and non-negligent man-slaughter	Forcible rape	Robbery	Aggravated assault	Property crime	Burglary	Larceny-theft	Motor vehicle theft
Springfield, MA M.S.A.	686,794									
Includes Franklin, Hampden, and Hampshire Counties										
City of Springfield	151,249	1,898	14	117	567	1,200	7,336	2,002	4,432	902
Total area actually reporting	98.1%	3,757	18	310	793	2,636	19,857	5,134	12,987	1,736
Estimated total	100.0%	3,795	18	313	800	2,664	20,122	5,199	13,168	1,755
Rate per 100,000 inhabitants		552.6	2.6	45.6	116.5	387.9	2,929.8	757.0	1,917.3	255.5
Springfield, MO M.S.A.[4]	426,242									
Includes Christian, Dallas,[4] Greene, Polk, and Webster Counties										
City of Springfield	155,106	1,068	9	95	289	675	14,514	2,128	11,357	1,029
Total area actually reporting	100.0%		11	133	326		19,386	3,257	14,786	1,343
Rate per 100,000 inhabitants			2.6	31.2	76.5		4,548.1	764.1	3,468.9	315.1
Springfield, OH M.S.A.	139,989									
Includes Clark County										
City of Springfield	61,999	319	9	34	138	138	4,547	816	3,385	346
Total area actually reporting	99.8%	345	10	38	146	151	6,218	1,214	4,586	418
Estimated total	100.0%	345	10	38	146	151	6,226	1,216	4,592	418
Rate per 100,000 inhabitants		246.4	7.1	27.1	104.3	107.9	4,447.5	868.6	3,280.3	298.6
State College, PA M.S.A.	145,722									
Includes Centre County										
City of State College	54,065	44	0	6	12	26	983	144	828	11
Total area actually reporting	98.0%	127	0	20	24	83	2,555	486	2,002	67
Estimated total	100.0%	134	0	20	26	88	2,615	495	2,050	70
Rate per 100,000 inhabitants		92.0	0.0	13.7	17.8	60.4	1,794.5	339.7	1,406.8	48.0
St. Cloud, MN M.S.A.[5]	187,379									
Includes Benton and Stearns Counties[5]										
City of St. Cloud[5]	67,404		0		51	164	3,097	358	2,646	93
Total area actually reporting	100.0%		1		62	237	4,912	610	4,122	180
Rate per 100,000 inhabitants			0.5		33.1	126.5	2,621.4	325.5	2,199.8	96.1
St. George, UT M.S.A.	142,153									
Includes Washington County										
City of St. George	74,356	161	1	20	26	114	2,105	441	1,547	117
Total area actually reporting	100.0%	269	2	32	32	203	3,197	684	2,334	179
Rate per 100,000 inhabitants		189.2	1.4	22.5	22.5	142.8	2,249.0	481.2	1,641.9	125.9
St. Joseph, MO-KS M.S.A.[2]	123,101									
Includes Doniphan County, KS and Andrew, Buchanan, and De Kalb Counties, MO										
City of St. Joseph, MO[2]	76,377	353	3	13	88	249	3,634	770	2,643	221
Total area actually reporting	98.4%	427	3	20	92	312	4,495	1,037	3,196	262
Estimated total	100.0%	434	3	21	93	317	4,547	1,046	3,236	265
Rate per 100,000 inhabitants		352.6	2.4	17.1	75.5	257.5	3,693.7	849.7	2,628.7	215.3
St. Louis, MO-IL M.S.A.	2,820,831									
Includes Bond, Calhoun, Clinton, Jersey, Macoupin, Madison, Monroe, and St. Clair Counties, IL and Franklin, Jefferson, Lincoln, St. Charles, St. Louis, Warren, and Washington Counties and St. Louis City, MO										
City of St. Louis, MO	356,204	7,383	167	237	2,634	4,345	30,443	7,274	17,328	5,841
City of St. Charles, MO	64,012	151	1	13	33	104	2,432	308	2,025	99
Total area actually reporting	75.4%	12,887	228	572	3,789	8,298	83,700	16,842	56,883	9,975
Estimated total	100.0%	14,833	233	572	4,222	9,806	95,909	19,311	65,915	10,683
Rate per 100,000 inhabitants		525.8	8.3	20.3	149.7	347.6	3,400.0	684.6	2,336.7	378.7
Stockton, CA M.S.A.	681,786									
Includes San Joaquin County										
City of Stockton	293,073	4,322	24	112	1,558	2,628	17,955	4,353	11,102	2,500
Total area actually reporting	100.0%	6,156	35	171	2,024	3,926	33,567	7,660	21,467	4,440
Rate per 100,000 inhabitants		902.9	5.1	25.1	296.9	575.8	4,923.4	1,123.5	3,148.6	651.2
Sumter, SC M.S.A.	104,311									
Includes Sumter County										
City of Sumter	38,547	577	5	13	129	430	2,745	674	1,852	219
Total area actually reporting	100.0%	772	13	23	174	562	3,893	1,254	2,264	375
Rate per 100,000 inhabitants		740.1	12.5	22.0	166.8	538.8	3,732.1	1,202.2	2,170.4	359.5

[2] Because of changes in the state/local agency's reporting practices, figures are not comparable to previous years' data.
[4] It was determined that the agency did not follow national Uniform Crime Reporting (UCR) Program guidelines for reporting an offense. Consequently, this figure is not included in this table.
[5] The data collection methodology for the offense of forcible rape used by the Minnesota state UCR Program (with the exception of Minneapolis and St. Paul, MN) does not comply with national UCR Program guidelines. Consequently, their figures for forcible rape and violent crime (of which forcible rape is a part) are not published in this table.

Table 6. Crime, by Metropolitan Statistical Area, 2008—*Continued*

(Number, percent, rate per 100,000 population.)

Area	Population	Violent crime	Murder and non-negligent man-slaughter	Forcible rape	Robbery	Aggravated assault	Property crime	Burglary	Larceny-theft	Motor vehicle theft
Syracuse, NY M.S.A.	644,461									
Includes Madison, Onondaga, and Oswego Counties										
City of Syracuse	138,211	1,366	24	71	419	852	6,165	1,938	3,725	502
Total area actually reporting	99.0%	1,971	31	163	530	1,247	15,365	3,672	10,917	776
Estimated total	100.0%	1,983	31	164	534	1,254	15,494	3,692	11,021	781
Rate per 100,000 inhabitants		307.7	4.8	25.4	82.9	194.6	2,404.2	572.9	1,710.1	121.2
Tallahassee, FL M.S.A.	352,043									
Includes Gadsden, Jefferson, Leon, and Wakulla Counties										
City of Tallahassee	168,984	1,908	8	133	642	1,125	8,968	2,804	5,660	504
Total area actually reporting	100.0%	3,149	15	182	796	2,156	13,756	4,688	8,320	748
Rate per 100,000 inhabitants		894.5	4.3	51.7	226.1	612.4	3,907.5	1,331.7	2,363.3	212.5
Tampa-St. Petersburg-Clearwater, FL M.S.A.	2,734,761									
Includes Hernando, Hillsborough, Pasco, and Pinellas Counties										
City of Tampa	336,911	2,975	27	83	1,056	1,809	15,498	4,098	9,648	1,752
City of St. Petersburg	243,111	3,368	20	110	1,095	2,143	15,404	4,232	9,711	1,461
City of Clearwater	104,986	991	11	38	318	624	4,785	856	3,678	251
City of Largo	72,298	553	3	40	134	376	3,219	608	2,404	207
Total area actually reporting	100.0%	18,071	153	949	4,828	12,141	112,538	28,483	75,151	8,904
Rate per 100,000 inhabitants		660.8	5.6	34.7	176.5	444.0	4,115.1	1,041.5	2,748.0	325.6
Texarkana, TX-Texarkana, AR M.S.A.	134,769									
Includes Miller County, AR and Bowie County, TX										
City of Texarkana, TX	36,300	467	2	18	74	373	2,264	626	1,519	119
City of Texarkana, AR	29,855	513	2	16	75	420	1,812	450	1,249	113
Total area actually reporting	90.3%	1,138	5	45	160	928	5,098	1,420	3,350	328
Estimated total	100.0%	1,177	5	50	163	959	5,377	1,535	3,490	352
Rate per 100,000 inhabitants		873.3	3.7	37.1	120.9	711.6	3,989.8	1,139.0	2,589.6	261.2
Toledo, OH M.S.A.	650,080									
Includes Fulton, Lucas, Ottawa, and Wood Counties										
City of Toledo	317,401	3,621	18	132	1,383	2,088	18,670	6,522	10,671	1,477
Total area actually reporting	93.9%	3,893	19	185	1,455	2,234	26,815	7,966	17,066	1,783
Estimated total	100.0%	3,964	20	197	1,483	2,264	27,970	8,188	17,942	1,840
Rate per 100,000 inhabitants		609.8	3.1	30.3	228.1	348.3	4,302.5	1,259.5	2,760.0	283.0
Topeka, KS M.S.A.	229,726									
Includes Jackson, Jefferson, Osage, Shawnee, and Wabaunsee Counties										
City of Topeka	122,554	609	10	35	275	289	7,316	1,561	5,067	688
Total area actually reporting	97.8%	845	10	55	283	497	10,014	2,275	6,909	830
Estimated total	100.0%	863	10	57	285	511	10,151	2,298	7,015	838
Rate per 100,000 inhabitants		375.7	4.4	24.8	124.1	222.4	4,418.7	1,000.3	3,053.6	364.8
Trenton-Ewing, NJ M.S.A.	365,688									
Includes Mercer County										
City of Trenton	82,140	989	19	23	546	401	2,636	724	1,404	508
City of Ewing Township	36,483	99	3	0	39	57	623	127	441	55
Total area actually reporting	100.0%	1,478	24	55	730	669	8,106	1,752	5,492	862
Rate per 100,000 inhabitants		404.2	6.6	15.0	199.6	182.9	2,216.6	479.1	1,501.8	235.7
Tucson, AZ M.S.A.[4]	1,010,650									
Includes Pima County										
City of Tucson[4]	528,917	4,252	65	246	1,451	2,490		5,157		5,808
Total area actually reporting	100.0%	5,241	96	338	1,798	3,009		8,479		7,576
Rate per 100,000 inhabitants		518.6	9.5	33.4	177.9	297.7		839.0		749.6
Tulsa, OK M.S.A.	912,415									
Includes Creek, Okmulgee, Osage, Pawnee, Rogers, Tulsa, and Wagoner Counties										
City of Tulsa	382,954	4,922	50	252	1,096	3,524	22,769	6,725	13,746	2,298
Total area actually reporting	100.0%	6,260	73	389	1,232	4,566	33,374	9,643	20,599	3,132
Rate per 100,000 inhabitants		686.1	8.0	42.6	135.0	500.4	3,657.8	1,056.9	2,257.6	343.3
Tuscaloosa, AL M.S.A.	207,198									
Includes Greene, Hale, and Tuscaloosa Counties										
City of Tuscaloosa	90,157	470	11	28	199	232	5,396	1,513	3,553	330
Total area actually reporting	98.8%	1,045	17	66	307	655	9,510	2,726	6,104	680
Estimated total	100.0%	1,056	17	67	311	661	9,626	2,753	6,185	688
Rate per 100,000 inhabitants		509.7	8.2	32.3	150.1	319.0	4,645.8	1,328.7	2,985.1	332.0

[4] It was determined that the agency did not follow national Uniform Crime Reporting (UCR) Program guidelines for reporting an offense. Consequently, this figure is not included in this table.

Table 6. Crime, by Metropolitan Statistical Area, 2008—*Continued*

(Number, percent, rate per 100,000 population.)

Area	Population	Violent crime	Murder and non-negligent man-slaughter	Forcible rape	Robbery	Aggravated assault	Property crime	Burglary	Larceny-theft	Motor vehicle theft
Tyler, TX M.S.A.	201,817									
Includes Smith County										
City of Tyler	98,042	656	5	46	129	476	4,463	767	3,484	212
Total area actually reporting	99.0%	984	13	80	156	735	6,822	1,553	4,848	421
Estimated total	100.0%	991	13	81	158	739	6,894	1,568	4,900	426
Rate per 100,000 inhabitants		491.0	6.4	40.1	78.3	366.2	3,416.0	776.9	2,427.9	211.1
Utica-Rome, NY M.S.A.	294,181									
Includes Herkimer and Oneida Counties										
City of Utica	58,234	479	4	21	181	273	2,778	729	1,929	120
City of Rome	33,746	41	2	8	14	17	611	111	466	34
Total area actually reporting	98.5%	856	8	59	225	564	6,931	1,523	5,180	228
Estimated total	100.0%	864	8	59	228	569	7,016	1,536	5,249	231
Rate per 100,000 inhabitants		293.7	2.7	20.1	77.5	193.4	2,384.9	522.1	1,784.3	78.5
Valdosta, GA M.S.A.	130,908									
Includes Brooks, Echols, Lanier, and Lowndes Counties										
City of Valdosta	47,989	280	1	30	114	135	2,388	548	1,686	154
Total area actually reporting	93.0%	499	4	41	147	307	4,248	1,016	2,966	266
Estimated total	100.0%	546	4	43	163	336	4,667	1,102	3,266	299
Rate per 100,000 inhabitants		417.1	3.1	32.8	124.5	256.7	3,565.1	841.8	2,494.9	228.4
Vallejo-Fairfield, CA M.S.A.	408,066									
Includes Solano County										
City of Vallejo	115,330	1,100	13	34	435	618	5,653	2,155	2,112	1,386
City of Fairfield	104,927	546	5	28	238	275	4,026	736	2,703	587
Total area actually reporting	100.0%	2,354	24	123	905	1,302	14,781	3,911	8,275	2,595
Rate per 100,000 inhabitants		576.9	5.9	30.1	221.8	319.1	3,622.2	958.4	2,027.9	635.9
Victoria, TX M.S.A.	114,072									
Includes Calhoun, Goliad, and Victoria Counties										
City of Victoria	62,464	435	1	40	66	328	3,339	824	2,404	111
Total area actually reporting	99.4%	587	2	61	72	452	4,478	1,200	3,099	179
Estimated total	100.0%	589	2	61	73	453	4,503	1,205	3,117	181
Rate per 100,000 inhabitants		516.3	1.8	53.5	64.0	397.1	3,947.5	1,056.4	2,732.5	158.7
Vineland-Millville-Bridgeton, NJ M.S.A.	156,078									
Includes Cumberland County										
City of Vineland	58,606	316	3	16	136	161	2,491	589	1,804	98
City of Millville	28,551	237	3	5	85	144	1,333	291	995	47
City of Bridgeton	24,714	334	6	4	113	211	1,091	337	709	45
Total area actually reporting	100.0%	1,004	15	25	350	614	5,845	1,495	4,096	254
Rate per 100,000 inhabitants		643.3	9.6	16.0	224.2	393.4	3,744.9	957.9	2,624.3	162.7
Virginia Beach-Norfolk-Newport News, VA-NC M.S.A.	1,663,408									
Includes Currituck County, NC and Gloucester, Isle of Wight, James City, Mathews, Surry, and York Counties and Chesapeake, Hampton, Newport News, Norfolk, Poquoson, Portsmouth, Suffolk, Virginia Beach, and Williamsburg Cities, VA										
City of Virginia Beach, VA	434,163	1,043	14	73	537	419	12,609	1,921	10,046	642
City of Norfolk, VA	235,067	1,951	28	86	1,050	787	12,195	1,868	9,212	1,115
City of Newport News, VA	178,308	1,235	16	73	509	637	7,348	1,460	5,388	500
City of Hampton, VA	145,897	472	8	42	211	211	5,127	761	3,963	403
City of Portsmouth, VA	101,782	719	15	59	348	297	5,650	1,123	4,182	345
Total area actually reporting	100.0%	7,077	106	478	3,218	3,275	57,550	9,750	44,007	3,793
Rate per 100,000 inhabitants		425.5	6.4	28.7	193.5	196.9	3,459.8	586.1	2,645.6	228.0
Visalia-Porterville, CA M.S.A.	426,568									
Includes Tulare County										
City of Visalia	121,850	675	10	46	194	425	5,719	1,238	3,774	707
City of Porterville	52,308	283	1	7	63	212	1,880	389	1,166	325
Total area actually reporting	100.0%	2,257	43	104	469	1,641	16,890	3,930	10,169	2,791
Rate per 100,000 inhabitants		529.1	10.1	24.4	109.9	384.7	3,959.5	921.3	2,383.9	654.3
Waco, TX M.S.A.	229,941									
Includes McLennan County										
City of Waco	123,208	1,031	11	75	252	693	7,393	2,090	4,915	388
Total area actually reporting	100.0%	1,415	15	153	294	953	10,768	2,792	7,431	545
Rate per 100,000 inhabitants		615.4	6.5	66.5	127.9	414.5	4,682.9	1,214.2	3,231.7	237.0
Warner Robins, GA M.S.A.	133,071									
Includes Houston County										
City of Warner Robins	61,443	330	4	18	90	218	3,779	845	2,759	175
Total area actually reporting	100.0%	471	8	22	109	332	5,790	1,229	4,284	277
Rate per 100,000 inhabitants		353.9	6.0	16.5	81.9	249.5	4,351.1	923.6	3,219.3	208.2

Table 6. Crime, by Metropolitan Statistical Area, 2008—*Continued*

(Number, percent, rate per 100,000 population.)

Area	Population	Violent crime	Murder and non-negligent man-slaughter	Forcible rape	Robbery	Aggravated assault	Property crime	Burglary	Larceny-theft	Motor vehicle theft
Washington-Arlington-Alexandria, DC-VA-MD-WV M.S.A.	5,363,413									
Includes the Metropolitan Divisions of Bethesda-Frederick-Rockville, MD and Washington-Arlington-Alexandria, DC-VA-MD-WV										
City of Washington, DC	591,833	8,135	186	186	4,154	3,609	28,759	3,781	18,787	6,191
City of Alexandria, VA	140,891	324	3	30	149	142	3,389	294	2,713	382
City of Frederick, MD	60,034	471	2	12	126	331	1,849	379	1,326	144
Total area actually reporting	100.0%	23,483	401	987	10,975	11,120	160,970	22,622	115,514	22,834
Rate per 100,000 inhabitants		437.8	7.5	18.4	204.6	207.3	3,001.3	421.8	2,153.7	425.7
Bethesda-Frederick-Rockville, MD M.D.	1,169,906									
Includes Frederick and Montgomery Counties										
Total area actually reporting	100.0%	3,024	25	159	1,346	1,494	30,002	4,501	22,878	2,623
Rate per 100,000 inhabitants		258.5	2.1	13.6	115.1	127.7	2,564.5	384.7	1,955.5	224.2
Washington-Arlington-Alexandria, DC-VA-MD-WV M.D.	4,193,507									
Includes District of Columbia; Calvert, Charles, and Prince George's Counties, MD; Arlington, Clarke, Fairfax, Fauquier, Loudoun, Prince William, Spotsylvania, Stafford, and Warren Counties and Alexandria, Fairfax, Falls Church, Fredericksburg, Manassas, and Manassas Park Cities, VA; and Jefferson County, WV										
Total area actually reporting	100.0%	20,459	376	828	9,629	9,626	130,968	18,121	92,636	20,211
Rate per 100,000 inhabitants		487.9	9.0	19.7	229.6	229.5	3,123.1	432.1	2,209.0	482.0
Waterloo-Cedar Falls, IA M.S.A.	163,606									
Includes Black Hawk, Bremer, and Grundy Counties										
City of Waterloo	66,098	510	2	43	112	353	2,824	779	1,874	171
City of Cedar Falls	37,759	129	0	12	10	107	671	113	536	22
Total area actually reporting	100.0%	765	3	66	123	573	4,269	1,089	2,945	235
Rate per 100,000 inhabitants		467.6	1.8	40.3	75.2	350.2	2,609.3	665.6	1,800.1	143.6
Wausau, WI M.S.A.	130,393									
Includes Marathon County										
City of Wausau	37,981	131	1	19	29	82	1,177	276	851	50
Total area actually reporting	100.0%	346	3	35	34	274	2,366	502	1,773	91
Rate per 100,000 inhabitants		265.4	2.3	26.8	26.1	210.1	1,814.5	385.0	1,359.7	69.8
Weirton-Steubenville, WV-OH M.S.A.	121,534									
Includes Jefferson County, OH and Brooke and Hancock Counties, WV										
City of Weirton, WV	18,660	23	0	0	7	16	243	43	180	20
City of Steubenville, OH	18,745	102	3	9	35	55	1,058	179	843	36
Total area actually reporting	93.9%	208	3	15	46	144	2,214	483	1,612	119
Estimated total	100.0%	224	3	17	51	153	2,450	525	1,793	132
Rate per 100,000 inhabitants		184.3	2.5	14.0	42.0	125.9	2,015.9	432.0	1,475.3	108.6
Wenatchee-East Wenatchee, WA M.S.A.	108,298									
Includes Chelan and Douglas Counties										
City of Wenatchee	29,976	99	1	21	12	65	1,207	212	934	61
City of East Wenatchee	12,328	24	2	7	1	14	600	66	515	19
Total area actually reporting	100.0%	206	5	50	22	129	3,108	518	2,420	170
Rate per 100,000 inhabitants		190.2	4.6	46.2	20.3	119.1	2,869.9	478.3	2,234.6	157.0
Wheeling, WV-OH M.S.A.	144,612									
Includes Belmont County, OH and Marshall and Ohio Counties, WV										
City of Wheeling, WV	28,838	141	1	16	37	87	875	186	632	57
Total area actually reporting	88.7%	280	3	44	59	174	2,394	551	1,674	169
Estimated total	100.0%	313	3	49	71	190	2,895	644	2,057	194
Rate per 100,000 inhabitants		216.4	2.1	33.9	49.1	131.4	2,001.9	445.3	1,422.4	134.2
Wichita, KS M.S.A.	601,018									
Includes Butler, Harvey, Sedgwick, and Sumner Counties										
City of Wichita	362,602	3,091	30	278	482	2,301	20,034	4,077	14,097	1,860
Total area actually reporting	99.6%	3,659	33	345	516	2,765	25,915	5,396	18,331	2,188
Estimated total	100.0%	3,668	33	346	517	2,772	25,981	5,407	18,382	2,192
Rate per 100,000 inhabitants		610.3	5.5	57.6	86.0	461.2	4,322.8	899.6	3,058.5	364.7
Wichita Falls, TX M.S.A.	147,728									
Includes Archer, Clay, and Wichita Counties										
City of Wichita Falls	101,279	557	4	46	208	299	6,980	1,515	4,936	529
Total area actually reporting	100.0%	635	7	56	213	359	7,811	1,822	5,418	571
Rate per 100,000 inhabitants		429.8	4.7	37.9	144.2	243.0	5,287.4	1,233.3	3,667.6	386.5

Table 6. Crime, by Metropolitan Statistical Area, 2008—*Continued*

(Number, percent, rate per 100,000 population.)

Area	Population	Violent crime	Murder and non-negligent man-slaughter	Forcible rape	Robbery	Aggravated assault	Property crime	Burglary	Larceny-theft	Motor vehicle theft
Williamsport, PA M.S.A.	116,368									
Includes Lycoming County										
City of Williamsport	29,380	99	2	5	51	41	1,174	269	849	56
Total area actually reporting	100.0%	180	2	17	60	101	2,401	536	1,778	87
Rate per 100,000 inhabitants		154.7	1.7	14.6	51.6	86.8	2,063.3	460.6	1,527.9	74.8
Wilmington, NC M.S.A.	349,460									
Includes Brunswick, New Hanover, and Pender Counties										
City of Wilmington	100,944	778	12	49	319	398	5,447	1,465	3,454	528
Total area actually reporting	98.3%	1,317	16	118	439	744	14,076	4,436	8,587	1,053
Estimated total	100.0%	1,342	16	120	446	760	14,373	4,505	8,801	1,067
Rate per 100,000 inhabitants		384.0	4.6	34.3	127.6	217.5	4,112.9	1,289.1	2,518.5	305.3
Winchester, VA-WV M.S.A.	123,259									
Includes Frederick County and Winchester City, VA and Hampshire County, WV										
City of Winchester, VA	25,904	86	1	8	36	41	1,316	202	1,060	54
Total area actually reporting	100.0%	250	2	60	54	134	3,254	676	2,358	220
Rate per 100,000 inhabitants		202.8	1.6	48.7	43.8	108.7	2,640.0	548.4	1,913.0	178.5
Winston-Salem, NC M.S.A.	469,651									
Includes Davie, Forsyth, Stokes, and Yadkin Counties										
City of Winston-Salem	226,460	2,079	19	104	723	1,233	14,995	4,670	9,234	1,091
Total area actually reporting	99.4%	2,824	23	167	827	1,807	22,642	6,665	14,472	1,505
Estimated total	100.0%	2,835	23	168	830	1,814	22,780	6,697	14,571	1,512
Rate per 100,000 inhabitants		603.6	4.9	35.8	176.7	386.2	4,850.4	1,426.0	3,102.5	321.9
Worcester, MA M.S.A.	789,453									
Includes Worcester County										
City of Worcester	177,151	1,718	6	42	373	1,297	6,356	1,701	3,983	672
Total area actually reporting	98.8%	3,236	15	164	552	2,505	16,339	4,314	10,681	1,344
Estimated total	100.0%	3,263	15	166	557	2,525	16,530	4,361	10,811	1,358
Rate per 100,000 inhabitants		413.3	1.9	21.0	70.6	319.8	2,093.9	552.4	1,369.4	172.0
Yakima, WA M.S.A.	234,618									
Includes Yakima County										
City of Yakima	83,027	429	8	49	133	239	5,940	1,233	3,907	800
Total area actually reporting	99.1%	774	19	99	242	414	12,137	3,034	7,303	1,800
Estimated total	100.0%	780	19	100	244	417	12,224	3,050	7,364	1,810
Rate per 100,000 inhabitants		332.5	8.1	42.6	104.0	177.7	5,210.2	1,300.0	3,138.7	771.5
York-Hanover, PA M.S.A.	425,908									
Includes York County										
City of York	40,221	473	11	27	322	113	2,150	462	1,440	248
City of Hanover	14,972	53	0	4	23	26	607	54	537	16
Total area actually reporting	100.0%	1,086	20	96	500	470	9,744	1,634	7,574	536
Rate per 100,000 inhabitants		255.0	4.7	22.5	117.4	110.4	2,287.8	383.7	1,778.3	125.8
Youngstown-Warren-Boardman, OH-PA M.S.A.	566,927									
Includes Mahoning and Trumbull Counties, OH and Mercer County, PA										
City of Youngstown, OH	72,887	733	29	34	252	418	4,030	1,684	1,853	493
City of Warren, OH	43,809	392	3	39	167	183	2,256	889	1,163	204
City of Boardman, OH	39,244	73	0	5	56	12	1,776	299	1,378	99
Total area actually reporting	95.4%	1,829	41	151	645	992	17,915	5,102	11,481	1,332
Estimated total	100.0%	1,875	41	159	663	1,012	18,678	5,249	12,059	1,370
Rate per 100,000 inhabitants		330.7	7.2	28.0	116.9	178.5	3,294.6	925.9	2,127.1	241.7
Yuba City, CA M.S.A.	166,703									
Includes Sutter and Yuba Counties										
City of Yuba City	62,595	231	4	14	65	148	1,999	383	1,384	232
Total area actually reporting	100.0%	695	10	53	130	502	4,831	1,320	2,925	586
Rate per 100,000 inhabitants		416.9	6.0	31.8	78.0	301.1	2,898.0	791.8	1,754.6	351.5
Yuma, AZ M.S.A.[2]	193,473									
Includes Yuma County[2]										
City of Yuma	90,245	511	4	25	56	426	3,203	638	2,196	369
Total area actually reporting	87.2%	637	6	32	68	531	4,376	1,090	2,771	515
Estimated total	100.0%	715	7	37	92	579	5,336	1,308	3,404	624
Rate per 100,000 inhabitants		369.6	3.6	19.1	47.6	299.3	2,758.0	676.1	1,759.4	322.5

[2] Because of changes in the state/local agency's reporting practices, figures are not comparable to previous years' data.

Table 6. Crime, by Metropolitan Statistical Area, 2008—*Continued*

(Number, percent, rate per 100,000 population.)

Area	Population	Violent crime	Murder and non-negligent man-slaughter	Forcible rape	Robbery	Aggravated assault	Property crime	Burglary	Larceny-theft	Motor vehicle theft
Aguadilla-Isabela-San Sebastian, Puerto Rico M.S.A.	339,523									
Includes Aguada, Aguadilla, Anasco, Isabela, Lares, Moca, Rincon, and San Sebastian Municipios										
Total area actually reporting	100.0%	323	21	5	151	146	3,359	1,544	1,623	192
Rate per 100,000 inhabitants		95.1	6.2	1.5	44.5	43.0	989.3	454.8	478.0	56.5
Fajardo, Puerto Rico M.S.A.	80,633									
Includes Ceiba, Fajardo, and Luquillo Municipios										
Total area actually reporting	100.0%	182	21	1	73	87	1,004	430	516	58
Rate per 100,000 inhabitants		225.7	26.0	1.2	90.5	107.9	1,245.1	533.3	639.9	71.9
Guayama, Puerto Rico M.S.A.	84,193									
Includes Arroyo, Guayama, and Patillas Municipios										
Total area actually reporting	100.0%	184	8	2	65	109	916	515	330	71
Rate per 100,000 inhabitants		218.5	9.5	2.4	77.2	129.5	1,088.0	611.7	392.0	84.3
Mayaguez, Puerto Rico M.S.A.	110,644									
Includes Hormigueros and Mayaguez Municipios										
Total area actually reporting	100.0%	239	11	1	126	101	2,863	833	1,916	114
Rate per 100,000 inhabitants		216.0	9.9	0.9	113.9	91.3	2,587.6	752.9	1,731.7	103.0
Ponce, Puerto Rico M.S.A.	262,943									
Includes Juana Diaz, Ponce, and Villalba Municipios										
Total area actually reporting	100.0%	902	89	14	374	425	3,758	942	2,523	293
Rate per 100,000 inhabitants		343.0	33.8	5.3	142.2	161.6	1,429.2	358.3	959.5	111.4
San German-Cabo Rojo, Puerto Rico M.S.A.	147,242									
Includes Cabo Rojo, Lajas, Sabana Grande, and San German Municipios										
Total area actually reporting	100.0%	119	3	1	77	38	840	417	381	42
Rate per 100,000 inhabitants		80.8	2.0	0.7	52.3	25.8	570.5	283.2	258.8	28.5
San Juan-Caguas-Guaynabo, Puerto Rico M.S.A.	2,608,375									
Includes Aguas Buenas, Aibonito, Arecibo, Barceloneta, Barranquitas, Bayamon, Caguas, Camuy, Canovanas, Carolina, Catano, Cayey, Ciales, Cidra, Comerio, Corozal, Dorado, Florida, Guaynabo, Gurabo, Hatillo, Humacao, Juncos, Las Piedras, Loiza, Manati, Maunabo, Morovis, Naguabo, Naranjito, Orocovis, Quebradillas, Rio Grande, San Juan, San Lorenzo, Toa Alta, Toa Baja, Trujillo Alto, Vega Alta, Vega Baja, and Yabucoa Municipios										
Total area actually reporting	100.0%	7,039	603	58	4,416	1,962	43,090	12,984	24,038	6,068
Rate per 100,000 inhabitants		269.9	23.1	2.2	169.3	75.2	1,652.0	497.8	921.6	232.6
Yauco, Puerto Rico M.S.A.	124,566									
Includes Guanica, Guayanilla, Penuelas, and Yauco Municipios										
Total area actually reporting	100.0%	179	20	9	63	87	1,070	421	600	49
Rate per 100,000 inhabitants		143.7	16.1	7.2	50.6	69.8	859.0	338.0	481.7	39.3

Table 7. Offense Analysis, 2004–2008

(Number.)

Classification	2004	2005	2006	2007	2008
Murder	16,148	16,740	17,030	16,929	16,272
Forcible rape	95,089	94,347	92,757	90,427	89,000
Robbery:[1]	401,470	417,438	447,403	445,125	441,855
By location:					
Street/highway	171,812	184,188	199,241	194,772	190,314
Commercial house	59,006	59,694	61,014	62,026	60,971
Gas or service station	10,893	11,889	12,075	11,766	11,424
Convenience store	24,653	23,822	24,921	24,933	24,300
Residence	55,525	59,207	64,024	67,508	71,939
Bank	9,775	8,766	9,591	9,252	8,962
Miscellaneous	69,806	69,871	76,537	74,868	73,946
Burglary:[1]	2,144,446	2,155,448	2,183,746	2,179,140	2,222,196
By location:					
Residence (dwelling):	1,409,253	1,417,440	1,445,557	1,478,901	1,562,976
Residence Night	405,556	402,881	411,558	421,855	437,007
Residence Day	666,345	669,579	705,175	738,654	805,193
Residence Unknown	337,351	344,980	328,824	318,392	320,776
Nonresidence (store, office, etc.):	735,193	738,008	738,189	700,239	659,220
Nonresidence Night	307,702	305,729	307,076	293,469	275,913
Nonresidence Day	223,012	221,183	234,458	227,092	222,633
Nonresidence Unknown	204,479	211,096	196,655	179,679	160,675
Larceny-theft (except motor vehicle theft):[1]	6,937,089	6,783,447	6,607,013	6,568,572	6,588,873
By type:					
Pocket-picking	29,840	29,221	28,770	27,408	27,151
Purse-snatching	42,345	42,040	39,997	38,058	33,327
Shoplifting	1,009,214	940,411	872,635	978,978	1,068,088
From motor vehicles (except accessories)	1,758,241	1,752,280	1,752,432	1,706,979	1,715,440
Motor vehicle accessories	749,173	693,225	638,678	599,063	643,225
Bicycles	249,813	248,792	231,238	224,345	221,936
From buildings	861,197	852,462	829,756	789,123	753,755
From coin-operated machines	45,927	40,885	35,264	31,036	26,910
All others	2,191,338	2,184,131	2,178,243	2,173,581	2,099,041
By value:					
Over $200	2,711,560	2,715,997	2,805,338	2,884,126	2,967,033
$50 to $200	1,562,672	1,522,810	1,474,693	1,471,078	1,465,595
Under $50	2,662,857	2,544,640	2,326,982	2,213,368	2,156,245
Motor vehicle theft	1,237,851	1,235,859	1,192,809	1,095,769	956,846

[1] Because of rounding, the number of offenses may not add to the total.

Table 8. Offenses Known to Law Enforcement, by State and City, 2008

(Number.)

State/City	Population	Violent crime	Murder and non-negligent man-slaughter	Forcible rape	Robbery	Aggravated assault	Property crime	Burglary	Larceny-theft	Motor vehicle theft	Arson[1]
ALABAMA											
Abbeville	2,939	16	0	1	2	13	79	21	54	4	
Addison	715	5	0	0	0	5	34	10	24	0	
Alexander City	14,917	204	3	14	47	140	1,024	190	790	44	
Aliceville	2,405	19	0	0	3	16	87	30	54	3	
Andalusia	8,689	56	0	8	4	44	477	94	361	22	
Anniston	23,620	572	13	30	179	350	2,429	788	1,478	163	
Arab	7,753	35	0	1	4	30	490	117	348	25	
Ardmore	1,209	1	0	0	0	1	20	3	15	2	
Argo	1,900	2	0	1	0	1	60	21	34	5	
Ashford	2,041	3	0	0	2	1	33	7	25	1	
Ashland	1,862	3	0	1	0	2	25	4	21	0	
Ashville	2,543	12	0	1	1	10	105	25	72	8	
Athens	23,432	53	0	4	19	30	849	141	675	33	
Atmore	7,391	77	3	5	19	50	542	108	403	31	
Attalla	6,515	60	0	5	7	48	363	47	308	8	
Auburn	55,649	181	2	17	56	106	2,894	1,022	1,818	54	
Autaugaville	877	0	0	0	0	0	15	8	7	0	
Bay Minette	7,710	67	0	7	15	45	391	56	318	17	
Bayou La Batre	2,716	22	1	0	10	11	275	73	184	18	
Bear Creek	999	4	0	0	0	4	30	8	20	2	
Berry	1,183	0	0	0	0	0	5	1	1	3	
Bessemer	28,479	579	5	28	193	353	3,716	1,046	2,392	278	
Birmingham	228,314	3,249	82	212	1,499	1,456	20,054	5,153	12,761	2,140	134
Blountsville	1,976	6	0	0	0	6	64	22	37	5	
Boaz	8,273	32	0	3	11	18	514	102	400	12	
Brent	4,384	21	0	1	3	17	114	26	86	2	
Brighton	3,247	2	0	0	1	1	11	4	7	0	
Brilliant	720	2	0	0	0	2	23	9	12	2	
Butler	1,699	0	0	0	0	0	18	7	9	2	
Calera	10,723	42	1	3	4	34	398	77	319	2	
Camden	2,210	6	0	0	0	6	23	6	17	0	
Carbon Hill	2,024	2	0	0	2	0	167	46	113	8	
Carrollton	929	0	0	0	0	0	10	4	5	1	
Centre	3,491	3	0	1	1	1	137	14	114	9	
Chatom	1,156	4	0	0	0	4	19	2	17	0	
Cherokee	1,167	3	0	0	1	2	11	4	7	0	
Chickasaw	5,935	45	2	3	17	23	428	143	240	45	
Clanton	8,849	54	0	5	8	41	480	80	374	26	
Clayhatchee	491	2	0	0	0	2	10	3	6	1	0
Clayton	1,358	13	0	0	1	12	37	6	28	3	
Coffeeville	344	1	0	0	0	1	3	0	2	1	
Collinsville	1,690	4	0	0	0	4	32	6	24	2	
Columbiana	3,839	11	0	1	3	7	152	32	119	1	
Coosada	1,645	2	0	0	1	1	28	5	22	1	
Cottonwood	1,176	3	0	0	0	3	21	6	14	1	
Courtland	762	2	0	0	0	2	12	2	8	2	
Crossville	1,464	0	0	0	0	0	13	3	7	3	
Dadeville	3,220	30	0	0	4	26	199	53	140	6	
Daleville	4,512	11	0	3	5	3	179	63	103	13	
Dauphin Island	1,605	1	0	0	1	0	65	24	39	2	
Decatur	55,941	291	3	29	123	136	3,996	976	2,889	131	
Demopolis	7,328	96	4	3	8	81	540	92	444	4	
Dora	2,411	4	0	0	1	3	103	33	55	15	
Dothan	66,412	400	3	30	189	178	3,513	859	2,506	148	
Double Springs	979	7	0	0	1	6	49	7	40	2	
Douglas	583	5	0	1	1	3	52	25	19	8	
Dozier	397	0	0	0	0	0	1	0	1	0	
East Brewton	2,489	9	0	1	2	6	112	28	75	9	
Eclectic	1,160	7	0	0	1	6	62	11	49	2	
Elba	4,124	15	0	2	1	12	185	48	134	3	
Elberta	582	10	0	1	2	7	125	35	79	11	
Enterprise	24,863	108	1	9	48	50	331	129	173	29	
Eutaw	2,941	26	0	0	7	19	105	39	59	7	
Evergreen	3,390	20	0	0	1	19	133	33	91	9	
Excel	600	2	0	0	0	2	9	2	7	0	
Fairfield	11,303	187	3	9	99	76	1,464	408	912	144	
Fairhope	17,180	10	0	5	3	2	419	95	308	16	
Falkville	1,166	1	0	0	0	1	34	9	25	0	
Fayette	4,672	16	1	1	5	9	181	26	142	13	
Flomaton	1,531	6	0	0	1	5	36	6	29	1	
Florala	1,899	5	0	0	2	3	60	14	43	3	
Florence	37,594	155	3	16	65	71	1,877	485	1,335	57	
Forkland	589	15	0	1	1	13	23	6	15	2	
Fort Payne	14,040	35	1	2	9	23	460	106	323	31	

[1] The FBI does not publish arson data unless it receives data from either the agency or the state for all 12 months of the calendar year.

Table 8. Offenses Known to Law Enforcement, by State and City, 2008—*Continued*

(Number.)

State/City	Population	Violent crime	Murder and non-negligent man-slaughter	Forcible rape	Robbery	Aggravated assault	Property crime	Burglary	Larceny-theft	Motor vehicle theft	Arson[1]
ALABAMA—*Continued*											
Gadsden	36,700	288	2	36	135	115	2,452	575	1,716	161	25
Gantt	240	0	0	0	0	0	4	2	2	0	
Gardendale	13,626	27	1	1	11	14	534	77	437	20	
Geneva	4,399	21	0	0	4	17	183	57	113	13	
Georgiana	1,557	15	0	0	1	14	49	12	35	2	
Geraldine	837	4	0	0	0	4	35	6	28	1	
Gordo	1,556	14	1	0	0	13	44	23	18	3	
Grant	693	1	0	0	0	1	4	2	1	1	
Greenville	6,974	35	1	0	12	22	393	66	313	14	
Grove Hill	1,338	2	0	0	0	2	8	3	5	0	
Guin	2,176	9	0	1	0	8	27	9	16	2	
Gulf Shores	10,985	33	1	19	6	7	562	57	497	8	
Guntersville	8,351	58	0	2	14	42	708	146	535	27	
Gurley	855	1	0	0	0	1	22	5	16	1	
Hackleburg	1,445	4	0	1	0	3	37	12	24	1	
Haleyville	4,054	25	1	3	2	19	303	65	223	15	
Hamilton	6,331	12	0	1	5	6	215	54	153	8	
Hammondville	544	0	0	0	0	0	4	1	3	0	
Hanceville	3,367	17	0	2	3	12	135	22	110	3	
Hartselle	13,815	16	0	6	3	7	447	89	341	17	
Hayneville	1,112	11	0	0	0	11	53	24	23	6	
Headland	4,045	19	0	4	2	13	200	56	139	5	
Heflin	3,543	19	1	2	1	15	102	17	74	11	
Helena	14,701	28	0	3	0	25	118	30	84	4	0
Henagar	2,558	4	0	0	0	4	31	6	25	0	
Highland Lake	502	0	0	0	0	0	2	1	1	0	
Hillsboro	588	1	0	0	0	1	6	1	4	1	
Hokes Bluff	4,452	3	0	0	1	2	55	9	45	1	
Hollywood	918	0	0	0	0	0	9	1	8	0	
Homewood	23,771	165	1	13	116	35	1,545	326	1,136	83	
Hoover	70,731	111	2	13	62	34	2,315	436	1,761	118	2
Hueytown	15,708	58	1	3	24	30	706	176	475	55	
Huntsville	172,794	1,222	18	93	412	699	10,647	2,369	7,196	1,082	
Hurtsboro	550	0	0	0	0	0	7	3	3	1	
Ider	716	0	0	0	0	0	14	3	9	2	
Irondale	9,426	63	0	5	29	29	527	160	336	31	
Jacksonville	9,881	71	0	2	34	35	666	251	397	18	
Jasper	13,956	92	1	8	39	44	1,321	241	1,006	74	
Killen	1,134	5	0	0	1	4	73	19	54	0	
Kimberly	2,743	2	0	1	0	1	49	11	33	5	
Kinston	612	0	0	0	0	0	4	2	1	1	
Lafayette	3,013	29	0	1	3	25	174	37	128	9	
Lake View	2,206	2	0	0	0	2	69	18	42	9	
Lanett	7,420	85	2	11	45	27	754	222	490	42	
Leeds	11,285	98	5	7	35	51	582	134	399	49	
Leighton	828	8	0	1	0	7	17	6	11	0	
Level Plains	1,502	17	0	0	5	12	51	17	34	0	
Lexington	837	3	0	0	0	3	6	1	4	1	
Lincoln	5,601	47	0	4	1	42	322	82	213	27	
Linden	2,268	0	0	0	0	0	37	8	28	1	
Littleville	950	1	0	0	0	1	26	5	18	3	
Lockhart	545	1	0	0	1	0	4	0	3	1	
Louisville	560	0	0	0	0	0	0	0	0	0	
Luverne	2,763	14	0	0	1	13	90	14	72	4	
Lynn	717	0	0	0	0	0	16	8	7	1	
Madison	39,529	96	0	7	38	51	1,082	270	767	45	
Maplesville	690	1	0	0	0	1	48	3	41	4	
Marion	3,133	40	0	1	3	36	174	40	130	4	
McIntosh	233	2	1	0	0	1	17	3	11	3	
McKenzie	604	2	0	0	0	2	9	3	4	2	
Mentone	481	0	0	0	0	0	5	1	4	0	
Midfield	5,158	51	0	1	33	17	440	160	243	37	
Millbrook	17,249	19	1	4	11	3	529	97	425	7	
Millry	588	0	0	0	0	0	8	0	8	0	
Mobile[2]	251,041	1,204	42	27	875	260	13,846	3,305	9,470	1,071	116
Monroeville	6,373	85	0	3	7	75	561	139	380	42	
Montevallo	6,030	17	0	0	9	8	277	84	178	15	
Montgomery	204,398	883	23	49	463	348	12,545	3,513	8,117	915	
Moody	13,588	1	1	0	0	0	293	69	183	41	
Morris	1,904	1	0	0	1	0	25	4	20	1	
Mosses	1,038	0	0	0	0	0	1	0	1	0	
Moundville	2,571	15	0	1	0	14	94	23	59	12	
Mountain Brook	21,057	3	0	0	3	0	407	100	303	4	

[1] The FBI does not publish arson data unless it receives data from either the agency or the state for all 12 months of the calendar year.

[2] The population for the city of Mobile, Alabama, includes 60,536 inhabitants from the jurisdiction of the Mobile County Sheriff's Department.

Table 8. Offenses Known to Law Enforcement, by State and City, 2008—*Continued*

(Number.)

State/City	Population	Violent crime	Murder and non-negligent man-slaughter	Forcible rape	Robbery	Aggravated assault	Property crime	Burglary	Larceny-theft	Motor vehicle theft	Arson[1]
ALABAMA—*Continued*											
Mount Vernon	817	22	0	1	2	19	30	5	24	1	
Muscle Shoals	12,925	78	0	3	19	56	635	128	487	20	0
Napier Field	394	2	0	1	0	1	9	7	1	1	
New Brockton	1,227	0	0	0	0	0	25	2	23	0	
New Hope	2,775	16	0	1	1	14	48	11	34	3	
Newton	1,648	3	0	0	0	3	69	12	51	6	
Newville	544	0	0	0	0	0	1	0	1	0	
North Courtland	797	1	0	0	0	1	16	4	11	1	
Northport	23,223	133	2	10	41	80	1,097	251	780	66	
Notasulga	832	6	0	1	0	5	22	10	12	0	
Oakman	924	1	0	0	0	1	28	5	23	0	
Odenville	1,264	9	0	2	1	6	54	12	37	5	
Oneonta	7,058	16	0	0	5	11	230	22	195	13	
Opelika	26,015	326	1	28	100	197	1,582	456	1,098	28	
Opp	6,662	18	0	3	3	12	182	23	159	0	
Orange Beach	6,589	15	0	5	0	10	344	57	281	6	
Owens Crossroads	1,491	3	0	0	0	3	37	11	24	2	
Oxford	20,511	103	1	12	47	43	1,191	179	957	55	
Ozark	14,584	89	0	7	23	59	713	154	514	45	
Pelham	21,532	31	1	5	12	13	485	50	406	29	
Pell City	12,898	66	0	9	8	49	681	85	578	18	
Phenix City	30,952	97	0	6	40	51	1,174	342	649	183	
Phil Campbell	1,035	0	0	0	0	0	19	4	14	1	
Piedmont	4,962	36	0	1	2	33	208	48	151	9	
Pine Hill	905	8	0	0	0	8	28	9	19	0	
Pisgah	693	0	0	0	0	0	4	0	4	0	
Pleasant Grove	10,299	15	1	0	5	9	247	87	139	21	
Powell	975	1	0	0	0	1	21	4	16	1	
Prattville	32,849	94	1	12	23	58	1,291	244	988	59	14
Priceville	2,659	4	0	0	1	3	76	8	67	1	
Prichard	27,691	331	11	3	161	156	1,845	602	923	320	
Ragland	2,125	3	0	1	0	2	16	1	13	2	
Rainbow City	9,276	3	1	0	2	0	265	41	215	9	
Rainsville	4,950	13	0	2	0	11	131	17	107	7	
Ranburne	481	0	0	0	0	0	23	5	17	1	
Red Bay	3,242	9	0	0	0	9	60	8	45	7	
Red Level	554	1	0	0	0	1	9	3	6	0	
Reform	1,786	11	0	0	2	9	61	18	40	3	
Riverside	2,023	10	0	1	0	9	18	6	11	1	
Roanoke	6,618	23	0	8	5	10	222	27	187	8	
Robertsdale	5,018	13	1	5	1	6	282	45	228	9	
Rockford	392	0	0	0	0	0	8	3	5	0	
Russellville	8,758	40	1	3	11	25	334	64	255	15	
Samson	2,006	3	0	1	0	2	46	13	29	4	
Saraland	12,893	37	0	0	18	19	321	89	214	18	
Sardis City	2,177	2	0	0	0	2	67	26	38	3	
Satsuma	6,029	11	0	2	1	8	120	21	81	18	
Selma	18,772	286	5	20	66	195	2,131	578	1,350	203	
Sheffield	9,118	69	2	7	27	33	671	169	474	28	
Silas	472	0	0	0	0	0	5	4	1	0	
Silverhill	695	1	0	1	0	0	15	8	7	0	
Sipsey	540	1	0	0	1	0	30	8	19	3	
Skyline	831	1	0	0	0	1	16	2	14	0	
Slocomb	2,033	7	0	0	2	5	57	13	40	4	
Snead	846	5	0	0	0	5	25	4	18	3	
Southside	8,441	9	0	2	0	7	86	18	64	4	
Spanish Fort	5,831	13	0	1	6	6	220	38	181	1	
Stevenson	2,003	36	0	0	0	36	108	19	73	16	
St. Florian	491	3	0	1	0	2	16	10	6	0	
Sulligent	1,960	5	0	0	1	4	51	11	33	7	
Sumiton	2,541	7	0	2	5	0	327	47	256	24	
Sylacauga	12,876	57	0	7	14	36	836	214	600	22	
Sylvania	1,266	0	0	0	0	0	16	8	8	0	
Tallassee	5,144	44	1	2	5	36	331	64	254	13	
Taylor	1,980	0	0	0	0	0	6	2	4	0	
Thomasville	4,474	32	0	2	0	30	236	37	189	10	
Thorsby	2,068	0	0	0	0	0	13	5	7	1	
Town Creek	1,206	0	0	0	0	0	31	9	22	0	
Triana	493	1	0	0	0	1	20	12	6	2	
Trinity	1,914	5	1	1	0	3	38	11	19	8	
Troy	14,538	72	2	1	45	24	877	222	626	29	
Trussville	19,199	28	0	2	22	4	951	101	811	39	
Tuscaloosa	90,157	470	11	28	199	232	5,396	1,513	3,553	330	
Tuscumbia	8,275	15	0	1	7	7	240	73	161	6	

[1] The FBI does not publish arson data unless it receives data from either the agency or the state for all 12 months of the calendar year.

Table 8. Offenses Known to Law Enforcement, by State and City, 2008—*Continued*

(Number.)

State/City	Population	Violent crime	Murder and non-negligent man-slaughter	Forcible rape	Robbery	Aggravated assault	Property crime	Burglary	Larceny-theft	Motor vehicle theft	Arson[1]
ALABAMA—*Continued*											
Tuskegee	11,287	163	4	10	29	120	873	362	494	17	
Union Springs	4,566	17	0	0	6	11	156	34	114	8	
Uniontown	1,413	37	0	1	9	27	63	23	33	7	
Valley	8,774	59	0	8	18	33	638	146	475	17	
Valley Head	649	1	0	0	0	1	19	6	12	1	
Vance	839	3	0	0	0	3	39	11	25	3	
Vernon	1,886	5	0	0	3	2	26	10	14	2	
Vestavia Hills	31,055	28	0	3	13	12	328	106	204	18	
Warrior	3,003	6	0	0	3	3	78	9	62	7	
Weaver	2,686	4	0	0	0	4	60	20	39	1	
Webb	1,361	1	0	0	0	1	5	1	4	0	
Wedowee	815	0	0	0	0	0	0	0	0	0	
West Blocton	1,425	0	0	0	0	0	1	0	1	0	
Wetumpka	7,840	23	0	1	3	19	427	95	325	7	
Winfield	4,651	13	0	2	0	11	185	26	142	17	
Woodstock	1,023	3	0	2	1	0	98	26	54	18	
York	2,489	10	0	0	0	10	75	20	52	3	
ALASKA											
Anchorage	280,068	2,647	10	263	544	1,830	9,211	1,191	7,254	766	106
Bethel	6,557	50	0	5	4	41	94	45	33	16	2
Bristol Bay Borough	963	0	0	0	0	0	52	18	17	17	0
Cordova	2,227	16	0	0	0	16	10	2	7	1	0
Craig	1,153	16	0	0	0	16	25	7	15	3	0
Dillingham	2,506	47	0	12	3	32	59	9	30	20	0
Fairbanks	35,131	272	3	41	28	200	1,189	141	921	127	3
Haines	2,255	8	0	0	0	8	37	6	31	0	0
Homer	5,808	51	1	0	2	48	282	67	198	17	0
Houston	2,153	3	0	0	0	3	29	9	17	3	0
Juneau	30,692	122	0	27	9	86	1,161	141	974	46	5
Kenai	7,784	50	0	2	2	46	313	42	256	15	1
Ketchikan	7,305	28	1	12	2	13	426	36	367	23	0
Kodiak	6,159	37	1	1	3	32	215	32	161	22	2
Kotzebue	3,160	12	0	5	1	6	17	7	5	5	0
North Pole	2,276	10	0	4	3	3	104	12	78	14	0
North Slope Borough	6,419	60	0	1	0	59	108	37	58	13	2
Palmer	8,292	60	0	2	3	55	304	32	262	10	0
Petersburg	2,839	20	1	0	0	19	148	27	118	3	0
Seward	3,092	3	0	0	0	3	115	9	102	4	1
Sitka	8,879	13	1	3	0	9	332	18	273	41	0
Skagway	818	6	0	1	0	5	58	5	53	0	0
Soldotna	4,360	12	0	1	0	11	256	18	231	7	0
St. Paul	432	2	0	1	0	1	3	3	0	0	0
Unalaska	3,789	14	0	0	1	13	0	9	54	3	2
Wasilla	10,497	64	0	0	4	60	417	38	360	19	2
Wrangell	1,998	3	0	0	0	3	112	18	90	4	0
ARIZONA											
Apache Junction	31,521	123	2	6	31	84	1,447	319	920	208	16
Avondale	85,376	457	12	10	147	288	4,701	1,020	2,929	752	15
Benson	4,995	10	0	2	2	6	154	48	98	8	0
Bisbee	5,958	48	0	1	1	46	254	32	222	0	1
Buckeye	32,070	51	1	4	13	33	1,542	472	929	141	1
Bullhead City	41,976	61	0	2	23	36	1,702	452	1,126	124	8
Camp Verde	11,011	33	0	1	0	32	232	51	170	11	0
Casa Grande	39,928	220	0	4	45	171	2,956	1,069	1,629	258	16
Chandler	253,076	801	6	56	241	498	7,984	1,414	5,768	802	92
Chino Valley	11,326	59	0	1	0	58	265	52	200	13	2
Clarkdale	4,328	9	0	0	1	8	96	52	37	7	0
Clifton	2,354	13	0	0	1	12	66	25	40	1	2
Colorado City	4,999	3	0	0	0	3	8	3	4	1	0
Coolidge	9,904	91	1	3	8	79	662	170	437	55	11
Cottonwood	11,520	48	0	1	4	43	532	79	424	29	3
Douglas	17,007	31	0	4	6	21	656	146	438	72	1
Eagar	4,536	6	0	0	0	6	105	25	73	7	0
El Mirage	27,543	72	1	6	38	27	1,060	275	670	115	8
Eloy	12,214	91	0	13	16	62	627	226	343	58	6
Flagstaff	60,400	262	3	43	61	155	3,364	409	2,867	88	27
Florence	17,880	51	0	0	3	48	283	49	210	24	1
Fredonia	1,108	1	0	1	0	0	30	9	20	1	0
Gilbert	220,373	238	0	26	63	149	4,933	1,113	3,429	391	21
Glendale	256,659	1,330	17	66	588	659	13,435	2,665	8,389	2,381	80
Globe	7,080	52	0	4	1	47	320	75	223	22	0
Goodyear	58,732	144	6	19	33	86	2,387	1,153	961	273	8
Holbrook	5,094	70	1	2	7	60	378	126	237	15	3

[1] The FBI does not publish arson data unless it receives data from either the agency or the state for all 12 months of the calendar year.

Table 8. Offenses Known to Law Enforcement, by State and City, 2008—*Continued*

(Number.)

State/City	Population	Violent crime	Murder and non-negligent man-slaughter	Forcible rape	Robbery	Aggravated assault	Property crime	Burglary	Larceny-theft	Motor vehicle theft	Arson[1]
ARIZONA—*Continued*											
Huachuca City	1,989	6	0	0	1	5	39	15	20	4	4
Jerome	357	2	0	0	1	1	23	4	19	0	0
Kingman	28,725	95	0	15	17	63	1,587	301	1,186	100	4
Lake Havasu City	57,616	100	1	18	10	71	1,385	244	1,056	85	8
Mammoth	2,534	4	0	0	0	4	18	9	6	3	1
Marana	34,549	33	0	4	15	14	1,083	165	817	101	1
Mesa	456,821	2,289	16	161	656	1,456	17,516	2,866	12,603	2,047	73
Miami	1,786	30	0	1	3	26	87	36	45	6	7
Nogales	19,757	69	0	0	10	59	836	163	470	203	0
Oro Valley	40,785	26	1	6	7	12	740	138	564	38	4
Paradise Valley	15,134	9	0	0	1	8	351	237	101	13	0
Parker	3,193	24	0	0	4	20	210	69	117	24	2
Peoria	151,493	315	8	50	104	153	5,339	1,197	3,572	570	18
Phoenix	1,585,838	10,465	167	481	4,825	4,992	82,689	18,783	48,685	15,221	473
Pima	2,077	4	0	0	0	4	67	30	34	3	0
Prescott	43,190	119	1	2	22	94	1,230	244	946	40	15
Prescott Valley	39,856	165	0	16	11	138	807	154	607	46	4
Quartzsite	3,544	9	0	0	0	9	86	10	69	7	0
Sahuarita	22,389	26	1	3	6	16	523	78	421	24	3
Scottsdale	238,905	423	5	28	130	260	7,903	1,488	5,897	518	36
Sedona	11,580	22	0	2	1	19	277	88	185	4	4
Show Low	12,394	114	0	6	3	105	591	182	394	15	4
Sierra Vista	43,642	111	1	13	24	73	1,418	261	1,056	101	13
Snowflake-Taylor	9,683	57	0	0	2	55	222	98	99	25	1
Somerton	11,837	26	0	1	1	24	190	41	122	27	3
South Tucson	5,606	211	1	4	80	126	854	116	665	73	1
Surprise	101,141	115	0	8	45	62	2,555	594	1,753	208	35
Tempe	176,388	856	6	34	323	493	10,242	1,545	7,584	1,113	54
Thatcher	4,874	5	0	0	0	5	132	42	83	7	1
Tolleson	7,232	66	0	4	28	34	962	241	620	101	3
Tucson[3]	528,917	4,252	65	246	1,451	2,490		5,157		5,808	318
Wellton	1,909	4	0	1	1	2	49	17	31	1	0
Wickenburg	6,716	13	0	0	0	13	195	72	114	9	0
Willcox	3,799	15	1	2	4	8	173	26	133	14	10
Winslow	9,842	66	0	3	9	54	544	56	464	24	2
Youngtown	5,301	17	0	0	3	14	89	26	45	18	3
Yuma	90,245	511	4	25	56	426	3,203	638	2,196	369	26
ARKANSAS											
Arkadelphia	10,826	45	0	7	8	30	402	146	243	13	2
Ashdown	4,407	12	1	2	1	8	161	28	121	12	2
Atkins	2,963	1	0	0	1	0	86	25	58	3	0
Augusta	2,278	12	0	0	0	12	45	8	37	0	0
Austin	1,719	0	0	0	0	0	21	3	18	0	0
Bald Knob	3,389	10	0	2	1	7	134	36	93	5	0
Barling	4,475	13	0	2	0	11	65	16	47	2	1
Bay	2,038	1	0	0	0	1	14	7	7	0	0
Bearden	992	8	0	0	0	8	37	20	16	1	0
Beebe	6,883	40	0	10	2	28	452	211	229	12	3
Bella Vista	16,120	14	0	5	2	7	144	50	93	1	1
Benton	29,121	97	1	6	18	72	1,421	358	988	75	5
Bentonville[4]	35,970	53	0	3	5	45	616	88	508	20	3
Berryville	5,284	21	0	7	4	10	340	99	223	18	3
Blytheville	15,829	194	4	11	56	123	1,241	469	685	87	17
Booneville	4,070	24	0	3	2	19	129	38	89	2	4
Brinkley	3,215	2	0	0	2	0	104	26	76	2	1
Bryant	15,218	38	0	10	4	24	777	164	575	38	2
Bull Shoals	2,109	6	0	0	0	6	34	7	27	0	0
Cabot	24,387	59	0	9	4	46	831	355	449	27	2
Camden	11,489	57	2	2	20	33	717	206	479	32	0
Cammack Village	775	0	0	0	0	0	18	12	5	1	0
Carlisle	2,369	2	0	1	1	0	106	64	40	2	0
Cave City	2,057	2	0	0	0	2	44	4	40	0	1
Cave Springs	1,620	2	0	0	0	2	29	1	28	0	0
Centerton	9,522	13	0	3	0	10	69	25	41	3	0
Charleston	3,013	1	0	0	1	0	29	8	21	0	1
Cherokee Village	4,799	4	0	0	0	4	113	34	77	2	0
Clarendon	1,680	0	0	0	0	0	0	0	0	0	0
Clarksville[4]	8,621	17	0	7	0	10	353	47	298	8	1
Clinton	2,388	3	0	0	0	3	59	10	47	2	0
Conway[4]	58,945	230	0	32	62	136	2,778	906	1,743	129	6

[1] The FBI does not publish arson data unless it receives data from either the agency or the state for all 12 months of the calendar year.
[3] The FBI determined that the agency did not follow national Uniform Crime Reporting (UCR) Program guidelines for reporting an offense. Consequently, this figure is not included in this table.
[4] Because of changes in the state/local agency's reporting practices, figures are not comparable to previous years' data.

Table 8. Offenses Known to Law Enforcement, by State and City, 2008—*Continued*

(Number.)

State/City	Population	Violent crime	Murder and non-negligent man-slaughter	Forcible rape	Robbery	Aggravated assault	Property crime	Burglary	Larceny-theft	Motor vehicle theft	Arson[1]
ARIZONA—*Continued*											
Corning	3,330	6	0	3	0	3	40	21	18	1	1
Cotter	1,083	4	0	0	0	4	36	5	29	2	0
Crossett	5,474	32	0	1	6	25	230	87	139	4	2
Dardanelle	4,422	22	0	5	5	12	138	82	54	2	1
Decatur	1,948	4	0	0	0	4	22	10	10	2	0
De Queen	5,899	24	0	6	3	15	268	97	159	12	1
Des Arc	1,720	6	0	1	1	4	14	8	6	0	0
De Witt	3,249	11	0	1	3	7	132	35	85	12	2
Dover	1,405	9	0	0	0	9	24	15	8	1	0
Dumas	4,592	21	0	1	6	14	185	56	122	7	4
Earle	2,763	3	0	0	3	0	60	43	17	0	0
El Dorado	19,706	208	2	3	38	165	1,358	572	712	74	4
Elkins	2,624	6	0	2	0	4	17	5	10	2	0
Eureka Springs	2,356	7	0	1	1	5	122	23	95	4	0
Fairfield Bay	2,491	5	0	1	0	4	35	10	24	1	0
Farmington	4,802	7	0	2	0	5	81	26	55	0	2
Fayetteville	73,999	334	1	38	44	251	2,757	568	2,072	117	7
Fordyce	4,226	31	0	1	12	18	140	75	52	13	1
Forrest City	13,391	114	0	7	43	64	1,061	243	763	55	2
Fort Smith	84,847	660	2	90	107	461	4,711	1,068	3,386	257	10
Gassville	2,178	1	0	0	0	1	32	10	21	1	0
Gentry	2,885	2	0	0	0	2	28	15	11	2	0
Glenwood	2,017	7	0	0	0	7	29	24	5	0	0
Gosnell	3,609	29	0	1	1	27	93	44	47	2	1
Gravette	2,657	15	0	0	1	14	29	18	10	1	0
Greenbrier	4,414	0	0	0	0	0	4	1	3	0	0
Green Forest	3,027	16	0	2	0	14	71	41	27	3	1
Greenland	1,292	0	0	0	0	0	21	3	16	2	0
Greenwood	8,661	13	0	4	0	9	118	39	78	1	0
Greers Ferry	970	2	0	1	0	1	11	3	7	1	0
Gurdon	2,296	15	0	1	1	13	64	28	35	1	1
Hamburg	2,696	15	0	0	2	13	75	17	58	0	1
Harrisburg	2,108	14	0	3	0	11	110	35	67	8	0
Harrison	13,221	83	0	19	5	59	578	222	331	25	10
Hazen	1,471	4	0	1	0	3	26	5	19	2	0
Heber Springs	7,262	21	0	6	0	15	297	111	181	5	2
Helena-West Helena	12,147	305	2	17	44	242	1,043	564	445	34	8
Highland	1,084	0	0	0	0	0	24	9	14	1	0
Hope	10,463	96	0	5	12	79	618	160	428	30	4
Horseshoe Bend	2,208	0	0	0	0	0	31	9	21	1	0
Hot Springs	39,451	513	1	19	104	389	3,922	737	2,996	189	9
Hoxie	2,627	3	0	0	0	3	25	9	13	3	1
Jacksonville[4]	31,316	286	4	20	46	216	1,593	407	1,141	45	15
Jonesboro	64,187	278	5	32	89	152	3,227	1,269	1,853	105	17
Judsonia	2,169	2	0	0	0	2	15	2	12	1	0
Kensett	1,820	7	0	3	0	4	29	9	17	3	0
Lakeview	857	0	0	0	0	0	3	0	2	1	0
Lake Village	2,413	57	1	3	1	52	72	45	27	0	4
Leachville	1,781	4	0	3	0	1	23	9	12	2	0
Lepanto	2,020	3	0	1	0	2	43	23	17	3	1
Lincoln	2,077	5	0	1	0	4	22	6	16	0	1
Little Flock	3,132	4	0	3	0	1	22	7	15	0	0
Little Rock	187,978	2,356	40	132	819	1,365	15,003	3,576	10,272	1,155	89
Lonoke	4,536	13	0	1	4	8	178	55	117	6	1
Lowell	7,274	20	1	3	0	16	122	41	72	9	1
Luxora	1,202	6	0	1	1	4	15	7	5	3	0
Magnolia	11,083	69	0	5	15	49	487	234	225	28	6
Marked Tree	2,632	1	0	0	1	0	66	10	55	1	0
Marmaduke	1,176	4	1	1	0	2	60	21	36	3	0
Maumelle	16,657	30	0	3	4	23	328	166	145	17	0
Mayflower	2,207	5	0	0	0	5	101	22	75	4	0
McCrory	1,560	0	0	0	0	0	17	6	10	1	1
McRae	701	1	0	0	0	1	43	20	19	4	1
Mena[4]	5,581	17	0	4	0	13	273	83	187	3	0
Mineral Springs	1,255	2	0	0	0	2	23	13	9	1	0
Monette	1,223	0	0	0	0	0	17	4	12	1	0
Monticello	9,379	31	0	4	6	21	442	133	275	34	2
Morrilton	6,582	27	0	7	2	18	524	107	399	18	3
Mountain Home	12,637	4	0	3	1	0	482	56	412	14	0
Mountain View	3,081	5	0	0	2	3	88	22	62	4	0
Mulberry	1,732	2	0	0	0	2	16	8	8	0	0
Nashville	4,746	21	1	1	2	17	286	92	184	10	0
Newport[4]	7,493	42	0	9	5	28	468	94	362	12	3

[1] The FBI does not publish arson data unless it receives data from either the agency or the state for all 12 months of the calendar year.
[4] Because of changes in the state/local agency's reporting practices, figures are not comparable to previous years' data.

Table 8. Offenses Known to Law Enforcement, by State and City, 2008—*Continued*

(Number.)

State/City	Population	Violent crime	Murder and non-negligent man-slaughter	Forcible rape	Robbery	Aggravated assault	Property crime	Burglary	Larceny-theft	Motor vehicle theft	Arson[1]
ARIZONA—*Continued*											
North Little Rock	59,369	810	11	36	274	489	6,107	1,527	4,137	443	12
Ola	1,230	8	0	0	0	8	24	19	5	0	0
Osceola	7,760	165	3	13	16	133	414	155	237	22	5
Ozark	3,562	19	1	2	0	16	95	15	72	8	1
Paragould	24,816	114	0	9	7	98	1,776	582	1,122	72	3
Paris	3,612	18	1	1	1	15	146	44	89	13	2
Pea Ridge	4,686	6	0	2	0	4	85	40	42	3	0
Piggott	3,515	7	0	1	1	5	71	42	29	0	0
Pine Bluff	50,144	819	16	71	248	484	4,674	1,596	2,648	430	27
Plummerville	867	4	0	1	0	3	18	11	7	0	0
Pottsville	2,838	13	0	1	0	12	50	36	12	2	0
Prairie Grove	3,754	13	0	2	0	11	51	14	34	3	0
Prescott[4]	4,571	6	0	0	0	6	90	47	36	7	0
Quitman	739	0	0	0	0	0	22	6	14	2	0
Rison	1,306	2	0	0	2	0	28	14	13	1	0
Rogers[4]	57,205	142	2	39	15	86	1,939	399	1,494	46	5
Rose Bud	453	0	0	0	0	0	5	2	2	1	0
Russellville	27,059	109	0	19	15	75	1,376	300	989	87	4
Searcy[4]	22,062	48	0	8	10	30	1,212	419	774	19	3
Sheridan	4,668	10	0	2	0	8	127	38	87	2	0
Sherwood	24,486	91	0	11	16	64	1,017	199	743	75	4
Siloam Springs[4]	14,988	31	0	11	1	19	398	100	272	26	2
Springdale	69,759	295	1	65	21	208	2,527	587	1,790	150	20
Star City	2,213	3	0	1	0	2	28	10	18	0	0
Stuttgart	8,969	65	1	6	13	45	579	210	355	14	10
Texarkana	29,855	513	2	16	75	420	1,812	450	1,249	113	12
Trumann	6,792	69	2	14	3	50	518	169	346	3	4
Van Buren	22,396	43	0	5	5	33	763	203	546	14	4
Vilonia	3,515	12	0	3	0	9	113	28	84	1	1
Waldron	3,597	21	0	0	0	21	84	54	27	3	2
Walnut Ridge	4,640	20	0	0	0	20	81	42	39	0	1
Ward	3,806	21	1	2	0	18	120	40	77	3	1
Warren	6,115	36	0	4	5	27	133	88	38	7	0
West Fork	2,358	3	0	0	0	3	36	15	21	0	0
West Memphis	27,446	623	3	32	121	467	2,551	1,188	1,185	178	17
White Hall[4]	5,152	15	0	0	0	15	129	13	101	15	1
Wynne	8,334	50	0	7	8	35	377	155	209	13	2
CALIFORNIA											
Adelanto	29,214	185	2	9	30	144	822	348	361	113	12
Agoura Hills	22,619	43	0	2	9	32	376	96	257	23	0
Alameda	69,998	210	2	9	107	92	1,875	325	1,278	272	9
Albany	15,909	50	0	3	30	17	650	88	435	127	0
Alhambra	86,404	276	1	8	156	111	2,082	447	1,270	365	9
Aliso Viejo	41,593	36	0	2	18	16	505	91	384	30	12
Alturas	2,784	25	0	3	2	20	71	16	50	5	1
American Canyon	17,321	53	0	2	19	32	517	137	331	49	0
Anaheim	333,746	1,312	11	83	573	645	8,331	1,604	5,633	1,094	44
Anderson	10,739	90	0	14	10	66	563	162	377	24	2
Antioch	100,702	875	8	29	398	440	2,850	923	1,241	686	38
Apple Valley	72,591	338	3	17	79	239	1,791	570	1,015	206	19
Arcadia	56,605	128	2	4	62	60	1,550	343	1,084	123	9
Arcata	17,073	43	0	1	13	29	565	164	368	33	7
Arroyo Grande	17,051	29	0	8	6	15	375	81	266	28	1
Artesia	16,348	69	3	2	27	37	327	97	154	76	1
Arvin	15,219	124	1	6	23	94	757	278	360	119	22
Atascadero	28,200	81	1	13	15	52	544	156	354	34	3
Atherton	7,352	38	0	1	2	35	230	51	172	7	6
Atwater	27,450	156	2	7	24	123	1,141	296	720	125	17
Auburn	13,084	47	0	5	8	34	363	58	263	42	5
Avalon	3,121	45	0	0	3	42	109	21	61	27	2
Avenal	17,711	77	0	2	8	67	168	71	81	16	7
Azusa	46,840	208	2	7	68	131	1,304	250	823	231	10
Bakersfield	326,046	2,077	25	48	708	1,296	16,160	4,168	9,476	2,516	161
Baldwin Park	78,031	267	8	9	106	144	1,759	356	812	591	10
Banning	29,816	166	0	6	24	136	742	293	356	93	0
Barstow	24,942	339	5	11	116	207	1,333	495	573	265	10
Bear Valley	4,592	0	0	0	0	0	56	10	45	1	0
Beaumont	34,208	72	1	7	16	48	811	173	554	84	1
Bell	36,877	185	3	13	71	98	648	162	307	179	0
Bellflower	73,488	507	7	11	228	261	2,182	432	1,085	665	18
Bell Gardens	44,939	255	4	11	115	125	885	169	304	412	2
Belmont[5]	24,588	25	0	3	7	15			242	42	3

[1] The FBI does not publish arson data unless it receives data from either the agency or the state for all 12 months of the calendar year.
[4] Because of changes in the state/local agency's reporting practices, figures are not comparable to previous years' data.
[5] The FBI determined that the agency's data were overreported. Consequently, those data are not included in this table.

Table 8. Offenses Known to Law Enforcement, by State and City, 2008—*Continued*

(Number.)

State/City	Population	Violent crime	Murder and non-negligent man-slaughter	Forcible rape	Robbery	Aggravated assault	Property crime	Burglary	Larceny-theft	Motor vehicle theft	Arson[1]
CALIFORNIA—*Continued*											
Belvedere	2,050	0	0	0	0	0	21	4	16	1	0
Benicia	26,255	46	1	6	14	25	512	179	264	69	10
Berkeley	101,170	652	8	25	496	123	6,837	1,095	4,790	952	28
Beverly Hills	34,684	126	2	11	61	52	1,071	296	733	42	3
Big Bear Lake	6,222	41	1	8	5	27	294	88	195	11	3
Biggs	1,817	17	0	0	0	17	38	9	23	6	0
Bishop	3,444	27	0	0	1	26	174	43	121	10	0
Blythe	23,042	62	1	2	10	49	587	188	368	31	13
Bradbury	1,066	0	0	0	0	0	6	3	3	0	0
Brawley	22,611	75	3	4	18	50	1,063	473	478	112	8
Brea	38,762	83	0	7	34	42	1,428	167	1,156	105	0
Brentwood	52,741	128	0	6	47	75	1,162	187	874	101	8
Brisbane	3,641	9	0	0	2	7	125	21	97	7	1
Broadmoor	4,369	19	0	2	8	9	98	44	44	10	1
Buellton	4,366	5	0	3	0	2	86	20	64	2	1
Buena Park	79,431	262	2	12	106	142	2,139	418	1,206	515	34
Burbank	103,640	235	2	17	86	130	2,941	589	1,834	518	26
Burlingame	27,474	68	0	4	25	39	854	134	626	94	3
Calabasas	22,511	19	0	2	6	11	370	67	271	32	3
Calexico	39,134	92	3	0	39	50	1,408	469	500	439	16
California City	14,652	75	0	8	19	48	415	192	181	42	2
Calimesa	7,462	14	0	1	4	9	191	56	115	20	0
Calipatria	7,676	0	0	0	0	0	56	37	11	8	0
Calistoga	5,165	12	0	1	1	10	120	33	84	3	0
Camarillo	63,843	77	2	9	25	41	1,038	220	756	62	11
Campbell	37,649	88	0	7	32	49	1,377	208	1,035	134	24
Canyon Lake	11,414	6	0	0	0	6	167	28	110	29	0
Capitola	9,457	99	0	5	18	76	609	70	525	14	2
Carlsbad	97,670	227	2	24	51	150	2,358	507	1,662	189	7
Carmel	3,870	8	0	0	0	8	139	35	102	2	0
Carpinteria	13,638	24	0	5	5	14	286	62	213	11	1
Carson	93,170	565	8	19	215	323	2,528	445	1,433	650	26
Cathedral City	53,601	241	2	22	54	163	1,633	554	825	254	5
Ceres	43,819	183	1	11	70	101	1,946	372	1,154	420	18
Cerritos	51,655	140	1	6	90	43	1,893	306	1,317	270	8
Chico	84,086	304	2	31	101	170	2,700	874	1,540	286	41
Chino	84,595	199	2	14	90	93	2,317	532	1,497	288	28
Chino Hills	75,297	67	1	5	22	39	1,203	277	822	104	12
Chowchilla	19,268	28	1	1	5	21	350	193	143	14	7
Chula Vista	223,408	832	6	55	321	450	6,514	1,008	3,339	2,167	27
Citrus Heights	84,361	419	1	20	140	258	3,694	668	2,377	649	12
City of Angels	3,825	8	2	0	1	5	80	32	43	5	0
Claremont	35,121	64	0	7	27	30	1,075	337	684	54	22
Clayton	11,217	8	0	0	3	5	235	50	174	11	0
Clearlake	15,117	81	2	14	17	48	532	181	269	82	11
Cloverdale	8,333	14	0	2	1	11	117	28	84	5	1
Clovis	93,848	148	2	19	51	76	3,209	665	2,267	277	15
Coachella	41,382	213	4	6	59	144	1,651	454	800	397	12
Coalinga	18,691	71	0	3	8	60	524	99	399	26	5
Colma	1,440	26	0	0	8	18	277	9	248	20	1
Colton	51,177	269	3	6	121	139	1,825	417	1,029	379	11
Colusa	5,829	10	0	3	2	5	135	44	83	8	0
Commerce	13,565	143	1	1	59	82	1,041	155	472	414	9
Compton	94,519	1,738	28	48	595	1,067	3,333	896	1,409	1,028	95
Concord	120,679	425	6	12	216	191	4,448	802	2,667	979	25
Corcoran	25,235	69	0	1	6	62	209	86	99	24	4
Corning	7,178	63	0	1	6	56	303	67	213	23	3
Corona	153,193	283	4	25	133	121	4,093	680	2,875	538	28
Coronado	22,694	28	0	2	12	14	583	103	435	45	3
Costa Mesa	108,898	350	1	39	120	190	3,367	516	2,547	304	12
Cotati	7,267	39	0	6	2	31	111	38	63	10	1
Covina	47,291	148	10	5	59	74	1,630	371	1,036	223	20
Crescent City	7,980	34	0	2	6	26	241	52	168	21	1
Cudahy	24,541	164	2	8	60	94	432	44	206	182	2
Culver City	38,850	141	0	0	103	38	1,378	171	1,061	146	2
Cupertino	53,385	52	0	2	19	31	1,065	169	851	45	11
Cypress	47,212	118	1	6	33	78	817	165	546	106	4
Daly City	100,542	283	1	25	143	114	2,045	276	1,425	344	21
Dana Point	35,737	48	0	4	9	35	581	96	448	37	8
Danville	40,874	26	0	1	5	20	562	115	426	21	5
Davis	63,179	128	0	20	30	78	2,338	400	1,794	144	25
Delano	54,273	247	5	11	54	177	1,974	857	575	542	105
Del Mar	4,430	14	0	3	5	6	173	51	107	15	1
Del Rey Oaks	1,523	6	0	0	5	1	47	12	35	0	0
Desert Hot Springs	25,471	315	4	13	74	224	1,570	613	586	371	4

[1] The FBI does not publish arson data unless it receives data from either the agency or the state for all 12 months of the calendar year.

Table 8. Offenses Known to Law Enforcement, by State and City, 2008—*Continued*

(Number.)

State/City	Population	Violent crime	Murder and non-negligent man-slaughter	Forcible rape	Robbery	Aggravated assault	Property crime	Burglary	Larceny-theft	Motor vehicle theft	Arson[1]
CALIFORNIA—*Continued*											
Diamond Bar	57,492	84	0	4	42	38	1,032	334	610	88	8
Dinuba	20,366	169	1	4	20	144	954	371	443	140	16
Dixon	17,716	65	1	7	20	37	800	96	643	61	5
Dorris	827	2	0	0	0	2	10	5	5	0	1
Dos Palos	4,992	36	2	0	1	33	127	39	74	14	0
Downey	108,184	451	3	24	252	172	3,980	712	2,038	1,230	8
Duarte	21,973	68	0	1	28	39	497	144	287	66	0
Dublin	45,995	88	0	11	31	46	753	148	526	79	5
Dunsmuir	1,781	7	0	1	0	6	44	17	26	1	2
East Palo Alto	33,513	368	5	18	106	239	821	276	212	333	1
El Cajon	92,225	528	1	35	204	288	3,355	571	1,905	879	16
El Centro	39,865	169	0	10	52	107	2,230	509	1,412	309	7
El Cerrito	22,116	132	0	0	98	34	1,076	217	666	193	7
Elk Grove	139,395	660	0	22	149	489	3,590	882	2,359	349	12
El Monte	123,049	800	12	32	265	491	2,666	632	1,333	701	28
El Segundo	16,310	44	0	2	22	20	633	148	433	52	4
Emeryville	9,704	131	1	2	97	31	976	119	675	182	0
Encinitas	60,211	132	0	15	33	84	1,033	275	669	89	3
Escalon	7,447	30	0	0	2	28	271	68	180	23	1
Escondido	136,508	567	4	31	195	337	4,182	898	2,405	879	27
Etna	766	1	0	0	0	1	6	1	5	0	0
Eureka	25,313	230	2	8	64	156	1,241	365	680	196	15
Exeter	10,108	38	1	1	2	34	302	89	182	31	4
Fairfax	7,039	8	0	1	1	6	108	21	77	10	5
Fairfield	104,927	546	5	28	238	275	4,026	736	2,703	587	28
Farmersville	10,170	66	0	0	13	53	258	84	127	47	2
Ferndale	1,391	3	0	0	0	3	17	6	10	1	0
Fillmore	15,194	34	0	1	7	26	271	54	190	27	3
Firebaugh	6,950	12	0	1	2	9	158	18	120	20	0
Folsom	69,523	96	0	13	29	54	1,546	244	1,219	83	19
Fontana	189,253	868	12	49	282	525	4,471	1,006	2,239	1,226	25
Fort Bragg	6,599	41	0	2	5	34	276	61	204	11	3
Fort Jones	644	4	0	0	0	4	12	6	6	0	0
Fortuna	11,388	23	0	7	3	13	443	94	321	28	5
Foster City	28,927	17	0	1	3	13	415	62	326	27	4
Fountain Valley	55,524	104	0	2	36	66	1,376	276	1,006	94	9
Fowler	5,467	8	0	0	1	7	163	30	94	39	0
Fremont	200,964	575	2	37	232	304	4,893	1,097	3,099	697	26
Fresno	475,723	2,782	40	80	984	1,678	22,056	4,173	14,106	3,777	224
Fullerton	132,776	410	2	36	145	227	4,143	816	2,935	392	17
Galt	24,503	49	0	3	11	35	699	150	476	73	9
Gardena	58,814	369	3	11	229	126	1,567	306	879	382	8
Garden Grove	165,629	609	3	20	248	338	3,848	828	2,454	566	28
Gilroy	50,136	237	3	13	86	135	1,561	258	1,113	190	24
Glendale	197,182	351	3	21	151	176	4,105	708	2,891	506	2
Glendora	49,738	68	1	3	27	37	1,421	236	1,085	100	4
Goleta	29,551	24	0	2	6	16	386	103	263	20	1
Gonzales	8,681	29	0	3	6	20	131	32	87	12	0
Grand Terrace	12,339	28	1	2	5	20	264	74	138	52	3
Grass Valley	12,345	58	0	6	9	43	453	71	350	32	1
Greenfield	15,145	90	0	3	36	51	465	190	225	50	1
Gridley	6,350	109	0	5	4	100	208	61	118	29	0
Grover Beach	13,030	90	0	3	7	80	316	106	200	10	3
Guadalupe	6,745	16	1	2	0	13	66	17	42	7	1
Gustine	5,120	18	1	1	3	13	142	44	83	15	2
Half Moon Bay	12,394	19	0	5	4	10	271	48	213	10	1
Hanford	50,602	227	2	12	66	147	1,899	371	1,316	212	16
Hawaiian Gardens	15,337	127	3	3	68	53	384	61	175	148	7
Hawthorne	84,445	746	4	18	378	346	2,166	561	1,050	555	4
Hayward	140,984	868	7	57	517	287	4,537	1,080	2,114	1,343	72
Healdsburg	10,913	25	1	2	5	17	270	63	192	15	3
Hemet	71,789	427	2	28	136	261	3,356	786	2,106	464	17
Hercules	25,214	75	0	4	30	41	456	138	218	100	3
Hermosa Beach	19,513	69	0	6	25	38	509	110	370	29	1
Hesperia	88,853	283	3	17	89	174	2,079	500	1,240	339	15
Hidden Hills	2,036	1	0	0	0	1	28	8	19	1	0
Highland	52,178	236	3	15	105	113	1,319	330	725	264	11
Hillsborough	10,725	3	0	0	1	2	74	33	41	0	0
Hollister	34,917	176	2	10	28	136	898	392	411	95	12
Holtville	5,376	3	0	0	2	1	108	51	31	26	0
Hughson	6,672	14	0	2	4	8	145	38	90	17	1
Huntington Beach	193,241	388	3	33	118	234	4,328	749	3,265	314	34
Huntington Park	61,307	554	3	14	378	159	2,684	301	1,396	987	15
Huron	7,288	59	0	3	19	37	126	41	69	16	4

[1] The FBI does not publish arson data unless it receives data from either the agency or the state for all 12 months of the calendar year.

Table 8. Offenses Known to Law Enforcement, by State and City, 2008—*Continued*

(Number.)

State/City	Population	Violent crime	Murder and non-negligent man-slaughter	Forcible rape	Robbery	Aggravated assault	Property crime	Burglary	Larceny-theft	Motor vehicle theft	Arson[1]
CALIFORNIA—*Continued*											
Imperial	13,669	8	0	1	1	6	158	30	102	26	1
Imperial Beach	26,335	182	0	12	69	101	746	165	338	243	9
Indian Wells	5,270	1	0	0	1	0	212	66	139	7	0
Indio	89,486	390	2	30	119	239	2,827	876	1,430	521	3
Industry	919	113	1	4	56	52	1,541	171	1,067	303	6
Inglewood	113,454	986	13	30	494	449	3,080	710	1,515	855	13
Ione	7,906	15	0	1	1	13	97	25	66	6	1
Irvine	209,278	129	1	18	54	56	3,211	452	2,556	203	44
Irwindale	1,451	28	0	0	8	20	237	60	138	39	2
Isleton	800	10	0	0	0	10	62	41	16	5	2
Jackson	4,398	34	0	2	4	28	201	82	107	12	0
Kensington	5,357	6	0	0	1	5	126	34	72	20	2
Kerman	13,092	27	0	1	5	21	452	85	290	77	1
King City	11,571	72	2	5	13	52	300	96	181	23	4
Kingsburg	11,336	22	1	2	2	17	417	96	245	76	3
La Canada Flintridge	20,817	22	0	0	7	15	374	156	201	17	5
Lafayette	24,865	23	0	4	12	7	565	127	400	38	2
Laguna Beach	24,035	79	0	10	6	63	587	154	411	22	2
Laguna Hills	31,861	41	0	0	13	28	580	100	444	36	10
Laguna Niguel	64,563	52	1	1	19	31	621	124	464	33	15
Laguna Woods	18,298	6	1	0	3	2	121	14	98	9	2
La Habra	59,202	177	0	14	58	105	1,310	308	869	133	1
La Habra Heights	5,942	4	0	0	2	2	62	21	39	2	0
Lake Elsinore	52,138	167	2	15	42	108	1,719	433	1,032	254	3
Lake Forest	75,637	108	1	7	32	68	921	178	680	63	21
Lakeport[5]	5,167	19	0	4	3	12			167	19	0
Lake Shastina	2,377	0	0	0	0	0	13	5	6	2	4
Lakewood	78,894	371	2	13	225	131	2,076	313	1,389	374	7
La Mesa	53,893	239	0	14	122	103	2,042	305	1,403	334	10
La Mirada	50,170	137	0	7	37	93	992	230	632	130	5
Lancaster	147,017	1,190	10	61	354	765	4,532	1,562	2,465	505	63
La Palma	15,652	31	0	1	17	13	261	81	161	19	0
La Puente	40,907	274	3	7	117	147	642	163	306	173	5
La Quinta	46,306	202	2	5	31	164	1,563	526	913	124	7
La Verne	33,298	58	0	5	20	33	691	181	482	28	5
Lawndale	31,541	221	3	9	113	96	522	135	254	133	5
Lemon Grove	23,937	153	0	17	58	78	668	208	288	172	8
Lemoore	24,207	63	2	4	12	45	651	132	438	81	11
Lincoln	49,608	55	0	7	12	36	482	171	261	50	6
Lindsay	10,680	65	3	2	3	57	345	61	173	111	0
Livermore	80,258	180	1	18	49	112	1,915	420	1,360	135	20
Livingston	13,548	84	0	9	13	62	384	184	149	51	0
Lodi	62,251	257	1	10	92	154	2,881	463	1,958	460	26
Loma Linda	22,024	43	0	7	12	24	591	135	352	104	6
Lomita	20,276	116	2	4	34	76	379	83	232	64	4
Lompoc	40,344	277	0	18	27	232	807	181	577	49	9
Long Beach	467,055	3,158	40	120	1,487	1,511	12,991	3,080	7,039	2,872	130
Los Alamitos	11,687	24	0	1	14	9	290	53	190	47	5
Los Altos	27,989	13	0	2	8	3	370	136	224	10	3
Los Altos Hills	8,396	1	0	0	0	1	54	33	21	0	1
Los Angeles	3,850,920	26,553	384	949	13,422	11,798	100,821	19,726	58,472	22,623	1,967
Los Banos	36,101	166	0	7	18	141	840	203	532	105	3
Los Gatos	29,233	32	1	5	9	17	660	108	501	51	19
Lynwood	70,381	660	9	23	234	394	1,762	441	457	864	22
Madera	57,636	464	7	24	153	280	1,199	330	669	200	2
Malibu	13,100	28	0	1	7	20	326	92	212	22	1
Mammoth Lakes	7,469	34	0	3	5	26	301	82	208	11	0
Manhattan Beach	36,866	52	0	2	29	21	930	144	736	50	3
Manteca	65,989	212	1	15	81	115	2,553	490	1,749	314	9
Marina	17,865	54	1	5	26	22	531	152	342	37	4
Martinez	34,985	105	3	11	32	59	1,331	262	881	188	0
Marysville	11,766	110	0	13	20	77	665	187	381	97	3
Maywood	28,411	194	4	5	92	93	545	116	215	214	0
Menlo Park	29,862	57	1	1	31	24	721	180	492	49	2
Merced	78,598	612	11	30	153	418	3,453	720	2,382	351	56
Millbrae	20,681	35	1	2	19	13	412	123	258	31	3
Mill Valley	13,205	10	0	0	2	8	203	63	128	12	1
Milpitas	67,282	149	0	10	66	73	2,072	228	1,592	252	22
Mission Viejo	94,702	101	0	3	40	58	1,206	204	936	66	22
Modesto	205,750	1,439	18	65	429	927	10,874	2,393	7,014	1,467	74
Monrovia	37,679	97	2	6	46	43	1,067	148	796	123	1
Montague	1,451	11	0	3	2	6	27	9	17	1	1
Montclair	36,643	225	2	13	112	98	2,234	349	1,569	316	13

[1] The FBI does not publish arson data unless it receives data from either the agency or the state for all 12 months of the calendar year.
[5] The FBI determined that the agency's data were overreported. Consequently, those data are not included in this table.

Table 8. Offenses Known to Law Enforcement, by State and City, 2008—*Continued*

(Number.)

State/City	Population	Violent crime	Murder and non-negligent man-slaughter	Forcible rape	Robbery	Aggravated assault	Property crime	Burglary	Larceny-theft	Motor vehicle theft	Arson[1]
CALIFORNIA—*Continued*											
Montebello	62,318	213	5	10	110	88	1,896	527	837	532	43
Monterey	28,326	165	0	11	38	116	1,032	184	796	52	4
Monterey Park	61,664	114	2	1	78	33	1,242	309	698	235	1
Monte Sereno	3,566	0	0	0	0	0	40	15	24	1	1
Moorpark	36,789	52	0	5	22	25	560	131	410	19	5
Moraga	16,956	6	0	2	1	3	204	45	149	10	2
Moreno Valley	195,649	1,082	10	66	538	468	6,264	2,192	3,052	1,020	13
Morgan Hill	38,051	81	0	7	21	53	764	165	506	93	25
Morro Bay	10,257	19	0	2	3	14	190	61	122	7	1
Mountain View	70,401	289	6	7	55	221	1,820	233	1,444	143	7
Mount Shasta	3,509	7	0	0	3	4	86	24	59	3	6
Murrieta	105,666	89	1	12	25	51	1,511	448	897	166	15
Napa	74,420	249	1	25	46	177	1,907	368	1,360	179	9
National City	59,390	486	0	25	183	278	2,182	365	1,024	793	4
Needles	5,344	22	1	0	7	14	205	54	129	22	4
Nevada City	2,933	23	0	1	3	19	88	20	63	5	0
Newark	41,558	174	0	13	68	93	1,870	330	1,340	200	9
Newman	10,416	25	0	2	6	17	328	99	190	39	15
Newport Beach	79,821	151	0	5	44	102	2,197	454	1,629	114	12
Norco	27,254	58	0	3	23	32	764	197	496	71	2
Norwalk	103,612	520	6	12	209	293	2,460	493	1,296	671	16
Novato	52,662	119	1	9	22	87	946	244	596	106	11
Oakdale	20,611	43	1	3	18	21	951	336	537	78	3
Oakland	401,587	7,905	115	338	3,323	4,129	21,488	4,488	8,915	8,085	299
Oakley	31,036	77	0	7	25	45	693	183	414	96	4
Oceanside	169,502	808	5	61	193	549	4,172	836	2,800	536	37
Ojai	7,781	15	0	1	3	11	172	32	133	7	2
Ontario	172,543	882	5	63	379	435	5,466	1,000	3,279	1,187	40
Orange	134,852	220	1	8	100	111	3,022	426	2,207	389	41
Orinda	18,350	6	0	0	4	2	277	92	168	17	1
Orland	7,215	29	1	2	7	19	207	82	114	11	4
Oroville	14,563	187	3	17	30	137	963	221	632	110	2
Oxnard	186,434	817	14	21	452	330	4,299	895	2,876	528	54
Pacifica	37,145	66	0	4	20	42	742	91	588	63	3
Pacific Grove	14,567	18	0	2	6	10	357	93	250	14	3
Palmdale	144,109	876	5	55	304	512	3,932	1,033	2,297	602	44
Palm Desert	51,556	64	3	9	42	10	2,622	778	1,695	149	5
Palm Springs	48,558	364	2	16	134	212	2,672	795	1,591	286	27
Palo Alto	58,203	83	2	5	42	34	1,744	366	1,307	71	13
Palos Verdes Estates	13,665	2	0	0	0	2	146	65	76	5	1
Paradise	26,466	63	1	13	7	42	729	157	517	55	4
Paramount	55,636	396	5	14	189	188	1,956	379	848	729	16
Parlier	13,443	132	2	6	18	106	535	131	307	97	17
Pasadena	144,545	621	3	21	260	337	4,182	858	2,957	367	18
Paso Robles	29,183	121	0	19	22	80	835	216	559	60	3
Patterson	20,338	55	0	4	20	31	557	185	288	84	4
Perris	56,285	257	3	14	121	119	1,917	638	894	385	6
Petaluma	54,454	213	0	20	29	164	902	149	698	55	12
Pico Rivera	63,399	247	2	14	102	129	1,567	252	868	447	14
Piedmont	10,417	4	0	0	4	0	239	52	143	44	0
Pinole	18,643	152	4	6	54	88	816	169	496	151	2
Pismo Beach	8,506	25	0	2	6	17	353	64	274	15	0
Pittsburg	63,227	204	3	3	130	68	2,354	439	1,337	578	8
Placentia	50,043	108	1	4	29	74	839	196	553	90	11
Placerville	9,929	62	0	1	8	53	272	88	151	33	3
Pleasant Hill	32,664	115	0	4	50	61	1,650	262	1,222	166	2
Pleasanton	66,829	75	0	6	22	47	1,488	186	1,188	114	4
Pomona	153,201	1,158	20	37	463	638	4,939	1,101	2,663	1,175	22
Porterville	52,308	283	1	7	63	212	1,880	389	1,166	325	4
Port Hueneme	21,497	82	2	5	23	52	335	87	189	59	14
Poway	48,772	95	0	8	20	67	876	211	570	95	1
Rancho Cucamonga	176,307	395	2	17	148	228	3,806	793	2,572	441	14
Rancho Mirage	17,220	14	1	3	9	1	898	245	605	48	2
Rancho Palos Verdes	41,410	40	0	1	13	26	479	145	311	23	0
Rancho Santa Margarita	49,936	26	0	2	6	18	532	96	413	23	6
Red Bluff	14,033	113	0	10	13	90	687	232	414	41	5
Redding	90,881	635	3	86	75	471	3,168	742	2,175	251	21
Redlands	70,730	253	1	19	111	122	2,771	540	1,868	363	11
Redondo Beach	67,469	186	0	12	78	96	1,564	282	1,140	142	6
Redwood City	73,369	250	1	22	75	152	2,122	343	1,447	332	9
Reedley	23,277	130	1	10	17	102	638	105	414	119	12
Rialto	99,485	558	11	17	230	300	2,233	660	824	749	11
Richmond	101,680	1,093	27	37	523	506	4,961	1,222	1,844	1,895	38
Ridgecrest	25,539	122	1	19	13	89	553	155	342	56	13

[1] The FBI does not publish arson data unless it receives data from either the agency or the state for all 12 months of the calendar year.

Table 8. Offenses Known to Law Enforcement, by State and City, 2008—*Continued*

(Number.)

State/City	Population	Violent crime	Murder and non-negligent man-slaughter	Forcible rape	Robbery	Aggravated assault	Property crime	Burglary	Larceny-theft	Motor vehicle theft	Arson[1]
CALIFORNIA—*Continued*											
Rio Dell	3,194	11	0	3	2	6	63	19	39	5	3
Rio Vista	7,980	42	0	1	3	38	136	56	70	10	1
Ripon	14,770	21	0	0	4	17	405	38	336	31	1
Riverbank	21,097	53	0	2	11	40	642	150	379	113	11
Riverside	299,384	1,922	19	109	726	1,068	11,059	2,208	7,230	1,621	125
Rocklin	53,803	73	0	13	20	40	1,207	260	864	83	9
Rohnert Park	40,431	215	0	11	19	185	766	142	552	72	10
Rolling Hills	1,920	0	0	0	0	0	18	8	10	0	0
Rolling Hills Estates	7,849	34	0	2	8	24	162	39	120	3	0
Rosemead	54,633	198	6	8	98	86	1,271	379	648	244	6
Roseville	112,817	325	0	25	70	230	4,099	629	3,089	381	13
Ross	2,277	0	0	0	0	0	32	12	18	2	0
Sacramento	467,065	4,660	49	168	1,761	2,682	22,499	5,216	12,373	4,910	210
Salinas	143,520	1,050	25	38	337	650	5,299	1,415	2,646	1,238	40
San Anselmo	11,916	12	0	1	2	9	281	77	199	5	4
San Bernardino	200,617	2,074	32	65	779	1,198	9,438	2,215	5,073	2,150	78
San Bruno	39,999	120	1	0	44	75	930	89	708	133	3
San Carlos	26,922	20	0	3	5	12	477	71	369	37	12
San Clemente	62,719	74	5	3	15	51	796	201	540	55	9
Sand City	379	4	0	0	1	3	123	4	118	1	0
San Diego	1,271,655	6,047	55	376	2,019	3,597	40,365	7,743	21,945	10,677	190
San Dimas	35,289	80	1	6	20	53	775	177	528	70	6
San Fernando	23,842	110	0	7	44	59	466	101	232	133	3
San Francisco	798,144	6,744	98	166	4,108	2,372	36,301	5,401	25,142	5,758	235
San Gabriel	40,691	152	1	2	80	69	754	191	483	80	3
Sanger	26,255	120	0	9	15	96	733	181	460	92	2
San Jacinto	39,358	161	0	5	49	107	1,509	455	796	258	2
San Jose	945,197	3,643	31	220	1,124	2,268	22,298	3,457	13,612	5,229	288
San Juan Capistrano	34,713	62	0	2	16	44	508	107	362	39	12
San Leandro	77,474	513	1	17	356	139	3,894	652	2,231	1,011	13
San Luis Obispo	43,421	136	0	32	38	66	1,717	334	1,328	55	40
San Marcos	81,683	213	1	8	55	149	1,609	401	934	274	2
San Marino	12,902	19	0	0	6	13	239	65	166	8	0
San Mateo	91,650	360	1	28	118	213	2,288	234	1,766	288	17
San Pablo	30,736	323	7	13	140	163	1,670	435	613	622	5
San Rafael	55,589	202	2	13	78	109	1,573	297	1,002	274	15
San Ramon	49,457	54	1	4	15	34	1,000	184	751	65	9
Santa Ana	339,674	1,726	30	66	842	788	6,980	1,097	4,348	1,535	125
Santa Barbara	85,791	492	2	26	117	347	2,512	488	1,911	113	32
Santa Clara	110,712	231	4	20	83	124	3,024	450	2,172	402	14
Santa Clarita	171,821	417	2	19	128	268	3,133	638	2,034	461	22
Santa Cruz	55,255	446	2	19	112	313	2,091	412	1,534	145	24
Santa Fe Springs	17,145	123	1	7	65	50	1,367	233	860	274	8
Santa Maria	86,744	622	9	57	100	456	2,591	528	1,573	490	19
Santa Monica	87,572	536	4	21	218	293	2,904	557	2,104	243	5
Santa Paula	28,617	118	1	10	47	60	769	130	577	62	1
Santa Rosa	154,874	751	8	49	149	545	3,681	791	2,520	370	19
Santee	53,186	159	1	12	34	112	1,167	222	756	189	3
Saratoga	30,346	13	0	1	2	10	309	93	204	12	7
Sausalito	7,139	12	0	2	0	10	193	51	128	14	0
Scotts Valley	11,129	10	0	4	4	2	272	53	213	6	3
Seal Beach	24,139	58	0	3	12	43	472	109	317	46	5
Seaside	33,659	186	1	13	43	129	625	167	401	57	3
Sebastopol	7,445	11	0	0	2	9	184	43	129	12	1
Selma	23,221	84	0	6	27	51	1,244	230	756	258	7
Shafter	15,892	45	2	4	7	32	518	194	251	73	17
Sierra Madre	10,908	13	0	0	1	12	133	42	84	7	0
Signal Hill	11,134	59	1	1	22	35	462	86	318	58	4
Simi Valley	121,572	183	4	13	59	107	1,985	403	1,437	145	23
Solana Beach	12,756	45	0	2	9	34	307	117	167	23	2
Soledad	28,685	86	1	3	20	62	312	127	156	29	0
Solvang	5,134	11	0	1	1	9	109	32	74	3	0
Sonoma	9,929	37	0	5	6	26	262	57	196	9	4
Sonora	4,617	19	0	3	4	12	592	96	487	9	1
South El Monte	21,590	124	3	4	46	71	536	105	245	186	7
South Gate	97,179	598	4	19	344	231	2,774	477	1,004	1,293	26
South Lake Tahoe	23,341	154	1	11	31	111	569	260	274	35	2
South Pasadena	24,608	40	1	7	23	9	503	154	271	78	5
South San Francisco	62,027	152	2	11	61	78	1,639	392	996	251	17
Stallion Springs	1,652	3	0	0	0	3	8	3	5	0	0
Stanton	37,557	167	2	6	78	81	743	185	435	123	12
St. Helena	5,808	3	0	0	0	3	89	26	46	17	1
Stockton	293,073	4,322	24	112	1,558	2,628	17,955	4,353	11,102	2,500	59

[1] The FBI does not publish arson data unless it receives data from either the agency or the state for all 12 months of the calendar year.

Table 8. Offenses Known to Law Enforcement, by State and City, 2008—*Continued*

(Number.)

State/City	Population	Violent crime	Murder and non-negligent man-slaughter	Forcible rape	Robbery	Aggravated assault	Property crime	Burglary	Larceny-theft	Motor vehicle theft	Arson[1]
CALIFORNIA—*Continued*											
Suisun City	27,093	139	2	9	52	76	958	215	611	132	5
Sunnyvale	131,052	184	2	17	65	100	2,590	350	1,894	346	33
Susanville	17,791	87	1	6	9	71	289	77	203	9	0
Sutter Creek	2,791	16	0	2	0	14	109	26	72	11	0
Taft	9,108	40	0	0	4	36	393	95	264	34	0
Temecula	98,663	151	3	15	54	79	2,432	704	1,482	246	4
Temple City	38,627	66	0	4	21	41	484	206	233	45	6
Thousand Oaks	124,106	148	2	16	37	93	1,769	308	1,367	94	17
Tiburon	8,682	9	0	3	1	5	130	21	107	2	0
Torrance	141,819	306	2	21	175	108	3,071	509	2,109	453	19
Tracy	82,960	132	0	4	69	59	2,635	405	1,944	286	34
Trinidad	312	2	0	0	0	2	20	5	15	0	0
Truckee	16,317	18	0	0	2	16	241	60	164	17	0
Tulare	56,624	408	3	13	83	309	2,612	561	1,553	498	33
Tulelake	954	3	0	0	0	3	9	3	6	0	0
Turlock	69,738	458	6	17	129	306	3,177	653	1,827	697	56
Tustin	71,272	109	1	11	52	45	1,555	210	1,193	152	10
Twentynine Palms	31,397	107	0	6	17	84	590	175	342	73	6
Twin Cities	20,924	26	0	2	4	20	520	128	337	55	5
Ukiah	14,971	151	1	22	16	112	479	213	237	29	2
Union City	70,409	422	3	25	170	224	2,228	517	1,340	371	20
Upland	72,929	252	1	13	115	123	2,654	527	1,802	325	7
Vacaville	92,424	292	1	29	117	145	2,128	297	1,585	246	17
Vallejo	115,330	1,100	13	34	435	618	5,653	2,155	2,112	1,386	56
Ventura	103,483	397	2	23	156	216	3,288	669	2,387	232	11
Vernon	90	54	0	2	36	16	429	43	226	160	10
Victorville	114,305	683	4	33	254	392	4,188	1,384	2,290	514	34
Villa Park	5,969	5	0	0	3	2	148	31	116	1	0
Visalia	121,850	675	10	46	194	425	5,719	1,238	3,774	707	17
Vista	90,919	513	1	37	154	321	2,528	757	1,320	451	12
Walnut	31,035	51	0	1	18	32	456	138	261	57	4
Walnut Creek	63,122	144	1	3	57	83	2,707	568	1,952	187	6
Waterford	9,193	31	1	1	5	24	263	77	154	32	3
Watsonville	50,211	353	3	14	81	255	1,872	290	1,358	224	14
Weed	2,977	26	0	3	5	18	124	40	74	10	0
West Covina	106,524	398	3	15	168	212	3,765	548	2,522	695	6
West Hollywood	36,130	327	1	9	158	159	1,478	270	1,065	143	5
Westlake Village	8,516	8	0	0	2	6	147	37	107	3	1
Westminster	88,730	238	1	11	98	128	2,634	509	1,782	343	12
Westmorland	2,199	6	0	0	1	5	26	11	6	9	0
West Sacramento[4]	48,715	175	2	19	75	79	1,371	333	810	228	27
Wheatland	3,784	3	0	1	0	2	53	17	30	6	0
Whittier	82,727	307	3	11	105	188	2,188	425	1,446	317	7
Williams	4,985	10	1	0	1	8	82	32	46	4	3
Willits	4,915	23	1	1	2	19	108	25	67	16	2
Willows	6,298	25	0	4	3	18	227	60	153	14	0
Windsor	25,600	87	0	11	13	63	250	60	173	17	3
Winters	7,101	5	0	1	0	4	193	55	130	8	0
Woodlake	7,316	34	0	2	3	29	214	59	120	35	10
Woodland	54,210	183	0	18	63	102	1,955	487	1,250	218	20
Yorba Linda	66,272	46	4	3	13	26	972	141	778	53	3
Yountville	3,272	1	0	1	0	0	45	14	26	5	0
Yreka	7,358	44	0	5	4	35	222	49	161	12	3
Yuba City	62,595	231	4	14	65	148	1,999	383	1,384	232	13
Yucaipa	51,202	83	1	9	38	35	938	252	549	137	20
Yucca Valley	20,814	70	0	4	8	58	651	179	373	99	8
COLORADO											
Alamosa	8,599	60	1	7	5	47	442	72	359	11	7
Arvada	106,847	215	1	27	62	125	2,703	416	2,039	248	31
Aspen	5,767	32	0	4	2	26	385	48	321	16	0
Ault	1,400	9	0	2	0	7	49	13	35	1	0
Aurora	316,323	1,622	18	188	555	861	10,660	2,216	7,146	1,298	98
Avon	6,685	21	0	4	2	15	207	41	151	15	0
Basalt	3,224	4	0	0	0	4	110	3	105	2	0
Bayfield	2,015	0	0	0	0	0	11	1	8	2	0
Berthoud	5,339	2	0	0	0	2	125	26	94	5	2
Black Hawk	103	0	0	0	0	0	129	3	126	0	0
Boulder	93,410	201	0	40	33	128	2,913	486	2,305	122	27
Bow Mar	809	0	0	0	0	0	18	4	12	2	1
Breckenridge	3,439	11	0	0	2	9	411	27	382	2	0
Brighton	32,171	94	1	14	7	72	1,154	165	891	98	18
Broomfield	55,820	37	0	10	7	20	1,247	98	1,083	66	21
Brush	5,390	7	0	0	2	5	78	14	61	3	0

[1] The FBI does not publish arson data unless it receives data from either the agency or the state for all 12 months of the calendar year.
[4] Because of changes in the state/local agency's reporting practices, figures are not comparable to previous years' data.

Table 8. Offenses Known to Law Enforcement, by State and City, 2008—*Continued*

(Number.)

State/City	Population	Violent crime	Murder and non-negligent man-slaughter	Forcible rape	Robbery	Aggravated assault	Property crime	Burglary	Larceny-theft	Motor vehicle theft	Arson[1]
COLORADO—*Continued*											
Buena Vista	2,122	0	0	0	0	0	16	7	9	0	0
Burlington	3,945	8	0	0	0	8	91	10	77	4	0
Canon City	15,885	83	2	27	4	50	568	80	465	23	9
Carbondale	6,221	31	0	8	0	23	185	34	143	8	0
Castle Rock	46,423	32	0	1	5	26	523	95	404	24	1
Cedaredge	2,250	3	0	0	0	3	29	5	22	2	0
Centennial	98,749	125	1	14	18	92	1,557	289	1,174	94	37
Center	2,373	4	1	0	1	2	34	7	25	2	1
Central City	548	3	0	0	0	3	31	3	28	0	0
Cherry Hills Village	6,329	1	0	0	1	0	63	27	33	3	0
Colorado Springs	378,403	1,999	24	335	518	1,122	16,067	3,402	11,541	1,124	108
Columbine Valley	1,315	0	0	0	0	0	14	2	12	0	0
Commerce City	44,451	162	2	21	18	121	1,385	284	912	189	9
Cortez	8,599	16	2	1	1	12	287	16	262	9	1
Craig	9,160	41	0	6	6	29	259	49	198	12	2
Crested Butte	1,648	0	0	0	0	0	23	2	19	2	0
Cripple Creek	1,024	6	0	0	0	6	51	3	46	2	0
Dacono	4,079	6	0	0	0	6	57	13	38	6	1
De Beque	496	0	0	0	0	0	11	5	5	1	0
Delta	8,728	42	0	10	0	32	325	70	239	16	5
Denver	592,881	3,361	40	282	951	2,088	19,316	5,173	10,547	3,596	147
Dillon	806	2	0	0	0	2	4	1	2	1	0
Durango	16,205	111	0	12	10	89	829	130	649	50	4
Eagle	5,963	8	0	0	0	8	106	14	87	5	0
Eaton	4,379	4	0	0	0	4	21	6	14	1	0
Edgewater	5,088	13	0	0	5	8	431	47	353	31	3
Elizabeth	1,449	2	0	0	0	2	52	13	35	4	2
Empire	324	1	0	0	0	1	6	0	6	0	0
Englewood	32,605	130	1	20	34	75	1,916	220	1,453	243	8
Erie	17,519	1	0	0	0	1	111	19	81	11	6
Estes Park	6,367	4	0	1	0	3	105	27	77	1	1
Evans	19,244	20	0	0	9	11	398	82	287	29	6
Federal Heights	11,620	50	0	12	11	27	563	82	418	63	2
Firestone	8,997	8	0	0	3	5	210	30	166	14	3
Florence	3,612	4	0	2	1	1	54	10	41	3	0
Fort Collins	135,785	549	2	75	39	433	4,607	784	3,582	241	23
Fort Lupton	7,527	15	0	1	3	11	170	38	119	13	2
Fort Morgan	10,582	24	0	2	3	19	333	66	256	11	2
Fountain	20,136	29	0	13	11	5	508	114	359	35	22
Fowler	1,094	3	0	0	0	3	26	4	22	0	0
Fraser/Winter Park	1,770	20	0	0	0	20	101	25	71	5	0
Frederick	8,908	19	0	0	0	19	141	23	113	5	1
Frisco	2,681	7	0	0	2	5	233	13	216	4	1
Fruita	7,346	9	0	4	1	4	248	65	169	14	1
Glendale	4,822	40	0	3	14	23	410	44	335	31	1
Glenwood Springs	9,089	52	0	4	6	42	491	54	416	21	6
Golden	17,175	41	0	1	5	35	484	54	404	26	3
Grand Junction	48,870	288	5	46	29	208	2,501	365	1,960	176	51
Greeley	91,900	518	4	46	69	399	3,415	748	2,461	206	29
Green Mountain Falls	800	9	0	0	0	9	20	12	6	2	0
Greenwood Village	14,285	26	0	3	10	13	636	107	486	43	9
Gunnison	5,407	25	0	1	3	21	330	46	276	8	2
Haxtun	971	2	0	0	0	2	1	0	1	0	0
Hotchkiss	1,081	8	0	5	0	3	38	9	25	4	0
Idaho Springs	1,734	20	0	1	1	18	87	10	69	8	0
Ignacio	627	6	0	0	0	6	4	3	1	0	0
Johnstown	9,608	20	0	3	2	15	116	30	79	7	1
Kersey	1,450	2	0	0	0	2	34	5	26	3	0
Kiowa	576	8	0	0	1	7	17	7	10	0	0
Lafayette	25,091	47	0	2	6	39	502	81	397	24	14
La Junta	6,974	25	0	5	2	18	311	79	216	16	5
Lakeside	19	1	0	0	1	0	25	2	20	3	0
Lakewood	139,803	723	1	86	194	442	5,959	909	4,390	660	43
Lamar	7,905	27	0	1	4	22	291	58	224	9	2
La Salle	1,966	5	0	0	0	5	36	3	29	4	0
Las Animas	2,289	10	0	1	1	8	74	15	56	3	0
La Veta	849	0	0	0	0	0	2	2	0	0	0
Leadville	2,719	15	0	0	0	15	57	10	46	1	0
Limon	1,731	9	0	1	2	6	13	0	11	2	0
Littleton	40,676	64	0	9	24	31	1,267	217	916	134	5
Log Lane Village	981	1	0	1	0	0	0	0	0	0	0
Lone Tree	9,488	12	0	6	4	2	553	51	484	18	0
Louisville	18,794	9	0	0	4	5	258	49	189	20	5

[1] The FBI does not publish arson data unless it receives data from either the agency or the state for all 12 months of the calendar year.

Table 8. Offenses Known to Law Enforcement, by State and City, 2008—*Continued*

(Number.)

State/City	Population	Violent crime	Murder and non-negligent man-slaughter	Forcible rape	Robbery	Aggravated assault	Property crime	Burglary	Larceny-theft	Motor vehicle theft	Arson[1]
COLORADO—*Continued*											
Loveland	66,204	109	1	23	20	65	1,797	291	1,431	75	19
Mancos	1,255	25	0	1	2	22	27	8	18	1	0
Manitou Springs	5,130	14	0	3	2	9	144	23	119	2	1
Meeker	2,333	16	0	0	0	16	90	18	68	4	0
Milliken	6,584	12	0	2	0	10	47	8	38	1	0
Minturn	1,187	3	0	0	1	2	16	4	8	4	2
Monte Vista	3,954	21	1	5	3	12	102	29	72	1	0
Montrose	17,895	48	0	6	8	34	805	114	661	30	4
Monument	2,651	9	0	4	0	5	164	35	129	0	1
Morrison	411	0	0	0	0	0	3	0	2	1	0
Mountain View	514	0	0	0	0	0	11	2	4	5	0
Mount Crested Butte	849	7	0	0	0	7	31	3	25	3	1
New Castle	3,809	19	0	1	0	18	89	19	63	7	4
Northglenn	33,668	119	1	25	19	74	1,310	194	950	166	9
Olathe	1,750	0	0	0	0	0	27	6	17	4	0
Ouray	913	3	0	2	0	1	22	6	16	0	0
Pagosa Springs	1,735	2	0	0	0	2	92	14	63	15	0
Palmer Lake	2,316	2	0	0	0	2	29	6	19	4	0
Parachute	1,295	5	0	2	1	2	48	9	26	13	2
Parker	45,825	49	2	11	6	30	653	148	470	35	6
Platteville	2,641	3	0	3	0	0	51	7	35	9	0
Rangely	2,106	7	0	1	0	6	33	4	27	2	0
Rocky Ford	3,948	11	0	0	0	11	104	34	68	2	5
Salida	5,320	4	0	1	0	3	143	33	105	5	0
Sheridan	5,395	25	0	2	5	18	360	42	265	53	4
Silt	2,663	3	0	0	0	3	47	11	34	2	1
Silverthorne	4,024	12	0	2	1	9	370	6	362	2	1
Snowmass Village	1,832	1	0	0	0	1	87	10	75	2	0
Steamboat Springs	9,470	56	0	6	0	50	470	99	346	25	0
Sterling	12,932	34	0	6	1	27	353	72	267	14	9
Telluride	2,378	11	0	0	1	10	168	10	147	11	0
Thornton	114,923	371	4	55	74	238	3,724	672	2,660	392	24
Trinidad	9,101	40	3	1	4	32	279	65	204	10	2
Vail	4,760	9	0	0	0	9	366	35	320	11	1
Victor	407	1	0	0	0	1	6	1	4	1	0
Westminster	106,810	284	2	44	62	176	3,534	467	2,622	445	19
Wheat Ridge	30,582	150	0	22	29	99	1,348	231	933	184	12
Wiggins	956	2	0	0	0	2	3	2	0	1	0
Windsor	18,476	15	1	1	2	11	322	68	238	16	4
Woodland Park	6,568	2	0	0	0	2	100	18	77	5	2
Wray	2,098	0	0	0	0	0	4	0	4	0	0
Yuma	3,258	7	0	0	1	6	89	37	48	4	2
CONNECTICUT											
Ansonia	18,547	26	1	3	12	10	347	43	268	36	2
Avon	17,522	4	0	1	0	3	135	7	125	3	0
Berlin	20,515	21	0	2	9	10	479	82	366	31	3
Bethel	18,566	4	0	0	3	1	167	30	128	9	0
Bloomfield	20,833	32	0	4	12	16	553	77	423	53	1
Branford	29,020	45	0	13	9	23	806	77	670	59	1
Bridgeport	136,327	1,638	20	58	737	823	6,174	1,269	3,768	1,137	61
Bristol	60,994	236	1	27	51	157	1,462	348	1,027	87	0
Brookfield	16,504	6	0	1	4	1	167	27	131	9	0
Canton	10,251	3	0	0	1	2	126	16	105	5	0
Cheshire	28,864	7	0	0	2	5	293	50	232	11	0
Clinton	13,636	17	0	7	2	8	369	16	344	9	2
Coventry	12,278	12	0	1	0	11	137	33	98	6	0
Cromwell	13,631	17	2	0	3	12	315	29	265	21	1
Danbury	79,753	109	1	15	41	52	1,626	275	1,237	114	3
Darien	20,322	7	0	0	4	3	207	37	164	6	0
Derby	12,438	21	0	6	8	7	344	61	256	27	2
East Hampton	12,756	8	0	2	0	6	151	39	103	9	0
East Hartford	48,586	222	1	22	88	111	1,611	361	1,069	181	9
East Haven	28,686	50	0	4	22	24	819	121	590	108	3
Easton	7,374	1	0	0	0	1	29	6	23	0	0
East Windsor	10,717	17	0	3	7	7	400	43	329	28	2
Enfield	44,982	51	2	0	23	26	1,030	162	814	54	4
Fairfield	57,568	39	2	5	12	20	1,081	152	881	48	0
Farmington	25,262	10	0	0	7	3	681	71	577	33	4
Glastonbury	33,323	21	1	3	4	13	308	73	229	6	0
Granby	11,323	6	0	2	1	3	133	18	111	4	2
Greenwich	61,953	15	2	2	5	6	481	83	362	36	0
Groton	9,345	21	0	4	2	15	189	45	139	5	1
Groton Long Point	680	1	0	0	0	1	8	2	5	1	0

[1] The FBI does not publish arson data unless it receives data from either the agency or the state for all 12 months of the calendar year.

Table 8. Offenses Known to Law Enforcement, by State and City, 2008—*Continued*

(Number.)

State/City	Population	Violent crime	Murder and non-negligent man-slaughter	Forcible rape	Robbery	Aggravated assault	Property crime	Burglary	Larceny-theft	Motor vehicle theft	Arson[1]
CONNECTICUT—*Continued*											
Groton Town	32,617	29	3	5	10	11	593	147	429	17	3
Guilford	22,491	30	0	5	3	22	382	59	309	14	0
Hamden	57,803	107	0	5	73	29	1,477	165	1,192	120	2
Hartford	124,610	1,503	31	61	629	782	6,374	1,000	4,048	1,326	97
Madison	18,901	5	0	1	3	1	218	53	156	9	2
Manchester	55,993	140	0	6	30	104	2,045	268	1,684	93	14
Meriden	59,345	172	2	10	72	88	2,043	409	1,473	161	4
Middlebury	7,356	2	0	0	0	2	63	12	47	4	0
Middletown	48,048	78	1	4	52	21	1,644	220	1,329	95	4
Milford	55,837	68	0	6	28	34	1,988	152	1,753	83	4
Monroe	19,415	17	0	1	3	13	184	42	135	7	0
Naugatuck	32,046	33	1	10	9	13	605	74	494	37	1
New Britain	70,553	278	1	11	146	120	3,514	788	2,096	630	3
New Canaan	19,946	4	0	1	1	2	150	15	132	3	0
Newington	29,653	24	1	5	15	3	847	88	694	65	2
New London	25,891	199	1	15	22	161	952	165	712	75	8
New Milford	28,601	12	0	4	1	7	306	73	212	21	0
Newtown	27,007	2	0	1	1	0	248	41	202	5	1
North Branford	14,468	14	0	3	2	9	214	37	164	13	1
North Haven	24,119	13	0	0	9	4	613	88	483	42	1
Norwalk	83,503	415	2	12	125	276	1,915	284	1,426	205	4
Norwich	36,471	178	1	28	49	100	944	272	610	62	19
Old Saybrook	10,559	4	0	0	1	3	217	24	187	6	0
Orange	13,887	4	0	0	3	1	473	45	420	8	0
Plainfield	15,552	13	0	1	2	10	130	36	77	17	1
Plainville	17,190	17	0	0	11	6	637	83	515	39	1
Plymouth	12,055	14	0	2	5	7	289	40	241	8	4
Portland	9,638	6	0	1	3	2	92	27	62	3	0
Putnam	9,329	24	0	7	3	14	183	27	146	10	2
Redding	8,909	0	0	0	0	0	51	7	44	0	0
Ridgefield	23,893	3	0	0	1	2	83	16	67	0	4
Rocky Hill	18,910	7	0	4	3	0	261	25	220	16	0
Seymour	16,338	35	0	13	4	18	222	31	174	17	0
Shelton	40,243	19	0	3	7	9	563	116	395	52	1
Simsbury	23,709	4	0	2	1	1	227	31	191	5	1
Southington	42,434	17	0	7	5	5	932	238	645	49	12
South Windsor	26,131	14	0	3	7	4	430	53	358	19	0
Stamford	118,597	390	5	27	172	186	2,131	325	1,590	216	8
Stonington	18,394	7	1	0	1	5	329	19	307	3	0
Stratford	48,891	144	2	4	59	79	1,548	208	1,159	181	20
Suffield	15,303	9	0	1	2	6	124	46	70	8	0
Thomaston	7,854	2	0	0	1	1	126	17	91	18	2
Torrington	35,478	54	1	11	11	31	734	156	540	38	7
Trumbull	34,807	21	0	0	15	6	742	61	637	44	0
Vernon	29,815	27	0	5	10	12	331	68	235	28	1
Wallingford	44,880	23	0	6	4	13	802	131	636	35	2
Waterbury	107,157	384	5	19	170	190	5,658	651	4,575	432	0
Waterford	18,788	58	0	4	6	48	496	50	432	14	1
Watertown	22,182	49	0	4	4	41	353	62	282	9	1
West Hartford	60,411	104	0	4	62	38	1,640	254	1,211	175	3
West Haven	52,714	383	0	0	60	323	1,587	235	1,166	186	6
Weston	10,217	1	0	0	0	1	72	8	63	1	2
Westport	26,596	28	0	2	4	22	435	72	348	15	3
Wethersfield	25,718	36	0	4	19	13	485	63	384	38	2
Willimantic	16,267	57	0	6	31	20	524	116	365	43	1
Wilton	17,720	3	0	0	2	1	109	19	89	1	1
Winchester	10,758	15	0	3	2	10	251	76	167	8	2
Windsor	28,813	24	1	6	13	4	610	59	489	62	3
Windsor Locks	12,544	16	0	5	7	4	202	30	162	10	0
Wolcott	16,557	2	0	0	1	1	258	47	188	23	2
Woodbridge	9,227	4	0	0	3	1	111	12	96	3	0
DELAWARE											
Bethany Beach	958	2	0	0	0	2	142	13	129	0	1
Blades	1,017	1	0	0	0	1	3	2	1	0	0
Bridgeville	1,620	12	0	0	3	9	99	22	76	1	0
Camden	2,574	15	0	4	3	8	181	13	163	5	0
Cheswold	472	2	0	0	1	1	33	12	20	1	0
Clayton	1,480	8	0	1	1	6	42	6	32	4	0
Dagsboro	574	2	0	1	0	1	17	3	14	0	0
Delaware City	1,523	3	0	0	1	2	34	10	20	4	0
Delmar	1,517	3	0	0	2	1	66	14	48	4	0
Dewey Beach	316	13	0	0	2	11	78	9	67	2	1
Dover	36,291	298	4	19	81	194	2,016	186	1,705	125	13

[1] The FBI does not publish arson data unless it receives data from either the agency or the state for all 12 months of the calendar year.

Table 8. Offenses Known to Law Enforcement, by State and City, 2008—*Continued*

(Number.)

State/City	Population	Violent crime	Murder and non-negligent man-slaughter	Forcible rape	Robbery	Aggravated assault	Property crime	Burglary	Larceny-theft	Motor vehicle theft	Arson[1]
DELAWARE—*Continued*											
Ellendale	352	0	0	0	0	0	0	0	0	0	0
Elsmere	5,701	39	1	2	11	25	219	46	150	23	0
Felton	876	1	0	0	0	1	7	3	4	0	0
Fenwick Island	363	0	0	0	0	0	18	3	14	1	0
Georgetown	5,196	64	0	8	29	27	272	70	191	11	0
Greenwood	902	2	0	0	1	1	8	1	7	0	0
Harrington	3,326	38	0	3	6	29	162	54	102	6	0
Laurel	3,891	68	0	2	24	42	216	51	157	8	1
Lewes	3,101	5	0	0	1	4	99	28	70	1	0
Middletown	12,006	87	0	3	26	58	388	79	288	21	2
Milford	8,472	107	0	6	41	60	576	94	447	35	3
Millsboro	2,560	10	0	1	0	9	183	39	144	0	1
Milton	1,823	10	0	3	1	6	83	45	38	0	0
Newark	30,115	172	0	9	57	106	1,157	192	888	77	11
New Castle	4,972	24	0	2	5	17	190	21	152	17	0
Newport	1,108	11	0	0	2	9	47	4	39	4	0
Ocean View	1,124	2	0	0	0	2	36	16	20	0	0
Rehoboth Beach	1,577	13	0	2	5	6	215	38	173	4	0
Seaford	7,231	76	0	4	31	41	385	82	297	6	0
Selbyville	1,783	7	0	0	2	5	128	45	79	4	0
Smyrna	8,581	73	0	8	15	50	288	57	221	10	0
South Bethany	522	0	0	0	0	0	23	6	17	0	0
Wilmington	72,888	1,410	26	27	573	784	3,806	834	2,333	639	3
Wyoming	1,392	5	0	0	2	3	14	2	11	1	0
DISTRICT OF COLUMBIA											
Washington	591,833	8,135	186	186	4,154	3,609	28,759	3,781	18,787	6,191	51
FLORIDA											
Alachua	9,398	43	0	1	6	36	359	96	247	16	0
Altamonte Springs	39,672	190	1	12	68	109	1,847	272	1,438	137	3
Altha	516	0	0	0	0	0	4	3	1	0	0
Apalachicola	2,197	4	0	0	0	4	52	16	35	1	0
Apopka	38,368	348	3	9	151	185	1,783	508	1,156	119	14
Arcadia	6,875	76	0	3	21	52	254	88	150	16	0
Astatula	1,815	1	0	0	0	1	12	6	6	0	0
Atlantic Beach	13,106	65	0	3	24	38	473	131	313	29	3
Atlantis	2,062	5	0	0	1	4	25	13	8	4	0
Auburndale	14,179	93	0	6	37	50	930	247	635	48	2
Aventura	29,683	68	0	2	41	25	2,295	105	2,114	76	0
Bal Harbour Village	3,083	4	0	0	0	4	58	5	51	2	0
Bartow	16,762	160	0	10	39	111	1,326	308	967	51	4
Bay Harbor Islands	4,893	4	0	0	0	4	86	40	38	8	0
Belleair	4,055	4	1	1	0	2	68	20	43	5	0
Belleair Beach	1,575	0	0	0	0	0	32	5	26	1	0
Belleair Bluffs	2,147	3	0	0	2	1	54	11	39	4	0
Belle Glade	16,494	415	8	12	84	311	1,362	416	850	96	10
Belleview	4,446	21	0	1	7	13	275	95	172	8	0
Biscayne Park	2,922	16	0	0	5	11	60	21	35	4	0
Blountstown	2,429	9	0	0	2	7	50	9	40	1	0
Boca Raton	84,630	210	1	15	74	120	3,254	564	2,505	185	1
Bonifay	2,749	4	0	2	1	1	28	8	19	1	0
Bowling Green	2,930	5	0	0	1	4	74	23	46	5	0
Boynton Beach	68,033	709	2	6	205	496	3,667	869	2,526	272	5
Bradenton	53,244	483	2	12	160	309	2,371	553	1,652	166	10
Bradenton Beach	1,534	7	0	0	1	6	56	10	45	1	0
Brooksville	7,898	72	2	4	14	52	369	77	269	23	2
Bunnell	1,879	44	0	0	12	32	105	30	51	24	0
Bushnell	2,223	16	0	2	2	12	153	28	119	6	0
Cape Coral	163,403	363	7	31	93	232	5,061	1,353	3,485	223	13
Carrabelle	1,233	9	0	1	0	8	46	16	20	10	0
Casselberry	24,527	145	1	3	36	105	1,076	219	784	73	7
Cedar Key	985	1	0	0	0	1	21	7	9	5	1
Center Hill	1,025	1	0	0	0	1	4	4	0	0	0
Chattahoochee	4,077	13	0	0	1	12	45	16	25	4	0
Chiefland	2,081	31	0	0	1	30	96	28	67	1	0
Chipley	3,697	18	0	3	2	13	79	25	50	4	0
Clearwater	104,986	991	11	38	318	624	4,785	856	3,678	251	21
Clermont	13,220	136	0	9	23	104	762	211	506	45	7
Clewiston	7,167	84	0	2	23	59	350	127	196	27	1
Cocoa	16,327	493	2	15	100	376	1,423	507	837	79	5
Cocoa Beach	11,817	105	1	4	20	80	868	128	705	35	1
Coconut Creek	50,511	104	1	10	30	63	1,432	249	1,085	98	1
Cooper City	29,060	95	0	2	16	77	722	123	569	30	9
Coral Gables	41,502	116	0	2	55	59	2,192	379	1,693	120	0

[1] The FBI does not publish arson data unless it receives data from either the agency or the state for all 12 months of the calendar year.

Table 8. Offenses Known to Law Enforcement, by State and City, 2008—*Continued*

(Number.)

State/City	Population	Violent crime	Murder and non-negligent man-slaughter	Forcible rape	Robbery	Aggravated assault	Property crime	Burglary	Larceny-theft	Motor vehicle theft	Arson[1]
FLORIDA—*Continued*											
Coral Springs	126,222	312	4	2	99	207	2,950	549	2,178	223	5
Crescent City	1,800	9	0	0	3	6	59	26	31	2	0
Crestview	19,865	102	0	16	22	64	683	43	600	40	1
Cross City	1,812	13	0	1	5	7	97	32	63	2	0
Crystal River	3,509	20	0	1	4	15	218	47	159	12	0
Cutler Bay	28,760	202	0	14	68	120	1,900	332	1,407	161	0
Dade City	7,102	102	1	2	15	84	423	132	277	14	4
Dania	28,052	341	1	10	128	202	1,685	404	1,121	160	6
Davenport	2,188	4	0	0	2	2	77	50	24	3	0
Davie	90,268	394	2	27	129	236	3,420	586	2,508	326	15
Daytona Beach	63,642	995	8	30	362	595	4,644	1,051	3,131	462	10
Daytona Beach Shores	5,130	24	0	1	1	22	232	119	103	10	0
Deerfield Beach	73,665	524	0	14	139	371	2,691	576	1,899	216	5
De Funiak Springs	4,905	90	0	6	7	77	121	44	72	5	5
Deland	27,343	232	3	4	62	163	1,525	400	1,023	102	4
Delray Beach	63,795	676	2	23	208	443	3,527	763	2,541	223	9
Doral	22,898	111	0	9	22	80	2,730	287	2,196	247	2
Dunedin	35,844	125	1	14	26	84	1,163	223	893	47	3
Dunnellon	1,986	16	0	2	1	13	105	32	73	0	0
Eatonville	2,343	62	2	7	14	39	142	48	73	21	1
Edgewater	21,743	45	0	5	4	36	698	216	448	34	9
Edgewood	2,077	3	0	0	2	1	108	27	72	9	0
El Portal	2,290	9	0	0	0	9	50	19	29	2	0
Eustis	19,139	81	0	8	22	51	618	136	431	51	0
Fellsmere	4,710	13	0	0	6	7	91	47	35	9	0
Fernandina Beach	11,505	46	0	4	17	25	458	87	362	9	0
Flagler Beach	3,276	15	0	1	5	9	137	26	101	10	0
Florida City	9,730	269	1	1	78	189	1,144	230	857	57	8
Fort Lauderdale	182,932	1,628	22	73	848	685	10,419	2,633	6,939	847	57
Fort Myers	65,107	797	11	35	231	520	3,342	642	2,346	354	18
Fort Pierce	39,861	791	4	39	234	514	2,622	815	1,628	179	6
Fort Walton Beach	18,831	93	0	9	21	63	792	178	574	40	2
Fruitland Park	4,293	19	0	2	2	15	128	20	99	9	0
Gainesville	113,286	1,046	3	87	235	721	5,961	1,382	4,165	414	18
Golden Beach	862	2	0	0	0	2	18	6	10	2	0
Graceville	2,404	0	0	0	0	0	65	20	42	3	0
Greenacres City	32,448	235	2	16	79	138	1,305	334	882	89	4
Green Cove Springs	6,461	76	0	14	12	50	291	135	144	12	8
Greensboro	593	5	0	0	1	4	28	10	15	3	0
Gretna	1,576	21	0	1	2	18	11	6	4	1	0
Groveland	6,484	23	0	0	5	18	161	47	103	11	0
Gulf Breeze	6,559	5	0	1	2	2	175	12	159	4	0
Gulfport	12,245	63	0	2	27	34	573	132	393	48	1
Gulf Stream	732	1	0	0	0	1	12	4	8	0	0
Haines City	18,921	129	1	5	54	69	932	308	559	65	1
Hallandale	38,722	411	2	18	125	266	1,811	389	1,254	168	8
Hampton	452	0	0	0	0	0	8	2	5	1	0
Havana	1,666	14	0	0	3	11	77	16	57	4	0
Hialeah	207,908	1,149	8	38	404	699	9,751	1,624	6,393	1,734	27
Hialeah Gardens	19,441	73	1	3	27	42	996	188	658	150	3
Highland Beach	3,966	0	0	0	0	0	49	11	38	0	0
High Springs	4,479	23	0	0	4	19	150	45	97	8	0
Hillsboro Beach	2,260	0	0	0	0	0	37	17	18	2	0
Holly Hill	13,299	112	0	7	31	74	732	187	462	83	3
Hollywood	141,048	800	13	53	394	340	7,066	1,650	4,643	773	10
Holmes Beach	4,973	12	0	0	3	9	170	34	136	0	0
Homestead	60,184	850	1	25	279	545	3,014	1,017	1,734	263	11
Howey-in-the-Hills	1,273	4	0	1	1	2	9	3	6	0	0
Hypoluxo	2,582	6	0	1	1	4	51	13	29	9	0
Indialantic	2,909	7	0	0	3	4	132	42	86	4	0
Indian Creek Village	38	0	0	0	0	0	4	0	4	0	0
Indian Harbour Beach	8,292	10	0	0	3	7	213	55	146	12	1
Indian River Shores	3,377	1	0	0	0	1	35	11	21	3	0
Indian Rocks Beach	5,106	13	0	1	2	10	175	35	136	4	2
Indian Shores	4,222	4	0	0	0	4	69	21	44	4	0
Inglis	1,622	6	0	1	0	5	49	11	35	3	0
Jacksonville	806,080	8,032	115	262	2,938	4,717	46,198	12,012	30,157	4,029	122
Jacksonville Beach	21,686	159	1	4	65	89	1,548	244	1,203	101	4
Jasper	1,775	16	0	1	5	10	117	35	75	7	0
Jennings	833	12	0	0	3	9	14	6	8	0	0
Juno Beach	3,312	5	0	2	0	3	98	24	73	1	0
Jupiter	49,429	169	0	8	49	112	1,430	253	1,112	65	6
Jupiter Inlet Colony	383	0	0	0	0	0	1	1	0	0	0

[1] The FBI does not publish arson data unless it receives data from either the agency or the state for all 12 months of the calendar year.

Table 8. Offenses Known to Law Enforcement, by State and City, 2008—*Continued*

(Number.)

State/City	Population	Violent crime	Murder and non-negligent man-slaughter	Forcible rape	Robbery	Aggravated assault	Property crime	Burglary	Larceny-theft	Motor vehicle theft	Arson[1]
FLORIDA—*Continued*											
Jupiter Island	653	0	0	0	0	0	13	6	5	2	0
Kenneth City	4,273	24	0	0	8	16	211	42	157	12	0
Key Biscayne	9,592	4	0	0	0	4	223	8	204	11	0
Key Colony Beach	760	0	0	0	0	0	20	3	17	0	0
Key West	22,084	210	0	29	75	106	1,848	396	1,266	186	0
Kissimmee	62,815	581	1	16	154	410	2,777	746	1,817	214	9
Lady Lake	13,687	48	0	1	3	44	277	56	202	19	1
Lake Alfred	4,471	8	0	0	1	7	147	26	110	11	0
Lake City	12,416	208	0	12	35	161	1,102	259	789	54	2
Lake Clarke Shores	3,291	4	0	1	2	1	93	40	41	12	0
Lake Hamilton	1,415	1	0	0	0	1	104	42	42	20	1
Lakeland	92,669	528	10	36	199	283	5,249	1,029	3,879	341	11
Lake Mary	15,426	23	0	0	7	16	333	149	173	11	0
Lake Park	8,618	115	2	2	45	66	957	161	729	67	2
Lake Placid	1,875	16	1	1	7	7	165	57	103	5	1
Lake Wales	14,675	72	0	0	30	42	944	192	727	25	1
Lake Worth	35,119	529	11	21	287	210	2,244	770	1,260	214	10
Lantana	10,111	69	0	8	27	34	617	179	373	65	0
Largo	72,298	553	3	40	134	376	3,219	608	2,404	207	9
Lauderdale-by-the-Sea	5,795	16	1	1	4	10	189	58	117	14	0
Lauderdale Lakes	30,910	395	2	22	143	228	1,636	350	1,129	157	5
Lauderhill	66,802	626	7	22	218	379	2,549	815	1,471	263	8
Lawtey	691	6	0	0	1	5	2	2	0	0	0
Leesburg	21,766	316	2	15	65	234	1,362	349	934	79	2
Lighthouse Point	11,113	10	0	1	5	4	309	42	256	11	0
Live Oak	7,184	123	2	3	33	85	302	146	143	13	0
Longboat Key	7,216	1	0	0	0	1	83	15	66	2	0
Longwood	13,374	92	1	3	22	66	719	256	436	27	1
Lynn Haven	15,369	49	2	3	2	42	475	112	342	21	1
Madeira Beach	4,306	41	0	1	9	31	260	41	214	5	0
Madison	3,010	36	2	2	11	21	208	64	137	7	0
Maitland	14,406	41	0	2	17	22	530	176	304	50	0
Manalapan	335	1	0	0	0	1	17	8	9	0	0
Mangonia Park	1,218	72	2	2	23	45	262	75	163	24	0
Marco Island	15,703	13	0	2	2	9	204	19	182	3	0
Margate	54,002	200	0	9	64	127	1,099	268	717	114	1
Marianna	6,219	66	0	3	10	53	309	69	229	11	0
Mascotte	5,777	29	1	4	1	23	118	43	64	11	0
Medley	1,016	12	0	0	2	10	455	63	311	81	0
Melbourne	77,286	969	8	31	222	708	4,202	977	2,991	234	13
Melbourne Beach	3,117	1	0	0	0	1	54	9	43	2	0
Melbourne Village	667	0	0	0	0	0	13	3	10	0	0
Mexico Beach	1,288	10	0	0	0	10	63	19	42	2	1
Miami	427,740	5,709	63	42	2,415	3,189	22,198	4,941	13,591	3,666	196
Miami Beach	83,609	990	6	50	405	529	8,215	1,279	6,144	792	13
Miami Gardens[4]	108,657	1,096	21	42	551	482	6,600	1,723	4,024	853	21
Miami Lakes	21,405	65	0	1	27	37	977	126	734	117	1
Miami Shores	9,424	56	1	8	27	20	580	140	398	42	1
Miami Springs	12,349	44	1	2	19	22	545	136	357	52	3
Milton	8,611	28	0	1	2	25	439	88	333	18	4
Minneola	9,503	10	0	1	2	7	147	62	81	4	0
Miramar	112,055	547	5	48	197	297	3,726	1,030	2,361	335	14
Monticello	2,487	41	0	1	4	36	40	35	2	3	1
Mount Dora	12,284	104	0	2	22	80	613	100	477	36	0
Mulberry	3,147	24	0	1	8	15	286	87	186	13	1
Naples	21,460	51	2	1	8	40	825	83	730	12	0
Neptune Beach	6,732	22	0	2	8	12	333	52	269	12	0
New Port Richey	17,352	182	1	16	42	123	1,087	357	661	69	6
New Smyrna Beach	23,218	120	0	2	22	96	1,016	235	737	44	5
Niceville	12,290	26	0	1	5	20	205	35	162	8	0
North Bay Village	8,015	20	0	2	0	18	202	65	113	24	0
North Lauderdale	41,734	281	0	18	94	169	1,087	340	644	103	2
North Miami	55,057	712	13	31	336	332	3,932	865	2,625	442	12
North Miami Beach	37,424	387	2	20	192	173	2,396	637	1,550	209	11
North Palm Beach	12,088	21	0	1	10	10	299	70	213	16	0
North Port	59,721	137	1	24	20	92	1,491	406	1,057	28	2
North Redington Beach	1,470	6	0	2	0	4	18	0	16	2	0
Oak Hill	1,591	12	0	0	1	11	28	15	11	2	1
Oakland	1,149	8	0	1	3	4	58	16	36	6	0
Oakland Park	41,630	408	2	24	125	257	2,507	584	1,717	206	8
Ocala	53,799	600	7	53	187	353	3,049	690	2,234	125	8
Ocean Ridge	1,627	1	0	0	0	1	39	12	25	2	0

[1] The FBI does not publish arson data unless it receives data from either the agency or the state for all 12 months of the calendar year.
[4] Because of changes in the state/local agency's reporting practices, figures are not comparable to previous years' data.

Table 8. Offenses Known to Law Enforcement, by State and City, 2008—*Continued*

(Number.)

State/City	Population	Violent crime	Murder and non-negligent man-slaughter	Forcible rape	Robbery	Aggravated assault	Property crime	Burglary	Larceny-theft	Motor vehicle theft	Arson[1]
FLORIDA—*Continued*											
Ocoee	32,482	211	1	12	46	152	1,701	335	1,196	170	6
Okeechobee	5,937	35	0	0	10	25	397	96	290	11	0
Oldsmar	13,478	37	1	7	13	16	594	122	448	24	7
Opa Locka	15,243	432	13	10	206	203	1,716	818	570	328	8
Orange City	9,567	99	0	1	24	74	1,009	194	782	33	2
Orange Park	8,878	32	0	3	8	21	271	41	217	13	1
Orlando	229,808	3,829	43	131	1,320	2,335	19,703	4,279	13,693	1,731	33
Ormond Beach	38,173	125	0	16	27	82	1,255	274	921	60	1
Oviedo	31,022	84	0	8	13	63	651	159	466	26	0
Pahokee	6,595	112	0	5	33	74	370	129	174	67	7
Palatka	10,769	156	0	4	38	114	1,011	145	824	42	3
Palm Bay	101,759	539	4	24	74	437	2,424	757	1,515	152	42
Palm Beach	9,445	4	0	0	0	4	161	22	134	5	0
Palm Beach Gardens	50,154	106	1	10	38	57	1,631	258	1,296	77	4
Palm Beach Shores	1,558	6	0	0	1	5	50	7	32	11	0
Palmetto	14,277	253	2	9	86	156	798	284	468	46	2
Palmetto Bay	22,415	55	0	3	22	30	998	162	754	82	1
Palm Springs	16,144	137	1	3	64	69	1,001	272	575	154	10
Panama City	36,339	426	3	10	86	327	2,197	453	1,609	135	16
Panama City Beach	15,453	81	0	16	17	48	993	198	795	0	4
Parker	4,503	19	0	5	3	11	208	42	148	18	0
Parkland	25,375	19	0	0	3	16	309	42	247	20	1
Pembroke Park	4,769	56	0	1	26	29	404	110	232	62	4
Pembroke Pines	146,108	400	3	15	151	231	5,817	917	4,511	389	9
Pensacola	53,385	502	4	34	136	328	2,696	528	2,024	144	17
Perry	6,713	187	1	9	14	163	310	128	167	15	7
Pinellas Park	46,913	319	4	23	79	213	2,848	546	2,134	168	6
Plantation	83,480	357	4	23	156	174	4,127	729	3,147	251	6
Plant City	32,228	240	2	11	88	139	1,900	310	1,422	168	7
Pompano Beach	101,769	1,208	9	58	422	719	5,690	1,232	3,906	552	20
Ponce Inlet	3,217	2	0	0	0	2	48	18	28	2	0
Port Orange	55,358	66	0	1	12	53	1,389	245	1,073	71	1
Port Richey	3,393	26	0	1	10	15	372	82	276	14	1
Port St. Joe	3,522	21	0	1	1	19	35	17	16	2	0
Port St. Lucie	159,735	387	3	38	44	302	3,970	1,114	2,760	96	9
Punta Gorda	16,699	28	0	0	4	24	471	191	272	8	0
Quincy	6,780	101	0	6	14	81	413	163	241	9	2
Redington Beaches	1,471	4	0	2	0	2	31	4	26	1	1
Riviera Beach	37,039	656	12	9	149	486	2,531	879	1,350	302	8
Rockledge	24,929	59	0	1	7	51	701	124	548	29	3
Royal Palm Beach	31,339	146	1	2	40	103	1,340	217	1,057	66	4
Safety Harbor	16,991	34	0	5	3	26	381	101	267	13	2
Sanford	51,464	354	8	23	185	138	3,189	725	2,095	369	3
Sanibel	5,586	5	0	0	0	5	105	20	81	4	0
Sarasota	51,818	582	8	22	196	356	3,666	815	2,662	189	12
Satellite Beach	11,636	25	0	4	4	17	263	88	162	13	1
Sea Ranch Lakes	733	1	0	0	1	0	10	0	9	1	0
Sebastian	20,667	47	0	5	3	39	556	148	399	9	4
Sebring	10,746	85	0	5	17	63	682	282	376	24	11
Seminole	19,031	70	0	5	18	47	747	131	582	34	3
Sewall's Point	1,989	2	0	0	0	2	24	2	21	1	0
Shalimar	699	0	0	0	0	0	12	3	9	0	0
Sneads	1,928	4	0	0	1	3	15	1	11	3	0
South Bay	4,541	60	0	2	8	50	175	54	107	14	0
South Daytona	13,690	54	0	6	13	35	494	162	290	42	0
South Miami	10,644	111	1	3	46	61	773	137	597	39	1
South Palm Beach	1,453	0	0	0	0	0	4	0	3	1	0
South Pasadena	5,507	12	0	0	4	8	196	28	163	5	1
Southwest Ranches	7,191	30	0	0	5	25	202	39	147	16	0
Springfield	8,742	74	0	3	16	55	393	180	178	35	0
Starke	5,892	30	0	0	3	27	200	19	168	13	0
St. Augustine	12,191	140	0	6	8	126	844	102	715	27	2
St. Augustine Beach	6,099	16	0	2	1	13	206	36	164	6	0
St. Cloud	27,810	196	0	7	17	172	1,005	266	694	45	16
St. Pete Beach	9,870	59	0	2	14	43	546	191	349	6	1
St. Petersburg	243,111	3,368	20	110	1,095	2,143	15,404	4,232	9,711	1,461	83
Stuart	15,938	82	1	7	22	52	856	128	684	44	3
Sunny Isles Beach	16,185	33	1	6	11	15	641	129	474	38	0
Sunrise	89,139	416	1	15	186	214	3,900	771	2,844	285	8
Surfside	4,439	34	0	1	2	31	136	21	107	8	0
Sweetwater	12,897	49	0	2	9	38	253	52	150	51	0
Tallahassee	168,984	1,908	8	133	642	1,125	8,968	2,804	5,660	504	57

[1] The FBI does not publish arson data unless it receives data from either the agency or the state for all 12 months of the calendar year.

Table 8. Offenses Known to Law Enforcement, by State and City, 2008—*Continued*

(Number.)

State/City	Population	Violent crime	Murder and non-negligent man-slaughter	Forcible rape	Robbery	Aggravated assault	Property crime	Burglary	Larceny-theft	Motor vehicle theft	Arson[1]
FLORIDA—*Continued*											
Tamarac	59,423	265	1	18	90	156	1,415	393	892	130	2
Tampa	336,911	2,975	27	83	1,056	1,809	15,498	4,098	9,648	1,752	131
Tarpon Springs	23,564	193	1	8	34	150	795	195	568	32	4
Tavares	14,037	69	2	5	12	50	314	64	228	22	0
Temple Terrace	22,304	156	0	6	56	94	927	230	629	68	0
Tequesta	5,855	9	0	0	1	8	113	31	79	3	0
Titusville	43,769	344	3	39	86	216	1,983	569	1,099	315	12
Treasure Island	7,412	20	0	2	8	10	270	52	211	7	0
Trenton	1,848	9	0	0	5	4	83	35	43	5	0
Umatilla	2,943	10	0	0	1	9	88	11	73	4	0
Valparaiso	6,224	4	0	1	0	3	76	20	53	3	0
Venice	21,086	48	0	1	5	42	679	109	545	25	4
Vero Beach	16,689	86	0	4	29	53	689	147	526	16	0
Village of Pinecrest	18,416	34	0	2	22	10	787	84	655	48	0
Virginia Gardens	2,143	2	0	0	0	2	34	5	26	3	0
Wauchula	4,509	23	0	3	3	17	173	65	101	7	0
Webster	889	14	0	0	0	14	40	10	26	4	0
Welaka	809	0	0	0	0	0	12	6	5	1	0
Wellington	56,081	191	0	11	49	131	1,766	347	1,325	94	8
West Melbourne	15,745	49	0	0	17	32	655	367	248	40	5
West Miami	5,484	19	0	0	10	9	205	65	115	25	1
Weston	65,288	89	0	2	22	65	993	163	789	41	0
West Palm Beach	100,434	967	18	47	446	456	5,845	1,445	3,887	513	20
West Park	14,371	129	1	5	37	86	670	184	400	86	1
White Springs	818	12	0	0	0	12	38	15	22	1	0
Wildwood	3,760	51	0	5	5	41	227	71	145	11	2
Williston	2,783	38	0	1	0	37	127	21	96	10	0
Wilton Manors	12,567	104	0	3	50	51	700	168	485	47	1
Windermere	2,032	0	0	0	0	0	61	1	56	4	0
Winter Garden	30,577	264	2	12	49	201	1,297	282	905	110	4
Winter Haven	32,886	287	5	20	78	184	2,273	472	1,598	203	19
Winter Park	27,613	120	1	8	46	65	1,232	312	859	61	6
Winter Springs	32,789	62	0	5	6	51	485	111	334	40	3
Zephyrhills	13,092	69	0	8	20	41	964	184	748	32	0
Zolfo Springs	1,740	2	0	0	0	2	25	8	15	2	0
GEORGIA											
Acworth	19,929	121	0	1	16	104	535	77	432	26	
Adairsville	3,256	21	0	0	3	18	220	37	164	19	
Alma	3,526	26	0	3	11	12	233	76	147	10	
Alpharetta	50,051	98	0	7	31	60	1,878	266	1,544	68	
Americus	16,483	198	1	12	49	136	1,086	380	666	40	
Aragon	1,076	0	0	0	0	0	30	0	30	0	0
Arcade	1,972	5	0	0	1	4	38	6	30	2	
Athens-Clarke County	113,950	535	2	54	204	275	6,445	1,706	4,374	365	26
Atlanta	533,016	7,403	105	126	3,308	3,864	38,978	9,989	22,499	6,490	147
Auburn	7,516	11	0	5	1	5	76	31	41	4	
Austell	7,202	69	2	0	5	62	283	46	201	36	
Bainbridge	12,133	106	0	2	19	85	747	143	584	20	
Baldwin	2,999	0	0	0	0	0	49	1	46	2	
Ball Ground	949	0	0	0	0	0	22	7	15	0	0
Barnesville[5]	5,956		0	1	12		248	50	192	6	1
Blackshear	3,508	13	0	3	4	6	193	50	129	14	
Blakely	5,285	33	1	1	2	29	134	48	83	3	
Bloomingdale	2,666	13	0	1	0	12	79	24	50	5	
Blythe	818	0	0	0	0	0	13	4	8	1	0
Braselton	3,300	7	0	1	2	4	163	38	120	5	
Bremen[4]	5,696	46	0	2	2	42	349	55	277	17	
Brooklet	1,337	5	0	0	2	3	16	5	8	3	0
Buchanan	1,150	6	0	0	0	6	46	17	28	1	
Butler	1,815	20	0	1	0	19	39	12	21	6	
Byron	4,295	19	0	0	6	13	153	34	110	9	
Calhoun	15,024	60	1	5	8	46	889	129	737	23	
Camilla	5,706	113	0	0	7	106	241	40	192	9	
Carrollton	23,259	415	2	13	55	345	1,342	234	1,045	63	
Cartersville	18,839	92	0	13	26	53	1,170	205	893	72	
Cave Spring	1,020	1	0	0	1	0	9	2	6	1	0
Cedartown	9,915	54	0	10	23	21	519	117	387	15	
Centerville	7,380	19	0	1	1	17	350	47	296	7	0
Chamblee	11,250	115	2	1	94	18	828	166	598	64	
Clarkston	7,635	100	3	3	66	28	296	131	114	51	
Claxton	2,417	4	0	0	1	3	91	17	73	1	
Cleveland	2,664	47	2	0	1	44	155	39	109	7	0
Cochran	4,904	20	0	3	6	11	298	58	230	10	1

[1] The FBI does not publish arson data unless it receives data from either the agency or the state for all 12 months of the calendar year.
[5] The FBI determined that the agency's data were overreported. Consequently, those data are not included in this table.

Table 8. Offenses Known to Law Enforcement, by State and City, 2008—*Continued*

(Number.)

State/City	Population	Violent crime	Murder and non-negligent man-slaughter	Forcible rape	Robbery	Aggravated assault	Property crime	Burglary	Larceny-theft	Motor vehicle theft	Arson[1]
GEORGIA—*Continued*											
College Park	20,094	385	13	20	196	156	2,279	655	1,237	387	9
Columbus	186,217	1,274	30	72	635	537	14,537	3,271	9,656	1,610	80
Commerce	6,443	51	1	2	2	46	247	31	195	21	1
Conyers	13,598	93	0	7	44	42	1,033	210	724	99	
Cordele	11,436	143	2	13	54	74	996	258	703	35	
Covington	15,126	54	2	5	23	24	865	228	583	54	0
Cumming	6,076	23	0	6	9	8	392	59	310	23	
Dallas	10,833	163	0	5	15	143	394	81	291	22	
Dalton	34,095	127	0	10	32	85	1,214	206	953	55	
Danielsville	451	1	0	0	0	1	32	8	22	2	
Decatur	19,287	48	1	1	35	11	895	200	626	69	
Donalsonville	2,711	15	0	1	3	11	112	22	85	5	
Doraville	10,408	78	2	0	43	33	442	93	290	59	
Douglas	11,255	133	0	7	19	107	1,515	243	1,190	82	
Dublin	17,628	192	1	3	48	140	1,266	210	991	65	1
Duluth	26,345	73	0	4	24	45	737	133	573	31	1
East Dublin	2,749	27	0	1	5	21	114	25	87	2	
Eastman	5,654	97	0	2	10	85	347	68	269	10	
East Point	43,253	420	6	11	241	162	3,144	952	1,722	470	
Eatonton	6,766	41	0	1	6	34	161	23	129	9	
Elberton	4,546	36	0	1	8	27	587	168	409	10	
Ellaville	1,797	10	1	0	0	9	30	7	23	0	0
Emerson	1,413	4	0	1	1	2	56	4	46	6	0
Euharlee	4,215	2	0	1	0	1	46	19	23	4	
Fairburn	11,555	54	1	0	25	28	634	233	328	73	1
Fayetteville	15,675	47	0	7	12	28	544	53	457	34	
Folkston	3,225	17	0	1	3	13	79	20	58	1	
Forest Park	21,855	153	2	11	95	45	1,379	409	831	139	
Fort Valley	8,133	110	4	0	18	88	433	113	306	14	
Franklin	861	8	0	3	1	4	46	7	37	2	
Glennville	5,210	13	1	3	7	2	176	43	132	1	
Gordon	2,114	0	0	0	0	0	27	3	20	4	0
Gray	2,239	11	1	2	0	8	50	1	49	0	
Greensboro	3,337	30	0	2	8	20	203	46	147	10	
Greenville	919	2	0	0	0	2	68	14	54	0	0
Griffin	23,561	159	2	12	67	78	1,671	328	1,242	101	
Grovetown	9,143	43	1	5	3	34	245	77	154	14	
Guyton	1,993	4	0	2	1	1	26	5	17	4	
Hahira	2,353	1	0	0	1	0	44	3	38	3	
Hartwell	4,310	24	0	2	8	14	346	47	296	3	
Helen	850	11	1	0	0	10	91	3	84	4	0
Hephzibah	4,506	11	0	2	0	9	125	35	77	13	
Hiawassee	874	5	0	0	0	5	34	9	25	0	
Hinesville	30,523	188	1	6	53	128	1,802	539	1,202	61	
Hiram	2,058	35	0	3	5	27	400	38	346	16	
Holly Springs	8,806	11	0	2	2	7	109	25	80	4	
Irwinton	585	0	0	0	0	0	0	0	0	0	0
Jackson	4,466	5	0	0	2	3	215	24	172	19	0
Jonesboro	3,923	37	0	2	14	21	227	74	128	25	0
Kennesaw	33,221	31	0	2	13	16	555	118	409	28	
Keysville	251	0	0	0	0	0	0	0	0	0	0
Kingsland	13,645	115	4	3	16	92	598	128	443	27	
Lafayette	6,911	38	0	3	3	32	392	51	323	18	
LaGrange	28,190	173	3	17	70	83	1,622	315	1,235	72	
Lake City	2,693	19	0	0	13	6	258	26	190	42	
Lawrenceville[4]	29,813	170	2	7	69	92	1,127	242	793	92	
Lilburn	11,546	52	0	2	30	20	600	127	423	50	
Lithonia	2,391	19	0	0	6	13	136	45	68	23	
Locust Grove	4,832	25	0	1	10	14	283	45	230	8	
Loganville	10,997	17	0	2	3	12	381	36	334	11	
Lumpkin	1,198	9	0	1	0	8	20	8	12	0	0
Macon	92,576	884	19	41	370	454	7,758	1,963	4,972	823	113
Madison	3,929	19	0	0	8	11	165	47	105	13	
Manchester	3,765	18	0	1	5	12	176	36	122	18	0
Marietta	67,492	399	3	15	248	133	2,522	616	1,606	300	
McDonough	20,236	179	0	8	21	150	776	154	550	72	0
McRae	4,682	27	0	0	4	23	116	23	88	5	
Midway	1,065	4	0	1	0	3	31	8	22	1	0
Milledgeville	20,194	78	0	5	35	38	1,046	212	799	35	7
Milton	15,054	14	1	2	3	8	445	81	346	18	
Molena	477	0	0	0	0	0	0	0	0	0	0
Monroe	13,707	87	1	7	31	48	609	171	407	31	0
Montezuma	3,845	32	1	1	2	28	177	50	120	7	

[1] The FBI does not publish arson data unless it receives data from either the agency or the state for all 12 months of the calendar year.
[4] Because of changes in the state/local agency's reporting practices, figures are not comparable to previous years' data.

Table 8. Offenses Known to Law Enforcement, by State and City, 2008—*Continued*

(Number.)

State/City	Population	Violent crime	Murder and non-negligent man-slaughter	Forcible rape	Robbery	Aggravated assault	Property crime	Burglary	Larceny-theft	Motor vehicle theft	Arson[1]
GEORGIA—*Continued*											
Monticello	2,615	14	0	1	2	11	107	23	77	7	
Morrow	5,534	48	0	3	26	19	1,085	65	959	61	
Moultrie	15,294	135	1	6	58	70	1,106	215	865	26	8
Mount Airy	1,018	5	0	0	0	5	0	8	13	0	
Mount Zion	1,595	0	0	0	0	0	8	5	3	0	
Nashville	4,840	23	0	3	7	13	252	70	175	7	4
Newnan	30,967	155	0	1	38	116	1,188	250	875	63	3
Newton	788	1	0	0	1	0	2	0	0	2	0
Norcross	10,782	92	2	5	57	28	457	130	282	45	1
Oakwood	4,208	21	0	0	8	13	237	59	164	14	
Ocilla	3,153	25	0	5	3	17	217	56	155	6	
Oxford	2,586	2	0	0	0	2	32	11	20	1	
Palmetto	5,245	11	0	3	2	6	185	60	108	17	0
Peachtree City	34,882	15	0	0	8	7	618	60	470	88	
Pembroke	2,499	32	1	0	2	29	93	21	65	7	
Pine Mountain	1,278	2	0	0	0	2	67	17	48	2	
Pooler	14,813	21	0	0	9	12	593	82	480	31	0
Portal	613	0	0	0	0	0	0	0	0	0	0
Port Wentworth	4,307	9	0	1	2	6	149	16	106	27	0
Powder Springs	15,719	95	0	4	15	76	416	110	269	37	3
Reidsville	2,448	18	0	0	2	16	136	35	95	6	
Richland	1,566	19	0	1	1	17	47	14	32	1	
Rincon[4]	7,948	23	0	1	8	14	249	37	200	12	
Ringgold	2,788	14	0	0	1	13	178	27	143	8	
Rockmart	4,566	16	1	0	2	13	168	27	136	5	0
Rossville	3,442	25	0	1	4	20	203	46	141	16	
Roswell	88,069	174	1	14	99	60	2,479	528	1,807	144	0
Royston	2,742	1	0	0	0	1	70	0	70	0	0
Sandersville	6,172	43	0	5	13	25	396	118	257	21	
Sandy Springs	82,953	223	0	17	161	45	3,118	885	1,953	280	
Savannah-Chatham Metropolitan	211,475	1,285	26	37	804	418	11,250	2,974	7,064	1,212	62
Screven	788	5	0	0	1	4	13	7	5	1	0
Shiloh	425	1	0	0	0	1	8	6	1	1	0
Smyrna[4]	50,196	313	1	7	108	197	1,673	427	1,096	150	
Snellville	20,467	52	0	2	19	31	807	80	678	49	0
Springfield	2,115	4	0	0	0	4	73	12	53	8	
Statesboro	27,119	388	1	7	57	323	1,465	325	1,088	52	
Statham	2,934	15	0	1	0	14	125	35	78	12	
St. Marys	16,916	101	0	5	19	77	505	92	404	9	
Stone Mountain	7,714	7	0	1	3	3	243	94	47	102	
Suwanee	15,848	27	0	1	11	15	510	75	399	36	
Sylvania	2,489	19	1	0	3	15	123	26	94	3	0
Tallapoosa	3,110	5	0	0	2	3	128	26	88	14	
Tallulah Falls	158	0	0	0	0	0	3	2	1	0	0
Temple	4,710	21	0	1	2	18	142	26	98	18	
Thomaston	9,134	31	0	1	7	23	391	69	312	10	
Thomasville	19,108	74	0	2	38	34	1,233	289	891	53	
Thunderbolt	2,666	10	0	4	5	1	130	43	78	9	
Tifton	16,611	207	2	7	65	133	1,207	271	881	55	5
Tignall	625	1	0	0	0	1	16	10	6	0	0
Tyrone	6,811	4	0	2	1	1	116	21	88	7	1
Union City	17,487	300	1	1	85	213	1,705	452	1,015	238	
Valdosta	47,989	280	1	30	114	135	2,388	548	1,686	154	
Vidalia	11,312	134	0	7	52	75	896	192	647	57	6
Villa Rica	14,072	101	0	5	2	94	551	80	440	31	
Warner Robins	61,859	333	4	18	91	220	3,805	851	2,778	176	22
Waverly Hall	809	7	0	1	1	5	4	3	1	0	0
Waycross	14,695	151	0	4	32	115	1,024	126	866	32	
West Point	3,365	49	0	9	8	32	249	64	160	25	5
Willacoochee	1,554	0	0	0	0	0	9	6	3	0	0
Winder	14,068	78	0	7	7	64	847	134	683	30	
Woodbury	1,060	5	1	0	2	2	38	11	24	3	
Wrens	2,209	17	0	1	7	9	135	39	91	5	0
Zebulon	1,239	10	0	0	1	9	23	7	15	1	0
HAWAII											
Honolulu	906,349	2,575	18	203	928	1,426	31,781	6,370	21,473	3,938	365
IDAHO											
Aberdeen	1,750	0	0	0	0	0	8	2	6	0	0
American Falls	4,080	11	0	2	1	8	104	9	92	3	1
Bellevue	2,207	10	0	0	0	10	43	15	26	2	0
Blackfoot	10,917	27	0	11	1	15	394	39	338	17	3
Boise	203,770	551	1	81	64	405	5,896	1,105	4,576	215	48
Bonners Ferry	2,636	3	0	1	0	2	38	6	30	2	0

[1] The FBI does not publish arson data unless it receives data from either the agency or the state for all 12 months of the calendar year.
[4] Because of changes in the state/local agency's reporting practices, figures are not comparable to previous years' data.

Table 8. Offenses Known to Law Enforcement, by State and City, 2008—*Continued*

(Number.)

State/City	Population	Violent crime	Murder and non-negligent man-slaughter	Forcible rape	Robbery	Aggravated assault	Property crime	Burglary	Larceny-theft	Motor vehicle theft	Arson[1]
IDAHO—*Continued*											
Buhl	4,044	8	0	1	0	7	117	24	87	6	0
Caldwell	41,766	165	0	26	12	127	1,416	259	1,059	98	13
Cascade	1,003	1	0	0	0	1	3	0	3	0	0
Challis	869	6	0	2	0	4	21	1	20	0	0
Chubbuck	11,800	42	0	5	3	34	570	44	513	13	2
Cottonwood	1,034	5	0	0	0	5	8	4	4	0	0
Emmett	6,428	15	0	3	0	12	192	42	143	7	2
Filer	2,050	1	0	1	0	0	6	0	4	2	0
Fruitland	4,709	12	0	1	0	11	99	21	70	8	0
Garden City	11,676	31	0	5	3	23	405	107	272	26	7
Gooding	3,186	12	0	2	0	10	65	14	48	3	1
Grangeville	3,076	5	0	1	0	4	111	22	85	4	0
Hagerman	770	0	0	0	0	0	8	2	4	2	0
Hailey	8,058	32	0	3	0	29	120	53	54	13	0
Heyburn	2,665	3	0	0	0	3	29	9	16	4	0
Idaho Falls	53,566	219	1	30	12	176	1,669	306	1,282	81	6
Jerome	8,923	28	2	1	4	21	197	44	140	13	1
Kamiah	1,085	1	0	0	0	1	27	7	18	2	1
Kellogg	2,205	2	0	1	0	1	70	12	53	5	1
Ketchum	3,263	10	0	2	0	8	109	23	80	6	1
Kimberly	3,065	7	0	0	0	7	45	16	28	1	0
Lewiston	31,911	45	1	9	7	28	1,059	237	774	48	1
McCall	2,663	16	0	10	0	6	149	36	110	3	0
Meridian	69,466	108	1	7	13	87	1,146	266	843	37	12
Montpelier	2,323	3	0	1	0	2	65	8	57	0	0
Moscow	23,470	20	0	4	4	12	588	61	512	15	0
Mountain Home	12,328	43	0	2	5	36	382	43	328	11	5
Nampa	83,007	274	0	64	20	190	2,378	502	1,714	162	22
Orofino	3,052	20	0	1	1	18	99	38	55	6	4
Osburn	1,376	2	0	1	0	1	8	2	6	0	0
Parma	1,838	6	0	0	0	6	31	3	28	0	0
Payette	7,679	12	0	2	1	9	160	34	120	6	1
Pinehurst	1,544	0	0	0	0	0	16	1	11	4	0
Pocatello	54,946	185	1	37	11	136	1,654	260	1,328	66	11
Ponderay	704	4	0	0	1	3	82	8	73	1	1
Post Falls	26,473	79	0	13	4	62	591	95	464	32	4
Preston	4,980	3	0	0	0	3	84	12	72	0	3
Priest River	1,928	5	0	0	1	4	36	9	24	3	0
Rathdrum	6,876	10	0	1	0	9	137	19	106	12	1
Rexburg	29,177	8	0	0	0	8	229	42	176	11	1
Rigby	3,351	7	0	2	0	5	95	21	72	2	0
Rupert	5,010	12	0	3	0	9	98	17	76	5	0
Salmon	2,945	5	0	1	1	3	27	14	13	0	0
Sandpoint	8,402	13	0	1	0	12	237	48	181	8	0
Shelley	4,187	5	0	1	0	4	52	2	45	5	0
Soda Springs	3,065	4	0	0	1	3	35	5	28	2	0
Spirit Lake	1,744	8	0	0	0	8	34	13	18	3	1
St. Anthony	3,410	3	0	1	0	2	33	6	27	0	0
St. Maries	2,619	16	0	3	0	13	33	7	24	2	0
Sun Valley	1,450	4	0	1	1	2	28	9	18	1	0
Twin Falls	42,417	137	1	26	11	99	1,567	277	1,212	78	14
Weiser	5,318	10	0	0	1	9	102	29	65	8	0
Wendell	2,425	8	0	1	0	7	37	13	23	1	1
Wilder	1,431	1	0	0	0	1	26	3	23	0	0
ILLINOIS[6]											
Aurora	174,488		2		154	537	4,347	879	3,216	252	33
Chicago	2,829,304		510		16,653	17,032	131,053	26,041	86,043	18,969	637
Elgin	105,535		2		84	164	2,351	473	1,716	162	4
Joliet	149,617		5		167	368	3,971	844	2,985	142	30
Naperville	144,205		2		23	92	2,431	322	2,037	72	10
Rockford	157,262	2,209	20	125	582	1,482	9,862	2,867	6,262	733	58
INDIANA											
Albion	2,328	0	0	0	0	0	0	0	0	0	0
Alexandria	5,839	5	0	2	1	2	242	34	205	3	1
Anderson	57,019	199	3	29	97	70	2,893	569	2,073	251	20
Angola	7,951	8	0	0	3	5	463	31	420	12	5
Auburn	12,926	10	0	4	2	4	416	48	356	12	1
Aurora	4,072	34	0	2	1	31	90	17	70	3	0
Bargersville	2,730	4	0	0	0	4	0	0	0	0	0
Batesville	6,420	6	0	0	0	6	95	20	75	0	1

[1] The FBI does not publish arson data unless it receives data from either the agency or the state for all 12 months of the calendar year.
[6] The data collection methodology for the offense of forcible rape used by the Illinois and the Minnesota state UCR Programs (with the exception of Rockford, Illinois and Minneapolis and St. Paul, Minnesota) does not comply with national UCR Program guidelines. Consequently, their figures for forcible rape and violent crime (of which forcible rape is a part) are not published in this table.

Table 8. Offenses Known to Law Enforcement, by State and City, 2008—*Continued*

(Number.)

State/City	Population	Violent crime	Murder and non-negligent man-slaughter	Forcible rape	Robbery	Aggravated assault	Property crime	Burglary	Larceny-theft	Motor vehicle theft	Arson[1]
INDIANA—*Continued*											
Bedford	13,458	30	1	6	5	18	559	72	466	21	3
Beech Grove	14,191	34	0	4	22	8	523	107	342	74	0
Berne	4,243	0	0	0	0	0	55	9	44	2	1
Bloomington	72,337	268	3	31	43	191	2,782	635	1,997	150	24
Bluffton	9,333	2	0	1	1	0	285	58	220	7	0
Boonville	6,713	0	0	0	0	0	181	5	167	9	0
Brazil	8,212	77	0	0	2	75	278	54	211	13	2
Bremen	4,659	1	0	0	0	1	73	21	46	6	0
Brownsburg	20,122	28	0	1	3	24	335	45	268	22	1
Burns Harbor	1,122	2	0	0	0	2	43	8	32	3	0
Carmel	65,982	23	0	3	5	15	970	134	788	48	2
Cedar Lake	10,817	10	0	3	3	4	314	55	231	28	2
Charlestown	7,252	4	0	1	1	2	313	74	232	7	0
Chesterfield	2,738	4	0	0	1	3	58	8	49	1	0
Chesterton	12,830	11	0	2	5	4	352	60	284	8	2
Clarks Hill	689	1	0	0	0	1	5	3	1	1	1
Clinton	4,817	13	0	2	1	10	97	30	59	8	3
Columbia City	8,307	9	0	2	1	6	166	25	128	13	0
Columbus	39,889	46	1	5	13	27	1,978	177	1,695	106	2
Corydon	2,755	0	0	0	0	0	39	9	23	7	0
Crawfordsville	15,061	29	0	3	9	17	770	139	606	25	2
Crown Point	24,479	10	0	2	6	2	643	48	545	50	5
Culver	1,494	1	0	0	0	1	21	7	14	0	0
Danville	8,229	7	0	0	0	7	117	15	91	11	0
Decatur	9,484	8	0	0	2	6	88	12	67	9	
Dyer	15,924	10	0	2	6	2	376	24	335	17	1
East Chicago	29,890	300	17	7	162	114	1,889	407	1,272	210	5
Elkhart	52,654	210	7	33	161	9	3,567	906	2,464	197	31
Elwood	8,968	6	1	0	4	1	670	188	455	27	0
Evansville	115,639	462	5	65	124	268	5,433	1,104	4,083	246	96
Fairmount	2,711	7	0	0	0	7	77	14	60	3	0
Fishers	70,594	26	0	4	12	10	936	89	804	43	1
Fort Wayne	251,194	816	25	96	479	216	10,314	2,410	7,238	666	96
Franklin	23,088	91	0	11	5	75	1,086	106	962	18	1
Gary	95,699	890	49	51	254	536	4,148	1,406	1,766	976	
Gas City	5,662	5	0	0	0	5	173	29	137	7	0
Georgetown	3,034	2	0	0	1	1	21	4	16	1	0
Goshen	32,152	45	0	13	21	11	1,282	196	1,048	38	17
Greendale	4,370	14	0	0	2	12	68	30	35	3	0
Greenfield	18,872	12	0	2	6	4	339	48	275	16	3
Greenwood	47,770	189	0	5	15	169	1,831	106	1,623	102	10
Griffith	16,216	39	2	5	13	19	728	119	560	49	1
Hagerstown	1,628	1	0	0	0	1	42	17	23	2	0
Hammond	76,498	671	13	37	232	389	3,921	1,020	2,399	502	56
Hartford City	6,281	10	0	2	3	5	212	63	139	10	0
Highland	22,608	36	0	3	20	13	899	108	736	55	0
Hobart	28,139	75	1	5	24	45	1,463	186	1,167	110	6
Huntington	16,537	30	0	8	2	20	400	63	321	16	5
Indianapolis	808,329	9,735	114	475	4,023	5,123	49,177	14,267	28,466	6,444	367
Jasper	14,039	7	0	0	1	6	182	23	152	7	0
Kokomo	45,779	217	3	19	59	136	2,684	519	2,078	87	5
Lafayette	63,990	325	3	24	53	245	3,000	610	2,191	199	16
La Porte	21,031	47	0	10	17	20	1,476	226	1,192	58	10
Ligonier	4,517	2	0	0	0	2	66	13	46	7	0
Logansport	18,626	20	0	7	8	5	904	139	731	34	2
Lowell	8,386	3	0	0	1	2	142	14	123	5	0
Marion	30,127	78	1	14	49	14	1,565	326	1,115	124	23
Martinsville	11,717	19	0	2	6	11	928	84	811	33	0
Merrillville	32,353	50	4	0	24	22	961	121	733	107	5
Michigan City	31,726	123	5	8	64	46	1,770	315	1,315	140	11
Mishawaka	49,756	189	0	16	75	98	3,482	500	2,776	206	18
Monticello	5,245	3	0	0	2	1	202	28	169	5	1
Mooresville	11,788	10	0	0	4	6	355	41	278	36	0
Muncie	65,084	349	0	30	78	241	2,627	494	2,003	130	43
Munster	22,217	7	0	0	6	1	529	56	445	28	0
Nappanee	7,164	1	0	0	1	0	195	11	178	6	1
New Albany	36,934	125	0	7	39	79	2,244	351	1,755	138	29
New Castle	18,229	18	0	6	11	1	1,572	344	1,160	68	4
New Haven	13,735	13	0	3	5	5	372	72	263	37	0
New Whiteland	5,851	13	0	0	0	13	112	8	103	1	0
Noblesville	43,333	56	0	18	11	27	986	176	771	39	5
North Liberty	1,339	2	0	0	0	2	8	1	6	1	0
North Manchester	5,836	17	0	4	3	10	148	23	124	1	0

[1] The FBI does not publish arson data unless it receives data from either the agency or the state for all 12 months of the calendar year.

Table 8. Offenses Known to Law Enforcement, by State and City, 2008—*Continued*

(Number.)

State/City	Population	Violent crime	Murder and non-negligent man-slaughter	Forcible rape	Robbery	Aggravated assault	Property crime	Burglary	Larceny-theft	Motor vehicle theft	Arson[1]
INDIANA—*Continued*											
North Vernon	6,294	10	0	0	2	8	269	44	219	6	0
Oakland City	2,521	3	0	0	1	2	67	15	51	1	0
Plainfield[4]	26,769	63	0	10	7	46	945	95	783	67	1
Plymouth	11,126	9	0	5	1	3	456	60	377	19	2
Portage	36,887	173	1	6	10	156	1,462	248	1,148	66	2
Portland	6,163	8	1	0	0	7	311	31	275	5	1
Richmond	36,738	153	0	16	42	95	1,706	433	1,088	185	58
Rushville	6,090	6	0	0	0	6	182	34	144	4	0
Salem	6,535	5	0	0	0	5	19	7	12	0	0
Schererville	29,320	19	0	3	8	8	864	80	729	55	0
Scottsburg	5,939	40	0	2	4	34	363	78	279	6	0
Seymour	19,269	95	0	4	5	86	1,283	132	1,076	75	5
South Bend	103,561	819	15	73	409	322	6,965	2,284	4,179	502	75
South Whitley	1,859	0	0	0	0	0	15	3	12	0	0
Speedway	12,527	59	1	2	47	9	584	81	456	47	0
St. John	12,871	1	0	0	1	0	128	19	105	4	1
Sullivan	4,464	2	0	0	1	1	56	4	49	3	0
Tell City	7,518	6	0	1	2	3	190	50	135	5	0
Terre Haute	58,860	155	1	21	90	43	4,985	1,135	3,415	435	55
Tipton	5,026	8	0	0	5	3	187	32	152	3	1
Valparaiso	30,169	103	1	3	3	96	872	130	700	42	2
Vincennes	17,863	26	0	3	13	10	1,376	261	1,037	78	4
Wabash	10,764	21	0	5	10	6	215	62	142	11	1
Walkerton	2,170	18	0	0	1	17	67	17	47	3	0
Warsaw	13,484	12	0	9	3	0	685	92	571	22	12
Waterloo	2,176	14	0	0	2	12	87	44	41	2	0
Westfield	21,121	20	1	7	2	10	569	76	475	18	8
West Lafayette	31,384	65	1	7	5	52	577	125	416	36	0
Westville	4,971	3	0	1	1	1	84	14	67	3	0
Whiting	4,726	8	0	0	4	4	214	31	172	11	0
Winchester	4,573	12	0	2	0	10	267	52	208	7	1
Winona Lake	4,255	13	0	2	0	11	54	8	44	2	0
IOWA											
Adel	4,188	6	0	0	0	6	83	20	54	9	0
Algona	5,316	13	0	1	0	12	40	16	23	1	1
Altoona	14,355	17	0	5	2	10	472	49	407	16	2
Ames	55,249	173	4	26	10	133	1,636	346	1,228	62	2
Anamosa	5,749	4	0	0	0	4	127	24	97	6	2
Ankeny	42,632	34	1	9	6	18	641	89	536	16	3
Atlantic	6,725	8	0	1	0	7	114	17	93	4	1
Belmond	2,315	0	0	0	0	0	12	5	6	1	0
Bettendorf	32,592	28	0	3	1	24	595	136	442	17	9
Bloomfield	2,573	8	0	1	0	7	5	1	4	0	2
Boone	12,611	81	0	14	1	66	284	88	186	10	4
Burlington	25,214	198	1	9	44	144	1,136	208	859	69	26
Camanche	4,266	2	0	0	0	2	38	6	31	1	0
Carlisle	3,670	6	0	1	0	5	49	22	26	1	1
Carroll	9,992	7	0	3	0	4	153	22	124	7	2
Carter Lake	3,227	15	0	2	2	11	166	34	120	12	1
Cedar Falls	37,759	129	0	12	10	107	671	113	536	22	12
Cedar Rapids	126,984	448	3	34	136	275	5,949	1,252	4,353	344	26
Centerville	5,466	26	1	3	1	21	224	62	154	8	3
Chariton	4,454	20	0	2	0	18	180	40	125	15	1
Charles City	7,516	10	1	0	0	9	113	15	93	5	4
Cherokee	4,720	0	0	0	0	0	79	6	68	5	0
Clarinda	5,501	12	0	1	0	11	211	77	117	17	9
Clarion	2,723	4	0	0	1	3	70	8	60	2	0
Clinton	26,483	152	0	9	16	127	1,075	253	751	71	14
Clive	14,717	32	0	5	1	26	335	59	256	20	3
Coralville	18,672	42	0	12	15	15	647	94	530	23	2
Council Bluffs	60,108	415	3	68	66	278	4,237	866	2,957	414	54
Cresco	3,732	5	0	2	0	3	66	11	52	3	1
Creston	7,483	16	0	0	5	11	234	46	174	14	0
Davenport	99,070	794	6	46	199	543	5,747	1,283	4,153	311	33
Decorah	7,916	3	0	0	0	3	14	1	11	2	0
Denison	7,265	10	0	0	0	10	76	9	62	5	2
Des Moines	196,680	1,330	12	171	319	828	10,016	1,999	7,253	764	43
De Witt	5,276	12	0	0	0	12	117	70	44	3	1
Dubuque	57,262	356	0	21	25	310	1,915	487	1,357	71	24
Dyersville	4,178	1	0	1	0	0	46	7	37	2	0
Eldora	2,734	8	0	0	0	8	31	2	27	2	1
Eldridge	4,900	5	0	1	0	4	93	8	77	8	0
Emmetsburg	3,621	3	0	0	0	3	18	8	10	0	0

[1] The FBI does not publish arson data unless it receives data from either the agency or the state for all 12 months of the calendar year.

[4] Because of changes in the state/local agency's reporting practices, figures are not comparable to previous years' data.

Table 8. Offenses Known to Law Enforcement, by State and City, 2008—*Continued*

(Number.)

State/City	Population	Violent crime	Murder and non-negligent man-slaughter	Forcible rape	Robbery	Aggravated assault	Property crime	Burglary	Larceny-theft	Motor vehicle theft	Arson[1]
IOWA—*Continued*											
Estherville	6,247	12	0	0	0	12	124	35	82	7	0
Evansdale	5,065	6	0	2	0	4	147	47	94	6	1
Fairfield	9,113	13	0	1	0	12	283	67	208	8	1
Forest City	4,094	8	0	0	0	8	37	17	19	1	1
Fort Dodge	25,100	172	1	7	26	138	1,529	386	1,044	99	8
Fort Madison	10,808	58	0	11	5	42	352	84	246	22	2
Garner	2,937	0	0	0	0	0	37	18	18	1	1
Glenwood	5,687	6	0	0	0	6	102	14	82	6	1
Grinnell	9,216	19	0	4	2	13	274	70	199	5	8
Grundy Center	2,515	2	0	0	0	2	14	3	11	0	0
Hampton	4,159	0	0	0	0	0	8	1	7	0	0
Hawarden	2,373	0	0	0	0	0	23	8	14	1	0
Humboldt	4,213	1	0	0	0	1	27	4	19	4	0
Independence	6,106	6	0	1	0	5	194	56	128	10	2
Indianola	14,572	28	0	8	1	19	269	54	199	16	0
Iowa City	67,600	257	7	24	55	171	1,692	388	1,232	72	13
Iowa Falls	5,007	3	0	1	0	2	130	11	117	2	0
Jefferson	4,184	3	0	0	1	2	82	44	25	13	0
Johnston	16,354	17	0	6	2	9	243	43	197	3	1
Keokuk	10,381	143	0	9	1	133	543	87	427	29	12
Le Mars	9,178	21	1	4	0	16	256	64	174	18	1
Manchester	4,854	19	0	0	0	19	68	22	42	4	0
Maquoketa	5,891	11	0	3	2	6	162	46	107	9	2
Marion	32,954	32	1	4	5	22	625	175	415	35	11
Marshalltown	25,792	157	0	2	10	145	1,016	258	700	58	3
Mason City	27,305	33	1	6	3	23	900	142	720	38	4
Missouri Valley	2,769	1	0	0	0	1	67	8	55	4	0
Monticello	3,719	4	0	0	0	4	32	5	22	5	0
Mount Pleasant	8,783	25	0	2	0	23	242	58	168	16	2
Mount Vernon	4,258	2	0	1	0	1	77	4	68	5	0
Muscatine	22,383	116	0	20	4	92	771	161	565	45	6
Nevada	6,639	39	1	2	0	36	162	21	121	20	2
New Hampton	3,439	5	0	0	0	5	22	6	15	1	1
Newton	15,111	21	1	0	1	19	428	74	343	11	2
North Liberty	11,990	25	0	5	4	16	45	18	19	8	0
Norwalk	8,709	21	0	0	1	20	175	29	141	5	1
Oelwein	6,064	2	0	0	0	2	98	44	51	3	2
Osage	3,425	8	0	0	0	8	63	26	33	4	0
Osceola	4,697	2	0	0	0	2	115	13	97	5	0
Oskaloosa	11,040	26	0	6	6	14	338	73	248	17	2
Ottumwa	24,479	147	0	13	7	127	1,073	247	780	46	9
Pella	10,470	32	0	0	0	32	186	35	149	2	7
Perry	9,049	27	0	0	0	27	149	20	119	10	1
Pleasant Hill	8,292	10	0	1	0	9	113	37	65	11	0
Polk City	3,202	1	0	0	0	1	16	5	11	0	0
Prairie City	1,436	0	0	0	0	0	7	2	5	0	0
Red Oak	5,699	11	0	0	2	9	196	54	133	9	4
Sac City	2,127	1	0	0	0	1	10	3	7	0	0
Sergeant Bluff	4,017	13	0	1	0	12	75	16	58	1	2
Sheldon	4,740	6	0	0	0	6	78	13	59	6	0
Shenandoah	4,995	0	0	0	0	0	96	20	68	8	2
Sioux City	82,404	327	5	38	55	229	2,699	522	2,024	153	25
Spencer	10,952	0	0	0	0	0	384	135	247	2	2
Spirit Lake	4,695	4	0	0	0	4	186	38	146	2	0
State Center	1,351	1	0	0	0	1	20	0	19	1	1
Storm Lake	9,664	43	0	2	0	41	390	92	282	16	7
Story City	3,347	1	0	0	0	1	37	14	22	1	0
Urbandale	39,345	42	1	6	8	27	678	134	524	20	4
Vinton	5,106	4	0	1	0	3	95	26	67	2	0
Waterloo	66,098	510	2	43	112	353	2,824	779	1,874	171	38
Waukee	13,279	11	0	0	1	10	231	103	125	3	2
Waverly	9,307	58	0	3	1	54	151	29	113	9	0
Webster City	7,736	47	0	6	3	38	180	29	145	6	0
West Burlington	3,317	14	0	1	1	12	271	29	232	10	0
West Des Moines	55,765	131	1	18	28	84	1,746	217	1,482	47	9
West Union	2,436	5	0	0	1	4	15	3	11	1	1
Williamsburg	2,815	3	0	0	0	3	23	7	16	0	0
Wilton	2,820	10	0	1	0	9	25	10	14	1	0
Windsor Heights	4,536	14	0	0	3	11	272	27	239	6	0
Winterset	4,856	6	0	1	0	5	63	13	49	1	0
KANSAS											
Abilene	6,274	14	0	2	0	12	311	41	259	11	5
Andover	10,308	12	0	4	0	8	461	52	405	4	0
Anthony	2,169	3	0	0	1	2	51	24	25	2	0

[1] The FBI does not publish arson data unless it receives data from either the agency or the state for all 12 months of the calendar year.

Table 8. Offenses Known to Law Enforcement, by State and City, 2008—*Continued*

(Number.)

State/City	Population	Violent crime	Murder and non-negligent man-slaughter	Forcible rape	Robbery	Aggravated assault	Property crime	Burglary	Larceny-theft	Motor vehicle theft	Arson[1]
KANSAS—*Continued*											
Arkansas City	11,073	81	0	10	7	64	415	82	313	20	4
Arma	1,520	8	0	0	0	8	34	11	22	1	3
Atchison	10,059	52	0	11	10	31	427	54	352	21	2
Atwood	1,071	1	0	0	0	1	8	0	8	0	0
Augusta	8,707	28	0	3	2	23	352	52	280	20	2
Baldwin City	4,307	8	0	2	0	6	80	9	66	5	0
Basehor	3,966	4	0	1	0	3	44	5	32	7	1
Baxter Springs	4,157	9	0	2	0	7	165	32	123	10	1
Bel Aire	6,787	9	0	1	0	8	71	13	55	3	0
Beloit	3,603	13	1	1	0	11	53	10	41	2	0
Bonner Springs	7,106	36	1	4	1	30	329	67	232	30	9
Bucklin	726	0	0	0	0	0	0	0	0	0	0
Canton	793	1	0	0	0	1	14	7	7	0	1
Chanute	8,788	21	0	4	0	17	312	47	247	18	1
Chapman	1,290	2	0	0	0	2	15	5	10	0	0
Cherryvale	2,248	3	0	0	0	3	60	15	39	6	1
Chetopa	1,218	4	0	1	0	3	36	13	23	0	0
Clay Center	4,342	20	0	3	0	17	113	38	70	5	0
Clearwater	2,354	3	0	0	0	3	27	6	20	1	0
Coffeyville	10,266	81	2	8	16	55	520	140	353	27	6
Colby	4,754	18	0	5	1	12	116	19	91	6	2
Colony	371	0	0	0	0	0	0	0	0	0	0
Columbus	3,202	6	0	3	0	3	79	12	63	4	0
Concordia	5,110	16	0	6	2	8	211	40	164	7	5
Council Grove	2,244	5	0	0	0	5	31	10	21	0	1
Derby	22,578	39	0	4	2	33	644	93	522	29	11
Dodge City	25,797	142	3	5	17	117	883	131	696	56	3
Edwardsville	4,498	23	0	1	3	19	127	36	79	12	2
El Dorado	12,569	89	0	7	3	79	496	120	332	44	4
Ellinwood[4]	2,036	1	0	0	0	1	21	3	16	2	1
Ellis	1,919	1	0	0	0	1	25	4	20	1	0
Ellsworth	2,871	4	0	0	0	4	70	15	54	1	0
Elwood	1,122	5	0	0	0	5	46	22	21	3	1
Eudora	6,339	18	0	1	0	17	125	14	105	6	0
Fairway	3,818	1	0	0	1	0	40	10	28	2	0
Fort Scott	7,869	47	0	2	5	40	303	70	218	15	2
Fredonia	2,404	5	0	0	0	5	64	19	38	7	0
Frontenac	3,219	4	0	2	0	2	94	32	57	5	1
Galena	3,149	7	0	0	0	7	97	17	70	10	0
Garden City	28,636	189	1	25	20	143	1,116	232	838	46	10
Gardner	17,598	49	1	6	4	38	399	83	301	15	7
Garnett	3,188	21	0	2	1	18	89	19	64	6	1
Girard	2,745	14	0	0	0	14	45	10	33	2	0
Goddard	3,967	0	0	0	0	0	86	26	55	5	1
Goodland	4,281	9	0	2	0	7	114	33	75	6	0
Grandview Plaza	973	12	0	1	1	10	34	6	27	1	0
Great Bend[4]	15,583	87	1	8	1	77	719	110	581	28	12
Halstead	1,888	4	0	1	0	3	9	3	6	0	0
Harper	1,395	3	0	2	0	1	17	6	10	1	0
Haven	1,158	1	0	0	0	1	4	0	4	0	0
Hays	20,115	58	0	8	3	47	580	81	481	18	2
Haysville	10,390	38	0	9	1	28	308	57	232	19	6
Herington	2,404	20	0	2	0	18	55	9	44	2	0
Hesston	3,715	4	0	1	0	3	114	40	73	1	0
Hiawatha	3,161	13	0	2	0	11	78	10	64	4	3
Hill City	1,378	2	0	0	0	2	38	9	28	1	0
Hillsboro	2,643	7	0	1	0	6	68	25	39	4	0
Holton	3,307	6	0	0	0	6	44	6	36	2	0
Hoxie	1,092	1	0	0	0	1	16	10	5	1	0
Independence	9,210	46	0	3	5	38	439	85	333	21	4
Inman	1,187	0	0	0	0	0	17	7	7	3	0
Iola	5,788	29	0	3	1	25	336	57	266	13	1
Junction City	20,265	169	0	15	19	135	881	171	661	49	6
Kechi	1,740	0	0	0	0	0	18	1	15	2	0
Kingman	3,014	13	0	1	0	12	43	10	30	3	0
La Harpe	641	3	0	0	0	3	1	0	1	0	0
Lansing	10,815	33	1	4	4	24	223	58	147	18	1
Larned	3,612	10	0	2	0	8	132	37	90	5	0
Lawrence	91,089	412	4	40	78	290	4,656	801	3,656	199	26
Leavenworth	34,702	321	2	13	68	238	1,243	271	870	102	16
Leawood	31,442	15	0	1	4	10	399	51	336	12	2
Lenexa	46,392	86	0	11	11	64	1,231	182	945	104	12

[1] The FBI does not publish arson data unless it receives data from either the agency or the state for all 12 months of the calendar year.

[4] Because of changes in the state/local agency's reporting practices, figures are not comparable to previous years' data.

Table 8. Offenses Known to Law Enforcement, by State and City, 2008—*Continued*

(Number.)

State/City	Population	Violent crime	Murder and non-negligent man-slaughter	Forcible rape	Robbery	Aggravated assault	Property crime	Burglary	Larceny-theft	Motor vehicle theft	Arson[1]
KANSAS—*Continued*											
Liberal	20,183	98	0	6	11	81	593	122	437	34	5
Lindsborg	3,254	1	0	1	0	0	71	14	57	0	1
Linn Valley	586	3	0	0	0	3	17	6	7	4	0
Louisburg	3,959	3	0	0	0	3	36	7	27	2	1
Lyons	3,435	6	0	0	0	6	18	8	10	0	0
Maize	2,950	6	0	2	0	4	70	20	49	1	0
Marion	1,872	9	0	1	0	8	37	11	20	6	0
Marysville	3,073	5	0	0	0	5	38	7	24	7	1
McPherson	13,450	26	0	4	1	21	295	42	237	16	5
Merriam	10,764	95	1	14	11	69	649	80	545	24	1
Minneapolis	1,976	5	0	0	0	5	45	12	32	1	0
Mission	9,709	17	0	1	3	13	420	49	302	69	1
Moran	522	0	0	0	0	0	0	0	0	0	0
Moundridge	1,625	2	0	0	0	2	10	7	3	0	0
Mulberry	573	1	0	0	0	1	8	0	6	2	0
Mulvane	5,921	7	0	0	1	6	132	20	111	1	2
Neodesha	2,628	6	0	0	0	6	71	13	51	7	2
Newton	18,052	96	1	14	14	67	562	112	436	14	10
Nickerson	1,140	4	0	0	0	4	16	2	14	0	0
Norton	2,642	2	0	1	0	1	38	12	22	4	0
Oakley	1,835	2	0	0	0	2	50	6	42	2	0
Oberlin	1,645	2	0	0	0	2	18	9	9	0	0
Osage City	2,825	17	0	2	1	14	98	29	64	5	0
Osawatomie	4,516	20	1	5	1	13	130	24	100	6	2
Oswego	1,977	2	0	0	0	2	20	2	18	0	0
Ottawa	12,937	42	0	10	2	30	315	57	245	13	2
Overland Park	171,909	305	1	35	60	209	4,093	507	3,226	360	44
Oxford[5]	1,068	1	0	0	0	1			20	0	0
Paola	5,409	9	0	1	0	8	155	13	134	8	3
Park City	7,781	6	0	0	1	5	219	40	159	20	1
Parsons	11,078	90	0	4	4	82	628	142	473	13	9
Peabody	1,200	0	0	0	0	0	14	2	11	1	1
Pittsburg	19,571	91	1	8	8	74	1,229	262	898	69	23
Pleasanton	1,330	1	0	0	0	1	16	10	6	0	0
Prairie Village	21,344	34	0	1	8	25	299	86	185	28	8
Pratt	6,387	15	1	1	1	12	115	26	85	4	0
Roeland Park	6,920	35	0	7	4	24	290	43	240	7	
Rose Hill	4,026	7	0	0	0	7	88	15	70	3	0
Russell	4,233	20	0	2	0	18	81	29	44	8	0
Sabetha	2,482	3	0	1	0	2	22	5	16	1	0
Salina	46,542	178	4	35	24	115	2,458	305	2,064	89	23
Scott City	3,448	14	0	3	1	10	42	9	29	4	0
Seneca	2,017	5	0	0	0	5	40	9	29	2	0
Shawnee	61,553	94	2	6	14	72	1,220	176	896	148	24
South Hutchinson	2,542	6	0	0	0	6	82	7	75	0	0
Spring Hill	5,427	10	0	2	0	8	113	27	80	6	1
Stafford	1,030	4	0	0	0	4	17	7	9	1	0
Sterling	2,523	4	0	1	0	3	47	12	33	2	1
St. Marys	2,254	4	0	0	0	4	33	15	16	2	0
Stockton	1,391	0	0	0	0	0	0	0	0	0	0
Tonganoxie	4,371	5	0	1	0	4	95	25	65	5	3
Topeka	122,554	609	10	35	275	289	7,316	1,561	5,067	688	10
Towanda	1,356	1	0	0	0	1	32	7	25	0	0
Ulysses	5,590	11	0	0	0	11	74	23	51	0	0
Valley Center	6,394	7	0	1	0	6	117	16	94	7	4
Wa Keeney	1,676	5	0	0	0	5	21	8	12	1	0
Wakefield	856	0	0	0	0	0	11	4	5	2	0
Wamego	4,276	3	0	2	0	1	77	9	66	2	0
Wathena	1,286	4	0	0	0	4	31	10	19	2	0
Wellington	7,712	33	1	3	1	28	399	78	302	19	6
Wellsville	1,746	7	0	2	1	4	52	11	39	2	0
Westwood	1,832	5	0	1	0	4	69	14	46	9	0
Wichita	362,602	3,091	30	278	482	2,301	20,034	4,077	14,097	1,860	187
Yates Center	1,367	0	0	0	0	0	12	6	5	1	0
KENTUCKY											
Albany	2,316	4	0	0	0	4	14	6	8	0	
Alexandria	8,452	20	0	0	2	18	179	24	146	9	
Anchorage	3,092	1	0	0	1	0	44	10	32	2	
Auburn	1,499	2	0	0	0	2	9	4	5	0	
Audubon Park	1,622	7	0	0	2	5	48	14	27	7	
Barbourville	3,575	2	0	0	0	2	27	3	19	5	
Bardstown	11,194	33	0	5	9	19	399	84	300	15	
Beattyville	1,104	1	0	0	0	1	9	3	5	1	

[1] The FBI does not publish arson data unless it receives data from either the agency or the state for all 12 months of the calendar year.

Table 8. Offenses Known to Law Enforcement, by State and City, 2008—*Continued*

(Number.)

State/City	Population	Violent crime	Murder and non-negligent man-slaughter	Forcible rape	Robbery	Aggravated assault	Property crime	Burglary	Larceny-theft	Motor vehicle theft	Arson[1]
KENTUCKY—*Continued*											
Beaver Dam	3,121	0	0	0	0	0	2	0	2	0	
Bellevue	5,818	3	0	0	2	1	61	6	53	2	
Berea	14,558	23	0	2	6	15	433	134	285	14	
Bowling Green	54,865	336	0	47	90	199	2,998	569	2,313	116	1
Brandenburg	2,168	2	0	0	0	2	71	10	59	2	
Burkesville	1,685	0	0	0	0	0	2	2	0	0	
Burnside	689	0	0	0	0	0	21	7	12	2	
Cadiz	2,626	15	0	0	1	14	78	17	59	2	
Calhoun	790	0	0	0	0	0	2	0	2	0	
Campbellsville	11,009	39	1	4	12	22	363	93	248	22	
Carlisle	2,101	1	0	0	0	1	21	3	16	2	
Carrollton	3,893	7	1	1	1	4	110	36	68	6	3
Catlettsburg	1,954	12	0	1	1	10	146	28	106	12	
Cave City	2,006	7	0	1	1	5	92	22	66	4	
Central City	5,715	9	0	1	3	5	34	6	25	3	
Clarkson	836	1	0	0	0	1	7	3	3	1	
Clay City	1,362	3	0	1	1	1	49	18	30	1	
Clinton	1,321	0	0	0	0	0	5	2	3	0	
Cloverport	1,234	0	0	0	0	0	3	2	1	0	
Cold Spring	6,003	9	0	2	1	6	199	15	182	2	
Columbia	4,247	7	0	2	0	5	31	10	21	0	
Corbin	8,394	21	0	5	6	10	358	83	264	11	
Covington	43,018	457	1	44	215	197	2,450	678	1,561	211	
Cumberland	2,265	2	0	0	0	2	16	10	4	2	
Cynthiana	6,264	24	1	1	7	15	356	86	259	11	
Danville	15,437	42	0	4	10	28	555	122	409	24	
Dawson Springs	2,900	3	0	0	0	3	65	31	33	1	
Dayton	5,420	21	0	0	6	15	124	24	90	10	
Earlington	1,566	0	0	0	0	0	2	0	2	0	
Edgewood	8,831	11	0	0	2	9	130	18	108	4	
Edmonton	1,642	0	0	0	0	0	16	6	10	0	
Elizabethtown	23,926	80	1	9	25	45	1,091	192	863	36	
Elkhorn City	1,003	0	0	0	0	0	8	0	8	0	
Elkton	1,959	1	0	0	1	0	23	7	16	0	
Elsmere	7,860	19	0	1	12	6	109	21	74	14	
Eminence	2,216	5	1	0	2	2	34	7	23	4	
Erlanger	17,164	28	0	4	10	14	553	129	395	29	
Evarts	1,034	8	0	0	1	7	34	12	22	0	
Falmouth	2,077	2	0	1	0	1	79	29	47	3	
Flatwoods	7,621	11	0	1	5	5	132	55	71	6	
Fleming-Neon	787	0	0	0	0	0	11	4	7	0	
Flemingsburg	2,683	4	0	0	1	3	51	15	36	0	
Fort Mitchell	7,493	15	0	2	7	6	256	43	197	16	
Fort Thomas	15,157	13	0	4	4	5	235	48	175	12	
Fort Wright	5,411	14	0	1	9	4	420	43	364	13	
Frankfort	27,014	90	0	12	36	42	1,091	247	793	51	
Franklin	8,007	32	1	2	19	10	325	72	235	18	
Fulton	2,374	11	0	1	1	9	121	26	91	4	
Glasgow	14,343	32	0	11	4	17	491	108	371	12	
Graymoor-Devondale	3,110	0	0	0	0	0	61	10	46	5	
Grayson	4,004	7	0	2	2	3	149	47	91	11	
Greensburg	2,394	0	0	0	0	0	2	1	1	0	
Greenville	4,235	0	0	0	0	0	11	6	5	0	
Guthrie	1,435	2	0	1	1	0	10	5	2	3	
Hardinsburg	2,442	1	0	0	0	1	2	0	0	2	
Harlan	1,858	7	0	0	3	4	79	13	62	4	
Harrodsburg	8,169	20	0	4	7	9	208	61	132	15	
Hartford	2,650	1	0	0	0	1	22	10	11	1	
Hawesville	979	0	0	0	0	0	2	1	1	0	
Hazard	4,781	22	0	5	13	4	213	32	174	7	
Heritage Creek	1,676	0	0	0	0	0	16	4	11	1	
Hickman	2,191	2	0	0	0	2	48	19	26	3	
Hillview	7,558	17	0	2	5	10	177	45	120	12	
Hodgenville	2,765	3	0	1	0	2	11	4	4	3	
Hopkinsville	31,823	187	0	14	65	108	1,657	438	1,135	84	
Horse Cave	2,319	1	0	0	1	0	14	3	11	0	
Independence	22,106	20	2	3	3	12	417	104	284	29	
Indian Hills	3,343	0	0	0	0	0	39	15	24	0	
Irvine	2,659	1	0	0	1	0	82	25	55	2	
Irvington	1,415	0	0	0	0	0	12	3	8	1	
Jackson	2,354	3	0	0	2	1	67	18	46	3	
Jamestown	1,741	4	0	0	0	4	61	18	43	0	
Jeffersontown	26,112	65	0	7	37	21	616	141	403	72	
Jenkins	2,239	3	0	1	1	1	26	10	14	2	

[1] The FBI does not publish arson data unless it receives data from either the agency or the state for all 12 months of the calendar year.

Table 8. Offenses Known to Law Enforcement, by State and City, 2008—*Continued*

(Number.)

State/City	Population	Violent crime	Murder and non-negligent man-slaughter	Forcible rape	Robbery	Aggravated assault	Property crime	Burglary	Larceny-theft	Motor vehicle theft	Arson[1]
KENTUCKY—*Continued*											
Junction City	2,197	2	0	0	1	1	9	2	6	1	
La Grange	6,355	10	0	1	6	3	197	59	129	9	
Lakeside Park-Crestview Hills	6,355	1	0	0	0	1	154	10	142	2	
Lancaster	4,473	4	0	1	1	2	73	18	55	0	
Lawrenceburg	10,024	13	0	3	1	9	111	25	79	7	
Lebanon	5,949	31	0	5	10	16	229	57	160	12	
Lebanon Junction	2,014	3	0	0	1	2	20	12	5	3	
Leitchfield	6,539	5	0	2	3	0	128	23	102	3	
Lewisburg	917	0	0	0	0	0	2	0	2	0	
Lewisport	1,652	0	0	0	0	0	2	0	2	0	
Lexington	281,473	1,780	12	137	529	1,102	9,724	2,259	6,878	587	44
Liberty	1,884	7	0	0	2	5	22	9	13	0	
London	7,993	17	1	1	9	6	478	91	352	35	
Lone Oak	435	0	0	0	0	0	1	1	0	0	
Louisa	2,078	5	0	0	2	3	69	14	49	6	
Louisville Metro	629,679	4,306	71	220	1,762	2,253	29,420	7,278	19,523	2,619	222
Ludlow	4,888	17	0	6	4	7	126	50	66	10	
Lynnview	1,011	1	0	0	1	0	6	5	1	0	
Manchester	1,917	0	0	0	0	0	42	12	25	5	
Marion	3,053	1	0	0	0	1	71	13	55	3	
Mayfield	10,208	42	0	5	9	28	322	98	217	7	
Maysville	9,183	31	0	3	13	15	582	180	386	16	
Middlesboro	9,862	15	0	2	6	7	305	39	257	9	
Millersburg	862	0	0	0	0	0	11	5	5	1	
Monticello	6,191	18	0	3	6	9	237	93	139	5	
Morgantown	2,571	2	0	0	0	2	14	9	4	1	
Mortons Gap	936	0	0	0	0	0	3	2	1	0	
Mount Sterling	6,886	31	1	5	10	15	468	83	371	14	
Mount Vernon	2,595	4	0	0	0	4	35	12	22	1	
Mount Washington	12,354	5	0	2	1	2	162	36	108	18	
Munfordville	1,605	1	0	0	0	1	24	7	17	0	
Murray	16,482	31	0	7	4	20	581	143	422	16	
New Castle	909	0	0	0	0	0	1	1	0	0	
New Haven	878	0	0	0	0	0	3	0	3	0	
Newport	15,409	83	2	9	43	29	1,097	177	854	66	6
Nicholasville	26,558	78	0	16	27	35	1,238	283	885	70	
Northfield	1,062	0	0	0	0	0	2	1	1	0	
Nortonville	1,229	0	0	0	0	0	6	3	3	0	
Oak Grove	9,806	38	0	4	16	18	400	161	214	25	
Olive Hill	1,817	6	0	0	4	2	96	32	59	5	
Owenton	1,487	0	0	0	0	0	8	2	6	0	
Owingsville	1,580	4	0	1	0	3	70	22	42	6	
Paintsville	4,120	4	0	0	2	2	101	16	78	7	
Paris	9,268	34	0	1	12	21	220	71	143	6	
Park Hills	2,758	1	0	0	1	0	36	11	24	1	
Pewee Valley	1,607	0	0	0	0	0	6	2	4	0	
Pikeville	6,277	13	0	2	5	6	421	41	373	7	
Pineville	1,967	8	0	0	1	7	48	5	39	4	
Pioneer Village	2,706	2	0	0	0	2	10	2	7	1	
Powderly	889	2	0	0	1	1	29	6	23	0	
Prestonsburg	3,843	11	0	1	4	6	163	29	123	11	
Princeton	6,328	29	1	11	0	17	186	53	120	13	
Providence	3,456	6	0	0	0	6	57	16	35	6	
Raceland	2,588	0	0	0	0	0	11	6	5	0	
Radcliff[7]	21,918		0	24	22		645	141	480	24	0
Russell	3,566	7	0	1	5	1	157	34	114	9	
Russell Springs	2,574	11	0	3	1	7	174	26	134	14	
Sadieville	316	1	0	0	0	1	3	2	1	0	
Science Hill	669	0	0	0	0	0	6	3	3	0	
Scottsville	4,573	5	0	2	0	3	23	7	16	0	
Shelbyville	11,300	39	0	3	18	18	340	87	234	19	
Shepherdsville	9,199	27	0	7	6	14	519	81	427	11	0
Shively	16,210	137	2	3	97	35	904	256	517	131	
Smiths Grove	761	0	0	0	0	0	3	2	1	0	
Somerset	12,438	25	0	2	12	11	675	94	562	19	
Southgate	3,275	0	0	0	0	0	22	1	18	3	
Springfield	2,880	6	0	0	2	4	65	23	35	7	
Stamping Ground	673	0	0	0	0	0	2	0	2	0	
Stanford	3,434	1	0	0	0	1	24	9	12	3	
Stanton	3,150	2	0	1	0	1	38	14	24	0	
St. Matthews	18,279	51	0	2	35	14	773	88	652	33	
Sturgis	1,921	2	0	1	0	1	24	5	18	1	
Taylor Mill	6,723	2	0	0	0	2	52	15	34	3	
Taylorsville	1,234	4	0	0	0	4	34	11	19	4	

[1] The FBI does not publish arson data unless it receives data from either the agency or the state for all 12 months of the calendar year.

[7] The data collection methodology for the offense of aggravated assault used by this agency does not comply with national UCR Program guidelines. Consequently, the figures for aggravated assault and violent crime (of which aggravated assault is a part) are not included in this table.

Table 8. Offenses Known to Law Enforcement, by State and City, 2008—*Continued*

(Number.)

State/City	Population	Violent crime	Murder and non-negligent man-slaughter	Forcible rape	Robbery	Aggravated assault	Property crime	Burglary	Larceny-theft	Motor vehicle theft	Arson[1]
KENTUCKY—*Continued*											
Tompkinsville	2,631	4	0	0	1	3	41	17	22	2	
Uniontown	1,022	0	0	0	0	0	2	1	1	0	
Vanceburg	1,703	4	0	2	0	2	23	10	13	0	
Villa Hills	7,702	1	0	0	1	0	59	10	47	2	
Vine Grove	4,192	2	0	2	0	0	88	18	63	7	
Warsaw	1,796	2	0	0	0	2	14	2	12	0	
West Liberty	3,345	3	0	0	0	3	39	4	35	0	
West Point	975	1	0	0	0	1	16	5	8	3	
Whitesburg	1,476	0	0	0	0	0	29	2	26	1	
Wilder	2,995	2	0	0	0	2	42	2	36	4	
Williamsburg	5,206	19	0	0	15	4	119	16	91	12	
Williamstown	3,516	4	0	1	1	2	104	25	72	7	
Wilmore	5,917	3	0	2	0	1	99	16	75	8	0
Winchester	16,555	41	2	5	10	24	644	117	517	10	
LOUISIANA											
Addis	3,590	13	0	0	0	13	5	0	5	0	0
Amite	4,322	90	0	0	7	83	424	100	299	25	7
Baker	13,550	24	1	0	2	21	500	105	379	16	4
Basile	2,390	8	0	1	0	7	14	6	8	0	1
Baton Rouge	226,920	2,690	67	65	1,032	1,526	12,468	3,783	7,711	974	225
Bernice	1,635	17	0	0	3	14	8	2	6	0	0
Blanchard	2,590	0	0	0	0	0	51	15	32	4	0
Bogalusa	12,607	147	5	13	40	89	789	281	457	51	4
Bossier City	62,500	1,173	6	24	104	1,039	2,704	431	2,095	178	2
Breaux Bridge	8,059	18	0	0	1	17	26	9	13	4	
Brusly	2,151	0	0	0	0	0	0	0	0	0	0
Clinton	1,878	31	0	1	1	29	49	19	29	1	0
Coushatta	2,095	13	0	1	2	10	46	8	38	0	0
Covington	9,553	38	1	1	7	29	265	61	195	9	1
Cullen	1,379	14	0	2	1	11	12	4	7	1	0
Denham Springs	10,269	71	0	10	35	26	893	286	601	6	0
De Quincy	3,214	9	0	1	0	8	89	18	69	2	0
De Ridder	10,134	51	0	2	1	48	210	70	139	1	
Elton	1,232	3	0	1	0	2	28	6	22	0	
Farmerville	3,637	45	0	0	7	38	160	41	116	3	1
Franklin	7,694	98	0	2	11	85	477	62	413	2	
Franklinton	3,719	55	2	2	8	43	263	49	209	5	0
French Settlement	1,071	4	0	0	0	4	20	1	19	0	0
Golden Meadow	2,122	9	0	0	0	9	7	2	2	3	0
Gonzales	9,252	35	1	1	4	29	247	7	226	14	0
Gramercy	6,798	32	1	0	1	30	144	17	118	9	0
Gretna	15,821	194	5	9	42	138	704	144	463	97	0
Hammond	19,825	431	0	15	73	343	2,488	1,000	1,319	169	0
Harahan	8,976	16	1	1	2	12	138	26	105	7	5
Houma	32,592	286	0	11	80	195	1,458	302	1,082	74	16
Iowa	2,599	10	0	0	3	7	119	25	86	8	1
Jennings	10,496	60	3	5	6	46	322	78	230	14	6
Kenner	64,597	376	7	20	129	220	2,623	528	1,848	247	26
Kentwood	2,259	0	0	0	0	0	180	45	134	1	0
Lafayette	113,770	1,276	10	73	307	886	6,766	1,421	4,839	506	34
Lake Providence	4,232	44	1	0	2	41	31	9	22	0	0
Mamou	3,438	43	0	3	2	38	128	19	103	6	2
Mandeville	12,047	32	0	1	3	28	347	52	283	12	1
Mansfield	5,395	61	0	1	1	59	224	40	177	7	0
Many	2,741	6	0	0	0	6	34	7	25	2	0
Marksville	5,676	64	1	0	4	59	413	105	296	12	
Minden	13,019	23	0	2	6	15	208	50	148	10	0
Monroe	50,988	493	11	21	141	320	4,360	1,219	3,010	131	0
Moreauville	927	4	0	0	0	4	12	3	9	0	0
Morgan City	11,626	79	1	7	17	54	523	87	418	18	0
New Orleans	281,440	2,869	179	65	1,085	1,540	14,880	4,591	7,081	3,208	
Olla	1,345	2	1	0	0	1	35	8	25	2	0
Pearl River	2,220	21	0	2	2	17	113	25	82	6	0
Pineville	14,725	42	0	4	7	31	827	217	569	41	0
Plaquemine	6,688	75	2	1	2	70	376	47	315	14	0
Pollock	381	6	0	0	1	5	11	5	6	0	0
Ponchatoula	6,482	95	0	3	14	78	531	177	325	29	0
Port Allen	5,034	23	0	2	3	18	184	50	121	13	0
Ruston	21,056	158	1	14	36	107	1,135	289	806	40	1
Shreveport	199,434	1,897	27	105	474	1,291	10,553	2,512	7,182	859	94
Slidell	27,379	129	0	11	23	95	1,799	230	1,492	77	0
Sterlington	1,341	5	0	1	0	4	23	8	15	0	0
Stonewall	1,913	2	0	0	0	2	12	5	6	1	3

[1] The FBI does not publish arson data unless it receives data from either the agency or the state for all 12 months of the calendar year.

Table 8. Offenses Known to Law Enforcement, by State and City, 2008—*Continued*

(Number.)

State/City	Population	Violent crime	Murder and non-negligent man-slaughter	Forcible rape	Robbery	Aggravated assault	Property crime	Burglary	Larceny-theft	Motor vehicle theft	Arson[1]
LOUISIANA—*Continued*											
Tallulah	7,539	66	0	4	8	54	262	105	152	5	3
Thibodaux	14,126	98	2	3	19	74	595	107	476	12	0
Tickfaw	694	0	0	0	0	0	30	2	24	4	0
Vinton	3,140	12	1	1	1	9	107	20	86	1	0
Westlake	4,565	15	0	1	4	10	141	32	94	15	0
West Monroe	12,916	79	0	2	7	70	1,057	196	816	45	2
Westwego	9,711	36	0	0	3	33	237	60	161	16	0
Zachary	14,445	48	0	0	7	41	198	19	162	17	0
MAINE											
Ashland	1,446	1	0	0	0	1	11	10	1	0	0
Auburn	23,205	44	1	8	14	21	743	120	595	28	4
Augusta	18,344	59	3	9	4	43	1,202	183	979	40	13
Baileyville	1,560	2	0	0	0	2	81	23	58	0	0
Bangor	31,902	51	1	4	21	25	2,018	255	1,715	48	7
Bar Harbor	5,166	0	0	0	0	0	48	17	28	3	0
Bath	8,925	7	0	3	1	3	306	28	271	7	1
Belfast	6,795	12	1	5	0	6	219	51	162	6	0
Berwick	7,654	2	0	2	0	0	150	32	105	13	0
Bethel	2,669	3	0	1	1	1	92	16	73	3	0
Biddeford	21,663	66	0	20	28	18	1,050	180	847	23	5
Boothbay Harbor	2,272	3	0	0	0	3	60	9	48	3	1
Brewer	9,091	8	0	1	5	2	344	23	316	5	0
Bridgton	5,460	9	0	5	0	4	98	18	77	3	0
Brownville	1,296	2	0	0	0	2	56	12	44	0	0
Brunswick	21,885	20	0	9	3	8	444	73	361	10	1
Bucksport	4,913	10	0	1	0	9	90	17	71	2	2
Buxton	8,179	2	0	0	0	2	67	15	51	1	2
Calais	3,188	43	0	1	0	42	167	17	150	0	0
Camden	5,232	4	0	1	0	3	123	20	100	3	0
Cape Elizabeth	8,802	0	0	0	0	0	73	14	57	2	1
Caribou	8,135	4	0	0	3	1	211	44	160	7	1
Carrabassett Valley	478	1	0	1	0	0	98	1	92	5	0
Clinton	3,338	5	0	3	1	1	73	23	49	1	0
Cumberland	7,770	1	0	1	0	0	32	9	20	3	0
Damariscotta	1,923	3	0	2	0	1	45	4	41	0	0
Dexter	3,697	10	0	0	1	9	141	30	104	7	0
Dixfield	2,541	1	0	1	0	0	46	7	36	3	0
Dover-Foxcroft	4,276	6	1	2	0	3	125	26	94	5	1
East Millinocket	3,181	0	0	0	0	0	19	3	16	0	0
Eastport	1,546	0	0	0	0	0	22	1	21	0	0
Eliot	6,371	3	0	1	0	2	58	20	37	1	0
Ellsworth	7,149	5	0	0	0	5	311	34	271	6	0
Fairfield	6,755	7	0	0	4	3	222	56	162	4	4
Falmouth	10,693	2	0	1	1	0	139	22	113	4	0
Farmington	7,576	9	0	6	0	3	246	23	219	4	1
Fort Fairfield	3,455	4	0	0	0	4	25	8	17	0	0
Fort Kent	4,187	1	0	0	0	1	33	10	20	3	0
Freeport	8,241	1	0	1	0	0	172	28	140	4	0
Fryeburg	3,358	6	0	2	1	3	46	11	33	2	0
Gardiner	6,115	6	0	3	0	3	158	37	117	4	0
Gorham	15,665	10	0	3	1	6	173	63	105	5	4
Gouldsboro	2,009	1	0	0	1	0	27	3	24	0	1
Greenville	1,730	1	0	0	1	0	53	9	42	2	0
Hallowell	2,451	2	0	0	2	0	111	14	94	3	0
Hampden	6,919	1	0	0	1	0	86	17	67	2	0
Holden	3,001	4	0	0	1	3	48	7	39	2	0
Houlton	6,133	8	0	1	1	6	130	17	109	4	1
Jay	4,795	0	0	0	0	0	71	17	50	4	2
Kennebunk	11,489	5	0	1	0	4	144	23	121	0	2
Kennebunkport	4,024	3	0	3	0	0	65	8	57	0	0
Kittery	10,307	4	0	3	1	0	146	19	119	8	0
Lewiston	35,183	94	1	22	34	37	1,065	204	830	31	13
Limestone	2,267	0	0	0	0	0	30	20	10	0	0
Lincoln	5,263	3	0	1	0	2	186	29	154	3	1
Lincolnville	2,195	2	0	0	0	2	20	5	11	4	0
Lisbon	9,360	2	0	1	0	1	112	11	92	9	0
Livermore Falls	3,140	7	0	2	0	5	95	28	66	1	2
Machias	2,133	4	0	1	0	3	59	13	45	1	1
Madawaska	4,342	0	0	0	0	0	59	3	54	2	0
Madison	4,601	8	0	2	1	5	129	25	100	4	0
Mechanic Falls	3,220	0	0	0	0	0	46	8	38	0	0
Mexico	2,872	3	0	3	0	0	119	26	89	4	2
Milbridge	1,313	0	0	0	0	0	17	0	17	0	0

[1] The FBI does not publish arson data unless it receives data from either the agency or the state for all 12 months of the calendar year.

Table 8. Offenses Known to Law Enforcement, by State and City, 2008—*Continued*

(Number.)

State/City	Population	Violent crime	Murder and non-negligent man-slaughter	Forcible rape	Robbery	Aggravated assault	Property crime	Burglary	Larceny-theft	Motor vehicle theft	Arson[1]
MAINE—*Continued*											
Millinocket	4,913	3	0	0	1	2	111	17	89	5	2
Milo	2,351	7	0	0	0	7	61	13	47	1	0
Monmouth	3,846	3	0	1	0	2	50	8	41	1	0
Mount Desert	2,181	3	0	2	0	1	39	2	36	1	0
Newport	3,120	4	0	3	0	1	108	11	95	2	0
North Berwick	4,888	0	0	0	0	0	33	16	17	0	0
Norway	4,784	8	0	4	1	3	99	29	67	3	0
Oakland	6,204	4	0	3	0	1	121	29	89	3	0
Ogunquit	1,273	2	0	0	0	2	53	3	50	0	0
Old Orchard Beach	9,400	36	4	10	4	18	215	39	165	11	1
Old Town	7,723	5	0	0	2	3	159	25	132	2	2
Orono	9,751	6	0	0	3	3	210	33	175	2	2
Oxford	3,917	7	0	4	0	3	135	14	117	4	0
Paris	4,990	3	0	2	1	0	79	15	62	2	1
Phippsburg	2,170	0	0	0	0	0	14	1	13	0	0
Pittsfield	4,246	3	0	0	1	2	79	8	67	4	3
Portland	62,656	254	4	42	107	101	2,769	483	2,157	129	34
Presque Isle	9,056	12	0	3	1	8	356	50	300	6	1
Rangeley	1,181	2	0	0	0	2	31	8	22	1	0
Richmond	3,421	2	0	0	1	1	15	2	13	0	0
Rockland	7,464	2	1	0	0	1	465	37	421	7	1
Rockport	3,551	1	0	0	0	1	41	3	38	0	0
Rumford	6,336	19	0	8	2	9	206	43	159	4	1
Sabattus	4,645	2	0	1	0	1	56	15	36	5	0
Saco	18,323	14	0	7	2	5	504	88	395	21	6
Sanford	21,294	41	0	16	7	18	723	123	577	23	6
Scarborough	19,228	13	0	1	8	4	348	61	278	9	1
Searsport	2,605	0	0	0	0	0	40	17	23	0	0
Skowhegan	8,751	16	1	7	2	6	388	50	327	11	4
South Berwick	7,253	4	0	2	1	1	71	15	55	1	0
South Portland	23,796	54	0	4	19	31	1,116	125	969	22	0
Southwest Harbor	1,953	0	0	0	0	0	94	17	77	0	0
Swan's Island	303	0	0	0	0	0	0	0	0	0	0
Thomaston	3,666	1	0	0	0	1	81	13	62	6	0
Topsham	9,972	2	0	1	1	0	191	24	158	9	0
Van Buren	2,482	0	0	0	0	0	9	0	8	1	0
Veazie	1,862	1	0	1	0	0	28	6	21	1	0
Waldoboro	5,049	2	0	1	0	1	103	26	74	3	0
Washburn	1,586	0	0	0	0	0	30	5	25	0	0
Waterville	15,964	32	0	12	8	12	730	95	625	10	1
Wells	10,012	5	0	3	0	2	244	46	187	11	2
Westbrook	16,310	40	0	8	8	24	715	91	599	25	3
Wilton	4,188	24	1	8	1	14	127	24	100	3	0
Windham	16,838	7	0	3	2	2	340	72	255	13	3
Winslow	7,895	5	0	4	0	1	203	30	168	5	0
Winter Harbor	959	1	0	0	0	1	4	1	3	0	0
Winthrop	6,467	6	0	1	1	4	78	21	53	4	0
Wiscasset	3,815	1	0	1	0	0	47	12	34	1	0
Yarmouth	8,095	1	0	1	0	0	87	12	71	4	3
York	13,840	5	1	3	0	1	213	27	177	9	2
MARYLAND											
Aberdeen	13,995	99	0	4	31	64	624	86	501	37	16
Annapolis	36,683	320	8	8	130	174	1,585	293	1,153	139	10
Baltimore	634,549	10,080	234	137	4,026	5,683	30,570	7,832	17,230	5,508	430
Baltimore City Sheriff	0	0	0	0	0	0	0	0	0	0	0
Bel Air	9,892	72	0	2	27	43	533	45	465	23	12
Berlin	4,023	18	1	0	4	13	143	25	117	1	1
Berwyn Heights	2,975	12	0	0	5	7	80	12	61	7	0
Bladensburg	7,677	102	2	1	64	35	584	106	312	166	0
Boonsboro	3,448	0	0	0	0	0	32	7	24	1	0
Bowie	53,311	103	0	2	64	37	988	258	611	119	4
Brunswick	5,270	5	0	0	1	4	131	19	111	1	1
Cambridge	11,901	133	1	6	40	86	729	214	491	24	9
Capitol Heights	4,156	8	1	1	2	4	42	7	17	18	0
Centreville	3,546	1	0	0	0	1	52	6	46	0	0
Chestertown	4,916	74	1	3	14	56	161	48	103	10	1
Cheverly	6,466	41	0	1	25	15	221	55	123	43	0
Chevy Chase Village	2,761	1	0	1	0	0	61	7	50	4	2
Colmar Manor	1,275	6	0	0	4	2	22	0	18	4	0
Cottage City	1,139	4	0	0	2	2	68	9	41	18	0
Crisfield	2,800	17	0	2	3	12	92	13	79	0	0
Cumberland	20,558	170	1	13	27	129	1,217	298	899	20	10
Delmar	3,407	26	0	1	2	23	102	24	66	12	0

[1] The FBI does not publish arson data unless it receives data from either the agency or the state for all 12 months of the calendar year.

Table 8. Offenses Known to Law Enforcement, by State and City, 2008—*Continued*

(Number.)

State/City	Population	Violent crime	Murder and non-negligent man-slaughter	Forcible rape	Robbery	Aggravated assault	Property crime	Burglary	Larceny-theft	Motor vehicle theft	Arson[1]
MARYLAND—*Continued*											
Denton	3,951	22	0	0	10	12	258	46	204	8	0
District Heights	6,122	31	2	1	16	12	194	47	108	39	0
Easton	14,730	107	1	8	24	74	552	105	434	13	0
Edmonston	1,349	8	1	0	4	3	79	16	51	12	0
Elkton	15,228	287	1	7	71	208	1,181	279	804	98	16
Fairmount Heights	1,517	1	0	0	0	1	20	7	4	9	0
Federalsburg	2,611	22	0	2	4	16	142	33	97	12	1
Forest Heights	2,591	6	0	0	2	4	38	22	8	8	0
Frederick	60,034	471	2	12	126	331	1,849	379	1,326	144	19
Frostburg	7,758	13	0	1	0	12	211	37	169	5	2
Fruitland	4,412	63	0	0	11	52	291	38	240	13	2
Glenarden	6,399	10	0	0	4	6	81	18	44	19	0
Greenbelt	21,582	215	2	10	152	51	1,262	122	870	270	0
Greensboro	2,013	9	0	0	1	8	82	22	57	3	0
Hagerstown	40,002	206	3	1	83	119	1,482	294	1,058	130	32
Hampstead	5,506	7	0	1	2	4	128	14	110	4	0
Hancock	1,741	13	0	0	1	12	42	7	34	1	0
Havre de Grace	13,055	64	2	3	15	44	458	78	367	13	2
Hurlock	1,989	8	0	0	2	6	74	29	35	10	1
Hyattsville	15,591	171	4	1	125	41	1,670	203	1,321	146	0
Landover Hills	1,537	5	0	0	1	4	22	4	11	7	0
La Plata	9,101	42	0	0	14	28	237	28	195	14	2
Laurel	21,676	158	2	6	68	82	1,144	158	771	215	2
Lonaconing	1,130	0	0	0	0	0	2	0	2	0	0
Luke	73	0	0	0	0	0	0	0	0	0	0
Manchester	3,572	5	0	0	0	5	41	13	25	3	0
Morningside	1,325	13	0	0	6	7	48	3	33	12	0
Mount Rainier	8,442	102	1	1	81	19	400	79	201	120	3
New Carrollton	12,640	64	0	3	36	25	359	117	186	56	0
North Brentwood	471	1	0	0	1	0	18	5	9	4	0
North East	2,840	7	0	0	1	6	176	38	126	12	1
Oakland	1,843	0	0	0	0	0	59	5	51	3	1
Ocean City	7,090	88	0	3	37	48	1,452	236	1,181	35	7
Ocean Pines	11,164	3	0	0	0	3	119	24	89	6	0
Oxford	716	0	0	0	0	0	0	0	0	0	0
Perryville	3,817	12	1	0	7	4	165	28	135	2	3
Pocomoke City	3,869	31	0	3	9	19	239	31	200	8	2
Port Deposit	703	3	1	0	0	2	23	4	17	2	0
Preston	686	2	0	0	0	2	9	2	4	3	0
Princess Anne	3,003	37	1	0	9	27	190	61	120	9	1
Ridgely	1,535	6	0	0	2	4	57	20	35	2	1
Rising Sun	1,817	3	0	0	1	2	78	12	59	7	3
Riverdale Park	6,513	93	2	3	62	26	322	75	188	59	0
Rock Hall	1,425	2	0	0	0	2	30	8	21	1	0
Salisbury	28,455	661	4	18	155	484	2,244	534	1,618	92	23
Seat Pleasant	4,899	63	0	0	26	37	206	39	118	49	0
Smithsburg	3,009	8	0	0	0	8	23	8	13	2	0
Snow Hill	2,315	13	0	0	0	13	57	6	51	0	1
St. Michaels	1,079	8	0	0	1	7	64	12	50	2	0
Sykesville	4,444	5	0	0	3	2	74	19	52	3	7
Takoma Park	17,493	120	0	4	79	37	617	135	383	99	3
Taneytown	5,461	7	0	0	1	6	119	16	102	1	2
Thurmont	6,085	10	0	0	1	9	98	15	80	3	1
Trappe	1,151	0	0	0	0	0	14	1	7	6	0
University Park	2,316	4	0	0	3	1	62	10	47	5	0
Upper Marlboro	667	1	0	0	0	1	28	3	21	4	0
Westernport	1,950	2	0	0	0	2	44	13	29	2	0
Westminster	17,829	109	0	0	8	101	673	96	558	19	13
MASSACHUSETTS											
Abington	16,590	56	1	10	5	40	360	119	213	28	0
Acton	20,795	21	0	5	2	14	273	46	223	4	0
Acushnet	10,474	24	0	2	1	21	173	70	91	12	3
Adams	8,145	39	0	6	0	33	251	83	161	7	2
Agawam	28,353	43	0	6	7	30	325	80	206	39	5
Amesbury	16,421	46	0	6	3	37	291	40	241	10	3
Amherst	36,106	86	0	13	9	64	470	211	235	24	2
Andover	33,442	10	0	0	2	8	441	61	360	20	1
Aquinnah	355	0	0	0	0	0	7	0	7	0	0
Arlington	40,989	55	0	3	14	38	661	185	441	35	16
Ashburnham	6,009	6	0	0	1	5	45	18	25	2	4
Ashfield	1,817	3	0	0	0	3	16	5	11	0	
Ashland	15,927	20	0	3	1	16	163	56	98	9	0
Athol	11,637	47	0	7	3	37	291	109	172	10	2

[1] The FBI does not publish arson data unless it receives data from either the agency or the state for all 12 months of the calendar year.

Table 8. Offenses Known to Law Enforcement, by State and City, 2008—*Continued*

(Number.)

State/City	Population	Violent crime	Murder and non-negligent man-slaughter	Forcible rape	Robbery	Aggravated assault	Property crime	Burglary	Larceny-theft	Motor vehicle theft	Arson[1]
MASSACHUSETTS—*Continued*											
Attleboro	43,228	143	0	8	31	104	956	223	662	71	9
Auburn[7]	16,298		0	4	13		503	83	393	27	8
Avon	4,285	6	0	0	2	4	195	23	161	11	
Ayer	7,378	24	0	3	5	16	148	50	88	10	3
Barnstable	47,828	372	1	39	41	291	1,638	450	1,105	83	14
Barre	5,455	20	0	2	2	16	72	21	47	4	
Becket	1,803	2	0	0	0	2	50	26	24	0	
Bedford	13,215	4	0	2	0	2	185	29	153	3	0
Belchertown	14,094	19	0	1	0	18	164	36	111	17	2
Belmont	23,252	38	0	5	8	25	263	96	152	15	1
Berkley	6,519	7	0	0	1	6	75	39	33	3	0
Berlin	2,740	0	0	0	0	0	18	1	16	1	0
Bernardston	2,234	3	0	0	0	3	24	7	14	3	0
Beverly	39,435	122	0	10	20	92	695	107	548	40	0
Blackstone	9,058	20	0	1	1	18	145	37	93	15	1
Bolton	4,522	2	0	0	0	2	61	29	31	1	2
Boston	604,465	6,676	62	237	2,398	3,979	22,429	3,493	16,531	2,405	
Bourne	19,048	63	0	5	10	48	580	258	313	9	3
Boxborough	5,124	11	0	2	2	7	52	14	34	4	1
Boxford	8,088	0	0	0	0	0	65	9	54	2	0
Boylston	4,298	2	0	0	0	2	32	10	21	1	0
Braintree	34,495	45	0	5	6	34	912	76	806	30	1
Brewster	10,009	16	0	0	0	16	129	35	87	7	2
Bridgewater	25,546	51	0	4	5	42	236	59	166	11	2
Brookline[7]	54,527		0	3	30		861	156	683	22	2
Buckland	1,990	7	0	1	0	6	17	4	13	0	0
Burlington	25,319	23	0	1	5	17	688	191	470	27	1
Cambridge	101,362	414	2	14	155	243	3,138	396	2,500	242	10
Canton	22,054	54	0	3	3	48	301	66	218	17	3
Carlisle	4,900	2	0	1	0	1	15	10	5	0	0
Carver	11,592	20	0	1	3	16	100	30	62	8	3
Charlemont	1,368	0	0	0	0	0	10	3	7	0	0
Charlton	12,740	15	0	1	2	12	131	40	74	17	2
Chatham	6,735	5	0	0	0	5	191	44	146	1	0
Chelmsford	34,187	45	0	2	8	35	651	68	557	26	1
Chelsea	38,621	669	2	25	212	430	1,635	407	979	249	1
Cheshire	3,287	0	0	0	0	0	12	8	4	0	
Chicopee	53,777	323	2	25	57	239	1,678	470	1,059	149	5
Chilmark	978	1	0	0	0	1	16	5	11	0	0
Clinton	14,101	4	0	0	0	4	122	23	92	7	0
Cohasset	7,171	7	0	1	1	5	128	62	64	2	0
Concord	17,543	13	0	0	2	11	273	88	182	3	2
Dalton	6,546	21	0	4	1	16	84	24	59	1	6
Danvers	26,958	52	0	2	9	41	945	65	845	35	1
Dartmouth	34,446	74	0	5	11	58	1,069	157	869	43	7
Dedham	24,217	37	0	3	20	14	593	74	492	27	1
Dennis	15,406	79	0	5	7	67	518	166	333	19	4
Dighton	6,819	13	0	0	0	13	27	10	15	2	
Douglas	8,033	12	0	3	0	9	34	12	15	7	0
Dover	5,634	4	0	0	0	4	21	4	16	1	0
Dracut	29,608	32	0	2	11	19	280	45	235	0	1
Dudley	11,181	23	0	3	2	18	52	32	17	3	1
East Bridgewater	13,988	23	0	4	2	17	206	42	148	16	1
East Brookfield	2,065	6	0	0	1	5	49	7	39	3	1
Eastham	5,440	0	0	0	0	0	80	26	54	0	0
Easthampton	16,072	43	0	1	2	40	179	63	109	7	6
East Longmeadow	15,363	23	0	1	2	20	369	64	290	15	2
Easton	23,047	15	0	0	4	11	211	44	159	8	0
Edgartown	3,935	8	0	0	0	8	103	25	69	9	0
Egremont	1,351	2	0	0	0	2	22	5	17	0	0
Erving	1,546	6	0	1	0	5	38	14	22	2	0
Everett	37,172	188	2	15	50	121	1,352	325	874	153	1
Fairhaven	16,115	51	1	0	10	40	558	146	389	23	2
Fall River	90,760	1,088	3	65	240	780	3,528	842	2,337	349	37
Falmouth	33,302	125	1	15	9	100	1,110	552	520	38	16
Fitchburg[7]	40,377		4	24	62		1,182	316	761	105	12
Framingham	64,519	196	1	11	40	144	1,600	268	1,166	166	
Franklin	31,608	3	0	0	2	1	96	15	78	3	1
Freetown	8,990	17	0	0	1	16	163	58	90	15	3
Gardner	20,587	88	0	11	8	69	557	190	331	36	3
Georgetown	8,241	2	0	0	0	2	41	5	35	1	
Gill	1,381	1	0	0	0	1	16	5	11	0	0
Gloucester	30,303	26	0	10	1	15	624	103	504	17	1

[1] The FBI does not publish arson data unless it receives data from either the agency or the state for all 12 months of the calendar year.

[7] The data collection methodology for the offense of aggravated assault used by this agency does not comply with national UCR Program guidelines. Consequently, the figures for aggravated assault and violent crime (of which aggravated assault is a part) are not included in this table.

Table 8. Offenses Known to Law Enforcement, by State and City, 2008—*Continued*

(Number.)

State/City	Population	Violent crime	Murder and non-negligent man-slaughter	Forcible rape	Robbery	Aggravated assault	Property crime	Burglary	Larceny-theft	Motor vehicle theft	Arson[1]
MASSACHUSETTS—*Continued*											
Goshen	960	1	0	0	0	1	2	2	0	0	0
Grafton	17,872	7	0	0	0	7	136	58	61	17	1
Granby	6,303	7	0	1	0	6	102	12	83	7	0
Granville	1,695	2	0	0	0	2	25	9	16	0	
Great Barrington	7,353	13	0	2	2	9	126	37	85	4	1
Greenfield	17,651	121	0	18	6	97	563	258	278	27	3
Groton	10,776	2	0	1	0	1	39	12	27	0	1
Groveland	7,041	3	0	0	0	3	48	8	39	1	0
Hadley	4,786	16	0	1	4	11	186	30	149	7	1
Halifax	7,722	20	0	3	0	17	70	16	48	6	0
Hamilton	8,170	0	0	0	0	0	61	11	49	1	0
Hampden	5,321	9	0	3	1	5	45	13	31	1	0
Hanover	14,064	4	0	0	1	3	368	42	321	5	0
Hanson[7]	10,010		1	2	2		166	45	109	12	4
Hardwick	2,653	10	0	0	0	10	25	4	19	2	1
Harvard	6,001	2	0	0	0	2	49	19	29	1	1
Harwich	12,381	32	0	2	2	28	273	114	153	6	3
Hatfield	3,259	2	0	0	0	2	4	1	3	0	
Haverhill	60,001	403	1	11	60	331	1,476	677	667	132	5
Hingham	22,724	7	0	0	3	4	358	74	279	5	0
Hinsdale	1,945	6	0	0	0	6	5	4	1	0	
Holden	16,695	10	0	0	1	9	91	19	68	4	1
Holliston	13,953	9	0	0	1	8	69	14	52	3	0
Holyoke	39,722	451	2	44	65	340	2,347	461	1,650	236	20
Hopedale	6,195	8	1	1	0	6	47	15	28	4	1
Hopkinton	14,419	2	0	0	0	2	84	3	78	3	0
Hubbardston	4,531	8	0	0	0	8	36	7	22	7	1
Hudson	19,766	2	0	1	0	1	172	22	137	13	0
Hull	11,064	42	0	0	3	39	150	51	88	11	1
Kingston	12,405	43	0	3	4	36	387	39	332	16	4
Lakeville	10,678	4	0	0	0	4	184	95	78	11	1
Lancaster	7,130	9	0	1	1	7	50	8	35	7	1
Lawrence	69,812	456	4	14	104	334	1,979	615	1,023	341	
Lee	5,782	8	0	0	0	8	53	4	38	11	0
Leicester	11,042	24	0	2	2	20	170	34	122	14	3
Lenox	5,106	9	0	2	0	7	91	21	68	2	1
Leominster	41,095	224	1	8	19	196	1,246	220	964	62	8
Leverett	1,753	0	0	0	0	0	7	4	3	0	0
Lexington	30,321	23	0	0	2	21	325	55	262	8	0
Lincoln	7,984	0	0	0	0	0	61	17	42	2	0
Littleton	8,776	15	0	4	0	11	93	24	65	4	1
Longmeadow	15,275	6	0	0	0	6	297	60	226	11	1
Lowell[4]	110,136	1,167	6	42	225	894	3,750	1,073	2,227	450	33
Ludlow	22,530	15	0	2	5	8	306	84	206	16	3
Lunenburg	10,012	24	0	1	2	21	174	37	124	13	0
Lynn	90,042	816	6	36	182	592	3,014	1,133	1,408	473	8
Lynnfield	11,360	12	0	2	3	7	152	29	114	9	1
Manchester-by-the-Sea	5,268	0	0	0	0	0	12	2	9	1	0
Marblehead	19,994	35	0	2	2	31	196	31	157	8	2
Marion	5,226	10	0	0	1	9	116	35	74	7	0
Marlborough	38,253	147	0	11	15	121	732	108	572	52	3
Marshfield	24,600	47	0	6	11	30	306	64	215	27	0
Mashpee	14,417	46	0	2	6	38	354	116	226	12	4
Mattapoisett	6,468	5	0	0	0	5	100	6	91	3	0
Maynard	10,144	13	0	0	1	12	16	2	13	1	0
Medfield	12,261	7	1	0	0	6	68	12	55	1	2
Medford	55,555	89	0	2	44	43	1,466	205	1,166	95	
Medway	12,782	3	0	1	0	2	113	25	86	2	0
Melrose	26,737	30	0	1	9	20	336	75	235	26	2
Mendon	5,823	8	0	1	0	7	43	12	29	2	1
Merrimac	6,459	2	0	1	0	1	32	17	12	3	2
Methuen	43,987	129	1	4	14	110	1,035	221	696	118	1
Middleboro	21,402	92	0	7	12	73	509	129	335	45	1
Millbury	13,551	35	0	0	1	34	282	74	194	14	2
Millis	7,928	1	0	0	0	1	51	13	36	2	0
Millville	2,857	5	0	0	0	5	35	8	26	1	0
Milton	26,298	16	2	0	6	8	280	67	207	6	
Monson	8,841	28	0	4	0	24	133	38	90	5	0
Montague	8,318	49	0	7	2	40	186	59	116	11	6
Monterey	963	0	0	0	0	0	0	0	0	0	0
Nahant	3,505	9	0	1	0	8	30	5	22	3	0
Natick	31,943	60	0	3	4	53	817	65	727	25	0
Needham	28,231	5	0	1	3	1	237	41	191	5	0

[1] The FBI does not publish arson data unless it receives data from either the agency or the state for all 12 months of the calendar year.
[7] The data collection methodology for the offense of aggravated assault used by this agency does not comply with national UCR Program guidelines. Consequently, the figures for aggravated assault and violent crime (of which aggravated assault is a part) are not included in this table.

Table 8. Offenses Known to Law Enforcement, by State and City, 2008—*Continued*

(Number.)

State/City	Population	Violent crime	Murder and non-negligent man-slaughter	Forcible rape	Robbery	Aggravated assault	Property crime	Burglary	Larceny-theft	Motor vehicle theft	Arson[1]
MASSACHUSETTS—*Continued*											
New Bedford	91,473	1,191	4	59	301	827	3,353	1,056	1,978	319	43
Newbury	6,950	3	0	2	0	1	49	15	30	4	1
Newburyport	17,133	19	0	1	1	17	249	31	202	16	0
New Salem	998	0	0	0	0	0	1	0	1	0	0
Newton	83,191	117	0	8	19	90	1,111	186	896	29	4
Norfolk	10,666	11	1	1	0	9	87	45	41	1	0
North Adams	13,781	85	1	4	5	75	634	251	355	28	4
Northampton	28,341	97	0	9	12	76	813	143	624	46	3
North Andover	27,775	13	2	0	3	8	222	26	186	10	1
North Attleboro	27,994	30	0	2	7	21	635	94	519	22	2
Northborough	14,683	8	0	0	1	7	101	16	80	5	1
Northbridge	14,526	33	0	2	0	31	237	69	161	7	3
North Brookfield[7]	4,834		0	2	0		38	9	23	6	0
Northfield	2,990	11	0	1	0	10	70	24	43	3	
North Reading	14,040	11	0	1	0	10	122	29	91	2	2
Norton	19,366	12	0	5	0	7	104	35	68	1	0
Norwell	10,329	10	0	2	1	7	107	18	85	4	0
Norwood	28,119	35	1	4	11	19	594	93	460	41	3
Oak Bluffs	3,731	6	0	0	0	6	110	12	97	1	0
Orange	7,831	24	0	2	2	20	194	93	95	6	0
Orleans	6,309	7	0	1	0	6	196	45	147	4	2
Oxford	13,671	44	0	1	4	39	169	47	102	20	3
Palmer	12,891	37	0	1	1	35	182	67	105	10	3
Paxton	4,546	3	0	0	1	2	27	10	17	0	0
Peabody	51,846	144	1	9	22	112	1,318	171	1,024	123	6
Pembroke	18,806	41	0	6	3	32	252	57	172	23	0
Pepperell	11,438	27	0	1	2	24	172	32	133	7	0
Pittsfield	42,597	298	0	53	16	229	1,105	374	672	59	6
Plainville	8,388	9	0	0	1	8	118	24	87	7	2
Plymouth	55,608	87	0	4	14	69	995	195	769	31	4
Princeton	3,510	0	0	0	0	0	32	19	13	0	0
Provincetown	3,383	17	0	2	0	15	189	10	177	2	0
Quincy	95,061	347	2	15	105	225	1,872	598	1,139	135	8
Randolph	30,068	150	0	7	22	121	756	138	547	71	1
Raynham	13,893	21	0	9	6	6	455	84	337	34	1
Reading	23,055	13	0	0	3	10	265	44	214	7	0
Rehoboth	11,649	10	0	1	0	9	163	41	105	17	1
Revere	56,445	237	2	15	51	169	1,594	291	1,063	240	2
Rochester	5,301	11	0	1	0	10	77	26	48	3	1
Rockland	17,789	19	0	3	3	13	302	44	241	17	
Rockport	7,615	10	0	4	0	6	23	6	15	2	1
Rowley	5,881	5	0	1	1	3	29	8	14	7	2
Royalston	1,396	2	0	0	0	2	12	6	6	0	0
Rutland	8,049	16	0	0	2	14	47	18	25	4	0
Salem	41,531	86	0	10	15	61	846	175	584	87	
Salisbury	8,609	46	0	6	1	39	191	79	95	17	1
Sandwich	20,258	26	0	1	3	22	351	90	253	8	4
Saugus	27,327	101	0	5	23	73	1,115	206	831	78	1
Savoy	722	1	0	0	0	1	3	2	1	0	0
Scituate	17,879	19	0	2	1	16	196	46	140	10	2
Seekonk	13,610	36	0	2	5	29	512	63	426	23	2
Sharon	16,984	5	0	0	0	5	114	34	80	0	1
Shelburne	2,034	0	0	0	0	0	15	1	14	0	0
Sherborn	4,218	0	0	0	0	0	22	11	11	0	0
Shirley	7,738	7	0	1	0	6	58	14	42	2	0
Shrewsbury	33,706	7	0	0	1	6	439	106	314	19	0
Somerset	18,265	49	0	3	8	38	307	38	260	9	0
Somerville	74,012	304	2	20	112	170	2,313	450	1,614	249	7
Southampton[7]	6,036		0	1	0		53	12	36	5	1
Southborough	9,569	0	0	0	0	0	55	14	36	5	0
Southbridge	16,886	80	0	4	10	66	401	172	199	30	5
South Hadley	16,921	33	0	3	7	23	257	66	185	6	2
Southwick	9,507	11	0	0	0	11	132	42	76	14	0
Springfield	151,249	1,898	14	117	567	1,200	7,336	2,002	4,432	902	61
Stockbridge	2,227	2	0	2	0	0	121	49	69	3	0
Stoughton	26,924	88	0	8	22	58	500	197	276	27	0
Stow	6,378	4	0	0	0	4	46	15	28	3	1
Sturbridge	9,266	20	0	6	0	14	163	33	122	8	1
Sudbury	17,190	4	0	2	0	2	112	21	90	1	0
Sunderland	3,714	14	0	0	1	13	43	21	19	3	0
Sutton	9,107	11	0	1	0	10	82	26	47	9	0

[1] The FBI does not publish arson data unless it receives data from either the agency or the state for all 12 months of the calendar year.

[7] The data collection methodology for the offense of aggravated assault used by this agency does not comply with national UCR Program guidelines. Consequently, the figures for aggravated assault and violent crime (of which aggravated assault is a part) are not included in this table.

Table 8. Offenses Known to Law Enforcement, by State and City, 2008—*Continued*

(Number.)

State/City	Population	Violent crime	Murder and non-negligent man-slaughter	Forcible rape	Robbery	Aggravated assault	Property crime	Burglary	Larceny-theft	Motor vehicle theft	Arson[1]
MASSACHUSETTS—*Continued*											
Swampscott	13,940	14	0	2	2	10	245	38	202	5	0
Swansea	16,274	49	0	3	3	43	306	48	231	27	3
Taunton	55,745	305	6	10	51	238	1,267	543	626	98	12
Templeton	7,911	14	1	3	1	9	100	44	49	7	1
Tewksbury	29,692	59	0	15	5	39	501	109	356	36	0
Tisbury	3,809	7	1	0	1	5	121	22	84	15	0
Topsfield	6,056	1	0	0	0	1	67	9	55	3	0
Townsend	9,394	5	0	1	0	4	149	96	48	5	0
Truro	2,139	2	0	1	0	1	23	6	16	1	0
Tyngsboro	11,955	13	0	3	4	6	195	49	126	20	1
Upton	6,629	5	1	0	0	4	53	12	30	11	0
Uxbridge	12,820	20	0	2	0	18	142	58	76	8	3
Wales	1,857	1	0	0	0	1	3	0	3	0	0
Walpole	23,113	25	0	3	6	16	356	59	285	12	3
Waltham	60,459	89	0	9	15	65	848	108	696	44	1
Ware	9,961	43	0	3	5	35	186	29	146	11	2
Warren	5,108	25	0	0	0	25	59	30	19	10	0
Watertown	32,462	52	0	3	6	43	563	101	433	29	1
Wellesley	26,975	14	0	2	4	8	215	51	155	9	0
Wellfleet	2,746	10	0	0	0	10	66	24	40	2	1
Wenham	4,608	7	0	1	2	4	30	3	25	2	0
Westborough	18,509	13	0	2	4	7	278	80	180	18	2
West Boylston	8,302	15	0	5	3	7	177	32	138	7	0
West Bridgewater	6,682	7	0	0	1	6	133	24	101	8	2
West Brookfield	3,827	8	0	0	1	7	55	15	37	3	0
Westfield	40,857	106	0	21	9	76	648	251	371	26	5
Westford	21,913	5	0	0	1	4	133	29	95	9	0
Westhampton	1,601	1	0	0	0	1	5	1	3	1	0
Westminster	7,446	7	0	1	0	6	144	18	116	10	0
West Newbury	4,283	6	0	0	0	6	25	3	22	0	0
Westport	15,253	55	0	2	0	53	183	74	81	28	1
West Tisbury	2,646	0	0	0	0	0	15	2	11	2	0
Westwood	13,995	12	0	2	2	8	156	32	114	10	5
Weymouth	53,180	106	0	8	20	78	859	173	630	56	
Wilbraham	14,098	12	0	1	4	7	187	37	139	11	0
Williamsburg	2,442	3	0	1	0	2	48	34	14	0	0
Williamstown	8,071	13	0	3	0	10	146	21	121	4	2
Wilmington	21,712	46	1	0	1	44	395	94	289	12	4
Winchendon	10,192	50	0	3	3	44	242	44	181	17	2
Winchester	21,171	5	0	1	1	3	295	49	238	8	1
Winthrop	20,404	70	0	3	8	59	279	100	160	19	2
Woburn	37,005	74	0	3	10	61	888	96	719	73	2
Worcester	177,151	1,718	6	42	373	1,297	6,356	1,701	3,983	672	10
Wrentham	11,181	2	0	1	1	0	43	7	36	0	0
Yarmouth	23,903	166	0	7	17	142	949	240	675	34	7
MICHIGAN											
Adrian	21,241	96	2	31	13	50	776	149	601	26	3
Algonac	4,571	9	0	1	1	7	43	8	31	4	0
Allegan	4,849	63	0	7	0	56	61	7	52	2	1
Alma	9,144	10	0	6	0	4	112	44	66	2	1
Almont	2,785	11	0	1	0	10	89	14	72	3	0
Alpena	10,395	43	1	9	1	32	336	70	247	19	4
Ann Arbor	115,148	295	0	32	66	197	3,121	622	2,353	146	13
Armada	1,662	0	0	0	0	0	14	0	14	0	0
Auburn Hills	20,952	66	0	15	19	32	1,056	123	877	56	6
Bad Axe	3,076	1	0	0	1	0	147	10	136	1	6
Bangor	1,839	10	0	0	0	10	70	9	59	2	1
Bath Township	11,846	10	0	0	3	7	102	32	67	3	1
Battle Creek	61,405	702	4	62	118	518	3,449	1,056	2,245	148	16
Bay City	33,703	198	3	30	35	130	1,120	328	725	67	8
Beaverton	1,073	7	0	0	0	7	25	6	17	2	0
Belding	5,727	24	0	12	0	12	290	37	242	11	1
Belleville	3,593	9	0	0	3	6	104	7	95	2	0
Benton Harbor	10,677	120	0	9	20	91	250	84	140	26	5
Benton Township	15,136	146	0	17	34	95	1,379	238	1,072	69	8
Berkley	14,770	10	0	1	3	6	181	26	140	15	3
Berrien Springs-Oronoko Township	9,436	10	0	2	2	6	220	24	185	11	1
Beverly Hills	9,856	7	0	0	4	3	123	17	102	4	0
Big Rapids	10,565	22	0	5	3	14	392	57	325	10	5
Birch Run	1,648	4	0	0	1	3	109	9	97	3	0
Birmingham	19,010	21	0	1	7	13	415	70	326	19	15
Blissfield	3,202	1	0	0	0	1	49	5	43	1	0

[1] The FBI does not publish arson data unless it receives data from either the agency or the state for all 12 months of the calendar year.

Table 8. Offenses Known to Law Enforcement, by State and City, 2008—*Continued*

(Number.)

State/City	Population	Violent crime	Murder and non-negligent man-slaughter	Forcible rape	Robbery	Aggravated assault	Property crime	Burglary	Larceny-theft	Motor vehicle theft	Arson[1]
MICHIGAN—*Continued*											
Bloomfield Hills	3,770	2	0	1	1	0	44	10	30	4	1
Bloomfield Township	40,866	28	0	4	11	13	646	139	476	31	1
Bridgeport Township	10,855	56	1	6	11	38	329	105	208	16	3
Bridgman	2,396	1	0	0	0	1	60	6	52	2	0
Brighton	7,237	25	0	7	3	15	210	22	175	13	0
Brown City	1,265	0	0	0	0	0	23	0	20	3	0
Buchanan	4,343	21	0	8	2	11	203	20	178	5	0
Buena Vista Township	9,374	129	0	13	25	91	500	227	243	30	9
Burton	30,303	151	1	13	52	85	1,416	326	980	110	12
Cadillac	10,351	53	0	10	1	42	480	76	391	13	2
Calumet	792	0	0	0	0	0	28	4	20	4	0
Cambridge Township	5,928	0	0	0	0	0	4	0	4	0	0
Canton Township	84,506	120	0	14	27	79	1,546	256	1,167	123	11
Capac	2,179	4	0	1	0	3	61	17	41	3	0
Caro[4]	4,044	2	0	1	0	1	31	5	26	0	0
Carrollton Township	5,973	18	0	1	3	14	178	48	123	7	1
Caseville	842	1	0	0	0	1	36	5	29	2	0
Cassopolis	1,856	6	0	0	1	5	20	3	17	0	0
Cedar Springs	3,280	6	0	2	0	4	102	18	79	5	0
Center Line	8,127	24	0	0	8	16	218	47	128	43	0
Central Lake	974	0	0	0	0	0	11	1	10	0	0
Charlevoix	2,654	8	0	4	0	4	82	12	69	1	1
Charlotte	9,045	28	0	10	2	16	286	41	236	9	2
Chelsea	5,095	8	0	2	0	6	109	15	92	2	1
Chesaning	2,345	8	0	1	0	7	37	10	25	2	0
Chesterfield Township	45,492	183	1	8	15	159	1,270	204	974	92	15
Chikaming Township	3,643	1	0	0	0	1	62	11	49	2	0
Chocolay Township	6,017	0	0	0	0	0	47	3	44	0	2
Clare	3,125	9	0	2	0	7	165	20	143	2	1
Clarkston	913	1	0	0	0	1	7	1	6	0	0
Clawson	12,213	14	0	1	6	7	115	12	93	10	1
Clayton Township	7,830	4	0	1	0	3	73	27	45	1	0
Clay Township	9,564	8	0	4	2	2	169	39	109	21	0
Clinton	2,428	3	0	0	0	3	43	6	35	2	1
Clinton Township	96,315	328	2	31	71	224	2,494	599	1,582	313	25
Clio	2,534	13	0	3	5	5	85	15	66	4	4
Coldwater	10,640	36	1	12	5	18	451	43	390	18	4
Coleman	1,127	9	0	1	0	8	50	4	43	3	0
Coloma Township	6,533	4	0	1	0	3	190	62	125	3	1
Columbia Township	7,656	4	0	2	0	2	213	52	150	11	8
Corunna	3,314	7	0	2	2	3	93	16	71	6	0
Covert Township	3,064	23	0	5	0	18	80	26	46	8	0
Davison	5,176	3	0	1	1	1	118	13	101	4	0
Davison Township	18,745	28	0	4	2	22	264	73	174	17	3
Dearborn	87,482	385	0	25	155	205	4,350	614	2,905	831	24
Dearborn Heights	52,538	208	1	13	62	132	1,396	376	726	294	14
Decatur	1,835	15	0	3	1	11	173	25	144	4	2
Denton Township	5,499	6	0	2	0	4	109	20	86	3	1
Detroit	905,783	17,428	306	330	6,115	10,677	53,095	17,818	18,836	16,441	691
Dewitt	4,394	6	0	0	0	6	46	6	39	1	0
Dewitt Township	13,222	22	0	2	5	15	129	27	93	9	1
Douglas	2,166	4	0	2	0	2	82	12	65	5	1
Dryden Township	4,655	7	0	1	0	6	51	11	37	3	0
Durand	3,773	4	0	2	0	2	92	17	72	3	1
East Grand Rapids	10,406	3	0	1	0	2	161	42	116	3	0
East Jordan	2,236	3	0	1	0	2	75	2	73	0	0
East Lansing[4]	46,215	188	0	17	27	144	1,038	270	718	50	28
Eastpointe	32,464	212	0	17	58	137	1,137	213	538	386	14
East Tawas	2,738	9	0	1	1	7	133	14	117	2	0
Eaton Rapids	5,295	18	0	2	0	16	141	12	127	2	2
Eau Claire	618	0	0	0	0	0	14	2	12	0	0
Elk Rapids	1,688	2	0	2	0	0	60	10	49	1	0
Elkton	759	0	0	0	0	0	19	4	15	0	0
Erie Township	4,707	2	0	0	0	2	50	11	35	4	0
Escanaba	12,198	34	0	7	2	25	740	125	598	17	2
Essexville	3,478	7	0	0	2	5	98	20	76	2	2
Farmington	9,826	16	1	2	5	8	185	29	135	21	2
Farmington Hills	78,602	144	0	17	24	103	1,621	341	1,118	162	10
Fenton	11,938	18	0	6	1	11	280	48	215	17	1
Ferndale	21,056	88	1	4	34	49	739	156	442	141	2
Flat Rock	9,016	27	0	2	2	23	193	55	125	13	1
Flint	113,462	2,297	32	103	686	1,476	6,889	3,273	2,707	909	145
Flushing	7,879	7	0	3	1	3	109	20	79	10	0

[1] The FBI does not publish arson data unless it receives data from either the agency or the state for all 12 months of the calendar year.
[4] Because of changes in the state/local agency's reporting practices, figures are not comparable to previous years' data.

Table 8. Offenses Known to Law Enforcement, by State and City, 2008—*Continued*

(Number.)

State/City	Population	Violent crime	Murder and non-negligent man-slaughter	Forcible rape	Robbery	Aggravated assault	Property crime	Burglary	Larceny-theft	Motor vehicle theft	Arson[1]
MICHIGAN—*Continued*											
Flushing Township	10,240	8	0	4	0	4	120	27	83	10	1
Forsyth Township	4,880	12	0	2	1	9	35	5	26	4	2
Fowlerville	3,092	14	0	1	1	12	112	6	101	5	0
Frankenmuth	4,687	8	1	0	0	7	75	6	69	0	0
Frankfort	1,460	0	0	0	0	0	38	8	30	0	1
Franklin	2,935	2	0	0	2	0	38	5	33	0	0
Fraser	14,919	35	0	5	4	26	620	222	362	36	2
Fremont	4,216	8	0	4	0	4	182	19	162	1	2
Fruitport[4]	1,075	15	0	2	7	6	566	47	511	8	0
Garden City	27,036	103	1	9	28	65	715	174	461	80	3
Gaylord	3,658	13	0	5	1	7	216	33	180	3	2
Genesee Township	23,362	94	0	14	18	62	479	157	267	55	14
Gerrish Township	3,125	1	0	1	0	0	36	5	31	0	0
Gibraltar	5,028	17	0	3	0	14	91	5	73	13	2
Gladstone	5,109	5	0	2	0	3	79	11	67	1	0
Gladwin	2,923	21	0	1	0	20	133	19	114	0	0
Grand Blanc	7,595	25	0	5	5	15	170	35	123	12	2
Grand Haven	10,486	47	0	10	6	31	314	37	274	3	0
Grand Ledge	7,735	4	0	1	1	2	162	20	136	6	0
Grand Rapids	193,096	1,981	15	81	767	1,118	9,209	2,286	6,470	453	97
Grandville	16,828	35	0	1	5	29	891	108	760	23	1
Grayling	1,837	1	0	0	0	1	72	5	66	1	0
Green Oak Township	17,964	16	0	1	1	14	265	42	206	17	1
Greenville	8,183	21	0	7	2	12	457	62	388	7	2
Grosse Pointe	5,057	5	0	0	4	1	109	4	88	17	0
Grosse Pointe Farms	8,699	14	0	1	4	9	163	12	119	32	0
Grosse Pointe Park	11,099	17	0	0	7	10	305	32	204	69	0
Grosse Pointe Shores	2,532	0	0	0	0	0	5	0	5	0	0
Grosse Pointe Woods	15,313	19	0	0	0	19	285	34	219	32	1
Hamburg Township	21,893	12	0	2	1	9	196	39	149	8	0
Hampton Township	9,704	11	0	3	0	8	449	57	379	13	0
Hamtramck	20,722	372	1	7	146	218	1,369	446	480	443	15
Hancock	4,129	5	0	1	0	4	70	13	50	7	0
Harbor Beach	1,621	0	0	0	0	0	43	10	33	0	0
Harbor Springs	1,543	0	0	0	0	0	32	0	31	1	0
Harper Woods	12,708	147	0	7	74	66	1,339	134	923	282	4
Hart	1,923	3	0	0	1	2	127	25	100	2	0
Hastings	6,915	23	1	8	0	14	277	36	231	10	1
Hazel Park	18,016	63	0	5	20	38	701	153	338	210	6
Hillsdale	7,841	10	0	2	4	4	160	22	138	0	0
Holland	33,874	135	1	30	23	81	1,207	186	989	32	5
Holly	6,342	23	0	3	0	20	159	38	116	5	0
Houghton	6,910	12	0	1	0	11	132	10	119	3	1
Howell	9,830	32	0	3	1	28	320	54	250	16	1
Hudson	2,328	4	0	2	0	2	83	8	73	2	1
Huntington Woods	5,806	3	0	0	2	1	46	8	37	1	1
Huron Township	15,731	32	0	8	1	23	313	88	201	24	1
Imlay City	3,725	11	0	0	0	11	88	9	77	2	0
Inkster	26,899	439	2	33	118	286	1,035	434	411	190	21
Ionia	12,689	15	0	10	0	5	238	33	198	7	0
Iron Mountain[4]	7,776	0	0	0	0	0	3	0	3	0	0
Iron River	3,007	7	0	1	1	5	82	18	63	1	0
Ishpeming	6,449	7	0	2	1	4	144	20	120	4	0
Ishpeming Township	3,606	1	0	1	0	0	24	6	18	0	0
Ithaca	3,024	0	0	0	0	0	71	3	68	0	0
Jackson	33,755	323	2	62	57	202	1,893	408	1,392	93	13
Jonesville	2,248	2	0	1	0	1	89	13	75	1	2
Kalamazoo	72,110	742	1	60	221	460	4,244	1,170	2,806	268	44
Kalkaska	2,182	5	1	0	0	4	110	15	94	1	0
Keego Harbor	2,852	7	0	0	0	7	36	9	27	0	0
Kentwood	47,573	280	0	28	68	184	1,716	335	1,308	73	7
Kinross Township	8,778	2	0	0	1	1	22	3	18	1	0
Laingsburg	1,263	6	0	0	0	6	18	4	14	0	0
Lake Odessa	2,228	0	0	0	0	0	2	1	1	0	0
Lake Orion	2,723	5	0	1	1	3	98	13	80	5	1
Lakeview	1,091	1	0	0	0	1	33	9	23	1	1
L'anse	1,867	0	0	0	0	0	37	15	22	0	1
Lansing	114,415	1,181	11	95	269	806	4,261	1,462	2,484	315	54
Lapeer	9,145	41	0	7	2	32	345	35	298	12	2
Lathrup Village	4,064	24	2	2	5	15	94	26	52	16	0
Lennon	494	0	0	0	0	0	11	4	7	0	0
Leoni Township	13,701	15	0	1	0	14	305	76	213	16	0
Leslie	2,330	0	0	0	0	0	19	4	15	0	0

[1] The FBI does not publish arson data unless it receives data from either the agency or the state for all 12 months of the calendar year.
[4] Because of changes in the state/local agency's reporting practices, figures are not comparable to previous years' data.

Table 8. Offenses Known to Law Enforcement, by State and City, 2008—*Continued*

(Number.)

State/City	Population	Violent crime	Murder and non-negligent man-slaughter	Forcible rape	Robbery	Aggravated assault	Property crime	Burglary	Larceny-theft	Motor vehicle theft	Arson[1]
MICHIGAN—*Continued*											
Lexington	1,059	4	0	1	0	3	14	1	12	1	0
Lincoln Park	35,673	123	0	15	41	67	1,728	388	1,103	237	10
Lincoln Township	14,312	17	0	4	2	11	237	24	209	4	2
Linden	3,474	2	0	0	1	1	37	4	33	0	0
Litchfield	1,403	2	0	0	0	2	36	8	28	0	1
Livonia	92,329	132	0	13	43	76	2,103	318	1,526	259	26
Lowell	4,181	6	0	0	1	5	31	4	26	1	1
Ludington	8,329	32	0	15	2	15	301	35	257	9	3
Luna Pier	1,541	3	0	1	0	2	62	11	49	2	0
Mackinac Island	467	4	0	2	0	2	400	2	397	1	0
Mackinaw City	841	0	0	0	0	0	25	0	25	0	0
Madison Heights	29,516	96	0	11	25	60	1,139	183	769	187	3
Madison Township	8,090	1	0	0	1	0	43	3	39	1	0
Manistee	6,508	5	0	3	0	2	193	21	169	3	0
Marquette	20,793	17	0	12	2	3	400	56	335	9	3
Marysville	10,067	6	0	2	0	4	231	35	192	4	0
Mason	8,269	17	0	4	1	12	209	37	164	8	1
Mattawan	2,862	0	0	0	0	0	112	5	106	1	0
Memphis	1,111	1	0	0	0	1	55	11	42	2	0
Meridian Township[4]	38,465	90	0	11	20	59	1,185	193	959	33	15
Metamora Township	4,691	3	0	0	0	3	69	10	54	5	0
Midland	40,962	50	0	22	11	17	807	87	698	22	3
Milan	5,780	5	0	0	0	5	185	25	152	8	0
Milford	16,697	15	0	3	1	11	125	25	97	3	4
Monroe	21,461	88	0	15	19	54	723	181	512	30	9
Montrose Township	7,775	12	0	4	0	8	128	33	83	12	0
Morenci	2,276	1	0	0	0	1	72	8	63	1	1
Mount Morris	3,223	19	0	2	4	13	80	16	56	8	0
Mount Morris Township	22,432	141	0	13	56	72	1,002	442	466	94	21
Mount Pleasant	26,565	54	0	13	3	38	560	125	418	17	2
Mundy Township	14,340	20	1	3	5	11	482	131	332	19	4
Muskegon[4]	39,319	384	1	36	101	246	2,367	566	1,658	143	15
Muskegon Heights[4]	11,596	214	1	20	39	154	1,008	290	634	84	9
Muskegon Township[4]	18,424	56	0	15	16	25	864	89	744	31	4
Napoleon Township	7,057	4	0	2	0	2	70	17	49	4	0
Nashville	1,663	2	0	1	0	1	22	2	18	2	0
Negaunee	4,436	1	0	1	0	0	59	9	50	0	1
New Baltimore	11,949	13	0	3	3	7	256	46	203	7	0
New Buffalo	2,435	4	0	2	0	2	61	16	45	0	1
Niles	11,229	65	0	16	18	31	482	90	367	25	5
North Branch	987	5	0	2	0	3	21	4	17	0	0
Northfield Township	8,578	33	0	6	2	25	199	52	128	19	2
North Muskegon[4]	3,916	1	0	0	1	0	104	5	98	1	0
Northville	6,028	7	0	2	0	5	93	12	77	4	0
Northville Township	25,742	15	0	3	1	11	486	73	395	18	1
Norton Shores	23,408	39	0	8	6	25	794	94	677	23	3
Norway	2,827	2	0	1	0	1	60	10	48	2	0
Novi	54,980	64	3	5	10	46	1,304	173	1,080	51	1
Oak Park	30,509	167	0	10	62	95	1,087	330	534	223	12
Ontwa Township-Edwardsburg	5,912	12	0	3	1	8	168	41	108	19	2
Orchard Lake	2,201	4	0	0	3	1	43	4	37	2	0
Oscoda Township	6,857	12	0	5	0	7	253	94	155	4	2
Otsego	3,824	7	0	1	2	4	77	11	65	1	0
Ovid	1,395	3	0	0	0	3	19	6	12	1	0
Owosso	15,094	58	0	8	11	39	607	104	492	11	1
Oxford	3,545	2	0	0	0	2	59	6	51	2	0
Parchment	1,801	6	0	2	0	4	60	1	58	1	0
Parma-Sandstone	6,850	3	0	0	0	3	42	6	32	4	0
Paw Paw	3,223	14	0	2	0	12	138	20	114	4	1
Pentwater	947	0	0	0	0	0	19	1	18	0	0
Perry	2,044	1	0	0	0	1	33	2	28	3	0
Petoskey	6,009	6	0	0	1	5	125	23	94	8	0
Pinckney	2,460	7	0	4	0	3	91	16	71	4	0
Pinconning	1,310	0	0	0	0	0	25	5	19	1	0
Pittsfield Township	35,064	80	1	10	33	36	1,144	215	839	90	2
Pleasant Ridge	2,469	3	0	0	3	0	15	2	13	0	0
Plymouth	8,622	6	0	1	2	3	147	22	111	14	3
Plymouth Township	25,676	19	1	2	6	10	354	62	272	20	1
Pontiac	66,366	1,253	21	73	315	844	2,539	1,034	998	507	39
Portage	46,210	85	0	16	22	47	1,934	277	1,594	63	8
Port Huron	30,937	230	0	17	43	170	1,467	390	1,003	74	7
Portland	3,697	7	0	1	1	5	68	5	62	1	1
Potterville	2,169	7	0	1	0	6	67	8	57	2	1

[1] The FBI does not publish arson data unless it receives data from either the agency or the state for all 12 months of the calendar year.
[4] Because of changes in the state/local agency's reporting practices, figures are not comparable to previous years' data.

Table 8. Offenses Known to Law Enforcement, by State and City, 2008—*Continued*

(Number.)

State/City	Population	Violent crime	Murder and non-negligent man-slaughter	Forcible rape	Robbery	Aggravated assault	Property crime	Burglary	Larceny-theft	Motor vehicle theft	Arson[1]
MICHIGAN—*Continued*											
Prairieville Township	3,540	0	0	0	0	0	20	8	11	1	1
Raisin Township	7,364	10	0	0	0	10	30	5	25	0	0
Reed City	2,344	0	0	0	0	0	46	7	39	0	0
Richfield Township, Genesee County	8,708	15	1	2	1	11	132	38	84	10	1
Richland Township, Saginaw County	4,242	1	0	0	0	1	16	5	11	0	0
Riverview	11,916	10	0	1	0	9	222	19	169	34	1
Rochester	11,098	18	0	2	2	14	182	32	143	7	0
Rockford	5,422	9	0	3	0	6	97	11	84	2	3
Rogers City	3,054	2	0	2	0	0	68	2	63	3	0
Romeo	3,762	9	0	1	0	8	93	8	78	7	0
Roosevelt Park	3,771	8	1	0	1	6	261	18	237	6	0
Roseville	46,834	233	0	21	45	167	2,269	461	1,485	323	10
Rothbury	438	1	0	0	0	1	24	0	24	0	1
Royal Oak	57,098	113	0	20	34	59	1,144	217	797	130	19
Saginaw	55,634	1,833	21	50	309	1,453	2,644	1,508	915	221	234
Saginaw Township	38,815	102	0	9	24	69	1,155	239	872	44	2
Saline	9,068	16	1	1	0	14	143	26	115	2	6
Sand Lake	518	0	0	0	0	0	10	1	7	2	0
Sandusky	2,631	5	0	1	0	4	132	22	107	3	3
Sault Ste. Marie	13,970	38	0	5	2	31	532	73	436	23	4
Scottville	1,247	11	0	3	0	8	38	4	32	2	0
Shelby Township	72,030	108	1	13	12	82	1,181	316	794	71	8
Somerset Township	4,745	0	0	0	0	0	26	3	21	2	0
Southfield	75,024	507	0	28	149	330	3,068	660	1,859	549	11
Southgate	28,055	93	0	9	24	60	1,111	142	838	131	5
South Haven	5,128	17	0	3	4	10	243	41	196	6	2
South Lyon	11,106	11	0	4	0	7	132	21	108	3	3
South Rockwood	1,632	2	0	1	0	1	25	4	16	5	0
Sparta	4,057	4	0	0	1	3	108	11	94	3	0
Spring Arbor Township	8,487	4	0	1	0	3	53	10	43	0	1
Spring Lake-Ferrysburg	5,462	8	0	3	0	5	95	19	76	0	1
Standish	1,940	2	0	1	0	1	36	3	31	2	0
St. Charles	2,058	4	0	0	0	4	64	14	50	0	0
St. Clair	5,815	3	0	2	1	0	89	15	73	1	0
St. Clair Shores	60,335	137	0	20	33	84	1,148	201	791	156	8
Sterling Heights	127,697	228	2	26	49	151	2,834	467	2,166	201	8
St. Johns	7,257	12	0	5	0	7	132	19	107	6	0
St. Joseph	8,453	15	0	3	4	8	309	30	272	7	1
St. Joseph Township	9,621	19	0	0	6	13	169	25	139	5	0
St. Louis	6,854	5	0	3	1	1	69	11	56	2	1
Stockbridge	1,286	7	0	2	1	4	49	5	43	1	1
Sturgis	10,914	36	0	6	4	26	344	64	268	12	1
Summit Township	21,912	45	0	2	4	39	292	97	172	23	1
Sumpter Township	11,383	22	1	2	1	18	252	84	134	34	3
Swartz Creek	5,308	9	0	3	1	5	146	31	105	10	3
Sylvan Lake	1,642	1	0	0	1	0	19	6	9	4	0
Tecumseh	8,724	8	0	3	0	5	89	10	75	4	0
Thetford Township	7,899	1	0	0	0	1	35	6	26	3	0
Thomas Township[4]	12,379	14	0	1	3	10	356	38	308	10	4
Tittabawassee Township	8,884	11	0	2	0	9	100	21	75	4	0
Trenton	18,222	18	0	1	1	16	216	27	165	24	1
Troy	80,491	94	2	13	15	64	1,852	307	1,380	165	6
Tuscarora Township	3,069	5	0	1	1	3	148	19	124	5	0
Unadilla Township	3,452	7	0	1	0	6	47	14	31	2	1
Utica	4,987	21	0	0	1	20	239	28	200	11	1
Van Buren Township	27,264	96	3	8	29	56	925	183	623	119	7
Walker	23,928	66	0	21	7	38	935	98	809	28	2
Walled Lake	6,956	16	0	0	1	15	156	29	120	7	1
Warren[5]	133,721	661	4	60	181	416		769	1,786		32
Waterford Township	70,676	232	2	34	60	136	1,822	436	1,253	133	12
Waterloo Township	3,000	5	0	0	0	5	19	6	13	0	0
Watervliet	1,733	6	1	0	0	5	60	5	54	1	0
Wayne	17,395	116	0	9	36	71	577	108	389	80	11
West Bloomfield Township	63,993	45	0	3	8	34	858	178	644	36	3
West Branch	1,835	0	0	0	0	0	41	0	40	1	0
Westland	79,944	431	2	48	104	277	2,643	638	1,581	424	29
White Cloud	1,396	9	0	3	1	5	112	17	93	2	1
Whitehall	2,801	4	0	2	0	2	132	3	125	4	0
White Lake Township	30,318	35	2	5	2	26	591	88	480	23	2
Wixom	13,485	20	0	4	6	10	335	64	242	29	2
Wolverine Lake	4,314	11	0	1	0	10	46	12	29	5	1
Wyandotte	25,120	55	0	2	8	45	573	90	395	88	5
Wyoming	70,552	269	0	45	82	142	1,784	486	1,122	176	14
Ypsilanti	21,766	285	3	13	74	195	1,024	278	649	97	6

[1] The FBI does not publish arson data unless it receives data from either the agency or the state for all 12 months of the calendar year.
[4] Because of changes in the state/local agency's reporting practices, figures are not comparable to previous years' data.
[5] The FBI determined that the agency's data were overreported. Consequently, those data are not included in this table.

Table 8. Offenses Known to Law Enforcement, by State and City, 2008—*Continued*

(Number.)

State/City	Population	Violent crime	Murder and non-negligent man-slaughter	Forcible rape	Robbery	Aggravated assault	Property crime	Burglary	Larceny-theft	Motor vehicle theft	Arson[1]
MINNESOTA[6]											
Albany	2,132		0		0	1	10	1	8	1	0
Albert Lea	17,447		0		7	22	367	41	313	13	1
Alexandria	11,373		0		1	13	455	41	407	7	1
Annandale	3,126		0		0	5	116	8	103	5	0
Anoka	17,161		1		9	17	830	112	684	34	3
Appleton	3,121		0		0	4	31	5	24	2	0
Apple Valley	50,619		0		22	40	1,477	161	1,281	35	5
Arden Hills	9,920		0		2	3	142	23	104	15	2
Austin	22,875		0		8	27	865	129	703	33	3
Avon	1,320		0		0	1	38	19	19	0	0
Babbitt	1,579		0		0	0	0	0	0	0	0
Baxter	8,464		0		0	8	299	21	276	2	1
Bayport	3,254		0		0	0	51	12	35	4	0
Becker	4,308		0		0	1	3	0	3	0	0
Belgrade	710		0		0	0	0	0	0	0	0
Belle Plaine	5,146		0		1	3	92	11	79	2	1
Bemidji	13,574		0		3	35	1,004	77	894	33	2
Benson	3,045		0		1	3	61	15	43	3	0
Big Lake	10,135		0		0	12	249	29	212	8	2
Biwabik	959		0		0	1	12	5	7	0	0
Blackduck	766		0		0	0	31	2	29	0	0
Blaine	56,808		1		7	39	2,353	227	2,053	73	10
Bloomington	80,996		1		51	60	3,213	255	2,798	160	12
Blue Earth	3,263		0		0	8	46	12	32	2	1
Brainerd	13,733		1		3	45	613	98	489	26	4
Breckenridge	3,225		0		0	2	68	17	50	1	0
Brooklyn Center	27,289		2		92	85	2,038	287	1,598	153	18
Brooklyn Park	71,891		1		118	154	3,059	606	2,241	212	20
Browns Valley	604		0		0	4	17	4	12	1	0
Brownton	785		0		0	1	5	4	1	0	0
Buffalo	14,614		0		0	10	372	28	332	12	3
Burnsville	58,974		0		34	20	2,076	266	1,736	74	4
Caledonia	2,848		0		0	3	59	8	49	2	0
Cambridge	7,907		0		2	5	421	33	371	17	0
Cannon Falls	4,053		0		3	4	157	14	138	5	2
Centennial Lakes	11,261		0		2	7	213	16	193	4	0
Champlin	23,785		0		4	9	518	74	427	17	1
Chaska	24,847		1		3	15	352	34	309	9	7
Chisholm	4,571		0		1	5	179	55	121	3	0
Cloquet	11,369		0		1	17	509	50	427	32	0
Cold Spring	3,788		0		0	6	74	10	63	1	0
Columbia Heights	17,894		2		37	32	890	158	646	86	10
Coon Rapids	61,776		0		33	69	2,899	208	2,592	99	14
Corcoran	5,762		0		0	1	80	12	62	6	1
Cottage Grove	33,396		0		4	14	723	92	604	27	4
Crookston	7,668		0		1	6	29	11	15	3	2
Crosby	2,218		0		0	2	94	5	81	8	1
Crystal	21,503		0		18	20	779	149	596	34	7
Dawson	1,355		0		0	0	8	2	5	1	0
Dayton	4,675		0		0	2	44	13	26	5	0
Deephaven-Woodland	4,204		0		0	2	38	4	34	0	0
Detroit Lakes	8,094		0		1	12	308	35	260	13	1
Dilworth	3,674		0		0	3	96	1	94	1	0
Duluth	84,171		2		128	195	4,211	520	3,524	167	18
Eagan	63,754		0		21	27	1,627	190	1,398	39	3
Eagle Lake	2,202		0		0	1	13	4	7	2	0
East Grand Forks	7,768		0		1	7	225	32	183	10	1
Eden Prairie	62,516		0		10	33	1,333	138	1,166	29	8
Elk River	23,659		0		4	14	810	91	694	25	9
Elmore	657		0		0	4	6	2	4	0	0
Ely	3,487		0		0	3	70	12	54	4	1
Eveleth	3,561		0		2	11	128	27	94	7	0
Fairmont	10,173		0		1	10	348	29	315	4	0
Falcon Heights	5,465		0		0	1	122	24	91	7	0
Faribault	22,082		0		2	44	678	122	518	38	11
Farmington	19,634		0		1	6	232	49	177	6	2
Fergus Falls	13,699		0		1	31	423	81	332	10	3
Floodwood	490		0		0	0	14	2	12	0	0
Forest Lake	17,965		0		2	7	587	69	465	53	1
Fridley	25,746		1		38	48	1,517	151	1,261	105	11
Gilbert	1,743		0		0	1	34	10	23	1	0
Glencoe	5,602		0		1	5	130	8	120	2	0
Glenwood	2,525		0		0	4	27	6	20	1	0
Golden Valley	19,969		0		18	19	586	124	440	22	3

[1] The FBI does not publish arson data unless it receives data from either the agency or the state for all 12 months of the calendar year.

[6] The data collection methodology for the offense of forcible rape used by the Illinois and the Minnesota state UCR Programs (with the exception of Rockford, Illinois and Minneapolis and St. Paul, Minnesota) does not comply with national UCR Program guidelines. Consequently, their figures for forcible rape and violent crime (of which forcible rape is a part) are not published in this table.

Table 8. Offenses Known to Law Enforcement, by State and City, 2008—*Continued*

(Number.)

State/City	Population	Violent crime	Murder and non-negligent man-slaughter	Forcible rape	Robbery	Aggravated assault	Property crime	Burglary	Larceny-theft	Motor vehicle theft	Arson[1]
MINNESOTA[6]—*Continued*											
Goodview	3,460		0		1	5	46	12	28	6	0
Grand Rapids	8,715		0		0	10	317	29	271	17	1
Granite Falls	2,869		0		0	4	41	3	33	5	0
Hallock	1,007		0		0	0	0	0	0	0	0
Hastings	22,125		1		5	12	670	90	552	28	6
Hermantown	9,435		1		0	5	307	43	250	14	1
Hibbing	16,155		1		0	6	165	54	106	5	0
Hilltop	734		0		2	8	73	10	52	11	0
Hokah	567		0		0	0	15	3	12	0	0
Hopkins	16,756		1		25	22	517	117	357	43	1
Houston	969		0		0	1	19	1	15	3	0
Hoyt Lakes	1,947		0		0	0	1	0	1	0	0
Hutchinson	14,023		0		4	12	415	41	364	10	7
International Falls	5,964		0		0	8	180	39	131	10	0
Inver Grove Heights	34,007		0		10	17	797	137	588	72	8
Jackson	3,333		0		1	8	68	14	50	4	1
Janesville	2,227		0		0	0	22	8	14	0	0
Jordan	5,647		0		0	4	96	8	85	3	0
Kasson	5,649		0		0	1	36	4	26	6	0
Kimball	713		0		0	3	9	1	6	2	0
Lake City	5,327		0		0	3	116	14	94	8	0
Lake Crystal	2,629		0		0	3	63	7	55	1	1
Lakefield	1,631		0		1	2	10	2	8	0	0
Lakes Area	8,349		0		1	10	183	23	149	11	4
Lakeville	55,600		1		6	20	1,039	120	899	20	4
Lauderdale	2,193		0		2	1	40	9	26	5	0
Lester Prairie	1,796		0		0	0	42	13	28	1	0
Le Sueur	4,302		0		0	1	84	10	72	2	0
Lewiston	1,495		0		0	0	1	0	0	1	0
Lino Lakes	20,282		0		1	11	280	34	238	8	10
Litchfield	6,595		0		1	4	119	19	97	3	1
Little Canada	9,634		1		3	9	266	32	193	41	2
Little Falls	8,116		0		1	9	193	15	172	6	0
Long Prairie	2,817		0		0	8	69	4	65	0	0
Madison	1,562		0		0	0	14	8	5	1	0
Mankato	36,316		0		13	53	1,785	255	1,472	58	18
Maple Grove	63,335		0		17	30	1,535	194	1,310	31	2
Mapleton	1,660		0		0	1	39	7	29	3	0
Maplewood	36,249		0		30	38	2,473	318	1,990	165	12
Marshall	12,468		0		4	34	496	77	400	19	1
Medina	5,181		0		0	1	125	15	104	6	0
Melrose	3,156		0		0	1	27	3	23	1	1
Mendota Heights	11,616		0		2	6	301	31	263	7	0
Milaca	3,073		0		0	6	130	9	119	2	0
Minneapolis	376,753	4,779	37	367	2,005	2,370	20,777	5,591	12,776	2,410	160
Minnetonka	50,231		1		5	14	1,084	222	830	32	3
Minnetrista	8,541		0		0	1	75	10	62	3	0
Montevideo	5,181		0		0	8	155	18	125	12	0
Montgomery	3,338		0		0	6	99	10	88	1	0
Moorhead	35,704		0		5	29	871	124	713	34	7
Moose Lake	2,575		0		0	6	82	2	80	0	0
Mora	3,455		0		0	7	128	12	114	2	0
Morris	4,946		0		0	7	140	9	130	1	0
Mound	9,568		0		0	2	160	28	122	10	0
Mounds View	12,081		3		2	10	447	73	340	34	1
Mountain Lake	1,923		0		0	3	14	1	10	3	0
New Brighton	20,897		1		8	13	567	76	445	46	5
New Hope	20,540		0		14	32	646	90	520	36	7
Newport	3,558		0		1	6	147	27	110	10	0
New Prague	7,374		0		1	4	163	18	143	2	2
New Richland	1,165		0		0	1	11	5	5	1	0
New Ulm	13,105		0		0	5	265	53	203	9	2
North Branch	10,713		0		1	6	339	33	292	14	1
Northfield	19,610		0		3	9	379	66	304	9	0
North Mankato	12,467		0		0	2	197	4	177	16	6
North Oaks	4,240		0		0	0	33	3	30	0	1
North St. Paul	11,356		0		3	4	452	70	350	32	2
Oakdale	27,108		0		23	25	1,085	100	908	77	12
Oak Park Heights	4,078		0		1	3	280	17	249	14	0
Olivia	2,381		1		0	5	103	18	80	5	0
Orono	12,415		0		0	1	202	25	163	14	0
Osakis	1,575		0		0	1	35	6	28	1	1
Owatonna[8]	24,999		0		1	19			357	15	4

[1] The FBI does not publish arson data unless it receives data from either the agency or the state for all 12 months of the calendar year.

[6] The data collection methodology for the offense of forcible rape used by the Illinois and the Minnesota state UCR Programs (with the exception of Rockford, Illinois and Minneapolis and St. Paul, Minnesota) does not comply with national UCR Program guidelines. Consequently, their figures for forcible rape and violent crime (of which forcible rape is a part) are not published in this table.

[8] The FBI determined that the agency's data were underreported. Consequently, those data are not included in this table.

Table 8. Offenses Known to Law Enforcement, by State and City, 2008—*Continued*

(Number.)

State/City	Population	Violent crime	Murder and non-negligent man-slaughter	Forcible rape	Robbery	Aggravated assault	Property crime	Burglary	Larceny-theft	Motor vehicle theft	Arson[1]
MINNESOTA[6]—*Continued*											
Park Rapids	3,600		0		3	9	243	40	189	14	0
Paynesville	2,271		0		0	3	95	19	76	0	1
Plymouth	71,713		0		16	33	1,664	299	1,309	56	4
Princeton	4,885		0		3	3	195	17	171	7	1
Prior Lake	24,219		1		5	20	466	83	367	16	5
Proctor	2,815		0		0	0	115	12	99	4	0
Ramsey	23,791		0		2	11	638	53	558	27	1
Red Wing	15,655		1		6	19	448	88	336	24	5
Redwood Falls	5,050		0		0	17	226	28	187	11	4
Richfield	33,260		2		38	33	1,130	186	886	58	4
Richmond	1,275		0		0	0	1	0	1	0	0
Robbinsdale	13,430		1		23	18	566	143	391	32	2
Rochester	100,589		4		65	133	2,853	534	2,133	186	27
Rogers	7,269		0		1	6	82	2	80	0	0
Roseau	2,776		0		0	5	65	6	54	5	0
Rosemount	21,944		1		2	9	380	51	318	11	0
Roseville	32,324		0		19	29	1,600	186	1,265	149	3
Sartell	14,319		0		2	4	229	16	208	5	3
Sauk Centre	3,945		0		1	3	122	22	95	5	0
Sauk Rapids	12,069		0		1	9	89	15	70	4	0
Savage	28,504		0		9	33	810	126	651	33	8
Shakopee	35,464		0		8	39	939	124	781	34	5
Silver Lake	804		0		0	0	7	1	4	2	0
Slayton	1,840		0		0	1	34	1	31	2	0
South Eastern Faribault County	1,112		0		0	0	0	0	0	0	0
South Lake Minnetonka	12,264		0		0	13	176	23	149	4	2
South St. Paul	19,156		0		11	17	659	134	455	70	0
Springfield	2,149		0		0	0	0	0	0	0	0
Spring Lake Park	6,539		0		7	15	465	56	378	31	2
St. Anthony	7,794		0		13	2	290	34	250	6	3
Staples	3,030		0		0	0	114	16	96	2	0
St. Charles	3,617		0		0	5	54	14	38	2	0
St. Cloud	67,404		0		51	164	3,097	358	2,646	93	11
St. Francis	7,676		0		0	8	179	30	141	8	1
Stillwater	18,053		0		2	8	442	68	356	18	4
St. James	4,306		0		1	5	107	13	93	1	0
St. Louis Park	44,011		2		35	20	1,438	248	1,121	69	3
St. Paul	276,083	2,199	18	147	765	1,269	11,524	2,936	6,770	1,818	172
St. Paul Park	5,290		0		2	9	180	39	129	12	4
St. Peter	10,969		0		1	15	293	39	244	10	0
Thief River Falls	8,488		0		2	9	215	28	177	10	2
Two Harbors	3,325		0		0	3	64	12	45	7	0
Vadnais Heights	12,745		0		0	7	240	21	185	34	0
Virginia	8,433		0		4	23	628	89	525	14	2
Wabasha	2,518		0		0	1	75	5	65	5	0
Wadena	3,946		0		0	6	112	7	100	5	0
Waite Park	6,815		0		10	17	557	32	507	18	0
Warroad	1,647		0		0	5	53	4	49	0	1
Waseca	9,488		0		0	13	224	16	197	11	1
Wayzata	3,937		0		1	1	135	17	115	3	1
Wells	2,367		0		0	0	14	4	7	3	1
West Hennepin	5,716		0		0	3	78	17	56	5	0
West St. Paul	18,756		0		18	15	1,001	98	838	65	4
Wheaton	1,428		0		0	1	31	3	26	2	0
White Bear Lake	23,771		1		10	34	981	188	736	57	12
Willmar	17,786		1		7	33	663	77	567	19	3
Windom	4,191		0		0	9	116	29	81	6	0
Winnebago	1,342		0		0	2	23	9	12	2	0
Winona	26,682		0		5	32	592	81	470	41	7
Winsted	2,470		0		0	2	52	17	35	0	0
Woodbury	56,619		0		13	26	1,272	200	1,018	54	1
Worthington	10,878		1		8	23	270	84	177	9	1
Wyoming	3,898		0		1	2	108	11	96	1	0
Zumbrota	3,103		0		0	2	41	4	34	3	0
MISSISSIPPI											
Aberdeen	6,025	30	0	2	9	19	135	42	84	9	0
Ackerman	1,504	2	1	0	0	1	4	0	3	1	0
Amory	7,219	17	0	2	11	4	293	55	231	7	1
Batesville	7,815	40	0	7	11	22	529	133	376	20	0
Bay St. Louis	8,200	10	0	3	4	3	322	59	242	21	2
Booneville	8,532	10	0	3	1	6	291	69	222	0	2
Brandon	21,151	10	0	4	3	3	240	60	169	11	5
Brookhaven	9,997	27	0	0	23	4	342	38	296	8	0

[1] The FBI does not publish arson data unless it receives data from either the agency or the state for all 12 months of the calendar year.

[6] The data collection methodology for the offense of forcible rape used by the Illinois and the Minnesota state UCR Programs (with the exception of Rockford, Illinois and Minneapolis and St. Paul, Minnesota) does not comply with national UCR Program guidelines. Consequently, their figures for forcible rape and violent crime (of which forcible rape is a part) are not published in this table.

Table 8. Offenses Known to Law Enforcement, by State and City, 2008—*Continued*

(Number.)

State/City	Population	Violent crime	Murder and non-negligent man-slaughter	Forcible rape	Robbery	Aggravated assault	Property crime	Burglary	Larceny-theft	Motor vehicle theft	Arson[1]
MISSISSIPPI—*Continued*											
Byhalia	1,300	7	1	0	0	6	60	15	41	4	0
Canton	12,469	66	1	13	16	36	481	235	225	21	0
Charleston	1,884	31	1	0	21	9	87	26	61	0	0
Clarksdale	18,029	139	5	14	56	64	998	495	432	71	9
Cleveland	12,292	74	0	0	33	41	942	159	771	12	10
Clinton	26,564	33	0	9	16	8	501	144	305	52	2
Collins	2,746	9	0	1	2	6	175	25	139	11	0
Columbus	23,802	97	1	16	45	35	966	199	725	42	7
Drew	2,174	26	0	5	3	18	77	54	22	1	
Edwards	1,302	1	0	0	0	1	7	5	1	1	0
Florence	3,520	0	0	0	0	0	18	7	6	5	1
Flowood	7,156	36	0	4	6	26	521	123	383	15	0
Fulton	4,067	2	0	0	2	0	83	14	64	5	0
Greenville	35,573	91	7	9	51	24	2,112	910	1,154	48	37
Greenwood	15,886	118	2	8	43	65	1,149	454	636	59	0
Grenada	14,664	83	0	4	38	41	698	204	465	29	1
Gulfport	65,704	221	8	20	122	71	3,997	946	2,824	227	19
Heidelberg	802	0	0	0	0	0	44	8	32	4	0
Hernando	11,694	14	0	5	2	7	290	62	214	14	0
Hollandale	2,942	6	0	0	2	4	60	25	34	1	1
Holly Springs	8,037	88	1	2	19	66	309	132	151	26	0
Horn Lake	24,692	36	3	1	23	9	784	124	598	62	5
Iuka	2,933	15	1	0	1	13	83	23	52	8	0
Jackson	174,734	1,652	63	136	942	511	13,035	4,334	6,990	1,711	81
Kosciusko	7,362	19	1	7	5	6	197	68	129	0	0
Laurel	18,415	101	4	3	51	43	1,015	269	683	63	5
Leakesville	1,023	0	0	0	0	0	0	0	0	0	0
Leland	4,783	13	0	0	3	10	145	70	74	1	0
Lexington	1,856	2	0	0	0	2	16	11	4	1	0
Long Beach	17,528	9	0	1	3	5	272	43	209	20	0
Louisville	6,633	15	0	1	9	5	76	66	10	0	0
Lucedale	3,065	18	0	0	2	16	120	26	80	14	0
Madison	17,858	18	0	5	0	13	202	13	183	6	0
Magnolia	2,091	6	0	0	0	6	44	19	21	4	0
McComb	13,587	56	3	2	27	24	653	150	466	37	0
Meridian	38,123	207	7	30	86	84	1,921	732	1,066	123	16
Morton	3,436	12	0	1	4	7	40	21	15	4	1
Natchez	16,433	52	2	5	16	29	795	238	533	24	1
New Albany	8,106	10	0	0	7	3	95	33	52	10	0
Newton	3,680	4	0	0	1	3	26	8	16	2	1
Ocean Springs[8]	17,247	26	0	3	12	11			519	26	3
Olive Branch	32,060	79	0	13	28	38	1,394	262	1,063	69	6
Oxford	15,334	17	0	7	5	5	458	98	335	25	0
Pascagoula	23,139	96	0	13	61	22	1,417	301	990	126	7
Pass Christian	7,008	5	0	1	0	4	159	32	119	8	2
Petal	10,717	9	1	2	1	5	98	58	34	6	4
Picayune	11,733	34	1	1	13	19	359	56	273	30	2
Poplarville	2,993	14	0	0	2	12	68	24	42	2	0
Port Gibson	1,647	7	0	2	1	4	22	4	18	0	0
Purvis	2,653	0	0	0	0	0	0	0	0	0	0
Raymond	1,675	2	0	0	1	1	10	4	6	0	0
Ridgeland	21,645	38	0	0	17	21	835	93	694	48	0
Ripley	5,682	4	0	1	1	2	112	38	61	13	0
Senatobia	7,197	7	0	0	4	3	259	81	173	5	0
Shelby	2,593	8	0	1	3	4	26	21	3	2	1
Southaven	44,570	84	6	5	37	36	1,927	212	1,603	112	2
Starkville	24,099	41	1	2	10	28	608	184	405	19	1
Summit	1,633	2	0	0	2	0	47	14	32	1	0
Vicksburg	25,345	248	7	25	55	161	1,743	374	1,266	103	11
Waveland	7,212	11	0	0	2	9	392	65	300	27	0
Waynesboro	5,649	21	1	0	13	7	112	65	43	4	0
West Point	11,281	36	0	6	9	21	376	101	274	1	0
Wiggins	4,872	22	0	3	2	17	256	82	171	3	0
Winona	4,579	10	0	1	6	3	21	3	16	2	0
MISSOURI											
Adrian	1,894	5	0	0	0	5	26	6	19	1	1
Advance	1,219	0	0	0	0	0	18	6	10	2	0
Alton	638	2	0	1	0	1	3	2	1	0	0
Anderson	1,930	6	0	1	0	5	58	19	32	7	0
Appleton City	1,279	5	0	0	0	5	30	17	13	0	1
Arbyrd	489	0	0	0	0	0	3	3	0	0	0
Archie	994	1	0	0	0	1	25	3	21	1	0
Arnold	20,669	50	2	1	6	41	1,252	57	1,169	26	0

[1] The FBI does not publish arson data unless it receives data from either the agency or the state for all 12 months of the calendar year.
[8] The FBI determined that the agency's data were underreported. Consequently, those data are not included in this table.

Table 8. Offenses Known to Law Enforcement, by State and City, 2008—*Continued*

(Number.)

State/City	Population	Violent crime	Murder and non-negligent man-slaughter	Forcible rape	Robbery	Aggravated assault	Property crime	Burglary	Larceny-theft	Motor vehicle theft	Arson[1]
MISSOURI—*Continued*											
Ash Grove	1,549	4	0	0	0	4	23	5	17	1	0
Ashland	2,200	6	0	0	0	6	48	5	37	6	0
Aurora	7,493	52	0	3	2	47	485	100	362	23	2
Auxvasse	999	1	0	0	0	1	29	6	21	2	1
Ava	3,110	16	0	0	0	16	214	46	161	7	0
Ballwin	29,978	20	2	3	1	14	283	42	234	7	0
Bates City	268	1	0	1	0	0	12	0	11	1	1
Battlefield	4,496	2	0	2	0	0	67	18	49	0	0
Bella Villa	636	4	0	0	1	3	4	3	0	1	0
Belle	1,385	1	0	0	0	1	4	1	2	1	0
Bellefontaine Neighbors	10,163	72	0	4	16	52	456	162	203	91	1
Bellerive	254	0	0	0	0	0	4	2	2	0	0
Bellflower	392	3	0	0	0	3	6	3	3	0	0
Bel-Nor	1,481	5	0	0	4	1	38	11	22	5	0
Bel-Ridge	2,895	55	2	1	10	42	179	72	79	28	2
Belton	24,771	48	0	4	11	33	612	122	431	59	4
Berkeley	9,367	116	2	6	35	73	765	320	300	145	5
Bernie	1,800	3	0	1	0	2	35	8	26	1	0
Bethany	3,072	3	0	0	0	3	98	27	66	5	0
Beverly Hills	558	0	0	0	0	0	0	0	0	0	0
Billings	1,113	3	0	0	0	3	36	3	33	0	0
Birch Tree	623	3	0	0	0	3	4	2	1	1	1
Birmingham	219	0	0	0	0	0	4	3	0	1	0
Bismarck	1,543	1	0	1	0	0	4	4	0	0	0
Bland	563	6	0	0	1	5	14	6	8	0	0
Bloomfield	1,879	3	0	0	0	3	28	6	21	1	0
Blue Springs	55,913	126	1	17	34	74	1,933	378	1,394	161	7
Bolivar[3]	11,129		0	6	3		325	55	265	5	0
Bonne Terre	7,369	14	0	0	1	13	74	13	48	13	0
Boonville	8,830	12	0	0	1	11	267	20	243	4	3
Bowling Green	5,260	6	0	3	0	3	142	19	122	1	0
Branson	7,572	132	0	8	8	116	1,046	119	905	22	2
Branson West	547	4	0	0	0	4	33	3	30	0	0
Breckenridge Hills	4,478	45	0	5	8	32	240	64	150	26	3
Brentwood	7,170	2	1	0	1	0	322	36	274	12	0
Bridgeton	15,030	82	0	3	33	46	1,056	103	879	74	15
Brookfield	4,311	6	0	1	0	5	80	28	48	4	1
Bucklin	474	2	0	0	0	2	7	5	2	0	0
Buckner	2,792	5	0	1	0	4	134	11	119	4	1
Buffalo	3,338	7	0	0	2	5	138	29	105	4	0
Butler	4,276	4	0	0	1	3	163	16	138	9	1
Butterfield Village	422	0	0	0	0	0	0	0	0	0	0
Cabool	2,134	1	0	0	1	0	39	12	26	1	0
California	4,172	13	0	0	7	6	81	19	57	5	1
Calverton Park	1,274	5	0	0	3	2	33	13	16	4	0
Camden Point	545	0	0	0	0	0	1	1	0	0	0
Camdenton	3,450	22	0	2	0	20	145	18	125	2	2
Cameron	9,064	8	0	0	0	8	165	31	131	3	4
Campbell	1,806	0	0	0	0	0	44	11	33	0	0
Canton	2,471	11	0	3	0	8	81	23	58	0	1
Cape Girardeau	37,374	177	3	18	56	100	2,234	338	1,868	28	25
Cardwell	722	4	0	1	0	3	9	1	8	0	0
Carl Junction	7,440	8	0	1	0	7	145	26	118	1	1
Carterville	1,969	13	0	0	0	13	12	3	7	2	0
Carthage	13,824	35	0	6	4	25	446	100	333	13	2
Caruthersville	6,177	65	0	7	8	50	230	75	147	8	0
Cassville	3,275	9	0	0	0	9	150	21	123	6	0
Center	642	1	0	0	0	1	16	8	8	0	0
Centralia	3,664	4	0	1	0	3	85	22	59	4	0
Chaffee	2,942	15	0	1	0	14	76	10	65	1	0
Charlack	1,344	7	0	0	2	5	91	14	71	6	0
Charleston	5,256	28	0	0	3	25	135	38	94	3	1
Chesterfield	46,200	45	1	2	8	34	1,007	124	863	20	0
Clarkton	1,232	4	0	1	0	3	21	9	9	3	3
Claycomo	1,303	6	0	1	1	4	28	9	17	2	1
Clayton	16,094	24	0	1	6	17	321	30	263	28	1
Cleveland	690	1	0	0	1	0	6	2	3	1	0
Clever	1,470	3	0	0	0	3	3	1	2	0	1
Clinton	9,445	27	0	2	4	21	354	74	264	16	1
Cole Camp	1,149	2	0	0	0	2	12	4	8	0	0
Columbia	101,033	392	5	19	138	230	3,951	836	2,968	147	10
Concordia	2,367	4	0	1	1	2	72	13	56	3	1
Conway	787	0	0	0	0	0	8	1	6	1	0

[1] The FBI does not publish arson data unless it receives data from either the agency or the state for all 12 months of the calendar year.
[3] The FBI determined that the agency did not follow national Uniform Crime Reporting (UCR) Program guidelines for reporting an offense. Consequently, this figure is not included in this table.

Table 8. Offenses Known to Law Enforcement, by State and City, 2008—*Continued*

(Number.)

State/City	Population	Violent crime	Murder and non-negligent man-slaughter	Forcible rape	Robbery	Aggravated assault	Property crime	Burglary	Larceny-theft	Motor vehicle theft	Arson[1]
MISSOURI—*Continued*											
Cool Valley	1,004	4	0	0	0	4	99	24	66	9	0
Cooter	419	2	0	0	0	2	1	0	0	1	0
Cottleville	2,919	9	0	0	0	9	31	1	30	0	0
Country Club Hills	1,279	5	0	1	2	2	67	26	31	10	0
Country Club Village	1,936	0	0	0	0	0	11	4	7	0	0
Crane	1,427	10	0	0	0	10	23	8	13	2	0
Crestwood	11,426	17	1	0	3	13	577	25	543	9	0
Creve Coeur	16,956	17	1	1	4	11	355	47	291	17	0
Crocker	992	6	0	0	0	6	23	8	12	3	1
Crystal City	4,585	9	0	3	0	6	107	10	91	6	1
Cuba	3,600	6	0	0	0	6	240	32	202	6	0
Deepwater	496	0	0	0	0	0	19	1	17	1	2
Dellwood	4,891	25	0	1	6	18	151	75	62	14	0
Delta	543	0	0	0	0	0	0	0	0	0	0
Desloge	5,190	28	0	4	4	20	236	21	210	5	0
De Soto	6,509	28	1	1	2	24	258	32	215	11	1
Des Peres	8,616	6	0	0	6	0	433	23	409	1	1
Dexter	7,723	15	0	1	0	14	234	47	179	8	2
Diamond	899	0	0	0	0	0	0	0	0	0	0
Dixon	1,528	2	0	0	0	2	68	10	55	3	0
Doniphan	1,890	4	0	0	0	4	135	31	102	2	0
Doolittle	665	0	0	0	0	0	16	5	10	1	1
Drexel	1,095	1	0	0	0	1	40	9	30	1	0
Duenweg	1,249	1	0	0	0	1	74	11	57	6	0
Duquesne	1,741	9	0	2	1	6	30	13	15	2	0
East Prairie	3,112	17	0	0	1	16	106	12	91	3	1
Edgerton	550	1	0	0	0	1	2	1	1	0	1
Edina	1,123	0	0	0	0	0	2	0	2	0	0
Edmundson	781	9	0	0	3	6	86	18	33	35	0
Eldon	4,976	15	0	2	0	13	209	36	163	10	2
El Dorado Springs	3,724	18	0	2	0	16	141	36	102	3	0
Ellington	991	4	0	1	0	3	32	15	16	1	0
Ellisville	9,249	10	0	2	1	7	128	15	97	16	0
Ellsinore	364	0	0	0	0	0	0	0	0	0	0
Elsberry	2,661	1	0	1	0	0	33	11	22	0	0
Eminence	556	0	0	0	0	0	1	0	0	1	0
Eureka	9,319	11	0	2	0	9	216	23	186	7	1
Everton	307	0	0	0	0	0	6	4	0	2	0
Excelsior Springs	11,965	64	0	2	7	55	401	93	295	13	7
Exeter	753	0	0	0	0	0	1	1	0	0	0
Fair Grove	1,436	0	0	0	0	0	17	2	13	2	1
Fair Play	457	0	0	0	0	0	25	11	14	0	0
Farber	392	0	0	0	0	0	0	0	0	0	0
Farmington	16,125	55	0	0	5	50	592	42	535	15	0
Fayette	2,674	3	0	1	0	2	8	0	8	0	0
Ferguson	20,967	163	1	7	68	87	1,291	376	701	214	1
Ferrelview	577	3	0	1	0	2	6	2	4	0	0
Festus	11,411	74	2	4	7	61	274	36	215	23	0
Fleming	118	0	0	0	0	0	0	0	0	0	0
Flordell Hills	861	14	0	1	1	12	47	26	16	5	2
Florissant	50,560	139	0	8	74	57	1,548	356	996	196	5
Foley	212	0	0	0	0	0	0	0	0	0	0
Fordland	764	1	0	1	0	0	1	1	0	0	0
Foristell	332	1	0	0	0	1	36	6	30	0	0
Forsyth	1,701	2	0	1	1	0	35	5	28	2	0
Fredericktown	4,119	25	0	1	2	22	134	31	98	5	1
Freeman	602	0	0	0	0	0	0	0	0	0	0
Frontenac	3,548	4	0	0	0	4	70	6	64	0	0
Fulton	12,904	47	0	3	3	41	578	113	448	17	5
Galena	522	0	0	0	0	0	0	0	0	0	0
Gallatin	1,736	3	0	0	0	3	23	7	13	3	0
Garden City	1,674	2	0	1	0	1	26	6	17	3	1
Gerald	1,234	2	0	0	0	2	17	6	10	1	0
Gideon	957	0	0	0	0	0	1	0	1	0	0
Gladstone	28,151	65	0	16	15	34	637	144	424	69	10
Glasgow	1,188	0	0	0	0	0	8	2	6	0	0
Glendale	5,494	1	0	0	0	1	56	11	43	2	0
Glen Echo Park	158	0	0	0	0	0	0	0	0	0	0
Goodman	1,268	0	0	0	0	0	18	8	7	3	0
Gower	1,440	1	0	0	0	1	25	5	20	0	0
Granby	2,246	18	0	0	0	18	27	7	18	2	2
Grandin	237	0	0	0	0	0	0	0	0	0	0
Grandview	24,020	186	1	17	53	115	1,065	281	632	152	7
Greendale	691	1	0	0	0	1	11	0	9	2	0

[1] The FBI does not publish arson data unless it receives data from either the agency or the state for all 12 months of the calendar year.

Table 8. Offenses Known to Law Enforcement, by State and City, 2008—*Continued*

(Number.)

State/City	Population	Violent crime	Murder and non-negligent man-slaughter	Forcible rape	Robbery	Aggravated assault	Property crime	Burglary	Larceny-theft	Motor vehicle theft	Arson[1]
MISSOURI—*Continued*											
Greenfield	1,236	6	0	0	0	6	11	4	6	1	0
Greenwood	4,725	0	0	0	0	0	63	22	32	9	1
Hallsville	958	1	0	0	0	1	35	6	29	0	0
Hamilton	1,792	4	0	1	0	3	37	5	30	2	0
Hannibal	17,418	144	1	11	25	107	1,554	172	1,352	30	0
Hardin	555	0	0	0	0	0	0	0	0	0	0
Harrisonville	9,849	11	1	0	1	9	414	56	332	26	1
Hartville	599	2	0	1	0	1	0	0	0	0	0
Hawk Point	560	0	0	0	0	0	0	0	0	0	0
Hayti	2,946	6	1	1	1	3	160	18	137	5	0
Hayti Heights	753	6	0	0	0	6	4	3	1	0	0
Hazelwood	25,398	137	0	5	44	88	1,347	222	1,019	106	1
Henrietta	431	0	0	0	0	0	0	0	0	0	0
Herculaneum	3,467	0	0	0	0	0	345	17	318	10	0
Hermann	2,736	5	0	0	0	5	68	25	43	0	0
Higginsville	4,533	7	1	0	0	6	178	36	136	6	1
High Hill	214	0	0	0	0	0	3	1	2	0	0
Highlandville	912	0	0	0	0	0	1	0	1	0	0
Hillsboro	2,033	19	0	0	2	17	111	16	91	4	1
Hillsdale	1,382	49	0	1	7	41	69	41	22	6	0
Holcomb	672	0	0	0	0	0	0	0	0	0	0
Holden	2,573	2	0	0	0	2	93	17	74	2	4
Hollister	3,897	65	0	5	4	56	174	34	125	15	0
Holts Summit	3,736	13	0	1	0	12	114	24	88	2	1
Hornersville	657	2	0	0	0	2	0	0	0	0	0
Houston	2,018	2	0	0	0	2	47	8	36	3	1
Humansville	1,023	1	0	0	0	1	6	2	4	0	0
Huntsville	1,646	0	0	0	0	0	6	2	4	0	0
Hurley	158	0	0	0	0	0	0	0	0	0	0
Iberia	680	4	0	0	0	4	1	1	0	0	0
Independence	110,376	824	9	57	163	595	8,096	1,413	5,904	779	27
Indian Point	748	1	0	0	0	1	2	0	2	0	0
Iron Mountain Lake	699	1	0	0	0	1	12	2	7	3	0
Ironton	1,319	6	0	2	0	4	32	6	22	4	0
Jackson	13,715	19	0	0	1	18	424	74	334	16	0
JASCO Metropolitan	2,937	6	0	1	0	5	24	4	19	1	0
Jasper	1,064	2	0	0	0	2	17	14	3	0	0
Jennings	14,603	238	3	5	54	176	1,294	440	641	213	4
Jonesburg	731	1	0	0	0	1	17	3	14	0	0
Joplin	49,551	356	3	42	55	256	4,312	692	3,308	312	46
Kahoka	2,169	0	0	0	0	0	7	3	4	0	0
Kansas City	451,454	6,269	115	248	2,090	3,816	28,277	7,467	16,463	4,347	299
Kearney	8,614	9	0	4	2	3	137	13	117	7	1
Kennett	10,689	43	2	3	8	30	665	138	512	15	2
Kimberling City	2,558	5	0	0	0	5	40	10	28	2	0
Kimmswick	93	0	0	0	0	0	0	0	0	0	0
Kirksville[4]	17,120	66	0	1	7	58	402	50	337	15	0
Kirkwood	26,755	41	6	2	8	25	840	77	739	24	11
Knob Noster	3,357	14	1	1	0	12	108	15	92	1	1
Ladue	8,191	9	0	2	1	6	141	19	119	3	0
La Grange	923	2	0	0	0	2	1	1	0	0	0
Lake Lafayette	369	1	0	0	0	1	18	6	12	0	0
Lake Lotawana	1,957	0	0	0	0	0	26	8	16	2	0
Lake Ozark	1,996	17	0	1	0	16	70	17	51	2	0
Lakeshire	1,284	5	0	0	1	4	14	4	10	0	0
Lake St. Louis	14,451	16	0	1	4	11	253	31	216	6	1
Lake Tapawingo	783	2	0	0	0	2	19	3	15	1	0
Lake Waukomis	896	2	0	0	0	2	5	2	3	0	0
Lake Winnebago	1,143	0	0	0	0	0	6	0	6	0	0
Lamar	4,541	25	0	2	1	22	121	15	105	1	2
La Monte	1,096	1	0	0	0	1	26	9	17	0	0
Lanagan	437	0	0	0	0	0	2	1	1	0	0
La Plata	1,430	1	0	0	0	1	7	2	5	0	0
Lathrop	2,353	7	0	1	0	6	32	18	13	1	0
Laurie	723	2	0	1	0	1	54	6	47	1	0
Lawson	2,354	6	0	1	0	5	45	17	25	3	0
Leadington	217	1	0	0	0	1	4	0	4	0	0
Leadwood	1,156	7	0	0	0	7	17	5	10	2	0
Lebanon	14,379	75	0	7	2	66	831	120	684	27	2
Lee's Summit	84,399	108	2	6	34	66	2,283	421	1,729	133	4
Leeton	634	0	0	0	0	0	16	3	13	0	0
Lexington	4,508	8	0	1	1	6	117	27	85	5	0
Liberal	787	2	0	0	0	2	6	4	1	1	0

[1] The FBI does not publish arson data unless it receives data from either the agency or the state for all 12 months of the calendar year.
[4] Because of changes in the state/local agency's reporting practices, figures are not comparable to previous years' data.

Table 8. Offenses Known to Law Enforcement, by State and City, 2008—*Continued*

(Number.)

State/City	Population	Violent crime	Murder and non-negligent man-slaughter	Forcible rape	Robbery	Aggravated assault	Property crime	Burglary	Larceny-theft	Motor vehicle theft	Arson[1]
MISSOURI—*Continued*											
Liberty	30,479	58	0	12	7	39	555	83	431	41	7
Licking	1,505	4	0	0	1	3	59	4	51	4	0
Lincoln	1,088	0	0	0	0	0	17	4	12	1	0
Linn	1,422	3	0	0	0	3	26	1	24	1	0
Linn Creek	301	2	0	0	0	2	8	1	7	0	0
Lockwood	915	0	0	0	0	0	3	0	3	0	0
Lone Jack	954	3	0	0	0	3	29	16	12	1	0
Louisiana	3,773	8	1	1	0	6	33	8	25	0	0
Lowry City	738	2	0	1	0	1	36	15	21	0	0
Macon	5,452	9	0	0	0	9	153	24	119	10	5
Malden	4,471	8	0	0	0	8	87	27	60	0	0
Manchester	18,595	11	0	3	1	7	330	41	282	7	0
Mansfield	1,349	0	0	0	0	0	39	14	23	2	0
Maplewood	8,625	44	1	5	8	30	445	64	350	31	2
Marble Hill	1,489	3	0	0	0	3	40	10	30	0	0
Marceline	2,298	4	0	0	0	4	36	12	21	3	0
Marionville	2,181	4	1	0	0	3	93	12	76	5	0
Marquand	265	0	0	0	0	0	0	0	0	0	0
Marshall	12,153	27	0	5	3	19	347	56	278	13	1
Marshfield	7,306	10	0	1	1	8	181	25	146	10	1
Marthasville	862	0	0	0	0	0	5	0	5	0	0
Martinsburg	325	0	0	0	0	0	0	0	0	0	0
Maryland Heights	25,977	35	0	4	19	12	976	132	773	71	2
Maryville	10,850	30	0	0	0	30	241	24	211	6	0
Matthews	528	1	0	0	0	1	8	4	4	0	0
Maysville	1,128	2	0	0	0	2	4	2	2	0	0
Memphis	1,953	2	0	0	0	2	22	10	12	0	0
Mexico	10,939	11	0	3	7	1	244	67	174	3	0
Milan	1,764	3	0	0	1	2	22	5	16	1	0
Miller	800	4	0	1	0	3	18	4	13	1	0
Miner	1,332	7	0	0	1	6	61	8	48	5	0
Moberly	14,138	34	0	0	9	25	543	76	451	16	2
Moline Acres	2,517	20	0	0	11	9	156	26	117	13	0
Monett	8,980	8	1	1	2	4	337	79	243	15	2
Monroe City	2,481	17	0	1	0	16	100	34	63	3	0
Montgomery City	2,503	2	0	0	0	2	61	18	40	3	0
Montrose	425	0	0	0	0	0	7	5	2	0	0
Morehouse	922	6	0	1	1	4	16	8	6	2	0
Mosby	248	0	0	0	0	0	3	1	2	0	0
Moscow Mills	2,506	15	0	0	1	14	53	7	45	1	0
Mound City	1,073	2	0	1	0	1	14	5	9	0	0
Mountain Grove[3]	4,629		3	1	0		161	38	117	6	0
Mountain View	2,619	6	0	1	0	5	79	15	61	3	2
Mount Vernon	4,640	11	1	0	0	10	195	11	177	7	0
Napoleon	194	0	0	0	0	0	2	1	1	0	0
Neosho	11,371	23	0	1	2	20	585	84	483	18	1
Nevada	8,286	34	0	2	4	28	515	59	426	30	8
New Bloomfield	750	0	0	0	0	0	5	2	3	0	0
Newburg	473	7	0	0	0	7	21	10	9	2	1
New Florence	749	1	0	0	0	1	17	4	13	0	0
New Haven	2,042	10	0	0	0	10	50	22	25	3	1
New London	1,005	4	0	1	0	3	24	9	15	0	0
New Madrid	2,999	1	0	0	0	1	23	3	20	0	0
New Melle	283	1	0	0	0	1	2	1	1	0	0
Niangua	494	0	0	0	0	0	1	0	1	0	0
Nixa	19,162	11	1	1	2	7	323	59	243	21	1
Noel	1,602	18	0	0	0	18	33	5	25	3	0
Norborne	757	0	0	0	0	0	1	0	0	1	0
Normandy	4,899	66	0	4	16	46	211	60	88	63	2
North Kansas City	5,676	35	0	3	12	20	414	36	322	56	0
Northmoor	400	1	0	0	0	1	31	10	16	5	0
Northwoods	4,309	25	1	0	10	14	168	66	65	37	2
Norwood	576	1	0	0	0	1	0	0	0	0	0
Oakland	1,565	1	0	0	0	1	20	2	18	0	0
Oakview Village	394	0	0	0	0	0	3	1	2	0	0
Odessa	4,706	2	0	0	1	1	103	20	78	5	3
O'Fallon	78,837	66	3	7	11	45	1,531	203	1,294	34	3
Olivette	7,472	30	0	0	5	25	231	45	160	26	0
Oran	1,244	0	0	0	0	0	39	4	35	0	0
Oregon	875	0	0	0	0	0	8	4	3	1	0
Orrick	822	5	0	1	1	3	19	11	6	2	0
Osage Beach	4,748	23	0	0	2	21	378	43	332	3	0
Osceola	792	1	0	0	0	1	17	1	16	0	0

[1] The FBI does not publish arson data unless it receives data from either the agency or the state for all 12 months of the calendar year.
[3] The FBI determined that the agency did not follow national Uniform Crime Reporting (UCR) Program guidelines for reporting an offense. Consequently, this figure is not included in this table.

Table 8. Offenses Known to Law Enforcement, by State and City, 2008—*Continued*

(Number.)

State/City	Population	Violent crime	Murder and non-negligent man-slaughter	Forcible rape	Robbery	Aggravated assault	Property crime	Burglary	Larceny-theft	Motor vehicle theft	Arson[1]
MISSOURI—*Continued*											
Overland	15,622	53	1	2	18	32	681	113	524	44	0
Owensville	2,474	2	0	0	0	2	135	23	107	5	0
Ozark	18,332	39	0	0	4	35	469	93	356	20	0
Pacific	7,288	29	0	3	2	24	283	47	217	19	1
Pagedale	3,402	41	2	3	12	24	210	84	113	13	0
Palmyra	3,410	3	0	0	0	3	72	9	61	2	0
Park Hills	8,965	5	0	0	2	3	133	18	106	9	0
Parkville	5,398	1	0	0	1	0	145	14	125	6	1
Parma	756	2	0	0	1	1	23	5	17	1	0
Pasadena Park	458	2	0	0	2	0	14	3	3	8	0
Peculiar	4,757	4	0	1	0	3	75	16	58	1	0
Perry	663	0	0	0	0	0	2	1	1	0	3
Perryville	8,195	3	0	1	0	2	186	36	138	12	1
Pevely	4,676	12	0	2	1	9	163	24	128	11	2
Piedmont	1,902	7	0	1	0	6	93	9	83	1	0
Pierce City	1,466	1	0	0	0	1	45	8	36	1	1
Pilot Grove	749	1	0	0	0	1	25	7	18	0	0
Pine Lawn	3,997	43	0	1	7	35	241	84	108	49	1
Pineville	872	0	0	0	0	0	2	1	0	1	0
Platte City	4,933	6	0	0	0	6	102	12	85	5	1
Platte Woods	455	1	0	0	0	1	9	1	5	3	0
Plattsburg	2,424	5	0	3	0	2	35	6	28	1	1
Pleasant Hill	7,223	3	1	0	0	2	151	34	113	4	0
Pleasant Hope	601	0	0	0	0	0	7	1	5	1	0
Pleasant Valley	3,517	4	0	2	1	1	63	30	30	3	2
Polo	607	0	0	0	0	0	3	1	2	0	0
Poplar Bluff	17,035	107	0	6	19	82	1,273	267	974	32	10
Purdy	1,164	2	0	1	0	1	26	10	15	1	1
Queen City	607	0	0	0	0	0	1	1	0	0	0
Qulin	482	1	0	0	0	1	1	0	1	0	0
Randolph	50	1	0	0	1	0	0	0	0	0	0
Raymore	18,181	7	0	1	0	6	336	36	294	6	1
Raytown	28,086	102	0	7	52	43	1,005	310	537	158	8
Republic	13,643	68	1	2	2	63	421	73	336	12	1
Rich Hill	1,496	8	0	0	0	8	38	9	27	2	0
Richland	1,769	2	0	0	1	1	50	10	36	4	0
Richmond	5,864	11	0	1	2	8	234	47	183	4	3
Richmond Heights	9,105	28	0	2	12	14	788	49	707	32	1
Riverside	2,986	16	0	1	3	12	265	27	208	30	1
Riverview	2,918	36	1	3	3	29	185	84	74	27	1
Rockaway Beach	591	4	0	0	0	4	9	2	5	2	0
Rock Hill	4,591	4	0	0	1	3	94	24	64	6	0
Rock Port	1,303	0	0	0	0	0	6	3	2	1	0
Rogersville	3,127	8	0	2	1	5	65	12	47	6	1
Rolla[4]	18,703	51	1	6	17	27	918	141	752	25	3
Rosebud	375	0	0	0	0	0	4	1	3	0	0
Salem	4,816	22	0	0	3	19	183	19	154	10	0
Salisbury	1,559	1	0	0	0	1	28	8	20	0	0
Sarcoxie	1,370	6	0	1	0	5	15	5	8	2	0
Savannah	5,073	6	0	0	0	6	92	23	68	1	0
Scott City	4,542	5	0	0	1	4	15	5	8	2	2
Sedalia	20,930	159	0	11	24	124	1,485	310	1,114	61	9
Seligman	924	0	0	0	0	0	0	0	0	0	0
Seneca	2,276	1	0	0	0	1	76	20	48	8	0
Seymour	2,046	5	0	1	0	4	52	9	41	2	0
Shrewsbury	6,234	6	0	0	5	1	117	14	89	14	0
Sikeston	17,053	226	1	18	43	164	879	216	628	35	13
Silex	247	1	0	0	0	1	3	1	1	1	1
Slater	1,901	0	0	0	0	0	44	2	39	3	2
Smithville	8,192	6	0	1	0	5	92	16	69	7	0
Southwest City	925	8	0	0	0	8	29	6	20	3	0
Sparta	1,199	4	0	0	0	4	23	5	15	3	0
Springfield	155,106	1,068	9	95	289	675	14,514	2,128	11,357	1,029	93
St. Ann	12,772	93	0	9	21	63	611	73	503	35	1
St. Charles	64,012	151	1	13	33	104	2,432	308	2,025	99	4
St. Clair	4,427	58	0	3	1	54	376	58	306	12	0
Steele	2,108	20	0	0	8	12	103	35	66	2	0
Steelville	1,484	13	0	1	0	12	30	6	21	3	0
Ste. Genevieve[4]	4,435	7	0	0	0	7	55	9	35	11	0
St. George	1,211	3	0	0	0	3	25	3	19	3	0
St. James	4,124	15	0	0	0	15	193	32	158	3	1
St. John	6,381	30	0	2	2	26	222	30	177	15	1
St. Joseph[4]	76,377	353	3	13	88	249	3,634	770	2,643	221	23

[1] The FBI does not publish arson data unless it receives data from either the agency or the state for all 12 months of the calendar year.

[4] Because of changes in the state/local agency's reporting practices, figures are not comparable to previous years' data.

Table 8. Offenses Known to Law Enforcement, by State and City, 2008—*Continued*

(Number.)

State/City	Population	Violent crime	Murder and non-negligent man-slaughter	Forcible rape	Robbery	Aggravated assault	Property crime	Burglary	Larceny-theft	Motor vehicle theft	Arson[1]
MISSOURI—*Continued*											
St. Louis	356,204	7,383	167	237	2,634	4,345	30,443	7,274	17,328	5,841	325
St. Marys	383	1	0	0	0	1	6	0	6	0	0
Stover	1,050	6	0	0	0	6	46	18	28	0	0
St. Peters	55,545	181	0	14	16	151	1,598	155	1,388	55	19
Strafford	2,175	2	0	0	0	2	124	4	113	7	0
Strasburg	136	0	0	0	0	0	0	0	0	0	0
St. Robert	3,493	62	0	3	4	55	309	39	254	16	2
Sugar Creek	3,504	14	0	2	2	10	181	37	125	19	2
Sullivan	6,738	11	0	1	0	10	317	52	255	10	0
Summersville	555	1	0	0	0	1	15	8	7	0	0
Sunset Hills	8,226	19	0	1	4	14	233	27	192	14	1
Sweet Springs	1,518	1	0	0	1	0	38	15	23	0	0
Tarkio	1,815	3	0	0	0	3	12	2	7	3	0
Thayer	2,152	3	0	0	0	3	21	6	14	1	0
Theodosia	251	0	0	0	0	0	0	0	0	0	1
Tipton	3,314	0	0	0	0	0	32	10	22	0	0
Town and Country	10,720	5	0	0	4	1	172	14	155	3	0
Tracy	209	2	0	0	0	2	12	1	11	0	0
Trenton	5,996	23	1	5	0	17	170	29	132	9	1
Trimble	479	0	0	0	0	0	0	0	0	0	0
Troy[4]	12,541	32	1	1	2	28	440	41	392	7	1
Truesdale	669	3	0	0	0	3	11	5	6	0	0
Union	9,715	76	0	1	2	73	463	52	399	12	1
Unionville	1,863	1	0	0	0	1	16	3	11	2	0
University City	36,402	302	2	8	77	215	1,944	353	1,382	209	17
Uplands Park	438	2	0	0	0	2	15	5	2	8	0
Urbana	436	4	0	0	0	4	9	3	6	0	2
Van Buren	817	1	0	0	0	1	5	1	4	0	0
Vandalia	4,420	16	0	0	0	16	50	8	39	3	0
Velda City	1,496	13	0	1	3	9	67	19	42	6	0
Velda Village Hills	1,036	0	0	0	0	0	0	0	0	0	0
Verona	726	1	0	1	0	0	8	4	2	2	0
Versailles	2,729	6	0	0	0	6	91	5	86	0	0
Viburnum	785	2	0	0	0	2	8	5	2	1	0
Vienna	645	3	0	0	0	3	12	0	12	0	0
Vinita Park	1,783	12	0	1	0	11	88	12	68	8	2
Walnut Grove	676	0	0	0	0	0	3	2	1	0	0
Wardell	249	0	0	0	0	0	1	1	0	0	0
Warrensburg	18,928	36	0	7	9	20	638	123	490	25	4
Warrenton	7,415	45	0	3	2	40	506	26	476	4	1
Warsaw	2,246	10	0	0	0	10	89	17	65	7	0
Warson Woods	1,859	0	0	0	0	0	28	2	25	1	0
Washburn	475	2	2	0	0	0	0	0	0	0	1
Washington	14,394	31	0	0	2	29	417	59	348	10	1
Waverly	782	1	0	0	0	1	10	6	4	0	0
Waynesville	3,829	28	0	0	6	22	162	12	145	5	2
Weatherby Lake	1,849	2	0	0	0	2	18	0	17	1	0
Webb City	11,496	7	0	0	4	3	444	51	378	15	0
Webster Groves	22,402	13	0	1	4	8	345	77	247	21	2
Wellston	2,309	66	1	4	11	50	145	57	46	42	4
Wellsville	1,333	1	0	0	0	1	11	3	6	2	0
Wentzville	25,842	42	0	11	3	28	568	66	492	10	3
Weston	1,652	8	0	2	0	6	38	5	33	0	1
West Plains	11,763	43	0	2	7	34	941	204	702	35	0
Westwood	291	0	0	0	0	0	2	1	1	0	0
Wheaton	742	0	0	0	0	0	0	0	0	0	0
Willard	3,373	5	0	0	0	5	99	12	85	2	1
Willow Springs	2,144	8	0	0	0	8	87	14	66	7	0
Winfield	913	1	0	0	0	1	10	1	7	2	1
Winona	1,332	3	1	0	1	1	26	10	13	3	0
Woodson Terrace	4,013	18	0	0	10	8	185	42	74	69	0
Wright City	2,989	8	1	0	1	6	128	18	105	5	0
MONTANA											
Baker	1,609	1	0	0	0	1	15	6	9	0	0
Belgrade	8,361	37	0	8	3	26	282	28	236	18	1
Billings[4]	103,196	272	2	40	54	176	4,261	618	3,367	276	22
Boulder	1,443	2	0	0	0	2	9	1	5	3	0
Bozeman	39,408	89	1	14	12	62	1,380	119	1,181	80	13
Colstrip	2,321	5	0	0	0	5	40	7	32	1	3
Columbia Falls	5,296	17	0	2	0	15	208	11	189	8	1
Columbus	1,957	0	0	0	0	0	44	3	39	2	0
Conrad	2,517	9	0	2	1	6	33	3	26	4	1
Cut Bank	3,129	36	0	2	0	34	78	11	63	4	2

[1] The FBI does not publish arson data unless it receives data from either the agency or the state for all 12 months of the calendar year.
[4] Because of changes in the state/local agency's reporting practices, figures are not comparable to previous years' data.

Table 8. Offenses Known to Law Enforcement, by State and City, 2008—*Continued*

(Number.)

State/City	Population	Violent crime	Murder and non-negligent man-slaughter	Forcible rape	Robbery	Aggravated assault	Property crime	Burglary	Larceny-theft	Motor vehicle theft	Arson[1]
MONTANA—*Continued*											
Dillon	4,091	10	0	0	0	10	74	11	61	2	1
East Helena	2,149	4	0	0	0	4	33	14	18	1	1
Ennis	1,036	0	0	0	0	0	18	12	6	0	0
Eureka	1,009	0	0	0	0	0	30	13	17	0	0
Fort Benton	1,443	3	0	0	0	3	35	8	24	3	0
Glasgow	2,885	7	0	1	0	6	52	8	42	2	0
Glendive	4,585	6	1	0	0	5	169	13	149	7	0
Great Falls	59,093	162	1	8	30	123	2,791	281	2,381	129	15
Hamilton	4,824	16	0	4	1	11	258	25	223	10	0
Havre	9,621	51	0	8	0	43	425	32	362	31	1
Helena	29,054	86	0	14	7	65	1,007	121	832	54	15
Hot Springs	568	2	0	0	0	2	4	1	2	1	1
Joliet	620	0	0	0	0	0	7	1	6	0	0
Kalispell	21,056	72	0	12	9	51	1,360	151	1,160	49	3
Laurel	6,525	13	0	3	0	10	213	23	186	4	0
Lewistown	5,899	17	0	4	0	13	93	12	81	0	1
Libby	2,886	10	0	1	1	8	102	17	82	3	0
Livingston	7,457	23	0	2	2	19	175	28	134	13	1
Manhattan	1,559	5	0	0	0	5	22	3	19	0	0
Missoula	68,445	181	1	17	22	141	2,463	225	2,131	107	10
Plains	1,254	3	0	0	0	3	48	7	38	3	0
Polson	5,170	28	0	1	0	27	229	29	186	14	0
Ronan City	2,028	15	0	1	1	13	94	19	73	2	0
Stevensville	2,023	10	0	0	0	10	46	6	35	5	2
St. Ignatius	814	4	0	0	1	3	28	6	22	0	1
Thompson Falls	1,436	6	0	0	0	6	40	13	23	4	0
Three Forks	1,941	2	0	1	0	1	16	2	13	1	0
Troy	985	1	0	0	0	1	5	0	5	0	0
West Yellowstone	1,471	0	0	0	0	0	11	0	8	3	0
Whitefish	8,433	12	0	0	1	11	288	24	247	17	1
Wolf Point	2,508	16	1	2	1	12	48	6	38	4	0
NEBRASKA											
Alliance	7,963	30	1	0	6	23	154	14	131	9	2
Ashland	2,587	1	0	0	0	1	12	6	6	0	0
Auburn	3,241	2	0	0	1	1	78	12	62	4	0
Aurora	4,180	4	0	2	0	2	33	13	18	2	1
Bayard	1,119	1	0	0	0	1	16	6	9	1	0
Beatrice	12,913	55	0	24	2	29	561	93	447	21	8
Bellevue	48,894	77	0	14	11	52	1,374	192	1,095	87	11
Blair	7,914	9	0	4	0	5	96	7	80	9	1
Bridgeport	1,443	0	0	0	0	0	18	3	15	0	0
Broken Bow	3,115	6	0	1	0	5	41	2	35	4	1
Central City	2,729	3	0	3	0	0	59	8	48	3	1
Chadron	5,473	14	1	5	1	7	174	35	120	19	1
Columbus	21,438	23	0	4	2	17	550	114	414	22	2
Cozad	4,264	6	0	2	0	4	66	8	55	3	0
Crete	6,292	28	0	3	2	23	224	52	163	9	0
David City	2,470	3	0	0	0	3	39	7	32	0	0
Emerson	821	1	0	0	0	1	0	0	0	0	0
Falls City	3,976	1	0	0	0	1	72	18	53	1	0
Fremont	25,362	53	0	20	5	28	980	228	717	35	3
Gering	7,633	4	0	0	0	4	183	35	137	11	0
Gordon	1,504	16	0	4	0	12	56	7	48	1	0
Gothenburg	3,710	0	0	0	0	0	53	3	49	1	0
Grand Island	45,022	188	2	17	24	145	2,217	326	1,787	104	12
Hastings	25,428	48	1	10	7	30	986	154	805	27	8
Holdrege	5,116	7	0	2	3	2	111	9	101	1	0
Imperial	1,774	0	0	0	0	0	4	1	3	0	0
Kearney	30,472	65	1	15	5	44	845	129	678	38	6
La Vista	17,103	10	0	4	0	6	290	51	224	15	2
Lexington	10,172	26	2	5	4	15	405	51	331	23	0
Lincoln	251,550	1,282	4	113	213	952	10,168	1,569	8,251	348	
Lyons	850	1	0	1	0	0	6	1	5	0	0
Madison	2,183	0	0	0	0	0	35	5	27	3	2
Milford	2,014	2	0	1	0	1	26	9	17	0	0
Minden	2,840	3	0	2	1	0	67	9	58	0	0
Nebraska City	7,049	8	0	3	0	5	192	39	148	5	1
Norfolk	23,096	34	0	16	5	13	764	97	643	24	4
Ogallala	4,474	5	1	2	1	1	183	18	160	5	3
Omaha	437,238	2,648	44	180	949	1,475	18,792	3,175	12,892	2,725	
O'Neill	3,293	0	0	0	0	0	11	2	8	1	0
Ord	2,041	1	0	0	0	1	7	4	3	0	0
Papillion	22,833	14	1	2	1	10	367	22	331	14	4

[1] The FBI does not publish arson data unless it receives data from either the agency or the state for all 12 months of the calendar year.

Table 8. Offenses Known to Law Enforcement, by State and City, 2008—*Continued*

(Number.)

State/City	Population	Violent crime	Murder and non-negligent man-slaughter	Forcible rape	Robbery	Aggravated assault	Property crime	Burglary	Larceny-theft	Motor vehicle theft	Arson[1]
NEBRASKA—*Continued*											
Plainview	1,197	2	0	0	0	2	9	1	7	1	0
Ralston	6,087	8	0	0	1	7	181	37	134	10	1
Scottsbluff	14,667	55	1	10	6	38	850	145	678	27	9
Seward	6,759	4	0	2	0	2	98	11	83	4	1
Sidney	6,492	5	0	2	0	3	129	15	111	3	0
South Sioux City	12,005	15	0	1	1	13	233	17	194	22	2
St. Paul	2,205	0	0	0	0	0	1	0	1	0	0
Superior	1,793	1	0	1	0	0	8	7	1	0	0
Valentine	2,619	9	0	0	1	8	63	10	50	3	0
Valley	1,864	3	0	0	1	2	39	11	25	3	1
Wahoo	4,000	4	0	1	0	3	48	7	39	2	0
Wayne	5,257	6	0	5	0	1	107	25	81	1	0
West Point	3,340	2	0	1	0	1	30	8	22	0	0
Wilber	1,734	0	0	0	0	0	9	0	9	0	0
Wymore	1,597	4	0	1	0	3	34	9	25	0	0
York	7,884	3	0	1	0	2	219	27	187	5	0
NEVADA											
Boulder City	14,810	9	0	0	2	7	146	66	68	12	10
Carlin	2,119	17	0	2	1	14	48	19	23	6	0
Elko	17,449	71	0	15	19	37	557	149	378	30	5
Fallon	8,599	33	0	0	4	29	424	59	343	22	6
Henderson	256,091	529	5	90	212	222	5,814	1,542	3,443	829	61
Las Vegas Metropolitan Police Department	1,353,175	13,324	120	729	4,932	7,543	53,160	14,902	26,856	11,402	319
Lovelock	1,893	17	0	0	0	17	51	23	21	7	0
Mesquite	16,470	23	0	2	8	13	369	42	292	35	1
North Las Vegas	228,363	1,620	11	57	554	998	7,416	2,208	3,591	1,617	32
Reno	218,556	1,532	15	83	488	946	9,714	1,975	6,757	982	43
Sparks	88,913	410	0	51	128	231	3,486	903	2,279	304	53
West Wendover	5,090	18	1	4	2	11	153	38	99	16	1
Winnemucca	8,097	22	2	0	0	20	107	36	64	7	2
Yerington	3,992	0	0	0	0	0	36	21	15	0	0
NEW HAMPSHIRE											
Alexandria	1,546	2	0	1	0	1	15	2	12	1	1
Alstead	2,114	0	0	0	0	0	24	6	18	0	0
Alton	5,142	5	1	0	1	3	100	37	60	3	4
Amherst	11,829	3	0	1	1	1	204	14	187	3	3
Antrim	2,640	2	0	1	0	1	65	11	53	1	0
Ashland	2,033	0	0	0	0	0	53	5	47	1	0
Auburn	5,217	3	0	0	0	3	35	3	30	2	0
Barnstead	4,656	5	0	1	0	4	72	29	37	6	0
Barrington	8,521	4	0	2	0	2	124	52	66	6	1
Bartlett	2,947	2	0	1	0	1	49	14	35	0	0
Bedford	21,505	7	0	3	3	1	280	22	251	7	7
Belmont	7,215	18	0	6	2	10	222	45	159	18	2
Bennington	1,484	1	0	0	0	1	47	3	39	5	0
Berlin	10,082	11	0	1	2	8	154	48	99	7	7
Bethlehem	2,468	3	0	0	1	2	37	13	19	5	2
Boscawen	3,994	5	0	0	1	4	46	11	33	2	0
Bow	8,170	5	0	1	0	4	92	9	78	5	0
Bradford	1,532	0	0	0	0	0	5	1	3	1	0
Brentwood	3,999	5	0	3	0	2	53	10	33	10	0
Bristol	3,123	8	0	1	0	7	89	12	74	3	1
Campton	3,019	1	0	0	0	1	68	22	42	4	1
Candia	4,213	4	0	0	0	4	71	7	61	3	3
Carroll	748	1	0	0	0	1	44	3	40	1	0
Charlestown	4,882	7	0	2	0	5	29	8	19	2	1
Claremont	13,090	26	0	7	2	17	357	34	308	15	0
Colebrook	2,366	4	0	1	0	3	45	7	34	4	1
Concord	42,603	89	0	18	26	45	1,211	127	1,049	35	11
Conway	9,247	33	0	6	10	17	450	58	379	13	7
Dalton	897	0	0	0	0	0	18	7	8	3	0
Danville	4,375	5	1	2	0	2	49	9	38	2	0
Deerfield	4,246	3	0	0	0	3	39	8	29	2	1
Deering	2,069	2	0	1	0	1	30	8	21	1	1
Derry	33,981	57	0	8	10	39	748	147	547	54	25
Dover	29,005	15	1	3	5	6	610	68	528	14	3
Dublin	1,589	1	0	1	0	0	21	5	16	0	0
Dunbarton	2,659	0	0	0	0	0	16	4	11	1	0
Enfield	4,858	6	0	3	1	2	60	13	46	1	1
Epping	6,252	5	0	1	0	4	164	25	135	4	1
Epsom	4,636	0	0	0	0	0	48	8	34	6	2
Exeter	14,817	15	0	3	3	9	160	26	129	5	2
Farmington	6,777	15	0	7	2	6	150	32	100	18	1
Fitzwilliam	2,311	0	0	0	0	0	39	5	7	27	0

[1] The FBI does not publish arson data unless it receives data from either the agency or the state for all 12 months of the calendar year.

Table 8. Offenses Known to Law Enforcement, by State and City, 2008—*Continued*

(Number.)

State/City	Population	Violent crime	Murder and non-negligent man-slaughter	Forcible rape	Robbery	Aggravated assault	Property crime	Burglary	Larceny-theft	Motor vehicle theft	Arson[1]
NEW HAMPSHIRE—*Continued*											
Franconia	1,055	0	0	0	0	0	26	4	20	2	0
Freedom	1,447	0	0	0	0	0	19	8	11	0	1
Fremont	4,148	5	0	1	1	3	47	8	36	3	0
Gilford	7,475	11	0	3	2	6	205	17	185	3	1
Gilmanton	3,572	1	0	0	0	1	37	14	23	0	1
Goffstown	17,716	6	0	2	3	1	251	40	204	7	2
Gorham	2,818	0	0	0	0	0	41	13	27	1	0
Grantham	2,567	1	0	0	0	1	23	5	17	1	1
Greenland	3,417	3	0	1	0	2	44	4	39	1	0
Hampstead	8,998	11	0	4	0	7	112	21	87	4	0
Hampton	15,443	29	0	9	8	12	346	37	298	11	1
Hancock	1,813	0	0	0	0	0	15	2	12	1	0
Hanover	11,092	6	0	5	1	0	207	11	195	1	1
Haverhill	4,636	17	1	3	1	12	131	28	99	4	0
Henniker	5,147	2	0	0	1	1	115	14	98	3	0
Hillsborough	5,599	16	0	1	3	12	147	23	113	11	5
Hinsdale	4,206	5	0	1	1	3	98	11	86	1	0
Hooksett	13,934	7	0	2	2	3	275	26	235	14	2
Hopkinton	5,642	0	0	0	0	0	55	10	40	5	0
Hudson	25,009	26	0	6	3	17	431	71	330	30	7
Jaffrey	5,703	7	0	1	0	6	65	18	41	6	1
Keene	22,931	55	0	12	16	27	742	83	638	21	10
Kingston	6,269	9	0	2	1	6	60	10	42	8	1
Laconia	17,008	57	1	7	9	40	680	96	559	25	10
Lancaster	3,292	4	0	0	0	4	91	11	76	4	2
Lebanon	12,749	22	0	6	2	14	462	37	418	7	3
Lee	4,483	1	0	0	0	1	24	8	15	1	0
Lincoln	1,339	5	0	1	0	4	109	7	97	5	0
Lisbon	1,669	1	0	1	0	0	31	6	22	3	0
Litchfield	8,798	3	0	0	0	3	110	26	79	5	3
Littleton	6,215	1	0	0	0	1	119	13	99	7	1
Londonderry	25,182	16	0	2	4	10	384	41	324	19	4
Loudon	5,221	3	0	0	0	3	94	9	80	5	0
Madison	2,332	0	0	0	0	0	67	19	45	3	0
Manchester[4]	109,083	518	2	71	166	279	3,538	577	2,696	265	55
Marlborough	2,094	3	0	2	0	1	48	4	40	4	0
Meredith	6,701	6	0	1	1	4	155	31	119	5	4
Merrimack	26,725	8	0	0	2	6	291	18	260	13	1
Middleton	1,829	1	0	0	0	1	25	10	15	0	0
Milford	15,197	21	0	5	7	9	316	50	251	15	5
Milton	4,604	8	0	5	0	3	72	15	51	6	3
Mont Vernon	2,414	0	0	0	0	0	7	4	2	1	0
Moultonborough	5,010	1	0	1	0	0	87	19	64	4	1
New Boston	5,160	1	1	0	0	0	32	6	22	4	0
Newbury	2,127	0	0	0	0	0	21	0	19	2	0
New Durham	2,568	4	0	0	0	4	41	8	31	2	0
Newfields	1,620	0	0	0	0	0	24	5	19	0	0
New Hampton	2,263	3	0	1	0	2	44	13	29	2	0
Newington	806	6	0	1	0	5	179	1	175	3	0
New Ipswich	5,307	3	0	0	1	2	64	16	48	0	2
Newmarket	9,679	8	0	2	1	5	44	10	31	3	0
Newport	6,498	10	0	2	0	8	240	24	204	12	6
Newton	4,546	2	0	0	0	2	34	9	21	4	0
Northfield	5,222	15	0	4	0	11	88	17	69	2	0
North Hampton	4,558	3	0	1	0	2	95	19	73	3	2
Northumberland	2,337	4	0	1	0	3	40	7	31	2	0
Northwood	4,136	7	0	1	0	6	57	21	34	2	0
Ossipee	4,727	9	0	1	1	7	141	23	106	12	1
Pelham	12,706	13	0	3	3	7	226	47	166	13	6
Pembroke	7,410	4	0	0	0	4	122	19	93	10	1
Peterborough	6,171	4	0	1	0	3	104	12	89	3	2
Pittsfield	4,431	9	0	3	1	5	100	13	82	5	0
Plaistow	7,644	3	0	0	2	1	168	12	142	14	1
Plymouth	6,425	16	0	6	2	8	181	40	132	9	1
Portsmouth	20,455	37	1	6	7	23	548	44	481	23	8
Raymond	10,259	17	0	2	2	13	190	19	160	11	1
Rindge	6,688	7	0	2	0	5	93	27	64	2	1
Rochester	30,781	58	0	16	7	35	982	122	813	47	6
Rollinsford	2,641	1	0	0	0	1	17	5	11	1	0
Rye	5,171	0	0	0	0	0	67	7	60	0	2
Sandown	5,900	1	0	0	0	1	53	15	36	2	1
Sandwich	1,329	0	0	0	0	0	44	10	34	0	0
Seabrook	8,578	26	0	0	7	19	275	30	232	13	0

[1] The FBI does not publish arson data unless it receives data from either the agency or the state for all 12 months of the calendar year.
[4] Because of changes in the state/local agency's reporting practices, figures are not comparable to previous years' data.

Table 8. Offenses Known to Law Enforcement, by State and City, 2008—*Continued*

(Number.)

State/City	Population	Violent crime	Murder and non-negligent man-slaughter	Forcible rape	Robbery	Aggravated assault	Property crime	Burglary	Larceny-theft	Motor vehicle theft	Arson[1]
NEW HAMPSHIRE—*Continued*											
Somersworth	11,905	35	0	11	3	21	344	80	258	6	2
South Hampton	885	0	0	0	0	0	2	1	1	0	0
Strafford	4,101	1	0	0	1	0	31	5	24	2	0
Stratham	7,315	2	0	2	0	0	72	11	59	2	1
Sugar Hill	611	0	0	0	0	0	5	2	3	0	0
Sunapee	3,392	1	0	0	0	1	10	4	5	1	0
Thornton	2,129	5	0	0	0	5	7	0	4	3	1
Tilton	3,586	12	0	4	4	4	189	22	162	5	0
Troy	2,080	4	0	1	0	3	31	10	21	0	0
Wakefield	5,487	4	0	2	0	2	106	30	70	6	2
Walpole	3,705	2	0	0	0	2	45	9	33	3	0
Waterville Valley	272	0	0	0	0	0	52	0	51	1	0
Weare	9,251	8	0	2	0	6	61	17	40	4	2
Webster	1,892	3	0	2	0	1	16	2	14	0	1
Wilton	3,970	5	1	2	0	2	63	18	43	2	0
Windham	13,457	13	0	1	5	7	182	58	117	7	2
Wolfeboro	6,581	10	0	4	0	6	101	16	81	4	3
Woodstock	1,173	4	0	0	1	3	36	8	28	0	0
NEW JERSEY											
Aberdeen Township	18,527	18	0	1	3	14	223	45	160	18	0
Absecon	8,096	27	0	3	11	13	357	92	255	10	0
Alexandria Township	5,141	0	0	0	0	0	0	0	0	0	0
Allendale	6,579	0	0	0	0	0	109	16	87	6	0
Allenhurst	698	1	0	0	0	1	37	2	35	0	0
Allentown	1,848	0	0	0	0	0	28	7	21	0	0
Alpha	2,368	13	0	0	1	12	14	3	10	1	0
Alpine	2,475	0	0	0	0	0	14	2	12	0	0
Andover Township	6,552	6	0	0	0	6	49	9	40	0	1
Asbury Park	16,459	319	1	6	153	159	946	268	622	56	2
Atlantic City[8]	39,425	654	12	37	288	317			1,748	160	6
Atlantic Highlands	4,601	5	0	1	0	4	71	17	53	1	0
Audubon	8,809	1	0	0	0	1	356	30	316	10	0
Audubon Park	1,049	1	0	0	1	0	22	3	18	1	0
Avalon	2,089	2	0	0	0	2	245	40	203	2	0
Avon-by-the-Sea	2,168	0	0	0	0	0	48	13	35	0	0
Barnegat Light	840	0	0	0	0	0	12	4	8	0	0
Barnegat Township	22,762	22	0	1	1	20	263	67	191	5	2
Barrington	6,877	6	0	1	3	2	67	19	44	4	0
Bay Head	1,263	0	0	0	0	0	81	11	69	1	0
Bayonne	57,170	209	0	7	106	96	994	237	636	121	4
Beach Haven	1,386	1	0	0	0	1	136	16	120	0	0
Beachwood	10,795	12	0	1	3	8	224	30	188	6	0
Bedminster Township	8,343	0	0	0	0	0	60	14	44	2	0
Belleville	33,679	118	1	0	64	53	814	138	501	175	9
Bellmawr	11,055	22	0	1	7	14	308	79	202	27	1
Belmar	5,885	32	0	1	3	28	309	95	211	3	1
Belvidere	2,620	3	0	0	0	3	17	0	16	1	1
Bergenfield	25,666	26	0	3	14	9	217	38	168	11	14
Berkeley Heights Township	13,337	4	0	0	0	4	87	15	66	6	0
Berkeley Township	42,799	41	0	9	7	25	677	144	503	30	6
Berlin	8,075	16	0	0	4	12	190	29	152	9	2
Berlin Township	5,370	14	0	0	7	7	209	27	175	7	0
Bernards Township	26,641	0	0	0	0	0	172	26	134	12	0
Bernardsville	7,767	2	0	0	0	2	46	5	40	1	1
Beverly	2,568	17	0	3	3	11	53	34	14	5	1
Blairstown Township	5,924	10	0	2	0	8	72	16	54	2	0
Bloomfield	43,827	106	0	3	77	26	1,160	202	796	162	5
Bloomingdale	7,449	10	0	0	2	8	74	22	50	2	0
Bogota	7,927	14	0	0	3	11	86	12	70	4	1
Boonton	8,446	8	0	0	1	7	87	23	60	4	1
Boonton Township	4,396	2	0	1	0	1	35	9	26	0	0
Bordentown	3,825	4	0	0	1	3	62	14	45	3	0
Bordentown Township	10,385	20	0	1	6	13	134	37	85	12	0
Bound Brook	10,165	24	0	0	18	6	216	72	137	7	0
Bradley Beach	4,797	15	0	3	5	7	135	25	108	2	0
Branchburg Township	15,005	1	0	0	0	1	102	16	83	3	0
Brick Township	78,218	105	0	4	19	82	1,617	279	1,292	46	3
Bridgeton	24,714	334	6	4	113	211	1,091	337	709	45	15
Bridgewater Township	44,434	15	0	1	5	9	673	75	568	30	3
Brielle	4,856	4	0	0	0	4	47	12	35	0	0
Brigantine	12,705	5	0	1	1	3	198	51	144	3	1
Brooklawn	2,246	20	0	1	12	7	302	26	268	8	0

[1] The FBI does not publish arson data unless it receives data from either the agency or the state for all 12 months of the calendar year.
[8] The FBI determined that the agency's data were underreported. Consequently, those data are not included in this table.

Table 8. Offenses Known to Law Enforcement, by State and City, 2008—*Continued*

(Number.)

State/City	Population	Violent crime	Murder and non-negligent man-slaughter	Forcible rape	Robbery	Aggravated assault	Property crime	Burglary	Larceny-theft	Motor vehicle theft	Arson[1]
NEW JERSEY—*Continued*											
Buena	3,717	12	0	2	0	10	105	32	65	8	0
Burlington	9,416	53	1	4	20	28	197	39	148	10	4
Burlington Township	21,388	43	0	3	25	15	485	44	423	18	4
Butler	8,130	9	0	1	2	6	97	21	67	9	0
Byram Township	8,491	3	0	0	0	3	66	8	55	3	3
Caldwell	7,145	1	0	0	1	0	30	10	19	1	0
Califon	1,026	0	0	0	0	0	5	2	3	0	0
Camden	76,182	1,777	54	70	815	838	4,912	1,221	2,693	998	120
Cape May	3,677	2	0	0	0	2	225	13	212	0	0
Cape May Point	223	0	0	0	0	0	21	0	21	0	0
Carlstadt	6,011	10	0	2	3	5	179	15	142	22	1
Carney's Point Township	7,923	20	0	1	8	11	151	50	90	11	1
Carteret	22,878	52	0	4	24	24	329	56	242	31	2
Cedar Grove Township	12,697	10	1	1	4	4	157	29	122	6	1
Chatham	8,209	1	0	0	1	0	56	9	44	3	1
Chatham Township	10,118	0	0	0	0	0	34	6	26	2	0
Cherry Hill Township	70,946	112	1	9	45	57	2,313	298	1,906	109	3
Chesilhurst	1,917	4	0	3	0	1	70	26	39	5	1
Chester	1,634	1	0	0	0	1	31	11	20	0	0
Chesterfield Township	7,023	1	0	0	1	0	31	1	26	4	0
Chester Township	7,822	1	0	0	0	1	34	7	27	0	0
Cinnaminson Township	15,259	20	0	1	10	9	351	62	276	13	0
Clark Township	14,326	6	0	0	0	6	148	22	117	9	0
Clayton	7,528	15	0	1	6	8	188	39	141	8	1
Clementon	4,849	40	0	1	13	26	221	44	165	12	2
Cliffside Park	22,713	17	0	0	5	12	240	59	171	10	0
Clifton	78,180	199	5	9	84	101	1,937	297	1,446	194	4
Clinton	2,544	2	0	1	0	1	14	4	10	0	0
Clinton Township	13,957	6	0	1	0	5	68	12	54	2	1
Closter	8,682	2	0	0	1	1	74	7	65	2	0
Collingswood	13,694	42	0	6	15	21	446	88	309	49	3
Colts Neck Township	10,116	4	0	0	0	4	76	11	63	2	1
Cranbury Township	4,027	2	0	0	1	1	45	21	23	1	0
Cranford Township	21,839	11	0	0	4	7	315	45	262	8	1
Cresskill	8,622	1	0	0	0	1	26	12	13	1	0
Deal	1,040	2	0	1	0	1	37	16	20	1	0
Delanco Township	4,529	10	0	2	2	6	72	17	53	2	1
Delaware Township	4,692	1	0	0	0	1	34	9	22	3	1
Delran Township	17,038	15	0	1	4	10	268	39	209	20	0
Demarest	5,135	2	0	0	0	2	16	6	10	0	0
Denville Township	16,549	5	0	0	1	4	151	37	103	11	1
Deptford Township	30,899	126	0	1	43	82	1,674	260	1,336	78	14
Dover	17,900	44	1	1	21	21	307	49	229	29	1
Dumont	16,984	16	0	0	2	14	187	13	170	4	4
Dunellen	6,950	7	0	0	3	4	148	25	121	2	0
Eastampton Township	6,544	11	0	0	3	8	134	32	92	10	0
East Brunswick Township	47,299	38	1	3	10	24	891	79	779	33	7
East Greenwich Township	7,491	14	0	2	2	10	158	34	116	8	2
East Hanover Township	11,382	5	0	0	2	3	177	14	151	12	0
East Newark	2,141	2	0	0	0	2	24	3	13	8	0
East Orange	65,218	470	6	21	177	266	1,641	508	767	366	16
East Rutherford	8,771	5	0	0	0	5	289	23	223	43	0
East Windsor Township	26,786	19	0	3	3	13	326	48	260	18	1
Eatontown	14,058	34	1	3	15	15	659	60	585	14	0
Edgewater	9,770	4	0	0	2	2	201	22	169	10	0
Edgewater Park Township	7,719	20	0	1	12	7	172	31	127	14	0
Edison Township	99,562	234	1	6	80	147	2,179	447	1,563	169	5
Egg Harbor City	4,363	26	0	2	6	18	178	52	119	7	1
Egg Harbor Township	40,550	78	1	5	35	37	883	166	650	67	16
Elizabeth	124,823	1,124	13	28	749	334	5,744	958	3,492	1,294	13
Elk Township	3,945	6	0	2	0	4	94	30	57	7	1
Elmer	1,332	0	0	0	0	0	28	4	24	0	0
Elmwood Park	18,667	20	0	0	8	12	428	57	323	48	0
Elsinboro Township	1,046	0	0	0	0	0	22	6	16	0	0
Emerson	7,330	6	0	1	1	4	44	4	40	0	0
Englewood	28,132	57	1	2	23	31	533	161	335	37	1
Englewood Cliffs	5,807	0	0	0	0	0	100	23	70	7	0
Englishtown	1,901	0	0	0	0	0	17	4	12	1	0
Essex Fells	2,001	0	0	0	0	0	14	2	12	0	0
Evesham Township	45,837	38	1	10	9	18	651	101	533	17	3
Ewing Township	36,483	99	3	0	39	57	623	127	441	55	6
Fairfield Township, Essex County	7,585	25	0	1	4	20	302	36	242	24	3
Fair Haven	5,891	1	0	0	0	1	66	7	59	0	0

[1] The FBI does not publish arson data unless it receives data from either the agency or the state for all 12 months of the calendar year.

Table 8. Offenses Known to Law Enforcement, by State and City, 2008—*Continued*

(Number.)

State/City	Population	Violent crime	Murder and non-negligent man-slaughter	Forcible rape	Robbery	Aggravated assault	Property crime	Burglary	Larceny-theft	Motor vehicle theft	Arson[1]
NEW JERSEY—*Continued*											
Fair Lawn	30,550	20	0	0	9	11	353	45	292	16	3
Fairview	13,517	50	0	0	21	29	252	117	125	10	0
Fanwood	7,108	5	0	0	4	1	83	7	70	6	0
Far Hills	904	0	0	0	0	0	6	0	6	0	0
Flemington	4,223	14	0	6	1	7	132	28	96	8	0
Florence Township	11,478	22	0	4	7	11	162	36	116	10	1
Florham Park	12,596	2	0	0	1	1	111	10	96	5	0
Fort Lee	36,474	10	0	0	4	6	319	61	247	11	1
Franklin	5,100	8	0	1	0	7	98	20	76	2	0
Franklin Lakes	11,677	3	0	0	3	0	127	33	93	1	0
Franklin Township, Gloucester County	17,288	29	0	3	7	19	411	141	242	28	6
Franklin Township, Hunterdon County	3,121	1	0	0	0	1	46	2	44	0	0
Franklin Township, Somerset County	59,965	83	1	6	36	40	917	237	617	63	7
Freehold	11,478	59	1	4	26	28	346	71	269	6	0
Freehold Township	35,161	55	0	6	26	23	994	79	900	15	0
Frenchtown	1,456	3	0	0	0	3	21	4	16	1	0
Galloway Township	36,577	74	2	3	18	51	838	198	606	34	9
Garfield	29,012	46	0	0	16	30	449	113	284	52	0
Garwood	4,311	0	0	0	0	0	44	6	38	0	0
Gibbsboro	2,416	4	0	0	2	2	36	8	26	2	0
Glassboro	19,573	68	0	3	28	37	477	123	331	23	7
Glen Ridge	6,662	7	0	0	3	4	123	32	77	14	1
Glen Rock	11,147	3	0	1	2	0	80	11	69	0	0
Gloucester City	11,318	20	0	4	10	6	372	92	236	44	1
Gloucester Township	64,946	212	0	28	60	124	1,731	508	1,094	129	20
Green Brook Township	7,055	6	0	0	4	2	130	14	106	10	0
Greenwich Township, Gloucester County	4,983	7	0	0	0	7	165	42	118	5	1
Greenwich Township, Warren County	5,201	2	0	0	0	2	117	7	109	1	0
Guttenberg	10,526	52	0	0	30	22	164	54	95	15	1
Hackensack	42,775	148	0	2	58	88	1,175	80	987	108	1
Hackettstown	9,431	8	0	0	0	8	208	46	155	7	0
Haddonfield	11,335	13	0	1	2	10	204	26	175	3	4
Haddon Heights	7,222	5	0	1	0	4	146	23	120	3	0
Haddon Township	14,260	27	1	0	11	15	426	73	341	12	3
Haledon	8,370	16	0	0	6	10	153	24	104	25	0
Hamburg	3,512	4	0	1	0	3	45	7	38	0	1
Hamilton Township, Atlantic County	24,995	89	2	6	30	51	1,225	207	969	49	13
Hamilton Township, Mercer County	90,282	176	1	9	93	73	1,878	460	1,254	164	6
Hammonton	13,558	22	0	0	1	21	211	48	148	15	0
Hanover Township	13,695	3	0	0	2	1	137	17	107	13	1
Harding Township	3,323	2	0	1	0	1	17	3	13	1	1
Hardyston Township	8,614	10	1	3	1	5	117	48	63	6	0
Harrington Park	4,879	0	0	0	0	0	15	1	14	0	0
Harrison	14,059	38	2	2	23	11	271	52	181	38	0
Harrison Township	12,695	15	0	5	1	9	220	44	171	5	2
Harvey Cedars	394	0	0	0	0	0	35	6	29	0	0
Hasbrouck Heights	11,423	7	0	0	2	5	104	6	95	3	0
Haworth	3,398	0	0	0	0	0	10	3	7	0	0
Hawthorne	18,015	14	0	0	6	8	311	38	258	15	0
Hazlet Township	20,910	12	0	0	6	6	299	39	244	16	3
Helmetta	2,026	1	0	0	0	1	8	4	4	0	0
High Bridge	3,676	3	0	1	0	2	51	12	39	0	0
Highland Park	14,166	11	0	1	8	2	249	29	211	9	0
Highlands	5,315	8	0	0	0	8	56	10	45	1	0
Hightstown	5,255	10	1	0	6	3	78	13	63	2	1
Hillsborough Township	38,718	13	0	4	2	7	322	61	259	2	0
Hillsdale	9,845	6	0	3	1	2	65	9	56	0	0
Hillside Township	21,177	112	0	12	80	20	659	163	378	118	2
Hi-Nella	989	6	0	0	3	3	20	5	13	2	2
Hoboken	40,618	149	1	3	56	89	986	203	672	111	2
Ho-Ho-Kus	4,017	0	0	0	0	0	31	9	21	1	0
Holland Township	5,236	2	0	0	0	2	23	5	18	0	0
Holmdel Township	16,991	11	1	0	2	8	280	22	255	3	0
Hopatcong	15,490	8	0	0	1	7	122	14	105	3	0
Hopewell	1,988	0	0	0	0	0	14	6	8	0	0
Hopewell Township	17,968	8	0	0	2	6	138	33	100	5	1
Howell Township	51,433	64	0	2	22	40	714	115	567	32	5
Independence Township	5,665	1	0	0	1	0	36	5	29	2	0
Interlaken	878	0	0	0	0	0	9	6	3	0	0
Irvington	56,237	1,200	24	41	573	562	3,173	965	1,332	876	15
Island Heights	1,883	3	0	0	0	3	25	3	21	1	0
Jackson Township	53,641	33	0	0	13	20	714	151	520	43	10
Jamesburg	6,404	8	0	3	2	3	73	16	54	3	0

[1] The FBI does not publish arson data unless it receives data from either the agency or the state for all 12 months of the calendar year.

Table 8. Offenses Known to Law Enforcement, by State and City, 2008—*Continued*

(Number.)

State/City	Population	Violent crime	Murder and non-negligent man-slaughter	Forcible rape	Robbery	Aggravated assault	Property crime	Burglary	Larceny-theft	Motor vehicle theft	Arson[1]
NEW JERSEY—*Continued*											
Jefferson Township	21,904	12	1	1	3	7	303	130	166	7	0
Jersey City	241,588	2,280	25	49	1,252	954	7,461	1,869	4,426	1,166	83
Keansburg	10,516	35	0	1	6	28	239	38	194	7	3
Kearny	36,759	118	2	5	55	56	1,018	170	716	132	6
Kenilworth	7,611	10	0	0	5	5	166	9	143	14	0
Keyport	7,460	11	0	1	2	8	115	28	79	8	2
Kinnelon	9,583	1	0	0	1	0	63	23	36	4	0
Lacey Township	26,327	29	0	2	7	20	759	81	662	16	1
Lake Como	1,771	3	0	0	0	3	29	9	19	1	0
Lakehurst	2,705	13	0	2	2	9	60	11	47	2	0
Lakewood Township[5]	70,864		3	4	93		1,424	526	805	93	15
Lambertville	3,712	8	0	0	0	8	65	16	48	1	0
Laurel Springs	1,886	8	0	0	3	5	60	10	48	2	1
Lavallette	2,757	4	0	0	0	4	65	8	55	2	0
Lawnside	2,818	20	0	0	5	15	99	6	86	7	1
Lawrence Township, Mercer County	32,059	59	0	7	19	33	891	110	735	46	8
Lebanon Township	6,229	4	0	2	0	2	57	6	46	5	1
Leonia	8,609	5	0	0	1	4	73	24	49	0	1
Lincoln Park	10,631	4	0	0	0	4	77	17	60	0	0
Linden	39,197	156	2	3	93	58	1,372	239	923	210	2
Lindenwold	17,077	159	3	5	88	63	694	266	348	80	11
Linwood	7,229	6	0	0	2	4	116	56	57	3	0
Little Egg Harbor Township	21,067	34	0	7	7	20	433	78	342	13	18
Little Falls Township[8]	11,631	20	0	1	2	17		46		25	1
Little Ferry	10,495	14	0	0	3	11	104	13	80	11	0
Little Silver	6,096	2	0	1	0	1	101	17	84	0	0
Livingston Township	27,945	22	0	0	12	10	486	31	435	20	0
Loch Arbour	273	1	0	0	1	0	4	3	1	0	0
Lodi	23,871	33	0	0	12	21	362	60	274	28	1
Logan Township	6,191	12	0	3	1	8	166	30	124	12	1
Long Beach Township[5]	3,538	7	0	0	0	7			142	1	0
Long Branch	32,331	111	1	2	64	44	825	180	606	39	2
Long Hill Township	8,601	2	0	0	2	0	76	11	63	2	0
Longport	1,080	0	0	0	0	0	13	2	11	0	0
Lopatcong Township	8,713	1	0	0	0	1	109	7	101	1	0
Lower Alloways Creek Township	1,879	1	0	0	0	1	29	6	20	3	1
Lower Township	19,963	39	0	3	6	30	457	94	353	10	7
Lumberton Township	12,258	29	0	4	11	14	357	59	286	12	7
Lyndhurst Township	19,397	12	0	0	9	3	342	43	265	34	2
Madison	16,056	12	0	2	2	8	114	23	89	2	0
Magnolia	4,307	27	1	0	9	17	92	23	53	16	1
Mahwah Township	24,225	7	0	0	1	6	195	13	155	27	1
Manalapan Township	39,115	24	0	5	5	14	418	75	317	26	0
Manasquan	6,208	8	0	2	1	5	205	33	171	1	0
Manchester Township	41,877	10	0	0	0	10	354	79	262	13	7
Mansfield Township, Burlington County	8,359	3	1	1	0	1	109	7	93	9	0
Mansfield Township, Warren County	8,098	12	0	1	1	10	140	15	121	4	0
Mantoloking	453	1	0	0	1	0	16	1	15	0	0
Mantua Township	15,262	21	0	5	10	6	375	74	294	7	2
Manville	10,869	3	0	0	2	1	195	17	168	10	1
Maple Shade Township	19,132	26	2	8	13	3	481	76	341	64	12
Maplewood Township	21,970	66	0	1	38	27	442	62	322	58	1
Margate City	8,545	10	0	1	3	6	129	23	104	2	2
Marlboro Township	41,011	25	0	0	10	15	382	105	253	24	2
Matawan[5]	8,753	11	0	0	2	9			93	2	0
Maywood	9,156	9	0	0	3	6	86	25	59	2	0
Medford Lakes	4,074	3	0	0	0	3	41	9	32	0	0
Medford Township	22,809	18	0	1	3	14	315	66	244	5	3
Mendham	5,049	3	0	1	0	2	35	0	34	1	0
Mendham Township	5,531	4	0	0	0	4	27	4	23	0	0
Merchantville	3,743	2	0	1	1	0	74	9	60	5	0
Metuchen	13,121	10	0	0	5	5	260	47	204	9	0
Middlesex	13,632	8	0	0	3	5	143	23	108	12	0
Middle Township	16,077	73	0	5	8	60	735	152	559	24	5
Middletown Township	66,105	42	0	3	10	29	1,031	147	856	28	0
Midland Park	6,776	4	0	0	2	2	75	20	54	1	0
Millburn Township[8]	18,557	19	0	0	11	8		50	478		0
Milltown	6,968	3	0	1	1	1	117	16	100	1	0
Millville	28,551	237	3	5	85	144	1,333	291	995	47	3
Mine Hill Township	3,589	0	0	0	0	0	35	7	27	1	0
Monmouth Beach	3,564	3	0	3	0	0	41	6	35	0	0
Monroe Township, Gloucester County	32,951	52	0	5	12	35	749	167	543	39	3

[1] The FBI does not publish arson data unless it receives data from either the agency or the state for all 12 months of the calendar year.
[5] The FBI determined that the agency's data were overreported. Consequently, those data are not included in this table.
[8] The FBI determined that the agency's data were underreported. Consequently, those data are not included in this table.

Table 8. Offenses Known to Law Enforcement, by State and City, 2008—*Continued*

(Number.)

State/City	Population	Violent crime	Murder and non-negligent man-slaughter	Forcible rape	Robbery	Aggravated assault	Property crime	Burglary	Larceny-theft	Motor vehicle theft	Arson[1]
NEW JERSEY—*Continued*											
Monroe Township, Middlesex County	37,412	11	0	0	0	11	255	47	193	15	2
Montclair	36,707	86	1	2	43	40	692	221	428	43	4
Montgomery Township	23,570	5	0	0	2	3	213	44	161	8	1
Montvale	7,344	4	0	0	4	0	39	4	31	4	0
Montville Township	21,097	8	0	1	0	7	255	53	191	11	0
Moonachie	2,742	2	0	0	0	2	55	12	33	10	0
Moorestown Township	19,613	13	0	1	9	3	477	71	396	10	2
Morris Plains	5,550	3	0	0	2	1	62	8	52	2	0
Morristown	19,117	115	1	2	45	67	543	86	438	19	0
Morris Township	20,966	22	0	4	4	14	154	24	117	13	1
Mountain Lakes	4,260	0	0	0	0	0	68	28	38	2	1
Mountainside	6,526	4	0	0	1	3	54	3	47	4	1
Mount Arlington	5,813	2	0	0	1	1	42	2	39	1	1
Mount Ephraim	4,359	11	0	0	3	8	161	21	132	8	0
Mount Holly Township	10,246	43	0	1	20	22	311	50	242	19	0
Mount Laurel Township	39,148	29	1	7	14	7	806	81	696	29	2
Mount Olive Township	26,042	18	0	3	3	12	282	40	234	8	1
Mullica Township	6,024	12	0	0	2	10	86	42	41	3	0
National Park	3,220	12	0	0	2	10	111	28	76	7	0
Neptune City	5,120	10	0	0	1	9	184	29	150	5	0
Neptune Township	28,356	185	1	10	78	96	1,458	285	1,081	92	9
Netcong	3,228	22	0	4	1	17	69	14	45	10	1
Newark	279,788	2,660	67	51	1,387	1,155	9,750	2,000	3,996	3,754	92
New Brunswick	50,605	319	5	18	122	174	2,242	667	1,375	200	7
Newfield	1,670	4	0	0	0	4	11	1	10	0	0
New Hanover Township	9,364	0	0	0	0	0	10	3	7	0	0
New Milford	15,942	8	0	1	5	2	100	18	81	1	0
New Providence	11,790	4	0	0	1	3	105	23	82	0	0
Newton	8,122	7	0	0	1	6	152	35	113	4	0
North Arlington	14,732	13	0	0	4	9	221	22	182	17	5
North Bergen Township	55,652	120	0	7	61	52	864	185	557	122	8
North Brunswick Township	39,878	71	1	1	29	40	861	177	593	91	4
North Caldwell	7,028	2	1	0	0	1	41	10	31	0	0
Northfield	7,901	3	0	0	3	0	144	42	99	3	0
North Haledon	9,039	8	0	0	1	7	63	4	57	2	1
North Hanover Township	7,393	5	0	0	2	3	58	19	36	3	0
North Plainfield	21,087	88	0	4	43	41	470	105	324	41	1
Northvale	4,539	2	0	0	0	2	17	0	16	1	0
North Wildwood	4,819	17	0	3	6	8	313	51	256	6	2
Norwood	6,246	1	0	0	0	1	19	2	16	1	0
Nutley Township	26,178	32	0	2	6	24	388	59	284	45	3
Oakland	13,454	4	0	0	1	3	106	12	89	5	0
Oaklyn	3,994	12	0	2	2	8	159	34	118	7	1
Ocean City	14,802	31	0	8	6	17	892	138	747	7	0
Ocean Gate	2,128	1	0	0	0	1	40	5	34	1	0
Oceanport	5,737	3	0	0	0	3	74	14	60	0	0
Ocean Township, Monmouth County	28,298	61	0	2	21	38	801	124	648	29	1
Ocean Township, Ocean County	8,926	3	0	0	0	3	171	25	142	4	0
Ogdensburg	2,548	4	0	0	0	4	33	6	26	1	0
Old Bridge Township	66,463	48	1	4	14	29	799	178	554	67	5
Old Tappan	6,071	0	0	0	0	0	39	3	36	0	0
Oradell	7,789	0	0	0	0	0	48	5	41	2	0
Orange	30,979	326	4	11	175	136	1,415	488	557	370	2
Oxford Township	2,596	1	0	0	0	1	27	11	14	2	0
Palisades Park	19,563	17	0	0	9	8	220	70	138	12	0
Palmyra	7,424	26	1	0	6	19	208	47	141	20	0
Paramus	26,232	88	0	3	36	49	1,709	90	1,556	63	6
Park Ridge	8,932	3	0	0	0	3	43	3	36	4	0
Parsippany-Troy Hills Township	50,990	30	0	1	7	22	724	167	495	62	1
Passaic	66,723	674	5	3	323	343	1,483	318	923	242	4
Paterson	145,542	1,456	17	23	771	645	4,560	1,563	2,020	977	18
Paulsboro	6,046	39	0	0	15	24	278	82	171	25	0
Peapack and Gladstone	2,558	0	0	0	0	0	14	3	9	2	0
Pemberton	1,503	6	0	1	3	2	12	0	11	1	0
Pemberton Township	27,995	58	3	8	11	36	459	128	298	33	5
Pennington	2,653	1	0	0	1	0	23	2	18	3	1
Pennsauken Township	34,897	139	3	10	61	65	1,441	348	937	156	8
Penns Grove	4,663	20	0	2	6	12	179	48	120	11	1
Pennsville Township	13,332	14	0	0	1	13	372	63	299	10	5
Pequannock Township	17,102	6	0	0	0	6	176	52	118	6	0
Perth Amboy	48,853	216	1	2	109	104	1,135	216	785	134	5
Phillipsburg	14,406	35	0	4	18	13	293	73	201	19	4
Pine Beach	2,067	0	0	0	0	0	40	1	37	2	0
Pine Hill	11,231	42	0	4	12	26	309	71	225	13	11

[1] The FBI does not publish arson data unless it receives data from either the agency or the state for all 12 months of the calendar year.

Table 8. Offenses Known to Law Enforcement, by State and City, 2008—*Continued*

(Number.)

State/City	Population	Violent crime	Murder and non-negligent man-slaughter	Forcible rape	Robbery	Aggravated assault	Property crime	Burglary	Larceny-theft	Motor vehicle theft	Arson[1]
NEW JERSEY—*Continued*											
Pine Valley	23	0	0	0	0	0	0	0	0	0	0
Piscataway Township	52,585	52	2	1	27	22	694	131	503	60	1
Pitman	9,169	10	0	0	5	5	137	11	118	8	0
Plainfield	46,124	461	5	14	212	230	1,539	390	1,011	138	5
Plainsboro Township	21,219	9	0	1	2	6	170	16	141	13	1
Pleasantville	18,713	181	1	5	87	88	764	262	446	56	6
Plumsted Township	8,253	5	0	3	0	2	114	29	75	10	0
Pohatcong Township	3,320	12	0	0	2	10	81	8	72	1	0
Point Pleasant	19,959	14	0	0	1	13	447	33	411	3	0
Point Pleasant Beach	5,401	9	0	2	2	5	236	41	193	2	0
Pompton Lakes	11,106	5	0	0	0	5	126	9	113	4	0
Princeton	13,456	14	0	0	4	10	326	65	257	4	3
Princeton Township	17,512	10	0	3	4	3	155	48	104	3	2
Prospect Park	5,592	8	0	0	5	3	120	27	80	13	0
Rahway	28,286	89	0	2	64	23	654	112	477	65	2
Ramsey	14,620	13	0	1	2	10	220	12	201	7	0
Randolph Township	25,293	5	0	0	1	4	187	28	153	6	3
Raritan	7,033	11	0	0	5	6	164	26	133	5	0
Raritan Township	22,712	5	1	2	0	2	199	23	170	6	2
Readington Township	16,010	7	0	4	1	2	188	42	142	4	2
Red Bank	11,843	57	0	4	39	14	265	31	227	7	0
Ridgefield	10,854	5	0	0	1	4	101	19	77	5	2
Ridgefield Park	12,383	9	0	0	3	6	194	38	137	19	1
Ridgewood	24,165	5	0	1	2	2	240	38	199	3	0
Ringwood	12,688	3	0	0	1	2	88	22	66	0	0
Riverdale	2,909	7	0	0	1	6	111	10	96	5	0
River Edge	10,648	6	0	1	3	2	97	35	60	2	1
Riverside Township	7,717	22	0	0	11	11	103	33	66	4	1
Riverton	2,629	0	0	0	0	0	77	19	58	0	4
River Vale Township	9,648	3	0	0	1	2	45	12	33	0	0
Robbinsville Township	12,157	11	0	3	0	8	108	18	88	2	0
Rochelle Park Township	6,166	2	0	0	1	1	95	17	74	4	0
Rockaway	6,268	1	0	0	0	1	60	5	51	4	0
Rockaway Township	25,606	17	0	2	9	6	455	36	409	10	2
Rockleigh	388	2	0	0	0	2	2	1	1	0	0
Roseland	5,343	1	0	0	1	0	25	7	17	1	0
Roselle	20,593	87	1	1	56	29	554	193	316	45	4
Roselle Park	12,775	23	0	1	7	15	208	43	152	13	1
Roxbury Township	23,278	15	0	0	1	14	300	37	252	11	0
Rumson	7,205	2	0	0	1	1	66	24	40	2	1
Runnemede	8,338	20	0	0	14	6	377	44	315	18	1
Rutherford	17,487	11	0	0	2	9	383	29	327	27	0
Saddle Brook Township	13,593	10	1	0	5	4	343	39	279	25	0
Saddle River	3,839	2	0	0	0	2	12	3	7	2	0
Salem	5,634	91	3	0	37	51	332	118	190	24	8
Sayreville	42,408	81	0	6	30	45	720	147	522	51	8
Scotch Plains Township	22,911	16	0	1	4	11	263	33	221	9	2
Sea Bright	1,804	6	0	0	0	6	49	1	48	0	0
Sea Girt	2,030	6	0	1	1	4	34	4	30	0	0
Sea Isle City[5]	2,927	10	0	2	2	6			172	3	0
Seaside Heights	3,326	34	0	6	3	25	219	25	184	10	1
Seaside Park	2,301	2	0	1	1	0	77	15	57	5	0
Secaucus	15,254	21	0	0	8	13	644	29	553	62	2
Ship Bottom	1,440	1	0	0	0	1	91	31	60	0	0
Shrewsbury	3,763	5	0	1	2	2	95	10	83	2	1
Somerdale	5,045	17	0	1	5	11	154	44	95	15	1
Somers Point	11,351	50	1	0	16	33	369	71	292	6	4
Somerville	12,675	20	1	0	10	9	224	27	183	14	0
South Amboy	7,773	15	0	0	2	13	121	32	78	11	2
South Bound Brook	4,884	2	0	0	0	2	37	11	26	0	0
South Brunswick Township	40,941	41	2	4	13	22	453	60	367	26	3
South Hackensack Township	2,274	13	0	1	6	6	82	8	60	14	0
South Harrison Township	3,141	5	0	0	0	5	12	3	8	1	0
South Orange	15,885	49	2	0	34	13	365	75	222	68	1
South Plainfield	22,708	32	1	0	20	11	475	74	376	25	4
South River	15,716	42	0	2	8	32	231	49	173	9	5
South Toms River	3,707	8	0	2	2	4	114	36	69	9	0
Sparta Township	19,262	0	0	0	0	0	138	10	126	2	0
Spotswood	8,151	6	0	0	3	3	125	31	93	1	2
Springfield	14,710	19	0	0	5	14	259	31	203	25	1
Springfield Township	3,509	1	0	0	0	1	61	15	37	9	0
Spring Lake	3,486	2	0	0	0	2	91	19	71	1	0
Spring Lake Heights	5,102	1	0	0	0	1	27	6	20	1	0
Stafford Township	26,659	29	0	1	3	25	542	72	459	11	4

[1] The FBI does not publish arson data unless it receives data from either the agency or the state for all 12 months of the calendar year.
[5] The FBI determined that the agency's data were overreported. Consequently, those data are not included in this table.

Table 8. Offenses Known to Law Enforcement, by State and City, 2008—*Continued*

(Number.)

State/City	Population	Violent crime	Murder and non-negligent man-slaughter	Forcible rape	Robbery	Aggravated assault	Property crime	Burglary	Larceny-theft	Motor vehicle theft	Arson[1]
NEW JERSEY—*Continued*											
Stanhope	3,577	3	0	1	1	1	66	15	48	3	1
Stillwater Township	4,299	0	0	0	0	0	46	14	30	2	0
Stone Harbor	1,004	4	0	0	1	3	92	17	74	1	0
Stratford	6,988	18	0	1	5	12	212	46	158	8	0
Summit	20,560	12	0	1	6	5	317	34	267	16	0
Surf City	1,556	1	0	0	0	1	53	11	42	0	0
Swedesboro	2,066	7	0	0	2	5	61	18	40	3	1
Tavistock	29	0	0	0	0	0	2	1	1	0	0
Teaneck Township	38,828	93	0	5	30	58	691	143	501	47	6
Tenafly	14,303	11	3	0	2	6	95	22	70	3	0
Teterboro	18	1	0	0	0	1	23	1	16	6	0
Tewksbury Township	6,085	1	0	0	0	1	17	7	10	0	0
Tinton Falls	19,409	18	0	3	9	6	337	50	277	10	3
Toms River Township	95,410	110	2	9	49	50	2,538	453	2,029	56	14
Totowa	10,649	17	1	1	6	9	384	26	314	44	1
Trenton	82,140	989	19	23	546	401	2,636	724	1,404	508	27
Tuckerton	3,874	6	0	0	0	6	47	11	34	2	1
Union Beach	6,638	6	0	0	1	5	81	23	58	0	0
Union City	61,931	341	1	4	157	179	1,518	367	991	160	1
Union Township	53,777	127	1	8	64	54	1,383	239	1,008	136	3
Upper Saddle River	8,545	4	0	1	0	3	45	7	35	3	0
Ventnor City	12,195	15	2	1	7	5	396	108	284	4	1
Vernon Township	24,943	14	1	3	0	10	420	81	327	12	3
Verona	12,494	9	0	1	0	8	160	35	118	7	2
Vineland	58,606	316	3	16	136	161	2,491	589	1,804	98	21
Voorhees Township	31,210	58	0	9	15	34	711	79	608	24	3
Waldwick	9,452	8	1	0	0	7	101	17	82	2	1
Wallington	11,273	15	0	0	4	11	195	32	140	23	1
Wall Township	26,287	13	0	0	5	8	454	106	338	10	3
Wanaque	11,787	3	0	1	1	1	106	10	96	0	0
Warren Township	16,052	2	0	0	0	2	97	7	87	3	0
Washington	6,665	7	0	0	3	4	183	27	151	5	0
Washington Township, Bergen County	9,621	1	0	0	0	1	39	15	24	0	0
Washington Township, Gloucester County	51,670	91	0	5	24	62	1,273	229	970	74	10
Washington Township, Morris County	18,493	13	0	0	0	13	110	29	76	5	0
Washington Township, Warren County	6,905	5	0	1	0	4	82	9	67	6	0
Watchung	6,727	6	0	0	6	0	337	21	310	6	0
Waterford Township	10,609	18	0	2	1	15	222	61	142	19	1
Wayne Township	53,956	48	0	2	16	30	1,415	143	1,214	58	0
Weehawken Township	12,265	25	0	0	13	12	388	76	270	42	3
Wenonah	2,334	3	0	0	0	3	22	5	17	0	0
Westampton Township	8,775	27	1	1	18	7	157	22	132	3	0
West Amwell Township	2,992	2	0	0	0	2	36	9	26	1	1
West Caldwell Township	10,442	6	0	0	2	4	91	8	77	6	1
West Cape May	970	3	0	0	1	2	48	10	38	0	0
West Deptford Township	22,266	38	0	1	10	27	511	105	364	42	2
Westfield	29,419	6	0	0	2	4	286	48	229	9	0
West Long Branch	8,361	12	0	1	5	6	204	19	176	9	0
West Milford Township	27,892	36	0	7	2	27	405	109	279	17	3
West New York	46,286	181	3	3	94	81	883	241	511	131	4
West Orange	42,470	97	0	6	42	49	751	178	496	77	2
Westville	4,453	27	0	1	10	16	196	55	126	15	0
West Wildwood	399	1	0	0	0	1	20	4	15	1	0
West Windsor Township	26,949	17	0	1	9	7	522	55	435	32	0
Westwood	10,707	9	0	0	1	8	98	14	83	1	2
Wharton	6,081	6	0	4	1	1	103	15	86	2	0
Wildwood	5,253	71	0	4	32	35	638	194	421	23	1
Wildwood Crest	4,046	6	0	2	2	2	203	71	132	0	0
Willingboro Township	37,258	141	3	12	64	62	641	168	407	66	5
Winfield Township	1,443	2	0	1	1	0	25	6	16	3	0
Winslow Township	39,622	154	1	5	29	119	773	217	501	55	11
Woodbridge Township	98,154	192	1	12	94	85	2,712	447	2,105	160	23
Woodbury	10,433	50	0	2	23	25	471	97	352	22	2
Woodbury Heights	3,036	8	0	0	4	4	115	24	83	8	0
Woodcliff Lake	5,937	2	0	0	0	2	53	4	47	2	0
Woodland Park	11,592	10	0	1	3	6	276	34	214	28	0
Woodlynne	2,663	22	0	7	8	7	145	44	83	18	2
Wood-Ridge	7,457	1	0	0	0	1	63	11	52	0	0
Woodstown	3,330	3	0	1	0	2	60	21	37	2	0
Woolwich Township	10,144	4	0	0	0	4	94	18	74	2	0
Wyckoff Township	16,964	11	0	0	1	10	119	23	94	2	1
NEW MEXICO											
Alamogordo	35,660	112	3	15	8	86	983	136	815	32	6
Albuquerque	527,464	4,718	38	370	1,350	2,960	31,994	6,224	21,098	4,672	132

[1] The FBI does not publish arson data unless it receives data from either the agency or the state for all 12 months of the calendar year.

Table 8. Offenses Known to Law Enforcement, by State and City, 2008—*Continued*

(Number.)

State/City	Population	Violent crime	Murder and non-negligent man-slaughter	Forcible rape	Robbery	Aggravated assault	Property crime	Burglary	Larceny-theft	Motor vehicle theft	Arson[1]
NEW MEXICO—*Continued*											
Angel Fire	1,127	0	0	0	0	0	41	25	16	0	0
Artesia	10,460	26	0	10	0	16	582	303	253	26	0
Aztec	6,851	34	0	13	3	18	203	47	133	23	11
Bayard	2,358	10	0	0	0	10	28	5	23	0	1
Belen	7,159	59	4	3	9	43	480	175	247	58	6
Bernalillo	7,179	155	3	2	16	134	275	103	139	33	2
Bloomfield[4]	7,181	44	1	11	2	30	156	65	81	10	2
Bosque Farms	4,010	5	0	0	0	5	58	18	32	8	0
Carlsbad	24,966	194	2	30	10	152	1,111	265	801	45	14
Carrizozo	1,028	3	0	0	1	2	21	6	15	0	0
Clayton	2,054	2	0	0	0	2	69	36	33	0	0
Clovis	33,263	272	3	29	52	188	2,226	613	1,506	107	32
Corrales	7,930	5	0	0	0	5	95	46	46	3	2
Deming	15,430	26	0	1	8	17	419	163	231	25	0
Dexter	1,245	1	0	0	0	1	23	7	16	0	0
Espanola	9,530	224	0	2	20	202	669	281	346	42	5
Estancia	1,522	5	0	0	0	5	31	3	28	0	0
Eunice	2,668	7	0	0	1	6	78	35	40	3	2
Farmington[5]	42,956		3	91	38		1,689	781	772	136	17
Gallup	18,642	294	1	24	34	235	1,436	238	1,096	102	1
Grants	8,883	62	0	4	13	45	285	149	116	20	0
Hatch	1,642	8	0	1	1	6	15	1	12	2	0
Hobbs	29,751	283	1	23	35	224	1,515	364	1,070	81	8
Jal	2,072	0	0	0	0	0	20	10	10	0	0
Las Cruces	91,982	491	4	37	78	372	4,419	869	3,312	238	7
Las Vegas	13,419	126	2	7	11	106	487	167	298	22	9
Lordsburg	2,598	3	0	0	0	3	1	1	0	0	0
Los Alamos	18,541	69	1	10	1	57	228	36	188	4	7
Los Lunas[5]	12,395		0	4	11		613	84	448	81	
Lovington	9,843	44	1	3	1	39	374	199	167	8	0
Milan	2,586	13	0	1	1	11	84	26	53	5	0
Moriarty	1,758	3	0	0	0	3	70	24	40	6	0
Portales	12,107	86	1	6	5	74	433	121	290	22	0
Raton[5]	6,500		0	1	1				127	12	3
Red River	485	1	0	0	0	1	16	10	5	1	0
Rio Rancho	79,647	233	1	23	35	174	2,028	393	1,400	235	15
Roswell	45,619	381	7	31	42	301	2,843	779	1,931	133	19
Ruidoso	9,031	29	1	3	7	18	287	141	135	11	2
Ruidoso Downs	2,656	18	0	1	1	16	106	30	73	3	0
Santa Fe	74,496	331	10	29	76	216	3,647	1,778	1,675	194	19
Santa Rosa	2,508	61	0	0	1	60	56	19	34	3	0
Silver City	9,915	84	1	5	5	73	574	174	372	28	0
Sunland Park	14,341	39	0	3	3	33	246	74	143	29	0
Taos	5,332	58	1	7	6	44	448	125	300	23	0
Tatum	726	0	0	0	0	0	18	7	11	0	0
Texico	1,032	3	1	1	0	1	11	6	5	0	0
Truth or Consequences	6,617	30	0	1	1	28	276	72	190	14	0
Tucumcari	5,030	64	0	4	2	58	217	69	139	9	0
Tularosa	2,850	12	0	1	1	10	55	34	20	1	0
NEW YORK											
Adams Village	1,681	0	0	0	0	0	8	3	4	1	0
Addison Town and Village	2,511	12	0	0	0	12	11	1	10	0	0
Akron Village	2,973	3	0	0	0	3	48	4	44	0	0
Albany	94,152	1,033	9	48	361	615	4,405	1,027	3,153	225	25
Albion Village	5,553	28	0	1	8	19	343	71	259	13	1
Alexandria Bay Village	1,109	2	0	1	0	1	20	7	12	1	0
Alfred Village	4,970	1	0	0	0	1	58	10	47	1	0
Allegany Village	1,764	3	0	0	0	3	23	7	16	0	0
Altamont Village	1,708	0	0	0	0	0	24	2	22	0	0
Amherst Town	110,351	141	0	2	45	94	2,082	206	1,819	57	8
Amity Town and Belmont Village	2,128	0	0	0	0	0	5	3	2	0	0
Amityville Village	9,247	6	0	0	4	2	193	21	163	9	0
Amsterdam	17,481	99	1	0	0	98	119	41	78	0	0
Andover Village	1,007	0	0	0	0	0	3	1	2	0	0
Arcade Village	1,890	2	0	0	0	2	60	11	49	0	0
Ardsley Village	4,933	2	0	0	1	1	39	3	35	1	0
Asharoken Village	637	0	0	0	0	0	1	0	1	0	0
Athens Village	1,713	0	0	0	0	0	0	0	0	0	0
Auburn	27,173	103	0	11	13	79	1,021	213	791	17	6
Avon Village	2,905	1	0	0	0	1	50	6	42	2	0
Baldwinsville Village	7,165	11	0	0	2	9	176	13	160	3	0
Ballston Spa Village	5,477	1	0	0	0	1	118	18	100	0	1

[1] The FBI does not publish arson data unless it receives data from either the agency or the state for all 12 months of the calendar year.
[4] Because of changes in the state/local agency's reporting practices, figures are not comparable to previous years' data.
[5] The FBI determined that the agency's data were overreported. Consequently, those data are not included in this table.

Table 8. Offenses Known to Law Enforcement, by State and City, 2008—*Continued*

(Number.)

State/City	Population	Violent crime	Murder and non-negligent man-slaughter	Forcible rape	Robbery	Aggravated assault	Property crime	Burglary	Larceny-theft	Motor vehicle theft	Arson[1]
NEW YORK—*Continued*											
Batavia	15,156	36	0	4	7	25	470	83	378	9	7
Bath Village	5,428	19	0	4	1	14	161	20	137	4	2
Beacon	14,522	63	0	0	20	43	352	107	225	20	1
Bedford Town	18,626	6	0	0	0	6	121	23	94	4	2
Bethlehem Town	33,349	20	0	4	4	12	502	75	419	8	0
Binghamton	44,746	276	1	11	84	180	2,389	342	2,000	47	2
Blooming Grove Town	12,348	8	0	1	1	6	151	18	117	16	2
Bolivar Village	1,108	0	0	0	0	0	8	2	6	0	0
Bolton Town	2,165	2	0	0	0	2	18	4	14	0	0
Boonville Village	2,054	0	0	0	0	0	41	2	39	0	0
Brant Town	1,827	1	0	0	0	1	19	5	12	2	0
Brewster	2,119	9	0	0	2	7	18	3	14	1	0
Briarcliff Manor Village	7,981	0	0	0	0	0	36	6	29	1	0
Brighton Town	34,226	31	0	2	13	16	988	123	833	32	1
Brockport Village	8,108	21	0	2	3	16	188	47	135	6	1
Bronxville Village	6,561	3	0	1	1	1	50	16	30	4	0
Buffalo	270,289	3,716	37	174	1,539	1,966	15,474	4,112	9,503	1,859	126
Cairo Town	6,582	6	0	0	1	5	65	9	53	3	0
Caledonia Village	2,136	0	0	0	0	0	25	1	24	0	0
Cambridge Village	1,813	1	0	1	0	0	39	4	35	0	0
Camden Village	2,257	6	0	0	0	6	59	12	46	1	0
Camillus Town and Village	23,231	7	0	0	3	4	293	38	249	6	4
Canandaigua	11,159	20	0	2	9	9	233	36	192	5	1
Canisteo Village	2,218	3	0	0	0	3	68	11	56	1	0
Canton Village	6,075	5	0	0	0	5	121	11	109	1	0
Cape Vincent Village	787	0	0	0	0	0	7	4	3	0	0
Carmel Town	34,545	10	0	0	1	9	316	52	255	9	2
Carroll Town	3,431	2	0	0	0	2	7	2	5	0	0
Carthage Village	3,801	15	0	2	0	13	103	18	81	4	1
Catskill Village	4,241	10	0	0	2	8	178	19	157	2	0
Cattaraugus Village	984	2	0	0	0	2	2	1	1	0	0
Cayuga Heights Village	3,667	0	0	0	0	0	43	14	29	0	0
Cazenovia Village	2,861	0	0	0	0	0	66	7	59	0	1
Central Square Village	1,634	3	0	0	0	3	29	2	26	1	0
Centre Island Village	428	0	0	0	0	0	4	3	1	0	0
Chatham Village	1,694	14	0	0	3	11	55	12	41	2	0
Cheektowaga Town	78,303	208	0	18	73	117	2,596	408	2,048	140	12
Chester Town	9,973	2	0	0	0	2	41	4	35	2	0
Chester Village	3,585	2	0	0	1	1	138	7	129	2	0
Chittenango Village	4,890	4	0	1	1	2	134	18	112	4	0
Cicero Town	28,331	10	0	1	4	5	482	65	404	13	2
Clarkstown Town	78,869	103	0	9	26	68	1,778	119	1,613	46	2
Clifton Springs Village	2,141	2	0	2	0	0	27	0	27	0	0
Clyde Village	2,082	3	0	1	1	1	76	14	61	1	1
Cobleskill Village	4,715	2	0	1	1	0	191	28	163	0	1
Coeymans Town	8,043	26	0	0	2	24	72	16	52	4	3
Cohoes	15,032	61	0	3	6	52	189	42	127	20	0
Colonie Town	78,272	54	0	1	33	20	2,310	239	2,032	39	9
Copake Town	3,283	3	0	0	1	2	17	4	12	1	0
Corning	10,259	33	0	5	2	26	354	72	276	6	2
Cornwall-on-Hudson Village	3,066	0	0	0	0	0	28	2	26	0	0
Cornwall Town	9,825	10	0	1	3	6	135	25	104	6	0
Cortland	18,342	71	0	6	7	58	331	86	238	7	4
Coxsackie Village	2,768	5	0	0	0	5	59	13	44	2	0
Crawford Town	9,528	12	0	1	2	9	197	22	171	4	0
Cuba Town	3,312	11	0	0	0	11	46	6	39	1	0
Dansville Village	4,464	3	0	0	1	2	118	6	111	1	0
Deerpark Town	8,456	4	0	0	1	3	141	30	108	3	1
Delhi Village	2,735	1	0	0	1	0	24	3	21	0	0
Depew Village	15,275	27	0	1	12	14	390	65	314	11	2
Deposit Village	1,592	3	0	0	0	3	27	12	15	0	1
Dewitt Town	21,397	28	0	2	8	18	510	70	420	20	0
Dexter Village	1,157	0	0	0	0	0	6	0	6	0	0
Dobbs Ferry Village	11,251	6	0	1	1	4	128	16	109	3	1
Dryden Village	1,825	7	0	1	0	6	74	5	69	0	0
Dunkirk	12,012	41	1	3	9	28	273	84	179	10	2
Durham Town	2,699	0	0	0	0	0	6	0	6	0	0
East Aurora-Aurora Town	13,491	4	0	0	2	2	145	15	124	6	1
Eastchester Town	18,793	9	0	0	5	4	233	12	216	5	1
East Greenbush Town	17,057	13	0	0	4	9	376	28	338	10	
East Hampton Town	18,998	20	0	2	4	14	477	92	366	19	0
East Hampton Village	1,330	0	0	0	0	0	120	13	107	0	0
East Rochester Village	6,221	10	0	2	3	5	187	31	144	12	0
East Syracuse Village	2,974	14	0	0	7	7	172	21	143	8	2

[1] The FBI does not publish arson data unless it receives data from either the agency or the state for all 12 months of the calendar year.

Table 8. Offenses Known to Law Enforcement, by State and City, 2008—*Continued*

(Number.)

State/City	Population	Violent crime	Murder and non-negligent man-slaughter	Forcible rape	Robbery	Aggravated assault	Property crime	Burglary	Larceny-theft	Motor vehicle theft	Arson[1]
NEW YORK—*Continued*											
Eden Town	7,734	0	0	0	0	0	52	13	37	2	0
Ellenville Village	3,877	24	0	2	1	21	105	34	70	1	1
Ellicott Town	5,229	13	0	0	3	10	268	43	215	10	0
Ellicottville	1,877	1	0	0	0	1	155	8	147	0	0
Elmira	29,255	108	3	4	34	67	1,168	276	872	20	2
Elmira Heights Village	3,886	1	0	0	0	1	77	17	58	2	0
Elmsford Village	4,779	5	0	0	1	4	38	11	22	5	0
Endicott Village	12,428	39	0	4	13	22	481	83	385	13	3
Evans Town	16,827	27	0	3	5	19	296	58	229	9	0
Fairport Village	5,442	5	0	1	0	4	58	17	39	2	0
Fallsburg Town	12,283	16	0	3	2	11	217	66	141	10	2
Fishkill Town	19,113	7	0	1	4	2	243	20	210	13	2
Fishkill Village	1,700	1	0	0	0	1	22	3	18	1	0
Floral Park Village	15,256	9	0	0	7	2	83	11	65	7	0
Florida Village	2,780	2	0	0	0	2	40	7	33	0	0
Fort Edward Village	3,023	4	0	0	0	4	32	9	22	1	0
Fort Plain Village	2,179	1	0	1	0	0	19	9	10	0	0
Frankfort Town	4,865	2	0	0	2	0	38	8	30	0	0
Franklinville Village	1,699	0	0	0	0	0	33	9	24	0	0
Fredonia Village	11,097	18	0	1	1	16	225	12	206	7	1
Freeport Village	42,249	201	1	4	108	88	1,032	216	696	120	3
Friendship Town	1,837	2	0	0	0	2	6	0	5	1	0
Fulton City	11,209	21	1	1	5	14	427	56	366	5	0
Garden City Village	21,741	11	0	0	10	1	265	22	233	10	
Gates Town	28,383	62	0	4	30	28	939	123	779	37	2
Geddes Town	10,482	5	0	0	4	1	220	29	187	4	0
Geneseo Village	7,669	6	0	2	1	3	102	20	82	0	0
Geneva	13,156	24	0	1	12	11	330	66	257	7	3
Germantown Town	1,982	1	0	0	0	1	1	0	1	0	0
Glen Cove	25,982	27	0	0	15	12	258	51	196	11	0
Glen Park Village	503	0	0	0	0	0	4	0	4	0	0
Glens Falls	13,923	16	0	0	1	15	520	46	468	6	0
Glenville Town	21,444	9	0	3	0	6	294	40	243	11	0
Gloversville	14,989	56	1	6	2	47	666	108	533	25	2
Goshen Town	8,534	4	0	0	0	4	95	13	76	6	0
Goshen Village	5,531	7	0	0	0	7	101	20	79	2	1
Gouverneur Village	4,005	14	0	4	1	9	182	21	161	0	0
Gowanda Village	2,606	2	0	0	1	1	122	29	93	0	0
Granville Village	2,541	3	0	2	1	0	40	19	20	1	0
Great Neck Estates Village	2,668	0	0	0	0	0	4	1	3	0	0
Greece Town	92,932	131	1	8	45	77	2,294	266	1,932	96	4
Greenburgh Town	43,808	50	0	3	11	36	757	99	629	29	1
Greene Village	1,654	0	0	0	0	0	0	0	0	0	0
Green Island Village	2,591	4	0	3	1	0	63	14	45	4	0
Greenport Town	4,262	1	0	0	0	1	105	6	99	0	0
Greenwich Village	1,825	4	0	0	0	4	36	6	27	3	0
Greenwood Lake Village	3,428	17	0	1	0	16	49	8	40	1	0
Groton Village	2,401	2	0	0	0	2	51	16	34	1	0
Guilderland Town	33,215	24	0	0	17	7	842	74	757	11	1
Hamburg Town	43,980	35	0	1	7	27	878	149	694	35	0
Hamburg Village	9,349	5	0	0	0	5	199	23	172	4	1
Hamilton Village	3,819	0	0	0	0	0	22	4	16	2	0
Hancock Village	1,090	6	0	0	0	6	7	6	1	0	0
Harriman Village	2,253	1	0	0	0	1	42	5	36	1	0
Hastings-on-Hudson Village	7,981	29	0	3	2	24	113	15	98	0	0
Haverstraw Town	36,019	64	0	6	19	39	520	140	364	16	1
Hempstead Village	51,613	341	10	10	192	129	897	197	469	231	16
Herkimer Village	6,973	87	0	6	5	76	391	49	340	2	0
Highlands Town	9,067	0	0	0	0	0	11	1	10	0	0
Homer Village	3,255	1	0	0	0	1	62	14	48	0	0
Hoosick Falls Village	3,269	4	0	1	0	3	75	16	48	11	0
Hornell	8,498	22	0	2	2	18	179	31	145	3	1
Horseheads Village	6,208	11	0	1	1	9	162	13	148	1	11
Hudson	6,788	27	1	0	3	23	222	37	185	0	0
Hudson Falls Village	6,645	10	0	2	1	7	46	11	33	2	1
Hunter Town	2,707	3	0	0	0	3	19	6	10	3	0
Huntington Bay Village	1,446	0	0	0	0	0	4	0	4	0	0
Hyde Park Town	20,355	5	0	1	1	3	207	32	171	4	0
Ilion Village	8,033	23	0	1	4	18	188	29	153	6	0
Independence Town	1,037	0	0	0	0	0	0	0	0	0	0
Inlet Town	381	0	0	0	0	0	4	0	4	0	0
Irondequoit Town	49,767	87	0	1	39	47	1,384	211	1,096	77	0
Irvington Village	6,688	1	0	0	0	1	40	13	26	1	1
Ithaca	30,114	58	0	1	28	29	1,094	207	861	26	0

[1] The FBI does not publish arson data unless it receives data from either the agency or the state for all 12 months of the calendar year.

Table 8. Offenses Known to Law Enforcement, by State and City, 2008—*Continued*

(Number.)

State/City	Population	Violent crime	Murder and non-negligent man-slaughter	Forcible rape	Robbery	Aggravated assault	Property crime	Burglary	Larceny-theft	Motor vehicle theft	Arson[1]
NEW YORK—*Continued*											
Jamestown	29,279	184	3	20	40	121	1,180	344	810	26	17
Johnson City Village	14,745	75	0	7	17	51	868	96	758	14	0
Johnstown	8,428	6	0	1	0	5	278	26	247	5	1
Jordan Village	1,320	0	0	0	0	0	6	1	5	0	0
Kenmore Village	14,973	33	0	2	11	20	281	39	230	12	4
Kensington Village	1,160	0	0	0	0	0	0	0	0	0	0
Kent Town	14,247	3	1	0	1	1	115	31	82	2	1
Kings Point Village	5,126	4	0	0	0	4	5	3	2	0	0
Kingston	22,520	69	0	5	48	16	645	115	510	20	
Kirkland Town	8,376	0	0	0	0	0	124	20	103	1	1
Lackawanna	17,549	91	0	6	16	69	476	115	336	25	1
Lake Placid Village	2,777	2	0	0	0	2	72	10	61	1	0
Lake Success Village	2,792	1	0	0	0	1	73	12	55	6	0
Lakewood-Busti	7,356	4	0	0	0	4	280	22	254	4	0
Lancaster Town	23,329	24	0	1	7	16	508	62	435	11	0
Larchmont Village	6,598	2	0	0	1	1	138	27	107	4	0
Le Roy Village	4,147	4	0	0	2	2	86	22	63	1	2
Lewisboro Town	12,607	0	0	0	0	0	84	9	75	0	0
Lewiston Town and Village	16,697	7	0	1	1	5	167	32	123	12	5
Liberty Village	3,881	20	1	4	4	11	159	35	118	6	0
Little Falls	4,878	45	0	0	0	45	144	28	111	5	0
Liverpool Village	2,348	2	0	0	2	0	58	5	52	1	0
Lloyd Harbor Village	3,597	0	0	0	0	0	10	2	8	0	0
Lloyd Town	10,853	10	0	3	1	6	132	21	109	2	0
Lockport	20,597	48	0	1	12	35	837	188	615	34	7
Long Beach	34,478	13	0	0	6	7	252	23	229	0	0
Lowville Village	3,184	5	0	0	1	4	101	14	87	0	0
Lynbrook Village	19,132	20	0	0	13	7	170	23	134	13	2
Lyons Village	3,395	21	0	0	5	16	200	29	169	2	0
Macedon Town and Village	8,785	4	0	0	1	3	49	13	35	1	0
Malone Village	5,782	13	0	1	2	10	223	36	187	0	0
Malverne Village	8,551	7	0	0	6	1	44	12	31	1	0
Mamaroneck Town	11,535	4	0	0	2	2	166	31	128	7	1
Mamaroneck Village	18,450	24	0	0	6	18	240	58	174	8	1
Manlius Town	24,954	24	0	3	3	18	467	49	409	9	
Massena Village	10,530	20	0	3	1	16	141	45	93	3	0
Maybrook Village	4,133	1	0	0	1	0	31	5	26	0	0
McGraw Village	956	0	0	0	0	0	3	0	3	0	0
Mechanicville	4,876	15	0	1	4	10	105	22	78	5	0
Medina Village	6,011	24	0	3	8	13	262	63	194	5	0
Menands Village	3,798	10	0	2	4	4	138	30	103	5	0
Middleport Village	1,778	2	0	0	0	2	61	4	55	2	0
Middletown	25,928	177	5	14	75	83	1,016	216	755	45	3
Millbrook Village	1,532	1	0	0	0	1	3	0	3	0	0
Monroe Village	8,174	22	0	0	8	14	224	24	196	4	
Montgomery Village	4,683	0	0	0	0	0	55	0	55	0	0
Monticello Village	6,551	36	0	3	15	18	275	85	184	6	2
Moravia Village	1,287	1	0	0	0	1	15	5	10	0	0
Moriah Town	3,468	2	0	0	0	2	6	2	4	0	0
Mount Hope Town	7,533	1	0	1	0	0	52	9	37	6	0
Mount Kisco Village	10,484	8	0	0	4	4	110	16	93	1	0
Mount Morris Village	2,867	4	0	0	1	3	53	11	42	0	0
Mount Pleasant Town	26,477	15	0	0	4	11	248	39	202	7	0
Mount Vernon	67,810	667	10	10	347	300	1,716	452	1,102	162	12
New Berlin Town	1,709	0	0	0	0	0	15	3	12	0	0
Newburgh	28,180	476	7	13	162	294	1,063	333	640	90	
Newburgh Town	31,111	29	0	3	17	9	1,116	116	951	49	3
New Castle Town	17,806	3	0	0	0	3	105	29	73	3	0
New Hartford Town and Village	19,231	11	0	0	5	6	803	53	744	6	0
New Paltz Town and Village	13,930	47	0	6	5	36	291	63	220	8	
New Rochelle	73,376	191	0	1	118	72	1,565	184	1,290	91	
New Windsor Town	25,279	28	0	0	10	18	526	89	425	12	2
New York	8,345,075	48,430	523	890	22,186	24,831	149,989	19,867	117,682	12,440	
New York Mills Village	3,326	2	0	0	1	1	75	7	67	1	0
Niagara Falls	51,192	562	3	24	171	364	2,747	827	1,759	161	29
Niagara Town	8,401	11	0	0	5	6	336	74	248	14	2
Niskayuna Town	21,925	11	0	0	5	6	378	25	343	10	0
Nissequogue Village	1,534	0	0	0	0	0	8	0	8	0	0
North Castle Town	12,237	3	0	0	0	3	75	12	59	4	1
North Greenbush Town	11,888	10	0	1	1	8	229	36	191	2	0
Northport Village	7,376	1	0	0	1	0	71	11	58	2	1
North Syracuse Village	6,596	9	0	1	2	6	105	17	85	3	0
North Tonawanda	31,199	35	0	1	10	24	521	121	380	20	1

[1] The FBI does not publish arson data unless it receives data from either the agency or the state for all 12 months of the calendar year.

Table 8. Offenses Known to Law Enforcement, by State and City, 2008—*Continued*

(Number.)

State/City	Population	Violent crime	Murder and non-negligent man-slaughter	Forcible rape	Robbery	Aggravated assault	Property crime	Burglary	Larceny-theft	Motor vehicle theft	Arson[1]
NEW YORK—*Continued*											
Northville Village	1,157	0	0	0	0	0	10	0	10	0	0
Norwich	7,021	16	0	7	1	8	317	49	261	7	
Nunda Town and Village	2,900	4	0	4	0	0	13	3	8	2	0
Ocean Beach Village	143	1	0	0	0	1	96	7	89	0	0
Ogdensburg	11,032	20	0	2	1	17	579	108	454	17	1
Ogden Town	19,263	15	0	1	2	12	257	34	209	14	0
Old Brookville Village	2,222	2	0	0	1	1	117	32	83	2	1
Old Westbury Village	5,362	3	0	1	1	1	33	4	28	1	1
Olean	14,165	89	0	11	8	70	463	47	413	3	6
Oneida	10,768	27	0	7	3	17	423	76	345	2	0
Oneonta City	13,224	48	0	6	5	37	327	84	235	8	0
Orangetown Town	36,759	51	0	1	17	33	547	49	487	11	0
Orchard Park Town	28,599	17	0	1	3	13	453	56	382	15	0
Oriskany Village	1,408	0	0	0	0	0	16	5	10	1	0
Ossining Town	5,764	1	0	0	0	1	45	5	39	1	0
Ossining Village	23,907	45	0	4	18	23	313	70	234	9	2
Oswego City	17,303	64	0	14	7	43	533	86	437	10	1
Owego Village	3,676	9	0	1	0	8	18	3	15	0	1
Oxford Village	1,542	0	0	0	0	0	16	2	14	0	0
Oyster Bay Cove Village	2,212	0	0	0	0	0	10	2	8	0	0
Painted Post Village	1,751	2	0	1	0	1	54	3	51	0	0
Peekskill	24,820	54	4	0	24	26	231	28	191	12	2
Pelham Manor Village	5,490	4	0	0	1	3	84	15	67	2	0
Pelham Village	6,479	8	0	0	3	5	140	22	116	2	0
Penn Yan Village	5,153	5	0	3	1	1	102	11	90	1	0
Perry Village	3,667	3	0	0	0	3	91	21	68	2	0
Philmont Village	1,368	4	0	0	0	4	3	2	1	0	0
Piermont Village	2,570	0	0	0	0	0	64	10	53	1	0
Pine Plains Town	2,721	0	0	0	0	0	25	3	22	0	0
Plattekill Town	10,925	15	0	1	1	13	102	32	66	4	1
Plattsburgh City	19,521	25	0	7	1	17	672	97	559	16	7
Pleasantville Village	7,164	0	0	0	0	0	0	0	0	0	0
Port Byron Village	1,234	0	0	0	0	0	0	0	0	0	0
Port Chester Village	28,237	69	0	1	47	21	636	88	509	39	2
Port Dickinson Village	1,597	1	0	0	0	1	12	6	6	0	0
Port Jervis	9,152	24	0	3	4	17	205	37	165	3	3
Portville Village	952	0	0	0	0	0	3	1	2	0	0
Port Washington	18,237	9	0	0	5	4	127	22	101	4	3
Potsdam Village	9,798	14	0	1	0	13	118	10	105	3	0
Poughkeepsie	29,606	394	5	23	162	204	1,122	261	784	77	8
Poughkeepsie Town	43,453	57	0	1	31	25	1,484	126	1,339	19	2
Pulaski Village	2,280	4	0	0	0	4	45	8	36	1	0
Quogue Village	1,114	2	0	0	0	2	40	8	30	2	0
Ramapo Town	75,433	78	1	6	19	52	722	121	573	28	0
Rensselaer City	7,926	30	0	3	9	18	246	58	175	13	0
Rhinebeck Village	3,064	3	0	0	1	2	67	5	62	0	0
Riverhead Town	34,618	113	2	4	36	71	1,085	192	864	29	0
Rochester	205,341	2,302	42	98	1,059	1,103	11,130	2,808	7,060	1,262	215
Rockville Centre Village	23,513	14	1	1	11	1	285	41	225	19	0
Rome	33,746	41	2	8	14	17	611	111	466	34	2
Rosendale Town	6,253	3	0	0	0	3	42	11	29	2	0
Rotterdam Town	29,689	41	0	4	12	25	842	97	722	23	10
Rouses Point Village	2,344	0	0	0	0	0	15	7	8	0	0
Rye	15,275	7	0	0	0	7	200	42	146	12	0
Rye Brook Village	9,720	0	0	0	0	0	91	19	67	5	0
Sackets Harbor Village	1,434	0	0	0	0	0	10	1	9	0	0
Sag Harbor Village	2,333	6	0	0	0	6	59	8	48	3	0
Salamanca	5,577	28	0	3	5	20	253	60	189	4	1
Sands Point Village	2,795	0	0	0	0	0	11	2	9	0	0
Saranac Lake Village	4,801	10	0	2	0	8	127	29	96	2	0
Saratoga Springs	29,091	23	0	1	6	16	602	78	503	21	3
Saugerties Town	15,791	13	0	3	1	9	327	179	145	3	3
Saugerties Village	3,862	4	0	0	0	4	83	9	70	4	1
Scarsdale Village	17,739	7	0	0	2	5	186	25	155	6	0
Schenectady	61,506	654	9	35	288	322	3,054	925	1,905	224	39
Schodack Town	11,533	6	0	0	2	4	108	26	81	1	0
Schoharie Village	996	0	0	0	0	0	20	11	9	0	0
Scotia Village	8,093	10	0	1	4	5	179	22	146	11	0
Seneca Falls Village	6,673	7	0	1	0	6	58	8	50	0	4
Shandaken Town	3,073	3	0	1	1	1	34	11	23	0	0
Shawangunk Town	12,792	9	0	0	2	7	141	22	118	1	1
Shelter Island Town	2,453	0	0	0	0	0	63	14	48	1	0
Sherburne Village	1,419	0	0	0	0	0	47	4	43	0	0
Sherrill	3,120	2	0	0	0	2	11	0	11	0	0

[1] The FBI does not publish arson data unless it receives data from either the agency or the state for all 12 months of the calendar year.

Table 8. Offenses Known to Law Enforcement, by State and City, 2008—*Continued*

(Number.)

State/City	Population	Violent crime	Murder and non-negligent man-slaughter	Forcible rape	Robbery	Aggravated assault	Property crime	Burglary	Larceny-theft	Motor vehicle theft	Arson[1]
NEW YORK—*Continued*											
Shortsville Village	1,319	0	0	0	0	0	0	0	0	0	0
Sidney Village	3,692	13	0	0	2	11	212	29	182	1	1
Silver Creek Village	2,798	2	0	1	0	1	57	2	53	2	0
Skaneateles Village	2,550	0	0	0	0	0	12	3	9	0	0
Sodus Point Village	1,104	0	0	0	0	0	5	1	4	0	0
Sodus Village	1,598	0	0	0	0	0	49	10	38	1	0
Solvay Village	6,429	27	0	5	6	16	162	35	117	10	1
Southampton Town	50,089	87	0	10	25	52	1,200	273	852	75	3
Southampton Village	4,049	3	1	0	1	1	186	22	164	0	0
South Glens Falls Village	3,401	5	0	2	1	2	143	19	122	2	0
South Nyack Village	3,374	3	0	0	1	2	70	11	55	4	1
Spring Valley Village	26,337	200	0	7	63	130	516	85	407	24	1
Stillwater Town	6,560	0	0	0	0	0	28	3	23	2	0
Stockport Town	2,824	0	0	0	0	0	4	2	2	0	0
Stony Point Town	15,226	7	0	0	2	5	146	16	128	2	0
Suffern Village	10,957	4	0	0	2	2	58	8	45	5	0
Syracuse	138,211	1,366	24	71	419	852	6,165	1,938	3,725	502	70
Tarrytown Village	11,435	4	0	0	4	0	146	15	126	5	2
Ticonderoga Town	4,995	9	0	0	0	9	67	14	50	3	1
Tonawanda	14,792	19	0	1	6	12	396	41	333	22	2
Tonawanda Town	56,605	136	1	8	37	90	1,160	222	882	56	6
Troy	47,567	392	5	19	152	216	2,363	600	1,650	113	15
Trumansburg Village	1,594	2	0	0	0	2	82	14	67	1	0
Tuckahoe Village	6,253	0	0	0	0	0	51	11	35	5	1
Tupper Lake Village	3,824	12	0	1	0	11	178	24	154	0	0
Tuxedo Park Village	720	0	0	0	0	0	0	0	0	0	0
Tuxedo Town	3,003	1	0	0	0	1	14	2	11	1	0
Ulster Town	12,733	9	0	1	6	2	284	35	238	11	3
Utica	58,234	479	4	21	181	273	2,778	729	1,929	120	20
Vernon Village	1,154	2	0	1	0	1	16	7	8	1	0
Vestal Town	27,412	18	0	0	0	18	592	44	545	3	0
Walden Village	7,035	20	0	1	4	15	114	8	102	4	0
Wallkill Town	27,643	28	0	3	16	9	781	90	667	24	
Walton Village	2,824	7	0	0	0	7	52	14	35	3	0
Wappingers Falls Village	5,386	3	0	1	2	0	139	12	123	4	1
Warsaw Village	3,632	11	0	2	5	4	64	7	54	3	0
Washingtonville Village	6,185	3	0	0	1	2	82	4	77	1	0
Waterford Town and Village	8,579	0	0	0	0	0	68	11	55	2	0
Waterloo Village	5,020	5	0	0	1	4	216	14	196	6	0
Watertown	27,546	143	0	12	20	111	1,286	194	1,035	57	9
Watervliet	9,788	32	0	1	8	23	272	48	214	10	1
Watkins Glen Village	2,032	2	0	0	1	1	79	3	75	1	1
Waverly Village	4,338	1	0	0	0	1	133	26	103	4	0
Wayland Village	1,787	0	0	0	0	0	14	0	14	0	0
Webster Town and Village	41,735	27	1	2	7	17	564	92	449	23	3
Weedsport Village	1,913	0	0	0	0	0	44	3	41	0	0
Wellsville Village	4,874	25	0	0	0	25	111	31	73	7	1
West Carthage Village	2,183	5	0	1	0	4	16	2	14	0	0
Westfield Village	3,361	4	0	0	0	4	55	18	36	1	0
Westhampton Beach Village	1,937	7	0	2	1	4	36	9	27	0	0
West Seneca Town	43,837	64	0	7	12	45	911	136	729	46	5
Whitehall Village	2,565	5	0	1	0	4	36	4	28	4	0
White Plains	57,932	86	0	1	20	65	1,167	40	1,103	24	1
Whitesboro Village	3,772	12	0	0	1	11	49	8	38	3	0
Whitestown Town	9,310	0	0	0	0	0	97	14	78	5	0
Windham Town	1,928	1	0	0	0	1	61	21	39	1	0
Woodbury Town	10,309	6	0	2	3	1	380	22	352	6	0
Woodstock Town	6,166	2	0	0	0	2	77	20	52	5	1
Yonkers	199,615	914	9	42	447	416	3,126	653	2,121	352	40
Yorktown Town	37,928	33	0	3	3	27	450	65	378	7	1
Yorkville Village	2,565	1	0	0	1	0	80	17	60	3	0
Youngstown Village	1,862	0	0	0	0	0	8	6	2	0	0
NORTH CAROLINA											
Aberdeen	5,662	35	0	1	19	15	294	49	226	19	5
Albemarle	15,423	121	1	7	39	74	1,114	287	761	66	14
Angier	4,414	38	1	0	6	31	196	71	110	15	3
Archdale	9,291	27	0	1	11	15	362	110	231	21	5
Asheboro	24,458	79	2	14	30	33	1,592	372	1,142	78	1
Asheville	74,215	535	2	33	251	249	4,268	907	2,951	410	62
Atlantic Beach	1,811	26	0	1	4	21	207	70	124	13	0
Ayden	5,020	19	0	0	7	12	285	73	202	10	1
Bailey	681	5	0	3	2	0	54	9	43	2	0
Bald Head Island	305	0	0	0	0	0	38	17	20	1	0
Beaufort	4,245	20	0	3	3	14	170	59	102	9	1

[1] The FBI does not publish arson data unless it receives data from either the agency or the state for all 12 months of the calendar year.

Table 8. Offenses Known to Law Enforcement, by State and City, 2008—*Continued*

(Number.)

State/City	Population	Violent crime	Murder and non-negligent man-slaughter	Forcible rape	Robbery	Aggravated assault	Property crime	Burglary	Larceny-theft	Motor vehicle theft	Arson[1]
NORTH CAROLINA—*Continued*											
Beech Mountain	330	0	0	0	0	0	30	6	22	2	0
Belmont	9,263	53	1	3	10	39	527	75	417	35	2
Benson	3,471	33	0	3	8	22	203	46	145	12	1
Bethel	1,739	6	0	0	1	5	83	12	68	3	0
Beulaville	1,121	11	0	0	1	10	55	17	38	0	0
Biscoe	1,680	4	0	1	3	0	166	18	144	4	0
Black Mountain	7,892	8	0	0	4	4	156	57	94	5	1
Bladenboro	1,667	17	0	0	3	14	117	33	83	1	0
Boiling Springs	3,796	1	0	1	0	0	48	17	30	1	2
Boone	13,885	25	1	4	7	13	425	60	355	10	1
Brevard	6,674	25	0	2	6	17	289	75	209	5	0
Broadway	1,151	3	0	0	1	2	16	0	16	0	0
Burgaw	4,160	13	0	0	3	10	151	23	120	8	1
Burlington	50,058	378	3	15	117	243	3,300	924	2,231	145	11
Butner	6,636	39	0	1	5	33	328	107	206	15	4
Candor	834	3	0	0	2	1	15	4	8	3	0
Canton	3,882	25	0	0	1	24	247	53	179	15	2
Cape Carteret	1,433	2	0	0	0	2	35	4	30	1	0
Carolina Beach	5,989	17	0	4	2	11	280	59	210	11	1
Carrboro	17,958	72	1	4	36	31	759	256	448	55	2
Carthage	2,027	6	0	0	0	6	69	22	41	6	1
Cary	125,277	107	3	12	47	45	2,342	503	1,761	78	13
Catawba	806	0	0	0	0	0	16	2	14	0	0
Chadbourn	2,063	31	0	0	12	19	273	62	201	10	2
Chapel Hill	52,034	152	2	9	74	67	1,882	531	1,261	90	3
Charlotte-Mecklenburg	758,769	7,070	83	272	2,984	3,731	46,934	11,933	29,735	5,266	336
Cherryville	5,554	15	0	0	2	13	275	87	179	9	0
China Grove	3,722	11	0	0	2	9	88	23	63	2	0
Claremont	1,143	7	1	1	3	2	59	15	38	6	0
Clayton	16,013	34	0	5	8	21	426	107	301	18	2
Cleveland	833	2	0	0	2	0	57	17	40	0	0
Clinton	8,876	98	0	4	40	54	543	125	385	33	6
Coats	2,115	8	0	0	2	6	41	12	28	1	0
Columbus	977	7	0	0	2	5	61	6	55	0	0
Concord	65,725	183	9	19	82	73	3,105	527	2,340	238	16
Cornelius	24,983	76	1	6	11	58	417	138	257	22	4
Cramerton	3,109	7	0	0	3	4	100	33	62	5	1
Creedmoor	3,606	12	0	3	2	7	107	28	69	10	2
Dobson	1,454	2	0	0	1	1	62	16	46	0	0
Dunn	10,004	96	1	6	33	56	933	174	698	61	1
Durham	221,785	1,815	24	75	886	830	11,958	3,490	7,584	884	30
East Spencer	1,777	13	0	1	3	9	59	32	21	6	2
Eden	15,393	72	2	1	20	49	869	215	606	48	
Edenton	4,992	33	0	2	10	21	215	43	168	4	2
Elizabeth City	19,813	155	0	6	55	94	909	216	665	28	1
Elkin	4,079	9	0	1	2	6	163	28	130	5	1
Elon	6,986	14	0	2	2	10	120	32	88	0	0
Emerald Isle	3,672	6	0	0	2	4	215	92	119	4	0
Enfield	2,331	56	1	3	8	44	139	84	51	4	2
Erwin	4,807	21	0	0	5	16	156	61	80	15	0
Farmville	4,630	27	0	0	4	23	244	86	151	7	1
Fayetteville	171,457	1,621	23	72	653	873	13,499	3,920	8,684	895	45
Fletcher	4,725	6	0	0	3	3	135	22	106	7	1
Forest City	7,086	41	1	3	10	27	692	130	532	30	11
Franklin	3,953	15	0	0	3	12	158	35	114	9	1
Franklinton	1,972	7	0	2	3	2	63	10	48	5	0
Fuquay-Varina	16,674	52	0	2	12	38	598	108	463	27	3
Garner	26,378	106	3	11	62	30	1,344	195	1,079	70	5
Gastonia	71,486	646	7	21	237	381	5,326	1,210	3,678	438	53
Gibsonville	4,732	16	0	3	0	13	160	47	108	5	1
Goldsboro	37,445	330	5	4	117	204	2,869	746	1,929	194	2
Graham	14,543	84	0	6	20	58	730	204	488	38	1
Granite Falls	4,570	15	1	5	2	7	277	51	220	6	0
Greensboro	249,561	2,157	24	109	998	1,026	15,809	4,942	9,759	1,108	108
Greenville	77,960	632	6	13	243	370	5,105	1,538	3,304	263	12
Grifton	2,234	5	0	0	2	3	68	14	50	4	0
Hamlet	5,749	29	0	1	15	13	408	143	254	11	7
Henderson	15,841	204	3	2	87	112	1,836	555	1,203	78	7
Hendersonville	12,027	74	2	5	12	55	888	131	715	42	8
Hertford	2,149	16	1	1	5	9	82	47	33	2	1
Hickory	41,414	331	3	22	116	190	3,180	615	2,361	204	
Highlands	950	1	0	0	0	1	53	19	34	0	0
High Point	102,298	718	11	30	310	367	6,108	1,953	3,755	400	33
Holden Beach	858	2	0	2	0	0	57	31	26	0	0

[1] The FBI does not publish arson data unless it receives data from either the agency or the state for all 12 months of the calendar year.

Table 8. Offenses Known to Law Enforcement, by State and City, 2008—*Continued*

(Number.)

State/City	Population	Violent crime	Murder and non-negligent man-slaughter	Forcible rape	Robbery	Aggravated assault	Property crime	Burglary	Larceny-theft	Motor vehicle theft	Arson[1]
NORTH CAROLINA—*Continued*											
Holly Ridge	830	9	0	0	0	9	44	9	30	5	0
Hope Mills	13,004	101	0	3	34	64	1,115	291	775	49	1
Hudson	3,023	9	0	2	2	5	115	19	89	7	0
Huntersville	45,273	71	1	4	20	46	1,122	224	833	65	10
Indian Beach	93	0	0	0	0	0	9	0	7	2	0
Jacksonville	75,770	286	5	29	89	163	2,545	505	1,921	119	5
Jefferson	1,361	1	0	0	1	0	16	3	10	3	0
Kannapolis	42,065	167	4	10	50	103	1,167	391	643	133	4
Kenansville	904	3	1	0	2	0	31	5	25	1	0
Kernersville	22,782	128	1	8	30	89	1,310	212	1,043	55	8
Kill Devil Hills[5]	6,670		0	3	3		592	168	406	18	2
King	6,863	13	0	0	1	12	267	52	204	11	3
Kings Mountain	11,136	24	0	1	8	15	510	139	348	23	1
Kinston	22,168	262	6	12	69	175	1,766	484	1,213	69	6
Kitty Hawk	3,344	3	0	1	1	1	152	38	110	4	0
Knightdale	7,571	29	0	7	12	10	349	74	262	13	3
La Grange	2,745	23	0	1	4	18	156	29	125	2	1
Lake Lure	1,005	1	0	0	0	1	40	16	23	1	0
Lake Royale	0	3	0	1	0	2	75	23	50	2	0
Landis	3,111	0	0	0	0	0	82	14	64	4	1
Laurel Park	2,151	3	0	1	1	1	13	1	11	1	0
Laurinburg	15,442	132	2	7	46	77	1,034	387	588	59	9
Leland	4,992	16	0	0	7	9	282	86	188	8	0
Lenoir	17,843	64	4	1	21	38	971	198	708	65	6
Lexington	20,375	118	1	4	35	78	959	309	598	52	4
Liberty	2,726	5	0	0	2	3	35	6	28	1	1
Lincolnton	10,779	60	0	0	9	51	881	258	592	31	2
Long View	4,940	47	1	2	13	31	315	129	161	25	1
Louisburg	3,764	19	2	1	6	10	188	57	121	10	1
Lumberton	21,849	446	4	9	176	257	2,951	775	1,950	226	12
Madison	2,256	50	0	1	1	48	125	32	92	1	0
Magnolia	989	3	0	0	0	3	38	4	32	2	0
Maiden	3,461	11	0	1	6	4	128	13	105	10	0
Manteo	1,330	3	0	1	1	1	74	16	49	9	0
Marion	5,112	33	1	0	9	23	455	160	269	26	5
Mars Hill	1,770	0	0	0	0	0	39	10	29	0	1
Marshville	3,198	17	0	1	4	12	78	30	43	5	0
Matthews	27,140	61	0	3	33	25	1,157	209	900	48	7
Mayodan	2,600	12	0	1	1	10	205	23	182	0	0
Maysville	963	0	0	0	0	0	15	2	12	1	0
Mebane	10,534	49	0	2	14	33	330	70	248	12	0
Middlesex	857	0	0	0	0	0	41	13	26	2	0
Mint Hill	20,096	52	0	5	14	33	399	241	118	40	7
Mocksville	4,634	16	1	3	5	7	263	36	214	13	1
Monroe	32,216	199	2	7	66	124	2,139	505	1,481	153	10
Morehead City	9,683	66	0	7	10	49	723	113	600	10	3
Morganton	17,069	60	0	3	14	43	668	209	428	31	0
Morrisville	14,976	15	0	2	9	4	350	54	287	9	1
Mount Airy	8,729	62	0	1	16	45	629	123	471	35	2
Mount Holly	9,982	55	1	6	10	38	347	79	229	39	3
Mount Olive	4,380	40	2	0	6	32	376	95	262	19	3
Murfreesboro	2,333	2	0	0	0	2	150	40	109	1	0
Murphy	1,565	10	0	0	0	10	120	24	94	2	1
Nags Head	3,064	10	0	1	2	7	321	133	179	9	1
Newland	649	0	0	0	0	0	19	0	19	0	0
Newport	4,318	7	0	2	1	4	68	11	56	1	0
Newton	13,359	31	0	1	12	18	763	211	507	45	1
North Topsail Beach	976	0	0	0	0	0	16	7	9	0	0
North Wilkesboro	4,139	18	0	3	9	6	251	64	177	10	0
Norwood	2,131	5	0	0	1	4	120	51	63	6	0
Oak Island	8,397	23	0	2	7	14	409	161	245	3	1
Old Fort	961	3	0	0	3	0	31	11	18	2	0
Oxford	8,628	110	0	6	33	71	628	303	301	24	1
Pilot Mountain	1,269	3	0	0	2	1	156	38	111	7	1
Pinebluff	1,419	1	0	0	0	1	28	14	14	0	0
Pinehurst	12,422	5	0	3	0	2	112	2	104	6	1
Pine Knoll Shores	1,553	1	0	1	0	0	33	10	23	0	0
Pine Level	1,551	1	0	1	0	0	61	7	54	0	0
Pinetops	1,252	9	0	0	5	4	81	20	57	4	0
Pineville	6,642	63	1	1	23	38	1,078	99	914	65	11
Pittsboro	2,582	12	0	1	3	8	80	17	57	6	0
Plymouth	3,826	66	0	0	14	52	257	107	144	6	0
Raeford	3,466	36	2	1	11	22	314	116	183	15	0
Raleigh	388,661	2,245	34	95	1,025	1,091	13,220	3,095	9,178	947	68

[1] The FBI does not publish arson data unless it receives data from either the agency or the state for all 12 months of the calendar year.

Table 8. Offenses Known to Law Enforcement, by State and City, 2008—*Continued*

(Number.)

State/City	Population	Violent crime	Murder and non-negligent man-slaughter	Forcible rape	Robbery	Aggravated assault	Property crime	Burglary	Larceny-theft	Motor vehicle theft	Arson[1]
NORTH CAROLINA—*Continued*											
Ramseur	1,715	3	0	0	1	2	93	24	66	3	0
Randleman	3,678	25	0	4	9	12	320	69	242	9	0
Red Springs	3,502	34	0	3	13	18	318	143	150	25	4
Reidsville	15,027	100	2	6	28	64	1,171	367	763	41	3
Richlands	913	5	0	0	1	4	39	6	31	2	0
Roanoke Rapids	16,347	84	0	6	40	38	1,016	249	711	56	5
Robbins	1,218	1	0	0	0	1	45	12	32	1	0
Robersonville	1,548	27	0	2	8	17	121	37	79	5	0
Rockingham	8,802	61	2	5	15	39	915	184	699	32	1
Rockwell	1,998	3	0	1	1	1	67	14	51	2	1
Rolesville	2,519	5	0	1	1	3	73	15	58	0	0
Rowland	1,148	4	1	0	3	0	67	34	29	4	0
Roxboro	8,681	83	1	3	16	63	617	189	404	24	5
Rutherfordton	4,019	1	0	0	1	0	154	27	124	3	0
Salisbury	28,747	327	4	15	145	163	2,345	583	1,592	170	8
Scotland Neck	2,163	34	0	3	10	21	186	66	116	4	0
Selma	6,921	76	1	9	27	39	501	276	199	26	4
Shallotte	1,759	14	0	1	5	8	251	116	124	11	2
Sharpsburg	2,400	14	0	2	5	7	73	37	30	6	1
Siler City	8,725	35	0	3	13	19	386	73	291	22	2
Smithfield	12,759	141	0	5	57	79	963	213	679	71	3
Southern Pines	12,604	155	1	4	43	107	710	209	467	34	5
Southern Shores	2,670	1	0	0	0	1	59	23	33	3	0
Southport	3,108	9	0	0	5	4	152	43	103	6	1
Sparta	1,778	3	0	0	0	3	27	8	16	3	0
Spencer	3,370	40	0	0	3	37	207	106	100	1	5
Stallings	8,960	22	0	1	5	16	301	67	226	8	0
Stanley	3,299	11	0	2	1	8	137	69	58	10	2
Star	797	2	0	0	0	2	22	5	17	0	0
St. Pauls	2,035	12	0	0	9	3	111	39	63	9	2
Sunset Beach	2,348	1	0	0	0	1	81	48	31	2	0
Surf City	1,986	9	0	1	0	8	182	87	94	1	0
Swansboro	1,915	10	0	0	4	6	94	16	69	9	1
Sylva	2,427	20	0	5	3	12	236	37	196	3	0
Tabor City	2,636	23	0	0	6	17	255	21	220	14	1
Tarboro	10,187	64	1	0	15	48	421	108	299	14	0
Taylorsville	1,828	9	1	0	2	6	211	39	167	5	0
Thomasville	26,528	155	1	3	41	110	1,642	392	1,176	74	5
Trent Woods	3,962	2	0	1	0	1	62	12	49	1	0
Troutman	1,819	6	0	0	4	2	129	53	69	7	0
Troy	3,373	26	0	1	5	20	185	30	147	8	1
Tryon	1,714	2	0	0	0	2	68	23	43	2	0
Valdese	4,523	6	1	0	2	3	102	40	61	1	0
Vass	780	3	0	0	0	3	53	12	40	1	0
Wadesboro	5,061	63	0	8	23	32	516	162	341	13	2
Wake Forest	27,532	52	0	3	17	32	650	120	511	19	0
Wallace	3,611	9	0	1	4	4	151	43	97	11	1
Warsaw	3,164	28	2	2	10	14	152	23	125	4	0
Washington	10,097	133	0	6	38	89	772	208	536	28	5
Waxhaw	3,665	13	1	0	5	7	192	39	148	5	0
Waynesville	9,921	37	0	8	8	21	347	117	215	15	1
Weldon	1,279	14	0	1	10	3	150	3	145	2	1
Wendell	5,260	12	0	2	3	7	184	60	119	5	0
West Jefferson	1,120	2	0	0	0	2	75	19	50	6	0
Whispering Pines	2,139	0	0	0	0	0	11	0	11	0	0
Whitakers	767	5	0	0	1	4	41	23	17	1	0
White Lake	565	2	0	0	0	2	82	15	62	5	0
Whiteville	5,226	75	0	4	27	44	765	146	583	36	2
Wilkesboro	3,168	19	0	3	2	14	357	62	283	12	0
Williamston	5,362	61	0	1	22	38	453	151	288	14	4
Wilmington	100,944	778	12	49	319	398	5,447	1,465	3,454	528	15
Wilson's Mills	1,587	7	0	1	0	6	63	29	28	6	0
Windsor	2,110	6	0	0	2	4	57	22	33	2	0
Winston-Salem	226,460	2,079	19	104	723	1,233	14,995	4,670	9,234	1,091	114
Winterville	4,803	35	0	0	3	32	271	95	163	13	2
Woodland	757	10	0	0	3	7	67	37	27	3	1
Wrightsville Beach	2,680	7	0	2	0	5	175	44	125	6	0
Yadkinville	2,862	10	0	2	1	7	164	35	124	5	1
Youngsville	748	8	0	0	2	6	77	12	64	1	0
Zebulon	4,566	33	0	1	7	25	446	34	404	8	5
NORTH DAKOTA											
Beulah	2,877	7	0	3	0	4	37	4	30	3	3
Bismarck	59,988	155	2	16	10	127	1,629	211	1,324	94	5
Burlington	993	0	0	0	0	0	4	3	1	0	0

[1] The FBI does not publish arson data unless it receives data from either the agency or the state for all 12 months of the calendar year.

Table 8. Offenses Known to Law Enforcement, by State and City, 2008—*Continued*

(Number.)

State/City	Population	Violent crime	Murder and non-negligent man-slaughter	Forcible rape	Robbery	Aggravated assault	Property crime	Burglary	Larceny-theft	Motor vehicle theft	Arson[1]
NORTH DAKOTA—*Continued*											
Cando	1,030	0	0	0	0	0	14	0	14	0	0
Carrington	2,080	0	0	0	0	0	11	7	3	1	1
Cavalier	1,333	1	0	1	0	0	19	1	16	2	0
Devils Lake	6,610	12	1	1	0	10	283	31	234	18	2
Dickinson[4]	15,910	30	0	0	1	29	320	39	250	31	2
Emerado	472	1	0	1	0	0	8	1	6	1	0
Fargo	92,883	273	0	52	27	194	2,906	442	2,252	212	20
Fessenden	499	1	0	0	0	1	3	0	3	0	0
Grafton	3,991	6	0	1	0	5	164	45	111	8	2
Grand Forks	52,064	142	0	25	14	103	1,769	273	1,391	105	15
Harvey	1,610	8	0	3	0	5	26	9	17	0	0
Jamestown	14,578	47	0	15	2	30	321	65	239	17	8
Lincoln	2,660	0	0	0	0	0	23	5	16	2	0
Lisbon	2,182	5	0	0	1	4	19	7	7	5	0
Mandan	17,860	34	0	15	4	15	383	43	311	29	7
Mayville	1,986	1	0	1	0	0	9	2	4	3	1
Minot	35,124	76	0	20	3	53	733	128	558	47	7
Northwood	871	0	0	0	0	0	3	2	1	0	0
Rolla	1,423	4	0	0	0	4	27	2	22	3	0
Steele	649	0	0	0	0	0	3	0	3	0	0
Thompson	949	0	0	0	0	0	10	3	6	1	0
Valley City	6,242	7	0	5	1	1	83	24	54	5	0
Wahpeton	7,603	11	0	1	1	9	162	13	145	4	2
Watford City	1,367	1	0	0	0	1	5	0	5	0	0
West Fargo	24,266	41	0	12	3	26	547	125	375	47	1
Williston	12,387	29	0	14	2	13	199	16	156	27	1
OHIO											
Aberdeen	1,540	4	0	0	2	2	81	22	56	3	0
Ada	5,793	0	0	0	0	0	61	12	46	3	0
Akron	206,845	1,897	17	167	801	912	10,721	3,770	6,001	950	109
Alliance	22,285	87	0	22	26	39	1,080	274	786	20	30
Amberley Village	3,565	3	0	0	0	3	64	15	44	5	0
Amelia	3,626	4	0	3	1	0	87	16	70	1	0
Amherst	11,683	6	0	1	4	1	250	27	214	9	1
Arcanum	1,969	0	0	0	0	0	25	4	21	0	1
Archbold	4,468	4	0	2	0	2	121	21	98	2	0
Ashland	21,900	19	0	12	5	2	600	86	504	10	1
Athens	21,981	21	0	1	4	16	485	69	400	16	1
Aurora	14,659	11	0	3	0	8	169	30	128	11	1
Austintown	35,185	19	1	1	16	1	1,525	297	1,150	78	2
Bainbridge Township	11,225	6	0	0	0	6	280	31	245	4	0
Barberton	26,637	63	1	18	21	23	1,202	247	893	62	22
Barnesville	4,054	5	0	0	2	3	19	12	6	1	0
Batavia	1,698	5	0	5	0	0	115	23	90	2	0
Bath Township, Summit County	10,257	11	0	2	7	2	176	30	140	6	0
Bay Village	14,598	1	0	0	0	1	6	2	4	0	0
Bazetta Township	6,011	0	0	0	0	0	63	11	49	3	0
Beavercreek	39,965	49	0	7	14	28	1,120	135	954	31	9
Beaver Township	6,087	2	0	0	0	2	161	31	123	7	1
Bedford	12,975	46	0	3	17	26	492	38	392	62	0
Bedford Heights	10,513	28	0	5	16	7	282	40	187	55	0
Bellaire	4,560	12	0	4	3	5	40	4	35	1	0
Bellbrook	6,969	1	0	0	0	1	129	24	103	2	1
Bellefontaine	12,697	47	0	8	8	31	708	66	622	20	1
Bellville	1,710	4	0	0	0	4	80	11	67	2	0
Belpre	6,498	10	0	8	2	0	129	29	97	3	2
Berea	17,679	26	0	4	14	8	292	27	247	18	2
Bethel	2,622	3	0	0	2	1	179	30	144	5	2
Bethesda	1,358	1	0	0	0	1	4	1	3	0	0
Beverly	1,338	3	0	1	0	2	28	0	26	2	0
Bexley	12,261	28	0	1	16	11	408	115	275	18	0
Blanchester	4,326	8	0	4	1	3	88	13	75	0	0
Blendon Township	7,775	11	0	3	6	2	257	44	197	16	1
Blue Ash	12,798	5	0	0	3	2	312	35	266	11	0
Bluffton	3,973	2	0	0	0	2	98	27	67	4	0
Boardman	39,244	73	0	5	56	12	1,776	299	1,378	99	4
Bowling Green	29,919	25	0	2	8	15	971	96	842	33	1
Brecksville	12,903	1	0	0	0	1	72	13	54	5	0
Broadview Heights	17,577	9	0	0	3	6	62	15	35	12	0
Brooklyn	10,408	37	0	3	16	18	648	66	530	52	0
Brooklyn Heights	1,452	0	0	0	0	0	37	6	28	3	0
Brookville	5,381	8	0	7	0	1	61	11	48	2	0
Bryan	8,263	10	0	4	0	6	103	22	78	3	1
Buckeye Lake	3,046	31	0	8	4	19	143	31	105	7	0

[1] The FBI does not publish arson data unless it receives data from either the agency or the state for all 12 months of the calendar year.
[4] Because of changes in the state/local agency's reporting practices, figures are not comparable to previous years' data.

Table 8. Offenses Known to Law Enforcement, by State and City, 2008—*Continued*

(Number.)

State/City	Population	Violent crime	Murder and non-negligent man-slaughter	Forcible rape	Robbery	Aggravated assault	Property crime	Burglary	Larceny-theft	Motor vehicle theft	Arson[1]
OHIO—*Continued*											
Butler Township	8,147	9	0	1	5	3	292	25	252	15	0
Cadiz	3,308	3	0	1	1	1	112	21	87	4	5
Cambridge	11,251	59	0	8	5	46	702	166	505	31	2
Campbell	8,432	30	1	1	19	9	275	124	122	29	0
Canal Fulton	5,015	9	0	4	1	4	124	23	101	0	2
Canfield	6,876	0	0	0	0	0	66	10	56	0	0
Canton	78,006	699	8	65	361	265	5,298	1,638	3,281	379	31
Cardington	2,022	2	0	0	0	2	31	9	21	1	0
Celina	10,243	18	0	2	4	12	426	50	370	6	0
Centerville	22,926	15	0	3	4	8	464	65	378	21	3
Champion Township	9,236	4	0	0	3	1	225	56	157	12	1
Chardon	5,243	2	0	0	0	2	59	11	48	0	0
Cheviot	8,200	11	0	1	7	3	227	32	185	10	0
Cincinnati	332,608	4,204	73	269	2,419	1,443	20,264	6,330	12,328	1,606	225
Circleville	13,667	25	0	7	9	9	1,054	198	829	27	4
Clay Township, Ottawa County	2,728	5	0	2	0	3	9	0	9	0	0
Cleveland	433,452	6,193	102	423	3,804	1,864	25,071	9,102	10,686	5,283	532
Cleves	2,605	3	0	0	1	2	79	20	57	2	1
Clinton Township	4,012	46	0	4	25	17	395	70	294	31	1
Clyde	6,165	4	0	1	2	1	250	40	207	3	0
Coldwater	4,409	3	0	3	0	0	36	10	23	3	0
Columbus	751,887	5,821	109	615	3,590	1,507	48,282	14,708	28,263	5,311	470
Conneaut	12,343	23	1	4	2	16	364	93	254	17	0
Cortland	6,386	2	0	1	0	1	119	30	84	5	3
Covington	2,540	2	0	1	0	1	52	4	48	0	0
Creston	2,115	1	0	1	0	0	79	5	73	1	0
Cridersville	1,700	1	0	0	0	1	34	7	27	0	0
Danville	1,071	0	0	0	0	0	19	1	18	0	0
Dayton	154,218	1,672	37	105	808	722	9,466	3,237	5,061	1,168	169
Deer Park	5,615	11	0	4	6	1	165	21	139	5	0
Defiance	15,926	37	0	11	4	22	654	74	576	4	2
Delaware	34,028	80	0	45	16	19	910	230	647	33	18
Delhi Township	31,362	21	0	3	2	16	393	93	290	10	4
Delphos	6,709	8	0	2	3	3	169	47	121	1	3
Delta	2,904	1	0	0	1	0	94	16	78	0	1
Dover	12,494	11	0	5	3	3	129	26	97	6	0
Dublin	38,825	18	0	6	9	3	733	110	605	18	1
Eastlake	19,503	24	0	0	12	12	521	28	464	29	3
Eaton	8,022	25	0	4	2	19	387	75	290	22	1
Edgerton	1,967	0	0	0	0	0	52	7	45	0	0
Elida	1,902	0	0	0	0	0	13	1	9	3	0
Elmwood Place	2,425	5	0	1	2	2	35	8	24	3	0
Elyria	54,931	183	1	20	65	97	2,339	615	1,616	108	16
Englewood	12,767	28	0	4	14	10	412	33	369	10	1
Euclid	47,387	174	1	19	105	49	1,516	550	797	169	9
Fairborn	32,463	64	1	29	20	14	1,110	250	808	52	2
Fairfield	42,315	165	3	12	55	95	1,466	244	1,158	64	4
Fairfield Township	17,374	25	0	4	7	14	649	78	557	14	3
Fairlawn	7,050	17	0	0	6	11	335	22	304	9	0
Fairport Harbor	3,219	10	0	3	0	7	170	44	119	7	1
Findlay	37,291	92	0	25	29	38	1,705	330	1,318	57	4
Forest Park	18,117	59	0	11	42	6	628	90	504	34	2
Fort Recovery	1,342	0	0	0	0	0	16	8	7	1	0
Franklin	12,996	32	0	4	8	20	644	106	511	27	3
Fredericktown	2,473	1	0	1	0	0	82	20	61	1	1
Fremont	16,682	48	1	3	18	26	1,063	144	892	27	5
Gahanna	33,828	30	0	5	13	12	940	155	747	38	9
Galion	10,843	12	0	4	5	3	497	102	383	12	1
Garfield Heights	27,746	121	0	8	46	67	1,081	333	668	80	4
Gates Mills	2,276	0	0	0	0	0	15	5	10	0	0
Geneva-on-the-Lake	1,491	3	0	2	0	1	16	5	9	2	1
Genoa	2,294	0	0	0	0	0	59	9	50	0	0
Georgetown	3,488	8	0	0	3	5	265	62	199	4	2
Germantown	5,072	6	0	2	1	3	89	29	60	0	0
German Township, Clark County	7,247	5	0	0	3	2	261	36	218	7	1
German Township, Montgomery County	3,277	2	0	0	0	2	47	20	22	5	1
Gibsonburg	2,449	2	0	0	0	2	94	13	81	0	0
Girard	10,097	63	0	3	8	52	519	152	314	53	5
Glendale	2,175	1	0	0	0	1	19	3	16	0	0
Goshen Township, Clermont County	16,462	8	0	7	1	0	297	79	212	6	1
Goshen Township, Mahoning County	3,450	4	0	0	0	4	111	33	73	5	0
Grandview Heights	6,251	3	0	0	2	1	190	44	141	5	1
Granville	5,399	2	0	0	0	2	72	13	57	2	1
Greenfield	5,120	11	0	4	5	2	321	52	261	8	2

[1] The FBI does not publish arson data unless it receives data from either the agency or the state for all 12 months of the calendar year.

Table 8. Offenses Known to Law Enforcement, by State and City, 2008—*Continued*

(Number.)

State/City	Population	Violent crime	Murder and non-negligent man-slaughter	Forcible rape	Robbery	Aggravated assault	Property crime	Burglary	Larceny-theft	Motor vehicle theft	Arson[1]
OHIO—*Continued*											
Greenhills	3,753	0	0	0	0	0	17	3	13	1	1
Greenville	12,772	38	0	6	12	20	562	89	438	35	6
Greenwich	1,510	0	0	0	0	0	7	3	4	0	0
Grove City	33,869	57	0	14	37	6	1,060	139	862	59	9
Groveport	5,352	7	0	2	1	4	189	35	142	12	2
Hamilton	62,498	414	4	73	159	178	4,105	1,007	2,832	266	38
Harrison	9,117	6	1	0	3	2	267	16	244	7	3
Hartville	2,584	1	0	0	1	0	49	11	37	1	0
Heath	8,926	18	0	5	7	6	447	53	387	7	4
Hebron	2,160	2	0	0	2	0	43	8	35	0	0
Highland Heights	8,636	2	0	0	1	1	80	21	55	4	0
Hilliard	27,936	26	0	6	14	6	893	159	698	36	2
Hillsboro	6,705	10	0	3	1	6	348	44	295	9	1
Holland	1,330	5	0	0	2	3	176	6	166	4	1
Howland Township	16,435	29	0	2	10	17	562	116	428	18	2
Hubbard Township	5,712	4	0	0	1	3	251	64	170	17	0
Huber Heights	37,284	85	0	16	39	30	1,539	216	1,238	85	26
Hudson	23,144	2	0	2	0	0	220	48	168	4	1
Huron	7,311	7	0	3	1	3	142	18	124	0	0
Independence	6,785	8	0	1	1	6	181	10	159	12	0
Indian Hill	5,895	5	0	2	3	0	42	8	34	0	0
Ironton	11,321	15	0	1	3	11	254	83	161	10	0
Jackson Township, Mahoning County	2,266	3	0	0	0	3	74	21	52	1	0
Jackson Township, Montgomery County	3,835	1	0	1	0	0	33	18	11	4	0
Jackson Township, Stark County	40,942	54	0	8	30	16	1,402	165	1,186	51	6
Jamestown	1,848	3	0	0	2	1	71	18	51	2	1
Jefferson	3,420	3	0	2	0	1	57	8	48	1	1
Jewett	772	0	0	0	0	0	12	7	5	0	0
Johnstown	4,062	0	0	0	0	0	7	1	6	0	0
Kent	28,265	67	0	7	20	40	639	165	436	38	39
Kenton	8,015	13	2	4	4	3	626	122	497	7	1
Kettering	53,714	62	0	20	32	10	1,525	309	1,129	87	9
Kirtland	7,428	4	0	0	0	4	50	8	39	3	0
Kirtland Hills	805	1	0	0	0	1	17	4	13	0	0
Lake Township	7,438	3	0	2	0	1	136	18	113	5	0
Lakewood	50,690	101	1	5	55	40	1,249	322	803	124	8
Lancaster	37,134	106	1	20	43	42	1,946	380	1,507	59	15
Lawrence Township	8,469	3	0	0	0	3	71	22	44	5	0
Lebanon	20,850	22	0	5	7	10	443	70	355	18	3
Lexington	4,121	3	0	0	1	2	102	18	82	2	0
Liberty Township	11,884	9	0	0	4	5	105	24	71	10	0
Lima	37,507	498	2	67	157	272	2,959	953	1,812	194	34
Lockland	3,394	21	0	2	14	5	196	49	115	32	0
Logan	7,474	12	0	3	6	3	468	75	377	16	1
London	9,645	7	0	3	2	2	279	39	229	11	3
Lorain	70,302	360	3	41	158	158	3,100	1,240	1,693	167	30
Lordstown	3,546	1	0	0	1	0	68	14	54	0	0
Loudonville	2,999	1	0	0	0	1	84	20	63	1	0
Louisville	9,501	5	0	0	2	3	161	23	133	5	1
Lynchburg	1,414	0	0	0	0	0	60	10	46	4	0
Lyndhurst	13,842	1	0	0	0	1	0	0	0	0	0
Madeira	9,090	4	0	0	2	2	45	8	36	1	0
Madison Township, Franklin County	18,111	6	0	0	4	2	185	59	116	10	0
Madison Township, Lake County	17,001	52	0	7	2	43	441	68	363	10	3
Manchester	2,094	2	0	0	0	2	27	8	18	1	2
Mansfield	49,428	183	3	30	83	67	2,639	799	1,774	66	10
Mariemont	3,116	0	0	0	0	0	66	5	60	1	0
Marietta	14,095	23	0	8	9	6	363	77	273	13	0
Marion	35,489	69	1	17	28	23	1,567	400	1,141	26	9
Martins Ferry	6,648	8	0	3	0	5	50	11	36	3	1
Marysville	17,804	8	0	3	3	2	457	67	386	4	5
Mason	30,582	17	5	2	5	5	494	76	407	11	2
Maumee	13,848	8	0	0	6	2	641	68	559	14	2
Mayfield Heights	17,715	17	1	3	5	8	321	16	285	20	2
Mayfield Village	3,115	0	0	0	0	0	79	21	56	2	0
McConnelsville	1,695	2	0	1	0	1	16	4	11	1	1
Medina Township	8,928	3	0	3	0	0	134	18	101	15	0
Mentor	51,917	43	0	11	11	21	1,175	135	969	71	8
Mentor-on-the-Lake	8,308	3	0	0	2	1	58	6	49	3	0
Miamisburg	19,874	31	0	4	10	17	739	158	547	34	2
Miami Township, Clermont County	39,711	23	0	5	9	9	895	136	740	19	7
Middlefield	2,406	5	1	1	0	3	72	5	66	1	0
Middletown	51,266	320	2	52	115	151	3,820	894	2,737	189	7
Milford	6,315	17	1	7	1	8	283	24	253	6	1

[1] The FBI does not publish arson data unless it receives data from either the agency or the state for all 12 months of the calendar year.

Table 8. Offenses Known to Law Enforcement, by State and City, 2008—*Continued*

(Number.)

State/City	Population	Violent crime	Murder and non-negligent man-slaughter	Forcible rape	Robbery	Aggravated assault	Property crime	Burglary	Larceny-theft	Motor vehicle theft	Arson[1]
OHIO—*Continued*											
Millersburg	3,614	5	0	1	0	4	74	12	62	0	1
Milton Township	2,848	3	1	0	1	1	61	22	34	5	0
Minerva	3,908	16	0	2	0	14	138	28	103	7	0
Mingo Junction	3,301	30	0	1	0	29	71	21	46	4	0
Monroe	15,025	40	0	2	11	27	558	77	466	15	2
Montgomery	10,221	2	0	0	2	0	211	20	183	8	0
Montpelier	4,016	8	0	2	1	5	190	49	136	5	2
Mount Gilead	3,538	3	0	2	0	1	113	18	93	2	1
Mount Orab	2,793	1	0	0	1	0	55	10	43	2	0
Mount Sterling	1,818	1	0	1	0	0	18	5	12	1	0
Napoleon	8,837	16	0	11	2	3	481	101	371	9	0
Navarre	1,421	0	0	0	0	0	25	9	15	1	1
Nelsonville	5,420	6	0	1	2	3	326	82	236	8	1
New Albany	7,034	0	0	0	0	0	101	23	75	3	0
Newark	47,283	140	4	40	53	43	2,269	536	1,650	83	38
New Boston	2,143	9	1	1	7	0	309	71	224	14	0
New Bremen	3,046	1	0	1	0	0	87	9	77	1	0
Newcomerstown	3,888	16	0	2	1	13	151	22	118	11	0
New Franklin	15,021	2	0	1	0	1	135	65	64	6	5
New Lebanon	4,116	3	0	0	1	2	86	25	58	3	1
New Lexington	4,525	5	0	0	3	2	157	25	121	11	0
New London	2,606	0	0	0	0	0	19	6	10	3	0
New Middletown	1,558	0	0	0	0	0	21	6	14	1	0
New Philadelphia	17,366	8	0	2	5	1	134	14	115	5	0
New Richmond	2,531	5	0	1	3	1	126	28	94	4	1
Newtown	4,112	2	0	0	0	2	66	6	60	0	0
New Vienna	1,392	0	0	0	0	0	19	4	14	1	0
New Washington	914	5	0	0	0	5	25	3	22	0	1
Niles	19,307	81	0	12	39	30	1,150	222	861	67	0
North Canton	16,886	7	0	6	1	0	272	60	201	11	1
North College Hill	9,355	34	0	5	23	6	424	125	279	20	3
Northfield	3,659	8	0	3	1	4	44	13	29	2	0
North Olmsted	31,347	35	0	5	16	14	625	86	502	37	1
North Ridgeville	28,301	16	0	2	4	10	271	76	179	16	0
Northwood	5,525	11	0	3	3	5	182	11	170	1	0
Norton	11,477	3	0	0	0	3	41	8	29	4	1
Oakwood, Montgomery County	8,437	11	0	1	1	9	119	17	98	4	0
Oberlin	8,350	20	0	3	3	14	221	46	168	7	0
Olmsted Falls	8,258	2	0	1	0	1	117	17	91	9	0
Ontario	5,234	9	0	2	5	2	580	32	545	3	1
Orange Village	3,280	4	0	1	0	3	44	8	34	2	0
Oregon	18,948	22	0	2	4	16	901	134	744	23	7
Orrville	8,378	7	1	2	4	0	187	64	121	2	3
Orwell	1,471	4	0	0	0	4	28	7	21	0	0
Oxford	22,243	96	0	16	6	74	676	134	517	25	10
Parma Heights	19,778	30	1	8	2	19	385	90	274	21	4
Pataskala	12,964	4	0	2	0	2	231	64	158	9	1
Paulding	3,342	5	0	3	1	1	17	3	14	0	0
Peebles	1,836	2	0	2	0	0	13	8	5	0	1
Peninsula	695	0	0	0	0	0	15	3	12	0	0
Pepper Pike	5,697	1	0	0	0	1	62	8	49	5	0
Perrysburg	17,043	18	0	5	4	9	493	69	409	15	0
Perry Township, Franklin County	3,615	0	0	0	0	0	50	8	42	0	1
Perry Township, Montgomery County	3,816	1	0	0	0	1	37	19	15	3	0
Perry Township, Stark County	28,063	67	3	3	20	41	767	186	528	53	5
Pickerington	18,435	9	0	2	1	6	328	50	267	11	4
Pierce Township	11,075	11	0	2	5	4	361	55	300	6	2
Piqua	20,609	34	0	14	9	11	1,142	182	932	28	5
Plain City	3,633	4	0	2	0	2	26	8	17	1	0
Poland Township	11,123	0	0	0	0	0	30	9	19	2	0
Poland Village	2,669	1	0	0	0	1	10	2	8	0	0
Port Clinton	6,175	16	0	4	3	9	216	31	182	3	0
Portsmouth	20,043	114	2	8	60	44	2,045	562	1,421	62	3
Powell	13,205	0	0	0	0	0	113	23	89	1	1
Powhatan Point	1,659	0	0	0	0	0	25	9	16	0	0
Ravenna	11,375	26	0	4	10	12	674	81	564	29	0
Reading	10,288	30	1	16	10	3	422	70	324	28	4
Reminderville	2,604	3	0	0	0	3	14	5	8	1	0
Reynoldsburg	33,727	94	1	13	58	22	1,303	279	945	79	9
Richmond Heights	10,148	4	0	1	1	2	335	23	297	15	0
Rittman	6,267	3	0	0	3	0	130	38	86	6	1
Riverside	25,357	76	0	7	17	52	778	166	548	64	6
Roaming Shores Village	1,196	0	0	0	0	0	12	4	7	1	0
Roseville	1,885	0	0	0	0	0	13	6	6	1	0

[1] The FBI does not publish arson data unless it receives data from either the agency or the state for all 12 months of the calendar year.

Table 8. Offenses Known to Law Enforcement, by State and City, 2008—*Continued*

(Number.)

State/City	Population	Violent crime	Murder and non-negligent man-slaughter	Forcible rape	Robbery	Aggravated assault	Property crime	Burglary	Larceny-theft	Motor vehicle theft	Arson[1]
OHIO—*Continued*											
Rossford	6,401	2	0	0	1	1	218	45	168	5	0
Russell Township	5,597	3	0	0	0	3	10	4	4	2	1
Salem	11,763	0	0	0	0	0	111	2	106	3	0
Sandusky	25,625	193	1	8	51	133	1,480	393	1,049	38	3
Sardinia	845	1	0	1	0	0	35	5	29	1	0
Sebring	4,534	1	0	0	0	1	40	13	25	2	0
Shelby	9,330	4	0	1	2	1	462	143	310	9	0
Smith Township	4,835	2	0	2	0	0	54	10	42	2	0
Smithville	1,296	1	0	0	1	0	38	12	26	0	1
Solon	22,057	18	0	4	9	5	206	37	167	2	1
South Euclid	21,196	40	3	11	23	3	502	136	314	52	1
South Russell	3,929	1	0	0	0	1	8	3	5	0	0
South Solon	385	0	0	0	0	0	0	0	0	0	0
Spencerville	2,158	0	0	0	0	0	36	6	30	0	4
Springdale	10,144	44	1	8	28	7	728	39	667	22	1
Springfield	61,999	319	9	34	138	138	4,547	816	3,385	346	9
Springfield Township, Hamilton County	40,018	85	1	8	55	21	768	210	519	39	5
Springfield Township, Mahoning County	6,009	5	0	2	1	2	133	49	83	1	2
St. Clair Township	7,668	1	0	0	1	0	73	0	73	0	0
Steubenville	18,745	102	3	9	35	55	1,058	179	843	36	0
Stow	34,260	24	0	14	8	2	765	111	646	8	6
Strasburg	2,721	3	0	1	2	0	81	20	58	3	0
Struthers	10,755	15	0	0	5	10	362	76	268	18	2
Sugarcreek Township	6,991	2	0	0	2	0	145	11	132	2	0
Sylvania Township	26,135	25	0	0	15	10	666	133	510	23	3
Tallmadge	17,405	12	0	0	7	5	424	106	302	16	9
Tipp City	9,267	8	0	3	3	2	160	19	137	4	2
Toledo	317,401	3,621	18	132	1,383	2,088	18,670	6,522	10,671	1,477	447
Twinsburg	17,520	7	0	0	2	5	140	18	112	10	2
Union	6,388	3	0	0	0	3	64	7	54	3	1
Uniontown	2,835	0	0	0	0	0	124	40	83	1	1
University Heights	12,592	21	0	4	11	6	233	40	185	8	2
Urbana	11,383	30	0	9	6	15	407	69	325	13	2
Vandalia	14,106	21	0	6	6	9	368	62	287	19	4
Van Wert	10,195	23	1	8	4	10	559	100	452	7	1
Vermilion	10,756	10	0	0	0	10	263	53	196	14	4
Wadsworth	20,657	8	0	5	1	2	431	53	352	26	6
Walbridge	3,095	2	1	1	0	0	111	26	80	5	0
Walton Hills	2,284	0	0	0	0	0	36	6	24	6	0
Wapakoneta	9,418	5	0	2	1	2	220	28	189	3	3
Warren	43,809	392	3	39	167	183	2,256	889	1,163	204	51
Warrensville Heights	13,594	57	0	7	41	9	511	174	241	96	8
Warren Township	6,045	8	0	0	1	7	80	26	46	8	0
Washington Court House	13,666	32	0	8	10	14	474	88	372	14	4
Waterville Township	5,694	0	0	0	0	0	27	7	20	0	0
Wauseon	7,299	8	0	3	1	4	234	24	208	2	1
Waynesburg	967	1	0	1	0	0	25	8	14	3	0
Wells Township	2,831	0	0	0	0	0	58	18	37	3	0
West Alexandria	1,296	1	0	0	1	0	38	8	29	1	0
West Carrollton	12,762	33	0	11	9	13	454	121	271	62	3
West Chester Township	55,672	87	1	23	34	29	1,545	281	1,218	46	15
Westerville	35,773	26	0	7	13	6	1,017	158	844	15	10
West Union	3,100	6	0	2	0	4	149	43	104	2	1
Whitehall	17,995	190	2	13	124	51	1,682	320	1,240	122	2
Willard	6,690	4	0	1	1	2	255	22	225	8	0
Williamsburg	2,365	5	0	2	1	2	79	17	58	4	0
Willoughby	22,384	16	0	3	10	3	374	72	267	35	3
Willoughby Hills	8,545	15	0	4	7	4	174	30	122	22	1
Willowick	13,692	11	0	0	2	9	182	47	118	17	0
Wilmington	12,571	32	0	7	10	15	694	70	621	3	0
Wintersville	3,786	2	0	1	0	1	80	13	66	1	1
Woodlawn	2,586	14	0	0	6	8	201	42	148	11	1
Wooster	26,105	59	1	15	19	24	1,112	263	831	18	7
Wyoming	8,374	8	0	0	6	2	129	28	94	7	0
Xenia	27,740	37	1	7	22	7	1,161	182	938	41	3
Yellow Springs	3,589	5	0	0	0	5	109	13	95	1	0
Youngstown	72,887	733	29	34	252	418	4,030	1,684	1,853	493	262
Zanesville	25,060	100	3	18	62	17	1,679	312	1,308	59	13
OKLAHOMA											
Achille	531	1	0	0	0	1	24	8	14	2	2
Ada	16,599	143	1	15	9	118	882	153	685	44	6
Altus	19,097	62	0	7	23	32	686	247	427	12	5
Alva	4,677	13	1	0	1	11	206	34	152	20	1

[1] The FBI does not publish arson data unless it receives data from either the agency or the state for all 12 months of the calendar year.

Table 8. Offenses Known to Law Enforcement, by State and City, 2008—*Continued*

(Number.)

State/City	Population	Violent crime	Murder and non-negligent man-slaughter	Forcible rape	Robbery	Aggravated assault	Property crime	Burglary	Larceny-theft	Motor vehicle theft	Arson[1]
OKLAHOMA—*Continued*											
Anadarko	6,301	40	0	1	4	35	343	108	217	18	21
Antlers	2,477	21	0	2	1	18	70	24	42	4	2
Apache	1,538	4	0	1	0	3	26	4	18	4	1
Ardmore	24,738	267	1	14	28	224	1,404	335	1,012	57	2
Arkoma	2,181	13	0	2	2	9	19	6	11	2	0
Atoka	3,081	5	0	0	1	4	132	34	94	4	3
Beaver	1,389	2	0	1	0	1	11	4	6	1	0
Beggs	1,364	5	0	1	1	3	40	20	19	1	1
Bethany	19,522	91	0	9	36	46	713	218	427	68	1
Bixby	21,114	22	0	5	3	14	285	71	198	16	1
Blackwell	7,117	25	0	2	0	23	143	39	98	6	1
Blanchard	6,616	5	0	1	0	4	108	30	59	19	1
Boise City	1,211	5	0	0	0	5	8	3	5	0	0
Boley	1,087	0	0	0	0	0	3	3	0	0	0
Bristow	4,388	19	0	1	2	16	150	35	99	16	1
Broken Arrow	92,075	190	4	16	36	134	2,162	476	1,515	171	31
Broken Bow	4,137	34	1	5	3	25	223	82	116	25	7
Caddo	983	5	0	0	0	5	2	0	2	0	0
Calera	1,820	13	0	3	0	10	32	11	20	1	0
Carnegie	1,544	9	0	1	0	8	17	9	7	1	1
Catoosa	6,724	56	2	3	6	45	152	52	79	21	0
Chandler	2,835	8	0	1	2	5	100	23	74	3	0
Checotah	3,474	3	0	0	0	3	99	3	87	9	2
Chelsea	2,237	6	0	1	0	5	22	10	10	2	1
Cherokee	1,415	1	0	1	0	0	27	10	14	3	0
Chickasha	17,218	134	1	5	11	117	778	218	494	66	14
Choctaw	11,337	3	0	0	0	3	179	54	115	10	0
Chouteau	2,008	7	0	2	0	5	63	14	44	5	0
Claremore	17,491	47	1	11	7	28	544	124	390	30	0
Clayton	725	3	0	0	0	3	9	4	5	0	0
Cleveland	3,151	6	0	1	1	4	70	15	50	5	0
Clinton	8,638	38	0	2	6	30	209	31	171	7	1
Coalgate	1,858	0	0	0	0	0	7	0	7	0	0
Colbert	1,117	1	1	0	0	0	29	13	13	3	0
Collinsville	4,821	5	0	2	0	3	77	35	39	3	2
Comanche	1,517	2	0	0	1	1	50	20	29	1	1
Coweta	9,043	23	0	1	3	19	199	39	144	16	1
Crescent	1,372	3	0	0	0	3	23	8	15	0	0
Cushing	9,631	16	0	2	1	13	223	56	147	20	0
Davenport	877	2	0	0	0	2	8	3	5	0	0
Davis	2,616	10	0	3	0	7	79	15	58	6	0
Del City	22,052	159	2	16	47	94	1,346	441	824	81	18
Dewey	3,321	15	0	6	1	8	118	19	97	2	2
Drumright	2,878	4	0	1	0	3	54	14	37	3	0
Duncan	22,535	44	1	3	6	34	993	189	768	36	2
Durant	16,432	58	0	11	7	40	836	269	508	59	3
Edmond	79,529	80	0	15	22	43	1,781	345	1,369	67	10
Elk City	11,180	18	2	2	0	14	230	39	181	10	0
El Reno	16,295	77	0	8	11	58	567	213	330	24	5
Enid	47,017	212	0	26	35	151	2,289	610	1,575	104	3
Eufaula	2,771	7	0	0	0	7	101	28	67	6	0
Fairfax	1,464	3	0	0	0	3	16	6	8	2	0
Fairview	2,534	12	0	1	1	10	110	42	67	1	0
Fort Gibson	4,367	9	0	3	1	5	66	16	46	4	0
Frederick	3,929	23	0	1	0	22	76	32	40	4	0
Geary	1,216	4	0	0	1	3	49	19	23	7	0
Glenpool	9,697	15	0	3	3	9	182	35	133	14	3
Goodwell	1,134	1	0	1	0	0	8	4	4	0	0
Grandfield	956	0	0	0	0	0	15	5	9	1	0
Grove	6,374	8	0	0	0	8	132	26	104	2	0
Guthrie	11,195	18	0	1	1	16	243	51	182	10	1
Guymon	10,580	28	1	3	3	21	282	79	197	6	2
Harrah	5,200	14	0	0	1	13	96	31	63	2	0
Hartshorne	2,055	5	0	1	0	4	59	17	32	10	3
Haskell	1,781	0	0	0	0	0	4	2	2	0	0
Healdton	2,761	5	1	0	0	4	41	17	19	5	1
Henryetta	6,043	21	0	2	1	18	129	46	63	20	3
Hinton	2,134	3	0	1	1	1	21	12	6	3	0
Hobart	3,613	11	0	2	0	9	63	19	43	1	1
Holdenville	5,453	25	2	0	0	23	118	30	80	8	4
Hollis	1,922	4	0	0	2	2	62	28	32	2	1
Hominy	3,651	4	0	0	0	4	19	4	13	2	1
Hooker	1,698	1	0	0	0	1	17	8	8	1	0

[1] The FBI does not publish arson data unless it receives data from either the agency or the state for all 12 months of the calendar year.

Table 8. Offenses Known to Law Enforcement, by State and City, 2008—*Continued*

(Number.)

State/City	Population	Violent crime	Murder and non-negligent man-slaughter	Forcible rape	Robbery	Aggravated assault	Property crime	Burglary	Larceny-theft	Motor vehicle theft	Arson[1]
OKLAHOMA—*Continued*											
Hugo	5,431	19	1	1	2	15	165	40	120	5	0
Hulbert	535	1	0	0	0	1	8	2	5	1	0
Hydro	1,008	13	0	0	0	13	13	4	8	1	0
Idabel	6,841	41	3	2	7	29	226	61	149	16	3
Jay	3,084	8	0	1	0	7	46	16	29	1	0
Jenks	15,703	13	1	2	4	6	279	56	207	16	2
Jones	2,712	2	0	0	0	2	28	5	21	2	0
Kiefer	1,545	5	0	0	0	5	10	3	5	2	1
Kingfisher	4,516	5	0	2	0	3	86	24	56	6	0
Kingston	1,591	3	0	1	0	2	19	4	11	4	0
Kiowa	700	3	0	0	0	3	21	4	15	2	0
Konawa	1,387	0	0	0	0	0	5	1	4	0	0
Krebs	2,118	2	0	0	0	2	37	16	18	3	2
Lawton	91,459	1,001	6	78	201	716	4,248	1,445	2,574	229	45
Lexington	2,102	2	0	2	0	0	47	9	37	1	0
Lindsay	2,899	2	0	0	0	2	67	21	46	0	0
Locust Grove	1,584	5	0	2	1	2	61	22	36	3	2
Lone Grove	5,281	10	0	1	1	8	115	24	87	4	1
Luther	1,116	6	0	2	0	4	12	3	9	0	0
Madill	3,790	7	1	0	0	6	130	35	91	4	4
Mangum	2,689	10	0	1	1	8	103	21	82	0	7
Mannford	2,845	3	0	2	0	1	21	8	10	3	0
Marietta	2,540	8	0	1	0	7	65	14	48	3	0
Marlow	4,580	12	0	4	1	7	136	30	105	1	1
Maysville	1,293	1	0	0	0	1	18	3	14	1	0
McAlester	18,291	50	1	4	9	36	890	171	685	34	4
McLoud	4,178	7	0	0	0	7	51	17	32	2	2
Meeker	981	4	0	0	2	2	34	10	24	0	0
Miami	13,321	59	0	13	5	41	666	121	516	29	12
Midwest City	56,168	252	3	26	64	159	2,462	598	1,724	140	9
Minco	1,795	0	0	0	0	0	3	3	0	0	0
Moore	52,494	93	1	16	23	53	2,077	485	1,431	161	16
Mooreland	1,242	0	0	0	0	0	31	10	21	0	0
Morris	1,310	3	0	0	1	2	12	5	6	1	0
Mountain View	785	1	0	0	0	1	4	2	2	0	0
Muldrow	3,176	9	0	1	0	8	58	21	36	1	0
Muskogee	40,115	391	0	26	60	305	1,752	631	1,037	84	23
Mustang	17,763	55	0	3	3	49	465	84	359	22	1
Newcastle	7,228	13	0	0	3	10	161	24	124	13	1
Newkirk	2,117	8	0	0	0	8	61	14	47	0	2
Nichols Hills	4,015	3	1	0	0	2	97	11	79	7	0
Nicoma Park	2,383	8	0	1	0	7	30	7	18	5	0
Noble	5,764	0	0	0	0	0	69	17	50	2	1
Norman	108,016	167	2	44	55	66	3,362	727	2,435	200	9
Nowata	3,984	18	0	3	1	14	124	28	84	12	2
Oilton	1,119	4	0	0	0	4	20	9	9	2	0
Okemah	2,921	7	0	4	1	2	91	20	69	2	3
Oklahoma City	552,452	5,400	57	318	1,524	3,501	32,563	9,225	19,439	3,899	125
Okmulgee	12,585	69	4	4	10	51	420	122	272	26	3
Oologah	1,159	1	0	0	0	1	40	16	21	3	0
Owasso	27,460	87	0	13	8	66	711	111	551	49	1
Pauls Valley	6,097	34	0	3	2	29	409	82	310	17	3
Pawhuska	3,452	70	0	1	2	67	91	41	43	7	0
Pawnee	2,169	5	0	0	3	2	26	12	11	3	0
Perkins	2,615	6	0	4	0	2	98	15	77	6	1
Perry	5,018	19	0	1	0	18	106	24	75	7	0
Piedmont	5,505	7	0	1	0	6	52	23	29	0	0
Pocola	4,491	10	0	2	1	7	68	26	26	16	1
Ponca City	24,435	111	0	5	12	94	1,278	236	963	79	13
Porum	735	1	0	0	0	1	8	3	4	1	0
Poteau	8,277	38	1	10	0	27	169	27	110	32	1
Prague	2,130	14	1	2	0	11	58	19	34	5	0
Pryor	9,291	89	0	6	7	76	313	76	212	25	1
Purcell	6,143	7	0	0	2	5	237	53	176	8	0
Ringling	1,043	2	0	0	0	2	16	6	8	2	0
Roland	3,299	7	0	3	0	4	55	11	42	2	0
Rush Springs	1,349	1	0	0	0	1	15	5	8	2	0
Sallisaw	8,831	26	0	0	5	21	286	72	198	16	1
Sand Springs	18,572	35	1	6	8	20	643	136	462	45	1
Sapulpa	20,991	45	0	8	5	32	715	144	495	76	1
Sayre	3,113	17	3	1	0	13	58	16	36	6	3
Seminole	6,801	28	0	1	2	25	308	69	225	14	3
Shawnee	30,398	245	2	21	27	195	1,827	403	1,280	144	7
Skiatook	6,707	16	0	4	0	12	223	68	147	8	2

[1] The FBI does not publish arson data unless it receives data from either the agency or the state for all 12 months of the calendar year.

Table 8. Offenses Known to Law Enforcement, by State and City, 2008—*Continued*

(Number.)

State/City	Population	Violent crime	Murder and non-negligent man-slaughter	Forcible rape	Robbery	Aggravated assault	Property crime	Burglary	Larceny-theft	Motor vehicle theft	Arson[1]
OKLAHOMA—*Continued*											
Snyder	1,375	1	0	0	0	1	10	2	6	2	0
Spencer	4,027	17	0	0	2	15	117	52	53	12	3
Spiro	2,328	7	0	1	0	6	48	14	32	2	1
Stigler	2,836	11	0	2	1	8	92	25	62	5	0
Stillwater	48,045	131	0	22	17	92	1,307	285	972	50	14
Stilwell	3,472	9	0	4	1	4	126	14	106	6	0
Stratford	1,484	1	0	0	0	1	20	6	13	1	1
Stringtown	419	0	0	0	0	0	14	10	4	0	1
Stroud	2,739	4	0	0	0	4	53	11	40	2	2
Sulphur	4,810	8	0	1	0	7	63	20	40	3	3
Tahlequah	16,663	45	0	7	3	35	578	126	425	27	4
Talihina	1,237	17	0	0	2	15	64	18	39	7	1
Tecumseh	6,746	22	0	5	2	15	222	64	140	18	3
Texhoma	926	0	0	0	0	0	8	2	6	0	0
The Village	9,759	30	0	1	5	24	309	75	209	25	4
Tishomingo	3,216	9	0	0	0	9	75	31	41	3	2
Tonkawa	3,014	4	0	2	0	2	87	25	49	13	0
Tulsa	382,954	4,922	50	252	1,096	3,524	22,769	6,725	13,746	2,298	250
Tushka	369	0	0	0	0	0	2	1	1	0	0
Tuttle	6,067	5	0	2	0	3	86	33	45	8	1
Valliant	741	1	0	0	0	1	28	7	20	1	0
Vian	1,456	10	0	2	0	8	16	2	13	1	0
Vinita	6,028	26	0	1	8	17	174	38	128	8	4
Wagoner	8,016	81	0	3	5	73	314	80	226	8	1
Walters	2,461	3	0	0	0	3	38	20	16	2	0
Warner	1,447	5	0	0	0	5	11	4	3	4	0
Warr Acres	9,422	63	0	4	24	35	560	154	336	70	4
Washington	542	0	0	0	0	0	2	2	0	0	0
Watonga	5,635	3	0	1	0	2	95	39	53	3	6
Waukomis	1,200	3	0	0	0	3	20	5	15	0	0
Waynoka	896	3	0	2	0	1	28	9	19	0	0
Weatherford	10,129	89	0	0	5	84	273	55	203	15	5
Weleetka	922	7	1	0	1	5	32	15	13	4	2
Westville	1,651	13	0	0	0	13	66	11	51	4	1
Wetumka	1,399	2	0	0	0	2	25	16	8	1	3
Wewoka	3,298	14	0	0	3	11	122	35	79	8	3
Wilburton	2,864	17	0	1	1	15	58	10	43	5	1
Woodward	12,257	43	0	10	0	33	627	168	432	27	2
Wright City	789	4	0	0	0	4	23	5	18	0	0
Yale	1,480	1	0	0	0	1	10	3	4	3	1
Yukon	22,686	20	0	4	5	11	581	108	452	21	7
OREGON											
Albany	48,075	65	0	11	29	25	1,803	157	1,532	114	9
Amity	1,482	0	0	0	0	0	28	7	20	1	0
Ashland	21,535	29	0	11	6	12	713	98	599	16	6
Astoria	9,891	27	0	2	8	17	437	77	331	29	6
Aumsville	3,440	7	0	0	0	7	90	30	56	4	1
Aurora	1,042	2	0	0	0	2	16	5	11	0	0
Baker City	9,355	12	0	0	1	11	105	31	69	5	0
Bandon	2,837	2	0	1	0	1	74	11	63	0	0
Banks	1,630	2	0	0	1	1	38	5	30	3	0
Beaverton	92,198	200	0	24	41	135	2,072	296	1,566	210	21
Bend	77,898	139	0	25	35	79	2,513	471	1,914	128	22
Black Butte	0	0	0	0	0	0	7	3	4	0	0
Boardman	2,947	11	0	0	1	10	64	11	49	4	0
Burns	2,639	2	0	0	0	2	92	22	66	4	0
Canby	15,985	15	0	1	3	11	404	50	342	12	3
Cannon Beach	1,742	1	0	0	1	0	27	8	19	0	0
Carlton	1,591	0	0	0	0	0	33	13	19	1	0
Central Point	16,966	7	0	1	2	4	343	35	297	11	3
Clatskanie	1,635	4	0	1	0	3	26	8	16	2	0
Coburg	1,028	1	0	0	1	0	23	7	15	1	1
Condon	643	0	0	0	0	0	1	0	1	0	0
Coos Bay	15,818	34	0	8	9	17	708	130	525	53	6
Coquille	4,159	1	0	1	0	0	32	13	18	1	2
Cornelius	11,589	23	0	1	8	14	269	52	191	26	4
Corvallis	51,343	60	0	11	15	34	1,341	200	1,073	68	11
Cottage Grove	9,118	11	0	1	5	5	476	77	360	39	13
Creswell	5,113	28	0	4	1	23	137	31	83	23	2
Dallas	15,892	18	0	3	1	14	308	37	253	18	25
Eagle Point	8,714	8	0	2	1	5	153	28	122	3	1
Elgin	1,651	0	0	0	0	0	44	5	38	1	0
Enterprise	1,698	1	0	0	0	1	38	7	31	0	0

[1] The FBI does not publish arson data unless it receives data from either the agency or the state for all 12 months of the calendar year.

Table 8. Offenses Known to Law Enforcement, by State and City, 2008—*Continued*

(Number.)

State/City	Population	Violent crime	Murder and non-negligent man-slaughter	Forcible rape	Robbery	Aggravated assault	Property crime	Burglary	Larceny-theft	Motor vehicle theft	Arson[1]
OREGON—*Continued*											
Estacada	2,446	4	0	0	3	1	74	21	48	5	0
Eugene	150,297	496	2	60	223	211	9,821	1,704	6,814	1,303	76
Florence	8,469	11	0	3	7	1	295	41	242	12	2
Forest Grove	20,743	22	0	2	5	15	665	79	552	34	0
Gaston	801	1	0	0	0	1	12	5	7	0	0
Gearhart	1,134	0	0	0	0	0	14	4	10	0	0
Gervais	2,470	10	0	0	2	8	53	13	33	7	0
Gladstone	12,080	27	0	7	5	15	366	51	294	21	2
Gold Beach	1,841	2	0	0	0	2	38	8	29	1	0
Grants Pass	33,673	58	0	8	28	22	1,837	256	1,460	121	7
Gresham	100,935	495	6	72	156	261	3,889	703	2,502	684	47
Hermiston	15,186	49	0	2	11	36	711	123	540	48	3
Hillsboro	94,373	162	0	36	62	64	2,536	293	2,079	164	16
Hines	1,392	1	0	0	0	1	12	2	10	0	0
Hood River	6,822	9	0	1	2	6	219	34	172	13	2
Hubbard	2,789	2	0	0	1	1	32	3	25	4	0
Independence	9,579	13	0	2	1	10	210	29	174	7	1
Jacksonville	2,178	0	0	0	0	0	30	4	26	0	0
John Day	1,486	2	1	1	0	0	23	4	17	2	0
Junction City	5,434	0	0	0	0	0	116	17	93	6	1
Keizer	35,698	64	0	5	10	49	942	136	724	82	9
King City	2,418	2	0	0	2	0	62	8	49	5	1
Klamath Falls	19,676	82	0	17	26	39	579	121	422	36	8
La Grande	12,524	17	1	2	2	12	406	52	329	25	7
Lake Oswego	36,864	26	1	4	3	18	520	98	406	16	10
Lakeview	2,330	22	0	0	0	22	71	27	43	1	0
Lebanon	15,068	24	0	2	8	14	807	160	603	44	6
Lincoln City	8,018	39	0	5	7	27	426	64	352	10	5
Madras	5,433	16	2	1	2	11	341	106	216	19	7
Malin	630	1	0	0	0	1	1	1	0	0	0
Manzanita	630	0	0	0	0	0	13	5	8	0	0
McMinnville	31,470	74	0	15	10	49	879	104	731	44	15
Medford	73,019	282	0	44	41	197	2,882	300	2,453	129	36
Milton-Freewater	6,318	11	0	0	1	10	179	48	119	12	3
Milwaukie	20,684	26	1	7	5	13	621	110	442	69	1
Molalla	7,304	9	0	2	1	6	261	31	208	22	2
Monmouth	9,709	19	0	3	2	14	223	57	156	10	2
Mount Angel	3,468	9	0	0	1	8	69	20	44	5	2
Myrtle Creek	3,528	1	0	0	0	1	67	2	64	1	1
Newberg-Dundee	25,878	22	1	4	5	12	523	39	447	37	15
Newport	9,896	38	0	8	6	24	526	87	412	27	2
North Bend	9,690	12	0	0	6	6	363	72	279	12	4
North Plains	1,838	0	0	0	0	0	17	2	12	3	0
Oakridge	3,165	1	1	0	0	0	71	22	48	1	1
Ontario	11,092	132	0	4	4	124	759	130	605	24	10
Oregon City	31,683	61	0	11	22	28	900	111	734	55	10
Pendleton	16,490	96	1	18	21	56	778	127	616	35	0
Philomath	4,504	15	0	2	1	12	89	19	60	10	1
Phoenix	4,319	5	0	1	1	3	130	16	109	5	0
Pilot Rock	1,491	1	0	0	0	1	16	6	7	3	0
Portland	553,023	3,445	26	250	1,132	2,037	29,243	4,307	21,597	3,339	303
Prineville	10,307	13	0	0	0	13	344	41	293	10	6
Redmond	25,092	58	0	9	10	39	1,221	196	961	64	14
Reedsport	4,274	3	0	1	0	2	104	11	87	6	0
Rockaway Beach	1,394	0	0	0	0	0	59	39	17	3	0
Rogue River	1,946	3	0	0	2	1	69	9	56	4	0
Roseburg	21,009	35	0	10	13	12	825	74	720	31	10
Salem	153,831	572	9	58	136	369	7,173	1,094	5,428	651	40
Sandy	9,127	13	0	6	2	5	259	41	196	22	0
Scappoose	6,377	4	0	0	3	1	150	16	126	8	0
Seaside	6,262	19	0	3	6	10	495	81	398	16	7
Shady Cove	2,296	2	0	0	1	1	45	9	34	2	0
Sherwood	18,023	5	0	2	2	1	181	29	145	7	5
Silverton	9,682	6	1	0	1	4	171	33	131	7	1
Springfield	57,081	245	1	14	41	189	3,858	506	2,843	509	39
Stayton	7,377	28	0	4	1	23	374	78	282	14	13
St. Helens	12,655	14	0	3	4	7	336	53	255	28	7
Sunriver	0	5	0	1	0	4	79	10	67	2	0
Sutherlin	7,266	8	0	4	0	4	189	35	145	9	1
Sweet Home	8,869	7	0	0	2	5	353	89	257	7	0
Talent	6,222	3	0	2	1	0	119	20	96	3	0
The Dalles	11,913	25	1	7	4	13	542	80	438	24	3
Tigard	50,536	91	0	6	51	34	1,651	227	1,341	83	9
Tillamook	4,502	4	0	0	1	3	234	25	198	11	1

[1] The FBI does not publish arson data unless it receives data from either the agency or the state for all 12 months of the calendar year.

Table 8. Offenses Known to Law Enforcement, by State and City, 2008—*Continued*

(Number.)

State/City	Population	Violent crime	Murder and non-negligent man-slaughter	Forcible rape	Robbery	Aggravated assault	Property crime	Burglary	Larceny-theft	Motor vehicle theft	Arson[1]
OREGON—*Continued*											
Toledo	3,318	5	0	0	2	3	145	28	107	10	0
Troutdale	15,571	25	1	3	6	15	576	96	426	54	12
Tualatin	26,758	48	0	9	8	31	751	100	613	38	1
Turner	1,741	7	0	0	2	5	50	6	39	5	1
Umatilla	6,504	5	0	1	0	4	125	14	102	9	2
Veneta	4,326	40	0	3	3	34	222	76	120	26	3
Vernonia	2,281	1	0	0	0	1	37	12	23	2	4
Warrenton	4,503	1	1	0	0	0	171	27	139	5	1
West Linn	25,299	3	1	2	0	0	277	30	239	8	2
Weston	698	0	0	0	0	0	15	5	10	0	0
Wilsonville	19,462	21	0	8	6	7	541	49	461	31	3
Winston	4,776	9	0	3	3	3	145	29	105	11	2
Woodburn	22,365	78	6	7	20	45	795	131	589	75	9
Yamhill	868	0	0	0	0	0	16	3	13	0	0
PENNSYLVANIA											
Abington Township	53,937	67	0	0	34	33	1,582	121	1,412	49	3
Adamstown	1,473	1	0	0	1	0	42	5	34	3	0
Adams Township, Butler County	9,296	7	0	1	0	6	76	9	64	3	0
Adams Township, Cambria County	6,065	0	0	0	0	0	46	4	41	1	0
Akron	4,020	2	0	2	0	0	39	4	35	0	2
Alburtis	2,448	6	0	0	1	5	28	8	19	1	0
Aldan	4,245	8	0	0	2	6	105	10	88	7	0
Aliquippa	10,659	49	0	0	14	35	235	48	155	32	0
Allegheny Township, Blair County	6,903	27	0	1	2	24	155	27	124	4	1
Allegheny Township, Westmoreland County	8,182	14	1	0	1	12	111	16	91	4	0
Allentown	107,335	805	16	33	497	259	5,653	1,423	3,738	492	27
Altoona	46,236	183	2	13	67	101	1,218	369	793	56	13
Ambler	6,192	13	0	0	6	7	123	15	101	7	2
Ambridge	7,006	67	0	2	24	41	284	56	210	18	8
Amity Township	11,874	12	0	4	2	6	158	31	117	10	2
Annville Township	4,745	0	0	0	0	0	71	7	64	0	1
Archbald	6,488	4	1	0	0	3	4	2	2	0	1
Arnold	5,210	26	0	3	18	5	94	40	37	17	1
Ashland	3,103	1	0	0	1	0	94	14	76	4	0
Ashley	2,672	1	0	0	0	1	21	0	14	7	0
Ashville	260	0	0	0	0	0	0	0	0	0	0
Aspinwall	2,699	1	0	0	1	0	39	7	30	2	0
Aston Township	16,864	21	0	1	5	15	286	37	232	17	2
Atglen	1,370	6	0	4	0	2	8	1	7	0	0
Athens	3,217	8	0	3	0	5	103	5	97	1	1
Athens Township	5,018	10	0	3	1	6	155	9	144	2	0
Auburn	800	5	0	0	0	5	7	1	5	1	0
Avalon	4,804	8	0	0	4	4	62	14	43	5	0
Avoca	2,666	4	0	1	0	3	39	18	21	0	0
Avondale	1,087	0	0	0	0	0	1	0	1	0	0
Avonmore Boro	761	0	0	0	0	0	0	0	0	0	0
Baldwin Borough	18,430	16	0	1	5	10	138	20	104	14	0
Baldwin Township	2,034	6	0	0	0	6	27	4	21	2	0
Bally	1,100	0	0	0	0	0	0	0	0	0	0
Bangor	5,257	4	0	0	0	4	118	9	99	10	0
Barrett Township	4,293	19	0	2	0	17	51	16	34	1	0
Beaver	4,364	4	0	1	1	2	123	15	104	4	0
Beaver Falls	9,024	95	4	3	26	62	443	57	359	27	1
Beaver Meadows	952	1	0	0	0	1	8	3	5	0	0
Bedford	2,996	4	0	1	0	3	30	4	25	1	0
Bedminster Township	6,228	8	0	1	0	7	57	3	54	0	0
Bell Acres	1,372	1	0	0	0	1	3	0	1	2	0
Bellefonte	6,166	2	0	0	0	2	69	20	47	2	0
Bellevue	7,968	30	0	3	12	15	190	33	140	17	2
Bellwood	1,872	2	0	0	1	1	20	3	17	0	1
Ben Avon	1,744	0	0	0	0	0	5	1	3	1	0
Ben Avon Heights	353	0	0	0	0	0	0	0	0	0	0
Bendersville	603	1	0	0	0	1	5	0	5	0	0
Bensalem Township	58,400	102	2	7	44	49	2,492	310	1,984	198	43
Berks-Lehigh Regional	28,644	17	1	0	3	13	348	35	291	22	0
Berlin	2,085	6	0	2	1	3	22	3	19	0	0
Bern Township	7,180	11	0	0	0	11	66	8	52	6	1
Bernville	883	0	0	0	0	0	3	1	1	1	0
Berwick	10,199	25	0	7	4	14	399	73	320	6	2
Bessemer	1,099	0	0	0	0	0	11	2	9	0	0
Bethel Park	31,477	27	0	4	0	23	279	33	229	17	1
Bethel Township, Armstrong County	1,203	0	0	0	0	0	0	0	0	0	0
Bethel Township, Berks County	4,539	1	0	0	1	0	48	5	42	1	0
Bethlehem	72,537	225	0	12	107	106	2,422	399	1,885	138	5

[1] The FBI does not publish arson data unless it receives data from either the agency or the state for all 12 months of the calendar year.

Table 8. Offenses Known to Law Enforcement, by State and City, 2008—*Continued*

(Number.)

State/City	Population	Violent crime	Murder and non-negligent man-slaughter	Forcible rape	Robbery	Aggravated assault	Property crime	Burglary	Larceny-theft	Motor vehicle theft	Arson[1]
PENNSYLVANIA—*Continued*											
Bethlehem Township	23,807	21	1	3	4	13	608	65	526	17	2
Biglerville	1,150	1	0	0	0	1	21	2	18	1	0
Birdsboro	5,193	6	0	0	1	5	81	15	63	3	2
Birmingham Township	4,256	1	0	0	0	1	25	3	19	3	0
Blacklick Township	2,059	0	0	0	0	0	1	0	1	0	0
Blair Township	4,734	6	0	1	0	5	66	13	51	2	0
Blairsville	3,383	12	0	4	2	6	89	19	66	4	0
Blakely	6,765	3	0	1	0	2	81	18	60	3	2
Blawnox	1,436	3	0	0	0	3	2	1	1	0	0
Bloomsburg Town	12,601	19	0	2	4	13	247	40	200	7	1
Blythe Township	903	0	0	0	0	0	0	0	0	0	0
Bolivar	464	0	0	0	0	0	0	0	0	0	0
Boyertown	3,941	3	0	0	2	1	114	15	85	14	3
Brackenridge	3,222	11	0	2	1	8	131	23	104	4	0
Braddock Hills	1,826	2	0	0	1	1	62	6	47	9	0
Bradford	8,368	50	0	4	3	43	337	32	292	13	1
Bradford Township	4,768	12	0	2	0	10	38	6	31	1	0
Brandywine Regional	10,069	26	0	7	1	18	98	5	90	3	0
Brecknock Township, Berks County	4,926	7	0	0	0	7	36	6	27	3	0
Briar Creek Township	3,069	2	0	0	0	2	20	5	15	0	0
Bridgeport	4,371	15	1	0	3	11	142	29	104	9	0
Bridgeville	4,868	1	0	0	0	1	71	16	51	4	0
Bridgewater	877	7	0	0	1	6	39	6	30	3	0
Brighton Township	7,903	10	0	0	0	10	46	3	43	0	0
Bristol Township	53,748	150	1	9	82	58	1,895	288	1,405	202	16
Brockway	2,052	2	0	1	0	1	16	2	14	0	0
Brookville	3,984	6	2	1	1	2	91	2	88	1	0
Brownsville	2,631	5	0	0	0	5	61	11	45	5	0
Bryn Athyn	1,309	0	0	0	0	0	15	0	15	0	0
Buckingham Township	19,437	6	0	1	0	5	143	31	110	2	0
Buffalo Township	7,261	10	0	1	0	9	61	24	36	1	0
Bushkill Township	8,179	11	0	0	0	11	65	8	51	6	0
Butler	13,921	125	0	0	29	96	743	143	600	0	5
Butler Township, Butler County	16,554	38	0	3	8	27	370	44	318	8	2
Butler Township, Luzerne County	9,278	34	0	1	2	31	122	33	83	6	0
Butler Township, Schuylkill County	6,142	7	0	2	0	5	32	13	17	2	0
Caernarvon Township, Berks County	3,461	2	0	0	1	1	99	13	83	3	0
California	6,597	11	0	0	1	10	127	23	102	2	1
Caln Township	12,148	57	0	3	12	42	423	35	374	14	3
Cambria Township	6,327	6	2	0	1	3	107	10	95	2	0
Cambridge Springs	2,240	3	1	0	0	2	22	0	22	0	1
Camp Hill	7,384	9	0	2	1	6	109	2	106	1	1
Canonsburg	8,711	43	0	1	5	37	226	37	181	8	0
Carbondale	9,228	24	0	1	4	19	151	28	116	7	1
Carlisle	18,427	75	0	7	49	19	647	82	548	17	5
Carnegie	7,926	29	0	3	15	11	187	19	162	6	2
Carrolltown	959	0	0	0	0	0	29	2	27	0	0
Carroll Township, Washington County	5,455	11	0	0	0	11	62	10	47	5	0
Carroll Township, York County	5,811	2	0	1	0	1	128	21	103	4	0
Carroll Valley	3,542	1	0	0	0	1	51	4	47	0	0
Castle Shannon	8,016	16	0	1	0	15	147	21	117	9	0
Catasauqua	6,567	21	0	1	0	20	172	23	144	5	0
Catawissa	1,535	2	0	0	0	2	51	2	49	0	0
Cecil Township	10,367	8	0	0	2	6	21	12	9	0	0
Center Township	11,680	25	0	2	8	15	403	44	353	6	0
Centerville	3,200	1	0	0	1	0	16	5	11	0	0
Central Berks Regional	7,468	15	0	1	8	6	184	34	127	23	0
Chalfont	4,186	2	0	0	0	2	28	0	28	0	0
Chambersburg	17,947	68	2	6	18	42	912	121	757	34	5
Charleroi	5,694	29	0	0	8	21	223	52	160	11	1
Chartiers Township	7,381	6	0	3	0	3	41	7	32	2	6
Cheltenham Township	36,027	100	0	5	62	33	980	185	747	48	5
Chester	36,638	1,055	17	42	237	759	1,388	450	714	224	30
Chester Township	4,454	58	0	0	9	49	56	21	22	13	0
Cheswick	1,739	1	0	0	0	1	11	2	9	0	0
Chippewa Township	9,688	1	0	0	1	0	181	18	158	5	0
Christiana	1,112	1	0	0	0	1	24	3	21	0	0
Churchill	3,246	43	0	0	3	40	20	4	15	1	0
Clairton	7,830	47	2	0	6	39	31	11	19	1	0
Clarion	5,226	4	0	2	0	2	101	24	72	5	1
Clarks Summit	6,530	1	0	0	0	1	50	3	45	2	0
Claysville	673	2	0	0	0	2	3	1	2	0	0
Clay Township	5,849	1	0	0	0	1	60	7	52	1	0
Clearfield	6,170	31	0	3	1	27	288	34	249	5	2

[1] The FBI does not publish arson data unless it receives data from either the agency or the state for all 12 months of the calendar year.

Table 8. Offenses Known to Law Enforcement, by State and City, 2008—*Continued*

(Number.)

State/City	Population	Violent crime	Murder and non-negligent man-slaughter	Forcible rape	Robbery	Aggravated assault	Property crime	Burglary	Larceny-theft	Motor vehicle theft	Arson[1]
PENNSYLVANIA—*Continued*											
Cleona	2,116	0	0	0	0	0	15	3	12	0	0
Clifton Heights	6,551	58	0	0	8	50	209	30	164	15	3
Coal Township	10,259	42	0	0	2	40	254	26	223	5	3
Coatesville	11,689	176	3	9	101	63	418	99	269	50	24
Cochranton	1,066	0	0	0	0	0	9	1	8	0	0
Colebrookdale District	6,434	4	0	1	0	3	139	5	130	4	0
Collegeville	4,968	1	0	1	0	0	100	11	87	2	0
Collier Township	6,477	6	0	1	0	5	170	14	152	4	1
Collingdale	8,378	120	0	1	23	96	271	37	199	35	0
Colonial Regional	20,091	12	0	3	5	4	581	40	531	10	3
Columbia	10,023	27	0	8	4	15	249	59	176	14	0
Conemaugh Township, Cambria County	2,462	4	0	0	0	4	7	1	6	0	0
Conemaugh Township, Somerset County	7,253	5	0	0	1	4	50	11	36	3	0
Conewago Township, Adams County	6,108	3	0	1	0	2	98	3	93	2	0
Conewango Township	3,550	8	0	3	1	4	102	13	87	2	1
Conneaut Lake Regional	3,510	2	0	0	0	2	58	4	53	1	0
Connellsville	8,475	19	0	4	2	13	341	99	237	5	0
Conoy Township	3,336	1	0	1	0	0	52	18	32	2	0
Conshohocken	8,639	23	0	1	1	21	206	34	164	8	0
Conyngham	1,839	0	0	0	0	0	0	0	0	0	0
Coopersburg	2,562	1	0	0	0	1	39	4	35	0	0
Coplay	3,371	1	0	0	1	0	46	4	42	0	0
Coraopolis	5,604	42	0	0	1	41	153	20	129	4	0
Cornwall	3,490	1	0	0	0	1	3	3	0	0	0
Corry	6,305	25	0	5	0	20	81	11	67	3	1
Covington Township	2,188	1	0	0	0	1	55	8	40	7	1
Crafton	6,527	11	0	0	4	7	140	18	115	7	0
Cranberry Township	27,315	33	0	5	4	24	448	30	411	7	2
Crescent Township	2,823	4	0	0	0	4	43	20	21	2	1
Cresson	1,481	3	0	0	0	3	53	8	45	0	0
Cresson Township	4,264	1	0	0	0	1	28	12	16	0	0
Croyle Township	2,216	2	0	0	0	2	21	0	21	0	0
Cumberland Township, Adams County	6,318	1	0	0	0	1	47	12	34	1	0
Cumru Township	17,542	17	0	0	9	8	380	62	286	32	2
Curwensville	2,460	6	0	0	1	5	52	9	42	1	2
Dale	1,359	9	0	0	0	9	4	2	2	0	0
Dallas	2,481	2	0	0	0	2	42	5	35	2	0
Dallas Township	8,691	0	0	0	0	0	63	25	37	1	0
Dalton	1,218	4	0	0	0	4	17	3	14	0	0
Danville	4,475	7	0	4	1	2	123	10	112	1	0
Darby	9,913	436	1	6	74	355	497	148	283	66	2
Darby Township	9,534	24	2	2	8	12	145	19	101	25	0
Darlington Township	1,998	0	0	0	0	0	0	0	0	0	0
Delaware Water Gap	800	0	0	0	0	0	0	0	0	0	0
Delmont	2,419	3	0	0	2	1	58	7	48	3	0
Denver	3,676	4	0	0	3	1	49	12	33	4	3
Derry	2,778	14	0	1	0	13	45	3	39	3	0
Derry Township, Dauphin County	22,050	48	1	4	6	37	825	72	737	16	3
Donegal Township	2,625	2	0	0	1	1	21	7	13	1	0
Donora	5,245	13	0	1	2	10	87	32	53	2	0
Dormont	8,406	50	0	1	11	38	161	32	118	11	1
Douglass Township, Berks County	3,526	0	0	0	0	0	19	6	12	1	0
Douglass Township, Montgomery County	10,153	6	0	0	1	5	115	13	90	12	1
Downingtown	7,889	33	0	0	7	26	309	38	251	20	4
Doylestown	8,142	24	0	0	11	13	228	19	206	3	0
Doylestown Township	18,752	30	0	2	5	23	248	36	208	4	2
Dublin Borough	2,142	2	0	0	1	1	10	1	9	0	0
Du Bois	7,653	40	0	5	3	32	308	35	260	13	0
Duboistown	1,188	0	0	0	0	0	0	0	0	0	0
Duncannon	1,502	1	0	0	0	1	45	5	40	0	0
Duncansville	1,169	2	0	1	1	0	27	5	21	1	0
Dunmore	13,909	16	0	4	6	6	204	42	141	21	0
Dupont	2,582	14	0	0	0	14	61	12	46	3	0
Duquesne	6,663	97	2	6	41	48	295	129	139	27	5
Duryea	4,344	2	0	0	0	2	73	22	48	3	0
Earl Township	6,907	1	0	0	1	0	66	19	44	3	1
East Bangor	1,090	0	0	0	0	0	3	0	2	1	0
East Berlin	1,430	0	0	0	0	0	0	0	0	0	0
East Buffalo Township	5,945	6	1	5	0	0	29	1	28	0	0
East Cocalico Township	10,484	2	0	0	2	0	159	27	121	11	0
East Conemaugh	1,163	1	0	0	0	1	4	2	2	0	0
East Coventry Township	6,795	3	0	0	1	2	53	16	34	3	0
East Deer Township	1,321	3	0	0	0	3	17	3	14	0	0
East Earl Township	6,543	3	0	2	1	0	72	19	47	6	0

[1] The FBI does not publish arson data unless it receives data from either the agency or the state for all 12 months of the calendar year.

Table 8. Offenses Known to Law Enforcement, by State and City, 2008—*Continued*

(Number.)

State/City	Population	Violent crime	Murder and non-negligent man-slaughter	Forcible rape	Robbery	Aggravated assault	Property crime	Burglary	Larceny-theft	Motor vehicle theft	Arson[1]
PENNSYLVANIA—*Continued*											
Eastern Adams Regional	9,915	5	0	3	0	2	64	8	50	6	0
Eastern Pike Regional	5,495	27	0	0	0	27	229	15	208	6	1
East Fallowfield Township	7,458	7	0	1	0	6	106	14	91	1	0
East Franklin Township	3,944	1	0	0	0	1	22	0	22	0	0
East Hempfield Township	23,515	12	0	4	6	2	613	79	518	16	1
East Lampeter Township	14,968	14	1	5	5	3	628	44	568	16	2
East Lansdowne	2,476	35	0	0	10	25	126	27	90	9	0
East McKeesport	2,796	9	0	0	2	7	27	7	19	1	0
East Norriton Township	13,575	4	0	0	2	2	349	37	295	17	0
East Norwegian Township	833	0	0	0	0	0	0	0	0	0	0
Easton	26,072	157	2	13	78	64	1,023	157	800	66	11
East Pennsboro Township	19,890	18	1	9	3	5	292	52	236	4	2
East Petersburg	4,344	7	0	0	3	4	46	7	36	3	0
East Pikeland Township	6,804	4	0	1	0	3	105	15	88	2	0
East Rochester	562	1	0	0	1	0	48	7	40	1	0
East Taylor Township	2,522	3	0	0	0	3	19	3	15	1	0
Easttown Township	10,536	6	0	2	1	3	116	31	83	2	0
East Vincent Township	6,454	7	0	0	3	4	61	18	38	5	0
East Washington	1,855	5	0	1	1	3	34	13	20	1	0
East Whiteland Township	10,684	7	0	0	0	7	141	12	124	5	1
Ebensburg	2,950	6	0	1	1	4	68	9	54	5	2
Economy	9,084	2	0	0	0	2	57	8	49	0	0
Eddystone	2,344	47	0	2	11	34	310	11	292	7	1
Edgewood	3,011	9	0	1	5	3	329	9	313	7	1
Edgeworth	1,589	0	0	0	0	0	0	0	0	0	0
Edinboro	6,562	5	0	4	0	1	102	14	87	1	0
Edwardsville	4,669	23	0	1	5	17	170	13	143	14	0
Elizabeth	1,457	3	0	0	1	2	52	11	37	4	0
Elizabethtown	12,110	15	0	7	2	6	201	27	171	3	2
Elizabeth Township	12,820	33	0	0	2	31	115	22	86	7	1
Elkland	1,659	3	0	0	0	3	12	2	10	0	0
Ellwood City	7,972	31	0	1	9	21	268	72	182	14	1
Emlenton Borough	734	1	0	0	0	1	10	2	6	2	0
Emmaus	11,359	18	0	1	7	10	350	46	288	16	7
Emporium	2,216	4	0	3	0	1	44	13	31	0	1
Emsworth	2,373	0	0	0	0	0	1	0	1	0	0
Ephrata Township	9,655	6	0	1	2	3	176	10	161	5	2
Erie	103,881	646	7	88	317	234	3,554	1,111	2,280	163	48
Etna	3,556	18	0	0	1	17	122	29	82	11	0
Everett	1,846	7	0	1	0	6	26	5	20	1	1
Everson	787	0	0	0	0	0	0	0	0	0	0
Exeter	5,930	13	0	0	0	13	101	13	82	6	0
Exeter Township, Berks County	26,988	16	0	1	5	10	521	64	430	27	5
Exeter Township, Luzerne County	2,532	3	0	0	0	3	32	6	22	4	0
Fairfield	511	0	0	0	0	0	3	1	2	0	0
Fairview Township, Luzerne County	4,298	3	0	0	0	3	41	4	37	0	0
Fairview Township, York County	16,897	21	0	2	4	15	329	51	272	6	1
Fallowfield Township	4,188	13	0	0	0	13	33	8	24	1	1
Falls Township, Bucks County	33,696	46	0	0	26	20	933	106	726	101	1
Falls Township, Wyoming County	1,949	2	0	0	0	2	9	1	8	0	0
Fawn Township	2,305	5	0	0	0	5	40	6	31	3	0
Ferguson Township	16,590	11	0	1	2	8	216	30	178	8	2
Ferndale	1,653	1	0	1	0	0	1	0	1	0	0
Findlay Township	5,034	13	0	0	0	13	62	5	55	2	0
Fleetwood	4,014	6	0	0	0	6	74	5	64	5	1
Folcroft	6,837	38	0	3	7	28	119	13	93	13	0
Ford City	3,157	4	0	0	2	2	85	14	67	4	0
Forest City	1,732	1	0	0	0	1	33	7	25	1	0
Forest Hills	6,231	3	0	0	2	1	76	19	54	3	0
Forks Township	14,603	8	0	3	0	5	176	10	163	3	0
Forty Fort	4,250	8	0	0	0	8	105	15	85	5	2
Foster Township	4,223	2	0	1	1	0	43	7	36	0	0
Fountain Hill	4,578	5	1	1	2	1	146	21	116	9	1
Fox Chapel	5,130	0	0	0	0	0	11	3	8	0	0
Frackville	4,127	6	0	0	1	5	5	5	0	0	0
Franconia Township	12,624	10	0	1	0	9	82	7	75	0	0
Franklin	6,667	25	0	3	1	21	180	27	149	4	0
Franklin Park	12,109	12	0	2	0	10	75	15	60	0	0
Franklin Township, Beaver County	4,290	6	0	1	1	4	51	11	38	2	0
Franklin Township, Carbon County	4,914	13	0	0	0	13	98	22	69	7	0
Freeland	3,390	18	0	0	3	15	79	9	66	4	0
Gaines Township	560	0	0	0	0	0	0	0	0	0	0
Galeton	1,214	0	0	0	0	0	23	5	18	0	0
Gallitzin	1,874	0	0	0	0	0	35	11	24	0	0
Gallitzin Township	1,294	0	0	0	0	0	4	2	2	0	0

[1] The FBI does not publish arson data unless it receives data from either the agency or the state for all 12 months of the calendar year.

Table 8. Offenses Known to Law Enforcement, by State and City, 2008—*Continued*

(Number.)

State/City	Population	Violent crime	Murder and non-negligent man-slaughter	Forcible rape	Robbery	Aggravated assault	Property crime	Burglary	Larceny-theft	Motor vehicle theft	Arson[1]
PENNSYLVANIA—*Continued*											
Geistown	2,354	3	0	0	1	2	45	10	31	4	0
Gettysburg	8,097	25	0	9	9	7	204	26	167	11	1
Gilpin Township	2,514	0	0	0	0	0	23	4	18	1	0
Girard	2,924	0	0	0	0	0	37	15	20	2	0
Glassport	4,542	23	0	0	3	20	92	31	56	5	0
Glenolden	7,213	16	0	2	6	8	219	32	176	11	0
Granville Township	4,925	3	0	0	0	3	124	23	99	2	0
Greencastle	4,100	13	0	2	0	11	162	15	145	2	1
Greenfield Township, Blair County	3,742	14	0	1	0	13	172	22	149	1	0
Greensburg	15,283	40	0	4	8	28	528	51	462	15	2
Green Tree	4,326	4	0	0	3	1	125	9	115	1	0
Greenville	6,094	12	2	4	2	4	164	28	130	6	1
Greenwood Township	2,068	0	0	0	0	0	0	0	0	0	0
Grove City	7,742	4	0	1	1	2	133	29	102	2	0
Halifax Regional	4,240	0	0	0	0	0	5	1	4	0	0
Hamburg	4,178	13	0	1	1	11	90	13	73	4	0
Hamiltonban Township	2,734	4	0	0	0	4	10	3	5	2	0
Hampden Township	27,012	4	0	0	4	0	194	27	160	7	2
Hampton Township	17,210	7	0	1	1	5	142	16	123	3	0
Hanover	14,972	53	0	4	23	26	607	54	537	16	7
Hanover Township, Luzerne County	11,008	9	0	1	4	4	215	33	172	10	4
Harleton	263	0	0	0	0	0	0	0	0	0	0
Harmar Township	3,017	13	0	1	3	9	94	4	83	7	0
Harmony Township	3,050	2	0	0	2	0	69	9	60	0	0
Harrisburg	47,118	780	9	46	483	242	2,615	743	1,637	235	31
Harrison Township	9,963	13	1	2	0	10	86	32	50	4	0
Harveys Lake	2,936	1	0	0	1	0	3	0	3	0	0
Hastings	1,289	4	0	0	0	4	40	12	27	1	0
Hatboro	7,123	28	3	0	1	24	128	20	104	4	0
Haverford Township	48,044	47	0	2	16	29	713	94	600	19	1
Hawley	1,294	0	0	0	0	0	21	2	19	0	0
Hazleton	21,788	69	0	6	18	45	470	158	265	47	5
Heidelberg Township, Berks County	1,764	2	0	1	0	1	9	4	4	1	0
Heidelberg Township, Lebanon County	4,148	0	0	0	0	0	38	4	32	2	0
Hellertown	5,658	26	0	2	0	24	98	12	84	2	0
Hemlock Township	2,242	2	0	1	0	1	167	6	161	0	0
Hempfield Township, Mercer County	3,855	6	0	0	0	6	101	14	82	5	0
Hermitage	16,315	27	0	3	7	17	672	56	608	8	1
Hickory Township	2,273	2	0	0	0	2	3	0	2	1	0
Highland Township	1,204	0	0	0	0	0	15	3	12	0	0
Highspire	2,604	16	0	0	1	15	25	1	23	1	0
Hilltown Township	13,494	23	0	2	5	16	246	38	202	6	1
Hollidaysburg	5,530	7	0	0	1	6	94	12	79	3	0
Homer City	1,714	9	0	0	0	9	20	0	20	0	0
Homestead	3,501	57	2	4	31	20	289	60	212	17	0
Honesdale	4,706	8	0	6	0	2	127	16	110	1	2
Honey Brook	1,516	0	0	0	0	0	1	1	0	0	0
Hopewell Township	12,303	48	0	2	6	40	286	42	225	19	0
Horsham Township	24,734	16	0	2	2	12	291	32	243	16	1
Houston	1,242	1	0	0	0	1	18	4	12	2	0
Hulmeville	873	0	0	0	0	0	1	0	1	0	0
Hummelstown	4,431	17	0	0	1	16	51	6	45	0	0
Huntingdon	6,799	11	0	0	1	10	96	20	76	0	0
Independence Township, Beaver County	2,681	1	0	0	0	1	28	3	22	3	0
Indiana	14,823	46	0	7	7	32	290	33	252	5	6
Indiana Township	7,026	5	0	3	0	2	70	24	44	2	0
Industry	1,790	2	0	0	0	2	33	6	26	1	1
Ingram	3,366	15	0	0	2	13	42	5	33	4	0
Irwin	4,046	6	0	0	0	6	72	9	60	3	0
Ivyland	842	0	0	0	0	0	13	2	11	0	0
Jackson Township, Butler County	3,724	2	0	0	1	1	73	11	61	1	0
Jackson Township, Cambria County	4,713	13	0	4	2	7	114	26	84	4	4
Jackson Township, Luzerne County	4,765	4	1	2	0	1	15	7	7	1	0
Jamestown	576	1	0	0	0	1	24	5	19	0	0
Jeannette	9,863	61	1	0	3	57	197	61	136	0	3
Jefferson Hills Borough	9,644	14	0	1	1	12	76	8	57	11	0
Jefferson Township, Mercer County	2,308	0	0	0	0	0	7	2	5	0	0
Jenkins Township	4,903	4	0	0	0	4	121	25	90	6	2
Jermyn	2,222	29	0	0	5	24	61	24	30	7	0
Jersey Shore	4,290	31	0	1	0	30	106	17	81	8	0
Jim Thorpe	4,889	21	0	2	2	17	98	20	74	4	1
Johnsonburg	2,687	3	0	0	1	2	52	18	33	1	1
Johnstown	23,172	114	2	3	42	67	756	212	501	43	12
Juniata Valley Regional	2,688	1	0	0	0	1	2	0	2	0	0

[1] The FBI does not publish arson data unless it receives data from either the agency or the state for all 12 months of the calendar year.

Table 8. Offenses Known to Law Enforcement, by State and City, 2008—*Continued*

(Number.)

State/City	Population	Violent crime	Murder and non-negligent man-slaughter	Forcible rape	Robbery	Aggravated assault	Property crime	Burglary	Larceny-theft	Motor vehicle theft	Arson[1]
PENNSYLVANIA—*Continued*											
Kane	3,762	4	0	1	0	3	33	2	31	0	0
Kennedy Township	9,765	20	0	0	6	14	167	22	133	12	0
Kennett Square	5,276	25	0	3	9	13	109	19	79	11	1
Kidder Township	1,424	12	0	0	0	12	132	31	100	1	0
Kingston	12,968	30	1	5	10	14	423	65	330	28	0
Kingston Township	7,087	16	0	1	0	15	73	11	61	1	0
Kiskiminetas Township	4,755	6	0	0	0	6	67	19	47	1	0
Kline Township	1,496	0	0	0	0	0	32	6	26	0	0
Knox	1,097	30	0	3	0	27	106	12	85	9	1
Koppel	772	4	0	1	0	3	23	3	20	0	0
Kulpmont	2,744	5	0	1	0	4	37	7	25	5	0
Kutztown	5,091	9	0	3	1	5	157	33	122	2	3
Laceyville	368	1	0	0	0	1	1	0	1	0	1
Laflin Borough	1,493	12	0	1	0	11	34	6	27	1	0
Lake City	2,883	4	0	0	0	4	37	6	30	1	0
Lamar Township	2,418	0	0	0	0	0	7	2	5	0	0
Lancaster	54,595	534	3	36	240	255	3,075	609	2,284	182	28
Lancaster Township, Butler County	2,568	1	0	1	0	0	13	1	12	0	1
Lancaster Township, Lancaster County	14,415	29	0	2	12	15	394	83	284	27	2
Lansdale	15,515	45	0	11	16	18	375	55	306	14	5
Lansdowne	10,660	66	0	1	21	44	406	105	282	19	1
Larksville	4,446	3	0	1	0	2	84	13	60	11	0
Latrobe	8,358	15	1	1	0	13	245	17	216	12	2
Laureldale	3,770	6	0	1	1	4	62	3	44	15	0
Lawrence Park Township	3,687	6	0	1	0	5	48	8	37	3	0
Lawrence Township, Clearfield County	7,476	43	0	2	1	40	276	28	245	3	0
Lawrence Township, Tioga County	1,684	8	0	0	0	8	0	0	0	0	0
Lebanon	24,212	114	1	8	38	67	810	162	604	44	5
Leechburg	2,203	1	0	0	0	1	44	5	31	8	0
Leetsdale	1,114	0	0	0	0	0	0	0	0	0	0
Leet Township	1,496	0	0	0	0	0	0	0	0	0	0
Lehighton	5,463	15	0	1	5	9	211	43	158	10	0
Lehigh Township, Northampton County	10,847	11	0	1	1	9	157	35	117	5	2
Lewisburg	5,515	21	1	1	1	18	62	9	53	0	0
Liberty	2,432	6	0	0	0	6	8	2	6	0	0
Liberty Township, Adams County	1,284	0	0	0	0	0	4	1	2	1	0
Liberty Township, Bedford County	1,434	0	0	0	0	0	0	0	0	0	0
Ligonier	1,608	3	0	0	1	2	25	0	22	3	1
Ligonier Township	6,754	12	0	1	0	11	45	10	35	0	0
Limerick Township	16,941	10	0	0	1	9	381	48	319	14	1
Lincoln	1,120	0	0	0	0	0	8	2	4	2	0
Linesville	1,093	0	0	0	0	0	0	0	0	0	0
Lititz	9,054	5	0	1	2	2	113	23	88	2	0
Littlestown	4,128	9	0	0	0	9	86	23	62	1	0
Lock Haven	8,616	19	0	4	3	12	309	41	264	4	2
Locust Township	2,524	5	0	1	0	4	53	7	42	4	0
Logan Township	11,859	70	1	1	12	56	348	73	268	7	4
Lower Allen Township	17,862	3	0	1	0	2	282	22	254	6	0
Lower Burrell	12,098	11	0	1	3	7	148	30	110	8	0
Lower Frederick Township	4,817	2	0	0	0	2	27	6	19	2	0
Lower Gwynedd Township	11,375	17	0	0	3	14	190	15	171	4	0
Lower Heidelberg Township	5,369	4	0	0	1	3	26	5	21	0	0
Lower Makefield Township	32,212	15	0	0	1	14	364	49	303	12	0
Lower Merion Township	57,367	26	0	1	18	7	949	147	766	36	0
Lower Milford Township	3,901	2	0	0	0	2	26	6	20	0	0
Lower Moreland Township	12,609	2	0	1	1	0	250	46	204	0	0
Lower Paxton Township	45,354	90	3	11	36	40	1,126	133	964	29	7
Lower Pottsgrove Township	12,210	13	0	1	0	12	272	21	244	7	1
Lower Providence Township	26,430	9	0	2	2	5	341	62	259	20	1
Lower Salford Township	14,520	1	0	0	0	1	89	9	76	4	0
Lower Saucon Township	11,343	51	0	3	2	46	116	22	92	2	1
Lower Southampton Township	19,084	62	0	2	12	48	450	68	357	25	5
Lower Swatara Township	8,514	5	0	2	2	1	130	11	114	5	2
Lower Windsor Township	7,836	4	1	1	0	2	107	31	70	6	1
Luzerne Township	6,637	2	0	0	0	2	38	6	29	3	0
Lykens	1,850	1	0	0	0	1	13	1	12	0	0
Macungie	3,123	1	0	0	0	1	53	7	46	0	1
Madison Township	1,595	0	0	0	0	0	0	0	0	0	0
Mahanoy City	4,380	3	0	0	0	3	42	11	31	0	0
Mahanoy Township	3,727	0	0	0	0	0	7	1	6	0	0
Mahoning Township, Carbon County	4,405	22	0	1	0	21	103	16	81	6	0
Mahoning Township, Montour County	4,283	38	0	1	0	37	20	1	19	0	0
Main Township	1,296	0	0	0	0	0	0	0	0	0	0
Malvern	3,104	2	0	0	0	2	22	4	18	0	0

[1] The FBI does not publish arson data unless it receives data from either the agency or the state for all 12 months of the calendar year.

Table 8. Offenses Known to Law Enforcement, by State and City, 2008—*Continued*

(Number.)

State/City	Population	Violent crime	Murder and non-negligent man-slaughter	Forcible rape	Robbery	Aggravated assault	Property crime	Burglary	Larceny-theft	Motor vehicle theft	Arson[1]
PENNSYLVANIA—*Continued*											
Manheim	4,635	3	1	0	2	0	102	17	80	5	0
Manheim Township	36,306	49	0	2	12	35	808	103	682	23	5
Manor	2,901	1	0	0	0	1	5	1	3	1	0
Manor Township, Armstrong County	3,934	0	0	0	0	0	1	1	0	0	0
Manor Township, Lancaster County	19,128	2	0	0	1	1	151	24	119	8	4
Mansfield	3,192	4	0	0	0	4	8	2	6	0	0
Marietta	2,591	2	0	0	0	2	84	16	67	1	0
Marion Center	417	0	0	0	0	0	0	0	0	0	0
Marion Township, Beaver County	880	0	0	0	0	0	5	1	4	0	0
Marion Township, Berks County	1,745	0	0	0	0	0	8	1	7	0	0
Marlborough Township	3,263	3	0	0	0	3	42	13	26	3	1
Marple Township	23,452	15	0	0	7	8	339	49	276	14	0
Martinsburg	2,120	2	0	0	0	2	42	2	39	1	0
Marysville	2,436	0	0	0	0	0	40	3	35	2	0
Masontown	3,395	6	0	0	2	4	63	15	46	2	1
McAdoo	2,090	0	0	0	0	0	4	0	4	0	0
McCandless	27,235	13	0	0	1	12	287	29	246	12	0
McKeesport	22,076	331	3	17	72	239	851	301	499	51	6
McKees Rocks	6,011	97	1	2	51	43	257	74	162	21	0
McSherrystown	2,800	5	0	0	0	5	51	6	45	0	1
Meadville	13,208	18	0	0	9	9	356	43	313	0	3
Mechanicsburg	8,772	41	0	0	6	35	230	24	201	5	1
Media	5,407	12	0	0	6	6	24	12	12	0	1
Mercer	2,211	2	0	0	0	2	35	4	30	1	0
Mercersburg	1,604	0	0	0	0	0	3	1	2	0	0
Meshoppen	427	0	0	0	0	0	0	0	0	0	0
Meyersdale	2,281	0	0	0	0	0	36	11	25	0	0
Middleburg	1,333	0	0	0	0	0	33	7	24	2	0
Middlesex Township, Butler County	5,469	2	0	1	0	1	32	4	23	5	0
Middlesex Township, Cumberland County	6,832	9	0	2	5	2	194	17	170	7	1
Middletown	8,823	20	0	4	3	13	156	27	128	1	0
Middletown Township	46,788	73	0	4	19	50	1,692	140	1,472	80	6
Midland	2,841	13	0	2	2	9	102	37	60	5	0
Midway	923	0	0	0	0	0	0	0	0	0	0
Mifflin	607	0	0	0	0	0	0	0	0	0	0
Mifflinburg	3,520	0	0	0	0	0	26	4	22	0	0
Mifflin County Regional	26,321	90	0	7	10	73	694	78	571	45	1
Mifflin Township	2,250	0	0	0	0	0	0	0	0	0	0
Milford	2,861	2	0	0	1	1	28	0	25	3	0
Millbourne	907	11	0	0	4	7	19	1	16	2	1
Millcreek Township, Erie County	51,622	37	0	4	16	17	1,003	225	743	35	4
Millcreek Township, Lebanon County	3,174	4	0	2	0	2	40	19	20	1	0
Millersburg	2,462	18	0	2	2	14	63	9	51	3	3
Millersville	7,196	9	0	2	1	6	110	33	70	7	0
Millvale	3,650	2	0	0	0	2	25	0	15	10	0
Millville	943	0	0	0	0	0	0	0	0	0	0
Milton	6,331	16	0	2	1	13	124	19	100	5	0
Minersville	4,223	6	0	0	1	5	50	4	46	0	0
Mohnton	3,093	1	0	0	0	1	29	6	20	3	0
Monaca	5,737	16	0	0	7	9	184	23	141	20	0
Monessen	8,015	51	0	2	7	42	182	50	125	7	1
Monongahela	4,405	19	0	1	6	12	165	26	123	16	0
Monroeville	27,531	99	2	3	29	65	674	70	564	40	3
Montgomery	5,067	0	0	0	0	0	45	8	37	0	0
Montgomery Township	24,166	9	1	0	5	3	508	33	469	6	1
Montoursville	4,590	2	0	0	2	0	84	5	79	0	0
Montrose	1,536	3	0	0	0	3	16	2	13	1	0
Moon Township	22,677	18	1	3	6	8	351	58	272	21	1
Moore Township	9,458	5	0	0	0	5	71	12	57	2	0
Moosic	5,777	29	0	1	3	25	293	30	253	10	1
Morrisville	9,604	35	0	2	6	27	296	53	205	38	1
Morton	2,631	10	0	0	1	9	116	10	103	3	0
Moscow	1,958	5	0	0	0	5	41	5	36	0	0
Mount Carmel	5,859	30	0	0	2	28	136	16	117	3	2
Mount Carmel Township	2,566	5	0	0	1	4	20	1	17	2	3
Mount Gretna Borough	234	0	0	0	0	0	1	0	1	0	0
Mount Holly Springs	1,914	1	0	0	0	1	52	9	42	1	0
Mount Jewett	994	2	0	0	0	2	30	3	27	0	0
Mount Joy	7,306	6	0	1	2	3	161	22	129	10	2
Mount Lebanon	30,326	16	0	1	5	10	287	38	241	8	1
Mount Oliver	3,647	52	2	4	28	18	191	64	91	36	1
Mount Pleasant Township	3,632	0	0	0	0	0	16	0	15	1	0
Mount Union	2,339	23	0	0	2	21	57	6	49	2	0
Muhlenberg Township	18,589	33	0	0	25	8	766	58	648	60	6

[1] The FBI does not publish arson data unless it receives data from either the agency or the state for all 12 months of the calendar year.

Table 8. Offenses Known to Law Enforcement, by State and City, 2008—*Continued*

(Number.)

State/City	Population	Violent crime	Murder and non-negligent man-slaughter	Forcible rape	Robbery	Aggravated assault	Property crime	Burglary	Larceny-theft	Motor vehicle theft	Arson[1]
PENNSYLVANIA—*Continued*											
Muncy	2,461	0	0	0	0	0	0	0	0	0	0
Munhall	11,185	21	0	0	9	12	146	40	95	11	0
Murrysville	19,511	2	0	0	0	2	140	40	99	1	0
Myerstown	3,114	1	0	0	0	1	41	4	36	1	0
Nanticoke	10,205	76	0	7	9	60	387	82	277	28	3
Narberth	4,039	5	0	0	2	3	44	10	31	3	0
Nazareth Area	6,053	8	0	0	1	7	140	15	120	5	0
Nelson Township	566	0	0	0	0	0	1	1	0	0	0
Nescopeck	1,427	0	0	0	0	0	12	0	12	0	0
Neshannock Township	9,341	5	0	0	1	4	146	29	116	1	0
Nesquehoning	3,325	16	0	0	2	14	48	8	38	2	1
Nether Providence Township	13,160	22	0	3	1	18	208	25	173	10	1
Neville Township	1,121	2	0	0	0	2	7	3	2	2	0
New Berlin	817	0	0	0	0	0	6	0	6	0	0
Newberry Township	15,531	25	0	7	5	13	383	70	301	12	0
New Bethlehem	980	7	0	0	0	7	36	7	29	0	0
New Brighton	9,320	56	0	2	9	45	480	79	397	4	2
New Britain	2,270	7	0	1	0	6	35	3	32	0	0
New Britain Township	11,003	5	0	0	0	5	107	16	89	2	1
New Castle	24,232	230	1	12	72	145	1,112	438	628	46	20
New Castle Township	395	0	0	0	0	0	38	1	34	3	0
New Cumberland	7,073	0	0	0	0	0	0	0	0	0	0
New Garden Township	11,857	8	0	1	4	3	181	26	135	20	5
New Hanover Township	9,285	10	0	0	1	9	89	28	57	4	1
New Holland	5,152	9	0	1	3	5	128	21	103	4	1
New Hope	2,272	8	0	0	1	7	56	14	42	0	0
New Kensington	13,594	52	0	6	23	23	444	107	311	26	6
Newport	1,469	20	0	0	0	20	55	6	49	0	0
Newport Township	4,770	34	0	2	0	32	71	10	50	11	0
New Sewickley Township	7,586	12	0	0	3	9	99	19	76	4	0
Newton Township	2,787	3	0	0	0	3	7	4	3	0	0
Newtown	2,371	3	0	0	0	3	20	1	19	0	0
Newtown Township, Bucks County	18,966	32	0	2	1	29	227	33	188	6	1
Newtown Township, Delaware County	11,817	8	0	0	2	6	128	19	97	12	1
Newville	1,311	2	0	0	0	2	40	3	34	3	0
New Wilmington	2,378	0	0	0	0	0	37	4	31	2	1
Norristown	31,195	406	4	12	184	206	1,219	365	726	128	7
Northampton	9,890	22	0	1	10	11	199	44	152	3	2
Northampton Township	40,879	10	0	2	3	5	266	51	206	9	2
North Belle Vernon	1,951	9	0	1	2	6	113	19	92	2	0
North Braddock	5,811	18	1	0	2	15	8	5	1	2	0
North Catasauqua	2,839	2	0	0	0	2	122	6	112	4	0
North Charleroi	1,307	1	0	0	1	0	13	7	6	0	0
North Cornwall Township	6,558	21	0	1	2	18	99	6	86	7	0
North Coventry Township	7,702	11	0	1	1	9	266	26	232	8	0
North East, Erie County	4,186	9	0	2	0	7	131	12	118	1	1
Northern Berks Regional	12,425	10	0	1	3	6	282	40	218	24	2
Northern Cambria Borough	3,922	3	0	1	1	1	110	33	69	8	2
Northern Regional	27,783	12	0	2	1	9	332	22	298	12	0
Northern York Regional	65,214	67	2	2	23	40	1,104	122	926	56	7
North Fayette Township	13,054	15	0	0	2	13	338	16	318	4	1
North Franklin Township	4,639	10	0	1	3	6	134	11	117	6	1
North Huntingdon Township	29,381	14	0	1	6	7	444	63	350	31	5
North Lebanon Township	10,939	52	0	0	5	47	296	44	246	6	1
North Londonderry Township	6,976	6	0	0	2	4	110	9	101	0	0
North Middleton Township	11,252	9	1	4	2	2	64	5	52	7	0
North Sewickley Township	5,620	5	0	0	1	4	31	3	27	1	0
North Strabane Township	12,288	21	0	1	1	19	202	16	177	9	1
Northumberland	3,495	9	0	3	1	5	95	28	63	4	0
North Union Township	1,260	0	0	0	0	0	3	3	0	0	0
North Versailles Township	12,200	66	0	1	8	57	338	45	282	11	0
North Wales	3,229	2	0	0	0	2	81	15	61	5	1
Northwest Lancaster County Regional	17,962	9	0	3	0	6	144	4	135	5	0
Northwest Lawrence County Regional	6,687	7	0	1	1	5	109	38	65	6	0
Norwood	5,782	16	0	0	1	15	122	10	105	7	0
Oakmont	6,413	20	0	1	2	17	141	30	100	11	1
O'Hara Township	9,536	17	0	0	2	15	86	17	64	5	0
Ohio Township	4,116	2	0	0	0	2	28	3	25	0	0
Ohioville	3,611	12	0	2	0	10	44	5	37	2	0
Oil City	10,608	6	0	0	1	5	169	17	144	8	2
Old Forge	8,521	16	0	0	0	16	29	2	20	7	0
Old Lycoming Township	5,273	8	0	3	1	4	99	16	83	0	0
Oliver Township	2,072	4	0	0	0	4	19	4	13	2	0
Olyphant	4,944	4	0	0	0	4	70	24	40	6	2

[1] The FBI does not publish arson data unless it receives data from either the agency or the state for all 12 months of the calendar year.

Table 8. Offenses Known to Law Enforcement, by State and City, 2008—*Continued*

(Number.)

State/City	Population	Violent crime	Murder and non-negligent man-slaughter	Forcible rape	Robbery	Aggravated assault	Property crime	Burglary	Larceny-theft	Motor vehicle theft	Arson[1]
PENNSYLVANIA—*Continued*											
Orangeville Area	1,635	0	0	0	0	0	18	1	17	0	0
Orwigsburg	2,972	3	0	0	0	3	39	5	33	1	0
Oxford	4,662	27	0	1	3	23	137	24	105	8	3
Paint Township	3,153	5	0	0	0	5	14	3	11	0	0
Palmerton	5,244	8	0	0	0	8	117	21	96	0	0
Palmer Township	20,311	17	0	0	8	9	489	44	437	8	0
Palmyra	6,981	8	0	0	3	5	121	14	102	5	0
Parker	745	1	0	0	0	1	0	0	0	0	0
Parkesburg	3,439	13	0	6	3	4	73	15	49	9	1
Parkside	2,178	8	0	0	1	7	51	12	38	1	1
Patterson Area	3,566	2	0	0	0	2	60	9	50	1	3
Patton	1,845	2	0	0	0	2	5	2	2	1	0
Patton Township	13,258	6	0	0	1	5	155	29	123	3	0
Paxtang	1,486	3	0	0	1	2	51	13	37	1	1
Pen Argyl	3,643	5	0	0	0	5	61	13	47	1	1
Penbrook	2,915	7	0	0	3	4	56	17	36	3	0
Penn Hills	43,835	218	6	16	94	102	1,142	318	709	115	10
Pennridge Regional	10,479	14	0	0	1	13	123	19	101	3	1
Penn Township, Butler County	5,150	0	0	0	0	0	43	8	35	0	1
Penn Township, Lancaster County	8,495	13	0	0	1	12	137	29	83	25	0
Penn Township, Westmoreland County	20,221	4	0	0	1	3	22	18	4	0	0
Penn Township, York County	15,931	20	0	0	7	13	269	37	227	5	4
Pequea Township	4,533	4	0	0	0	4	55	8	42	5	2
Perkasie	8,633	5	0	0	0	5	334	45	283	6	1
Perryopolis	1,718	2	0	0	0	2	24	9	15	0	0
Peters Township	20,244	13	0	2	2	9	175	35	128	12	1
Philadelphia	1,441,117	20,771	331	1,038	9,618	9,784	62,584	12,845	40,681	9,058	
Phoenixville	16,410	44	0	3	12	29	367	27	334	6	0
Pine Creek Township	3,192	3	1	0	0	2	19	1	18	0	0
Pittsburgh	309,757	3,358	72	136	1,541	1,609	12,625	3,108	8,258	1,259	98
Plainfield Township	6,152	1	0	0	0	1	53	2	48	3	0
Plains Township	10,452	16	0	0	1	15	143	16	117	10	2
Pleasant Hills	7,734	0	0	0	0	0	109	14	91	4	0
Plum	26,108	21	0	3	8	10	153	56	96	1	0
Plumstead Township	11,825	1	0	0	1	0	127	19	99	9	5
Plymouth	6,055	53	1	1	7	44	95	26	63	6	1
Plymouth Township, Montgomery County	16,323	39	0	2	30	7	692	86	572	34	3
Pocono Mountain Regional	35,481	85	0	23	26	36	1,052	409	601	42	7
Pocono Township	11,214	17	0	1	8	8	403	62	321	20	0
Point Township	3,828	23	0	1	0	22	32	5	25	2	0
Port Allegany	2,188	0	0	0	0	0	0	0	0	0	0
Port Carbon	1,749	0	0	0	0	0	6	2	4	0	0
Pottstown	21,285	202	2	16	81	103	1,244	181	973	90	17
Pottsville	14,416	40	2	2	0	36	232	27	189	16	3
Prospect Park	6,386	32	0	0	1	31	152	16	126	10	0
Punxsutawney	5,937	52	0	0	8	44	146	24	119	3	0
Pymatuning Township	3,559	8	0	3	1	4	115	37	70	8	0
Quarryville	2,166	7	0	0	2	5	50	5	44	1	0
Radnor Township	31,231	23	0	1	5	17	352	28	312	12	0
Ralpho Township	3,884	3	0	0	0	3	10	4	6	0	0
Rankin	2,105	34	1	2	4	27	60	26	27	7	0
Reading	80,860	868	10	33	452	373	4,208	1,268	2,150	790	40
Redstone Township	6,051	6	0	0	0	6	17	3	14	0	0
Resa Regional	2,549	4	0	0	0	4	18	8	10	0	0
Reserve Township	3,525	5	0	0	1	4	40	3	35	2	0
Reynoldsville	2,546	2	0	0	1	1	26	0	26	0	0
Rice Township	2,919	4	0	0	0	4	9	1	8	0	0
Richland	1,488	0	0	0	0	0	0	0	0	0	0
Richland Township, Bucks County	12,700	10	0	2	3	5	259	24	230	5	1
Richland Township, Cambria County	12,342	13	0	0	2	11	603	15	581	7	0
Ridgway	4,104	14	0	1	1	12	122	30	90	2	3
Ridley Park	6,993	14	0	1	2	11	63	7	54	2	1
Ridley Township	29,895	63	1	9	17	36	569	67	468	34	3
Ringtown	763	0	0	0	0	0	2	0	2	0	0
Riverside	1,821	0	0	0	0	0	3	0	3	0	0
Roaring Brook Township	1,809	0	0	0	0	0	38	4	33	1	0
Roaring Spring	2,257	1	0	1	0	0	54	5	47	2	0
Robesonia	2,058	4	0	0	2	2	34	6	25	3	0
Robeson Township	7,640	12	0	0	3	9	86	32	50	4	0
Robinson Township, Allegheny County	13,373	22	0	1	3	18	412	31	364	17	0
Rochester	3,644	19	0	2	6	11	200	33	149	18	0
Rochester Township	2,862	3	0	0	0	3	71	11	55	5	1
Rockledge	2,478	8	0	0	0	8	45	8	31	6	0
Roseto	1,643	0	0	0	0	0	8	3	4	1	0

[1] The FBI does not publish arson data unless it receives data from either the agency or the state for all 12 months of the calendar year.

Table 8. Offenses Known to Law Enforcement, by State and City, 2008—*Continued*

(Number.)

State/City	Population	Violent crime	Murder and non-negligent man-slaughter	Forcible rape	Robbery	Aggravated assault	Property crime	Burglary	Larceny-theft	Motor vehicle theft	Arson[1]
PENNSYLVANIA—*Continued*											
Rosslyn Farms	424	0	0	0	0	0	0	0	0	0	0
Ross Township	30,448	45	0	1	15	29	889	98	771	20	4
Rostraver Township	11,625	12	0	1	7	4	545	38	495	12	3
Royersford	4,356	7	0	2	0	5	79	10	65	4	2
Rush Township	3,724	1	0	0	0	1	109	8	99	2	0
Rye Township	2,534	0	0	0	0	0	14	6	8	0	0
Sadsbury Township, Chester County	3,385	0	0	0	0	0	1	0	1	0	0
Salem Township, Luzerne County	4,114	8	0	0	0	8	54	9	45	0	0
Salisbury Township	14,057	9	0	2	2	5	320	30	275	15	0
Saltsburg	885	2	0	0	0	2	5	1	4	0	0
Sandy Township	11,550	14	0	2	0	12	259	37	209	13	0
Sankertown	622	0	0	0	0	0	1	1	0	0	0
Saxonburg	1,596	1	0	0	0	1	6	1	5	0	0
Saxton	755	0	0	0	0	0	0	0	0	0	0
Sayre	5,457	17	0	3	0	14	162	21	138	3	0
Schuylkill Haven	5,164	5	0	1	1	3	123	21	99	3	1
Scottdale	4,410	15	1	2	3	9	102	9	91	2	0
Scott Township, Allegheny County	15,850	51	0	1	5	45	241	35	199	7	0
Scott Township, Columbia County	5,033	2	0	0	0	2	46	7	39	0	0
Scott Township, Lackawanna County	4,928	0	0	0	0	0	7	2	1	4	0
Scranton	72,247	238	5	30	97	106	2,629	639	1,851	139	23
Selinsgrove	5,283	115	0	8	3	104	255	56	187	12	5
Seward	453	0	0	0	0	0	0	0	0	0	0
Sewickley	4,077	5	0	1	1	3	50	6	43	1	0
Sewickley Heights	916	0	0	0	0	0	0	0	0	0	0
Shaler Township	27,911	13	0	0	4	9	273	44	214	15	1
Shamokin Dam	1,438	1	0	1	0	0	30	0	29	1	1
Sharon	14,853	138	1	8	30	99	589	136	424	29	2
Sharon Hill	5,317	22	1	0	1	20	182	17	148	17	1
Sharpsburg	3,258	26	0	4	4	18	51	16	22	13	1
Sheffield Township	2,203	4	0	0	0	4	11	6	5	0	0
Shenandoah	5,157	26	1	1	9	15	218	65	145	8	7
Shillington	5,022	5	0	0	2	3	94	15	72	7	0
Shippensburg	5,611	3	0	1	1	1	82	15	64	3	0
Shippingport	219	0	0	0	0	0	2	0	2	0	0
Shiremanstown	1,469	2	0	0	0	2	5	2	3	0	0
Shohola Township	2,426	0	0	0	0	0	16	5	9	2	0
Silver Lake Township	1,732	1	0	0	0	1	12	2	9	1	0
Silver Spring Township	13,110	2	0	1	1	0	187	15	166	6	0
Sinking Spring	3,603	3	0	0	2	1	91	17	67	7	0
Slatington	4,405	9	0	0	0	9	90	18	71	1	0
Slippery Rock	3,320	2	0	1	0	1	48	9	39	0	0
Smethport	1,561	0	0	0	0	0	33	12	20	1	0
Solebury Township	8,795	2	0	1	0	1	72	26	45	1	0
Somerset	6,366	28	1	3	8	16	218	34	178	6	2
Souderton	6,553	26	0	2	3	21	108	12	94	2	0
South Abington Township	9,528	18	0	0	0	18	128	20	102	6	2
South Beaver Township	2,819	2	0	0	0	2	29	4	24	1	0
South Buffalo Township	2,794	0	0	0	0	0	19	1	15	3	1
South Centre Township	1,909	1	0	0	0	1	77	7	66	4	0
South Coatesville	1,078	7	0	1	0	6	15	5	7	3	0
South Connellsville Borough	2,153	4	0	0	0	4	13	3	9	1	0
Southern Regional Lancaster County	3,841	4	0	1	1	2	32	5	25	2	0
Southern Regional York County	10,007	11	1	4	4	2	336	41	289	6	1
South Fayette Township	13,213	38	0	0	1	37	90	4	82	4	1
South Fork	1,025	0	0	0	0	0	0	0	0	0	5
South Greensburg	2,219	1	0	1	0	0	39	11	28	0	0
South Heidelberg Township	7,264	10	0	0	2	8	75	12	60	3	0
South Heights	491	0	0	0	0	0	0	0	0	0	0
South Lebanon Township	8,637	4	0	0	0	4	97	23	74	0	0
South Londonderry Township	7,336	5	0	1	2	2	48	5	40	3	0
South Park Township	13,811	6	0	0	5	1	51	19	25	7	0
South Pymatuning Township	2,801	0	0	0	0	0	0	0	0	0	0
South Strabane Township	8,767	23	1	6	5	11	361	20	332	9	2
South Waverly	963	0	0	0	0	0	27	4	22	1	0
Southwestern Regional	18,269	11	0	1	2	8	167	25	139	3	3
Southwest Greensburg	2,200	6	0	0	1	5	49	7	41	1	0
Southwest Mercer County Regional	11,149	27	0	4	7	16	287	33	227	27	1
Southwest Regional	2,159	15	0	0	1	14	12	1	6	5	0
South Whitehall Township	19,679	43	0	3	11	29	686	73	599	14	2
South Williamsport	6,008	18	0	0	3	15	137	8	123	6	0
Spring City	3,407	8	0	2	1	5	92	33	57	2	1
Springdale	3,482	12	0	0	1	11	61	9	45	7	0

[1] The FBI does not publish arson data unless it receives data from either the agency or the state for all 12 months of the calendar year.

Table 8. Offenses Known to Law Enforcement, by State and City, 2008—*Continued*

(Number.)

State/City	Population	Violent crime	Murder and non-negligent man-slaughter	Forcible rape	Robbery	Aggravated assault	Property crime	Burglary	Larceny-theft	Motor vehicle theft	Arson[1]
PENNSYLVANIA—*Continued*											
Springettsbury Township	24,957	50	0	3	32	15	1,105	91	988	26	6
Springfield Township, Bucks County	5,084	1	0	0	0	1	51	8	42	1	1
Springfield Township, Montgomery County	18,843	13	0	0	3	10	246	18	219	9	1
Spring Garden Township	12,146	37	3	1	19	14	373	73	283	17	3
Spring Township, Berks County	26,765	15	0	1	8	6	352	49	285	18	1
Spring Township, Centre County	6,866	5	0	1	0	4	58	6	49	3	0
Spring Township, Snyder County	1,552	1	0	0	0	1	1	0	1	0	0
State College	54,065	44	0	6	12	26	983	144	828	11	11
St. Clair Boro	2,989	2	0	0	0	2	63	3	60	0	1
St. Clair Township	1,339	1	0	0	0	1	0	0	0	0	1
Steelton	5,590	38	1	2	23	12	231	42	180	9	3
St. Marys City	13,432	11	0	1	1	9	259	53	203	3	2
Stoneboro	1,013	2	0	0	0	2	4	0	3	1	0
Stonycreek Township	2,903	7	0	0	0	7	38	14	24	0	0
Strasburg	2,747	4	0	1	1	2	13	2	11	0	0
Stroud Area Regional	34,393	98	1	17	43	37	1,562	195	1,335	32	7
Sugarcreek	4,968	5	0	0	0	5	41	0	41	0	1
Sugarloaf Township, Luzerne County	4,053	4	0	0	2	2	213	17	195	1	0
Summerhill Township	2,576	0	0	0	0	0	24	2	22	0	1
Summit Hill	2,978	0	0	0	0	0	14	4	10	0	0
Summit Township	2,251	8	0	0	0	8	3	0	2	1	0
Sunbury	9,768	81	2	6	2	71	255	46	196	13	2
Susquehanna Depot	1,566	0	0	0	0	0	1	0	1	0	0
Susquehanna Regional	6,711	4	0	0	0	4	110	18	86	6	0
Susquehanna Township, Cambria County	2,039	3	0	0	0	3	6	0	5	1	0
Susquehanna Township, Dauphin County	22,920	43	0	5	18	20	446	70	353	23	3
Swarthmore	6,074	13	0	1	0	12	94	18	74	2	1
Swatara Township	22,413	155	0	0	41	114	695	130	542	23	8
Sweden Township	710	0	0	0	0	0	0	0	0	0	0
Swissvale	8,751	117	1	0	26	90	248	61	184	3	0
Swoyersville	7,605	18	0	0	2	16	146	33	112	1	1
Sykesville	1,167	0	0	0	0	0	0	0	0	0	0
Tamaqua	6,583	8	0	1	2	5	189	14	173	2	0
Tarentum	4,526	14	0	2	1	11	267	41	219	7	1
Tatamy	1,101	0	0	0	0	0	4	0	4	0	0
Telford	4,617	10	2	0	0	8	71	8	61	2	0
Terre Hill	1,247	3	0	1	2	0	22	5	16	1	1
Throop	4,056	15	0	3	0	12	67	14	49	4	0
Tidioute	717	1	0	1	0	0	3	0	3	0	0
Tilden Township	3,831	4	0	0	2	2	97	6	91	0	0
Tinicum Township, Bucks County	4,224	1	0	0	0	1	36	2	34	0	0
Tinicum Township, Delaware County	4,201	20	0	3	1	16	189	9	159	21	3
Titusville	5,751	12	0	4	0	8	151	23	121	7	0
Towamencin Township	17,601	15	0	2	5	8	231	29	196	6	3
Towanda	2,833	6	0	5	0	1	78	23	54	1	0
Trafford	3,008	7	0	0	0	7	50	6	43	1	0
Trainer	1,833	23	0	0	4	19	91	23	52	16	0
Tredyffrin Township	28,963	19	0	2	5	12	278	50	218	10	0
Troy	1,464	1	0	0	0	1	35	1	32	2	0
Tullytown	1,961	1	0	0	0	1	59	8	47	4	0
Tulpehocken Township	3,564	2	0	0	2	0	18	8	10	0	1
Tunkhannock	1,772	2	0	0	0	2	10	1	6	3	1
Tunkhannock Township, Wyoming County	4,285	5	0	0	0	5	68	17	49	2	1
Union Dale	342	0	0	0	0	0	0	0	0	0	0
Uniontown	11,670	71	0	4	47	20	425	102	292	31	1
Union Township, Lawrence County	5,025	11	0	0	8	3	115	12	100	3	0
Upland	2,868	32	0	6	2	24	60	17	40	3	0
Upper Burrell Township	2,128	0	0	0	0	0	20	2	18	0	0
Upper Chichester Township	17,705	55	0	2	15	38	739	83	604	52	4
Upper Darby Township	78,550	507	7	17	259	224	2,384	331	1,851	202	10
Upper Dublin Township	25,860	50	0	3	4	43	370	44	303	23	1
Upper Gwynedd Township	15,978	24	0	1	2	21	158	26	128	4	2
Upper Leacock Township	8,644	13	0	0	2	11	100	21	67	12	2
Upper Makefield Township	8,509	9	0	0	0	9	73	17	56	0	0
Upper Merion Township	26,457	35	0	1	15	19	1,474	88	1,344	42	0
Upper Moreland Township	24,166	28	0	1	6	21	510	58	439	13	2
Upper Nazareth Township	5,877	13	0	1	0	12	80	4	73	3	0
Upper Perkiomen	6,350	25	0	3	4	18	150	26	111	13	1
Upper Pottsgrove Township	5,201	12	0	0	0	12	61	6	48	7	0
Upper Providence Township, Delaware County	11,078	7	0	0	0	7	36	11	24	1	0
Upper Providence Township, Montgomery County	19,516	4	0	0	0	4	322	34	281	7	1
Upper Saucon Township	14,888	6	0	2	0	4	169	28	137	4	0
Upper Southampton Township	15,249	7	0	1	0	6	171	33	130	8	0
Upper St. Clair Township	18,812	10	0	2	4	4	100	14	84	2	0

[1] The FBI does not publish arson data unless it receives data from either the agency or the state for all 12 months of the calendar year.

Table 8. Offenses Known to Law Enforcement, by State and City, 2008—*Continued*

(Number.)

State/City	Population	Violent crime	Murder and non-negligent man-slaughter	Forcible rape	Robbery	Aggravated assault	Property crime	Burglary	Larceny-theft	Motor vehicle theft	Arson[1]
PENNSYLVANIA—*Continued*											
Upper Uwchlan Township	11,351	3	0	0	0	3	78	7	70	1	0
Upper Yoder Township	5,494	8	2	1	0	5	13	4	9	0	2
Uwchlan Township	18,715	15	0	1	3	11	304	54	245	5	5
Valley Township	6,609	9	0	0	1	8	18	5	13	0	0
Vandergrift	4,998	3	0	1	0	2	9	4	5	0	0
Vandling	703	0	0	0	0	0	7	1	6	0	2
Vernon Township	5,415	2	0	0	1	1	47	6	41	0	0
Verona	2,837	20	0	0	2	18	115	18	94	3	1
Vintondale	478	0	0	0	0	0	0	0	0	0	0
Walker Township	980	0	0	0	0	0	1	0	1	0	0
Walnutport	2,214	3	0	1	1	1	62	11	51	0	0
Wampum	625	2	0	0	0	2	6	2	4	0	0
Warminster Township	33,702	35	0	7	13	15	593	68	508	17	5
Warren	9,378	133	0	6	2	125	231	30	195	6	2
Warrington Township	23,162	51	0	5	4	42	318	26	273	19	3
Warwick Township, Bucks County	14,715	7	0	0	1	6	113	19	94	0	6
Warwick Township, Lancaster County	17,221	8	0	1	4	3	83	15	65	3	0
Washington, Washington County	14,586	186	1	18	63	104	834	121	618	95	13
Washington Township, Fayette County	4,158	13	0	0	0	13	51	17	32	2	0
Washington Township, Franklin County	11,893	15	1	4	1	9	310	34	266	10	4
Washington Township, Northampton County	4,897	0	0	0	0	0	69	16	49	4	1
Washington Township, Westmoreland County	7,360	13	0	0	2	11	57	15	42	0	0
Watsontown	2,090	6	0	1	1	4	62	6	56	0	2
Waymart	3,796	1	0	0	0	1	0	0	0	0	0
Waynesburg	4,169	4	0	1	2	1	108	21	82	5	0
Weatherly	2,604	17	0	0	0	17	59	19	36	4	1
Wellsboro	3,228	3	1	0	0	2	43	4	39	0	0
Wernersville	2,501	1	0	0	0	1	39	4	33	2	0
Wesleyville	3,301	7	0	0	1	6	48	6	41	1	1
West Alexander	300	0	0	0	0	0	2	1	1	0	0
West Brandywine Township	7,756	10	0	0	1	9	71	9	54	8	0
West Brownsville	1,021	0	0	0	0	0	2	2	0	0	0
West Caln Township	8,430	5	0	0	2	3	96	23	70	3	2
West Chester	18,273	112	0	17	47	48	477	79	358	40	3
West Cocalico Township	7,177	1	1	0	0	0	72	17	47	8	1
West Conshohocken	1,515	5	0	1	1	3	55	4	50	1	0
West Cornwall Township	1,992	4	0	0	0	4	2	0	2	0	0
West Deer Township	11,949	2	0	0	0	2	125	34	85	6	0
West Earl Township	7,724	4	0	2	2	0	93	17	68	8	0
West Fallowfield Township	2,596	0	0	0	0	0	14	4	10	0	0
Westfield	1,115	1	0	0	0	1	4	0	4	0	0
West Goshen Township	21,168	34	0	1	4	29	506	46	441	19	0
West Grove Borough	2,771	2	0	0	1	1	29	8	18	3	0
West Hazleton	3,313	9	0	1	2	6	151	27	107	17	0
West Hempfield Township	16,059	8	0	1	1	6	311	42	258	11	1
West Hills Regional	10,667	2	0	0	0	2	147	22	123	2	1
West Homestead	1,994	17	1	1	0	15	32	4	28	0	0
West Lampeter Township	15,609	5	0	1	1	3	176	17	153	6	2
West Lebanon Township	842	8	0	0	0	8	56	5	49	2	0
West Manchester Township	18,433	43	0	4	17	22	737	94	624	19	3
West Manheim Township	7,477	4	0	2	0	2	60	11	44	5	5
West Mayfield Borough	1,076	3	0	0	0	3	11	5	2	4	0
West Mead Township	5,075	0	0	0	0	0	0	0	0	0	0
West Newton	2,849	7	0	0	2	5	64	8	56	0	0
West Norriton Township	14,533	34	0	6	4	24	361	51	301	9	2
West Pikeland Township	4,069	1	0	0	0	1	66	9	57	0	0
West Pike Run	1,834	0	0	0	0	0	11	3	6	2	0
West Pittston	4,913	9	0	1	2	6	127	31	90	6	2
West Pottsgrove Township	3,777	17	1	2	3	11	150	18	121	11	1
West Reading	4,050	24	0	3	4	17	259	35	207	17	0
West Sadsbury Township	2,501	3	0	1	0	2	84	0	82	2	0
West Salem Township	3,334	8	0	2	0	6	38	11	27	0	0
West Shore Regional	6,621	17	0	0	2	15	36	28	4	4	1
Westtown-East Goshen Regional	31,632	24	1	2	1	20	381	49	317	15	0
West View	6,669	8	0	0	2	6	178	6	165	7	0
West Vincent Township	4,251	1	1	0	0	0	41	9	30	2	0
West Whiteland Township	18,190	15	0	2	8	5	533	33	488	12	2
West Wyoming	2,689	4	0	0	0	4	55	9	41	5	0
West York	4,210	16	0	0	9	7	87	29	50	8	0
Whitaker Borough	1,214	8	0	0	8	0	42	11	26	5	0
Whitehall	13,379	7	0	3	0	4	62	5	52	5	0
Whitehall Township	27,037	40	0	3	23	14	1,410	122	1,250	38	8
White Haven Borough	1,144	2	0	0	0	2	11	3	6	2	0
Whitemarsh Township	17,634	16	0	1	1	14	271	28	233	10	3

[1] The FBI does not publish arson data unless it receives data from either the agency or the state for all 12 months of the calendar year.

Table 8. Offenses Known to Law Enforcement, by State and City, 2008—*Continued*

(Number.)

State/City	Population	Violent crime	Murder and non-negligent man-slaughter	Forcible rape	Robbery	Aggravated assault	Property crime	Burglary	Larceny-theft	Motor vehicle theft	Arson[1]
PENNSYLVANIA—*Continued*											
White Oak	7,995	10	0	1	3	6	70	9	54	7	0
White Township	1,309	4	0	1	0	3	16	7	6	3	0
Whitpain Township	18,800	19	0	3	6	10	221	37	178	6	0
Wiconisco Township	1,106	0	0	0	0	0	4	0	4	0	0
Wilkes-Barre	40,976	180	2	17	104	57	1,521	250	1,170	101	6
Wilkes-Barre Township	3,045	4	0	0	2	2	764	12	745	7	2
Wilkinsburg	17,504	184	2	11	65	106	628	261	279	88	11
Wilkins Township	6,298	7	0	0	3	4	120	10	106	4	1
Williamsburg	1,251	2	0	0	0	2	20	2	17	1	0
Williamsport	29,380	99	2	5	51	41	1,174	269	849	56	9
Willistown Township	10,755	5	0	1	0	4	62	9	51	2	0
Windber	4,025	10	0	1	0	9	36	9	24	3	2
Wind Gap	2,791	7	0	1	1	5	53	2	50	1	0
Womelsdorf	2,824	3	0	0	1	2	37	6	26	5	0
Woodward Township	2,265	0	0	0	0	0	4	4	0	0	0
Wrightsville	2,260	5	0	0	0	5	22	4	18	0	0
Wright Township	5,885	1	0	1	0	0	79	5	74	0	0
Wyoming	3,003	4	0	0	2	2	113	20	89	4	0
Wyomissing	10,448	14	0	2	7	5	503	26	460	17	1
Yardley	2,502	2	0	0	0	2	12	2	7	3	0
Yeadon	11,385	81	2	5	31	43	330	110	179	41	2
York	40,221	473	11	27	322	113	2,150	462	1,440	248	19
York Area Regional	58,148	111	1	17	17	76	752	163	566	23	3
Youngsville	1,666	4	0	1	0	3	9	0	9	0	0
Zelienople	3,926	14	0	1	0	13	78	5	69	4	0
RHODE ISLAND											
Barrington	16,272	2	0	1	0	1	219	36	181	2	3
Bristol	22,387	12	0	1	2	9	450	61	368	21	4
Burrillville	16,465	9	0	1	1	7	159	31	119	9	2
Central Falls	18,667	109	3	18	23	65	493	121	266	106	5
Charlestown	8,087	8	0	2	0	6	119	30	88	1	1
Coventry	34,342	27	0	5	3	19	644	121	501	22	12
Cranston	79,987	136	1	16	55	64	2,184	331	1,605	248	8
Cumberland	34,359	31	1	5	10	15	506	99	359	48	7
East Greenwich	13,294	5	0	1	3	1	199	35	156	8	2
East Providence	48,413	70	0	10	16	44	782	136	587	59	13
Foster	4,505	1	0	0	0	1	48	24	24	0	0
Glocester	10,528	7	0	0	0	7	64	15	45	4	2
Hopkinton	7,961	6	0	4	0	2	109	23	81	5	2
Jamestown	5,458	2	0	0	0	2	87	10	72	5	0
Johnston	28,515	27	0	6	4	17	626	94	469	63	5
Lincoln	22,075	34	0	4	7	23	470	55	380	35	1
Little Compton	3,500	3	0	0	1	2	60	23	37	0	0
Middletown	16,004	13	0	5	2	6	361	56	294	11	1
Narragansett	16,399	13	1	2	1	9	320	63	246	11	1
Newport	25,030	121	0	16	20	85	1,091	229	828	34	6
New Shoreham	1,014	0	0	0	0	0	85	3	77	5	0
North Kingstown	26,547	24	0	4	4	16	490	115	346	29	5
North Providence	32,689	45	0	5	9	31	478	132	291	55	4
North Smithfield	11,292	5	0	0	0	5	191	31	141	19	2
Pawtucket	71,712	268	3	25	109	131	2,498	653	1,477	368	19
Portsmouth	16,879	16	0	5	0	11	290	55	228	7	5
Providence	170,965	1,162	12	44	498	608	9,063	1,875	5,701	1,487	31
Richmond	7,652	3	0	0	1	2	123	20	100	3	0
Scituate	10,853	1	0	0	0	1	126	20	98	8	1
Smithfield	21,198	9	1	3	0	5	289	33	243	13	4
South Kingstown	29,218	22	0	2	8	12	355	72	273	10	2
Tiverton	14,935	9	0	1	0	8	352	85	245	22	0
Warren	10,965	15	0	4	1	10	227	35	176	16	2
Warwick	84,326	83	0	19	21	43	2,737	300	2,291	146	21
Westerly	23,276	27	0	5	4	18	531	79	425	27	3
West Greenwich	6,527	1	0	0	0	1	97	17	76	4	3
West Warwick	29,029	57	3	13	12	29	675	122	504	49	8
Woonsocket	43,301	181	2	28	58	93	1,394	368	902	124	12
SOUTH CAROLINA											
Abbeville	5,529	83	0	4	2	77	144	23	111	10	0
Aiken	29,630	157	1	9	49	98	1,377	219	1,085	73	3
Allendale	3,664	46	0	1	9	36	197	84	103	10	2
Anderson	26,498	195	4	14	62	115	1,837	341	1,344	152	12
Andrews	2,940	21	1	0	4	16	221	44	162	15	0
Atlantic Beach	395	12	0	1	4	7	21	6	13	2	0
Aynor	588	30	0	0	1	29	31	7	22	2	0
Bamberg	3,432	35	0	2	7	26	184	51	128	5	0
Barnwell	4,785	52	0	0	12	40	389	118	259	12	1

[1] The FBI does not publish arson data unless it receives data from either the agency or the state for all 12 months of the calendar year.

Table 8. Offenses Known to Law Enforcement, by State and City, 2008—*Continued*

(Number.)

State/City	Population	Violent crime	Murder and non-negligent man-slaughter	Forcible rape	Robbery	Aggravated assault	Property crime	Burglary	Larceny-theft	Motor vehicle theft	Arson[1]
SOUTH CAROLINA—*Continued*											
Batesburg-Leesville	5,545	47	0	3	9	35	300	67	210	23	0
Beaufort	11,772	171	0	7	41	123	837	162	641	34	2
Belton	4,639	24	1	1	3	19	126	19	103	4	0
Bennettsville	8,854	181	2	4	27	148	574	119	441	14	6
Bishopville	3,918	38	1	1	2	34	244	42	190	12	0
Blacksburg	1,900	17	0	0	4	13	154	30	119	5	0
Blackville	2,841	29	0	0	13	16	126	39	79	8	0
Bluffton	4,386	49	0	3	16	30	366	66	287	13	5
Branchville	1,034	4	0	0	1	3	10	4	5	1	1
Brunson	573	0	0	0	0	0	1	0	1	0	0
Burnettown	2,658	2	0	0	0	2	31	5	21	5	0
Calhoun Falls	2,178	14	0	1	1	12	58	13	41	4	0
Camden	7,073	82	0	0	11	71	473	117	325	31	0
Cameron	411	0	0	0	0	0	3	0	2	1	0
Campobello	596	0	0	0	0	0	0	0	0	0	0
Cayce	12,605	123	0	12	32	79	833	164	611	58	4
Central	4,147	21	0	2	3	16	179	33	137	9	0
Chapin	704	12	0	0	2	10	44	5	38	1	0
Charleston	111,645	800	14	60	288	438	4,535	724	3,399	412	19
Cheraw	5,397	44	0	3	6	35	404	43	351	10	1
Chesnee	1,069	6	0	1	0	5	74	12	57	5	0
Chester	5,988	102	2	4	33	63	347	105	218	24	5
Chesterfield	1,308	4	0	0	2	2	48	10	35	3	0
Clemson	12,941	43	0	4	3	36	308	48	243	17	2
Clinton	8,930	124	0	8	25	91	560	141	401	18	1
Clio	727	1	0	0	0	1	17	4	13	0	0
Clover	4,772	112	0	1	1	110	173	34	134	5	1
Columbia	125,485	1,079	13	56	334	676	6,825	1,182	4,998	645	25
Cottageville	680	2	0	1	0	1	27	11	13	3	0
Cowpens	2,391	16	0	1	5	10	145	55	82	8	0
Darlington	6,598	136	1	7	9	119	663	154	484	25	2
Denmark	3,002	32	2	0	7	23	97	33	58	6	1
Due West	1,269	5	0	1	1	3	21	2	19	0	0
Duncan	3,058	27	0	0	4	23	125	24	93	8	0
Edgefield	4,412	19	0	2	2	15	94	11	78	5	0
Edisto Beach	722	3	0	0	1	2	60	11	47	2	0
Elgin	1,114	4	0	0	0	4	39	3	34	2	0
Elloree	696	4	0	0	1	3	11	1	10	0	0
Estill	2,332	42	1	0	5	36	106	39	66	1	1
Eutawville	328	3	1	0	2	0	19	3	16	0	0
Fairfax	3,094	17	0	1	3	13	34	20	13	1	0
Florence	31,508	533	8	27	111	387	3,088	526	2,374	188	16
Folly Beach	2,359	15	0	3	0	12	209	29	168	12	0
Forest Acres	9,889	72	0	0	29	43	639	109	501	29	1
Fort Lawn	803	6	0	0	0	6	76	32	40	4	0
Fountain Inn	7,560	42	0	4	3	35	142	19	107	16	1
Gaffney	12,942	125	0	8	27	90	812	159	584	69	4
Georgetown	8,470	172	1	3	22	146	780	146	590	44	2
Goose Creek	37,227	111	0	4	30	77	755	147	548	60	7
Great Falls	2,023	40	0	1	10	29	170	41	123	6	2
Greeleyville	397	11	0	0	3	8	24	9	15	0	0
Greenville	59,038	592	2	21	157	412	3,705	659	2,681	365	10
Greenwood	22,399	277	0	6	38	233	1,673	355	1,263	55	5
Greer	24,220	121	1	6	23	91	768	132	553	83	3
Hampton	2,766	12	0	1	2	9	120	37	75	8	0
Hanahan	15,950	79	0	7	17	55	610	140	413	57	2
Hardeeville	1,947	38	1	2	14	21	216	30	174	12	0
Harleyville	687	3	0	0	2	1	36	12	22	2	0
Hartsville	7,419	235	1	7	34	193	1,165	248	876	41	3
Hemingway	499	3	0	1	2	0	83	24	50	9	0
Holly Hill	1,344	9	0	0	3	6	94	44	45	5	0
Honea Path	3,649	46	0	1	4	41	215	47	153	15	2
Inman	1,963	11	0	2	1	8	78	8	64	6	0
Irmo	11,584	42	1	1	13	27	319	57	251	11	0
Isle of Palms	4,686	8	0	0	1	7	197	71	111	15	0
Iva	1,193	1	0	0	1	0	12	2	6	4	0
Jackson	1,642	5	0	1	0	4	33	9	23	1	0
Jamestown	100	0	0	0	0	0	1	0	1	0	0
Johnsonville	1,452	7	0	0	2	5	52	11	37	4	0
Johnston	2,331	22	0	2	3	17	125	22	90	13	0
Jonesville	893	1	0	0	0	1	29	8	18	3	1
Kingstree	3,243	28	0	0	10	18	303	66	220	17	0
Lake City	6,689	109	0	10	14	85	513	113	361	39	3
Lamar	987	13	0	0	0	13	37	10	21	6	1

[1] The FBI does not publish arson data unless it receives data from either the agency or the state for all 12 months of the calendar year.

Table 8. Offenses Known to Law Enforcement, by State and City, 2008—*Continued*

(Number.)

State/City	Population	Violent crime	Murder and non-negligent man-slaughter	Forcible rape	Robbery	Aggravated assault	Property crime	Burglary	Larceny-theft	Motor vehicle theft	Arson[1]
SOUTH CAROLINA—*Continued*											
Lancaster	9,913	222	3	6	31	182	653	167	447	39	4
Landrum	2,583	7	0	1	0	6	88	15	70	3	0
Latta	1,483	51	0	0	8	43	86	17	62	7	0
Laurens	9,706	139	0	2	26	111	689	181	481	27	1
Lexington	15,673	46	0	3	14	29	551	53	479	19	0
Liberty	3,057	8	0	1	1	6	159	25	120	14	0
Loris	2,330	23	0	0	5	18	114	19	91	4	0
Lyman	2,842	12	0	1	3	8	93	12	73	8	0
Manning	3,937	56	0	5	13	38	324	63	247	14	2
Marion	6,782	94	1	1	19	73	585	148	398	39	0
Mauldin	20,891	74	0	5	18	51	490	74	384	32	3
McColl	2,327	25	2	0	1	22	118	45	67	6	3
McCormick	2,677	36	0	1	1	34	71	15	53	3	0
Moncks Corner	6,996	59	0	3	15	41	426	92	297	37	1
Mount Pleasant	67,027	215	0	17	32	166	1,404	202	1,114	88	1
Mullins	4,689	69	1	2	17	49	588	199	364	25	3
Myrtle Beach	30,850	532	2	37	217	276	4,834	782	3,587	465	7
Newberry	10,942	49	0	1	12	36	504	77	416	11	1
New Ellenton	2,231	23	0	0	7	16	100	39	51	10	2
Ninety Six	1,916	12	0	1	1	10	43	8	34	1	0
North	775	5	0	0	0	5	34	7	26	1	0
North Augusta	20,616	62	2	5	26	29	1,005	145	790	70	1
North Charleston	92,749	1,375	14	69	570	722	6,705	1,202	4,721	782	20
North Myrtle Beach	16,073	78	2	6	28	42	1,733	350	1,348	35	2
Orangeburg	12,755	112	0	8	39	65	866	209	594	63	5
Pacolet	2,790	8	1	0	1	6	81	17	57	7	1
Pageland	2,509	42	0	1	4	37	184	36	142	6	3
Pamplico	1,153	10	0	0	1	9	13	6	6	1	0
Pawleys Island	141	0	0	0	0	0	26	4	22	0	0
Pelion	597	1	0	0	0	1	42	1	40	1	0
Pickens	3,006	15	0	1	2	12	141	26	109	6	1
Pine Ridge	1,775	4	0	0	0	4	13	4	9	0	0
Port Royal	10,331	35	0	4	7	24	274	49	210	15	0
Prosperity	1,060	8	0	2	1	5	31	6	24	1	0
Ridgeland	2,632	36	1	2	15	18	192	23	156	13	0
Ridgeville	2,076	0	0	0	0	0	0	0	0	0	0
Rock Hill	66,906	749	4	43	102	600	2,970	596	2,137	237	19
Salem	132	0	0	0	0	0	4	0	4	0	0
Saluda	2,920	56	0	0	4	52	84	7	71	6	0
Santee	712	20	0	1	9	10	81	14	61	6	0
Scranton	996	1	0	0	0	1	24	5	18	1	0
Simpsonville	17,033	111	0	4	13	94	794	134	618	42	5
Society Hill	683	1	0	0	0	1	14	4	9	1	0
South Congaree	2,385	7	0	0	1	6	63	15	43	5	0
Spartanburg	38,726	802	6	23	203	570	3,572	953	2,352	267	38
Springdale	2,916	9	0	0	2	7	112	8	90	14	0
Springfield	481	2	0	0	1	1	6	1	2	3	0
St. George	2,108	8	0	1	1	6	119	29	84	6	0
St. Matthews	1,965	33	0	3	4	26	104	18	81	5	0
St. Stephen	1,756	6	1	0	0	5	100	22	73	5	0
Sullivans Island	1,874	1	0	0	0	1	50	16	33	1	0
Summerton	1,023	36	0	0	8	28	89	27	58	4	2
Summerville	46,405	163	1	8	57	97	1,511	164	1,204	143	1
Sumter	38,547	577	5	13	129	430	2,745	674	1,852	219	14
Surfside Beach	4,782	18	0	2	6	10	326	79	196	51	0
Swansea	790	6	0	0	1	5	43	6	35	2	0
Tega Cay	4,799	10	0	1	0	9	71	14	55	2	0
Timmonsville	2,381	44	0	1	7	36	195	67	110	18	2
Travelers Rest	4,523	8	1	0	3	4	230	24	195	11	2
Turbeville	704	9	0	1	6	2	34	16	16	2	0
Union	7,999	127	2	3	15	107	409	98	302	9	7
Wagener	874	12	0	2	2	8	54	22	30	2	0
Walhalla	3,626	35	1	4	1	29	150	36	107	7	0
Walterboro	5,777	115	0	4	37	74	629	78	512	39	5
Ware Shoals	2,343	11	0	1	0	10	111	20	88	3	0
Wellford	2,330	10	0	1	2	7	73	14	50	9	0
West Columbia	13,983	176	2	8	46	120	1,032	139	828	65	1
Westminster	2,658	27	0	0	1	26	117	32	83	2	0
West Pelzer	909	2	0	0	1	1	24	4	15	5	0
Whitmire	1,528	6	0	2	0	4	36	7	28	1	0
Williamston	3,936	34	0	1	12	21	121	25	86	10	1
Williston	3,194	8	0	0	3	5	102	25	70	7	1
Winnsboro	3,545	52	0	6	3	43	283	46	228	9	1

[1] The FBI does not publish arson data unless it receives data from either the agency or the state for all 12 months of the calendar year.

Table 8. Offenses Known to Law Enforcement, by State and City, 2008—*Continued*

(Number.)

State/City	Population	Violent crime	Murder and non-negligent man-slaughter	Forcible rape	Robbery	Aggravated assault	Property crime	Burglary	Larceny-theft	Motor vehicle theft	Arson[1]
SOUTH CAROLINA—*Continued*											
Woodruff	4,065	20	0	4	1	15	183	49	122	12	0
Yemassee	866	1	0	0	0	1	21	2	18	1	0
York	7,834	108	2	6	21	79	376	84	276	16	1
SOUTH DAKOTA											
Aberdeen	24,382	45	0	19	3	23	503	91	389	23	7
Armour	659	2	0	2	0	0	5	4	1	0	0
Avon	518	0	0	0	0	0	0	0	0	0	0
Belle Fourche	4,926	11	0	2	0	9	60	15	42	3	1
Bonesteel	253	0	0	0	0	0	0	0	0	0	0
Box Elder	3,312	7	0	2	1	4	83	11	67	5	0
Brandon	7,445	2	0	0	0	2	51	2	49	0	0
Brookings	19,546	10	0	6	0	4	248	23	211	14	0
Burke	565	0	0	0	0	0	0	0	0	0	0
Canton	4,275	4	0	2	0	2	41	8	30	3	1
Centerville	843	1	0	0	0	1	0	0	0	0	0
Chamberlain	2,249	12	0	1	0	11	37	7	24	6	1
Deadwood	1,283	0	0	0	0	0	48	2	38	8	0
Delmont	216	0	0	0	0	0	0	0	0	0	0
Eagle Butte	953	0	0	0	0	0	14	4	10	0	0
Estelline	662	0	0	0	0	0	8	1	7	0	0
Eureka	927	0	0	0	0	0	0	0	0	0	0
Freeman	1,182	0	0	0	0	0	0	0	0	0	0
Gettysburg	1,061	1	0	0	0	1	7	2	5	0	0
Hermosa	355	0	0	0	0	0	0	0	0	0	0
Hot Springs	4,040	2	0	0	0	2	49	19	29	1	0
Hoven	395	0	0	0	0	0	0	0	0	0	0
Irene	401	0	0	0	0	0	2	1	1	0	0
Jefferson	596	0	0	0	0	0	1	0	1	0	0
Kadoka	647	1	0	0	0	1	2	0	2	0	0
Kimball	682	0	0	0	0	0	0	0	0	0	0
Lead	2,874	1	0	0	0	1	12	3	9	0	0
Lemmon	1,167	2	0	1	0	1	11	4	6	1	0
Lennox	2,846	3	0	0	0	3	7	1	6	0	0
Leola	382	0	0	0	0	0	0	0	0	0	0
Madison	6,294	2	0	0	0	2	107	14	91	2	0
Martin	1,002	4	0	0	0	4	3	2	1	0	0
McIntosh	208	0	0	0	0	0	0	0	0	0	0
Menno	664	0	0	0	0	0	0	0	0	0	0
Mitchell	14,861	35	0	7	2	26	476	59	397	20	8
Mobridge	3,086	5	0	1	0	4	74	9	63	2	0
New Effington	224	0	0	0	0	0	0	0	0	0	0
North Sioux City	2,549	4	0	0	0	4	45	1	44	0	0
Parkston	1,489	0	0	0	0	0	3	0	3	0	0
Pierre	14,051	46	0	14	3	29	527	83	389	55	5
Rapid City	64,556	346	2	73	50	221	2,572	392	2,035	145	22
Rosholt	428	0	0	0	0	0	0	0	0	0	0
Scotland	792	0	0	0	0	0	0	0	0	0	0
Sioux Falls	155,110	522	5	130	46	341	3,937	659	3,030	248	38
Sisseton	2,447	9	0	1	0	8	16	1	12	3	0
Spearfish	10,144	12	2	8	0	2	283	66	203	14	0
Springfield	1,490	0	0	0	0	0	0	0	0	0	0
Sturgis	5,937	10	0	1	0	9	144	23	116	5	0
Summerset	451	0	0	0	0	0	0	0	0	0	0
Tripp	633	0	0	0	0	0	0	0	0	0	0
Tyndall	1,103	0	0	0	0	0	0	0	0	0	0
Vermillion	10,251	7	0	0	1	6	112	15	92	5	2
Viborg	771	3	0	0	0	3	1	1	0	0	0
Wagner	1,545	1	0	1	0	0	1	1	0	0	0
Watertown	20,565	35	0	17	0	18	579	71	462	46	8
Wilmot	512	0	0	0	0	0	0	0	0	0	0
Winner	2,768	5	0	0	0	5	31	4	24	3	0
Yankton[4]	13,660	18	1	4	1	12	357	60	285	12	0
TENNESSEE											
Adamsville	2,118	9	0	0	1	8	58	11	40	7	0
Alamo	2,317	10	0	1	2	7	43	18	25	0	0
Alcoa	8,625	116	1	3	18	94	512	79	401	32	6
Alexandria	872	1	0	0	0	1	15	10	4	1	0
Algood	3,366	17	0	0	1	16	130	16	108	6	0
Ardmore	1,151	11	0	0	0	11	36	7	27	2	0
Ashland City	4,658	18	0	2	0	16	245	41	199	5	1
Athens	14,237	194	0	5	34	155	1,239	282	914	43	7
Atoka	7,500	10	0	1	1	8	148	25	119	4	0
Baileyton	494	0	0	0	0	0	18	3	14	1	0
Baneberry	470	0	0	0	0	0	0	0	0	0	0

[1] The FBI does not publish arson data unless it receives data from either the agency or the state for all 12 months of the calendar year.
[4] Because of changes in the state/local agency's reporting practices, figures are not comparable to previous years' data.

Table 8. Offenses Known to Law Enforcement, by State and City, 2008—*Continued*

(Number.)

State/City	Population	Violent crime	Murder and non-negligent man-slaughter	Forcible rape	Robbery	Aggravated assault	Property crime	Burglary	Larceny-theft	Motor vehicle theft	Arson[1]
TENNESSEE—*Continued*											
Bartlett	48,044	126	1	4	17	104	1,047	189	802	56	2
Baxter	1,379	7	0	1	0	6	44	11	31	2	1
Belle Meade	3,454	2	0	0	0	2	23	6	16	1	0
Bells	2,252	12	0	1	0	11	58	25	27	6	0
Benton	1,119	4	0	0	0	4	35	9	23	3	0
Berry Hill	745	6	0	0	2	4	93	9	70	14	0
Bethel Springs	775	0	0	0	0	0	9	2	7	0	0
Big Sandy	511	3	0	0	0	3	6	3	3	0	0
Blaine	1,757	1	0	0	0	1	7	2	4	1	0
Bluff City	1,618	2	1	0	0	1	66	17	48	1	0
Bolivar	5,586	54	0	4	9	41	402	97	275	30	6
Bradford	1,059	2	0	0	0	2	19	2	13	4	0
Brentwood	36,341	30	0	6	4	20	459	96	350	13	1
Brighton	2,672	7	0	0	0	7	39	8	29	2	0
Bristol	25,485	124	7	11	7	99	1,328	176	1,053	99	6
Bruceton	1,453	3	0	0	0	3	12	1	11	0	0
Burns	1,409	1	0	1	0	0	28	7	19	2	0
Calhoun	522	4	0	1	0	3	11	4	7	0	0
Camden	3,662	6	0	0	1	5	198	31	160	7	1
Carthage	2,224	12	0	0	1	11	79	16	59	4	1
Caryville	2,395	32	0	2	5	25	106	40	58	8	0
Celina	1,345	5	0	0	0	5	18	6	12	0	0
Centerville	3,998	3	0	0	1	2	104	26	74	4	0
Chapel Hill	1,317	13	0	0	0	13	28	12	14	2	0
Chattanooga	171,611	1,875	20	63	511	1,281	12,864	2,843	8,937	1,084	16
Church Hill	6,771	8	0	2	0	6	135	27	103	5	0
Clarksburg	372	0	0	0	0	0	3	3	0	0	0
Clarksville	121,386	953	6	59	209	679	4,693	1,386	3,045	262	21
Cleveland	39,420	453	1	17	44	391	2,306	432	1,783	91	10
Clifton	2,693	1	0	0	0	1	14	4	8	2	0
Clinton	9,554	50	0	0	4	46	523	110	383	30	6
Collegedale	7,599	8	0	1	2	5	325	33	284	8	0
Collierville	40,001	70	1	5	15	49	801	110	660	31	2
Collinwood	1,017	0	0	0	0	0	4	0	2	2	0
Columbia	34,080	421	7	18	69	327	1,657	459	1,127	71	16
Cookeville	29,276	133	1	18	26	88	1,758	357	1,326	75	5
Coopertown	3,356	7	0	0	1	6	46	18	24	4	0
Copperhill	447	5	0	0	1	4	15	8	6	1	1
Cornersville	953	2	0	0	0	2	10	1	6	3	0
Covington	9,175	91	0	1	15	75	504	148	338	18	1
Cowan	1,736	4	0	1	0	3	61	9	43	9	1
Cross Plains	1,647	3	0	0	0	3	25	5	17	3	0
Crossville	11,563	106	1	11	10	84	951	238	664	49	1
Crump	1,453	18	0	0	1	17	79	24	55	0	0
Cumberland City	327	12	0	0	0	12	14	5	9	0	0
Cumberland Gap	202	0	0	0	0	0	7	2	4	1	0
Dandridge	2,619	9	0	1	2	6	119	13	97	9	0
Dayton	6,676	22	1	1	3	17	350	78	259	13	2
Decatur	1,463	2	0	0	0	2	65	13	50	2	0
Decaturville	822	0	0	0	0	0	3	3	0	0	0
Decherd	2,135	10	0	0	0	10	59	12	42	5	0
Dickson	13,861	96	0	4	11	81	831	85	704	42	2
Dover	1,592	4	0	0	0	4	22	2	18	2	0
Dresden	2,605	14	0	0	1	13	64	14	50	0	0
Dyer	2,397	2	0	0	0	2	25	9	15	1	0
Dyersburg	17,222	156	2	13	32	109	1,340	323	946	71	3
East Ridge	19,630	174	1	8	33	132	1,297	358	863	76	5
Elizabethton	13,909	77	0	3	7	67	748	127	587	34	8
Elkton	605	2	0	0	1	1	12	2	7	3	0
Englewood	1,741	6	0	0	0	6	46	10	31	5	0
Erin	1,449	6	0	0	1	5	38	5	33	0	0
Erwin	5,805	8	0	2	2	4	132	15	114	3	0
Estill Springs	2,265	5	0	1	0	4	41	8	32	1	0
Ethridge	555	0	0	0	0	0	11	2	7	2	0
Etowah	3,768	31	0	2	2	27	191	35	139	17	3
Fairview	7,917	23	1	1	1	20	132	28	89	15	0
Fayetteville	7,102	63	1	2	9	51	406	61	336	9	3
Franklin	58,997	116	1	13	18	84	908	142	739	27	2
Friendship	594	1	0	0	0	1	14	1	11	2	0
Gadsden	537	2	0	0	0	2	10	4	4	2	0
Gainesboro	836	2	0	0	0	2	24	3	18	3	0
Gallatin	29,507	125	1	9	23	92	614	90	489	35	5
Gallaway	707	12	0	0	0	12	34	8	24	2	0

[1] The FBI does not publish arson data unless it receives data from either the agency or the state for all 12 months of the calendar year.

Table 8. Offenses Known to Law Enforcement, by State and City, 2008—*Continued*

(Number.)

State/City	Population	Violent crime	Murder and non-negligent man-slaughter	Forcible rape	Robbery	Aggravated assault	Property crime	Burglary	Larceny-theft	Motor vehicle theft	Arson[1]
TENNESSEE—*Continued*											
Gates	847	2	0	0	1	1	11	9	1	1	0
Gatlinburg	5,755	37	0	6	6	25	569	243	306	20	4
Germantown	41,160	26	0	3	5	18	610	114	484	12	7
Gibson	399	0	0	0	0	0	17	5	9	3	0
Gleason	1,387	10	0	0	0	10	39	10	24	5	1
Goodlettsville	16,781	89	0	5	21	63	799	132	614	53	0
Gordonsville	1,316	6	0	0	0	6	32	8	23	1	0
Grand Junction	307	2	0	0	0	2	7	2	4	1	0
Graysville	1,427	9	0	0	1	8	27	2	22	3	1
Greenbrier	6,575	31	0	0	1	30	133	33	95	5	0
Greenfield	2,019	11	0	1	1	9	37	7	29	1	0
Halls	2,181	12	0	0	1	11	64	17	42	5	0
Harriman	6,659	44	0	7	7	30	339	86	227	26	3
Henderson	6,374	28	0	0	4	24	230	39	187	4	1
Hendersonville	47,819	189	0	24	24	141	1,146	166	919	61	3
Henning	1,276	17	0	0	1	16	50	25	22	3	0
Henry	548	2	0	0	0	2	10	3	7	0	0
Hohenwald	3,822	27	0	2	2	23	123	29	88	6	0
Hollow Rock	938	1	0	0	0	1	16	3	13	0	0
Hornbeak	418	1	0	0	0	1	1	1	0	0	0
Humboldt	9,072	74	1	5	13	55	578	130	409	39	10
Huntingdon	4,132	7	0	0	2	5	126	32	92	2	0
Huntland	870	0	0	0	0	0	23	13	10	0	1
Jacksboro	2,054	12	0	0	1	11	275	21	253	1	0
Jackson	63,620	707	7	28	244	428	4,630	1,093	3,124	413	17
Jamestown	1,899	9	0	0	1	8	160	31	123	6	2
Jasper	3,107	15	0	0	0	15	63	13	44	6	0
Jefferson City	8,127	31	0	3	3	25	501	70	407	24	0
Jellico	2,528	13	0	0	5	8	166	26	129	11	0
Johnson City	61,690	309	0	20	51	238	2,849	535	2,203	111	15
Jonesborough	5,165	6	0	0	1	5	66	11	54	1	0
Kenton	1,294	4	0	0	0	4	13	6	7	0	0
Kimball	1,399	8	0	0	0	8	95	3	83	9	1
Kingsport	44,350	374	2	18	53	301	2,764	542	2,083	139	25
Kingston Springs	2,941	0	0	0	0	0	39	3	34	2	0
Knoxville	184,559	1,992	28	140	668	1,156	12,186	2,661	8,383	1,142	101
Lafayette	4,383	15	1	0	1	13	85	27	54	4	0
La Follette	8,195	82	1	2	6	73	604	200	370	34	3
La Grange	146	0	0	0	0	0	1	0	0	1	0
Lake City	1,837	2	0	0	0	2	133	23	100	10	1
Lakewood	2,594	9	0	1	2	6	44	18	16	10	0
La Vergne	30,638	182	0	7	20	155	864	248	539	77	3
Lawrenceburg	10,784	122	1	5	13	103	565	111	430	24	3
Lebanon	24,599	186	2	9	37	138	1,106	167	860	79	11
Lenoir City	7,978	75	0	5	5	65	466	70	366	30	1
Lewisburg	10,888	73	0	2	6	65	345	87	235	23	2
Livingston	3,553	31	0	0	1	30	105	32	72	1	1
Lookout Mountain	1,863	1	0	0	0	1	12	1	11	0	0
Loretto	1,706	8	0	0	0	8	15	3	12	0	0
Loudon	4,850	18	0	0	4	14	70	8	59	3	0
Lynnville	335	0	0	0	0	0	0	0	0	0	0
Madisonville	4,638	20	0	2	4	14	250	44	193	13	0
Martin	10,080	46	0	7	3	36	447	67	370	10	0
Maryville	27,259	52	0	5	13	34	774	189	545	40	2
Mason	1,216	10	0	0	0	10	32	6	23	3	0
Maury City	692	2	0	0	1	1	13	5	8	0	0
Maynardville	1,899	6	0	0	0	6	82	10	62	10	0
McEwen	1,658	5	0	0	2	3	14	4	8	2	0
McKenzie	5,405	19	1	1	4	13	253	62	183	8	0
McMinnville	13,251	68	0	11	7	50	613	108	465	40	0
Medina	2,022	6	0	0	1	5	27	11	14	2	1
Memphis	672,046	12,937	138	366	4,787	7,646	53,839	15,874	32,548	5,417	190
Middleton	614	0	0	0	0	0	18	5	11	2	1
Milan	7,854	50	0	4	2	44	311	85	213	13	1
Millersville	6,361	15	0	0	3	12	117	37	72	8	2
Millington	10,282	104	1	7	18	78	599	97	467	35	1
Minor Hill	447	2	0	0	0	2	13	2	10	1	0
Monteagle	1,200	9	0	0	3	6	17	3	10	4	0
Morristown	27,579	237	0	19	52	166	2,087	202	1,766	119	13
Moscow	569	3	0	0	0	3	24	8	14	2	0
Mountain City	2,397	7	0	0	0	7	66	15	49	2	1
Mount Carmel	5,478	7	0	0	0	7	68	8	59	1	0
Mount Juliet	21,177	57	0	2	5	50	537	108	404	25	4
Mount Pleasant	4,401	14	0	0	0	14	192	21	158	13	1
Munford	6,538	13	0	1	1	11	166	33	119	14	0

[1] The FBI does not publish arson data unless it receives data from either the agency or the state for all 12 months of the calendar year.

Table 8. Offenses Known to Law Enforcement, by State and City, 2008—*Continued*

(Number.)

State/City	Population	Violent crime	Murder and non-negligent man-slaughter	Forcible rape	Robbery	Aggravated assault	Property crime	Burglary	Larceny-theft	Motor vehicle theft	Arson[1]
TENNESSEE—*Continued*											
Murfreesboro	102,536	646	6	31	162	447	4,439	1,029	3,217	193	8
Nashville	602,181	8,404	76	301	2,384	5,643	32,347	6,326	23,764	2,257	116
Newbern	3,140	40	1	0	4	35	120	25	86	9	0
New Hope	1,036	1	0	0	0	1	4	2	2	0	0
New Market	1,335	1	0	0	0	1	4	1	3	0	0
Newport	7,466	85	3	4	16	62	711	124	532	55	3
New Tazewell	2,874	14	0	0	6	8	129	24	102	3	0
Niota	800	0	0	0	0	0	4	0	3	1	0
Nolensville	2,662	7	0	0	0	7	39	6	33	0	0
Norris	1,469	0	0	0	0	0	13	3	8	2	0
Oakland	4,825	5	0	0	1	4	35	6	26	3	0
Oak Ridge	27,540	123	0	11	34	78	1,504	443	979	82	9
Obion	1,073	0	0	0	0	0	22	0	22	0	1
Oliver Springs	3,314	3	0	0	0	3	108	21	76	11	0
Oneida	3,854	27	0	0	1	26	229	59	167	3	0
Paris	9,941	53	0	4	9	40	539	168	360	11	2
Parsons	2,353	4	0	0	0	4	38	8	27	3	0
Petersburg	598	1	0	0	0	1	12	3	7	2	0
Pigeon Forge	6,237	72	0	10	15	47	715	270	392	53	6
Pikeville	1,899	4	0	0	0	4	24	0	22	2	0
Piperton	1,207	1	0	0	0	1	30	9	17	4	0
Pittman Center	666	0	0	0	0	0	21	16	5	0	0
Pleasant View	4,074	1	0	0	1	0	93	32	58	3	0
Portland	11,321	50	1	4	2	43	355	130	204	21	3
Powells Crossroads	1,221	0	0	0	0	0	4	2	1	1	0
Pulaski	7,797	59	1	6	11	41	444	107	323	14	2
Puryear	673	2	0	0	0	2	14	4	9	1	0
Red Bank	11,512	63	0	7	9	47	531	137	362	32	0
Red Boiling Springs	1,060	2	0	0	0	2	11	3	7	1	0
Ridgely	1,521	8	1	0	0	7	26	9	17	0	0
Ridgetop	1,711	6	0	0	1	5	30	15	15	0	1
Rockwood	5,575	7	0	1	0	6	344	63	262	19	0
Rogersville	4,331	31	1	0	7	23	333	70	249	14	1
Rossville	522	0	0	0	0	0	11	0	10	1	0
Rutherford	1,243	5	0	0	0	5	18	5	13	0	0
Savannah	7,293	87	1	6	10	70	650	137	478	35	5
Scotts Hill	911	7	0	0	0	7	15	4	11	0	0
Selmer	4,684	29	0	4	1	24	230	46	176	8	0
Sevierville	16,652	97	1	5	23	68	1,109	163	874	72	3
Sewanee	2,579	0	0	0	0	0	84	23	60	1	0
Shelbyville	19,902	109	0	9	18	82	608	171	409	28	1
Signal Mountain	7,089	1	0	0	0	1	74	16	58	0	2
Smithville	4,345	36	0	4	10	22	225	46	166	13	0
Sneedville	1,320	2	0	0	0	2	40	14	25	1	0
Soddy-Daisy	12,407	73	0	7	9	57	480	118	328	34	1
Somerville	2,966	24	0	0	3	21	81	8	71	2	0
South Carthage	1,315	15	0	0	2	13	30	6	20	4	0
South Fulton	2,403	4	0	0	0	4	71	29	36	6	0
South Pittsburg	3,128	4	0	0	1	3	94	20	67	7	1
Sparta	4,928	15	0	1	10	4	404	83	301	20	6
Spencer	1,682	0	0	0	0	0	28	3	21	4	0
Spring City	1,999	1	0	0	0	1	56	6	45	5	1
Springfield	17,210	235	1	10	67	157	811	126	642	43	4
Spring Hill	27,290	48	0	6	4	38	282	39	233	10	1
St. Joseph	857	0	0	0	0	0	24	15	8	1	0
Surgoinsville	1,774	0	0	0	0	0	21	2	19	0	0
Sweetwater	6,638	56	0	0	4	52	286	65	210	11	2
Tazewell	2,143	12	0	0	4	8	118	46	68	4	0
Tellico Plains	963	12	0	0	0	12	40	10	30	0	0
Toone	350	0	0	0	0	0	5	1	4	0	0
Townsend	263	1	0	0	0	1	8	3	5	0	0
Tracy City	1,656	11	0	0	0	11	30	9	17	4	1
Trenton	4,477	35	0	0	3	32	187	45	135	7	2
Trezevant	885	8	0	0	1	7	22	6	16	0	1
Trimble	720	2	0	0	0	2	6	2	3	1	1
Troy	1,213	4	0	0	0	4	22	3	19	0	0
Tullahoma	18,776	109	0	5	18	86	890	185	648	57	0
Tusculum	2,296	4	0	0	2	2	30	7	23	0	0
Union City	10,612	84	0	8	10	66	622	105	504	13	0
Vonore	1,517	15	0	1	1	13	102	18	81	3	0
Wartburg	920	2	0	0	0	2	8	3	5	0	0
Wartrace	580	0	0	0	0	0	3	2	1	0	0
Watertown	1,410	8	0	1	1	6	28	5	20	3	1
Waverly	4,172	4	0	0	0	4	87	13	68	6	0

[1] The FBI does not publish arson data unless it receives data from either the agency or the state for all 12 months of the calendar year.

Table 8. Offenses Known to Law Enforcement, by State and City, 2008—*Continued*

(Number.)

State/City	Population	Violent crime	Murder and non-negligent man-slaughter	Forcible rape	Robbery	Aggravated assault	Property crime	Burglary	Larceny-theft	Motor vehicle theft	Arson[1]
TENNESSEE—*Continued*											
Waynesboro	2,117	10	0	0	0	10	38	7	26	5	0
Westmoreland	2,189	13	0	0	0	13	41	16	24	1	1
White Bluff	2,528	2	0	1	0	1	41	13	24	4	0
White House	9,973	26	1	3	0	22	163	29	129	5	0
White Pine	2,101	17	0	2	1	14	128	14	100	14	2
Whiteville	4,459	4	0	0	1	3	80	16	54	10	0
Whitwell	1,595	5	1	0	0	4	80	20	54	6	3
Winchester	7,898	66	0	4	3	59	409	92	298	19	5
Winfield	1,000	11	0	1	0	10	72	27	44	1	1
Woodbury	2,555	4	0	1	1	2	56	14	35	7	1
TEXAS											
Abernathy	2,746	4	0	0	2	2	38	8	28	2	0
Abilene	116,267	648	7	88	180	373	4,500	1,206	3,061	233	41
Addison	13,837	94	1	7	29	57	925	142	704	79	0
Alamo	16,686	98	0	9	18	71	1,146	159	886	101	4
Alamo Heights	7,454	11	0	2	6	3	298	41	249	8	2
Alice	19,855	181	0	8	11	162	1,684	387	1,224	73	19
Allen	83,242	66	1	7	13	45	1,484	298	1,137	49	3
Alpine	6,227	12	0	3	1	8	80	32	41	7	3
Alto	1,187	5	0	0	0	5	46	14	32	0	0
Alton	10,876	21	0	1	5	15	308	80	191	37	0
Alvarado	4,198	15	2	1	3	9	128	37	83	8	1
Alvin	22,847	65	2	4	23	36	892	163	682	47	2
Amarillo	187,674	1,474	13	122	324	1,015	10,310	2,419	7,150	741	48
Andrews	9,708	51	0	13	2	36	259	75	171	13	2
Angleton	18,703	86	1	9	18	58	582	144	415	23	3
Anna	1,905	3	0	0	0	3	165	19	144	2	0
Anson	2,285	6	0	0	0	6	13	4	9	0	0
Anthony	4,149	29	0	0	5	24	193	15	172	6	0
Aransas Pass	8,957	39	0	6	12	21	661	169	459	33	0
Arcola	1,256	6	0	0	1	5	26	11	13	2	0
Argyle	3,548	3	0	1	0	2	36	9	24	3	0
Arlington	375,836	2,262	23	141	694	1,404	20,149	4,461	14,140	1,548	63
Arp	958	0	0	0	0	0	7	4	3	0	1
Athens	12,348	66	0	11	14	41	583	188	370	25	1
Atlanta	5,482	40	0	4	5	31	205	59	138	8	0
Austin	753,535	3,935	23	273	1,333	2,306	44,801	8,586	33,582	2,633	87
Azle	11,371	45	0	3	14	28	494	92	390	12	6
Baird	1,668	0	0	0	0	0	6	1	2	3	0
Balch Springs	20,011	175	2	21	56	96	1,679	275	1,278	126	2
Balcones Heights	2,971	42	0	6	9	27	486	55	396	35	0
Ballinger	3,720	5	0	0	0	5	83	19	62	2	0
Bangs	1,591	3	0	0	0	3	10	3	7	0	0
Bastrop	8,190	26	1	3	7	15	384	39	333	12	2
Bay City	17,705	102	1	8	45	48	893	194	689	10	5
Bayou Vista	1,697	0	0	0	0	0	3	0	3	0	0
Baytown	70,596	324	6	41	100	177	3,457	741	2,371	345	18
Beaumont	109,103	1,015	7	75	331	602	6,404	1,925	4,170	309	34
Bedford	49,210	247	0	21	25	201	1,784	308	1,377	99	8
Bee Cave	2,852	4	1	1	2	0	132	24	103	5	1
Beeville	12,697	69	0	10	8	51	417	118	277	22	1
Bellaire	18,316	28	0	1	22	5	407	96	296	15	1
Bellmead	9,593	130	1	19	21	89	1,000	123	856	21	3
Bellville	4,448	16	0	7	0	9	102	13	87	2	0
Belton	17,536	37	0	0	5	32	519	113	383	23	1
Benbrook	23,017	28	1	6	4	17	416	109	280	27	9
Bertram	1,405	2	0	0	0	2	18	7	7	4	0
Beverly Hills	2,049	3	0	0	0	3	74	22	49	3	0
Big Sandy	1,353	5	0	1	1	3	6	6	0	0	0
Big Spring	23,952	159	2	16	33	108	1,589	410	1,103	76	17
Bishop	3,132	10	0	2	0	8	123	10	111	2	0
Blanco	1,604	8	0	0	0	8	44	6	36	2	0
Bloomburg	360	0	0	0	0	0	0	0	0	0	0
Blue Mound	2,357	14	0	0	2	12	60	26	27	7	1
Boerne	9,875	21	0	7	5	9	308	44	249	15	1
Bogata	1,254	0	0	0	0	0	18	4	12	2	2
Bonham	10,669	40	1	7	6	26	370	116	235	19	4
Borger	12,744	202	0	9	7	186	569	138	405	26	1
Bowie	5,565	14	0	1	2	11	270	53	206	11	0
Brady	5,252	13	0	0	3	10	154	39	112	3	1
Brazoria	2,988	16	0	5	1	10	92	20	66	6	0
Breckenridge	5,578	15	0	1	3	11	115	34	76	5	1
Bremond	861	3	0	0	0	3	14	10	1	3	1
Brenham	15,237	72	2	15	11	44	449	128	294	27	0
Bridge City	8,550	20	0	2	3	15	168	47	103	18	0

[1] The FBI does not publish arson data unless it receives data from either the agency or the state for all 12 months of the calendar year.

Table 8. Offenses Known to Law Enforcement, by State and City, 2008—*Continued*

(Number.)

State/City	Population	Violent crime	Murder and non-negligent man-slaughter	Forcible rape	Robbery	Aggravated assault	Property crime	Burglary	Larceny-theft	Motor vehicle theft	Arson[1]
TEXAS—*Continued*											
Bridgeport	6,146	8	0	3	1	4	160	43	115	2	0
Brookshire	3,955	32	1	4	14	13	164	57	91	16	2
Brookside Village	2,004	12	1	0	2	9	33	18	13	2	0
Brownfield	8,947	28	0	1	7	20	124	46	68	10	1
Brownsville	176,893	634	4	26	173	431	10,139	1,590	8,205	344	38
Brownwood	19,597	87	0	5	5	77	831	179	625	27	2
Bruceville-Eddy	1,543	6	0	0	1	5	70	17	50	3	0
Bryan	72,815	573	4	41	100	428	3,665	1,029	2,441	195	20
Bullard	1,839	4	0	2	0	2	78	15	62	1	0
Bulverde	4,624	3	0	0	1	2	79	9	68	2	0
Burkburnett	10,506	14	0	1	0	13	166	69	95	2	1
Burleson	35,166	72	0	12	16	44	925	174	695	56	1
Burnet	5,835	15	0	6	0	9	112	26	79	7	0
Cactus	2,602	12	0	1	1	10	14	7	6	1	0
Caddo Mills	1,212	1	0	0	0	1	25	12	9	4	0
Caldwell	3,734	9	0	0	2	7	29	9	17	3	0
Calvert	1,361	7	0	0	0	7	43	19	18	6	0
Cameron	5,771	16	0	0	4	12	242	35	195	12	0
Canton	3,666	13	0	0	2	11	197	15	171	11	0
Canyon	14,202	9	0	2	0	7	124	15	102	7	2
Carrollton	125,607	293	4	17	134	138	3,935	1,017	2,556	362	25
Carthage	6,600	20	0	0	1	19	112	26	76	10	0
Castle Hills	4,175	7	0	0	4	3	343	66	270	7	0
Castroville	3,074	9	0	2	0	7	64	6	56	2	0
Cedar Hill	46,153	123	4	11	42	66	1,512	384	986	142	1
Cedar Park	64,020	63	0	10	9	44	986	228	709	49	14
Celina	5,716	8	0	2	1	5	79	17	57	5	2
Center	5,775	37	0	4	4	29	346	59	268	19	2
Childress	6,497	28	0	0	0	28	115	44	61	10	0
Chillicothe	702	1	0	0	1	0	5	2	3	0	0
Cibolo	14,734	14	0	3	0	11	163	34	122	7	1
Cisco	3,759	5	0	0	2	3	68	11	54	3	0
Clarksville	3,464	0	0	0	0	0	53	26	27	0	0
Cleburne	29,954	131	1	19	16	95	1,130	217	850	63	4
Cleveland	8,021	89	2	15	9	63	750	117	598	35	4
Clifton	3,617	3	0	0	0	3	69	21	45	3	1
Clint	974	0	0	0	0	0	13	0	8	5	0
Clute	10,777	54	0	9	9	36	398	90	289	19	3
Clyde	3,754	6	0	0	1	5	89	21	66	2	1
Cockrell Hill	4,275	23	0	4	7	12	141	34	83	24	3
Coffee City	209	0	0	0	0	0	10	3	7	0	0
Coleman	4,626	7	0	0	0	7	179	77	97	5	2
College Station	81,925	245	1	42	55	147	3,012	628	2,283	101	2
Colleyville	24,472	4	0	0	0	4	281	63	209	9	0
Collinsville	1,523	7	0	0	0	7	24	12	11	1	1
Colorado City	3,883	18	0	4	2	12	127	15	105	7	1
Columbus	3,905	58	0	13	5	40	208	64	140	4	3
Comanche	4,194	6	0	0	0	6	92	18	66	8	2
Combes	2,837	12	0	0	0	12	70	30	32	8	1
Commerce	9,497	49	0	3	9	37	359	100	246	13	0
Conroe	54,554	255	3	27	78	147	2,518	558	1,783	177	5
Converse	16,057	24	0	2	11	11	460	79	356	25	4
Coppell	39,541	27	0	2	13	12	718	177	501	40	2
Copperas Cove	30,052	127	0	5	19	103	977	297	641	39	19
Corinth	21,890	21	0	4	2	15	312	64	224	24	0
Corpus Christi	286,558	2,226	19	192	490	1,525	17,652	3,464	13,503	685	96
Corrigan	1,906	4	0	0	0	4	22	10	10	2	0
Corsicana	26,711	97	0	16	31	50	1,312	306	948	58	4
Cottonwood Shores	1,202	0	0	0	0	0	10	6	2	2	0
Crandall	3,796	19	0	0	3	16	66	10	47	9	0
Crane	3,050	6	0	2	0	4	23	8	14	1	1
Crockett	6,880	32	1	1	4	26	286	66	199	21	2
Crowell	980	0	0	0	0	0	7	4	3	0	0
Crowley	12,680	18	0	3	2	13	266	62	204	0	0
Crystal City	7,127	17	0	0	1	16	177	63	105	9	0
Cuero	6,453	17	0	5	0	12	182	39	143	0	2
Daingerfield	2,476	9	0	1	2	6	79	32	40	7	1
Dalhart	6,882	15	0	0	0	15	140	39	92	9	1
Dallas	1,276,214	11,420	170	499	6,466	4,285	75,759	21,149	42,402	12,208	900
Dalworthington Gardens	2,429	8	0	1	0	7	63	12	44	7	0
Danbury	1,682	1	0	0	0	1	4	1	3	0	0
Dayton	7,399	26	0	2	3	21	189	45	123	21	0
Decatur	6,413	16	0	8	1	7	186	22	152	12	0
Deer Park	30,900	85	1	12	11	61	809	117	629	63	3

[1] The FBI does not publish arson data unless it receives data from either the agency or the state for all 12 months of the calendar year.

Table 8. Offenses Known to Law Enforcement, by State and City, 2008—*Continued*

(Number.)

State/City	Population	Violent crime	Murder and non-negligent man-slaughter	Forcible rape	Robbery	Aggravated assault	Property crime	Burglary	Larceny-theft	Motor vehicle theft	Arson[1]
TEXAS—*Continued*											
De Kalb	1,802	7	0	1	1	5	66	34	31	1	0
De Leon	2,347	16	1	1	0	14	52	23	25	4	0
Del Rio	36,922	92	2	0	9	81	908	180	656	72	16
Denison	24,276	112	2	1	24	85	951	221	687	43	6
Denton	120,295	357	0	70	93	194	3,333	667	2,507	159	24
Denver City	4,017	16	0	0	0	16	73	12	59	2	0
DeSoto	48,131	163	6	8	46	103	1,698	641	935	122	3
Devine	4,508	12	1	0	2	9	94	22	67	5	0
Diboll	5,550	12	0	6	0	6	137	42	86	9	0
Dickinson	17,884	62	0	5	18	39	601	170	384	47	0
Dilley	3,592	8	0	0	0	8	34	15	16	3	0
Dimmitt	3,676	5	0	0	0	5	130	45	81	4	0
Donna	16,984	117	1	4	17	95	1,013	240	721	52	7
Double Oak	3,331	1	0	0	0	1	16	3	12	1	0
Driscoll	803	3	0	0	0	3	46	7	39	0	0
Dublin	3,823	5	0	0	0	5	61	23	30	8	1
Dumas	13,698	55	0	12	7	36	501	75	403	23	5
Duncanville	36,221	138	1	6	74	57	1,501	435	902	164	6
Eagle Lake	3,684	8	0	0	0	8	39	9	30	0	1
Eagle Pass	26,766	66	0	0	8	58	983	149	807	27	4
Early	2,769	6	0	2	0	4	67	10	55	2	0
Eastland	3,907	6	0	0	0	6	129	28	98	3	0
East Mountain	627	1	0	0	0	1	9	2	6	1	0
Edcouch	4,506	7	0	0	0	7	99	40	55	4	1
Eden	2,356	3	0	0	0	3	31	10	21	0	0
Edgewood	1,446	6	0	0	1	5	20	6	11	3	2
Edinburg	71,734	285	3	21	69	192	4,306	846	3,082	378	27
Edna	5,780	24	0	4	2	18	150	50	91	9	0
El Campo	10,612	31	0	4	4	23	334	108	206	20	1
Electra	2,921	14	0	0	1	13	125	49	67	9	0
Elgin	10,486	33	0	9	6	18	259	75	167	17	0
El Paso	612,374	2,825	17	181	456	2,171	19,702	2,079	14,870	2,753	118
Elsa	6,771	23	0	0	6	17	297	72	209	16	1
Ennis	19,646	123	5	1	28	89	979	221	704	54	1
Euless	53,157	134	0	18	53	63	1,851	394	1,286	171	6
Everman	5,750	38	0	2	7	29	170	46	105	19	0
Fairfield	3,648	10	0	1	1	8	50	8	42	0	0
Fair Oaks Ranch	6,341	1	0	0	0	1	34	17	17	0	0
Falfurrias	4,932	41	1	0	0	40	192	72	109	11	11
Farmers Branch	26,362	76	1	4	44	27	1,448	242	1,049	157	4
Farmersville	3,472	2	0	1	0	1	40	10	29	1	0
Farwell	1,264	1	0	0	0	1	30	6	22	2	0
Ferris	2,539	11	0	2	0	9	114	34	72	8	2
Flatonia	1,432	1	1	0	0	0	10	3	6	1	0
Florence	1,127	1	0	0	0	1	19	3	13	3	0
Floresville	7,594	2	1	0	0	1	228	25	200	3	2
Flower Mound	70,761	54	0	2	13	39	639	110	510	19	3
Floydada	3,094	10	1	2	1	6	33	19	14	0	0
Forest Hill	13,926	97	0	10	34	53	451	131	272	48	1
Forney	15,855	18	0	3	4	11	434	160	241	33	1
Fort Stockton	7,293	22	1	0	3	18	289	117	157	15	0
Fort Worth	701,345	4,601	49	350	1,706	2,496	35,325	9,018	23,562	2,745	216
Frankston	1,234	3	0	0	1	2	34	6	28	0	0
Fredericksburg	11,110	10	0	2	3	5	244	22	219	3	1
Freeport	12,539	37	2	1	6	28	418	132	254	32	1
Freer	2,950	8	0	1	0	7	45	17	27	1	0
Friendswood	34,066	36	1	3	6	26	460	105	337	18	3
Friona	3,574	9	0	2	0	7	36	12	23	1	0
Frisco	99,472	106	1	15	11	79	2,552	504	1,992	56	4
Gainesville	16,650	78	1	17	23	37	683	205	447	31	0
Galena Park	10,243	16	1	3	4	8	277	87	158	32	0
Galveston	56,870	443	4	78	145	216	3,085	748	2,079	258	29
Ganado	1,824	2	0	0	1	1	7	4	3	0	0
Garland	219,135	773	10	81	325	357	9,241	2,265	6,243	733	45
Gatesville	15,139	21	0	5	3	13	380	114	236	30	5
Georgetown	49,644	66	1	12	9	44	722	134	545	43	1
Giddings	5,470	35	0	5	1	29	201	27	170	4	2
Gilmer	5,260	34	0	0	3	31	242	49	179	14	1
Gladewater	6,317	36	0	5	9	22	356	72	267	17	4
Glenn Heights	11,339	41	1	3	3	34	292	127	143	22	5
Godley	1,024	1	0	0	0	1	17	1	14	2	0
Gonzales	7,374	103	0	4	11	88	272	94	177	1	0
Gorman	1,243	2	1	0	0	1	9	2	6	1	0
Graham	8,496	21	0	6	1	14	199	74	113	12	0
Granbury	8,315	18	2	0	1	15	461	36	406	19	6

[1] The FBI does not publish arson data unless it receives data from either the agency or the state for all 12 months of the calendar year.

Table 8. Offenses Known to Law Enforcement, by State and City, 2008—*Continued*

(Number.)

State/City	Population	Violent crime	Murder and non-negligent man-slaughter	Forcible rape	Robbery	Aggravated assault	Property crime	Burglary	Larceny-theft	Motor vehicle theft	Arson[1]
TEXAS—*Continued*											
Grand Prairie	162,706	545	7	49	216	273	7,571	1,777	4,486	1,308	22
Grand Saline	3,224	5	0	0	0	5	73	15	55	3	0
Granger	1,357	4	0	0	1	3	50	14	33	3	0
Granite Shoals	2,829	8	0	0	1	7	79	29	50	0	1
Grapeland	1,376	9	1	0	0	8	39	23	13	3	0
Grapevine	51,136	102	0	14	20	68	1,754	226	1,408	120	5
Greenville	25,886	264	0	17	73	174	1,490	398	981	111	5
Gregory	2,211	6	0	2	0	4	75	7	67	1	2
Groesbeck	4,297	16	0	1	5	10	71	22	49	0	0
Groves	14,321	43	0	6	16	21	504	133	330	41	0
Gun Barrel City	6,083	59	0	2	4	53	318	49	260	9	0
Hale Center	2,138	12	0	0	0	12	23	11	12	0	0
Hallettsville	2,498	8	0	0	1	7	76	8	66	2	0
Hallsville	2,998	2	0	0	0	2	46	17	27	2	0
Haltom City	40,239	190	3	15	44	128	1,913	422	1,274	217	18
Hamlin	1,887	3	0	0	0	3	7	1	6	0	1
Harker Heights	25,579	48	1	3	24	20	757	187	534	36	0
Harlingen	64,922	455	4	33	88	330	4,387	1,016	3,181	190	53
Haskell	2,591	2	0	0	0	2	52	18	34	0	1
Hawk Cove	620	0	0	0	0	0	18	2	9	7	2
Hawkins	1,531	4	0	0	1	3	43	12	28	3	0
Hawley	572	0	0	0	0	0	10	2	7	1	0
Hearne	4,601	50	3	2	9	36	173	33	131	9	1
Heath	7,863	11	0	0	0	11	99	18	75	6	0
Hedwig Village	2,354	1	0	0	1	0	193	17	166	10	2
Helotes	7,033	2	0	0	0	2	113	26	82	5	1
Hemphill	1,029	0	0	0	0	0	18	2	15	1	1
Hempstead	7,599	63	0	1	11	51	236	95	114	27	1
Henderson	11,644	98	0	6	20	72	706	107	564	35	3
Hereford	14,444	77	2	1	8	66	434	150	265	19	4
Hewitt	13,788	25	0	1	4	20	200	48	140	12	2
Hickory Creek	3,864	3	0	0	0	3	84	5	73	6	0
Hidalgo	12,238	14	0	1	1	12	172	51	77	44	1
Highland Park	9,105	4	0	0	3	1	252	37	202	13	0
Highland Village	17,004	13	1	1	1	10	142	16	122	4	1
Hill Country Village	1,109	3	0	1	2	0	76	24	49	3	0
Hillsboro	8,972	25	0	7	4	14	284	49	217	18	1
Hitchcock	7,254	30	1	6	14	9	217	57	133	27	3
Holliday	1,785	0	0	0	0	0	17	11	6	0	0
Hollywood Park	3,306	2	0	0	0	2	135	11	119	5	0
Hondo	9,035	36	1	5	3	27	339	56	273	10	4
Hooks	2,935	8	0	0	0	8	28	15	11	2	0
Horizon City	13,488	19	0	1	3	15	211	78	95	38	3
Horseshoe Bay	2,473	2	0	1	0	1	57	28	27	2	0
Houston	2,238,895	24,779	294	750	10,603	13,132	110,759	26,947	68,598	15,214	956
Howe	2,730	4	0	1	0	3	19	6	12	1	1
Hubbard	1,769	3	0	0	0	3	3	0	3	0	1
Hudson	4,277	11	0	3	0	8	61	18	39	4	0
Hudson Oaks	1,988	2	0	1	0	1	58	8	47	3	0
Humble	15,026	116	0	8	59	49	1,727	188	1,341	198	3
Huntington	2,104	1	0	0	0	1	20	9	9	2	0
Huntsville	38,097	176	0	13	35	128	1,189	238	883	68	5
Hurst	38,702	192	1	16	40	135	2,188	276	1,826	86	3
Hutchins	3,104	14	0	4	1	9	184	34	134	16	1
Hutto	15,488	12	1	0	0	11	131	35	91	5	1
Idalou	2,101	7	0	4	0	3	35	11	22	2	0
Ingleside	9,023	15	0	8	1	6	256	64	177	15	2
Ingram	1,910	5	4	0	0	1	63	12	49	2	0
Iowa Park	6,292	8	0	2	1	5	55	16	37	2	1
Irving	200,470	722	7	31	238	446	8,560	1,819	5,867	874	31
Italy	2,137	6	0	1	2	3	41	12	26	3	0
Itasca	1,673	3	0	0	0	3	13	3	9	1	0
Jacinto City	9,949	38	0	1	14	23	320	77	210	33	1
Jacksboro	4,513	1	0	0	0	1	81	18	55	8	0
Jacksonville	14,302	118	0	12	27	79	749	198	512	39	1
Jamaica Beach	1,107	2	0	1	0	1	28	7	16	5	0
Jarrell	1,439	1	0	0	1	0	14	9	4	1	0
Jasper	7,228	37	1	3	6	27	303	79	217	7	2
Jefferson	1,946	10	0	0	2	8	94	31	62	1	0
Jersey Village	7,299	20	0	0	6	14	223	41	159	23	1
Johnson City	1,565	2	0	0	0	2	33	7	24	2	0
Jones Creek	2,107	0	0	0	0	0	12	8	3	1	0
Jonestown	2,472	11	0	0	2	9	96	30	62	4	0
Joshua	5,788	13	0	0	4	9	152	99	46	7	0
Jourdanton	4,367	4	0	2	0	2	31	13	17	1	0

[1] The FBI does not publish arson data unless it receives data from either the agency or the state for all 12 months of the calendar year.

Table 8. Offenses Known to Law Enforcement, by State and City, 2008—*Continued*

(Number.)

State/City	Population	Violent crime	Murder and non-negligent man-slaughter	Forcible rape	Robbery	Aggravated assault	Property crime	Burglary	Larceny-theft	Motor vehicle theft	Arson[1]
TEXAS—*Continued*											
Junction	2,569	15	0	3	0	12	51	14	37	0	0
Karnes City	3,345	16	0	1	2	13	94	23	65	6	4
Katy	14,106	42	0	0	9	33	620	68	511	41	2
Kaufman	8,775	17	0	0	3	14	233	45	176	12	0
Keene	6,408	3	0	0	1	2	111	32	71	8	0
Keller	39,598	17	0	4	5	8	532	81	437	14	0
Kemah	2,482	15	0	6	2	7	145	18	118	9	0
Kemp	1,300	1	0	0	0	1	25	9	16	0	0
Kempner	1,186	0	0	0	0	0	0	0	0	0	0
Kenedy	3,311	9	1	2	0	6	120	59	60	1	0
Kennedale	7,108	23	1	1	3	18	308	86	183	39	0
Kerens	1,840	3	0	0	2	1	65	26	33	6	1
Kermit	5,078	9	0	2	0	7	48	17	30	1	0
Kerrville	22,942	73	0	9	10	54	770	151	581	38	6
Kilgore	12,120	50	0	2	17	31	758	129	568	61	0
Killeen	115,906	885	10	66	216	593	4,757	1,711	2,877	169	40
Kingsville	24,253	208	1	21	16	170	1,291	414	845	32	1
Kirby	8,568	10	0	1	6	3	174	84	76	14	3
Kirbyville	1,949	0	0	0	0	0	12	5	5	2	0
Kountze	2,167	6	0	0	0	6	62	24	38	0	1
Kress	766	1	0	0	0	1	6	4	1	1	0
Kyle	28,543	33	0	2	0	31	372	81	276	15	2
Lacy-Lakeview	5,864	26	1	10	1	14	217	49	152	16	3
La Feria	6,972	12	0	0	2	10	341	86	252	3	0
Lago Vista	6,305	9	0	2	0	7	145	44	97	4	3
La Grange	4,690	10	0	1	3	6	85	25	57	3	0
Laguna Vista	3,534	6	0	2	0	4	85	29	48	8	1
La Joya	4,923	0	0	0	0	0	52	19	33	0	0
Lake Dallas	7,724	19	0	8	1	10	165	25	118	22	0
Lake Jackson	27,603	47	0	10	15	22	827	133	667	27	1
Lakeside	1,328	0	0	0	0	0	31	5	20	6	0
Lakeview	6,518	17	0	1	1	15	93	27	60	6	0
Lakeway	10,976	18	0	2	1	15	156	42	103	11	0
Lake Worth	4,792	16	0	0	5	11	354	49	293	12	0
La Marque	14,072	145	1	26	44	74	627	241	337	49	10
Lamesa	8,890	30	0	3	2	25	268	86	166	16	6
Lampasas	8,000	17	0	0	1	16	207	41	158	8	2
Lancaster	36,584	131	3	11	43	74	1,643	729	678	236	5
La Porte	34,552	166	0	5	11	150	607	196	344	67	17
Laredo	222,870	1,357	10	78	311	958	14,340	2,091	10,522	1,727	43
La Vernia	1,214	2	0	0	0	2	35	5	28	2	1
Lavon	421	0	0	0	0	0	17	8	7	2	0
League City	71,651	96	3	17	32	44	1,718	400	1,239	79	7
Leander	26,680	32	0	0	3	29	367	52	295	20	7
Leon Valley	10,152	32	0	4	15	13	834	136	644	54	1
Levelland	12,399	96	0	16	8	72	466	151	293	22	3
Lewisville	100,947	234	1	25	90	118	3,270	612	2,329	329	11
Lexington	1,238	2	0	0	0	2	8	1	7	0	0
Liberty	8,403	41	0	1	3	37	395	80	290	25	0
Lindale	4,811	8	0	1	2	5	180	28	139	13	0
Linden	2,129	2	0	0	0	2	48	17	31	0	0
Little Elm	29,616	21	0	1	4	16	309	58	231	20	1
Littlefield	6,027	33	1	0	1	31	204	56	139	9	2
Live Oak	12,958	23	0	3	9	11	609	101	468	40	4
Livingston	6,345	38	0	7	10	21	380	61	307	12	7
Llano	3,254	2	0	1	0	1	84	20	63	1	0
Lockhart	13,869	77	0	8	7	62	293	75	214	4	1
Lockney	1,692	9	0	2	0	7	47	15	29	3	1
Lone Star	1,606	9	1	1	1	6	49	25	24	0	0
Longview	77,272	806	9	45	219	533	5,101	1,143	3,563	395	50
Lorena	1,702	0	0	0	0	0	37	5	31	1	0
Lorenzo	1,189	2	0	0	0	2	9	7	1	1	1
Los Fresnos	5,469	2	0	0	1	1	75	18	57	0	0
Lubbock	219,594	2,098	8	82	298	1,710	12,271	3,109	8,564	598	51
Lufkin	34,214	176	1	12	48	115	2,192	590	1,513	89	2
Luling	5,483	38	0	3	5	30	210	55	148	7	2
Lumberton	10,243	9	0	0	3	6	271	61	193	17	1
Lytle	2,786	1	0	0	0	1	118	16	98	4	1
Madisonville	4,392	33	0	4	2	27	166	34	127	5	0
Magnolia	1,267	7	0	0	0	7	61	12	48	1	0
Malakoff	2,331	23	0	4	1	18	103	37	56	10	0
Manor	3,711	15	0	1	3	11	85	14	68	3	0
Mansfield	46,560	79	1	9	27	42	1,060	229	762	69	10
Manvel	5,353	32	0	5	3	24	84	19	45	20	0
Marble Falls	7,638	32	0	7	2	23	364	36	316	12	0

[1] The FBI does not publish arson data unless it receives data from either the agency or the state for all 12 months of the calendar year.

Table 8. Offenses Known to Law Enforcement, by State and City, 2008—*Continued*

(Number.)

State/City	Population	Violent crime	Murder and non-negligent man-slaughter	Forcible rape	Robbery	Aggravated assault	Property crime	Burglary	Larceny-theft	Motor vehicle theft	Arson[1]
TEXAS—*Continued*											
Marfa	1,860	2	0	0	0	2	25	10	15	0	0
Marion	1,147	2	0	1	0	1	19	6	13	0	7
Marlin	5,950	14	0	3	3	8	59	33	25	1	0
Marshall	23,874	157	3	8	35	111	1,138	335	749	54	11
Mart	2,591	10	0	1	1	8	29	12	16	1	1
Martindale	1,150	0	0	0	0	0	7	4	3	0	0
Mathis	5,331	26	0	1	5	20	204	65	138	1	4
McAllen	130,039	371	9	18	135	209	7,875	818	6,599	458	14
McGregor	4,890	11	0	0	1	10	139	29	97	13	0
McKinney	126,659	267	3	51	42	171	2,744	503	2,136	105	28
Meadows Place	6,688	6	0	2	4	0	89	20	59	10	1
Melissa	4,362	3	0	0	0	3	88	22	61	5	0
Memorial Villages	11,907	9	0	1	7	1	169	53	109	7	1
Memphis	2,230	2	0	0	0	2	85	50	33	2	1
Mercedes	15,066	111	2	8	15	86	798	221	504	73	6
Meridian	1,514	2	0	0	0	2	6	2	4	0	0
Merkel	2,625	4	0	0	0	4	35	22	12	1	1
Mesquite	132,600	492	3	10	170	309	6,126	1,029	4,399	698	17
Mexia	6,610	44	0	5	7	32	359	68	282	9	4
Midland	105,049	420	4	66	94	256	3,486	836	2,492	158	9
Midlothian	16,847	42	0	6	6	30	299	79	195	25	2
Milford	744	1	0	0	0	1	17	7	9	1	0
Mineral Wells	16,804	92	0	23	9	60	666	143	490	33	2
Mission	68,236	118	5	2	53	58	2,846	438	2,042	366	0
Missouri City	77,075	169	4	20	58	87	1,204	304	809	91	14
Monahans	6,282	64	0	2	3	59	265	90	172	3	0
Mont Belvieu	2,677	9	0	5	1	3	123	24	81	18	0
Montgomery	588	2	0	0	0	2	9	3	6	0	0
Morgans Point Resort	4,529	3	0	1	0	2	47	14	30	3	1
Mount Pleasant	14,853	70	1	1	14	54	489	114	346	29	5
Muleshoe	4,297	15	0	6	1	8	103	28	65	10	1
Munday	1,222	10	0	3	0	7	16	4	11	1	0
Murphy	16,612	9	0	1	1	7	172	20	141	11	2
Mustang Ridge	941	4	0	0	0	4	18	8	10	0	0
Nacogdoches	32,265	97	0	14	21	62	1,149	281	827	41	2
Nash	2,423	8	0	0	1	7	46	17	28	1	0
Nassau Bay	4,059	6	0	2	3	1	127	32	85	10	1
Navasota	7,522	39	0	0	11	28	288	68	209	11	3
Nederland	16,033	28	1	5	4	18	582	146	414	22	0
Needville	3,550	4	0	0	0	4	21	11	10	0	0
New Boston	4,641	7	0	1	2	4	207	31	157	19	2
New Braunfels	53,803	134	4	5	33	92	2,144	342	1,715	87	33
New Deal	744	0	0	0	0	0	0	0	0	0	0
Nocona	3,250	6	0	0	0	6	38	21	13	4	0
Nolanville	2,829	17	0	2	2	13	81	17	59	5	0
Northlake	1,205	1	0	0	0	1	30	4	23	3	0
North Richland Hills	65,552	272	2	20	49	201	2,197	434	1,618	145	1
Oak Ridge	249	2	0	0	1	1	11	7	4	0	0
Oak Ridge North	3,420	9	0	1	3	5	71	9	55	7	2
Odessa	97,644	675	7	2	73	593	3,970	893	2,809	268	32
O'Donnell	915	1	0	1	0	0	5	3	0	2	1
Olmos Park	2,304	3	0	0	2	1	86	17	65	4	0
Olney	3,250	12	1	2	0	9	103	48	50	5	0
Olton	2,187	4	0	1	0	3	21	8	8	5	0
Onalaska	1,507	4	0	1	0	3	25	5	20	0	0
Orange	17,287	212	0	21	75	116	1,198	434	651	113	37
Orange Grove	1,423	4	0	0	0	4	38	12	25	1	0
Overton	2,360	12	0	6	1	5	50	11	36	3	1
Ovilla	3,966	4	0	0	0	4	25	6	16	3	0
Oyster Creek	1,251	17	0	1	1	15	48	23	24	1	0
Paducah	1,229	2	0	0	0	2	13	9	4	0	2
Palacios	5,038	45	0	6	2	37	276	109	158	9	5
Palestine	18,197	140	1	13	19	107	943	245	646	52	1
Palmer	2,252	3	0	0	1	2	58	20	38	0	0
Pampa	17,140	141	2	3	6	130	836	189	610	37	2
Panhandle	2,515	7	0	1	0	6	21	5	15	1	0
Pantego	2,368	8	0	1	5	2	139	19	116	4	0
Paris	26,121	160	1	5	45	109	1,491	393	1,057	41	22
Parker	2,896	0	0	0	0	0	30	3	27	0	0
Pasadena	147,114	645	11	60	164	410	4,954	971	3,640	343	9
Pearland	83,185	108	1	21	21	65	1,804	348	1,347	109	6
Pearsall	7,663	25	4	0	2	19	224	66	153	5	0
Pecos	7,726	15	2	0	1	12	165	41	112	12	1
Pelican Bay	1,616	10	0	0	2	8	64	23	39	2	1
Penitas	1,181	3	0	0	0	3	36	21	9	6	1

[1] The FBI does not publish arson data unless it receives data from either the agency or the state for all 12 months of the calendar year.

Table 8. Offenses Known to Law Enforcement, by State and City, 2008—*Continued*

(Number.)

State/City	Population	Violent crime	Murder and non-negligent man-slaughter	Forcible rape	Robbery	Aggravated assault	Property crime	Burglary	Larceny-theft	Motor vehicle theft	Arson[1]
TEXAS—*Continued*											
Perryton	8,331	3	0	1	0	2	62	17	39	6	0
Pflugerville	37,454	38	0	12	7	19	886	146	708	32	8
Pharr	66,084	260	3	20	80	157	3,731	868	2,503	360	9
Pilot Point	4,454	10	0	3	1	6	38	11	26	1	0
Pinehurst	2,153	9	0	0	1	8	87	13	70	4	1
Pittsburg	4,684	23	0	5	6	12	167	45	118	4	1
Plainview	21,574	82	1	9	7	65	1,066	251	783	32	12
Plano	265,739	602	7	48	144	403	8,132	1,549	6,171	412	18
Pleasanton	9,762	38	0	7	6	25	388	83	292	13	3
Ponder	1,396	1	0	0	1	0	9	1	8	0	0
Port Aransas	3,826	22	0	5	1	16	335	82	245	8	2
Port Arthur	55,032	403	9	35	126	233	2,410	957	1,265	188	61
Port Isabel	5,301	30	0	11	3	16	329	51	276	2	0
Portland	16,604	17	0	4	2	11	418	71	337	10	1
Port Lavaca	11,379	36	0	2	1	33	288	79	193	16	1
Port Neches	12,574	35	0	4	5	26	395	97	283	15	0
Poteet	3,663	14	0	0	1	13	60	13	39	8	1
Pottsboro	2,157	7	0	0	0	7	43	9	29	5	0
Premont	2,815	6	0	1	2	3	38	14	20	4	0
Presidio	4,841	6	0	0	2	4	25	9	15	1	0
Primera	3,491	4	0	1	0	3	99	31	62	6	2
Princeton	6,072	19	0	5	3	11	160	36	120	4	0
Progreso	5,449	12	0	1	1	10	132	37	84	11	1
Prosper	7,007	0	0	0	0	0	104	45	58	1	0
Queen City	1,542	25	0	6	5	14	62	28	32	2	1
Quinlan	1,447	8	0	0	1	7	57	12	40	5	0
Quitman	2,260	8	0	0	1	7	28	12	14	2	0
Ralls	1,994	4	1	0	0	3	21	6	14	1	0
Ransom Canyon	1,120	0	0	0	0	0	11	0	10	1	0
Raymondville	9,475	259	1	1	15	242	570	212	350	8	14
Red Oak	9,323	20	0	2	6	12	238	83	140	15	1
Refugio	2,701	3	0	0	0	3	39	4	32	3	0
Reno	3,077	12	0	1	0	11	41	18	20	3	1
Richardson	100,597	269	4	23	112	130	3,379	850	2,282	247	4
Richland Hills	8,099	13	0	1	4	8	276	77	169	30	0
Richmond	13,637	54	0	10	10	34	294	63	201	30	5
Richwood	3,446	6	0	1	2	3	63	17	44	2	1
Riesel	1,017	1	0	1	0	0	12	2	10	0	0
Rio Grande City	14,080	57	0	5	5	47	569	175	314	80	3
Rising Star	837	3	0	0	0	3	6	0	4	2	0
River Oaks	6,932	12	0	6	2	4	202	60	126	16	0
Roanoke	3,852	6	1	1	3	1	103	12	89	2	0
Robinson	10,358	28	1	3	1	23	245	23	220	2	0
Robstown	12,132	22	0	0	11	11	736	307	408	21	5
Rockdale	5,920	26	0	0	6	20	244	61	165	18	0
Rockport	9,622	19	1	3	2	13	417	115	285	17	1
Rockwall	36,467	51	1	7	11	32	1,035	116	853	66	0
Rollingwood	1,414	1	0	0	0	1	41	13	28	0	0
Roma	11,377	22	0	5	1	16	267	77	109	81	3
Roman Forest	4,045	0	0	0	0	0	2	2	0	0	0
Roscoe	1,240	1	0	0	0	1	10	9	1	0	0
Rosebud	1,332	4	0	0	0	4	19	2	17	0	0
Rose City	501	0	0	0	0	0	2	0	0	2	0
Rosenberg	34,273	87	0	18	24	45	710	175	485	50	2
Round Rock	102,411	128	0	19	30	79	2,689	396	2,213	80	9
Rowlett	57,010	76	0	16	16	44	984	213	710	61	3
Royse City	9,597	38	0	6	3	29	194	32	151	11	0
Runaway Bay	1,404	2	0	0	0	2	24	2	20	2	0
Rusk	5,216	9	0	3	0	6	124	45	77	2	0
Sabinal	1,635	5	0	0	1	4	38	6	32	0	0
Sachse	19,651	22	0	2	8	12	281	74	195	12	0
Saginaw	20,765	53	1	3	12	37	570	97	424	49	2
Salado	2,055	1	0	0	1	0	36	6	29	1	0
San Angelo	90,739	369	6	63	66	234	4,476	1,046	3,198	232	24
San Antonio	1,351,244	9,699	116	424	2,743	6,416	97,564	18,908	70,651	8,005	521
San Augustine	2,352	21	0	0	3	18	47	15	32	0	0
San Benito	24,807	87	1	9	17	60	1,045	255	729	61	5
San Diego	4,445	30	0	0	1	29	219	105	109	5	3
Sanger	8,013	11	0	2	1	8	118	31	75	12	0
San Juan	34,103	128	1	3	36	88	1,647	384	1,140	123	8
San Marcos	52,473	161	0	14	34	113	1,682	278	1,293	111	3
San Saba	2,535	2	0	0	0	2	15	3	11	1	0
Sansom Park Village	4,167	24	1	2	2	19	157	57	82	18	0
Santa Anna	1,006	4	0	1	0	3	10	6	4	0	0
Santa Fe	10,603	23	0	6	5	12	255	75	163	17	1

[1] The FBI does not publish arson data unless it receives data from either the agency or the state for all 12 months of the calendar year.

Table 8. Offenses Known to Law Enforcement, by State and City, 2008—*Continued*

(Number.)

State/City	Population	Violent crime	Murder and non-negligent man-slaughter	Forcible rape	Robbery	Aggravated assault	Property crime	Burglary	Larceny-theft	Motor vehicle theft	Arson[1]
TEXAS—*Continued*											
Santa Rosa	3,164	9	0	1	2	6	45	17	26	2	0
Schertz	30,609	81	0	20	15	46	661	90	529	42	0
Seabrook	11,760	20	0	5	3	12	231	52	163	16	0
Seadrift	1,436	0	0	0	0	0	32	16	15	1	1
Seagoville	11,867	29	1	1	8	19	498	136	299	63	0
Seagraves	2,332	6	0	2	0	4	25	9	14	2	0
Sealy	6,320	16	0	2	1	13	198	46	124	28	1
Seguin	26,348	136	0	11	32	93	1,415	253	1,113	49	4
Selma	4,881	16	0	0	4	12	285	40	228	17	1
Seminole	6,078	2	0	0	0	2	110	19	85	6	0
Seven Points	1,238	7	0	1	0	6	64	11	47	6	0
Seymour	2,663	24	1	4	3	16	54	15	39	0	1
Shallowater	2,292	0	0	0	0	0	33	2	30	1	0
Shamrock	1,809	5	0	0	1	4	15	3	10	2	2
Shavano Park	3,255	1	0	0	0	1	73	7	63	3	0
Shenandoah	2,022	9	0	0	5	4	194	14	174	6	1
Sherman	38,039	153	0	3	18	132	1,560	366	1,141	53	0
Silsbee	6,834	16	0	0	4	12	174	49	123	2	0
Sinton	5,360	22	0	1	2	19	159	43	113	3	0
Slaton	5,739	30	0	10	0	20	153	52	98	3	0
Smithville	4,501	21	0	2	0	19	83	21	62	0	0
Snyder	10,418	126	0	11	1	114	308	83	215	10	1
Socorro	32,444	81	0	3	18	60	767	171	506	90	7
Somerset	1,862	9	0	0	1	8	38	12	23	3	0
Somerville	1,683	17	0	4	3	10	35	15	17	3	1
Sonora	3,082	19	1	4	0	14	28	5	22	1	1
Sour Lake	1,738	2	0	1	0	1	31	4	26	1	0
South Houston	16,496	126	0	7	44	75	618	137	368	113	3
Southlake	26,837	13	0	0	4	9	633	122	501	10	0
South Padre Island	2,797	50	0	11	8	31	701	134	549	18	0
Southside Place	1,669	6	0	0	3	3	5	1	4	0	0
Spearman	2,909	4	0	1	0	3	44	11	30	3	0
Springtown	3,167	12	0	0	0	12	79	24	47	8	0
Spring Valley	3,803	1	0	0	1	0	144	19	122	3	0
Stafford	20,051	65	1	7	27	30	974	172	681	121	2
Stamford	3,080	17	0	1	3	13	84	27	50	7	1
Stanton	2,205	6	0	2	1	3	19	5	12	2	0
Stephenville	16,945	46	0	13	2	31	601	78	507	16	0
Stratford	1,872	3	0	1	0	2	8	3	5	0	1
Sudan	994	6	0	0	1	5	6	1	5	0	0
Sugar Land	81,763	138	0	5	46	87	1,729	253	1,381	95	0
Sullivan City	4,440	3	0	2	1	0	39	24	12	3	0
Sulphur Springs	15,493	53	0	7	12	34	257	79	161	17	5
Sunrise Beach Village	755	1	0	0	0	1	15	3	12	0	0
Sunset Valley	870	2	0	0	2	0	182	12	164	6	0
Surfside Beach	891	1	0	0	0	1	33	9	20	4	0
Sweeny	3,591	9	0	0	2	7	74	13	56	5	0
Sweetwater	10,365	139	0	10	7	122	357	83	259	15	3
Taft	3,348	29	0	6	0	23	70	24	44	2	1
Tahoka	2,528	5	0	2	0	3	51	14	37	0	1
Tatum	1,205	4	0	0	0	4	22	8	13	1	1
Taylor	16,048	11	1	2	4	4	435	91	336	8	5
Teague	4,765	11	0	0	0	11	101	29	67	5	0
Temple	58,812	243	3	27	107	106	2,794	557	2,082	155	5
Terrell	19,722	101	3	7	47	44	920	278	577	65	3
Terrell Hills	5,197	7	0	1	4	2	100	22	76	2	0
Texarkana	36,300	467	2	18	74	373	2,264	626	1,519	119	11
Texas City	44,768	184	5	13	92	74	2,085	555	1,405	125	5
The Colony	43,724	55	1	11	15	28	803	171	565	67	8
Thorndale	1,321	2	0	0	0	2	8	0	7	1	0
Thrall	897	4	0	0	0	4	13	7	6	0	0
Three Rivers	1,677	6	0	0	0	6	63	32	28	3	0
Tioga	931	0	0	0	0	0	9	4	4	1	1
Tolar	680	1	0	0	0	1	1	1	0	0	0
Tomball	10,412	43	0	8	11	24	400	72	308	20	1
Tool	2,459	5	0	0	0	5	40	12	26	2	0
Trinity	2,736	6	2	0	1	3	61	11	44	6	0
Trophy Club	8,141	0	0	0	0	0	71	13	56	2	0
Troy	1,410	2	0	0	0	2	33	11	21	1	0
Tulia	4,575	14	1	2	1	10	114	26	77	11	0
Tye	1,141	2	0	0	2	0	25	6	18	1	0
Tyler	98,042	656	5	46	129	476	4,463	767	3,484	212	7
Universal City	18,430	47	1	2	12	32	435	118	296	21	4
University Park	24,561	5	0	2	2	1	457	88	348	21	1
Uvalde	16,263	86	0	8	17	61	942	227	692	23	2

[1] The FBI does not publish arson data unless it receives data from either the agency or the state for all 12 months of the calendar year.

Table 8. Offenses Known to Law Enforcement, by State and City, 2008—*Continued*

(Number.)

State/City	Population	Violent crime	Murder and non-negligent man-slaughter	Forcible rape	Robbery	Aggravated assault	Property crime	Burglary	Larceny-theft	Motor vehicle theft	Arson[1]
TEXAS—*Continued*											
Van	2,592	8	0	1	1	6	55	14	37	4	0
Van Alstyne	2,987	8	0	1	0	7	50	7	42	1	1
Vernon	10,998	44	0	6	3	35	327	57	257	13	2
Victoria	62,464	435	1	40	66	328	3,339	824	2,404	111	11
Vidor	10,901	40	0	3	7	30	364	94	230	40	1
Waco	123,208	1,031	11	75	252	693	7,393	2,090	4,915	388	35
Waelder	996	3	0	0	2	1	2	2	0	0	1
Wake Village	5,562	0	0	0	0	0	64	26	32	6	0
Waller	2,073	16	1	3	3	9	114	37	75	2	1
Wallis	1,306	3	0	0	0	3	8	3	1	4	0
Watauga	24,114	80	0	2	14	64	556	138	375	43	4
Waxahachie	28,110	119	2	7	27	83	1,016	241	711	64	9
Weatherford	26,696	48	1	15	7	25	682	108	546	28	4
Webster	10,196	47	1	7	24	15	772	57	648	67	1
Weimar	2,004	1	0	0	1	0	16	7	5	4	0
Wells	793	12	0	0	0	12	10	3	7	0	0
Weslaco	33,096	162	3	14	48	97	1,979	413	1,386	180	11
West	2,701	2	0	0	0	2	30	5	21	4	0
West Columbia	4,191	8	0	1	2	5	62	8	49	5	1
West Lake Hills	3,145	0	0	0	0	0	116	25	89	2	0
West Orange	3,827	11	0	0	5	6	225	33	185	7	2
Westover Hills	697	0	0	0	0	0	18	1	16	1	0
West Tawakoni	1,754	7	0	1	0	6	48	16	27	5	0
West University Place	15,578	11	0	2	4	5	203	55	141	7	0
Westworth	3,113	8	0	0	5	3	105	34	70	1	0
Wharton	9,221	64	0	4	11	49	391	67	312	12	4
Whitehouse	7,791	3	0	1	1	1	81	11	63	7	1
White Oak	6,326	6	0	3	0	3	190	36	118	36	2
Whitesboro	4,043	4	0	1	0	3	76	12	63	1	0
White Settlement	16,330	28	1	1	6	20	467	124	310	33	4
Whitney	2,051	3	0	0	0	3	71	10	58	3	0
Wichita Falls	101,279	557	4	46	208	299	6,980	1,515	4,936	529	42
Willis	4,320	36	1	3	10	22	175	52	111	12	0
Willow Park	4,431	5	0	1	1	3	64	11	48	5	0
Wills Point	3,884	12	0	3	2	7	92	20	66	6	0
Wilmer	3,599	13	0	0	1	12	105	44	56	5	0
Windcrest	5,259	20	1	2	12	5	413	35	360	18	1
Wink	882	0	0	0	0	0	13	0	13	0	0
Winnsboro	3,950	34	0	0	0	34	75	40	29	6	0
Winters	2,545	6	0	0	0	6	26	17	8	1	2
Wolfe City	1,648	2	0	0	0	2	32	14	17	1	0
Wolfforth	3,538	3	0	0	1	2	42	18	24	0	0
Woodville	2,261	3	0	1	2	0	31	6	25	0	0
Woodway	8,776	22	0	4	3	15	157	21	131	5	0
Wortham	1,079	2	0	1	0	1	12	4	5	3	0
Wylie	38,693	48	0	10	4	34	712	183	504	25	0
Yoakum	5,477	21	0	0	2	19	131	45	82	4	0
Yorktown	2,155	3	0	0	1	2	30	14	15	1	1
UTAH											
Alpine/Highland	25,593	11	0	3	1	7	325	95	219	11	0
American Fork/Cedar Hills	37,173	35	0	10	8	17	1,302	222	1,041	39	4
Big Water	394	3	0	0	0	3	5	3	1	1	0
Blanding	3,181	3	0	0	0	3	42	3	39	0	0
Bountiful	44,098	42	1	10	16	15	905	134	743	28	4
Brian Head	126	0	0	0	0	0	28	3	25	0	0
Brigham City	18,682	43	0	3	5	35	516	78	421	17	7
Cedar City	28,883	32	0	8	3	21	855	133	682	40	1
Centerville	15,488	7	0	2	0	5	367	38	311	18	0
Clearfield	27,649	46	0	6	10	30	856	122	709	25	8
Clinton	20,646	16	0	7	3	6	270	46	214	10	0
Draper	40,607	24	0	5	3	16	965	226	678	61	1
Enoch	5,130	3	0	2	0	1	30	14	14	2	0
Farmington	17,185	9	0	2	1	6	174	37	130	7	1
Grantsville	8,815	5	0	3	0	2	178	36	136	6	2
Gunnison	2,781	15	0	1	1	13	131	28	92	11	0
Harrisville	5,748	20	0	0	12	8	263	26	232	5	0
Heber	10,024	9	0	5	0	4	69	15	52	2	1
Helper	1,863	3	0	0	0	3	27	12	13	2	1
Hildale	1,993	2	0	0	0	2	4	4	0	0	0
Hurricane	13,622	30	0	3	3	24	356	72	259	25	0
Ivins	8,148	5	0	1	0	4	116	35	80	1	0
Kanab	3,794	9	0	0	1	8	56	16	38	2	0
Kaysville	25,672	7	0	2	1	4	450	61	358	31	0
La Verkin	4,583	7	0	0	0	7	49	14	28	7	1

[1] The FBI does not publish arson data unless it receives data from either the agency or the state for all 12 months of the calendar year.

Table 8. Offenses Known to Law Enforcement, by State and City, 2008—*Continued*

(Number.)

State/City	Population	Violent crime	Murder and non-negligent man-slaughter	Forcible rape	Robbery	Aggravated assault	Property crime	Burglary	Larceny-theft	Motor vehicle theft	Arson[1]
UTAH—*Continued*											
Layton	65,029	100	1	25	26	48	2,148	380	1,689	79	11
Leeds	775	0	0	0	0	0	4	1	3	0	0
Lehi	48,465	22	1	12	5	4	833	111	692	30	0
Logan	48,670	44	1	13	2	28	943	218	694	31	3
Mapleton	7,775	0	0	0	0	0	76	9	61	6	0
Midvale	27,875	83	0	21	12	50	1,555	371	974	210	0
Moab	4,877	17	0	1	2	14	212	38	169	5	0
Monticello	1,957	3	0	0	0	3	23	6	17	0	0
Murray	45,760	153	1	17	38	97	3,262	538	2,480	244	5
Naples	1,597	2	0	0	0	2	50	3	40	7	0
Nephi	5,295	7	0	1	0	6	148	45	88	15	0
North Ogden	17,441	7	0	2	2	3	196	35	156	5	0
North Park	12,272	11	0	4	0	7	255	41	210	4	1
North Salt Lake	13,217	15	0	5	2	8	383	134	231	18	3
Ogden	83,353	386	4	42	127	213	4,200	699	3,154	347	22
Orem	94,228	66	2	22	9	33	2,584	246	2,222	116	2
Park City	8,104	15	0	3	3	9	514	96	395	23	0
Parowan	2,638	2	0	1	1	0	28	12	14	2	0
Payson	17,703	4	0	0	1	3	544	100	407	37	0
Perry	3,962	4	0	1	1	2	91	6	84	1	0
Pleasant Grove/Lindon	32,755	22	0	5	4	13	549	57	461	31	2
Pleasant View	6,906	6	0	2	1	3	112	15	90	7	0
Price	8,146	17	0	5	0	12	411	64	329	18	3
Provo	119,189	184	0	40	21	123	2,994	451	2,401	142	11
Richfield	7,152	6	0	3	2	1	296	37	251	8	1
Riverdale	8,015	14	1	3	6	4	525	28	489	8	1
Roosevelt	4,928	5	0	1	1	3	172	21	144	7	1
Roy	35,279	49	1	18	7	23	802	126	645	31	3
Salem	6,082	1	0	0	0	1	83	30	51	2	0
Salina	2,391	7	0	0	0	7	98	15	76	7	0
Salt Lake City	180,514	1,420	12	75	486	847	16,169	2,044	12,282	1,843	58
Sandy	96,998	158	0	22	36	100	3,748	589	2,912	247	11
Santaquin/Genola	8,861	2	0	0	0	2	112	27	80	5	0
Saratoga Springs	19,624	9	0	2	2	5	141	30	100	11	1
Smithfield	9,448	3	0	2	0	1	127	34	90	3	1
South Jordan	51,044	44	0	10	7	27	1,118	178	882	58	4
South Ogden	15,783	25	0	7	10	8	572	74	480	18	2
South Salt Lake	21,490	221	4	37	61	119	1,889	288	1,310	291	4
Spanish Fork	29,880	13	0	7	1	5	578	109	453	16	2
Springville	27,753	37	0	16	9	12	723	103	598	22	1
St. George	74,356	161	1	20	26	114	2,105	441	1,547	117	7
Stockton	583	1	0	1	0	0	7	3	2	2	0
Sunset	4,887	1	0	0	0	1	169	64	105	0	0
Syracuse	23,333	7	0	4	0	3	332	44	281	7	2
Taylorsville City	58,600	202	0	24	71	107	2,940	446	2,196	298	6
Tooele	30,364	66	0	13	5	48	1,116	259	794	63	5
Tremonton	6,579	15	0	2	3	10	222	49	162	11	0
Vernal	8,496	32	0	8	3	21	345	57	261	27	2
Washington	18,184	26	0	5	2	19	442	79	342	21	0
West Bountiful	5,350	7	0	3	1	3	202	33	162	7	0
West Jordan	105,772	214	0	39	29	146	3,201	470	2,472	259	16
West Valley	124,128	595	2	95	167	331	6,473	804	4,805	864	20
Woods Cross	8,671	8	0	2	2	4	238	31	193	14	0
VERMONT											
Barre	8,860	5	0	0	0	5	205	21	178	6	0
Barre Town	8,037	0	0	0	0	0	128	14	106	8	2
Bellows Falls	2,908	13	0	4	0	9	43	10	33	0	1
Bennington	15,087	33	0	4	3	26	470	77	377	16	4
Berlin	2,818	8	0	0	0	8	30	1	28	1	0
Bradford	819	0	0	0	0	0	23	2	20	1	0
Brandon	3,882	1	0	0	0	1	105	30	72	3	0
Brattleboro	11,542	30	0	2	2	26	347	63	272	12	1
Burlington	38,370	152	0	19	23	110	1,654	253	1,358	43	6
Castleton	4,373	1	0	0	0	1	2	2	0	0	0
Chester	3,029	2	0	1	0	1	42	9	30	3	1
Colchester	17,245	20	0	4	3	13	950	149	782	19	4
Dover	1,440	3	0	0	0	3	142	28	113	1	0
Essex	19,564	26	0	1	3	22	514	117	389	8	1
Fair Haven	2,929	3	0	1	0	2	88	16	65	7	0
Hardwick	3,231	10	0	0	0	10	116	22	89	5	1
Hartford	10,739	14	0	1	0	13	237	51	172	14	1
Hinesburg	4,653	8	0	0	0	8	63	16	42	5	0
Ludlow	2,679	0	0	0	0	0	67	15	51	1	0
Lyndonville	1,228	0	0	0	0	0	0	0	0	0	0

[1] The FBI does not publish arson data unless it receives data from either the agency or the state for all 12 months of the calendar year.

Table 8. Offenses Known to Law Enforcement, by State and City, 2008—*Continued*

(Number.)

State/City	Population	Violent crime	Murder and non-negligent man-slaughter	Forcible rape	Robbery	Aggravated assault	Property crime	Burglary	Larceny-theft	Motor vehicle theft	Arson[1]
VERMONT—*Continued*											
Manchester	4,293	7	0	0	0	7	102	20	80	2	0
Middlebury	8,208	8	0	5	2	1	299	45	254	0	0
Milton	10,671	12	0	2	0	10	447	105	323	19	1
Montpelier	7,779	10	0	0	3	7	354	31	308	15	2
Morristown	5,570	8	0	1	0	7	144	27	117	0	0
Newport	5,206	13	0	2	0	11	122	21	100	1	0
Northfield	5,743	10	0	1	0	9	68	15	48	5	0
Norwich	3,502	1	0	0	0	1	12	4	8	0	0
Randolph	5,068	3	0	1	0	2	44	7	36	1	0
Richmond	4,180	0	0	0	0	0	23	18	2	3	0
Rutland	16,775	40	1	8	6	25	956	151	772	33	5
Shelburne	7,160	7	0	0	0	7	118	34	80	4	1
South Burlington	17,785	16	0	7	2	7	687	78	590	19	2
Springfield	8,616	22	0	4	2	16	308	62	232	14	3
St. Albans	7,263	47	0	1	11	35	484	62	407	15	0
St. Johnsbury	7,455	6	0	0	1	5	114	30	83	1	1
Stowe	4,955	2	0	0	0	2	213	24	186	3	1
Swanton	6,458	4	0	0	2	2	82	20	61	1	0
Thetford	2,799	0	0	0	0	0	4	0	4	0	0
Vergennes	2,691	3	0	0	0	3	45	13	30	2	0
Vernon	2,045	0	0	0	0	0	6	2	3	1	0
Waterbury	5,404	3	0	0	1	2	61	5	54	2	0
Weathersfield	2,848	1	0	1	0	0	50	19	30	1	0
Williston	8,458	4	0	0	0	4	358	48	303	7	0
Wilmington	2,370	8	0	1	0	7	59	12	43	4	0
Windsor	3,618	5	0	0	2	3	50	14	36	0	0
Winhall	787	2	0	0	0	2	51	4	47	0	0
Winooski	6,434	27	1	5	4	17	580	85	477	18	11
Woodstock	3,132	0	0	0	0	0	45	8	37	0	0
VIRGINIA											
Abingdon	7,991	15	0	5	3	7	346	35	304	7	1
Alexandria	140,891	324	3	30	149	142	3,389	294	2,713	382	6
Altavista	3,371	16	0	0	4	12	114	18	83	13	1
Amherst	2,203	0	0	0	0	0	28	1	25	2	0
Appalachia	1,735	8	1	1	0	6	50	9	39	2	0
Ashland	7,125	24	0	3	8	13	255	25	210	20	1
Bedford	6,260	13	1	2	0	10	226	28	191	7	0
Berryville	3,177	6	0	0	3	3	89	12	73	4	0
Big Stone Gap	5,661	5	0	3	0	2	124	16	106	2	2
Blacksburg	41,509	55	0	8	11	36	656	127	503	26	8
Blackstone	3,511	7	0	1	3	3	135	41	88	6	0
Bluefield	5,163	13	0	1	1	11	159	15	138	6	0
Bowling Green	1,029	0	0	0	0	0	3	0	3	0	0
Boykins	602	0	0	0	0	0	3	1	2	0	0
Bridgewater	5,404	0	0	0	0	0	26	0	21	5	0
Bristol	17,563	72	0	14	15	43	709	129	541	39	4
Broadway	3,031	0	0	0	0	0	8	3	5	0	0
Brookneal	1,250	2	0	0	0	2	21	9	9	3	0
Buena Vista	6,475	4	0	1	0	3	52	0	51	1	0
Burkeville	467	0	0	0	0	0	11	1	10	0	0
Cape Charles	1,518	0	0	0	0	0	9	1	8	0	0
Cedar Bluff	1,042	0	0	0	0	0	23	4	18	1	0
Charlottesville	41,216	219	5	23	79	112	1,950	186	1,616	148	13
Chase City	2,310	6	0	0	2	4	74	14	58	2	1
Chatham	1,259	1	0	0	1	0	8	0	8	0	0
Chesapeake	220,812	969	12	65	363	529	6,868	1,216	5,225	427	38
Chilhowie	1,746	2	1	0	0	1	32	4	28	0	0
Chincoteague	4,306	3	0	0	0	3	79	22	54	3	0
Christiansburg	19,466	50	2	14	9	25	789	126	632	31	3
Clarksville	1,252	3	1	0	1	1	34	1	33	0	1
Clifton Forge	3,946	6	0	1	0	5	63	18	44	1	1
Clinchco	404	0	0	0	0	0	0	0	0	0	0
Clintwood	1,498	2	0	0	0	2	47	10	37	0	1
Coeburn	1,982	2	0	0	0	2	56	12	44	0	1
Colonial Beach	3,784	13	0	2	1	10	126	27	96	3	0
Colonial Heights	17,843	45	0	2	19	24	795	69	692	34	9
Courtland	1,246	0	0	0	0	0	0	0	0	0	0
Covington	6,130	13	1	2	0	10	171	36	129	6	4
Crewe	2,255	9	0	0	6	3	80	19	58	3	1
Culpeper	14,072	59	0	3	20	36	481	43	416	22	11
Damascus	1,084	0	0	0	0	0	34	3	30	1	0
Danville	44,383	262	11	7	110	134	2,704	510	2,097	97	12
Dayton	1,354	0	0	0	0	0	11	1	9	1	0
Dublin	2,199	1	0	1	0	0	61	6	54	1	1
Dumfries	4,805	10	0	1	4	5	168	36	110	22	2

[1] The FBI does not publish arson data unless it receives data from either the agency or the state for all 12 months of the calendar year.

Table 8. Offenses Known to Law Enforcement, by State and City, 2008—*Continued*

(Number.)

State/City	Population	Violent crime	Murder and non-negligent man-slaughter	Forcible rape	Robbery	Aggravated assault	Property crime	Burglary	Larceny-theft	Motor vehicle theft	Arson[1]
VIRGINIA—*Continued*											
Edinburg	874	0	0	0	0	0	5	0	5	0	0
Elkton	2,619	2	0	0	1	1	28	4	23	1	0
Emporia	5,593	43	1	3	12	27	341	68	266	7	4
Exmore	1,346	2	0	0	2	0	51	7	42	2	0
Fairfax City	23,486	32	1	4	19	8	643	47	573	23	9
Falls Church	10,979	17	0	0	12	5	375	31	323	21	0
Farmville	7,216	17	2	1	8	6	148	21	122	5	0
Franklin	8,955	45	0	2	11	32	500	114	360	26	1
Fredericksburg	22,740	139	2	15	44	78	1,116	95	961	60	1
Fries	552	0	0	0	0	0	1	0	1	0	0
Front Royal	14,688	35	0	8	11	16	718	73	614	31	0
Galax	6,796	32	0	12	2	18	265	30	222	13	0
Gate City	2,040	3	0	1	1	1	56	10	44	2	1
Glade Spring	1,543	1	0	1	0	0	3	0	3	0	0
Glasgow	1,009	0	0	0	0	0	5	1	3	1	0
Glen Lyn	164	0	0	0	0	0	11	2	7	2	0
Gordonsville	1,700	3	0	0	0	3	29	4	24	1	0
Gretna	1,187	0	0	0	0	0	17	7	10	0	0
Grottoes	2,182	6	0	1	2	3	16	1	15	0	1
Grundy	961	0	0	0	0	0	6	2	4	0	0
Halifax	1,259	1	0	0	0	1	21	0	19	2	0
Hampton	145,897	472	8	42	211	211	5,127	761	3,963	403	15
Harrisonburg	44,346	142	1	12	25	104	1,224	246	903	75	6
Haymarket	1,265	2	0	0	0	2	9	0	9	0	1
Haysi	177	1	0	0	0	1	0	0	0	0	0
Herndon	21,900	43	0	2	11	30	450	39	393	18	1
Hillsville	2,644	4	0	1	2	1	52	7	44	1	0
Honaker	1,444	0	0	0	0	0	13	5	7	1	0
Hopewell	23,035	278	3	12	76	187	998	293	596	109	6
Hurt	1,208	1	0	0	1	0	12	4	8	0	0
Independence	895	1	0	0	0	1	9	1	7	1	0
Jonesville	966	3	0	0	0	3	26	5	21	0	0
Kenbridge	1,290	7	3	0	0	4	14	3	11	0	0
Kilmarnock	1,188	0	0	0	0	0	27	3	23	1	0
La Crosse	587	2	0	0	0	2	14	0	14	0	0
Lawrenceville	1,353	6	0	0	0	6	31	11	20	0	0
Lebanon	3,163	6	0	2	2	2	114	7	104	3	0
Leesburg	39,899	59	1	7	22	29	802	62	715	25	2
Lexington	7,026	3	0	0	1	2	70	5	64	1	0
Louisa	1,568	4	0	0	1	3	38	9	25	4	0
Luray	4,856	7	0	2	0	5	134	15	113	6	0
Lynchburg	71,805	347	4	30	101	212	2,739	425	2,160	154	16
Manassas	35,290	148	4	20	49	75	1,079	180	810	89	5
Manassas Park	11,528	23	0	6	4	13	191	17	153	21	3
Marion	6,013	35	1	1	3	30	190	35	149	6	3
Martinsville	14,430	59	1	2	25	31	546	102	420	24	4
Middleburg	959	0	0	0	0	0	10	0	9	1	0
Middletown	1,148	2	0	1	0	1	43	5	36	2	0
Mount Jackson	1,791	3	0	0	1	2	35	5	30	0	0
Narrows	2,155	1	0	1	0	0	22	7	13	2	0
New Market	1,859	1	0	0	0	1	18	4	14	0	0
Newport News	178,308	1,235	16	73	509	637	7,348	1,460	5,388	500	89
Norfolk	235,067	1,951	28	86	1,050	787	12,195	1,868	9,212	1,115	57
Norton	3,691	11	0	1	1	9	282	27	252	3	1
Occoquan	830	2	0	0	0	2	10	0	9	1	0
Onancock	1,392	2	0	0	0	2	23	10	11	2	0
Onley	475	1	0	0	1	0	21	3	18	0	0
Orange	4,639	8	0	2	0	6	110	29	79	2	0
Parksley	797	0	0	0	0	0	44	6	35	3	0
Pearisburg	2,770	3	0	1	0	2	58	5	52	1	0
Pembroke	1,167	0	0	0	0	0	15	2	12	1	0
Pennington Gap	1,726	0	0	0	0	0	38	16	22	0	0
Petersburg	32,677	615	5	30	256	324	2,479	871	1,296	312	10
Pocahontas	419	0	0	0	0	0	1	1	0	0	0
Poquoson	11,850	15	0	4	0	11	207	33	165	9	5
Portsmouth	101,782	719	15	59	348	297	5,650	1,123	4,182	345	8
Pound	1,073	3	0	0	0	3	25	4	21	0	0
Pulaski	8,997	30	0	4	5	21	401	87	295	19	4
Purcellville	5,175	7	0	1	1	5	86	7	74	5	2
Quantico	613	0	0	0	0	0	7	2	5	0	0
Radford	16,109	79	1	4	8	66	537	166	356	15	5
Remington	678	0	0	0	0	0	5	0	5	0	0
Rich Creek	683	2	0	1	0	1	13	5	8	0	0
Richlands	3,997	15	0	3	5	7	221	36	180	5	1
Richmond	199,674	1,588	31	53	779	725	8,148	1,787	5,331	1,030	51

[1] The FBI does not publish arson data unless it receives data from either the agency or the state for all 12 months of the calendar year.

Table 8. Offenses Known to Law Enforcement, by State and City, 2008—*Continued*

(Number.)

State/City	Population	Violent crime	Murder and non-negligent man-slaughter	Forcible rape	Robbery	Aggravated assault	Property crime	Burglary	Larceny-theft	Motor vehicle theft	Arson[1]
VIRGINIA—*Continued*											
Roanoke	91,983	745	11	48	213	473	5,090	983	3,811	296	39
Rocky Mount	4,546	15	0	2	3	10	145	16	123	6	0
Salem	25,193	36	2	1	7	26	761	121	605	35	2
Saltville	2,220	10	0	1	0	9	40	7	32	1	0
Shenandoah	1,862	0	0	0	0	0	33	8	22	3	0
Smithfield	7,071	14	0	0	10	4	288	34	237	17	1
South Boston	7,856	31	2	5	16	8	417	77	324	16	3
South Hill	4,556	38	1	2	13	22	217	24	185	8	1
Stanley	1,328	1	0	0	0	1	32	3	27	2	0
Staunton	23,746	58	2	5	13	38	607	59	523	25	5
Stephens City	1,479	2	0	0	2	0	42	8	30	4	0
St. Paul	966	0	0	0	0	0	28	2	26	0	0
Strasburg	4,334	18	0	3	0	15	132	20	107	5	0
Suffolk	83,470	310	5	29	90	186	2,147	386	1,617	144	31
Tappahannock	2,177	6	0	1	3	2	137	10	126	1	2
Tazewell	4,268	12	0	2	1	9	79	11	65	3	0
Timberville	1,714	0	0	0	0	0	12	3	9	0	0
Victoria	1,747	3	0	2	0	1	21	6	13	2	0
Vienna	14,889	7	0	1	0	6	246	32	209	5	2
Vinton	7,876	21	0	5	5	11	298	37	254	7	1
Virginia Beach	434,163	1,043	14	73	537	419	12,609	1,921	10,046	642	135
Warrenton	9,190	25	0	2	5	18	269	16	238	15	2
Warsaw	1,360	4	0	0	0	4	11	0	11	0	0
Waverly	2,160	16	0	0	4	12	22	6	11	5	0
Waynesboro	21,846	93	1	4	21	67	635	107	494	34	5
Weber City	1,310	1	0	0	0	1	32	5	27	0	0
West Point	3,145	3	0	0	1	2	41	9	29	3	0
White Stone	340	0	0	0	0	0	5	0	5	0	0
Williamsburg	12,445	22	0	3	9	10	250	13	224	13	1
Winchester	25,904	86	1	8	36	41	1,316	202	1,060	54	6
Wise	3,232	4	0	2	0	2	104	10	92	2	1
Woodstock	4,297	8	0	0	1	7	59	1	55	3	0
Wytheville	8,148	3	1	0	2	0	314	20	283	11	2
WASHINGTON											
Aberdeen	16,116	39	0	4	12	23	990	174	744	72	5
Airway Heights	5,239	26	1	5	4	16	151	26	108	17	0
Algona	2,764	12	0	1	1	10	44	15	24	5	0
Anacortes	17,020	27	0	3	5	19	504	109	364	31	1
Arlington	17,187	34	0	1	11	22	752	108	556	88	3
Auburn	50,660	275	0	14	102	159	3,613	630	2,343	640	23
Bainbridge Island	22,041	29	0	4	6	19	317	77	233	7	7
Battle Ground	14,099	38	0	13	5	20	369	65	276	28	0
Bellevue	122,459	168	0	33	72	63	4,289	687	3,327	275	18
Bellingham	78,804	181	2	23	59	97	4,358	641	3,515	202	23
Bingen	681	1	0	0	0	1	19	5	12	2	0
Black Diamond	3,979	14	0	1	0	13	57	20	32	5	0
Blaine	4,948	9	0	2	2	5	251	51	197	3	1
Bonney Lake	16,482	33	2	4	4	23	432	86	314	32	5
Bothell	32,464	37	0	1	19	17	843	156	591	96	5
Bremerton	33,735	308	1	52	53	202	1,564	383	1,076	105	20
Brewster	2,075	7	0	1	0	6	122	35	78	9	2
Brier	6,362	4	0	0	2	2	93	23	64	6	3
Buckley	5,488	13	0	1	1	11	97	19	71	7	5
Burien	31,342	189	4	28	71	86	1,477	380	844	253	12
Burlington	8,869	27	1	3	9	14	1,021	104	856	61	2
Camas	18,527	20	0	11	3	6	443	73	349	21	5
Carnation	1,831	2	0	1	1	0	25	10	15	0	0
Castle Rock	2,118	9	0	3	3	3	68	10	53	5	0
Centralia	15,772	107	1	13	23	70	1,029	162	789	78	8
Chehalis	7,243	16	0	3	5	8	642	78	537	27	5
Cheney	10,653	15	0	1	3	11	298	45	241	12	0
Chewelah	2,291	4	0	2	2	0	116	31	81	4	0
Clarkston	7,123	21	0	0	4	17	347	38	302	7	0
Cle Elum	3,480	6	0	2	0	4	185	37	139	9	0
Clyde Hill	3,049	4	0	0	0	4	35	15	18	2	1
College Place	9,159	3	0	2	0	1	213	28	175	10	0
Colville	4,939	5	0	1	2	2	191	8	182	1	0
Connell	3,018	1	0	0	0	1	37	5	30	2	0
Cosmopolis	1,687	1	0	1	0	0	21	5	15	1	1
Coulee Dam	1,057	3	0	1	0	2	13	3	7	3	0
Coupeville	1,860	5	0	1	2	2	67	23	40	4	0
Covington	18,158	39	0	6	23	10	554	128	356	70	17
Des Moines	29,013	116	1	14	59	42	1,080	255	616	209	4
Dupont	7,407	12	0	2	1	9	54	15	36	3	0
Duvall	6,171	0	0	0	0	0	33	6	27	0	1

[1] The FBI does not publish arson data unless it receives data from either the agency or the state for all 12 months of the calendar year.

Table 8. Offenses Known to Law Enforcement, by State and City, 2008—*Continued*

(Number.)

State/City	Population	Violent crime	Murder and non-negligent man-slaughter	Forcible rape	Robbery	Aggravated assault	Property crime	Burglary	Larceny-theft	Motor vehicle theft	Arson[1]
WASHINGTON—*Continued*											
East Wenatchee	12,328	24	2	7	1	14	600	66	515	19	1
Eatonville	2,495	4	0	1	0	3	70	20	48	2	6
Edgewood	9,833	18	0	0	2	16	225	84	130	11	2
Edmonds	40,214	63	0	4	21	38	964	231	671	62	7
Ellensburg	17,540	47	0	21	1	25	970	184	740	46	7
Elma	3,146	12	0	0	2	10	213	50	154	9	1
Enumclaw	11,066	2	0	0	1	1	274	39	210	25	2
Ephrata	7,298	24	0	2	11	11	576	164	390	22	6
Everett	98,552	584	1	76	223	284	7,542	1,251	5,108	1,183	18
Everson	2,159	5	0	1	0	4	104	15	85	4	0
Federal Way	84,775	323	8	30	170	115	4,549	800	2,933	816	13
Ferndale	11,325	21	0	4	6	11	326	79	229	18	6
Fife	8,322	47	0	2	10	35	565	85	361	119	6
Fircrest	6,299	8	0	1	1	6	159	38	106	15	0
Forks	3,221	39	0	7	5	27	146	27	118	1	0
Gig Harbor	6,631	13	0	2	5	6	348	40	281	27	3
Goldendale	3,720	9	0	1	1	7	167	40	118	9	1
Grand Coulee	1,920	9	0	3	0	6	52	20	31	1	0
Grandview	9,418	14	1	0	1	12	363	88	219	56	2
Granger	2,968	10	0	4	2	4	134	55	55	24	2
Granite Falls	3,055	14	0	1	0	13	145	28	100	17	2
Hoquiam	8,902	20	0	1	3	16	394	71	305	18	2
Ilwaco	999	11	0	0	1	10	34	4	29	1	0
Issaquah	24,326	17	1	1	6	9	814	103	638	73	3
Kalama	2,182	2	0	2	0	0	67	7	58	2	0
Kelso	12,063	70	0	27	12	31	845	129	641	75	3
Kenmore	20,688	38	1	7	8	22	319	89	203	27	3
Kennewick	62,930	235	1	38	40	156	2,382	409	1,810	163	30
Kent	84,966	543	2	84	171	286	4,649	1,112	2,702	835	23
Kettle Falls	1,577	0	0	0	0	0	82	22	57	3	0
Kirkland	47,619	97	0	11	35	51	1,928	255	1,499	174	16
Kittitas	1,225	2	0	1	1	0	63	15	46	2	0
La Center	1,953	6	0	0	0	6	48	4	42	2	1
Lacey	39,037	98	1	16	24	57	1,731	236	1,403	92	3
Lake Forest Park	12,562	11	0	0	4	7	275	60	194	21	0
Lake Stevens	13,698	28	0	3	5	20	544	111	372	61	6
Lakewood	57,081	532	3	57	145	327	3,442	691	2,350	401	25
Langley	1,035	0	0	0	0	0	71	32	34	5	0
Liberty Lake	6,947	2	0	0	1	1	79	13	56	10	0
Long Beach	1,380	4	0	2	0	2	92	49	41	2	0
Longview	36,887	150	1	34	43	72	1,925	310	1,453	162	27
Lynden	11,812	8	0	1	3	4	196	35	159	2	3
Lynnwood	33,602	146	1	6	62	77	2,293	258	1,849	186	6
Maple Valley	17,626	20	0	4	4	12	355	99	223	33	11
Marysville	34,192	75	0	12	19	44	1,214	247	782	185	12
McCleary	1,593	3	0	0	0	3	25	9	16	0	0
Medical Lake	4,709	4	0	2	0	2	36	13	22	1	1
Medina	3,626	1	0	0	0	1	82	11	61	10	0
Mercer Island	24,134	13	0	0	3	10	419	79	310	30	4
Mill Creek	15,776	25	0	3	9	13	464	93	308	63	1
Milton	6,927	30	0	1	12	17	256	58	166	32	0
Monroe	16,764	55	1	7	11	36	462	64	347	51	4
Montesano	3,613	0	0	0	0	0	128	21	105	2	0
Morton	1,091	7	0	1	0	6	73	12	54	7	0
Moses Lake	18,283	103	2	10	23	68	1,739	338	1,316	85	4
Mountlake Terrace	20,015	40	0	6	17	17	555	106	393	56	7
Mount Vernon	31,237	91	0	19	26	46	1,732	275	1,374	83	28
Moxee	2,251	3	0	1	1	1	10	6	3	1	0
Mukilteo	20,870	18	0	3	5	10	498	137	299	62	2
Newcastle	10,080	6	0	1	2	3	202	50	126	26	5
Normandy Park	6,222	3	0	0	2	1	165	58	102	5	1
North Bend	4,622	15	0	5	4	6	152	26	118	8	1
North Bonneville	807	0	0	0	0	0	17	2	13	2	0
Oakesdale	389	0	0	0	0	0	6	3	3	0	0
Oak Harbor	23,068	61	0	24	3	34	569	125	406	38	7
Oakville	731	0	0	0	0	0	15	7	5	3	0
Ocean Shores	4,964	5	0	2	1	2	120	40	77	3	0
Odessa	911	5	0	0	0	5	13	6	7	0	0
Olympia	45,189	149	3	24	42	80	2,192	366	1,676	150	8
Omak	4,685	22	0	5	7	10	240	87	140	13	0
Oroville	1,564	8	0	2	0	6	84	17	64	3	0
Orting	6,262	2	0	0	1	1	96	8	83	5	1
Othello	6,429	30	0	4	4	22	527	74	410	43	3
Pacific	6,076	13	1	1	4	7	144	37	74	33	2
Palouse	930	0	0	0	0	0	9	3	5	1	0

[1] The FBI does not publish arson data unless it receives data from either the agency or the state for all 12 months of the calendar year.

Table 8. Offenses Known to Law Enforcement, by State and City, 2008—*Continued*

(Number.)

State/City	Population	Violent crime	Murder and non-negligent man-slaughter	Forcible rape	Robbery	Aggravated assault	Property crime	Burglary	Larceny-theft	Motor vehicle theft	Arson[1]
WASHINGTON—*Continued*											
Pasco	55,612	166	1	19	46	100	1,664	468	1,030	166	24
Port Angeles	18,835	67	1	16	14	36	914	145	735	34	17
Port Orchard	7,960	50	2	9	6	33	461	127	312	22	4
Port Townsend	9,161	18	0	1	0	17	378	70	301	7	4
Poulsbo	7,991	42	0	7	3	32	303	44	257	2	0
Prosser	5,097	7	0	1	1	5	207	47	141	19	1
Pullman	26,587	20	0	3	2	15	391	108	273	10	1
Puyallup	36,860	153	0	18	51	84	2,624	264	1,950	410	19
Quincy	5,553	13	0	5	1	7	249	56	179	14	0
Rainier	1,613	2	0	1	1	0	22	10	12	0	0
Raymond	2,917	12	0	0	0	12	100	21	72	7	1
Reardan	597	0	0	0	0	0	10	5	5	0	0
Redmond	49,921	65	2	17	20	26	1,681	175	1,420	86	5
Republic	951	2	0	0	0	2	18	5	12	1	0
Richland	45,522	101	0	25	14	62	1,048	206	788	54	7
Ridgefield	4,547	2	0	0	2	0	104	11	86	7	0
Ritzville	1,720	0	0	0	0	0	67	16	48	3	0
Rosalia	586	0	0	0	0	0	7	1	6	0	0
Roy	810	9	0	1	0	8	19	3	14	2	0
Royal City	1,966	10	0	0	1	9	55	21	28	6	1
Ruston	880	2	0	0	1	1	31	10	15	6	1
Sammamish	35,395	18	0	6	3	9	422	103	307	12	4
SeaTac	25,743	160	2	16	79	63	1,513	406	805	302	3
Seattle	598,077	3,447	29	126	1,612	1,680	32,820	6,503	22,642	3,675	79
Sedro Woolley	10,902	14	1	5	3	5	536	107	389	40	3
Selah	7,136	5	0	5	0	0	213	54	145	14	0
Sequim	6,161	25	0	6	2	17	238	36	193	9	3
Shelton	9,322	56	0	14	5	37	883	164	643	76	2
Shoreline	52,571	97	0	13	45	39	1,673	362	1,131	180	17
Snohomish	8,822	32	0	2	12	18	381	65	281	35	18
Snoqualmie	9,103	3	0	1	0	2	113	18	88	7	0
Soap Lake	1,861	17	0	0	1	16	55	20	34	1	0
South Bend	1,807	1	0	0	0	1	50	9	37	4	1
Spokane	201,491	1,352	13	94	460	785	11,025	2,269	7,218	1,538	58
Spokane Valley	85,551	270	1	25	66	178	3,424	635	2,364	425	29
Stanwood	6,130	11	0	5	1	5	251	41	193	17	0
Steilacoom	6,124	8	0	2	1	5	87	18	63	6	1
Sumas	1,237	0	0	0	0	0	51	11	37	3	0
Sumner	9,723	48	0	5	7	36	488	104	317	67	6
Sunnyside	14,985	41	2	2	14	23	1,129	260	603	266	9
Tacoma	196,851	1,995	15	142	622	1,216	15,071	2,890	9,463	2,718	75
Tenino	2,229	4	0	0	1	3	67	19	46	2	0
Tieton	1,171	2	0	1	0	1	5	0	4	1	1
Toledo	680	3	0	2	1	0	14	11	0	3	0
Tonasket	941	0	0	0	0	0	69	10	56	3	0
Toppenish	9,236	64	1	7	26	30	613	147	344	122	12
Tukwila	17,237	180	6	15	91	68	2,821	374	2,038	409	13
Tumwater	13,564	38	0	8	11	19	592	127	428	37	0
Twisp	892	2	0	0	0	2	43	10	33	0	0
Union Gap	5,644	23	1	5	8	9	677	115	516	46	1
University Place	30,529	93	1	6	34	52	834	216	516	102	7
Vancouver	163,574	605	0	105	176	324	6,298	842	4,248	1,208	61
Walla Walla	30,830	134	1	31	12	90	1,388	264	1,052	72	11
Wapato	4,569	46	0	5	14	27	363	81	229	53	1
Washougal	12,256	35	0	10	3	22	273	60	200	13	3
Wenatchee	29,976	99	1	21	12	65	1,207	212	934	61	1
Westport	2,575	8	0	0	4	4	99	36	60	3	0
West Richland	10,689	5	0	2	0	3	131	30	98	3	1
White Salmon	2,348	3	0	0	1	2	58	12	39	7	0
Wilbur	873	1	0	0	0	1	12	2	10	0	0
Winlock	1,256	0	0	0	0	0	41	8	28	5	0
Winthrop	376	0	0	0	0	0	14	3	11	0	0
Woodinville	10,280	17	0	3	5	9	454	94	332	28	7
Woodland	4,894	16	0	3	2	11	195	40	129	26	7
Woodway	1,434	0	0	0	0	0	24	14	9	1	0
Yakima	83,027	429	8	49	133	239	5,940	1,233	3,907	800	27
Yarrow Point	1,059	0	0	0	0	0	9	0	8	1	0
Yelm	5,716	14	0	6	3	5	230	60	162	8	1
Zillah	2,669	5	0	3	1	1	181	52	121	8	2
WEST VIRGINIA											
Ansted	1,579	1	0	0	0	1	3	0	3	0	0
Barboursville	3,402	19	0	0	8	11	386	33	351	2	3
Bethlehem	2,492	0	0	0	0	0	11	1	10	0	0
Bluefield	11,018	36	0	5	12	19	242	84	145	13	4
Bridgeport	7,825	10	0	0	2	8	278	28	241	9	2

[1] The FBI does not publish arson data unless it receives data from either the agency or the state for all 12 months of the calendar year.

Table 8. Offenses Known to Law Enforcement, by State and City, 2008—*Continued*

(Number.)

State/City	Population	Violent crime	Murder and non-negligent man-slaughter	Forcible rape	Robbery	Aggravated assault	Property crime	Burglary	Larceny-theft	Motor vehicle theft	Arson[1]
WEST VIRGINIA—*Continued*											
Buckhannon	5,477	11	0	1	1	9	50	7	41	2	1
Cameron	1,080	1	0	0	0	1	0	0	0	0	0
Chapmanville	1,107	4	0	0	2	2	48	8	35	5	0
Charleston	50,132	592	3	21	125	443	2,997	608	2,177	212	34
Charles Town	4,283	10	0	2	1	7	118	27	85	6	0
Clarksburg	16,294	83	1	9	13	60	889	197	650	42	12
Dunbar	7,641	28	0	5	7	16	195	55	112	28	2
Elkins	6,986	30	0	0	4	26	232	47	179	6	7
Fairmont	19,075	52	0	0	9	43	403	120	258	25	12
Fayetteville	2,647	0	0	0	0	0	81	9	70	2	0
Follansbee	2,839	5	0	0	1	4	44	13	26	5	0
Glen Dale	1,402	0	0	0	0	0	40	7	32	1	1
Grafton	5,291	0	0	0	0	0	20	5	13	2	0
Granville	810	4	0	0	1	3	86	9	75	2	0
Hurricane	6,255	11	0	1	0	10	209	15	172	22	1
Kenova	3,258	20	1	2	10	7	203	40	145	18	0
Keyser	5,242	11	0	3	2	6	151	34	114	3	3
Lewisburg	3,528	1	0	0	0	1	39	4	35	0	1
Logan	1,491	17	0	0	2	15	300	38	255	7	1
Martinsburg	16,649	109	0	5	34	70	1,130	109	974	47	10
Montgomery	1,919	2	0	0	1	1	62	5	57	0	0
Moorefield	2,465	8	0	0	0	8	68	18	46	4	2
Moundsville	9,145	25	0	0	4	21	352	69	266	17	6
Nitro	6,773	4	0	0	3	1	182	28	149	5	2
Oceana	1,403	6	1	0	0	5	90	6	80	4	0
Philippi	2,764	4	1	0	0	3	43	3	38	2	0
Point Pleasant	4,401	14	0	0	7	7	215	48	155	12	0
Princeton	6,217	49	1	4	11	33	472	67	386	19	1
Ranson	4,570	18	0	0	4	14	40	8	28	4	0
Ravenswood	3,948	1	0	0	0	1	29	8	21	0	0
Ripley	3,246	6	0	1	0	5	64	10	51	3	0
Shinnston	2,222	2	0	0	0	2	55	9	46	0	0
South Charleston	12,371	46	2	1	18	25	631	108	484	39	5
Spencer	2,171	3	0	0	0	3	53	4	48	1	0
St. Albans	10,967	42	0	0	10	32	434	95	301	38	1
Summersville	3,316	7	0	1	1	5	78	8	67	3	0
Vienna	10,583	9	1	0	0	8	367	29	332	6	1
Weirton	18,660	23	0	0	7	16	243	43	180	20	2
Wellsburg	2,580	2	0	0	1	1	48	18	26	4	1
Weston	4,221	2	1	0	0	1	10	0	10	0	1
West Union	781	0	0	0	0	0	9	3	6	0	0
Wheeling	28,838	141	1	16	37	87	875	186	632	57	3
White Sulphur Springs	2,286	0	0	0	0	0	1	0	1	0	0
Williamson	3,074	15	0	2	0	13	46	9	32	5	0
Williamstown	2,972	1	0	1	0	0	28	3	25	0	0
WISCONSIN											
Adams	1,791	2	0	0	0	2	95	22	69	4	0
Albany	1,104	7	0	0	0	7	23	3	20	0	0
Algoma	3,166	2	0	1	0	1	104	5	98	1	1
Altoona	6,573	10	0	6	0	4	151	29	116	6	1
Amery	2,774	8	0	0	1	7	84	4	73	7	0
Antigo	8,031	13	0	1	1	11	576	50	512	14	0
Appleton	69,975	155	0	20	19	116	2,217	324	1,837	56	12
Arcadia	2,308	3	0	0	0	3	40	5	31	4	0
Ashland	7,999	22	0	1	2	19	492	81	393	18	1
Ashwaubenon	17,299	10	0	1	0	9	887	48	812	27	0
Bangor	1,368	2	0	0	1	1	17	1	16	0	0
Baraboo	11,089	25	2	0	2	21	120	10	104	6	6
Barron	3,143	5	0	3	0	2	39	7	31	1	0
Bayfield	574	1	0	0	0	1	34	5	29	0	0
Bayside	4,288	0	0	0	0	0	28	3	25	0	0
Beaver Dam	15,260	13	0	0	3	10	486	65	416	5	0
Belleville	2,336	1	0	1	0	0	35	0	33	2	0
Beloit	36,737	164	2	15	56	91	1,719	255	1,304	160	8
Beloit Town	7,468	11	0	4	3	4	188	40	136	12	2
Berlin	5,086	4	0	0	0	4	168	13	153	2	2
Big Bend	1,285	2	0	0	2	0	68	10	56	2	0
Black River Falls	3,435	4	0	0	0	4	140	19	117	4	0
Blair	1,253	1	0	0	0	1	30	6	21	3	0
Bloomer	3,342	0	0	0	0	0	64	4	60	0	0
Bloomfield	5,976	1	0	0	0	1	103	12	89	2	0
Boscobel	3,128	42	0	0	0	42	80	27	53	0	0
Brillion	2,815	2	0	0	0	2	19	3	14	2	0
Brodhead	3,068	2	0	0	0	2	110	6	103	1	1
Brookfield	39,267	19	0	2	7	10	1,379	129	1,245	5	1

[1] The FBI does not publish arson data unless it receives data from either the agency or the state for all 12 months of the calendar year.

Table 8. Offenses Known to Law Enforcement, by State and City, 2008—*Continued*

(Number.)

State/City	Population	Violent crime	Murder and non-negligent man-slaughter	Forcible rape	Robbery	Aggravated assault	Property crime	Burglary	Larceny-theft	Motor vehicle theft	Arson[1]
WISCONSIN—*Continued*											
Brookfield Township	6,149	9	0	0	2	7	161	1	156	4	0
Brown Deer	11,732	39	0	1	15	23	380	33	335	12	0
Burlington	10,473	2	0	1	1	0	345	28	305	12	0
Burlington Town	6,465	1	0	0	0	1	76	11	60	5	1
Butler	1,784	6	0	0	0	6	54	5	45	4	0
Caledonia	25,608	29	0	1	3	25	226	75	125	26	0
Campbellsport	1,967	0	0	0	0	0	25	2	23	0	0
Campbell Township	4,470	2	0	0	0	2	71	12	58	1	0
Cedarburg	11,043	9	0	0	1	8	137	14	120	3	0
Chenequa	586	0	0	0	0	0	5	0	5	0	0
Chetek	2,162	3	0	0	0	3	60	11	45	4	0
Chilton	3,598	4	0	2	0	2	43	5	35	3	0
Chippewa Falls	13,330	32	0	1	6	25	316	54	249	13	2
Cleveland	1,380	3	0	0	0	3	10	1	8	1	0
Clinton	2,271	0	0	0	0	0	54	4	50	0	0
Clintonville	4,330	18	0	3	0	15	215	30	177	8	1
Colby-Abbotsford	3,563	0	0	0	0	0	80	4	75	1	0
Columbus	5,032	6	0	0	0	6	117	13	103	1	0
Combined Locks	3,156	3	0	0	0	3	18	4	14	0	0
Coon Valley	697	0	0	0	0	0	12	3	2	7	0
Cornell	1,408	1	0	1	0	0	35	2	32	1	0
Cottage Grove	5,958	4	0	1	0	3	121	29	88	4	1
Crandon	1,852	2	0	0	0	2	52	18	31	3	0
Cross Plains	3,618	1	1	0	0	0	49	6	43	0	0
Cuba City	2,006	0	0	0	0	0	54	4	50	0	0
Cudahy	18,596	69	0	3	27	39	691	141	509	41	3
Cumberland	2,252	0	0	0	0	0	17	3	9	5	0
Dane	1,000	0	0	0	0	0	0	0	0	0	0
Darien	1,650	1	0	0	0	1	48	17	31	0	0
Darlington	2,238	7	0	1	0	6	42	2	36	4	0
DeForest	9,074	7	0	3	2	2	190	16	171	3	0
Delafield	6,901	12	0	0	3	9	125	5	119	1	0
Delavan	8,417	25	0	1	3	21	366	38	314	14	0
Delavan Town	4,839	8	0	2	0	6	121	23	90	8	0
Denmark	2,154	0	0	0	0	0	8	0	7	1	0
De Pere	23,015	12	0	5	2	5	402	62	331	9	0
Dodgeville	4,534	8	0	2	0	6	64	6	57	1	0
Durand	1,867	0	0	0	0	0	4	1	3	0	0
Eagle River	1,555	0	0	0	0	0	115	3	109	3	2
Eagle Village	1,846	4	0	0	2	2	27	1	24	2	0
East Troy	4,212	7	0	0	0	7	136	14	119	3	4
Eau Claire	65,344	84	1	13	14	56	1,827	362	1,406	59	2
Edgar	1,471	0	0	0	0	0	13	3	10	0	0
Edgerton	5,281	3	1	0	0	2	40	8	30	2	0
Eleva	642	0	0	0	0	0	12	1	9	2	0
Elkhart Lake	1,175	1	0	1	0	0	29	0	27	2	0
Elkhorn	9,317	8	0	2	0	6	235	34	189	12	0
Elk Mound	801	7	0	0	0	7	11	1	10	0	0
Ellsworth	3,141	1	0	0	0	1	107	7	97	3	0
Elm Grove	5,980	3	0	1	1	1	73	10	63	0	0
Elroy	1,447	1	0	0	0	1	29	4	22	3	0
Evansville	5,027	4	0	0	0	4	77	11	66	0	0
Everest	16,032	57	2	1	3	51	373	65	290	18	0
Fennimore	2,224	1	0	0	0	1	79	10	69	0	0
Fitchburg	23,599	69	0	2	28	39	828	96	699	33	2
Fond du Lac	42,037	144	0	27	7	110	1,232	120	1,069	43	8
Fontana	1,866	3	0	0	1	2	29	2	27	0	1
Fort Atkinson	12,004	15	0	1	0	14	245	23	219	3	2
Fox Lake	1,466	0	0	0	0	0	8	3	4	1	0
Fox Point	6,780	2	0	0	2	0	89	11	76	2	0
Fox Valley	17,562	9	0	0	0	9	446	74	357	15	0
Franklin	35,751	44	0	5	5	34	780	129	620	31	4
Frederic	1,192	0	0	0	0	0	14	5	8	1	0
Geneva Town	4,756	6	0	0	1	5	115	16	98	1	0
Genoa City	2,939	0	0	0	0	0	51	15	35	1	0
Germantown	19,508	30	0	0	5	25	453	53	389	11	2
Glendale	13,190	20	0	0	20	0	837	35	766	36	0
Grafton	11,533	12	0	0	3	9	214	10	200	4	0
Grand Chute	20,836	23	1	4	4	14	1,211	64	1,121	26	2
Grand Rapids	7,647	2	0	1	1	0	37	8	27	2	0
Grantsburg	1,423	5	0	0	0	5	39	6	30	3	0
Green Bay	100,531	502	2	76	104	320	3,107	651	2,303	153	17
Greendale	13,979	12	0	0	6	6	811	28	774	9	0
Greenfield	36,217	51	0	4	32	15	1,409	186	1,162	61	3
Green Lake	1,140	0	0	0	0	0	23	1	22	0	0

[1] The FBI does not publish arson data unless it receives data from either the agency or the state for all 12 months of the calendar year.

Table 8. Offenses Known to Law Enforcement, by State and City, 2008—*Continued*

(Number.)

State/City	Population	Violent crime	Murder and non-negligent man-slaughter	Forcible rape	Robbery	Aggravated assault	Property crime	Burglary	Larceny-theft	Motor vehicle theft	Arson[1]
WISCONSIN—*Continued*											
Hales Corners	7,715	7	0	1	4	2	172	12	154	6	0
Hartford	13,995	11	0	0	3	8	275	26	243	6	0
Hartland	8,717	9	0	1	0	8	108	13	92	3	0
Hayward	2,304	6	0	0	0	6	241	17	209	15	0
Hazel Green	1,108	2	0	0	0	2	2	2	0	0	0
Highland	819	0	0	0	0	0	7	2	4	1	0
Hillsboro	1,265	0	0	0	0	0	10	9	1	0	0
Hobart-Lawrence	10,388	0	0	0	0	0	63	10	50	3	0
Holmen	7,910	9	0	0	0	9	166	22	137	7	1
Horicon	3,553	2	0	1	0	1	30	6	20	4	1
Hortonville	2,788	0	0	0	0	0	144	8	135	1	0
Hudson	12,504	12	1	2	2	7	684	50	614	20	1
Hurley	1,560	9	0	0	0	9	69	3	58	8	0
Independence	1,213	3	0	0	0	3	8	3	4	1	0
Iron Ridge	987	0	0	0	0	0	11	1	10	0	0
Jackson	6,350	10	0	0	1	9	40	6	32	2	0
Janesville	63,353	172	1	23	53	95	2,796	507	2,215	74	17
Jefferson	7,845	11	0	1	0	10	229	26	196	7	0
Juneau	2,611	0	0	0	0	0	64	7	55	2	0
Kaukauna	15,519	9	0	2	1	6	365	33	323	9	0
Kenosha	96,977	343	3	40	129	171	2,920	590	2,123	207	10
Kewaskum	4,197	5	0	1	0	4	98	2	94	2	0
Kewaunee	2,814	3	0	1	0	2	51	3	47	1	0
Kiel	3,509	8	0	2	0	6	76	8	66	2	0
Kohler	1,968	0	0	0	0	0	55	1	54	0	0
La Crosse	50,569	206	1	16	32	157	1,891	308	1,495	88	8
Ladysmith	3,476	1	0	1	0	0	158	25	131	2	3
Lake Delton	2,938	13	0	1	2	10	515	21	488	6	0
Lake Geneva	8,203	10	0	0	0	10	402	23	375	4	1
Lake Hallie	6,065	4	0	0	0	4	225	35	182	8	0
Lake Mills	5,504	1	0	0	0	1	76	14	62	0	0
Lancaster	3,846	0	0	0	0	0	28	12	16	0	0
Lodi	2,937	1	0	0	0	1	76	10	66	0	0
Luxemburg	2,261	0	0	0	0	0	30	6	23	1	0
Madison	231,231	891	10	50	368	463	8,256	2,038	5,720	498	93
Manitowoc	32,891	53	0	6	4	43	662	77	579	6	1
Maple Bluff	1,306	0	0	0	0	0	34	7	24	3	0
Marathon City	1,546	11	0	0	0	11	29	6	23	0	0
Marinette	10,641	10	1	1	3	5	459	64	381	14	5
Marion	1,192	1	0	0	0	1	17	0	17	0	0
Markesan	1,289	0	0	0	0	0	20	7	12	1	0
Marshall Village	3,696	4	0	0	0	4	55	5	50	0	0
Marshfield	18,847	12	0	7	1	4	494	59	424	11	2
Mauston	4,332	26	0	0	1	25	162	30	124	8	0
Mayville	5,322	1	0	0	0	1	110	8	101	1	1
McFarland	7,827	7	0	2	0	5	175	26	147	2	0
Medford	4,012	10	0	2	0	8	180	16	163	1	0
Menasha	16,829	43	1	9	2	31	534	70	439	25	4
Menomonee Falls	34,590	14	0	2	3	9	514	60	434	20	2
Menomonie	15,477	40	0	3	0	37	439	57	372	10	4
Mequon	23,483	5	0	0	3	2	164	43	120	1	0
Merrill	9,587	36	0	6	3	27	313	38	267	8	0
Middleton	17,059	19	0	3	4	12	532	88	428	16	5
Milton	5,832	3	0	0	0	3	87	10	76	1	1
Milwaukee	602,131	7,339	71	208	3,207	3,853	36,562	6,409	23,615	6,538	317
Mineral Point	2,529	1	0	0	0	1	57	5	48	4	0
Minocqua	4,947	5	0	0	0	5	247	14	220	13	0
Mishicot	1,368	0	0	0	0	0	7	1	6	0	0
Mondovi	2,604	0	0	0	0	0	53	16	37	0	0
Monona	8,047	15	0	2	7	6	421	22	387	12	4
Monroe	10,470	16	1	1	2	12	363	36	313	14	5
Mosinee	4,039	0	0	0	0	0	111	16	91	4	0
Mount Horeb	6,884	0	0	0	0	0	113	14	98	1	0
Mount Pleasant	26,193	39	0	1	21	17	832	137	677	18	2
Mukwonago	7,046	6	0	0	2	4	132	18	107	7	0
Muskego	23,025	4	0	3	1	0	157	37	110	10	0
Neenah	25,005	34	2	4	5	23	413	76	326	11	4
Neillsville	2,555	1	0	0	0	1	76	9	64	3	0
New Berlin	39,091	18	0	1	3	14	612	81	509	22	7
New Glarus	2,051	1	0	0	0	1	82	7	75	0	0
New Holstein	3,122	3	0	0	0	3	91	14	77	0	0
New Lisbon	2,542	3	0	0	1	2	16	0	16	0	0
New Richmond	8,273	0	0	0	0	0	300	40	255	5	3
Niagara	1,726	0	0	0	0	0	41	12	26	3	0

[1] The FBI does not publish arson data unless it receives data from either the agency or the state for all 12 months of the calendar year.

Table 8. Offenses Known to Law Enforcement, by State and City, 2008—*Continued*

(Number.)

State/City	Population	Violent crime	Murder and non-negligent man-slaughter	Forcible rape	Robbery	Aggravated assault	Property crime	Burglary	Larceny-theft	Motor vehicle theft	Arson[1]
WISCONSIN—*Continued*											
North Fond du Lac	5,118	5	0	0	0	5	101	9	87	5	0
North Hudson	3,790	0	0	0	0	0	12	1	10	1	0
North Prairie	2,076	0	0	0	0	0	15	1	13	1	0
Oak Creek	33,833	32	0	6	16	10	1,072	130	908	34	2
Oconomowoc	14,612	4	0	2	0	2	146	22	119	5	0
Oconomowoc Town	8,178	4	0	0	0	4	41	10	25	6	0
Oconto	4,595	9	0	5	0	4	161	23	132	6	2
Oconto Falls	2,782	2	0	0	2	0	56	4	50	2	1
Omro	3,379	6	0	0	0	6	12	10	0	2	0
Onalaska	16,873	4	0	0	1	3	572	50	516	6	0
Oregon	9,445	6	0	2	0	4	195	45	150	0	1
Osceola	2,723	17	0	0	0	17	45	7	37	1	0
Oshkosh	64,747	186	0	13	29	144	2,294	460	1,767	67	6
Osseo	1,608	1	0	0	0	1	52	13	37	2	0
Palmyra	1,749	5	0	2	0	3	81	6	75	0	0
Park Falls	2,323	1	0	1	0	0	44	3	40	1	0
Pepin	928	0	0	0	0	0	24	0	24	0	0
Peshtigo	3,208	0	0	0	0	0	84	16	64	4	0
Pewaukee	13,229	9	0	0	3	6	169	17	144	8	3
Pewaukee Village	8,997	5	0	0	3	2	137	18	115	4	0
Phillips	1,461	6	0	1	0	5	52	2	50	0	0
Platteville	9,600	6	0	1	0	5	140	23	106	11	0
Pleasant Prairie	20,126	3	0	1	0	2	402	27	373	2	0
Plover	11,796	8	0	0	0	8	316	52	254	10	0
Plymouth	8,304	5	0	2	0	3	226	29	192	5	3
Portage	9,811	33	0	6	1	26	354	44	307	3	0
Port Washington	11,086	1	1	0	0	0	140	11	125	4	1
Poynette	2,548	0	0	0	0	0	27	11	16	0	0
Prescott	4,029	4	0	0	0	4	146	20	125	1	0
Pulaski	3,556	5	0	0	0	5	48	2	45	1	0
Racine	82,226	542	10	19	293	220	3,930	1,299	2,431	200	26
Reedsburg	8,687	15	0	5	0	10	156	15	134	7	0
Rhinelander	7,641	8	0	2	0	6	283	23	252	8	0
Rice Lake	8,284	18	0	3	3	12	339	51	277	11	5
Richland Center	5,068	8	0	1	0	7	127	7	119	1	0
Ripon	7,204	19	1	0	2	16	139	13	124	2	0
River Falls	14,093	44	0	4	7	33	496	68	420	8	2
River Hills	1,649	2	0	1	1	0	20	3	16	1	0
Rome Town	3,045	3	0	0	0	3	44	9	31	4	0
Rothschild	5,370	1	0	0	0	1	142	6	133	3	0
Sauk Prairie	4,189	2	0	0	1	1	382	38	341	3	1
Saukville	4,327	4	0	2	0	2	102	5	92	5	0
Seymour	3,446	5	0	1	0	4	47	3	40	4	0
Shawano	8,670	26	1	1	1	23	406	43	356	7	1
Sheboygan	47,813	80	0	10	27	43	2,188	349	1,772	67	10
Sheboygan Falls	7,815	0	0	0	0	0	116	1	115	0	1
Shiocton	928	1	0	0	0	1	8	1	7	0	0
Shorewood	13,426	16	0	2	8	6	425	57	353	15	3
Shorewood Hills	1,653	1	0	1	0	0	50	4	46	0	0
Silver Lake	2,518	2	0	0	0	2	28	10	17	1	0
Siren	814	1	0	0	0	1	48	3	44	1	0
Slinger	4,566	0	0	0	0	0	74	4	70	0	0
Somerset	2,397	0	0	0	0	0	42	2	40	0	0
South Milwaukee	21,114	19	0	3	10	6	510	72	406	32	3
Sparta	9,007	18	0	0	5	13	294	88	202	4	5
Spencer	1,822	0	0	0	0	0	15	2	13	0	0
Spooner	2,557	3	0	2	0	1	90	10	77	3	1
Spring Green	1,429	0	0	0	0	0	32	7	25	0	0
Stanley	3,615	4	0	0	0	4	101	10	91	0	0
St. Croix Falls	2,148	1	0	0	1	0	69	7	61	1	0
St. Francis	9,173	10	0	3	5	2	313	47	253	13	1
Stoughton	12,934	7	0	1	1	5	259	43	199	17	0
Strum	1,024	0	0	0	0	0	1	0	1	0	0
Sturgeon Bay	8,915	3	0	1	0	2	151	15	134	2	1
Sturtevant	6,780	14	0	0	3	11	37	9	26	2	0
Summit	5,128	3	0	1	0	2	31	6	22	3	0
Sun Prairie	28,793	70	0	1	7	62	681	95	557	29	0
Superior	26,530	82	0	12	28	42	1,490	197	1,217	76	11
Theresa	1,299	1	0	0	0	1	42	2	39	1	0
Thiensville	3,196	4	0	0	1	3	20	3	16	1	0
Three Lakes	2,238	2	0	0	0	2	21	3	17	1	0
Tomah	8,812	20	0	5	1	14	396	46	343	7	0
Tomahawk	3,647	9	1	0	1	7	134	23	105	6	0
Town of East Troy	3,893	0	0	0	0	0	38	6	32	0	0
Town of Madison	5,941	53	0	6	20	27	233	46	160	27	3

[1] The FBI does not publish arson data unless it receives data from either the agency or the state for all 12 months of the calendar year.

Table 8. Offenses Known to Law Enforcement, by State and City, 2008—*Continued*

(Number.)

State/City	Population	Violent crime	Murder and non-negligent man-slaughter	Forcible rape	Robbery	Aggravated assault	Property crime	Burglary	Larceny-theft	Motor vehicle theft	Arson[1]
WISCONSIN—*Continued*											
Town of Menasha	17,392	23	0	2	4	17	249	50	182	17	0
Trempealeau	1,508	0	0	0	0	0	3	2	1	0	0
Twin Lakes	5,660	9	0	2	2	5	145	12	129	4	0
Two Rivers	11,680	30	0	1	3	26	183	31	146	6	0
Valders	969	0	0	0	0	0	2	0	2	0	0
Verona	11,262	11	0	1	2	8	179	18	159	2	0
Viroqua	4,316	13	0	0	0	13	99	3	94	2	0
Walworth	2,667	7	0	0	0	7	38	1	36	1	0
Washburn	2,084	6	0	0	0	6	104	1	102	1	0
Waterloo	3,235	2	0	0	0	2	40	4	33	3	0
Watertown	23,130	72	0	7	6	59	501	97	384	20	7
Waukesha	66,984	84	0	23	24	37	1,443	320	1,050	73	11
Waunakee	11,341	6	1	1	2	2	174	18	152	4	0
Waupaca	5,865	10	0	0	0	10	266	29	230	7	0
Waupun	10,642	24	0	5	0	19	221	18	198	5	0
Wausau	37,981	131	1	19	29	82	1,177	276	851	50	6
Wautoma	2,076	0	0	0	0	0	30	6	24	0	0
Wauwatosa	45,298	111	1	10	65	35	1,747	233	1,417	97	0
West Allis	59,602	220	2	6	108	104	3,154	569	2,382	203	27
West Bend	29,958	30	1	1	8	20	852	36	795	21	2
Westby	2,134	2	0	0	0	2	31	6	23	2	0
West Milwaukee	4,051	27	0	1	15	11	340	59	254	27	0
West Salem	4,825	4	0	0	0	4	61	7	52	2	0
Whitefish Bay	13,702	10	0	1	7	2	246	29	209	8	0
Whitehall	1,601	0	0	0	0	0	44	1	43	0	0
Whitewater	14,122	20	0	3	3	14	321	51	262	8	1
Williams Bay	2,676	2	0	1	0	1	54	10	39	5	1
Winneconne	2,508	2	0	0	0	2	7	5	2	0	0
Wisconsin Dells	2,484	23	0	5	1	17	265	34	221	10	2
Wisconsin Rapids	17,372	8	1	3	2	2	843	158	675	10	6
Woodruff	2,005	0	0	0	0	0	48	2	44	2	0
WYOMING											
Afton	1,774	0	0	0	0	0	14	1	13	0	0
Basin	1,234	3	0	0	0	3	27	3	24	0	0
Buffalo	4,690	27	0	0	0	27	107	11	92	4	0
Casper	53,430	159	1	30	19	109	2,289	368	1,805	116	31
Cheyenne	55,931	122	2	24	25	71	2,565	284	2,171	110	16
Cody	9,225	28	0	16	3	9	295	57	233	5	3
Diamondville	649	1	0	0	0	1	15	5	10	0	0
Douglas	5,722	6	0	0	1	5	211	22	187	2	2
Evanston	11,492	14	2	1	5	6	367	49	297	21	1
Evansville	2,338	11	0	0	1	10	93	10	81	2	1
Gillette	25,678	37	0	7	1	29	856	106	706	44	14
Glenrock	2,387	4	0	0	0	4	27	4	20	3	0
Green River	12,113	88	0	1	1	86	315	46	250	19	3
Greybull	1,728	7	0	0	0	7	18	7	10	1	0
Guernsey	1,082	2	0	0	0	2	10	4	6	0	0
Hanna	861	1	0	0	0	1	3	3	0	0	0
Jackson	9,753	44	0	11	1	32	415	57	354	4	0
Kemmerer	2,401	9	0	0	0	9	41	5	35	1	0
Lander	7,158	12	0	3	1	8	246	23	211	12	1
Laramie	27,260	29	0	5	2	22	811	112	663	36	4
Lovell	2,246	29	0	1	0	28	53	15	37	1	0
Lusk	1,327	1	0	0	0	1	31	7	19	5	0
Mills	3,169	7	0	0	0	7	113	11	96	6	0
Moorcroft	858	3	1	1	0	1	41	20	20	1	0
Newcastle	3,334	12	0	0	0	12	135	20	108	7	0
Pine Bluffs	1,140	5	0	0	0	5	27	8	18	1	1
Powell	5,370	20	0	5	2	13	192	27	158	7	2
Rawlins	8,651	27	0	3	1	23	284	37	237	10	2
Riverton	9,907	33	1	10	3	19	460	31	414	15	5
Rock Springs	19,800	119	0	6	6	107	751	92	601	58	1
Saratoga	1,739	3	0	1	0	2	11	1	9	1	0
Sheridan	16,827	27	0	5	5	17	474	73	386	15	3
Sundance	1,211	1	0	1	0	0	28	6	22	0	0
Thermopolis	2,897	16	0	2	0	14	58	9	47	2	0
Torrington	5,396	11	0	3	0	8	158	25	131	2	0
Wheatland	3,327	4	0	2	0	2	99	12	82	5	2
Worland	4,901	16	0	0	0	16	38	10	27	1	0

[1] The FBI does not publish arson data unless it receives data from either the agency or the state for all 12 months of the calendar year.

Table 9. Offenses Known to Law Enforcement, by State and University and College, 2008

(Number.)

State and University/College	Campus	Student enroll-ment[1]	Violent crime	Murder and non-negligent man-slaughter	Forcible rape	Robbery	Aggra-vated assault	Property crime	Burglary	Larceny-theft	Motor vehicle theft	Arson[2]
ALABAMA												
Alabama State University		5,608	17	0	0	15	2	160	22	134	4	
Auburn University	Montgomery	5,138	1	0	1	0	0	60	11	48	1	
Calhoun Community College[3]			1	0	0	0	1	8	0	8	0	
Jacksonville State University		9,077	5	0	1	0	4	137	24	112	1	
Troy University		28,955	3	0	0	3	0	171	30	132	9	
University of Alabama:	Huntsville	7,264	1	0	0	0	1	72	5	67	0	
	Tuscaloosa	25,544	13	0	1	8	4	423	97	321	5	
University of Montevallo		2,949	1	0	0	0	1	32	3	29	0	
University of North Alabama		7,097	2	0	0	0	2	77	19	58	0	
University of South Alabama		13,779	16	0	3	9	4	209	49	157	3	
University of West Alabama		4,011	1	0	0	1	0	3	0	3	0	
ALASKA												
University of Alaska:	Anchorage	16,463	3	0	0	0	3	130	4	123	3	0
	Fairbanks	8,618	6	0	0	0	6	104	9	94	1	0
ARIZONA												
Arizona State University	Main Campus	51,481	25	0	0	5	20	1,029	130	842	57	9
Central Arizona College		4,951	1	0	0	0	1	51	11	38	2	0
Northern Arizona University		21,347	15	0	7	1	7	363	36	318	9	10
Pima Community College		32,982	4	0	0	1	3	162	2	147	13	0
University of Arizona		37,217	15	0	3	4	8	1,006	61	897	48	0
Yavapai College		9,060	0	0	0	0	0	37	0	37	0	0
ARKANSAS												
Arkansas State University:	Beebe	4,311	0	0	0	0	0	1	0	1	0	0
	Jonesboro	11,130	8	0	2	0	6	188	74	114	0	0
Arkansas Tech University		7,476	0	0	0	0	0	117	29	86	2	0
University of Arkansas:	Fayetteville	18,648	14	0	5	2	7	234	50	177	7	0
	Little Rock	12,135	8	0	2	5	1	189	87	99	3	0
	Medical Sciences	2,538	19	0	1	0	18	267	3	257	7	0
	Monticello	3,187	1	0	0	0	1	21	6	15	0	0
	Pine Bluff	3,200	5	0	0	4	1	122	44	74	4	1
University of Central Arkansas		12,619	6	0	1	1	4	198	57	133	8	0
CALIFORNIA												
Allan Hancock College		13,176	0	0	0	0	0	35	6	27	2	0
California State Polytechnic University:	Pomona	21,477	3	0	1	0	2	170	12	143	15	0
	San Luis Obispo	19,777	0	0	0	0	0	213	3	209	1	10
California State University:	Bakersfield	7,700	4	0	0	0	4	93	25	65	3	0
	Channel Islands	3,599	1	0	0	0	1	35	0	34	1	0
	Chico	17,034	5	0	3	1	1	313	27	284	2	4
	Dominguez Hills	12,082	4	0	2	0	2	113	41	57	15	0
	East Bay	13,124	7	0	1	5	1	112	23	82	7	0
	Fresno	22,383	11	0	1	6	4	416	79	324	13	0
	Fullerton	37,130	5	0	0	0	5	234	39	180	15	0
	Long Beach	36,868	0	0	0	0	0	206	32	147	27	1
	Los Angeles	21,051	7	0	1	2	4	290	28	252	10	1
	Monterey Bay	4,080	14	0	1	2	11	122	19	97	6	1
	Northridge	35,446	14	0	1	6	7	320	47	259	14	0
	Sacramento	28,829	4	0	0	1	3	149	15	126	8	2
	San Bernardino	17,066	5	0	3	1	1	110	25	74	11	0
	San Jose[3]		31	0	9	18	4	401	30	361	10	1
	San Marcos	9,159	4	0	1	0	3	61	10	51	0	0
	Stanislaus	8,836	3	0	3	0	0	76	26	46	4	0
College of the Sequoias		11,697	2	0	0	0	2	71	37	34	0	1
Contra Costa Community College		7,147	15	0	0	14	1	180	1	144	35	0
Cuesta College		10,920	0	0	0	0	0	15	0	15	0	0
El Camino College		24,895	8	0	1	7	0	157	11	128	18	1
Foothill-De Anza College		42,247	0	0	0	0	0	104	38	61	5	0
Fresno Community College		21,624	4	0	0	2	2	158	14	131	13	0
Humboldt State University		7,773	7	0	5	0	2	150	12	135	3	2
Marin Community College		6,476	1	0	0	1	0	49	3	45	1	0
Pasadena Community College		26,672	1	0	0	0	1	214	9	183	22	1
Reedley Community College		12,158	0	0	0	0	0	39	0	39	0	1
Riverside Community College		30,961	5	0	1	3	1	149	21	123	5	3
San Bernardino Community College		12,839	1	0	0	0	1	110	34	65	11	0
San Diego State University		35,695	37	0	8	10	19	649	91	468	90	3
San Francisco State University		30,125	14	0	0	13	1	271	48	203	20	3
San Jose/Evergreen Community College		18,512	0	0	0	0	0	60	4	53	3	0
Santa Rosa Junior College		25,626	0	0	0	0	0	92	8	84	0	1
Solano Community College		11,163	0	0	0	0	0	57	0	55	2	0
Sonoma State University		8,770	7	0	4	0	3	93	10	83	0	5

Note: Caution should be exercised in making any intercampus comparisons or ranking schools because university/college crime statistics are affected by a variety of factors. These include demographic characteristics of the surrounding community, ratio of male to female students, number of on-campus residents, accessibility of the campus to outside visitors, size of enrollment, etc.

[1] The student enrollment figures provided by the United States Department of Education are for the 2007 school year, the most recent available. The enrollment figures include full-time and part-time students.

[2] The FBI does not publish arson data unless it receives data from either the agency or the state for all 12 months of the calendar year.

[3] Student enrollment figures were not available.

Table 9. Offenses Known to Law Enforcement, by State and University and College, 2008—*Continued*

(Number.)

State and University/College	Campus	Student enrollment[1]	Violent crime	Murder and nonnegligent manslaughter	Forcible rape	Robbery	Aggravated assault	Property crime	Burglary	Larceny-theft	Motor vehicle theft	Arson[2]
University of California:	Berkeley	34,940	46	0	2	21	23	901	74	804	23	3
	Davis	29,796	11	0	3	3	5	1,049	74	961	14	1
	Hastings College of Law	1,262	9	0	0	2	7	41	21	16	4	0
	Irvine	26,483	7	0	2	3	2	551	68	452	31	1
	Los Angeles	37,476	58	0	10	27	21	845	191	611	43	4
	Medical Center, Sacramento[3]		5	0	0	1	4	195	21	161	13	0
	Merced	1,871	0	0	0	0	0	36	5	31	0	0
	Riverside	17,187	18	0	3	8	7	362	48	302	12	2
	San Diego	27,020	6	0	3	1	2	514	53	429	32	4
	San Francisco	2,999	6	0	0	6	0	295	18	267	10	0
	Santa Barbara	21,410	8	0	2	3	3	518	29	487	2	2
	Santa Cruz	15,825	6	0	3	0	3	303	66	234	3	2
Ventura County Community College District		12,603	0	0	0	0	0	154	0	149	5	2
West Valley-Mission College		20,042	2	0	0	0	2	125	10	108	7	0
COLORADO												
Adams State College		2,830	9	0	3	2	4	35	10	25	0	0
Arapahoe Community College		6,538	0	0	0	0	0	26	1	25	0	0
Auraria Higher Education Center[3]			1	0	0	1	0	172	10	157	5	0
Colorado School of Mines		4,560	3	0	0	0	3	43	6	36	1	1
Colorado State University:	Fort Collins	27,569	6	0	2	0	4	401	13	386	2	6
	Pueblo	5,908	0	0	0	0	0	80	8	68	4	0
Fort Lewis College		3,928	2	0	1	0	1	72	10	61	1	2
Pikes Peak Community College		11,407	3	0	0	0	3	27	2	24	1	1
Red Rocks Community College		7,223	0	0	0	0	0	35	2	33	0	0
University of Colorado:	Boulder	31,796	17	0	7	3	7	491	45	443	3	6
	Colorado Springs	8,660	0	0	0	0	0	60	6	54	0	0
	Denver	21,658	0	0	0	0	0	48	0	47	1	0
	Health Sciences Center[3]		0	0	0	0	0	14	0	14	0	0
University of Northern Colorado		12,702	6	0	2	1	3	213	43	169	1	2
CONNECTICUT												
Central Connecticut State University		12,106	4	0	3	1	0	71	8	55	8	0
Eastern Connecticut State University		5,137	2	0	0	2	0	96	4	90	2	0
Southern Connecticut State University		11,930	2	0	2	0	0	122	13	101	8	0
University of Connecticut:	Health Center[3]		0	0	0	0	0	62	12	49	1	0
	Storrs, Avery Point, and Hartford[3]		6	0	3	1	2	221	39	181	1	0
Western Connecticut State University		6,211	3	0	3	0	0	59	30	29	0	0
Yale University		11,454	6	0	1	3	2	290	55	231	4	0
DELAWARE												
Delaware State University		3,756	7	0	2	2	3	75	41	34	0	0
University of Delaware		20,342	13	0	3	7	3	364	32	330	2	2
FLORIDA												
Florida A&M University		11,562	24	0	3	15	6	274	28	239	7	0
Florida Atlantic University		26,193	7	0	2	1	4	241	39	185	17	0
Florida Gulf Coast University		9,339	1	0	0	0	1	51	6	45	0	0
Florida International University		38,182	14	0	1	4	9	481	80	364	37	2
Florida State University:	Panama City[3]		0	0	0	0	0	15	0	15	0	0
	Tallahassee	40,555	25	0	2	14	9	557	60	486	11	1
New College of Florida		767	2	0	1	1	0	37	6	30	1	1
Pensacola Junior College		10,728	2	0	0	1	1	82	26	56	0	0
Santa Fe College		14,824	2	0	0	0	2	42	0	42	0	1
Tallahassee Community College		13,776	7	0	0	2	5	143	3	134	6	0
University of Central Florida		48,398	13	0	3	3	7	536	56	425	55	0
University of Florida		51,725	10	0	0	3	7	676	49	612	15	1
University of North Florida		16,406	4	0	1	2	1	243	21	218	4	0
University of South Florida:	St. Petersburg[3]		2	0	0	1	1	34	4	21	9	1
	Tampa	44,870	9	0	2	5	2	379	104	260	15	3
University of West Florida		10,358	1	0	0	0	1	106	22	80	4	0
GEORGIA												
Abraham Baldwin Agricultural College		3,665	2	0	1	0	1	77	20	57	0	0
Augusta State University		6,588	0	0	0	0	0	44	1	43	0	
Clark Atlanta University		4,271	19	0	1	18	0	186	65	110	11	
Coastal Georgia Community College		2,942	0	0	0	0	0	8	0	8	0	
Columbus State University		7,593	1	0	0	0	1	54	2	51	1	
Emory University		12,570	2	0	0	2	0	449	44	384	21	1
Georgia Institute of Technology		18,742	21	0	1	12	8	752	113	586	53	0
Georgia Perimeter College		21,473	3	0	0	1	2	172	6	158	8	1
Georgia State University		27,134	16	0	1	9	6	250	1	241	8	

Note: Caution should be exercised in making any intercampus comparisons or ranking schools because university/college crime statistics are affected by a variety of factors. These include demographic characteristics of the surrounding community, ratio of male to female students, number of on-campus residents, accessibility of the campus to outside visitors, size of enrollment, etc.

[1] The student enrollment figures provided by the United States Department of Education are for the 2007 school year, the most recent available. The enrollment figures include full-time and part-time students.

[2] The FBI does not publish arson data unless it receives data from either the agency or the state for all 12 months of the calendar year.

[3] Student enrollment figures were not available.

Table 9. Offenses Known to Law Enforcement, by State and University and College, 2008—*Continued*

(Number.)

State and University/College	Campus	Student enrollment[1]	Violent crime	Murder and nonnegligent manslaughter	Forcible rape	Robbery	Aggravated assault	Property crime	Burglary	Larceny-theft	Motor vehicle theft	Arson[2]
Kennesaw State University		20,607	3	0	1	1	1	136	25	109	2	0
Medical College of Georgia		2,392	0	0	0	0	0	117	0	107	10	
Middle Georgia College		3,444	0	0	0	0	0	60	6	52	2	
Morehouse College		2,810	4	0	0	3	1	185	16	165	4	
Morris-Brown College[3]			1	0	0	0	1	17	3	14	0	
North Georgia College and State University		5,227	0	0	0	0	0	39	2	37	0	
Savannah State University		3,169	5	0	1	4	0	228	79	147	2	0
South Georgia College		1,754	0	0	0	0	0	20	9	11	0	0
University of Georgia		33,831	1	0	0	0	1	372	47	320	5	
University of West Georgia		10,677	6	0	0	2	4	162	30	129	3	
Valdosta State University		11,280	3	0	0	1	2	183	0	182	1	6
INDIANA												
Ball State University		19,849	9	0	3	3	3	314	62	246	6	3
Indiana State University		10,543	11	0	0	1	10	200	17	180	3	0
Indiana University:	Bloomington	38,990	2	0	1	1	0	435	57	367	11	
	Gary	4,790	0	0	0	0	0	71	3	67	1	0
	Indianapolis[3]		5	0	0	3	2	385	70	296	19	1
	New Albany	6,241	0	0	0	0	0	32	2	30	0	0
Marian College		2,043	1	0	1	0	0	20	6	13	1	0
Purdue University		40,534	5	0	1	2	2	526	73	447	6	3
IOWA												
Iowa State University		26,160	21	0	7	0	14	274	36	236	2	6
University of Iowa		29,117	14	0	1	1	12	242	32	208	2	1
University of Northern Iowa		12,692	4	0	1	0	3	83	5	77	1	0
KANSAS												
Emporia State University		6,354	1	0	1	0	0	34	8	26	0	0
Fort Hays State University		9,588	3	0	2	0	1	41	11	29	1	0
Kansas State University		23,332	3	0	0	1	2	148	32	115	1	0
Pittsburg State University		7,087	1	0	0	0	1	84	16	68	0	0
University of Kansas	Medical Center[3]		6	0	2	1	3	185	4	172	9	0
Washburn University		6,901	0	0	0	0	0	69	15	52	2	5
Wichita State University		14,226	5	0	2	3	0	137	3	133	1	3
KENTUCKY												
Eastern Kentucky University		15,839	6	0	2	1	3	348	85	261	2	
Kentucky State University		2,696	5	0	2	3	0	117	45	72	0	
Morehead State University		8,897	2	0	1	0	1	64	14	49	1	
Murray State University		10,778	1	0	0	1	0	161	22	135	4	4
Northern Kentucky University		14,785	2	0	2	0	0	133	19	114	0	
University of Kentucky		25,856	12	0	2	4	6	524	27	475	22	
University of Louisville		20,592	7	0	0	7	0	326	29	289	8	
Western Kentucky University		19,258	8	0	5	1	2	194	31	157	6	
LOUISIANA												
Delgado Community College		13,210	0	0	0	0	0	47	9	37	1	0
Grambling State University		5,161	23	0	1	13	9	150	75	71	4	0
Louisiana State University:	Baton Rouge[3]		19	0	1	6	12	401	78	302	21	1
	Eunice	2,864	0	0	0	0	0	0	0	0	0	0
	Health Sciences Center, New Orleans	2,234	0	0	0	0	0	7	0	7	0	0
	Health Sciences Center, Shreveport	800	12	0	0	0	12	64	1	61	2	57
	Shreveport	3,948	6	0	0	0	6	25	3	22	0	0
Louisiana Tech University		10,564	5	0	0	2	3	184	37	146	1	1
McNeese State University		8,095	1	0	0	1	0	49	1	45	3	0
Nicholls State University		6,864	4	0	0	0	4	32	5	24	3	0
Northwestern State University		9,037	3	0	0	0	3	23	13	10	0	0
Southeastern Louisiana University		14,744	10	0	1	3	6	126	13	110	3	3
Southern University and A&M College:	Baton Rouge	8,288	5	0	0	2	3	149	26	117	6	0
	New Orleans	2,648	0	0	0	0	0	7	1	6	0	0
Tulane University		10,125	15	0	11	2	2	157	36	118	3	1
University of Louisiana	Monroe	8,541	3	0	0	1	2	142	11	128	3	0
University of New Orleans		11,363	9	0	0	0	9	110	8	97	5	1
MAINE												
University of Maine:	Farmington	2,351	1	0	0	1	0	43	7	36	0	0
	Orono	11,912	5	0	3	1	1	254	40	213	1	10
University of Southern Maine		10,453	2	0	1	0	1	76	6	70	0	3
MARYLAND												
Bowie State University		5,464	13	0	1	5	7	96	39	55	2	0
Coppin State University		3,932	4	0	0	0	4	56	10	46	0	0
Frostburg State University		4,993	8	0	0	2	6	87	17	69	1	0

Note: Caution should be exercised in making any intercampus comparisons or ranking schools because university/college crime statistics are affected by a variety of factors. These include demographic characteristics of the surrounding community, ratio of male to female students, number of on-campus residents, accessibility of the campus to outside visitors, size of enrollment, etc.

[1] The student enrollment figures provided by the United States Department of Education are for the 2007 school year, the most recent available. The enrollment figures include full-time and part-time students.

[2] The FBI does not publish arson data unless it receives data from either the agency or the state for all 12 months of the calendar year.

[3] Student enrollment figures were not available.

Table 9. Offenses Known to Law Enforcement, by State and University and College, 2008—*Continued*

(Number.)

State and University/College	Campus	Student enroll-ment[1]	Violent crime	Murder and non-negligent man-slaughter	Forcible rape	Robbery	Aggra-vated assault	Property crime	Burglary	Larceny-theft	Motor vehicle theft	Arson[2]
Morgan State University		7,208	31	0	0	25	6	136	33	97	6	0
Salisbury University		7,581	4	0	1	2	1	126	23	102	1	0
St. Mary's College		2,002	1	0	0	0	1	74	6	68	0	0
Towson University		19,758	10	0	0	3	7	172	35	136	1	2
University of Baltimore		5,421	2	0	0	1	1	81	5	76	0	0
University of Maryland:	Baltimore City	5,884	8	0	0	4	4	140	0	136	4	0
	Baltimore County	12,041	3	0	1	2	0	155	19	135	1	1
	College Park	36,014	20	0	1	10	9	547	141	363	43	1
	Eastern Shore	4,086	7	0	0	3	4	150	31	118	1	1
MASSACHUSETTS												
Amherst College		1,683	0	0	0	0	0	94	0	94	0	0
Bentley College		5,636	9	0	6	0	3	77	15	60	2	
Boston College		14,621	15	0	7	0	8	159	48	110	1	
Boston University		32,053	27	0	7	12	8	405	61	340	4	1
Brandeis University		5,333	3	0	1	0	2	88	16	71	1	
Bridgewater State College		9,934	9	0	4	0	5	73	7	62	4	0
Bristol Community College		7,388	1	0	0	0	1	13	0	13	0	0
Clark University		3,210	5	0	1	2	2	35	5	29	1	0
Emerson College		4,380	3	0	1	1	1	51	9	42	0	
Fitchburg State College		6,692	3	0	0	0	3	63	4	59	0	0
Harvard University		25,690	8	0	1	4	3	494	287	203	4	
Holyoke Community College		6,461	1	0	0	1	0	19	0	19	0	
Lasell College		1,403	2	0	0	0	2	46	10	36	0	0
Massachusetts College of Art		2,312	1	0	0	1	0	29	3	26	0	0
Massachusetts College of Liberal Arts		1,841	0	0	0	0	0	49	21	28	0	0
Massachusetts Institute of Technology		10,220	5	0	0	3	2	237	86	148	3	0
Merrimack College		2,098	2	0	0	0	2	52	12	39	1	
Northeastern University		24,434	7	0	3	3	1	315	34	280	1	
North Shore Community College		7,107	1	0	0	0	1	31	0	30	1	
Salem State College		10,085	1	0	1	0	0	112	38	74	0	0
Smith College		3,065	2	0	1	1	0	68	3	65	0	0
Springfield College		4,755	14	0	4	1	9	60	20	40	0	0
Tufts University:	Medford	9,758	7	0	3	0	4	122	32	89	1	1
	Suffolk[3]		0	0	0	0	0	19	2	17	0	0
	Worcester[3]		1	0	1	0	0	24	2	22	0	0
University of Massachusetts:	Amherst	25,873	17	0	3	0	14	301	58	243	0	2
	Dartmouth	9,080	12	0	1	3	8	210	66	141	3	
	Harbor Campus, Boston	13,433	5	0	0	1	4	88	7	80	1	0
Wellesley College		2,380	0	0	0	0	0	56	17	39	0	
Western New England College		3,657	1	0	1	0	0	56	4	52	0	0
Westfield State College		5,392	3	0	2	0	1	64	3	61	0	0
Worcester Polytechnic Institute		4,158	0	0	0	0	0	49	3	46	0	0
MICHIGAN												
Central Michigan University		26,611	8	0	5	0	3	217	30	185	2	0
Eastern Michigan University		22,837	8	0	2	4	2	243	45	194	4	0
Grand Rapids Community College		15,212	0	0	0	0	0	147	0	147	0	0
Lansing Community College		19,465	1	0	0	0	1	133	0	133	0	0
Michigan State University		46,045	23	0	8	5	10	1,034	140	881	13	2
Michigan Technological University		6,744	1	0	0	0	1	73	1	72	0	0
Mott Community College		10,455	1	0	0	0	1	81	4	77	0	2
Northern Michigan University		9,358	3	0	1	0	2	112	46	65	1	0
Oakland Community College		24,532	1	0	0	1	0	59	1	56	2	0
Oakland University		18,081	4	0	0	1	3	70	4	63	3	1
Saginaw Valley State University		9,662	3	0	0	0	3	153	33	119	1	0
University of Michigan:	Ann Arbor	41,042	15	0	0	3	12	771	26	728	17	2
	Dearborn	8,336	0	0	0	0	0	48	0	39	9	0
	Flint	6,883	4	0	1	0	3	97	16	79	2	0
Western Michigan University		24,433	8	0	3	2	3	200	13	186	1	6
MINNESOTA[4]												
University of Minnesota:	Duluth	11,184		0		0	0	74	6	68	0	0
	Morris	1,686		0		0	0	21	2	19	0	0
	Twin Cities	50,883		0		7	4	614	36	568	10	1
MISSISSIPPI												
Coahoma Community College		2,216	2	0	0	1	1	16	16	0	0	0
Jackson State University		8,698	5	0	0	3	2	162	15	140	7	1
Mississippi State University		17,039	2	0	0	1	1	162	5	154	3	0
University of Mississippi:	Medical Center	1,702	0	0	0	0	0	159	1	157	1	0
	Oxford	15,129	0	0	0	0	0	127	28	96	3	0

Note: Caution should be exercised in making any intercampus comparisons or ranking schools because university/college crime statistics are affected by a variety of factors. These include demographic characteristics of the surrounding community, ratio of male to female students, number of on-campus residents, accessibility of the campus to outside visitors, size of enrollment, etc.

[1] The student enrollment figures provided by the United States Department of Education are for the 2007 school year, the most recent available. The enrollment figures include full-time and part-time students.

[2] The FBI does not publish arson data unless it receives data from either the agency or the state for all 12 months of the calendar year.

[3] Student enrollment figures were not available.

[4] The data collection methodology for the offense of forcible rape used by the Minnesota state Uniform Crime Reporting (UCR) program does not comply with national UCR guidelines. Consequently, their figures for forcible rape and violent crime (of which forcible rape is a part) are not published in this table.

Table 9. Offenses Known to Law Enforcement, by State and University and College, 2008—*Continued*

(Number.)

State and University/College	Campus	Student enrollment[1]	Violent crime	Murder and nonnegligent manslaughter	Forcible rape	Robbery	Aggravated assault	Property crime	Burglary	Larceny-theft	Motor vehicle theft	Arson[2]
MISSOURI												
Lincoln University		3,156	5	0	0	1	4	51	24	27	0	0
Missouri University of Science and Technology		6,166	0	0	0	0	0	61	3	58	0	0
Missouri Western State University		5,342	1	0	0	0	1	69	13	56	0	0
Northwest Missouri State University		6,511	5	0	4	0	1	63	9	53	1	0
Southeast Missouri State University		10,624	5	0	4	1	0	55	9	46	0	0
St. Louis Community College:	Florissant Valley	6,250	0	0	0	0	0	108	27	80	1	0
	Meramec	10,168	0	0	0	0	0	16	1	15	0	0
Truman State University		5,920	1	0	1	0	0	96	21	74	1	1
University of Central Missouri		10,918	1	0	0	0	1	105	26	77	2	0
University of Missouri:	Columbia	28,405	10	0	1	3	6	357	23	332	2	1
	Kansas City	14,442	4	0	0	3	1	180	19	158	3	0
	St. Louis	15,527	14	0	0	3	11	116	18	90	8	0
Washington University		13,382	2	0	0	1	1	150	30	118	2	0
MONTANA												
Montana State University		11,932	10	0	5	0	5	155	8	145	2	2
NEBRASKA												
University of Nebraska:	Kearney	6,478	0	0	0	0	0	41	13	27	1	0
	Lincoln	22,973	4	0	0	3	1	334	39	293	2	0
NEVADA												
Truckee Meadows Community College		12,166	0	0	0	0	0	30	2	27	1	1
University of Nevada:	Las Vegas	27,960	4	0	0	1	3	292	48	221	23	3
	Reno	16,681	9	0	6	1	2	159	20	136	3	1
NEW JERSEY												
Brookdale Community College		14,025	2	0	0	1	1	50	0	47	3	0
Essex County College		10,995	2	0	1	1	0	61	1	60	0	0
Kean University		13,394	2	0	1	0	1	154	52	100	2	0
Middlesex County College		12,097	0	0	0	0	0	25	0	24	1	0
Monmouth University		6,494	5	0	1	0	4	47	10	35	2	4
Montclair State University		16,736	6	0	1	2	3	238	3	234	1	1
New Jersey Institute of Technology		8,288	11	0	0	6	5	105	2	87	16	0
Richard Stockton College of New Jersey		7,355	3	0	0	0	3	105	17	86	2	0
Rowan University		10,091	8	0	3	3	2	139	28	109	2	1
Rutgers University:	Camden	5,159	6	0	0	4	2	120	29	87	4	0
	Newark	10,553	5	0	0	4	1	151	21	118	12	0
	New Brunswick	34,804	9	0	1	3	5	554	115	427	12	4
Stevens Institute of Technology		5,241	2	0	0	1	1	21	12	8	1	1
The College of New Jersey		6,964	3	0	0	1	2	127	29	81	17	0
University of Medicine and Dentistry:	Camden[3]		0	0	0	0	0	0	0	0	0	0
	Newark	5,617	27	0	0	14	13	283	2	258	23	0
	New Brunswick[3]		0	0	0	0	0	51	1	50	0	0
William Paterson University		10,443	4	0	1	3	0	116	25	87	4	0
NEW MEXICO												
Eastern New Mexico University		4,173	3	0	3	0	0	43	7	36	0	0
New Mexico State University		16,722	16	0	1	3	12	325	22	289	14	3
University of New Mexico		25,672	17	0	2	8	7	638	56	511	71	7
NEW YORK												
Ithaca College		6,660	6	0	3	1	2	116	10	104	2	0
Rensselaer Polytechnic Institute		6,566	1	0	0	1	0	78	6	72	0	0
State University of New York:	Buffalo	28,054	10	0	2	2	6	418	76	335	7	2
	Maritime College	1,487	1	0	1	0	0	30	6	24	0	0
	Upstate Medical Center[3]		0	0	0	0	0	122	4	118	0	0
State University of New York Agricultural and Technical College:	Alfred	3,184	4	0	1	0	3	71	12	58	1	1
	Canton	2,737	3	0	2	0	1	87	2	85	0	0
	Cobleskill	2,592	2	0	1	1	0	82	17	64	1	0
	Farmingdale[3]		0	0	0	0	0	41	2	39	0	0
	Morrisville[3]		0	0	0	0	0	91	8	82	1	0
State University of New York College:	Brockport	8,303	3	0	2	0	1	136	23	113	0	0
	Buffalo	10,993	4	0	1	1	2	220	48	166	6	0
	Cortland	7,056	2	0	2	0	0	98	26	70	2	0
	Environmental Science and Forestry	2,299	0	0	0	0	0	11	2	9	0	0
	Fredonia[3]		1	0	0	0	1	107	16	91	0	1
	Geneseo[3]		0	0	0	0	0	83	15	68	0	0
	New Paltz	7,690	0	0	0	0	0	85	11	73	1	0
	Old Westbury	3,565	5	0	0	1	4	70	14	56	0	1
	Optometry	299	0	0	0	0	0	2	0	2	0	0

Note: Caution should be exercised in making any intercampus comparisons or ranking schools because university/college crime statistics are affected by a variety of factors. These include demographic characteristics of the surrounding community, ratio of male to female students, number of on-campus residents, accessibility of the campus to outside visitors, size of enrollment, etc.

[1] The student enrollment figures provided by the United States Department of Education are for the 2007 school year, the most recent available. The enrollment figures include full-time and part-time students.

[2] The FBI does not publish arson data unless it receives data from either the agency or the state for all 12 months of the calendar year.

[3] Student enrollment figures were not available.

Table 9. Offenses Known to Law Enforcement, by State and University and College, 2008—*Continued*

(Number.)

State and University/College	Campus	Student enroll-ment[1]	Violent crime	Murder and non-negligent man-slaughter	Forcible rape	Robbery	Aggra-vated assault	Property crime	Burglary	Larceny-theft	Motor vehicle theft	Arson[2]
	Oswego	8,660	0	0	0	0	0	140	44	95	1	0
	Plattsburgh	6,259	5	0	1	2	2	133	37	96	0	0
	Potsdam	4,338	2	0	0	0	2	82	14	67	1	0
	Purchase	4,251	4	0	0	1	3	104	20	84	0	0
	Utica-Rome[3]		1	0	1	0	0	20	3	17	0	0
United States Merchant Marine Academy		933	0	0	0	0	0	17	10	7	0	0
NORTH CAROLINA												
Appalachian State University		15,871	1	0	1	0	0	123	13	110	0	0
Duke University		13,598	10	0	1	3	6	832	51	776	5	2
East Carolina University		25,990	7	0	1	1	5	266	17	247	2	0
Elizabeth City State University		3,061	2	0	0	2	0	56	3	53	0	0
Elon University		5,456	0	0	0	0	0	61	13	48	0	0
Fayetteville State University		6,692	4	0	0	3	1	164	13	146	5	0
Methodist College		2,118	1	0	0	0	1	25	0	25	0	0
North Carolina Agricultural and Technical State University[5]		10,498	6	0	0	5	1		23		3	2
North Carolina Central University		8,383	21	0	0	10	11	218	33	171	14	0
North Carolina School of the Arts		867	0	0	0	0	0	27	2	22	3	0
North Carolina State University	Raleigh	31,802	20	0	3	9	8	430	51	371	8	0
University of North Carolina:	Chapel Hill	28,136	5	0	0	4	1	340	10	324	6	3
	Charlotte	22,388	11	0	2	4	5	348	20	319	9	2
	Greensboro	18,627	4	0	0	1	3	183	1	178	4	2
	Pembroke	5,937	0	0	0	0	0	63	0	62	1	0
	Wilmington	12,180	3	0	1	0	2	279	16	260	3	0
Wake Forest University		6,788	4	0	1	2	1	110	17	90	3	0
Western Carolina University		9,056	8	0	0	0	8	132	12	120	0	1
NORTH DAKOTA												
North Dakota State College of Science		2,417	0	0	0	0	0	37	12	25	0	0
North Dakota State University		12,527	0	0	0	0	0	136	15	119	2	0
University of North Dakota		12,559	1	0	0	0	1	141	4	135	2	0
OHIO												
Bowling Green State University		18,619	1	0	0	1	0	235	22	212	1	3
Cleveland State University		15,038	4	0	1	2	1	216	13	201	2	0
Cuyahoga Community College		24,563	4	0	0	1	3	174	6	167	1	0
Kent State University		22,819	5	0	0	3	2	216	19	197	0	0
Lakeland Community College		8,934	0	0	0	0	0	49	3	42	4	0
Miami University		15,968	7	0	3	1	3	170	12	158	0	1
Ohio State University	Columbus	52,568	16	0	7	8	1	1,065	183	865	17	9
Ohio University		21,089	7	0	6	0	1	193	29	163	1	1
University of Akron		23,007	6	0	3	3	0	358	21	331	6	1
University of Cincinnati		29,319	9	0	3	3	3	615	55	556	4	1
Wright State University		16,151	10	0	4	5	1	168	33	132	3	1
Youngstown State University		13,595	0	0	0	0	0	148	18	122	8	0
OKLAHOMA												
Cameron University		5,469	0	0	0	0	0	28	5	23	0	0
East Central University		4,463	0	0	0	0	0	22	4	18	0	0
Murray State College		2,281	0	0	0	0	0	4	4	0	0	0
Northeastern Oklahoma A&M College		1,913	2	0	0	0	2	32	21	11	0	0
Northeastern State University:	Broken Arrow[3]		0	0	0	0	0	5	0	5	0	0
	Tahlequah[3]		2	0	1	0	1	61	11	49	1	1
Oklahoma State University:	Main Campus	23,213	10	0	2	0	8	315	45	270	0	1
	Okmulgee	3,301	1	0	1	0	0	9	0	6	3	0
	Tulsa[3]		1	0	0	0	1	6	1	5	0	0
Rogers State University		3,903	3	0	3	0	0	13	4	9	0	0
Seminole State College		2,068	0	0	0	0	0	15	1	14	0	0
Southeastern Oklahoma State University		3,893	1	0	1	0	0	39	16	23	0	0
Southwestern Oklahoma State University		4,989	0	0	0	0	0	25	7	18	0	0
Tulsa Community College		16,881	0	0	0	0	0	36	0	34	2	0
University of Central Oklahoma		15,495	2	0	1	0	1	120	21	97	2	0
University of Oklahoma:	Health Sciences Center	3,754	5	0	0	1	4	168	4	160	4	0
	Norman	26,068	3	0	1	1	1	271	34	231	6	1
PENNSYLVANIA												
Bloomsburg University		8,745	3	0	2	0	1	86	2	84	0	1
California University		8,206	0	0	0	0	0	48	3	45	0	0
Cheyney University		1,438	9	0	0	2	7	75	29	45	1	1
Clarion University		6,795	3	0	0	0	3	59	14	43	2	0
Dickinson College		2,381	3	0	1	2	0	55	1	54	0	0
East Stroudsburg University		7,053	7	0	0	2	5	106	30	76	0	0
Elizabethtown College		2,360	3	0	3	0	0	23	0	23	0	0

Note: Caution should be exercised in making any intercampus comparisons or ranking schools because university/college crime statistics are affected by a variety of factors. These include demographic characteristics of the surrounding community, ratio of male to female students, number of on-campus residents, accessibility of the campus to outside visitors, size of enrollment, etc.

[1] The student enrollment figures provided by the United States Department of Education are for the 2007 school year, the most recent available. The enrollment figures include full-time and part-time students.

[2] The FBI does not publish arson data unless it receives data from either the agency or the state for all 12 months of the calendar year.

[3] Student enrollment figures were not available.

[5] The FBI determined that the agency's data were underreported. Consequently, those data are not included in this table.

Table 9. Offenses Known to Law Enforcement, by State and University and College, 2008—*Continued*

(Number.)

State and University/College	Campus	Student enroll-ment[1]	Violent crime	Murder and non-negligent man-slaughter	Forcible rape	Robbery	Aggra-vated assault	Property crime	Burglary	Larceny-theft	Motor vehicle theft	Arson[2]
Indiana University		14,018	4	0	2	1	1	99	13	86	0	0
Kutztown University		10,295	7	0	6	1	0	120	3	117	0	0
Lehigh University		6,845	5	0	0	5	0	92	5	85	2	1
Mansfield University		3,338	1	0	0	0	1	18	3	15	0	0
Millersville University		8,306	8	0	0	1	7	90	27	63	0	0
Moravian College		1,989	1	0	0	0	1	61	13	47	1	0
Pennsylvania State University:	Altoona	4,034	2	0	0	0	2	35	3	32	0	1
	Beaver	793	0	0	0	0	0	11	1	10	0	0
	Behrend	4,171	0	0	0	0	0	29	5	24	0	0
	Berks	2,824	0	0	0	0	0	29	4	24	1	0
	Harrisburg	3,907	0	0	0	0	0	13	0	13	0	0
	Hazelton	1,232	0	0	0	0	0	18	3	15	0	0
	McKeesport[3]		2	0	0	0	2	6	1	5	0	0
	Mont Alto	1,204	0	0	0	0	0	16	0	16	0	0
	University Park	43,252	12	0	0	3	9	465	50	411	4	3
Shippensburg University		7,765	3	0	2	0	1	67	26	41	0	0
Slippery Rock University		8,325	1	0	0	0	1	52	10	42	0	0
University of Pittsburgh	Pittsburgh	27,020	12	0	1	3	8	386	35	351	0	1
West Chester University		13,219	5	0	5	0	0	123	62	60	1	2
RHODE ISLAND												
Brown University		8,167	1	0	0	0	1	233	83	150	0	1
University of Rhode Island		15,650	7	0	5	2	0	229	29	192	8	2
SOUTH CAROLINA												
Benedict College		2,641	20	0	0	4	16	258	147	109	2	2
Bob Jones University[3]			0	0	0	0	0	36	15	21	0	0
Clemson University		17,585	8	0	1	1	6	252	31	218	3	2
Coastal Carolina University		7,872	18	0	7	8	3	124	31	93	0	1
College of Charleston		11,316	8	0	3	0	5	150	15	134	1	0
Columbia College		1,510	0	0	0	0	0	19	3	16	0	0
Denmark Technical College		1,571	1	0	0	1	0	0	0	0	0	0
Erskine College		892	0	0	0	0	0	10	0	10	0	0
Francis Marion University		3,864	1	0	0	1	0	85	12	71	2	0
Greenville Technical College		14,300	8	0	1	1	6	82	15	66	1	0
Lander University		2,408	2	0	2	0	0	30	4	26	0	0
Medical University of South Carolina		2,537	5	0	1	1	3	197	2	195	0	0
Midlands Technical College		10,706	1	0	0	0	1	45	0	42	3	0
Presbyterian College		1,180	0	0	0	0	0	14	1	13	0	0
South Carolina State University		4,933	16	0	0	6	10	248	127	113	8	0
Spartanburg Methodist College		797	0	0	0	0	0	16	10	5	1	0
The Citadel		3,300	3	0	0	2	1	39	8	31	0	0
Trident Technical College		12,076	1	0	0	1	0	34	1	32	1	0
University of South Carolina:	Aiken	3,267	0	0	0	0	0	20	0	19	1	0
	Columbia	27,272	12	0	2	4	6	219	72	133	14	0
	Upstate	4,916	1	0	0	0	1	45	4	41	0	0
Winthrop University		6,382	3	0	1	0	2	77	17	58	2	0
SOUTH DAKOTA												
South Dakota State University		11,645	0	0	0	0	0	0	0	0	0	0
Austin Peay State University		9,094	11	0	1	1	9	138	27	111	0	1
Christian Brothers University		1,874	2	0	0	1	1	26	3	22	1	0
East Tennessee State University		13,119	4	0	1	2	1	146	19	121	6	0
Middle Tennessee State University		23,246	15	0	1	5	9	329	57	267	5	2
Northeast State Technical Community College		5,237	0	0	0	0	0	7	0	7	0	0
Southwest Tennessee Community College		10,617	1	0	0	1	0	37	2	34	1	0
Tennessee State University		9,065	8	0	1	3	4	176	0	174	2	0
Tennessee Technological University		10,321	6	0	1	0	5	95	16	79	0	2
University of Memphis		20,379	3	0	0	2	1	161	38	117	6	0
University of Tennessee:	Chattanooga	9,558	1	0	0	0	1	182	43	136	3	0
	Knoxville	29,937	3	0	1	2	0	270	5	260	5	2
	Martin	7,171	1	0	0	0	1	89	7	82	0	0
	Memphis[3]		5	0	0	2	3	99	6	89	4	0
Vanderbilt University		11,847	14	0	1	2	11	468	28	434	6	0
Volunteer State Community College		7,065	0	0	0	0	0	11	0	11	0	0
Walters State Community College		5,825	0	0	0	0	0	10	0	10	0	0
TEXAS												
Abilene Christian University		4,675	0	0	0	0	0	108	19	87	2	0
Alamo Community College District[3]			11	1	2	6	2	372	5	335	32	0
Alvin Community College		4,169	0	0	0	0	0	8	0	7	1	0
Amarillo College		10,387	0	0	0	0	0	31	4	27	0	0
Angelo State University		6,239	2	0	1	0	1	63	2	58	3	0
Austin College		1,339	0	0	0	0	0	31	1	29	1	0

Note: Caution should be exercised in making any intercampus comparisons or ranking schools because university/college crime statistics are affected by a variety of factors. These include demographic characteristics of the surrounding community, ratio of male to female students, number of on-campus residents, accessibility of the campus to outside visitors, size of enrollment, etc.

[1] The student enrollment figures provided by the United States Department of Education are for the 2007 school year, the most recent available. The enrollment figures include full-time and part-time students.

[2] The FBI does not publish arson data unless it receives data from either the agency or the state for all 12 months of the calendar year.

[3] Student enrollment figures were not available.

Table 9. Offenses Known to Law Enforcement, by State and University and College, 2008—*Continued*

(Number.)

State and University/College	Campus	Student enrollment[1]	Violent crime	Murder and nonnegligent manslaughter	Forcible rape	Robbery	Aggravated assault	Property crime	Burglary	Larceny-theft	Motor vehicle theft	Arson[2]
Baylor Health Care System[3]			7	0	0	3	4	472	21	438	13	0
Baylor University	Waco	14,174	5	0	0	1	4	201	10	189	2	0
Central Texas College		21,532	3	0	0	0	3	18	1	17	0	0
College of the Mainland		3,521	0	0	0	0	0	19	0	18	1	1
Eastfield College		10,653	1	0	0	0	1	55	1	52	2	0
El Paso Community College		25,023	3	0	0	1	2	166	10	146	10	0
Grayson County College		3,811	1	0	0	0	1	16	7	9	0	0
Hardin-Simmons University		2,435	1	0	0	0	1	32	8	24	0	0
Houston Baptist University		2,339	0	0	0	0	0	18	2	16	0	0
Lamar University	Beaumont	10,213	11	0	0	5	6	125	8	115	2	0
Laredo Community College		7,831	0	0	0	0	0	21	2	19	0	0
McLennan Community College		8,079	0	0	0	0	0	28	0	27	1	0
Midwestern State University		6,027	0	0	0	0	0	51	4	46	1	0
Mountain View College		7,009	0	0	0	0	0	46	0	34	12	0
North Lake College		9,835	0	0	0	0	0	36	3	32	1	0
Paris Junior College		4,343	1	0	1	0	0	23	11	11	1	0
Prairie View A&M University		8,382	10	0	2	5	3	210	72	127	11	0
Rice University		5,161	5	0	0	4	1	249	12	234	3	0
Richland College		15,311	1	0	0	0	1	101	5	95	1	0
Southern Methodist University		10,829	8	0	3	3	2	205	35	165	5	1
South Plains College		6,602	1	0	0	0	1	13	3	10	0	0
Southwestern University		1,294	2	0	0	0	2	22	1	21	0	0
Stephen F. Austin State University		11,607	7	0	6	0	1	224	38	178	8	1
St. Mary's University		3,920	1	0	0	0	1	70	4	61	5	0
Sul Ross State University		2,717	1	0	1	0	0	27	9	18	0	0
Tarleton State University		9,460	0	0	0	0	0	63	33	30	0	1
Texas A&M International University		5,179	1	0	0	0	1	45	5	39	1	0
Texas A&M University:	College Station	46,542	9	0	4	1	4	491	18	469	4	0
	Commerce	8,813	1	0	0	0	1	54	6	47	1	0
	Corpus Christi	8,563	2	0	1	0	1	69	16	53	0	0
	Galveston	1,614	0	0	0	0	0	21	0	21	0	0
	Kingsville	6,567	1	0	1	0	0	65	17	47	1	0
Texas Christian University		8,668	2	0	0	0	2	178	3	173	2	0
Texas Southern University		9,540	11	0	1	4	6	239	69	154	16	1
Texas State Technical College:	Harlingen	4,957	0	0	0	0	0	25	2	23	0	0
	Marshall	705	0	0	0	0	0	15	4	11	0	0
	Waco	4,210	2	0	0	0	2	137	49	86	2	0
Texas State University	San Marcos	28,121	2	0	0	0	2	282	38	241	3	2
Texas Technological University	Lubbock	28,260	6	0	0	2	4	348	25	321	2	1
Texas Woman's University		12,168	1	0	1	0	0	55	7	48	0	1
Trinity University		2,686	1	0	1	0	0	159	29	126	4	0
Tyler Junior College		8,217	1	0	0	0	1	69	3	64	2	0
University of Houston:	Central Campus	34,663	19	0	3	8	8	409	22	361	26	1
	Clearlake	7,522	0	0	0	0	0	20	1	19	0	0
	Downtown Campus	11,793	1	0	0	0	1	63	0	61	2	0
University of Mary Hardin-Baylor		2,651	0	0	0	0	0	44	2	41	1	0
University of North Texas:	Denton	34,710	7	0	0	0	7	227	27	193	7	2
	Health Science Center	1,153	0	0	0	0	0	14	1	13	0	0
University of Texas:	Arlington	24,889	18	0	2	7	9	327	50	271	6	0
	Austin	50,170	11	0	2	6	3	657	36	611	10	1
	Brownsville	17,215	3	0	0	1	2	50	4	42	4	0
	Dallas	14,556	4	0	0	0	4	94	17	75	2	0
	El Paso	20,154	4	0	0	1	3	197	39	150	8	1
	Health Science Center, San Antonio	2,868	0	0	0	0	0	88	4	83	1	0
	Health Science Center, Tyler[3]		0	0	0	0	0	7	0	7	0	0
	Houston[3]		0	0	0	0	0	321	27	288	6	0
	Medical Branch	2,422	0	0	0	0	0	165	1	160	4	0
	Pan American	17,435	4	0	0	1	3	109	18	88	3	0
	Permian Basin	3,559	5	0	2	0	3	39	5	32	2	0
	San Antonio	28,533	5	0	1	0	4	190	5	184	1	0
	Southwestern Medical School	2,253	0	0	0	0	0	227	21	198	8	0
	Tyler	6,137	3	0	1	0	2	36	21	15	0	0
Western Texas College		1,844	1	0	0	1	0	7	3	4	0	0
West Texas A&M University		7,502	5	0	2	1	2	44	5	39	0	0

Note: Caution should be exercised in making any intercampus comparisons or ranking schools because university/college crime statistics are affected by a variety of factors. These include demographic characteristics of the surrounding community, ratio of male to female students, number of on-campus residents, accessibility of the campus to outside visitors, size of enrollment, etc.

[1] The student enrollment figures provided by the United States Department of Education are for the 2007 school year, the most recent available. The enrollment figures include full-time and part-time students.

[2] The FBI does not publish arson data unless it receives data from either the agency or the state for all 12 months of the calendar year.

[3] Student enrollment figures were not available.

Table 9. Offenses Known to Law Enforcement, by State and University and College, 2008—*Continued*

(Number.)

State and University/College	Campus	Student enroll-ment[1]	Violent crime	Murder and non-negligent man-slaughter	Forcible rape	Robbery	Aggra-vated assault	Property crime	Burglary	Larceny-theft	Motor vehicle theft	Arson[2]
UTAH												
Brigham Young University		34,174	0	0	0	0	0	318	13	299	6	0
College of Eastern Utah		2,085	0	0	0	0	0	25	12	13	0	0
Southern Utah University		7,057	0	0	0	0	0	59	12	45	2	0
University of Utah		28,025	6	0	0	2	4	599	35	549	15	0
Utah State University		14,893	1	0	1	0	0	103	14	89	0	0
Utah Valley University		23,840	1	0	0	0	1	70	2	68	0	0
Weber State University		18,081	1	0	0	0	1	51	12	39	0	0
VERMONT												
University of Vermont		12,239	0	0	0	0	0	181	33	148	0	2
VIRGINIA												
Christopher Newport University		4,884	5	0	1	3	1	114	5	109	0	0
College of William and Mary		7,795	4	0	3	0	1	236	21	215	0	0
Emory and Henry College		1,026	0	0	0	0	0	3	1	2	0	0
Ferrum College		1,233	0	0	0	0	0	21	1	20	0	0
George Mason University		30,276	4	0	0	2	2	226	13	208	5	0
Hampton University		5,658	6	0	0	3	3	87	24	63	0	0
James Madison University		17,918	2	0	1	0	1	190	7	181	2	0
Longwood University		4,727	5	0	3	1	1	52	14	38	0	0
Norfolk State University		6,155	17	0	2	11	4	176	41	125	10	4
Northern Virginia Community College		41,266	0	0	0	0	0	152	1	151	0	0
Old Dominion University		22,287	15	1	1	8	5	278	31	241	6	1
Radford University		9,122	5	0	2	0	3	90	12	77	1	5
Thomas Nelson Community College		9,368	0	0	0	0	0	21	0	21	0	0
University of Richmond		4,324	2	0	0	0	2	92	27	63	2	1
University of Virginia		24,257	5	0	3	0	2	367	68	294	5	0
University of Virginia's College at Wise		1,803	0	0	0	0	0	0	0	0	0	0
Virginia Commonwealth University		31,700	23	0	1	5	17	617	13	588	16	2
Virginia Military Institute		1,378	3	0	0	0	3	23	10	13	0	0
Virginia Polytechnic Institute and State University		29,898	3	0	1	1	1	277	61	213	3	2
Virginia State University		4,720	14	0	0	4	10	191	4	182	5	0
Virginia Western Community College		8,653	0	0	0	0	0	9	0	9	0	0
WASHINGTON												
Central Washington University		10,505	2	0	2	0	0	152	38	112	2	0
Eastern Washington University		10,686	1	0	0	0	1	106	7	99	0	0
Evergreen State College		4,586	1	0	1	0	0	137	27	106	4	1
University of Washington		40,218	15	0	1	9	5	549	84	446	19	1
Washington State University:	Pullman	24,396	5	0	3	0	2	149	24	124	1	7
	Vancouver[3]		0	0	0	0	0	16	0	14	2	0
Western Washington University		14,276	1	0	0	1	0	175	36	135	4	0
WEST VIRGINIA												
Concord University		2,735	2	0	0	0	2	17	3	14	0	0
Marshall University		13,808	11	0	1	3	7	170	13	156	1	0
Potomac State College		1,608	1	0	1	0	0	7	1	6	0	0
Shepherd University		4,119	1	0	1	0	0	31	1	30	0	2
West Virginia State University		3,218	4	0	1	0	3	27	3	23	1	0
West Virginia Tech		1,453	1	0	0	0	1	20	3	17	0	1
WISCONSIN												
University of Wisconsin:	Eau Claire	10,854	0	0	0	0	0	87	0	86	1	0
	Green Bay	6,110	2	0	1	0	1	49	2	45	2	0
	La Crosse	9,994	1	0	1	0	0	56	10	45	1	0
	Madison	41,563	8	0	1	1	6	431	58	363	10	2
	Milwaukee	29,338	6	0	4	2	0	283	23	257	3	1
	Oshkosh	12,772	1	0	0	1	0	66	9	57	0	0
	Parkside	5,010	1	0	1	0	0	73	5	68	0	0
	Platteville	7,189	3	0	0	0	3	83	11	72	0	0
	Stevens Point	9,115	0	0	0	0	0	96	0	96	0	0
	Stout	8,477	1	0	1	0	0	115	20	95	0	0
	Superior	2,753	1	0	1	0	0	30	6	23	1	0
	Whitewater	10,737	1	0	0	0	1	99	8	91	0	0
WYOMING												
Sheridan College		3,277	1	0	1	0	0	3	0	3	0	0
University of Wyoming		12,875	0	0	0	0	0	147	7	137	3	0

Note: Caution should be exercised in making any intercampus comparisons or ranking schools because university/college crime statistics are affected by a variety of factors. These include demographic characteristics of the surrounding community, ratio of male to female students, number of on-campus residents, accessibility of the campus to outside visitors, size of enrollment, etc.

[1] The student enrollment figures provided by the United States Department of Education are for the 2007 school year, the most recent available. The enrollment figures include full-time and part-time students.

[2] The FBI does not publish arson data unless it receives data from either the agency or the state for all 12 months of the calendar year.

[3] Student enrollment figures were not available.

Table 10. Offenses Known to Law Enforcement, by State Metropolitan and Nonmetropolitan Counties, 2008

(Number.)

State/County	Violent crime	Murder and non-negligent man-slaughter	Forcible rape	Robbery	Aggravated assault	Property crime	Burglary	Larceny-theft	Motor vehicle theft	Arson[1]
ALABAMA-Metropolitan Counties										
Bibb	20	0	2	1	17	138	54	71	13	
Chilton	328	0	9	3	316	477	159	312	6	
Colbert	169	0	6	4	159	563	122	418	23	
Elmore	58	0	13	16	29	688	231	420	37	
Geneva	28	0	5	2	21	226	82	118	26	
Hale	63	2	3	7	51	219	86	99	34	
Henry	22	1	2	0	19	119	34	74	11	
Houston	31	0	10	10	11	525	103	364	58	
Jefferson	637	5	62	282	288	5,960	2,358	3,103	499	
Lauderdale	61	1	13	3	44	972	323	594	55	
Lawrence	35	0	1	3	31	505	179	310	16	
Lee	103	3	20	24	56	1,850	643	1,095	112	
Limestone	38	1	6	8	23	380	103	241	36	
Madison	224	0	20	38	166	2,506	810	1,464	232	
Mobile	223	9	24	84	106	2,431	778	1,385	268	
Montgomery	52	0	6	9	37	720	225	405	90	
Morgan	28	2	3	4	19	388	231	155	2	
Russell	97	2	5	8	82	336	137	163	36	
Shelby	77	0	15	15	47	1,029	428	517	84	
St. Clair	38	0	8	5	25	324	119	181	24	
Tuscaloosa	229	2	21	32	174	1,807	570	1,041	196	
Walker	46	1	8	14	23	1,024	279	673	72	
ALABAMA-Nonmetropolitan Counties										
Baldwin	137	3	18	22	94	1,094	339	685	70	
Barbour	18	0	1	0	17	60	57	0	3	
Butler	21	0	2	1	18	226	95	124	7	
Chambers	20	0	4	3	13	186	69	108	9	
Cherokee	15	0	0	0	15	150	37	113	0	
Clay	10	0	3	0	7	128	55	66	7	
Cleburne	27	0	0	3	24	211	76	113	22	
Conecuh	7	1	0	0	6	87	37	48	2	
Coosa	24	0	3	1	20	260	100	155	5	
Covington	12	2	6	1	3	67	33	33	1	
Crenshaw	11	1	2	0	8	170	59	94	17	
Cullman	134	1	29	5	99	1,249	351	828	70	
Dale	47	0	2	1	44	165	57	102	6	
Dallas	53	0	4	9	40	586	168	364	54	
Escambia	26	0	2	6	18	163	48	105	10	
Fayette	7	0	2	2	3	103	40	49	14	
Franklin	15	0	4	0	11	123	47	67	9	
Jackson	53	0	9	0	44	558	180	281	97	
Macon	53	1	5	3	44	315	131	130	54	
Marengo	20	0	3	3	14	164	54	92	18	
Marshall	64	2	13	5	44	656	244	364	48	
Monroe	34	2	0	1	31	105	54	46	5	
Perry	5	1	0	0	4	102	41	49	12	
Pickens	14	1	4	1	8	63	26	32	5	
Pike	6	0	0	3	3	85	38	43	4	
Talladega	72	0	7	24	41	1,107	303	767	37	
Washington	82	0	6	2	74	164	43	112	9	
Wilcox	6	0	0	0	6	19	3	11	5	
Winston	17	0	1	0	16	235	58	169	8	
ARIZONA-Metropolitan Counties										
Coconino	123	0	15	3	105	559	171	373	15	16
Maricopa	1,018	26	23	121	848	7,260	2,050	4,303	907	153
Mohave	191	7	16	15	153	2,411	894	1,303	214	22
Pima	674	28	72	234	340	11,987	2,762	7,754	1,471	126
Pinal	198	7	39	36	116	3,930	493	2,731	706	24
Yavapai	302	3	20	6	273	1,568	536	893	139	9
Yuma[2]	96	2	5	10	79	934	394	422	118	9
ARIZONA-Nonmetropolitan Counties										
Apache	28	0	6	0	22	234	102	126	6	0
Cochise	446	4	16	14	412	1,027	360	527	140	10
Gila	66	0	2	2	62	386	130	201	55	11
Graham	276	0	0	0	276	248	101	131	16	16
La Paz	70	0	0	2	68	368	100	232	36	8
Navajo	58	0	10	1	47	636	323	241	72	4
Santa Cruz	5	0	0	3	2	437	181	154	102	0
ARKANSAS-Metropolitan Counties										
Benton	129	1	33	0	95	500	221	240	39	3
Cleveland	2	1	1	0	0	130	55	67	8	3
Craighead	21	0	1	1	19	316	134	149	33	5
Crawford	16	0	5	1	10	300	113	157	30	1

[1] The FBI does not publish arson data unless it receives data from either the agency or the state for all 12 months of the calendar year.

[2] Because of changes in the state/local agency's reporting practices, figures are not comparable to previous years' data.

Table 10. Offenses Known to Law Enforcement, by State Metropolitan and Nonmetropolitan Counties, 2008—*Continued*

(Number.)

State/County	Violent crime	Murder and non-negligent man-slaughter	Forcible rape	Robbery	Aggravated assault	Property crime	Burglary	Larceny-theft	Motor vehicle theft	Arson[1]
Crittenden	80	0	3	8	69	406	117	255	34	10
Faulkner	50	2	13	0	35	716	187	458	71	10
Franklin	24	0	1	0	23	196	78	107	11	2
Garland	129	3	25	14	87	2,504	1,152	1,170	182	21
Grant	21	0	3	0	18	169	68	84	17	2
Jefferson	84	4	9	6	65	535	240	229	66	10
Lincoln	14	0	2	0	12	93	56	33	4	2
Lonoke	128	0	22	5	101	624	280	266	78	4
Madison	30	1	4	1	24	75	36	34	5	0
Perry	14	0	1	0	13	69	34	32	3	1
Poinsett	49	0	2	1	46	76	69	3	4	4
Pulaski[2]	374	2	22	44	306	1,964	858	889	217	16
Saline	131	3	27	10	91	1,044	327	668	49	6
Sebastian	79	0	6	4	69	399	147	232	20	2
Washington	132	0	15	2	115	526	200	284	42	5
ARKANSAS-Nonmetropolitan Counties										
Arkansas	1	0	0	0	1	93	30	51	12	0
Ashley[2]	10	0	2	2	6	201	81	113	7	4
Baxter	37	1	6	1	29	607	118	459	30	1
Boone[2]	33	0	5	0	28	238	57	179	2	7
Bradley	9	1	1	0	7	51	23	18	10	0
Calhoun	0	0	0	0	0	28	12	10	6	0
Carroll	27	0	0	0	27	230	49	151	30	3
Chicot[2]	8	0	0	3	5	74	43	27	4	1
Clark	16	0	1	3	12	148	58	84	6	2
Cleburne	60	2	7	3	48	293	129	142	22	7
Columbia	26	0	1	1	24	206	81	112	13	1
Cross	62	0	5	0	57	233	34	185	14	1
Dallas	2	0	0	0	2	30	14	14	2	0
Drew	38	0	1	1	36	177	83	81	13	7
Fulton	17	1	1	0	15	108	49	51	8	1
Greene	15	2	3	0	10	157	39	114	4	0
Hempstead	31	3	4	0	24	207	69	100	38	1
Howard	9	0	1	0	8	63	32	30	1	5
Independence[2]	186	2	18	14	152	1,199	493	616	90	18
Izard	5	0	2	0	3	70	35	32	3	4
Jackson	47	0	5	1	41	168	62	89	17	6
Johnson[2]	20	0	1	0	19	194	130	64	0	9
Lawrence	16	1	2	0	13	145	60	85	0	0
Little River	10	0	4	0	6	55	33	19	3	0
Logan	19	1	4	1	13	270	73	162	35	2
Marion	43	0	2	2	39	218	74	141	3	2
Mississippi	29	3	11	4	11	366	81	231	54	3
Nevada[2]	1	0	0	0	1	19	11	4	4	0
Newton	23	2	1	0	20	96	39	47	10	2
Ouachita	21	1	2	1	17	122	56	58	8	0
Polk	20	0	5	2	13	118	69	43	6	1
Pope	29	0	11	0	18	449	183	230	36	4
Prairie	1	0	0	0	1	83	25	49	9	0
Randolph	0	0	0	0	0	59	3	55	1	2
Sevier	26	1	1	1	23	247	115	110	22	0
St. Francis	28	0	3	9	16	482	149	333	0	1
Union	34	1	8	5	20	415	72	307	36	2
White	42	3	10	4	25	808	283	423	102	3
Yell	40	1	6	1	32	172	94	59	19	4
CALIFORNIA-Metropolitan Counties										
Alameda	728	5	24	287	412	2,829	626	1,386	817	24
Butte	145	1	22	25	97	1,373	509	850	14	13
Contra Costa	548	16	29	204	299	3,359	1,169	2,179	11	27
El Dorado	235	7	17	21	190	2,038	738	1,286	14	20
Fresno	652	19	30	126	477	6,121	1,735	3,472	914	280
Imperial	121	2	7	14	98	976	315	633	28	9
Kern	1,891	23	137	461	1,270	10,541	3,272	5,814	1,455	389
Kings	177	3	8	18	148	607	213	332	62	10
Los Angeles	7,362	135	232	1,967	5,028	19,893	5,311	9,200	5,382	417
Madera	252	2	12	27	211	1,388	520	849	19	2
Marin	148	2	10	27	109	961	286	673	2	10
Merced	469	5	16	55	393	2,392	775	1,603	14	8
Monterey	187	6	15	53	113	1,569	526	1,029	14	18
Napa	60	0	5	4	51	507	187	316	4	2

[1] The FBI does not publish arson data unless it receives data from either the agency or the state for all 12 months of the calendar year.
[2] Because of changes in the state/local agency's reporting practices, figures are not comparable to previous years' data.

Table 10. Offenses Known to Law Enforcement, by State Metropolitan and Nonmetropolitan Counties, 2008—*Continued*

(Number.)

State/County	Violent crime	Murder and non-negligent man-slaughter	Forcible rape	Robbery	Aggravated assault	Property crime	Burglary	Larceny-theft	Motor vehicle theft	Arson[1]
Orange	163	0	5	27	131	1,425	298	982	145	5
Placer	296	3	21	34	238	1,939	691	1,209	39	9
Riverside	1,515	24	82	387	1,022	13,387	3,577	7,412	2,398	43
Sacramento	3,282	47	194	1,274	1,767	15,525	4,580	10,771	174	195
San Benito	66	1	10	1	54	294	111	172	11	2
San Bernardino	1,295	23	69	206	997	6,866	2,153	3,326	1,387	130
San Diego	1,516	14	93	262	1,147	7,454	2,010	3,783	1,661	43
San Joaquin	1,085	9	27	205	844	5,388	1,676	3,576	136	24
San Luis Obispo	210	2	26	14	168	1,340	474	859	7	11
San Mateo	221	5	12	45	159	1,760	190	1,293	277	9
Santa Barbara	171	2	19	33	117	1,884	569	1,307	8	19
Santa Clara	286	1	27	46	212	1,817	465	1,144	208	5
Santa Cruz	332	3	32	61	236	2,298	692	1,595	11	27
Shasta	447	1	33	19	394	1,104	526	551	27	11
Solano	123	1	9	26	87	418	177	231	10	13
Sonoma	631	3	34	48	546	1,628	667	940	21	19
Stanislaus	522	4	30	118	370	3,561	1,315	1,877	369	169
Sutter	109	0	7	9	93	719	229	449	41	5
Tulare[3]	514	24	29	88	373		1,040	2,414		58
Ventura	212	4	20	35	153	1,326	345	891	90	24
Yolo	45	2	5	9	29	344	125	210	9	2
Yuba	240	6	18	36	180	1,177	503	658	16	11
CALIFORNIA-Nonmetropolitan Counties										
Alpine	14	1	2	0	11	72	14	58	0	0
Amador	62	0	14	5	43	609	229	366	14	3
Calaveras	83	0	6	14	63	650	290	351	9	4
Colusa	21	0	0	5	16	254	87	163	4	3
Del Norte	79	0	16	9	54	293	155	134	4	4
Glenn	8	0	0	0	8	141	51	88	2	0
Humboldt	137	1	13	20	103	954	273	654	27	8
Inyo	58	0	1	2	55	178	66	110	2	4
Lake	198	3	10	21	164	859	417	435	7	9
Lassen	34	0	7	3	24	148	54	92	2	5
Mariposa	42	1	3	0	38	257	96	159	2	2
Mendocino	336	5	16	34	281	632	297	331	4	17
Modoc	18	0	3	0	15	88	34	54	0	2
Mono	15	0	2	1	12	97	40	57	0	0
Nevada	164	1	14	11	138	538	205	327	6	1
Plumas	138	3	13	3	119	290	139	145	6	0
Sierra	6	0	0	1	5	35	19	16	0	1
Siskiyou	47	1	6	3	37	219	88	129	2	4
Tehama	212	0	6	8	198	369	230	139	0	14
Trinity	22	0	1	2	19	66	37	29	0	0
Tuolumne	114	1	20	11	82	802	356	438	8	13
COLORADO-Metropolitan Counties										
Adams	420	4	71	58	287	2,718	685	1,497	536	34
Arapahoe	202	2	22	30	148	1,381	325	937	119	30
Boulder	46	1	11	2	32	659	199	420	40	17
Clear Creek	17	0	0	0	17	94	31	61	2	1
Douglas	233	1	73	18	141	2,098	498	1,520	80	22
El Paso	822	7	60	18	737	1,802	638	963	201	38
Gilpin	9	0	1	0	8	39	7	32	0	0
Jefferson	250	0	38	17	195	2,844	517	2,148	179	39
Larimer	118	2	29	9	78	1,067	279	706	82	13
Mesa	174	2	32	14	126	1,394	386	895	113	10
Park	20	0	0	0	20	120	55	57	8	1
Pueblo	19	2	0	3	14	1,383	305	1,021	57	2
Teller	14	0	0	0	14	74	26	44	4	2
Weld	109	1	13	4	91	956	327	531	98	8
COLORADO-Nonmetropolitan Counties										
Alamosa	5	0	0	0	5	35	9	26	0	0
Archuleta	12	0	1	0	11	113	30	71	12	0
Bent	0	0	0	0	0	15	7	7	1	1
Chaffee	15	0	2	1	12	125	32	89	4	0
Crowley	6	0	2	0	4	0	0	0	0	0
Custer	14	0	4	1	9	45	10	29	6	1
Delta	27	0	5	1	21	158	44	107	7	2
Dolores	0	0	0	0	0	16	5	11	0	0
Eagle	56	1	2	1	52	543	67	471	5	6
Fremont	58	1	5	0	52	235	66	160	9	1
Grand	14	0	0	0	14	156	31	121	4	0

[1] The FBI does not publish arson data unless it receives data from either the agency or the state for all 12 months of the calendar year.
[3] The motor vehicle thefts for this county are collected by the Tulare County Highway Patrol. These data can be found in Table 11.

Table 10. Offenses Known to Law Enforcement, by State Metropolitan and Nonmetropolitan Counties, 2008—*Continued*

(Number.)

State/County	Violent crime	Murder and non-negligent man-slaughter	Forcible rape	Robbery	Aggravated assault	Property crime	Burglary	Larceny-theft	Motor vehicle theft	Arson[1]
Gunnison	19	0	1	0	18	19	1	16	2	0
Hinsdale	1	1	0	0	0	10	1	8	1	0
Jackson	3	0	0	0	3	7	2	5	0	0
Kiowa	0	0	0	0	0	0	0	0	0	0
Kit Carson	6	0	0	0	6	29	10	18	1	0
Lake	6	0	0	0	6	24	9	8	7	0
La Plata	31	1	15	0	15	343	115	202	26	4
Las Animas	5	0	0	0	5	4	1	3	0	0
Logan	6	0	1	0	5	36	7	28	1	1
Mineral	0	0	0	0	0	1	0	0	1	0
Moffat	0	0	0	0	0	29	3	25	1	1
Montezuma	66	1	1	1	63	181	73	86	22	2
Montrose	28	0	5	0	23	180	60	102	18	1
Morgan	2	0	0	1	1	79	12	59	8	1
Ouray	10	0	0	0	10	26	5	20	1	0
Phillips	0	0	0	0	0	5	0	4	1	0
Pitkin	18	0	4	0	14	111	14	82	15	0
Prowers	18	0	1	0	17	40	20	19	1	0
Rio Grande	5	0	0	0	5	37	16	19	2	1
Routt	19	0	6	0	13	62	12	46	4	0
Saguache	11	0	0	0	11	25	7	15	3	0
San Juan	4	0	0	0	4	29	9	19	1	0
San Miguel	2	0	0	0	2	56	15	40	1	0
Sedgwick	7	0	0	0	7	22	5	14	3	0
Summit	48	0	3	6	39	579	63	505	11	6
Washington	8	0	2	0	6	56	20	31	5	1
Yuma	5	0	1	0	4	30	4	25	1	1
DELAWARE-Metropolitan Counties										
New Castle County Police Department	1,544	14	97	430	1,003	7,719	1,992	4,986	741	9
FLORIDA-Metropolitan Counties										
Alachua	878	1	46	105	726	3,389	1,175	2,010	204	23
Baker	75	1	3	5	66	276	37	219	20	2
Bay	417	6	57	48	306	2,381	611	1,618	152	4
Brevard	1,089	4	61	127	897	5,709	1,309	4,047	353	26
Broward	344	4	16	114	210	1,011	193	731	87	3
Charlotte	500	3	15	68	414	4,535	1,083	3,234	218	2
Clay	819	5	51	90	673	4,576	1,058	3,281	237	28
Collier	1,110	6	53	224	827	5,154	1,258	3,590	306	22
Escambia	2,217	18	127	554	1,518	9,468	2,417	6,364	687	24
Flagler	214	0	13	39	162	1,943	484	1,358	101	6
Gadsden	379	1	2	24	352	802	536	248	18	2
Gilchrist	36	2	0	0	34	197	76	109	12	0
Hernando	576	2	75	77	422	5,841	1,662	3,848	331	11
Hillsborough	4,927	46	241	1,089	3,551	29,113	7,505	19,144	2,464	82
Indian River	327	4	30	64	229	2,913	735	2,063	115	5
Jefferson	174	0	7	6	161	125	50	67	8	2
Lake	897	7	56	57	777	3,673	1,229	2,166	278	21
Lee	1,665	28	91	450	1,096	12,468	4,174	7,394	900	98
Leon	343	6	16	59	262	1,592	792	674	126	44
Manatee	2,130	8	70	508	1,544	11,288	2,870	7,784	634	27
Marion	1,438	15	109	117	1,197	4,908	1,548	2,990	370	6
Martin	401	1	10	142	248	3,293	749	2,418	126	14
Miami-Dade	8,749	95	339	2,552	5,763	51,712	9,284	36,211	6,217	82
Nassau	606	1	6	22	577	1,496	482	905	109	12
Okaloosa	462	3	29	91	339	3,769	767	2,799	203	4
Orange	6,991	74	372	2,316	4,229	33,577	9,907	19,981	3,689	0
Osceola	799	9	28	138	624	6,732	2,631	3,716	385	0
Palm Beach	2,895	33	182	892	1,788	18,782	4,814	12,034	1,934	124
Pasco	1,497	22	111	315	1,049	14,588	4,040	9,452	1,096	64
Pinellas	1,271	8	126	245	892	8,386	2,077	5,831	478	43
Polk	1,525	28	86	254	1,157	11,265	3,874	6,537	854	0
Santa Rosa	247	2	15	22	208	1,513	418	992	103	5
Sarasota	739	7	53	173	506	8,770	2,195	6,163	412	7
Seminole	735	4	33	105	593	4,243	1,166	2,712	365	4
St. Johns	545	4	13	61	467	4,301	945	3,125	231	7
St. Lucie	329	4	21	70	234	1,901	628	1,155	118	12
Volusia	1,044	4	88	152	800	5,906	1,945	3,474	487	30
Wakulla	88	0	11	8	69	648	167	437	44	6
FLORIDA-Nonmetropolitan Counties										
Bradford	116	1	7	3	105	406	199	163	44	2
Calhoun	21	0	2	1	18	89	32	55	2	1
Citrus	457	7	21	55	374	2,865	728	1,940	197	20
Columbia	237	2	14	20	201	1,457	505	872	80	0

[1] The FBI does not publish arson data unless it receives data from either the agency or the state for all 12 months of the calendar year.

Table 10. Offenses Known to Law Enforcement, by State Metropolitan and Nonmetropolitan Counties, 2008—*Continued*

(Number.)

State/County	Violent crime	Murder and non-negligent man-slaughter	Forcible rape	Robbery	Aggravated assault	Property crime	Burglary	Larceny-theft	Motor vehicle theft	Arson[1]
DeSoto	179	2	4	39	134	833	300	473	60	5
Dixie	82	0	8	8	66	615	238	340	37	6
Franklin	17	0	0	0	17	76	14	57	5	0
Glades	56	0	3	3	50	330	123	170	37	3
Gulf	53	0	2	1	50	187	42	133	12	0
Hamilton	59	1	6	8	44	272	85	165	22	0
Hardee	65	0	6	21	38	598	119	409	70	0
Hendry	259	4	4	46	205	1,136	504	528	104	17
Highlands	181	5	11	21	144	1,912	601	1,202	109	5
Holmes	41	0	4	0	37	271	79	154	38	0
Jackson	193	6	13	11	163	565	221	300	44	2
Lafayette	19	0	0	0	19	30	13	14	3	0
Levy	205	0	26	14	165	1,033	373	557	103	3
Madison	146	0	4	9	133	359	157	183	19	1
Monroe	182	4	13	15	150	2,144	479	1,580	85	3
Okeechobee	260	2	19	26	213	1,060	493	525	42	2
Putnam	617	7	28	64	518	3,003	1,399	1,385	219	6
Sumter	142	2	14	22	104	842	257	529	56	1
Suwannee	120	1	8	1	110	507	160	300	47	1
Taylor	98	0	11	0	87	255	127	115	13	1
Union	58	1	1	4	52	130	60	55	15	2
Walton	163	1	9	11	142	1,006	254	682	70	2
Washington	31	0	2	2	27	241	72	143	26	0
GEORGIA-Metropolitan Counties										
Augusta-Richmond	1,124	20	143	723	238	13,911	3,502	8,755	1,654	184
Barrow	225	2	7	10	206	974	195	689	90	
Bibb	176	1	16	68	91	2,487	544	1,705	238	
Brooks	78	0	0	3	75	252	61	153	38	0
Burke[4]		5	0	0		705	242	430	33	
Butts	61	0	10	4	47	769	151	542	76	
Carroll	403	1	24	21	357	1,992	615	1,178	199	
Catoosa	74	3	4	9	58	1,131	276	705	150	
Cherokee	127	2	2	16	107	1,605	389	1,144	72	8
Clayton County Police Department	1,424	27	74	669	654	10,067	4,023	4,602	1,442	60
Cobb	3	0	1	0	2	0	0	0	0	0
Cobb County Police Department	1,236	18	96	555	567	12,765	3,477	7,969	1,319	39
Columbia	93	0	21	25	47	2,278	346	1,831	101	8
Coweta	138	4	16	32	86	1,425	382	900	143	
Crawford	26	0	1	0	25	391	114	248	29	
Dade[5]		0	1	0		197	59	112	26	
Dawson	19	1	4	2	12	409	82	290	37	1
DeKalb County Police Department	4,600	102	180	2,933	1,385	37,343	11,461	19,336	6,546	216
Dougherty County Police Department	21	0	0	5	16	511	187	279	45	
Douglas	164	1	11	47	105	2,551	753	1,537	261	1
Echols	11	2	0	0	9	47	25	18	4	0
Fayette	33	1	3	8	21	652	213	394	45	1
Floyd	18	0	0	0	18	6	2	2	2	
Forsyth	121	5	21	23	72	1,971	503	1,332	136	6
Fulton County Police Department	904	12	55	457	380	7,118	2,545	3,405	1,168	28
Gwinnett County Police Department[2]	1,068	33	12	726	297	18,094	5,726	10,389	1,979	103
Hall	236	3	29	46	158	2,448	651	1,526	271	17
Haralson	75	1	4	1	69	397	112	251	34	
Heard	11	0	1	0	10	162	44	91	27	
Henry County Police Department	309	3	13	130	163	4,351	1,035	2,865	451	6
Jasper	12	0	0	0	12	268	101	153	14	
Jones	31	1	2	5	23	561	172	341	48	0
Lamar	34	1	1	2	30	226	68	136	22	
Lanier	13	0	1	0	12	166	66	89	11	
Liberty	89	2	2	16	69	648	242	377	29	
Long	26	2	9	2	13	260	119	118	23	
Lowndes	111	1	10	26	74	1,154	306	794	54	
Madison	88	0	1	5	82	591	82	467	42	6
Marion	7	0	1	0	6	28	6	18	4	0
McDuffie	41	4	0	13	24	350	93	222	35	0
Murray	45	0	4	4	37	678	141	477	60	
Newton	346	8	8	38	292	1,985	770	992	223	
Oglethorpe	48	1	3	1	43	447	143	274	30	0
Paulding	189	0	16	25	148	2,557	608	1,692	257	19
Rockdale	329	4	24	69	232	2,548	556	1,718	274	13
Spalding	127	2	11	16	98	1,645	477	1,048	120	0
Terrell	18	1	1	0	16	139	58	70	11	

[1] The FBI does not publish arson data unless it receives data from either the agency or the state for all 12 months of the calendar year.
[2] Because of changes in the state/local agency's reporting practices, figures are not comparable to previous years' data.
[4] The FBI determined that the agency did not follow national Uniform Crime Reporting (UCR) Program guidelines for reporting an offense. Consequently, this figure is not included in this table.
[5] The FBI determined that the agency's data were overreported. Consequently, those data are not included in this table.

Table 10. Offenses Known to Law Enforcement, by State Metropolitan and Nonmetropolitan Counties, 2008—*Continued*

(Number.)

State/County	Violent crime	Murder and non-negligent man-slaughter	Forcible rape	Robbery	Aggravated assault	Property crime	Burglary	Larceny-theft	Motor vehicle theft	Arson[1]
Twiggs	23	1	0	0	22	201	44	133	24	
Walker	287	1	7	9	270	1,120	346	697	77	
Walton	110	3	9	17	81	1,019	290	596	133	
Whitfield	252	1	11	14	226	1,737	417	1,246	74	
GEORGIA-Nonmetropolitan Counties										
Baldwin[5]		0	5	15		894	305	552	37	
Banks	129	0	3	8	118	707	130	539	38	
Ben Hill	16	0	3	1	12	319	68	234	17	
Bleckley	14	2	0	1	11	99	24	68	7	0
Bulloch	42	0	5	10	27	783	238	481	64	
Calhoun	4	0	0	0	4	66	26	34	6	0
Camden[5]		4	1	6		495	166	308	21	
Charlton	7	0	1	0	6	100	28	66	6	
Chattooga	46	0	1	3	42	309	99	201	9	
Decatur	41	2	1	4	34	310	97	197	16	
Dodge	9	0	0	1	8	40	13	23	4	
Early	33	1	4	3	25	207	56	141	10	
Evans	4	0	1	1	2	167	61	80	26	
Franklin	27	0	3	3	21	405	142	205	58	
Gordon	46	0	8	5	33	649	176	440	33	
Grady	12	1	1	2	8	184	63	110	11	
Habersham	54	0	10	0	44	512	167	329	16	0
Hart	77	2	2	1	72	447	154	270	23	
Irwin	7	0	2	0	5	128	46	67	15	4
Jackson	46	0	3	4	39	1,132	289	787	56	
Jeff Davis	43	1	3	1	38	378	53	288	37	
Jefferson	22	0	1	2	19	188	83	81	24	
Laurens	49	1	9	3	36	598	169	364	65	
Lincoln[4]	5	0	0	0	5		42		7	
Lumpkin	49	0	10	1	38	405	99	285	21	
Miller	6	0	0	1	5	59	13	42	4	
Mitchell	41	1	0	2	38	105	30	70	5	0
Polk County Police Department	67	0	6	11	50	719	253	360	106	11
Pulaski	2	0	0	0	2	88	31	54	3	
Putnam	61	1	0	1	59	330	123	193	14	
Rabun	11	0	1	2	8	200	45	148	7	0
Screven	23	0	0	4	19	130	43	79	8	
Seminole	16	0	2	1	13	90	28	56	6	
Stephens	27	0	2	4	21	660	97	538	25	
Taliaferro	2	0	0	0	2	65	37	26	2	
Taylor	2	1	0	1	0	74	14	55	5	0
Thomas[4]	62	1	4	7	50			355	25	4
Tift	103	2	7	18	76	963	265	616	82	
Toombs	28	0	1	5	22	261	91	139	31	
Towns	11	0	0	0	11	170	52	109	9	
Treutlen	22	0	0	0	22	133	27	103	3	
Turner	9	0	2	1	6	101	21	72	8	1
Upson	55	0	2	4	49	409	117	278	14	
Ware	55	2	10	6	37	743	176	519	48	0
Washington	37	1	1	4	31	280	90	183	7	
Wheeler	1	0	0	0	1	68	22	38	8	
White	19	2	1	2	14	296	111	156	29	
Wilcox	4	0	0	0	4	47	30	14	3	
Wilkes	1	0	0	0	1	13	5	5	3	0
HAWAII-Nonmetropolitan Counties										
Hawaii Police Department	441	4	78	73	286	5,494	1,208	3,796	490	67
Kauai Police Department	208	2	52	20	134	2,584	710	1,718	156	10
IDAHO-Metropolitan Counties										
Ada	164	2	17	12	133	1,068	326	693	49	8
Bannock	11	0	1	1	9	127	23	100	4	2
Boise	11	0	0	0	11	136	52	80	4	1
Bonneville	100	1	16	3	80	858	199	605	54	5
Canyon	75	1	10	3	61	675	214	392	69	9
Franklin	4	0	2	0	2	43	5	35	3	2
Gem	6	0	5	0	1	30	11	17	2	0
Jefferson	18	0	3	0	15	204	56	135	13	0
Kootenai	122	2	18	7	95	945	297	582	66	9
Nez Perce	5	1	1	0	3	66	17	49	0	1
Owyhee	20	0	13	0	7	157	38	109	10	1
Power	1	0	0	0	1	33	3	28	2	0

[1] The FBI does not publish arson data unless it receives data from either the agency or the state for all 12 months of the calendar year.
[4] The FBI determined that the agency did not follow national Uniform Crime Reporting (UCR) Program guidelines for reporting an offense. Consequently, this figure is not included in this table.
[5] The FBI determined that the agency's data were overreported. Consequently, those data are not included in this table.

Table 10. Offenses Known to Law Enforcement, by State Metropolitan and Nonmetropolitan Counties, 2008—*Continued*

(Number.)

State/County	Violent crime	Murder and non-negligent man-slaughter	Forcible rape	Robbery	Aggravated assault	Property crime	Burglary	Larceny-theft	Motor vehicle theft	Arson[1]
IDAHO-Nonmetropolitan Counties										
Adams	7	0	0	0	7	52	10	40	2	1
Bear Lake	2	0	1	0	1	38	10	26	2	0
Benewah	17	1	1	1	14	22	7	12	3	0
Bingham	17	2	1	1	13	241	57	170	14	0
Blaine	4	0	0	0	4	48	30	16	2	0
Bonner	33	1	3	0	29	388	85	266	37	3
Boundary	6	0	1	0	5	71	25	42	4	2
Butte	19	0	0	3	16	9	7	1	1	0
Camas	1	0	0	0	1	24	8	15	1	0
Caribou	1	0	1	0	0	20	6	14	0	0
Clark	0	0	0	0	0	16	5	11	0	0
Clearwater	13	0	0	0	13	114	17	94	3	0
Custer	5	0	1	0	4	49	6	43	0	0
Elmore	11	0	2	0	9	77	14	58	5	0
Fremont	4	0	1	0	3	100	20	79	1	0
Gooding	13	0	5	0	8	40	13	18	9	0
Idaho	9	0	1	0	8	88	17	58	13	0
Jerome	8	1	2	0	5	120	36	74	10	1
Latah	21	0	2	0	19	151	65	73	13	2
Lemhi	2	0	0	0	2	9	4	4	1	0
Lewis	4	0	1	0	3	28	14	11	3	1
Lincoln	2	0	0	0	2	5	1	3	1	0
Madison	20	0	7	0	13	79	17	61	1	1
Minidoka	19	1	5	0	13	178	37	123	18	2
Oneida	7	0	0	0	7	40	8	29	3	0
Payette	4	0	2	0	2	62	18	35	9	0
Teton	10	0	0	1	9	25	7	16	2	0
Twin Falls	41	0	4	0	37	280	109	132	39	3
Valley	9	0	5	0	4	88	31	50	7	2
Washington	3	0	0	0	3	26	10	12	4	0
INDIANA-Metropolitan Counties										
Allen	56	0	18	13	25	1,110	219	815	76	4
Bartholomew	22	1	0	1	20	394	40	333	21	0
Boone	3	1	0	2	0	282	66	190	26	3
Brown	3	1	0	0	2	95	26	66	3	1
Carroll	7	0	0	1	6	193	55	122	16	2
Clark	33	0	6	7	20	654	244	356	54	5
Delaware	27	1	4	4	18	521	125	341	55	0
Elkhart	58	1	23	21	13	2,123	656	1,236	231	19
Floyd	1	0	0	1	0	733	143	538	52	0
Gibson	8	0	2	0	6	196	40	151	5	0
Greene	5	0	1	1	3	143	38	89	16	0
Hancock	7	0	2	2	3	317	124	177	16	0
Harrison	10	0	2	3	5	461	114	308	39	2
Howard	41	0	4	2	35	630	243	355	32	0
Johnson	10	1	0	1	8	799	119	665	15	0
Lake	22	1	5	9	7	1,019	160	766	93	0
La Porte	22	0	5	8	9	835	288	507	40	2
Monroe	50	0	9	9	32	817	277	482	58	5
Newton	5	0	1	0	4	190	75	101	14	1
Porter	43	1	2	1	39	1,074	211	823	40	0
Putnam	22	0	4	3	15	243	92	115	36	0
Shelby	36	0	4	4	28	362	108	232	22	0
St. Joseph	107	1	9	21	76	1,990	610	1,280	100	15
Tippecanoe	35	0	6	3	26	889	251	593	45	11
Tipton	12	0	1	2	9	140	63	73	4	0
Vanderburgh	66	3	4	9	50	1,318	173	1,100	45	8
Warrick	134	0	8	0	126	707	134	551	22	2
Wells	0	0	0	0	0	135	41	82	12	2
INDIANA-Nonmetropolitan Counties										
Blackford	0	0	0	0	0	58	14	40	4	0
Daviess	5	0	0	0	5	71	20	37	14	1
Grant	13	0	3	3	7	429	99	290	40	0
Henry	3	1	2	0	0	675	258	377	40	1
Huntington	7	0	2	2	3	138	35	94	9	0
Jackson	15	0	3	2	10	382	88	285	9	0
Jennings	52	0	7	2	43	148	126	14	8	1
Knox	3	0	0	0	3	23	14	6	3	0
LaGrange	2	0	0	1	1	244	63	169	12	0
Lawrence	8	0	1	1	6	297	103	166	28	4

[1] The FBI does not publish arson data unless it receives data from either the agency or the state for all 12 months of the calendar year.

Table 10. Offenses Known to Law Enforcement, by State Metropolitan and Nonmetropolitan Counties, 2008—*Continued*

(Number.)

State/County	Violent crime	Murder and non-negligent man-slaughter	Forcible rape	Robbery	Aggravated assault	Property crime	Burglary	Larceny-theft	Motor vehicle theft	Arson[1]
Martin	1	0	1	0	0	64	10	36	18	2
Noble	9	0	2	0	7	158	72	70	16	1
Parke	11	0	1	10	0	190	49	135	6	4
Pulaski	11	1	0	2	8	214	46	154	14	4
Randolph	13	0	13	0	0	146	51	92	3	0
Ripley	2	0	0	0	2	187	39	138	10	0
Starke	18	0	1	3	14	462	152	265	45	4
Steuben	14	0	6	2	6	614	136	433	45	1
Wabash	0	0	0	0	0	178	56	122	0	2
Wayne	4	0	4	0	0	134	43	77	14	0
White	0	0	0	0	0	21	21	0	0	0
IOWA-Metropolitan Counties										
Benton	0	0	0	0	0	98	23	74	1	0
Black Hawk	39	0	5	0	34	263	88	157	18	4
Bremer	16	1	0	0	15	47	11	36	0	0
Dallas	3	0	1	0	2	79	18	55	6	0
Dubuque	60	0	4	0	56	251	82	146	23	4
Grundy	1	0	0	0	1	69	14	47	8	0
Guthrie	2	0	0	1	1	64	31	30	3	0
Harrison	7	0	2	0	5	119	31	77	11	1
Johnson	58	1	4	0	53	231	105	106	20	4
Jones	2	0	2	0	0	52	15	30	7	0
Linn	18	1	5	0	12	286	122	133	31	13
Madison	2	0	1	0	1	21	9	10	2	0
Mills	24	0	4	1	19	192	56	113	23	5
Polk	91	1	10	7	73	741	175	495	71	3
Pottawattamie	45	1	10	1	33	513	127	319	67	1
Scott	11	1	1	1	8	214	43	154	17	1
Story	11	0	3	0	8	188	82	90	16	3
Warren	22	0	7	0	15	243	64	165	14	2
Washington	23	0	5	0	18	123	73	41	9	0
Woodbury	17	1	2	0	14	107	56	48	3	1
IOWA-Nonmetropolitan Counties										
Adair	6	0	1	0	5	46	9	35	2	1
Adams	3	0	1	0	2	57	14	39	4	0
Allamakee	2	0	0	0	2	25	2	22	1	0
Appanoose	12	1	0	0	11	63	26	33	4	6
Audubon	6	0	0	0	6	15	0	12	3	0
Buchanan	9	1	1	0	7	89	24	61	4	2
Buena Vista	3	0	0	0	3	69	30	34	5	0
Butler	4	0	0	0	4	24	8	15	1	0
Calhoun	6	0	0	0	6	123	37	80	6	0
Carroll	3	0	0	0	3	36	3	31	2	0
Cass	8	0	1	1	6	110	39	66	5	0
Cedar	16	0	0	0	16	88	19	65	4	2
Cerro Gordo	8	0	0	0	8	107	36	65	6	0
Cherokee	1	0	0	0	1	37	11	26	0	0
Clarke	10	0	0	0	10	71	19	47	5	2
Clay	2	0	0	0	2	50	31	17	2	1
Clayton	13	0	3	0	10	45	20	21	4	1
Clinton	45	1	3	0	41	150	49	79	22	2
Davis	9	0	1	0	8	9	5	4	0	0
Des Moines	27	0	1	1	25	184	43	122	19	2
Emmet	1	0	0	0	1	38	21	15	2	0
Fayette	15	0	2	1	12	30	9	16	5	0
Floyd	1	0	1	0	0	21	12	9	0	0
Hamilton	12	1	0	0	11	88	44	39	5	1
Hancock	3	0	0	0	3	76	17	57	2	0
Hardin	8	0	3	0	5	92	39	44	9	1
Henry	29	0	3	1	25	126	46	71	9	1
Howard	2	0	0	0	2	66	17	46	3	1
Humboldt	2	1	0	0	1	32	9	20	3	0
Ida	9	0	2	0	7	63	10	52	1	0
Iowa	8	0	0	0	8	105	26	72	7	1
Jasper	16	0	1	1	14	131	40	79	12	3
Jefferson	5	0	0	0	5	79	29	43	7	0
Keokuk	0	0	0	0	0	14	0	13	1	0
Lee	27	0	6	0	21	119	31	76	12	1
Louisa	5	1	4	0	0	33	0	28	5	2
Lyon	13	0	3	0	10	87	28	49	10	1
Mahaska	22	0	0	0	22	82	34	41	7	2
Marion	31	1	10	0	20	73	25	41	7	0

[1] The FBI does not publish arson data unless it receives data from either the agency or the state for all 12 months of the calendar year.

Table 10. Offenses Known to Law Enforcement, by State Metropolitan and Nonmetropolitan Counties, 2008—*Continued*

(Number.)

State/County	Violent crime	Murder and non-negligent man-slaughter	Forcible rape	Robbery	Aggravated assault	Property crime	Burglary	Larceny-theft	Motor vehicle theft	Arson[1]
Marshall	31	2	4	0	25	93	43	42	8	1
Mitchell	1	0	0	0	1	8	3	3	2	0
Monona	0	0	0	0	0	2	0	1	1	0
Monroe	5	0	0	0	5	27	7	17	3	1
Muscatine	20	1	2	3	14	128	51	69	8	4
O'Brien	4	0	0	0	4	51	21	25	5	2
Osceola	2	0	0	0	2	11	3	8	0	0
Plymouth	7	0	2	0	5	45	13	26	6	0
Pocahontas	1	0	1	0	0	34	18	15	1	0
Poweshiek	9	0	3	0	6	131	45	71	15	1
Sac	2	0	0	0	2	44	25	17	2	0
Sioux	6	0	1	0	5	79	30	43	6	1
Tama	28	0	2	1	25	135	65	59	11	1
Taylor	0	0	0	0	0	46	15	29	2	0
Union	1	0	0	0	1	32	9	19	4	1
Van Buren	7	0	0	1	6	98	44	52	2	0
Wapello	8	0	1	0	7	124	44	66	14	0
Wayne	9	0	1	0	8	51	20	26	5	1
Webster	24	0	0	1	23	238	53	151	34	3
Winneshiek	1	0	0	0	1	32	9	23	0	0
Worth	0	0	0	0	0	114	23	81	10	1
Wright	1	0	0	0	1	47	24	20	3	0
KANSAS-Metropolitan Counties										
Butler	42	1	6	1	34	524	201	278	45	2
Doniphan	4	0	2	0	2	99	33	59	7	3
Douglas	16	0	4	0	12	260	64	183	13	4
Franklin	32	0	7	0	25	187	74	100	13	3
Geary	8	0	2	0	6	43	9	33	1	2
Harvey	23	0	2	0	21	94	16	73	5	2
Jackson	30	0	2	0	28	173	62	99	12	1
Jefferson	12	0	1	0	11	347	102	222	23	5
Leavenworth	74	0	4	1	69	345	133	180	32	14
Linn	19	1	4	0	14	85	26	42	17	1
Miami	19	0	3	0	16	178	59	100	19	13
Osage	9	0	2	0	7	77	39	32	6	5
Pottawattamie	26	1	3	2	20	227	69	143	15	2
Riley County Police Department	225	3	42	30	150	1,765	336	1,358	71	13
Shawnee	131	0	11	7	113	1,563	382	1,103	78	12
Sumner	16	0	1	0	15	144	50	84	10	0
Wabaunsee	13	0	1	0	12	93	35	49	9	0
Wyandotte	6	0	0	1	5	6	0	4	2	0
KANSAS-Nonmetropolitan Counties										
Allen	19	0	3	0	16	107	23	72	12	3
Anderson	4	0	0	1	3	48	16	30	2	1
Atchison	5	0	0	0	5	54	20	29	5	5
Barber	4	0	2	0	2	13	0	10	3	0
Barton[2]	4	0	2	0	2	136	49	80	7	0
Bourbon	2	0	1	0	1	55	20	30	5	1
Brown	24	0	1	0	23	53	17	32	4	0
Chautauqua	11	0	1	0	10	45	16	28	1	0
Cherokee	18	0	2	2	14	195	51	113	31	5
Cheyenne	1	0	0	0	1	17	2	14	1	0
Clark	1	0	0	0	1	23	10	12	1	0
Clay	8	0	1	0	7	54	18	27	9	0
Cloud	2	0	0	0	2	29	13	16	0	0
Coffey	12	0	4	0	8	47	11	35	1	0
Cowley	35	0	1	0	34	246	98	137	11	2
Crawford	41	0	1	1	39	296	90	189	17	12
Dickinson	17	0	5	0	12	132	30	96	6	3
Edwards	2	0	0	0	2	23	9	14	0	0
Elk	2	0	1	0	1	28	7	21	0	0
Ellis	10	0	2	0	8	75	18	53	4	1
Ellsworth	7	1	0	0	6	58	20	35	3	0
Finney	46	0	8	3	35	258	65	178	15	2
Ford	16	0	0	1	15	55	17	29	9	0
Graham	4	0	0	0	4	30	11	17	2	1
Grant	8	2	0	0	6	23	9	14	0	0
Gray	2	0	1	0	1	24	4	18	2	1
Greenwood	25	0	1	2	22	212	58	149	5	1
Harper	1	0	0	0	1	18	7	9	2	0
Hodgeman	5	0	0	0	5	26	9	16	1	0

[1] The FBI does not publish arson data unless it receives data from either the agency or the state for all 12 months of the calendar year.
[2] Because of changes in the state/local agency's reporting practices, figures are not comparable to previous years' data.

Table 10. Offenses Known to Law Enforcement, by State Metropolitan and Nonmetropolitan Counties, 2008—*Continued*

(Number.)

State/County	Violent crime	Murder and non-negligent man-slaughter	Forcible rape	Robbery	Aggravated assault	Property crime	Burglary	Larceny-theft	Motor vehicle theft	Arson[1]
Kearny	13	0	1	0	12	91	16	72	3	1
Kingman	3	0	1	0	2	55	21	28	6	2
Kiowa	5	0	2	0	3	36	12	21	3	0
Labette	15	0	1	0	14	118	44	68	6	8
Lane	3	0	1	0	2	22	8	12	2	0
Lincoln	5	0	0	0	5	45	12	31	2	1
Lyon	15	0	3	0	12	104	16	81	7	5
McPherson	9	0	2	1	6	99	33	63	3	2
Mitchell	4	0	1	0	3	60	28	27	5	2
Morris	2	0	1	0	1	39	16	23	0	0
Morton	10	0	0	0	10	39	13	23	3	0
Nemaha	9	0	2	0	7	52	13	38	1	0
Neosho	13	0	1	1	11	99	40	50	9	8
Osborne	4	1	0	0	3	56	25	29	2	1
Ottawa	9	0	1	0	8	72	29	40	3	1
Pawnee	15	0	2	0	13	36	14	21	1	1
Phillips	6	0	0	0	6	13	2	9	2	0
Pratt	5	0	1	0	4	50	16	30	4	3
Rawlins	3	0	1	0	2	17	2	14	1	0
Reno	39	0	4	2	33	297	111	174	12	13
Republic	2	0	0	0	2	55	18	33	4	1
Rice	9	0	1	0	8	46	16	27	3	1
Rooks	2	0	0	0	2	7	3	4	0	0
Rush	2	0	0	0	2	25	13	8	4	0
Russell	6	0	0	0	6	38	15	21	2	1
Saline	22	1	6	0	15	156	51	97	8	7
Scott	0	0	0	0	0	23	2	17	4	2
Seward	9	0	1	0	8	49	9	35	5	1
Sherman	9	0	0	0	9	23	6	16	1	0
Smith	1	0	0	0	1	24	14	8	2	0
Stafford	4	0	0	0	4	44	11	29	4	0
Stanton	1	0	0	1	0	24	4	18	2	0
Thomas	11	0	4	2	5	32	2	28	2	0
Washington	6	0	0	0	6	11	4	6	1	0
Wichita	10	0	0	0	10	20	2	16	2	0
Wilson	6	0	1	0	5	67	39	26	2	3
Woodson	10	0	5	0	5	39	9	29	1	1
KENTUCKY-Metropolitan Counties										
Bourbon	2	0	0	0	2	80	25	48	7	
Boyd	32	0	0	15	17	316	83	207	26	
Bracken	5	0	1	1	3	71	29	38	4	
Bullitt	35	1	11	4	19	560	243	284	33	
Christian	24	1	4	7	12	422	173	215	34	
Clark	15	1	4	5	5	322	126	179	17	
Daviess	31	0	4	2	25	578	147	404	27	3
Edmonson	3	0	0	0	3	48	15	30	3	
Gallatin	1	0	1	0	0	33	10	22	1	
Grant	1	0	1	0	0	92	34	54	4	
Greenup	16	0	1	5	10	64	38	19	7	
Hancock	1	0	0	0	1	15	7	7	1	
Hardin	5	0	3	0	2	127	55	65	7	
Jefferson	0	0	0	0	0	12	2	9	1	
Jessamine	10	0	2	6	2	202	69	107	26	
Kenton	1	0	0	0	1	6	1	5	0	
Larue	12	0	3	0	9	51	17	33	1	
McLean	4	0	0	0	4	16	5	8	3	
Meade	6	0	1	2	3	183	79	82	22	
Nelson	21	0	3	3	15	277	95	169	13	
Oldham	0	0	0	0	0	1	0	1	0	
Oldham County Police Department	26	0	12	8	6	472	117	339	16	
Pendleton	1	0	0	0	1	87	20	56	11	
Scott	17	0	2	3	12	411	134	251	26	
Shelby	33	0	4	7	22	399	101	276	22	
Spencer	3	0	1	1	1	41	24	12	5	
Trigg	2	0	0	0	2	92	44	37	11	
Trimble	0	0	0	0	0	16	1	9	6	
Warren	14	0	1	3	10	486	138	319	29	
KENTUCKY-Nonmetropolitan Counties										
Adair	1	0	0	0	1	12	6	4	2	
Allen	11	1	1	1	8	91	33	49	9	
Anderson	5	0	0	2	3	57	16	37	4	
Ballard	8	0	3	0	5	104	34	67	3	

[1] The FBI does not publish arson data unless it receives data from either the agency or the state for all 12 months of the calendar year.

Table 10. Offenses Known to Law Enforcement, by State Metropolitan and Nonmetropolitan Counties, 2008—*Continued*

(Number.)

State/County	Violent crime	Murder and non-negligent man-slaughter	Forcible rape	Robbery	Aggravated assault	Property crime	Burglary	Larceny-theft	Motor vehicle theft	Arson[1]
Barren	11	1	5	2	3	232	90	126	16	
Bell	5	0	0	1	4	58	15	38	5	
Boyle	5	0	1	1	3	127	38	75	14	
Breckinridge	2	0	0	0	2	35	13	16	6	
Butler	2	0	0	0	2	40	18	16	6	
Caldwell	5	0	0	0	5	58	30	23	5	
Calloway	14	1	3	1	9	448	163	250	35	
Carroll	0	0	0	0	0	3	0	3	0	
Carter	2	0	0	1	1	175	69	91	15	
Casey	4	0	0	0	4	116	40	67	9	
Clay	6	0	1	0	5	116	42	49	25	
Clinton	0	0	0	0	0	0	0	0	0	
Crittenden	0	0	0	0	0	17	4	12	1	
Cumberland	0	0	0	0	0	4	1	1	2	
Estill	2	0	0	2	0	242	69	154	19	
Fleming	9	0	2	0	7	46	15	18	13	
Floyd	1	0	0	0	1	151	39	96	16	
Franklin	20	0	3	11	6	110	57	45	8	
Fulton	1	0	1	0	0	54	15	33	6	
Garrard	0	0	0	0	0	133	43	86	4	
Graves	13	2	2	1	8	143	63	71	9	
Grayson	11	0	3	0	8	159	63	85	11	
Harlan	14	0	1	0	13	57	23	34	0	
Harrison	8	0	0	3	5	210	84	116	10	
Hart	2	0	1	0	1	25	18	6	1	
Hopkins	10	0	1	0	9	247	84	140	23	
Jackson	3	0	1	0	2	65	21	38	6	
Johnson	1	0	0	0	1	40	5	29	6	
Knott	0	0	0	0	0	77	13	57	7	
Knox	12	0	3	0	9	324	112	181	31	
Laurel	19	0	3	3	13	430	131	240	59	
Lawrence	3	0	0	0	3	21	11	10	0	
Letcher	2	0	0	0	2	100	38	57	5	
Lewis	10	0	2	5	3	67	30	31	6	
Lincoln	4	0	0	2	2	114	58	41	15	
Livingston	5	0	0	1	4	117	53	58	6	
Logan	20	0	2	9	9	212	89	111	12	
Lyon	3	0	0	0	3	34	12	19	3	
Madison	9	1	0	0	8	342	124	199	19	
Magoffin	2	0	0	0	2	26	8	13	5	
Marion	0	0	0	0	0	114	31	76	7	
Martin	2	0	1	0	1	91	33	45	13	
Mason	14	0	1	5	8	189	75	111	3	
McCracken	44	0	14	10	20	601	188	360	53	
McCreary	6	0	0	1	5	200	71	108	21	
Mercer	0	0	0	0	0	53	22	24	7	
Metcalfe	3	0	0	0	3	48	15	25	8	
Montgomery	10	0	0	2	8	456	164	269	23	
Muhlenberg	1	0	0	0	1	38	20	13	5	
Nicholas	0	0	0	0	0	11	4	6	1	
Ohio	13	1	2	0	10	125	52	66	7	
Owen	2	0	0	0	2	54	28	23	3	
Owsley	0	0	0	0	0	21	12	8	1	
Perry	2	0	0	0	2	26	10	12	4	
Pike	11	0	0	1	10	50	11	35	4	
Pulaski	44	1	5	6	32	1,047	364	654	29	
Rockcastle	7	0	1	2	4	47	23	12	12	
Rowan	3	0	0	1	2	34	7	27	0	
Russell	5	0	0	0	5	64	16	43	5	
Simpson	11	0	0	9	2	144	46	84	14	
Taylor	14	1	5	1	7	153	57	87	9	
Todd	1	0	0	0	1	22	5	14	3	
Union	2	0	0	0	2	59	11	48	0	
Washington	2	0	0	0	2	49	25	20	4	
Wayne	6	0	2	2	2	80	53	23	4	
Whitley	2	0	0	0	2	108	47	44	17	
LOUISIANA-Metropolitan Counties										
Ascension	370	3	17	33	317	2,660	550	1,928	182	14
Bossier	277	3	2	2	270	495	68	388	39	1
Caddo	158	0	13	14	131	959	223	635	101	12
Cameron	49	1	1	0	47	163	28	113	22	0
East Baton Rouge	766	18	26	232	490	8,066	2,238	5,390	438	37

[1] The FBI does not publish arson data unless it receives data from either the agency or the state for all 12 months of the calendar year.

Table 10. Offenses Known to Law Enforcement, by State Metropolitan and Nonmetropolitan Counties, 2008—*Continued*

(Number.)

State/County	Violent crime	Murder and non-negligent man-slaughter	Forcible rape	Robbery	Aggravated assault	Property crime	Burglary	Larceny-theft	Motor vehicle theft	Arson[1]
Grant	17	0	2	0	15	272	105	139	28	2
Jefferson	2,243	36	70	593	1,544	15,047	3,675	9,832	1,540	136
Lafayette	363	1	21	62	279	1,465	382	884	199	14
Lafourche	166	4	8	15	139	1,400	146	1,168	86	0
Livingston	175	5	14	15	141	2,547	785	1,524	238	0
Ouachita	178	0	4	33	141	3,008	944	1,906	158	6
Plaquemines	54	0	1	1	52	388	44	325	19	3
Pointe Coupee[4]	56	3	2	2	49		84	203		4
Rapides	324	5	33	6	280	1,528	346	993	189	3
St. Charles	172	4	14	31	123	1,359	434	822	103	15
St. John the Baptist	161	11	6	85	59	1,653	382	1,108	163	
St. Martin	93	1	13	16	63	274	27	247	0	
St. Tammany	401	4	42	23	332	2,914	775	1,916	223	24
Terrebonne	359	5	30	59	265	2,957	501	2,202	254	14
Union	25	0	0	0	25	45	17	28	0	5
West Baton Rouge	69	1	7	11	50	564	47	477	40	1
West Feliciana	52	0	4	2	46	125	29	80	16	1
LOUISIANA-Nonmetropolitan Counties										
Acadia	108	0	4	1	103	609	110	437	62	0
Assumption	151	0	4	1	146	375	72	271	32	0
Beauregard	61	1	5	2	53	336	125	177	34	3
Caldwell	62	1	0	1	60	351	116	210	25	2
Concordia	78	3	11	5	59	265	106	146	13	0
East Carroll	17	0	1	2	14	50	16	30	4	0
Evangeline	39	0	3	1	35	419	100	299	20	1
Franklin	11	0	0	3	8	159	58	93	8	0
Jackson	7	2	0	0	5	146	40	91	15	1
Jefferson Davis	68	2	7	3	56	378	52	297	29	0
Lincoln	31	0	3	2	26	242	90	127	25	0
Madison	77	0	1	1	75	157	42	100	15	1
Morehouse	30	2	2	5	21	544	82	429	33	2
Natchitoches	111	0	3	4	104	408	96	278	34	1
Red River	19	0	1	0	18	90	20	63	7	0
Richland	8	0	1	0	7	173	30	127	16	0
Sabine	34	1	0	2	31	322	96	202	24	0
St. James	172	2	2	6	162	628	159	429	40	3
St. Mary	228	2	14	47	165	918	213	654	51	1
Tangipahoa	1,042	3	25	73	941	4,583	1,851	2,594	138	1
Vermilion	278	3	10	2	263	265	54	211	0	0
Washington	134	5	9	15	105	687	202	435	50	0
Webster	45	0	4	0	41	202	97	79	26	1
West Carroll	28	3	0	0	25	264	72	176	16	4
MAINE-Metropolitan Counties										
Androscoggin	6	0	2	0	4	229	66	155	8	1
Cumberland	28	0	5	4	19	567	251	279	37	3
Penobscot	6	0	0	1	5	711	206	461	44	0
Sagadahoc	5	0	2	1	2	149	57	86	6	1
York	23	0	7	1	15	512	183	294	35	0
MAINE-Nonmetropolitan Counties										
Aroostook	2	0	0	0	2	74	20	50	4	0
Franklin	2	0	0	0	2	117	68	46	3	0
Hancock	5	0	1	1	3	241	50	183	8	0
Kennebec	8	0	7	0	1	299	63	218	18	3
Knox	10	0	1	0	9	225	63	150	12	0
Lincoln	13	0	5	0	8	235	74	152	9	3
Oxford	18	0	10	0	8	270	101	157	12	1
Piscataquis	4	0	3	0	1	110	40	58	12	1
Somerset	13	0	8	1	4	376	126	217	33	1
Waldo	7	0	0	0	7	138	79	48	11	1
Washington	43	0	1	1	41	200	61	128	11	0
MARYLAND-Metropolitan Counties										
Allegany	2	0	0	0	2	77	16	61	0	0
Anne Arundel	0	0	0	0	0	0	0	0	0	0
Anne Arundel County Police Department	2,603	10	101	680	1,812	17,627	3,124	13,105	1,398	132
Baltimore County	0	0	0	0	0	0	0	0	0	0
Baltimore County Police Department	4,901	30	148	1,725	2,998	26,611	4,393	19,340	2,878	333
Calvert	294	1	6	15	272	1,495	352	1,051	92	1
Carroll	70	0	19	6	45	375	87	276	12	3
Cecil	92	2	7	19	64	1,223	510	600	113	1
Charles	741	10	26	173	532	4,016	725	2,922	369	0
Frederick	238	1	8	16	213	1,599	252	1,282	65	21
Harford	433	3	54	128	248	2,966	770	1,945	251	20

[1] The FBI does not publish arson data unless it receives data from either the agency or the state for all 12 months of the calendar year.
[4] The FBI determined that the agency did not follow national Uniform Crime Reporting (UCR) Program guidelines for reporting an offense. Consequently, this figure is not included in this table.

Table 10. Offenses Known to Law Enforcement, by State Metropolitan and Nonmetropolitan Counties, 2008—*Continued*

(Number.)

State/County	Violent crime	Murder and non-negligent man-slaughter	Forcible rape	Robbery	Aggravated assault	Property crime	Burglary	Larceny-theft	Motor vehicle theft	Arson[1]
Howard	0	0	0	0	0	0	0	0	0	0
Howard County Police Department	703	4	36	259	404	8,205	1,376	6,317	512	82
Montgomery	0	0	0	0	0	0	0	0	0	0
Montgomery County Police Department	2,087	21	131	1,100	835	24,888	3,603	19,027	2,258	252
Prince George's	93	0	0	0	93	0	0	0	0	0
Prince George's County Police Department	5,966	102	215	2,954	2,695	34,856	6,636	20,046	8,174	355
Queen Anne's	101	1	10	11	79	707	149	521	37	3
Somerset	0	0	0	0	0	46	8	37	1	0
Washington	165	0	12	23	130	1,349	335	924	90	0
Wicomico	136	1	13	29	93	881	287	534	60	4
MARYLAND-Nonmetropolitan Counties										
Caroline	39	1	4	7	27	393	156	225	12	0
Dorchester	26	0	4	3	19	324	117	189	18	0
Garrett	29	0	0	1	28	301	97	193	11	0
Kent	21	0	1	3	17	163	73	88	2	1
St. Mary's	268	2	8	40	218	1,946	466	1,364	116	5
Talbot	18	0	3	0	15	288	60	221	7	0
Worcester	55	2	1	0	52	163	41	110	12	0
MICHIGAN-Metropolitan Counties										
Barry	29	0	13	1	15	420	83	315	22	3
Bay	51	0	12	12	27	648	97	525	26	1
Berrien	126	0	24	10	92	876	264	570	42	4
Cass	44	2	19	0	23	713	230	441	42	3
Ingham	107	0	16	13	78	1,023	234	740	49	5
Ionia[2]	61	1	15	3	42	381	131	229	21	4
Jackson	101	1	18	3	79	481	132	323	26	4
Kalamazoo	236	1	37	58	140	2,520	736	1,672	112	23
Kent	336	1	58	46	231	3,852	956	2,730	166	26
Lapeer	47	0	9	0	38	472	106	339	27	1
Livingston	55	0	5	2	48	847	174	619	54	5
Macomb	370	0	65	50	255	2,671	527	1,937	207	17
Monroe[2]	240	2	56	37	145	2,658	658	1,861	139	48
Newaygo	58	0	5	0	53	410	164	235	11	2
Oakland	285	3	45	44	193	4,105	868	3,042	195	61
Ottawa	268	3	87	29	149	2,962	682	2,182	98	22
Saginaw	134	1	5	13	115	642	165	436	41	1
St. Clair	206	2	29	15	160	1,783	434	1,214	135	17
Van Buren	103	2	28	5	68	677	141	451	85	7
Washtenaw	520	5	55	109	351	2,419	895	1,307	217	30
Wayne	13	0	0	9	4	17	2	13	2	0
MICHIGAN-Nonmetropolitan Counties										
Alcona	9	0	0	0	9	165	55	107	3	1
Alger	0	0	0	0	0	3	2	1	0	0
Allegan	90	1	27	9	53	730	170	510	50	2
Benzie	30	0	5	3	22	186	58	118	10	2
Charlevoix	12	0	4	0	8	156	49	105	2	5
Cheboygan	8	1	3	0	4	97	41	53	3	0
Chippewa	7	0	0	0	7	93	33	59	1	0
Crawford	23	0	6	1	16	186	62	107	17	0
Delta	5	0	1	0	4	51	12	36	3	2
Gladwin	23	0	3	1	19	146	52	83	11	3
Gratiot	16	0	8	1	7	189	43	137	9	0
Hillsdale	34	0	10	0	24	226	66	143	17	0
Huron	16	1	3	0	12	195	79	111	5	5
Iosco	0	0	0	0	0	0	0	0	0	0
Iron	6	0	4	0	2	30	6	23	1	0
Isabella	43	0	14	3	26	530	171	328	31	5
Kalkaska	24	0	1	1	22	249	79	160	10	2
Keweenaw	1	0	1	0	0	39	5	34	0	2
Lake	24	1	2	1	20	256	117	129	10	4
Luce	6	0	0	0	6	97	54	42	1	0
Mackinac	2	0	0	1	1	60	22	38	0	1
Manistee	14	0	4	0	10	129	20	104	5	0
Marquette	3	0	0	0	3	167	19	146	2	0
Mason	42	0	8	1	33	521	87	425	9	2
Mecosta	56	0	5	1	50	496	134	345	17	4
Menominee	4	0	1	0	3	57	27	29	1	0
Midland	60	0	22	1	37	424	77	323	24	4
Missaukee	0	0	0	0	0	22	8	14	0	0
Montcalm	56	1	28	2	25	506	153	325	28	7
Montmorency	11	0	1	0	10	57	24	25	8	0

[1] The FBI does not publish arson data unless it receives data from either the agency or the state for all 12 months of the calendar year.

[2] Because of changes in the state/local agency's reporting practices, figures are not comparable to previous years' data.

Table 10. Offenses Known to Law Enforcement, by State Metropolitan and Nonmetropolitan Counties, 2008—*Continued*

(Number.)

State/County	Violent crime	Murder and non-negligent man-slaughter	Forcible rape	Robbery	Aggravated assault	Property crime	Burglary	Larceny-theft	Motor vehicle theft	Arson[1]
Oceana	26	1	11	0	14	331	110	210	11	1
Ogemaw	13	0	2	0	11	215	91	117	7	3
Ontonagon	2	0	0	0	2	18	6	12	0	0
Osceola	31	0	6	0	25	235	80	151	4	1
Otsego	9	0	0	0	9	80	24	53	3	0
Roscommon	17	0	4	1	12	205	47	129	29	0
Sanilac	22	2	4	1	15	194	62	121	11	1
Schoolcraft	0	0	0	0	0	1	0	1	0	0
St. Joseph	39	0	9	0	30	317	109	196	12	2
Tuscola	24	0	6	0	18	368	144	192	32	4
Wexford	26	1	5	0	20	392	69	309	14	3
MINNESOTA-Metropolitan Counties[6]										
Anoka		2		4	54	1,870	381	1,393	96	14
Benton		0		1	9	308	54	219	35	7
Blue Earth		0		0	3	181	52	114	15	5
Carlton		0		0	8	335	75	244	16	0
Carver		0		3	18	994	118	837	39	5
Chisago		0		1	13	517	100	386	31	1
Clay[5]		0		1	3			43	7	0
Dakota		0		1	19	211	55	136	20	4
Dodge[5]		1		0		250	44	197	9	3
Hennepin		0		2	16	136	17	110	9	4
Houston		0		0	5	113	33	74	6	0
Isanti		0		1	10	438	120	282	36	3
Nicollet		0		0	5	90	25	59	6	1
Olmsted		0		2	19	408	112	257	39	7
Polk		1		0	28	223	55	158	10	2
Scott		0		0	9	166	37	112	17	1
Sherburne		1		2	27	627	116	478	33	1
Stearns		1		1	30	466	82	363	21	2
St. Louis		0		5	39	788	242	449	97	6
Washington		0		10	21	1,151	253	853	45	6
Wright		0		6	50	2,021	212	1,716	93	6
MINNESOTA-Nonmetropolitan Counties[6]										
Aitkin		2		1	16	412	138	246	28	2
Becker		0		1	20	181	85	74	22	1
Beltrami		0		2	38	413	89	269	55	6
Brown		0		0	0	3	1	0	2	2
Cass		0		1	21	446	128	253	65	2
Chippewa		0		1	8	69	2	63	4	0
Clearwater		0		0	19	118	29	84	5	4
Cook		0		1	9	122	24	87	11	1
Cottonwood		0		0	2	47	22	22	3	0
Crow Wing		0		0	31	387	93	259	35	2
Douglas		0		0	4	342	75	250	17	6
Faribault		0		0	0	69	38	28	3	2
Fillmore		0		0	3	111	34	68	9	2
Freeborn		0		2	6	117	14	90	13	0
Goodhue		0		2	8	207	60	126	21	2
Grant		0		0	8	110	32	70	8	0
Hubbard		1		0	3	310	120	169	21	1
Itasca		0		0	17	375	101	253	21	3
Jackson		0		0	0	38	7	28	3	0
Kanabec		0		2	17	257	94	144	19	7
Kandiyohi		0		3	13	320	47	261	12	1
Kittson		0		0	0	78	15	62	1	0
Koochiching		0		0	8	141	42	89	10	1
Lac Qui Parle		0		0	3	50	7	42	1	1
Lake		1		0	4	86	40	46	0	0
Lake of the Woods		0		0	5	51	14	33	4	0
Le Sueur[5]		0		0	10			109	6	2
Lincoln		0		0	1	5	0	5	0	0
Lyon		0		0	4	55	22	29	4	2
Marshall		0		0	5	108	8	98	2	0
Martin		0		0	5	57	17	38	2	1
McLeod		1		0	10	107	40	61	6	0
Meeker		0		0	9	205	48	145	12	0
Mille Lacs		0		0	24	373	90	252	31	2
Morrison		1		0	10	360	73	269	18	1
Mower		0		1	11	202	58	117	27	1
Murray		0		0	0	63	25	33	5	2

[1] The FBI does not publish arson data unless it receives data from either the agency or the state for all 12 months of the calendar year.
[5] The FBI determined that the agency's data were overreported. Consequently, those data are not included in this table.
[6] The data collection methodology for the offense of forcible rape used by the Minnesota state UCR Program does not comply with national UCR Program guidelines. Consequently, its figures for forcible rape and violent crime (of which forcible rape is a part) are not published in this table.

Table 10. Offenses Known to Law Enforcement, by State Metropolitan and Nonmetropolitan Counties, 2008—*Continued*

(Number.)

State/County	Violent crime	Murder and non-negligent man-slaughter	Forcible rape	Robbery	Aggravated assault	Property crime	Burglary	Larceny-theft	Motor vehicle theft	Arson[1]
Nobles		0		0	3	40	22	17	1	0
Norman		0		0	3	43	14	26	3	0
Otter Tail		0		1	7	489	154	305	30	3
Pennington		0		0	1	52	13	34	5	0
Pine		0		3	27	851	300	486	65	9
Pipestone		0		0	4	77	17	58	2	0
Pope		0		0	2	58	21	32	5	0
Red Lake		0		0	0	11	2	7	2	0
Redwood		0		0	5	108	33	70	5	3
Renville		0		1	4	94	24	65	5	2
Roseau		0		0	4	96	18	74	4	1
Steele		1		0	4	115	32	74	9	2
Stevens		0		0	3	21	9	11	1	0
Swift		0		0	3	47	21	22	4	0
Todd		0		0	9	227	77	141	9	0
Traverse		0		0	4	23	6	16	1	0
Wadena		0		2	9	74	32	40	2	1
Waseca		0		0	2	89	35	43	11	4
Watonwan		0		0	4	67	20	44	3	0
Wilkin		0		0	0	37	10	25	2	0
Winona		0		0	3	100	28	62	10	5
MISSISSIPPI-Metropolitan Counties										
DeSoto	30	1	4	8	17	736	91	541	104	3
Forrest	10	0	1	1	8	71	39	27	5	0
Harrison	44	7	10	19	8	1,700	396	1,128	176	7
Jackson	122	2	26	12	82	1,819	478	1,121	220	0
Lamar	68	2	20	15	31	690	229	412	49	4
Madison	40	4	7	6	23	410	119	250	41	2
Marshall	75	0	2	13	60	603	230	315	58	
Rankin	40	0	3	5	32	784	216	538	30	4
Tate	11	0	1	1	9	295	109	136	50	0
MISSISSIPPI-Nonmetropolitan Counties										
Adams	51	1	3	3	44	575	149	378	48	6
Bolivar	2	1	0	1	0	1	0	1	0	1
Choctaw	11	0	3	0	8	86	34	45	7	0
Claiborne[5]		1	2	11		116	55	57	4	0
Coahoma	10	1	0	2	7	128	62	53	13	3
Greene	9	2	1	2	4	24	15	8	1	1
Grenada	15	0	2	2	11	164	74	73	17	0
Jefferson	38	0	1	1	36	50	17	33	0	2
Lauderdale	38	1	11	12	14	524	236	252	36	3
Leake	0	0	0	0	0	24	14	10	0	1
Lee	64	0	5	7	52	670	265	372	33	8
Leflore	104	1	6	7	90	505	234	261	10	2
Lincoln	16	1	0	0	15	340	88	225	27	0
Lowndes	75	3	20	10	42	476	151	296	29	7
Oktibbeha	61	3	2	5	51	184	82	92	10	2
Panola	46	1	1	2	42	498	243	231	24	0
Pearl River	37	0	15	8	14	705	283	365	57	5
Pike	23	2	1	3	17	469	189	246	34	
Sunflower	160	2	16	75	67	101	82	12	7	0
Union	4	1	0	1	2	199	87	96	16	10
Warren	21	2	5	4	10	305	104	171	30	1
Washington	13	0	3	4	6	425	169	224	32	9
Winston	8	0	0	2	6	13	8	3	2	0
MISSOURI-Metropolitan Counties										
Andrew	17	0	0	1	16	107	33	69	5	0
Bates	34	1	5	0	28	155	62	84	9	0
Bollinger	9	1	1	1	6	83	30	51	2	1
Boone	111	1	5	11	94	794	236	508	50	11
Buchanan	20	0	1	2	17	226	75	137	14	2
Caldwell	9	0	1	0	8	70	20	38	12	2
Callaway	25	2	4	2	17	807	199	566	42	3
Cape Girardeau	117	0	1	4	112	281	116	151	14	0
Cass	71	0	6	3	62	347	128	188	31	1
Christian	108	0	2	0	106	293	98	173	22	1
Clay	21	0	2	2	17	216	98	99	19	6
Clinton	13	0	3	0	10	93	24	53	16	1
Cole	46	0	3	3	40	496	152	327	17	3
Dallas[4]		0	0	1		146	47	90	9	1
De Kalb	11	0	4	1	6	92	34	50	8	2

[1] The FBI does not publish arson data unless it receives data from either the agency or the state for all 12 months of the calendar year.

[4] The FBI determined that the agency did not follow national Uniform Crime Reporting (UCR) Program guidelines for reporting an offense. Consequently, this figure is not included in this table.

[5] The FBI determined that the agency's data were overreported. Consequently, those data are not included in this table.

Table 10. Offenses Known to Law Enforcement, by State Metropolitan and Nonmetropolitan Counties, 2008—*Continued*

(Number.)

State/County	Violent crime	Murder and non-negligent man-slaughter	Forcible rape	Robbery	Aggravated assault	Property crime	Burglary	Larceny-theft	Motor vehicle theft	Arson[1]
Franklin	63	2	8	3	50	845	174	623	48	2
Greene	87	0	16	21	50	1,440	337	954	149	16
Howard	3	1	0	0	2	54	14	40	0	0
Jackson	60	3	4	14	39	602	186	341	75	2
Jasper	103	2	12	4	85	618	204	368	46	8
Jefferson	434	1	49	25	359	3,507	431	2,884	192	35
Lafayette	19	1	0	0	18	158	54	93	11	0
Lincoln	57	0	0	0	57	286	100	147	39	5
McDonald	76	1	7	1	67	389	91	256	42	7
Moniteau	9	0	2	0	7	67	28	29	10	0
Newton	86	2	9	1	74	789	207	496	86	13
Osage	7	0	1	2	4	153	46	97	10	1
Platte	41	0	2	2	37	337	81	248	8	3
Polk	31	0	4	0	27	318	145	155	18	0
Ray[2]	19	0	0	0	19	98	42	49	7	0
St. Charles	203	1	6	17	179	1,293	301	920	72	13
St. Louis County Police Department	1,165	15	83	328	739	11,407	2,530	7,767	1,110	75
Warren	110	0	2	3	105	232	72	138	22	5
Washington	34	2	0	0	32	189	48	105	36	0
Webster	45	0	0	0	45	240	77	144	19	2
MISSOURI-Nonmetropolitan Counties										
Adair	14	0	2	0	12	12	8	2	2	0
Atchison	0	0	0	0	0	26	7	17	2	0
Audrain	12	0	0	2	10	160	58	96	6	0
Barry	83	0	4	0	79	361	107	245	9	0
Barton	13	0	3	1	9	83	25	58	0	4
Benton	53	0	4	1	48	190	56	129	5	0
Butler	53	0	0	2	51	545	149	355	41	0
Camden	39	0	0	0	39	459	123	301	35	2
Carroll	6	0	2	1	3	43	7	25	11	0
Carter	0	0	0	0	0	33	11	16	6	0
Cedar	3	0	0	0	3	82	24	57	1	0
Clark	9	0	1	1	7	50	25	20	5	0
Cooper	8	0	1	0	7	184	69	100	15	1
Crawford	5	0	0	0	5	127	43	74	10	0
Dade	3	0	0	0	3	58	12	33	13	0
Daviess	2	0	0	0	2	66	33	27	6	0
Dent	9	1	0	0	8	110	44	61	5	1
Douglas[4]		2	0	0		97	40	39	18	2
Dunklin	24	0	1	1	22	245	58	173	14	1
Gasconade	5	0	0	0	5	141	49	81	11	0
Gentry	3	0	1	1	1	48	21	25	2	2
Grundy	4	0	1	0	3	42	18	20	4	0
Harrison	4	0	0	0	4	53	23	29	1	0
Henry	40	0	6	0	34	277	95	155	27	1
Hickory	3	1	0	0	2	121	43	65	13	0
Holt	9	0	0	1	8	64	28	32	4	0
Howell	57	2	4	0	51	394	130	235	29	3
Iron	20	0	0	0	20	73	20	39	14	0
Johnson	34	0	0	0	34	307	100	180	27	0
Knox	4	0	0	0	4	105	18	87	0	0
Laclede	33	1	5	0	27	305	88	177	40	5
Lawrence	48	0	1	2	45	307	107	175	25	3
Lewis	6	0	0	1	5	56	15	39	2	0
Linn	17	0	0	0	17	65	34	24	7	2
Livingston	1	0	0	0	1	61	28	31	2	0
Macon[4]		0	0	0		55	25	27	3	0
Madison	12	0	1	0	11	61	22	31	8	0
Maries	8	0	0	1	7	65	31	29	5	0
Marion	4	0	0	0	4	70	14	53	3	1
Mercer	3	0	0	0	3	28	18	7	3	1
Miller	62	2	4	0	56	223	67	130	26	0
Mississippi	19	1	0	0	18	57	17	38	2	0
Monroe	15	0	1	1	13	80	38	38	4	0
Montgomery	13	1	0	0	12	99	54	38	7	0
Morgan	73	0	1	1	71	267	117	135	15	0
New Madrid	38	3	0	1	34	56	17	33	6	1
Nodaway	12	1	0	0	11	146	55	78	13	0
Oregon	22	1	0	1	20	35	4	29	2	1
Ozark[4]		4	2	1		152	78	67	7	0
Pemiscot	12	2	3	2	5	109	33	69	7	0

[1] The FBI does not publish arson data unless it receives data from either the agency or the state for all 12 months of the calendar year.
[2] Because of changes in the state/local agency's reporting practices, figures are not comparable to previous years' data.
[4] The FBI determined that the agency did not follow national Uniform Crime Reporting (UCR) Program guidelines for reporting an offense. Consequently, this figure is not included in this table.

Table 10. Offenses Known to Law Enforcement, by State Metropolitan and Nonmetropolitan Counties, 2008—*Continued*

(Number.)

State/County	Violent crime	Murder and non-negligent man-slaughter	Forcible rape	Robbery	Aggravated assault	Property crime	Burglary	Larceny-theft	Motor vehicle theft	Arson[1]
Perry	9	0	0	0	9	88	20	61	7	1
Pettis	37	0	0	0	37	249	63	171	15	1
Phelps	52	0	3	1	48	323	85	219	19	2
Pike	12	0	0	0	12	101	39	44	18	4
Pulaski	103	2	15	4	82	298	119	160	19	1
Putnam	1	0	0	0	1	12	9	3	0	0
Ralls	23	0	3	0	20	116	45	63	8	3
Randolph[2]	7	0	0	0	7	82	32	44	6	0
Reynolds	6	0	1	0	5	18	12	1	5	0
Ripley	23	1	1	2	19	207	62	135	10	2
Saline	14	0	4	0	10	125	44	66	15	0
Schuyler	5	0	2	0	3	9	1	5	3	1
Scotland	1	1	0	0	0	26	9	15	2	1
Scott	24	0	1	2	21	145	35	102	8	1
Shannon	11	0	1	0	10	40	14	23	3	0
Shelby	0	0	0	0	0	66	32	32	2	0
St. Clair	6	2	0	1	3	138	50	86	2	0
Ste. Genevieve	22	1	0	0	21	163	50	96	17	4
St. Francois	76	0	4	2	70	607	191	361	55	5
Stoddard	23	0	1	2	20	143	76	66	1	0
Stone	104	1	2	3	98	604	189	347	68	2
Sullivan	11	0	2	0	9	71	27	31	13	1
Taney	98	0	8	1	89	584	147	390	47	0
Texas	20	0	3	0	17	188	50	123	15	4
Vernon	34	0	3	1	30	238	58	153	27	4
Wayne	27	0	0	0	27	94	35	49	10	0
Worth	6	0	0	0	6	22	8	13	1	0
Wright	24	1	0	1	22	95	34	54	7	0
MONTANA-Metropolitan Counties										
Cascade	48	1	3	1	43	327	48	254	25	2
Missoula	114	1	14	2	97	659	136	470	53	9
Yellowstone	60	0	10	0	50	596	120	424	52	3
MONTANA-Nonmetropolitan Counties										
Beaverhead	14	0	0	0	14	49	10	36	3	0
Big Horn	58	0	1	1	56	166	8	138	20	1
Blaine	4	0	1	0	3	27	7	18	2	0
Broadwater	10	1	4	0	5	91	2	87	2	1
Carter	0	0	0	0	0	2	1	1	0	0
Chouteau	1	0	0	0	1	20	2	14	4	2
Dawson	6	0	4	0	2	83	6	73	4	0
Deer Lodge	27	0	1	0	26	135	18	97	20	1
Fallon	0	0	0	0	0	7	0	7	0	0
Fergus	7	0	0	0	7	30	8	19	3	0
Flathead	197	3	18	7	169	1,201	211	896	94	6
Gallatin	49	0	19	1	29	423	71	309	43	5
Garfield	0	0	0	0	0	0	0	0	0	0
Glacier	9	0	1	0	8	40	3	32	5	0
Granite	0	0	0	0	0	33	4	27	2	0
Hill	32	1	4	2	25	145	9	125	11	2
Jefferson	15	0	3	0	12	48	12	31	5	1
Judith Basin	3	0	0	0	3	13	4	9	0	0
Lake	53	1	7	0	45	291	66	188	37	6
Lewis and Clark	36	0	3	0	33	270	65	178	27	4
Lincoln	25	1	5	0	19	239	51	169	19	1
Madison	13	1	1	0	11	83	23	55	5	2
McCone	1	0	0	0	1	18	2	9	7	0
Meagher	4	0	1	0	3	14	1	13	0	0
Mineral	13	0	0	1	12	11	4	5	2	0
Musselshell	9	0	0	0	9	58	2	56	0	1
Park	29	1	4	0	24	74	25	42	7	2
Phillips	5	0	0	0	5	56	18	34	4	0
Pondera	1	0	1	0	0	11	1	9	1	0
Powell	25	0	0	1	24	123	20	100	3	1
Ravalli	41	0	6	0	35	345	68	265	12	3
Roosevelt	18	0	0	0	18	29	7	19	3	0
Rosebud	14	0	1	1	12	67	7	54	6	0
Sanders	27	2	4	1	20	122	10	101	11	1
Sheridan	8	0	1	0	7	74	16	53	5	0
Silver Bow	148	0	8	4	136	1,473	196	1,139	138	5
Stillwater	8	0	0	0	8	42	16	22	4	0
Sweet Grass	12	0	1	0	11	22	3	16	3	0

[1] The FBI does not publish arson data unless it receives data from either the agency or the state for all 12 months of the calendar year.

[2] Because of changes in the state/local agency's reporting practices, figures are not comparable to previous years' data.

Table 10. Offenses Known to Law Enforcement, by State Metropolitan and Nonmetropolitan Counties, 2008—*Continued*

(Number.)

State/County	Violent crime	Murder and non-negligent man-slaughter	Forcible rape	Robbery	Aggravated assault	Property crime	Burglary	Larceny-theft	Motor vehicle theft	Arson[1]
Teton	2	0	0	0	2	56	10	45	1	0
Toole	15	0	2	0	13	86	10	72	4	2
Valley	3	0	0	0	3	26	4	19	3	0
Wibaux	0	0	0	0	0	3	0	3	0	0
NEBRASKA-Metropolitan Counties										
Cass	10	0	1	1	8	245	72	162	11	2
Dakota	8	0	0	1	7	27	9	14	4	0
Dixon	4	0	2	0	2	76	25	44	7	0
Douglas	165	0	5	9	151	1,151	273	795	83	0
Lancaster	22	2	3	1	16	347	82	255	10	3
Sarpy	21	0	12	1	8	767	124	593	50	3
Saunders	6	0	0	0	6	75	29	45	1	0
Washington	1	0	0	1	0	119	22	86	11	2
NEBRASKA-Nonmetropolitan Counties										
Adams	3	0	1	2	0	149	44	101	4	2
Antelope	1	0	0	0	1	24	8	15	1	0
Arthur	0	0	0	0	0	0	0	0	0	0
Box Butte	1	0	0	0	1	7	2	4	1	0
Boyd	1	0	0	0	1	13	6	7	0	0
Brown	1	0	0	0	1	51	9	40	2	0
Buffalo	12	0	5	0	7	126	25	89	12	1
Burt	7	0	1	0	6	37	15	22	0	0
Butler	9	0	1	4	4	22	4	18	0	0
Cedar	0	0	0	0	0	1	0	1	0	0
Chase	1	0	0	0	1	14	4	9	1	0
Cherry	3	0	0	0	3	8	3	4	1	0
Colfax	9	0	0	0	9	45	5	37	3	0
Cuming	0	0	0	0	0	10	1	9	0	0
Custer	3	0	1	0	2	51	8	37	6	0
Dawes	1	0	0	0	1	11	4	7	0	0
Dawson	10	1	3	0	6	83	17	54	12	0
Deuel	0	0	0	0	0	31	6	21	4	1
Dodge	9	0	0	2	7	175	44	120	11	0
Franklin	0	0	0	0	0	19	1	15	3	0
Frontier	0	0	0	0	0	27	5	20	2	0
Furnas	2	0	0	0	2	33	5	22	6	0
Gosper	0	0	0	0	0	13	1	12	0	0
Hall	12	0	1	2	9	225	57	152	16	2
Hamilton	2	0	1	1	0	50	8	40	2	0
Harlan	2	0	2	0	0	4	1	0	3	0
Hitchcock	1	0	0	0	1	4	4	0	0	0
Hooker	0	0	0	0	0	0	0	0	0	0
Jefferson	0	0	0	0	0	87	21	61	5	0
Kearney	3	0	1	0	2	59	7	49	3	0
Keith	0	0	0	0	0	56	12	42	2	0
Keya Paha	1	0	0	0	1	9	3	6	0	0
Knox	0	0	0	0	0	37	15	22	0	0
Lincoln	18	1	2	1	14	191	30	159	2	0
Madison	7	0	2	1	4	74	15	52	7	3
Merrick	8	0	0	0	8	54	14	36	4	0
Morrill	2	0	0	0	2	29	4	22	3	0
Nance	4	0	0	0	4	11	1	10	0	0
Otoe	3	1	0	1	1	64	11	47	6	1
Pawnee	2	0	0	0	2	57	10	38	9	0
Perkins	2	0	1	0	1	36	16	16	4	0
Phelps	0	0	0	0	0	33	2	26	5	1
Platte	4	0	0	0	4	161	51	103	7	1
Polk	0	0	0	0	0	60	7	52	1	0
Red Willow	0	0	0	0	0	35	7	25	3	0
Richardson	3	0	0	0	3	98	28	64	6	0
Rock	0	0	0	0	0	9	3	6	0	0
Saline	3	0	1	0	2	66	31	29	6	1
Scotts Bluff	9	1	4	0	4	104	21	74	9	0
Sheridan	3	0	0	0	3	50	13	35	2	0
Sherman	2	0	0	0	2	12	3	8	1	0
Sioux	0	0	0	0	0	0	0	0	0	0
Stanton	3	0	0	0	3	42	9	31	2	0
Thayer	2	0	0	0	2	96	21	69	6	1
Wayne	2	0	0	0	2	14	3	10	1	0
Webster	2	0	0	0	2	34	9	21	4	0
Wheeler	1	0	0	0	1	5	1	4	0	0
York	2	0	1	0	1	54	7	41	6	0

[1] The FBI does not publish arson data unless it receives data from either the agency or the state for all 12 months of the calendar year.

Table 10. Offenses Known to Law Enforcement, by State Metropolitan and Nonmetropolitan Counties, 2008—*Continued*

(Number.)

State/County	Violent crime	Murder and non-negligent man-slaughter	Forcible rape	Robbery	Aggravated assault	Property crime	Burglary	Larceny-theft	Motor vehicle theft	Arson[1]
NEVADA-Metropolitan Counties										
Carson City	231	0	0	24	207	1,265	291	874	100	8
Storey	12	0	0	2	10	64	23	37	4	0
Washoe	239	0	1	14	224	1,516	530	824	162	8
NEVADA-Nonmetropolitan Counties										
Churchill	20	1	3	1	15	205	68	119	18	1
Douglas	62	1	7	5	49	747	193	509	45	7
Elko	24	0	9	1	14	188	91	80	17	4
Esmeralda	3	0	0	0	3	10	5	3	2	1
Eureka	6	0	1	0	5	17	6	9	2	0
Humboldt	59	0	0	1	58	48	27	18	3	4
Lander	49	0	10	2	37	118	28	78	12	0
Lincoln	6	1	0	1	4	34	7	22	5	2
Lyon	83	0	1	5	77	781	253	455	73	4
Mineral	15	0	0	0	15	24	14	7	3	0
Nye	124	4	23	20	77	892	275	507	110	14
Pershing	33	0	4	2	27	51	25	23	3	0
White Pine	20	2	1	3	14	111	45	55	11	0
NEW HAMPSHIRE-Metropolitan Counties										
Rockingham	44	0	0	0	44	1	0	1	0	0
NEW HAMPSHIRE-Nonmetropolitan Counties										
Carroll	3	0	1	0	2	33	11	17	5	1
Cheshire	2	0	0	0	2	8	0	8	0	0
Merrimack	6	0	1	0	5	4	0	4	0	1
NEW MEXICO-Metropolitan Counties										
Bernalillo	942	10	54	137	741	2,733	940	1,369	424	60
Dona Ana	304	5	26	8	265	1,348	431	757	160	21
Sandoval	36	0	2	1	33	183	120	62	1	0
San Juan	258	4	35	6	213	920	266	559	95	3
Santa Fe	179	3	27	13	136	778	551	210	17	11
Valencia	108	5	13	12	78	991	458	306	227	27
NEW MEXICO-Nonmetropolitan Counties										
Catron	2	0	0	0	2	19	9	10	0	0
Chaves	56	2	11	3	40	417	227	149	41	1
Cibola	14	0	0	0	14	85	48	29	8	0
Colfax	4	0	0	0	4	12	6	6	0	0
Curry[7]	17	0	0	2	15		56		16	2
Eddy	67	0	19	5	43	445	165	259	21	0
Grant	13	2	0	0	11	70	38	32	0	0
Lincoln	52	0	0	0	52	131	57	71	3	0
Luna	77	2	2	1	72	328	153	133	42	0
Otero[5]		1	8	3		243	124	106	13	0
Quay	4	0	0	0	4	16	10	5	1	0
Roosevelt	7	0	2	0	5	67	30	31	6	0
Socorro	21	0	0	2	19	79	41	33	5	1
NEW YORK-Metropolitan Counties										
Albany	33	0	4	3	26	103	28	74	1	0
Broome	56	1	9	7	39	1,001	197	780	24	3
Chemung	15	1	3	1	10	339	77	251	11	3
Dutchess	60	0	2	4	54	815	195	584	36	2
Erie	128	1	15	10	102	966	197	735	34	5
Herkimer	0	0	0	0	0	5	0	5	0	0
Livingston	34	0	6	1	27	482	90	385	7	3
Madison	12	0	3	0	9	274	79	191	4	3
Monroe	195	3	16	51	125	3,779	588	3,054	137	8
Nassau	1,602	14	58	748	782	14,847	1,929	11,900	1,018	
Niagara	78	2	9	8	59	1,387	378	960	49	6
Oneida	26	1	4	2	19	421	133	276	12	5
Onondaga	188	1	27	40	120	1,873	360	1,427	86	10
Ontario	44	0	10	6	28	970	187	760	23	1
Orange	11	0	1	1	9	47	23	22	2	1
Orleans	17	1	2	2	12	292	88	182	22	2
Oswego	36	1	8	6	21	385	123	232	30	0
Putnam	33	1	2	8	22	345	84	251	10	4
Rockland	9	0	1	1	7	44	2	41	1	0
Saratoga	49	0	8	6	35	1,281	238	1,009	34	7
Schenectady	3	0	0	1	2	47	2	44	1	0
Schoharie	2	0	0	0	2	105	34	70	1	2
Suffolk	122	0	0	2	120	4	0	4	0	0
Suffolk County Police Department	2,166	39	91	890	1,146	26,235	3,805	20,490	1,940	265
Tioga	15	0	4	1	10	253	60	183	10	4
Tompkins	28	1	6	2	19	407	83	307	17	0

[1] The FBI does not publish arson data unless it receives data from either the agency or the state for all 12 months of the calendar year.
[5] The FBI determined that the agency's data were overreported. Consequently, those data are not included in this table.
[7] The FBI determined that the agency's data were underreported. Consequently, those data are not included in this table.

Table 10. Offenses Known to Law Enforcement, by State Metropolitan and Nonmetropolitan Counties, 2008—*Continued*

(Number.)

State/County	Violent crime	Murder and non-negligent man-slaughter	Forcible rape	Robbery	Aggravated assault	Property crime	Burglary	Larceny-theft	Motor vehicle theft	Arson[1]
Warren	51	0	7	8	36	738	89	640	9	4
Washington	31	2	9	2	18	355	78	270	7	1
Wayne	50	0	7	7	36	618	149	443	26	8
Westchester Public Safety	41	0	1	1	39	136	9	125	2	0
NEW YORK-Nonmetropolitan Counties										
Allegany	0	0	0	0	0	1	0	1	0	0
Cattaraugus	44	2	3	2	37	552	173	348	31	2
Cayuga	25	0	2	1	22	354	74	274	6	0
Chautauqua	30	2	10	2	16	823	251	550	22	7
Chenango	4	1	0	1	2	322	61	251	10	1
Clinton	4	0	0	0	4	9	1	8	0	0
Columbia	25	1	2	0	22	320	83	230	7	0
Cortland	12	1	8	1	2	300	47	239	14	0
Delaware	11	0	3	1	7	110	53	53	4	0
Essex	0	0	0	0	0	0	0	0	0	0
Franklin	0	0	0	0	0	0	0	0	0	0
Fulton	13	0	0	2	11	324	87	224	13	0
Genesee	48	1	10	2	35	663	135	501	27	0
Greene	11	0	0	0	11	78	43	27	8	0
Lewis	12	0	1	0	11	188	89	89	10	2
Montgomery	25	0	0	4	21	404	65	327	12	1
Otsego	12	0	2	0	10	216	87	123	6	1
Schuyler	8	0	1	0	7	87	26	60	1	0
Seneca	13	0	3	1	9	203	38	151	14	2
Steuben	6	0	2	0	4	69	9	60	0	0
St. Lawrence	13	0	1	1	11	52	16	34	2	0
Sullivan	28	1	1	4	22	477	134	325	18	10
Wyoming	13	0	0	0	13	217	55	154	8	0
Yates	6	0	0	2	4	152	55	96	1	0
NORTH CAROLINA-Metropolitan Counties										
Alamance	161	1	5	16	139	1,275	493	712	70	5
Alexander	78	3	9	10	56	758	298	418	42	7
Anson	83	4	4	15	60	608	247	300	61	1
Brunswick	162	2	21	27	112	2,147	961	1,036	150	32
Buncombe	194	5	24	50	115	2,462	877	1,356	229	7
Burke	100	3	7	18	72	1,295	545	649	101	3
Cabarrus	73	4	11	16	42	1,160	519	583	58	7
Caldwell	63	3	2	12	46	1,472	519	856	97	17
Cumberland	740	13	34	182	511	4,852	1,335	3,164	353	41
Currituck	44	1	4	2	37	514	170	325	19	2
Davie	43	1	4	7	31	671	259	380	32	2
Durham	60	1	1	19	39	922	309	542	71	2
Edgecombe	71	4	8	13	46	586	292	229	65	7
Franklin[5]		1	5	14		868	382	387	99	6
Gaston	16	0	0	0	16	4	0	3	1	0
Guilford	216	2	22	41	151	2,154	870	1,117	167	33
Haywood	98	0	6	4	88	958	390	517	51	5
Henderson	71	0	12	17	42	1,582	626	816	140	1
Hoke	26	2	1	16	7	789	558	193	38	1
Johnston	187	3	25	35	124	2,691	1,001	1,436	254	11
Madison	4	0	2	0	2	217	91	113	13	1
Nash	79	2	7	25	45	842	374	319	149	17
New Hanover	184	1	25	50	108	2,635	676	1,823	136	11
Onslow	289	6	31	49	203	3,148	1,127	1,812	209	22
Orange	50	5	5	29	11	822	427	345	50	3
Person	67	2	5	6	54	626	231	351	44	1
Pitt	255	1	10	36	208	1,835	736	984	115	6
Randolph	124	1	3	22	98	2,208	647	1,411	150	8
Rockingham	72	1	3	18	50	1,517	532	864	121	1
Stokes	101	1	4	7	89	973	336	557	80	4
Union	311	5	17	22	267	2,104	894	1,087	123	11
Wake	165	3	15	34	113	1,903	677	1,010	216	13
Wayne	171	4	1	32	134	2,101	819	1,066	216	2
Yadkin	103	0	13	5	85	621	235	325	61	7
NORTH CAROLINA-Nonmetropolitan Counties										
Alleghany	1	0	0	1	0	28	2	26	0	0
Ashe	23	0	4	2	17	413	206	180	27	
Avery	20	0	4	0	16	195	64	120	11	1
Beaufort	130	1	8	13	108	778	325	391	62	14
Bertie	26	1	5	6	14	289	132	131	26	2
Bladen	139	2	1	19	117	1,074	381	637	56	11
Camden	9	0	2	1	6	98	30	65	3	1
Cherokee	39	0	2	1	36	549	171	366	12	3

[1] The FBI does not publish arson data unless it receives data from either the agency or the state for all 12 months of the calendar year.
[5] The FBI determined that the agency's data were overreported. Consequently, those data are not included in this table.

Table 10. Offenses Known to Law Enforcement, by State Metropolitan and Nonmetropolitan Counties, 2008—*Continued*

(Number.)

State/County	Violent crime	Murder and non-negligent man-slaughter	Forcible rape	Robbery	Aggravated assault	Property crime	Burglary	Larceny-theft	Motor vehicle theft	Arson[1]
Chowan	24	0	1	2	21	170	75	91	4	3
Clay	11	0	0	0	11	153	35	106	12	1
Cleveland	52	0	27	21	4	1,537	665	691	181	2
Columbus	161	3	3	36	119	1,705	767	758	180	5
Dare	41	0	6	2	33	706	179	491	36	4
Gates	9	0	3	1	5	227	62	145	20	2
Granville	60	0	7	12	41	891	336	482	73	8
Halifax	161	3	8	30	120	1,103	563	432	108	16
Hertford	30	3	2	9	16	398	166	192	40	2
Iredell	225	3	25	20	177	1,914	705	1,058	151	10
Lee	41	3	3	9	26	734	287	364	83	12
Lenoir	170	0	2	14	154	1,051	359	638	54	13
Lincoln	98	1	14	10	73	1,819	681	1,060	78	8
Martin[5]		1	3	6		448	202	195	51	9
McDowell	54	5	2	12	35	661	266	345	50	5
Montgomery	64	2	3	6	53	482	172	266	44	1
Moore	56	2	12	5	37	866	395	385	86	12
Pasquotank	76	1	8	14	53	344	143	187	14	3
Perquimans	4	0	2	0	2	146	73	69	4	1
Richmond	150	5	2	31	112	1,160	478	606	76	13
Robeson	628	17	18	139	454	4,085	2,137	1,524	424	34
Rowan	199	3	16	26	154	1,468	493	882	93	13
Rutherford	157	0	11	23	123	1,373	480	783	110	20
Sampson	144	6	14	35	89	1,434	739	554	141	9
Scotland	55	6	2	12	35	754	445	259	50	19
Stanly	36	2	7	6	21	549	243	281	25	4
Transylvania	36	0	2	1	33	385	169	186	30	5
Tyrrell	7	0	2	1	4	64	3	58	3	1
Vance	83	5	1	17	60	1,398	721	594	83	8
Warren	39	1	6	10	22	553	240	270	43	5
Watauga	22	1	0	3	18	497	185	288	24	1
Wilkes	174	2	3	18	151	1,332	555	689	88	4
Wilson	98	1	1	15	81	777	245	457	75	9
Yancey	14	0	0	1	13	144	71	65	8	1
NORTH DAKOTA-Metropolitan Counties										
Burleigh	22	0	9	0	13	157	46	101	10	1
Cass	4	0	1	0	3	185	57	112	16	2
Grand Forks	6	0	0	0	6	69	18	39	12	0
Morton	11	0	6	0	5	78	14	59	5	0
NORTH DAKOTA-Nonmetropolitan Counties										
Barnes	1	0	0	0	1	28	8	17	3	0
Bottineau	0	0	0	0	0	21	9	11	1	0
Burke	0	0	0	0	0	21	10	10	1	0
Cavalier	2	0	0	0	2	37	3	30	4	0
Dickey	0	0	0	0	0	16	2	13	1	0
Eddy	1	0	0	0	1	9	4	5	0	0
Emmons	1	0	0	0	1	29	14	14	1	0
Griggs	0	0	0	0	0	0	0	0	0	0
Hettinger	0	0	0	0	0	9	1	6	2	0
Kidder	0	0	0	0	0	2	1	1	0	0
Lamoure	2	0	0	0	2	4	1	2	1	0
Logan	0	0	0	0	0	4	0	4	0	0
McHenry	0	0	0	0	0	24	5	16	3	0
McIntosh	1	0	0	0	1	5	0	5	0	0
McKenzie	0	0	0	0	0	31	4	24	3	0
McLean	14	0	4	0	10	125	39	80	6	0
Mercer	2	0	0	0	2	19	7	8	4	0
Mountrail	3	0	0	0	3	56	10	41	5	0
Nelson	2	0	0	0	2	21	4	10	7	0
Oliver	0	0	0	0	0	4	0	4	0	0
Pembina	3	0	0	0	3	27	6	15	6	0
Pierce	0	0	0	0	0	1	1	0	0	0
Ramsey	1	0	0	0	1	32	5	20	7	0
Renville	0	0	0	0	0	6	1	5	0	0
Richland	14	0	1	1	12	84	25	54	5	0
Sargent	1	0	0	0	1	25	0	25	0	0
Sheridan	0	0	0	0	0	9	2	6	1	0
Stark	6	0	1	0	5	78	4	54	20	1
Stutsman	3	0	3	0	0	52	13	35	4	2
Towner	0	0	0	0	0	24	11	13	0	0
Traill	0	0	0	0	0	29	7	13	9	2
Walsh	5	0	3	0	2	110	44	51	15	1

[1] The FBI does not publish arson data unless it receives data from either the agency or the state for all 12 months of the calendar year.

[5] The FBI determined that the agency's data were overreported. Consequently, those data are not included in this table.

Table 10. Offenses Known to Law Enforcement, by State Metropolitan and Nonmetropolitan Counties, 2008—*Continued*

(Number.)

State/County	Violent crime	Murder and non-negligent man-slaughter	Forcible rape	Robbery	Aggravated assault	Property crime	Burglary	Larceny-theft	Motor vehicle theft	Arson[1]
Ward	17	0	4	0	13	111	39	61	11	1
Wells	0	0	0	0	0	36	23	13	0	0
Williams	12	0	2	0	10	105	41	52	12	2
OHIO-Metropolitan Counties										
Allen	55	0	12	22	21	1,273	270	969	34	2
Belmont	28	0	12	6	10	562	162	350	50	6
Brown	9	0	3	2	4	471	174	281	16	2
Carroll	1	0	1	0	0	90	25	58	7	2
Clark	19	1	4	5	9	1,359	346	948	65	7
Clermont	61	1	28	13	19	1,788	492	1,203	93	12
Erie	33	1	2	5	25	593	177	377	39	1
Fairfield	26	1	8	10	7	1,202	309	846	47	4
Fulton	18	0	8	2	8	360	111	225	24	2
Geauga	6	1	1	1	3	224	50	166	8	1
Greene	22	0	7	3	12	425	157	247	21	6
Hamilton	317	3	51	185	78	6,621	1,110	5,292	219	50
Jefferson	25	0	3	1	21	408	109	274	25	3
Licking	23	0	1	10	12	1,107	321	688	98	4
Lorain	39	0	13	14	12	789	417	353	19	19
Lucas	85	0	13	16	56	1,409	338	957	114	12
Mahoning	10	0	0	3	7	252	60	182	10	0
Miami	5	0	4	0	1	561	155	372	34	9
Morrow	4	0	1	2	1	255	94	146	15	0
Ottawa	5	0	4	1	0	352	68	274	10	0
Pickaway	45	0	6	4	35	1,093	408	658	27	11
Portage	27	0	8	14	5	1,799	516	1,177	106	11
Preble	22	0	5	1	16	428	152	256	20	5
Richland	41	0	15	5	21	1,249	403	789	57	12
Summit	41	3	9	14	15	1,161	247	838	76	9
Trumbull	27	2	6	1	18	505	147	295	63	2
Union	11	0	2	0	9	352	98	244	10	2
Washington	75	2	14	1	58	396	121	256	19	1
Wood	2	0	0	2	0	471	183	268	20	3
OHIO-Nonmetropolitan Counties										
Adams	7	1	2	1	3	441	172	255	14	2
Ashland	10	0	1	0	9	271	113	145	13	4
Athens	11	0	2	0	9	46	10	36	0	2
Auglaize	5	0	3	0	2	294	67	222	5	0
Champaign	13	0	7	0	6	426	139	244	43	8
Coshocton	18	2	5	1	10	783	183	578	22	11
Crawford	5	0	1	1	3	245	71	165	9	0
Darke	49	0	13	2	34	391	142	236	13	5
Fayette	18	0	8	5	5	576	128	434	14	2
Guernsey	14	0	10	0	4	366	153	199	14	3
Hancock	7	0	2	0	5	325	111	205	9	7
Hardin	5	0	1	2	2	336	119	209	8	0
Harrison	7	0	1	1	5	125	40	68	17	2
Highland	11	0	1	0	10	404	144	245	15	2
Hocking	10	0	3	1	6	417	193	206	18	7
Holmes	9	1	3	1	4	220	59	144	17	0
Huron	12	0	1	0	11	454	156	255	43	1
Marion	12	0	3	5	4	716	118	588	10	0
Meigs	14	0	5	5	4	362	177	165	20	2
Mercer	13	5	2	1	5	237	44	180	13	1
Morgan	6	1	1	0	4	221	88	116	17	2
Muskingum	57	2	34	13	8	1,290	322	884	84	10
Paulding	10	0	2	0	8	202	68	134	0	3
Pike	8	0	2	3	3	303	77	204	22	3
Ross	38	1	15	11	11	1,860	506	1,237	117	13
Van Wert	2	0	1	0	1	259	93	163	3	0
Wayne	34	0	13	2	19	686	344	321	21	6
Williams	12	0	8	1	3	291	44	214	33	6
OKLAHOMA-Metropolitan Counties										
Canadian	42	0	9	1	32	76	39	26	11	0
Cleveland	47	1	7	0	39	291	112	136	43	6
Comanche	13	0	2	2	9	149	78	62	9	0
Creek	47	1	11	4	31	547	223	290	34	10
Grady	10	1	2	1	6	311	86	191	34	6
Le Flore	63	1	5	0	57	244	88	103	53	5
Lincoln	38	2	7	0	29	265	79	145	41	4
Logan	47	1	9	0	37	240	67	151	22	8
McClain	14	0	4	0	10	164	48	91	25	2
Oklahoma	33	3	1	2	27	278	89	140	49	0

[1] The FBI does not publish arson data unless it receives data from either the agency or the state for all 12 months of the calendar year.

Table 10. Offenses Known to Law Enforcement, by State Metropolitan and Nonmetropolitan Counties, 2008—*Continued*

(Number.)

State/County	Violent crime	Murder and non-negligent man-slaughter	Forcible rape	Robbery	Aggravated assault	Property crime	Burglary	Larceny-theft	Motor vehicle theft	Arson[1]
Okmulgee	13	0	1	2	10	116	53	49	14	6
Pawnee	26	1	1	1	23	133	45	78	10	1
Rogers	5	1	1	0	3	291	121	128	42	1
Sequoyah	214	2	16	6	190	278	119	122	37	6
Tulsa	311	5	16	15	275	1,066	380	601	85	6
Wagoner	36	1	6	1	28	387	146	183	58	4
OKLAHOMA-Nonmetropolitan Counties										
Adair[5]		4	1	0		141	57	51	33	12
Alfalfa	1	0	0	0	1	40	6	26	8	3
Atoka	24	0	6	0	18	149	52	76	21	9
Beaver	1	0	0	1	0	31	5	24	2	0
Beckham	11	1	3	0	7	72	16	44	12	1
Blaine	12	1	2	0	9	58	11	42	5	0
Bryan	41	0	5	2	34	354	150	161	43	11
Carter	39	0	4	1	34	177	66	93	18	5
Cherokee	99	1	2	0	96	502	224	223	55	2
Choctaw	22	2	0	3	17	170	58	93	19	4
Cimarron	0	0	0	0	0	0	0	0	0	0
Coal	12	1	0	0	11	112	13	89	10	2
Cotton	1	0	0	0	1	6	2	3	1	0
Craig	4	2	0	1	1	122	51	64	7	1
Custer	11	0	1	1	9	67	14	53	0	5
Delaware	84	0	15	1	68	457	229	197	31	9
Dewey	0	0	0	0	0	19	6	13	0	0
Ellis	3	0	0	0	3	19	8	8	3	1
Garfield	3	0	0	1	2	102	22	65	15	2
Garvin	26	0	5	2	19	160	37	113	10	6
Grant	3	0	0	0	3	53	11	41	1	0
Harmon	0	0	0	0	0	16	9	7	0	0
Harper	4	0	0	0	4	23	4	14	5	0
Hughes	1	1	0	0	0	134	41	67	26	1
Jackson	5	1	0	0	4	69	30	32	7	1
Jefferson	10	0	1	0	9	26	11	14	1	0
Johnston	13	1	0	0	12	8	6	2	0	1
Kingfisher	11	0	0	0	11	89	29	48	12	2
Kiowa	14	0	0	0	14	49	18	28	3	1
Latimer	21	1	0	1	19	84	22	37	25	3
Love	7	0	1	0	6	86	21	47	18	1
Major	1	0	0	0	1	34	5	28	1	0
Marshall	41	0	3	0	38	109	30	61	18	3
Mayes	16	0	1	0	15	217	89	115	13	0
McIntosh	35	0	6	2	27	339	132	187	20	7
Murray	11	0	1	0	10	46	21	23	2	2
Muskogee	67	0	5	4	58	300	108	143	49	15
Noble	4	0	1	0	3	84	21	56	7	1
Nowata	28	0	1	0	27	75	31	33	11	1
Okfuskee	17	2	2	1	12	58	27	23	8	4
Payne	28	0	2	1	25	202	87	94	21	10
Pittsburg[5]		2	3	1		474	192	260	22	23
Pontotoc[5]		0	2	1		210	80	115	15	7
Pottawatomie	56	1	7	0	48	558	203	300	55	6
Pushmataha	4	0	1	0	3	111	55	36	20	5
Roger Mills	2	0	0	0	2	51	11	38	2	2
Seminole	46	1	1	2	42	266	71	184	11	13
Stephens	44	0	7	0	37	134	39	78	17	11
Texas	5	0	2	0	3	50	12	36	2	0
Tillman	1	0	1	0	0	32	18	13	1	4
Washita	13	1	5	0	7	46	13	25	8	4
Woods	5	1	2	0	2	28	3	22	3	2
Woodward	13	0	0	1	12	101	36	51	14	1
OREGON-Metropolitan Counties										
Benton	27	1	6	0	20	281	90	177	14	5
Clackamas	237	4	39	108	86	5,548	849	4,215	484	21
Deschutes	87	0	18	3	66	903	222	627	54	11
Jackson	122	2	13	13	94	868	195	609	64	8
Lane	300	4	25	21	250	1,485	567	708	210	17
Marion	92	0	15	36	41	2,663	615	1,748	300	5
Multnomah	39	1	3	8	27	920	127	722	71	5
Polk	31	0	4	1	26	335	85	222	28	10
Washington	270	1	73	68	128	3,341	699	2,369	273	31
Yamhill	33	0	7	3	23	563	121	389	53	7

[1] The FBI does not publish arson data unless it receives data from either the agency or the state for all 12 months of the calendar year.
[5] The FBI determined that the agency's data were overreported. Consequently, those data are not included in this table.

Table 10. Offenses Known to Law Enforcement, by State Metropolitan and Nonmetropolitan Counties, 2008—*Continued*

(Number.)

State/County	Violent crime	Murder and non-negligent man-slaughter	Forcible rape	Robbery	Aggravated assault	Property crime	Burglary	Larceny-theft	Motor vehicle theft	Arson[1]
OREGON-Nonmetropolitan Counties										
Clatsop	14	0	2	1	11	187	46	128	13	1
Crook	25	0	7	1	17	137	57	75	5	4
Curry	32	1	1	1	29	191	38	141	12	1
Douglas	41	0	14	5	22	949	259	641	49	17
Gilliam	0	0	0	0	0	46	7	32	7	1
Grant	0	0	0	0	0	70	10	58	2	1
Harney	0	0	0	0	0	21	3	15	3	0
Hood River	13	0	0	3	10	261	71	178	12	1
Jefferson	6	0	1	2	3	225	50	143	32	3
Klamath	61	0	9	8	44	648	172	418	58	4
Lake	0	0	0	0	0	47	7	36	4	0
Lincoln	25	0	4	1	20	433	146	266	21	3
Linn	11	2	1	4	4	979	315	594	70	6
Malheur	8	0	3	0	5	169	50	106	13	4
Morrow	23	0	1	0	22	194	39	142	13	3
Sherman	1	0	0	0	1	45	11	32	2	1
Tillamook	12	0	2	1	9	258	94	145	19	4
Umatilla	38	1	8	1	28	355	109	178	68	6
Union	5	0	0	0	5	129	32	88	9	0
Wallowa	0	0	0	0	0	53	10	36	7	1
Wasco	6	0	0	1	5	176	42	114	20	0
PENNSYLVANIA-Metropolitan Counties										
Allegheny County Police Department	46	0	7	1	38	218	5	193	20	92
Beaver	0	0	0	0	0	5	0	5	0	0
Cumberland	0	0	0	0	0	0	0	0	0	0
Luzerne	2	0	0	0	2	8	0	8	0	0
Montgomery	0	0	0	0	0	0	0	0	0	0
Pike	0	0	0	0	0	0	0	0	0	0
Washington	0	0	0	0	0	0	0	0	0	0
York	2	0	0	1	1	2	1	1	0	0
PENNSYLVANIA-Nonmetropolitan Counties										
Bradford	0	0	0	0	0	0	0	0	0	0
Clarion	0	0	0	0	0	4	2	2	0	0
Elk	0	0	0	0	0	0	0	0	0	0
Franklin	0	0	0	0	0	0	0	0	0	0
Greene	0	0	0	0	0	0	0	0	0	0
Jefferson	0	0	0	0	0	0	0	0	0	0
Snyder	0	0	0	0	0	3	1	1	1	0
Tioga	0	0	0	0	0	0	0	0	0	0
SOUTH CAROLINA-Metropolitan Counties										
Aiken	432	4	49	108	271	3,431	1,096	1,911	424	16
Anderson[5]	895	13	38	121	723			4,069	800	23
Berkeley	597	9	41	107	440	3,599	1,041	2,101	457	12
Calhoun	39	0	1	3	35	352	100	178	74	6
Dorchester	433	4	12	95	322	2,276	711	1,331	234	13
Edgefield	28	1	4	4	19	376	78	260	38	1
Fairfield	216	3	9	15	189	581	153	344	84	0
Florence	580	5	30	120	425	2,971	721	1,944	306	18
Greenville	2,242	28	108	518	1,588	10,891	2,945	6,708	1,238	32
Horry	0	0	0	0	0	41	0	41	0	0
Horry County Police Department	1,245	12	44	151	1,038	8,153	2,045	5,145	963	37
Kershaw	214	2	13	23	176	1,369	405	802	162	14
Laurens	316	2	22	31	261	1,430	444	752	234	12
Pickens	248	0	24	12	212	1,751	489	1,049	213	13
Richland	2,438	15	77	496	1,850	9,785	2,414	6,050	1,321	35
Saluda	50	0	12	5	33	226	58	153	15	2
Spartanburg	908	12	88	197	611	7,098	1,838	4,569	691	65
York	552	4	47	57	444	3,192	938	2,021	233	11
SOUTH CAROLINA-Nonmetropolitan Counties										
Abbeville	53	1	4	3	45	340	77	234	29	4
Bamberg	40	0	2	2	36	288	90	156	42	4
Barnwell	128	0	4	5	119	428	125	273	30	3
Beaufort	710	6	17	130	557	4,286	1,236	2,780	270	21
Cherokee	118	4	0	24	90	1,312	436	765	111	5
Chester	211	2	9	29	171	920	307	558	55	9
Chesterfield	157	0	7	7	143	897	252	577	68	3
Clarendon	182	1	11	29	141	1,013	250	623	140	1
Dillon	329	2	11	56	260	1,073	328	645	100	7
Georgetown	296	2	20	25	249	1,704	476	1,113	115	6
Greenwood	301	2	11	9	279	1,600	347	1,150	103	4
Hampton	104	1	5	7	91	343	118	201	24	0

[1] The FBI does not publish arson data unless it receives data from either the agency or the state for all 12 months of the calendar year.

[5] The FBI determined that the agency's data were overreported. Consequently, those data are not included in this table.

Table 10. Offenses Known to Law Enforcement, by State Metropolitan and Nonmetropolitan Counties, 2008—*Continued*

(Number.)

State/County	Violent crime	Murder and non-negligent man-slaughter	Forcible rape	Robbery	Aggravated assault	Property crime	Burglary	Larceny-theft	Motor vehicle theft	Arson[1]
Jasper	134	5	11	23	95	791	211	481	99	9
Lancaster	269	2	27	32	208	2,064	751	1,168	145	8
Lee	89	2	5	7	75	545	165	301	79	5
Marion	161	0	2	11	148	837	257	501	79	5
Marlboro	156	2	6	9	139	694	211	421	62	5
McCormick	44	1	6	2	35	97	22	61	14	2
Newberry	68	0	3	5	60	461	72	364	25	0
Oconee	279	2	23	18	236	1,419	447	875	97	7
Orangeburg	456	7	32	84	333	3,905	1,337	2,013	555	7
Union	101	2	3	11	85	460	146	277	37	7
Williamsburg	168	5	5	40	118	877	287	479	111	18
SOUTH DAKOTA-Metropolitan Counties										
Lincoln	4	0	1	0	3	75	23	44	8	0
Minnehaha	36	1	13	1	21	333	104	192	37	1
Pennington	105	1	56	2	46	360	104	245	11	4
Turner	9	1	0	0	8	28	6	18	4	1
Union	2	0	1	0	1	42	12	30	0	0
SOUTH DAKOTA-Nonmetropolitan Counties										
Aurora	2	0	0	0	2	1	0	1	0	0
Beadle	1	0	0	0	1	25	2	23	0	1
Bennett	9	0	0	0	9	21	8	9	4	1
Bon Homme	0	0	0	0	0	3	0	3	0	0
Brookings	7	0	3	0	4	79	16	60	3	0
Brown	5	0	2	0	3	43	16	27	0	0
Butte	4	0	2	0	2	22	8	13	1	0
Campbell	0	0	0	0	0	0	0	0	0	0
Charles Mix	13	0	2	0	11	51	29	11	11	1
Clay	0	0	0	0	0	17	5	12	0	0
Codington	4	0	3	0	1	44	19	22	3	0
Corson	0	0	0	0	0	9	1	8	0	0
Custer	7	0	1	0	6	85	30	51	4	0
Davison	0	0	0	0	0	6	2	3	1	0
Deuel	1	1	0	0	0	24	12	12	0	0
Edmunds	0	0	0	0	0	3	3	0	0	0
Faulk	3	0	0	0	3	13	4	8	1	0
Hamlin	4	0	1	0	3	37	14	20	3	0
Harding	0	0	0	0	0	0	0	0	0	0
Hughes	2	0	1	0	1	9	5	4	0	0
Lawrence	4	0	0	1	3	52	18	31	3	0
Marshall	10	0	1	0	9	50	23	25	2	0
Moody	3	0	0	0	3	29	1	26	2	0
Potter	0	0	0	0	0	1	1	0	0	0
Roberts	9	0	2	0	7	11	7	3	1	0
Sanborn	4	0	3	0	1	12	6	4	2	0
Spink	8	0	1	1	6	40	9	25	6	1
Stanley	3	0	0	0	3	40	6	32	2	0
Sully	1	0	0	0	1	2	1	0	1	0
Tripp	0	0	0	0	0	10	2	8	0	0
Walworth	2	0	0	0	2	4	2	2	0	0
Yankton	2	0	0	0	2	15	2	13	0	0
Ziebach	1	0	0	0	1	1	1	0	0	0
TENNESSEE-Metropolitan Counties										
Anderson	136	1	15	9	111	924	360	472	92	15
Blount	290	2	31	15	242	1,694	776	781	137	6
Bradley	285	1	18	8	258	1,075	323	675	77	5
Cannon	27	1	0	1	25	136	63	49	24	1
Carter	52	1	4	1	46	635	204	372	59	3
Chester	30	0	5	0	25	152	48	88	16	1
Dickson	121	2	9	3	107	792	300	416	76	4
Fayette	127	2	1	11	113	581	196	316	69	4
Hamilton	293	2	17	14	260	2,082	608	1,322	152	1
Hartsville-Trousdale	35	0	2	3	30	172	53	109	10	1
Hawkins	83	0	3	12	68	1,109	415	593	101	2
Hickman	44	1	6	1	36	326	95	186	45	5
Jefferson	89	1	10	8	70	887	388	418	81	10
Knox	557	6	23	116	412	5,604	1,709	3,487	408	30
Loudon	71	1	1	7	62	607	164	398	45	6
Madison	159	3	9	11	136	926	306	521	99	4
Marion	54	0	2	5	47	284	82	161	41	3
Montgomery	139	0	12	4	123	839	214	538	87	4
Polk	39	1	1	1	36	269	80	153	36	6
Robertson	83	0	6	7	70	490	172	280	38	1
Rutherford	263	3	24	5	231	1,329	432	757	140	9

[1] The FBI does not publish arson data unless it receives data from either the agency or the state for all 12 months of the calendar year.

Table 10. Offenses Known to Law Enforcement, by State Metropolitan and Nonmetropolitan Counties, 2008—*Continued*

(Number.)

State/County	Violent crime	Murder and non-negligent man-slaughter	Forcible rape	Robbery	Aggravated assault	Property crime	Burglary	Larceny-theft	Motor vehicle theft	Arson[1]
Sequatchie	20	1	3	0	16	106	24	52	30	3
Shelby	488	4	38	82	364	3,696	1,295	2,155	246	21
Stewart	42	0	4	0	38	181	99	65	17	3
Sullivan	269	1	44	14	210	1,782	696	926	160	17
Sumner	143	0	13	8	122	784	238	482	64	8
Tipton	275	0	13	8	254	654	188	357	109	2
Unicoi	9	0	0	0	9	61	12	48	1	0
Washington	249	2	14	10	223	961	367	531	63	7
Williamson	71	1	2	5	63	518	160	327	31	5
Wilson	253	1	20	3	229	1,158	408	653	97	6
TENNESSEE-Nonmetropolitan Counties										
Bedford	32	0	1	0	31	355	131	204	20	8
Benton	22	0	0	0	22	183	36	130	17	0
Bledsoe	14	0	0	0	14	93	16	66	11	0
Campbell	166	1	5	9	151	1,108	432	587	89	15
Carroll	29	0	0	1	28	150	40	80	30	1
Claiborne	103	1	6	9	87	736	304	384	48	8
Clay	13	1	1	1	10	63	32	28	3	1
Coffee	55	0	0	3	52	453	50	358	45	0
Crockett	19	0	1	2	16	104	29	63	12	0
Decatur	28	0	2	0	26	201	73	113	15	5
DeKalb	38	0	5	4	29	352	142	179	31	0
Dyer	49	0	3	2	44	340	94	215	31	0
Fentress	52	0	2	1	49	386	196	164	26	3
Franklin	32	0	6	3	23	283	73	183	27	4
Gibson	43	0	3	0	40	303	86	177	40	2
Giles	54	0	0	2	52	308	123	167	18	2
Greene	221	1	14	7	199	1,068	413	541	114	25
Grundy	35	2	0	0	33	169	50	85	34	5
Hancock	1	0	0	1	0	132	54	69	9	1
Hardin	109	2	2	4	101	498	181	275	42	4
Haywood	55	0	4	7	44	266	109	127	30	0
Henderson	69	0	8	2	59	305	100	181	24	2
Henry	75	1	6	2	66	510	172	315	23	2
Houston	24	1	1	0	22	165	77	78	10	1
Humphreys	17	1	1	1	14	114	47	59	8	0
Jackson	20	0	3	1	16	141	49	76	16	0
Johnson	64	0	0	0	64	176	79	80	17	0
Lake	2	0	0	0	2	37	6	28	3	0
Lauderdale	62	1	4	2	55	277	94	146	37	0
Lawrence	90	2	10	4	74	621	240	318	63	12
Lewis	36	0	3	1	32	170	65	95	10	3
Lincoln	111	1	0	2	108	485	215	246	24	2
Marshall	48	0	0	0	48	190	51	122	17	0
Maury	143	0	11	11	121	893	249	553	91	8
McMinn	99	0	4	5	90	833	251	501	81	6
McNairy	40	0	4	1	35	317	127	167	23	4
Meigs	37	0	4	1	32	312	89	180	43	9
Monroe	103	2	0	1	100	625	242	317	66	10
Moore	15	1	6	0	8	102	30	60	12	0
Obion	21	0	2	0	19	219	40	165	14	4
Overton	31	1	0	4	26	292	121	164	7	4
Perry	21	0	1	2	18	177	63	100	14	0
Pickett	1	0	0	0	1	72	12	59	1	0
Putnam	82	2	5	6	69	709	185	458	66	3
Roane	53	1	2	5	45	865	227	569	69	7
Scott	97	0	7	0	90	577	212	337	28	0
Sevier	136	0	19	6	111	2,111	1,109	876	126	2
Van Buren	6	0	0	0	6	60	13	40	7	1
Warren	49	0	1	3	45	416	158	211	47	3
Wayne	18	0	1	0	17	80	26	49	5	6
Weakley	43	3	4	2	34	223	90	112	21	1
White	112	1	0	2	109	375	82	258	35	1
TEXAS-Metropolitan Counties										
Aransas	27	1	2	3	21	455	172	253	30	0
Archer	10	2	0	1	7	77	24	46	7	0
Armstrong	0	0	0	0	0	10	4	6	0	0
Atascosa	43	4	0	7	32	312	135	150	27	1
Austin	8	1	0	0	7	127	46	64	17	0
Bandera	12	1	2	0	9	209	76	132	1	3
Bastrop	201	2	21	7	171	870	332	446	92	5
Bell	88	2	35	3	48	883	242	604	37	45
Bexar	650	19	90	123	418	7,303	2,391	4,436	476	137

[1] The FBI does not publish arson data unless it receives data from either the agency or the state for all 12 months of the calendar year.

Table 10. Offenses Known to Law Enforcement, by State Metropolitan and Nonmetropolitan Counties, 2008—*Continued*

(Number.)

State/County	Violent crime	Murder and non-negligent man-slaughter	Forcible rape	Robbery	Aggravated assault	Property crime	Burglary	Larceny-theft	Motor vehicle theft	Arson[1]
Bowie	128	1	9	7	111	611	221	323	67	6
Brazoria	72	0	3	21	48	1,320	523	697	100	0
Brazos	61	0	5	1	55	463	174	264	25	2
Burleson	32	2	14	0	16	164	88	60	16	3
Caldwell	45	0	5	6	34	162	78	81	3	3
Calhoun	21	1	3	0	17	162	61	89	12	0
Callahan	4	0	0	0	4	15	8	6	1	0
Cameron	352	4	39	24	285	1,726	806	804	116	6
Carson	11	0	1	1	9	50	19	28	3	0
Chambers	70	1	4	8	57	499	224	233	42	1
Clay	16	1	5	1	9	187	62	114	11	0
Collin	79	2	18	2	57	840	385	385	70	0
Comal	169	2	17	5	145	945	284	602	59	7
Coryell	10	0	1	1	8	152	78	70	4	0
Crosby	4	0	1	0	3	7	2	2	3	0
Dallas	28	0	1	6	21	378	81	259	38	18
Delta	8	0	0	1	7	77	48	22	7	1
Denton	79	1	11	8	59	901	268	570	63	18
Ector	58	3	0	14	41	1,111	302	703	106	9
Ellis	70	0	3	1	66	1,202	441	611	150	5
El Paso	224	2	27	32	163	1,221	294	735	192	24
Fort Bend	1,041	6	51	141	843	3,910	1,521	2,071	318	10
Galveston	144	5	16	19	104	982	398	506	78	19
Goliad	6	0	2	2	2	49	20	27	2	1
Grayson	39	1	8	5	25	705	253	406	46	4
Gregg	104	4	14	13	73	715	179	430	106	7
Guadalupe	88	1	5	2	80	775	304	417	54	1
Hardin	43	0	6	4	33	416	126	221	69	2
Harris	7,924	74	351	2,441	5,058	47,432	13,017	28,560	5,855	424
Hays	182	0	8	7	167	1,165	401	760	4	2
Hidalgo	887	24	72	181	610	7,055	2,678	3,731	646	156
Hunt	59	3	0	11	45	1,207	449	683	75	5
Irion	6	0	0	0	6	26	8	18	0	0
Jefferson	33	0	2	3	28	463	150	264	49	3
Johnson	225	0	0	3	222	1,241	367	741	133	20
Jones	6	0	2	1	3	70	23	39	8	0
Kaufman	265	1	4	19	241	1,648	664	833	151	13
Kendall	16	1	4	3	8	163	42	113	8	2
Lampasas	8	0	3	0	5	74	30	38	6	0
Liberty	150	2	13	10	125	1,221	444	597	180	23
Lubbock	112	0	11	11	90	746	362	312	72	6
McLennan	113	1	39	8	65	799	287	441	71	12
Medina	43	0	6	3	34	230	121	99	10	15
Midland	90	0	5	5	80	547	209	314	24	4
Montgomery	706	8	41	132	525	6,957	2,196	4,399	362	65
Nueces	81	0	10	4	67	287	120	154	13	5
Orange	97	1	8	7	81	620	236	307	77	4
Parker	61	1	7	1	52	1,097	390	649	58	0
Potter	19	2	1	1	15	226	67	142	17	3
Randall	33	0	5	2	26	306	88	182	36	8
Robertson	12	0	1	0	11	131	38	77	16	4
Rockwall	52	0	5	2	45	331	107	193	31	0
Rusk	105	2	3	2	98	642	259	302	81	4
San Jacinto	55	0	1	4	50	589	226	271	92	3
San Patricio	26	0	0	3	23	375	119	235	21	3
Smith	309	8	29	24	248	1,903	704	1,013	186	17
Tarrant	121	0	24	25	72	1,307	410	787	110	3
Taylor	19	0	4	1	14	131	69	57	5	1
Tom Green	21	0	5	0	16	256	73	169	14	3
Travis	290	2	30	33	225	3,576	1,107	2,271	198	13
Upshur	55	0	13	4	38	632	254	322	56	0
Victoria	89	0	14	3	72	608	200	371	37	2
Waller	28	1	1	3	23	243	125	98	20	0
Webb	78	1	4	11	62	344	140	165	39	3
Wichita	16	0	2	1	13	153	72	71	10	3
Williamson	188	1	32	19	136	1,526	378	1,063	85	10
Wilson	60	2	4	1	53	208	67	123	18	0
Wise	141	0	14	5	122	505	166	325	14	0
TEXAS-Nonmetropolitan Counties										
Anderson	50	1	5	2	42	381	186	156	39	2
Andrews	9	0	1	0	8	68	20	46	2	2
Angelina	124	0	7	5	112	287	120	148	19	0
Bailey	1	0	0	0	1	25	11	12	2	0

[1] The FBI does not publish arson data unless it receives data from either the agency or the state for all 12 months of the calendar year.

Table 10. Offenses Known to Law Enforcement, by State Metropolitan and Nonmetropolitan Counties, 2008—*Continued*

(Number.)

State/County	Violent crime	Murder and non-negligent man-slaughter	Forcible rape	Robbery	Aggravated assault	Property crime	Burglary	Larceny-theft	Motor vehicle theft	Arson[1]
Baylor	0	0	0	0	0	23	17	6	0	0
Bee	22	0	3	2	17	166	61	92	13	1
Blanco	4	0	1	0	3	34	17	15	2	0
Borden	0	0	0	0	0	5	2	3	0	1
Bosque	23	1	6	2	14	82	27	53	2	0
Brewster	10	1	1	1	7	31	13	18	0	0
Briscoe	0	0	0	0	0	15	2	11	2	0
Brooks	0	0	0	0	0	15	6	6	3	0
Brown	21	2	1	1	17	154	70	82	2	5
Burnet	48	1	3	1	43	318	112	183	23	3
Camp	8	0	2	2	4	152	60	79	13	2
Cass	18	1	3	1	13	336	146	153	37	7
Castro	7	1	1	0	5	99	35	57	7	0
Cherokee	66	1	10	2	53	420	144	216	60	4
Childress	0	0	0	0	0	15	0	14	1	0
Cochran	7	0	1	2	4	77	30	42	5	6
Coke	5	0	0	0	5	5	4	1	0	1
Coleman	0	0	0	0	0	32	10	20	2	1
Collingsworth	4	0	3	1	0	3	3	0	0	0
Colorado	17	0	2	2	13	123	31	82	10	2
Comanche	4	1	2	0	1	78	31	45	2	1
Concho	2	0	0	0	2	16	9	6	1	0
Cooke	23	1	2	1	19	269	133	111	25	2
Cottle	2	1	0	0	1	8	8	0	0	0
Crane	2	1	0	0	1	33	11	21	1	3
Crockett	11	1	4	0	6	56	15	38	3	1
Culberson	1	0	0	1	0	2	2	0	0	0
Dallam	0	0	0	0	0	23	17	5	1	1
Dawson	0	0	0	0	0	32	13	17	2	0
Deaf Smith	7	0	0	1	6	102	32	61	9	1
Dewitt	10	0	2	0	8	89	33	52	4	0
Dickens	0	0	0	0	0	2	0	2	0	0
Dimmit	87	0	5	5	77	278	110	160	8	3
Donley	4	0	0	0	4	54	13	38	3	0
Duval	27	1	2	2	22	120	57	59	4	1
Eastland	3	0	0	2	1	32	11	19	2	1
Edwards	3	0	0	0	3	51	27	22	2	1
Erath	28	0	11	0	17	169	54	95	20	3
Falls	9	0	1	0	8	43	9	22	12	1
Fannin	26	1	4	1	20	245	95	140	10	4
Fayette	4	1	0	0	3	161	34	119	8	2
Fisher	15	0	8	0	7	51	15	32	4	2
Floyd	4	0	0	0	4	15	2	12	1	1
Foard	0	0	0	0	0	5	0	5	0	0
Franklin	8	0	0	2	6	117	61	43	13	0
Freestone	8	0	0	1	7	138	40	82	16	0
Frio	5	0	0	0	5	43	21	22	0	1
Gaines	6	1	1	0	4	60	5	53	2	3
Garza	3	0	1	0	2	58	16	36	6	0
Gillespie	5	0	2	0	3	92	23	67	2	0
Glasscock	1	1	0	0	0	4	1	3	0	0
Gonzales	11	0	0	2	9	81	37	41	3	1
Gray	12	0	1	2	9	95	23	66	6	0
Grimes	24	0	4	2	18	402	140	242	20	0
Hale	3	0	1	1	1	81	35	44	2	0
Hall	3	2	0	0	1	23	14	6	3	0
Hamilton	18	0	0	0	18	156	58	80	18	0
Hansford	9	0	0	0	9	19	6	10	3	1
Hardeman	9	0	3	2	4	98	50	44	4	2
Harrison	84	1	1	7	75	789	347	402	40	0
Hartley	0	0	0	0	0	20	8	11	1	1
Haskell	0	0	0	0	0	21	3	17	1	1
Hemphill	12	0	2	0	10	61	13	41	7	2
Henderson	147	3	1	6	137	1,046	441	485	120	3
Hill	6	0	0	2	4	320	146	156	18	3
Hockley	10	0	4	0	6	71	26	38	7	3
Hood	47	0	0	3	44	608	181	386	41	14
Hopkins	40	0	13	0	27	219	85	107	27	0
Houston	15	0	2	1	12	191	63	96	32	1
Howard	26	0	3	3	20	117	45	62	10	0
Hudspeth	3	0	0	1	2	34	18	16	0	0
Hutchinson	14	0	0	0	14	87	40	41	6	0
Jack	3	0	2	0	1	44	20	19	5	0

[1] The FBI does not publish arson data unless it receives data from either the agency or the state for all 12 months of the calendar year.

Table 10. Offenses Known to Law Enforcement, by State Metropolitan and Nonmetropolitan Counties, 2008—*Continued*

(Number.)

State/County	Violent crime	Murder and non-negligent man-slaughter	Forcible rape	Robbery	Aggravated assault	Property crime	Burglary	Larceny-theft	Motor vehicle theft	Arson[1]
Jackson	15	0	1	0	14	93	28	59	6	0
Jasper	42	0	2	4	36	282	110	143	29	0
Jeff Davis	8	0	3	0	5	11	6	5	0	0
Jim Hogg	10	0	0	0	10	83	22	50	11	0
Jim Wells	94	0	6	3	85	455	213	211	31	4
Karnes	11	1	2	0	8	72	22	41	9	0
Kenedy	3	0	1	1	1	9	3	4	2	0
Kent	7	0	1	0	6	11	2	9	0	1
Kerr	39	1	5	3	30	330	111	193	26	6
Kimble	3	0	1	0	2	6	6	0	0	0
King	0	0	0	0	0	3	1	2	0	0
Kinney	4	0	0	0	4	28	12	16	0	0
Kleberg	13	0	3	0	10	414	34	377	3	1
Knox	2	0	1	0	1	19	3	14	2	0
La Salle	4	0	0	1	3	108	40	68	0	2
Lamar	26	0	4	1	21	317	116	181	20	0
Lamb	4	0	0	1	3	50	11	39	0	0
Lavaca	6	0	0	0	6	47	20	24	3	0
Lee	14	0	3	1	10	95	36	55	4	0
Leon	26	0	5	3	18	106	45	50	11	0
Limestone	35	1	17	5	12	265	91	160	14	3
Lipscomb	3	0	0	0	3	13	9	4	0	0
Live Oak	2	0	0	0	2	29	16	10	3	0
Llano	20	0	2	0	18	267	70	187	10	0
Loving	0	0	0	0	0	12	0	12	0	0
Lynn	0	0	0	0	0	20	8	12	0	0
Madison	9	1	0	0	8	109	41	54	14	1
Marion	24	2	3	2	17	157	72	77	8	0
Martin	1	1	0	0	0	14	3	8	3	0
Mason	6	0	0	0	6	30	9	21	0	0
Matagorda	50	0	0	0	50	270	96	160	14	3
Maverick	205	1	6	7	191	722	264	427	31	2
McCulloch	8	0	4	1	3	37	15	17	5	0
McMullen	1	0	0	0	1	0	0	0	0	0
Menard	3	0	0	0	3	8	1	7	0	0
Milam	5	1	0	1	3	222	59	144	19	3
Mills	3	0	0	0	3	34	11	22	1	0
Mitchell	0	0	0	0	0	24	4	18	2	0
Montague	10	1	0	0	9	180	66	98	16	2
Moore	5	0	1	0	4	75	24	42	9	3
Morris	25	0	2	1	22	129	63	47	19	0
Motley	2	0	0	0	2	10	7	2	1	3
Nacogdoches	109	2	9	6	92	507	173	268	66	8
Navarro	34	2	10	3	19	652	257	367	28	0
Newton	15	2	3	2	8	158	41	112	5	1
Nolan	9	0	0	0	9	39	12	23	4	0
Ochiltree	8	0	3	0	5	36	10	24	2	0
Oldham	4	0	0	0	4	26	11	14	1	0
Palo Pinto	15	2	1	1	11	172	77	78	17	0
Panola	28	1	5	1	21	292	62	179	51	1
Parmer	2	0	1	0	1	55	20	35	0	0
Pecos	5	0	0	0	5	29	16	13	0	0
Polk	53	1	14	3	35	717	239	414	64	2
Presidio	1	0	0	0	1	3	0	3	0	0
Rains	22	3	6	0	13	129	41	81	7	0
Reagan	1	0	0	0	1	20	6	13	1	0
Real	2	1	0	0	1	7	4	3	0	1
Red River	8	0	0	1	7	78	11	58	9	1
Reeves	5	0	0	0	5	57	20	34	3	1
Refugio	13	0	0	2	11	70	20	44	6	0
Roberts	2	0	1	0	1	18	1	17	0	1
Runnels	0	0	0	0	0	10	0	10	0	0
Sabine	35	0	2	1	32	97	46	43	8	1
San Augustine	17	1	0	1	15	97	35	48	14	1
San Saba	1	0	0	0	1	24	13	9	2	0
Schleicher	1	0	0	0	1	17	8	9	0	0
Scurry	5	1	0	0	4	52	21	28	3	0
Shackelford	0	0	0	0	0	15	7	6	2	0
Shelby	55	1	7	3	44	272	71	176	25	1
Sherman	0	0	0	0	0	0	0	0	0	0
Somervell	8	0	0	0	8	100	26	70	4	0
Starr	102	6	12	11	73	404	175	155	74	1
Stephens	1	0	0	0	1	36	19	15	2	0

[1] The FBI does not publish arson data unless it receives data from either the agency or the state for all 12 months of the calendar year.

Table 10. Offenses Known to Law Enforcement, by State Metropolitan and Nonmetropolitan Counties, 2008—*Continued*

(Number.)

State/County	Violent crime	Murder and non-negligent man-slaughter	Forcible rape	Robbery	Aggravated assault	Property crime	Burglary	Larceny-theft	Motor vehicle theft	Arson[1]
Sterling	2	0	0	0	2	13	4	9	0	0
Stonewall	3	0	0	0	3	9	4	4	1	0
Sutton	4	0	1	0	3	13	0	12	1	0
Swisher	5	0	0	0	5	41	14	25	2	0
Terrell	2	0	0	0	2	17	4	9	4	0
Terry	1	0	0	0	1	23	9	10	4	0
Throckmorton	1	0	1	0	0	5	4	1	0	0
Titus	87	1	10	2	74	305	121	162	22	6
Trinity	28	0	0	1	27	112	45	52	15	5
Tyler	53	1	8	6	38	281	164	94	23	4
Upton	6	0	0	0	6	14	2	12	0	0
Uvalde	20	0	3	0	17	138	42	83	13	2
Val Verde	2	1	0	0	1	121	36	75	10	0
Van Zandt	66	3	0	5	58	800	311	415	74	1
Walker	47	1	6	4	36	434	176	225	33	0
Ward	18	0	1	0	17	100	31	66	3	1
Washington	33	1	2	0	30	155	70	79	6	0
Wharton	76	0	1	4	71	437	232	177	28	8
Wheeler	4	0	0	0	4	33	8	19	6	0
Wilbarger	1	0	1	0	0	29	13	15	1	0
Willacy	16	0	1	0	15	91	42	46	3	2
Winkler	2	0	1	0	1	45	2	41	2	0
Wood	73	1	1	5	66	544	176	325	43	3
Yoakum	5	0	1	0	4	33	6	24	3	0
Young	14	0	0	0	14	91	42	44	5	2
Zapata	46	1	1	3	41	145	75	56	14	0
Zavala	30	0	1	2	27	115	44	62	9	2
UTAH-Metropolitan Counties										
Cache	25	1	14	0	10	495	75	408	12	1
Davis	32	0	10	0	22	216	70	137	9	0
Juab	5	0	0	2	3	83	31	49	3	0
Morgan	1	0	0	1	0	61	13	40	8	0
Salt Lake	654	2	71	114	467	8,300	1,505	5,999	796	32
Summit	14	0	5	0	9	596	110	460	26	0
Tooele	45	1	6	6	32	387	45	308	34	4
Utah	47	0	12	3	32	392	99	263	30	6
Washington	39	1	4	1	33	121	38	75	8	2
Weber	41	1	8	13	19	1,052	170	811	71	6
UTAH-Nonmetropolitan Counties										
Beaver	9	0	0	0	9	74	16	57	1	0
Box Elder	4	0	1	0	3	222	60	154	8	0
Carbon	15	0	7	1	7	131	47	70	14	2
Daggett	1	0	0	1	0	25	4	20	1	0
Duchesne	17	0	4	0	13	142	36	95	11	1
Emery	6	0	1	2	3	150	51	95	4	0
Grand	7	0	0	0	7	67	21	37	9	0
Iron	19	0	5	1	13	144	60	75	9	3
Kane	8	0	4	1	3	55	34	21	0	0
Millard	20	0	2	2	16	265	55	198	12	0
Rich	2	0	0	0	2	45	11	33	1	0
San Juan	12	0	2	1	9	34	11	23	0	0
Sevier	11	0	2	0	9	213	58	148	7	2
Uintah	20	0	4	0	16	240	47	164	29	5
Wasatch	7	0	3	0	4	143	22	109	12	1
Wayne	2	0	0	0	2	72	8	62	2	0
VERMONT-Metropolitan Counties										
Chittenden	0	0	0	0	0	1	0	1	0	0
Franklin	17	0	3	5	9	289	62	207	20	1
Grand Isle	0	0	0	0	0	84	38	42	4	1
VERMONT-Nonmetropolitan Counties										
Addison	0	0	0	0	0	0	0	0	0	0
Bennington	0	0	0	0	0	0	0	0	0	0
Caledonia	1	0	0	0	1	4	1	3	0	0
Lamoille	9	0	2	0	7	128	28	96	4	0
Orange	0	0	0	0	0	46	9	37	0	0
Orleans	0	0	0	0	0	35	7	28	0	0
Rutland	3	0	0	0	3	111	12	98	1	0
Washington	1	0	0	0	1	0	0	0	0	0
Windham	0	0	0	0	0	1	0	1	0	0
Windsor	0	0	0	0	0	0	0	0	0	0
VIRGINIA-Metropolitan Counties										
Albemarle County Police Department	128	3	24	37	64	1,929	239	1,588	102	18
Amelia	15	0	3	0	12	156	38	95	23	2
Amherst	32	1	7	6	18	529	59	435	35	7

[1] The FBI does not publish arson data unless it receives data from either the agency or the state for all 12 months of the calendar year.

Table 10. Offenses Known to Law Enforcement, by State Metropolitan and Nonmetropolitan Counties, 2008—*Continued*

(Number.)

State/County	Violent crime	Murder and non-negligent man-slaughter	Forcible rape	Robbery	Aggravated assault	Property crime	Burglary	Larceny-theft	Motor vehicle theft	Arson[1]
Appomattox	10	0	4	2	4	125	31	84	10	2
Arlington County Police Department	316	3	22	145	146	4,818	390	4,116	312	6
Bedford	51	0	18	4	29	774	119	601	54	2
Botetourt	20	0	6	1	13	357	46	294	17	3
Campbell	77	2	19	11	45	833	166	616	51	5
Caroline	66	0	12	13	41	440	87	348	5	13
Charles City	6	1	0	1	4	29	14	9	6	0
Chesterfield County Police Department	609	11	64	321	213	7,213	1,575	5,172	466	93
Clarke	10	1	2	0	7	172	17	141	14	3
Cumberland	14	0	3	2	9	65	17	41	7	0
Dinwiddie	45	0	10	6	29	486	129	306	51	6
Fairfax County Police Department	714	19	60	333	302	18,216	1,375	15,760	1,081	105
Fauquier	39	1	9	6	23	609	80	471	58	7
Fluvanna	18	1	3	2	12	219	62	137	20	4
Franklin	36	1	7	7	21	575	119	425	31	1
Frederick	127	1	46	14	66	1,589	366	1,088	135	9
Giles	15	0	3	1	11	180	54	112	14	0
Gloucester	21	1	5	5	10	489	40	427	22	9
Greene	35	0	5	5	25	218	52	155	11	3
Hanover	39	1	8	10	20	1,133	110	969	54	7
Henrico County Police Department	582	17	35	331	199	9,062	1,486	7,005	571	93
Isle of Wight	45	2	5	13	25	476	138	308	30	5
James City County Police Department	71	1	13	18	39	924	200	691	33	21
King and Queen	8	0	1	0	7	41	9	31	1	1
King William	4	0	0	3	1	79	9	55	15	1
Loudoun	269	3	47	35	184	3,116	280	2,657	179	42
Louisa	40	1	16	5	18	452	78	359	15	6
Mathews	5	0	2	0	3	87	23	60	4	1
Montgomery	47	1	7	2	37	547	159	337	51	8
Nelson	8	0	1	1	6	261	70	171	20	3
New Kent	33	0	3	8	22	248	51	173	24	4
Pittsylvania	73	2	12	16	43	582	229	325	28	2
Powhatan	11	4	1	3	3	318	79	211	28	0
Prince George County Police Department	41	0	8	13	20	438	85	325	28	3
Prince William County Police Department	560	12	24	261	263	7,555	1,081	5,840	634	74
Pulaski	65	1	11	5	48	616	106	485	25	6
Roanoke County Police Department	116	2	15	18	81	1,199	223	906	70	14
Rockingham	20	1	7	0	12	273	112	153	8	1
Scott	39	2	6	1	30	468	104	332	32	2
Spotsylvania	288	1	41	46	200	2,473	297	2,038	138	5
Stafford	181	2	46	40	93	1,702	213	1,353	136	12
Surry	16	1	0	2	13	89	41	43	5	1
Sussex	25	0	1	4	20	174	49	107	18	2
Warren	14	2	5	1	6	423	38	357	28	3
Washington	57	2	13	7	35	1,143	253	842	48	9
York	65	1	8	26	30	1,277	201	1,038	38	16
VIRGINIA-Nonmetropolitan Counties										
Accomack	69	2	11	30	26	600	182	377	41	0
Alleghany	9	0	1	0	8	103	28	69	6	0
Augusta	82	0	9	8	65	802	148	605	49	9
Bath	1	0	0	0	1	32	7	25	0	0
Bland	0	0	0	0	0	51	12	36	3	1
Brunswick	17	1	1	3	12	134	34	77	23	0
Buchanan	44	1	6	2	35	468	147	276	45	6
Buckingham	30	0	3	6	21	196	65	107	24	3
Carroll	52	2	4	2	44	399	144	216	39	4
Charlotte	33	2	2	7	22	170	60	97	13	3
Culpeper	27	0	5	1	21	335	33	263	39	1
Dickenson	27	2	5	3	17	214	63	135	16	4
Essex	13	0	5	3	5	87	11	60	16	2
Floyd	8	1	1	0	6	155	38	104	13	2
Grayson	20	5	2	1	12	144	49	77	18	1
Greensville	15	1	3	6	5	199	67	121	11	1
Halifax	35	1	5	6	23	414	142	236	36	4
Henry	158	6	9	35	108	1,211	366	762	83	8
Highland	0	0	0	0	0	15	7	8	0	0
King George	33	0	9	4	20	416	78	317	21	3
Lancaster	10	1	1	0	8	116	30	75	11	0
Lee	20	1	2	2	15	368	100	253	15	0
Lunenburg	13	0	1	2	10	105	38	50	17	3
Mecklenburg	32	1	4	5	22	433	125	278	30	8
Northampton	17	0	1	6	10	229	76	134	19	0

[1] The FBI does not publish arson data unless it receives data from either the agency or the state for all 12 months of the calendar year.

Table 10. Offenses Known to Law Enforcement, by State Metropolitan and Nonmetropolitan Counties, 2008—*Continued*

(Number.)

State/County	Violent crime	Murder and non-negligent man-slaughter	Forcible rape	Robbery	Aggravated assault	Property crime	Burglary	Larceny-theft	Motor vehicle theft	Arson[1]
Northumberland	12	0	2	2	8	181	67	105	9	0
Nottoway	19	0	1	1	17	56	17	36	3	1
Orange	15	1	3	1	10	254	51	179	24	5
Page	19	0	6	0	13	254	84	157	13	3
Patrick	18	0	4	2	12	406	109	252	45	2
Prince Edward	15	0	2	3	10	79	33	39	7	0
Rappahannock	4	0	2	0	2	47	10	33	4	1
Richmond	7	1	3	0	3	47	6	37	4	0
Rockbridge	19	0	9	1	9	254	57	185	12	3
Russell	27	0	3	3	21	289	79	190	20	7
Shenandoah	39	0	6	2	31	330	91	215	24	0
Smyth	32	5	4	0	23	320	63	241	16	4
Southampton	30	1	2	14	13	381	96	254	31	0
Tazewell	42	2	4	4	32	541	134	378	29	2
Westmoreland	8	1	0	1	6	157	31	117	9	1
Wise	46	0	7	3	36	366	118	221	27	13
Wythe	25	2	7	2	14	129	22	103	4	0
WASHINGTON-Metropolitan Counties										
Asotin	14	1	2	0	11	192	39	148	5	0
Benton	68	0	9	5	54	551	206	310	35	4
Chelan	35	2	15	3	15	878	120	698	60	2
Clark	276	2	66	47	161	4,396	813	2,919	664	37
Cowlitz	50	1	25	2	22	710	240	407	63	5
Douglas	48	0	7	6	35	420	119	272	29	4
Franklin	13	0	1	1	11	163	52	95	16	1
King	549	8	107	181	253	7,040	2,407	3,729	904	104
Kitsap	674	2	123	44	505	3,760	1,045	2,538	177	29
Pierce	1,147	10	107	204	826	10,037	2,535	6,077	1,425	63
Skagit	80	7	18	11	44	1,491	461	906	124	10
Skamania	11	0	3	1	7	196	55	124	17	0
Spokane	247	4	9	25	209	2,473	646	1,599	228	13
Thurston	320	0	32	30	258	3,282	865	2,239	178	23
Whatcom	131	0	35	5	91	1,376	493	761	122	5
Yakima	132	6	17	42	67	2,509	943	1,157	409	67
WASHINGTON-Nonmetropolitan Counties										
Adams	27	0	5	1	21	302	93	173	36	2
Clallam	51	2	17	2	30	585	166	380	39	7
Columbia	2	0	0	0	2	206	29	170	7	0
Ferry	7	1	0	0	6	20	11	8	1	0
Garfield	2	0	0	0	2	56	20	34	2	0
Grant	81	4	8	17	52	1,480	529	817	134	15
Grays Harbor	32	2	4	4	22	370	138	192	40	1
Island	39	0	13	4	22	1,130	456	643	31	1
Jefferson	34	0	7	0	27	431	164	255	12	1
Kittitas	19	0	2	1	16	487	134	311	42	0
Klickitat	10	0	0	1	9	151	103	16	32	0
Lewis	70	0	14	3	53	851	264	528	59	8
Lincoln	8	0	5	1	2	160	43	114	3	2
Mason	140	0	31	11	98	1,639	641	844	154	9
Okanogan	13	0	3	2	8	470	171	269	30	0
Pacific	22	0	4	1	17	380	158	204	18	3
Pend Oreille	7	0	1	2	4	394	107	257	30	0
San Juan	6	1	0	0	5	259	86	153	20	1
Stevens	37	1	15	3	18	633	243	331	59	3
Wahkiakum	6	0	0	1	5	50	19	28	3	0
Walla Walla	19	0	8	1	10	336	83	238	15	0
Whitman	5	0	2	0	3	73	27	38	8	1
WEST VIRGINIA-Metropolitan Counties										
Berkeley	53	2	0	21	30	1,208	351	792	65	12
Boone	14	0	0	1	13	87	23	39	25	2
Brooke	9	0	0	1	8	116	43	62	11	1
Cabell	61	1	9	22	29	846	211	571	64	6
Hampshire	24	0	2	1	21	110	56	45	9	0
Jefferson	37	0	2	12	23	471	135	312	24	8
Kanawha	202	6	15	35	146	1,474	495	845	134	21
Marshall	18	0	4	1	13	251	63	165	23	1
Mineral	148	4	1	1	142	64	15	46	3	1
Morgan	7	0	1	2	4	58	19	33	6	1
Putnam	55	0	10	5	40	922	159	688	75	7
Wayne	2	0	0	1	1	143	60	72	11	0

[1] The FBI does not publish arson data unless it receives data from either the agency or the state for all 12 months of the calendar year.

Table 10. Offenses Known to Law Enforcement, by State Metropolitan and Nonmetropolitan Counties, 2008—*Continued*

(Number.)

State/County	Violent crime	Murder and non-negligent man-slaughter	Forcible rape	Robbery	Aggravated assault	Property crime	Burglary	Larceny-theft	Motor vehicle theft	Arson[1]
WEST VIRGINIA-Nonmetropolitan Counties										
Braxton	13	0	0	0	13	33	15	16	2	0
Fayette	53	2	6	5	40	274	122	116	36	3
Greenbrier	11	0	1	1	9	144	41	92	11	0
Hardy	12	0	0	1	11	57	27	27	3	0
Harrison	44	0	0	7	37	418	126	262	30	8
Jackson	13	0	1	1	11	153	45	88	20	0
Lewis	8	0	0	1	7	18	1	14	3	1
Mason	10	0	0	0	10	184	0	158	26	1
Mercer	127	5	3	8	111	535	240	243	52	8
Monroe	8	0	0	0	8	25	14	10	1	0
Raleigh	83	1	5	18	59	1,046	334	647	65	11
Randolph	12	0	0	0	12	49	15	31	3	0
Upshur	6	0	3	0	3	94	15	71	8	0
Wyoming	3	0	0	1	2	231	167	59	5	0
WISCONSIN-Metropolitan Counties										
Brown	46	0	14	4	28	1,342	289	1,011	42	4
Calumet	8	1	2	0	5	175	40	129	6	0
Chippewa	14	0	6	1	7	378	69	292	17	0
Columbia	38	0	7	0	31	389	134	238	17	4
Dane	57	1	13	7	36	1,163	297	805	61	4
Douglas	10	0	3	2	5	230	102	117	11	2
Eau Claire	11	1	3	2	5	259	96	158	5	0
Fond du Lac	37	0	9	1	27	289	84	185	20	1
Iowa	10	1	1	3	5	171	43	123	5	1
Kenosha	42	1	6	8	27	807	209	552	46	4
Kewaunee	3	0	0	0	3	84	15	62	7	2
La Crosse	22	0	1	2	19	198	53	133	12	2
Marathon	146	0	15	2	129	464	125	323	16	1
Milwaukee	1	0	0	1	0	17	0	17	0	0
Oconto	1	0	0	0	1	468	121	303	44	0
Outagamie	23	0	7	0	16	461	76	360	25	1
Ozaukee	10	0	0	1	9	156	20	128	8	4
Pierce	9	0	0	0	9	160	49	96	15	0
Racine	15	0	3	10	2	689	85	557	47	0
Rock	40	0	14	2	24	496	153	319	24	3
Sheboygan	32	0	3	2	27	548	87	446	15	6
St. Croix	31	0	6	2	23	480	110	343	27	2
Washington	32	0	9	6	17	620	112	487	21	10
Waukesha	21	0	6	0	15	682	99	562	21	0
Winnebago	26	0	1	1	24	411	138	249	24	1
WISCONSIN-Nonmetropolitan Counties										
Adams	26	0	4	1	21	479	259	205	15	0
Ashland	11	0	0	0	11	48	10	28	10	0
Barron	2	0	0	2	0	251	81	151	19	2
Bayfield	21	0	0	0	21	273	91	176	6	0
Buffalo	2	0	1	0	1	45	10	28	7	1
Burnett	9	1	1	0	7	279	113	157	9	0
Clark	19	0	4	0	15	379	101	265	13	1
Crawford	20	0	8	0	12	157	35	122	0	1
Dodge	45	1	2	1	41	263	81	160	22	3
Door	12	0	1	2	9	224	41	173	10	0
Dunn	38	0	4	1	33	221	72	132	17	0
Florence	6	1	1	0	4	117	29	85	3	0
Forest	6	0	0	1	5	122	22	94	6	1
Grant	19	1	0	0	18	205	72	119	14	0
Green	9	0	1	0	8	162	26	125	11	1
Green Lake	2	0	1	0	1	85	22	59	4	0
Iron	8	0	0	1	7	55	19	36	0	0
Jackson	8	1	5	0	2	240	79	132	29	0
Jefferson	36	1	4	5	26	400	117	255	28	3
Juneau	27	0	4	3	20	211	76	118	17	0
Lafayette	1	0	1	0	0	149	34	108	7	1
Langlade	16	0	2	0	14	248	69	166	13	1
Lincoln	4	0	2	0	2	151	50	85	16	0
Manitowoc	23	0	3	0	20	194	50	139	5	3
Marinette	11	3	4	0	4	462	211	228	23	0
Marquette	16	0	2	1	13	190	55	115	20	0
Menominee	2	0	0	1	1	71	27	43	1	0
Monroe	5	0	0	1	4	260	53	183	24	0
Oneida	11	0	0	0	11	276	76	189	11	1
Pepin	4	0	1	0	3	18	11	5	2	0
Polk	67	1	15	0	51	393	137	223	33	2

[1] The FBI does not publish arson data unless it receives data from either the agency or the state for all 12 months of the calendar year.

Table 10. Offenses Known to Law Enforcement, by State Metropolitan and Nonmetropolitan Counties, 2008—*Continued*

(Number.)

State/County	Violent crime	Murder and non-negligent man-slaughter	Forcible rape	Robbery	Aggravated assault	Property crime	Burglary	Larceny-theft	Motor vehicle theft	Arson[1]
Portage	7	0	2	1	4	364	105	248	11	5
Price	37	1	1	0	35	78	34	40	4	0
Richland	13	0	0	0	13	127	51	67	9	0
Rusk	9	0	1	0	8	157	53	96	8	1
Sauk	30	0	7	2	21	616	129	466	21	2
Sawyer	24	0	5	0	19	246	51	173	22	3
Shawano	3	0	1	1	1	401	113	253	35	0
Taylor	12	1	5	0	6	183	47	124	12	0
Trempealeau	5	0	2	0	3	136	35	91	10	0
Vernon	8	1	1	0	6	167	51	97	19	0
Vilas	10	0	5	0	5	233	53	167	13	1
Walworth	19	0	8	4	7	354	54	281	19	1
Washburn	8	0	2	0	6	256	98	144	14	0
Waupaca	37	0	9	1	27	463	138	291	34	7
Waushara	7	0	1	0	6	272	48	211	13	0
Wood	4	0	1	0	3	196	69	116	11	0
WYOMING-Metropolitan Counties										
Laramie	58	1	5	5	47	551	120	398	33	2
Natrona	17	0	6	1	10	278	111	139	28	1
WYOMING-Nonmetropolitan Counties										
Albany	5	1	0	0	4	68	15	42	11	0
Big Horn	7	0	4	0	3	22	16	4	2	0
Campbell	30	0	1	0	29	237	55	161	21	2
Carbon	9	0	0	0	9	47	7	38	2	0
Converse	3	0	0	0	3	39	4	32	3	0
Crook	1	0	1	0	0	72	15	55	2	0
Fremont	18	0	1	0	17	179	50	114	15	5
Goshen	20	0	2	0	18	67	4	60	3	1
Hot Springs	1	0	0	0	1	31	7	23	1	1
Johnson	0	0	0	0	0	30	4	25	1	0
Lincoln	8	0	2	0	6	106	22	76	8	2
Niobrara	1	0	1	0	0	5	1	4	0	0
Park	28	0	5	0	23	100	23	72	5	0
Platte	1	0	0	0	1	31	7	24	0	1
Sheridan	14	0	4	0	10	60	12	47	1	0
Sublette	22	0	3	2	17	221	48	156	17	1
Sweetwater	22	0	2	0	20	141	35	91	15	1
Teton	8	1	1	0	6	122	13	103	6	1
Uinta	3	0	1	0	2	75	3	62	10	0
Washakie	7	0	0	0	7	10	0	8	2	0
Weston	0	0	0	0	0	7	4	2	1	0

[1] The FBI does not publish arson data unless it receives data from either the agency or the state for all 12 months of the calendar year.

Table 11. Offenses Known to Law Enforcement, by State and Agency, 2008

(Number.)

State/Agency Type	Unit/Office	Violent crime	Murder and non-negligent man-slaughter	Forcible rape	Robbery	Aggra-vated assault	Property crime	Burglary	Larceny-theft	Motor vehicle theft	Arson[1]
ALABAMA—State Agencies											
Alabama Alcoholic Beverage Control Board		0	0	0	0	0	0	0	0	0	
ALABAMA—Other Agencies											
22nd Judicial Circuit Drug Task Force		1	0	0	0	1	0	0	0	0	
24th Judicial Circuit Drug and Violent Crime Task Force		0	0	0	0	0	0	0	0	0	
Marshall County Drug Enforcement Unit		0	0	0	0	0	0	0	0	0	
ALASKA—State Agencies											
Alaska State Troopers		771	9	52	33	677	4,174	1,181	2,598	395	41
Alcohol Beverage Control Board		0	0	0	0	0	5	0	5	0	0
ALASKA—Other Agencies											
Anchorage International Airport		1	0	0	0	1	81	2	72	7	0
Fairbanks International Airport		2	0	0	0	2	40	1	36	3	0
ARIZONA—State Agencies											
Arizona Department of Public Safety		7	0	0	0	7	4	0	3	1	0
ARKANSAS—State Agencies											
State Capitol Police		1	0	0	1	0	15	3	11	1	0
CALIFORNIA—State Agencies											
Agnews Developmental Center		0	0	0	0	0	12	4	6	2	0
Atascadero State Hospital		60	1	0	1	58	17	0	17	0	3
California State Fair		4	0	0	1	3	83	4	73	6	0
Coalinga State Hospital		25	0	1	1	23	27	4	23	0	0
Department of Parks and Recreation:	Angeles	0	0	0	0	0	2	0	2	0	0
	Bay Area	0	0	0	0	0	3	0	3	0	0
	Calaveras County	2	0	0	0	2	0	0	0	0	0
	Capital	0	0	0	0	0	9	4	5	0	0
	Channel Coast	1	0	0	1	0	54	4	50	0	0
	Colorado	0	0	0	0	0	0	0	0	0	0
	Four Rivers District	0	0	0	0	0	9	1	8	0	0
	Gold Fields District	5	0	0	1	4	88	0	88	0	3
	Hollister Hills	1	0	0	0	1	3	0	0	3	0
	Hungry Valley	0	0	0	0	0	3	1	2	0	0
	Inland Empire	0	0	0	0	0	5	3	1	1	0
	Marin County	0	0	0	0	0	0	0	0	0	0
	Mendocino Headquarters	6	0	1	0	5	2	1	1	0	0
	Monterey County	0	0	0	0	0	50	4	46	0	0
	North Coast Redwoods	2	0	0	0	2	57	6	48	3	0
	Northern Buttes	1	0	0	0	1	11	1	7	3	0
	Oceano Dunes	7	0	0	0	7	97	18	67	12	0
	Ocotillo Wells	0	0	0	0	0	2	0	2	0	1
	Orange Coast	1	0	0	0	1	75	18	55	2	0
	Russian River	0	0	0	0	0	55	3	52	0	1
	San Diego Coast	3	0	0	2	1	59	3	55	1	0
	San Joaquin	0	0	0	0	0	9	2	7	0	0
	San Luis Obispo Coast	0	0	0	0	0	14	3	11	0	0
	Santa Cruz Mountains	0	0	0	0	0	88	2	85	1	0
	Sierra	0	0	0	0	0	16	0	16	0	0
	Silverado	0	0	0	0	0	10	0	10	0	0
	Twin Cities	1	0	0	0	1	4	1	3	0	0
Fairview Developmental Center		0	0	0	0	0	5	1	4	0	0
Highway Patrol:	Alameda County	1	0	0	0	1	262	0	18	244	0
	Alpine County	0	0	0	0	0	1	0	0	1	0
	Amador County	0	0	0	0	0	43	0	0	43	0
	Butte County	2	0	1	1	0	322	1	39	282	0
	Calaveras County	0	0	0	0	0	99	0	16	83	0
	Colusa County	1	0	0	0	1	19	0	1	18	0
	Contra Costa County	0	0	0	0	0	898	0	4	894	0
	Del Norte County	1	0	0	0	1	46	1	0	45	0
	El Dorado County	0	0	0	0	0	201	0	39	162	0
	Fresno County	0	0	0	0	0	224	0	13	211	0
	Glenn County	0	0	0	0	0	28	0	0	28	0
	Humboldt County	0	0	0	0	0	130	0	5	125	0
	Imperial County	0	0	0	0	0	146	0	16	130	0
	Inyo County	0	0	0	0	0	25	1	6	18	0
	Kern County	3	0	0	0	3	426	0	34	392	0
	Kings County	1	0	0	0	1	102	0	0	102	0
	Lake County	0	0	0	0	0	126	0	20	106	0
	Lassen County	0	0	0	0	0	11	0	6	5	0
	Los Angeles County	20	0	0	2	18	455	10	23	422	1
	Madera County	0	0	0	0	0	320	0	45	275	0
	Marin County	0	0	0	0	0	120	0	0	120	0
	Mariposa County	1	0	0	0	1	25	0	8	17	0

[1] The FBI does not publish arson data unless it receives data from either the agency or the state for all 12 months of the calendar year.

Table 11. Offenses Known to Law Enforcement, by State and Agency, 2008—*Continued*

(Number.)

State/Agency Type	Unit/Office	Violent crime	Murder and non-negligent man-slaughter	Forcible rape	Robbery	Aggra-vated assault	Property crime	Burglary	Larceny-theft	Motor vehicle theft	Arson[1]
	Mendocino County	3	0	0	0	3	83	0	21	62	0
	Merced County	0	0	0	0	0	483	0	60	423	0
	Modoc County	0	0	0	0	0	6	0	3	3	0
	Mono County	0	0	0	0	0	1	0	0	1	0
	Monterey County	4	0	0	1	3	377	0	20	357	0
	Napa County	0	0	0	0	0	58	0	8	50	0
	Nevada County	0	0	0	0	0	101	0	19	82	0
	Orange County	3	0	0	0	3	46	3	23	20	0
	Placer County	1	0	0	0	1	219	0	59	160	0
	Plumas County	0	0	0	0	0	40	0	9	31	0
	Riverside County	8	0	0	1	7	96	20	3	73	0
	Sacramento County	11	0	1	2	8	3,676	20	527	3,129	0
	San Benito County	0	0	0	0	0	35	0	0	35	0
	San Bernardino County	10	0	0	0	10	60	4	3	53	0
	San Diego County	18	0	0	0	18	168	6	22	140	0
	San Francisco County	0	0	0	0	0	23	0	3	20	0
	San Joaquin County	0	0	0	0	0	823	0	142	681	0
	San Luis Obispo County	2	0	1	0	1	136	0	20	116	0
	San Mateo County	6	0	0	0	6	30	0	0	30	0
	Santa Barbara County	3	0	1	0	2	123	0	18	105	0
	Santa Clara County	1	0	0	0	1	71	0	14	57	0
	Santa Cruz County	1	0	0	0	1	349	0	57	292	0
	Shasta County	1	0	0	0	1	174	0	30	144	0
	Sierra County	2	0	0	0	2	0	0	0	0	0
	Siskiyou County	0	0	0	0	0	25	0	4	21	0
	Solano County	1	0	0	0	1	92	0	0	92	0
	Sonoma County	1	0	1	0	0	277	1	47	229	0
	Stanislaus County	1	0	1	0	0	645	0	16	629	0
	Sutter County	0	0	0	0	0	28	0	4	24	0
	Tehama County	4	0	0	2	2	84	4	11	69	0
	Trinity County	0	0	0	0	0	20	0	0	20	0
	Tulare County	3	0	0	0	3	1,080	0	183	897	0
	Tuolumne County	1	0	0	0	1	109	0	12	97	0
	Ventura County	0	0	0	0	0	39	0	9	30	0
	Yolo County	0	0	0	0	0	33	0	0	33	0
	Yuba County	2	0	0	0	2	187	1	16	170	0
Napa State Hospital[2]			0	5	0		10	3	7	0	0
Patton State Hospital		511	0	0	1	510	12	3	9	0	2
Porterville Developmental Center		0	0	0	0	0	0	0	0	0	0
Sonoma Developmental Center		0	0	0	0	0	1	0	1	0	0
CALIFORNIA—Other Agencies											
East Bay Municipal Utility		0	0	0	0	0	26	0	26	0	0
East Bay Regional Parks:	Alameda County	5	1	2	2	0	114	4	106	4	8
	Contra Costa County	11	0	0	8	3	218	7	202	9	6
Fontana Unified School District		36	0	2	7	27	207	70	133	4	5
Los Angeles County Metropolitan Transportation Authority		7	0	0	0	7	48	8	40	0	0
Los Angeles Transportation Services Bureau		445	1	6	273	165	803	16	610	177	2
Monterey Peninsula Airport		0	0	0	0	0	12	0	10	2	0
Port of San Diego Harbor		22	0	3	6	13	527	15	512	0	1
San Bernardino Unified School District		131	0	1	119	11	396	195	183	18	6
San Francisco Bay Area Rapid Transit:	Alameda County	140	1	0	119	20	1,329	4	1,110	215	2
	Contra Costa County	44	0	1	38	5	956	9	723	224	0
	San Francisco County	35	0	1	31	3	162	4	157	1	0
	San Mateo County	5	0	0	4	1	163	1	132	30	1
Santa Clara Transit District		36	0	0	22	14	101	0	98	3	0
Stockton Unified School District		87	0	3	13	71	529	86	434	9	12
Twin Rivers Unified School District		44	0	2	16	26	100	44	51	5	1
Union Pacific Railroad:	Alameda County	4	0	0	0	4	219	197	22	0	0
	Amador County	0	0	0	0	0	0	0	0	0	0
	Butte County	3	0	0	0	3	6	0	6	0	0
	Calaveras County	0	0	0	0	0	0	0	0	0	0
	Colusa County	0	0	0	0	0	0	0	0	0	0
	Contra Costa County	2	0	0	0	2	5	1	4	0	0
	El Dorado County	0	0	0	0	0	0	0	0	0	0
	Fresno County	0	0	0	0	0	0	0	0	0	0
	Glenn County	0	0	0	0	0	0	0	0	0	0
	Humboldt County	0	0	0	0	0	0	0	0	0	0
	Imperial County	0	0	0	0	0	57	53	4	0	0
	Inyo County	0	0	0	0	0	0	0	0	0	0
	Kern County	0	0	0	0	0	13	3	10	0	0
	Kings County	0	0	0	0	0	0	0	0	0	0
	Lassen County	0	0	0	0	0	1	0	1	0	0

[1] The FBI does not publish arson data unless it receives data from either the agency or the state for all 12 months of the calendar year.
[2] The FBI determined that the agency's data were overreported. Consequently, those data are not included in this table.

Table 11. Offenses Known to Law Enforcement, by State and Agency, 2008—*Continued*

(Number.)

State/Agency Type	Unit/Office	Violent crime	Murder and non-negligent man-slaughter	Forcible rape	Robbery	Aggra-vated assault	Property crime	Burglary	Larceny-theft	Motor vehicle theft	Arson[1]
	Los Angeles County	6	0	0	0	6	128	98	30	0	0
	Madera County	0	0	0	0	0	0	0	0	0	0
	Marin County	0	0	0	0	0	0	0	0	0	0
	Mendocino County	0	0	0	0	0	0	0	0	0	0
	Merced County	0	0	0	0	0	16	0	16	0	0
	Modoc County	0	0	0	0	0	0	0	0	0	0
	Monterey County	0	0	0	0	0	0	0	0	0	0
	Napa County	0	0	0	0	0	0	0	0	0	0
	Nevada County	0	0	0	0	0	1	0	1	0	0
	Orange County	0	0	0	0	0	0	0	0	0	0
	Placer County	4	0	0	0	4	19	3	16	0	0
	Plumas County	0	0	0	0	0	0	0	0	0	0
	Riverside County	0	0	0	0	0	112	102	10	0	0
	Sacramento County	9	0	0	0	9	20	0	20	0	0
	San Benito County	0	0	0	0	0	0	0	0	0	0
	San Bernardino County	0	0	0	0	0	46	32	14	0	0
	San Francisco County	0	0	0	0	0	0	0	0	0	0
	San Joaquin County	10	0	0	0	10	127	81	46	0	0
	San Luis Obispo County	0	0	0	0	0	8	1	7	0	0
	San Mateo County	0	0	0	0	0	0	0	0	0	0
	Santa Barbara County	0	0	0	0	0	5	0	5	0	0
	Santa Clara County	0	0	0	0	0	2	0	2	0	0
	Santa Cruz County	0	0	0	0	0	0	0	0	0	0
	Shasta County	1	0	0	0	1	4	3	1	0	0
	Sierra County	0	0	0	0	0	0	0	0	0	0
	Siskiyou County	0	0	0	0	0	3	2	1	0	0
	Solano County	0	0	0	0	0	1	0	1	0	0
	Sonoma County	0	0	0	0	0	0	0	0	0	0
	Stanislaus County	2	0	0	0	2	13	2	11	0	0
	Sutter County	0	0	0	0	0	1	0	1	0	0
	Tehama County	1	0	0	0	1	0	0	0	0	0
	Trinity County	0	0	0	0	0	0	0	0	0	0
	Tulare County	0	0	0	0	0	1	1	0	0	0
	Ventura County	0	0	0	0	0	0	0	0	0	0
	Yolo County	2	0	0	0	2	2	0	2	0	0
	Yuba County	0	0	0	0	0	2	0	2	0	0
COLORADO—State Agencies											
Colorado Mental Health Institute		0	0	0	0	0	21	0	21	0	0
State Patrol		19	0	0	0	19	51	0	15	36	0
CONNECTICUT—State Agencies											
Connecticut State Police		396	9	63	53	271	5,288	1,530	3,352	406	111
State Capitol Police		0	0	0	0	0	2	0	2	0	0
CONNECTICUT—Other Agencies											
Metropolitan Transportation Authority		2	0	0	2	0	63	1	62	0	0
DELAWARE—State Agencies											
Attorney General:	Kent County	0	0	0	0	0	0	0	0	0	0
	New Castle County	0	0	0	0	0	1	0	1	0	0
	Sussex County	0	0	0	0	0	2	0	2	0	0
Division of Alcohol and Tobacco Enforcement		0	0	0	0	0	0	0	0	0	0
Environmental Control		0	0	0	0	0	0	0	0	0	0
Fish and Wildlife		5	0	0	0	5	18	0	18	0	0
Park Rangers		2	0	0	0	2	93	15	78	0	2
River and Bay Authority		1	0	0	0	1	17	3	13	1	0
State Capitol Police		0	0	0	0	0	36	6	28	2	0
State Fire Marshal		51	0	0	0	51	25	24	1	0	263
State Police:	Kent County	489	4	58	66	361	2,140	687	1,270	183	3
	New Castle County	705	2	27	314	362	5,778	665	4,786	327	6
	Sussex County	731	6	74	93	558	3,801	1,193	2,337	271	5
DELAWARE—Other Agencies											
Amtrak Police		0	0	0	0	0	0	0	0	0	0
Drug Enforcement Administration	Wilmington Resident Office	0	0	0	0	0	0	0	0	0	0
Wilmington Fire Department		10	0	0	0	10	3	2	1	0	24
DISTRICT OF COLUMBIA—Other Agencies											
Metro Transit Police		374	0	0	276	98	1,420	2	1,144	274	0
National Zoological Park		0	0	0	0	0	32	5	27	0	0
FLORIDA—State Agencies											
Capitol Police		0	0	0	0	0	26	1	25	0	0
Department of Environmental Protection, Division of Law Enforcement:	Alachua County	0	0	0	0	0	6	0	6	0	0
	Bay County	0	0	0	0	0	0	0	0	0	0
	Brevard County	0	0	0	0	0	5	0	5	0	0
	Broward County	0	0	0	0	0	0	0	0	0	0
	Charlotte County	0	0	0	0	0	0	0	0	0	0

[1] The FBI does not publish arson data unless it receives data from either the agency or the state for all 12 months of the calendar year.

Table 11. Offenses Known to Law Enforcement, by State and Agency, 2008—*Continued*

(Number.)

State/Agency Type	Unit/Office	Violent crime	Murder and non-negligent man-slaughter	Forcible rape	Robbery	Aggra-vated assault	Property crime	Burglary	Larceny-theft	Motor vehicle theft	Arson[1]
	Citrus County	0	0	0	0	0	1	1	0	0	0
	Collier County	0	0	0	0	0	0	0	0	0	0
	Columbia County	0	0	0	0	0	3	3	0	0	0
	DeSoto County	0	0	0	0	0	0	0	0	0	0
	Dixie County	0	0	0	0	0	0	0	0	0	0
	Duval County	0	0	0	0	0	6	2	4	0	0
	Escambia County	0	0	0	0	0	0	0	0	0	0
	Franklin County	0	0	0	0	0	0	0	0	0	0
	Gadsden County	0	0	0	0	0	1	1	0	0	0
	Gilchrist County	0	0	0	0	0	0	0	0	0	0
	Hamilton County	0	0	0	0	0	2	1	1	0	0
	Hillsborough County	0	0	0	0	0	0	0	0	0	0
	Indian River County	0	0	0	0	0	0	0	0	0	0
	Jefferson County	0	0	0	0	0	0	0	0	0	0
	Lake County	0	0	0	0	0	0	0	0	0	0
	Lee County	0	0	0	0	0	0	0	0	0	0
	Leon County	0	0	0	0	0	0	0	0	0	0
	Levy County	0	0	0	0	0	0	0	0	0	0
	Madison County	0	0	0	0	0	0	0	0	0	0
	Manatee County	0	0	0	0	0	0	0	0	0	0
	Marion County	0	0	0	0	0	0	0	0	0	0
	Martin County	0	0	0	0	0	2	2	0	0	0
	Miami-Dade County	0	0	0	0	0	0	0	0	0	0
	Monroe County	0	0	0	0	0	9	2	7	0	0
	Nassau County	0	0	0	0	0	0	0	0	0	0
	Okaloosa County	0	0	0	0	0	2	1	1	0	0
	Okeechobee County	0	0	0	0	0	0	0	0	0	0
	Orange County	0	0	0	0	0	3	3	0	0	0
	Palm Beach County	0	0	0	0	0	0	0	0	0	0
	Pasco County	0	0	0	0	0	0	0	0	0	0
	Pinellas County	0	0	0	0	0	0	0	0	0	0
	Putnam County	0	0	0	0	0	0	0	0	0	0
	Santa Rosa County	0	0	0	0	0	0	0	0	0	0
	Sarasota County	0	0	0	0	0	0	0	0	0	0
	Seminole County	0	0	0	0	0	0	0	0	0	0
	St. Johns County	0	0	0	0	0	5	2	3	0	0
	St. Lucie County	0	0	0	0	0	4	2	2	0	0
	Taylor County	0	0	0	0	0	1	1	0	0	0
	Volusia County	0	0	0	0	0	18	6	12	0	0
	Wakulla County	0	0	0	0	0	0	0	0	0	0
	Walton County	0	0	0	0	0	1	0	1	0	0
Department of Insurance:	Broward County	0	0	0	0	0	0	0	0	0	0
	Duval County	0	0	0	0	0	0	0	0	0	0
	Escambia County	0	0	0	0	0	0	0	0	0	0
	Hillsborough County	0	0	0	0	0	0	0	0	0	0
	Lee County	0	0	0	0	0	0	0	0	0	0
	Miami-Dade County	0	0	0	0	0	0	0	0	0	0
	Orange County	0	0	0	0	0	0	0	0	0	0
	Palm Beach County	0	0	0	0	0	0	0	0	0	0
	Pinellas County	0	0	0	0	0	0	0	0	0	0
Department of Law Enforcement:	Duval County, Jacksonville	0	0	0	0	0	0	0	0	0	0
	Escambia County, Pensacola	0	0	0	0	0	0	0	0	0	0
	Hillsborough County, Tampa	0	0	0	0	0	0	0	0	0	0
	Lee County, Fort Myers	0	0	0	0	0	0	0	0	0	0
	Leon County, Tallahassee	0	0	0	0	0	2	0	2	0	0
	Miami-Dade County, Miami	0	0	0	0	0	2	0	2	0	0
	Orange County, Orlando	0	0	0	0	0	0	0	0	0	0
Florida Game Commission:	Alachua County	0	0	0	0	0	0	0	0	0	0
	Baker County	0	0	0	0	0	0	0	0	0	0
	Bay County	0	0	0	0	0	0	0	0	0	0
	Bradford County	0	0	0	0	0	0	0	0	0	0
	Brevard County	0	0	0	0	0	0	0	0	0	0
	Broward County	0	0	0	0	0	0	0	0	0	0
	Calhoun County	0	0	0	0	0	0	0	0	0	0
	Charlotte County	0	0	0	0	0	0	0	0	0	0
	Citrus County	0	0	0	0	0	0	0	0	0	0
	Clay County	0	0	0	0	0	0	0	0	0	0
	Collier County	0	0	0	0	0	0	0	0	0	0

[1] The FBI does not publish arson data unless it receives data from either the agency or the state for all 12 months of the calendar year.

Table 11. Offenses Known to Law Enforcement, by State and Agency, 2008—*Continued*

(Number.)

State/Agency Type	Unit/Office	Violent crime	Murder and non-negligent man-slaughter	Forcible rape	Robbery	Aggra-vated assault	Property crime	Burglary	Larceny-theft	Motor vehicle theft	Arson[1]
	Columbia County	0	0	0	0	0	0	0	0	0	0
	DeSoto County	0	0	0	0	0	0	0	0	0	0
	Dixie County	0	0	0	0	0	0	0	0	0	0
	Duval County	0	0	0	0	0	0	0	0	0	0
	Escambia County	0	0	0	0	0	0	0	0	0	0
	Flagler County	0	0	0	0	0	0	0	0	0	0
	Franklin County	0	0	0	0	0	0	0	0	0	0
	Gadsden County	0	0	0	0	0	0	0	0	0	0
	Gilchrist County	0	0	0	0	0	0	0	0	0	0
	Glades County	0	0	0	0	0	0	0	0	0	0
	Gulf County	0	0	0	0	0	0	0	0	0	0
	Hamilton County	0	0	0	0	0	0	0	0	0	0
	Hardee County	0	0	0	0	0	0	0	0	0	0
	Hendry County	0	0	0	0	0	0	0	0	0	0
	Hernando County	0	0	0	0	0	0	0	0	0	0
	Highlands County	0	0	0	0	0	0	0	0	0	0
	Hillsborough County	0	0	0	0	0	0	0	0	0	0
	Holmes County	0	0	0	0	0	0	0	0	0	0
	Indian River County	0	0	0	0	0	0	0	0	0	0
	Jackson County	0	0	0	0	0	0	0	0	0	0
	Jefferson County	0	0	0	0	0	0	0	0	0	0
	Lafayette County	0	0	0	0	0	0	0	0	0	0
	Lake County	0	0	0	0	0	0	0	0	0	0
	Lee County	0	0	0	0	0	0	0	0	0	0
	Leon County	0	0	0	0	0	0	0	0	0	0
	Levy County	0	0	0	0	0	0	0	0	0	0
	Liberty County	0	0	0	0	0	0	0	0	0	0
	Madison County	0	0	0	0	0	0	0	0	0	0
	Manatee County	0	0	0	0	0	0	0	0	0	0
	Marion County	0	0	0	0	0	0	0	0	0	0
	Martin County	0	0	0	0	0	0	0	0	0	0
	Miami-Dade County	0	0	0	0	0	0	0	0	0	0
	Monroe County	0	0	0	0	0	0	0	0	0	0
	Nassau County	0	0	0	0	0	0	0	0	0	0
	Okaloosa County	0	0	0	0	0	0	0	0	0	0
	Okeechobee County	0	0	0	0	0	0	0	0	0	0
	Orange County	0	0	0	0	0	0	0	0	0	0
	Osceola County	0	0	0	0	0	0	0	0	0	0
	Palm Beach County	0	0	0	0	0	0	0	0	0	0
	Pasco County	0	0	0	0	0	0	0	0	0	0
	Pinellas County	0	0	0	0	0	0	0	0	0	0
	Polk County	0	0	0	0	0	0	0	0	0	0
	Putnam County	0	0	0	0	0	0	0	0	0	0
	Santa Rosa County	0	0	0	0	0	0	0	0	0	0
	Sarasota County	0	0	0	0	0	0	0	0	0	0
	Seminole County	0	0	0	0	0	0	0	0	0	0
	St. Johns County	0	0	0	0	0	0	0	0	0	0
	St. Lucie County	0	0	0	0	0	0	0	0	0	0
	Suwannee County	0	0	0	0	0	0	0	0	0	0
	Taylor County	0	0	0	0	0	0	0	0	0	0
	Union County	0	0	0	0	0	0	0	0	0	0
	Volusia County	0	0	0	0	0	0	0	0	0	0
	Wakulla County	0	0	0	0	0	0	0	0	0	0
	Walton County	0	0	0	0	0	0	0	0	0	0
	Washington County	0	0	0	0	0	0	0	0	0	0
Highway Patrol:	Alachua County	1	0	0	0	1	0	0	0	0	0
	Baker County	0	0	0	0	0	0	0	0	0	0
	Bay County	0	0	0	0	0	0	0	0	0	0
	Bradford County	0	0	0	0	0	0	0	0	0	0
	Brevard County	0	0	0	0	0	0	0	0	0	0
	Broward County	50	0	0	1	49	116	0	24	92	0
	Calhoun County	0	0	0	0	0	0	0	0	0	0
	Charlotte County	2	0	0	0	2	1	0	0	1	0
	Citrus County	1	0	0	0	1	0	0	0	0	0
	Clay County	0	0	0	0	0	0	0	0	0	0
	Collier County	0	0	0	0	0	0	0	0	0	0
	Columbia County	2	0	0	1	1	1	0	1	0	0
	DeSoto County	0	0	0	0	0	0	0	0	0	0
	Dixie County	0	0	0	0	0	0	0	0	0	0
	Duval County	2	0	0	0	2	3	0	3	0	0
	Escambia County	5	0	0	1	4	1	0	1	0	0
	Flagler County	0	0	0	0	0	0	0	0	0	0
	Franklin County	0	0	0	0	0	0	0	0	0	0
	Gadsden County	4	0	0	1	3	1	0	1	0	0

[1] The FBI does not publish arson data unless it receives data from either the agency or the state for all 12 months of the calendar year.

Table 11. Offenses Known to Law Enforcement, by State and Agency, 2008—*Continued*

(Number.)

State/Agency Type	Unit/Office	Violent crime	Murder and non-negligent man-slaughter	Forcible rape	Robbery	Aggra-vated assault	Property crime	Burglary	Larceny-theft	Motor vehicle theft	Arson[1]
	Gilchrist County	0	0	0	0	0	0	0	0	0	0
	Glades County	0	0	0	0	0	0	0	0	0	0
	Gulf County	0	0	0	0	0	0	0	0	0	0
	Hamilton County	0	0	0	0	0	0	0	0	0	0
	Hardee County	0	0	0	0	0	0	0	0	0	0
	Hendry County	1	0	0	0	1	0	0	0	0	0
	Hernando County	1	0	0	0	1	0	0	0	0	0
	Highlands County	0	0	0	0	0	0	0	0	0	0
	Hillsborough County	16	0	0	1	15	4	0	4	0	0
	Holmes County	0	0	0	0	0	0	0	0	0	0
	Indian River County	0	0	0	0	0	1	0	1	0	0
	Jackson County	0	0	0	0	0	1	0	1	0	0
	Jefferson County	0	0	0	0	0	0	0	0	0	0
	Lafayette County	0	0	0	0	0	0	0	0	0	0
	Lake County	3	0	0	0	3	0	0	0	0	0
	Lee County	2	0	0	1	1	3	0	2	1	0
	Leon County	1	0	0	0	1	3	0	3	0	0
	Levy County	0	0	0	0	0	0	0	0	0	0
	Liberty County	0	0	0	0	0	0	0	0	0	0
	Madison County	0	0	0	0	0	0	0	0	0	0
	Manatee County	1	0	0	0	1	0	0	0	0	0
	Marion County	1	0	0	0	1	1	0	0	1	0
	Martin County	1	0	0	0	1	1	0	0	1	0
	Miami-Dade County	28	0	0	1	27	106	0	30	76	0
	Monroe County	0	0	0	0	0	0	0	0	0	0
	Nassau County	0	0	0	0	0	0	0	0	0	0
	Okaloosa County	2	0	0	0	2	0	0	0	0	0
	Okeechobee County	0	0	0	0	0	1	0	1	0	0
	Orange County	6	0	0	0	6	8	0	6	2	0
	Osceola County	2	0	0	0	2	2	0	2	0	0
	Palm Beach County	28	0	0	2	26	38	0	8	30	0
	Pasco County	3	0	0	0	3	0	0	0	0	0
	Pinellas County	3	0	0	0	3	1	0	1	0	0
	Polk County	0	0	0	0	0	0	0	0	0	0
	Putnam County	1	0	0	0	1	0	0	0	0	0
	Santa Rosa County	0	0	0	0	0	0	0	0	0	0
	Sarasota County	4	0	0	1	3	4	0	4	0	0
	Seminole County	1	0	0	0	1	0	0	0	0	0
	St. Johns County	2	0	0	1	1	3	0	1	2	0
	St. Lucie County	1	0	0	0	1	3	0	3	0	0
	Sumter County	0	0	0	0	0	0	0	0	0	0
	Suwannee County	0	0	0	0	0	1	0	1	0	0
	Taylor County	0	0	0	0	0	0	0	0	0	0
	Union County	0	0	0	0	0	0	0	0	0	0
	Volusia County	7	0	0	0	7	1	0	1	0	0
	Wakulla County	1	0	0	0	1	0	0	0	0	0
	Walton County	0	0	0	0	0	0	0	0	0	0
	Washington County	0	0	0	0	0	0	0	0	0	0
State Treasurer's Office	Division of Insurance Fraud	0	0	0	0	0	0	0	0	0	0
FLORIDA—Other Agencies											
Duval County Schools		104	0	4	24	76	939	211	696	32	3
Florida School for the Deaf and Blind		0	0	0	0	0	2	0	2	0	0
Fort Lauderdale Airport		3	0	0	0	3	336	3	294	39	0
Jacksonville Airport Authority		0	0	0	0	0	110	9	59	42	0
Lee County Port Authority		1	0	0	0	1	182	4	167	11	0
Melbourne International Airport		0	0	0	0	0	3	0	3	0	0
Miami-Dade County Public Schools		452	0	24	209	219	2,482	915	1,544	23	15
Miccosukee Tribal		25	0	2	0	23	113	42	61	10	0
Palm Beach County School District		92	0	2	28	62	825	152	668	5	1
Port Everglades		3	0	0	0	3	39	1	37	1	0
Sarasota-Bradenton International Airport		0	0	0	0	0	15	0	7	8	0
Seminole Tribal		71	0	5	23	43	684	76	545	63	2
St. Petersburg-Clearwater International Airport		0	0	0	0	0	1	0	1	0	0
Tampa International Airport		1	0	0	0	1	212	25	157	30	0
Volusia County Beach Management		17	0	0	11	6	151	0	149	2	0
GEORGIA—State Agencies											
Atlanta State Farmers Market		1	0	0	0	1	55	1	39	15	
Department of Natural Resources	Social Circle	0	0	0	0	0	0	0	0	0	0
Department of Transportation	Office of Investigations	0	0	0	0	0	11	0	11	0	0
Ports Authority	Savannah	0	0	0	0	0	16	1	14	1	0
GEORGIA—Other Agencies											
Bibb County Board of Education		7	0	0	1	6	147	29	114	4	
Chatham County Board of Education		18	0	1	6	11	240	18	215	7	

[1] The FBI does not publish arson data unless it receives data from either the agency or the state for all 12 months of the calendar year.

Table 11. Offenses Known to Law Enforcement, by State and Agency, 2008—*Continued*

(Number.)

State/Agency Type	Unit/Office	Violent crime	Murder and non-negligent man-slaughter	Forcible rape	Robbery	Aggra-vated assault	Property crime	Burglary	Larceny-theft	Motor vehicle theft	Arson[1]
Cherokee County Marshall		0	0	0	0	0	0	0	0	0	0
Cobb County Board of Education		21	0	1	4	16	424	47	373	4	
Fulton County School System		15	0	0	0	15	205	12	188	5	
Gwinnett County Public Schools		6	0	0	1	5	351	29	316	6	7
Hartsfield-Jackson Atlanta International Airport		13	0	0	2	11	307	0	245	62	
Metropolitan Atlanta Rapid Transit Authority		185	0	1	63	121	320	7	260	53	
IDAHO—State Agencies											
Idaho State Police		14	2	1	0	11	13	4	4	5	0
INDIANA—State Agencies											
Northern Indiana Commuter Transportation District		3	0	0	3	0	93	0	87	6	0
State Police:	Adams County	0	0	0	0	0	0	0	0	0	0
	Allen County	0	0	0	0	0	0	0	0	0	0
	Bartholomew County	2	0	0	0	2	5	0	4	1	0
	Benton County	1	0	0	0	1	1	0	1	0	0
	Blackford County	1	0	0	0	1	1	0	1	0	0
	Boone County	0	0	0	0	0	1	1	0	0	0
	Brown County	10	1	0	0	9	38	14	19	5	0
	Carroll County	3	0	1	0	2	10	3	6	1	0
	Cass County	32	0	6	8	18	144	20	112	12	0
	Clark County	2	0	0	0	2	2	0	2	0	0
	Clay County	2	0	0	0	2	10	2	8	0	0
	Clinton County	4	0	0	0	4	38	14	22	2	0
	Crawford County	2	0	0	0	2	18	7	11	0	1
	Daviess County	0	0	0	0	0	0	0	0	0	0
	Dearborn County	0	0	0	0	0	0	0	0	0	0
	Decatur County	3	0	1	0	2	6	1	5	0	1
	De Kalb County	4	0	0	1	3	19	0	18	1	0
	Delaware County	4	0	2	0	2	43	3	39	1	0
	Dubois County	1	1	0	0	0	3	0	3	0	0
	Elkhart County	0	0	0	0	0	0	0	0	0	0
	Fayette County	5	0	1	1	3	62	9	39	14	0
	Floyd County	4	0	1	0	3	12	2	10	0	0
	Fountain County	0	0	0	0	0	0	0	0	0	3
	Franklin County	4	0	0	0	4	19	5	13	1	0
	Fulton County	3	0	0	0	3	40	4	36	0	0
	Gibson County	1	0	1	0	0	11	2	8	1	0
	Grant County	4	0	0	0	4	22	11	9	2	0
	Greene County	5	1	0	2	2	10	0	9	1	0
	Hamilton County	1	0	0	0	1	15	1	9	5	0
	Hancock County	14	0	1	2	11	100	31	66	3	0
	Harrison County	3	0	1	1	1	17	0	13	4	0
	Hendricks County	0	0	0	0	0	1	0	1	0	0
	Henry County	1	0	1	0	0	27	8	18	1	0
	Howard County	1	0	0	0	1	4	0	4	0	0
	Huntington County	11	0	0	0	11	81	22	51	8	0
	Jackson County	2	0	0	0	2	9	1	6	2	0
	Jasper County	1	0	0	0	1	6	2	4	0	1
	Jay County	0	0	0	0	0	0	0	0	0	0
	Jefferson County	7	0	2	0	5	17	4	12	1	1
	Jennings County	0	0	0	0	0	1	0	0	1	0
	Johnson County	6	0	0	0	6	44	8	36	0	0
	Knox County	0	0	0	0	0	3	0	3	0	1
	Kosciusko County	2	0	0	0	2	34	9	24	1	0
	LaGrange County	12	0	3	1	8	86	5	30	51	2
	Lake County	3	0	2	0	1	15	2	8	5	0
	La Porte County	6	0	3	0	3	34	7	25	2	0
	Lawrence County	13	0	1	0	12	21	4	15	2	1
	Madison County	2	0	0	1	1	8	0	6	2	0
	Marion County	0	0	0	0	0	3	0	3	0	0
	Marshall County	1	0	1	0	0	16	5	9	2	0
	Martin County	14	0	2	1	11	52	22	24	6	0
	Miami County	8	0	1	0	7	33	4	28	1	0
	Monroe County	8	0	0	1	7	16	4	12	0	0
	Montgomery County	6	0	0	0	6	38	5	21	12	1
	Morgan County	0	0	0	0	0	7	2	3	2	0
	Newton County	5	1	0	0	4	30	4	24	2	0
	Noble County	0	0	0	0	0	0	0	0	0	1
	Ohio County	10	0	5	0	5	21	5	15	1	0
	Orange County	5	0	2	0	3	5	1	4	0	0
	Owen County	1	0	0	0	1	0	0	0	0	0
	Parke County	5	0	1	0	4	25	8	16	1	0
	Perry County	10	0	4	0	6	7	3	4	0	0
	Pike County	5	0	0	0	5	17	0	9	8	0
	Porter County	8	1	0	3	4	29	3	26	0	0

[1] The FBI does not publish arson data unless it receives data from either the agency or the state for all 12 months of the calendar year.

Table 11. Offenses Known to Law Enforcement, by State and Agency, 2008—*Continued*

(Number.)

State/Agency Type	Unit/Office	Violent crime	Murder and non-negligent man-slaughter	Forcible rape	Robbery	Aggra-vated assault	Property crime	Burglary	Larceny-theft	Motor vehicle theft	Arson[1]
	Posey County	1	0	1	0	0	1	0	1	0	0
	Pulaski County	11	0	3	0	8	22	3	15	4	0
	Putnam County	1	0	0	0	1	2	0	2	0	0
	Randolph County	0	0	0	0	0	0	0	0	0	0
	Ripley County	0	0	0	0	0	0	0	0	0	1
	Rush County	2	1	1	0	0	4	0	4	0	0
	Scott County	0	0	0	0	0	0	0	0	0	0
	Shelby County	7	0	0	0	7	18	3	14	1	0
	Spencer County	1	1	0	0	0	7	2	5	0	0
	Starke County	5	0	0	0	5	10	0	10	0	1
	Steuben County	2	0	0	0	2	1	1	0	0	1
	St. Joseph County	15	0	0	1	14	74	12	51	11	0
	Sullivan County	2	2	0	0	0	0	0	0	0	0
	Switzerland County	14	0	1	0	13	58	4	49	5	0
	Tippecanoe County	2	0	1	0	1	6	2	3	1	0
	Tipton County	0	0	0	0	0	0	0	0	0	0
	Union County	3	0	2	0	1	42	1	41	0	0
	Vanderburgh County	0	0	0	0	0	1	0	1	0	0
	Vermillion County	6	0	0	0	6	7	0	7	0	1
	Vigo County	2	0	1	0	1	7	3	4	0	0
	Wabash County	0	0	0	0	0	3	3	0	0	0
	Warren County	3	0	1	1	1	21	2	19	0	1
	Warrick County	10	0	2	0	8	34	5	27	2	0
	Washington County	1	1	0	0	0	0	0	0	0	0
	Wayne County	2	0	0	0	2	5	2	3	0	0
	Wells County	8	0	3	1	4	37	7	27	3	0
	White County	5	1	0	0	4	15	1	12	2	0
	Whitley County	0	0	0	0	0	0	0	0	0	0
INDIANA—Other Agencies											
St. Joseph County Airport Authority		1	0	0	0	1	20	0	8	12	0
KANSAS—State Agencies											
Kansas Bureau of Investigation		2	0	1	0	1	1	0	1	0	0
Kansas Department of Wildlife and Parks		3	0	0	0	3	48	9	39	0	1
Kansas Highway Patrol		30	1	2	4	23	66	5	47	14	1
Kansas Lottery Security Division		0	0	0	0	0	0	0	0	0	0
KANSAS—Other Agencies											
Blue Valley School District		0	0	0	0	0	29	1	28	0	1
Johnson County Park		3	0	0	0	3	36	7	28	1	2
Metropolitan Topeka Airport Authority		1	0	0	0	1	12	3	9	0	0
Potawatomi Tribal		1	0	0	0	1	33	3	30	0	0
Shawnee Mission Public Schools		0	0	0	0	0	13	1	12	0	0
Unified School District:	Goddard	0	0	0	0	0	35	1	34	0	0
	Topeka	9	0	0	0	9	111	8	101	2	1
Wyandotte County Parks and Recreation		1	0	0	0	1	24	1	22	1	1
KENTUCKY—State Agencies											
Alcohol Beverage Control		0	0	0	0	0	0	0	0	0	
Fish and Wildlife Enforcement		0	0	0	0	0	4	0	4	0	
Kentucky Horse Park		0	0	0	0	0	52	0	52	0	
Motor Vehicle Enforcement		7	0	0	0	7	9	1	7	1	
Park Security		1	0	0	0	1	25	2	22	1	
State Police		1,192	68	398	116	610	7,459	3,195	3,550	714	
Unlawful Narcotics Investigation	Treatment and Education	1	0	0	0	1	4	0	4	0	
KENTUCKY—Other Agencies											
Barren County Drug Task Force		0	0	0	0	0	0	0	0	0	
Buffalo Trace-Gateway Narcotics Task Force		0	0	0	0	0	0	0	0	0	
Central Kentucky Area Drug Task Force		0	0	0	0	0	0	0	0	0	
Cincinnati-Northern Kentucky International Airport		0	0	0	0	0	102	0	78	24	
Clark County School System		0	0	0	0	0	7	0	7	0	
FIVCO Area Drug Task Force		0	0	0	0	0	1	0	1	0	
Greater Hardin County Narcotics Task Force		1	0	0	0	1	0	0	0	0	
Jefferson County Board of Education		39	0	0	2	37	142	86	56	0	
Lake Cumberland Area Drug Enforcement Task Force		0	0	0	0	0	0	0	0	0	
Lexington Bluegrass Airport		0	0	0	0	0	1	0	0	1	
Louisville Regional Airport Authority		0	0	0	0	0	16	0	8	8	
Montgomery County School District		1	0	0	0	1	16	0	16	0	
Northern Kentucky Narcotics Enforcement Unit		0	0	0	0	0	3	0	3	0	
Pennyrile Narcotics Task Force		0	0	0	0	0	1	0	1	0	
LOUISIANA—State Agencies											
Department of Public Safety	State Capitol Detail	10	0	0	1	9	21	4	16	1	0
Tensas Basin Levee District		0	0	0	0	0	9	1	8	0	1

[1] The FBI does not publish arson data unless it receives data from either the agency or the state for all 12 months of the calendar year.

Table 11. Offenses Known to Law Enforcement, by State and Agency, 2008—*Continued*

(Number.)

State/Agency Type	Unit/Office	Violent crime	Murder and non-negligent man-slaughter	Forcible rape	Robbery	Aggra-vated assault	Property crime	Burglary	Larceny-theft	Motor vehicle theft	Arson[1]
MAINE—State Agencies											
Drug Enforcement Agency:	Androscoggin County	0	0	0	0	0	0	0	0	0	0
	Aroostook County	0	0	0	0	0	0	0	0	0	0
	Cumberland County	0	0	0	0	0	0	0	0	0	0
	Franklin County	0	0	0	0	0	0	0	0	0	0
	Hancock County	0	0	0	0	0	0	0	0	0	0
	Kennebec County	0	0	0	0	0	0	0	0	0	0
	Knox County	0	0	0	0	0	0	0	0	0	0
	Lincoln County	0	0	0	0	0	0	0	0	0	0
	Oxford County	0	0	0	0	0	0	0	0	0	0
	Penobscot County	0	0	0	0	0	0	0	0	0	0
	Piscataquis County	0	0	0	0	0	0	0	0	0	0
	Sagadahoc County	0	0	0	0	0	0	0	0	0	0
	Somerset County	0	0	0	0	0	0	0	0	0	0
	Waldo County	0	0	0	0	0	0	0	0	0	0
	Washington County	0	0	0	0	0	0	0	0	0	0
	York County	0	0	0	0	0	0	0	0	0	0
State Police:	Androscoggin County	5	0	0	0	5	120	40	60	20	0
	Aroostook County	9	1	3	2	3	303	96	186	21	0
	Cumberland County	14	2	1	0	11	131	60	59	12	0
	Franklin County	0	0	0	0	0	64	30	31	3	0
	Hancock County	10	0	2	0	8	191	46	138	7	6
	Kennebec County	8	0	4	1	3	376	129	231	16	0
	Knox County	2	2	0	0	0	78	18	53	7	0
	Lincoln County	0	0	0	0	0	16	8	8	0	0
	Oxford County	13	2	1	0	10	220	120	91	9	0
	Penobscot County	6	1	1	1	3	407	116	260	31	3
	Piscataquis County	0	0	0	0	0	8	6	2	0	0
	Sagadahoc County	0	0	0	0	0	6	3	2	1	0
	Somerset County	4	0	1	0	3	219	83	116	20	0
	Waldo County	14	0	0	0	14	172	51	114	7	0
	Washington County	8	3	2	0	3	224	82	137	5	0
	York County	5	0	0	1	4	250	69	165	16	0
MARYLAND—State Agencies											
Comptroller of the Treasury	Field Enforcement Division	0	0	0	0	0	0	0	0	0	0
Department of Public Safety and Correctional Services	Internal Investigations Unit	183	4	0	0	179	0	0	0	0	0
General Services:	Annapolis, Anne Arundel County	0	0	0	0	0	25	1	22	2	0
	Baltimore City	2	0	0	2	0	50	0	50	0	0
Maryland State Police Statewide		6	0	0	1	5	10	0	8	2	0
Natural Resources Police		0	0	0	0	0	304	22	280	2	113
Rosewood		1	0	1	0	0	8	0	7	1	0
Springfield Hospital		0	0	0	0	0	13	1	12	0	0
State Fire Marshal		0	0	0	0	0	0	0	0	0	0
State Police:	Allegany County	37	0	3	3	31	499	115	367	17	10
	Anne Arundel County	8	0	0	0	8	65	1	22	42	0
	Baltimore City	5	0	0	0	5	0	0	0	0	0
	Baltimore County	16	1	2	0	13	103	1	43	59	0
	Calvert County	73	1	1	7	64	379	81	282	16	10
	Caroline County	23	1	4	4	14	147	49	81	17	2
	Carroll County	157	1	1	20	135	1,470	351	1,037	82	3
	Cecil County	136	3	1	12	120	965	316	573	76	46
	Charles County	11	0	0	0	11	58	0	54	4	43
	Dorchester County	20	0	2	5	13	96	40	47	9	4
	Frederick County	69	1	3	10	55	503	76	401	26	18
	Garrett County	42	2	2	4	34	181	69	97	15	5
	Harford County	211	1	3	44	163	640	176	385	79	77
	Howard County	2	0	0	0	2	51	0	29	22	0
	Kent County	16	0	3	2	11	63	29	22	12	7
	Montgomery County	4	0	0	0	4	25	0	11	14	0
	Prince George's County	9	0	0	0	9	129	2	34	93	0
	Queen Anne's County	59	0	5	2	52	192	55	118	19	9
	Somerset County	33	1	2	5	25	226	68	134	24	4
	St. Mary's County	35	0	3	4	28	201	47	135	19	17
	Talbot County	25	1	2	9	13	137	33	86	18	2
	Washington County	50	0	2	9	39	253	50	181	22	23
	Wicomico County	120	1	2	12	105	347	130	178	39	15
	Worcester County	26	1	1	3	21	235	60	157	18	5
Transit Administration		0	0	0	0	0	0	0	0	0	0
Transportation Authority		4	1	0	2	1	235	14	192	29	0

[1] The FBI does not publish arson data unless it receives data from either the agency or the state for all 12 months of the calendar year.

Table 11. Offenses Known to Law Enforcement, by State and Agency, 2008—*Continued*

(Number.)

State/Agency Type	Unit/Office	Violent crime	Murder and non-negligent man-slaughter	Forcible rape	Robbery	Aggra-vated assault	Property crime	Burglary	Larceny-theft	Motor vehicle theft	Arson[1]
MARYLAND—Other Agencies											
Maryland-National Capital Park Police:	Montgomery County	19	0	0	13	6	231	15	207	9	1
	Prince George's County	77	3	3	43	28	275	16	244	15	0
MASSACHUSETTS—State Agencies											
Massachusetts Bay Transportation Authority:	Bristol County	0	0	0	0	0	4	0	4	0	0
	Essex County	0	0	0	0	0	20	0	19	1	0
	Middlesex County	22	0	0	9	13	171	3	161	7	0
	Norfolk County	12	0	0	8	4	96	3	84	9	0
	Plymouth County	0	0	0	0	0	58	1	53	4	0
	Suffolk County	279	1	2	182	94	344	5	333	6	0
	Worcester County	0	0	0	0	0	13	1	12	0	0
State Police:	Barnstable County	5	0	0	0	5	4	1	2	1	0
	Berkshire County	2	1	0	0	1	96	53	38	5	0
	Bristol County	32	0	0	0	32	9	3	3	3	0
	Dukes County	0	0	0	0	0	0	0	0	0	0
	Essex County	2	0	0	2	0	1	0	1	0	
	Franklin County	19	0	2	0	17	5	4	0	1	0
	Hampden County	30	0	1	5	24	34	6	12	16	3
	Hampshire County	5	0	0	0	5	10	2	6	2	0
	Middlesex County	1	0	0	0	1	4	0	4	0	
	Norfolk County	16	0	0	0	16	19	1	11	7	0
	Plymouth County	14	0	1	0	13	3	1	1	1	0
	Worcester County	35	0	0	0	35	16	3	11	2	0
MICHIGAN—State Agencies											
State Police:	Alcona County	3	0	1	0	2	14	5	9	0	0
	Alger County	10	0	5	0	5	75	36	35	4	0
	Allegan County	57	0	18	1	38	392	105	258	29	0
	Alpena County	30	0	8	2	20	184	42	132	10	3
	Antrim County	3	0	3	0	0	23	6	15	2	3
	Arenac County	10	0	8	0	2	20	7	13	0	0
	Baraga County	8	0	2	0	6	50	19	26	5	1
	Barry County	48	0	11	1	36	329	108	203	18	1
	Bay County	75	0	22	7	46	411	121	262	28	1
	Benzie County	4	0	2	0	2	34	9	25	0	0
	Berrien County	60	1	22	5	32	370	125	230	15	4
	Branch County	22	0	9	0	13	185	43	117	25	3
	Calhoun County	37	0	16	0	21	260	94	149	17	3
	Cass County	15	0	8	0	7	112	41	64	7	2
	Charlevoix County	5	0	2	0	3	17	2	11	4	0
	Cheboygan County	18	0	6	0	12	175	84	85	6	1
	Chippewa County	24	0	4	0	20	127	49	69	9	3
	Clare County	11	0	7	1	3	83	35	41	7	0
	Clinton County	6	1	4	0	1	31	14	15	2	0
	Crawford County	10	0	9	0	1	25	6	18	1	1
	Delta County	17	0	10	0	7	86	38	48	0	2
	Dickinson County	11	0	10	0	1	45	13	32	0	1
	Eaton County	16	0	8	1	7	94	29	61	4	1
	Emmet County	10	0	3	0	7	162	48	109	5	1
	Genesee County	57	1	10	6	40	208	61	111	36	2
	Gladwin County	15	0	10	0	5	65	15	46	4	1
	Gogebic County	7	0	2	1	4	33	7	22	4	0
	Grand Traverse County	20	0	7	1	12	205	33	162	10	0
	Gratiot County	22	0	9	2	11	127	29	88	10	1
	Hillsdale County	24	0	11	0	13	201	86	105	10	3
	Houghton County	14	0	7	0	7	125	30	87	8	4
	Huron County	8	0	1	0	7	101	43	54	4	0
	Ingham County	15	0	7	1	7	112	22	85	5	0
	Ionia County	38	0	7	1	30	308	66	209	33	4
	Iosco County	32	1	10	2	19	242	100	129	13	4
	Iron County	10	0	2	0	8	53	16	36	1	2
	Isabella County	34	0	12	1	21	204	63	130	11	1
	Jackson County	65	1	21	5	38	335	102	205	28	7
	Kalamazoo County	8	0	3	0	5	18	4	13	1	0
	Kalkaska County	17	0	10	0	7	88	34	50	4	1
	Kent County	20	0	5	1	14	55	4	46	5	0
	Lake County	17	1	7	0	9	70	40	28	2	3
	Lapeer County	49	0	36	0	13	98	42	46	10	2
	Leelanau County	1	0	1	0	0	9	0	9	0	0
	Lenawee County	49	0	2	0	47	201	70	114	17	2
	Livingston County	36	0	21	2	13	442	97	314	31	3
	Luce County	28	0	8	1	19	84	40	41	3	0
	Mackinac County	12	0	2	0	10	99	41	51	7	3
	Macomb County	13	1	5	0	7	39	6	29	4	0
	Manistee County	14	0	5	0	9	207	66	127	14	3

[1] The FBI does not publish arson data unless it receives data from either the agency or the state for all 12 months of the calendar year.

Table 11. Offenses Known to Law Enforcement, by State and Agency, 2008—*Continued*

(Number.)

State/Agency Type	Unit/Office	Violent crime	Murder and non-negligent man-slaughter	Forcible rape	Robbery	Aggra-vated assault	Property crime	Burglary	Larceny-theft	Motor vehicle theft	Arson[1]
	Marquette County	39	0	16	1	22	383	146	218	19	4
	Mason County	14	0	11	0	3	69	20	46	3	0
	Mecosta County	12	0	3	0	9	136	43	85	8	0
	Menominee County	10	1	5	0	4	94	41	51	2	0
	Midland County	6	0	4	0	2	66	16	43	7	0
	Missaukee County	11	1	4	0	6	31	7	19	5	2
	Monroe County	38	0	14	6	18	179	56	104	19	3
	Montcalm County	42	1	18	1	22	301	105	184	12	3
	Montmorency County	6	1	2	0	3	37	17	17	3	1
	Muskegon County	37	1	16	1	19	351	77	256	18	2
	Newaygo County	29	0	14	0	15	376	103	238	35	4
	Oakland County	62	1	7	5	49	328	124	168	36	3
	Oceana County	13	0	7	1	5	125	29	89	7	2
	Ogemaw County	36	0	14	1	21	185	69	105	11	2
	Ontonagon County	2	0	1	0	1	18	5	13	0	0
	Osceola County	13	0	5	2	6	170	58	107	5	3
	Oscoda County	3	0	3	0	0	26	13	12	1	0
	Otsego County	37	0	12	2	23	251	93	141	17	2
	Ottawa County	2	0	0	0	2	51	10	38	3	0
	Presque Isle County	4	0	1	0	3	17	10	7	0	1
	Roscommon County	15	0	7	0	8	131	29	88	14	0
	Saginaw County	49	0	20	3	26	269	84	165	20	8
	Sanilac County	41	0	25	1	15	179	75	89	15	3
	Schoolcraft County	10	1	6	0	3	74	39	31	4	0
	Shiawassee County	33	0	23	1	9	132	44	81	7	0
	St. Clair County	39	1	5	1	32	317	95	191	31	4
	St. Joseph County	32	1	7	2	22	251	87	148	16	3
	Tuscola County	31	1	12	0	18	173	71	86	16	3
	Van Buren County	62	2	15	3	42	547	198	301	48	5
	Washtenaw County	57	1	7	5	44	231	111	104	16	3
	Wayne County	44	0	9	3	32	117	11	77	29	0
	Wexford County	18	1	8	0	9	140	34	99	7	1
MICHIGAN—Other Agencies											
Huron-Clinton Metropolitan Authority	Hudson Mills Metropark	0	0	0	0	0	2	0	2	0	0
	Stony Creek Metropark	2	0	0	0	2	39	3	35	1	0
Wayne County Airport		14	0	0	1	13	339	2	243	94	0
MINNESOTA—State Agencies[3]											
Capitol Security	St. Paul		0		0	0	32	0	32	0	0
Minnesota State Patrol			0		0	0	0	0	0	0	0
State Patrol:	Brainerd		0		0	0	0	0	0	0	0
	Detroit Lakes		0		0	0	0	0	0	0	0
	Duluth		0		0	0	0	0	0	0	0
	Golden Valley		0		0	0	0	0	0	0	0
	Mankato		0		0	0	0	0	0	0	0
	Marshall		0		0	0	0	0	0	0	0
	Oakdale		0		0	0	0	0	0	0	0
	Rochester		0		0	0	0	0	0	0	0
	St. Cloud		0		0	0	0	0	0	0	0
	Thief River Falls		0		0	0	0	0	0	0	0
	Virginia		0		0	0	0	0	0	0	0
MINNESOTA—Other Agencies[3]											
Minneapolis-St. Paul International Airport			0		0	0	0	0	0	0	0
MISSOURI—State Agencies											
Capitol Police		0	0	0	0	0	46	0	46	0	0
Department of Conservation		0	0	0	0	0	0	0	0	0	0
Division of Alcohol and Tobacco Control		0	0	0	0	0	0	0	0	0	0
Gaming Commission	Enforcement Division	6	0	0	0	6	276	0	276	0	0
State Highway Patrol:	Jefferson City	6	1	1	1	3	11	3	3	5	0
	Kirkwood	8	1	2	0	5	19	0	14	5	0
	Lee's Summit	10	2	0	0	8	28	6	12	10	0
	Macon	6	1	1	0	4	10	5	3	2	0
	Poplar Bluff	11	0	0	1	10	10	1	5	4	0
	Rolla	5	1	0	0	4	6	1	3	2	0
	Springfield	4	0	0	0	4	8	0	4	4	0
	St. Joseph	25	0	0	2	23	33	8	19	6	0
	Willow Springs	6	0	0	2	4	5	0	3	2	0
State Fire Marshal		0	0	0	0	0	0	0	0	0	293
State Park Rangers		0	0	0	0	0	80	11	68	1	0
State Water Patrol		4	0	2	0	2	169	0	168	1	0
MISSOURI—Other Agencies											
Bootheel Drug Task Force		0	0	0	0	0	0	0	0	0	0
Clay County Drug Task Force		0	0	0	0	0	0	0	0	0	0
Clay County Park Authority		2	0	1	0	1	25	4	19	2	0

[1] The FBI does not publish arson data unless it receives data from either the agency or the state for all 12 months of the calendar year.

[3] The data collection methodology for the offense of forcible rape used by the Minnesota state UCR Program does not comply with national UCR Program guidelines. Consequently, its figures for forcible rape and violent crime (of which forcible rape is a part) are not published in this table.

Table 11. Offenses Known to Law Enforcement, by State and Agency, 2008—*Continued*

(Number.)

State/Agency Type	Unit/Office	Violent crime	Murder and non-negligent man-slaughter	Forcible rape	Robbery	Aggra-vated assault	Property crime	Burglary	Larceny-theft	Motor vehicle theft	Arson[1]
Jackson County Drug Task Force		0	0	0	0	0	0	0	0	0	0
Jackson County Park Rangers		0	0	0	0	0	0	0	0	0	0
Lambert-St. Louis International Airport		18	0	0	0	18	256	0	256	0	0
Platte County Multi-Jurisdictional Enforcement Group		0	0	0	0	0	0	0	0	0	0
Springfield-Branson Airport		0	0	0	0	0	16	0	15	1	0
St. Charles County Park Rangers		0	0	0	0	0	1	0	1	0	0
St. Peters Ranger Division		2	0	0	0	2	48	1	46	1	0
NEBRASKA—State Agencies											
Nebraska State Patrol		8	0	1	0	7	1	1	0	0	0
State Patrol:	Adams County	0	0	0	0	0	0	0	0	0	0
	Antelope County	0	0	0	0	0	0	0	0	0	0
	Arthur County	0	0	0	0	0	0	0	0	0	0
	Banner County	0	0	0	0	0	1	0	1	0	0
	Blaine County	0	0	0	0	0	0	0	0	0	0
	Boone County	0	0	0	0	0	0	0	0	0	0
	Box Butte County	0	0	0	0	0	0	0	0	0	0
	Boyd County	0	0	0	0	0	0	0	0	0	0
	Brown County	0	0	0	0	0	0	0	0	0	0
	Buffalo County	1	0	0	0	1	0	0	0	0	0
	Burt County	0	0	0	0	0	0	0	0	0	0
	Butler County	1	0	0	0	1	0	0	0	0	0
	Cass County	0	0	0	0	0	0	0	0	0	0
	Cedar County	1	0	0	0	1	0	0	0	0	0
	Chase County	0	0	0	0	0	0	0	0	0	0
	Cherry County	0	0	0	0	0	0	0	0	0	0
	Cheyenne County	0	0	0	0	0	0	0	0	0	0
	Clay County	0	0	0	0	0	1	0	1	0	0
	Colfax County	0	0	0	0	0	0	0	0	0	0
	Cuming County	0	0	0	0	0	0	0	0	0	0
	Custer County	1	0	0	0	1	0	0	0	0	0
	Dakota County	0	0	0	0	0	1	0	1	0	0
	Dawes County	0	0	0	0	0	0	0	0	0	0
	Dawson County	0	0	0	0	0	1	0	0	1	0
	Deuel County	0	0	0	0	0	0	0	0	0	0
	Dixon County	0	0	0	0	0	0	0	0	0	0
	Dodge County	0	0	0	0	0	0	0	0	0	0
	Douglas County	0	0	0	0	0	1	0	1	0	0
	Dundy County	0	0	0	0	0	0	0	0	0	0
	Fillmore County	0	0	0	0	0	0	0	0	0	0
	Franklin County	0	0	0	0	0	1	0	1	0	0
	Frontier County	0	0	0	0	0	0	0	0	0	0
	Furnas County	0	0	0	0	0	0	0	0	0	0
	Gage County	0	0	0	0	0	0	0	0	0	0
	Garden County	1	0	0	0	1	0	0	0	0	0
	Garfield County	0	0	0	0	0	0	0	0	0	0
	Gosper County	0	0	0	0	0	0	0	0	0	0
	Grant County	0	0	0	0	0	0	0	0	0	0
	Greeley County	0	0	0	0	0	0	0	0	0	0
	Hall County	2	0	0	0	2	2	2	0	0	0
	Hamilton County	0	0	0	0	0	0	0	0	0	0
	Harlan County	0	0	0	0	0	0	0	0	0	0
	Hayes County	0	0	0	0	0	0	0	0	0	0
	Hitchcock County	0	0	0	0	0	0	0	0	0	0
	Holt County	0	0	0	0	0	0	0	0	0	0
	Hooker County	0	0	0	0	0	0	0	0	0	0
	Howard County	0	0	0	0	0	1	1	0	0	0
	Jefferson County	0	0	0	0	0	0	0	0	0	0
	Johnson County	0	0	0	0	0	0	0	0	0	0
	Kearney County	0	0	0	0	0	0	0	0	0	0
	Keith County	0	0	0	0	0	0	0	0	0	0
	Keya Paha County	0	0	0	0	0	0	0	0	0	0
	Kimball County	0	0	0	0	0	0	0	0	0	0
	Knox County	0	0	0	0	0	0	0	0	0	0
	Lancaster County	0	0	0	0	0	6	0	6	0	0
	Lincoln County	0	0	0	0	0	1	0	0	1	0
	Logan County	1	0	0	1	0	0	0	0	0	0
	Loup County	0	0	0	0	0	0	0	0	0	0
	Madison County	1	0	0	0	1	3	1	2	0	0
	McPherson County	0	0	0	0	0	0	0	0	0	0
	Merrick County	0	0	0	0	0	1	1	0	0	0
	Morrill County	0	0	0	0	0	0	0	0	0	0
	Nance County	0	0	0	0	0	0	0	0	0	0
	Nemaha County	0	0	0	0	0	0	0	0	0	0

[1] The FBI does not publish arson data unless it receives data from either the agency or the state for all 12 months of the calendar year.

Table 11. Offenses Known to Law Enforcement, by State and Agency, 2008—*Continued*

(Number.)

State/Agency Type	Unit/Office	Violent crime	Murder and non-negligent man-slaughter	Forcible rape	Robbery	Aggra-vated assault	Property crime	Burglary	Larceny-theft	Motor vehicle theft	Arson[1]
	Nuckolls County	1	0	1	0	0	0	0	0	0	0
	Otoe County	0	0	0	0	0	1	0	0	1	0
	Pawnee County	0	0	0	0	0	1	0	0	1	0
	Perkins County	0	0	0	0	0	0	0	0	0	0
	Phelps County	0	0	0	0	0	0	0	0	0	0
	Pierce County	0	0	0	0	0	0	0	0	0	0
	Platte County	0	0	0	0	0	0	0	0	0	0
	Polk County	0	0	0	0	0	0	0	0	0	0
	Red Willow County	0	0	0	0	0	0	0	0	0	0
	Richardson County	0	0	0	0	0	1	0	1	0	0
	Rock County	0	0	0	0	0	1	1	0	0	0
	Saline County	0	0	0	0	0	0	0	0	0	0
	Sarpy County	1	0	0	0	1	0	0	0	0	0
	Saunders County	0	0	0	0	0	0	0	0	0	0
	Scotts Bluff County	0	0	0	0	0	0	0	0	0	0
	Seward County	1	0	0	0	1	0	0	0	0	0
	Sheridan County	1	0	0	0	1	0	0	0	0	0
	Sherman County	0	0	0	0	0	0	0	0	0	0
	Sioux County	1	0	0	0	1	0	0	0	0	0
	Stanton County	1	0	0	0	1	0	0	0	0	0
	Thayer County	0	0	0	0	0	0	0	0	0	0
	Thomas County	0	0	0	0	0	0	0	0	0	0
	Thurston County	0	0	0	0	0	0	0	0	0	0
	Valley County	0	0	0	0	0	0	0	0	0	0
	Washington County	0	0	0	0	0	0	0	0	0	0
	Wayne County	0	0	0	0	0	0	0	0	0	0
	Webster County	0	0	0	0	0	0	0	0	0	0
	Wheeler County	0	0	0	0	0	0	0	0	0	0
	York County	0	0	0	0	0	0	0	0	0	0
NEVADA—State Agencies											
Taxicab Authority		98	0	0	6	92	296	1	294	1	0
NEVADA—Other Agencies											
Clark County School District		99	0	3	34	62	1,053	174	845	34	48
Washoe County School District		16	0	0	0	16	258	47	209	2	16
NEW HAMPSHIRE—State Agencies											
Liquor Commission		4	1	0	1	2	4	0	4	0	0
NEW JERSEY—State Agencies											
Department of Human Services		56	0	6	1	49	125	0	125	0	0
New Jersey Transit Police		93	1	0	49	43	340	6	330	4	1
Palisades Interstate Parkway		4	0	0	0	4	0	0	0	0	0
Port Authority of New York and New Jersey[4]		43	0	0	10	33		6		28	0
State Police:	Atlantic County	54	0	1	17	36	1,073	119	932	22	4
	Bergen County	6	0	0	1	5	106	2	91	13	2
	Burlington County	51	1	3	14	33	584	152	397	35	0
	Cape May County	45	0	4	8	33	437	103	312	22	3
	Cumberland County	117	3	0	16	98	930	278	588	64	17
	Hudson County	4	0	0	1	3	25	0	25	0	0
	Hunterdon County	20	0	2	0	18	216	54	155	7	3
	Mercer County	6	0	0	2	4	136	14	119	3	1
	Monmouth County	25	0	0	1	24	242	66	167	9	2
	Morris County	11	0	0	1	10	25	7	12	6	0
	Ocean County	9	0	0	0	9	105	14	90	1	1
	Salem County	45	1	0	11	33	471	126	303	42	6
	Sussex County	32	0	1	2	29	487	105	359	23	0
	Union County	5	0	0	3	2	29	1	23	5	0
	Warren County	15	0	0	1	14	240	45	175	20	3
NEW JERSEY—Other Agencies											
Park Police:	Camden County	11	0	0	2	9	22	6	16	0	2
NEW MEXICO—Other Agencies											
Acoma Tribal		17	0	0	0	17	20	7	12	1	0
Laguna Tribal		98	0	15	0	83	76	14	57	5	1
NEW YORK—State Agencies											
State Park:	Long Island Region	12	1	0	3	8	152	7	140	5	0
	New York City Region	10	0	0	6	4	122	1	120	1	0
	Saratoga/Capital Region	4	0	0	1	3	29	3	26	0	0
	Taconic Region	1	0	0	0	1	23	6	17	0	0
State Police:	Albany County	18	0	4	1	13	221	18	199	4	
	Allegany County	48	0	9	4	35	249	109	133	7	
	Broome County	72	0	42	6	24	672	152	498	22	
	Cattaraugus County	48	0	7	5	36	219	74	131	14	0
	Cayuga County	18	0	1	2	15	268	64	203	1	
	Chautauqua County	21	0	4	0	17	116	37	74	5	0
	Chemung County	69	0	10	1	58	386	58	323	5	

[1] The FBI does not publish arson data unless it receives data from either the agency or the state for all 12 months of the calendar year.

[4] The FBI determined that the agency's data were underreported. Consequently, those data are not included in this table.

Table 11. Offenses Known to Law Enforcement, by State and Agency, 2008—*Continued*

(Number.)

State/Agency Type	Unit/Office	Violent crime	Murder and non-negligent man-slaughter	Forcible rape	Robbery	Aggra-vated assault	Property crime	Burglary	Larceny-theft	Motor vehicle theft	Arson[1]
	Chenango County	21	1	11	1	8	152	60	90	2	2
	Clinton County	106	1	22	3	80	845	209	615	21	
	Columbia County	56	0	2	2	52	444	121	315	8	1
	Cortland County	26	0	1	0	25	199	32	160	7	2
	Delaware County	36	0	2	3	31	247	104	136	7	
	Dutchess County	126	0	15	14	97	813	183	602	28	1
	Erie County	42	0	6	2	34	544	128	410	6	1
	Essex County	38	0	6	1	31	271	78	191	2	
	Franklin County	60	0	17	1	42	368	153	203	12	
	Fulton County	24	0	5	1	18	110	20	87	3	0
	Genesee County	25	1	4	3	17	109	15	88	6	1
	Greene County	66	1	2	2	61	853	151	680	22	
	Hamilton County	5	0	2	0	3	27	7	20	0	
	Herkimer County	36	0	4	3	29	234	93	136	5	
	Jefferson County	70	0	2	4	64	614	173	429	12	
	Lewis County	18	0	4	0	14	57	23	31	3	
	Livingston County	18	0	2	0	16	71	11	57	3	0
	Madison County	15	0	3	0	12	257	86	163	8	
	Monroe County	28	0	9	2	17	53	3	50	0	0
	Montgomery County	8	0	0	1	7	94	31	60	3	0
	Nassau County	10	2	0	1	7	24	0	22	2	1
	New York County	0	0	0	0	0	49	1	48	0	0
	Niagara County	15	0	1	4	10	264	37	223	4	
	Oneida County	76	1	13	6	56	685	181	485	19	
	Onondaga County	22	2	3	2	15	677	122	539	16	
	Ontario County	18	0	7	2	9	223	32	189	2	
	Orange County	129	1	22	16	90	846	93	722	31	
	Orleans County	2	0	0	1	1	71	15	50	6	0
	Oswego County	57	2	12	3	40	809	256	533	20	
	Otsego County	23	0	2	1	20	370	101	263	6	
	Putnam County	28	0	4	1	23	154	29	116	9	
	Rensselaer County	54	0	4	4	46	521	120	391	10	0
	Rockland County	18	0	2	0	16	13	0	13	0	
	Saratoga County	64	0	11	3	50	610	114	480	16	
	Schenectady County	12	0	0	1	11	99	13	78	8	1
	Schoharie County	16	0	2	0	14	185	61	114	10	
	Schuyler County	5	0	2	0	3	24	6	16	2	
	Seneca County	20	0	5	2	13	133	38	91	4	
	Steuben County	64	0	19	2	43	424	129	277	18	14
	St. Lawrence County	111	0	10	1	100	527	174	333	20	
	Suffolk County	17	0	2	1	14	38	6	28	4	
	Sullivan County	96	2	16	2	76	474	181	275	18	
	Tioga County	10	0	4	0	6	139	34	100	5	0
	Tompkins County	30	1	3	1	25	214	49	158	7	3
	Ulster County	185	5	26	2	152	401	148	229	24	
	Warren County	42	0	13	0	29	225	26	197	2	1
	Washington County	58	0	5	0	53	203	55	142	6	
	Wayne County	56	1	12	6	37	396	108	276	12	4
	Westchester County	67	2	3	7	55	675	100	567	8	
	Wyoming County	19	0	1	1	17	47	12	35	0	0
	Yates County	4	0	0	0	4	15	6	8	1	0
NEW YORK—Other Agencies											
Board of Water:	Delaware County	0	0	0	0	0	0	0	0	0	0
	Sullivan County	0	0	0	0	0	2	2	0	0	0
	Ulster County	2	0	0	0	2	5	0	5	0	0
	Westchester County	0	0	0	0	0	19	1	18	0	0
Broome County Special Investigations Task Force		0	0	0	0	0	1	0	1	0	0
CSX Transportation:	Albany County	0	0	0	0	0	5	0	5	0	0
	Bronx County	0	0	0	0	0	156	0	156	0	0
	Cattaraugus County	0	0	0	0	0	0	0	0	0	0
	Cayuga County	0	0	0	0	0	0	0	0	0	0
	Chautauqua County	0	0	0	0	0	2	0	2	0	0
	Columbia County	0	0	0	0	0	2	0	2	0	0
	Dutchess County	0	0	0	0	0	0	0	0	0	0
	Erie County	0	0	0	0	0	15	4	11	0	0
	Genesee County	0	0	0	0	0	1	0	1	0	0
	Greene County	0	0	0	0	0	0	0	0	0	0
	Herkimer County	0	0	0	0	0	2	0	2	0	0
	Jefferson County	0	0	0	0	0	1	0	1	0	0
	Madison County	0	0	0	0	0	5	0	5	0	0
	Monroe County	0	0	0	0	0	12	2	10	0	0
	Montgomery County	0	0	0	0	0	2	1	1	0	0
	Niagara County	0	0	0	0	0	4	0	4	0	0
	Oneida County	0	0	0	0	0	4	0	4	0	

[1] The FBI does not publish arson data unless it receives data from either the agency or the state for all 12 months of the calendar year.

Table 11. Offenses Known to Law Enforcement, by State and Agency, 2008—*Continued*

(Number.)

State/Agency Type	Unit/Office	Violent crime	Murder and non-negligent man-slaughter	Forcible rape	Robbery	Aggra-vated assault	Property crime	Burglary	Larceny-theft	Motor vehicle theft	Arson[1]
	Onondaga County	0	0	0	0	0	3	0	3	0	0
	Ontario County	0	0	0	0	0	0	0	0	0	0
	Orange County	0	0	0	0	0	2	0	2	0	0
	Orleans County	0	0	0	0	0	0	0	0	0	0
	Queens County	0	0	0	0	0	0	0	0	0	0
	Rensselaer County	0	0	0	0	0	0	0	0	0	0
	Rockland County	0	0	0	0	0	1	0	1	0	0
	Schenectady County	0	0	0	0	0	0	0	0	0	0
	Seneca County	0	0	0	0	0	0	0	0	0	0
	St. Lawrence County	0	0	0	0	0	0	0	0	0	0
	Ulster County	0	0	0	0	0	1	0	1	0	0
	Wayne County	0	0	0	0	0	4	0	4	0	0
	Westchester County	0	0	0	0	0	1	0	1	0	0
New York City Metropolitan Transportation Authority		108	0	2	64	42	581	23	552	6	2
Onondaga County Parks		1	0	0	0	1	36	9	26	1	0
Suffolk County Parks		1	0	0	1	0	50	3	47	0	0
NORTH CAROLINA—State Agencies											
North Carolina Highway Patrol		0	0	0	0	0	0	0	0	0	0
State Capitol Police		9	0	0	1	8	30	3	27	0	0
State Park Rangers:	Crowders Mountain	0	0	0	0	0	3	0	3	0	0
	Dismal Swamp	0	0	0	0	0	0	0	0	0	0
	Elk Knob	0	0	0	0	0	0	0	0	0	0
	Lake Norman	0	0	0	0	0	1	0	1	0	0
	Merchants Millpond	0	0	0	0	0	0	0	0	0	0
NORTH CAROLINA—Other Agencies											
Raleigh-Durham International Airport		1	0	1	0	0	89	8	71	10	0
OHIO—State Agencies											
Ohio Department of Natural Resources		0	0	0	0	0	40	5	31	4	0
Ohio State Highway Patrol		332	3	19	6	304	442	29	342	71	9
OHIO—Other Agencies											
Cleveland Metropolitan Park District		14	0	0	8	6	116	3	111	2	7
Hamilton County Park District		2	0	1	0	1	27	0	27	0	0
Lake Metroparks		1	0	0	0	1	23	0	23	0	0
Lorain County Metropolitan Park District		0	0	0	0	0	0	0	0	0	0
Port Columbus International Airport		2	0	0	0	2	145	5	130	10	0
OKLAHOMA—State Agencies											
Capitol Park Police		1	0	0	1	0	14	1	10	3	0
OKLAHOMA—Other Agencies											
Jenks Public Schools		2	0	0	0	2	27	2	25	0	0
Madill Public Schools		0	0	0	0	0	1	0	1	0	0
McAlester Public Schools		1	0	0	0	1	1	0	1	0	0
Norman Public Schools		0	0	0	0	0	29	6	23	0	0
Putnam City Campus		2	0	0	0	2	142	6	136	0	1
OREGON—Other Agencies											
Port of Portland		2	0	0	2	0	420	11	371	38	0
Siletz Tribal		1	0	0	1	0	43	17	24	2	0
PENNSYLVANIA—State Agencies											
Bureau of Narcotics:	Allegheny County	0	0	0	0	0	0	0	0	0	0
	Bedford County	0	0	0	0	0	0	0	0	0	0
	Blair County	0	0	0	0	0	0	0	0	0	0
	Cambria County	0	0	0	0	0	0	0	0	0	0
	Cameron County	0	0	0	0	0	0	0	0	0	0
	Centre County	0	0	0	0	0	0	0	0	0	0
	Chester County	0	0	0	0	0	0	0	0	0	0
	Clearfield County	0	0	0	0	0	0	0	0	0	0
	Clinton County	0	0	0	0	0	0	0	0	0	0
	Crawford County	0	0	0	0	0	0	0	0	0	0
	Delaware County	0	0	0	0	0	0	0	0	0	0
	Elk County	0	0	0	0	0	0	0	0	0	0
	Erie County	0	0	0	0	0	0	0	0	0	0
	Fayette County	0	0	0	0	0	0	0	0	0	0
	Forest County	0	0	0	0	0	0	0	0	0	0
	Greene County	0	0	0	0	0	0	0	0	0	0
	Huntingdon County	0	0	0	0	0	0	0	0	0	0
	Juniata County	0	0	0	0	0	0	0	0	0	0
	Lycoming County	0	0	0	0	0	0	0	0	0	0
	McKean County	0	0	0	0	0	0	0	0	0	0
	Mifflin County	0	0	0	0	0	0	0	0	0	0
	Montour County	0	0	0	0	0	0	0	0	0	0
	Northumberland County	0	0	0	0	0	0	0	0	0	0
	Philadelphia County	0	0	0	0	0	0	0	0	0	0
	Potter County	0	0	0	0	0	0	0	0	0	0
	Snyder County	0	0	0	0	0	0	0	0	0	0

[1] The FBI does not publish arson data unless it receives data from either the agency or the state for all 12 months of the calendar year.

Table 11. Offenses Known to Law Enforcement, by State and Agency, 2008—*Continued*

(Number.)

State/Agency Type	Unit/Office	Violent crime	Murder and non-negligent man-slaughter	Forcible rape	Robbery	Aggra-vated assault	Property crime	Burglary	Larceny-theft	Motor vehicle theft	Arson[1]
	Somerset County	0	0	0	0	0	0	0	0	0	0
	Tioga County	0	0	0	0	0	0	0	0	0	0
	Union County	0	0	0	0	0	0	0	0	0	0
	Venango County	0	0	0	0	0	0	0	0	0	0
	Warren County	0	0	0	0	0	0	0	0	0	0
	Washington County	0	0	0	0	0	0	0	0	0	0
	Westmoreland County	0	0	0	0	0	0	0	0	0	0
Department of Environmental Resources		0	0	0	0	0	7	0	7	0	0
State Capitol Police		3	0	0	2	1	51	2	48	1	1
State Park Police	Pymatuning	0	0	0	0	0	27	0	27	0	0
State Police, Bureau of Criminal Investigation:	Adams County	0	0	0	0	0	0	0	0	0	0
	Allegheny County	0	0	0	0	0	5	0	1	4	0
	Armstrong County	0	0	0	0	0	0	0	0	0	0
	Beaver County	0	0	0	0	0	0	0	0	0	0
	Bedford County	0	0	0	0	0	0	0	0	0	0
	Berks County	0	0	0	0	0	0	0	0	0	0
	Blair County	0	0	0	0	0	0	0	0	0	0
	Bradford County	0	0	0	0	0	0	0	0	0	0
	Bucks County	0	0	0	0	0	0	0	0	0	0
	Butler County	0	0	0	0	0	0	0	0	0	0
	Cambria County	0	0	0	0	0	0	0	0	0	0
	Cameron County	0	0	0	0	0	0	0	0	0	0
	Carbon County	0	0	0	0	0	0	0	0	0	0
	Centre County	0	0	0	0	0	0	0	0	0	0
	Chester County	0	0	0	0	0	5	0	5	0	0
	Clarion County	0	0	0	0	0	0	0	0	0	0
	Clearfield County	0	0	0	0	0	1	0	1	0	0
	Clinton County	0	0	0	0	0	0	0	0	0	0
	Columbia County	0	0	0	0	0	0	0	0	0	0
	Crawford County	0	0	0	0	0	0	0	0	0	0
	Cumberland County	0	0	0	0	0	0	0	0	0	0
	Dauphin County	0	0	0	0	0	2	0	2	0	0
	Delaware County	0	0	0	0	0	1	0	1	0	0
	Elk County	0	0	0	0	0	0	0	0	0	0
	Erie County	0	0	0	0	0	0	0	0	0	0
	Fayette County	0	0	0	0	0	2	0	1	1	0
	Forest County	0	0	0	0	0	0	0	0	0	0
	Franklin County	0	0	0	0	0	0	0	0	0	0
	Fulton County	0	0	0	0	0	0	0	0	0	0
	Greene County	0	0	0	0	0	0	0	0	0	0
	Huntingdon County	0	0	0	0	0	0	0	0	0	0
	Indiana County	0	0	0	0	0	0	0	0	0	0
	Jefferson County	0	0	0	0	0	0	0	0	0	0
	Juniata County	0	0	0	0	0	0	0	0	0	0
	Lackawanna County	0	0	0	0	0	0	0	0	0	0
	Lancaster County	0	0	0	0	0	0	0	0	0	0
	Lawrence County	0	0	0	0	0	0	0	0	0	0
	Lebanon County	0	0	0	0	0	2	0	1	1	0
	Lehigh County	0	0	0	0	0	0	0	0	0	0
	Luzerne County	0	0	0	0	0	0	0	0	0	0
	Lycoming County	0	0	0	0	0	0	0	0	0	0
	McKean County	0	0	0	0	0	0	0	0	0	0
	Mercer County	0	0	0	0	0	1	0	0	1	0
	Mifflin County	0	0	0	0	0	0	0	0	0	0
	Monroe County	0	0	0	0	0	0	0	0	0	0
	Montgomery County	0	0	0	0	0	0	0	0	0	0
	Montour County	0	0	0	0	0	0	0	0	0	0
	Northampton County	0	0	0	0	0	0	0	0	0	0
	Northumberland County	0	0	0	0	0	0	0	0	0	0
	Perry County	0	0	0	0	0	0	0	0	0	0
	Philadelphia County	1	0	0	0	1	0	0	0	0	0
	Pike County	0	0	0	0	0	0	0	0	0	0
	Potter County	0	0	0	0	0	0	0	0	0	0
	Schuylkill County	2	0	0	2	0	0	0	0	0	0
	Snyder County	0	0	0	0	0	0	0	0	0	0
	Somerset County	0	0	0	0	0	0	0	0	0	0
	Sullivan County	0	0	0	0	0	0	0	0	0	0
	Susquehanna County	0	0	0	0	0	1	0	1	0	0
	Tioga County	0	0	0	0	0	0	0	0	0	0
	Union County	0	0	0	0	0	0	0	0	0	0
	Venango County	0	0	0	0	0	0	0	0	0	0
	Warren County	0	0	0	0	0	0	0	0	0	0
	Washington County	0	0	0	0	0	1	0	0	1	0
	Wayne County	0	0	0	0	0	0	0	0	0	0

[1] The FBI does not publish arson data unless it receives data from either the agency or the state for all 12 months of the calendar year.

Table 11. Offenses Known to Law Enforcement, by State and Agency, 2008—*Continued*

(Number.)

State/Agency Type	Unit/Office	Violent crime	Murder and non-negligent man-slaughter	Forcible rape	Robbery	Aggra-vated assault	Property crime	Burglary	Larceny-theft	Motor vehicle theft	Arson[1]
	Westmoreland County	0	0	0	0	0	1	0	1	0	0
	Wyoming County	0	0	0	0	0	0	0	0	0	0
	York County	0	0	0	0	0	1	0	0	1	0
State Police:	Adams County	65	1	18	11	35	599	162	403	34	4
	Allegheny County	38	0	2	0	36	33	4	22	7	0
	Armstrong County	39	0	13	6	20	461	148	291	22	6
	Beaver County	21	0	3	2	16	233	84	130	19	31
	Bedford County	43	2	16	6	19	661	235	398	28	15
	Berks County	181	6	4	10	161	757	204	488	65	8
	Blair County	41	1	10	4	26	274	92	158	24	4
	Bradford County	44	0	25	1	18	612	220	372	20	6
	Bucks County	68	1	6	14	47	657	87	547	23	7
	Butler County	101	1	6	6	88	771	208	515	48	10
	Cambria County	44	0	8	4	32	321	109	190	22	14
	Cameron County	3	0	2	0	1	93	68	24	1	0
	Carbon County	50	1	8	5	36	362	143	203	16	15
	Centre County	47	0	12	6	29	609	207	366	36	9
	Chester County	127	1	20	26	80	1,374	525	767	82	43
	Clarion County	37	0	9	6	22	526	150	343	33	8
	Clearfield County	32	1	16	0	15	577	208	343	26	8
	Clinton County	18	0	4	6	8	446	118	312	16	1
	Columbia County	10	0	1	3	6	110	38	71	1	6
	Crawford County	47	0	13	4	30	782	326	391	65	2
	Cumberland County	66	0	17	5	44	644	187	433	24	5
	Delaware County	70	2	6	26	36	1,048	145	872	31	4
	Elizabethville	66	0	18	11	37	994	200	748	46	10
	Elk County	6	1	2	0	3	216	86	114	16	2
	Erie County	102	2	20	23	57	1,655	315	1,283	57	12
	Fayette County	219	2	22	63	132	1,920	557	1,194	169	107
	Franklin County	110	1	23	19	67	1,103	254	805	44	23
	Fulton County	26	0	2	2	22	263	91	161	11	1
	Greene County	37	1	8	10	18	473	151	282	40	12
	Huntingdon County	67	0	14	8	45	485	159	309	17	9
	Indiana County	71	0	23	19	29	1,199	299	838	62	24
	Jefferson County	20	2	2	3	13	291	109	165	17	6
	Juniata County	23	0	7	6	10	250	85	161	4	1
	Lackawanna County	21	3	5	0	13	239	100	123	16	41
	Lancaster County	74	1	28	18	27	869	280	542	47	38
	Lawrence County	32	0	6	4	22	528	144	343	41	33
	Lebanon County	71	0	7	7	57	374	85	268	21	1
	Lehigh County	43	1	9	9	24	883	180	665	38	7
	Luzerne County	215	10	13	7	185	1,010	253	700	57	29
	Lycoming County	21	0	7	3	11	711	208	486	17	10
	McKean County	10	0	4	2	4	213	89	116	8	6
	Mercer County	43	1	12	8	22	533	185	328	20	24
	Mifflin County	9	0	2	1	6	124	49	63	12	2
	Monroe County	158	3	14	23	118	1,381	451	828	102	14
	Montour County	5	0	1	0	4	83	22	59	2	5
	Northampton County	18	0	3	2	13	286	77	187	22	8
	Northumberland County	78	1	1	2	74	289	79	200	10	3
	Perry County	69	3	21	11	34	623	164	441	18	2
	Philadelphia County	11	0	0	0	11	7	0	5	2	0
	Pike County	78	0	15	13	50	689	291	361	37	17
	Potter County	31	2	26	0	3	217	117	94	6	6
	Schuylkill County	166	0	19	7	140	946	210	686	50	19
	Skippack	75	1	7	4	63	512	152	336	24	9
	Snyder County	23	2	5	0	16	376	95	255	26	2
	Somerset County	63	1	19	9	34	626	229	370	27	6
	Sullivan County	4	0	1	2	1	118	57	57	4	4
	Susquehanna County	41	3	16	1	21	497	152	292	53	7
	Tioga County	25	0	9	1	15	285	121	150	14	2
	Tionesta	40	0	7	1	32	164	93	68	3	2
	Union County	16	0	7	2	7	225	68	147	10	0
	Venango County	35	1	11	4	19	441	143	274	24	10
	Warren County	37	2	6	1	28	336	106	210	20	3
	Washington County	97	5	12	24	56	1,056	242	744	70	31
	Wayne County	123	2	15	5	101	647	184	426	37	9
	Westmoreland County	167	1	39	29	98	1,940	468	1,349	123	34
	Wyoming County	9	0	5	0	4	205	52	139	14	4
	York County	93	0	14	13	66	713	208	451	54	11
PENNSYLVANIA—Other Agencies											
Allegheny County Port Authority		100	0	0	28	72	109	3	94	12	0
County Detective:	Berks County	3	0	2	0	1	5	0	3	2	0
	Bucks County	2	0	0	0	2	11	1	10	0	0

[1] The FBI does not publish arson data unless it receives data from either the agency or the state for all 12 months of the calendar year.

Table 11. Offenses Known to Law Enforcement, by State and Agency, 2008—*Continued*

(Number.)

State/Agency Type	Unit/Office	Violent crime	Murder and non-negligent man-slaughter	Forcible rape	Robbery	Aggra-vated assault	Property crime	Burglary	Larceny-theft	Motor vehicle theft	Arson[1]
	Butler County	0	0	0	0	0	0	0	0	0	0
	Clinton County	0	0	0	0	0	0	0	0	0	0
	Dauphin County	26	0	1	1	24	40	1	39	0	0
	Lebanon County	4	1	2	0	1	5	0	5	0	0
	Lehigh County	1	0	1	0	0	58	1	0	57	1
	Pike County	0	0	0	0	0	27	0	27	0	0
	Schuylkill County	1	1	0	0	0	1	0	1	0	0
	Westmoreland County	9	0	0	0	9	77	0	77	0	0
	York County	0	0	0	0	0	8	0	1	7	0
Delaware County District Attorney	Criminal Investigation Division	4	0	0	0	4	0	0	0	0	0
Delaware County Park		15	0	1	0	14	116	0	116	0	0
Harrisburg International Airport		0	0	0	0	0	16	0	9	7	0
Wilkes-Barre Area School District		2	0	0	0	2	4	0	4	0	0
RHODE ISLAND—State Agencies											
Department of Environmental Management		1	0	0	1	0	49	2	45	2	0
Rhode Island State Airport		2	0	0	0	2	48	1	35	12	0
Rhode Island State Police Headquarters		15	2	5	0	8	75	0	32	43	0
State Police:	Chepachet	9	0	4	1	4	36	2	24	10	0
	Hope Valley	4	0	0	1	3	68	21	37	10	0
	Lincoln	12	0	6	0	6	83	1	57	25	0
	Portsmouth	3	0	1	0	2	7	1	5	1	1
	Wickford	3	0	1	1	1	29	2	22	5	0
SOUTH CAROLINA—State Agencies											
Bureau of Protective Services		1	0	0	0	1	37	1	33	3	0
Department of Mental Health		0	0	0	0	0	13	3	10	0	0
Department of Natural Resources:	Abbeville County	0	0	0	0	0	0	0	0	0	0
	Aiken County	0	0	0	0	0	0	0	0	0	0
	Allendale County	0	0	0	0	0	0	0	0	0	0
	Anderson County	0	0	0	0	0	0	0	0	0	0
	Bamberg County	0	0	0	0	0	0	0	0	0	0
	Barnwell County	0	0	0	0	0	0	0	0	0	0
	Beaufort County	0	0	0	0	0	0	0	0	0	0
	Berkeley County	0	0	0	0	0	0	0	0	0	0
	Calhoun County	0	0	0	0	0	0	0	0	0	0
	Charleston County	0	0	0	0	0	0	0	0	0	0
	Cherokee County	0	0	0	0	0	0	0	0	0	0
	Chester County	0	0	0	0	0	0	0	0	0	0
	Chesterfield County	0	0	0	0	0	0	0	0	0	0
	Clarendon County	0	0	0	0	0	0	0	0	0	0
	Colleton County	0	0	0	0	0	0	0	0	0	0
	Darlington County	0	0	0	0	0	0	0	0	0	0
	Dillon County	0	0	0	0	0	0	0	0	0	0
	Dorchester County	0	0	0	0	0	0	0	0	0	0
	Edgefield County	0	0	0	0	0	0	0	0	0	0
	Fairfield County	0	0	0	0	0	0	0	0	0	0
	Florence County	0	0	0	0	0	0	0	0	0	0
	Georgetown County	0	0	0	0	0	0	0	0	0	0
	Greenville County	0	0	0	0	0	0	0	0	0	0
	Greenwood County	0	0	0	0	0	0	0	0	0	0
	Hampton County	0	0	0	0	0	0	0	0	0	0
	Horry County	0	0	0	0	0	0	0	0	0	0
	Jasper County	0	0	0	0	0	0	0	0	0	0
	Kershaw County	0	0	0	0	0	0	0	0	0	0
	Lancaster County	0	0	0	0	0	0	0	0	0	0
	Laurens County	0	0	0	0	0	0	0	0	0	0
	Lee County	0	0	0	0	0	0	0	0	0	0
	Lexington County	0	0	0	0	0	0	0	0	0	0
	Marion County	0	0	0	0	0	0	0	0	0	0
	Marlboro County	0	0	0	0	0	0	0	0	0	0
	McCormick County	0	0	0	0	0	0	0	0	0	0
	Newberry County	0	0	0	0	0	0	0	0	0	0
	Oconee County	0	0	0	0	0	0	0	0	0	0
	Orangeburg County	0	0	0	0	0	0	0	0	0	0
	Pickens County	0	0	0	0	0	0	0	0	0	0
	Richland County	0	0	0	0	0	0	0	0	0	0
	Saluda County	0	0	0	0	0	0	0	0	0	0
	Spartanburg County	0	0	0	0	0	0	0	0	0	0
	Sumter County	0	0	0	0	0	0	0	0	0	0
	Union County	0	0	0	0	0	0	0	0	0	0
	Williamsburg County	0	0	0	0	0	0	0	0	0	0
	York County	0	0	0	0	0	0	0	0	0	0

[1] The FBI does not publish arson data unless it receives data from either the agency or the state for all 12 months of the calendar year.

Table 11. Offenses Known to Law Enforcement, by State and Agency, 2008—*Continued*

(Number.)

State/Agency Type	Unit/Office	Violent crime	Murder and non-negligent man-slaughter	Forcible rape	Robbery	Aggra-vated assault	Property crime	Burglary	Larceny-theft	Motor vehicle theft	Arson[1]
Employment Security Commission		0	0	0	0	0	0	0	0	0	0
Forestry Commission:	Abbeville County	0	0	0	0	0	0	0	0	0	0
	Aiken County	0	0	0	0	0	0	0	0	0	10
	Allendale County	0	0	0	0	0	0	0	0	0	1
	Anderson County	0	0	0	0	0	0	0	0	0	2
	Bamberg County	0	0	0	0	0	1	0	1	0	1
	Barnwell County	0	0	0	0	0	1	0	1	0	1
	Beaufort County	0	0	0	0	0	0	0	0	0	7
	Berkeley County	0	0	0	0	0	0	0	0	0	47
	Calhoun County	0	0	0	0	0	0	0	0	0	1
	Charleston County	0	0	0	0	0	0	0	0	0	7
	Cherokee County	0	0	0	0	0	0	0	0	0	0
	Chester County	0	0	0	0	0	0	0	0	0	0
	Chesterfield County	0	0	0	0	0	19	0	19	0	6
	Clarendon County	0	0	0	0	0	1	0	1	0	6
	Colleton County	0	0	0	0	0	0	0	0	0	7
	Darlington County	0	0	0	0	0	1	0	1	0	1
	Dillon County	0	0	0	0	0	0	0	0	0	7
	Dorchester County	0	0	0	0	0	0	0	0	0	4
	Edgefield County	0	0	0	0	0	1	0	1	0	0
	Fairfield County	0	0	0	0	0	2	0	2	0	0
	Georgetown County	0	0	0	0	0	0	0	0	0	0
	Greenville County	0	0	0	0	0	0	0	0	0	0
	Greenwood County	0	0	0	0	0	0	0	0	0	1
	Hampton County	0	0	0	0	0	0	0	0	0	6
	Horry County	0	0	0	0	0	0	0	0	0	20
	Jasper County	0	0	0	0	0	0	0	0	0	9
	Kershaw County	0	0	0	0	0	1	0	1	0	4
	Lancaster County	0	0	0	0	0	1	0	1	0	1
	Laurens County	0	0	0	0	0	1	0	1	0	0
	Lee County	0	0	0	0	0	0	0	0	0	1
	Lexington County	0	0	0	0	0	0	0	0	0	3
	Marion County	0	0	0	0	0	0	0	0	0	5
	Marlboro County	0	0	0	0	0	0	0	0	0	0
	McCormick County	0	0	0	0	0	0	0	0	0	8
	Newberry County	0	0	0	0	0	1	0	1	0	0
	Oconee County	0	0	0	0	0	0	0	0	0	4
	Orangeburg County	0	0	0	0	0	0	0	0	0	16
	Pickens County	0	0	0	0	0	1	0	1	0	1
	Richland County	0	0	0	0	0	3	0	3	0	0
	Saluda County	0	0	0	0	0	0	0	0	0	0
	Spartanburg County	0	0	0	0	0	0	0	0	0	2
	Sumter County	0	0	0	0	0	1	0	1	0	6
	Union County	0	0	0	0	0	0	0	0	0	0
	Williamsburg County	0	0	0	0	0	3	0	3	0	2
	York County	0	0	0	0	0	1	0	1	0	1
Highway Patrol:	Abbeville County	0	0	0	0	0	0	0	0	0	0
	Aiken County	0	0	0	0	0	1	0	0	1	0
	Anderson County	1	0	0	0	1	4	0	3	1	0
	Bamberg County	0	0	0	0	0	0	0	0	0	0
	Barnwell County	0	0	0	0	0	0	0	0	0	0
	Beaufort County	0	0	0	0	0	0	0	0	0	0
	Berkeley County	1	0	0	0	1	0	0	0	0	0
	Calhoun County	0	0	0	0	0	0	0	0	0	0
	Charleston County	0	0	0	0	0	0	0	0	0	0
	Cherokee County	0	0	0	0	0	0	0	0	0	0
	Chester County	0	0	0	0	0	0	0	0	0	0
	Chesterfield County	0	0	0	0	0	0	0	0	0	0
	Clarendon County	0	0	0	0	0	0	0	0	0	0
	Colleton County	0	0	0	0	0	0	0	0	0	0
	Darlington County	0	0	0	0	0	1	0	0	1	0
	Dillon County	0	0	0	0	0	0	0	0	0	0
	Dorchester County	0	0	0	0	0	0	0	0	0	0
	Edgefield County	0	0	0	0	0	0	0	0	0	0
	Fairfield County	0	0	0	0	0	0	0	0	0	0
	Florence County	0	0	0	0	0	0	0	0	0	0
	Georgetown County	0	0	0	0	0	0	0	0	0	0
	Greenville County	1	0	0	0	1	3	0	0	3	0
	Greenwood County	0	0	0	0	0	1	0	0	1	0
	Hampton County	0	0	0	0	0	0	0	0	0	0
	Horry County	0	0	0	0	0	1	0	0	1	0
	Jasper County	0	0	0	0	0	0	0	0	0	0
	Kershaw County	0	0	0	0	0	0	0	0	0	0

[1] The FBI does not publish arson data unless it receives data from either the agency or the state for all 12 months of the calendar year.

Table 11. Offenses Known to Law Enforcement, by State and Agency, 2008—*Continued*

(Number.)

State/Agency Type	Unit/Office	Violent crime	Murder and non-negligent man-slaughter	Forcible rape	Robbery	Aggra-vated assault	Property crime	Burglary	Larceny-theft	Motor vehicle theft	Arson[1]
	Lancaster County	0	0	0	0	0	0	0	0	0	0
	Laurens County	0	0	0	0	0	0	0	0	0	0
	Lee County	0	0	0	0	0	0	0	0	0	0
	Lexington County	0	0	0	0	0	1	0	0	1	0
	Marion County	0	0	0	0	0	0	0	0	0	0
	Marlboro County	0	0	0	0	0	0	0	0	0	0
	McCormick County	0	0	0	0	0	0	0	0	0	0
	Newberry County	0	0	0	0	0	0	0	0	0	0
	Oconee County	0	0	0	0	0	0	0	0	0	0
	Orangeburg County	0	0	0	0	0	1	0	1	0	0
	Pickens County	0	0	0	0	0	1	0	1	0	0
	Richland County	0	0	0	0	0	1	0	0	1	0
	Saluda County	0	0	0	0	0	0	0	0	0	0
	Spartanburg County	0	0	0	0	0	1	0	0	1	0
	Sumter County	0	0	0	0	0	0	0	0	0	0
	Union County	0	0	0	0	0	0	0	0	0	0
	Williamsburg County	0	0	0	0	0	0	0	0	0	0
	York County	1	0	0	0	1	0	0	0	0	0
South Carolina Law Enforcement Division Vice:	Abbeville County	0	0	0	0	0	0	0	0	0	0
	Aiken County	0	0	0	0	0	0	0	0	0	0
	Allendale County	0	0	0	0	0	0	0	0	0	0
	Anderson County	0	0	0	0	0	0	0	0	0	0
	Bamberg County	0	0	0	0	0	0	0	0	0	0
	Barnwell County	0	0	0	0	0	0	0	0	0	0
	Beaufort County	0	0	0	0	0	0	0	0	0	0
	Berkeley County	0	0	0	0	0	0	0	0	0	0
	Calhoun County	0	0	0	0	0	0	0	0	0	0
	Charleston County	0	0	0	0	0	0	0	0	0	0
	Cherokee County	0	0	0	0	0	0	0	0	0	0
	Chester County	0	0	0	0	0	0	0	0	0	0
	Chesterfield County	0	0	0	0	0	0	0	0	0	0
	Clarendon County	0	0	0	0	0	0	0	0	0	0
	Colleton County	0	0	0	0	0	0	0	0	0	0
	Darlington County	0	0	0	0	0	0	0	0	0	0
	Dillon County	0	0	0	0	0	0	0	0	0	0
	Dorchester County	0	0	0	0	0	0	0	0	0	0
	Edgefield County	0	0	0	0	0	0	0	0	0	0
	Fairfield County	0	0	0	0	0	0	0	0	0	0
	Florence County	0	0	0	0	0	0	0	0	0	0
	Georgetown County	0	0	0	0	0	0	0	0	0	0
	Greenville County	0	0	0	0	0	0	0	0	0	0
	Greenwood County	0	0	0	0	0	0	0	0	0	0
	Hampton County	0	0	0	0	0	0	0	0	0	0
	Horry County	0	0	0	0	0	0	0	0	0	0
	Jasper County	0	0	0	0	0	0	0	0	0	0
	Kershaw County	0	0	0	0	0	0	0	0	0	0
	Lancaster County	0	0	0	0	0	0	0	0	0	0
	Laurens County	0	0	0	0	0	0	0	0	0	0
	Lee County	0	0	0	0	0	0	0	0	0	0
	Lexington County	0	0	0	0	0	0	0	0	0	0
	Marion County	0	0	0	0	0	0	0	0	0	0
	Marlboro County	0	0	0	0	0	0	0	0	0	0
	McCormick County	0	0	0	0	0	0	0	0	0	0
	Newberry County	0	0	0	0	0	0	0	0	0	0
	Oconee County	0	0	0	0	0	0	0	0	0	0
	Orangeburg County	0	0	0	0	0	0	0	0	0	0
	Pickens County	0	0	0	0	0	0	0	0	0	0
	Richland County	0	0	0	0	0	0	0	0	0	0
	Saluda County	0	0	0	0	0	0	0	0	0	0
	Spartanburg County	0	0	0	0	0	0	0	0	0	0
	Sumter County	0	0	0	0	0	0	0	0	0	0
	Union County	0	0	0	0	0	0	0	0	0	0
	Williamsburg County	0	0	0	0	0	0	0	0	0	0
State Transport Police:	Abbeville County	0	0	0	0	0	0	0	0	0	0
	Aiken County	0	0	0	0	0	0	0	0	0	0
	Allendale County	0	0	0	0	0	0	0	0	0	0
	Bamberg County	0	0	0	0	0	0	0	0	0	0
	Barnwell County	0	0	0	0	0	0	0	0	0	0
	Beaufort County	0	0	0	0	0	0	0	0	0	0
	Berkeley County	0	0	0	0	0	0	0	0	0	0
	Calhoun County	0	0	0	0	0	0	0	0	0	0
	Charleston County	0	0	0	0	0	0	0	0	0	0
	Cherokee County	0	0	0	0	0	0	0	0	0	0
	Chester County	0	0	0	0	0	0	0	0	0	0

[1] The FBI does not publish arson data unless it receives data from either the agency or the state for all 12 months of the calendar year.

Table 11. Offenses Known to Law Enforcement, by State and Agency, 2008—*Continued*

(Number.)

State/Agency Type	Unit/Office	Violent crime	Murder and non-negligent man-slaughter	Forcible rape	Robbery	Aggra-vated assault	Property crime	Burglary	Larceny-theft	Motor vehicle theft	Arson[1]
	Chesterfield County	0	0	0	0	0	0	0	0	0	0
	Clarendon County	0	0	0	0	0	0	0	0	0	0
	Darlington County	0	0	0	0	0	0	0	0	0	0
	Dillon County	0	0	0	0	0	0	0	0	0	0
	Dorchester County	0	0	0	0	0	0	0	0	0	0
	Edgefield County	0	0	0	0	0	0	0	0	0	0
	Fairfield County	0	0	0	0	0	0	0	0	0	0
	Florence County	0	0	0	0	0	0	0	0	0	0
	Georgetown County	0	0	0	0	0	0	0	0	0	0
	Greenwood County	0	0	0	0	0	0	0	0	0	0
	Hampton County	0	0	0	0	0	0	0	0	0	0
	Jasper County	0	0	0	0	0	0	0	0	0	0
	Kershaw County	0	0	0	0	0	0	0	0	0	0
	Lancaster County	0	0	0	0	0	0	0	0	0	0
	Laurens County	0	0	0	0	0	0	0	0	0	0
	Lee County	0	0	0	0	0	0	0	0	0	0
	Lexington County	0	0	0	0	0	0	0	0	0	0
	Marion County	0	0	0	0	0	0	0	0	0	0
	Marlboro County	0	0	0	0	0	0	0	0	0	0
	McCormick County	0	0	0	0	0	0	0	0	0	0
	Newberry County	0	0	0	0	0	0	0	0	0	0
	Oconee County	0	0	0	0	0	0	0	0	0	0
	Orangeburg County	0	0	0	0	0	0	0	0	0	0
	Pickens County	0	0	0	0	0	0	0	0	0	0
	Saluda County	0	0	0	0	0	0	0	0	0	0
	Sumter County	0	0	0	0	0	0	0	0	0	0
	Union County	0	0	0	0	0	0	0	0	0	0
	Williamsburg County	0	0	0	0	0	0	0	0	0	0
	York County	0	0	0	0	0	0	0	0	0	0
South Carolina Law Enforcement Division Vehicle Crimes		0	0	0	0	0	0	0	0	0	0
South Carolina School for the Deaf and Blind		0	0	0	0	0	0	0	0	0	0
State Museum		0	0	0	0	0	0	0	0	0	0
State Ports Authority		0	0	0	0	0	1	0	1	0	0
United States Department of Energy	Savannah River Plant	0	0	0	0	0	22	0	22	0	0
SOUTH CAROLINA—Other Agencies											
Charleston County Aviation Authority		1	0	0	0	1	40	0	18	22	0
Columbia Metropolitan Airport		1	0	0	0	1	20	0	18	2	0
Greenville-Spartanburg International Airport		0	0	0	0	0	13	0	11	2	0
Whitten Center		1	0	0	0	1	1	0	1	0	0
Division of Criminal Investigation		43	8	11	4	20	25	8	17	0	5
Alcoholic Beverage Commission		0	0	0	0	0	0	0	0	0	0
Department of Correction	Internal Affairs	4	0	0	0	4	0	0	0	0	0
Department of Safety		7	0	0	1	6	21	0	1	20	0
State Fire Marshal		0	0	0	0	0	0	0	0	0	53
State Park Rangers:	Bicentennial Capitol Mall	0	0	0	0	0	5	0	4	1	0
	Big Hill Pond	0	0	0	0	0	0	0	0	0	0
	Big Ridge	0	0	0	0	0	1	0	1	0	0
	Bledsoe Creek	0	0	0	0	0	0	0	0	0	0
	Booker T. Washington	0	0	0	0	0	0	0	0	0	0
	Burgess Falls Natural Area	0	0	0	0	0	1	0	1	0	0
	Cedars of Lebanon	0	0	0	0	0	1	0	1	0	0
	Chickasaw	0	0	0	0	0	0	0	0	0	0
	Cove Lake	0	0	0	0	0	0	0	0	0	0
	Cumberland Mountain	0	0	0	0	0	0	0	0	0	0
	Cumberland Trail	0	0	0	0	0	0	0	0	0	0
	David Crockett	0	0	0	0	0	0	0	0	0	0
	Davy Crockett Birthplace	0	0	0	0	0	2	0	2	0	0
	Dunbar Cave Natural Area	0	0	0	0	0	0	0	0	0	0
	Edgar Evins	0	0	0	0	0	8	0	8	0	0
	Fall Creek Falls	0	0	0	0	0	1	0	1	0	0
	Fort Loudon State Historic Park	0	0	0	0	0	0	0	0	0	0
	Fort Pillow State Historic Park	0	0	0	0	0	0	0	0	0	0
	Frozen Head Natural Area	0	0	0	0	0	0	0	0	0	0
	Harpeth Scenic Rivers	0	0	0	0	0	1	1	0	0	0
	Harrison Bay	1	0	0	0	1	4	0	4	0	0
	Henry Horton	0	0	0	0	0	3	0	3	0	0

[1] The FBI does not publish arson data unless it receives data from either the agency or the state for all 12 months of the calendar year.

Table 11. Offenses Known to Law Enforcement, by State and Agency, 2008—*Continued*

(Number.)

State/Agency Type	Unit/Office	Violent crime	Murder and non-negligent man-slaughter	Forcible rape	Robbery	Aggra-vated assault	Property crime	Burglary	Larceny-theft	Motor vehicle theft	Arson[1]
	Hiwassee/Ocoee State Scenic Rivers	0	0	0	0	0	0	0	0	0	0
	Indian Mountain	0	0	0	0	0	0	0	0	0	0
	Johnsonville State Historic Park	0	0	0	0	0	0	0	0	0	0
	Long Hunter	0	0	0	0	0	0	0	0	0	0
	Meeman-Shelby Forest	0	0	0	0	0	1	0	1	0	0
	Montgomery Bell	0	0	0	0	0	2	0	2	0	0
	Mousetail Landing	0	0	0	0	0	2	2	0	0	0
	Natchez Trace	0	0	0	0	0	1	0	1	0	0
	Nathan Bedford Forrest	0	0	0	0	0	1	0	1	0	0
	Norris Dam	1	0	0	0	1	3	1	2	0	0
	Old Stone Fort State Archaeological Park	0	0	0	0	0	5	0	5	0	0
	Panther Creek	0	0	0	0	0	1	0	1	0	0
	Paris Landing	0	0	0	0	0	0	0	0	0	0
	Pickett	0	0	0	0	0	0	0	0	0	0
	Pickwick Landing	0	0	0	0	0	0	0	0	0	0
	Pinson Mounds State Archaeological Park	0	0	0	0	0	0	0	0	0	0
	Radnor Lake Natural Area	0	0	0	0	0	0	0	0	0	0
	Red Clay State Historic Park	0	0	0	0	0	0	0	0	0	0
	Reelfoot Lake	0	0	0	0	0	0	0	0	0	0
	Roan Mountain	0	0	0	0	0	0	0	0	0	0
	Rock Island	0	0	0	0	0	6	0	6	0	0
	Sgt. Alvin C. York	0	0	0	0	0	0	0	0	0	0
	South Cumberland Recreation Area	0	0	0	0	0	0	0	0	0	0
	Standing Stone	0	0	0	0	0	0	0	0	0	0
	Sycamore Shoals State Historic Park	0	0	0	0	0	0	0	0	0	0
	Tim's Ford	0	0	0	0	0	1	0	1	0	0
	T.O. Fuller	0	0	0	0	0	0	0	0	0	0
	Warrior's Path	0	0	0	0	0	7	0	7	0	0
TennCare Office of Inspector General		0	0	0	0	0	2	0	2	0	0
Tennessee Bureau of Investigation		0	0	0	0	0	1	0	1	0	0
Tennessee Department of Revenue	Special Investigations Unit	0	0	0	0	0	1	0	1	0	0
Wildlife Resources Agency:	Region 1	0	0	0	0	0	0	0	0	0	0
	Region 2	0	0	0	0	0	0	0	0	0	0
	Region 3	0	0	0	0	0	0	0	0	0	0
	Region 4	2	0	0	0	2	1	0	1	0	0
TENNESSEE—Other Agencies											
Chattanooga Metropolitan Airport		0	0	0	0	0	4	0	4	0	0
Dickson Parks and Recreation		0	0	0	0	0	0	0	0	0	0
Drug Task Force:	1st Judicial District	0	0	0	0	0	0	0	0	0	0
	2nd Judicial District	0	0	0	0	0	0	0	0	0	0
	3rd Judicial District	0	0	0	0	0	0	0	0	0	0
	4th Judicial District	0	0	0	0	0	1	0	0	1	0
	5th Judicial District	0	0	0	0	0	1	0	1	0	0
	8th Judicial District	0	0	0	0	0	0	0	0	0	0
	9th Judicial District	0	0	0	0	0	0	0	0	0	0
	10th Judicial District	0	0	0	0	0	1	0	1	0	0
	12th Judicial District	0	0	0	0	0	0	0	0	0	0
	13th Judicial District	0	0	0	0	0	0	0	0	0	0
	14th Judicial District	2	0	0	1	1	0	0	0	0	0
	15th Judicial District	0	0	0	0	0	0	0	0	0	0
	17th Judicial District	0	0	0	0	0	0	0	0	0	0
	18th Judicial District	0	0	0	0	0	1	0	0	1	0
	19th Judicial District	0	0	0	0	0	0	0	0	0	0
	21st Judicial District	0	0	0	0	0	0	0	0	0	0
	22nd Judicial District	0	0	0	0	0	0	0	0	0	0
	23rd Judicial District	0	0	0	0	0	1	0	1	0	0
	24th Judicial District	1	0	0	0	1	0	0	0	0	0
	25th Judicial District	0	0	0	0	0	4	0	4	0	0
	27th Judicial District	0	0	0	0	0	0	0	0	0	0
	31st Judicial District	0	0	0	0	0	0	0	0	0	0
Knoxville Metropolitan Airport		0	0	0	0	0	18	0	18	0	0
Memphis International Airport		4	0	0	1	3	207	0	204	3	0
Metropolitan Board of Parks and Recreation	Nashville-Davidson	8	0	0	3	5	97	6	86	5	6
Nashville International Airport		1	0	0	0	1	7	0	5	2	0

[1] The FBI does not publish arson data unless it receives data from either the agency or the state for all 12 months of the calendar year.

Table 11. Offenses Known to Law Enforcement, by State and Agency, 2008—*Continued*

(Number.)

State/Agency Type	Unit/Office	Violent crime	Murder and non-negligent man-slaughter	Forcible rape	Robbery	Aggra-vated assault	Property crime	Burglary	Larceny-theft	Motor vehicle theft	Arson[1]
Smyrna/Rutherford County Airport Authority		0	0	0	0	0	2	0	2	0	0
Tri-Cities Regional Airport		0	0	0	0	0	4	2	2	0	0
West Tennessee Violent Crime Task Force		1	0	0	0	1	0	0	0	0	0
TEXAS—Other Agencies											
Amarillo International Airport		0	0	0	0	0	3	0	3	0	0
Cameron County Park Rangers		10	0	0	2	8	51	12	37	2	0
Dallas-Fort Worth International Airport		8	0	1	2	5	675	13	626	36	0
Hospital District:	Dallas County	2	0	0	0	2	442	5	426	11	0
	Tarrant County	2	0	0	0	2	167	9	155	3	0
Houston Metropolitan Transit Authority		3	0	0	1	2	25	0	23	2	0
Independent School District:	Aldine	3	0	0	2	1	152	45	100	7	0
	Alvin	13	0	2	0	11	89	5	83	1	1
	Angleton	1	0	0	0	1	33	5	28	0	3
	Austin	19	0	1	3	15	623	74	547	2	8
	Cedar Hill	4	0	0	2	2	61	2	57	2	2
	Conroe	8	0	0	0	8	238	8	230	0	4
	Corpus Christi	38	0	0	3	35	238	28	210	0	4
	East Central	0	0	0	0	0	0	0	0	0	0
	Ector County	47	0	0	2	45	166	6	157	3	1
	El Paso	17	0	0	1	16	396	40	355	1	2
	Fort Bend	23	0	0	1	22	414	46	364	4	2
	Humble	8	0	2	0	6	113	22	90	1	0
	Judson	1	0	0	1	0	38	1	37	0	0
	Katy	9	0	4	1	4	400	14	384	2	1
	Kaufman	2	0	0	0	2	7	0	6	1	0
	Killeen	1	0	0	0	1	103	6	95	2	2
	Klein	2	0	0	2	0	213	7	205	1	0
	Mexia	0	0	0	0	0	12	3	9	0	0
	Midland	0	0	0	0	0	86	12	74	0	0
	Pasadena	5	0	0	3	2	156	10	142	4	0
	Socorro	40	0	0	0	40	198	8	188	2	5
	Spring	35	0	2	3	30	141	0	138	3	2
	Spring Branch	4	0	0	1	3	73	16	55	2	0
	Taft	0	0	0	0	0	8	1	7	0	0
UTAH—State Agencies											
Parks and Recreation		11	1	0	0	10	52	1	51	0	0
UTAH—Other Agencies											
Cache-Rich Drug Task Force		0	0	0	0	0	6	5	1	0	0
Davis Metropolitan Narcotics Strike Force		0	0	0	0	0	3	0	3	0	0
Granite School District		13	0	1	0	12	206	21	184	1	5
Utah County Attorney	Investigations Division	0	0	0	0	0	0	0	0	0	0
Utah County Major Crime Task Force		2	0	0	1	1	14	0	14	0	0
Utah Transit Authority		4	0	0	1	3	185	0	185	0	0
VERMONT—State Agencies											
Attorney General		0	0	0	0	0	4	0	4	0	0
Department of Motor Vehicles		0	0	0	0	0	1	0	1	0	0
Fish and Wildlife Department	Law Enforcement Division	2	0	0	0	2	2	0	2	0	0
State Police:	Bradford	17	1	5	0	11	138	53	72	13	2
	Brattleboro	19	4	1	1	13	210	104	101	5	0
	Derby	10	1	4	1	4	328	125	189	14	1
	Middlesex	18	1	2	1	14	341	140	194	7	0
	New Haven	5	0	2	0	3	244	82	149	13	2
	Rockingham	13	2	2	0	9	204	68	109	27	2
	Royalton	18	2	7	0	9	259	93	140	26	2
	Rutland	16	3	1	4	8	526	213	284	29	2
	Shaftsbury	17	0	4	1	12	161	61	91	9	0
	St. Albans	38	0	13	1	24	681	226	402	53	0
	St. Johnsbury	19	1	1	2	15	332	122	190	20	13
	Williston	20	0	3	3	14	280	100	167	13	10
Vermont State Police		0	0	0	0	0	0	0	0	0	0
Vermont State Police Headquarters	Bureau of Criminal Investigations	0	0	0	0	0	0	0	0	0	0
VIRGINIA—State Agencies											
Alcoholic Beverage Control Commission		0	0	0	0	0	38	0	38	0	0
Department of Conservation and Recreation		1	0	0	0	1	51	0	51	0	0
Southside Virginia Training Center		5	0	1	0	4	25	0	25	0	0
State Police:	Accomack County	3	1	0	1	1	12	0	10	2	0
	Albemarle County	0	0	0	0	0	7	0	6	1	0
	Alexandria	0	0	0	0	0	2	0	1	1	0
	Alleghany County	0	0	0	0	0	3	0	3	0	0
	Amelia County	1	0	0	0	1	4	0	3	1	0
	Amherst County	3	0	0	0	3	2	1	1	0	0
	Appomattox County	0	0	0	0	0	0	0	0	0	1

[1] The FBI does not publish arson data unless it receives data from either the agency or the state for all 12 months of the calendar year.

Table 11. Offenses Known to Law Enforcement, by State and Agency, 2008—*Continued*

(Number.)

State/Agency Type	Unit/Office	Violent crime	Murder and non-negligent man-slaughter	Forcible rape	Robbery	Aggra-vated assault	Property crime	Burglary	Larceny-theft	Motor vehicle theft	Arson[1]
	Augusta County	0	0	0	0	0	1	0	1	0	0
	Bath County	1	0	0	0	1	1	0	1	0	2
	Bedford County	2	0	0	0	2	9	0	7	2	0
	Bland County	1	0	1	0	0	7	0	6	1	0
	Botetourt County	1	0	0	0	1	2	0	2	0	0
	Brunswick County	0	0	0	0	0	0	0	0	0	0
	Buchanan County	1	0	0	0	1	5	1	4	0	3
	Buckingham County	1	0	0	0	1	9	0	6	3	0
	Campbell County	1	0	0	0	1	8	1	5	2	1
	Caroline County	0	0	0	0	0	53	1	21	31	2
	Carroll County	3	0	0	1	2	29	2	27	0	0
	Charlotte County	1	0	0	0	1	2	0	1	1	1
	Chesapeake	0	0	0	0	0	1	0	1	0	0
	Chesterfield County	11	0	1	0	10	12	0	9	3	0
	Clarke County	0	0	0	0	0	0	0	0	0	1
	Colonial Heights	0	0	0	0	0	0	0	0	0	0
	Craig County	2	1	0	0	1	1	0	0	1	1
	Culpeper County	16	0	0	0	16	6	1	3	2	0
	Cumberland County	1	0	0	1	0	1	0	1	0	0
	Danville	0	0	0	0	0	0	0	0	0	0
	Dickenson County	0	0	0	0	0	1	0	1	0	0
	Dinwiddie County	5	0	0	0	5	4	0	3	1	1
	Essex County	0	0	0	0	0	0	0	0	0	0
	Fairfax County	12	0	0	0	12	33	0	12	21	0
	Fauquier County	1	0	0	0	1	2	0	1	1	0
	Floyd County	2	1	0	0	1	4	1	1	2	0
	Fluvanna County	0	0	0	0	0	2	0	1	1	1
	Franklin County	0	0	0	0	0	8	0	4	4	1
	Frederick County	2	0	1	0	1	8	0	5	3	0
	Fredericksburg	0	0	0	0	0	0	0	0	0	0
	Galax	0	0	0	0	0	1	0	1	0	0
	Giles County	1	1	0	0	0	6	1	5	0	1
	Gloucester County	0	0	0	0	0	1	0	1	0	0
	Goochland County	1	1	0	0	0	3	0	3	0	0
	Grayson County	3	2	0	0	1	3	0	1	2	0
	Greene County	0	0	0	0	0	1	0	0	1	0
	Greensville County	0	0	0	0	0	5	1	4	0	0
	Halifax County	3	0	1	0	2	12	4	5	3	0
	Hampton	7	0	0	0	7	1	0	0	1	0
	Hanover County	10	0	0	0	10	2	0	2	0	0
	Harrisonburg	0	0	0	0	0	5	0	3	2	0
	Henrico County	4	1	1	0	2	13	0	13	0	0
	Henry County	1	1	0	0	0	6	0	2	4	0
	Highland County	2	0	0	0	2	1	0	1	0	0
	Isle of Wight County	0	0	0	0	0	3	0	2	1	0
	James City County	0	0	0	0	0	0	0	0	0	0
	King and Queen County	1	0	0	0	1	4	1	2	1	0
	King George County	0	0	0	0	0	2	0	1	1	0
	Lancaster County	0	0	0	0	0	1	1	0	0	0
	Lee County	1	0	0	0	1	7	0	4	3	3
	Loudoun County	1	0	1	0	0	21	0	4	17	0
	Louisa County	0	0	0	0	0	3	0	2	1	0
	Lunenburg County	0	0	0	0	0	6	1	1	4	0
	Lynchburg	0	0	0	0	0	3	0	3	0	0
	Madison County	0	0	0	0	0	0	0	0	0	0
	Mathews County	0	0	0	0	0	0	0	0	0	0
	Mecklenburg County	1	0	0	0	1	8	0	5	3	0
	Middlesex County	0	0	0	0	0	0	0	0	0	0
	Montgomery County	1	0	0	0	1	9	0	8	1	0
	New Kent County	2	0	0	0	2	3	1	2	0	0
	Newport News	0	0	0	0	0	0	0	0	0	0
	Norfolk	2	0	0	0	2	9	0	7	2	0
	Northampton County	1	0	0	1	0	4	0	4	0	0
	Northumberland County	0	0	0	0	0	2	0	2	0	0
	Orange County	0	0	0	0	0	1	1	0	0	2
	Page County	4	0	0	0	4	2	0	2	0	0
	Patrick County	1	0	1	0	0	3	0	2	1	0
	Petersburg	1	0	0	0	1	3	0	3	0	0
	Pittsylvania County	0	0	0	0	0	29	1	5	23	0
	Portsmouth	0	0	0	0	0	1	0	1	0	0
	Powhatan County	12	0	0	0	12	0	0	0	0	0
	Prince Edward County	0	0	0	0	0	0	0	0	0	0
	Prince George County	0	0	0	0	0	2	0	2	0	0
	Prince William County	5	0	0	0	5	19	0	9	10	0

[1] The FBI does not publish arson data unless it receives data from either the agency or the state for all 12 months of the calendar year.

Table 11. Offenses Known to Law Enforcement, by State and Agency, 2008—*Continued*

(Number.)

State/Agency Type	Unit/Office	Violent crime	Murder and non-negligent man-slaughter	Forcible rape	Robbery	Aggra-vated assault	Property crime	Burglary	Larceny-theft	Motor vehicle theft	Arson[1]
	Pulaski County	1	0	0	0	1	11	2	8	1	0
	Rappahannock County	0	0	0	0	0	1	0	1	0	0
	Richmond	3	0	0	0	3	11	0	7	4	0
	Richmond County	2	0	0	0	2	0	0	0	0	0
	Roanoke	5	0	0	0	5	1	0	0	1	0
	Roanoke County	1	0	0	0	1	1	0	1	0	0
	Rockbridge County	1	0	0	1	0	9	0	8	1	0
	Rockingham County	0	0	0	0	0	35	1	15	19	0
	Russell County	0	0	0	0	0	17	0	14	3	0
	Salem	0	0	0	0	0	1	0	1	0	0
	Scott County	0	0	0	0	0	8	1	3	4	1
	Shenandoah County	3	3	0	0	0	7	0	7	0	0
	Smyth County	3	1	0	0	2	12	2	8	2	2
	Southampton County	0	0	0	0	0	3	0	1	2	0
	Spotsylvania County	0	0	0	0	0	2	0	1	1	0
	Stafford County	0	0	0	0	0	2	0	2	0	0
	Surry County	0	0	0	0	0	4	0	4	0	1
	Sussex County	0	0	0	0	0	2	1	1	0	0
	Tazewell County	7	0	1	0	6	29	7	17	5	3
	Virginia Beach	4	0	0	0	4	4	0	1	3	0
	Warren County	1	0	0	0	1	1	0	1	0	0
	Washington County	2	0	0	0	2	12	1	10	1	1
	Westmoreland County	0	0	0	0	0	1	0	1	0	0
	Winchester	1	0	0	1	0	1	0	1	0	1
	Wise County	2	0	0	0	2	4	0	4	0	2
	Wythe County	4	1	0	0	3	22	0	22	0	2
	York County	0	0	0	0	0	0	0	0	0	0
Virginia State Capitol		0	0	0	0	0	59	0	59	0	0
VIRGINIA—Other Agencies											
Norfolk Airport Authority		0	0	0	0	0	63	0	59	4	0
Port Authority	Norfolk	0	0	0	0	0	6	0	6	0	0
Reagan National Airport		5	0	0	1	4	480	1	395	84	0
Richmond International Airport		1	0	0	0	1	57	0	46	11	0
WASHINGTON—Other Agencies											
Lummi Tribal		77	0	1	9	67	287	73	202	12	6
Nooksack Tribal		11	0	3	2	6	69	24	41	4	0
Port Of Seattle		11	0	1	2	8	1,034	50	843	141	9
Swinomish Tribal		4	0	2	1	1	66	13	50	3	0
WEST VIRGINIA—State Agencies											
Department of Natural Resources:	Greenbrier County	0	0	0	0	0	0	0	0	0	0
	Hampshire County	0	0	0	0	0	0	0	0	0	0
	Harrison County	0	0	0	0	0	0	0	0	0	0
	Marion County	0	0	0	0	0	0	0	0	0	0
	Mercer County	0	0	0	0	0	0	0	0	0	0
	Monongalia County	0	0	0	0	0	0	0	0	0	0
	Morgan County	0	0	0	0	0	0	0	0	0	0
	Preston County	0	0	0	0	0	0	0	0	0	0
	Raleigh County	0	0	0	0	0	0	0	0	0	0
	Ritchie County	0	0	0	0	0	0	0	0	0	0
	Roane County	0	0	0	0	0	0	0	0	0	0
	Summers County	0	0	0	0	0	0	0	0	0	0
	Taylor County	0	0	0	0	0	0	0	0	0	0
	Wood County	0	0	0	0	0	0	0	0	0	0
State Police:	Beckley	31	0	1	2	28	357	69	249	39	1
	Berkeley Springs	9	0	0	0	9	140	54	69	17	0
	Bridgeport	19	1	1	2	15	229	59	144	26	2
	Buckeye	23	0	0	0	23	79	27	50	2	3
	Buckhannon	7	0	3	0	4	114	12	87	15	1
	Clay	15	0	2	0	13	73	29	31	13	2
	Danville	24	0	1	2	21	231	47	166	18	1
	Elizabeth	11	1	1	0	9	90	37	45	8	1
	Elkins	35	0	3	3	29	217	59	143	15	6
	Fairmont	10	0	0	0	10	175	30	125	20	1
	Gilbert	17	0	1	2	14	116	25	81	10	0
	Glenville	12	0	1	0	11	31	11	19	1	1
	Grafton	0	0	0	0	0	23	8	14	1	0
	Grantsville	10	0	1	0	9	96	39	41	16	0
	Hamlin	48	2	6	2	38	293	83	170	40	3
	Harrisville	13	0	0	1	12	71	18	50	3	1
	Hinton	4	0	0	0	4	55	18	32	5	0
	Hundred	4	0	0	0	4	28	6	19	3	1
	Huntington	27	0	4	6	17	667	114	524	29	0
	Jesse	8	0	2	0	6	54	15	35	4	1
	Keyser	47	0	3	4	40	207	74	115	18	0

[1] The FBI does not publish arson data unless it receives data from either the agency or the state for all 12 months of the calendar year.

Table 11. Offenses Known to Law Enforcement, by State and Agency, 2008—*Continued*

(Number.)

State/Agency Type	Unit/Office	Violent crime	Murder and non-negligent man-slaughter	Forcible rape	Robbery	Aggra-vated assault	Property crime	Burglary	Larceny-theft	Motor vehicle theft	Arson[1]
	Kingwood	14	0	0	0	14	123	42	69	12	1
	Lewisburg	14	0	3	0	11	123	29	81	13	0
	Logan	75	1	10	9	55	746	176	497	73	13
	Moorefield	13	0	1	1	11	58	26	27	5	2
	Morgantown	34	0	4	7	23	543	139	370	34	3
	Moundsville	11	1	2	2	6	23	0	20	3	0
	New Cumberland	2	0	0	0	2	30	5	24	1	0
	Oak Hill	17	0	1	2	14	111	23	82	6	2
	Parkersburg	12	0	1	0	11	214	46	149	19	2
	Parsons	6	0	0	0	6	62	29	29	4	0
	Petersburg	7	0	0	0	7	32	9	20	3	0
	Philippi	21	0	1	0	20	87	30	48	9	2
	Point Pleasant	7	1	3	0	3	109	43	59	7	1
	Princeton	18	0	1	3	14	341	93	213	35	0
	Quincy	13	0	0	0	13	176	36	114	26	5
	Rainelle	3	0	0	2	1	84	21	60	3	1
	Richwood	2	0	0	0	2	35	7	25	3	0
	Ripley	3	0	0	0	3	50	11	37	2	0
	Romney	4	0	2	0	2	137	37	87	13	0
	Spencer	14	0	0	1	13	37	12	24	1	0
	St. Marys	2	0	0	0	2	20	2	16	2	0
	Summersville	2	0	0	0	2	63	12	48	3	0
	Sutton	27	1	0	0	26	103	18	76	9	4
	Union	14	0	0	0	14	83	29	47	7	0
	Upperglade	46	0	0	0	46	72	20	48	4	1
	Welch	21	1	1	0	19	58	18	38	2	0
	Wellsburg	3	0	1	0	2	16	5	8	3	0
	Weston	15	0	2	0	13	151	35	102	14	1
	West Union	3	0	0	0	3	22	9	10	3	0
	Wheeling	5	1	3	0	1	59	12	45	2	1
	Williamson	49	0	3	0	46	195	48	115	32	3
	Winfield	32	0	3	1	28	170	29	129	12	1
State Police, Bureau of Criminal Investigation:	Beckley	0	0	0	0	0	1	0	1	0	0
	Buckhannon	0	0	0	0	0	0	0	0	0	0
	Charleston	0	0	0	0	0	0	0	0	0	0
	Fairmont	0	0	0	0	0	0	0	0	0	0
State Police, Parkway Authority:	Kanawha County	2	0	0	0	2	4	0	4	0	0
	Raleigh County	1	0	0	1	0	8	0	8	0	0
WEST VIRGINIA—Other Agencies											
Eastern Panhandle Drug and Violent Crime Task Force		0	0	0	0	0	0	0	0	0	0
Harrison County Drug and Violent Crime Task Force		0	0	0	0	0	0	0	0	0	0
WISCONSIN—State Agencies											
Capitol Police		1	0	0	1	0	65	1	64	0	0
Department of Natural Resources		0	0	0	0	0	0	0	0	0	0
Wisconsin State Patrol		0	0	0	0	0	0	0	0	0	0
WISCONSIN—Other Agencies											
Lac du Flambeau Tribal		11	1	1	0	9	310	27	245	38	0
Menominee Tribal		44	2	3	2	37	147	19	100	28	4
Oneida Tribal		15	0	4	0	11	492	17	456	19	0
PUERTO RICO AND OTHER OUTLYING AREAS											
Puerto Rico		9,484	807	95	5,467	3,115	59,254	19,138	33,113	7,003	
FEDERAL AGENCIES											
National Institutes of Health		0	0	0	0	0	122	1	120	1	0
United States Department of the Interior:	Bureau of Indian Affairs	6,212	172	879	296	4,865	17,524	4,692	10,168	2,664	1,187
	Bureau of Land Management	14	2	0	0	12	398	15	354	29	51
	Bureau of Reclamation	0	0	0	0	0	3	0	0	3	0
	Fish and Wildlife Service	39	6	2	0	31	335	88	216	31	72
	National Park Service	367	5	37	66	259	3,278	342	2,833	103	100

[1] The FBI does not publish arson data unless it receives data from either the agency or the state for all 12 months of the calendar year.

Table 12. Crime Trends, by Population Group, 2007–2008

(Number, percent change.)

Population group	Violent crime	Murder and non-negligent man-slaughter	Forcible rape	Robbery	Aggra-vated assault	Property crime	Burglary	Larceny-theft	Motor vehicle theft	Arson	Number of agencies	2008 estimated population
TOTAL ALL AGENCIES:												
2007	1,325,306	16,107	80,800	428,740	799,659	9,114,239	2,017,411	6,054,038	1,042,790	63,340		
2008	1,292,673	15,433	78,833	423,771	774,636	9,004,837	2,049,232	6,046,758	908,847	61,050	13,865	278,355,520
Percent change	-2.5	-4.2	-2.4	-1.2	-3.1	-1.2	+1.6	-0.1	-12.8	-3.6		
Total Cities												
2007	1,056,651	12,623	59,707	374,129	610,192	7,123,311	1,484,130	4,808,063	831,118	47,266		
2008	1,030,681	11,922	58,251	369,384	591,124	7,005,641	1,502,430	4,784,605	718,606	45,539	9,872	188,370,552
Percent change	-2.5	-5.6	-2.4	-1.3	-3.1	-1.7	+1.2	-0.5	-13.5	-3.7		
GROUP I (250,000 and over)												
2007	501,856	6,857	19,985	206,542	268,472	2,488,280	537,931	1,539,319	411,030	18,499		
2008	489,075	6,502	19,145	203,730	259,698	2,411,508	541,896	1,520,608	349,004	17,706	76	56,533,626
Percent change	-2.5	-5.2	-4.2	-1.4	-3.3	-3.1	+0.7	-1.2	-15.1	-4.3		
1,000,000 and over (Group I subset)												
2007	209,001	2,789	6,203	94,385	105,624	923,358	187,272	579,090	156,996	6,343		
2008	205,683	2,670	6,136	93,467	103,410	904,743	186,911	582,015	135,817	5,963	10	25,543,437
Percent change	-1.6	-4.3	-1.1	-1.0	-2.1	-2.0	-0.2	+0.5	-13.5	-6.0		
500,000 to 999,999 (Group I subset)												
2007	166,502	2,325	7,037	64,756	92,384	887,207	197,684	543,906	145,617	6,396		
2008	162,302	2,151	6,720	63,351	90,080	863,699	203,220	537,518	122,961	5,872	25	16,970,506
Percent change	-2.5	-7.5	-4.5	-2.2	-2.5	-2.6	+2.8	-1.2	-15.6	-8.2		
250,000 to 499,999 (Group I subset)												
2007	126,353	1,743	6,745	47,401	70,464	677,715	152,975	416,323	108,417	5,760		
2008	121,090	1,681	6,289	46,912	66,208	643,066	151,765	401,075	90,226	5,871	41	14,019,683
Percent change	-4.2	-3.6	-6.8	-1.0	-6.0	-5.1	-0.8	-3.7	-16.8	+1.9		
GROUP II (100,000 to 249,999)												
2007	175,657	2,186	10,379	62,922	100,170	1,205,107	260,130	797,113	147,864	7,785		
2008	169,212	1,981	10,057	61,874	95,300	1,195,752	268,600	798,869	128,283	7,357	192	28,438,286
Percent change	-3.7	-9.4	-3.1	-1.7	-4.9	-0.8	+3.3	+0.2	-13.2	-5.5		
GROUP III (50,000 to 99,999)												
2007	136,981	1,434	9,231	45,126	81,190	1,077,362	226,799	738,847	111,716	7,031		
2008	134,031	1,360	9,119	44,032	79,520	1,064,589	225,361	740,309	98,919	6,838	444	30,327,776
Percent change	-2.2	-5.2	-1.2	-2.4	-2.1	-1.2	-0.6	+0.2	-11.5	-2.7		
GROUP IV (25,000 to 49,999)												
2007	92,211	876	7,473	27,474	56,388	836,207	166,258	603,044	66,905	5,099		
2008	91,541	831	7,276	27,221	56,213	828,384	167,855	600,722	59,807	5,002	745	25,544,892
Percent change	-0.7	-5.1	-2.6	-0.9	-0.3	-0.9	+1.0	-0.4	-10.6	-1.9		
GROUP V (10,000 to 24,999)												
2007	80,245	735	6,814	20,334	52,362	801,505	158,092	588,600	54,813	4,467		
2008	79,142	689	6,759	20,358	51,336	800,460	161,949	590,024	48,487	4,405	1,636	25,846,912
Percent change	-1.4	-6.3	-0.8	+0.1	-2.0	-0.1	+2.4	+0.2	-11.5	-1.4		
GROUP VI (under 10,000)												
2007	69,701	535	5,825	11,731	51,610	714,850	134,920	541,140	38,790	4,385		
2008	67,680	559	5,895	12,169	49,057	704,948	136,769	534,073	34,106	4,231	6,779	21,679,060
Percent change	-2.9	+4.5	+1.2	+3.7	-4.9	-1.4	+1.4	-1.3	-12.1	-3.5		
Metropolitan Counties												
2007	214,809	2,660	14,964	50,415	146,770	1,565,883	396,792	991,215	177,876	12,338		
2008	209,222	2,612	14,893	50,087	141,630	1,573,253	407,774	1,007,198	158,281	11,986	1,659	64,890,568
Percent change	-2.6	-1.8	-0.5	-0.7	-3.5	+0.5	+2.8	+1.6	-11.0	-2.9		
Nonmetropolitan Counties[1]												
2007	53,846	824	6,129	4,196	42,697	425,045	136,489	254,760	33,796	3,736		
2008	52,770	899	5,689	4,300	41,882	425,943	139,028	254,955	31,960	3,525	2,334	25,094,400
Percent change	-2.0	+9.1	-7.2	+2.5	-1.9	+0.2	+1.9	+0.1	-5.4	-5.6		
SUBURBAN AREAS[2]												
2007	362,044	3,913	26,443	91,111	240,577	3,067,134	680,382	2,092,372	294,380	20,970		
2008	353,894	3,831	26,316	90,417	233,330	3,072,578	697,477	2,113,639	261,462	20,262	7,321	116,592,948
Percent change	-2.3	-2.1	-0.5	-0.8	-3.0	+0.2	+2.5	+1.0	-11.2	-3.4		

[1] Includes state police agencies that report aggregately for the entire state.

[2] Suburban areas include law enforcement agencies in cities with less than 50,000 inhabitants and county law enforcement agencies that are within a Metropolitan Statistical Area. Suburban areas exclude all metropolitan agencies associated with a principal city. The agencies associated with suburban areas also appear in other groups within this table.

Table 13. Crime Trends, by Suburban and Nonsuburban Cities[1] and Population Group, 2007–2008

(Number, percent change.)

Population group	Violent crime	Murder and non-negligent man-slaughter	Forcible rape	Robbery	Aggra-vated assault	Property crime	Burglary	Larceny-theft	Motor vehicle theft	Arson	Number of agencies	2008 estimated population
TOTAL SUBURBAN CITIES:												
2007	147,235	1,253	11,479	40,696	93,807	1,501,251	283,590	1,101,157	116,504	8,632		
2008	144,672	1,219	11,423	40,330	91,700	1,499,325	289,703	1,106,441	103,181	8,276	5,662	51,702,380
Percent change	-1.7	-2.7	-0.5	-0.9	-2.2	-0.1	+2.2	+0.5	-11.4	-4.1		
GROUP IV (25,000 to 49,999)												
2007	56,321	533	4,236	18,013	33,539	539,118	105,124	385,203	48,791	3,140		
2008	55,620	494	4,142	17,642	33,342	537,683	106,531	387,708	43,444	2,960	561	19,044,685
Percent change	-1.2	-7.3	-2.2	-2.1	-0.6	-0.3	+1.3	+0.7	-11.0	-5.7		
GROUP V (10,000 to 24,999)												
2007	51,476	450	4,075	14,522	32,429	522,042	99,743	380,967	41,332	2,943		
2008	50,473	436	4,020	14,403	31,614	528,017	104,115	387,331	36,571	2,938	1,224	19,462,232
Percent change	-1.9	-3.1	-1.3	-0.8	-2.5	+1.1	+4.4	+1.7	-11.5	-0.2		
GROUP VI (under 10,000)												
2007	39,438	270	3,168	8,161	27,839	440,091	78,723	334,987	26,381	2,549		
2008	38,579	289	3,261	8,285	26,744	433,625	79,057	331,402	23,166	2,378	3,877	13,195,463
Percent change	-2.2	+7.0	+2.9	+1.5	-3.9	-1.5	+0.4	-1.1	-12.2	-6.7		
TOTAL NONSUBURBAN CITIES:												
2007	94,922	893	8,633	18,843	66,553	851,311	175,680	631,627	44,004	5,319		
2008	93,691	860	8,507	19,418	64,906	834,467	176,870	618,378	39,219	5,362	3,498	21,368,484
Percent change	-1.3	-3.7	-1.5	+3.1	-2.5	-2.0	+0.7	-2.1	-10.9	+0.8		
GROUP IV (25,000 to 49,999)												
2007	35,890	343	3,237	9,461	22,849	297,089	61,134	217,841	18,114	1,959		
2008	35,921	337	3,134	9,579	22,871	290,701	61,324	213,014	16,363	2,042	184	6,500,207
Percent change	+0.1	-1.7	-3.2	+1.2	+0.1	-2.2	+0.3	-2.2	-9.7	+4.2		
GROUP V (10,000 to 24,999)												
2007	28,769	285	2,739	5,812	19,933	279,463	58,349	207,633	13,481	1,524		
2008	28,669	253	2,739	5,955	19,722	272,443	57,834	202,693	11,916	1,467	412	6,384,680
Percent change	-0.3	-11.2	0.0	+2.5	-1.1	-2.5	-0.9	-2.4	-11.6	-3.7		
GROUP VI (under 10,000)												
2007	30,263	265	2,657	3,570	23,771	274,759	56,197	206,153	12,409	1,836		
2008	29,101	270	2,634	3,884	22,313	271,323	57,712	202,671	10,940	1,853	2,902	8,483,597
Percent change	-3.8	+1.9	-0.9	+8.8	-6.1	-1.3	+2.7	-1.7	-11.8	+0.9		

[1] Suburban cities include law enforcement agencies in cities with less than 50,000 inhabitants that are within a Metropolitan Statistical Area. Suburban cities exclude all metropolitan agencies associated with a principal city. Nonsuburban cities include law enforcement agencies in cities with less than 50,000 inhabitants that are not associated with a Metropolitan Statistical Area.

Table 14. Crime Trends, by Metropolitan and Nonmetropolitan Counties[1] and Population Group, 2007–2008

(Number, percent change.)

Population group and range	Violent crime	Murder and non-negligent man-slaughter	Forcible rape	Robbery	Aggra-vated assault	Property crime	Burglary	Larceny-theft	Motor vehicle theft	Arson	Number of agencies	2008 estimated population
METROPOLITAN COUNTIES												
100,000 and over												
2007	152,173	1,826	8,925	43,207	98,215	1,045,866	254,450	668,389	123,027	7,768		
2008	148,823	1,823	8,881	42,610	95,509	1,061,155	263,770	688,119	109,266	7,565	145	39,156,860
Percent change	-2.2	-0.2	-0.5	-1.4	-2.8	+1.5	+3.7	+3.0	-11.2	-2.6		
25,000 to 99,999												
2007	45,980	610	4,451	5,073	35,846	393,657	112,925	248,682	32,050	3,027		
2008	44,327	579	4,430	5,343	33,975	390,576	114,810	246,256	29,510	2,854	415	21,430,203
Percent change	-3.6	-5.1	-0.5	+5.3	-5.2	-0.8	+1.7	-1.0	-7.9	-5.7		
Under 25,000												
2007	16,877	224	1,588	2,135	12,930	126,360	29,417	74,144	22,799	1,572		
2008	16,587	210	1,582	2,134	12,661	121,522	29,194	72,823	19,505	1,567	1,099	4,303,505
Percent change	-1.7	-6.3	-0.4	*	-2.1	-3.8	-0.8	-1.8	-14.4	-0.3		
NONMETROPOLITAN COUNTIES												
25,000 and over												
2007	22,889	307	2,386	1,969	18,227	183,571	61,712	107,791	14,068	1,357		
2008	22,072	324	2,139	2,104	17,505	184,636	63,216	108,052	13,368	1,280	273	10,599,165
Percent change	-3.6	+5.5	-10.4	+6.9	-4.0	+0.6	+2.4	+0.2	-5.0	-5.7		
10,000 to 24,999												
2007	15,925	242	1,606	1,030	13,047	124,357	40,133	74,919	9,305	1,044		
2008	15,700	267	1,459	1,055	12,919	125,615	40,635	76,036	8,944	1,041	547	8,748,110
Percent change	-1.4	+10.3	-9.2	+2.4	-1.0	+1.0	+1.3	+1.5	-3.9	-0.3		
Under 10,000												
2007	9,049	137	1,405	377	7,130	65,145	19,694	39,772	5,679	1,001		
2008	8,771	165	1,260	395	6,951	63,691	19,535	38,893	5,263	782	1,357	3,816,787
Percent change	-3.1	+20.4	-10.3	+4.8	-2.5	-2.2	-0.8	-2.2	-7.3	-21.9		

[1] Metropolitan counties include sheriffs and county law enforcement agencies associated with a Metropolitan Statistical Area. Nonmetropolitan counties include sheriffs and county law enforcement agencies that are not associated with a Metropolitan Statistical Area. The offenses from state police agencies are not included in this table.

* Less than one-tenth of 1 percent.

Table 15. Crime Trends, by Population Group, 2007–2008

(Number, percent change.)

Population group	Forcible rape		Robbery				Aggravated assault			
	Rape by force	Assault to rape-attempts	Firearm	Knife or cutting instrument	Other weapon	Strong-arm	Firearm	Knife or cutting instrument	Other weapon	Hands, fists, feet, etc.
TOTAL ALL AGENCIES:										
2007	72,772	6,223	161,921	31,199	34,565	150,350	158,059	138,098	251,979	192,236
2008	71,264	5,803	161,283	28,649	32,556	149,367	153,476	135,306	240,996	189,334
Percent change	-2.1	-6.7	-0.4	-8.2	-5.8	-0.7	-2.9	-2.0	-4.4	-1.5
Total Cities										
2007	53,165	4,908	137,254	26,907	29,116	131,572	125,084	107,751	186,440	132,827
2008	52,068	4,560	136,086	24,712	27,588	130,169	120,215	106,152	178,256	131,758
Percent change	-2.1	-7.1	-0.9	-8.2	-5.2	-1.1	-3.9	-1.5	-4.4	-0.8
GROUP I (250,000 and over)										
2007	16,779	1,970	74,461	12,604	13,209	60,426	64,169	41,875	74,070	33,881
2008	16,055	1,850	72,978	11,533	12,146	59,179	61,613	40,964	71,925	33,781
Percent change	-4.3	-6.1	-2.0	-8.5	-8.0	-2.1	-4.0	-2.2	-2.9	-0.3
1,000,000 and over (Group I subset)										
2007	4,558	770	25,832	5,266	4,559	21,516	19,444	12,987	19,915	8,559
2008	4,477	769	24,427	4,793	4,269	21,139	17,617	13,163	20,691	10,076
Percent change	-1.8	-0.1	-5.4	-9.0	-6.4	-1.8	-9.4	+1.4	+3.9	+17.7
500,000 to 999,999 (Group I subset)										
2007	6,073	626	28,289	4,087	4,965	19,535	25,342	16,453	29,408	11,756
2008	5,828	569	27,684	3,770	4,535	19,182	25,075	15,812	28,525	11,376
Percent change	-4.0	-9.1	-2.1	-7.8	-8.7	-1.8	-1.1	-3.9	-3.0	-3.2
250,000 to 499,999 (Group I subset)										
2007	6,148	574	20,340	3,251	3,685	19,375	19,383	12,435	24,747	13,566
2008	5,750	512	20,867	2,970	3,342	18,858	18,921	11,989	22,709	12,329
Percent change	-6.5	-10.8	+2.6	-8.6	-9.3	-2.7	-2.4	-3.6	-8.2	-9.1
GROUP II (100,000 to 249,999)										
2007	9,163	837	24,562	5,089	5,515	24,464	22,443	20,132	35,797	18,098
2008	8,981	722	24,749	4,596	5,664	24,063	21,004	19,884	32,973	17,775
Percent change	-2.0	-13.7	+0.8	-9.7	+2.7	-1.6	-6.4	-1.2	-7.9	-1.8
GROUP III (50,000 to 99,999)										
2007	8,539	686	16,607	4,025	4,338	20,075	15,200	16,451	28,307	21,411
2008	8,490	613	15,952	3,743	4,090	20,178	14,758	16,416	26,814	21,987
Percent change	-0.6	-10.6	-3.9	-7.0	-5.7	+0.5	-2.9	-0.2	-5.3	+2.7
GROUP IV (25,000 to 49,999)										
2007	6,997	476	9,750	2,407	2,866	12,451	9,266	11,197	18,925	17,000
2008	6,838	438	10,123	2,306	2,737	12,055	9,381	11,248	18,507	17,077
Percent change	-2.3	-8.0	+3.8	-4.2	-4.5	-3.2	+1.2	+0.5	-2.2	+0.5
GROUP V (10,000 to 24,999)										
2007	6,369	432	7,826	1,742	2,072	8,651	7,791	9,828	16,151	18,506
2008	6,315	432	7,802	1,571	1,932	9,009	7,544	9,748	15,299	18,637
Percent change	-0.8	0.0	-0.3	-9.8	-6.8	+4.1	-3.2	-0.8	-5.3	+0.7
GROUP VI (under 10,000)										
2007	5,318	507	4,048	1,040	1,116	5,505	6,215	8,268	13,190	23,931
2008	5,389	505	4,482	963	1,019	5,685	5,915	7,892	12,738	22,501
Percent change	+1.3	-0.4	+10.7	-7.4	-8.7	+3.3	-4.8	-4.5	-3.4	-6.0
Metropolitan Counties										
2007	13,870	945	22,957	3,925	4,894	17,230	26,159	24,232	53,112	42,137
2008	13,871	898	23,431	3,602	4,382	17,614	26,189	23,295	50,656	40,801
Percent change	*	-5.0	+2.1	-8.2	-10.5	+2.2	+0.1	-3.9	-4.6	-3.2
Nonmetropolitan Counties										
2007	5,737	370	1,710	367	555	1,548	6,816	6,115	12,427	17,272
2008	5,325	345	1,766	335	586	1,584	7,072	5,859	12,084	16,775
Percent change	-7.2	-6.8	+3.3	-8.7	+5.6	+2.3	+3.8	-4.2	-2.8	-2.9
SUBURBAN AREAS[1]										
2007	24,548	1,735	38,093	7,308	8,880	35,390	39,531	40,756	82,725	76,396
2008	24,509	1,672	38,570	6,720	8,148	35,884	39,315	39,454	78,561	75,277
Percent change	-0.2	-3.6	+1.3	-8.0	-8.2	+1.4	-0.5	-3.2	-5.0	-1.5

[1] Suburban areas include law enforcement agencies in cities with less than 50,000 inhabitants and county law enforcement agencies that are within a Metropolitan Statistical Area. Suburban areas exclude all metropolitan agencies associated with a principal city. The agencies associated with suburban areas also appear in other groups within this table.

* Less than one-tenth of 1 percent.

Table 15. Crime Trends, by Population Group, 2007–2008—*Continued*

(Number, percent change.)

Population group	Burglary			Motor vehicle theft			Arson			Number of agencies	2008 estimated population
	Forcible entry	Unlawful entry	Attempted forcible entry	Autos	Trucks and buses	Other vehicles	Structure	Mobile	Other		
TOTAL ALL AGENCIES:											
2007	1,180,109	627,757	125,586	725,930	177,071	84,686	26,095	17,000	17,669		
2008	1,203,298	634,240	126,348	618,801	154,261	83,409	25,712	17,048	16,212	13,843	263,379,547
Percent change	+2.0	+1.0	+0.6	-14.8	-12.9	-1.5	-1.5	+0.3	-8.2		
Total Cities											
2007	861,304	450,815	97,410	586,909	138,776	53,928	19,776	12,023	12,799		
2008	874,323	455,234	97,516	496,920	119,254	53,139	19,420	12,109	11,783	9,857	174,498,252
Percent change	+1.5	+1.0	+0.1	-15.3	-14.1	-1.5	-1.8	+0.7	-7.9		
GROUP I (250,000 and over)											
2007	325,934	120,614	30,766	265,047	80,977	18,882	6,991	5,999	3,886		
2008	330,747	119,900	30,423	218,106	67,983	18,736	6,994	5,927	3,314	71	43,881,824
Percent change	+1.5	-0.6	-1.1	-17.7	-16.0	-0.8	*	-1.2	-14.7		
1,000,000 and over (Group I subset)											
2007	98,510	35,794	7,302	80,390	37,273	7,473	1,931	2,311	1,362		
2008	99,131	34,584	7,288	66,634	30,542	7,232	1,888	2,408	1,030	8	14,369,058
Percent change	+0.6	-3.4	-0.2	-17.1	-18.1	-3.2	-2.2	+4.2	-24.4		
500,000 to 999,999 (Group I subset)											
2007	130,898	41,584	13,901	99,918	25,658	6,902	2,587	1,775	1,314		
2008	135,481	42,669	13,457	81,371	22,893	6,998	2,403	1,644	1,134	23	15,744,124
Percent change	+3.5	+2.6	-3.2	-18.6	-10.8	+1.4	-7.1	-7.4	-13.7		
250,000 to 499,999 (Group I subset)											
2007	96,526	43,236	9,563	84,739	18,046	4,507	2,473	1,913	1,210		
2008	96,135	42,647	9,678	70,101	14,548	4,506	2,703	1,875	1,150	40	13,768,642
Percent change	-0.4	-1.4	+1.2	-17.3	-19.4	*	+9.3	-2.0	-5.0		
GROUP II (100,000 to 249,999)											
2007	149,767	79,449	17,905	110,747	22,695	9,342	3,324	1,863	1,951		
2008	154,367	82,558	18,122	93,895	20,388	9,235	3,121	1,956	1,861	185	27,258,935
Percent change	+3.1	+3.9	+1.2	-15.2	-10.2	-1.1	-6.1	+5.0	-4.6		
GROUP III (50,000 to 99,999)											
2007	130,586	79,470	16,394	88,252	15,052	8,245	2,951	1,745	2,244		
2008	129,594	79,061	16,288	76,909	13,696	8,075	2,947	1,741	2,127	444	30,327,776
Percent change	-0.8	-0.5	-0.6	-12.9	-9.0	-2.1	-0.1	-0.2	-5.2		
GROUP IV (25,000 to 49,999)											
2007	95,000	58,557	12,701	52,093	8,227	6,585	2,089	1,011	1,890		
2008	96,183	58,982	12,690	45,944	7,054	6,809	2,050	1,022	1,816	745	25,544,892
Percent change	+1.2	+0.7	-0.1	-11.8	-14.3	+3.4	-1.9	+1.1	-3.9		
GROUP V (10,000 to 24,999)											
2007	88,182	58,750	10,631	42,133	6,937	5,624	2,168	782	1,419		
2008	90,368	60,161	10,947	37,011	6,043	5,341	2,105	829	1,391	1,634	25,808,805
Percent change	+2.5	+2.4	+3.0	-12.2	-12.9	-5.0	-2.9	+6.0	-2.0		
GROUP VI (under 10,000)											
2007	71,835	53,975	9,013	28,637	4,888	5,250	2,253	623	1,409		
2008	73,064	54,572	9,046	25,055	4,090	4,943	2,203	634	1,274	6,778	21,676,020
Percent change	+1.7	+1.1	+0.4	-12.5	-16.3	-5.8	-2.2	+1.8	-9.6		
Metropolitan Counties											
2007	234,579	131,479	22,112	118,127	33,005	23,257	4,542	4,157	3,676		
2008	243,132	132,545	22,804	102,318	30,012	22,989	4,645	4,090	3,476	1,655	63,876,299
Percent change	+3.6	+0.8	+3.1	-13.4	-9.1	-1.2	+2.3	-1.6	-5.4		
Nonmetropolitan Counties											
2007	84,226	45,463	6,064	20,894	5,290	7,501	1,777	820	1,194		
2008	85,843	46,461	6,028	19,563	4,995	7,281	1,647	849	953	2,331	25,004,996
Percent change	+1.9	+2.2	-0.6	-6.4	-5.6	-2.9	-7.3	+3.5	-20.2		
SUBURBAN AREAS[1]											
2007	388,168	240,163	43,043	208,586	47,349	34,842	8,213	5,660	6,932		
2008	401,093	242,864	43,957	181,408	42,621	34,394	8,218	5,584	6,488	7,315	115,559,504
Percent change	+3.3	+1.1	+2.1	-13.0	-10.0	-1.3	+0.1	-1.3	-6.4		

[1] Suburban areas include law enforcement agencies in cities with less than 50,000 inhabitants and county law enforcement agencies that are within a Metropolitan Statistical Area. Suburban areas exclude all metropolitan agencies associated with a principal city. The agencies associated with suburban areas also appear in other groups within this table.

* Less than one-tenth of 1 percent.

Table 16. Crime Per 100,000 Population, by Population Group, 2008

(Number, rate.)

Population group	Violent crime		Murder and nonnegligent manslaughter		Forcible rape		Robbery		Aggravated assault	
	Number of offenses known	Rate	Number of offenses known	Rate	Number of offenses known	Rate	Number of offenses known	Rate	Number of offenses known	Rate
TOTAL ALL AGENCIES:	1,292,693	470.6	15,282	5.6	80,797	29.4	423,023	154.0	773,591	281.6
Total Cities	1,034,427	552.8	11,883	6.4	60,017	32.1	369,124	197.3	593,403	317.1
GROUP I (250,000 and over)	489,839	866.5	6,502	11.5	19,909	35.2	203,730	360.4	259,698	459.4
1,000,000 and over (Group I subset)	206,447	808.2	2,670	10.5	6,900	27.0	93,467	365.9	103,410	404.8
500,000 to 999,999 (Group I subset)	162,302	956.4	2,151	12.7	6,720	39.6	63,351	373.3	90,080	530.8
250,000 to 499,999 (Group I subset)	121,090	863.7	1,681	12.0	6,289	44.9	46,912	334.6	66,208	472.3
GROUP II (100,000 to 249,999)	170,997	599.2	2,000	7.0	10,438	36.6	62,536	219.1	96,023	336.5
GROUP III (50,000 to 99,999)	135,012	451.3	1,347	4.5	9,324	31.2	43,601	145.7	80,740	269.9
GROUP IV (25,000 to 49,999)	89,737	357.0	803	3.2	7,219	28.7	26,421	105.1	55,294	220.0
GROUP V (10,000 to 24,999)	81,012	313.7	684	2.6	7,077	27.4	20,595	79.7	52,656	203.9
GROUP VI (under 10,000)	67,830	320.5	547	2.6	6,050	28.6	12,241	57.8	48,992	231.5
Metropolitan Counties	206,994	324.5	2,548	4.0	14,998	23.5	49,706	77.9	139,742	219.1
Nonmetropolitan Counties[1]	51,272	215.3	851	3.6	5,782	24.3	4,193	17.6	40,446	169.8
SUBURBAN AREAS[2]	352,062	306.2	3,745	3.3	26,592	23.1	89,847	78.1	231,878	201.7

Population group	Property crime		Burglary		Larceny-theft		Motor vehicle theft		Number of agencies	2008 estimated population
	Number of offenses known	Rate	Number of offenses known	Rate	Number of offenses known	Rate	Number of offenses known	Rate		
TOTAL ALL AGENCIES:	8,994,167	3,274.0	2,042,369	743.4	6,043,976	2,200.1	907,822	330.5	13,416	274,715,428
Total Cities	7,033,769	3,759.1	1,506,589	805.2	4,805,734	2,568.3	721,446	385.6	9,602	187,114,108
GROUP I (250,000 and over)	2,428,800	4,296.2	541,896	958.5	1,537,900	2,720.3	349,004	617.3	76	56,533,626
1,000,000 and over (Group I subset)	904,743	3,542.0	186,911	731.7	582,015	2,278.5	135,817	531.7	10	25,543,437
500,000 to 999,999 (Group I subset)	880,991	5,191.3	203,220	1,197.5	554,810	3,269.3	122,961	724.6	25	16,970,506
250,000 to 499,999 (Group I subset)	643,066	4,586.9	151,765	1,082.5	401,075	2,860.8	90,226	643.6	41	14,019,683
GROUP II (100,000 to 249,999)	1,208,611	4,235.4	272,245	954.0	806,548	2,826.4	129,818	454.9	192	28,536,118
GROUP III (50,000 to 99,999)	1,062,532	3,551.6	226,010	755.5	736,161	2,460.7	100,361	335.5	438	29,917,008
GROUP IV (25,000 to 49,999)	816,451	3,248.0	164,788	655.6	592,757	2,358.1	58,906	234.3	733	25,136,755
GROUP V (10,000 to 24,999)	811,733	3,143.1	164,850	638.3	597,821	2,314.8	49,062	190.0	1,636	25,826,255
GROUP VI (under 10,000)	705,642	3,334.1	136,800	646.4	534,547	2,525.7	34,295	162.0	6,527	21,164,346
Metropolitan Counties	1,551,617	2,432.6	402,097	630.4	993,625	1,557.8	155,895	244.4	1,605	63,783,265
Nonmetropolitan Counties[1]	408,781	1,716.3	133,683	561.3	244,617	1,027.0	30,481	128.0	2,209	23,818,055
SUBURBAN AREAS[2]	3,052,865	2,655.3	692,128	602.0	2,101,656	1,828.0	259,081	225.3	7,164	114,971,924

[1] Includes state police agencies that report aggregately for the entire state.

[2] Suburban areas include law enforcement agencies in cities with less than 50,000 inhabitants and county law enforcement agencies that are within a Metropolitan Statistical Area. Suburban areas exclude all metropolitan agencies associated with a principal city. The agencies associated with suburban areas also appear in other groups within this table.

Table 17. Crime Per 100,000 Population, by Suburban and Nonsuburban Cities[1] and Population Group, 2008

(Number, rate.)

Population group	Violent crime		Murder and nonnegligent manslaughter		Forcible rape		Robbery		Aggravated assault	
	Number of offenses known	Rate	Number of offenses known	Rate	Number of offenses known	Rate	Number of offenses known	Rate	Number of offenses known	Rate
TOTAL SUBURBAN CITIES:	145,074	283.4	1,197	2.3	11,600	22.7	40,141	78.4	92,136	180.0
GROUP IV (25,000 to 49,999)	55,103	292.1	480	2.5	4,077	21.6	17,295	91.7	33,251	176.3
GROUP V (10,000 to 24,999)	51,198	264.5	437	2.3	4,164	21.5	14,521	75.0	32,076	165.7
GROUP VI (under 10,000)	38,773	299.0	280	2.2	3,359	25.9	8,325	64.2	26,809	206.8
TOTAL NONSUBURBAN CITIES:	93,488	446.5	837	4.0	8,729	41.7	19,116	91.3	64,806	309.5
GROUP IV (25,000 to 49,999)	34,609	551.9	323	5.2	3,117	49.7	9,126	145.5	22,043	351.5
GROUP V (10,000 to 24,999)	29,820	461.0	247	3.8	2,919	45.1	6,074	93.9	20,580	318.1
GROUP VI (under 10,000)	29,059	354.4	267	3.3	2,693	32.8	3,916	47.8	22,183	270.6

Population group	Property crime		Burglary		Larceny-theft		Motor vehicle theft		Number of agencies	2008 estimated population
	Number of offenses known	Rate	Number of offenses known	Rate	Number of offenses known	Rate	Number of offenses known	Rate		
TOTAL SUBURBAN CITIES:	1,501,248	2,932.8	290,031	566.6	1,108,031	2,164.6	103,186	201.6	5,559	51,188,659
GROUP IV (25,000 to 49,999)	533,905	2,830.1	105,916	561.4	384,920	2,040.3	43,069	228.3	555	18,865,496
GROUP V (10,000 to 24,999)	532,495	2,750.9	105,138	543.1	390,573	2,017.7	36,784	190.0	1,216	19,357,410
GROUP VI (under 10,000)	434,848	3,353.8	78,977	609.1	332,538	2,564.7	23,333	180.0	3,788	12,965,753
TOTAL NONSUBURBAN CITIES:	832,578	3,976.3	176,407	842.5	617,094	2,947.1	39,077	186.6	3,337	20,938,697
GROUP IV (25,000 to 49,999)	282,546	4,505.4	58,872	938.8	207,837	3,314.1	15,837	252.5	178	6,271,259
GROUP V (10,000 to 24,999)	279,238	4,316.7	59,712	923.1	207,248	3,203.8	12,278	189.8	420	6,468,845
GROUP VI (under 10,000)	270,794	3,302.9	57,823	705.3	202,009	2,463.9	10,962	133.7	2,739	8,198,593

[1] Suburban cities include law enforcement agencies in cities with less than 50,000 inhabitants that are within a Metropolitan Statistical Area. Suburban cities exclude all metropolitan agencies associated with a principal city. Nonsuburban cities include law enforcement agencies in cities with less than 50,000 inhabitants that are not associated with a Metropolitan Statistical Area.

Table 18. Crime Per 100,000 Population, by Metropolitan and Nonmetropolitan Counties[1] and Population Group, 2008

(Number, rate.)

Population group	Violent crime		Murder and nonnegligent manslaughter		Forcible rape		Robbery		Aggravated assault	
	Number of offenses known	Rate	Number of offenses known	Rate	Number of offenses known	Rate	Number of offenses known	Rate	Number of offenses known	Rate
METROPOLITAN COUNTIES										
100,000 and over	147,324	381.9	1,789	4.6	8,747	22.7	42,332	109.7	94,456	244.9
25,000 to 99,999	43,675	207.4	565	2.7	4,646	22.1	5,259	25.0	33,205	157.7
Under 25,000	16,462	396.6	194	4.7	1,623	39.1	2,115	51.0	12,530	301.9
NONMETROPOLITAN COUNTIES										
25,000 and over	21,544	212.7	307	3.0	2,158	21.3	2,087	20.6	16,992	167.8
10,000 to 24,999	15,202	181.4	243	2.9	1,496	17.9	1,084	12.9	12,379	147.7
Under 10,000	8,535	237.8	163	4.5	1,308	36.4	369	10.3	6,695	186.5

Population group	Property crime		Burglary		Larceny-theft		Motor vehicle theft		Number of agencies	2008 estimated population
	Number of offenses known	Rate	Number of offenses known	Rate	Number of offenses known	Rate	Number of offenses known	Rate		
METROPOLITAN COUNTIES										
100,000 and over	1,047,563	2,715.8	259,715	673.3	680,086	1,763.1	107,762	279.4	142	38,572,814
25,000 to 99,999	386,214	1,833.9	114,094	541.8	243,273	1,155.1	28,847	137.0	409	21,059,954
Under 25,000	117,850	2,839.4	28,291	681.6	70,273	1,693.1	19,286	464.7	1,054	4,150,497
NONMETROPOLITAN COUNTIES										
25,000 and over	180,446	1,781.8	61,686	609.1	105,755	1,044.3	13,005	128.4	261	10,127,065
10,000 to 24,999	121,462	1,449.4	39,267	468.6	73,564	877.9	8,631	103.0	523	8,379,992
Under 10,000	62,471	1,740.5	19,122	532.8	38,163	1,063.3	5,186	144.5	1,275	3,589,254

[1] Metropolitan counties include sheriffs and county law enforcement agencies associated with a Metropolitan Statistical Area. Nonmetropolitan counties include sheriffs and county law enforcement agencies that are not associated with a Metropolitan Statistical Area. The offenses from state police agencies are not included in this table.

Table 19. Crime Per 100,000 Population, Selected Known Offenses, by Population Group, 2008

(Number, rate.)

Population group	Forcible rape		Robbery				Aggravated assault			
	Rape by force	Assault to rape-attempts	Firearm	Knife or cutting instrument	Other weapon	Strong-arm	Firearm	Knife or cutting instrument	Other weapon	Hands, fists, feet, etc.
TOTAL ALL AGENCIES:										
Number of offenses known	72,389	5,888	163,163	28,754	32,693	150,874	154,145	136,025	241,311	189,094
Rate	27.8	2.3	62.7	11.1	12.6	58.0	59.2	52.3	92.7	72.7
Total Cities										
Number of offenses known	52,969	4,649	137,978	24,846	27,808	131,872	121,672	107,519	179,963	132,654
Rate	30.5	2.7	79.4	14.3	16.0	75.9	70.0	61.9	103.5	76.3
GROUP I (250,000 and over)										
Number of offenses known	16,215	1,876	74,719	11,753	12,318	61,200	62,451	42,014	73,196	34,231
Rate	36.5	4.2	168.0	26.4	27.7	137.6	140.4	94.5	164.6	77.0
1,000,000 and over (Group I subset)										
Number of offenses known	4,477	769	24,427	4,793	4,269	21,139	17,617	13,163	20,691	10,076
Rate	31.2	5.4	170.0	33.4	29.7	147.1	122.6	91.6	144.0	70.1
500,000 to 999,999 (Group I subset)										
Number of offenses known	5,988	595	29,425	3,990	4,707	21,203	25,913	16,862	29,796	11,826
Rate	36.7	3.6	180.1	24.4	28.8	129.8	158.6	103.2	182.4	72.4
250,000 to 499,999 (Group I subset)										
Number of offenses known	5,750	512	20,867	2,970	3,342	18,858	18,921	11,989	22,709	12,329
Rate	41.8	3.7	151.6	21.6	24.3	137.0	137.4	87.1	164.9	89.5
GROUP II (100,000 to 249,999)										
Number of offenses known	9,138	736	25,223	4,639	5,725	24,147	21,359	20,090	33,053	17,857
Rate	33.4	2.7	92.2	17.0	20.9	88.3	78.1	73.4	120.8	65.3
GROUP III (50,000 to 99,999)										
Number of offenses known	8,688	636	15,818	3,688	4,029	20,066	14,902	16,431	26,880	22,527
Rate	29.0	2.1	52.9	12.3	13.5	67.1	49.8	54.9	89.8	75.3
GROUP IV (25,000 to 49,999)										
Number of offenses known	6,793	426	9,780	2,217	2,751	11,673	9,125	11,086	18,315	16,768
Rate	27.0	1.7	38.9	8.8	10.9	46.4	36.3	44.1	72.9	66.7
GROUP V (10,000 to 24,999)										
Number of offenses known	6,605	460	7,926	1,584	1,958	9,054	7,832	9,998	15,782	18,938
Rate	25.6	1.8	30.8	6.1	7.6	35.1	30.4	38.8	61.2	73.5
GROUP VI (under 10,000)										
Number of offenses known	5,530	515	4,512	965	1,027	5,732	6,003	7,900	12,737	22,333
Rate	26.2	2.4	21.3	4.6	4.9	27.1	28.4	37.4	60.2	105.6
Metropolitan Counties										
Number of offenses known	14,008	906	23,476	3,576	4,344	17,540	25,661	22,852	49,899	40,394
Rate	22.3	1.4	37.4	5.7	6.9	27.9	40.9	36.4	79.5	64.4
Nonmetropolitan Counties										
Number of offenses known	5,412	333	1,709	332	541	1,462	6,812	5,654	11,449	16,046
Rate	22.9	1.4	7.2	1.4	2.3	6.2	28.8	23.9	48.4	67.8
SUBURBAN AREAS[1]										
Number of offenses known	24,810	1,686	38,600	6,657	8,098	35,656	38,923	39,127	78,148	74,651
Rate	21.8	1.5	33.9	5.8	7.1	31.3	34.2	34.4	68.6	65.5

[1] Suburban areas include law enforcement agencies in cities with less than 50,000 inhabitants and county law enforcement agencies that are within a Metropolitan Statistical Area. Suburban areas exclude all metropolitan agencies associated with a principal city. The agencies associated with suburban areas also appear in other groups within this table.

Table 19. Crime Per 100,000 Population, Selected Known Offenses, by Population Group, 2008—*Continued*

(Number, rate.)

Population group	Burglary			Motor vehicle theft			Number of agencies	2008 estimated population
	Forcible entry	Unlawful entry	Attempted forcible entry	Autos	Trucks and buses	Other vehicles		
TOTAL ALL AGENCIES:								
Number of offenses known	1,200,143	634,256	126,350	624,282	154,528	83,017	13,389	260,212,782
Rate	461.2	243.7	48.6	239.9	59.4	31.9		
Total Cities								
Number of offenses known	879,009	458,372	97,890	504,754	120,171	53,543	9,583	173,798,468
Rate	505.8	263.7	56.3	290.4	69.1	30.8		
GROUP I (250,000 and over)								
Number of offenses known	333,540	120,761	30,550	223,718	68,272	19,026	72	44,473,657
Rate	750.0	271.5	68.7	503.0	153.5	42.8		
1,000,000 and over (Group I subset)								
Number of offenses known	99,131	34,584	7,288	66,634	30,542	7,232	8	14,369,058
Rate	689.9	240.7	50.7	463.7	212.6	50.3		
500,000 to 999,999 (Group I subset)								
Number of offenses known	138,274	43,530	13,584	86,983	23,182	7,288	24	16,335,957
Rate	846.4	266.5	83.2	532.5	141.9	44.6		
250,000 to 499,999 (Group I subset)								
Number of offenses known	96,135	42,647	9,678	70,101	14,548	4,506	40	13,768,642
Rate	698.2	309.7	70.3	509.1	105.7	32.7		
GROUP II (100,000 to 249,999)								
Number of offenses known	157,019	83,291	18,382	95,245	20,481	9,327	185	27,356,767
Rate	574.0	304.5	67.2	348.2	74.9	34.1		
GROUP III (50,000 to 99,999)								
Number of offenses known	130,062	79,739	16,209	77,939	14,221	8,201	438	29,917,008
Rate	434.7	266.5	54.2	260.5	47.5	27.4		
GROUP IV (25,000 to 49,999)								
Number of offenses known	93,607	58,466	12,715	45,256	6,961	6,689	733	25,136,755
Rate	372.4	232.6	50.6	180.0	27.7	26.6		
GROUP V (10,000 to 24,999)								
Number of offenses known	91,762	61,451	11,061	37,357	6,171	5,401	1,633	25,771,354
Rate	356.1	238.4	42.9	145.0	23.9	21.0		
GROUP VI (under 10,000)								
Number of offenses known	73,019	54,664	8,973	25,239	4,065	4,899	6,522	21,142,927
Rate	345.4	258.5	42.4	119.4	19.2	23.2		
Metropolitan Counties								
Number of offenses known	240,803	130,827	22,791	101,128	29,670	22,588	1,600	62,755,364
Rate	383.7	208.5	36.3	161.1	47.3	36.0		
Nonmetropolitan Counties								
Number of offenses known	80,331	45,057	5,669	18,400	4,687	6,886	2,206	23,658,950
Rate	339.5	190.4	24.0	77.8	19.8	29.1		
SUBURBAN AREAS[1]								
Number of offenses known	398,660	241,317	43,997	180,117	42,324	33,935	7,154	113,895,695
Rate	350.0	211.9	38.6	158.1	37.2	29.8		

[1] Suburban areas include law enforcement agencies in cities with less than 50,000 inhabitants and county law enforcement agencies that are within a Metropolitan Statistical Area. Suburban areas exclude all metropolitan agencies associated with a principal city. The agencies associated with suburban areas also appear in other groups within this table.

Table 20. Murder, by State and Type of Weapon, 2008

(Number.)

State	Total murders[1]	Total firearms	Handguns	Rifles	Shotguns	Firearms (type unknown)	Knives or cutting instruments	Other weapons	Hands, fists, feet, etc.[2]
Alabama	338	262	241	1	20	0	24	35	17
Alaska	27	13	9	1	3	0	1	6	7
Arizona	405	290	243	15	16	16	45	45	25
Arkansas	157	110	65	1	9	35	17	25	5
California	2,142	1,487	1,156	48	64	219	294	241	120
Colorado	151	86	50	3	2	31	31	17	17
Connecticut	112	71	46	1	0	24	27	11	3
Delaware	57	44	29	0	2	13	6	5	2
Georgia	614	435	371	20	13	31	73	98	8
Hawaii	25	11	7	1	2	1	8	0	6
Idaho	23	14	9	2	3	0	0	3	6
Illinois[3]	530	421	412	3	1	5	48	50	11
Indiana	306	220	134	16	4	66	28	39	19
Iowa	74	25	13	2	4	6	16	20	13
Kansas	110	61	41	2	3	15	15	17	17
Kentucky	182	121	78	8	13	22	25	27	9
Louisiana	390	309	241	20	12	36	33	34	14
Maine	31	11	6	2	0	3	10	4	6
Maryland	493	353	328	4	13	8	61	51	28
Massachusetts	164	89	59	2	0	28	49	23	3
Michigan	536	375	165	16	8	186	40	94	27
Minnesota	106	54	51	1	2	0	22	22	8
Mississippi	184	142	115	4	11	12	15	20	7
Missouri	455	349	172	25	15	137	41	53	12
Montana	23	11	5	3	1	2	4	4	4
Nebraska	22	9	1	1	2	5	4	8	1
Nevada	163	93	60	1	6	26	27	35	8
New Hampshire	12	2	1	1	0	0	3	7	0
New Jersey	376	236	202	1	3	30	67	39	34
New Mexico	134	88	70	4	7	7	22	13	11
New York	835	475	107	12	20	336	184	147	29
North Carolina	586	362	261	22	25	54	54	102	68
North Dakota	3	0	0	0	0	0	2	0	1
Ohio	460	293	175	5	5	108	38	90	39
Oklahoma	212	128	106	6	10	6	33	28	23
Oregon	82	47	24	2	2	19	16	18	1
Pennsylvania	700	521	398	15	16	92	66	86	27
Rhode Island	29	18	9	0	0	9	6	4	1
South Carolina	304	206	125	9	18	54	31	43	24
South Dakota	22	13	4	0	2	7	1	7	1
Tennessee	408	240	170	11	19	40	53	91	24
Texas	1,372	895	706	58	52	79	230	140	107
Utah	41	19	16	0	0	3	8	8	6
Vermont	17	8	4	3	0	1	0	6	3
Virginia	366	240	121	12	13	94	54	61	11
Washington	190	110	82	2	10	16	32	25	23
West Virginia	55	33	14	2	10	7	5	13	4
Wisconsin	146	80	51	7	3	19	25	22	19
Wyoming	10	4	2	0	0	2	3	1	2

[1] Total number of murders for which supplemental homicide data were received.
[2] Pushed is included in hands, fists, feet, etc.
[3] Limited supplemental homicide data were received.

Table 21. Robbery, by State and Type of Weapon, 2008

(Number.)

State	Total robberies[1]	Firearms	Knives or cutting instruments	Other weapons	Strong-arm	Agency count	Population
Alabama	3,618	2,225	191	196	1,006	299	3,233,392
Alaska	642	167	60	71	344	33	673,786
Arizona	9,645	4,986	840	840	2,979	85	6,414,715
Arkansas	2,660	1,279	164	172	1,045	210	2,609,689
California	69,287	22,047	6,245	6,415	34,580	724	36,588,661
Colorado	3,148	1,191	306	353	1,298	199	4,637,260
Connecticut	3,129	994	313	336	1,486	101	3,377,299
Delaware	1,838	827	116	141	754	54	873,092
District of Columbia	4,430	1,811	234	181	2,204	3	591,833
Florida	36,224	16,915	2,267	3,075	13,967	591	18,294,452
Georgia	15,069	9,677	616	1,061	3,715	298	7,263,407
Hawaii	1,021	109	94	80	738	3	1,145,204
Idaho	215	64	32	29	90	102	1,444,155
Illinois[2]	582	261	37	51	233	1	157,262
Indiana	7,186	3,773	415	531	2,467	265	5,045,972
Iowa	1,234	295	109	160	670	194	2,765,774
Kansas	1,286	513	118	157	498	240	2,218,689
Kentucky	3,604	1,490	267	553	1,294	292	3,554,879
Louisiana	5,221	2,966	264	331	1,660	130	3,517,098
Maine	333	53	43	34	203	165	1,316,456
Maryland	9,175	4,243	833	478	3,621	156	4,999,048
Massachusetts	6,489	1,616	1,255	798	2,820	322	5,821,590
Michigan	12,459	6,295	592	1,095	4,477	480	8,705,522
Minnesota	4,142	1,322	265	635	1,920	303	4,955,284
Mississippi	2,198	1,316	124	222	536	104	1,667,671
Missouri	7,347	3,785	418	589	2,555	586	5,787,538
Montana	168	29	14	39	86	87	924,548
Nebraska	1,285	619	95	98	473	219	1,636,902
Nevada	6,473	2,693	593	557	2,630	36	2,600,167
New Hampshire	353	76	48	45	184	138	1,032,522
New Jersey	12,282	4,113	1,022	778	6,369	527	8,522,218
New Mexico	2,031	950	247	156	678	69	1,606,223
New York	9,524	2,831	959	1,186	4,548	587	10,739,528
North Carolina	12,862	7,288	894	1,059	3,621	324	7,452,925
North Dakota	70	9	10	11	40	71	580,591
Ohio	17,242	7,200	719	1,575	7,748	412	8,532,469
Oklahoma	3,639	1,764	286	261	1,328	281	3,418,015
Oregon	2,618	611	300	267	1,440	152	3,649,695
Pennsylvania	18,636	7,781	1,282	1,218	8,355	1,126	11,891,768
Rhode Island	879	215	116	108	440	48	1,050,788
South Carolina	6,000	3,402	417	490	1,691	454	3,848,869
South Dakota	116	25	19	15	57	98	652,677
Tennessee	10,666	6,416	697	852	2,701	433	5,845,629
Texas	37,718	17,962	3,218	3,398	13,140	987	24,292,555
Utah	1,415	450	152	157	656	118	2,687,888
Vermont	89	22	19	13	35	80	604,277
Virginia	7,390	4,166	489	664	2,071	377	7,694,707
Washington	6,116	1,481	551	611	3,473	234	6,125,943
West Virginia	521	166	46	90	219	155	1,046,031
Wisconsin	5,124	2,651	330	453	1,690	374	5,588,110
Wyoming	85	23	13	8	41	62	528,009

[1] The number of robberies for which breakdowns by type of weapon were received from agencies that submitted 12 months of data in 2008.
[2] Limited data were received.

Table 22. Aggravated Assault, by State and Type of Weapon, 2008

(Number.)

State	Total aggravated assaults[1]	Firearms	Knives or cutting instruments	Other weapons	Personal weapons	Agency count	Population
Alabama	7,659	2,258	1,107	1,672	2,622	299	3,233,392
Alaska	3,307	535	679	895	1,198	33	673,786
Arizona	16,974	4,842	2,954	5,141	4,037	85	6,414,715
Arkansas	9,641	2,316	1,605	2,168	3,552	210	2,609,689
California	103,892	19,126	16,601	37,917	30,248	724	36,588,661
Colorado	10,530	2,029	2,486	2,767	3,248	199	4,637,260
Connecticut	4,595	548	1,017	1,597	1,433	101	3,377,299
Delaware	3,880	971	864	1,624	421	54	873,092
District of Columbia	3,707	847	1,086	1,310	464	3	591,833
Florida	82,681	16,697	14,597	32,236	19,151	591	18,294,452
Georgia	20,206	5,476	3,650	5,251	5,829	298	7,263,407
Hawaii	1,846	182	413	602	649	3	1,145,204
Idaho	2,403	355	466	773	809	102	1,444,155
Illinois[2]	1,482	760	233	360	129	1	157,262
Indiana	10,655	1,735	1,486	3,367	4,067	265	5,045,972
Iowa	6,125	588	1,025	1,433	3,079	194	2,765,774
Kansas	6,801	1,786	1,367	2,265	1,383	240	2,218,689
Kentucky	5,913	1,224	885	2,371	1,433	292	3,554,879
Louisiana	16,643	4,335	2,593	4,368	5,347	130	3,517,098
Maine	808	59	206	210	333	165	1,316,456
Maryland	14,881	2,023	3,433	5,168	4,257	156	4,999,048
Massachusetts	18,739	1,859	4,357	9,863	2,660	322	5,821,590
Michigan	30,232	7,918	5,855	10,603	5,856	480	8,705,522
Minnesota	7,372	1,226	1,641	2,023	2,482	303	4,955,284
Mississippi	2,489	860	497	620	512	104	1,667,671
Missouri	19,953	5,904	2,719	5,384	5,946	586	5,787,538
Montana	1,939	264	272	588	815	87	924,548
Nebraska	3,353	499	598	1,516	740	219	1,636,902
Nevada	11,099	1,936	2,144	5,214	1,805	36	2,600,167
New Hampshire	1,023	167	343	277	236	138	1,032,522
New Jersey	13,561	2,063	3,062	4,183	4,253	527	8,522,218
New Mexico	7,676	1,742	1,333	2,278	2,323	69	1,606,223
New York	16,801	2,190	4,646	4,921	5,044	587	10,739,528
North Carolina	21,408	6,658	4,221	5,795	4,734	324	7,452,925
North Dakota	734	15	92	145	482	71	580,591
Ohio	14,131	3,370	2,963	4,436	3,362	412	8,532,469
Oklahoma	13,293	2,464	2,149	4,940	3,740	281	3,418,015
Oregon	5,766	680	1,030	1,971	2,085	152	3,649,695
Pennsylvania	27,141	5,348	4,098	6,787	10,908	1,126	11,891,768
Rhode Island	1,436	304	452	497	183	48	1,050,788
South Carolina	21,284	5,602	3,887	5,819	5,976	454	3,848,869
South Dakota	942	112	345	325	160	98	652,677
Tennessee	30,407	9,381	6,539	11,196	3,291	433	5,845,629
Texas	76,279	17,622	16,875	26,750	15,032	987	24,292,555
Utah	3,672	600	1,036	1,307	729	118	2,687,888
Vermont	609	60	134	143	272	80	604,277
Virginia	10,139	2,146	2,311	3,451	2,231	377	7,694,707
Washington	11,947	1,805	2,171	3,848	4,123	234	6,125,943
West Virginia	2,560	559	403	736	862	155	1,046,031
Wisconsin	9,012	2,003	926	1,916	4,167	374	5,588,110
Wyoming	949	96	173	284	396	62	528,009

[1] The number of aggravated assaults for which breakdowns by type of weapon were received from agencies that submitted 12 months of data in 2008.
[2] Limited data were received.

Table 23. Offense Analysis, Number and Percent Change, 2007–2008

(Number, percent, dollars; 13,845 agencies; 2008 estimated population 262,132,235.)

Classification	Number of offenses, 2008	Percent change from 2007	Percent distribution[1]	Average value
Murder	13,180	-5.4	-	
Forcible rape	75,068	-1.8	-	
Robbery:[1]	358,847	-1.6	100.0	$1,315
By location:				
Street/highway	154,561	-0.5	43.1	1,032
Commercial house	49,517	-2.1	13.8	1,651
Gas or service station	9,278	-4.8	2.6	1,007
Convenience store	19,735	-5.5	5.5	712
Residence	58,424	+2.5	16.3	1,589
Bank	7,278	-5.1	2.0	4,854
Miscellaneous	60,054	-5.3	16.7	1,317
Burglary:[1]	1,924,025	+1.5	100.0	2,079
By location:				
Residence (dwelling):	1,353,258	+5.1	70.3	2,060
Residence Night	378,370	+0.9	19.7	1,610
Residence Day	697,153	+6.4	36.2	2,170
Residence Unknown	277,735	+8.0	14.4	2,396
Nonresidence (store, office, etc.):	570,767	-6.0	29.7	2,123
Nonresidence Night	238,891	-6.1	12.4	1,747
Nonresidence Day	192,760	-7.1	10.0	2,087
Nonresidence Unknown	139,116	-4.5	7.2	2,819
Larceny-theft (except motor vehicle theft):[1]	5,602,099	+0.7	100.0	925
By type:				
Pocket-picking	23,085	-10.7	0.4	563
Purse-snatching	28,336	+9.2	0.5	427
Shoplifting	908,127	*	16.2	196
From motor vehicles (except accessories)	1,458,529	+6.2	26.0	724
Motor vehicle accessories	546,893	-0.2	9.8	532
Bicycles	188,698	-5.3	3.4	289
From buildings	640,870	-16.7	11.4	1,540
From coin-operated machines	22,880	-4.8	0.4	354
All others	1,784,681	-0.4	31.9	1,448
By value:				
Over $200	2,522,679	+2.4	45.0	1,987
$50 to $200	1,246,102	-0.8	22.2	109
Under $50	1,833,318	-3.8	32.7	18
Motor vehicle theft	825,527	-13.5	-	6,751

[1] Because of rounding, the percentages may not add to 100.0.
* Less than one-tenth of 1 percent.

Table 24. Property Stolen and Recovered, by Type and Value, 2008

(Dollars, percent; 13,301 agencies; 2008 estimated population 253,453,367.)

Type of property	Value of property		Percent recovered
	Stolen	Recovered	
Total	$14,832,665,848	$3,816,312,784	25.7
Currency, notes, etc.	1,151,853,609	40,571,672	3.5
Jewelry and precious metals	1,501,337,916	63,842,862	4.3
Clothing and furs	288,616,049	36,699,571	12.7
Locally stolen motor vehicles	5,640,153,991	3,224,301,776	57.2
Office equipment	876,730,353	34,020,122	3.9
Televisions, radios, stereos, etc.	966,272,029	51,089,823	5.3
Firearms	142,215,920	12,207,052	8.6
Household goods	337,571,821	10,569,384	3.1
Consumable goods	138,864,080	15,221,279	11.0
Livestock	22,826,952	2,496,863	10.9
Miscellaneous	3,766,223,128	325,292,380	8.6

SECTION III:
OFFENSES CLEARED

OFFENSES CLEARED

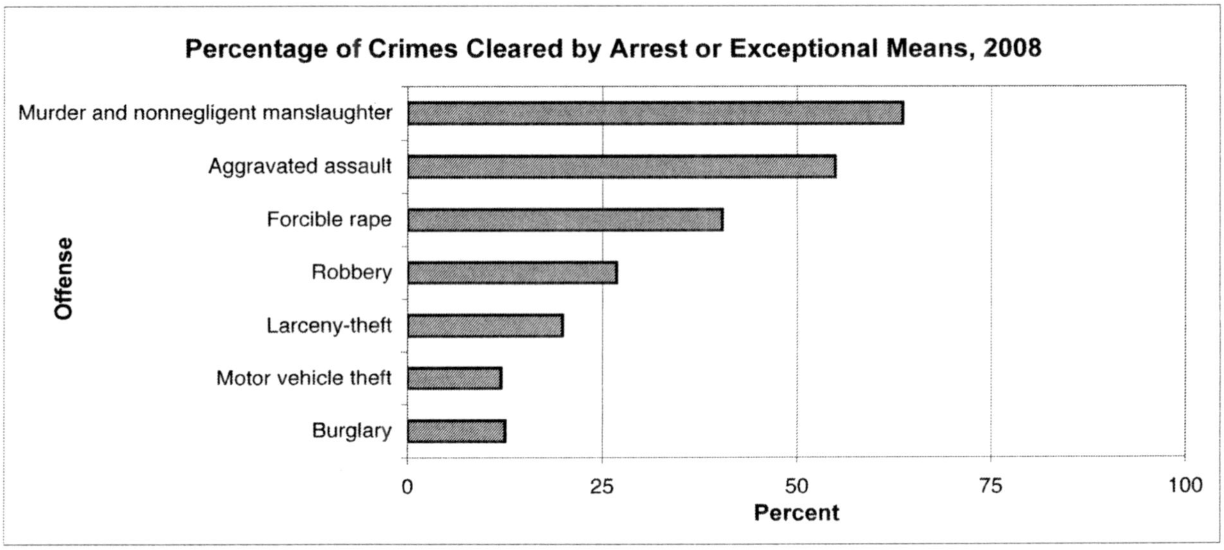

Law enforcement agencies that report crime to the Federal Bureau of Investigation (FBI) can clear, or "close," offenses in one of two ways: by arrest or by exceptional means. However, the administrative closing of a case by a local law enforcement agency does not necessarily mean that the agency can clear an offense for UCR purposes. To clear an offense within the program's guidelines, the reporting agency must adhere to certain criteria, which are outlined in this section. (*Note:* The UCR Program does not distinguish between offenses cleared by arrest and those cleared by exceptional means in its data presentations. The distinction is made solely for the purpose of a definition and not for data collection and publication.) See Appendix I for information on the UCR Program's statistical methodology.

Cleared by Arrest

In the UCR Program, a law enforcement agency reports that an offense is cleared by arrest, or solved for crime reporting purposes, when at least one person is arrested, charged with the commission of the offense, and turned over to the court for prosecution (whether following arrest, court summons, or police notice). To qualify as a clearance, *all* of these conditions must be met.

In its calculations, the UCR Program counts the number of offenses that are cleared, not the number of arrestees. Therefore, the arrest of one person may clear several crimes, and the arrest of many persons may clear only one offense. In addition, some clearances recorded by an agency during a particular calendar year, such as 2008, may pertain to offenses that occurred in previous years.

Cleared by Exceptional Means

In certain situations, elements beyond law enforcement's control prevent the agency from arresting and formally charging the offender. When this occurs, the agency can clear the offense *exceptionally*. There are four UCR Program requirements that law enforcement must meet in order to clear an offense by exceptional means. The agency must have:

- Identified the offender
- Gathered enough evidence to support an arrest, make a charge, and turn over the offender to the court for prosecution
- Identified the offender's exact location so that the suspect could be taken into custody immediately
- Encountered a circumstance outside the control of law enforcement that prohibits the agency from arresting, charging, and prosecuting the offender

Examples of exceptional clearances include, but are not limited to, the death of the offender (e.g., suicide or justifiably killed by a law enforcement officer or a citizen), the victim's refusal to cooperate with the prosecution after the offender has been identified, or the denial of extradition because the offender committed a crime in another jurisdiction and is being prosecuted for that offense. In the UCR Program, the recovery of property does not clear an offense.

National Clearances

A review of the data for 2008 revealed law enforcement agencies in the United States cleared 45.1 percent of violent crimes (murder, forcible rape, robbery, and aggravated assault) and 17.4 percent of property crimes (burglary, larceny-theft, and motor vehicle theft) brought to their attention. In

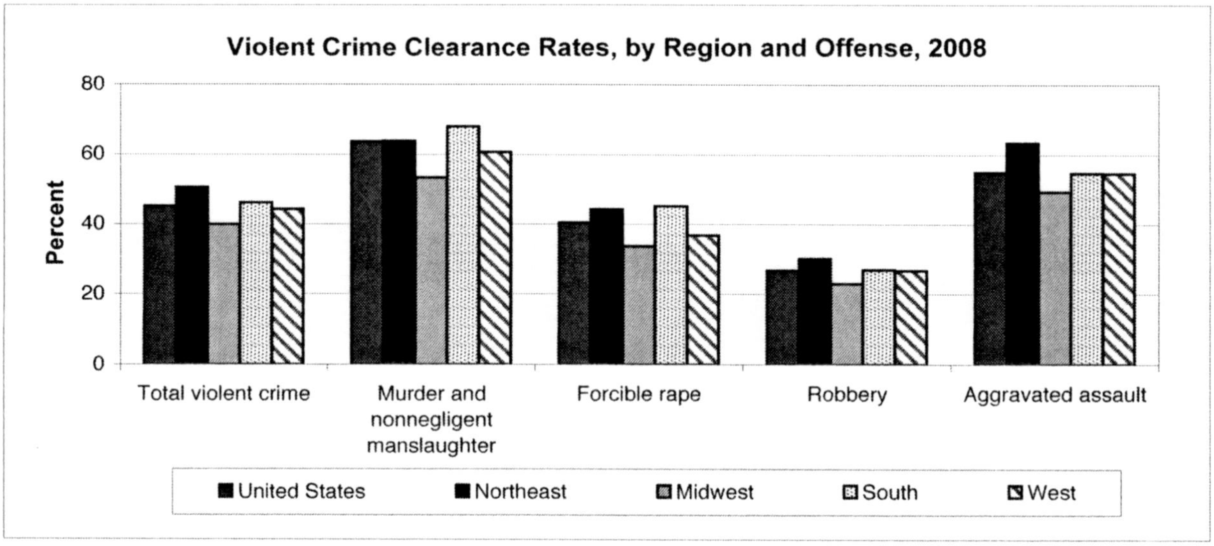

addition, law enforcement cleared 17.8 percent of arson offenses.

As in most years, law enforcement agencies cleared a higher percentage of violent crimes than property crimes in 2008. As a rule, this long-term trend is attributed to the more vigorous investigative efforts put forth for violent crimes. In addition, violent crimes more often involve victims and/or witnesses who are able to identify the perpetrators.

A breakdown of the clearances for violent crimes for 2008 revealed that the nation's law enforcement agencies cleared 63.6 percent of murder offenses, 54.9 percent of aggravated assault offenses, 40.4 percent of forcible rape offenses, and 26.8 percent of robbery offenses. The data for property crimes showed that agencies cleared 19.9 percent of larceny-theft offenses, 12.5 percent of burglary offenses, and 12.0 percent of motor vehicle theft offenses. (Table 25)

Law enforcement agencies throughout the nation collectively cleared 17.4 percent of property crime offenses in 2008, including 12.5 percent of burglary offenses, 19.9 percent of larceny-theft offenses, 12.0 percent of motor vehicle theft offenses, and 17.8 percent of arson offenses. (Table 25)

Regional Clearances

The UCR Program divides the nation into four regions: the Northeast, the Midwest, the South, and the West. (See Appendix III for further details.) A review of clearance data for 2008 by region showed that agencies in the Northeast cleared the greatest proportion of their violent crime offenses (50.4 percent). Law enforcement agencies in the South cleared 46.0 percent of their violent crimes, while agencies in the West and Midwest cleared 44.2 percent and 39.9 percent, respectively.

For murder and nonnegligent manslaughter, the South cleared 68.0 percent of offenses, followed by the Northeast (63.8 percent), the West (60.7 percent) and the Midwest (53.3 percent each). Forcible rape offenses were cleared 45.2 percent of the time in the South, 44.2 percent of the time in the Northeast, 36.8 percent in the West, and 33.7 percent in the Midwest. For robbery, the Northeast had the highest clearance rate, at 30.1 percent. The Northeast also had the highest proportion of clearances for aggravated assault (63.3 percent). (Table 26)

Clearance data for 2008 showed that, among the regions, law enforcement agencies in the Northeast cleared the highest percentage of their property crimes (20.5 percent). Agencies in the South and Midwest cleared 17.8 percent and 17.5 percent, respectively. Agencies in the West cleared 15.3 percent of their property crimes. (Table 26) The South cleared the highest number of offenses at nearly 4 million. Agencies in the Northeast cleared the highest percentage of burglary offenses at 15.6 percent, followed by the South at 13.0 percent, the West at 11.5 percent, and the Midwest at 10.7 percent. For larceny-theft, the Northeast (22.4 percent) was followed by the Midwest (20.3 percent), the South (20.0 percent), and the West (18.3 percent). The Northeast also cleared the highest proportion of motor vehicle thefts at 15.2 percent and the greatest percentage of arson offenses (23.6 percent). (Table 26)

Clearances by Population Groups

The UCR Program uses the following population group designations in its data presentations: cities (grouped according to population size) and counties (classified as either metropolitan or nonmetropolitan counties). (A breakdown of these classifications is furnished in Appendix III.)

Cities

In 2008, the clearance data collected showed that law enforcement agencies in the nation's cities cleared 43.1 percent of their violent crime offenses. Among the city population groups, agencies in the smallest cities, those with populations under 10,000 inhabitants, cleared the greatest proportion of their violent crime offenses (54.5 percent), and law enforcement in cities with 500,000 to 999,999 inhabitants cleared the smallest proportion of their violent crime offenses (36.9 percent).

The clearance data for murder showed that among the city population groups, cities with populations of 10,000 to 24,999 inhabitants cleared the greatest percentage of their murders (70.9 percent). Law enforcement agencies in cities with 500,000 to 999,000 inhabitants cleared the lowest percentage of their murders (53.6 percent). For forcible rape, cities with 1,000,000 or more inhabitants cleared the largest percentage of offenses at 47.6 percent, while cities with 25,000 to 49,999 inhabitants cleared the lowest percentage of offenses at 35.4 percent. Cities with fewer than 10,000 inhabitants cleared the greatest percentage of their robbery offenses at 34.0 percent, and cities with 500,000 to 999,999 inhabitants cleared the lowest proportion of their robbery offenses at 21.5 percent. For aggravated assault, cities with under 10,000 inhabitants cleared the highest proportion of offenses (61.2 percent); cities with 500,000 to 999,999 inhabitants cleared the lowest percentage of offenses (47.0 percent). (Table 25)

In 2008, agencies in the nation's cities collectively cleared 17.6 percent of their property crime offenses. Law enforcement in cities with 10,000 to 24,999 inhabitants cleared the highest proportion of the property crimes (22.2 percent) brought to their attention; cities with 500,000 to 999,999 inhabitants cleared the smallest proportion of their property crimes (12.3 percent). (Table 25)

Law enforcement agencies in cities cleared 12.0 percent of burglaries, 20.3 percent of larceny-thefts, 11.0 percent of motor vehicle thefts, and 17.7 percent of arsons in 2008. (Table 25) For burglaries, cities with under 10,000 inhabitants cleared the largest percentage of their offenses, at 16.3 percent, while cities with 1,000,000 or more inhabitants cleared the smallest percentage of their offenses, at 8.1 percent. Cities with 10,000 to 24,999 inhabitants cleared the greatest percentage of their larceny-theft offenses (22.5 percent), and cities with 500,000 to 999,999 inhabitants cleared the lowest proportion of larceny-theft offenses (14.4 percent). For motor vehicle theft and arson, cities with under 10,000 inhabitants cleared the highest percentages of their offenses, at 22.1 percent and 26.7 percent, respectively. (Table 25)

Metropolitan and Nonmetropolitan Counties

In 2008, law enforcement agencies in metropolitan counties cleared 51.2 percent of their violent crime offenses. Of the violent crimes made known to law enforcement agencies, murder offenses had the highest proportion of clearance (65.8 percent), followed by 59.8 percent of aggravated assaults, 44.0 percent of forcible rapes, and 28.3 percent of robberies being cleared. Law enforcement agencies in metropolitan counties cleared 16.7 percent of their total property crimes, 13.2 percent of burglaries, 18.5 percent of larceny-thefts, 14.3 percent of motor vehicle thefts, and 17.0 percent of their arsons. (Table 25)

Like their counterparts in metropolitan counties, nonmetropolitan counties collectively cleared a greater proportion of their violent crimes than did the nation as a whole in 2008. Nonmetropolitan counties cleared 57.7 percent of their violent crime offenses and 17.9 percent of property crimes. Of the violent crimes known to them, law enforcement in nonmetropolitan counties had the highest number of clearances for murder (68.1 percent), 44.9 percent of forcible rapes, 39.0 percent of robberies, and 61.3 percent of aggravated assaults being cleared. Agencies in nonmetropolitan counties reported clearing 16.0 percent of their burglaries, 18.1 percent of their larceny-thefts, 23.8 percent of their motor vehicle thefts, and 22.1 percent of their arsons. (Table 25)

Clearances by Classification Group and Type

For forcible rape, by classification group and type, law enforcement agencies cleared 40.5 percent of assault to rape attempts and 39.3 percent of rapes by force in 2008. Cleared robbery offenses included 30.8 percent of offenses involving strong-arm tactics, 29.4 percent of offenses involving knives or other cutting instruments, 21.0 percent of offenses involving firearms, and 28.8 percent of offenses involving other weapons. For aggravated assault, agencies cleared 59.4 percent of offenses involving hands, feet, fists, etc.; 61.8 percent of offenses involving knives or other cutting instruments; 39.5 percent of offenses involving firearms; and 55.3 percent of offenses involving other weapons. (Table 27)

For property crime clearances grouped by classification and type, data showed that the highest percentage of burglary clearances in the nation in 2008 (13.9 percent) were of offenses that involved unlawful entry of structures. Law enforcement agencies cleared 11.6 percent of burglaries involving forcible entry and 10.6 percent of attempted forcible entry offenses. For motor vehicle theft, agencies cleared 12.3 percent of motor vehicle theft offenses involving automobiles and 9.5 percent of motor vehicle theft offenses involving trucks and buses. (Table 27)

In 2008, 21.4 percent of structural arson offenses were cleared by arrest or exceptional means, while 8.8 percent of mobile arson offenses and 21.0 percent of other arson crimes were cleared. (Table 27)

Clearances and Juveniles

When an offender under 18 years of age is cited to appear in juvenile court or before other juvenile authorities, the

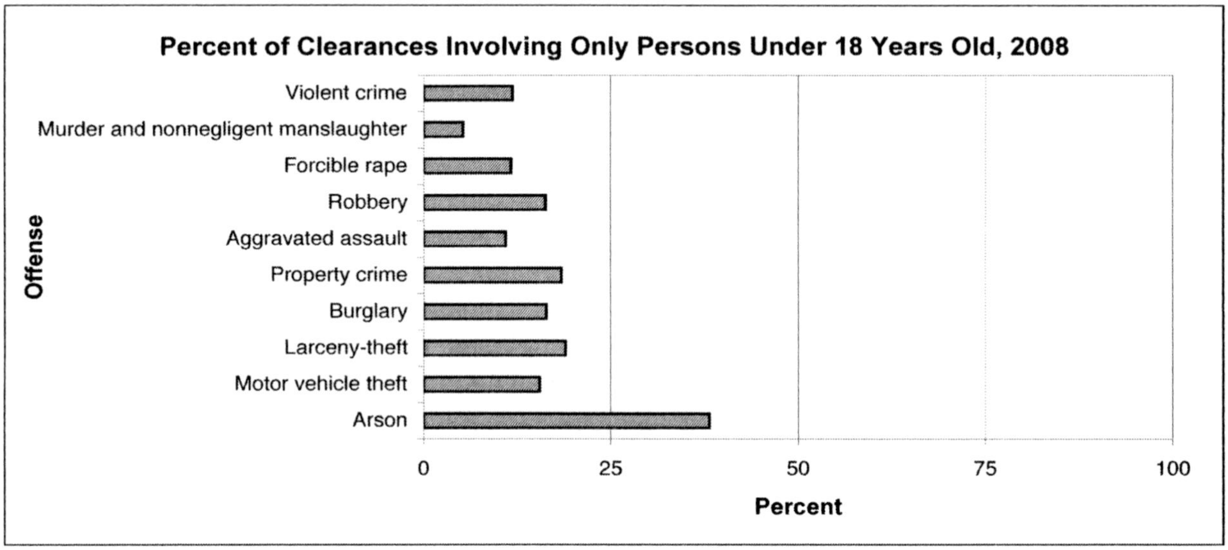

UCR Program considers the incident for which the juvenile is being held responsible to be cleared by arrest, although a physical arrest may not have occurred. In addition, according to program definitions, clearances that include both adult and juvenile offenders are classified as clearances for crimes committed by adults. Therefore, the juvenile clearance data are limited to those clearances involving juveniles only, and the figures in this publication should not be used to present a definitive picture of juvenile involvement in crime.

Of the clearances for violent crimes that were reported in the nation in 2008, 11.9 percent involved only juveniles, down from 12.3 percent in 2007. In the nation's cities, collectively, 12.1 percent of violent crime clearances involved only juveniles, with juveniles in cities exclusively involved in 5.7 percent of murder clearances, 11.0 percent of forcible rape clearances, 16.3 percent of robbery clearances, and 11.1 percent of aggravated assault clearances. Of the nation's city population groups, cities with 50,000 to 99,999 inhabitants had the highest percentage of overall clearances for violent crime only involving juveniles (13.4 percent); cities with 1,000,000 or more inhabitants had the lowest percentage (10.4 percent).

Law enforcement agencies in metropolitan counties reported that 12.3 percent of their violent crime clearances—including 4.1 percent of their murder clearances, 13.1 percent of their forcible rape clearances, 17.0 percent of their robbery clearances, and 11.6 percent of their aggravated assault clearances—involved only juveniles. Agencies in nonmetropolitan counties reported that 8.9 percent of their clearances for violent crime involved only juveniles, including 3.0 percent of their murder clearances, 14.8 percent of their forcible rape clearances, 7.8 percent of their robbery clearances, and 8.4 percent of their aggravated assault clearances. (Table 28)

In 2008, 18.4 percent of clearances for property crime involved only juveniles. Nineteen percent of all reported larceny-theft clearances involved only juveniles. In cities collectively, 19.0 percent of the clearances for property crime, 16.7 percent of clearances for burglary, 19.6 percent of clearances for larceny-theft, 15.7 percent of clearances for motor vehicle theft, and 39.9 percent of clearances for arson involved juveniles only. Among the population groups labeled *city*, the percentages of clearances involving only juveniles for overall property crime ranged from a low of 16.1 percent in cities with populations fewer than 10,000 inhabitants to a high of 21.2 percent in cities with populations of 100,000 to 249,999.

Metropolitan counties reported 16.7 percent of property crime clearances, 16.6 percent of burglary clearances, 16.9 percent of larceny-theft clearances, 15.2 percent of motor vehicle theft clearances, and 37.1 percent of arson clearances involved persons under 18 years of age. In nonmetropolitan counties, 13.3 percent of property crime clearances, 13.6 percent of burglary clearances, 13.1 percent of larceny-theft clearances, 14.1 percent of motor vehicle theft clearances, and 23.9 percent of arson clearances involved juveniles exclusively. In suburban areas, 42.1 percent of arson clearances involved only juveniles. (Table 28)

Arson offenses had the highest percentage of clearances involving only juveniles—38.2 percent—nationally in 2008. (Table 28) Of clearances for structural arsons, 37.4 percent involved only juveniles. Approximately 20.3 percent of clearances for mobile arsons and 48.7 percent of other property type arsons involved only juveniles. (Expanded Arson Table 2; see Section I for more information)

Table 25. Number and Percent of Offenses Cleared by Arrest or Exceptional Means, by Population Group, 2008

(Number, percent.)

Population group	Violent crime	Murder and non-negligent man-slaughter	Forcible rape	Robbery	Aggra-vated assault	Property crime	Burglary	Larceny-theft	Motor vehicle theft	Arson[1]	Number of agencies	2008 estimated population
TOTAL ALL AGENCIES:												
Offenses known	1,204,655	14,225	78,919	381,768	729,743	8,628,538	1,978,524	5,781,757	868,257	59,868	14,074	262,319,792
Percent cleared by arrest	45.1	63.6	40.4	26.8	54.9	17.4	12.5	19.9	12.0	17.8		
Total Cities												
Offenses known	945,218	10,795	58,111	327,781	548,531	6,673,088	1,445,576	4,546,371	681,141	44,295	10,155	174,772,477
Percent cleared by arrest	43.1	62.7	39.0	26.4	53.2	17.6	12.0	20.3	11.0	17.7		
GROUP I (250,000 and over)												
Offenses known	401,676	5,433	17,905	163,198	215,140	2,087,161	486,682	1,288,640	311,839	16,532	72	44,176,815
Percent cleared by arrest	37.9	58.6	42.2	23.6	47.8	13.2	9.5	15.7	8.6	13.2		
1,000,000 and over (Group I subset)												
Offenses known	123,058	1,637	5,246	54,628	61,547	623,701	141,003	378,290	104,408	5,326	8	14,369,058
Percent cleared by arrest	38.2	70.1	47.6	25.1	48.2	12.4	8.1	15.2	7.9	10.5		
500,000 to 999,999 (Group I subset)												
Offenses known	159,727	2,133	6,517	62,423	88,654	831,918	196,850	516,045	119,023	5,507	24	16,064,157
Percent cleared by arrest	36.9	53.6	41.6	21.5	47.0	12.3	9.1	14.4	8.7	14.2		
250,000 to 499,999 (Group I subset)												
Offenses known	118,891	1,663	6,142	46,147	64,939	631,542	148,829	394,305	88,408	5,699	40	13,743,600
Percent cleared by arrest	38.9	53.8	38.1	24.7	48.7	15.1	11.3	17.8	9.4	14.9		
GROUP II (100,000 to 249,999)												
Offenses known	168,868	1,993	10,229	62,075	94,571	1,201,078	269,014	801,783	130,281	7,209	190	28,236,007
Percent cleared by arrest	42.5	64.6	38.8	26.2	53.0	16.8	11.3	19.8	9.9	16.4		
GROUP III (50,000 to 99,999)												
Offenses known	133,570	1,316	9,277	42,981	79,996	1,052,700	223,771	731,207	97,722	6,925	436	29,790,618
Percent cleared by arrest	45.2	63.4	35.7	29.0	54.7	19.4	13.2	22.5	11.0	17.9		
GROUP IV (25,000 to 49,999)												
Offenses known	89,983	804	7,278	26,231	55,670	809,060	161,951	589,635	57,474	4,912	726	24,893,513
Percent cleared by arrest	48.1	71.4	35.4	30.9	57.6	20.3	12.5	23.1	13.3	19.7		
GROUP V (10,000 to 24,999)												
Offenses known	81,526	688	7,164	20,738	52,936	808,115	164,708	594,376	49,031	4,372	1,623	25,613,592
Percent cleared by arrest	51.6	70.9	38.4	32.7	60.5	22.2	14.7	24.6	17.9	25.7		
GROUP VI (under 10,000)												
Offenses known	69,595	561	6,258	12,558	50,218	714,974	139,450	540,730	34,794	4,345	7,108	22,061,932
Percent cleared by arrest	54.5	70.8	40.3	34.0	61.2	20.7	16.3	21.7	22.1	26.7		
Metropolitan Counties												
Offenses known	208,390	2,577	14,963	49,882	140,968	1,551,116	400,225	994,354	156,537	12,241	1,661	63,542,081
Percent cleared by arrest	51.2	65.8	44.0	28.3	59.8	16.7	13.2	18.5	14.3	17.0		
Nonmetropolitan Counties												
Offenses known	51,047	853	5,845	4,105	40,244	404,334	132,723	241,032	30,579	3,332	2,258	24,005,234
Percent cleared by arrest	57.7	68.1	44.9	39.0	61.3	17.9	16.0	18.1	23.8	22.1		
SUBURBAN AREAS[2]												
Offenses known	353,856	3,783	26,770	89,943	233,360	3,036,247	687,409	2,090,633	258,205	20,465	7,462	114,616,380
Percent cleared by arrest	51.1	66.7	41.4	29.7	60.2	18.6	13.6	20.7	14.6	19.8		

[1] Not all agencies submit reports for arson to the FBI. As a result, the number of reports the FBI uses to compute the percent of offenses cleared for arson is less than the number it uses to compute the percent of offenses cleared for all other offenses.

[2] Suburban areas include law enforcement agencies in cities with less than 50,000 inhabitants and county law enforcement agencies that are within a Metropolitan Statistical Area. Suburban areas exclude all metropolitan agencies associated with a principal city. The agencies associated with suburban areas also appear in other groups within this table.

Table 26. Number and Percent of Offenses Cleared by Arrest or Exceptional Means, by Region and Geographic Division, 2008

(Number, percent.)

Geographic region/division	Violent crime	Murder and non-negligent man-slaughter	Forcible rape	Robbery	Aggra-vated assault	Property crime	Burglary	Larceny-theft	Motor vehicle theft	Arson[1]	Number of agencies	2008 estimated population
TOTAL ALL AGENCIES:												
Offenses known	1,204,655	14,225	78,919	381,768	729,743	8,628,538	1,978,524	5,781,757	868,257	59,868	14,074	262,319,792
Percent cleared by arrest	45.1	63.6	40.4	26.8	54.9	17.4	12.5	19.9	12.0	17.8		
Northeast												
Offenses known	148,881	1,735	9,571	52,671	84,904	1,032,119	206,449	745,020	80,650	6,591	3,150	44,564,427
Percent cleared by arrest	50.4	63.8	44.2	30.1	63.3	20.5	15.6	22.4	15.2	23.6		
New England												
Offenses known	43,601	359	3,308	12,035	27,899	327,274	66,933	233,968	26,373	1,886	882	13,644,453
Percent cleared by arrest	48.0	53.8	30.4	26.0	59.5	15.4	12.3	16.9	9.8	21.8		
Middle Atlantic												
Offenses known	105,280	1,376	6,263	40,636	57,005	704,845	139,516	511,052	54,277	4,705	2,268	30,919,974
Percent cleared by arrest	51.3	66.4	51.5	31.4	65.2	22.8	17.2	24.9	17.8	24.3		
Midwest												
Offenses known	185,906	2,179	17,256	56,782	109,689	1,495,421	334,714	1,030,573	130,134	12,514	3,487	46,953,492
Percent cleared by arrest	39.9	53.3	33.7	22.9	49.4	17.5	10.7	20.3	13.1	15.9		
East North Central												
Offenses known	117,535	1,358	10,363	41,734	64,080	913,905	219,617	609,540	84,748	8,125	1,637	27,794,694
Percent cleared by arrest	35.4	47.9	30.5	21.7	44.8	16.3	10.0	19.2	11.6	14.4		
West North Central												
Offenses known	68,371	821	6,893	15,048	45,609	581,516	115,097	421,033	45,386	4,389	1,850	19,158,798
Percent cleared by arrest	47.7	62.4	38.3	26.1	56.0	19.4	12.0	21.8	15.8	18.6		
South												
Offenses known	567,472	6,979	31,859	171,636	356,998	3,981,945	984,104	2,652,643	345,198	22,581	5,540	103,539,490
Percent cleared by arrest	46.0	68.0	45.2	27.0	54.7	17.8	13.0	20.0	14.6	19.1		
South Atlantic												
Offenses known	310,043	3,740	15,041	99,273	191,989	2,098,721	508,101	1,400,199	190,421	11,506	2,755	54,995,451
Percent cleared by arrest	47.3	66.0	49.2	27.4	57.1	19.1	14.7	21.1	15.5	20.3		
East South Central												
Offenses known	79,379	1,060	5,211	23,241	49,867	564,622	149,021	373,566	42,035	2,271	1,165	15,265,637
Percent cleared by arrest	45.6	67.5	38.7	27.1	54.5	17.6	11.6	20.3	15.7	19.8		
West South Central												
Offenses known	178,050	2,179	11,607	49,122	115,142	1,318,602	326,982	878,878	112,742	8,804	1,620	33,278,402
Percent cleared by arrest	43.7	71.9	42.9	26.2	50.7	15.8	10.8	18.0	12.7	17.4		
West												
Offenses known	302,396	3,332	20,233	100,679	178,152	2,119,053	453,257	1,353,521	312,275	18,182	1,897	67,262,383
Percent cleared by arrest	44.2	60.7	36.8	26.7	54.6	15.3	11.5	18.3	7.9	15.5		
Mountain												
Offenses known	87,091	929	7,558	23,185	55,419	688,344	149,874	454,576	83,894	4,975	774	20,958,751
Percent cleared by arrest	44.5	67.1	32.8	24.0	54.3	16.9	9.5	20.8	9.2	18.4		
Pacific												
Offenses known	215,305	2,403	12,675	77,494	122,733	1,430,709	303,383	898,945	228,381	13,207	1,123	46,303,632
Percent cleared by arrest	44.1	58.2	39.1	27.5	54.7	14.5	12.5	17.0	7.4	14.4		

[1] Not all agencies submit reports for arson to the FBI. As a result, the number of reports the FBI uses to compute the percent of offenses cleared for arson is less than the number it uses to compute the percent of offenses cleared for all other offenses.

Table 27. Number and Percent of Offenses Cleared by Arrest or Exceptional Means, by Population Group, 2008

(Number, percent.)

Population group	Forcible rape		Robbery				Aggravated assault			
	Rape by force	Assault to rape-attempts	Firearm	Knife or cutting instrument	Other weapon	Strongarm	Firearm	Knife or cutting instrument	Other weapon	Hands, fists, feet, etc.
TOTAL ALL AGENCIES:										
Offenses known	66,958	5,502	145,944	26,407	29,502	135,712	138,167	121,413	210,134	169,256
Percent cleared by arrest	39.3	40.5	21.0	29.4	28.8	30.8	39.5	61.8	55.3	59.4
Total Cities										
Offenses known	50,184	4,377	126,207	23,322	25,725	121,074	111,844	98,634	163,569	122,123
Percent cleared by arrest	38.1	40.5	21.0	28.9	28.5	30.4	37.7	61.3	54.2	58.4
GROUP I (250,000 and over)										
Offenses known	15,526	1,828	70,741	11,232	11,785	58,130	58,866	39,426	69,598	31,592
Percent cleared by arrest	41.4	41.4	19.4	26.3	25.2	27.3	34.2	58.7	50.6	50.3
1,000,000 and over (Group I subset)										
Offenses known	4,477	769	24,427	4,793	4,269	21,139	17,617	13,163	20,691	10,076
Percent cleared by arrest	48.4	42.9	19.6	25.9	27.5	30.8	35.8	57.9	51.2	50.8
500,000 to 999,999 (Group I subset)										
Offenses known	5,545	573	27,386	3,759	4,396	19,918	23,652	15,632	27,980	10,990
Percent cleared by arrest	40.3	39.6	17.2	25.6	23.8	23.4	34.5	58.0	48.4	47.7
250,000 to 499,999 (Group I subset)										
Offenses known	5,504	486	18,928	2,680	3,120	17,073	17,597	10,631	20,927	10,526
Percent cleared by arrest	36.7	41.2	22.2	28.2	24.1	27.6	32.3	60.8	53.0	52.5
GROUP II (100,000 to 249,999)										
Offenses known	8,234	673	21,663	4,252	5,168	21,285	18,554	17,688	28,171	15,620
Percent cleared by arrest	37.7	39.1	20.4	27.3	28.3	30.7	37.5	62.4	54.6	61.5
GROUP III (50,000 to 99,999)										
Offenses known	8,040	569	13,607	3,404	3,549	17,595	13,230	14,610	22,992	20,205
Percent cleared by arrest	34.8	38.7	23.6	29.5	32.1	32.2	38.1	61.1	56.4	57.5
GROUP IV (25,000 to 49,999)										
Offenses known	6,451	390	8,583	2,054	2,444	10,392	8,196	10,095	16,370	15,447
Percent cleared by arrest	33.7	42.1	24.7	33.7	32.0	34.6	43.6	62.6	57.4	61.3
GROUP V (10,000 to 24,999)										
Offenses known	6,360	419	7,229	1,452	1,816	8,220	7,150	9,220	14,232	17,426
Percent cleared by arrest	37.7	40.1	26.4	38.4	33.1	37.3	49.5	66.5	60.9	62.0
GROUP VI (under 10,000)										
Offenses known	5,573	498	4,384	928	963	5,452	5,848	7,595	12,206	21,833
Percent cleared by arrest	39.9	40.6	26.8	38.8	38.5	37.8	50.5	65.2	58.1	63.9
Metropolitan Counties										
Offenses known	11,568	757	18,157	2,802	3,284	13,330	19,991	17,732	36,079	32,211
Percent cleared by arrest	41.9	42.3	19.5	32.3	30.6	33.4	43.7	63.1	58.4	62.9
Nonmetropolitan Counties										
Offenses known	5,206	368	1,580	283	493	1,308	6,332	5,047	10,486	14,922
Percent cleared by arrest	44.7	37.2	35.3	45.2	35.3	40.4	58.0	65.6	60.1	60.6
SUBURBAN AREAS[1]										
Offenses known	21,888	1,479	31,363	5,596	6,593	29,218	31,331	32,176	60,536	63,764
Percent cleared by arrest	39.5	41.4	21.6	34.4	32.2	34.8	44.9	64.6	59.3	63.6

[1] Suburban areas include law enforcement agencies in cities with less than 50,000 inhabitants and county law enforcement agencies that are within a Metropolitan Statistical Area. Suburban areas exclude all metropolitan agencies associated with a principal city. The agencies associated with suburban areas also appear in other groups within this table.

[2] Not all agencies submit reports for arson to the FBI. As a result, the number of reports the FBI uses to compute the percent of offenses cleared for arson is less than the number it uses to compute the percent of offenses cleared for all other offenses. Agencies must report arson clearances by detailed property classification as specified on the *Monthly Return of Arson Offenses Known to Law Enforcement* to be included in this table; therefore, clearances in this table may differ from other clearance tables.

Table 27. Number and Percent of Offenses Cleared by Arrest or Exceptional Means, by Population Group, 2008—*Continued*

(Number, percent.)

Population group	Burglary			Motor vehicle theft			Arson[2]			Number of agencies	2008 estimated population
	Forcible entry	Unlawful entry	Attempted forcible entry	Autos	Trucks and buses	Other vehicles	Structure	Mobile	Other		
TOTAL ALL AGENCIES:											
Offenses known	1,082,875	568,245	110,741	582,054	137,036	72,910	23,958	16,152	15,407	13,472	241,803,753
Percent cleared by arrest	11.6	13.9	10.6	12.3	9.5	10.5	21.4	8.8	21.0		
Total Cities											
Offenses known	811,363	422,617	86,993	475,228	110,045	47,961	18,280	11,531	11,332	9,823	164,394,139
Percent cleared by arrest	11.1	13.6	10.7	11.3	8.4	9.9	21.1	8.5	21.8		
GROUP I (250,000 and over)											
Offenses known	312,070	114,157	28,267	212,928	65,428	17,457	6,566	5,594	3,089	67	41,720,494
Percent cleared by arrest	8.6	10.9	9.9	9.2	6.2	8.8	18.2	5.7	17.8		
1,000,000 and over (Group I subset)											
Offenses known	99,131	34,584	7,288	66,634	30,542	7,232	1,888	2,408	1,030	8	14,369,058
Percent cleared by arrest	7.5	9.2	11.3	9.4	4.6	7.3	17.1	5.0	11.1		
500,000 to 999,999 (Group I subset)											
Offenses known	124,635	39,881	12,490	82,316	21,079	6,091	2,247	1,495	952	22	14,623,528
Percent cleared by arrest	8.4	10.4	9.4	8.5	6.8	9.7	18.4	5.5	19.3		
250,000 to 499,999 (Group I subset)											
Offenses known	88,304	39,692	8,489	63,978	13,807	4,134	2,431	1,691	1,107	37	12,727,908
Percent cleared by arrest	10.3	12.8	9.3	9.7	9.1	9.9	18.8	6.7	22.7		
GROUP II (100,000 to 249,999)											
Offenses known	139,449	74,139	14,811	89,573	17,449	8,071	2,791	1,887	1,814	170	25,118,296
Percent cleared by arrest	10.5	12.9	9.8	9.5	9.0	7.8	18.3	7.1	22.2		
GROUP III (50,000 to 99,999)											
Offenses known	117,106	72,461	14,677	71,800	12,041	6,905	2,806	1,683	2,075	406	27,823,891
Percent cleared by arrest	12.3	14.4	11.9	11.0	9.7	9.5	18.9	9.5	22.5		
GROUP IV (25,000 to 49,999)											
Offenses known	85,726	53,187	10,591	41,225	5,947	6,071	1,911	933	1,750	693	23,741,598
Percent cleared by arrest	11.6	13.7	10.5	13.4	13.1	9.7	22.1	11.9	19.9		
GROUP V (10,000 to 24,999)											
Offenses known	85,417	56,271	9,952	35,136	5,368	4,821	1,995	782	1,333	1,554	24,493,117
Percent cleared by arrest	14.3	16.0	11.3	19.0	16.0	13.2	27.6	16.9	28.3		
GROUP VI (under 10,000)											
Offenses known	71,595	52,402	8,695	24,566	3,812	4,636	2,211	652	1,271	6,933	21,496,743
Percent cleared by arrest	16.2	16.7	12.4	23.4	20.0	15.8	29.3	19.8	25.6		
Metropolitan Counties											
Offenses known	193,240	105,000	18,229	88,401	22,849	18,580	4,152	3,849	3,189	1,488	54,365,891
Percent cleared by arrest	12.1	14.4	9.7	14.5	12.2	10.2	21.6	8.1	17.6		
Nonmetropolitan Counties											
Offenses known	78,272	40,628	5,519	18,425	4,142	6,369	1,526	772	886	2,161	23,043,723
Percent cleared by arrest	15.8	15.9	12.6	25.7	23.3	16.0	24.9	15.7	22.5		
SUBURBAN AREAS[1]											
Offenses known	335,229	204,824	36,919	160,988	33,599	28,631	7,526	5,255	6,072	7,071	103,114,853
Percent cleared by arrest	12.7	15.0	10.4	15.0	12.7	10.7	24.2	9.8	20.5		

[1] Suburban areas include law enforcement agencies in cities with less than 50,000 inhabitants and county law enforcement agencies that are within a Metropolitan Statistical Area. Suburban areas exclude all metropolitan agencies associated with a principal city. The agencies associated with suburban areas also appear in other groups within this table.

[2] Not all agencies submit reports for arson to the FBI. As a result, the number of reports the FBI uses to compute the percent of offenses cleared for arson is less than the number it uses to compute the percent of offenses cleared for all other offenses. Agencies must report arson clearances by detailed property classification as specified on the *Monthly Return of Arson Offenses Known to Law Enforcement* to be included in this table; therefore, clearances in this table may differ from other clearance tables.

Table 28. Number of Offenses Cleared by Arrest or Exceptional Means and Percent Involving Persons Under 18 Years of Age, by Population Group, 2008

(Number, percent.)

Population group	Violent crime	Murder and non-negligent man-slaughter	Forcible rape	Robbery	Aggra-vated assault	Property crime	Burglary	Larceny-theft	Motor vehicle theft	Arson[1]	Number of agencies	2008 estimated population
TOTAL ALL AGENCIES:												
Offenses known	459,553	7,718	27,661	86,577	337,597	1,306,464	209,586	1,007,106	89,772	9,881	13,138	236,404,090
Percent under 18 years old	11.9	5.3	11.7	16.3	11.0	18.4	16.4	19.0	15.5	38.2		
Total Cities												
Offenses known	358,547	5,894	20,377	75,618	256,658	1,051,186	152,646	832,078	66,462	7,387	9,634	161,088,799
Percent under 18 years old	12.1	5.7	11.0	16.3	11.1	19.0	16.7	19.6	15.7	39.9		
GROUP I (250,000 and over)												
Offenses known	137,148	2,765	7,060	34,832	92,491	253,056	41,459	186,688	24,909	2,091	66	41,128,661
Percent under 18 years old	10.9	6.2	8.9	15.6	9.4	17.0	16.2	17.4	15.2	35.7		
1,000,000 and over (Group I subset)												
Offenses known	46,978	1,147	2,499	13,697	29,635	77,065	11,480	57,382	8,203	558	8	14,369,058
Percent under 18 years old	10.4	4.7	9.3	15.4	8.3	14.8	15.2	15.0	12.4	37.1		
500,000 to 999,999 (Group I subset)												
Offenses known	47,966	819	2,339	10,707	34,101	89,150	15,037	65,248	8,865	705	21	14,031,695
Percent under 18 years old	10.7	5.1	8.6	15.3	9.6	17.1	17.7	16.9	17.6	35.2		
250,000 to 499,999 (Group I subset)												
Offenses known	42,204	799	2,222	10,428	28,755	86,841	14,942	64,058	7,841	828	37	12,727,908
Percent under 18 years old	11.7	9.5	8.6	16.1	10.3	18.8	15.5	19.9	15.2	35.3		
GROUP II (100,000 to 249,999)												
Offenses known	60,214	1,069	3,320	13,447	42,378	173,206	25,296	137,330	10,580	1,059	169	25,004,526
Percent under 18 years old	12.5	6.7	12.0	18.1	10.9	21.2	18.6	22.0	16.9	36.6		
GROUP III (50,000 to 99,999)												
Offenses known	52,097	735	2,867	10,637	37,858	180,740	25,799	145,470	9,471	1,165	395	27,155,884
Percent under 18 years old	13.4	4.9	11.7	17.9	12.4	20.9	15.5	22.2	16.4	42.0		
GROUP IV (25,000 to 49,999)												
Offenses known	38,224	502	2,316	7,062	28,344	148,742	18,005	124,022	6,715	904	679	23,277,840
Percent under 18 years old	13.0	4.0	13.0	16.7	12.3	20.7	17.8	21.4	17.2	44.7		
GROUP V (10,000 to 24,999)												
Offenses known	36,647	441	2,464	5,857	27,885	160,214	21,387	131,012	7,815	1,055	1,495	23,600,543
Percent under 18 years old	12.5	5.0	11.7	14.1	12.4	18.3	16.7	18.7	15.4	45.1		
GROUP VI (under 10,000)												
Offenses known	34,217	382	2,350	3,783	27,702	135,228	20,700	107,556	6,972	1,113	6,830	20,921,345
Percent under 18 years old	12.7	3.9	12.4	15.1	12.5	16.1	15.9	16.3	13.7	39.5		
Metropolitan Counties												
Offenses known	76,081	1,332	5,037	9,688	60,024	192,275	38,667	136,684	16,924	1,790	1,417	52,838,171
Percent under 18 years old	12.3	4.1	13.1	17.0	11.6	16.7	16.6	16.9	15.2	37.1		
Nonmetropolitan Counties												
Offenses known	24,925	492	2,247	1,271	20,915	63,003	18,273	38,344	6,386	704	2,087	22,477,120
Percent under 18 years old	8.9	3.0	14.8	7.8	8.4	13.3	13.6	13.1	14.1	23.9		
SUBURBAN AREAS[2]												
Offenses known	139,617	2,055	9,025	20,336	108,201	461,595	74,124	357,170	30,301	3,627	6,882	100,147,163
Percent under 18 years old	13.0	4.2	12.7	16.7	12.6	18.0	16.9	18.5	14.9	42.1		

[1] Not all agencies submit reports for arson to the FBI. As a result, the number of reports the FBI uses to compute the percent of offenses cleared for arson is less than the number it uses to compute the percent of offenses cleared for all other offenses.

[2] Suburban areas include law enforcement agencies in cities with less than 50,000 inhabitants and county law enforcement agencies that are within a Metropolitan Statistical Area. Suburban areas exclude all metropolitan agencies associated with a principal city. The agencies associated with suburban areas also appear in other groups within this table.

SECTION IV:

PERSONS ARRESTED

PERSONS ARRESTED

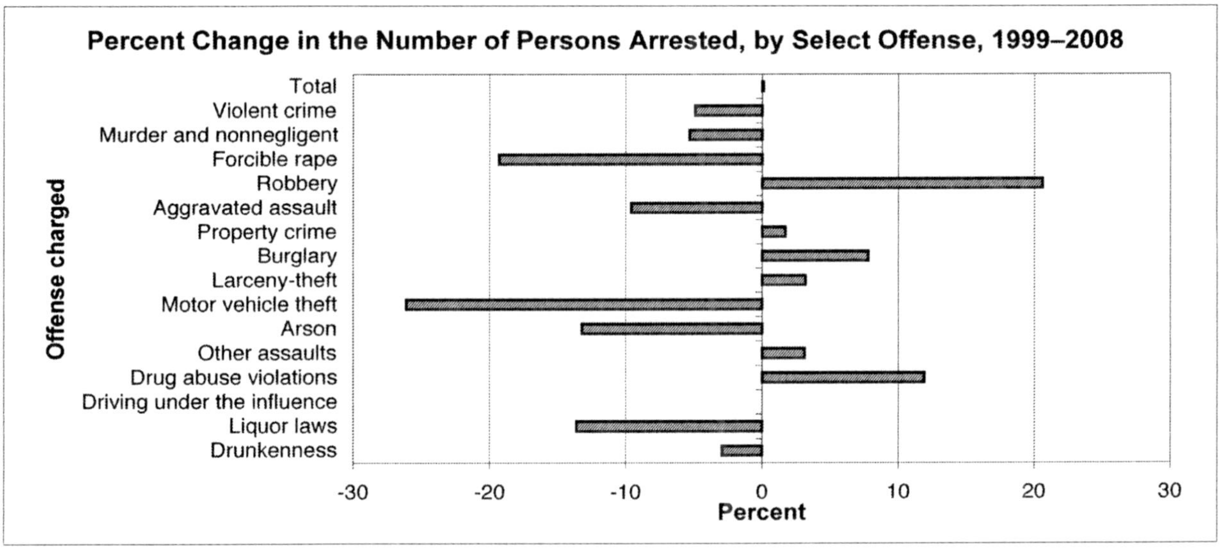

In the Uniform Crime Reporting (UCR) Program, one arrest is counted for each separate instance in which an individual is arrested, cited, or summoned for criminal acts in Part I and Part II crimes. (See Appendix II for additional information concerning Part I and Part II crimes.) One person may be arrested multiple times during the year; as a result, the arrest figures in this section should not be taken as the total number of individuals arrested. Instead, it provides the number of arrest occurrences reported by law enforcement. Information regarding the UCR Program's statistical methodology and table construction can be found in Appendix I.

National Volume, Trends, and Rates

Volume

The FBI estimated that 14,005,615 arrests occurred in 2008 for all offenses (except traffic violations). Of these arrests, 594,911 were for violent crimes and 1,687,345 were for property crimes. Of the total violent crimes in 2008, aggravated assaults accounted for 72.3 percent, or 429,969 incidents. Robbery had the next highest proportion with 21.8 percent, followed by forcible rape (3.8 percent) and murder and nonnegligent manslaughter (2.2 percent). Of the estimated 1,687,345 arrests for property crimes in 2008, 1,266,706 (75.1 percent) were for larceny-theft, 308,479 (18.3 percent) were for burglary, 98,035 (5.8 percent) were for motor vehicle theft, and 14,125 (0.8 percent) were for arson. (Table 29) The most frequent arrests made in 2008 were for drug abuse violations (estimated at 1,702,537 arrests). These arrests made up 12.2 percent of the total number of all arrests.

A comparison of arrest figures from 2007 to 2008 revealed a 1.5 percent decrease. Arrests for violent crimes decreased 0.6 percent, while arrests for property crimes increased 5.6 percent during the 2-year period. An examination of the 5-year and 10-year arrest trends showed that the total number of arrests in 2008 rose 1.7 percent from the 2004 total. Arrests for violent crimes showed a 1.5 percent increase from 2004 to 2008 and property crimes showed a 4.8 percent increase. In the 10-year trend data (1999 to 2008), the number of arrests increased by 0.1 percent. For violent crimes, the number of arrests fell 4.9 percent, while arrests for property crimes increased 1.7 percent. (Tables 32, 34, and 36)

The number of adults arrested for violent crime (arrestees age 18 years and over) decreased 1.3 percent from 2007 to 2008, increased 2.7 percent from 2004 to 2008, and increased 3.4 percent from 1999 to 2008 The number of juveniles arrested for violent crime (arrestees under 18 years of age) decreased 2.8 percent from 2007 to 2008, decreased 3.5 percent from 2004 to 2008, and decreased 15.7 percent from 1999 to 2008. (Tables 32, 34, and 36)

Trends

The trend data for murder showed that the number of arrests for this offense decreased 2.9 percent from 2007 to 2008, increased 0.5 percent from 2004 to 2008, and decreased 5.3 percent from 1999 to 2008. The number of adults arrested for murder declined 0.4 percent from 2007 to 2008, rose 0.9 percent from 2004 to 2008, and fell 4.9 percent from 1999 to 2008. The number of juveniles arrested for murder fell 1.9 percent from 2007 to 2008, rose 4.5 percent from 2004 to 2008, and fell 8.8 percent from 1999 to 2008. (Tables 32, 34, and 36)

For forcible rape, the 2-year trend data showed that arrests increased 1.2 percent from 2007 to 2008, with adult arrests increasing 1.8 percent and juvenile arrests dropping 2.0 percent. The 5-year trend data showed that arrests decreased 11.0 percent from 2004 to 2008; adult arrests decreased 8.9 percent and juvenile arrests declined 21.2 percent during this period. The 10-year trend data showed that forcible rape arrests dropped 19.3 percent from 1999 to 2008, with adult arrests falling 17.7 percent and juvenile arrests falling 27.2 percent. (Tables 32, 34, and 36)

For robbery, the 2-year trend data showed that arrests increased 2.6 percent from 2007 to 2008, with adult arrests rising 2.8 percent and juvenile arrests decreasing 2.3 percent. The 5-year trend data showed that total robbery arrests rose 22.1 percent from 2004 to 2008; adult arrests rose 15.4 percent and juvenile arrests rose 45.8 percent during this period. The 10-year trend data showed that arrests rose 20.6 percent from 1999 to 2008, with adult arrests increasing 18.9 percent and juvenile arrests increasing 25.4 percent. (Tables 32, 34, and 36)

The aggravated assault trend data showed that the number of arrests for this offense fell 1.6 percent from 2007 to 2008, dropped 2.5 percent from 2004 to 2008, and fell 9.6 percent from 1999 to 2008. The number of adults arrested for aggravated assault percent decreased 1.2 percent from 2007 to 2008, declined 1.4 percent from 2004 to 2008, and declined 7.8 percent from 1999 to 2008. The number of juveniles arrested for aggravated assault dropped 4.4 percent from 2007 to 2008, fell 9.4 percent from 2004 to 2008, and dropped 20.8 percent from 1999 to 2008. (Tables 32, 34, and 36)

The 2-year, 5-year, and 10-year trend data showed that the number of arrests for property crime increased 5.6 percent from 2007 to 2008, increased 4.8 percent from 2004 to 2008, and increased 1.7 percent from 1999 to 2008. The number of adults arrested for property crime offenses (arrestees age 18 years and over) increased 5.8 percent from 2007 to 2008, increased 7.4 percent from 2004 to 2008, and increased 12.1 percent from 1999 to 2008. The number of juveniles arrested for property crime (arrestees under 18 years of age) increased 5.1 percent from 2007 to 2008, decreased 2.0 percent from 2004 to 2008, and decreased 19.6 percent from 1999 to 2008. (Tables 32, 34, and 36)

The trend data for burglary showed that the number of arrests for this offense increased 2.5 percent from 2007 to 2008, increased 6.3 percent from 2004 to 2008, and increased 7.8 percent from 1999 to 2008. The number of adults arrested for burglary rose 2.5 percent from 2007 to 2008, rose 7.3 percent from 2004 to 2008, and rose 19.2 percent from 1999 to 2008. The number of juveniles arrested for burglary increased 2.7 percent from 2007 to 2008, increased 3.8 percent from 2004 to 2008, and fell 14.4 percent from 1999 to 2008. (Tables 32, 34, and 36)

For larceny-theft, the 2-year trend data showed that arrests increased 8.8 percent from 2007 to 2008, with adult arrests increasing 9.1 percent and juvenile arrests increasing 8.0 percent. The 5-year trend data showed that total larceny-theft arrests increased 8.2 percent from 2004 to 2008; adult arrests increased 11.4 percent and juvenile arrests rose 0.1 percent during this period. The 10-year trend data showed that larceny-theft arrests rose 3.2 percent from 1999 to 2008, with adult arrests increasing 12.9 percent and juvenile arrests falling 17.3 percent. (Tables 32, 34, and 36)

For motor vehicle theft, the 2-year trend data showed that arrests declined 18.3 percent from 2007 to 2008, with adult arrests decreasing 18.5 percent and juvenile arrests decreasing 17.3 percent. The 5-year trend data showed that total motor vehicle theft arrests fell 29.2 percent from 2004 to 2008; adult arrests declined 28.0 percent and juvenile arrests fell 32.6 percent during this period. The 10-year trend data showed that arrests dropped 26.1 percent from 1999 to 2008, with adult arrests falling 12.7 percent and juvenile arrests dropping 50.0 percent. (Tables 32, 34, and 36)

The arson trend data showed that the number of arrests for this offense decreased 3.4 percent from 2007 to 2008, fell 7.1 percent from 2004 to 2008, and fell 13.2 percent from 1999 to 2008. The number of adults arrested for arson rose 1.0 percent from 2007 to 2008, increased 2.2 percent from 2004 to 2008, and increased 0.1 percent from 1999 to 2008. The number of juveniles arrested for arson declined by 8.0 percent from 2007 to 2008, dropped 15.9 percent from 2004 to 2008, and dropped 24.0 percent from 1999 to 2008. (Tables 32, 34, and 36)

Rates

The rate of arrests was estimated at 4,637.7 arrests per 100,000 inhabitants in 2008. The arrest rate for violent crime was 198.2 per 100,000 inhabitants, and the arrest rate for property crime was 565.2 per 100,000 inhabitants. (Table 30) Law enforcement agencies throughout the nation reported 4.3 murder arrests, 7.5 forcible rape arrests, 43.6 robbery arrests, and 142.9 aggravated assault arrests per 100,000 inhabitants in 2008. Rates for all violent crimes, except robbery, were down from the 2007 rates. Law enforcement agencies throughout the nation reported 565.2 property crime arrests, 102.3 burglary arrests, 425.7 larceny-theft arrests, 32.5 motor vehicle theft arrests, and 4.7 arson arrests per 100,000 inhabitants in 2008. Larceny-theft and arson rates both fell from 2007 to 2008.

By Age, Sex, and Race

Law enforcement agencies that contributed arrest data to the UCR Program reported information on the age, sex, and race of the persons they arrested. According to the 2008 data, adults accounted for 84.8 percent of arrestees nationally. (Table 38)

A review of arrest data by age from 2007 to 2008 showed that arrests of adults decreased 1.3 percent during this

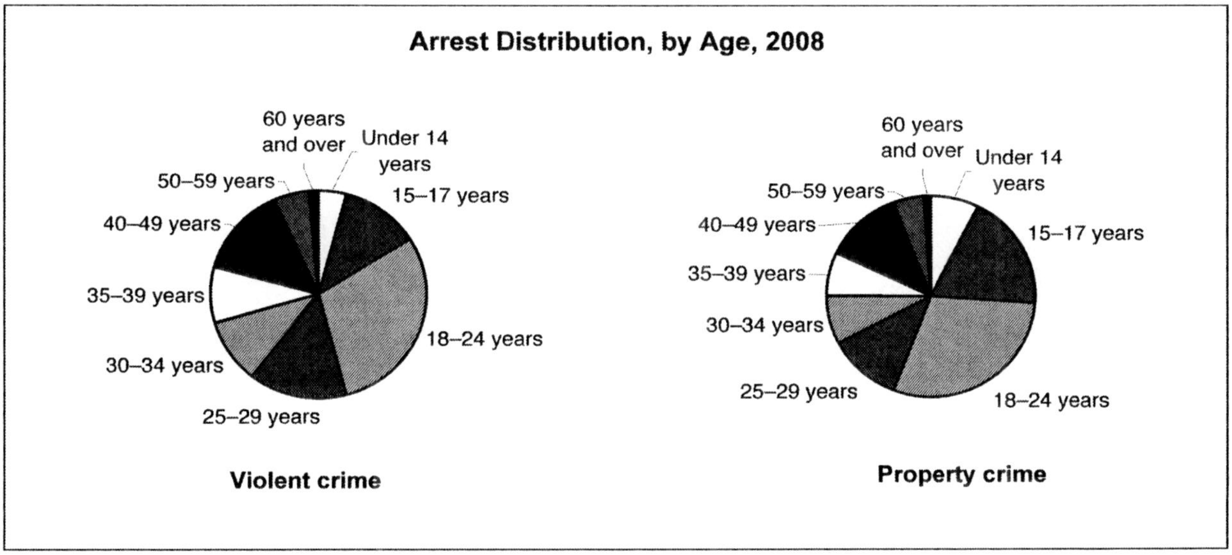

period. Arrests of adults for property crimes increased 5.8 percent, and arrests of adults for violent crimes decreased 0.4 percent over the same time span. The arrest total for juveniles (those under 18 years of age) decreased 2.8 percent from 2007 to 2008. Over the 2-year period, arrests of juveniles for violent crimes fell 1.9 percent; juvenile arrests property crimes increased 5.1 percent. (Table 36)

By sex, males accounted for 75.5 percent of all persons arrested. Males represented 81.7 percent of arrestees for violent crime, 89.2 percent of arrestees for murder, 98.8 percent of arrestees for forcible rape, 88.4 percent for robbery, and 78.5 percent for aggravated assault. Females accounted for 18.3 percent of violent crime arrestees, 10.8 percent of murder arrestees, 1.2 percent of forcible rape arrestees, 11.6 percent of robbery arrestees, and 21.5 percent of aggravated assault arrestees. (Tables 38 and 42)

In 2008, most arrestees for property crime (73.9 percent) were over 18 years of age. By sex, males accounted for 65.2 percent of arrestees for property crime, 85.4 percent of arrestees for burglary, 58.7 percent of arrestees for larceny-theft, 82.8 percent of arrestees for motor vehicle theft, and 84.1 percent of arrestees for arson. Females accounted for 12.2 percent of property crime arrestees. Of the four property crimes, larceny-theft had the highest proportion of female arrestees at 41.3 percent. (Tables 38 and 42)

In 2008, 69.2 percent of all persons arrested were White; 28.3 percent were Black; and the remaining 2.4 percent were of other races (American Indian or Alaskan Native and Asian or Pacific Islander). Of all arrestees for violent crimes, 58.3 percent were White, 39.4 percent were Black, and 2.3 percent were of other races. For murder, 47.9 percent of arrestees were White, 50.1 percent were Black, and 2.1 percent were of other races. For forcible rape, 65.2 percent of arrestees were White, 32.2 percent were Black, and 2.6 percent were of other races. For robbery, 41.7 percent of arrestees were White, 56.7 percent of arrestees were Black, and 1.6 percent were of other races. For aggravated assault, 63.3 percent of arrestees were White, 34.2 percent of arrestees were Black, and 2.6 percent were of other races. (Table 43)

Of all arrestees for property crimes, 67.4 percent were White, 30.1 percent were Black, and 2.5 percent were of other races. For burglary, 66.8 percent of arrestees were White, 31.4 percent were Black, and 1.8 percent were of other races. For larceny-theft, 68.1 percent of arrestees were White, 29.3 percent were Black, and 2.7 percent were of other races. For motor vehicle theft, 59.7 percent of arrestees were White, 38.1 percent of arrestees were Black, and 2.3 percent were of other races. For arson, 75.8 percent of arrestees were White, 21.7 percent of arrestees were Black, and 2.4 percent were of other races. (Table 43)

White adults were most commonly arrested for driving under the influence (964,583 arrests) and drug abuse violations (829,432 arrests). Black adults were most frequently arrested for drug abuse violations (452,590 arrests) and other assaults (simple) (319,498 arrests). (Table 43)

Regional Arrest Rates

The UCR Program divides the United States into four regions: the Northeast, the Midwest, the South, and the West. (Appendix III provides a more information about the regions.) Law enforcement agencies in the Northeast had an overall arrest rate of 3,743.9 arrests per 100,000 inhabitants, well below the national rate (4,637.7 arrests per 100,000 inhabitants). In this region, the arrest rate for violent crimes was 174.2 arrests per 100,000 inhabitants, and for property crime, the arrest rate was 463.0 arrests per 100,000 inhabitants. In the Midwest, law enforcement agencies reported an arrest rate of 4,717.5 arrests per 100,000 inhabitants. The arrest rate for violent crimes was 154.4 and

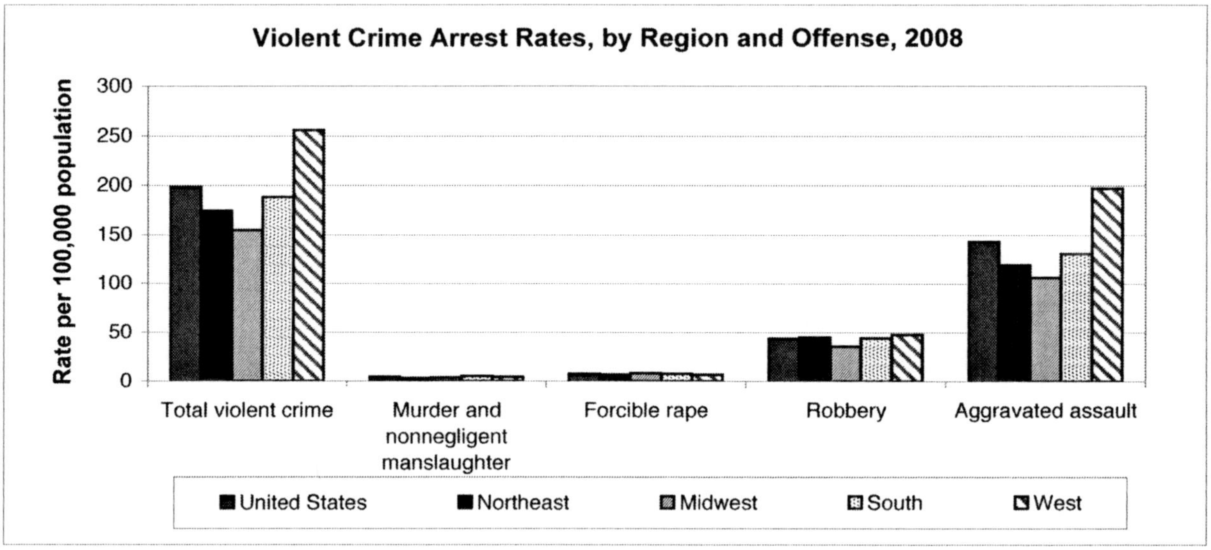

the arrest rate for property crime was 593.4. Law enforcement agencies in the South, the nation's most populous region, reported an arrest rate of 5,128.7 per 100,000 inhabitants. Arrests for violent crime occurred at a rate of 188.1 arrests per 100,000 residents, and for property crime, the arrest rate was 621.4 arrests per 100,000 inhabitants. In the Western states, law enforcement agencies reported an overall arrest rate of 4,602.2 arrests per 100,000 inhabitants. The region's violent crime arrest rate was 255.7, while its property crime arrest rate was 547.9. (Table 30)

The regional murder arrest rates were 3.2 in the Northeast, 3.8 in the Midwest, 5.2 in the South, and 4.3 in the West. For forcible rape, the regional arrest rates were 6.8 in the Northeast, 8.5 in the Midwest, 7.7 in the South, and 6.9 in the West. Regional arrest rates for robbery were 44.9 in the Northeast, 35.8 in the Midwest, 44.3 in the South, and 47.6 in the West. For aggravated assault, the regional arrest rates were 119.4 in the Northeast, 106.3 in the Midwest, 130.9 in the South, and 197.0 in the West. (Table 30)

The regional burglary arrest rates were 80.0 in the Northeast, 84.1 in the Midwest, 109.6 in the South, and 121.1 in the West. For larceny-theft, the regional arrest rates were 358.5 in the Northeast, 465.0 in the Midwest, 479.2 in the South, and 381.3 in the West. Regional arrest rates for motor vehicle theft were 19.8 in the Northeast, 39.6 in the Midwest, 28.1 in the South, and 40.6 in the West. For arson, the regional arrest rates were 4.6 in the Northeast, 4.6 in the Midwest, 4.6 in the South, and 4.9 in the West. (Table 30)

By population group, law enforcement agencies in the nation's cities collectively reported 222.6 violent crime arrests per 100,000 inhabitants in 2008. In the city population groups, cities with 250,000 or more inhabitants reported the highest violent crime arrest rate (310.5) and cities with 10,000 to 24,999 inhabitants reported the lowest violent crime arrest rate (150.3). Cities reported an overall murder arrest rate of 4.6 per 100,000 inhabitants; cities with 250,000 or more inhabitants had the highest murder arrest rate (8.0) and cities with under 10,000 inhabitants had the lowest murder arrest rate (2.0). The collective city forcible rape arrest rate was 7.9 per 100,000 inhabitants, with the highest rate in cities with 250,000 or more inhabitants (10.2) and the lowest rate in cities with 10,000 to 24,999 inhabitants (6.2). The overall robbery arrest rate for cities was 53.6 per 100,000 inhabitants; cities with 250,000 or more inhabitants had the highest robbery arrest rate (88.5) and cities with under 10,000 inhabitants had the lowest robbery arrest rate (22.7). For aggravated assault, the collective city arrest rate was 156.6 per 100,000 inhabitants, with the greatest arrest rate in cities with 250,000 or more inhabitants (203.8) and the lowest arrest rate in cities with 10,000 to 24,999 inhabitants (112.8). (Table 31)

Agencies in metropolitan counties reported a violent crime arrest rate of 152.7 per 100,000 inhabitants, with arrest rates of 3.8 for murder, 6.2 for forcible rape, 25.2 for robbery, and 117.6 for aggravated assault. Agencies in nonmetropolitan counties reported arrest rates of 114.3 for violent crime, 3.0 for murder, 7.2 for forcible rape, 8.8 for robbery, and 95.2 for aggravated assault. (Table 31)

By population group, law enforcement agencies in the nation's cities collectively reported 665.4 property crime arrests per 100,000 inhabitants in 2008. In the city population groups, cities with 100,000 to 249,999 inhabitants reported the highest property crime arrest rate (721.3) and cities with under 10,000 inhabitants reported the lowest property crime arrest rate (605.0). Cities reported an overall burglary arrest rate of 109.7 per 100,000 inhabitants; cities with 100,000 to 249,999 inhabitants had the highest burglary arrest rate (135.0) and cities with 25,000 to 49,999 inhabitants had the lowest burglary arrest rate (89.5). The collective city larceny-theft arrest rate was 514.6 per 100,000 inhabitants, with the highest rate in cities with 50,000 to 99,999 inhabitants (547.6) and the lowest rate in cities with fewer than 10,000 inhabitants (471.6). The overall motor vehicle theft arrest rate for cities was 35.9 per 100,000 inhabitants; cities with 250,000 or more inhabitants had the highest motor vehicle theft arrest rate (61.7), and cities with 25,000 to 49,999 inhabitants had the lowest motor vehicle theft arrest rate (20.7). For arson, the collective city arrest rate was 5.1 per 100,000 inhabitants, with the greatest arrest rate in cities with under 10,000 inhabitants (7.0) and the lowest arrest rate in cities with 250,000 or more inhabitants (4.5). (Table 31)

Agencies in metropolitan counties reported a property crime arrest rate of 356.8 per 100,000 inhabitants, with arrest rates of 84.2 for burglary, 242.8 for larceny-theft, 26.1 for motor vehicle theft, and 3.6 for arson. Agencies in nonmetropolitan counties reported arrest rates of 478.3 for property crime, 85.7 for burglary, 162.2 for larceny-theft, 20.9 for motor vehicle theft, and 3.9 for arson. (Table 31)

Community Types

In 2008, law enforcement agencies in the nation's cities reported that 83.5 percent of arrests in their jurisdictions were of adults and 16.5 percent of arrests were of juveniles. Adults accounted for 83.0 percent of arrestees for violent crimes, while juveniles accounted for 17.0 percent. Adults made up 73.2 percent of the arrestees for property crimes, and juveniles accounted for 26.8 percent. Of all arrests in the nation's cities in 2008, 45.9 percent were of individuals under 25 years of age. In metropolitan counties, 40.1 percent of arrests were of individuals under 25 years of age. In nonmetropolitan counties, 36.9 percent of persons arrested were of individuals under 25 years of age. (Tables 46, 47, 53, and 59)

Males accounted for 75.1 percent and females accounted for 24.9 percent of arrestees in the nation's cities in 2008. In metropolitan counties, males composed 76.7 percent of arrestees, and in nonmetropolitan counties, males represented 76.9 percent of all arrestees. (Tables 48, 54, and 60)

By race, 66.9 percent of arrestees in the nation's cities in 2008 were White, 30.5 percent were Black, and 2.5 percent were of other races (American Indian or Alaska Native and Asian or Pacific Islander). Whites accounted for 74.6 percent of arrestees in metropolitan counties in 2008, Blacks made up 24.1 percent of arrestees, and persons of other races made up 1.2 percent of the total. In nonmetropolitan counties, Whites made up 81.5 percent of arrestees, Blacks accounted for 13.9 percent of arrestees, and other races made up 4.6 percent of the total. (Tables 49, 55, and 61)

Population Groups: Trends and Rates

The national UCR Program aggregates data by various population groups, which include cities, metropolitan counties, and nonmetropolitan counties. Definitions of these groups can be found in Appendix III. The total number of arrests in U.S. cities fell 1.0 percent from 2007 to 2008. The number of arrests for violent crimes rose 0.3 percent and arrests for property crimes increased 5.8 percent during the 2-year time frame. (Table 44)

In 2008, law enforcement agencies in cities collectively recorded an arrest rate of 5,062.0 arrests per 100,000 inhabitants. The nation's smallest cities, those with fewer than 10,000 inhabitants, had the highest arrest rate among the city population groups with 6,032.8 arrests per 100,000 inhabitants. Law enforcement agencies in cities with 25,000 to 49,999 inhabitants recorded the lowest rate, 4,464.3. In the nation's metropolitan counties, law enforcement agencies reported an arrest rate of 3,610.9 per 100,000 inhabitants. Agencies in nonmetropolitan counties reported an arrest rate of 3,760.4. (Table 31)

Table 29. Estimated Number of Arrests, 2008

(Number.)

Offense	Arrests
TOTAL[1]	14,005,615
Violent Crime	594,911
Murder and nonnegligent manslaughter	12,955
Forcible rape	22,584
Robbery	129,403
Aggravated assault	429,969
Property Crime	1,687,345
Burglary	308,479
Larceny-theft	1,266,706
Motor vehicle theft	98,035
Arson	14,125
Other	
Other assaults	1,298,342
Forgery and counterfeiting	90,127
Fraud	234,199
Embezzlement	21,402
Stolen property; buying, receiving, possessing	111,319
Vandalism	285,012
Weapons; carrying, possessing, etc.	179,661
Prostitution and commercialized vice	75,004
Sex offenses (except forcible rape and prostitution)	79,914
Drug abuse violations	1,702,537
Gambling	9,811
Offenses against the family and children	118,419
Driving under the influence	1,483,396
Liquor laws	625,939
Drunkenness	611,069
Disorderly conduct	685,985
Vagrancy	33,852
All other offenses	3,835,083
Suspicion	1,650
Curfew and loitering law violations	133,063
Runaways	109,225

[1] Does not include suspicion.

Table 30. Number and Rate of Arrests, by Geographic Region, 2008

(Number, rate per 100,000.)

Offense charged	United States total (11,713 agencies; population 230,897,506)		Northeast (2,988 agencies; population 42,553,201)		Midwest (2,907 agencies; population 46,840,018)		South (4,064 agencies; population 74,688,005)		West (1,754 agencies; population 66,816,282)	
	Total	Rate	Total	Rate	Total	Rate	Total	Rate	Total	Rate
TOTAL[1]	10,708,399	4,637.7	1,593,164	3,743.9	2,209,670	4,717.5	3,830,554	5,128.7	3,075,011	4,602.2
Violent Crime	457,752	198.2	74,143	174.2	72,308	154.4	140,471	188.1	170,830	255.7
Murder and nonnegligent manslaughter	9,888	4.3	1,345	3.2	1,778	3.8	3,908	5.2	2,857	4.3
Forcible rape	17,213	7.5	2,906	6.8	3,975	8.5	5,754	7.7	4,578	6.9
Robbery	100,738	43.6	19,100	44.9	16,783	35.8	33,076	44.3	31,779	47.6
Aggravated assault	329,913	142.9	50,792	119.4	49,772	106.3	97,733	130.9	131,616	197.0
Property Crime	1,305,135	565.2	197,008	463.0	277,953	593.4	464,117	621.4	366,057	547.9
Burglary	236,219	102.3	34,059	80.0	39,399	84.1	81,823	109.6	80,938	121.1
Larceny-theft	982,997	425.7	152,561	358.5	217,819	465.0	357,872	479.2	254,745	381.3
Motor vehicle theft	75,135	32.5	8,446	19.8	18,559	39.6	21,015	28.1	27,115	40.6
Arson	10,784	4.7	1,942	4.6	2,176	4.6	3,407	4.6	3,259	4.9
Other										
Other assaults	994,804	430.8	162,314	381.4	214,321	457.6	384,715	515.1	233,454	349.4
Forgery and counterfeiting	68,976	29.9	10,347	24.3	11,779	25.1	28,221	37.8	18,629	27.9
Fraud	174,598	75.6	26,788	63.0	30,496	65.1	94,501	126.5	22,813	34.1
Embezzlement	16,458	7.1	1,446	3.4	2,258	4.8	8,781	11.8	3,973	5.9
Stolen property; buying, receiving, possessing	85,584	37.1	14,852	34.9	20,791	44.4	22,286	29.8	27,655	41.4
Vandalism	219,059	94.9	42,677	100.3	47,686	101.8	52,929	70.9	75,767	113.4
Weapons; carrying, possessing, etc.	138,255	59.9	16,671	39.2	27,631	59.0	46,466	62.2	47,487	71.1
Prostitution and commercialized vice	58,784	25.5	6,831	16.1	10,140	21.6	18,775	25.1	23,038	34.5
Sex offenses (except forcible rape and prostitution)	60,804	26.3	10,040	23.6	12,444	26.6	15,246	20.4	23,074	34.5
Drug abuse violations	1,304,098	564.8	211,851	497.8	239,846	512.1	447,300	598.9	405,101	606.3
Gambling	7,632	3.3	597	1.4	4,171	8.9	2,147	2.9	717	1.1
Offenses against the family and children	87,197	37.8	21,919	51.5	22,903	48.9	29,018	38.9	13,357	20.0
Driving under the influence	1,110,083	480.8	141,243	331.9	238,503	509.2	329,919	441.7	400,418	599.3
Liquor laws	478,800	207.4	55,886	131.3	168,088	358.9	116,728	156.3	138,098	206.7
Drunkenness	474,378	205.4	36,091	84.8	37,251	79.5	271,208	363.1	129,828	194.3
Disorderly conduct	529,929	229.5	130,961	307.8	168,735	360.2	153,168	205.1	77,065	115.3
Vagrancy	26,325	11.4	4,079	9.6	3,963	8.5	9,447	12.6	8,836	13.2
All other offenses (except traffic)	2,921,526	1,265.3	390,535	917.8	560,443	1,196.5	1,141,975	1,529.0	828,573	1,240.1
Suspicion	1,259	0.5	28	0.1	131	0.3	1,006	1.3	94	0.1
Curfew and loitering law violations	104,168	45.1	29,961	70.4	18,003	38.4	23,310	31.2	32,894	49.2
Runaways	84,054	36.4	6,924	16.3	19,957	42.6	29,826	39.9	27,347	40.9

[1] Does not include suspicion.

Table 31. Number and Rate of Arrests, by Population Group, 2008

(Number, rate per 100,000 population.)

Offense charged	Total (11,713 agencies; population 230,897,506)		Cities: Total cities (8,676 cities; population 161,327,084)		Cities: Group I (66 cities, 250,000 and over; population 44,061,178)		Cities: Group II (162 cities, 100,000 to 249,999; population 24,028,515)		Cities: Group III (389 cities, 50,000 to 99,999; population 26,564,793)	
	Total	Rate	Total	Rate	Total	Rate	Total	Rate	Total	Rate
TOTAL[1]	10,708,399	4,637.7	8,166,412	5,062.0	2,354,179	5,343.0	1,179,503	4,908.8	1,263,861	4,757.7
Violent Crime	457,752	198.2	359,178	222.6	136,796	310.5	60,740	252.8	56,631	213.2
Murder and nonnegligent manslaughter	9,888	4.3	7,406	4.6	3,506	8.0	1,402	5.8	924	3.5
Forcible rape	17,213	7.5	12,697	7.9	4,497	10.2	1,960	8.2	1,752	6.6
Robbery	100,738	43.6	86,484	53.6	38,978	88.5	15,100	62.8	12,865	48.4
Aggravated assault	329,913	142.9	252,591	156.6	89,815	203.8	42,278	175.9	41,090	154.7
Property Crime	1,305,135	565.2	1,073,444	665.4	290,061	658.3	173,326	721.3	185,113	696.8
Burglary	236,219	102.3	177,035	109.7	50,455	114.5	32,433	135.0	31,110	117.1
Larceny-theft	982,997	425.7	830,179	514.6	210,460	477.7	131,022	545.3	145,480	547.6
Motor vehicle theft	75,135	32.5	57,996	35.9	27,165	61.7	8,732	36.3	7,069	26.6
Arson	10,784	4.7	8,234	5.1	1,981	4.5	1,139	4.7	1,454	5.5
Other										
Other assaults	994,804	430.8	768,204	476.2	224,990	510.6	120,217	500.3	119,169	448.6
Forgery and counterfeiting	68,976	29.9	52,778	32.7	14,666	33.3	7,522	31.3	7,960	30.0
Fraud	174,598	75.6	104,394	64.7	17,697	40.2	13,391	55.7	15,858	59.7
Embezzlement	16,458	7.1	12,689	7.9	2,789	6.3	2,459	10.2	2,390	9.0
Stolen property; buying, receiving, possessing	85,584	37.1	66,673	41.3	21,587	49.0	9,790	40.7	11,396	42.9
Vandalism	219,059	94.9	175,343	108.7	46,811	106.2	24,384	101.5	28,633	107.8
Weapons; carrying, possessing, etc.	138,255	59.9	110,133	68.3	44,407	100.8	17,456	72.6	16,448	61.9
Prostitution and commercialized vice	58,784	25.5	55,447	34.4	39,402	89.4	7,771	32.3	4,450	16.8
Sex offenses (except forcible rape and prostitution)	60,804	26.3	44,101	27.3	15,760	35.8	5,936	24.7	7,047	26.5
Drug abuse violations	1,304,098	564.8	1,004,709	622.8	369,389	838.4	149,107	620.5	148,469	558.9
Gambling	7,632	3.3	6,911	4.3	5,515	12.5	417	1.7	244	0.9
Offenses against the family and children	87,197	37.8	40,252	25.0	6,603	15.0	6,339	26.4	6,215	23.4
Driving under the influence	1,110,083	480.8	699,851	433.8	153,625	348.7	87,259	363.1	102,635	386.4
Liquor laws	478,800	207.4	387,261	240.0	66,610	151.2	45,656	190.0	59,396	223.6
Drunkenness	474,378	205.4	411,455	255.0	107,621	244.3	65,153	271.1	67,779	255.1
Disorderly conduct	529,929	229.5	456,838	283.2	106,512	241.7	55,628	231.5	70,553	265.6
Vagrancy	26,325	11.4	23,629	14.6	13,796	31.3	2,196	9.1	2,836	10.7
All other offenses (except traffic)	2,921,526	1,265.3	2,149,220	1,332.2	594,008	1,348.1	304,495	1,267.2	326,124	1,227.7
Suspicion	1,259	0.5	939	0.6	11	0.0	148	0.6	345	1.3
Curfew and loitering law violations	104,168	45.1	99,044	61.4	53,546	121.5	9,146	38.1	12,785	48.1
Runaways	84,054	36.4	64,858	40.2	21,988	49.9	11,115	46.3	11,730	44.2

[1] Does not include suspicion.
[2] Suburban areas include law enforcement agencies in cities with less than 50,000 inhabitants and county law enforcement agencies that are within a metropolitan statistical area. Suburban areas exclude all metropolitan agencies associated with a principal city. The agencies associated with suburban areas also appear in other groups within this table.

Table 31. Number and Rate of Arrests, by Population Group, 2008—*Continued*

(Number, rate per 100,000 population.)

Offense charged	Cities						Counties				Suburban area[3] (6,405 agencies; population 101,327,487)	
	Group IV (673 cities, 25,000 to 49,999; population 23,142,316)		Group V (1,419 cities, 10,000 to 24,999; population 22,395,901)		Group VI (5,882 cities, under 10,000; population 19,772,026)		Metropolitan counties (1,201 agencies; population 49,582,436)		Nonmetropolitan counties (1,836 agencies; population 19,987,986)			
	Total	Rate	Total	Rate	Total	Rate	Total	Rate	Total	Rate	Total	Rate
TOTAL[1]	1,033,134	4,464.3	1,142,930	4,810.7	1,192,805	6,032.8	1,790,357	3,610.9	751,630	3,760.4	4,164,540	4,110.0
Violent Crime	38,097	164.6	35,700	150.3	31,214	157.9	75,734	152.7	22,840	114.3	151,654	149.7
Murder and nonnegligent manslaughter	640	2.8	535	2.3	399	2.0	1,875	3.8	607	3.0	2,972	2.9
Forcible rape	1,483	6.4	1,484	6.2	1,521	7.7	3,081	6.2	1,435	7.2	6,099	6.0
Robbery	8,166	35.3	6,882	29.0	4,493	22.7	12,490	25.2	1,764	8.8	28,029	27.7
Aggravated assault	27,808	120.2	26,799	112.8	24,801	125.4	58,288	117.6	19,034	95.2	114,554	113.1
Property Crime	151,380	654.1	153,951	648.0	119,613	605.0	176,897	356.8	54,794	274.1	484,666	478.3
Burglary	20,717	89.5	22,350	94.1	19,970	101.0	41,767	84.2	17,417	87.1	86,857	85.7
Larceny-theft	124,807	539.3	125,166	526.8	93,244	471.6	120,390	242.8	32,428	162.2	369,806	365.0
Motor vehicle theft	4,800	20.7	5,224	22.0	5,006	25.3	12,960	26.1	4,179	20.9	23,597	23.3
Arson	1,056	4.6	1,211	5.1	1,393	7.0	1,780	3.6	770	3.9	4,406	4.3
Other												
Other assaults	98,781	426.8	102,812	432.7	102,235	517.1	159,681	322.1	66,919	334.8	368,424	363.6
Forgery and counterfeiting	7,015	30.3	8,168	34.4	7,447	37.7	11,916	24.0	4,282	21.4	27,345	27.0
Fraud	13,975	60.4	18,139	76.3	25,334	128.1	46,375	93.5	23,829	119.2	82,906	81.8
Embezzlement	1,863	8.1	1,871	7.9	1,317	6.7	2,909	5.9	860	4.3	6,287	6.2
Stolen property; buying, receiving, possessing	8,463	36.6	8,669	36.5	6,768	34.2	14,489	29.2	4,422	22.1	33,541	33.1
Vandalism	24,226	104.7	25,574	107.6	25,715	130.1	30,820	62.2	12,896	64.5	84,055	83.0
Weapons; carrying, possessing, etc.	10,601	45.8	10,210	43.0	11,011	55.7	21,497	43.4	6,625	33.1	45,035	44.4
Prostitution and commercialized vice	2,419	10.5	887	3.7	518	2.6	3,129	6.3	208	1.0	6,505	6.4
Sex offenses (except forcible rape and prostitution)	5,154	22.3	5,280	22.2	4,924	24.9	11,732	23.7	4,971	24.9	22,806	22.5
Drug abuse violations	109,031	471.1	111,436	469.0	117,277	593.1	217,685	439.0	81,704	408.8	469,767	463.6
Gambling	183	0.8	207	0.9	345	1.7	513	1.0	208	1.0	1,008	1.0
Offenses against the family and children	6,399	27.7	7,537	31.7	7,159	36.2	34,862	70.3	12,083	60.5	48,629	48.0
Driving under the influence	96,281	416.0	122,641	516.2	137,410	695.0	252,529	509.3	157,703	789.0	507,664	501.0
Liquor laws	50,785	219.4	66,518	280.0	98,296	497.1	56,968	114.9	34,571	173.0	196,121	193.6
Drunkenness	53,985	233.3	57,276	241.1	59,641	301.6	45,085	90.9	17,838	89.2	160,349	158.2
Disorderly conduct	58,461	252.6	74,093	311.9	91,591	463.2	50,375	101.6	22,716	113.6	205,143	202.5
Vagrancy	1,931	8.3	876	3.7	1,994	10.1	2,443	4.9	253	1.3	6,112	6.0
All other offenses (except traffic)	279,174	1,206.3	314,966	1,325.7	330,453	1,671.3	555,203	1,119.8	217,103	1,086.2	1,207,516	1,191.7
Suspicion	119	0.5	69	0.3	247	1.2	225	0.5	95	0.5	592	0.6
Curfew and loitering law violations	6,990	30.2	8,505	35.8	8,072	40.8	4,662	9.4	462	2.3	21,747	21.5
Runaways	7,940	34.3	7,614	32.0	4,471	22.6	14,853	30.0	4,343	21.7	27,260	26.9

[1] Does not include suspicion.

[2] Suburban areas include law enforcement agencies in cities with less than 50,000 inhabitants and county law enforcement agencies that are within a metropolitan statistical area. Suburban areas exclude all metropolitan agencies associated with a principal city. The agencies associated with suburban areas also appear in other groups within this table.

Table 32. Ten-Year Arrest Trends, 1999 and 2008

(Number, percent change; 7,892 agencies; 2008 estimated population 175,783,510; 1999 estimated population 158,084,635.)

Offense charged	Number of persons arrested								
	Total all ages			Under 18 years of age			18 years of age and over		
	1999	2008	Percent change	1999	2008	Percent change	1999	2008	Percent change
TOTAL[1]	8,057,640	8,068,627	+0.1	1,389,081	1,171,365	-15.7	6,668,559	6,897,262	+3.4
Violent Crime	368,356	350,198	-4.9	58,886	53,819	-8.6	309,470	296,379	-4.2
Murder and nonnegligent manslaughter	7,467	7,072	-5.3	735	670	-8.8	6,732	6,402	-4.9
Forcible rape	15,631	12,622	-19.3	2,539	1,848	-27.2	13,092	10,774	-17.7
Robbery	60,919	73,459	+20.6	15,673	19,651	+25.4	45,246	53,808	+18.9
Aggravated assault	284,339	257,045	-9.6	39,939	31,650	-20.8	244,400	225,395	-7.8
Property Crime	970,803	987,171	+1.7	319,037	256,649	-19.6	651,766	730,522	+12.1
Burglary	172,981	186,396	+7.8	58,906	50,415	-14.4	114,075	135,981	+19.2
Larceny-theft	716,261	739,223	+3.2	228,980	189,259	-17.3	487,281	549,964	+12.9
Motor vehicle theft	71,871	53,145	-26.1	25,799	12,910	-50.0	46,072	40,235	-12.7
Arson	9,690	8,407	-13.2	5,352	4,065	-24.0	4,338	4,342	+0.1
Other									
Other assaults	734,320	756,803	+3.1	133,750	133,342	-0.3	600,570	623,461	+3.8
Forgery and counterfeiting	62,823	51,578	-17.9	4,063	1,471	-63.8	58,760	50,107	-14.7
Fraud	210,254	146,610	-30.3	5,531	4,541	-17.9	204,723	142,069	-30.6
Embezzlement	11,402	13,614	+19.4	1,129	777	-31.2	10,273	12,837	+25.0
Stolen property; buying, receiving, possessing	66,460	67,288	+1.2	16,364	12,607	-23.0	50,096	54,681	+9.2
Vandalism	159,463	165,378	+3.7	68,456	63,162	-7.7	91,007	102,216	+12.3
Weapons; carrying, possessing, etc.	95,282	100,592	+5.6	23,040	22,488	-2.4	72,242	78,104	+8.1
Prostitution and commercialized vice	45,002	37,297	-17.1	705	849	+20.4	44,297	36,448	-17.7
Sex offenses (except forcible rape and prostitution)	52,470	44,645	-14.9	9,616	7,849	-18.4	42,854	36,796	-14.1
Drug abuse violations	866,640	969,762	+11.9	109,884	101,977	-7.2	756,756	867,785	+14.7
Gambling	5,281	2,577	-51.2	488	241	-50.6	4,793	2,336	-51.3
Offenses against the family and children	83,653	68,571	-18.0	5,194	3,202	-38.4	78,459	65,369	-16.7
Driving under the influence	848,736	848,408	*	12,261	8,943	-27.1	836,475	839,465	+0.4
Liquor laws	383,318	331,327	-13.6	91,212	70,938	-22.2	292,106	260,389	-10.9
Drunkenness	426,594	414,282	-2.9	13,591	10,304	-24.2	413,003	403,978	-2.2
Disorderly conduct	345,045	333,395	-3.4	92,603	94,158	+1.7	252,442	239,237	-5.2
Vagrancy	16,432	15,587	-5.1	1,366	973	-28.8	15,066	14,614	-3.0
All other offenses (except traffic)	2,131,686	2,242,048	+5.2	248,285	201,579	-18.8	1,883,401	2,040,469	+8.3
Suspicion	4,508	987	-78.1	1,069	149	-86.1	3,439	838	-75.6
Curfew and loitering law violations	82,213	60,210	-26.8	82,213	60,210	-26.8	-	-	-
Runaways	91,407	61,286	-33.0	91,407	61,286	-33.0	-	-	-

[1] Does not include suspicion.

* Less than one-tenth of 1 percent.

Table 33. Ten-Year Arrest Trends, by Sex, 1999 and 2008

(Number, percent change; 7,892 agencies; 2008 estimated population 175,783,510; 1999 estimated population 158,084,635.)

Offense charged	Male						Female					
	Total			Under 18			Total			Under 18		
	1999	2008	Percent change	1999	2008	Percent change	1999	2008	Percent change	1999	2008	Percent change
TOTAL[1]	6,279,139	6,083,494	-3.1	1,007,838	819,807	-18.7	1,778,501	1,985,133	+11.6	381,243	351,558	-7.8
Violent Crime	305,271	286,255	-6.2	48,550	44,519	-8.3	63,085	63,943	+1.4	10,336	9,300	-10.0
Murder and nonnegligent manslaughter	6,636	6,292	-5.2	673	625	-7.1	831	780	-6.1	62	45	-27.4
Forcible rape	15,452	12,474	-19.3	2,487	1,824	-26.7	179	148	-17.3	52	24	-53.8
Robbery	54,658	64,844	+18.6	14,283	17,737	+24.2	6,261	8,615	+37.6	1,390	1,914	+37.7
Aggravated assault	228,525	202,645	-11.3	31,107	24,333	-21.8	55,814	54,400	-2.5	8,832	7,317	-17.2
Property Crime	680,364	639,470	-6.0	226,267	163,158	-27.9	290,439	347,701	+19.7	92,770	93,491	+0.8
Burglary	149,875	157,341	+5.0	52,009	43,702	-16.0	23,106	29,055	+25.7	6,897	6,713	-2.7
Larceny-theft	461,632	431,212	-6.6	148,181	105,099	-29.1	254,629	308,011	+21.0	80,799	84,160	+4.2
Motor vehicle theft	60,540	43,801	-27.6	21,344	10,774	-49.5	11,331	9,344	-17.5	4,455	2,136	-52.1
Arson	8,317	7,116	-14.4	4,733	3,583	-24.3	1,373	1,291	-6.0	619	482	-22.1
Other												
Other assaults	564,655	560,226	-0.8	93,177	87,815	-5.8	169,665	196,577	+15.9	40,573	45,527	+12.2
Forgery and counterfeiting	38,570	31,947	-17.2	2,612	979	-62.5	24,253	19,631	-19.1	1,451	492	-66.1
Fraud	114,020	80,973	-29.0	3,707	2,949	-20.4	96,234	65,637	-31.8	1,824	1,592	-12.7
Embezzlement	5,768	6,575	+14.0	595	435	-26.9	5,634	7,039	+24.9	534	342	-36.0
Stolen property; buying, receiving, possessing	56,110	53,172	-5.2	14,269	10,178	-28.7	10,350	14,116	+36.4	2,095	2,429	+15.9
Vandalism	135,146	137,165	+1.5	60,183	54,680	-9.1	24,317	28,213	+16.0	8,273	8,482	+2.5
Weapons; carrying, possessing, etc.	87,790	93,112	+6.1	20,957	20,420	-2.6	7,492	7,480	-0.2	2,083	2,068	-0.7
Prostitution and commercialized vice	19,762	12,133	-38.6	315	206	-34.6	25,240	25,164	-0.3	390	643	+64.9
Sex offenses (except forcible rape and prostitution)	48,800	40,876	-16.2	8,897	7,151	-19.6	3,670	3,769	+2.7	719	698	-2.9
Drug abuse violations	711,384	784,561	+10.3	93,229	85,601	-8.2	155,256	185,201	+19.3	16,655	16,376	-1.7
Gambling	4,481	2,227	-50.3	462	229	-50.4	800	350	-56.3	26	12	-53.8
Offenses against the family and children	65,172	51,268	-21.3	3,316	2,038	-38.5	18,481	17,303	-6.4	1,878	1,164	-38.0
Driving under the influence	714,457	667,017	-6.6	10,228	6,772	-33.8	134,279	181,391	+35.1	2,033	2,171	+6.8
Liquor laws	298,874	241,328	-19.3	63,176	44,707	-29.2	84,444	89,999	+6.6	28,036	26,231	-6.4
Drunkenness	370,924	347,399	-6.3	10,902	7,854	-28.0	55,670	66,883	+20.1	2,689	2,450	-8.9
Disorderly conduct	262,713	243,865	-7.2	66,044	62,816	-4.9	82,332	89,530	+8.7	26,559	31,342	+18.0
Vagrancy	13,302	12,037	-9.5	1,119	776	-30.7	3,130	3,550	+13.4	247	197	-20.2
All other offenses (except traffic)	1,687,374	1,724,690	+2.2	185,631	149,326	-19.6	444,312	517,358	+16.4	62,654	52,253	-16.6
Suspicion	3,563	790	-77.8	833	115	-86.2	945	197	-79.2	236	34	-85.6
Curfew and loitering law violations	56,843	40,275	-29.1	56,843	40,275	-29.1	25,370	19,935	-21.4	25,370	19,935	-21.4
Runaways	37,359	26,923	-27.9	37,359	26,923	-27.9	54,048	34,363	-36.4	54,048	34,363	-36.4

[1] Does not include suspicion.

Table 34. Five-Year Arrest Trends, by Age, 2004 and 2008

(Number, percent change; 9,651 agencies; 2008 estimated population 192,575,487; 2004 estimated population 186,517,601.)

Offense charged	Number of persons arrested								
	Total all ages			Under 18 years of age			18 years of age and over		
	2004	2008	Percent change	2004	2008	Percent change	2004	2008	Percent change
TOTAL[1]	8,795,070	8,945,033	+1.7	1,369,405	1,320,998	-3.5	7,425,665	7,624,035	+2.7
Violent Crime	360,341	365,654	+1.5	54,217	56,658	+4.5	306,124	308,996	+0.9
Murder and nonnegligent manslaughter	7,763	7,804	+0.5	618	735	+18.9	7,145	7,069	-1.1
Forcible rape	15,843	14,104	-11.0	2,626	2,068	-21.2	13,217	12,036	-8.9
Robbery	63,081	77,001	+22.1	13,927	20,301	+45.8	49,154	56,700	+15.4
Aggravated assault	273,654	266,745	-2.5	37,046	33,554	-9.4	236,608	233,191	-1.4
Property Crime	1,041,192	1,090,763	+4.8	289,928	284,235	-2.0	751,264	806,528	+7.4
Burglary	189,868	201,860	+6.3	52,413	54,429	+3.8	137,455	147,431	+7.3
Larceny-theft	758,552	820,992	+8.2	210,541	210,745	+0.1	548,011	610,247	+11.4
Motor vehicle theft	82,700	58,558	-29.2	21,759	14,673	-32.6	60,941	43,885	-28.0
Arson	10,072	9,353	-7.1	5,215	4,388	-15.9	4,857	4,965	+2.2
Other									
Other assaults	814,770	844,554	+3.7	155,135	147,780	-4.7	659,635	696,774	+5.6
Forgery and counterfeiting	77,097	56,862	-26.2	3,235	1,691	-47.7	73,862	55,171	-25.3
Fraud	203,602	158,133	-22.3	4,876	4,900	+0.5	198,726	153,233	-22.9
Embezzlement	12,176	14,645	+20.3	727	868	+19.4	11,449	13,777	+20.3
Stolen property; buying, receiving, possessing	86,298	74,677	-13.5	15,645	14,156	-9.5	70,653	60,521	-14.3
Vandalism	176,396	185,429	+5.1	67,768	69,903	+3.2	108,628	115,526	+6.4
Weapons; carrying, possessing, etc.	106,836	109,031	+2.1	24,894	23,829	-4.3	81,942	85,202	+4.0
Prostitution and commercialized vice	43,188	38,052	-11.9	863	740	-14.3	42,325	37,312	-11.8
Sex offenses (except forcible rape and prostitution)	54,507	48,879	-10.3	11,428	8,901	-22.1	43,079	39,978	-7.2
Drug abuse violations	1,059,458	1,051,161	-0.8	117,040	111,536	-4.7	942,418	939,625	-0.3
Gambling	3,648	2,841	-22.1	409	359	-12.2	3,239	2,482	-23.4
Offenses against the family and children	81,559	77,747	-4.7	4,328	3,726	-13.9	77,231	74,021	-4.2
Driving under the influence	918,288	944,937	+2.9	12,497	10,143	-18.8	905,791	934,794	+3.2
Liquor laws	391,638	397,742	+1.6	84,181	84,661	+0.6	307,457	313,081	+1.8
Drunkenness	361,814	404,479	+11.8	10,957	10,585	-3.4	350,857	393,894	+12.3
Disorderly conduct	420,574	430,656	+2.4	129,167	119,561	-7.4	291,407	311,095	+6.8
Vagrancy	19,463	19,928	+2.4	1,138	1,103	-3.1	18,325	18,825	+2.7
All other offenses (except traffic)	2,426,270	2,499,771	+3.0	245,017	236,571	-3.4	2,181,253	2,263,200	+3.8
Suspicion	4,499	1,029	-77.1	616	162	-73.7	3,883	867	-77.7
Curfew and loitering law violations	57,397	60,345	+5.1	57,397	60,345	+5.1	-	-	-
Runaways	78,558	68,747	-12.5	78,558	68,747	-12.5	-	-	-

[1] Does not include suspicion.

Table 35. Five-Year Arrest Trends, by Age and Sex, 2004 and 2008

(Number, percent change; 9,651 agencies; 2008 estimated population 192,575,487; 2004 estimated population 186,517,601.)

Offense charged	Male						Female					
	Total			Under 18			Total			Under 18		
	2004	2008	Percent change	2004	2008	Percent change	2004	2008	Percent change	2004	2008	Percent change
TOTAL[1]	6,678,189	6,721,064	+0.6	954,088	921,708	-3.4	2,116,881	2,223,969	+5.1	415,317	399,290	-3.9
Violent Crime	295,711	298,613	+1.0	44,021	46,913	+6.6	64,630	67,041	+3.7	10,196	9,745	-4.4
Murder and nonnegligent manslaughter	6,844	6,944	+1.5	555	686	+23.6	919	860	-6.4	63	49	-22.2
Forcible rape	15,585	13,938	-10.6	2,552	2,037	-20.2	258	166	-35.7	74	31	-58.1
Robbery	56,062	68,043	+21.4	12,598	18,448	+46.4	7,019	8,958	+27.6	1,329	1,853	+39.4
Aggravated assault	217,220	209,688	-3.5	28,316	25,742	-9.1	56,434	57,057	+1.1	8,730	7,812	-10.5
Property Crime	705,353	707,500	+0.3	190,929	181,075	-5.2	335,839	383,263	+14.1	98,999	103,160	+4.2
Burglary	161,913	171,488	+5.9	46,109	47,547	+3.1	27,955	30,372	+8.6	6,304	6,882	+9.2
Larceny-theft	466,717	479,769	+2.8	122,540	117,383	-4.2	291,835	341,223	+16.9	88,001	93,362	+6.1
Motor vehicle theft	68,276	48,373	-29.2	17,762	12,291	-30.8	14,424	10,185	-29.4	3,997	2,382	-40.4
Arson	8,447	7,870	-6.8	4,518	3,854	-14.7	1,625	1,483	-8.7	697	534	-23.4
Other												
Other assaults	612,141	624,548	+2.0	103,439	96,878	-6.3	202,629	220,006	+8.6	51,696	50,902	-1.5
Forgery and counterfeiting	46,069	34,619	-24.9	2,103	1,125	-46.5	31,028	22,243	-28.3	1,132	566	-50.0
Fraud	109,956	87,370	-20.5	3,041	3,160	+3.9	93,646	70,763	-24.4	1,835	1,740	-5.2
Embezzlement	5,969	7,010	+17.4	447	488	+9.2	6,207	7,635	+23.0	280	380	+35.7
Stolen property; buying, receiving, possessing	69,994	59,138	-15.5	13,005	11,431	-12.1	16,304	15,539	-4.7	2,640	2,725	+3.2
Vandalism	146,684	153,281	+4.5	58,036	60,422	+4.1	29,712	32,148	+8.2	9,732	9,481	-2.6
Weapons; carrying, possessing, etc.	97,887	100,627	+2.8	22,188	21,564	-2.8	8,949	8,404	-6.1	2,706	2,265	-16.3
Prostitution and commercialized vice	13,735	11,352	-17.3	255	184	-27.8	29,453	26,700	-9.3	608	556	-8.6
Sex offenses (except forcible rape and prostitution)	50,596	45,474	-10.1	10,435	8,086	-22.5	3,911	3,405	-12.9	993	815	-17.9
Drug abuse violations	853,350	850,523	-0.3	95,492	93,489	-2.1	206,108	200,638	-2.7	21,548	18,047	-16.2
Gambling	3,106	2,457	-20.9	382	345	-9.7	542	384	-29.2	27	14	-48.1
Offenses against the family and children	61,958	58,192	-6.1	2,693	2,396	-11.0	19,601	19,555	-0.2	1,635	1,330	-18.7
Driving under the influence	745,530	741,575	-0.5	9,853	7,637	-22.5	172,758	203,362	+17.7	2,644	2,506	-5.2
Liquor laws	290,682	287,781	-1.0	54,555	53,004	-2.8	100,956	109,961	+8.9	29,626	31,657	+6.9
Drunkenness	306,698	337,369	+10.0	8,372	7,990	-4.6	55,116	67,110	+21.8	2,585	2,595	+0.4
Disorderly conduct	308,955	314,696	+1.9	86,799	79,870	-8.0	111,619	115,960	+3.9	42,368	39,691	-6.3
Vagrancy	15,774	15,536	-1.5	895	876	-2.1	3,689	4,392	+19.1	243	227	-6.6
All other offenses (except traffic)	1,867,099	1,912,202	+2.4	176,206	173,574	-1.5	559,171	587,569	+5.1	68,811	62,997	-8.4
Suspicion	3,566	819	-77.0	450	122	-72.9	933	210	-77.5	166	40	-75.9
Curfew and loitering law violations	38,588	40,770	+5.7	38,588	40,770	+5.7	18,809	19,575	+4.1	18,809	19,575	+4.1
Runaways	32,354	30,431	-5.9	32,354	30,431	-5.9	46,204	38,316	-17.1	46,204	38,316	-17.1

[1] Does not include suspicion.

Table 36. Current Year Over Previous Year Arrest Trends, 2007–2008

(Number, percent change; 11,056 agencies; 2008 estimated population 217,449,129; 2007 estimated population 215,715,035.)

Offense charged	Number of persons arrested											
	Total all ages			Under 15 years of age			Under 18 years of age			18 years of age and over		
	2007	2008	Percent change	2007	2008	Percent change	2007	2008	Percent change	2007	2008	Percent change
TOTAL[1]	10,216,503	10,062,709	-1.5	443,677	420,970	-5.1	1,581,838	1,537,628	-2.8	8,634,665	8,525,081	-1.3
Violent Crime	426,254	423,560	-0.6	18,751	17,712	-5.5	68,039	66,717	-1.9	358,215	356,843	-0.4
Murder and nonnegligent manslaughter	9,089	8,823	-2.9	93	69	-25.8	899	853	-5.1	8,190	7,970	-2.7
Forcible rape	16,152	16,349	+1.2	849	853	+0.5	2,538	2,487	-2.0	13,614	13,862	+1.8
Robbery	89,577	91,946	+2.6	5,109	4,794	-6.2	24,079	24,621	+2.3	65,498	67,325	+2.8
Aggravated assault	311,436	306,442	-1.6	12,700	11,996	-5.5	40,523	38,756	-4.4	270,913	267,686	-1.2
Property Crime	1,160,094	1,224,765	+5.6	94,497	93,604	-0.9	306,076	321,542	+5.1	854,018	903,223	+5.8
Burglary	217,440	222,925	+2.5	17,673	17,432	-1.4	58,773	60,368	+2.7	158,667	162,557	+2.5
Larceny-theft	848,687	923,421	+8.8	69,170	70,002	+1.2	221,574	239,408	+8.0	627,113	684,013	+9.1
Motor vehicle theft	83,172	67,992	-18.3	4,485	3,406	-24.1	20,397	16,859	-17.3	62,775	51,133	-18.5
Arson	10,795	10,427	-3.4	3,169	2,764	-12.8	5,332	4,907	-8.0	5,463	5,520	+1.0
Other												
Other assaults	933,744	935,234	+0.2	65,909	62,951	-4.5	170,922	166,627	-2.5	762,822	768,607	+0.8
Forgery and counterfeiting	73,746	64,869	-12.0	289	232	-19.7	2,250	1,916	-14.8	71,496	62,953	-11.9
Fraud	185,130	173,538	-6.3	824	896	+8.7	5,400	5,567	+3.1	179,730	167,971	-6.5
Embezzlement	15,886	15,681	-1.3	43	26	-39.5	1,165	941	-19.2	14,721	14,740	+0.1
Stolen property; buying, receiving, possessing	87,085	80,058	-8.1	4,025	3,585	-10.9	16,210	15,244	-6.0	70,875	64,814	-8.6
Vandalism	212,485	207,610	-2.3	33,568	31,890	-5.0	82,153	78,776	-4.1	130,332	128,834	-1.1
Weapons; carrying, possessing, etc.	131,563	125,380	-4.7	9,836	9,155	-6.9	30,807	28,506	-7.5	100,756	96,874	-3.9
Prostitution and commercialized vice	51,806	49,065	-5.3	131	114	-13.0	1,041	1,032	-0.9	50,765	48,033	-5.4
Sex offenses (except forcible rape and prostitution)	58,546	56,510	-3.5	5,363	5,020	-6.4	11,125	10,548	-5.2	47,421	45,962	-3.1
Drug abuse violations	1,270,289	1,185,067	-6.7	20,218	18,965	-6.2	135,769	126,774	-6.6	1,134,520	1,058,293	-6.7
Gambling	4,576	3,604	-21.2	92	77	-16.3	500	407	-18.6	4,076	3,197	-21.6
Offenses against the family and children	85,259	82,154	-3.6	1,255	1,105	-12.0	4,135	4,042	-2.2	81,124	78,112	-3.7
Driving under the influence	1,035,769	1,048,196	+1.2	366	187	-48.9	13,297	11,498	-13.5	1,022,472	1,036,698	+1.4
Liquor laws	471,727	463,989	-1.6	9,563	9,084	-5.0	106,220	99,248	-6.6	365,507	364,741	-0.2
Drunkenness	439,131	455,272	+3.7	1,388	1,271	-8.4	12,627	11,651	-7.7	426,504	443,621	+4.0
Disorderly conduct	497,214	487,047	-2.0	54,397	50,350	-7.4	144,081	136,829	-5.0	353,133	350,218	-0.8
Vagrancy	24,950	24,383	-2.3	877	895	+2.1	2,844	3,014	+6.0	22,106	21,369	-3.3
All other offenses (except traffic)	2,859,003	2,776,193	-2.9	67,084	62,877	-6.3	274,931	266,215	-3.2	2,584,072	2,509,978	-2.9
Suspicion	1,472	1,040	-29.3	69	47	-31.9	275	195	-29.1	1,197	845	-29.4
Curfew and loitering law violations	109,877	102,117	-7.1	28,924	25,983	-10.2	109,877	102,117	-7.1	-	-	-
Runaways	82,369	78,417	-4.8	26,277	24,991	-4.9	82,369	78,417	-4.8	-	-	-

[1] Does not include suspicion.

Table 37. Current Year Over Previous Year Arrest Trends, by Age and Sex, 2007–2008

(Number, percent change; 11,056 agencies; 2008 estimated population 217,449,129; 2007 estimated population 215,715,035.)

Offense charged	Male						Female					
	Total			Under 18			Total			Under 18		
	2007	2008	Percent change	2007	2008	Percent change	2007	2008	Percent change	2007	2008	Percent change
TOTAL[1]	7,718,150	7,572,871	-1.9	1,110,502	1,073,916	-3.3	2,498,353	2,489,838	-0.3	471,336	463,712	-1.6
Violent Crime	348,490	345,946	-0.7	56,127	55,241	-1.6	77,764	77,614	-0.2	11,912	11,476	-3.7
Murder and nonnegligent manslaughter	8,149	7,855	-3.6	838	795	-5.1	940	968	+3.0	61	58	-4.9
Forcible rape	15,985	16,141	+1.0	2,495	2,446	-2.0	167	208	+24.6	43	41	-4.7
Robbery	79,082	81,108	+2.6	21,705	22,283	+2.7	10,495	10,838	+3.3	2,374	2,338	-1.5
Aggravated assault	245,274	240,842	-1.8	31,089	29,717	-4.4	66,162	65,600	-0.8	9,434	9,039	-4.2
Property Crime	770,438	795,093	+3.2	199,031	204,743	+2.9	389,656	429,672	+10.3	107,045	116,799	+9.1
Burglary	185,254	189,959	+2.5	51,792	52,865	+2.1	32,186	32,966	+2.4	6,981	7,503	+7.5
Larceny-theft	507,878	540,161	+6.4	125,651	133,438	+6.2	340,809	383,260	+12.5	95,923	105,970	+10.5
Motor vehicle theft	68,139	56,201	-17.5	16,878	14,136	-16.2	15,033	11,791	-21.6	3,519	2,723	-22.6
Arson	9,167	8,772	-4.3	4,710	4,304	-8.6	1,628	1,655	+1.7	622	603	-3.1
Other												
Other assaults	696,370	694,130	-0.3	113,150	109,615	-3.1	237,374	241,104	+1.6	57,772	57,012	-1.3
Forgery and counterfeiting	45,472	40,151	-11.7	1,534	1,271	-17.1	28,274	24,718	-12.6	716	645	-9.9
Fraud	101,903	96,178	-5.6	3,453	3,621	+4.9	83,227	77,360	-7.0	1,947	1,946	-0.1
Embezzlement	7,446	7,574	+1.7	680	533	-21.6	8,440	8,107	-3.9	485	408	-15.9
Stolen property; buying, receiving, .possessing	69,249	63,529	-8.3	13,229	12,353	-6.6	17,836	16,529	-7.3	2,981	2,891	-3.0
Vandalism	176,228	171,992	-2.4	71,062	68,133	-4.1	36,257	35,618	-1.8	11,091	10,643	-4.0
Weapons; carrying, possessing, etc.	121,251	115,784	-4.5	27,817	25,722	-7.5	10,312	9,596	-6.9	2,990	2,784	-6.9
Prostitution and commercialized vice	16,608	15,330	-7.7	223	261	+17.0	35,198	33,735	-4.2	818	771	-5.7
Sex offenses (except forcible rape and prostitution)	53,452	51,766	-3.2	10,056	9,519	-5.3	5,094	4,744	-6.9	1,069	1,029	-3.7
Drug abuse violations	1,025,066	961,308	-6.2	113,424	106,423	-6.2	245,223	223,759	-8.8	22,345	20,351	-8.9
Gambling	3,846	3,094	-19.6	477	386	-19.1	730	510	-30.1	23	21	-8.7
Offenses against the family and children	63,413	61,044	-3.7	2,513	2,584	+2.8	21,846	21,110	-3.4	1,622	1,458	-10.1
Driving under the influence	819,809	821,827	+0.2	10,060	8,663	-13.9	215,960	226,369	+4.8	3,237	2,835	-12.4
Liquor laws	339,246	333,662	-1.6	66,319	61,721	-6.9	132,481	130,327	-1.6	39,901	37,527	-5.9
Drunkenness	368,222	381,167	+3.5	9,428	8,828	-6.4	70,909	74,105	+4.5	3,199	2,823	-11.8
Disorderly conduct	363,144	356,305	-1.9	95,826	91,508	-4.5	134,070	130,742	-2.5	48,255	45,321	-6.1
Vagrancy	19,345	18,723	-3.2	2,003	2,151	+7.4	5,605	5,660	+1.0	841	863	+2.6
All other offenses (except traffic)	2,196,861	2,133,458	-2.9	201,799	195,830	-3.0	662,142	642,735	-2.9	73,132	70,385	-3.8
Suspicion	1,154	816	-29.3	205	150	-26.8	318	224	-29.6	70	45	-35.7
Curfew and loitering law violations	75,994	70,158	-7.7	75,994	70,158	-7.7	33,883	31,959	-5.7	33,883	31,959	-5.7
Runaways	36,297	34,652	-4.5	36,297	34,652	-4.5	46,072	43,765	-5.0	46,072	43,765	-5.0

[1] Does not include suspicion.

Table 38. Arrests, Distribution by Age, 2008

(Number, percent; 11,713 agencies; 2008 estimated population 230,897,506.)

Offense charged	Total all ages	Ages under 15	Ages under 18	Ages 18 and over	Under 10	10–12	13–14	15	16	17	18	19	20
TOTAL	10,709,361	442,038	1,623,083	9,086,278	11,226	88,568	342,244	318,635	404,507	457,903	521,457	526,789	485,219
Total percent distribution[1]	100.0	4.1	15.2	84.8	0.1	0.8	3.2	3.0	3.8	4.3	4.9	4.9	4.5
Violent Crime	457,455	19,675	73,970	383,485	469	4,072	15,134	14,402	18,603	21,290	23,673	22,752	20,124
Violent crime percent distribution[1]	100.0	4.3	16.2	83.8	0.1	0.9	3.3	3.1	4.1	4.7	5.2	5.0	4.4
Murder and nonnegligent manslaughter	9,888	79	974	8,914	1	8	70	150	296	449	654	738	648
Forcible rape	16,916	860	2,505	14,411	8	216	636	462	540	643	820	825	748
Robbery	100,738	5,384	27,522	73,216	61	672	4,651	5,517	7,717	8,904	9,464	8,056	6,197
Aggravated assault	329,913	13,352	42,969	286,944	399	3,176	9,777	8,273	10,050	11,294	12,735	13,133	12,531
Property Crime	1,305,135	98,100	339,990	965,145	2,345	20,665	75,090	68,015	83,794	90,081	92,132	74,921	59,317
Property crime percent distribution[1]	100.0	7.5	26.1	73.9	0.2	1.6	5.8	5.2	6.4	6.9	7.1	5.7	4.5
Burglary	236,219	18,538	64,418	171,801	554	3,692	14,292	13,252	15,634	16,994	18,997	15,506	11,844
Larceny-theft	982,997	72,921	251,483	731,514	1,480	15,687	55,754	49,373	62,106	67,083	67,388	54,850	43,726
Motor vehicle theft	75,135	3,819	19,068	56,067	20	401	3,398	4,489	5,359	5,401	5,277	4,134	3,430
Arson	10,784	2,822	5,021	5,763	291	885	1,646	901	695	603	470	431	317
Other													
Other assaults	994,804	66,557	177,519	817,285	1,932	16,571	48,054	35,107	38,762	37,093	33,582	33,575	33,543
Forgery and counterfeiting	68,976	239	2,003	66,973	9	47	183	223	489	1,052	2,355	2,992	3,151
Fraud	174,598	925	5,691	168,907	42	149	734	845	1,489	2,432	4,510	5,914	6,258
Embezzlement	16,458	28	993	15,465	4	3	21	43	287	635	1,173	1,251	1,106
Stolen property; buying, receiving, possessing	85,584	3,719	16,060	69,524	58	578	3,083	3,155	4,333	4,853	5,685	5,126	4,188
Vandalism	219,059	33,230	82,441	136,618	1,543	8,282	23,405	15,779	16,745	16,687	14,774	11,605	9,168
Weapons; carrying, possessing, etc.	138,255	9,695	30,804	107,451	391	2,376	6,928	5,607	7,171	8,331	9,521	8,476	7,109
Prostitution and commercialized vice	58,784	129	1,158	57,626	8	7	114	172	329	528	1,831	2,319	2,456
Sex offenses (except forcible rape and prostitution)	60,804	5,229	11,029	49,775	240	1,487	3,502	1,934	1,913	1,953	2,470	2,197	1,963
Drug abuse violations	1,304,098	20,357	137,958	1,166,140	192	2,176	17,989	23,031	37,641	56,929	82,608	82,123	72,956
Gambling	7,632	182	1,295	6,337	3	10	169	262	333	518	620	534	534
Offenses against the family and children	87,197	1,213	4,378	82,819	84	228	901	833	1,119	1,213	1,745	1,873	2,034
Driving under the influence	1,110,083	196	12,001	1,098,082	39	20	137	460	2,777	8,568	23,470	32,644	37,181
Liquor laws	478,800	9,211	100,844	377,956	128	695	8,388	14,843	28,652	48,138	79,697	83,998	69,000
Drunkenness	474,378	1,273	11,934	462,444	59	59	1,155	1,795	2,915	5,951	12,870	14,201	14,214
Disorderly conduct	529,929	52,645	144,932	384,997	881	11,920	39,844	30,326	32,183	29,778	24,253	21,118	19,644
Vagrancy	26,325	913	3,098	23,227	6	148	759	825	954	406	1,232	968	850
All other offenses (except traffic)	2,921,526	64,863	276,553	2,644,973	1,764	10,700	52,399	55,648	71,710	84,332	103,141	118,117	120,374
Suspicion	1,259	51	210	1,049	1	9	41	47	55	57	115	85	49
Curfew and loitering law violations	104,168	26,728	104,168	-	402	4,231	22,095	23,898	29,124	24,418	-	-	-
Runaways	84,054	26,880	84,054	-	626	4,135	22,119	21,385	23,129	12,660	-	-	-

[1] Because of rounding, the percentages may not add to 100.0.

Table 38. Arrests, Distribution by Age, 2008—*Continued*

(Number, percent; 11,713 agencies; 2008 estimated population 230,897,506.)

Offense charged	21	22	23	24	25–29	30–34	35–39	40–44	45–49	50–54	55–59	60–64	65 and over
TOTAL	438,772	409,282	384,447	354,459	1,523,228	1,053,380	938,036	864,786	747,575	454,674	218,928	95,312	69,934
Total percent distribution[1]	4.1	3.8	3.6	3.3	14.2	9.8	8.8	8.1	7.0	4.2	2.0	0.9	0.7
Violent Crime	18,937	17,604	16,802	15,646	67,020	46,294	39,761	34,957	28,753	16,504	7,884	3,687	3,087
Violent crime percent distribution[1]	4.1	3.8	3.7	3.4	14.7	10.1	8.7	7.6	6.3	3.6	1.7	0.8	0.7
Murder and nonnegligent manslaughter	532	494	483	411	1,689	918	753	555	416	272	176	85	90
Forcible rape	710	622	569	516	2,362	1,838	1,638	1,453	1,027	614	336	158	175
Robbery	4,829	4,014	3,515	3,069	11,645	6,695	5,511	4,579	3,258	1,561	569	162	92
Aggravated assault	12,866	12,474	12,235	11,650	51,324	36,843	31,859	28,370	24,052	14,057	6,803	3,282	2,730
Property Crime	48,876	43,053	38,187	34,428	145,737	101,133	93,813	86,610	71,554	41,538	18,980	8,183	6,683
Property crime percent distribution[1]	3.7	3.3	2.9	2.6	11.2	7.7	7.2	6.6	5.5	3.2	1.5	0.6	0.5
Burglary	9,695	8,377	7,361	6,506	27,075	17,530	15,705	13,965	10,642	5,461	2,005	705	427
Larceny-theft	35,856	31,785	28,149	25,462	107,996	76,180	71,665	67,382	57,205	34,323	16,288	7,197	6,062
Motor vehicle theft	3,015	2,623	2,451	2,282	9,843	6,781	5,946	4,748	3,252	1,447	517	195	126
Arson	310	268	226	178	823	642	497	515	455	307	170	86	68
Other													
Other assaults	35,726	34,754	34,237	32,511	146,974	107,287	97,040	85,328	69,806	39,582	18,038	8,182	7,120
Forgery and counterfeiting	2,885	2,828	2,880	2,764	13,426	9,604	8,374	6,503	4,861	2,650	1,038	404	258
Fraud	5,887	5,991	5,901	5,773	29,729	25,030	23,262	19,263	14,553	8,675	4,443	2,103	1,615
Embezzlement	911	803	697	596	2,378	1,843	1,484	1,292	905	539	294	106	87
Stolen property; buying, receiving, possessing	3,670	3,278	3,080	2,613	11,972	8,287	7,197	6,147	4,365	2,342	973	379	222
Vandalism	8,983	7,581	6,505	5,919	22,752	13,697	11,280	9,568	7,397	4,101	1,760	813	715
Weapons; carrying, possessing, etc.	6,771	6,157	5,650	5,054	19,677	11,189	8,183	6,569	5,701	3,664	1,931	978	821
Prostitution and commercialized vice	2,291	2,434	2,156	2,055	9,438	7,538	7,758	7,260	5,393	2,706	1,084	471	436
Sex offenses (except forcible rape and prostitution)	2,001	1,773	1,713	1,479	6,677	5,611	5,424	5,431	4,814	3,351	2,041	1,332	1,498
Drug abuse violations	65,242	59,071	54,401	49,985	207,658	130,463	106,789	96,509	81,548	46,887	20,181	6,674	3,045
Gambling	386	310	298	237	937	535	446	359	368	248	219	148	158
Offenses against the family and children	2,310	2,417	2,664	2,656	15,135	13,728	13,439	10,799	7,558	3,801	1,585	657	418
Driving under the influence	52,385	53,388	52,471	48,597	204,165	136,200	117,761	107,844	98,831	65,461	36,168	18,222	13,294
Liquor laws	12,047	8,415	6,769	5,573	21,049	15,170	14,940	17,350	19,030	13,125	6,998	2,890	1,905
Drunkenness	21,613	19,778	18,447	16,941	70,782	50,128	48,925	53,301	54,514	37,461	17,877	7,166	4,226
Disorderly conduct	23,849	21,108	18,544	16,086	63,228	40,516	35,539	34,180	31,377	19,252	9,085	4,094	3,124
Vagrancy	697	561	563	544	2,345	2,020	2,479	3,235	3,355	2,414	1,212	485	267
All other offenses (except traffic)	123,244	117,918	112,432	104,961	461,983	327,005	294,051	272,209	232,825	140,323	67,118	28,326	20,946
Suspicion	61	60	50	41	166	102	91	72	67	50	19	12	9
Curfew and loitering law violations	-	-	-	-	-	-	-	-	-	-	-	-	-
Runaways	-	-	-	-	-	-	-	-	-	-	-	-	-

[1] Because of rounding, the percentages may not add to 100.0.

Table 39. Male Arrests, Distribution by Age, 2008

(Number, percent; 11,713 agencies; 2008 estimated population 230,897,506.)

Offense charged	Total all ages	Ages under 15	Ages under 18	Ages 18 and over	Under 10	10–12	13–14	15	16	17	18	19	20
TOTAL	8,086,667	303,190	1,138,281	6,948,386	9,213	64,409	229,568	216,220	283,281	335,590	396,117	401,559	369,934
Total percent distribution[1]	100.0	3.7	14.1	85.9	0.1	0.8	2.8	2.7	3.5	4.1	4.9	5.0	4.6
Violent Crime	373,678	15,818	61,195	312,483	407	3,336	12,075	11,681	15,541	18,155	20,171	19,089	16,766
Violent crime percent distribution[1]	100.0	4.2	16.4	83.6	0.1	0.9	3.2	3.1	4.2	4.9	5.4	5.1	4.5
Murder and nonnegligent manslaughter	8,824	68	909	7,915	1	7	60	138	274	429	598	678	596
Forcible rape	16,712	847	2,465	14,247	8	213	626	450	534	634	817	816	740
Robbery	89,033	4,818	24,966	64,067	55	596	4,167	4,941	7,040	8,167	8,588	7,182	5,508
Aggravated assault	259,109	10,085	32,855	226,254	343	2,520	7,222	6,152	7,693	8,925	10,168	10,413	9,922
Property Crime	850,587	64,506	217,683	632,904	1,867	14,136	48,503	43,412	52,640	57,125	60,444	49,086	38,257
Property crime percent distribution[1]	100.0	7.6	25.6	74.4	0.2	1.7	5.7	5.1	6.2	6.7	7.1	5.8	4.5
Burglary	201,826	16,174	56,616	145,210	497	3,161	12,516	11,580	13,811	15,051	16,925	13,534	10,215
Larceny-theft	577,467	42,710	140,554	436,913	1,081	9,837	31,792	27,291	33,683	36,870	38,553	31,638	24,885
Motor vehicle theft	62,229	3,121	16,107	46,122	16	340	2,765	3,779	4,543	4,664	4,544	3,531	2,883
Arson	9,065	2,501	4,406	4,659	273	798	1,430	762	603	540	422	383	274
Other													
Other assaults	739,970	44,141	116,883	623,087	1,616	11,944	30,581	22,224	25,101	25,417	23,770	23,819	24,184
Forgery and counterfeiting	42,860	161	1,340	41,520	4	33	124	165	341	673	1,531	1,942	2,023
Fraud	98,712	591	3,726	94,986	28	95	468	559	983	1,593	2,907	3,554	3,749
Embezzlement	7,954	18	569	7,385	4	1	13	28	162	361	601	620	519
Stolen property; buying, receiving, possessing	68,174	2,961	13,064	55,110	53	455	2,453	2,539	3,546	4,018	4,737	4,217	3,454
Vandalism	181,526	28,612	71,434	110,092	1,396	7,087	20,129	13,794	14,572	14,456	12,682	9,782	7,587
Weapons; carrying, possessing, etc.	127,865	8,520	27,830	100,035	361	2,080	6,079	5,001	6,544	7,765	8,997	8,007	6,717
Prostitution and commercialized vice	18,012	29	280	17,732	3	3	23	39	70	142	284	363	432
Sex offenses (except forcible rape and prostitution)	55,631	4,775	9,950	45,681	220	1,390	3,165	1,693	1,733	1,749	2,180	1,949	1,759
Drug abuse violations	1,063,498	16,271	116,660	946,838	155	1,741	14,375	19,168	32,198	49,023	70,718	70,008	61,577
Gambling	7,021	177	1,269	5,752	3	10	164	259	329	504	606	510	506
Offenses against the family and children	64,918	760	2,795	62,123	58	159	543	477	718	840	1,214	1,282	1,363
Driving under the influence	872,399	137	9,063	863,336	31	14	92	339	2,050	6,537	18,197	25,424	29,049
Liquor laws	345,973	4,753	62,837	283,136	101	375	4,277	8,410	17,854	31,820	54,641	59,689	50,346
Drunkenness	397,888	828	9,099	388,789	46	40	742	1,294	2,197	4,780	10,585	11,736	11,856
Disorderly conduct	391,187	34,444	97,402	293,785	719	8,409	25,316	19,743	21,897	21,318	18,249	15,869	14,737
Vagrancy	20,417	606	2,209	18,208	6	104	496	573	700	330	984	714	623
All other offenses (except traffic)	2,248,826	45,714	204,249	2,044,577	1,419	7,904	36,391	39,690	53,474	65,371	82,529	93,832	94,386
Suspicion	991	41	164	827	1	7	33	41	40	42	90	67	44
Curfew and loitering law violations	71,675	17,647	71,675	-	304	2,935	14,408	15,989	20,311	17,728	-	-	-
Runaways	36,905	11,680	36,905	-	411	2,151	9,118	9,102	10,280	5,843	-	-	-

[1] Because of rounding, the percentages may not add to 100.0.

Table 39. Male Arrests, Distribution by Age, 2008—*Continued*

(Number, percent; 11,713 agencies; 2008 estimated population 230,897,506.)

Offense charged	21	22	23	24	25–29	30–34	35–39	40–44	45–49	50–54	55–59	60–64	65 and over
TOTAL	339,291	314,636	295,323	271,839	1,166,183	798,613	697,204	645,143	572,893	362,673	180,263	79,061	57,654
Total percent distribution[1]	4.2	3.9	3.7	3.4	14.4	9.9	8.6	8.0	7.1	4.5	2.2	1.0	0.7
Violent Crime	15,687	14,380	13,707	12,732	54,508	37,334	31,380	27,608	23,038	13,528	6,670	3,167	2,718
Violent crime percent distribution[1]	4.2	3.8	3.7	3.4	14.6	10.0	8.4	7.4	6.2	3.6	1.8	0.8	0.7
Murder and nonnegligent manslaughter	490	453	426	368	1,521	805	628	465	340	233	158	76	80
Forcible rape	700	615	562	506	2,339	1,816	1,608	1,439	1,012	610	335	157	175
Robbery	4,279	3,476	3,076	2,667	10,073	5,733	4,681	3,901	2,806	1,370	505	147	75
Aggravated assault	10,218	9,836	9,643	9,191	40,575	28,980	24,463	21,803	18,880	11,315	5,672	2,787	2,388
Property Crime	31,825	27,800	24,501	21,899	93,289	65,110	61,759	58,553	49,451	28,696	12,872	5,200	4,162
Property crime percent distribution[1]	3.7	3.3	2.9	2.6	11.0	7.7	7.3	6.9	5.8	3.4	1.5	0.6	0.5
Burglary	8,334	7,130	6,180	5,453	22,436	14,305	12,877	11,547	8,981	4,657	1,698	586	352
Larceny-theft	20,678	18,293	16,116	14,483	62,306	44,880	43,778	42,741	37,427	22,553	10,567	4,365	3,650
Motor vehicle theft	2,543	2,146	2,011	1,821	7,890	5,427	4,747	3,887	2,694	1,248	463	177	110
Arson	270	231	194	142	657	498	357	378	349	238	144	72	50
Other													
Other assaults	26,270	25,758	25,643	24,733	113,400	82,843	74,068	65,252	54,496	31,537	14,735	6,690	5,889
Forgery and counterfeiting	1,828	1,741	1,808	1,672	8,082	5,719	5,049	4,016	3,080	1,771	746	313	199
Fraud	3,458	3,487	3,347	3,232	16,093	13,242	12,229	10,800	8,515	5,327	2,723	1,321	1,002
Embezzlement	430	397	348	267	1,156	868	674	604	403	266	117	57	58
Stolen property; buying, receiving, possessing	2,930	2,537	2,400	1,976	9,263	6,300	5,593	4,916	3,538	1,936	801	325	187
Vandalism	7,362	6,174	5,219	4,780	18,076	10,771	8,692	7,282	5,763	3,241	1,418	671	592
Weapons; carrying, possessing, etc.	6,375	5,797	5,305	4,711	18,361	10,319	7,451	5,946	5,179	3,377	1,807	918	768
Prostitution and commercialized vice	480	584	582	555	2,989	2,616	2,258	2,036	1,751	1,246	738	402	416
Sex offenses (except forcible rape and prostitution)	1,805	1,597	1,535	1,318	6,060	5,125	4,944	4,995	4,474	3,166	1,989	1,301	1,484
Drug abuse violations	54,823	49,176	44,974	41,352	169,930	104,848	81,968	72,251	62,255	37,541	16,922	5,786	2,709
Gambling	371	298	286	227	872	489	374	307	305	197	168	109	127
Offenses against the family and children	1,556	1,596	1,778	1,799	10,668	10,315	10,339	8,665	6,182	3,168	1,324	536	338
Driving under the influence	40,370	41,089	40,985	38,383	162,817	109,603	92,035	81,885	75,135	51,762	29,773	15,398	11,431
Liquor laws	9,656	6,831	5,485	4,464	16,940	12,174	11,769	13,840	15,507	11,317	6,220	2,579	1,678
Drunkenness	18,152	16,766	15,690	14,422	60,159	42,283	40,071	43,176	44,979	32,305	16,125	6,552	3,932
Disorderly conduct	18,420	16,422	14,339	12,409	48,537	30,289	26,145	25,265	24,008	15,500	7,561	3,437	2,598
Vagrancy	569	440	449	429	1,728	1,465	1,818	2,482	2,725	2,027	1,081	430	244
All other offenses (except traffic)	96,874	91,714	86,897	80,449	353,119	246,821	218,519	205,213	182,063	114,726	56,458	23,862	17,115
Suspicion	50	52	45	30	136	79	69	51	46	39	15	7	7
Curfew and loitering law violations	-	-	-	-	-	-	-	-	-	-	-	-	-
Runaways	-	-	-	-	-	-	-	-	-	-	-	-	-

[1] Because of rounding, the percentages may not add to 100.0.

Table 40. Female Arrests, Distribution by Age, 2008

(Number, percent; 11,713 agencies; 2008 estimated population 230,897,506.)

Offense charged	Total all ages	Ages under 15	Ages under 18	Ages 18 and over	Under 10	10–12	13–14	15	16	17	18	19	20
TOTAL	2,622,694	138,848	484,802	2,137,892	2,013	24,159	112,676	102,415	121,226	122,313	125,340	125,230	115,285
Total percent distribution[1]	100.0	5.3	18.5	81.5	0.1	0.9	4.3	3.9	4.6	4.7	4.8	4.8	4.4
Violent Crime	83,777	3,857	12,775	71,002	62	736	3,059	2,721	3,062	3,135	3,502	3,663	3,358
Violent crime percent distribution[1]	100.0	4.6	15.2	84.8	0.1	0.9	3.7	3.2	3.7	3.7	4.2	4.4	4.0
Murder and nonnegligent manslaughter	1,064	11	65	999	0	1	10	12	22	20	56	60	52
Forcible rape	204	13	40	164	0	3	10	12	6	9	3	9	8
Robbery	11,705	566	2,556	9,149	6	76	484	576	677	737	876	874	689
Aggravated assault	70,804	3,267	10,114	60,690	56	656	2,555	2,121	2,357	2,369	2,567	2,720	2,609
Property Crime	454,548	33,594	122,307	332,241	478	6,529	26,587	24,603	31,154	32,956	31,688	25,835	21,060
Property crime percent distribution[1]	100.0	7.4	26.9	73.1	0.1	1.4	5.8	5.4	6.9	7.3	7.0	5.7	4.6
Burglary	34,393	2,364	7,802	26,591	57	531	1,776	1,672	1,823	1,943	2,072	1,972	1,629
Larceny-theft	405,530	30,211	110,929	294,601	399	5,850	23,962	22,082	28,423	30,213	28,835	23,212	18,841
Motor vehicle theft	12,906	698	2,961	9,945	4	61	633	710	816	737	733	603	547
Arson	1,719	321	615	1,104	18	87	216	139	92	63	48	48	43
Other													
Other assaults	254,834	22,416	60,636	194,198	316	4,627	17,473	12,883	13,661	11,676	9,812	9,756	9,359
Forgery and counterfeiting	26,116	78	663	25,453	5	14	59	58	148	379	824	1,050	1,128
Fraud	75,886	334	1,965	73,921	14	54	266	286	506	839	1,603	2,360	2,509
Embezzlement	8,504	10	424	8,080	0	2	8	15	125	274	572	631	587
Stolen property; buying, receiving, possessing	17,410	758	2,996	14,414	5	123	630	616	787	835	948	909	734
Vandalism	37,533	4,618	11,007	26,526	147	1,195	3,276	1,985	2,173	2,231	2,092	1,823	1,581
Weapons; carrying, possessing, etc.	10,390	1,175	2,974	7,416	30	296	849	606	627	566	524	469	392
Prostitution and commercialized vice	40,772	100	878	39,894	5	4	91	133	259	386	1,547	1,956	2,024
Sex offenses (except forcible rape and prostitution)	5,173	454	1,079	4,094	20	97	337	241	180	204	290	248	204
Drug abuse violations	240,600	4,086	21,298	219,302	37	435	3,614	3,863	5,443	7,906	11,890	12,115	11,379
Gambling	611	5	26	585	0	0	5	3	4	14	14	24	28
Offenses against the family and children	22,279	453	1,583	20,696	26	69	358	356	401	373	531	591	671
Driving under the influence	237,684	59	2,938	234,746	8	6	45	121	727	2,031	5,273	7,220	8,132
Liquor laws	132,827	4,458	38,007	94,820	27	320	4,111	6,433	10,798	16,318	25,056	24,309	18,654
Drunkenness	76,490	445	2,835	73,655	13	19	413	501	718	1,171	2,285	2,465	2,358
Disorderly conduct	138,742	18,201	47,530	91,212	162	3,511	14,528	10,583	10,286	8,460	6,004	5,249	4,907
Vagrancy	5,908	307	889	5,019	0	44	263	252	254	76	248	254	227
All other offenses (except traffic)	672,700	19,149	72,304	600,396	345	2,796	16,008	15,958	18,236	18,961	20,612	24,285	25,988
Suspicion	268	10	46	222	0	2	8	6	15	15	25	18	5
Curfew and loitering law violations	32,493	9,081	32,493	-	98	1,296	7,687	7,909	8,813	6,690	-	-	-
Runaways	47,149	15,200	47,149	-	215	1,984	13,001	12,283	12,849	6,817	-	-	-

[1] Because of rounding, the percentages may not add to 100.0.

Table 40. Female Arrests, Distribution by Age, 2008—*Continued*

(Number, percent; 11,713 agencies; 2008 estimated population 230,897,506.)

Offense charged	21	22	23	24	25–29	30–34	35–39	40–44	45–49	50–54	55–59	60–64	65 and over
TOTAL	99,481	94,646	89,124	82,620	357,045	254,767	240,832	219,643	174,682	92,001	38,665	16,251	12,280
Total percent distribution[1]	3.8	3.6	3.4	3.2	13.6	9.7	9.2	8.4	6.7	3.5	1.5	0.6	0.5
Violent Crime	3,250	3,224	3,095	2,914	12,512	8,960	8,381	7,349	5,715	2,976	1,214	520	369
Violent crime percent distribution[1]	3.9	3.8	3.7	3.5	14.9	10.7	10.0	8.8	6.8	3.6	1.4	0.6	0.4
Murder and nonnegligent manslaughter	42	41	57	43	168	113	125	90	76	39	18	9	10
Forcible rape	10	7	7	10	23	22	30	14	15	4	1	1	0
Robbery	550	538	439	402	1,572	962	830	678	452	191	64	15	17
Aggravated assault	2,648	2,638	2,592	2,459	10,749	7,863	7,396	6,567	5,172	2,742	1,131	495	342
Property Crime	17,051	15,253	13,686	12,529	52,448	36,023	32,054	28,057	22,103	12,842	6,108	2,983	2,521
Property crime percent distribution[1]	3.8	3.4	3.0	2.8	11.5	7.9	7.1	6.2	4.9	2.8	1.3	0.7	0.6
Burglary	1,361	1,247	1,181	1,053	4,639	3,225	2,828	2,418	1,661	804	307	119	75
Larceny-theft	15,178	13,492	12,033	10,979	45,690	31,300	27,887	24,641	19,778	11,770	5,721	2,832	2,412
Motor vehicle theft	472	477	440	461	1,953	1,354	1,199	861	558	199	54	18	16
Arson	40	37	32	36	166	144	140	137	106	69	26	14	18
Other													
Other assaults	9,456	8,996	8,594	7,778	33,574	24,444	22,972	20,076	15,310	8,045	3,303	1,492	1,231
Forgery and counterfeiting	1,057	1,087	1,072	1,092	5,344	3,885	3,325	2,487	1,781	879	292	91	59
Fraud	2,429	2,504	2,554	2,541	13,636	11,788	11,033	8,463	6,038	3,348	1,720	782	613
Embezzlement	481	406	349	329	1,222	975	810	688	502	273	177	49	29
Stolen property; buying, receiving, possessing	740	741	680	637	2,709	1,987	1,604	1,231	827	406	172	54	35
Vandalism	1,621	1,407	1,286	1,139	4,676	2,926	2,588	2,286	1,634	860	342	142	123
Weapons; carrying, possessing, etc.	396	360	345	343	1,316	870	732	623	522	287	124	60	53
Prostitution and commercialized vice	1,811	1,850	1,574	1,500	6,449	4,922	5,500	5,224	3,642	1,460	346	69	20
Sex offenses (except forcible rape and prostitution)	196	176	178	161	617	486	480	436	340	185	52	31	14
Drug abuse violations	10,419	9,895	9,427	8,633	37,728	25,615	24,821	24,258	19,293	9,346	3,259	888	336
Gambling	15	12	12	10	65	46	72	52	63	51	51	39	31
Offenses against the family and children	754	821	886	857	4,467	3,413	3,100	2,134	1,376	633	261	121	80
Driving under the influence	12,015	12,299	11,486	10,214	41,348	26,597	25,726	25,959	23,696	13,699	6,395	2,824	1,863
Liquor laws	2,391	1,584	1,284	1,109	4,109	2,996	3,171	3,510	3,523	1,808	778	311	227
Drunkenness	3,461	3,012	2,757	2,519	10,623	7,845	8,854	10,125	9,535	5,156	1,752	614	294
Disorderly conduct	5,429	4,686	4,205	3,677	14,691	10,227	9,394	8,915	7,369	3,752	1,524	657	526
Vagrancy	128	121	114	115	617	555	661	753	630	387	131	55	23
All other offenses (except traffic)	26,370	26,204	25,535	24,512	108,864	80,184	75,532	66,996	50,762	25,597	10,660	4,464	3,831
Suspicion	11	8	5	11	30	23	22	21	21	11	4	5	2
Curfew and loitering law violations	-	-	-	-	-	-	-	-	-	-	-	-	-
Runaways	-	-	-	-	-	-	-	-	-	-	-	-	-

[1] Because of rounding, the percentages may not add to 100.0.

Table 41. Arrests of Persons Under 15, 18, 21, and 25 Years of Age, 2008

(Number, percent; 11,713 agencies; 2008 estimated population 230,897,506.)

Offense charged	Total all ages	Number of persons arrested				Percent of total all ages			
		Under 15	Under 18	Under 21	Under 25	Under 15	Under 18	Under 21	Under 25
TOTAL	10,709,361	442,038	1,623,083	3,156,548	4,743,508	4.1	15.2	29.5	44.3
Violent Crime	457,455	19,675	73,970	140,519	209,508	4.3	16.2	30.7	45.8
Murder and nonnegligent manslaughter	9,888	79	974	3,014	4,934	0.8	9.9	30.5	49.9
Forcible rape	16,916	860	2,505	4,898	7,315	5.1	14.8	29.0	43.2
Robbery	100,738	5,384	27,522	51,239	66,666	5.3	27.3	50.9	66.2
Aggravated assault	329,913	13,352	42,969	81,368	130,593	4.0	13.0	24.7	39.6
Property Crime	1,305,135	98,100	339,990	566,360	730,904	7.5	26.1	43.4	56.0
Burglary	236,219	18,538	64,418	110,765	142,704	7.8	27.3	46.9	60.4
Larceny-theft	982,997	72,921	251,483	417,447	538,699	7.4	25.6	42.5	54.8
Motor vehicle theft	75,135	3,819	19,068	31,909	42,280	5.1	25.4	42.5	56.3
Arson	10,784	2,822	5,021	6,239	7,221	26.2	46.6	57.9	67.0
Other									
Other assaults	994,804	66,557	177,519	278,219	415,447	6.7	17.8	28.0	41.8
Forgery and counterfeiting	68,976	239	2,003	10,501	21,858	0.3	2.9	15.2	31.7
Fraud	174,598	925	5,691	22,373	45,925	0.5	3.3	12.8	26.3
Embezzlement	16,458	28	993	4,523	7,530	0.2	6.0	27.5	45.8
Stolen property; buying, receiving, possessing	85,584	3,719	16,060	31,059	43,700	4.3	18.8	36.3	51.1
Vandalism	219,059	33,230	82,441	117,988	146,976	15.2	37.6	53.9	67.1
Weapons; carrying, possessing, etc.	138,255	9,695	30,804	55,910	79,542	7.0	22.3	40.4	57.5
Prostitution and commercialized vice	58,784	129	1,158	7,764	16,700	0.2	2.0	13.2	28.4
Sex offenses (except forcible rape and prostitution)	60,804	5,229	11,029	17,659	24,625	8.6	18.1	29.0	40.5
Drug abuse violations	1,304,098	20,357	137,958	375,645	604,344	1.6	10.6	28.8	46.3
Gambling	7,632	182	1,295	2,983	4,214	2.4	17.0	39.1	55.2
Offenses against the family and children	87,197	1,213	4,378	10,030	20,077	1.4	5.0	11.5	23.0
Driving under the influence	1,110,083	196	12,001	105,296	312,137	*	1.1	9.5	28.1
Liquor laws	478,800	9,211	100,844	333,539	366,343	1.9	21.1	69.7	76.5
Drunkenness	474,378	1,273	11,934	53,219	129,998	0.3	2.5	11.2	27.4
Disorderly conduct	529,929	52,645	144,932	209,947	289,534	9.9	27.3	39.6	54.6
Vagrancy	26,325	913	3,098	6,148	8,513	3.5	11.8	23.4	32.3
All other offenses (except traffic)	2,921,526	64,863	276,553	618,185	1,076,740	2.2	9.5	21.2	36.9
Suspicion	1,259	51	210	459	671	4.1	16.7	36.5	53.3
Curfew and loitering law violations	104,168	26,728	104,168	104,168	104,168	25.7	100.0	100.0	100.0
Runaways	84,054	26,880	84,054	84,054	84,054	32.0	100.0	100.0	100.0

* Less than one-tenth of 1 percent.

Table 42. Arrests, Distribution by Sex, 2008

(Number, percent; 11,713 agencies; 2008 estimated population 230,897,506.)

Offense charged	Number of persons arrested			Percent male	Percent female	Percent distribution[1]		
	Total	Male	Female			Total	Male	Female
TOTAL	10,709,361	8,086,667	2,622,694	75.5	24.5	100.0	100.0	100.0
Violent Crime	457,455	373,678	83,777	81.7	18.3	4.3	4.6	3.2
Murder and nonnegligent manslaughter	9,888	8,824	1,064	89.2	10.8	0.1	0.1	*
Forcible rape	16,916	16,712	204	98.8	1.2	0.2	0.2	*
Robbery	100,738	89,033	11,705	88.4	11.6	0.9	1.1	0.4
Aggravated assault	329,913	259,109	70,804	78.5	21.5	3.1	3.2	2.7
Property Crime	1,305,135	850,587	454,548	65.2	34.8	12.2	10.5	17.3
Burglary	236,219	201,826	34,393	85.4	14.6	2.2	2.5	1.3
Larceny-theft	982,997	577,467	405,530	58.7	41.3	9.2	7.1	15.5
Motor vehicle theft	75,135	62,229	12,906	82.8	17.2	0.7	0.8	0.5
Arson	10,784	9,065	1,719	84.1	15.9	0.1	0.1	0.1
Other								
Other assaults	994,804	739,970	254,834	74.4	25.6	9.3	9.2	9.7
Forgery and counterfeiting	68,976	42,860	26,116	62.1	37.9	0.6	0.5	1.0
Fraud	174,598	98,712	75,886	56.5	43.5	1.6	1.2	2.9
Embezzlement	16,458	7,954	8,504	48.3	51.7	0.2	0.1	0.3
Stolen property; buying, receiving, possessing	85,584	68,174	17,410	79.7	20.3	0.8	0.8	0.7
Vandalism	219,059	181,526	37,533	82.9	17.1	2.0	2.2	1.4
Weapons; carrying, possessing, etc.	138,255	127,865	10,390	92.5	7.5	1.3	1.6	0.4
Prostitution and commercialized vice	58,784	18,012	40,772	30.6	69.4	0.5	0.2	1.6
Sex offenses (except forcible rape and prostitution)	60,804	55,631	5,173	91.5	8.5	0.6	0.7	0.2
Drug abuse violations	1,304,098	1,063,498	240,600	81.6	18.4	12.2	13.2	9.2
Gambling	7,632	7,021	611	92.0	8.0	0.1	0.1	*
Offenses against the family and children	87,197	64,918	22,279	74.4	25.6	0.8	0.8	0.8
Driving under the influence	1,110,083	872,399	237,684	78.6	21.4	10.4	10.8	9.1
Liquor laws	478,800	345,973	132,827	72.3	27.7	4.5	4.3	5.1
Drunkenness	474,378	397,888	76,490	83.9	16.1	4.4	4.9	2.9
Disorderly conduct	529,929	391,187	138,742	73.8	26.2	4.9	4.8	5.3
Vagrancy	26,325	20,417	5,908	77.6	22.4	0.2	0.3	0.2
All other offenses (except traffic)	2,921,526	2,248,826	672,700	77.0	23.0	27.3	27.8	25.6
Suspicion	1,259	991	268	78.7	21.3	*	*	*
Curfew and loitering law violations	104,168	71,675	32,493	68.8	31.2	1.0	0.9	1.2
Runaways	84,054	36,905	47,149	43.9	56.1	0.8	0.5	1.8

[1] Because of rounding, the percentages may not add to 100.0.
* Less than one-tenth of 1 percent.

Table 43. Arrests, Distribution by Race, 2008

(Number, percent; 11,711 agencies; 2008 estimated population 230,863,907.)

Offense charged	Total arrests					Percent distribution[1]					Arrests under 18				
	Total	White	Black	American Indian or Alaskan Native	Asian or Pacific Islander	Total	White	Black	American Indian or Alaskan Native	Asian or Pacific Islander	Total	White	Black	American Indian or Alaskan Native	Asian or Pacific Islander
TOTAL	10,662,206	7,382,063	3,015,905	142,908	121,330	100.0	69.2	28.3	1.3	1.1	1,616,672	1,073,970	498,970	19,154	24,578
Violent Crime	455,967	265,754	179,636	5,431	5,146	100.0	58.3	39.4	1.2	1.1	73,712	34,360	38,005	527	820
Murder and nonnegligent manslaughter	9,859	4,721	4,935	99	104	100.0	47.9	50.1	1.0	1.1	970	387	567	5	11
Forcible rape	16,847	10,990	5,428	198	231	100.0	65.2	32.2	1.2	1.4	2,487	1,539	912	20	16
Robbery	100,525	41,962	56,948	681	934	100.0	41.7	56.7	0.7	0.9	27,476	8,590	18,465	96	325
Aggravated assault	328,736	208,081	112,325	4,453	3,877	100.0	63.3	34.2	1.4	1.2	42,779	23,844	18,061	406	468
Property Crime	1,300,167	876,425	391,645	15,688	16,409	100.0	67.4	30.1	1.2	1.3	338,470	218,889	110,322	3,801	5,458
Burglary	235,407	157,252	73,960	2,077	2,118	100.0	66.8	31.4	0.9	0.9	64,198	40,436	22,545	538	679
Larceny-theft	979,145	666,360	286,844	12,684	13,257	100.0	68.1	29.3	1.3	1.4	250,281	164,660	78,212	2,972	4,437
Motor vehicle theft	74,881	44,674	28,510	795	902	100.0	59.7	38.1	1.1	1.2	19,002	9,936	8,564	239	263
Arson	10,734	8,139	2,331	132	132	100.0	75.8	21.7	1.2	1.2	4,989	3,857	1,001	52	79
Other															
Other assaults	991,225	645,870	319,498	14,237	11,620	100.0	65.2	32.2	1.4	1.2	176,903	103,993	69,110	1,749	2,051
Forgery and counterfeiting	68,586	46,425	21,073	334	754	100.0	67.7	30.7	0.5	1.1	1,993	1,325	626	16	26
Fraud	173,567	117,217	53,508	1,424	1,418	100.0	67.5	30.8	0.8	0.8	5,652	3,486	2,014	80	72
Embezzlement	16,314	10,517	5,455	95	247	100.0	64.5	33.4	0.6	1.5	987	596	369	8	14
Stolen property; buying, receiving, possessing	85,351	52,719	31,258	663	711	100.0	61.8	36.6	0.8	0.8	16,020	8,734	6,993	132	161
Vandalism	218,188	164,334	47,974	3,359	2,521	100.0	75.3	22.0	1.5	1.2	82,064	64,547	15,424	985	1,108
Weapons; carrying, possessing, etc.	137,869	78,114	57,454	1,010	1,291	100.0	56.7	41.7	0.7	0.9	30,701	18,536	11,583	225	357
Prostitution and commercialized vice	58,678	32,682	23,987	491	1,518	100.0	55.7	40.9	0.8	2.6	1,156	459	662	17	18
Sex offenses (except forcible rape and prostitution)	60,582	44,553	14,546	646	837	100.0	73.5	24.0	1.1	1.4	10,965	7,755	2,990	84	136
Drug abuse violations	1,299,708	829,432	452,590	8,408	9,278	100.0	63.8	34.8	0.6	0.7	137,495	97,257	37,806	1,146	1,286
Gambling	7,611	1,720	5,712	21	158	100.0	22.6	75.0	0.3	2.1	1,295	68	1,213	0	14
Offenses against the family and children	86,051	57,292	26,527	1,646	586	100.0	66.6	30.8	1.9	0.7	4,343	3,136	1,126	63	18
Driving under the influence	1,104,342	964,583	110,682	14,706	14,371	100.0	87.3	10.0	1.3	1.3	11,930	11,037	527	220	146
Liquor laws	475,198	400,995	54,878	13,997	5,328	100.0	84.4	11.5	2.9	1.1	100,204	90,378	5,761	2,906	1,159
Drunkenness	472,562	390,057	70,969	8,901	2,635	100.0	82.5	15.0	1.9	0.6	11,905	10,555	989	277	84
Disorderly conduct	527,626	334,697	180,073	8,641	4,215	100.0	63.4	34.1	1.6	0.8	144,470	82,714	59,206	1,419	1,131
Vagrancy	26,283	15,705	9,945	500	133	100.0	59.8	37.8	1.9	0.5	3,097	2,429	645	7	16
All other offenses (except traffic)	2,907,265	1,931,327	898,881	40,237	36,820	100.0	66.4	30.9	1.4	1.3	275,281	192,550	74,523	3,033	5,175
Suspicion	1,247	584	642	14	7	100.0	46.8	51.5	1.1	0.6	210	105	104	0	1
Curfew and loitering law violations	103,992	65,661	36,223	828	1,280	100.0	63.1	34.8	0.8	1.2	103,992	65,661	36,223	828	1,280
Runaways	83,827	55,400	22,749	1,631	4,047	100.0	66.1	27.1	1.9	4.8	83,827	55,400	22,749	1,631	4,047

[1] Because of rounding, the percentages may not add to 100.0.

Table 43. Arrests, Distribution by Race, 2008—*Continued*

(Number, percent; 11,711 agencies; 2008 estimated population 230,863,907.)

Offense charged	Percent distribution[1]					Arrests 18 and over					Percent distribution[1]				
	Total	White	Black	American Indian or Alaskan Native	Asian or Pacific Islander	Total	White	Black	American Indian or Alaskan Native	Asian or Pacific Islander	Total	White	Black	American Indian or Alaskan Native	Asian or Pacific Islander
TOTAL	100.0	66.4	30.9	1.2	1.5	9,045,534	6,308,093	2,516,935	123,754	96,752	100.0	69.7	27.8	1.4	1.1
Violent Crime	100.0	46.6	51.6	0.7	1.1	382,255	231,394	141,631	4,904	4,326	100.0	60.5	37.1	1.3	1.1
Murder and nonnegligent manslaughter	100.0	39.9	58.5	0.5	1.1	8,889	4,334	4,368	94	93	100.0	48.8	49.1	1.1	1.0
Forcible rape	100.0	61.9	36.7	0.8	0.6	14,360	9,451	4,516	178	215	100.0	65.8	31.4	1.2	1.5
Robbery	100.0	31.3	67.2	0.3	1.2	73,049	33,372	38,483	585	609	100.0	45.7	52.7	0.8	0.8
Aggravated assault	100.0	55.7	42.2	0.9	1.1	285,957	184,237	94,264	4,047	3,409	100.0	64.4	33.0	1.4	1.2
Property Crime	100.0	64.7	32.6	1.1	1.6	961,697	657,536	281,323	11,887	10,951	100.0	68.4	29.3	1.2	1.1
Burglary	100.0	63.0	35.1	0.8	1.1	171,209	116,816	51,415	1,539	1,439	100.0	68.2	30.0	0.9	0.8
Larceny-theft	100.0	65.8	31.2	1.2	1.8	728,864	501,700	208,632	9,712	8,820	100.0	68.8	28.6	1.3	1.2
Motor vehicle theft	100.0	52.3	45.1	1.3	1.4	55,879	34,738	19,946	556	639	100.0	62.2	35.7	1.0	1.1
Arson	100.0	77.3	20.1	1.0	1.6	5,745	4,282	1,330	80	53	100.0	74.5	23.2	1.4	0.9
Other															
Other assaults	100.0	58.8	39.1	1.0	1.2	814,322	541,877	250,388	12,488	9,569	100.0	66.5	30.7	1.5	1.2
Forgery and counterfeiting	100.0	66.5	31.4	0.8	1.3	66,593	45,100	20,447	318	728	100.0	67.7	30.7	0.5	1.1
Fraud	100.0	61.7	35.6	1.4	1.3	167,915	113,731	51,494	1,344	1,346	100.0	67.7	30.7	0.8	0.8
Embezzlement	100.0	60.4	37.4	0.8	1.4	15,327	9,921	5,086	87	233	100.0	64.7	33.2	0.6	1.5
Stolen property; buying, receiving, possessing	100.0	54.5	43.7	0.8	1.0	69,331	43,985	24,265	531	550	100.0	63.4	35.0	0.8	0.8
Vandalism	100.0	78.7	18.8	1.2	1.4	136,124	99,787	32,550	2,374	1,413	100.0	73.3	23.9	1.7	1.0
Weapons; carrying, possessing, etc.	100.0	60.4	37.7	0.7	1.2	107,168	59,578	45,871	785	934	100.0	55.6	42.8	0.7	0.9
Prostitution and commercialized vice	100.0	39.7	57.3	1.5	1.6	57,522	32,223	23,325	474	1,500	100.0	56.0	40.5	0.8	2.6
Sex offenses (except forcible rape and prostitution)	100.0	70.7	27.3	0.8	1.2	49,617	36,798	11,556	562	701	100.0	74.2	23.3	1.1	1.4
Drug abuse violations	100.0	70.7	27.5	0.8	0.9	1,162,213	732,175	414,784	7,262	7,992	100.0	63.0	35.7	0.6	0.7
Gambling	100.0	5.3	93.7	0.0	1.1	6,316	1,652	4,499	21	144	100.0	26.2	71.2	0.3	2.3
Offenses against the family and children	100.0	72.2	25.9	1.5	0.4	81,708	54,156	25,401	1,583	568	100.0	66.3	31.1	1.9	0.7
Driving under the influence	100.0	92.5	4.4	1.8	1.2	1,092,412	953,546	110,155	14,486	14,225	100.0	87.3	10.1	1.3	1.3
Liquor laws	100.0	90.2	5.7	2.9	1.2	374,994	310,617	49,117	11,091	4,169	100.0	82.8	13.1	3.0	1.1
Drunkenness	100.0	88.7	8.3	2.3	0.7	460,657	379,502	69,980	8,624	2,551	100.0	82.4	15.2	1.9	0.6
Disorderly conduct	100.0	57.3	41.0	1.0	0.8	383,156	251,983	120,867	7,222	3,084	100.0	65.8	31.5	1.9	0.8
Vagrancy	100.0	78.4	20.8	0.2	0.5	23,186	13,276	9,300	493	117	100.0	57.3	40.1	2.1	0.5
All other offenses (except traffic)	100.0	69.9	27.1	1.1	1.9	2,631,984	1,738,777	824,358	37,204	31,645	100.0	66.1	31.3	1.4	1.2
Suspicion	100.0	50.0	49.5	0.0	0.5	1,037	479	538	14	6	100.0	46.2	51.9	1.4	0.6
Curfew and loitering law violations	100.0	63.1	34.8	0.8	1.2	-	-	-	-	-	-	-	-	-	-
Runaways	100.0	66.1	27.1	1.9	4.8	-	-	-	-	-	-	-	-	-	-

[1] Because of rounding, the percentages may not add to 100.0.

Table 44. City Arrest Trends, 2007–2008

(Number, percent change; 8,075 agencies; 2008 estimated population 152,635,660; 2007 estimated population 150,965,405.)

Offense charged	Number of persons arrested								
	Total all ages			Under 18 years of age			18 years of age and over		
	2007	2008	Percent change	2007	2008	Percent change	2007	2008	Percent change
TOTAL[1]	7,754,942	7,675,570	-1.0	1,312,026	1,279,410	-2.5	6,442,916	6,396,160	-0.7
Violent Crime	336,403	337,519	+0.3	56,564	55,865	-1.2	279,839	281,654	+0.6
Murder and nonnegligent manslaughter	6,825	6,659	-2.4	739	703	-4.9	6,086	5,956	-2.1
Forcible rape	11,836	11,924	+0.7	1,884	1,863	-1.1	9,952	10,061	+1.1
Robbery	77,884	80,168	+2.9	21,441	21,768	+1.5	56,443	58,400	+3.5
Aggravated assault	239,858	238,768	-0.5	32,500	31,531	-3.0	207,358	207,237	-0.1
Property Crime	958,096	1,013,687	+5.8	259,680	274,445	+5.7	698,416	739,242	+5.8
Burglary	163,795	168,231	+2.7	45,523	47,107	+3.5	118,272	121,124	+2.4
Larceny-theft	720,573	785,293	+9.0	193,315	210,112	+8.7	527,258	575,181	+9.1
Motor vehicle theft	65,610	52,180	-20.5	16,568	13,243	-20.1	49,042	38,937	-20.6
Arson	8,118	7,983	-1.7	4,274	3,983	-6.8	3,844	4,000	+4.1
Other									
Other assaults	709,265	717,341	+1.1	132,665	130,581	-1.6	576,600	586,760	+1.8
Forgery and counterfeiting	57,440	50,232	-12.5	1,800	1,524	-15.3	55,640	48,708	-12.5
Fraud	105,276	102,425	-2.7	4,289	4,448	+3.7	100,987	97,977	-3.0
Embezzlement	12,380	12,251	-1.0	965	780	-19.2	11,415	11,471	+0.5
Stolen property; buying, receiving, possessing	68,490	63,387	-7.5	13,926	13,170	-5.4	54,564	50,217	-8.0
Vandalism	170,222	166,097	-2.4	67,929	65,300	-3.9	102,293	100,797	-1.5
Weapons; carrying, possessing, etc.	106,179	100,831	-5.0	25,693	23,709	-7.7	80,486	77,122	-4.2
Prostitution and commercialized vice	49,528	46,733	-5.6	990	975	-1.5	48,538	45,758	-5.7
Sex offenses (except forcible rape and prostitution)	42,081	40,946	-2.7	7,938	7,647	-3.7	34,143	33,299	-2.5
Drug abuse violations	977,064	914,851	-6.4	110,112	102,827	-6.6	866,952	812,024	-6.3
Gambling	3,807	3,013	-20.9	458	369	-19.4	3,349	2,644	-21.1
Offenses against the family and children	39,376	38,176	-3.0	2,837	2,555	-9.9	36,539	35,621	-2.5
Driving under the influence	659,844	671,542	+1.8	9,014	7,933	-12.0	650,830	663,609	+2.0
Liquor laws	379,495	372,693	-1.8	82,502	76,437	-7.4	296,993	296,256	-0.2
Drunkenness	378,408	394,081	+4.1	11,062	10,179	-8.0	367,346	383,902	+4.5
Disorderly conduct	426,732	417,677	-2.1	125,447	118,876	-5.2	301,285	298,801	-0.8
Vagrancy	22,506	21,811	-3.1	2,526	2,698	+6.8	19,980	19,113	-4.3
All other offenses (except traffic)	2,084,620	2,032,707	-2.5	227,899	221,522	-2.8	1,856,721	1,811,185	-2.5
Suspicion	815	775	-4.9	192	169	-12.0	623	606	-2.7
Curfew and loitering law violations	105,177	97,916	-6.9	105,177	97,916	-6.9	-	-	-
Runaways	62,553	59,654	-4.6	62,553	59,654	-4.6	-	-	-

[1] Does not include suspicion.

Table 45. City Arrest Trends, by Age and Sex, 2007–2008

(Number, percent change; 8,075 agencies; 2008 estimated population 152,635,660; 2007 estimated population 150,965,405.)

Offense charged	Male						Female					
	Total			Under 18			Total			Under 18		
	2007	2008	Percent change	2007	2008	Percent change	2007	2008	Percent change	2007	2008	Percent change
TOTAL[1]	5,830,468	5,746,787	-1.4	917,851	889,093	-3.1	1,924,474	1,928,783	+0.2	394,175	390,317	-1.0
Violent Crime	274,039	274,557	+0.2	46,615	46,187	-0.9	62,364	62,962	+1.0	9,949	9,678	-2.7
Murder and nonnegligent manslaughter	6,161	5,954	-3.4	694	652	-6.1	664	705	+6.2	45	51	+13.3
Forcible rape	11,725	11,778	+0.5	1,854	1,832	-1.2	111	146	+31.5	30	31	+3.3
Robbery	68,631	70,585	+2.8	19,288	19,657	+1.9	9,253	9,583	+3.6	2,153	2,111	-2.0
Aggravated assault	187,522	186,240	-0.7	24,779	24,046	-3.0	52,336	52,528	+0.4	7,721	7,485	-3.1
Property Crime	622,834	642,671	+3.2	164,879	170,433	+3.4	335,262	371,016	+10.7	94,801	104,012	+9.7
Burglary	138,542	142,453	+2.8	39,790	40,949	+2.9	25,253	25,778	+2.1	5,733	6,158	+7.4
Larceny-theft	423,736	450,394	+6.3	107,546	114,852	+6.8	296,837	334,899	+12.8	85,769	95,260	+11.1
Motor vehicle theft	53,677	43,084	-19.7	13,773	11,119	-19.3	11,933	9,096	-23.8	2,795	2,124	-24.0
Arson	6,879	6,740	-2.0	3,770	3,513	-6.8	1,239	1,243	+0.3	504	470	-6.7
Other												
Other assaults	528,249	532,036	+0.7	87,373	85,125	-2.6	181,016	185,305	+2.4	45,292	45,456	+0.4
Forgery and counterfeiting	35,629	31,304	-12.1	1,213	1,003	-17.3	21,811	18,928	-13.2	587	521	-11.2
Fraud	60,600	59,227	-2.3	2,714	2,912	+7.3	44,676	43,198	-3.3	1,575	1,536	-2.5
Embezzlement	5,796	5,809	+0.2	548	443	-19.2	6,584	6,442	-2.2	417	337	-19.2
Stolen property; buying, receiving, possessing	53,960	49,846	-7.6	11,287	10,574	-6.3	14,530	13,541	-6.8	2,639	2,596	-1.6
Vandalism	141,072	137,520	-2.5	58,875	56,535	-4.0	29,150	28,577	-2.0	9,054	8,765	-3.2
Weapons; carrying, possessing, etc.	97,969	93,166	-4.9	23,267	21,478	-7.7	8,210	7,665	-6.6	2,426	2,231	-8.0
Prostitution and commercialized vice	15,635	14,467	-7.5	199	242	+21.6	33,893	32,266	-4.8	791	733	-7.3
Sex offenses (except forcible rape and prostitution)	37,933	37,063	-2.3	7,097	6,823	-3.9	4,148	3,883	-6.4	841	824	-2.0
Drug abuse violations	791,813	745,626	-5.8	92,510	86,724	-6.3	185,251	169,225	-8.7	17,602	16,103	-8.5
Gambling	3,231	2,625	-18.8	437	352	-19.5	576	388	-32.6	21	17	-19.0
Offenses against the family and children	25,635	24,894	-2.9	1,618	1,540	-4.8	13,741	13,282	-3.3	1,219	1,015	-16.7
Driving under the influence	517,711	522,164	+0.9	6,773	5,930	-12.4	142,133	149,378	+5.1	2,241	2,003	-10.6
Liquor laws	273,496	268,588	-1.8	51,646	47,631	-7.8	105,999	104,105	-1.8	30,856	28,806	-6.6
Drunkenness	318,263	331,076	+4.0	8,275	7,722	-6.7	60,145	63,005	+4.8	2,787	2,457	-11.8
Disorderly conduct	311,392	305,206	-2.0	83,302	79,345	-4.8	115,340	112,471	-2.5	42,145	39,531	-6.2
Vagrancy	17,568	16,893	-3.8	1,782	1,925	+8.0	4,938	4,918	-0.4	744	773	+3.9
All other offenses (except traffic)	1,597,440	1,558,601	-2.4	167,238	162,721	-2.7	487,180	474,106	-2.7	60,661	58,801	-3.1
Suspicion	662	630	-4.8	148	133	-10.1	153	145	-5.2	44	36	-18.2
Curfew and loitering law violations	72,944	67,499	-7.5	72,944	67,499	-7.5	32,233	30,417	-5.6	32,233	30,417	-5.6
Runaways	27,259	25,949	-4.8	27,259	25,949	-4.8	35,294	33,705	-4.5	35,294	33,705	-4.5

[1] Does not include suspicion.

Table 46. City Arrests, Distribution by Age, 2008

(Number, percent; 8,676 agencies; 2008 estimated population 161,327,084.)

Offense charged	Total all ages	Ages under 15	Ages under 18	Ages 18 and over	Under 10	10–12	13–14	15	16	17	18	19	20
TOTAL	8,167,159	373,257	1,344,732	6,822,427	8,796	74,392	290,069	267,403	333,502	370,570	409,901	411,485	375,385
Total percent distribution[1]	100.0	4.6	16.5	83.5	0.1	0.9	3.6	3.3	4.1	4.5	5.0	5.0	4.6
Violent Crime	358,986	16,272	61,065	297,921	361	3,265	12,646	11,956	15,444	17,393	18,853	18,193	16,122
Violent crime percent distribution[1]	100.0	4.5	17.0	83.0	0.1	0.9	3.5	3.3	4.3	4.8	5.3	5.1	4.5
Murder and nonnegligent manslaughter	7,406	66	785	6,621	0	6	60	125	246	348	514	610	504
Forcible rape	12,505	660	1,887	10,618	4	166	490	338	411	478	577	605	559
Robbery	86,484	4,829	24,077	62,407	55	613	4,161	4,815	6,787	7,646	7,968	6,781	5,289
Aggravated assault	252,591	10,717	34,316	218,275	302	2,480	7,935	6,678	8,000	8,921	9,794	10,197	9,770
Property Crime	1,073,444	84,163	287,403	786,041	1,940	17,710	64,513	57,794	70,570	74,876	75,244	60,873	48,166
Property crime percent distribution[1]	100.0	7.8	26.8	73.2	0.2	1.6	6.0	5.4	6.6	7.0	7.0	5.7	4.5
Burglary	177,035	14,571	49,642	127,393	414	2,842	11,315	10,374	11,991	12,706	13,655	11,098	8,575
Larceny-theft	830,179	64,235	218,535	611,644	1,274	13,837	49,124	43,112	53,744	57,444	57,199	46,223	36,695
Motor vehicle theft	57,996	3,062	15,165	42,831	15	316	2,731	3,588	4,277	4,238	4,049	3,247	2,676
Arson	8,234	2,295	4,061	4,173	237	715	1,343	720	558	488	341	305	220
Other													
Other assaults	768,204	53,096	139,026	629,178	1,459	13,215	38,422	27,570	29,620	28,740	26,154	26,595	26,791
Forgery and counterfeiting	52,778	163	1,576	51,202	6	28	129	167	404	842	1,864	2,352	2,435
Fraud	104,394	738	4,477	99,917	19	122	597	686	1,142	1,911	3,395	4,259	4,429
Embezzlement	12,689	20	809	11,880	4	1	15	31	225	533	928	1,041	909
Stolen property; buying, receiving, possessing	66,673	3,268	13,647	53,026	50	512	2,706	2,710	3,664	4,005	4,508	4,005	3,292
Vandalism	175,343	27,950	68,088	107,255	1,201	6,913	19,836	13,271	13,569	13,298	11,450	9,171	7,270
Weapons; carrying, possessing, etc.	110,133	7,820	25,384	84,749	257	1,860	5,703	4,663	5,970	6,931	7,885	7,014	5,817
Prostitution and commercialized vice	55,447	108	1,069	54,378	8	6	94	167	302	492	1,729	2,183	2,318
Sex offenses (except forcible rape and prostitution)	44,101	3,725	7,931	36,170	142	1,038	2,545	1,440	1,382	1,384	1,691	1,565	1,412
Drug abuse violations	1,004,709	16,742	111,628	893,081	140	1,769	14,833	19,175	30,718	44,993	64,200	63,416	55,836
Gambling	6,911	171	1,256	5,655	2	10	159	251	324	510	597	508	500
Offenses against the family and children	40,252	819	2,825	37,427	48	159	612	545	707	754	1,146	1,221	1,279
Driving under the influence	699,851	147	8,178	691,673	31	14	102	331	1,941	5,759	15,365	21,261	24,006
Liquor laws	387,261	7,522	78,017	309,244	106	552	6,864	11,829	22,169	36,497	63,372	68,081	55,778
Drunkenness	411,455	1,124	10,438	401,017	50	53	1,021	1,560	2,558	5,196	10,797	12,028	12,117
Disorderly conduct	456,838	46,698	126,279	330,559	725	10,625	35,348	26,430	27,650	25,501	20,796	18,505	17,190
Vagrancy	23,629	853	2,770	20,859	6	139	708	753	849	315	1,140	880	754
All other offenses (except traffic)	2,149,220	54,856	228,785	1,920,435	1,371	8,962	44,523	46,898	59,280	67,751	78,722	88,266	88,924
Suspicion	939	38	179	760	0	8	30	40	50	51	65	68	40
Curfew and loitering law violations	99,044	25,527	99,044	-	373	4,066	21,088	22,714	27,491	23,312	-	-	-
Runaways	64,858	21,437	64,858	-	497	3,365	17,575	16,422	17,473	9,526	-	-	-

[1] Because of rounding, the percentages may not add to 100.0.

Table 46. City Arrests, Distribution by Age, 2008—*Continued*

(Number, percent; 8,676 agencies; 2008 estimated population 161,327,084.)

Offense charged	21	22	23	24	25–29	30–34	35–39	40–44	45–49	50–54	55–59	60–64	65 and over
TOTAL	337,213	311,874	290,708	266,992	1,133,174	771,986	685,670	638,803	560,084	343,933	164,767	70,149	50,303
Total percent distribution[1]	4.1	3.8	3.6	3.3	13.9	9.5	8.4	7.8	6.9	4.2	2.0	0.9	0.6
Violent Crime	15,166	13,988	13,205	12,357	52,652	35,691	30,219	26,605	21,812	12,536	5,808	2,591	2,123
Violent crime percent distribution[1]	4.2	3.9	3.7	3.4	14.7	9.9	8.4	7.4	6.1	3.5	1.6	0.7	0.6
Murder and nonnegligent manslaughter	398	395	360	331	1,291	662	487	378	282	178	124	50	57
Forcible rape	519	445	399	395	1,776	1,410	1,202	1,074	765	442	238	97	115
Robbery	4,104	3,398	2,930	2,577	9,863	5,728	4,757	3,993	2,891	1,393	503	151	81
Aggravated assault	10,145	9,750	9,516	9,054	39,722	27,891	23,773	21,160	17,874	10,523	4,943	2,293	1,870
Property Crime	39,703	34,784	30,800	27,860	116,907	81,330	76,194	71,165	59,522	35,052	16,071	6,824	5,546
Property crime percent distribution[1]	3.7	3.2	2.9	2.6	10.9	7.6	7.1	6.6	5.5	3.3	1.5	0.6	0.5
Burglary	6,966	6,132	5,450	4,773	19,720	12,900	12,012	10,881	8,401	4,364	1,593	562	311
Larceny-theft	30,196	26,434	23,325	21,221	89,109	62,806	59,287	56,267	48,350	29,376	13,975	6,075	5,106
Motor vehicle theft	2,320	2,026	1,846	1,730	7,485	5,143	4,549	3,635	2,451	1,089	371	129	85
Arson	221	192	179	136	593	481	346	382	320	223	132	58	44
Other													
Other assaults	28,762	27,841	27,510	25,976	115,874	82,566	72,655	63,290	51,971	29,501	13,165	5,709	4,818
Forgery and counterfeiting	2,232	2,207	2,208	2,146	10,328	7,336	6,356	4,904	3,638	1,964	752	300	180
Fraud	3,920	3,915	3,737	3,625	17,790	14,007	12,752	10,826	8,203	4,814	2,344	1,098	803
Embezzlement	749	646	555	458	1,839	1,383	1,094	956	638	365	194	71	54
Stolen property; buying, receiving, possessing	2,825	2,502	2,374	1,969	9,004	6,291	5,356	4,635	3,287	1,766	771	286	155
Vandalism	7,130	6,063	5,248	4,738	18,080	10,736	8,720	7,357	5,705	3,174	1,326	593	494
Weapons; carrying, possessing, etc.	5,529	4,979	4,581	4,044	15,701	8,738	6,210	4,846	4,112	2,685	1,393	680	535
Prostitution and commercialized vice	2,152	2,283	2,020	1,956	8,897	7,121	7,376	6,866	5,064	2,545	1,015	447	406
Sex offenses (except forcible rape and prostitution)	1,491	1,295	1,277	1,094	4,882	4,090	3,876	4,019	3,545	2,476	1,488	960	1,009
Drug abuse violations	49,791	44,924	41,344	37,918	157,686	99,384	81,671	74,332	63,124	36,334	15,669	5,105	2,347
Gambling	377	297	291	224	863	460	366	285	286	201	170	113	117
Offenses against the family and children	1,402	1,441	1,537	1,412	7,398	5,863	5,253	3,921	2,841	1,486	696	314	217
Driving under the influence	34,163	34,628	33,756	31,270	130,371	85,716	73,358	66,371	60,508	39,914	21,838	11,098	8,050
Liquor laws	9,938	6,920	5,610	4,534	17,166	12,316	12,379	14,724	16,602	11,581	6,180	2,506	1,557
Drunkenness	18,911	17,273	16,026	14,744	61,370	43,288	42,107	46,207	47,431	33,029	15,779	6,215	3,695
Disorderly conduct	21,255	18,666	16,228	14,067	54,875	34,560	29,871	28,473	26,424	16,193	7,626	3,344	2,486
Vagrancy	620	493	491	460	2,000	1,780	2,167	2,916	3,099	2,232	1,133	451	243
All other offenses (except traffic)	91,044	86,677	81,869	76,107	329,365	229,261	207,634	196,056	172,229	106,049	51,334	21,437	15,461
Suspicion	53	52	41	33	126	69	56	49	43	36	15	7	7
Curfew and loitering law violations	-	-	-	-	-	-	-	-	-	-	-	-	-
Runaways	-	-	-	-	-	-	-	-	-	-	-	-	-

[1] Because of rounding, the percentages may not add to 100.0.

Table 47. City Arrests of Persons Under 15, 18, 21, and 25 Years of Age, 2008

(Number, percent; 8,676 agencies; 2008 estimated population 161,327,084.)

Offense charged	Total all ages	Number of persons arrested				Percent of total all ages			
		Under 15	Under 18	Under 21	Under 25	Under 15	Under 18	Under 21	Under 25
TOTAL	8,167,159	373,257	1,344,732	2,541,503	3,748,290	4.6	16.5	31.1	45.9
Violent Crime	358,986	16,272	61,065	114,233	168,949	4.5	17.0	31.8	47.1
Murder and nonnegligent manslaughter	7,406	66	785	2,413	3,897	0.9	10.6	32.6	52.6
Forcible rape	12,505	660	1,887	3,628	5,386	5.3	15.1	29.0	43.1
Robbery	86,484	4,829	24,077	44,115	57,124	5.6	27.8	51.0	66.1
Aggravated assault	252,591	10,717	34,316	64,077	102,542	4.2	13.6	25.4	40.6
Property Crime	1,073,444	84,163	287,403	471,686	604,833	7.8	26.8	43.9	56.3
Burglary	177,035	14,571	49,642	82,970	106,291	8.2	28.0	46.9	60.0
Larceny-theft	830,179	64,235	218,535	358,652	459,828	7.7	26.3	43.2	55.4
Motor vehicle theft	57,996	3,062	15,165	25,137	33,059	5.3	26.1	43.3	57.0
Arson	8,234	2,295	4,061	4,927	5,655	27.9	49.3	59.8	68.7
Other									
Other assaults	768,204	53,096	139,026	218,566	328,655	6.9	18.1	28.5	42.8
Forgery and counterfeiting	52,778	163	1,576	8,227	17,020	0.3	3.0	15.6	32.2
Fraud	104,394	738	4,477	16,560	31,757	0.7	4.3	15.9	30.4
Embezzlement	12,689	20	809	3,687	6,095	0.2	6.4	29.1	48.0
Stolen property; buying, receiving, possessing	66,673	3,268	13,647	25,452	35,122	4.9	20.5	38.2	52.7
Vandalism	175,343	27,950	68,088	95,979	119,158	15.9	38.8	54.7	68.0
Weapons; carrying, possessing, etc.	110,133	7,820	25,384	46,100	65,233	7.1	23.0	41.9	59.2
Prostitution and commercialized vice	55,447	108	1,069	7,299	15,710	0.2	1.9	13.2	28.3
Sex offenses (except forcible rape and prostitution)	44,101	3,725	7,931	12,599	17,756	8.4	18.0	28.6	40.3
Drug abuse violations	1,004,709	16,742	111,628	295,080	469,057	1.7	11.1	29.4	46.7
Gambling	6,911	171	1,256	2,861	4,050	2.5	18.2	41.4	58.6
Offenses against the family and children	40,252	819	2,825	6,471	12,263	2.0	7.0	16.1	30.5
Driving under the influence	699,851	147	8,178	68,810	202,627	*	1.2	9.8	29.0
Liquor laws	387,261	7,522	78,017	265,248	292,250	1.9	20.1	68.5	75.5
Drunkenness	411,455	1,124	10,438	45,380	112,334	0.3	2.5	11.0	27.3
Disorderly conduct	456,838	46,698	126,279	182,770	252,986	10.2	27.6	40.0	55.4
Vagrancy	23,629	853	2,770	5,544	7,608	3.6	11.7	23.5	32.2
All other offenses (except traffic)	2,149,220	54,856	228,785	484,697	820,394	2.6	10.6	22.6	38.2
Suspicion	939	38	179	352	531	4.0	19.1	37.5	56.5
Curfew and loitering law violations	99,044	25,527	99,044	99,044	99,044	25.8	100.0	100.0	100.0
Runaways	64,858	21,437	64,858	64,858	64,858	33.1	100.0	100.0	100.0

* Less than one-tenth of 1 percent.

Table 48. City Arrests, Distribution by Sex, 2008

(Number, percent; 8,676 agencies; 2008 estimated population 161,327,084.)

Offense charged	Number of persons arrested			Percent male	Percent female	Percent distribution[1]		
	Total	Male	Female			Total	Male	Female
TOTAL	8,167,159	6,135,326	2,031,833	75.1	24.9	100.0	100.0	100.0
Violent Crime	358,986	292,211	66,775	81.4	18.6	4.4	4.8	3.3
Murder and nonnegligent manslaughter	7,406	6,636	770	89.6	10.4	0.1	0.1	*
Forcible rape	12,505	12,362	143	98.9	1.1	0.2	0.2	*
Robbery	86,484	76,312	10,172	88.2	11.8	1.1	1.2	0.5
Aggravated assault	252,591	196,901	55,690	78.0	22.0	3.1	3.2	2.7
Property Crime	1,073,444	684,441	389,003	63.8	36.2	13.1	11.2	19.1
Burglary	177,035	150,426	26,609	85.0	15.0	2.2	2.5	1.3
Larceny-theft	830,179	479,034	351,145	57.7	42.3	10.2	7.8	17.3
Motor vehicle theft	57,996	48,031	9,965	82.8	17.2	0.7	0.8	0.5
Arson	8,234	6,950	1,284	84.4	15.6	0.1	0.1	0.1
Other								
Other assaults	768,204	571,150	197,054	74.3	25.7	9.4	9.3	9.7
Forgery and counterfeiting	52,778	32,940	19,838	62.4	37.6	0.6	0.5	1.0
Fraud	104,394	61,656	42,738	59.1	40.9	1.3	1.0	2.1
Embezzlement	12,689	6,017	6,672	47.4	52.6	0.2	0.1	0.3
Stolen property; buying, receiving, possessing	66,673	52,601	14,072	78.9	21.1	0.8	0.9	0.7
Vandalism	175,343	145,193	30,150	82.8	17.2	2.1	2.4	1.5
Weapons; carrying, possessing, etc.	110,133	101,900	8,233	92.5	7.5	1.3	1.7	0.4
Prostitution and commercialized vice	55,447	16,897	38,550	30.5	69.5	0.7	0.3	1.9
Sex offenses (except forcible rape and prostitution)	44,101	39,856	4,245	90.4	9.6	0.5	0.6	0.2
Drug abuse violations	1,004,709	823,225	181,484	81.9	18.1	12.3	13.4	8.9
Gambling	6,911	6,465	446	93.5	6.5	0.1	0.1	*
Offenses against the family and children	40,252	26,378	13,874	65.5	34.5	0.5	0.4	0.7
Driving under the influence	699,851	545,026	154,825	77.9	22.1	8.6	8.9	7.6
Liquor laws	387,261	280,617	106,644	72.5	27.5	4.7	4.6	5.2
Drunkenness	411,455	346,176	65,279	84.1	15.9	5.0	5.6	3.2
Disorderly conduct	456,838	337,245	119,593	73.8	26.2	5.6	5.5	5.9
Vagrancy	23,629	18,481	5,148	78.2	21.8	0.3	0.3	0.3
All other offenses (except traffic)	2,149,220	1,649,706	499,514	76.8	23.2	26.3	26.9	24.6
Suspicion	939	762	177	81.2	18.8	*	*	*
Curfew and loitering law violations	99,044	68,374	30,670	69.0	31.0	1.2	1.1	1.5
Runaways	64,858	28,009	36,849	43.2	56.8	0.8	0.5	1.8

[1] Because of rounding, the percentages may not add to 100.0.
* Less than one-tenth of 1 percent.

Table 49. City Arrests, Distribution by Race, 2008

(Number, percent; 8,674 agencies; 2008 estimated population 161,293,485.)

Offense charged	Total arrests					Percent distribution[1]					Arrests under 18				
	Total	White	Black	American Indian or Alaskan Native	Asian or Pacific Islander	Total	White	Black	American Indian or Alaskan Native	Asian or Pacific Islander	Total	White	Black	American Indian or Alaskan Native	Asian or Pacific Islander
TOTAL	8,139,474	5,448,338	2,483,321	107,485	100,330	100.0	66.9	30.5	1.3	1.2	1,339,716	879,704	423,192	15,671	21,149
Violent Crime	357,858	198,644	151,045	3,794	4,375	100.0	55.5	42.2	1.1	1.2	60,855	27,681	32,047	408	719
Murder and nonnegligent manslaughter	7,392	3,215	4,022	62	93	100.0	43.5	54.4	0.8	1.3	783	305	464	3	11
Forcible rape	12,451	7,553	4,561	139	198	100.0	60.7	36.6	1.1	1.6	1,874	1,053	792	15	14
Robbery	86,352	35,502	49,455	562	833	100.0	41.1	57.3	0.7	1.0	24,045	7,594	16,072	91	288
Aggravated assault	251,663	152,374	93,007	3,031	3,251	100.0	60.5	37.0	1.2	1.3	34,153	18,729	14,719	299	406
Property Crime	1,069,810	710,548	331,734	13,261	14,267	100.0	66.4	31.0	1.2	1.3	286,097	185,023	92,982	3,283	4,809
Burglary	176,583	112,562	60,938	1,330	1,753	100.0	63.7	34.5	0.8	1.0	49,491	30,105	18,470	352	564
Larceny-theft	827,176	559,628	244,631	11,254	11,663	100.0	67.7	29.6	1.4	1.4	217,458	144,367	66,426	2,707	3,958
Motor vehicle theft	57,851	32,297	24,241	574	739	100.0	55.8	41.9	1.0	1.3	15,114	7,460	7,254	183	217
Arson	8,200	6,061	1,924	103	112	100.0	73.9	23.5	1.3	1.4	4,034	3,091	832	41	70
Other															
Other assaults	765,599	476,315	268,747	10,780	9,757	100.0	62.2	35.1	1.4	1.3	138,560	80,769	54,765	1,317	1,709
Forgery and counterfeiting	52,600	34,833	16,897	250	620	100.0	66.2	32.1	0.5	1.2	1,568	1,022	516	8	22
Fraud	103,834	67,208	34,609	929	1,088	100.0	64.7	33.3	0.9	1.0	4,456	2,611	1,718	69	58
Embezzlement	12,614	8,127	4,204	76	207	100.0	64.4	33.3	0.6	1.6	805	493	292	7	13
Stolen property; buying, receiving, possessing	66,525	38,992	26,446	466	621	100.0	58.6	39.8	0.7	0.9	13,617	7,172	6,184	114	147
Vandalism	174,644	129,052	40,802	2,640	2,150	100.0	73.9	23.4	1.5	1.2	67,779	53,036	12,945	821	977
Weapons; carrying, possessing, etc.	109,866	59,365	48,738	661	1,102	100.0	54.0	44.4	0.6	1.0	25,299	15,232	9,602	165	300
Prostitution and commercialized vice	55,351	30,625	22,915	468	1,343	100.0	55.3	41.4	0.8	2.4	1,067	415	622	15	15
Sex offenses (except forcible rape and prostitution)	43,978	31,046	11,748	472	712	100.0	70.6	26.7	1.1	1.6	7,889	5,431	2,287	54	117
Drug abuse violations	1,002,145	606,582	382,522	5,718	7,323	100.0	60.5	38.2	0.6	0.7	111,275	76,822	32,525	915	1,013
Gambling	6,897	1,256	5,523	7	111	100.0	18.2	80.1	0.1	1.6	1,256	53	1,196	0	7
Offenses against the family and children	40,028	28,127	10,681	799	421	100.0	70.3	26.7	2.0	1.1	2,799	1,926	807	51	15
Driving under the influence	696,998	603,440	73,883	9,406	10,269	100.0	86.6	10.6	1.3	1.5	8,140	7,493	382	153	112
Liquor laws	384,768	319,744	48,487	12,014	4,523	100.0	83.1	12.6	3.1	1.2	77,583	69,162	5,008	2,464	949
Drunkenness	410,424	334,786	65,579	7,634	2,425	100.0	81.6	16.0	1.9	0.6	10,420	9,182	910	248	80
Disorderly conduct	455,043	283,475	160,687	7,106	3,775	100.0	62.3	35.3	1.6	0.8	125,888	72,585	51,194	1,070	1,039
Vagrancy	23,593	13,892	9,088	484	129	100.0	58.9	38.5	2.1	0.5	2,769	2,149	597	7	16
All other offenses (except traffic)	2,142,371	1,368,859	714,573	28,318	30,621	100.0	63.9	33.4	1.3	1.4	227,821	158,355	62,609	2,313	4,544
Suspicion	934	412	505	13	4	100.0	44.1	54.1	1.4	0.4	179	82	96	0	1
Curfew and loitering law violations	98,900	61,823	35,148	780	1,149	100.0	62.5	35.5	0.8	1.2	98,900	61,823	35,148	780	1,149
Runaways	64,694	41,187	18,760	1,409	3,338	100.0	63.7	29.0	2.2	5.2	64,694	41,187	18,760	1,409	3,338

[1] Because of rounding, the percentages may not add to 100.0.

Table 49. City Arrests, Distribution by Race, 2008—*Continued*

(Number, percent; 8,674 agencies; 2008 estimated population 161,293,485.)

Offense charged	Percent distribution[1]					Arrests 18 years and over					Percent distribution[1]				
	Total	White	Black	American Indian or Alaskan Native	Asian or Pacific Islander	Total	White	Black	American Indian or Alaskan Native	Asian or Pacific Islander	Total	White	Black	American Indian or Alaskan Native	Asian or Pacific Islander
TOTAL	100.0	65.7	31.6	1.2	1.6	6,799,758	4,568,634	2,060,129	91,814	79,181	100.0	67.2	30.3	1.4	1.2
Violent Crime	100.0	45.5	52.7	0.7	1.2	297,003	170,963	118,998	3,386	3,656	100.0	57.6	40.1	1.1	1.2
Murder and nonnegligent manslaughter	100.0	39.0	59.3	0.4	1.4	6,609	2,910	3,558	59	82	100.0	44.0	53.8	0.9	1.2
Forcible rape	100.0	56.2	42.3	0.8	0.7	10,577	6,500	3,769	124	184	100.0	61.5	35.6	1.2	1.7
Robbery	100.0	31.6	66.8	0.4	1.2	62,307	27,908	33,383	471	545	100.0	44.8	53.6	0.8	0.9
Aggravated assault	100.0	54.8	43.1	0.9	1.2	217,510	133,645	78,288	2,732	2,845	100.0	61.4	36.0	1.3	1.3
Property Crime	100.0	64.7	32.5	1.1	1.7	783,713	525,525	238,752	9,978	9,458	100.0	67.1	30.5	1.3	1.2
Burglary	100.0	60.8	37.3	0.7	1.1	127,092	82,457	42,468	978	1,189	100.0	64.9	33.4	0.8	0.9
Larceny-theft	100.0	66.4	30.5	1.2	1.8	609,718	415,261	178,205	8,547	7,705	100.0	68.1	29.2	1.4	1.3
Motor vehicle theft	100.0	49.4	48.0	1.2	1.4	42,737	24,837	16,987	391	522	100.0	58.1	39.7	0.9	1.2
Arson	100.0	76.6	20.6	1.0	1.7	4,166	2,970	1,092	62	42	100.0	71.3	26.2	1.5	1.0
Other															
Other assaults	100.0	58.3	39.5	1.0	1.2	627,039	395,546	213,982	9,463	8,048	100.0	63.1	34.1	1.5	1.3
Forgery and counterfeiting	100.0	65.2	32.9	0.5	1.4	51,032	33,811	16,381	242	598	100.0	66.3	32.1	0.5	1.2
Fraud	100.0	58.6	38.6	1.5	1.3	99,378	64,597	32,891	860	1,030	100.0	65.0	33.1	0.9	1.0
Embezzlement	100.0	61.2	36.3	0.9	1.6	11,809	7,634	3,912	69	194	100.0	64.6	33.1	0.6	1.6
Stolen property; buying, receiving, possessing	100.0	52.7	45.4	0.8	1.1	52,908	31,820	20,262	352	474	100.0	60.1	38.3	0.7	0.9
Vandalism	100.0	78.2	19.1	1.2	1.4	106,865	76,016	27,857	1,819	1,173	100.0	71.1	26.1	1.7	1.1
Weapons; carrying, possessing, etc.	100.0	60.2	38.0	0.7	1.2	84,567	44,133	39,136	496	802	100.0	52.2	46.3	0.6	0.9
Prostitution and commercialized vice	100.0	38.9	58.3	1.4	1.4	54,284	30,210	22,293	453	1,328	100.0	55.7	41.1	0.8	2.4
Sex offenses (except forcible rape and prostitution)	100.0	68.8	29.0	0.7	1.5	36,089	25,615	9,461	418	595	100.0	71.0	26.2	1.2	1.6
Drug abuse violations	100.0	69.0	29.2	0.8	0.9	890,870	529,760	349,997	4,803	6,310	100.0	59.5	39.3	0.5	0.7
Gambling	100.0	4.2	95.2	0.0	0.6	5,641	1,203	4,327	7	104	100.0	21.3	76.7	0.1	1.8
Offenses against the family and children	100.0	68.8	28.8	1.8	0.5	37,229	26,201	9,874	748	406	100.0	70.4	26.5	2.0	1.1
Driving under the influence	100.0	92.1	4.7	1.9	1.4	688,858	595,947	73,501	9,253	10,157	100.0	86.5	10.7	1.3	1.5
Liquor laws	100.0	89.1	6.5	3.2	1.2	307,185	250,582	43,479	9,550	3,574	100.0	81.6	14.2	3.1	1.2
Drunkenness	100.0	88.1	8.7	2.4	0.8	400,004	325,604	64,669	7,386	2,345	100.0	81.4	16.2	1.8	0.6
Disorderly conduct	100.0	57.7	40.7	0.8	0.8	329,155	210,890	109,493	6,036	2,736	100.0	64.1	33.3	1.8	0.8
Vagrancy	100.0	77.6	21.6	0.3	0.6	20,824	11,743	8,491	477	113	100.0	56.4	40.8	2.3	0.5
All other offenses (except traffic)	100.0	69.5	27.5	1.0	2.0	1,914,550	1,210,504	651,964	26,005	26,077	100.0	63.2	34.1	1.4	1.4
Suspicion	100.0	45.8	53.6	0.0	0.6	755	330	409	13	3	100.0	43.7	54.2	1.7	0.4
Curfew and loitering law violations	100.0	62.5	35.5	0.8	1.2	-	-	-	-	-	-	-	-	-	-
Runaways	100.0	63.7	29.0	2.2	5.2	-	-	-	-	-	-	-	-	-	-

[1] Because of rounding, the percentages may not add to 100.0.

Table 50. Metropolitan County Arrest Trends, 2007–2008

(Number, percent change; 1,173 agencies; 2008 estimated population 44,481,258; 2007 estimated population 44,248,400.)

Offense charged	Number of persons arrested								
	Total all ages			Under 18 years of age			18 years of age and over		
	2007	2008	Percent change	2007	2008	Percent change	2007	2008	Percent change
TOTAL[1]	1,680,801	1,636,197	-2.7	200,532	193,133	-3.7	1,480,269	1,443,064	-2.5
Violent Crime	66,071	63,001	-4.6	9,291	8,807	-5.2	56,780	54,194	-4.6
Murder and nonnegligent manslaughter	1,669	1,572	-5.8	127	112	-11.8	1,542	1,460	-5.3
Forcible rape	2,824	2,869	+1.6	436	396	-9.2	2,388	2,473	+3.6
Robbery	9,875	10,104	+2.3	2,439	2,685	+10.1	7,436	7,419	-0.2
Aggravated assault	51,703	48,456	-6.3	6,289	5,614	-10.7	45,414	42,842	-5.7
Property Crime	147,606	155,285	+5.2	35,561	36,905	+3.8	112,045	118,380	+5.7
Burglary	36,185	37,114	+2.6	9,243	9,556	+3.4	26,942	27,558	+2.3
Larceny-theft	96,837	105,094	+8.5	22,772	23,968	+5.3	74,065	81,126	+9.5
Motor vehicle theft	12,802	11,434	-10.7	2,699	2,674	-0.9	10,103	8,760	-13.3
Arson	1,782	1,643	-7.8	847	707	-16.5	935	936	+0.1
Other									
Other assaults	154,274	148,748	-3.6	29,233	27,231	-6.8	125,041	121,517	-2.8
Forgery and counterfeiting	11,626	10,279	-11.6	342	288	-15.8	11,284	9,991	-11.5
Fraud	49,780	44,132	-11.3	774	782	1.0	49,006	43,350	-11.5
Embezzlement	2,586	2,556	-1.2	184	142	-22.8	2,402	2,414	+0.5
Stolen property; buying, receiving, possessing	13,877	12,394	-10.7	1,763	1,565	-11.2	12,114	10,829	-10.6
Vandalism	29,106	28,171	-3.2	10,474	9,887	-5.6	18,632	18,284	-1.9
Weapons; carrying, possessing, etc.	18,491	18,129	-2.0	4,293	4,011	-6.6	14,198	14,118	-0.6
Prostitution and commercialized vice	2,086	2,125	+1.9	45	51	+13.3	2,041	2,074	+1.6
Sex offenses (except forcible rape and prostitution)	11,042	10,533	-4.6	2,152	1,945	-9.6	8,890	8,588	-3.4
Drug abuse violations	202,673	189,035	-6.7	19,649	18,378	-6.5	183,024	170,657	-6.8
Gambling	509	403	-20.8	30	20	-33.3	479	383	-20.0
Offenses against the family and children	33,479	32,678	-2.4	930	1,115	+19.9	32,549	31,563	-3.0
Driving under the influence	236,690	240,553	+1.6	2,329	2,002	-14.0	234,361	238,551	+1.8
Liquor laws	55,628	56,238	+1.1	14,556	14,448	-0.7	41,072	41,790	+1.7
Drunkenness	40,690	41,575	+2.2	1,063	961	-9.6	39,627	40,614	+2.5
Disorderly conduct	47,404	46,931	-1.0	13,787	13,329	-3.3	33,617	33,602	*
Vagrancy	2,240	2,332	+4.1	310	289	-6.8	1,930	2,043	+5.9
All other offenses (except traffic)	535,848	513,043	-4.3	34,671	32,921	-5.0	501,177	480,122	-4.2
Suspicion	595	216	-63.7	56	13	-76.8	539	203	-62.3
Curfew and loitering law violations	4,100	3,702	-9.7	4,100	3,702	-9.7	-	-	-
Runaways	14,995	14,354	-4.3	14,995	14,354	-4.3	-	-	-

[1] Does not include suspicion.

* Less than one-tenth of 1 percent.

Table 51. Metropolitan County Arrest Trends, by Age and Sex, 2007–2008

(Number, percent change; 1,173 agencies; 2008 estimated population 44,481,258; 2007 estimated population 44,248,400.)

Offense charged	Male						Female					
	Total			Under 18			Total			Under 18		
	2007	2008	Percent change	2007	2008	Percent change	2007	2008	Percent change	2007	2008	Percent change
TOTAL[1]	1,289,154	1,252,213	-2.9	143,095	138,171	-3.4	391,647	383,984	-2.0	57,437	54,962	4.3
Violent Crime	54,573	52,115	-4.5	7,690	7,359	-4.3	11,498	10,886	-5.3	1,601	1,448	-9.6
Murder and nonnegligent manslaughter	1,473	1,382	-6.2	118	106	-10.2	196	190	-3.1	9	6	33.3
Forcible rape	2,794	2,832	+1.4	432	392	-9.3	30	37	+23.3	4	4	0.0
Robbery	8,847	9,048	+2.3	2,239	2,476	+10.6	1,028	1,056	+2.7	200	209	+4.5
Aggravated assault	41,459	38,853	-6.3	4,901	4,385	-10.5	10,244	9,603	-6.3	1,388	1,229	-11.5
Property Crime	105,464	109,614	+3.9	25,489	26,219	+2.9	42,142	45,671	+8.4	10,072	10,686	+6.1
Burglary	31,425	32,176	+2.4	8,345	8,582	+2.8	4,760	4,938	+3.7	898	974	+8.5
Larceny-theft	61,967	66,594	+7.5	14,169	14,794	+4.4	34,870	38,500	+10.4	8,603	9,174	+6.6
Motor vehicle theft	10,543	9,477	-10.1	2,224	2,237	+0.6	2,259	1,957	-13.4	475	437	-8.0
Arson	1,529	1,367	-10.6	751	606	-19.3	253	276	+9.1	96	101	+5.2
Other												
Other assaults	115,174	110,601	-4.0	19,592	18,457	-5.8	39,100	38,147	-2.4	9,641	8,774	-9.0
Forgery and counterfeiting	7,136	6,356	-10.9	253	205	-19.0	4,490	3,923	-12.6	89	83	-6.7
Fraud	26,146	23,320	-10.8	532	490	-7.9	23,634	20,812	-11.9	242	292	+20.7
Embezzlement	1,267	1,330	+5.0	119	82	-31.1	1,319	1,226	-7.1	65	60	-7.7
Stolen property; buying, receiving, possessing	11,421	10,139	-11.2	1,502	1,357	-9.7	2,456	2,255	-8.2	261	208	-20.3
Vandalism	24,203	23,395	-3.3	8,956	8,516	-4.9	4,903	4,776	-2.6	1,518	1,371	-9.7
Weapons; carrying, possessing, etc.	16,959	16,652	-1.8	3,818	3,537	-7.4	1,532	1,477	-3.6	475	474	-0.2
Prostitution and commercialized vice	848	748	-11.8	18	15	-16.7	1,238	1,377	+11.2	27	36	33.3
Sex offenses (except forcible rape and prostitution)	10,409	9,933	-4.6	2,014	1,799	-10.7	633	600	-5.2	138	146	+5.8
Drug abuse violations	162,009	151,881	-6.3	16,178	15,292	-5.5	40,664	37,154	-8.6	3,471	3,086	-11.1
Gambling	406	327	-19.5	29	18	-37.9	103	76	-26.2	1	2	+100.0
Offenses against the family and children	27,894	27,142	-2.7	643	794	+23.5	5,585	5,536	-0.9	287	321	+11.8
Driving under the influence	190,008	191,159	+0.6	1,778	1,546	-13.0	46,682	49,394	+5.8	551	456	-17.2
Liquor laws	39,584	40,029	+1.1	9,076	8,926	-1.7	16,044	16,209	+1.0	5,480	5,522	+0.8
Drunkenness	33,563	34,161	+1.8	780	728	-6.7	7,127	7,414	+4.0	283	233	-17.7
Disorderly conduct	34,741	34,598	-0.4	9,159	9,039	-1.3	12,663	12,333	-2.6	4,628	4,290	-7.3
Vagrancy	1,625	1,635	+0.6	216	205	-5.1	615	697	+13.3	94	84	-10.6
All other offenses (except traffic)	416,179	398,072	-4.4	25,708	24,581	-4.4	119,669	114,971	-3.9	8,963	8,340	-7.0
Suspicion	446	148	-66.8	38	7	-81.6	149	68	-54.4	18	6	-66.7
Curfew and loitering law violations	2,678	2,342	-12.5	2,678	2,342	-12.5	1,422	1,360	-4.4	1,422	1,360	-4.4
Runaways	6,867	6,664	-3.0	6,867	6,664	-3.0	8,128	7,690	-5.4	8,128	7,690	-5.4

[1] Does not include suspicion.

Table 52. Metropolitan County Arrests, Distribution by Age, 2008

(Number, percent; 1,201 agencies; 2008 estimated population 49,582,436.)

Offense charged	Total all ages	Ages under 15	Ages under 18	Ages 18 and over	Under 10	10–12	13–14	15	16	17	18	19	20
TOTAL	1,790,536	53,888	213,460	1,577,076	1,618	11,130	41,140	40,394	54,474	64,704	79,265	81,061	76,795
Total percent distribution[1]	100.0	3.0	11.9	88.1	0.1	0.6	2.3	2.3	3.0	3.6	4.4	4.5	4.3
Violent Crime	75,688	2,882	10,877	64,811	74	667	2,141	2,103	2,655	3,237	3,815	3,597	3,087
Violent crime percent distribution[1]	100.0	3.8	14.4	85.6	0.1	0.9	2.8	2.8	3.5	4.3	5.0	4.8	4.1
Murder and nonnegligent manslaughter	1,875	9	148	1,727	0	1	8	22	43	74	116	101	113
Forcible rape	3,035	126	419	2,616	2	28	96	88	88	117	170	164	131
Robbery	12,490	539	3,263	9,227	6	56	477	674	873	1,177	1,326	1,103	771
Aggravated assault	58,288	2,208	7,047	51,241	66	582	1,560	1,319	1,651	1,869	2,203	2,229	2,072
Property Crime	176,897	11,339	42,416	134,481	279	2,411	8,649	8,403	10,670	12,004	12,757	10,647	8,364
Property crime percent distribution[1]	100.0	6.4	24.0	76.0	0.2	1.4	4.9	4.8	6.0	6.8	7.2	6.0	4.7
Burglary	41,767	3,047	10,996	30,771	98	665	2,284	2,169	2,698	3,082	3,627	3,038	2,211
Larceny-theft	120,390	7,311	27,671	92,719	140	1,553	5,618	5,394	7,026	7,940	8,114	6,845	5,507
Motor vehicle theft	12,960	559	2,989	9,971	3	63	493	696	839	895	925	677	576
Arson	1,780	422	760	1,020	38	130	254	144	107	87	91	87	70
Other													
Other assaults	159,681	10,664	29,717	129,964	349	2,653	7,662	5,960	6,915	6,178	5,237	4,898	4,758
Forgery and counterfeiting	11,916	61	326	11,590	1	15	45	42	68	155	381	492	552
Fraud	46,375	122	871	45,504	4	19	99	113	268	368	755	1,021	1,209
Embezzlement	2,909	8	165	2,744	0	2	6	10	55	92	217	176	168
Stolen property; buying, receiving, possessing	14,489	358	1,890	12,599	4	47	307	375	513	644	922	845	678
Vandalism	30,820	3,962	10,807	20,013	203	1,011	2,748	1,930	2,407	2,508	2,350	1,622	1,274
Weapons; carrying, possessing, etc.	21,497	1,607	4,623	16,874	119	437	1,051	810	1,031	1,175	1,359	1,201	1,002
Prostitution and commercialized vice	3,129	20	83	3,046	0	1	19	4	26	33	97	127	131
Sex offenses (except forcible rape and prostitution)	11,732	1,095	2,166	9,566	59	337	699	349	341	381	511	408	372
Drug abuse violations	217,685	2,872	20,708	196,977	33	324	2,515	3,104	5,546	9,186	13,649	13,687	12,407
Gambling	513	6	23	490	1	0	5	6	7	4	13	15	19
Offenses against the family and children	34,862	259	1,166	33,696	8	42	209	218	319	370	412	431	525
Driving under the influence	252,529	24	2,075	250,454	4	4	16	63	427	1,561	4,874	6,995	8,198
Liquor laws	56,968	1,074	14,604	42,364	15	107	952	1,910	4,131	7,489	10,557	10,104	8,245
Drunkenness	45,085	101	997	44,088	3	5	93	158	251	487	1,505	1,572	1,479
Disorderly conduct	50,375	4,525	14,030	36,345	78	969	3,478	3,023	3,367	3,115	2,405	1,809	1,660
Vagrancy	2,443	57	300	2,143	0	7	50	69	96	78	79	77	84
All other offenses (except traffic)	555,203	7,552	36,084	519,119	250	1,313	5,989	6,793	9,484	12,255	17,324	21,322	22,577
Suspicion	225	6	17	208	0	1	5	5	3	3	46	15	6
Curfew and loitering law violations	4,662	1,069	4,662	-	26	143	900	1,104	1,504	985	-	-	-
Runaways	14,853	4,225	14,853	-	108	615	3,502	3,842	4,390	2,396	-	-	-

[1] Because of rounding, the percentages may not add to 100.0.

Table 52. Metropolitan County Arrests, Distribution by Age, 2008—*Continued*

(Number, percent; 1,201 agencies; 2008 estimated population 49,582,436.)

Offense charged	21	22	23	24	25–29	30–34	35–39	40–44	45–49	50–54	55–59	60–64	65 and over
TOTAL	71,586	68,522	65,826	61,542	273,527	196,932	176,144	157,576	129,250	75,210	35,825	15,971	12,044
Total percent distribution[1]	4.0	3.8	3.7	3.4	15.3	11.0	9.8	8.8	7.2	4.2	2.0	0.9	0.7
Violent Crime	2,937	2,796	2,801	2,529	10,852	7,967	7,177	6,288	5,144	2,935	1,477	756	653
Violent crime percent distribution[1]	3.9	3.7	3.7	3.3	14.3	10.5	9.5	8.3	6.8	3.9	2.0	1.0	0.9
Murder and nonnegligent manslaughter	108	81	102	64	302	179	198	132	90	61	33	24	23
Forcible rape	141	127	118	87	394	295	297	260	173	125	58	37	39
Robbery	622	532	515	423	1,495	787	627	504	302	147	56	9	8
Aggravated assault	2,066	2,056	2,066	1,955	8,661	6,706	6,055	5,392	4,579	2,602	1,330	686	583
Property Crime	6,890	6,096	5,484	4,831	21,344	14,882	13,187	11,836	9,197	4,957	2,180	980	849
Property crime percent distribution[1]	3.9	3.4	3.1	2.7	12.1	8.4	7.5	6.7	5.2	2.8	1.2	0.6	0.5
Burglary	1,886	1,535	1,297	1,167	5,143	3,222	2,566	2,226	1,630	764	285	95	79
Larceny-theft	4,412	4,063	3,693	3,227	14,311	10,307	9,463	8,690	6,890	3,881	1,764	829	723
Motor vehicle theft	539	447	461	408	1,750	1,253	1,061	845	595	254	107	45	28
Arson	53	51	33	29	140	100	97	75	82	58	24	11	19
Other													
Other assaults	4,842	4,751	4,670	4,514	21,599	17,019	16,873	15,182	12,386	6,910	3,261	1,593	1,471
Forgery and counterfeiting	480	444	470	435	2,246	1,625	1,504	1,208	917	506	206	65	59
Fraud	1,261	1,319	1,350	1,406	7,889	7,321	6,956	5,600	4,287	2,577	1,383	653	517
Embezzlement	135	127	113	108	414	330	296	254	184	129	58	19	16
Stolen property; buying, receiving, possessing	640	595	534	504	2,292	1,540	1,388	1,147	814	430	156	69	45
Vandalism	1,276	1,038	862	800	3,177	2,029	1,727	1,520	1,163	615	280	143	137
Weapons; carrying, possessing, etc.	996	933	822	785	3,008	1,803	1,369	1,191	1,044	669	344	178	170
Prostitution and commercialized vice	130	146	125	94	501	395	364	375	309	144	62	20	26
Sex offenses (except forcible rape and prostitution)	321	313	318	289	1,263	1,075	1,073	1,051	933	644	388	277	330
Drug abuse violations	11,240	10,156	9,344	8,672	35,934	22,327	18,120	16,066	13,239	7,472	3,143	1,058	463
Gambling	5	7	5	11	53	54	55	56	66	33	37	28	33
Offenses against the family and children	639	664	804	876	5,684	5,821	6,172	5,235	3,581	1,781	695	260	116
Driving under the influence	11,775	12,234	12,212	11,349	47,489	32,050	27,216	24,685	22,222	14,539	8,018	3,869	2,729
Liquor laws	1,217	823	696	587	2,290	1,623	1,498	1,540	1,438	927	446	202	171
Drunkenness	1,953	1,808	1,760	1,604	6,803	4,823	4,872	5,101	5,080	3,153	1,529	680	366
Disorderly conduct	1,728	1,650	1,539	1,391	5,546	3,912	3,827	3,762	3,257	2,035	960	481	383
Vagrancy	70	56	66	73	301	224	287	293	242	168	74	29	20
All other offenses (except traffic)	23,045	22,561	21,846	20,676	94,820	70,101	62,157	55,169	43,728	24,573	11,125	4,606	3,489
Suspicion	6	5	5	8	22	11	26	17	19	13	3	5	1
Curfew and loitering law violations	-	-	-	-	-	-	-	-	-	-	-	-	-
Runaways	-	-	-	-	-	-	-	-	-	-	-	-	-

[1] Because of rounding, the percentages may not add to 100.0.

Table 53. Metropolitan County Arrests of Persons Under 15, 18, 21, and 25 Years of Age, 2008

(Number, percent; 1,201 agencies; 2008 estimated population 49,582,436.)

Offense charged	Total all ages	Number of persons arrested				Percent of total all ages			
		Under 15	Under 18	Under 21	Under 25	Under 15	Under 18	Under 21	Under 25
TOTAL	1,790,536	53,888	213,460	450,581	718,057	3.0	11.9	25.2	40.1
Violent Crime	75,688	2,882	10,877	21,376	32,439	3.8	14.4	28.2	42.9
Murder and nonnegligent manslaughter	1,875	9	148	478	833	0.5	7.9	25.5	44.4
Forcible rape	3,035	126	419	884	1,357	4.2	13.8	29.1	44.7
Robbery	12,490	539	3,263	6,463	8,555	4.3	26.1	51.7	68.5
Aggravated assault	58,288	2,208	7,047	13,551	21,694	3.8	12.1	23.2	37.2
Property Crime	176,897	11,339	42,416	74,184	97,485	6.4	24.0	41.9	55.1
Burglary	41,767	3,047	10,996	19,872	25,757	7.3	26.3	47.6	61.7
Larceny-theft	120,390	7,311	27,671	48,137	63,532	6.1	23.0	40.0	52.8
Motor vehicle theft	12,960	559	2,989	5,167	7,022	4.3	23.1	39.9	54.2
Arson	1,780	422	760	1,008	1,174	23.7	42.7	56.6	66.0
Other									
Other assaults	159,681	10,664	29,717	44,610	63,387	6.7	18.6	27.9	39.7
Forgery and counterfeiting	11,916	61	326	1,751	3,580	0.5	2.7	14.7	30.0
Fraud	46,375	122	871	3,856	9,192	0.3	1.9	8.3	19.8
Embezzlement	2,909	8	165	726	1,209	0.3	5.7	25.0	41.6
Stolen property; buying, receiving, possessing	14,489	358	1,890	4,335	6,608	2.5	13.0	29.9	45.6
Vandalism	30,820	3,962	10,807	16,053	20,029	12.9	35.1	52.1	65.0
Weapons; carrying, possessing, etc.	21,497	1,607	4,623	8,185	11,721	7.5	21.5	38.1	54.5
Prostitution and commercialized vice	3,129	20	83	438	933	0.6	2.7	14.0	29.8
Sex offenses (except forcible rape and prostitution)	11,732	1,095	2,166	3,457	4,698	9.3	18.5	29.5	40.0
Drug abuse violations	217,685	2,872	20,708	60,451	99,863	1.3	9.5	27.8	45.9
Gambling	513	6	23	70	98	1.2	4.5	13.6	19.1
Offenses against the family and children	34,862	259	1,166	2,534	5,517	0.7	3.3	7.3	15.8
Driving under the influence	252,529	24	2,075	22,142	69,712	*	0.8	8.8	27.6
Liquor laws	56,968	1,074	14,604	43,510	46,833	1.9	25.6	76.4	82.2
Drunkenness	45,085	101	997	5,553	12,678	0.2	2.2	12.3	28.1
Disorderly conduct	50,375	4,525	14,030	19,904	26,212	9.0	27.9	39.5	52.0
Vagrancy	2,443	57	300	540	805	2.3	12.3	22.1	33.0
All other offenses (except traffic)	555,203	7,552	36,084	97,307	185,435	1.4	6.5	17.5	33.4
Suspicion	225	6	17	84	108	2.7	7.6	37.3	48.0
Curfew and loitering law violations	4,662	1,069	4,662	4,662	4,662	22.9	100.0	100.0	100.0
Runaways	14,853	4,225	14,853	14,853	14,853	28.4	100.0	100.0	100.0

* Less than one-tenth of 1 percent.

Table 54. Metropolitan County Arrests, Distribution by Sex, 2008

(Number, percent; 1,201 agencies; 2008 estimated population 49,582,436.)

Offense charged	Number of persons arrested			Percent male	Percent female	Percent distribution[1]		
	Total	Male	Female			Total	Male	Female
TOTAL	1,790,536	1,372,958	417,578	76.7	23.3	100.0	100.0	100.0
Violent Crime	75,688	62,425	13,263	82.5	17.5	4.2	4.5	3.2
Murder and nonnegligent manslaughter	1,875	1,657	218	88.4	11.6	0.1	0.1	0.1
Forcible rape	3,035	2,995	40	98.7	1.3	0.2	0.2	*
Robbery	12,490	11,160	1,330	89.4	10.6	0.7	0.8	0.3
Property Crime	176,897	124,004	52,893	70.1	29.9	9.9	9.0	12.7
Aggravated assault	58,288	46,613	11,675	80.0	20.0	3.3	3.4	2.8
Burglary	41,767	36,147	5,620	86.5	13.5	2.3	2.6	1.3
Larceny-theft	120,390	75,658	44,732	62.8	37.2	6.7	5.5	10.7
Motor vehicle theft	12,960	10,712	2,248	82.7	17.3	0.7	0.8	0.5
Arson	1,780	1,487	293	83.5	16.5	0.1	0.1	0.1
Other								
Other assaults	159,681	118,902	40,779	74.5	25.5	8.9	8.7	9.8
Forgery and counterfeiting	11,916	7,447	4,469	62.5	37.5	0.7	0.5	1.1
Fraud	46,375	24,752	21,623	53.4	46.6	2.6	1.8	5.2
Embezzlement	2,909	1,507	1,402	51.8	48.2	0.2	0.1	0.3
Stolen property; buying, receiving, possessing	14,489	11,906	2,583	82.2	17.8	0.8	0.9	0.6
Vandalism	30,820	25,636	5,184	83.2	16.8	1.7	1.9	1.2
Weapons; carrying, possessing, etc.	21,497	19,805	1,692	92.1	7.9	1.2	1.4	0.4
Prostitution and commercialized vice	3,129	995	2,134	31.8	68.2	0.2	0.1	0.5
Sex offenses (except forcible rape and prostitution)	11,732	11,058	674	94.3	5.7	0.7	0.8	0.2
Drug abuse violations	217,685	175,679	42,006	80.7	19.3	12.2	12.8	10.1
Gambling	513	397	116	77.4	22.6	*	*	*
Offenses against the family and children	34,862	28,850	6,012	82.8	17.2	1.9	2.1	1.4
Driving under the influence	252,529	201,151	51,378	79.7	20.3	14.1	14.7	12.3
Liquor laws	56,968	40,607	16,361	71.3	28.7	3.2	3.0	3.9
Drunkenness	45,085	37,159	7,926	82.4	17.6	2.5	2.7	1.9
Disorderly conduct	50,375	37,156	13,219	73.8	26.2	2.8	2.7	3.2
Vagrancy	2,443	1,730	713	70.8	29.2	0.1	0.1	0.2
All other offenses (except traffic)	555,203	431,737	123,466	77.8	22.2	31.0	31.4	29.6
Suspicion	225	155	70	68.9	31.1	*	*	*
Curfew and loitering law violations	4,662	3,013	1,649	64.6	35.4	0.3	0.2	0.4
Runaways	14,853	6,887	7,966	46.4	53.6	0.8	0.5	1.9

[1] Because of rounding, the percentages may not add to 100.0.

* Less than one-tenth of 1 percent.

Table 55. Metropolitan County Arrests, Distribution by Race, 2008

(Number, percent; 1,201 agencies; 2008 estimated population 49,582,436.)

Offense charged	Total arrests					Percent distribution[1]					Arrests under 18				
	Total	White	Black	American Indian or Alaskan Native	Asian or Pacific Islander	Total	White	Black	American Indian or Alaskan Native	Asian or Pacific Islander	Total	White	Black	American Indian or Alaskan Native	Asian or Pacific Islander
TOTAL	1,777,640	1,326,436	428,837	11,149	11,218	100.0	74.6	24.1	0.6	0.6	212,579	142,471	67,507	1,071	1,530
Violent Crime	75,501	50,474	23,968	511	548	100.0	66.9	31.7	0.7	0.7	10,856	5,317	5,430	47	62
Murder and nonnegligent manslaughter	1,864	1,128	718	9	9	100.0	60.5	38.5	0.5	0.5	147	63	83	1	0
Forcible rape	3,026	2,313	675	17	21	100.0	76.4	22.3	0.6	0.7	418	325	91	1	1
Robbery	12,437	5,593	6,738	36	70	100.0	45.0	54.2	0.3	0.6	3,257	925	2,301	4	27
Aggravated assault	58,174	41,440	15,837	449	448	100.0	71.2	27.2	0.8	0.8	7,034	4,004	2,955	41	34
Property Crime	175,974	121,411	52,418	797	1,348	100.0	69.0	29.8	0.5	0.8	42,283	25,593	16,136	155	399
Burglary	41,544	30,573	10,566	189	216	100.0	73.6	25.4	0.5	0.5	10,950	7,265	3,584	30	71
Larceny-theft	119,763	80,405	37,789	531	1,038	100.0	67.1	31.6	0.4	0.9	27,594	16,013	11,175	109	297
Motor vehicle theft	12,895	9,023	3,722	70	80	100.0	70.0	28.9	0.5	0.6	2,982	1,724	1,221	13	24
Arson	1,772	1,410	341	7	14	100.0	79.6	19.2	0.4	0.8	757	591	156	3	7
Other															
Other assaults	159,187	116,719	40,591	885	992	100.0	73.3	25.5	0.6	0.6	29,632	16,944	12,394	131	163
Forgery and counterfeiting	11,766	8,283	3,338	37	108	100.0	70.4	28.4	0.3	0.9	324	215	104	2	3
Fraud	46,135	31,504	14,222	207	202	100.0	68.3	30.8	0.4	0.4	859	589	257	8	5
Embezzlement	2,856	1,686	1,135	8	27	100.0	59.0	39.7	0.3	0.9	163	89	74	0	0
Stolen property; buying, receiving, possessing	14,430	10,285	3,993	76	76	100.0	71.3	27.7	0.5	0.5	1,885	1,152	712	7	14
Vandalism	30,749	24,463	5,881	213	192	100.0	79.6	19.1	0.7	0.6	10,768	8,437	2,212	55	64
Weapons; carrying, possessing, etc.	21,434	13,792	7,393	121	128	100.0	64.3	34.5	0.6	0.6	4,606	2,727	1,802	30	47
Prostitution and commercialized vice	3,120	1,910	1,047	9	154	100.0	61.2	33.6	0.3	4.9	83	40	40	0	3
Sex offenses (except forcible rape and prostitution)	11,669	9,215	2,298	71	85	100.0	79.0	19.7	0.6	0.7	2,150	1,540	589	9	12
Drug abuse violations	216,634	157,422	56,959	1,071	1,182	100.0	72.7	26.3	0.5	0.5	20,647	15,673	4,742	93	139
Gambling	507	318	154	11	24	100.0	62.7	30.4	2.2	4.7	23	7	16	0	0
Offenses against the family and children	34,027	21,057	12,678	152	140	100.0	61.9	37.3	0.4	0.4	1,158	872	279	5	2
Driving under the influence	250,869	222,885	24,606	1,359	2,019	100.0	88.8	9.8	0.5	0.8	2,052	1,953	76	12	11
Liquor laws	56,399	50,402	4,815	743	439	100.0	89.4	8.5	1.3	0.8	14,493	13,639	599	138	117
Drunkenness	44,443	39,863	3,935	462	183	100.0	89.7	8.9	1.0	0.4	991	913	66	8	4
Disorderly conduct	50,080	33,771	15,687	349	273	100.0	67.4	31.3	0.7	0.5	13,982	7,090	6,759	79	54
Vagrancy	2,440	1,632	801	3	4	100.0	66.9	32.8	0.1	0.2	300	256	44	0	0
All other offenses (except traffic)	549,747	394,853	148,061	3,943	2,890	100.0	71.8	26.9	0.7	0.5	35,855	25,026	10,428	171	230
Suspicion	221	101	117	0	3	100.0	45.7	52.9	0.0	1.4	17	9	8	0	0
Curfew and loitering law violations	4,635	3,486	1,059	18	72	100.0	75.2	22.8	0.4	1.6	4,635	3,486	1,059	18	72
Runaways	14,817	10,904	3,681	103	129	100.0	73.6	24.8	0.7	0.9	14,817	10,904	3,681	103	129

[1] Because of rounding, the percentages may not add to 100.0.

Table 55. Metropolitan County Arrests, Distribution by Race, 2008—*Continued*

(Number, percent; 1,201 agencies; 2008 estimated population 49,582,436.)

Offense charged	Percent distribution[1]					Arrests under 18					Percent distribution[1]				
	Total	White	Black	American Indian or Alaskan Native	Asian or Pacific Islander	Total	White	Black	American Indian or Alaskan Native	Asian or Pacific Islander	Total	White	Black	American Indian or Alaskan Native	Asian or Pacific Islander
TOTAL	100.0	67.0	31.8	0.5	0.7	1,565,061	1,183,965	361,330	10,078	9,688	100.0	75.6	23.1	0.6	0.6
Violent Crime	100.0	49.0	50.0	0.4	0.6	64,645	45,157	18,538	464	486	100.0	69.9	28.7	0.7	0.8
Murder and nonnegligent manslaughter	100.0	42.9	56.5	0.7	0.0	1,717	1,065	635	8	9	100.0	62.0	37.0	0.5	0.5
Forcible rape	100.0	77.8	21.8	0.2	0.2	2,608	1,988	584	16	20	100.0	76.2	22.4	0.6	0.8
Robbery	100.0	28.4	70.6	0.1	0.8	9,180	4,668	4,437	32	43	100.0	50.8	48.3	0.3	0.5
Aggravated assault	100.0	56.9	42.0	0.6	0.5	51,140	37,436	12,882	408	414	100.0	73.2	25.2	0.8	0.8
Property Crime	100.0	60.5	38.2	0.4	0.9	133,691	95,818	36,282	642	949	100.0	71.7	27.1	0.5	0.7
Burglary	100.0	66.3	32.7	0.3	0.6	30,594	23,308	6,982	159	145	100.0	76.2	22.8	0.5	0.5
Larceny-theft	100.0	58.0	40.5	0.4	1.1	92,169	64,392	26,614	422	741	100.0	69.9	28.9	0.5	0.8
Motor vehicle theft	100.0	57.8	40.9	0.4	0.8	9,913	7,299	2,501	57	56	100.0	73.6	25.2	0.6	0.6
Arson	100.0	78.1	20.6	0.4	0.9	1,015	819	185	4	7	100.0	80.7	18.2	0.4	0.7
Other															
Other assaults	100.0	57.2	41.8	0.4	0.6	129,555	99,775	28,197	754	829	100.0	77.0	21.8	0.6	0.6
Forgery and counterfeiting	100.0	66.4	32.1	0.6	0.9	11,442	8,068	3,234	35	105	100.0	70.5	28.3	0.3	0.9
Fraud	100.0	68.6	29.9	0.9	0.6	45,276	30,915	13,965	199	197	100.0	68.3	30.8	0.4	0.4
Embezzlement	100.0	54.6	45.4	0.0	0.0	2,693	1,597	1,061	8	27	100.0	59.3	39.4	0.3	1.0
Stolen property; buying, receiving, possessing	100.0	61.1	37.8	0.4	0.7	12,545	9,133	3,281	69	62	100.0	72.8	26.2	0.6	0.5
Vandalism	100.0	78.4	20.5	0.5	0.6	19,981	16,026	3,669	158	128	100.0	80.2	18.4	0.8	0.6
Weapons; carrying, possessing, etc.	100.0	59.2	39.1	0.7	1.0	16,828	11,065	5,591	91	81	100.0	65.8	33.2	0.5	0.5
Prostitution and commercialized vice	100.0	48.2	48.2	0.0	3.6	3,037	1,870	1,007	9	151	100.0	61.6	33.2	0.3	5.0
Sex offenses (except forcible rape and prostitution)	100.0	71.6	27.4	0.4	0.6	9,519	7,675	1,709	62	73	100.0	80.6	18.0	0.7	0.8
Drug abuse violations	100.0	75.9	23.0	0.5	0.7	195,987	141,749	52,217	978	1,043	100.0	72.3	26.6	0.5	0.5
Gambling	100.0	30.4	69.6	0.0	0.0	484	311	138	11	24	100.0	64.3	28.5	2.3	5.0
Offenses against the family and children	100.0	75.3	24.1	0.4	0.2	32,869	20,185	12,399	147	138	100.0	61.4	37.7	0.4	0.4
Driving under the influence	100.0	95.2	3.7	0.6	0.5	248,817	220,932	24,530	1,347	2,008	100.0	88.8	9.9	0.5	0.8
Liquor laws	100.0	94.1	4.1	1.0	0.8	41,906	36,763	4,216	605	322	100.0	87.7	10.1	1.4	0.8
Drunkenness	100.0	92.1	6.7	0.8	0.4	43,452	38,950	3,869	454	179	100.0	89.6	8.9	1.0	0.4
Disorderly conduct	100.0	50.7	48.3	0.6	0.4	36,098	26,681	8,928	270	219	100.0	73.9	24.7	0.7	0.6
Vagrancy	100.0	85.3	14.7	0.0	0.0	2,140	1,376	757	3	4	100.0	64.3	35.4	0.1	0.2
All other offenses (except traffic)	100.0	69.8	29.1	0.5	0.6	513,892	369,827	137,633	3,772	2,660	100.0	72.0	26.8	0.7	0.5
Suspicion	100.0	52.9	47.1	0.0	0.0	204	92	109	0	3	100.0	45.1	53.4	0.0	1.5
Curfew and loitering law violations	100.0	75.2	22.8	0.4	1.6	-	-	-	-	-	-	-	-	-	-
Runaways	100.0	73.6	24.8	0.7	0.9	-	-	-	-	-	-	-	-	-	-

[1] Because of rounding, the percentages may not add to 100.0.

Table 56. Nonmetropolitan County Arrest Trends, 2007–2008

(Number, percent change; 1,808 agencies; 2008 estimated population 20,332,211; 2007 estimated population 20,501,230.)

Offense charged	Number of persons arrested								
	Total all ages			Under 18 years of age			18 years of age and over		
	2007	2008	Percent change	2007	2008	Percent change	2007	2008	Percent change
TOTAL[1]	780,760	750,942	-3.8	69,280	65,085	-6.1	711,480	685,857	-3.6
Violent Crime	23,780	23,040	-3.1	2,184	2,045	-6.4	21,596	20,995	-2.8
Murder and nonnegligent manslaughter	595	592	-0.5	33	38	+15.2	562	554	-1.4
Forcible rape	1,492	1,556	+4.3	218	228	+4.6	1,274	1,328	+4.2
Robbery	1,818	1,674	-7.9	199	168	-15.6	1,619	1,506	-7.0
Aggravated assault	19,875	19,218	-3.3	1,734	1,611	-7.1	18,141	17,607	-2.9
Property Crime	54,392	55,793	+2.6	10,835	10,192	-5.9	43,557	45,601	+4.7
Burglary	17,460	17,580	+0.7	4,007	3,705	-7.5	13,453	13,875	+3.1
Larceny-theft	31,277	33,034	+5.6	5,487	5,328	-2.9	25,790	27,706	+7.4
Motor vehicle theft	4,760	4,378	-8.0	1,130	942	-16.6	3,630	3,436	-5.3
Arson	895	801	-10.5	211	217	+2.8	684	584	-14.6
Other									
Other assaults	70,205	69,145	-1.5	9,024	8,815	-2.3	61,181	60,330	-1.4
Forgery and counterfeiting	4,680	4,358	-6.9	108	104	-3.7	4,572	4,254	-7.0
Fraud	30,074	26,981	-10.3	337	337	+0.0	29,737	26,644	-10.4
Embezzlement	920	874	-5.0	16	19	+18.8	904	855	-5.4
Stolen property; buying, receiving, possessing	4,718	4,277	-9.3	521	509	-2.3	4,197	3,768	-10.2
Vandalism	13,157	13,342	+1.4	3,750	3,589	-4.3	9,407	9,753	+3.7
Weapons; carrying, possessing, etc.	6,893	6,420	-6.9	821	786	-4.3	6,072	5,634	-7.2
Prostitution and commercialized vice	192	207	+7.8	6	6	0.0	186	201	+8.1
Sex offenses (except forcible rape and prostitution)	5,423	5,031	-7.2	1,035	956	-7.6	4,388	4,075	-7.1
Drug abuse violations	90,552	81,181	-10.3	6,008	5,569	-7.3	84,544	75,612	-10.6
Gambling	260	188	-27.7	12	18	+50.0	248	170	-31.5
Offenses against the family and children	12,404	11,300	-8.9	368	372	+1.1	12,036	10,928	-9.2
Driving under the influence	139,235	136,101	-2.3	1,954	1,563	-20.0	137,281	134,538	-2.0
Liquor laws	36,604	35,058	-4.2	9,162	8,363	-8.7	27,442	26,695	-2.7
Drunkenness	20,033	19,616	-2.1	502	511	+1.8	19,531	19,105	-2.2
Disorderly conduct	23,078	22,439	-2.8	4,847	4,624	-4.6	18,231	17,815	-2.3
Vagrancy	204	240	+17.6	8	27	+237.5	196	213	+8.7
All other offenses (except traffic)	238,535	230,443	-3.4	12,361	11,772	-4.8	226,174	218,671	-3.3
Suspicion	62	49	-21.0	27	13	-51.9	35	36	+2.9
Curfew and loitering law violations	600	499	-16.8	600	499	-16.8	-	-	-
Runaways	4,821	4,409	-8.5	4,821	4,409	-8.5	-	-	-

[1] Does not include suspicion.

Table 57. Nonmetropolitan County Arrest Trends, by Age and Sex, 2007–2008

(Number, percent; 1,808 agencies; 2008 estimated population 20,332,211; 2007 estimated population 20,501,230.)

Offense charged	Male						Female					
	Total			Under 18			Total			Under 18		
	2007	2008	Percent change	2007	2008	Percent change	2007	2008	Percent change	2007	2008	Percent change
TOTAL[1]	598,528	573,871	-4.1	49,556	46,652	-5.9	182,232	177,071	-2.8	19,724	18,433	-6.5
Violent Crime	19,878	19,274	-3.0	1,822	1,695	-7.0	3,902	3,766	-3.5	362	350	-3.3
Murder and nonnegligent manslaughter	515	519	+0.8	26	37	+42.3	80	73	-8.8	7	1	-85.7
Forcible rape	1,466	1,531	+4.4	209	222	+6.2	26	25	-3.8	9	6	-33.3
Robbery	1,604	1,475	-8.0	178	150	-15.7	214	199	-7.0	21	18	-14.3
Aggravated assault	16,293	15,749	-3.3	1,409	1,286	-8.7	3,582	3,469	-3.2	325	325	0.0
Property Crime	42,140	42,808	+1.6	8,663	8,091	-6.6	12,252	12,985	+6.0	2,172	2,101	-3.3
Burglary	15,287	15,330	+0.3	3,657	3,334	-8.8	2,173	2,250	+3.5	350	371	+6.0
Larceny-theft	22,175	23,173	+4.5	3,936	3,792	-3.7	9,102	9,861	+8.3	1,551	1,536	-1.0
Motor vehicle theft	3,919	3,640	-7.1	881	780	-11.5	841	738	-12.2	249	162	-34.9
Arson	759	665	-12.4	189	185	-2.1	136	136	0.0	22	32	+45.5
Other												
Other assaults	52,947	51,493	-2.7	6,185	6,033	-2.5	17,258	17,652	+2.3	2,839	2,782	-2.0
Forgery and counterfeiting	2,707	2,491	-8.0	68	63	-7.4	1,973	1,867	-5.4	40	41	+2.5
Fraud	15,157	13,631	-10.1	207	219	+5.8	14,917	13,350	-10.5	130	118	-9.2
Embezzlement	383	435	+13.6	13	8	-38.5	537	439	-18.2	3	11	+266.7
Stolen property; buying, receiving, possessing	3,868	3,544	-8.4	440	422	-4.1	850	733	-13.8	81	87	+7.4
Vandalism	10,953	11,077	+1.1	3,231	3,082	-4.6	2,204	2,265	+2.8	519	507	-2.3
Weapons; carrying, possessing, etc.	6,323	5,966	-5.6	732	707	-3.4	570	454	-20.4	89	79	-11.2
Prostitution and commercialized vice	125	115	-8.0	6	4	-33.3	67	92	+37.3	0	2	-
Sex offenses (except forcible rape and prostitution)	5,110	4,770	-6.7	945	897	-5.1	313	261	-16.6	90	59	-34.4
Drug abuse violations	71,244	63,801	-10.4	4,736	4,407	-6.9	19,308	17,380	-10.0	1,272	1,162	-8.6
Gambling	209	142	-32.1	11	16	+45.5	51	46	-9.8	1	2	100.0
Offenses against the family and children	9,884	9,008	-8.9	252	250	-0.8	2,520	2,292	-9.0	116	122	+5.2
Driving under the influence	112,090	108,504	-3.2	1,509	1,187	-21.3	27,145	27,597	+1.7	445	376	-15.5
Liquor laws	26,166	25,045	-4.3	5,597	5,164	-7.7	10,438	10,013	-4.1	3,565	3,199	-10.3
Drunkenness	16,396	15,930	-2.8	373	378	+1.3	3,637	3,686	+1.3	129	133	+3.1
Disorderly conduct	17,011	16,501	-3.0	3,365	3,124	-7.2	6,067	5,938	-2.1	1,482	1,500	+1.2
Vagrancy	152	195	+28.3	5	21	+320.0	52	45	-13.5	3	6	+100.0
All other offenses (except traffic)	183,242	176,785	-3.5	8,853	8,528	-3.7	55,293	53,658	-3.0	3,508	3,244	-7.5
Suspicion	46	38	-17.4	19	10	-47.4	16	11	-31.3	8	3	-62.5
Curfew and loitering law violations	372	317	-14.8	372	317	-14.8	228	182	-20.2	228	182	-20.2
Runaways	2,171	2,039	-6.1	2,171	2,039	-6.1	2,650	2,370	-10.6	2,650	2,370	-10.6

[1] Does not include suspicion.

Table 58. Nonmetropolitan County Arrests, Distribution by Age, 2008

(Number, percent; 1,836 agencies; 2008 estimated population 19,987,986.)

Offense charged	Total all ages	Ages under 15	Ages under 18	Ages 18 and over	Under 10	10–12	13–14	15	16	17	18	19	20
TOTAL	751,666	14,893	64,891	686,775	812	3,046	11,035	10,838	16,531	22,629	32,291	34,243	33,039
Total percent distribution[1]	100.0	2.0	8.6	91.4	0.1	0.4	1.5	1.4	2.2	3.0	4.3	4.6	4.4
Violent Crime	22,781	521	2,028	20,753	34	140	347	343	504	660	1,005	962	915
Violent crime percent distribution[1]	100.0	2.3	8.9	91.1	0.1	0.6	1.5	1.5	2.2	2.9	4.4	4.2	4.0
Murder and nonnegligent manslaughter	607	4	41	566	1	1	2	3	7	27	24	27	31
Forcible rape	1,376	74	199	1,177	2	22	50	36	41	48	73	56	58
Robbery	1,764	16	182	1,582	0	3	13	28	57	81	170	172	137
Aggravated assault	19,034	427	1,606	17,428	31	114	282	276	399	504	738	707	689
Property Crime	54,794	2,598	10,171	44,623	126	544	1,928	1,818	2,554	3,201	4,131	3,401	2,787
Property crime percent distribution[1]	100.0	4.7	18.6	81.4	0.2	1.0	3.5	3.3	4.7	5.8	7.5	6.2	5.1
Burglary	17,417	920	3,780	13,637	42	185	693	709	945	1,206	1,715	1,370	1,058
Larceny-theft	32,428	1,375	5,277	27,151	66	297	1,012	867	1,336	1,699	2,075	1,782	1,524
Motor vehicle theft	4,179	198	914	3,265	2	22	174	205	243	268	303	210	178
Arson	770	105	200	570	16	40	49	37	30	28	38	39	27
Other													
Other assaults	66,919	2,797	8,776	58,143	124	703	1,970	1,577	2,227	2,175	2,191	2,082	1,994
Forgery and counterfeiting	4,282	15	101	4,181	2	4	9	14	17	55	110	148	164
Fraud	23,829	65	343	23,486	19	8	38	46	79	153	360	634	620
Embezzlement	860	0	19	841	0	0	0	2	7	10	28	34	29
Stolen property; buying, receiving, possessing	4,422	93	523	3,899	4	19	70	70	156	204	255	276	218
Vandalism	12,896	1,318	3,546	9,350	139	358	821	578	769	881	974	812	624
Weapons; carrying, possessing, etc.	6,625	268	797	5,828	15	79	174	134	170	225	277	261	290
Prostitution and commercialized vice	208	1	6	202	0	0	1	1	1	3	5	9	7
Sex offenses (except forcible rape and prostitution)	4,971	409	932	4,039	39	112	258	145	190	188	268	224	179
Drug abuse violations	81,704	743	5,622	76,082	19	83	641	752	1,377	2,750	4,759	5,020	4,713
Gambling	208	5	16	192	0	0	5	5	2	4	10	11	15
Offenses against the family and children	12,083	135	387	11,696	28	27	80	70	93	89	187	221	230
Driving under the influence	157,703	25	1,748	155,955	4	2	19	66	409	1,248	3,231	4,388	4,977
Liquor laws	34,571	615	8,223	26,348	7	36	572	1,104	2,352	4,152	5,768	5,813	4,977
Drunkenness	17,838	48	499	17,339	6	1	41	77	106	268	568	601	618
Disorderly conduct	22,716	1,422	4,623	18,093	78	326	1,018	873	1,166	1,162	1,052	804	794
Vagrancy	253	3	28	225	0	2	1	3	9	13	13	11	12
All other offenses (except traffic)	217,103	2,455	11,684	205,419	143	425	1,887	1,957	2,946	4,326	7,095	8,529	8,873
Suspicion	95	7	14	81	1	0	6	2	2	3	4	2	3
Curfew and loitering law violations	462	132	462	-	3	22	107	80	129	121	-	-	-
Runaways	4,343	1,218	4,343	-	21	155	1,042	1,121	1,266	738	-	-	-

[1] Because of rounding, the percentages may not add to 100.0.

Table 58. Nonmetropolitan County Arrests, Distribution by Age, 2008—*Continued*

(Number, percent; 1,836 agencies; 2008 estimated population 19,987,986.)

Offense charged	21	22	23	24	25–29	30–34	35–39	40–44	45–49	50–54	55–59	60–64	65 and over
TOTAL	29,973	28,886	27,913	25,925	116,527	84,462	76,222	68,407	58,241	35,531	18,336	9,192	7,587
Total percent distribution[1]	4.0	3.8	3.7	3.4	15.5	11.2	10.1	9.1	7.7	4.7	2.4	1.2	1.0
Violent Crime	834	820	796	760	3,516	2,636	2,365	2,064	1,797	1,033	599	340	311
Violent crime percent distribution[1]	3.7	3.6	3.5	3.3	15.4	11.6	10.4	9.1	7.9	4.5	2.6	1.5	1.4
Murder and nonnegligent manslaughter	26	18	21	16	96	77	68	45	44	33	19	11	10
Forcible rape	50	50	52	34	192	133	139	119	89	47	40	24	21
Robbery	103	84	70	69	287	180	127	82	65	21	10	2	3
Aggravated assault	655	668	653	641	2,941	2,246	2,031	1,818	1,599	932	530	303	277
Property Crime	2,283	2,173	1,903	1,737	7,486	4,921	4,432	3,609	2,835	1,529	729	379	288
Property crime percent distribution[1]	4.2	4.0	3.5	3.2	13.7	9.0	8.1	6.6	5.2	2.8	1.3	0.7	0.5
Burglary	843	710	614	566	2,212	1,408	1,127	858	611	333	127	48	37
Larceny-theft	1,248	1,288	1,131	1,014	4,576	3,067	2,915	2,425	1,965	1,066	549	293	233
Motor vehicle theft	156	150	144	144	608	385	336	268	206	104	39	21	13
Arson	36	25	14	13	90	61	54	58	53	26	14	17	5
Other													
Other assaults	2,122	2,162	2,057	2,021	9,501	7,702	7,512	6,856	5,449	3,171	1,612	880	831
Forgery and counterfeiting	173	177	202	183	852	643	514	391	306	180	80	39	19
Fraud	706	757	814	742	4,050	3,702	3,554	2,837	2,063	1,284	716	352	295
Embezzlement	27	30	29	30	125	130	94	82	83	45	42	16	17
Stolen property; buying, receiving, possessing	205	181	172	140	676	456	453	365	264	146	46	24	22
Vandalism	577	480	395	381	1,495	932	833	691	529	312	154	77	84
Weapons; carrying, possessing, etc.	246	245	247	225	968	648	604	532	545	310	194	120	116
Prostitution and commercialized vice	9	5	11	5	40	22	18	19	20	17	7	4	4
Sex offenses (except forcible rape and prostitution)	189	165	118	96	532	446	475	361	336	231	165	95	159
Drug abuse violations	4,211	3,991	3,713	3,395	14,038	8,752	6,998	6,111	5,185	3,081	1,369	511	235
Gambling	4	6	2	2	21	21	25	18	16	14	12	7	8
Offenses against the family and children	269	312	323	368	2,053	2,044	2,014	1,643	1,136	534	194	83	85
Driving under the influence	6,447	6,526	6,503	5,978	26,305	18,434	17,187	16,788	16,101	11,008	6,312	3,255	2,515
Liquor laws	892	672	463	452	1,593	1,231	1,063	1,086	990	617	372	182	177
Drunkenness	749	697	661	593	2,609	2,017	1,946	1,993	2,003	1,279	569	271	165
Disorderly conduct	866	792	777	628	2,807	2,044	1,841	1,945	1,696	1,024	499	269	255
Vagrancy	7	12	6	11	44	16	25	26	14	14	5	5	4
All other offenses (except traffic)	9,155	8,680	8,717	8,178	37,798	27,643	24,260	20,984	16,868	9,701	4,659	2,283	1,996
Suspicion	2	3	4	0	18	22	9	6	5	1	1	0	1
Curfew and loitering law violations	-	-	-	-	-	-	-	-	-	-	-	-	-
Runaways	-	-	-	-	-	-	-	-	-	-	-	-	-

[1] Because of rounding, the percentages may not add to 100.0.

Table 59. Nonmetropolitan County Arrests of Persons Under 15, 18, 21, and 25 Years of Age, 2008

(Number, percent; 1,836 agencies; 2008 estimated population 19,987,986.)

Offense charged	Total all ages	Number of persons arrested				Percent of total all ages			
		Under 15	Under 18	Under 21	Under 25	Under 15	Under 18	Under 21	Under 25
TOTAL	751,666	14,893	64,891	164,464	277,161	2.0	8.6	21.9	36.9
Violent Crime	22,781	521	2,028	4,910	8,120	2.3	8.9	21.6	35.6
Murder and nonnegligent manslaughter	607	4	41	123	204	0.7	6.8	20.3	33.6
Forcible rape	1,376	74	199	386	572	5.4	14.5	28.1	41.6
Robbery	1,764	16	182	661	987	0.9	10.3	37.5	56.0
Aggravated assault	19,034	427	1,606	3,740	6,357	2.2	8.4	19.6	33.4
Property Crime	54,794	2,598	10,171	20,490	28,586	4.7	18.6	37.4	52.2
Burglary	17,417	920	3,780	7,923	10,656	5.3	21.7	45.5	61.2
Larceny-theft	32,428	1,375	5,277	10,658	15,339	4.2	16.3	32.9	47.3
Motor vehicle theft	4,179	198	914	1,605	2,199	4.7	21.9	38.4	52.6
Arson	770	105	200	304	392	13.6	26.0	39.5	50.9
Other assaults	66,919	2,797	8,776	15,043	23,405	4.2	13.1	22.5	35.0
Forgery and counterfeiting	4,282	15	101	523	1,258	0.4	2.4	12.2	29.4
Fraud	23,829	65	343	1,957	4,976	0.3	1.4	8.2	20.9
Embezzlement	860	0	19	110	226	0.0	2.2	12.8	26.3
Stolen property; buying, receiving, possessing	4,422	93	523	1,272	1,970	2.1	11.8	28.8	44.5
Vandalism	12,896	1,318	3,546	5,956	7,789	10.2	27.5	46.2	60.4
Weapons; carrying, possessing, etc.	6,625	268	797	1,625	2,588	4.0	12.0	24.5	39.1
Prostitution and commercialized vice	208	1	6	27	57	0.5	2.9	13.0	27.4
Sex offenses (except forcible rape and prostitution)	4,971	409	932	1,603	2,171	8.2	18.7	32.2	43.7
Drug abuse violations	81,704	743	5,622	20,114	35,424	0.9	6.9	24.6	43.4
Gambling	208	5	16	52	66	2.4	7.7	25.0	31.7
Offenses against the family and children	12,083	135	387	1,025	2,297	1.1	3.2	8.5	19.0
Driving under the influence	157,703	25	1,748	14,344	39,798	*	1.1	9.1	25.2
Liquor laws	34,571	615	8,223	24,781	27,260	1.8	23.8	71.7	78.9
Drunkenness	17,838	48	499	2,286	4,986	0.3	2.8	12.8	28.0
Disorderly conduct	22,716	1,422	4,623	7,273	10,336	6.3	20.4	32.0	45.5
Vagrancy	253	3	28	64	100	1.2	11.1	25.3	39.5
All other offenses (except traffic)	217,103	2,455	11,684	36,181	70,911	1.1	5.4	16.7	32.7
Suspicion	95	7	14	23	32	7.4	14.7	24.2	33.7
Curfew and loitering law violations	462	132	462	462	462	28.6	100.0	100.0	100.0
Runaways	4,343	1,218	4,343	4,343	4,343	28.0	100.0	100.0	100.0

* Less than one-tenth of 1 percent.

Table 60. Nonmetropolitan County Arrests, Distribution by Sex, 2008

(Number, percent; 1,836 agencies; 2008 estimated population 19,987,986.)

Offense charged	Number of persons arrested			Percent male	Percent female	Percent distribution[1]		
	Total	Male	Female			Total	Male	Female
TOTAL	751,666	578,383	173,283	76.9	23.1	100.0	100.0	100.0
Violent Crime	22,781	19,042	3,739	83.6	16.4	3.0	3.3	2.2
Murder and nonnegligent manslaughter	607	531	76	87.5	12.5	0.1	0.1	*
Forcible rape	1,376	1,355	21	98.5	1.5	0.2	0.2	*
Robbery	1,764	1,561	203	88.5	11.5	0.2	0.3	0.1
Aggravated assault	19,034	15,595	3,439	81.9	18.1	2.5	2.7	2.0
Property Crime	54,794	42,142	12,652	76.9	23.1	7.3	7.3	7.3
Burglary	17,417	15,253	2,164	87.6	12.4	2.3	2.6	1.2
Larceny-theft	32,428	22,775	9,653	70.2	29.8	4.3	3.9	5.6
Motor vehicle theft	4,179	3,486	693	83.4	16.6	0.6	0.6	0.4
Arson	770	628	142	81.6	18.4	0.1	0.1	0.1
Other assaults	66,919	49,918	17,001	74.6	25.4	8.9	8.6	9.8
Forgery and counterfeiting	4,282	2,473	1,809	57.8	42.2	0.6	0.4	1.0
Fraud	23,829	12,304	11,525	51.6	48.4	3.2	2.1	6.7
Embezzlement	860	430	430	50.0	50.0	0.1	0.1	0.2
Stolen property; buying, receiving, possessing	4,422	3,667	755	82.9	17.1	0.6	0.6	0.4
Vandalism	12,896	10,697	2,199	82.9	17.1	1.7	1.8	1.3
Weapons; carrying, possessing, etc.	6,625	6,160	465	93.0	7.0	0.9	1.1	0.3
Prostitution and commercialized vice	208	120	88	57.7	42.3	*	*	0.1
Sex offenses (except forcible rape and prostitution)	4,971	4,717	254	94.9	5.1	0.7	0.8	0.1
Drug abuse violations	81,704	64,594	17,110	79.1	20.9	10.9	11.2	9.9
Gambling	208	159	49	76.4	23.6	*	*	*
Offenses against the family and children	12,083	9,690	2,393	80.2	19.8	1.6	1.7	1.4
Driving under the influence	157,703	126,222	31,481	80.0	20.0	21.0	21.8	18.2
Liquor laws	34,571	24,749	9,822	71.6	28.4	4.6	4.3	5.7
Drunkenness	17,838	14,553	3,285	81.6	18.4	2.4	2.5	1.9
Disorderly conduct	22,716	16,786	5,930	73.9	26.1	3.0	2.9	3.4
Vagrancy	253	206	47	81.4	18.6	*	*	*
All other offenses (except traffic)	217,103	167,383	49,720	77.1	22.9	28.9	28.9	28.7
Suspicion	95	74	21	77.9	22.1	*	*	*
Curfew and loitering law violations	462	288	174	62.3	37.7	0.1	*	0.1
Runaways	4,343	2,009	2,334	46.3	53.7	0.6	0.3	1.3

[1] Because of rounding, the percentages may not add to 100.0.
* Less than one-tenth of 1 percent.

Table 61. Nonmetropolitan County Arrests, Distribution by Race, 2008

(Number, percent; 1,836 agencies; 2008 estimated population 19,987,986.)

Offense charged	Total arrests					Percent distribution[1]					Arrests under 18				
	Total	White	Black	American Indian or Alaskan Native	Asian or Pacific Islander	Total	White	Black	American Indian or Alaskan Native	Asian or Pacific Islander	Total	White	Black	American Indian or Alaskan Native	Asian or Pacific Islander
TOTAL	745,092	607,289	103,747	24,274	9,782	100.0	81.5	13.9	3.3	1.3	64,377	51,795	8,271	2,412	1,899
Violent Crime	22,608	16,636	4,623	1,126	223	100.0	73.6	20.4	5.0	1.0	2,001	1,362	528	72	39
Murder and nonnegligent manslaughter	603	378	195	28	2	100.0	62.7	32.3	4.6	0.3	40	19	20	1	0
Forcible rape	1,370	1,124	192	42	12	100.0	82.0	14.0	3.1	0.9	195	161	29	4	1
Robbery	1,736	867	755	83	31	100.0	49.9	43.5	4.8	1.8	174	71	92	1	10
Aggravated assault	18,899	14,267	3,481	973	178	100.0	75.5	18.4	5.1	0.9	1,592	1,111	387	66	28
Property Crime	54,383	44,466	7,493	1,630	794	100.0	81.8	13.8	3.0	1.5	10,090	8,273	1,204	363	250
Burglary	17,280	14,117	2,456	558	149	100.0	81.7	14.2	3.2	0.9	3,757	3,066	491	156	44
Larceny-theft	32,206	26,327	4,424	899	556	100.0	81.7	13.7	2.8	1.7	5,229	4,280	611	156	182
Motor vehicle theft	4,135	3,354	547	151	83	100.0	81.1	13.2	3.7	2.0	906	752	89	43	22
Arson	762	668	66	22	6	100.0	87.7	8.7	2.9	0.8	198	175	13	8	2
Other															
Other assaults	66,439	52,836	10,160	2,572	871	100.0	79.5	15.3	3.9	1.3	8,711	6,280	1,951	301	179
Forgery and counterfeiting	4,220	3,309	838	47	26	100.0	78.4	19.9	1.1	0.6	101	88	6	6	1
Fraud	23,598	18,505	4,677	288	128	100.0	78.4	19.8	1.2	0.5	337	286	39	3	9
Embezzlement	844	704	116	11	13	100.0	83.4	13.7	1.3	1.5	19	14	3	1	1
Stolen property; buying, receiving, possessing	4,396	3,442	819	121	14	100.0	78.3	18.6	2.8	0.3	518	410	97	11	0
Vandalism	12,795	10,819	1,291	506	179	100.0	84.6	10.1	4.0	1.4	3,517	3,074	267	109	67
Weapons; carrying, possessing, etc.	6,569	4,957	1,323	228	61	100.0	75.5	20.1	3.5	0.9	796	577	179	30	10
Prostitution and commercialized vice	207	147	25	14	21	100.0	71.0	12.1	6.8	10.1	6	4	0	2	0
Sex offenses (except forcible rape and prostitution)	4,935	4,292	500	103	40	100.0	87.0	10.1	2.1	0.8	926	784	114	21	7
Drug abuse violations	80,929	65,428	13,109	1,619	773	100.0	80.8	16.2	2.0	1.0	5,573	4,762	539	138	134
Gambling	207	146	35	3	23	100.0	70.5	16.9	1.4	11.1	16	8	1	0	7
Offenses against the family and children	11,996	8,108	3,168	695	25	100.0	67.6	26.4	5.8	0.2	386	338	40	7	1
Driving under the influence	156,475	138,258	12,193	3,941	2,083	100.0	88.4	7.8	2.5	1.3	1,738	1,591	69	55	23
Liquor laws	34,031	30,849	1,576	1,240	366	100.0	90.6	4.6	3.6	1.1	8,128	7,577	154	304	93
Drunkenness	17,695	15,408	1,455	805	27	100.0	87.1	8.2	4.5	0.2	494	460	13	21	0
Disorderly conduct	22,503	17,451	3,699	1,186	167	100.0	77.5	16.4	5.3	0.7	4,600	3,039	1,253	270	38
Vagrancy	250	181	56	13	0	100.0	72.4	22.4	5.2	0.0	28	24	4	0	0
All other offenses (except traffic)	215,147	167,615	36,247	7,976	3,309	100.0	77.9	16.8	3.7	1.5	11,605	9,169	1,486	549	401
Suspicion	92	71	20	1	0	100.0	77.2	21.7	1.1	0.0	14	14	0	0	0
Curfew and loitering law violations	457	352	16	30	59	100.0	77.0	3.5	6.6	12.9	457	352	16	30	59
Runaways	4,316	3,309	308	119	580	100.0	76.7	7.1	2.8	13.4	4,316	3,309	308	119	580

[1] Because of rounding, the percentages may not add to 100.0.

Table 61. Nonmetropolitan County Arrests, Distribution by Race, 2008—*Continued*

(Number, percent; 1,836 agencies; 2008 estimated population 19,987,986.)

Offense charged	Percent distribution[1]					Arrests under 18					Percent distribution[1]				
	Total	White	Black	American Indian or Alaskan Native	Asian or Pacific Islander	Total	White	Black	American Indian or Alaskan Native	Asian or Pacific Islander	Total	White	Black	American Indian or Alaskan Native	Asian or Pacific Islander
TOTAL	100.0	80.5	12.8	3.7	2.9	680,715	555,494	95,476	21,862	7,883	100.0	81.6	14.0	3.2	1.2
Violent Crime	100.0	68.1	26.4	3.6	1.9	20,607	15,274	4,095	1,054	184	100.0	74.1	19.9	5.1	0.9
Murder and nonnegligent manslaughter	100.0	47.5	50.0	2.5	0.0	563	359	175	27	2	100.0	63.8	31.1	4.8	0.4
Forcible rape	100.0	82.6	14.9	2.1	0.5	1,175	963	163	38	11	100.0	82.0	13.9	3.2	0.9
Robbery	100.0	40.8	52.9	0.6	5.7	1,562	796	663	82	21	100.0	51.0	42.4	5.2	1.3
Aggravated assault	100.0	69.8	24.3	4.1	1.8	17,307	13,156	3,094	907	150	100.0	76.0	17.9	5.2	0.9
Property Crime	100.0	82.0	11.9	3.6	2.5	44,293	36,193	6,289	1,267	544	100.0	81.7	14.2	2.9	1.2
Burglary	100.0	81.6	13.1	4.2	1.2	13,523	11,051	1,965	402	105	100.0	81.7	14.5	3.0	0.8
Larceny-theft	100.0	81.9	11.7	3.0	3.5	26,977	22,047	3,813	743	374	100.0	81.7	14.1	2.8	1.4
Motor vehicle theft	100.0	83.0	9.8	4.7	2.4	3,229	2,602	458	108	61	100.0	80.6	14.2	3.3	1.9
Arson	100.0	88.4	6.6	4.0	1.0	564	493	53	14	4	100.0	87.4	9.4	2.5	0.7
Other															
Other assaults	100.0	72.1	22.4	3.5	2.1	57,728	46,556	8,209	2,271	692	100.0	80.6	14.2	3.9	1.2
Forgery and counterfeiting	100.0	87.1	5.9	5.9	1.0	4,119	3,221	832	41	25	100.0	78.2	20.2	1.0	0.6
Fraud	100.0	84.9	11.6	0.9	2.7	23,261	18,219	4,638	285	119	100.0	78.3	19.9	1.2	0.5
Embezzlement	100.0	73.7	15.8	5.3	5.3	825	690	113	10	12	100.0	83.6	13.7	1.2	1.5
Stolen property; buying, receiving, possessing	100.0	79.2	18.7	2.1	0.0	3,878	3,032	722	110	14	100.0	78.2	18.6	2.8	0.4
Vandalism	100.0	87.4	7.6	3.1	1.9	9,278	7,745	1,024	397	112	100.0	83.5	11.0	4.3	1.2
Weapons; carrying, possessing, etc.	100.0	72.5	22.5	3.8	1.3	5,773	4,380	1,144	198	51	100.0	75.9	19.8	3.4	0.9
Prostitution and commercialized vice	100.0	66.7	0.0	33.3	0.0	201	143	25	12	21	100.0	71.1	12.4	6.0	10.4
Sex offenses (except forcible rape and prostitution)	100.0	84.7	12.3	2.3	0.8	4,009	3,508	386	82	33	100.0	87.5	9.6	2.0	0.8
Drug abuse violations	100.0	85.4	9.7	2.5	2.4	75,356	60,666	12,570	1,481	639	100.0	80.5	16.7	2.0	0.8
Gambling	100.0	50.0	6.3	0.0	43.8	191	138	34	3	16	100.0	72.3	17.8	1.6	8.4
Offenses against the family and children	100.0	87.6	10.4	1.8	0.3	11,610	7,770	3,128	688	24	100.0	66.9	26.9	5.9	0.2
Driving under the influence	100.0	91.5	4.0	3.2	1.3	154,737	136,667	12,124	3,886	2,060	100.0	88.3	7.8	2.5	1.3
Liquor laws	100.0	93.2	1.9	3.7	1.1	25,903	23,272	1,422	936	273	100.0	89.8	5.5	3.6	1.1
Drunkenness	100.0	93.1	2.6	4.3	0.0	17,201	14,948	1,442	784	27	100.0	86.9	8.4	4.6	0.2
Disorderly conduct	100.0	66.1	27.2	5.9	0.8	17,903	14,412	2,446	916	129	100.0	80.5	13.7	5.1	0.7
Vagrancy	100.0	85.7	14.3	0.0	0.0	222	157	52	13	0	100.0	70.7	23.4	5.9	0.0
All other offenses (except traffic)	100.0	79.0	12.8	4.7	3.5	203,542	158,446	34,761	7,427	2,908	100.0	77.8	17.1	3.6	1.4
Suspicion	100.0	100.0	0.0	0.0	0.0	78	57	20	1	0	100.0	73.1	25.6	1.3	0.0
Curfew and loitering law violations	100.0	77.0	3.5	6.6	12.9	-	-	-	-	-	-	-	-	-	-
Runaways	100.0	76.7	7.1	2.8	13.4	-	-	-	-	-	-	-	-	-	-

[1] Because of rounding, the percentages may not add to 100.0.

Table 62. Suburban Area[1] Arrest Trends, 2007–2008

(Number, percent change; 5,889 agencies; 2008 estimated population 90,656,646; 2007 estimated population 90,106,531.)

Offense charged	Number of persons arrested								
	Total all ages			Under 18 years of age			18 years of age and over		
	2007	2008	Percent change	2007	2008	Percent change	2007	2008	Percent change
TOTAL[2]	3,716,948	3,650,091	-1.8	566,266	547,278	-3.4	3,150,682	3,102,813	-1.5
Violent Crime	129,897	125,433	-3.4	20,974	19,881	-5.2	108,923	105,552	-3.1
Murder and nonnegligent manslaughter	2,503	2,408	-3.8	214	192	-10.3	2,289	2,216	-3.2
Forcible rape	5,398	5,406	+0.1	898	825	-8.1	4,500	4,581	+1.8
Robbery	22,291	22,607	+1.4	5,802	6,007	+3.5	16,489	16,600	+0.7
Aggravated assault	99,705	95,012	-4.7	14,060	12,857	-8.6	85,645	82,155	-4.1
Property Crime	389,850	415,337	+6.5	102,377	108,640	+6.1	287,473	306,697	+6.7
Burglary	74,037	76,087	+2.8	20,462	21,093	+3.1	53,575	54,994	+2.6
Larceny-theft	287,842	314,592	+9.3	74,085	80,310	+8.4	213,757	234,282	+9.6
Motor vehicle theft	23,942	20,695	-13.6	5,613	5,174	-7.8	18,329	15,521	-15.3
Arson	4,029	3,963	-1.6	2,217	2,063	-6.9	1,812	1,900	+4.9
Other assaults	326,525	322,056	-1.4	66,916	64,803	-3.2	259,609	257,253	-0.9
Forgery and counterfeiting	25,520	23,230	-9.0	883	729	-17.4	24,637	22,501	-8.7
Fraud	85,146	79,059	-7.1	2,013	2,115	+5.1	83,133	76,944	-7.4
Embezzlement	5,312	5,231	-1.5	428	302	-29.4	4,884	4,929	+0.9
Stolen property; buying, receiving, possessing	31,468	28,830	-8.4	5,794	5,316	-8.2	25,674	23,514	-8.4
Vandalism	76,497	73,654	-3.7	31,895	29,953	-6.1	44,602	43,701	-2.0
Weapons; carrying, possessing, etc.	40,662	38,366	-5.6	10,494	9,549	-9.0	30,168	28,817	-4.5
Prostitution and commercialized vice	4,502	4,548	+1.0	105	133	+26.7	4,397	4,415	+0.4
Sex offenses (except forcible rape and prostitution)	20,593	19,894	-3.4	4,308	4,025	-6.6	16,285	15,869	-2.6
Drug abuse violations	430,800	406,182	-5.7	52,617	49,829	-5.3	378,183	356,353	-5.8
Gambling	1,064	853	-19.8	114	73	-36.0	950	780	-17.9
Offenses against the family and children	44,731	43,758	-2.2	1,885	2,032	+7.8	42,846	41,726	-2.6
Driving under the influence	459,850	465,391	+1.2	5,787	4,936	-14.7	454,063	460,455	+1.4
Liquor laws	180,225	176,250	-2.2	45,728	42,912	-6.2	134,497	133,338	-0.9
Drunkenness	133,396	135,069	+1.3	5,015	4,347	-13.3	128,381	130,722	+1.8
Disorderly conduct	180,540	177,760	-1.5	57,403	54,618	-4.9	123,137	123,142	*
Vagrancy	4,542	4,746	+4.5	592	614	+3.7	3,950	4,132	+4.6
All other offenses (except traffic)	1,099,273	1,060,930	-3.5	104,383	98,957	-5.2	994,890	961,973	-3.3
Suspicion	1,100	525	-52.3	151	87	-42.4	949	438	-53.8
Curfew and loitering law violations	20,497	19,156	-6.5	20,497	19,156	-6.5	-	-	-
Runaways	26,058	24,358	-6.5	26,058	24,358	-6.5	-	-	-

[1] Suburban areas include law enforcement agencies in cities with less than 50,000 inhabitants and county law enforcement agencies that are within a metropolitan statistical area. Suburban areas exclude all metropolitan agencies associated with a principal city.
[2] Does not include suspicion.
* Less than one-tenth of 1 percent.

Table 63. Suburban Area[1] Arrest Trends, by Age and Sex, 2007–2008

(Number, percent change; 5,889 agencies; 2008 estimated population 90,656,646; 2007 estimated population 90,106,531.)

Offense charged	Male						Female					
	Total			Under 18			Total			Under 18		
	2007	2008	Percent change	2007	2008	Percent change	2007	2008	Percent change	2007	2008	Percent change
TOTAL[2]	2,811,414	2,748,391	-2.2	402,213	388,447	-3.4	905,534	901,700	-0.4	164,053	158,831	-3.2
Violent Crime	106,646	103,029	-3.4	17,273	16,431	-4.9	23,251	22,404	-3.6	3,701	3,450	-6.8
Murder and nonnegligent manslaughter	2,222	2,129	-4.2	197	182	-7.6	281	279	-0.7	17	10	-41.2
Forcible rape	5,346	5,339	-0.1	887	815	-8.1	52	67	+28.8	11	10	-9.1
Robbery	19,842	20,100	+1.3	5,292	5,532	+4.5	2,449	2,507	+2.4	510	475	-6.9
Aggravated assault	79,236	75,461	-4.8	10,897	9,902	-9.1	20,469	19,551	-4.5	3,163	2,955	-6.6
Property Crime	262,357	274,655	+4.7	68,956	72,483	+5.1	127,493	140,682	+10.3	33,421	36,157	+8.2
Burglary	64,104	65,751	+2.6	18,347	18,825	+2.6	9,933	10,336	+4.1	2,115	2,268	+7.2
Larceny-theft	175,237	188,411	+7.5	44,099	47,540	+7.8	112,605	126,181	+12.1	29,986	32,770	+9.3
Motor vehicle theft	19,534	17,107	-12.4	4,551	4,301	-5.5	4,408	3,588	-18.6	1,062	873	-17.8
Arson	3,482	3,386	-2.8	1,959	1,817	-7.2	547	577	+5.5	258	246	-4.7
Other												
Other assaults	242,406	237,696	-1.9	44,946	43,441	-3.3	84,119	84,360	+0.3	21,970	21,362	-2.8
Forgery and counterfeiting	15,505	14,126	-8.9	619	483	-22.0	10,015	9,104	-9.1	264	246	-6.8
Fraud	45,957	43,165	-6.1	1,323	1,385	+4.7	39,189	35,894	-8.4	690	730	+5.8
Embezzlement	2,546	2,581	+1.4	266	177	-33.5	2,766	2,650	-4.2	162	125	-22.8
Stolen property; buying, receiving, possessing	25,134	22,995	-8.5	4,672	4,346	-7.0	6,334	5,835	-7.9	1,122	970	-13.5
Vandalism	64,213	61,596	-4.1	27,650	25,841	-6.5	12,284	12,058	-1.8	4,245	4,112	-3.1
Weapons; carrying, possessing, etc.	37,406	35,269	-5.7	9,452	8,559	-9.4	3,256	3,097	-4.9	1,042	990	-5.0
Prostitution and commercialized vice	1,763	1,713	-2.8	31	56	+80.6	2,739	2,835	+3.5	74	77	+4.1
Sex offenses (except forcible rape and prostitution)	19,374	18,606	-4.0	3,974	3,665	-7.8	1,219	1,288	+5.7	334	360	+7.8
Drug abuse violations	345,220	327,032	-5.3	43,192	41,226	-4.6	85,580	79,150	-7.5	9,425	8,603	-8.7
Gambling	877	694	-20.9	105	65	-38.1	187	159	-15.0	9	8	-11.1
Offenses against the family and children	35,447	34,573	-2.5	1,188	1,363	+14.7	9,284	9,185	-1.1	697	669	-4.0
Driving under the influence	362,563	363,313	+0.2	4,390	3,718	-15.3	97,287	102,078	+4.9	1,397	1,218	-12.8
Liquor laws	127,825	124,549	-2.6	28,476	26,606	-6.6	52,400	51,701	-1.3	17,252	16,306	-5.5
Drunkenness	109,937	110,914	+0.9	3,679	3,284	-10.7	23,459	24,155	+3.0	1,336	1,063	-20.4
Disorderly conduct	132,375	130,716	-1.3	39,077	37,470	-4.1	48,165	47,044	-2.3	18,326	17,148	-6.4
Vagrancy	3,526	3,628	+2.9	440	476	+8.2	1,016	1,118	+10.0	152	138	-9.2
All other offenses (except traffic)	844,645	813,466	-3.7	76,812	73,297	-4.6	254,628	247,464	-2.8	27,571	25,660	-6.9
Suspicion	860	397	-53.8	115	67	-41.7	240	128	-46.7	36	20	-44.4
Curfew and loitering law violations	13,955	12,873	-7.8	13,955	12,873	-7.8	6,542	6,283	-4.0	6,542	6,283	-4.0
Runaways	11,737	11,202	-4.6	11,737	11,202	-4.6	14,321	13,156	-8.1	14,321	13,156	-8.1

[1] Suburban areas include law enforcement agencies in cities with less than 50,000 inhabitants and county law enforcement agencies that are within a metropolitan statistical area. Suburban areas exclude all metropolitan agencies associated with a principal city.
[2] Does not include suspicion.

Table 64. Suburban Area[1] Arrests, Distribution by Age, 2008

(Number, percent; 6,405 agencies; 2008 estimated population 101,327,487.)

Offense charged	Total all ages	Ages under 15	Ages under 18	Ages 18 and over	Under 10	10–12	13–14	15	16	17	18	19	20
TOTAL	4,165,010	165,555	617,661	3,547,349	4,382	34,072	127,101	118,240	153,690	180,176	217,946	216,293	194,939
Total percent distribution[2]	100.0	4.0	14.8	85.2	0.1	0.8	3.1	2.8	3.7	4.3	5.2	5.2	4.7
Violent Crime	151,532	6,569	24,052	127,480	189	1,461	4,919	4,653	5,870	6,960	7,957	7,530	6,461
Violent crime percent distribution[2]	100.0	4.3	15.9	84.1	0.1	1.0	3.2	3.1	3.9	4.6	5.3	5.0	4.3
Murder and nonnegligent manslaughter	2,972	18	250	2,722	0	1	17	42	78	112	191	202	196
Forcible rape	5,977	301	905	5,072	3	74	224	168	198	238	349	321	274
Robbery	28,029	1,312	7,284	20,745	13	152	1,147	1,461	2,004	2,507	2,801	2,355	1,707
Aggravated assault	114,554	4,938	15,613	98,941	173	1,234	3,531	2,982	3,590	4,103	4,616	4,652	4,284
Property Crime	484,666	35,447	126,117	358,549	829	7,424	27,194	25,072	31,227	34,371	35,285	28,840	22,579
Property crime percent distribution[2]	100.0	7.3	26.0	74.0	0.2	1.5	5.6	5.2	6.4	7.1	7.3	6.0	4.7
Burglary	86,857	6,859	24,020	62,837	221	1,395	5,243	4,838	5,844	6,479	7,425	6,046	4,470
Larceny-theft	369,806	26,162	94,017	275,789	489	5,514	20,159	18,477	23,420	25,958	25,976	21,340	16,872
Motor vehicle theft	23,597	1,141	5,842	17,755	9	132	1,000	1,360	1,657	1,684	1,666	1,257	1,085
Arson	4,406	1,285	2,238	2,168	110	383	792	397	306	250	218	197	152
Other													
Other assaults	368,424	27,620	72,620	295,804	811	7,074	19,735	14,303	15,907	14,790	12,881	12,194	11,938
Forgery and counterfeiting	27,345	109	820	26,525	2	23	84	74	187	450	954	1,243	1,296
Fraud	82,906	354	2,421	80,485	15	59	280	319	638	1,110	1,998	2,529	2,823
Embezzlement	6,287	15	360	5,927	4	3	8	14	107	224	434	434	416
Stolen property; buying, receiving, possessing	33,541	1,368	6,114	27,427	15	223	1,130	1,207	1,650	1,889	2,355	2,044	1,670
Vandalism	84,055	13,438	33,268	50,787	625	3,386	9,427	6,101	6,666	7,063	6,378	4,612	3,528
Weapons; carrying, possessing, etc.	45,035	3,815	10,896	34,139	217	1,033	2,565	1,966	2,346	2,769	3,115	2,681	2,209
Prostitution and commercialized vice	6,505	29	172	6,333	0	3	26	20	52	71	193	242	253
Sex offenses (except forcible rape and prostitution)	22,806	2,200	4,603	18,203	105	616	1,479	788	777	838	1,008	873	801
Drug abuse violations	469,767	8,057	55,575	414,192	84	885	7,088	8,915	15,029	23,574	35,357	33,809	28,746
Gambling	1,008	24	79	929	2	3	19	18	22	15	39	41	37
Offenses against the family and children	48,629	592	2,394	46,235	30	109	453	478	623	701	818	775	923
Driving under the influence	507,664	66	5,298	502,366	13	7	46	166	1,133	3,933	10,944	15,080	16,945
Liquor laws	196,121	3,850	46,653	149,468	47	309	3,494	6,722	13,306	22,775	38,484	38,615	29,608
Drunkenness	160,349	478	4,647	155,702	21	25	432	716	1,216	2,237	5,379	5,700	5,138
Disorderly conduct	205,143	21,393	60,776	144,367	327	4,827	16,239	12,616	13,787	12,980	10,324	8,414	7,692
Vagrancy	6,112	160	691	5,421	0	25	135	152	204	175	301	232	209
All other offenses (except traffic)	1,207,516	26,357	110,987	1,096,529	787	4,622	20,948	21,660	28,734	34,236	43,682	50,367	51,649
Suspicion	592	32	111	481	0	5	27	31	28	20	60	38	18
Curfew and loitering law violations	21,747	5,627	21,747	-	74	779	4,774	5,173	6,368	4,579	-	-	-
Runaways	27,260	7,955	27,260	-	185	1,171	6,599	7,076	7,813	4,416	-	-	-

[1] Suburban areas include law enforcement agencies in cities with less than 50,000 inhabitants and county law enforcement agencies that are within a metropolitan statistical area. Suburban areas exclude all metropolitan agencies associated with a principal city.

[2] Because of rounding, the percentages may not add to 100.0.

Table 64. Suburban Area[1] Arrests, Distribution by Age, 2008—*Continued*

(Number, percent; 6,405 agencies; 2008 estimated population 101,327,487.)

Offense charged	21	22	23	24	25–29	30–34	35–39	40–44	45–49	50–54	55–59	60–64	65 and over
TOTAL	173,245	160,836	150,801	138,899	594,399	412,012	367,301	333,250	279,176	165,654	79,075	35,803	27,720
Total percent distribution[2]	4.2	3.9	3.6	3.3	14.3	9.9	8.8	8.0	6.7	4.0	1.9	0.9	0.7
Violent Crime	6,166	5,728	5,544	5,052	21,577	15,262	13,620	12,078	9,866	5,539	2,643	1,303	1,154
Violent crime percent distribution[2]	4.1	3.8	3.7	3.3	14.2	10.1	9.0	8.0	6.5	3.7	1.7	0.9	0.8
Murder and nonnegligent manslaughter	152	128	142	101	486	275	287	208	130	90	58	37	39
Forcible rape	271	226	218	185	775	594	559	492	339	224	111	54	80
Robbery	1,370	1,209	1,062	920	3,314	1,817	1,522	1,271	836	370	134	37	20
Aggravated assault	4,373	4,165	4,122	3,846	17,002	12,576	11,252	10,107	8,561	4,855	2,340	1,175	1,015
Property Crime	18,575	16,221	14,439	12,943	55,143	37,753	34,365	31,450	24,699	14,211	6,384	3,024	2,638
Property crime percent distribution[2]	3.8	3.3	3.0	2.7	11.4	7.8	7.1	6.5	5.1	2.9	1.3	0.6	0.5
Burglary	3,748	3,148	2,716	2,413	10,096	6,400	5,482	4,855	3,412	1,612	631	211	172
Larceny-theft	13,764	12,183	10,875	9,752	41,664	28,932	26,817	24,917	20,067	12,023	5,508	2,713	2,386
Motor vehicle theft	948	790	772	713	3,107	2,170	1,893	1,512	1,070	460	195	72	45
Arson	115	100	76	65	276	251	173	166	150	116	50	28	35
Other													
Other assaults	12,196	11,765	11,509	10,943	50,589	38,000	36,494	32,711	26,700	14,755	6,852	3,307	2,970
Forgery and counterfeiting	1,120	1,062	1,118	1,042	5,245	3,794	3,328	2,597	1,960	1,072	423	155	116
Fraud	2,639	2,682	2,618	2,592	13,994	12,107	11,369	9,525	7,166	4,299	2,246	1,053	845
Embezzlement	338	295	258	231	888	719	608	518	378	227	117	36	30
Stolen property; buying, receiving, possessing	1,426	1,325	1,167	1,025	4,760	3,261	2,793	2,359	1,715	910	377	151	89
Vandalism	3,392	2,750	2,351	2,054	7,895	4,744	4,109	3,545	2,634	1,545	616	328	306
Weapons; carrying, possessing, etc.	2,103	1,936	1,720	1,551	5,913	3,435	2,655	2,263	1,966	1,274	653	361	304
Prostitution and commercialized vice	245	294	241	187	1,055	832	764	782	607	318	159	70	91
Sex offenses (except forcible rape and prostitution)	729	643	644	555	2,439	1,948	1,939	1,949	1,685	1,142	724	502	622
Drug abuse violations	24,931	22,118	19,894	18,292	72,397	44,197	35,381	30,845	25,412	14,088	5,848	1,970	907
Gambling	18	23	13	24	116	95	119	95	93	55	68	46	47
Offenses against the family and children	1,078	1,121	1,316	1,308	8,026	7,728	7,987	6,690	4,592	2,317	975	368	213
Driving under the influence	24,027	24,522	24,218	22,206	92,545	61,464	53,485	49,799	45,889	30,415	16,653	8,229	5,945
Liquor laws	4,594	3,118	2,401	1,991	7,038	4,638	4,161	4,519	4,568	3,036	1,534	699	464
Drunkenness	7,797	6,889	6,306	5,695	23,381	16,530	16,292	17,601	17,811	11,742	5,567	2,363	1,511
Disorderly conduct	8,910	7,791	6,800	5,952	22,892	14,661	13,451	13,014	11,453	6,892	3,239	1,547	1,335
Vagrancy	171	141	172	162	759	569	628	719	596	420	204	84	54
All other offenses (except traffic)	52,768	50,389	48,054	45,080	197,676	140,237	123,704	110,152	89,350	51,364	23,783	10,198	8,076
Suspicion	22	23	18	14	71	38	49	39	36	33	10	9	3
Curfew and loitering law violations	-	-	-	-	-	-	-	-	-	-	-	-	-
Runaways	-	-	-	-	-	-	-	-	-	-	-	-	-

[1] Suburban areas include law enforcement agencies in cities with less than 50,000 inhabitants and county law enforcement agencies that are within a metropolitan statistical area. Suburban areas exclude all metropolitan agencies associated with a principal city.

[2] Because of rounding, the percentages may not add to 100.0.

Table 65. Suburban Area[1] Arrests of Persons Under 15, 18, 21, and 25 Years of Age, 2008

(Number, percent; 6,405 agencies; 2008 estimated population 101,327,487.)

Offense charged	Total all ages	Number of persons arrested				Percent of total all ages			
		Under 15	Under 18	Under 21	Under 25	Under 15	Under 18	Under 21	Under 25
TOTAL	4,165,010	165,555	617,661	1,246,839	1,870,620	4.0	14.8	29.9	44.9
Violent Crime	151,532	6,569	24,052	46,000	68,490	4.3	15.9	30.4	45.2
Murder and nonnegligent manslaughter	2,972	18	250	839	1,362	0.6	8.4	28.2	45.8
Forcible rape	5,977	301	905	1,849	2,749	5.0	15.1	30.9	46.0
Robbery	28,029	1,312	7,284	14,147	18,708	4.7	26.0	50.5	66.7
Aggravated assault	114,554	4,938	15,613	29,165	45,671	4.3	13.6	25.5	39.9
Property Crime	484,666	35,447	126,117	212,821	274,999	7.3	26.0	43.9	56.7
Burglary	86,857	6,859	24,020	41,961	53,986	7.9	27.7	48.3	62.2
Larceny-theft	369,806	26,162	94,017	158,205	204,779	7.1	25.4	42.8	55.4
Motor vehicle theft	23,597	1,141	5,842	9,850	13,073	4.8	24.8	41.7	55.4
Arson	4,406	1,285	2,238	2,805	3,161	29.2	50.8	63.7	71.7
Other									
Other assaults	368,424	27,620	72,620	109,633	156,046	7.5	19.7	29.8	42.4
Forgery and counterfeiting	27,345	109	820	4,313	8,655	0.4	3.0	15.8	31.7
Fraud	82,906	354	2,421	9,771	20,302	0.4	2.9	11.8	24.5
Embezzlement	6,287	15	360	1,644	2,766	0.2	5.7	26.1	44.0
Stolen property; buying, receiving, possessing	33,541	1,368	6,114	12,183	17,126	4.1	18.2	36.3	51.1
Vandalism	84,055	13,438	33,268	47,786	58,333	16.0	39.6	56.9	69.4
Weapons; carrying, possessing, etc.	45,035	3,815	10,896	18,901	26,211	8.5	24.2	42.0	58.2
Prostitution and commercialized vice	6,505	29	172	860	1,827	0.4	2.6	13.2	28.1
Sex offenses (except forcible rape and prostitution)	22,806	2,200	4,603	7,285	9,856	9.6	20.2	31.9	43.2
Drug abuse violations	469,767	8,057	55,575	153,487	238,722	1.7	11.8	32.7	50.8
Gambling	1,008	24	79	196	274	2.4	7.8	19.4	27.2
Offenses against the family and children	48,629	592	2,394	4,910	9,733	1.2	4.9	10.1	20.0
Driving under the influence	507,664	66	5,298	48,267	143,240	*	1.0	9.5	28.2
Liquor laws	196,121	3,850	46,653	153,360	165,464	2.0	23.8	78.2	84.4
Drunkenness	160,349	478	4,647	20,864	47,551	0.3	2.9	13.0	29.7
Disorderly conduct	205,143	21,393	60,776	87,206	116,659	10.4	29.6	42.5	56.9
Vagrancy	6,112	160	691	1,433	2,079	2.6	11.3	23.4	34.0
All other offenses (except traffic)	1,207,516	26,357	110,987	256,685	452,976	2.2	9.2	21.3	37.5
Suspicion	592	32	111	227	304	5.4	18.8	38.3	51.4
Curfew and loitering law violations	21,747	5,627	21,747	21,747	21,747	25.9	100.0	100.0	100.0
Runaways	27,260	7,955	27,260	27,260	27,260	29.2	100.0	100.0	100.0

[1] Suburban areas include law enforcement agencies in cities with less than 50,000 inhabitants and county law enforcement agencies that are within a metropolitan statistical area. Suburban areas exclude all metropolitan agencies associated with a principal city.
* Less than one-tenth of 1 percent.

Table 66. Suburban Area[1] Arrests, Distribution by Sex, 2008

(Number, percent; 6,405 agencies; 2008 estimated population 101,327,487.)

Offense charged	Number of persons arrested			Percent male	Percent female	Percent distribution[2]		
	Total	Male	Female			Total	Male	Female
TOTAL	4,165,010	3,135,905	1,029,105	75.3	24.7	100.0	100.0	100.0
Violent Crime	151,532	124,221	27,311	82.0	18.0	3.6	4.0	2.7
Murder and nonnegligent manslaughter	2,972	2,643	329	88.9	11.1	0.1	0.1	*
Forcible rape	5,977	5,902	75	98.7	1.3	0.1	0.2	*
Robbery	28,029	24,900	3,129	88.8	11.2	0.7	0.8	0.3
Aggravated assault	114,554	90,776	23,778	79.2	20.8	2.8	2.9	2.3
Property Crime	484,666	318,040	166,626	65.6	34.4	11.6	10.1	16.2
Burglary	86,857	75,064	11,793	86.4	13.6	2.1	2.4	1.1
Larceny-theft	369,806	219,724	150,082	59.4	40.6	8.9	7.0	14.6
Motor vehicle theft	23,597	19,483	4,114	82.6	17.4	0.6	0.6	0.4
Arson	4,406	3,769	637	85.5	14.5	0.1	0.1	0.1
Other								
Other assaults	368,424	272,036	96,388	73.8	26.2	8.8	8.7	9.4
Forgery and counterfeiting	27,345	16,701	10,644	61.1	38.9	0.7	0.5	1.0
Fraud	82,906	46,028	36,878	55.5	44.5	2.0	1.5	3.6
Embezzlement	6,287	3,070	3,217	48.8	51.2	0.2	0.1	0.3
Stolen property; buying, receiving, possessing	33,541	26,903	6,638	80.2	19.8	0.8	0.9	0.6
Vandalism	84,055	70,187	13,868	83.5	16.5	2.0	2.2	1.3
Weapons; carrying, possessing, etc.	45,035	41,425	3,610	92.0	8.0	1.1	1.3	0.4
Prostitution and commercialized vice	6,505	2,337	4,168	35.9	64.1	0.2	0.1	0.4
Sex offenses (except forcible rape and prostitution)	22,806	21,317	1,489	93.5	6.5	0.5	0.7	0.1
Drug abuse violations	469,767	378,861	90,906	80.6	19.4	11.3	12.1	8.8
Gambling	1,008	804	204	79.8	20.2	*	*	*
Offenses against the family and children	48,629	38,087	10,542	78.3	21.7	1.2	1.2	1.0
Driving under the influence	507,664	396,564	111,100	78.1	21.9	12.2	12.6	10.8
Liquor laws	196,121	138,991	57,130	70.9	29.1	4.7	4.4	5.6
Drunkenness	160,349	132,049	28,300	82.4	17.6	3.8	4.2	2.7
Disorderly conduct	205,143	150,773	54,370	73.5	26.5	4.9	4.8	5.3
Vagrancy	6,112	4,602	1,510	75.3	24.7	0.1	0.1	0.1
All other offenses (except traffic)	1,207,516	925,240	282,276	76.6	23.4	29.0	29.5	27.4
Suspicion	592	455	137	76.9	23.1	*	*	*
Curfew and loitering law violations	21,747	14,732	7,015	67.7	32.3	0.5	0.5	0.7
Runaways	27,260	12,482	14,778	45.8	54.2	0.7	0.4	1.4

[1] Suburban areas include law enforcement agencies in cities with less than 50,000 inhabitants and county law enforcement agencies that are within a metropolitan statistical area. Suburban areas exclude all metropolitan agencies associated with a principal city.
[2] Because of rounding, the percentages may not add to 100.0.
* Less than one-tenth of 1 percent.

Table 67. Suburban Area[1] Arrests, Distribution by Race, 2008

(Number, percent; 6,404 agencies; 2008 estimated population 101,304,348.)

Offense charged	Total arrests					Percent distribution[2]					Arrests under 18				
	Total	White	Black	American Indian or Alaskan Native	Asian or Pacific Islander	Total	White	Black	American Indian or Alaskan Native	Asian or Pacific Islander	Total	White	Black	American Indian or Alaskan Native	Asian or Pacific Islander
TOTAL	4,140,443	3,115,053	964,802	28,834	31,754	100.0	75.2	23.3	0.7	0.8	615,070	440,921	164,880	3,789	5,480
Violent Crime	151,038	99,266	49,470	1,071	1,231	100.0	65.7	32.8	0.7	0.8	23,976	12,428	11,263	129	156
Murder and nonnegligent manslaughter	2,960	1,718	1,210	13	19	100.0	58.0	40.9	0.4	0.6	249	111	134	2	2
Forcible rape	5,947	4,405	1,450	40	52	100.0	74.1	24.4	0.7	0.9	900	644	248	5	3
Robbery	27,937	12,941	14,728	112	156	100.0	46.3	52.7	0.4	0.6	7,272	2,355	4,846	15	56
Aggravated assault	114,194	80,202	32,082	906	1,004	100.0	70.2	28.1	0.8	0.9	15,555	9,318	6,035	107	95
Property Crime	482,091	342,024	132,584	2,904	4,579	100.0	70.9	27.5	0.6	0.9	125,422	83,250	40,000	671	1,501
Burglary	86,474	63,791	21,724	409	550	100.0	73.8	25.1	0.5	0.6	23,926	16,574	7,057	103	192
Larceny-theft	367,754	258,219	103,373	2,335	3,827	100.0	70.2	28.1	0.6	1.0	93,448	61,269	30,425	524	1,230
Motor vehicle theft	23,476	16,463	6,723	135	155	100.0	70.1	28.6	0.6	0.7	5,823	3,605	2,139	34	45
Arson	4,387	3,551	764	25	47	100.0	80.9	17.4	0.6	1.1	2,225	1,802	379	10	34
Other															
Other assaults	367,031	268,527	93,081	2,570	2,853	100.0	73.2	25.4	0.7	0.8	72,391	46,060	25,478	364	489
Forgery and counterfeiting	27,098	19,147	7,632	82	237	100.0	70.7	28.2	0.3	0.9	814	575	225	3	11
Fraud	82,422	56,540	25,064	331	487	100.0	68.6	30.4	0.4	0.6	2,399	1,558	807	15	19
Embezzlement	6,192	4,012	2,117	12	51	100.0	64.8	34.2	0.2	0.8	357	217	138	0	2
Stolen property; buying, receiving, possessing	33,409	22,717	10,290	174	228	100.0	68.0	30.8	0.5	0.7	6,100	3,714	2,302	27	57
Vandalism	83,709	67,468	15,026	617	598	100.0	80.6	18.0	0.7	0.7	33,132	27,098	5,598	201	235
Weapons; carrying, possessing, etc.	44,882	29,384	14,949	238	311	100.0	65.5	33.3	0.5	0.7	10,854	7,156	3,539	50	109
Prostitution and commercialized vice	6,486	4,209	1,939	32	306	100.0	64.9	29.9	0.5	4.7	172	102	64	1	5
Sex offenses (except forcible rape and prostitution)	22,698	17,836	4,489	151	222	100.0	78.6	19.8	0.7	1.0	4,567	3,394	1,122	20	31
Drug abuse violations	467,425	347,396	114,906	2,187	2,936	100.0	74.3	24.6	0.5	0.6	55,385	44,525	10,134	283	443
Gambling	1,000	556	371	12	61	100.0	55.6	37.1	1.2	6.1	79	20	58	0	1
Offenses against the family and children	47,703	31,592	15,529	298	284	100.0	66.2	32.6	0.6	0.6	2,376	1,784	575	13	4
Driving under the influence	504,697	449,805	46,882	3,163	4,847	100.0	89.1	9.3	0.6	1.0	5,260	4,977	209	33	41
Liquor laws	194,303	172,560	17,449	2,276	2,018	100.0	88.8	9.0	1.2	1.0	46,382	42,923	2,446	510	503
Drunkenness	159,139	139,206	17,398	1,770	765	100.0	87.5	10.9	1.1	0.5	4,634	4,223	317	66	28
Disorderly conduct	204,084	144,928	56,240	1,522	1,394	100.0	71.0	27.6	0.7	0.7	60,608	37,735	22,115	308	450
Vagrancy	6,104	4,080	1,987	14	23	100.0	66.8	32.6	0.2	0.4	691	562	126	0	3
All other offenses (except traffic)	1,199,476	857,367	325,152	9,056	7,901	100.0	71.5	27.1	0.8	0.7	110,487	82,401	26,361	751	974
Suspicion	583	264	304	10	5	100.0	45.3	52.1	1.7	0.9	111	50	60	0	1
Curfew and loitering law violations	21,682	16,230	5,176	96	180	100.0	74.9	23.9	0.4	0.8	21,682	16,230	5,176	96	180
Runaways	27,191	19,939	6,767	248	237	100.0	73.3	24.9	0.9	0.9	27,191	19,939	6,767	248	237

[1] Suburban areas include law enforcement agencies in cities with less than 50,000 inhabitants and county law enforcement agencies that are within a metropolitan statistical area. Suburban areas exclude all metropolitan agencies associated with a principal city.

[2] Because of rounding, the percentages may not add to 100.0.

Table 67. Suburban Area[1] Arrests, Distribution by Race, 2008—*Continued*

(Number, percent; 6,404 agencies; 2008 estimated population 101,304,348.)

Offense charged	Percent distribution[2]					Arrests under 18					Percent distribution[2]				
	Total	White	Black	American Indian or Alaskan Native	Asian or Pacific Islander	Total	White	Black	American Indian or Alaskan Native	Asian or Pacific Islander	Total	White	Black	American Indian or Alaskan Native	Asian or Pacific Islander
TOTAL	100.0	71.7	26.8	0.6	0.9	3,525,373	2,674,132	799,922	25,045	26,274	100.0	75.9	22.7	0.7	0.7
Violent Crime	100.0	51.8	47.0	0.5	0.7	127,062	86,838	38,207	942	1,075	100.0	68.3	30.1	0.7	0.8
Murder and nonnegligent manslaughter	100.0	44.6	53.8	0.8	0.8	2,711	1,607	1,076	11	17	100.0	59.3	39.7	0.4	0.6
Forcible rape	100.0	71.6	27.6	0.6	0.3	5,047	3,761	1,202	35	49	100.0	74.5	23.8	0.7	1.0
Robbery	100.0	32.4	66.6	0.2	0.8	20,665	10,586	9,882	97	100	100.0	51.2	47.8	0.5	0.5
Aggravated assault	100.0	59.9	38.8	0.7	0.6	98,639	70,884	26,047	799	909	100.0	71.9	26.4	0.8	0.9
Property Crime	100.0	66.4	31.9	0.5	1.2	356,669	258,774	92,584	2,233	3,078	100.0	72.6	26.0	0.6	0.9
Burglary	100.0	69.3	29.5	0.4	0.8	62,548	47,217	14,667	306	358	100.0	75.5	23.4	0.5	0.6
Larceny-theft	100.0	65.6	32.6	0.6	1.3	274,306	196,950	72,948	1,811	2,597	100.0	71.8	26.6	0.7	0.9
Motor vehicle theft	100.0	61.9	36.7	0.6	0.8	17,653	12,858	4,584	101	110	100.0	72.8	26.0	0.6	0.6
Arson	100.0	81.0	17.0	0.4	1.5	2,162	1,749	385	15	13	100.0	80.9	17.8	0.7	0.6
Other															
Other assaults	100.0	63.6	35.2	0.5	0.7	294,640	222,467	67,603	2,206	2,364	100.0	75.5	22.9	0.7	0.8
Forgery and counterfeiting	100.0	70.6	27.6	0.4	1.4	26,284	18,572	7,407	79	226	100.0	70.7	28.2	0.3	0.9
Fraud	100.0	64.9	33.6	0.6	0.8	80,023	54,982	24,257	316	468	100.0	68.7	30.3	0.4	0.6
Embezzlement	100.0	60.8	38.7	0.0	0.6	5,835	3,795	1,979	12	49	100.0	65.0	33.9	0.2	0.8
Stolen property; buying, receiving, possessing	100.0	60.9	37.7	0.4	0.9	27,309	19,003	7,988	147	171	100.0	69.6	29.3	0.5	0.6
Vandalism	100.0	81.8	16.9	0.6	0.7	50,577	40,370	9,428	416	363	100.0	79.8	18.6	0.8	0.7
Weapons; carrying, possessing, etc.	100.0	65.9	32.6	0.5	1.0	34,028	22,228	11,410	188	202	100.0	65.3	33.5	0.6	0.6
Prostitution and commercialized vice	100.0	59.3	37.2	0.6	2.9	6,314	4,107	1,875	31	301	100.0	65.0	29.7	0.5	4.8
Sex offenses (except forcible rape and prostitution)	100.0	74.3	24.6	0.4	0.7	18,131	14,442	3,367	131	191	100.0	79.7	18.6	0.7	1.1
Drug abuse violations	100.0	80.4	18.3	0.5	0.8	412,040	302,871	104,772	1,904	2,493	100.0	73.5	25.4	0.5	0.6
Gambling	100.0	25.3	73.4	0.0	1.3	921	536	313	12	60	100.0	58.2	34.0	1.3	6.5
Offenses against the family and children	100.0	75.1	24.2	0.5	0.2	45,327	29,808	14,954	285	280	100.0	65.8	33.0	0.6	0.6
Driving under the influence	100.0	94.6	4.0	0.6	0.8	499,437	444,828	46,673	3,130	4,806	100.0	89.1	9.3	0.6	1.0
Liquor laws	100.0	92.5	5.3	1.1	1.1	147,921	129,637	15,003	1,766	1,515	100.0	87.6	10.1	1.2	1.0
Drunkenness	100.0	91.1	6.8	1.4	0.6	154,505	134,983	17,081	1,704	737	100.0	87.4	11.1	1.1	0.5
Disorderly conduct	100.0	62.3	36.5	0.5	0.7	143,476	107,193	34,125	1,214	944	100.0	74.7	23.8	0.8	0.7
Vagrancy	100.0	81.3	18.2	0.0	0.4	5,413	3,518	1,861	14	20	100.0	65.0	34.4	0.3	0.4
All other offenses (except traffic)	100.0	74.6	23.9	0.7	0.9	1,088,989	774,966	298,791	8,305	6,927	100.0	71.2	27.4	0.8	0.6
Suspicion	100.0	45.0	54.1	0.0	0.9	472	214	244	10	4	100.0	45.3	51.7	2.1	0.8
Curfew and loitering law violations	100.0	74.9	23.9	0.4	0.8	-	-	-	-	-	-	-	-	-	-
Runaways	100.0	73.3	24.9	0.9	0.9	-	-	-	-	-	-	-	-	-	-

[1] Suburban areas include law enforcement agencies in cities with less than 50,000 inhabitants and county law enforcement agencies that are within a metropolitan statistical area. Suburban areas exclude all metropolitan agencies associated with a principal city.

[2] Because of rounding, the percentages may not add to 100.0.

Table 68. Police Disposition of Juvenile Offenders Taken into Custody, 2008

(Number, percent.)

Population group	Total[1]	Handled within department and released	Referred to juvenile court jurisdiction	Referred to welfare agency	Referred to other police agency	Referred to criminal or adult court	Number of agencies	2008 estimated population
TOTAL AGENCIES:								
Number	602,210	131,631	399,059	3,081	6,797	61,642	5,251	118,759,497
Percent[2]	100.0	21.9	66.3	0.5	1.1	10.2		
Total Cities								
Number	510,252	119,696	332,881	2,636	6,101	48,938	4,060	88,591,101
Percent[2]	100.0	23.5	65.2	0.5	1.2	9.6		
GROUP I (250,000 and over)								
Number	141,432	43,632	93,552	17	789	3,442	39	26,875,238
Percent[2]	100.0	30.9	66.1	*	0.6	2.4		
GROUP II (100,000 to 249,999)								
Number	71,987	17,768	48,745	478	1,523	3,473	86	12,710,757
Percent[2]	100.0	24.7	67.7	0.7	2.1	4.8		
GROUP III (50,000 to 99,999)								
Number	96,973	20,111	66,612	681	1,256	8,313	230	15,525,328
Percent[2]	100.0	20.7	68.7	0.7	1.3	8.6		
GROUP IV (25,000 to 49,999)								
Number	63,330	11,939	41,189	583	1,259	8,360	341	11,778,506
Percent[2]	100.0	18.9	65.0	0.9	2.0	13.2		
GROUP V (10,000 to 24,999)								
Number	71,991	13,299	45,174	507	559	12,452	776	12,367,656
Percent[2]	100.0	18.5	62.7	0.7	0.8	17.3		
GROUP VI (under 10,000)								
Number	64,539	12,947	37,609	370	715	12,898	2,588	9,333,616
Percent[2]	100.0	20.1	58.3	0.6	1.1	20.0		
Metropolitan Counties								
Number	71,773	9,165	52,602	257	575	9,174	545	22,370,406
Percent[2]	100.0	12.8	73.3	0.4	0.8	12.8		
Nonmetropolitan Counties								
Number	20,185	2,770	13,576	188	121	3,530	646	7,797,990
Percent[2]	100.0	13.7	67.3	0.9	0.6	17.5		
SUBURBAN AREAS[3]								
Number	250,877	48,450	160,812	1,497	2,311	37,807	3,266	56,299,487
Percent[2]	100.0	19.3	64.1	0.6	0.9	15.1		

[1] Includes all offenses except traffic and neglect cases.
[2] Because of rounding, the percentages may not add to 100.0.
[3] Suburban areas include law enforcement agencies in cities with less than 50,000 inhabitants and county law enforcement agencies that are within a metropolitan statistical area. Suburban areas exclude all metropolitan agencies associated with a principal city. The agencies associated with suburban areas also appear in other groups within this table.
* Less than one-tenth of 1 percent.

Table 69. State Arrests, 2008

(Number.)

State	Total all classes[1]	Violent crime[2]	Property crime[2]	Murder and non-negligent man-slaughter	Forcible rape	Robbery	Aggra-vated assault	Burglary	Larceny-theft	Motor vehicle theft	Arson	Other assaults
ALABAMA												
Under 18	12,832	719	3,773	21	26	351	321	760	2,844	137	32	1,957
Total all ages	212,192	6,541	24,496	315	356	2,047	3,823	4,110	19,192	1,067	127	26,590
ALASKA												
Under 18	3,951	212	1,288	0	2	44	166	145	1,055	63	25	368
Total all ages	38,294	2,121	4,108	22	54	275	1,770	457	3,337	268	46	4,076
ARIZONA												
Under 18	53,826	1,619	11,065	29	28	457	1,105	1,523	8,769	613	160	4,853
Total all ages	334,238	9,226	41,904	310	185	2,044	6,687	5,086	33,963	2,593	262	25,778
ARKANSAS												
Under 18	13,209	468	3,796	2	16	96	354	856	2,843	77	20	1,380
Total all ages	138,372	4,749	15,437	118	194	623	3,814	2,992	11,967	417	61	9,701
CALIFORNIA												
Under 18	227,754	17,172	47,793	224	235	6,879	9,834	15,658	27,836	3,477	822	21,371
Total all ages	1,547,811	125,235	170,546	1,850	2,088	22,391	98,906	56,409	95,447	17,203	1,487	93,284
COLORADO[3]												
Under 18	43,398	902	8,397	5	58	232	607	1,002	6,866	398	131	2,268
Total all ages	221,175	6,208	25,453	155	453	926	4,674	2,993	20,936	1,298	226	14,746
CONNECTICUT												
Under 18	19,458	1,186	4,093	12	48	299	827	666	3,179	199	49	3,780
Total all ages	123,405	5,934	17,141	110	244	1,245	4,335	2,846	13,466	711	118	20,336
DELAWARE												
Under 18	7,199	574	1,620	4	26	194	350	300	1,246	37	37	1,597
Total all ages	42,641	2,942	6,746	32	138	713	2,059	1,102	5,403	171	70	8,584
DISTRICT OF COLUMBIA[3,4]												
Under 18	524	30	50	0	0	19	11	0	31	19	0	56
Total all ages	7,297	74	104	0	0	39	35	0	73	31	0	200
FLORIDA[3,5]												
Under 18	118,296	8,373	36,701	81	242	2,960	5,090	9,753	24,657	2,147	144	15,368
Total all ages	1,149,818	52,740	149,942	882	1,770	11,870	38,218	31,468	109,021	9,073	380	90,504
GEORGIA												
Under 18	38,807	1,890	9,116	37	63	724	1,066	2,188	6,246	624	58	5,252
Total all ages	268,869	11,489	37,402	320	313	2,958	7,898	6,654	28,467	2,091	190	23,411
HAWAII												
Under 18	12,029	288	1,531	0	8	157	123	185	1,225	109	12	996
Total all ages	52,818	1,319	4,523	18	102	393	806	601	3,467	424	31	4,894
IDAHO												
Under 18	14,863	227	2,942	3	18	18	188	381	2,411	78	72	1,239
Total all ages	71,854	1,425	7,009	14	102	97	1,212	938	5,802	185	84	5,922
ILLINOIS[6]												
Under 18	33,161	3,503	6,078	54	74	1,529	1,846	1,087	3,345	1,619	27	5,688
Total all ages	172,433	8,711	23,372	364	452	2,922	4,973	2,894	15,889	4,514	75	26,438
INDIANA												
Under 18	38,675	1,498	8,963	18	52	385	1,043	1,276	6,902	673	112	4,603
Total all ages	220,709	8,351	30,527	268	262	1,930	5,891	4,475	23,865	1,970	217	20,268
IOWA												
Under 18	20,893	743	5,276	6	29	94	614	724	4,239	228	85	2,591
Total all ages	116,614	4,230	13,950	50	108	404	3,668	1,907	11,349	553	141	10,399
KANSAS												
Under 18	11,183	336	2,293	5	40	52	239	291	1,882	80	40	1,542
Total all ages	80,352	2,491	7,187	47	183	285	1,976	1,054	5,678	372	83	11,483
KENTUCKY												
Under 18	3,671	279	1,514	6	5	146	122	313	1,122	44	35	336
Total all ages	35,973	1,817	6,700	55	33	598	1,131	1,220	5,268	150	62	2,552
LOUISIANA												
Under 18	19,068	1,666	4,319	15	35	264	1,352	1,036	3,045	207	31	2,722
Total all ages	140,519	9,236	19,742	183	238	1,035	7,780	3,840	14,812	920	170	15,893
MAINE												
Under 18	6,990	86	2,125	0	10	24	52	372	1,632	93	28	907
Total all ages	57,060	735	8,325	8	72	184	471	1,352	6,580	330	63	6,849
MARYLAND												
Under 18	47,175	3,657	12,463	31	52	1,947	1,627	2,318	8,415	1,405	325	7,500
Total all ages	300,165	13,001	38,147	307	404	4,443	7,847	7,411	26,879	3,292	565	29,510
MASSACHUSETTS												
Under 18	17,974	1,964	3,411	8	31	529	1,396	761	2,469	131	50	2,517
Total all ages	149,582	12,474	18,471	77	310	2,065	10,022	3,725	13,906	707	133	21,337
MICHIGAN												
Under 18	36,027	2,187	10,382	12	114	772	1,289	1,729	7,676	845	132	3,685
Total all ages	276,904	12,398	35,166	142	578	2,488	9,190	6,251	25,696	2,919	300	26,868

[1] Does not include traffic arrests.
[2] Violent crimes are offenses of murder and nonnegligent manslaughter, forcible rape, robbery, and aggravated assault. Property crimes are offenses of burglary, larceny-theft, motor vehicle theft, and arson.
[3] See Appendix I for details.
[4] Includes arrests reported by the Metro Transit Police. This agency has no population associated with it.
[5] The arrest category *All other offenses* also includes the arrest counts for offenses against the family and children, drunkenness, disorderly conduct, vagrancy, suspicion, curfew and loitering law violations, and runaways.
[6] Forcible rape figures for Illinois include only those data provided by Rockford. The forcible rape figures for Minnesota include only those provided by the cities of St. Paul and Minneapolis. See Appendix I for details.

Table 69. State Arrests, 2008—*Continued*

(Number.)

State	Forgery and counter-feiting	Fraud	Embezzle-ment	Stolen property; buying, receiving, possessing	Vandal-ism	Weapons; carrying, possessing, etc.	Prostitu-tion and commer-cialized vice	Sex offenses (except forcible rape and prosti-tution)	Drug abuse violations	Gamb-ling	Offenses against the family and children	Driving under the influence
ALABAMA												
Under 18	23	60	3	240	322	190	0	26	987	8	15	93
Total all ages	1,818	8,381	153	2,295	2,277	1,546	260	582	16,488	58	1,055	14,991
ALASKA												
Under 18	5	24	8	4	210	33	2	42	265	0	2	89
Total all ages	87	275	106	38	879	345	159	166	1,716	0	320	5,538
ARIZONA												
Under 18	51	97	26	160	3,711	538	27	307	5,413	1	284	561
Total all ages	3,207	2,352	322	1,285	11,680	3,681	1,602	1,773	34,242	7	3,026	39,746
ARKANSAS												
Under 18	18	25	7	144	613	162	2	38	948	1	2	147
Total all ages	937	3,351	54	1,224	1,848	1,330	316	194	11,513	24	117	11,707
CALIFORNIA												
Under 18	293	590	85	3,089	16,286	8,131	487	2,184	21,661	33	10	1,468
Total all ages	9,078	10,294	2,159	18,831	33,056	31,800	13,385	14,502	268,763	615	380	214,828
COLORADO[3]												
Under 18	47	168	16	155	2,061	556	24	225	3,456	1	77	435
Total all ages	1,025	2,433	250	760	6,072	2,054	618	903	17,851	7	2,991	28,198
CONNECTICUT												
Under 18	13	76	2	57	1,155	316	4	140	1,604	2	87	86
Total all ages	789	1,471	181	433	3,001	1,399	523	579	16,132	37	1,154	8,235
DELAWARE												
Under 18	8	133	13	150	326	154	1	45	705	1	3	0
Total all ages	607	2,077	277	525	1,184	477	132	202	5,895	6	239	215
DISTRICT OF COLUMBIA[3, 4]												
Under 18	0	0	0	3	12	11	0	0	19	0	0	0
Total all ages	3	4	0	19	21	33	1	0	79	1	0	32
FLORIDA[3, 5]												
Under 18	170	723	44	315	2,698	1,852	53	310	13,011	69		498
Total all ages	5,157	17,336	1,160	3,446	8,966	8,092	6,059	3,452	159,916	464		61,852
GEORGIA												
Under 18	101	252	25	507	1,007	1,344	31	545	3,157	28	184	205
Total all ages	3,852	6,738	363	3,287	3,397	4,935	1,848	3,402	34,697	319	2,638	25,421
HAWAII												
Under 18	1	29	5	24	421	24	11	68	409	13	2	70
Total all ages	156	423	74	117	937	199	421	295	2,022	31	47	5,812
IDAHO												
Under 18	13	27	6	67	739	168	2	89	781	0	22	209
Total all ages	156	490	112	225	1,426	625	21	314	5,514	1	622	11,850
ILLINOIS[6]												
Under 18	5	18	0	17	1,879	1,098	37	84	6,055	864	8	32
Total all ages	346	330	2	56	5,172	4,117	3,616	965	45,612	3,604	362	4,909
INDIANA												
Under 18	29	70	0	1,907	1,322	297	2	247	2,380	5	346	167
Total all ages	1,443	1,978	15	7,142	2,775	1,921	1,256	1,516	22,671	38	1,790	23,475
IOWA												
Under 18	42	53	10	75	1,603	154	2	78	1,165	1	12	226
Total all ages	604	1,155	94	210	3,307	519	129	237	8,497	13	870	14,147
KANSAS												
Under 18	11	37	34	38	582	122	1	87	976	3	26	245
Total all ages	556	1,427	201	307	2,020	731	227	325	6,854	9	261	13,080
KENTUCKY												
Under 18	17	5	0	167	146	58	0	3	506	0	1	8
Total all ages	573	260	5	652	467	611	539	21	7,952	11	589	2,363
LOUISIANA												
Under 18	6	40	7	231	651	321	4	122	1,600	11	135	69
Total all ages	528	1,794	300	1,328	2,744	1,748	412	596	17,959	83	1,186	7,977
MAINE												
Under 18	12	22	3	39	444	46	0	51	561	1	1	95
Total all ages	311	886	51	189	1,492	356	26	275	5,778	4	93	7,270
MARYLAND												
Under 18	41	78	43	31	2,015	1,357	12	292	7,648	43	38	214
Total all ages	1,093	2,368	433	241	4,215	4,328	1,337	1,343	57,288	283	2,220	23,714
MASSACHUSETTS												
Under 18	22	48	6	224	906	265	6	87	2,115	0	103	101
Total all ages	623	1,518	155	1,337	3,448	1,405	1,229	696	19,825	35	1,295	12,941
MICHIGAN												
Under 18	38	433	42	415	1,175	824	16	237	3,278	17	11	482
Total all ages	915	5,800	1,176	1,851	3,569	4,617	761	962	31,775	136	2,610	35,534

[3] See Appendix I for details.
[4] Includes arrests reported by the Metro Transit Police. This agency has no population associated with it.
[5] The arrest category A*ll other offenses* also includes the arrest counts for offenses against the family and children, drunkenness, disorderly conduct, vagrancy, suspicion, curfew and loitering law violations, and runaways.
[6] Forcible rape figures for Illinois include only those data provided by Rockford. The forcible rape figures for Minnesota include only those provided by the cities of St. Paul and Minneapolis. See Appendix I for details.

Table 69. State Arrests, 2008—*Continued*

(Number.)

State	Liquor laws	Drunken-ness[7]	Disorderly conduct	Vagrancy	All other offenses (except traffic)	Suspi-cion	Curfew and loitering law violations	Run-aways	Number of agencies	2008 estimated population
ALABAMA										
Under 18	703	78	1,539	10	1,695	0	32	359	291	3,772,968
Total all ages	6,077	11,087	4,862	300	81,944	0	32	359		
ALASKA										
Under 18	281	10	52	0	718	0	1	337	32	666,481
Total all ages	1,692	108	836	3	15,379	4	1	337		
ARIZONA										
Under 18	5,789	4	3,388	15	5,628	0	5,066	5,223	85	6,414,715
Total all ages	29,984	12	18,150	1,535	94,437	0	5,066	5,223		
ARKANSAS										
Under 18	267	265	1,064	29	2,535	3	772	523	201	2,403,738
Total all ages	2,224	10,454	3,664	1,200	56,920	113	772	523		
CALIFORNIA										
Under 18	5,181	4,245	10,974	383	44,395	0	17,697	4,226	637	36,555,329
Total all ages	19,649	121,180	15,362	4,364	358,577	0	17,697	4,226		
COLORADO[3]										
Under 18	4,437	8	3,719	0	9,544	2	1,844	5,056	192	4,359,586
Total all ages	15,108	204	11,573	211	77,600	10	1,844	5,056		
CONNECTICUT										
Under 18	400	0	3,558	0	2,836	0	48	15	96	3,226,747
Total all ages	1,443	0	15,758	44	28,752	0	48	15		
DELAWARE										
Under 18	458	29	638	0	644	0	100	0	54	873,092
Total all ages	2,451	769	2,229	916	6,068	0	100	0		
DISTRICT OF COLUMBIA[3,4]										
Under 18	3	0	88	0	251	0	1	0	2	
Total all ages	2,083	54	240	147	4,201	0	1	0		
FLORIDA[3,5]										
Under 18	1,227				36,884				591	18,294,452
Total all ages	33,084				547,648					
GEORGIA										
Under 18	846	50	4,683	45	6,709	51	867	1,912	262	5,995,191
Total all ages	9,391	2,540	22,373	763	67,641	183	867	1,912		
HAWAII										
Under 18	216	0	120	0	3,157	0	283	4,361	3	1,145,204
Total all ages	1,185	0	771	0	24,948	0	283	4,361		
IDAHO										
Under 18	1,940	22	595	0	3,501	0	735	1,539	101	1,435,156
Total all ages	6,494	439	2,442	9	24,484	0	735	1,539		
ILLINOIS[6]										
Under 18	268	0	3,112	0	3,849	0	552	14	2	2,986,566
Total all ages	1,317	0	17,947	11	24,980	0	552	14		
INDIANA										
Under 18	2,657	490	2,622	8	7,073	6	730	3,253	155	4,658,523
Total all ages	9,883	18,536	8,158	36	54,870	77	730	3,253		
IOWA										
Under 18	2,055	367	2,386	0	2,694	0	812	548	194	2,765,774
Total all ages	8,846	12,320	6,642	28	29,057	0	812	548		
KANSAS										
Under 18	1,413	1	810	0	1,278	0	0	1,348	232	1,895,788
Total all ages	7,284	329	3,806	0	20,426	0	0	1,348		
KENTUCKY										
Under 18	39	36	110	6	409	0	8	23	3	660,796
Total all ages	97	3,487	694	383	6,169	0	8	23		
LOUISIANA										
Under 18	292	31	2,820	9	3,041	28	493	450	104	2,471,978
Total all ages	6,845	2,970	12,180	355	35,613	87	493	450		
MAINE										
Under 18	1,084	9	201	0	1,137	0	64	102	164	1,314,189
Total all ages	4,782	43	1,886	2	17,541	0	64	102		
MARYLAND										
Under 18	1,202	8	2,171	52	7,359	78	236	637	154	5,574,256
Total all ages	6,820	12	7,431	160	104,757	591	236	637		
MASSACHUSETTS										
Under 18	775	204	1,375	0	3,538	1	13	293	315	5,819,911
Total all ages	4,214	6,021	8,337	19	33,868	28	13	293		
MICHIGAN										
Under 18	4,033	6	1,384	0	5,380	0	802	1,200	485	8,664,761
Total all ages	20,242	343	9,247	254	80,678	0	802	1,200		

[3] See Appendix I for details.
[4] Includes arrests reported by the Metro Transit Police. This agency has no population associated with it.
[5] The arrest category *All other offenses* also includes the arrest counts for offenses against the family and children, drunkenness, disorderly conduct, vagrancy, suspicion, curfew and loitering law violations, and runaways.
[6] Forcible rape figures for Illinois include only those data provided by Rockford. The forcible rape figures for Minnesota include only those provided by the cities of St. Paul and Minneapolis. See Appendix I for details.
[7] Drunkenness is not considered a crime in some states; therefore, the figures vary widely from state to state.

Table 69. State Arrests, 2008—*Continued*

(Number.)

State	Total all classes[1]	Violent crime[2]	Property crime[2]	Murder and non-negligent man-slaughter	Forcible rape	Robbery	Aggra-vated assault	Burglary	Larceny-theft	Motor vehicle theft	Arson	Other assaults
MINNESOTA[6]												
Under 18	45,954	1,135	10,262	12	13	402	708	972	8,824	368	98	3,669
Total all ages	204,367	5,612	29,245	111	106	1,286	4,109	3,388	24,188	1,479	190	18,243
MISSISSIPPI												
Under 18	10,347	218	2,232	14	13	107	84	561	1,535	101	35	1,240
Total all ages	108,280	1,946	11,109	135	165	572	1,074	2,248	8,275	485	101	10,244
MISSOURI												
Under 18	45,321	1,642	11,574	35	62	543	1,002	1,799	8,861	767	147	6,554
Total all ages	332,126	12,520	45,261	356	548	2,419	9,197	7,085	34,447	3,343	386	36,334
MONTANA												
Under 18	7,251	109	1,782	1	4	6	98	138	1,503	108	33	682
Total all ages	32,378	852	4,617	11	25	47	769	360	3,973	227	57	4,071
NEBRASKA												
Under 18	15,375	247	3,570	5	18	75	149	331	3,063	129	47	1,961
Total all ages	89,301	1,967	9,602	43	146	397	1,381	908	8,242	374	78	9,072
NEVADA												
Under 18	24,656	939	4,808	11	31	369	528	1,000	3,435	254	119	2,639
Total all ages	166,395	6,516	17,542	146	263	1,835	4,272	3,492	12,712	1,118	220	18,585
NEW HAMPSHIRE												
Under 18	6,906	93	853	0	10	31	52	134	671	22	26	959
Total all ages	43,634	624	3,165	5	69	150	400	437	2,596	85	47	5,595
NEW JERSEY												
Under 18	51,527	2,980	8,307	26	61	1,461	1,432	1,503	6,335	233	236	4,171
Total all ages	386,427	13,948	34,665	276	372	4,371	8,929	6,419	26,932	917	397	26,380
NEW MEXICO												
Under 18	9,587	440	2,433	6	12	55	367	259	2,056	73	45	1,099
Total all ages	78,500	3,464	9,003	71	129	417	2,847	1,215	7,336	350	102	6,563
NEW YORK[3]												
Under 18	40,142	2,497	10,946	34	61	1,045	1,357	2,273	8,056	464	153	4,022
Total all ages	300,683	13,320	48,915	273	543	3,393	9,111	7,893	38,595	1,992	435	28,925
NORTH CAROLINA												
Under 18	40,840	2,119	11,202	49	43	864	1,163	3,023	7,767	303	109	6,315
Total all ages	413,895	18,852	60,398	578	520	4,364	13,390	14,459	44,112	1,511	316	49,545
NORTH DAKOTA												
Under 18	6,719	68	1,229	0	15	4	49	100	1,036	86	7	465
Total all ages	27,896	408	2,975	3	45	25	335	281	2,497	175	22	1,897
OHIO												
Under 18	38,975	1,196	8,129	16	92	600	488	1,479	6,204	335	111	5,948
Total all ages	249,113	6,808	35,461	186	487	2,615	3,520	6,211	27,928	1,081	241	30,596
OKLAHOMA												
Under 18	21,697	790	5,216	19	40	201	530	1,024	3,909	159	124	1,411
Total all ages	161,466	5,956	17,029	160	316	831	4,649	3,114	13,046	591	278	10,180
OREGON												
Under 18	28,909	720	7,179	13	35	212	460	813	5,925	261	180	2,203
Total all ages	147,653	4,844	27,202	95	276	1,187	3,286	2,816	22,590	1,452	344	15,447
PENNSYLVANIA												
Under 18	102,605	5,309	13,798	56	212	2,028	3,013	2,319	10,329	849	301	8,723
Total all ages	483,711	25,776	60,856	576	1,167	7,412	16,621	10,310	46,384	3,479	683	47,334
RHODE ISLAND												
Under 18	5,576	200	1,177	0	14	88	98	240	865	37	35	741
Total all ages	35,157	876	3,756	12	58	259	547	777	2,794	138	47	4,104
SOUTH CAROLINA												
Under 18	18,306	893	3,638	27	45	252	569	858	2,621	116	43	2,318
Total all ages	177,424	7,270	18,177	198	289	1,383	5,400	3,552	13,725	772	128	13,990
SOUTH DAKOTA												
Under 18	5,793	54	1,121	0	7	2	45	105	929	56	31	460
Total all ages	27,721	465	2,782	13	53	31	368	281	2,342	115	44	2,902
TENNESSEE												
Under 18	35,507	1,663	7,057	18	60	535	1,050	1,404	5,141	434	78	5,648
Total all ages	309,981	13,626	39,706	304	344	2,934	10,044	6,221	30,894	2,324	267	31,413
TEXAS												
Under 18	171,536	4,900	32,028	73	294	1,729	2,804	5,599	25,055	1,113	261	22,524
Total all ages	1,141,646	34,235	130,782	863	2,034	8,199	23,139	19,693	104,395	5,962	732	109,003

[1] Does not include traffic arrests.
[2] Violent crimes are offenses of murder and nonnegligent manslaughter, forcible rape, robbery, and aggravated assault. Property crimes are offenses of burglary, larceny-theft, motor vehicle theft, and arson.
[3] See Appendix I for details.
[6] Forcible rape figures for Illinois include only those data provided by Rockford. The forcible rape figures for Minnesota include only those provided by the cities of St. Paul and Minneapolis. See Appendix I for details.

Table 69. State Arrests, 2008—*Continued*

(Number.)

State	Forgery and counter-feiting	Fraud	Embezzle-ment	Stolen property; buying, receiving, possessing	Vandal-ism	Weapons; carrying, possessing, etc.	Prostitu-tion and commer-cialized vice	Sex offenses (except forcible rape and prosti-tution)	Drug abuse violations	Gamb-ling	Offenses against the family and children	Driving under the influence
MINNESOTA[6]												
Under 18	71	199	10	393	1,879	787	45	302	2,785	4	37	530
Total all ages	1,605	3,481	39	1,692	4,634	2,269	1,338	1,524	18,196	14	856	29,832
MISSISSIPPI												
Under 18	11	69	14	88	208	187	1	47	683	12	293	137
Total all ages	883	1,895	715	715	936	1,003	119	412	11,741	227	3,606	11,629
MISSOURI												
Under 18	74	109	31	539	2,403	728	8	432	3,398	14	90	425
Total all ages	2,515	3,638	223	3,066	7,352	4,058	635	2,434	35,990	125	4,636	34,004
MONTANA												
Under 18	6	9	5	10	460	20	0	20	297	0	50	63
Total all ages	64	166	32	33	1,119	121	11	64	1,620	0	313	4,240
NEBRASKA												
Under 18	18	92	17	209	1,030	198	1	123	1,166	1	37	281
Total all ages	446	1,691	113	830	2,698	1,108	212	595	10,432	19	1,539	13,692
NEVADA												
Under 18	19	54	31	249	1,591	444	63	153	1,723	2	8	124
Total all ages	1,017	1,942	523	1,606	2,983	2,051	4,659	1,594	14,886	35	1,491	14,445
NEW HAMPSHIRE												
Under 18	5	61	5	134	341	13	0	31	642	2	8	76
Total all ages	202	924	29	481	1,140	88	56	152	3,266	5	165	4,571
NEW JERSEY												
Under 18	52	139	5	1,038	3,110	1,422	30	302	5,766	18	152	342
Total all ages	1,729	4,992	162	4,027	6,914	5,059	1,453	1,527	52,749	158	15,113	24,313
NEW MEXICO												
Under 18	13	32	13	114	345	211	2	14	919	1	4	112
Total all ages	246	506	167	732	770	619	219	151	6,113	3	931	9,741
NEW YORK[3]												
Under 18	148	270	5	905	3,505	575	10	736	5,141	7	319	216
Total all ages	3,488	7,259	203	4,835	12,069	3,379	824	3,887	52,945	86	2,472	25,169
NORTH CAROLINA												
Under 18	41	385	91	755	1,919	1,370	12	121	3,174	3	101	517
Total all ages	2,396	19,035	1,723	5,263	7,886	7,434	1,408	1,362	36,571	138	6,534	49,599
NORTH DAKOTA												
Under 18	3	21	9	39	330	41	0	26	278	0	88	67
Total all ages	75	655	35	139	584	166	3	95	1,769	0	164	4,003
OHIO												
Under 18	78	190	4	664	1,705	592	5	217	2,691	10	690	158
Total all ages	1,323	3,180	44	3,622	4,496	2,999	1,266	964	30,580	76	6,705	19,088
OKLAHOMA												
Under 18	24	55	88	429	577	323	1	69	1,873	0	118	233
Total all ages	831	2,510	659	2,261	1,562	2,131	412	720	20,548	7	977	18,980
OREGON												
Under 18	25	105	5	70	2,134	328	23	180	2,303	1	10	161
Total all ages	986	1,684	54	374	5,418	1,777	752	1,334	16,723	3	611	17,015
PENNSYLVANIA												
Under 18	91	344	48	619	4,643	1,481	11	550	6,055	27	49	559
Total all ages	2,977	8,634	490	3,077	12,947	4,576	2,498	2,779	56,228	268	1,155	53,319
RHODE ISLAND												
Under 18	4	25	4	91	458	138	0	34	426	0	95	25
Total all ages	140	758	133	340	1,264	391	216	122	3,791	4	159	2,778
SOUTH CAROLINA												
Under 18	22	75	17	182	645	438	1	93	1,800	1	205	94
Total all ages	1,534	13,705	352	1,658	2,466	1,682	388	442	18,224	53	1,438	14,742
SOUTH DAKOTA												
Under 18	4	64	11	23	286	57	0	30	403	0	129	107
Total all ages	109	840	48	61	604	129	10	77	2,395	0	342	6,190
TENNESSEE												
Under 18	93	229	48	59	1,424	604	26	151	3,004	52	50	204
Total all ages	3,104	9,361	1,147	880	4,295	3,238	2,111	731	34,686	360	1,771	26,322
TEXAS												
Under 18	160	425	59	145	5,638	1,641	139	676	15,326	52	44	1,082
Total all ages	7,323	13,473	573	745	13,855	11,667	8,784	4,059	136,897	500	4,939	90,066

[3] See Appendix I for details.

[6] Forcible rape figures for Illinois include only those data provided by Rockford. The forcible rape figures for Minnesota include only those provided by the cities of St. Paul and Minneapolis. See Appendix I for details.

Table 69. State Arrests, 2008—*Continued*

(Number.)

State	Liquor laws	Drunken-ness[7]	Disorderly conduct	Vagrancy	All other offenses (except traffic)	Suspi-cion	Curfew and loitering law violations	Run-aways	Number of agencies	2008 estimated population
MINNESOTA[6]										
Under 18	6,359	0	4,356	14	5,756	0	3,882	3,479	321	5,074,064
Total all ages	27,458	0	14,227	360	36,381	0	3,882	3,479		
MISSISSIPPI										
Under 18	269	104	1,964	3	1,777	2	500	288	75	1,308,021
Total all ages	2,269	6,272	7,233	75	34,431	32	500	288		
MISSOURI										
Under 18	2,800	30	2,590	42	6,583	0	1,805	3,450	384	5,542,829
Total all ages	14,242	581	15,431	250	103,576	0	1,805	3,450		
MONTANA										
Under 18	1,394	0	511	0	910	0	518	405	88	932,625
Total all ages	5,471	0	3,032	9	5,620	0	518	405		
NEBRASKA										
Under 18	2,432	0	927	1	2,189	0	460	415	218	1,634,173
Total all ages	12,746	0	4,306	28	17,329	1	460	415		
NEVADA										
Under 18	2,203	83	1,019	89	4,025	14	3,189	1,187	34	2,545,496
Total all ages	10,011	201	3,156	2,438	56,321	17	3,189	1,187		
NEW HAMPSHIRE										
Under 18	1,036	304	211	0	1,795	0	33	304	138	1,032,522
Total all ages	4,909	4,168	1,200	45	12,512	0	33	304		
NEW JERSEY										
Under 18	2,560	0	4,366	32	7,958	0	4,728	4,049	526	8,355,142
Total all ages	7,683	0	23,314	1,897	151,567	0	4,728	4,049		
NEW MEXICO										
Under 18	722	14	531	1	2,230	0	64	273	54	1,445,951
Total all ages	3,389	746	2,700	2	32,066	32	64	273		
NEW YORK[3]										
Under 18	995	0	1,994	38	7,813	0	0	0	562	9,223,778
Total all ages	4,631	0	13,505	968	73,803	0	0	0		
NORTH CAROLINA										
Under 18	1,317	0	3,890	2	6,396	0	0	1,110	288	6,612,884
Total all ages	10,778	0	14,976	195	118,692	0	0	1,110		
NORTH DAKOTA										
Under 18	1,204	1	797	0	1,154	0	275	624	71	580,591
Total all ages	5,582	630	1,864	3	5,950	0	275	624		
OHIO										
Under 18	2,269	50	3,173	28	8,821	15	1,472	870	384	6,866,208
Total all ages	12,815	4,459	20,493	65	61,678	53	1,472	870		
OKLAHOMA										
Under 18	453	950	1,006	0	3,139	0	2,227	2,715	296	3,638,086
Total all ages	3,013	25,426	3,401	0	39,921	0	2,227	2,715		
OREGON										
Under 18	4,412	0	1,466	0	3,543	0	2,006	2,035	152	3,649,695
Total all ages	19,287	0	8,214	10	21,877	0	2,006	2,035		
PENNSYLVANIA										
Under 18	7,332	385	17,391	122	7,923	0	25,066	2,079	1,067	12,020,349
Total all ages	26,626	25,838	62,987	1,101	57,100	0	25,066	2,079		
RHODE ISLAND										
Under 18	113	2	966	0	988	0	9	80	47	1,050,788
Total all ages	936	12	3,120	2	12,166	0	9	80		
SOUTH CAROLINA										
Under 18	974	131	3,022	0	3,083	0	60	614	464	4,399,248
Total all ages	12,648	12,850	15,768	1,520	37,843	0	60	614		
SOUTH DAKOTA										
Under 18	1,498	14	254	0	458	0	167	653	94	630,213
Total all ages	5,745	53	1,746	133	2,270	0	167	653		
TENNESSEE										
Under 18	1,270	409	3,650	0	5,773	0	1,927	2,166	383	4,948,055
Total all ages	8,071	20,522	10,759	80	93,705	0	1,927	2,166		
TEXAS										
Under 18	5,601	3,141	20,305	1,901	29,338	0	13,164	13,247	964	23,376,796
Total all ages	29,859	140,094	40,371	3,224	334,786	0	13,164	13,247		

[3] See Appendix I for details.
[6] Forcible rape figures for Illinois include only those data provided by Rockford. The forcible rape figures for Minnesota include only those provided by the cities of St. Paul and Minneapolis. See Appendix I for details.
[7] Drunkenness is not considered a crime in some states; therefore, the figures vary widely from state to state.

Table 69. State Arrests, 2008—*Continued*

(Number.)

State	Total all classes[1]	Violent crime[2]	Property crime[2]	Murder and non-negligent man-slaughter	Forcible rape	Robbery	Aggra-vated assault	Burglary	Larceny-theft	Motor vehicle theft	Arson	Other assaults
UTAH												
Under 18	24,576	359	6,278	6	52	68	233	396	5,666	153	63	2,210
Total all ages	114,017	2,044	18,725	47	181	495	1,321	1,342	16,821	460	102	10,515
VERMONT												
Under 18	1,403	47	293	1	9	1	36	60	202	23	8	205
Total all ages	13,533	456	1,714	8	71	21	356	300	1,308	87	19	1,454
VIRGINIA												
Under 18	40,940	1,105	6,743	20	52	506	527	1,154	5,198	221	170	4,946
Total all ages	331,159	7,457	33,083	309	370	2,194	4,584	4,624	27,101	1,052	306	38,256
WASHINGTON												
Under 18	30,669	1,247	8,865	8	115	452	672	1,515	6,814	401	135	4,206
Total all ages	228,993	6,943	32,352	104	675	1,637	4,527	4,895	25,769	1,412	276	26,165
WEST VIRGINIA												
Under 18	2,317	77	620	0	2	16	59	70	517	28	5	388
Total all ages	41,681	1,280	5,059	31	40	143	1,066	583	4,263	179	34	5,643
WISCONSIN												
Under 18	100,121	1,644	15,265	31	156	646	811	1,628	12,744	767	126	3,862
Total all ages	411,968	8,050	42,425	195	710	1,981	5,164	4,664	35,698	1,664	399	19,821
WYOMING												
Under 18	6,861	73	1,097	1	7	12	53	90	944	51	12	742
Total all ages	40,979	633	3,073	14	45	35	539	334	2,592	125	22	3,408

[1] Does not include traffic arrests.

[2] Violent crimes are offenses of murder and nonnegligent manslaughter, forcible rape, robbery, and aggravated assault. Property crimes are offenses of burglary, larceny-theft, motor vehicle theft, and arson.

Table 69. State Arrests, 2008—*Continued*

(Number.)

State	Forgery and counter-feiting	Fraud	Embezzle-ment	Stolen property; buying, receiving, possessing	Vandal-ism	Weapons; carrying, possessing, etc.	Prostitu-tion and commer-cialized vice	Sex offenses (except forcible rape and prosti-tution)	Drug abuse violations	Gamb-ling	Offenses against the family and children	Driving under the influence
UTAH												
Under 18	25	53	1	184	1,799	355	23	314	1,663	1	127	98
Total all ages	927	1,031	22	787	3,999	1,200	463	811	9,242	7	1,667	6,894
VERMONT												
Under 18	4	7	1	20	116	15	0	2	141	0	10	24
Total all ages	88	346	42	133	402	18	6	23	1,137	0	313	2,647
VIRGINIA												
Under 18	54	136	99	190	1,523	558	4	209	2,736	4	22	183
Total all ages	2,433	8,818	1,936	989	4,979	4,035	558	1,068	32,513	58	1,643	27,732
WASHINGTON												
Under 18	61	43	6	424	2,212	634	54	183	2,555	0	15	488
Total all ages	1,567	991	147	2,792	6,539	2,879	694	994	23,440	1	691	34,952
WEST VIRGINIA												
Under 18	1	2	3	20	104	27	1	12	219	0	6	29
Total all ages	306	731	91	204	797	268	150	112	4,249	19	66	4,429
WISCONSIN												
Under 18	94	203	22	713	4,157	1,402	27	986	4,597	49	223	573
Total all ages	1,842	6,321	268	1,815	10,475	4,997	687	2,750	25,075	137	2,768	40,549
WYOMING												
Under 18	6	10	0	10	313	46	0	19	505	1	29	91
Total all ages	113	226	5	75	889	136	34	173	2,969	7	267	7,159

Table 69. State Arrests, 2008—*Continued*

(Number.)

State	Liquor laws	Drunken-ness[7]	Disorderly conduct	Vagrancy	All other offenses (except traffic)	Suspi-cion	Curfew and loitering law violations	Run-aways	Number of agencies	2008 estimated population
UTAH										
Under 18	2,146	197	1,900	163	5,040	0	1,015	625	106	2,376,842
Total all ages	9,577	4,181	4,563	189	35,533	0	1,015	625		
VERMONT										
Under 18	156	4	123	0	233	0	0	2	73	509,775
Total all ages	662	9	854	1	3,226	0	0	2		
VIRGINIA										
Under 18	2,284	208	1,515	0	9,848	0	2,854	5,719	375	7,543,553
Total all ages	12,885	30,407	5,912	111	107,713	0	2,854	5,719		
WASHINGTON										
Under 18	3,536	0	654	0	3,838	0	48	1,600	208	4,761,193
Total all ages	11,634	3	4,797	32	69,732	0	48	1,600		
WEST VIRGINIA										
Under 18	163	12	54	0	447	0	69	63	148	1,109,343
Total all ages	1,217	4,264	1,075	18	11,571	0	69	63		
WISCONSIN										
Under 18	9,776	0	18,662	84	26,633	0	7,046	4,103	367	5,540,528
Total all ages	41,928	0	64,868	2,795	123,248	0	7,046	4,103		
WYOMING										
Under 18	1,231	32	226	21	1,491	10	428	480	62	528,009
Total all ages	4,617	2,754	1,469	34	11,999	31	428	480		

[7] Drunkenness is not considered a crime in some states; therefore, the figures vary widely from state to state.

SECTION V:

LAW ENFORCEMENT PERSONNEL

LAW ENFORCEMENT PERSONNEL

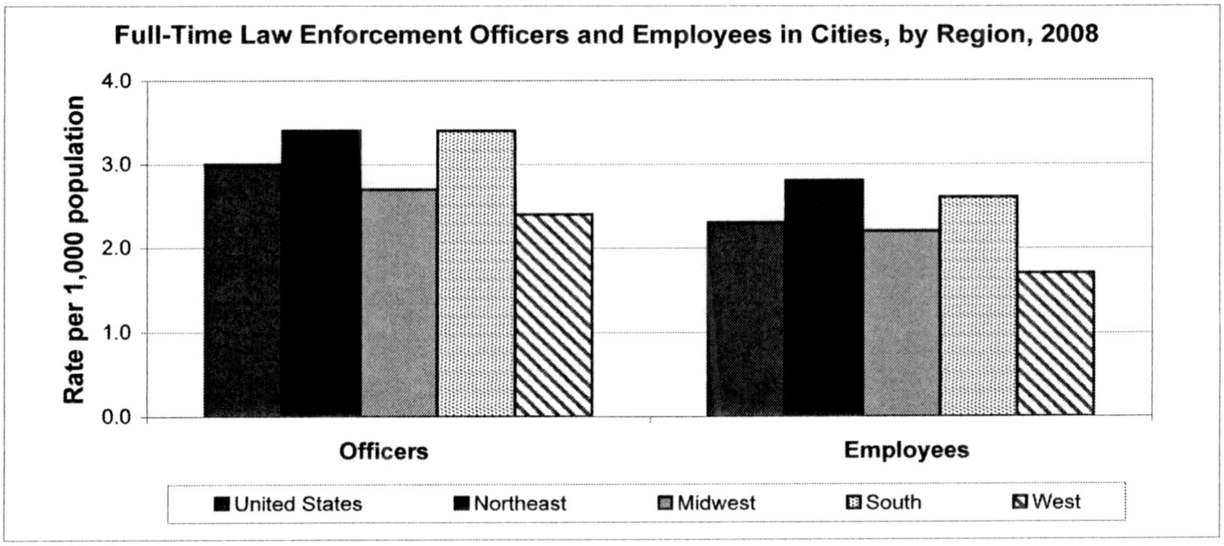

The Uniform Crime Reporting (UCR) Program defines law enforcement officers as individuals who ordinarily carry a firearm and a badge, have full arrest powers, and are paid from governmental funds set aside specifically for sworn law enforcement representatives. Because of law enforcement's varied service requirements and functions, as well as the distinct demographic traits and characteristics of jurisdictions, readers should use caution when drawing comparisons between agencies' staffing levels based upon police employment data from the UCR Program. In addition, the data presented here reflect existing staff levels and should not be interpreted as preferred officer strengths recommended by the FBI. Lastly, it should be noted that the totals given for sworn officers for any particular agency reflect not only the patrol officers on the street but also officers assigned to various other duties such as those in administrative and investigative positions and those assigned to special teams.

Each year, law enforcement agencies across the United States report the total number of sworn law enforcement officers and civilians in their agencies as of October 31 to the UCR Program. Civilian employees include personnel such as clerks, radio dispatchers, meter attendants, stenographers, jailers, correctional officers, and mechanics provided that they are full-time employees of the agency.

This section of *Crime in the United States* presents those data as the number and rate of law enforcement officers and civilian employees throughout the United States. In 2008, 14,169 state, city, university and college, metropolitan and nonmetropolitan county, and other law enforcement agencies employed 708,569 sworn officers and 315,659 civilians, who provided law enforcement services to more than 286 million people nationwide. (Table 74)

The data in this section are broken down by geographic region and division, population group, state, city, university and college, metropolitan and nonmetropolitan county, and other law enforcement agencies. (Information about geographic regions and divisions and population groups can be found in Appendix III.) UCR Program staff compute the rate of sworn officers and law enforcement employees by taking the number of employees (sworn officers only or in combination with civilians), dividing by the population for which the agency provides law enforcement service, and multiplying by 1,000.

- Tables 70 and 71 present the number and rate of law enforcement personnel per 1,000 inhabitants collectively employed by agencies, broken down by geographic region and division by population group.
- Tables 72 and 73 provide a count of law enforcement agencies by population group, based on the employment rate ranges for sworn officer and civilian employees per 1,000 inhabitants.
- Table 74 provides the number and percentage of male and female sworn officers and civilian employees by population group.
- Table 75 lists the percentage of full-time civilian law enforcement employees by population group.
- Table 76 breaks down by state the number of sworn law enforcement officers and civilians employed by state law enforcement agencies.
- Tables 78 to 80 list the number of law enforcement employees for cities, universities and colleges, and metropolitan and nonmetropolitan counties.

- Table 81 supplies employee data for those law enforcement agencies that serve the nation's transit systems, parks and forests, schools and school districts, hospitals, etc.

The demographic traits and characteristics of a jurisdiction affect its requirements for law enforcement service. For instance, a village between two large cities may require more law enforcement than a community of the same size with no urban center nearby. A town with legal gambling may have different law enforcement needs than a town near a military base. A city largely made up of college students may have different law enforcement needs than a city whose residents are mainly retirees.

Similarly, the functions of law enforcement agencies are diverse. Employees of these agencies patrol local streets and major highways, protect citizens in the nation's smallest towns and largest cities, and conduct investigations on offenses at the local and state level. State police in one area may enforce traffic laws on state highways and interstates; in another area, they may be responsible for investigating violent crimes. Sheriff's departments may collect tax monies, serve as the enforcement authority for local and state courts, administer jail facilities, or carry out some combination of these duties. This has an impact on an agency's staffing levels.

Because of the differing service requirements and functions, care should be taken when drawing comparisons between and among the staffing levels of law enforcement agencies. The data in this section are not intended as recommended or preferred officer strength; they should be used merely as guides. Adequate staffing levels can be determined only after careful study of the conditions that affect the service requirements in a particular jurisdiction.

Rate

The UCR Program computes these rates by taking the number of employees, dividing by the population of the agency's jurisdiction, and multiplying by 1,000. The rate of full-time law enforcement employees (civilian and sworn) per 1,000 inhabitants in the nation for 2008 was 3.6.

Among the nation's four regions, law enforcement agencies in the Northeast had the highest rate of law enforcement employees in 2008, with 3.4 per 1,000 inhabitants. Agencies in the South had 3.4 law enforcement employees per 1,000 inhabitants, followed by the Midwest (2.7) and the West (2.4). (Table 70)

An examination of the 2008 law enforcement employee data by population group showed that the nation's cities had a collective rate of 3.0 law enforcement employees per 1,000 inhabitants. Cities with fewer than 10,000 inhabitants had the highest rate of law enforcement employees, with 4.5 per 1,000 inhabitants. Cities with 25,000 to 49,999 inhabitants and cities with 50,000 to 99,999 inhabitants had the lowest rate of law enforcement employees (2.3 per 1,000 in population). The nation's largest cities, those with 250,000 or more inhabitants, averaged 3.7 law enforcement employees for every 1,000 inhabitants. (Table 70)

Sworn Personnel

An analysis of the 2008 data showed that law enforcement agencies in the cities in the Northeast had the highest rate of sworn officers—2.8 per 1,000 inhabitants, followed by the South (2.6), the Midwest (2.2), and the West (1.7). (Table 71)

By population group in 2008, there were 2.3 sworn officers for each 1,000 resident population in the nation's cities collectively. This rate was unchanged from the 2006 and 2007 data. Cities with fewer than 10,000 inhabitants had the highest rate at 3.5 sworn officers per 1,000 inhabitants. The nation's largest cities, those with 250,000 or more inhabitants, averaged 2.8 officers per 1,000 inhabitants. (Table 71)

Males accounted for 88.1 percent of all full-time sworn law enforcement officers in 2008. Cities with populations of 1 million and over employed the highest percentage (18.2) of full-time female officers. Of the city population groups, cities with populations of 10,000 to 24,999 inhabitants employed the highest percentage (92.2) of male officers. In metropolitan counties, 86.4 percent of officers were male, and in nonmetropolitan counties, 92.0 percent of officers were male. (Table 74)

Civilian Employees

Civilian employees provide a myriad of services to the nation's law enforcement and criminal justice agencies. Among other duties, they dispatch officers, provide administrative and record-keeping support, and query local, state, and national databases.

In 2008, 30.8 percent of all law enforcement employees in the nation were civilians. Female employees accounted for 61.6 percent of all full-time civilian law enforcement employees in 2008. In cities, civilians made up 22.6 percent of law enforcement agencies employees. Civilians made up 41.9 percent of law enforcement employees in metropolitan counties, 40.8 percent of law enforcement employees in nonmetropolitan counties, and 34.9 percent of law enforcement employees in suburban areas. (Table 74)

Table 70. Full-Time Law Enforcement Employees,[1] by Geographic Region and Division and Population Group, 2008

(Number, rate per 1,000 population.)

Geographic region/division	Total (10,915 cities; population 193,548,068)	Group I (75 cities, 250,000 and over; population 55,781,739)	Group II (189 cities, 100,000 to 249,999; population 27,940,012)	Group III (437 cities, 50,000 to 99,999; population 29,817,070)	Group IV (807 cities, 25,000 to 49,999; population 27,597,191)	Group V (1,807 cities, 10,000 to 24,999; population 28,634,261)
TOTAL						
Number of employees	581,504	203,685	69,458	68,260	64,319	69,817
Average number of employees per 1,000 inhabitants	3.0	3.7	2.5	2.3	2.3	2.4
Northeast						
Number of employees	148,946	63,711	9,727	16,191	18,715	19,836
Average number of employees per 1,000 inhabitants	3.4	5.7	3.5	2.6	2.4	2.2
New England						
Number of employees	34,498	2,862	4,784	6,073	7,082	7,360
Average number of employees per 1,000 inhabitants	2.7	4.7	3.3	2.4	2.3	2.2
Middle Atlantic						
Number of employees	114,448	60,849	4,943	10,118	11,633	12,476
Average number of employees per 1,000 inhabitants	3.7	5.7	3.6	2.8	2.4	2.2
Midwest						
Number of employees	119,708	34,738	9,181	14,185	17,047	19,453
Average number of employees per 1,000 inhabitants	2.7	3.9	2.3	2.0	2.1	2.2
East North Central						
Number of employees	86,804	26,719	6,306	10,101	13,594	13,987
Average number of employees per 1,000 inhabitants	2.8	4.1	2.4	2.1	2.1	2.3
West North Central						
Number of employees	32,904	8,019	2,875	4,084	3,453	5,466
Average number of employees per 1,000 inhabitants	2.5	3.2	2.1	1.7	2.0	2.2
South						
Number of employees	195,204	53,130	31,148	21,343	18,261	23,603
Average number of employees per 1,000 inhabitants	3.4	3.2	2.8	2.7	2.8	3.0
South Atlantic						
Number of employees	91,638	21,255	17,056	11,405	8,812	10,687
Average number of employees per 1,000 inhabitants	3.9	4.3	3.0	3.0	3.0	3.3
East South Central						
Number of employees	33,871	6,847	4,537	2,377	4,225	5,595
Average number of employees per 1,000 inhabitants	3.5	2.8	3.3	3.2	2.9	3.2
West South Central						
Number of employees	69,695	25,028	9,555	7,561	5,224	7,321
Average number of employees per 1,000 inhabitants	2.9	2.8	2.4	2.3	2.4	2.7
West						
Number of employees	117,646	52,106	19,402	16,541	10,296	6,925
Average number of employees per 1,000 inhabitants	2.4	2.7	1.9	1.9	2.0	2.2
Mountain						
Number of employees	40,986	17,802	6,176	4,698	3,990	2,501
Average number of employees per 1,000 inhabitants	2.6	2.7	2.1	2.1	2.1	2.5
Pacific						
Number of employees	76,660	34,304	13,226	11,843	6,306	4,424
Average number of employees per 1,000 inhabitants	2.3	2.7	1.8	1.8	1.9	2.0

Note: No 2008 police employee data were received for the state of West Virginia.

[1] Full-time law enforcement employees include civilians.

Table 70. Full-Time Law Enforcement Employees,[1] by Geographic Region and Division and Population Group, 2008—*Continued*

(Number, rate per 1,000 population.)

Geographic region/division	Group VI (7,600 cities, under 10,000; population 23,777,795)	Total city agencies	2008 estimated city population	County[2] (3,254 agencies; population 92,689,393)	Total city and county agencies	2008 estimated total agency population	Suburban Area[3] (7,412 agencies; population 121,966,483)
TOTAL							
Number of employees	105,965	10,915	193,548,068	442,724	14,169	286,237,461	475,575
Average number of employees per 1,000 inhabitants	4.5			4.8			3.9
Northeast							
Number of employees	20,766	2,448	43,249,515				
Average number of employees per 1,000 inhabitants	3.3						
New England							
Number of employees	6,337	760	12,565,101				
Average number of employees per 1,000 inhabitants	3.7						
Middle Atlantic							
Number of employees	14,429	1,688	30,684,414				
Average number of employees per 1,000 inhabitants	3.2						
Midwest							
Number of employees	25,104	3,302	44,263,045				
Average number of employees per 1,000 inhabitants	3.4						
East North Central							
Number of employees	16,097	2,072	31,160,435				
Average number of employees per 1,000 inhabitants	3.4						
West North Central							
Number of employees	9,007	1,230	13,102,610				
Average number of employees per 1,000 inhabitants	3.4						
South							
Number of employees	47,719	3,817	57,241,561				
Average number of employees per 1,000 inhabitants	6.3						
South Atlantic							
Number of employees	22,423	1,524	23,422,121				
Average number of employees per 1,000 inhabitants	8.0						
East South Central							
Number of employees	10,290	978	9,738,647				
Average number of employees per 1,000 inhabitants	5.3						
West South Central							
Number of employees	15,006	1,315	24,080,793				
Average number of employees per 1,000 inhabitants	5.3						
West							
Number of employees	12,376	1,348	48,793,947				
Average number of employees per 1,000 inhabitants	4.8						
Mountain							
Number of employees	5,819	583	15,768,765				
Average number of employees per 1,000 inhabitants	4.4						
Pacific							
Number of employees	6,557	765	33,025,182				
Average number of employees per 1,000 inhabitants	5.3						

Note: No 2008 police employee data were received for the state of West Virginia.

[1] Full-time law enforcement employees include civilians.

[2] The designation county is a combination of both metropolitan and nonmetropolitan counties.

[3] Suburban areas include law enforcement agencies in cities with less than 50,000 inhabitants and county law enforcement agencies that are within a Metropolitan Statistical Area. Suburban areas exclude all metropolitan agencies associated with a principal city. The agencies associated with suburban areas also appear in other groups within this table.

Table 71. Full-Time Law Enforcement Officers, by Geographic Region and Division and Population Group, 2008

(Number, rate per 1,000 population.)

Geographic region/division	Total (10,915 cities; population 193,548,068)	Group I (75 cities, 250,000 and over; population 55,781,739)	Group II (189 cities, 100,000 to 249,999; population 27,940,012)	Group III (437 cities, 50,000 to 99,999; population 29,817,070)	Group IV (807 cities, 25,000 to 49,999; population 27,597,191)	Group V (1,807 cities, 10,000 to 24,999; population 28,634,261)
TOTAL						
Number of officers	449,896	156,445	52,273	52,341	50,650	55,767
Average number of officers per 1,000 inhabitants	2.3	2.8	1.9	1.8	1.8	1.9
Northeast						
Number of officers	119,002	47,705	8,054	13,395	15,690	16,695
Average number of officers per 1,000 inhabitants	2.8	4.2	2.9	2.2	2.0	1.9
New England						
Number of officers	28,247	2,213	3,929	5,178	5,850	5,989
Average number of officers per 1,000 inhabitants	2.2	3.7	2.7	2.1	1.9	1.8
Middle Atlantic						
Number of officers	90,755	45,492	4,125	8,217	9,840	10,706
Average number of officers per 1,000 inhabitants	3.0	4.3	3.0	2.3	2.0	1.9
Midwest						
Number of officers	98,163	29,689	7,425	11,318	13,435	15,624
Average number of officers per 1,000 inhabitants	2.2	3.3	1.8	1.6	1.7	1.8
East North Central						
Number of officers	72,070	23,779	5,134	8,031	10,717	11,213
Average number of officers per 1,000 inhabitants	2.3	3.7	1.9	1.7	1.7	1.8
West North Central						
Number of officers	26,093	5,910	2,291	3,287	2,718	4,411
Average number of officers per 1,000 inhabitants	2.0	2.4	1.7	1.4	1.6	1.8
South						
Number of officers	148,143	40,836	23,278	16,119	14,135	18,315
Average number of officers per 1,000 inhabitants	2.6	2.5	2.1	2.1	2.2	2.3
South Atlantic						
Number of officers	69,370	15,846	12,756	8,517	6,939	8,473
Average number of officers per 1,000 inhabitants	3.0	3.2	2.2	2.2	2.4	2.6
East South Central						
Number of officers	26,480	5,595	3,395	1,817	3,349	4,328
Average number of officers per 1,000 inhabitants	2.7	2.3	2.5	2.4	2.3	2.4
West South Central						
Number of officers	52,293	19,395	7,127	5,785	3,847	5,514
Average number of officers per 1,000 inhabitants	2.2	2.1	1.8	1.8	1.8	2.0
West						
Number of officers	84,588	38,215	13,516	11,509	7,390	5,133
Average number of officers per 1,000 inhabitants	1.7	2.0	1.3	1.3	1.4	1.6
Mountain						
Number of officers	29,303	12,692	4,376	3,275	2,900	1,857
Average number of officers per 1,000 inhabitants	1.9	2.0	1.5	1.5	1.6	1.9
Pacific						
Number of officers	55,285	25,523	9,140	8,234	4,490	3,276
Average number of officers per 1,000 inhabitants	1.7	2.0	1.3	1.3	1.4	1.5

Note: No 2008 police employee data were received for the state of West Virginia.

Table 71. Full-Time Law Enforcement Officers, by Geographic Region and Division and Population Group, 2008—*Continued*

(Number, rate per 1,000 population.)

Geographic region/division	Group VI (7,600 cities, under 10,000; population 23,777,795)	Total city agencies	2008 estimated city population	County[1] (3,254 agencies; population 92,689,393)	Total city and county agencies	2008 estimated total agency population	Suburban area[2] (7,412 agencies; population 121,966,483)
TOTAL							
Number of officers	82,420	10,915	193,548,068	258,673	14,169	286,237,461	309,689
Average number of officers per 1,000 inhabitants	3.5			2.8			2.5
Northeast							
Number of officers	17,463	2,448	43,249,515				
Average number of officers per 1,000 inhabitants	2.8						
New England							
Number of officers	5,088	760	12,565,101				
Average number of officers per 1,000 inhabitants	3.0						
Middle Atlantic							
Number of officers	12,375	1,688	30,684,414				
Average number of officers per 1,000 inhabitants	2.7						
Midwest							
Number of officers	20,672	3,302	44,263,045				
Average number of officers per 1,000 inhabitants	2.8						
East North Central							
Number of officers	13,196	2,072	31,160,435				
Average number of officers per 1,000 inhabitants	2.8						
West North Central							
Number of officers	7,476	1,230	13,102,610				
Average number of officers per 1,000 inhabitants	2.9						
South							
Number of officers	35,460	3,817	57,241,561				
Average number of officers per 1,000 inhabitants	4.7						
South Atlantic							
Number of officers	16,839	1,524	23,422,121				
Average number of officers per 1,000 inhabitants	6.0						
East South Central							
Number of officers	7,996	978	9,738,647				
Average number of officers per 1,000 inhabitants	4.1						
West South Central							
Number of officers	10,625	1,315	24,080,793				
Average number of officers per 1,000 inhabitants	3.7						
West							
Number of officers	8,825	1,348	48,793,947				
Average number of officers per 1,000 inhabitants	3.4						
Mountain							
Number of officers	4,203	583	15,768,765				
Average number of officers per 1,000 inhabitants	3.2						
Pacific							
Number of officers	4,622	765	33,025,182				
Average number of officers per 1,000 inhabitants	3.7						

Note: No 2008 police employee data were received for the state of West Virginia.

[1] The designation county is a combination of both metropolitan and nonmetropolitan counties.

[2] Suburban areas include law enforcement agencies in cities with less than 50,000 inhabitants and county law enforcement agencies that are within a metropolitan statistical area. Suburban areas exclude all metropolitan agencies associated with a principal city. The agencies associated with suburban areas also appear in other groups within this table.

Table 72. Full-Time Law Enforcement Employees,[1] by Rate Range, 2008

(Number, rate per 1,000 population.)

Rate range	Total cities[2] (9,927 cities; population 193,548,068)	Group I (75 cities, 250,000 and over; population 55,781,739)	Group II (189 cities, 100,000 to 249,999; population 27,940,012)	Group III (437 cities, 50,000 to 99,999; population 29,817,070)	Group IV (807 cities, 25,000 to 49,999; population 27,597,191)	Group V (1,807 cities, 10,000 to 24,999; population 28,634,261)	Group VI (6,612 cities, under 10,000; population 23,777,795)
Total Cities							
Number	9,927	75	189	437	807	1,807	6,612
Percent[3]	100.0	100.0	100.0	100.0	100.0	100.0	100.0
0.1–0.5							
Number	99	0	0	0	1	5	93
Percent	1.0	0.0	0.0	0.0	0.1	0.3	1.4
0.6–1.0							
Number	444	0	0	5	21	42	376
Percent	4.5	0.0	0.0	1.1	2.6	2.3	5.7
1.1–1.5							
Number	1,068	1	15	60	92	189	711
Percent	10.8	1.3	7.9	13.7	11.4	10.5	10.8
1.6–2.0							
Number	1,825	10	58	125	203	383	1,046
Percent	18.4	13.3	30.7	28.6	25.2	21.2	15.8
2.1–2.5							
Number	1,971	20	45	126	249	470	1,061
Percent	19.9	26.7	23.8	28.8	30.9	26.0	16.0
2.6–3.0							
Number	1,434	19	34	58	116	328	879
Percent	14.4	25.3	18.0	13.3	14.4	18.2	13.3
3.1–3.5							
Number	968	6	17	32	68	207	638
Percent	9.8	8.0	9.0	7.3	8.4	11.5	9.6
3.6–4.0							
Number	593	6	12	12	30	81	452
Percent	6.0	8.0	6.3	2.7	3.7	4.5	6.8
4.1–4.5							
Number	442	4	5	12	17	55	349
Percent	4.5	5.3	2.6	2.7	2.1	3.0	5.3
4.6–5.0							
Number	283	1	2	2	6	25	247
Percent	2.9	1.3	1.1	0.5	0.7	1.4	3.7
5.1 and over							
Number	800	8	1	5	4	22	760
Percent	8.1	10.7	0.5	1.1	0.5	1.2	11.5

Note: No 2008 police employee data were received for the state of West Virginia.

[1] Full-time law enforcement employees include civilians.

[2] The number of agencies used to compile these figures differs from other tables that include data about law enforcement employees because agencies with no resident population are excluded from this table. These agencies include those associated with universities and colleges (see Table 79) and other agencies (see Table 81), as well as some state agencies that have concurrent jurisdiction with other local law enforcement.

[3] Because of rounding, the percentages may not add to 100.0.

Table 73. Full-Time Law Enforcement Officers, by Rate Range, 2008

(Number, rate per 1,000 population.)

Rate range	Total cities[1] (9,927 cities; population 193,548,068)	Group I (75 cities, 250,000 and over; population 55,781,739)	Group II (189 cities, 100,000 to 249,999; population 27,940,012)	Group III (437 cities, 50,000 to 99,999; population 29,817,070)	Group IV (807 cities, 25,000 to 49,999; population 27,597,191)	Group V (1,807 cities, 10,000 to 24,999; population 28,634,261)	Group VI (6,612 cities, under 10,000; population 23,777,795)
Total Cities							
Number	9,927	75	189	437	807	1,807	6,612
Percent[2]	100.0	100.0	100.0	100.0	100.0	100.0	100.0
0.1–0.5							
Number	113	0	0	0	1	5	107
Percent	1.1	0.0	0.0	0.0	0.1	0.3	1.6
0.6–1.0							
Number	619	0	11	36	55	84	433
Percent	6.2	0.0	5.8	8.2	6.8	4.6	6.5
1.1–1.5							
Number	1,814	13	68	141	223	394	975
Percent	18.3	17.3	36.0	32.3	27.6	21.8	14.7
1.6–2.0							
Number	2,562	27	53	151	292	650	1,389
Percent	25.8	36.0	28.0	34.6	36.2	36.0	21.0
2.1–2.5							
Number	1,817	12	30	68	132	375	1,200
Percent	18.3	16.0	15.9	15.6	16.4	20.8	18.1
2.6–3.0							
Number	1,091	9	13	23	73	174	799
Percent	11.0	12.0	6.9	5.3	9.0	9.6	12.1
3.1–3.5							
Number	651	4	10	10	21	74	532
Percent	6.6	5.3	5.3	2.3	2.6	4.1	8.0
3.6–4.0							
Number	392	3	4	3	7	35	340
Percent	3.9	4.0	2.1	0.7	0.9	1.9	5.1
4.1–4.5							
Number	241	1	0	4	1	7	228
Percent	2.4	1.3	0.0	0.9	0.1	0.4	3.4
4.6–5.0							
Number	152	4	0	0	0	5	143
Percent	1.5	5.3	0.0	0.0	0.0	0.3	2.2
5.1 and over							
Number	475	2	0	1	2	4	466
Percent	4.8	2.7	0.0	0.2	0.2	0.2	7.0

Note: No 2008 police employee data were received for the state of West Virginia.

[1] The number of agencies used to compile these figures differs from other tables that include data about law enforcement officers because agencies with no resident population are excluded from this table. These agencies include those associated with universities and colleges (see Table 79) and other agencies (see Table 81), as well as some state agencies that have concurrent jurisdiction with other local law enforcement.

[2] Because of rounding, the percentages may not add to 100.0.

Table 74. Full-Time Law Enforcement Employees, by Population Group, Percent Male and Female, 2008

(Number, percent.)

Population group	Total law enforcement employees	Percent law enforcement employees		Total officers	Percent officers		Total civilians	Percent civilians		Number of agencies	2008 estimated population
		Male	Female		Male	Female		Male	Female		
TOTAL AGENCIES:	1,024,228	72.8	27.2	708,569	88.1	11.9	315,659	38.4	61.6	14,169	286,237,461
Total Cities	581,504	75.0	25.0	449,896	88.1	11.9	131,608	30.2	69.8	10,915	193,548,068
GROUP I (250,000 and over)	203,685	70.9	29.1	156,445	83.0	17.0	47,240	30.8	69.2	75	55,781,739
1,000,000 and over (Group I subset)	109,612	69.5	30.5	84,091	81.8	18.2	25,521	29.2	70.8	10	25,543,437
500,000 to 999,999 (Group I subset)	54,659	73.5	26.5	42,616	84.0	16.0	12,043	36.4	63.6	24	16,218,619
250,000 to 499,999 (Group I subset)	39,414	71.2	28.8	29,738	85.2	14.8	9,676	28.2	71.8	41	14,019,683
GROUP II (100,000 to 249,999)	69,458	72.8	27.2	52,273	88.1	11.9	17,185	26.3	73.7	189	27,940,012
GROUP III (50,000 to 99,999)	68,260	75.9	24.1	52,341	90.5	9.5	15,919	27.8	72.2	437	29,817,070
GROUP IV (25,000 to 49,999)	64,319	77.8	22.2	50,650	91.4	8.6	13,669	27.2	72.8	807	27,597,191
GROUP V (10,000 to 24,999)	69,817	79.1	20.9	55,767	92.2	7.8	14,050	26.9	73.1	1,807	28,634,261
GROUP VI (under 10,000)	105,965	79.2	20.8	82,420	91.3	8.7	23,545	37.1	62.9	7,600	23,777,795
Metropolitan Counties	308,179	69.1	30.9	179,079	86.4	13.6	129,100	45.1	54.9	1,201	65,844,305
Nonmetropolitan Counties	134,545	71.8	28.2	79,594	92.0	8.0	54,951	42.5	57.5	2,053	26,845,088
SUBURBAN AREAS[1]	475,575	72.5	27.5	309,689	88.5	11.5	165,886	42.6	57.4	7,412	121,966,483

Note: No 2008 police employee data were received for the state of West Virginia.
[1] Suburban areas include law enforcement agencies in cities with less than 50,000 inhabitants and county law enforcement agencies that are within a Metropolitan Statistical Area. Suburban areas exclude all metropolitan agencies associated with a principal city. The agencies associated with suburban areas also appear in other groups within this table.

Table 75. Full-Time Civilian Law Enforcement Employees, by Population Group, 2008

(Number, percent.)

Population group	Percent civilian employees	Number of Agencies	2008 estimated population
TOTAL AGENCIES:	30.8	14,169	286,237,461
Total Cities	22.6	10,915	193,548,068
GROUP I (250,000 and over)	23.2	75	55,781,739
1,000,000 and over (Group I subset)	23.3	10	25,543,437
500,000 to 999,999 (Group I subset)	22.0	24	16,218,619
250,000 to 499,999 (Group I subset)	24.5	41	14,019,683
GROUP II (100,000 to 249,999)	24.7	189	27,940,012
GROUP III (50,000 to 99,999)	23.3	437	29,817,070
GROUP IV (25,000 to 49,999)	21.3	807	27,597,191
GROUP V (10,000 to 24,999)	20.1	1,807	28,634,261
GROUP VI (under 10,000)	22.2	7,600	23,777,795
Metropolitan Counties	41.9	1,201	65,844,305
Nonmetropolitan Counties	40.8	2,053	26,845,088
SUBURBAN AREAS[1]	34.9	7,412	121,966,483

Note: No 2008 police employee data were received for the state of West Virginia.
[1] Suburban areas include law enforcement agencies in cities with less than 50,000 inhabitants and county law enforcement agencies that are within a Metropolitan Statistical Area. Suburban areas exclude all metropolitan agencies associated with a principal city. The agencies associated with suburban areas also appear in other groups within this table.

Table 76. Full-Time State Law Enforcement Employees, by State, 2008

(Number.)

State/Agency	Total law enforcement employees	Total officers		Total civilians	
		Male	Female	Male	Female
Alabama					
Department of Public Safety	1,411	713	16	189	493
Other state agencies	251	195	10	7	39
Alaska					
State Troopers	567	324	15	107	121
Other state agencies	9	5	0	1	3
Arizona					
Department of Public Safety	2,152	1,176	68	372	536
Other state agencies	68	29	2	21	16
Arkansas					
State Police	957	527	23	119	288
Other state agencies	52	37	2	7	6
California					
Highway Patrol	10,677	6,516	629	1,603	1,929
Other state agencies	1,123	846	231	8	38
Colorado					
State Patrol	1,007	698	49	79	181
Other state agencies	78	15	3	39	21
Connecticut					
State Police	1,796	1,157	85	235	319
Other state agencies	38	27	1	8	2
Delaware					
State Police	919	604	75	109	131
Other state agencies	642	282	89	61	210
Florida					
Highway Patrol	2,089	1,376	179	173	361
Other state agencies	3,165	1,274	173	602	1,116
Georgia					
Department of Public Safety	993	765	22	127	79
Other state agencies	1,303	437	57	318	491
Idaho					
State Police	462	257	11	55	139
Illinois					
State Police	3,532	1,897	228	529	878
Other state agencies	448	282	25	88	53
Indiana					
State Police	2,034	1,254	67	295	418
Other state agencies	103	82	14	0	7
Iowa					
Department of Public Safety	983	625	44	136	178
Kansas					
Highway Patrol	840	524	17	116	183
Other state agencies	578	289	13	119	157
Kentucky					
State Police	1,891	886	30	585	390
Other state agencies	274	250	9	6	9
Louisiana					
State Police	1,762	1,224	51	113	374
Other state agencies	55	43	3	0	9
Maine					
State Police	551	296	23	114	118
Other state agencies[1]	53	24	1	17	11
Maryland					
State Police	2,230	1,363	117	413	337
Other state agencies	1,664	866	133	315	350
Massachusetts					
State Police	2,920	2,189	183	231	317
Other state agencies	257	221	27	3	6
Michigan					
State Police	2,907	1,620	210	397	680
Minnesota					
State Patrol	730	470	48	111	101
Other state agencies	55	10	1	35	9
Missouri					
State Highway Patrol	2,173	1,013	41	490	629
Other state agencies	582	499	30	7	46
Montana					
Highway Patrol	268	199	12	15	42
Other state agencies	23	20	0	0	3
Nebraska					
State Patrol	716	468	28	73	147

Note: Caution should be used when comparing data from one state to that of another. The responsibilities of the various state police, highway patrol, and department of public safety agencies range from full law enforcement duties to only traffic patrol, which can impact both the level of employment for agencies as well as the ratio of sworn officers to civilians employed. Any valid comparison must take these factors and the other identified variables affecting crime into consideration.

[1] The total employee count includes employees from agencies that are not represented in other law enforcement employee tables.

Table 76. Full-Time State Law Enforcement Employees, by State, 2008—*Continued*

(Number.)

State/Agency	Total law enforcement employees	Total officers		Total civilians	
		Male	Female	Male	Female
Nevada					
Highway Patrol	925	468	43	120	294
Other state agencies	63	34	3	10	16
New Hampshire					
State Police	529	331	37	47	114
Other state agencies	35	19	4	5	7
New Jersey					
State Police	4,499	2,921	119	696	763
Other state agencies	444	335	31	51	27
Port Authority of New York and New Jersey[2]	1,132	945	110	19	58
New Mexico					
State Police	675	525	15	41	94
New York					
State Police	6,102	4,519	425	489	669
Other state agencies	289	251	21	4	13
North Carolina					
Highway Patrol	2,256	1,698	45	273	240
Other state agencies	1,080	543	177	100	260
North Dakota					
Highway Patrol	187	132	6	19	30
Ohio					
Highway Patrol	2,630	1,417	139	510	564
Other state agencies	543	402	31	33	77
Oklahoma					
Department of Public Safety	1,488	809	16	289	374
Other state agencies	69	25	3	29	12
Oregon					
State Police	898	489	48	133	228
Other state agencies	54	31	13	0	10
Pennsylvania					
State Police	6,265	4,325	213	773	954
Other state agencies	157	136	7	9	5
Rhode Island					
State Police	247	185	17	31	14
Other state agencies	92	70	4	11	7
South Carolina					
Highway Patrol	1,151	897	27	94	133
Other state agencies[1]	1,535	893	141	176	325
South Dakota					
Highway Patrol	253	148	2	70	33
Other state agencies	149	40	3	39	67
Tennessee					
Department of Safety	1,683	819	112	249	503
Other state agencies	1,051	599	72	124	256
Texas					
Department of Public Safety	8,076	3,304	202	1,520	3,050
Utah					
Highway Patrol	535	438	20	31	46
Other state agencies	157	135	12	6	4
Vermont					
State Police	447	280	27	48	92
Other state agencies	47	31	1	5	10
Virginia					
State Police	2,560	1,776	102	212	470
Other state agencies	515	265	44	86	120
Washington					
State Patrol	2,303	996	84	595	628
Wisconsin					
State Patrol	665	457	52	64	92
Other state agencies	402	320	48	12	22
Wyoming					
Highway Patrol	370	192	8	63	107

Note: Caution should be used when comparing data from one state to that of another. The responsibilities of the various state police, highway patrol, and department of public safety agencies range from full law enforcement duties to only traffic patrol, which can impact both the level of employment for agencies as well as the ratio of sworn officers to civilians employed. Any valid comparison must take these factors and the other identified variables affecting crime into consideration.

[2] Data reported are the number of law enforcement employees for the state of New Jersey.

Table 77. Full-Time Law Enforcement Employees, by State, 2008

(Number.)

State	Total law enforcement employees	Total officers		Total civilians		Number of agencies	2008 estimated population
		Male	Female	Male	Female		
Alabama	16,172	9,988	787	2,005	3,392	350	4,437,374
Alaska	1,963	1,144	116	234	469	43	686,293
Arizona	22,912	11,520	1,380	4,537	5,475	95	6,382,545
Arkansas	9,678	5,560	504	1,326	2,288	275	2,850,876
California	123,506	70,594	10,692	14,739	27,481	459	31,804,738
Colorado	16,859	10,117	1,491	1,711	3,540	224	4,869,988
Connecticut	10,657	7,845	787	812	1,213	102	3,501,252
Delaware	3,159	1,998	298	323	540	52	871,838
District of Columbia	5,190	3,455	1,000	291	444	2	591,833
Florida	73,872	38,114	6,362	10,849	18,547	402	18,297,732
Georgia	33,209	20,514	3,775	2,996	5,924	427	8,931,253
Hawaii	3,795	2,687	310	245	553	4	1,288,198
Idaho	4,461	2,512	174	520	1,255	106	1,519,310
Illinois	52,561	31,496	5,752	7,392	7,921	749	12,846,505
Indiana	15,877	9,690	770	2,469	2,948	222	5,623,508
Iowa	8,031	4,770	398	1,093	1,770	232	2,967,083
Kansas	10,284	6,198	613	1,416	2,057	331	2,550,708
Kentucky	10,188	7,275	534	1,026	1,353	365	4,141,804
Louisiana	22,621	13,960	3,346	1,586	3,729	200	4,293,435
Maine	2,961	2,107	138	308	408	133	1,315,497
Maryland	20,797	13,538	2,081	1,988	3,190	132	5,456,159
Massachusetts	20,173	15,250	1,359	1,490	2,074	331	6,281,021
Michigan	26,495	17,010	2,494	3,028	3,963	618	9,948,437
Minnesota	13,697	7,805	1,063	2,005	2,824	320	5,145,905
Mississippi	8,243	4,648	429	1,271	1,895	167	2,489,444
Missouri	20,319	13,039	1,398	2,231	3,651	578	5,860,645
Montana	2,661	1,545	106	445	565	104	931,062
Nebraska	4,810	3,106	385	342	977	165	1,770,070
Nevada	8,841	5,194	534	866	2,247	37	2,600,167
New Hampshire	3,373	2,367	199	245	562	147	1,156,970
New Jersey	42,022	29,640	2,739	3,669	5,974	546	8,400,257
New Mexico	5,765	3,730	390	548	1,097	97	1,805,058
New York	80,949	52,722	8,607	5,780	13,840	342	18,103,583
North Carolina	32,028	19,488	2,563	4,368	5,609	499	9,189,952
North Dakota	1,673	1,110	114	179	270	100	640,830
Ohio	31,469	19,541	2,309	4,014	5,605	607	9,715,611
Oklahoma	11,553	7,002	693	1,578	2,280	304	3,642,361
Oregon	9,965	5,276	614	1,702	2,373	202	3,752,587
Pennsylvania	29,641	22,290	2,698	1,792	2,861	937	9,356,098
Rhode Island	3,240	2,403	180	299	358	48	1,050,788
South Carolina	15,316	10,061	1,288	1,395	2,572	381	4,479,234
South Dakota	2,273	1,347	85	344	497	142	800,171
Tennessee	25,067	14,016	1,513	4,366	5,172	449	6,209,570
Texas	87,479	46,909	5,766	14,755	20,049	1,004	24,229,899
Utah	7,719	4,362	344	1,516	1,497	131	2,735,255
Vermont	1,299	874	81	116	228	43	271,869
Virginia	23,748	16,265	2,193	1,446	3,844	279	7,767,656
Washington	14,980	9,605	1,000	1,471	2,904	245	6,538,812
West Virginia[1]							
Wisconsin	18,648	11,230	1,808	2,061	3,549	376	5,607,356
Wyoming	2,029	1,285	107	153	484	65	528,864

[1] No 2008 police employee data were received for the state of West Virginia.

Table 78. Full-Time Law Enforcement Employees, by State and City, 2008

(Number.)

State/City	Population	Total law enforcement employees	Total officers	Total civilians
ALABAMA				
Abbeville	2,939	19	10	9
Adamsville	4,722	29	17	12
Addison	715	3	3	0
Alabaster	29,328	88	69	19
Albertville	19,818	58	40	18
Alexander City	14,917	64	46	18
Aliceville	2,405	11	7	4
Andalusia	8,689	40	30	10
Anniston	23,620	119	84	35
Arab	7,753	36	24	12
Ardmore	1,209	11	7	4
Argo	1,900	6	6	0
Ariton	743	2	2	0
Ashford	2,041	8	4	4
Ashland	1,862	11	7	4
Ashville	2,543	6	6	0
Athens	23,432	54	43	11
Atmore	7,391	38	33	5
Attalla	6,515	26	20	6
Auburn	55,649	104	98	6
Autaugaville	877	1	1	0
Baker Hill	311	1	1	0
Bay Minette	7,710	33	23	10
Bayou La Batre	2,716	16	11	5
Bear Creek	999	1	1	0
Berry	1,183	3	3	0
Bessemer	28,479	141	105	36
Birmingham	228,314	1,085	789	296
Blountsville	1,976	6	6	0
Boaz	8,273	33	23	10
Brent	4,384	5	5	0
Brewton	5,256	32	25	7
Bridgeport	2,628	11	7	4
Brighton	3,247	11	6	5
Brookside	1,323	1	1	0
Brundidge	2,294	13	8	5
Butler	1,699	6	6	0
Calera	10,723	32	26	6
Camden	2,210	9	8	1
Carrollton	929	3	3	0
Cedar Bluff	1,657	4	4	0
Centre	3,491	11	10	1
Centreville	2,533	6	6	0
Chatom	1,156	6	6	0
Cherokee	1,167	4	4	0
Chickasaw	5,935	26	21	5
Citronelle	3,708	14	9	5
Clanton	8,849	25	22	3
Clayhatchee	491	1	1	0
Clayton	1,358	4	4	0
Clio	2,212	3	3	0
Coffeeville	344	1	1	0
Collinsville	1,690	9	4	5
Columbiana	3,839	12	8	4
Coosada	1,645	3	3	0
Cordova	2,267	5	4	1
Cottonwood	1,176	3	3	0
Creola	2,082	12	7	5
Cullman	15,074	66	49	17
Dadeville	3,220	13	12	1
Daleville	4,512	23	17	6
Daphne	19,245	71	44	27
Dauphin Island	1,605	13	10	3
Decatur	55,941	147	127	20
Demopolis	7,328	23	20	3
Dora	2,411	7	4	3
Dothan	66,412	224	152	72
Double Springs	979	5	5	0
Douglas	583	3	3	0
East Brewton	2,489	6	4	2
Eclectic	1,160	10	6	4
Elba	4,124	22	14	8
Elberta	582	6	5	1
Enterprise	24,863	70	53	17
Eufaula	14,560	55	38	17
Eutaw	2,941	11	10	1
Evergreen	3,390	17	15	2
Excel	600	1	1	0
Fairfield	11,303	51	38	13
Fairhope	17,180	55	32	23
Falkville	1,166	8	8	0
Fayette	4,672	12	11	1
Flomaton	1,531	11	6	5
Florala	1,899	6	6	0
Florence	37,594	119	92	27
Foley	14,157	88	58	30
Fort Payne	14,040	38	34	4
Fultondale	6,945	31	23	8
Gadsden	36,700	133	101	32
Gardendale	13,626	36	28	8
Geneva	4,399	15	11	4
Georgiana	1,557	10	7	3
Geraldine	837	3	3	0
Glencoe	5,356	10	7	3
Goodwater	1,516	8	4	4
Gordo	1,556	4	4	0
Grant	693	5	5	0
Greensboro	2,541	9	9	0
Greenville	6,974	35	27	8
Grove Hill	1,338	8	7	1
Guin	2,176	4	4	0
Gulf Shores	10,985	54	40	14
Guntersville	8,351	43	32	11
Gurley	855	4	4	0
Hackleburg	1,445	2	2	0
Haleyville	4,054	16	11	5
Hamilton	6,331	13	12	1
Hammondville	544	2	2	0
Hanceville	3,367	15	11	4
Harpersville	1,689	9	9	0
Hartford	2,408	12	7	5
Hartselle	13,815	37	29	8
Headland	4,045	14	10	4
Heflin	3,543	11	10	1
Helena	14,701	26	22	4
Henagar	2,558	6	2	4
Hillsboro	588	1	1	0
Hokes Bluff	4,452	7	5	2
Hollywood	918	3	2	1
Homewood	23,771	105	75	30
Hoover	70,731	216	158	58
Hueytown	15,708	38	32	6
Huntsville	172,794	512	398	114
Ider	716	4	3	1
Irondale	9,426	35	28	7
Jackson	5,091	25	19	6
Jacksonville	9,881	31	26	5
Jasper	13,956	73	46	27
Jemison	2,661	12	11	1
Killen	1,134	5	5	0
Kimberly	2,743	7	5	2
Kinsey	1,969	3	2	1
Lafayette	3,013	16	15	1
Lake View	2,206	5	4	1
Lanett	7,420	31	27	4
Leeds	11,285	26	22	4
Leesburg	822	3	3	0
Leighton	828	3	3	0
Level Plains	1,502	6	6	0
Lexington	837	2	2	0
Lincoln	5,601	22	17	5
Linden	2,268	7	7	0
Lineville	2,363	11	7	4
Littleville	950	8	5	3
Livingston	2,969	12	7	5
Lockhart	545	1	1	0
Loxley	1,659	17	12	5

Table 78. Full-Time Law Enforcement Employees, by State and City, 2008—*Continued*

(Number.)

State/City	Population	Total law enforcement employees	Total officers	Total civilians
Luverne	2,763	14	10	4
Lynn	717	2	1	1
Madison	39,529	97	71	26
Maplesville	690	5	5	0
Marion	3,133	13	6	7
McIntosh	233	9	9	0
McKenzie	604	1	1	0
Mentone	481	2	2	0
Midfield	5,158	16	12	4
Midland City	1,865	11	5	6
Millbrook	17,249	39	30	9
Millport	1,007	1	1	0
Millry	588	4	3	1
Mobile	251,041	686	512	174
Monroeville	6,373	29	23	6
Montevallo	6,030	18	14	4
Montgomery	204,398	654	499	155
Moody	13,588	19	18	1
Morris	1,904	8	6	2
Moulton	3,262	11	11	0
Moundville	2,571	8	7	1
Mountain Brook	21,057	62	49	13
Mount Vernon	817	6	5	1
Muscle Shoals	12,925	43	34	9
Myrtlewood	131	1	1	0
Napier Field	394	2	2	0
New Brockton	1,227	5	3	2
New Hope	2,775	7	7	0
New Site	828	1	1	0
Newton	1,648	5	4	1
North Courtland	797	2	1	1
Northport	23,223	79	60	19
Notasulga	832	6	3	3
Oakman	924	3	3	0
Odenville	1,264	9	9	0
Ohatchee	1,237	6	6	0
Oneonta	7,058	19	18	1
Opelika	26,015	96	75	21
Opp	6,662	29	22	7
Orange Beach	6,589	57	36	21
Owens Crossroads	1,491	4	4	0
Oxford	20,511	62	50	12
Ozark	14,584	40	34	6
Pelham	21,532	80	65	15
Pell City	12,898	33	30	3
Phenix City	30,952	99	78	21
Phil Campbell	1,035	2	2	0
Pickensville	632	2	1	1
Piedmont	4,962	19	14	5
Pinckard	623	2	2	0
Pine Hill	905	4	4	0
Pleasant Grove	10,299	26	20	6
Powell	975	2	1	1
Prattville	32,849	86	76	10
Priceville	2,659	4	4	0
Prichard	27,691	67	45	22
Ragland	2,125	4	3	1
Rainbow City	9,276	32	22	10
Rainsville	4,950	15	11	4
Ranburne	481	2	2	0
Red Bay	3,242	11	7	4
Reform	1,786	5	5	0
Riverside	2,023	4	4	0
Roanoke	6,618	29	24	5
Robertsdale	5,018	27	14	13
Rockford	392	2	1	1
Russellville	8,758	28	24	4
Samson	2,006	6	5	1
Saraland	12,893	49	38	11
Sardis City	2,177	4	4	0
Scottsboro	14,870	66	44	22
Selma	18,772	72	48	24
Sheffield	9,118	35	29	6
Shorter	352	11	4	7
Silas	472	2	1	1
Silverhill	695	2	2	0
Sipsey	540	1	1	0
Skyline	831	3	1	2
Slocomb	2,033	7	6	1
Snead	846	5	5	0
Southside	8,441	15	9	6
Spanish Fort	5,831	15	14	1
Springville	3,618	12	12	0
Steele	1,214	3	2	1
Stevenson	2,003	6	4	2
Sulligent	1,960	7	7	0
Sumiton	2,541	11	7	4
Summerdale	714	6	5	1
Sylacauga	12,876	48	41	7
Sylvania	1,266	2	2	0
Talladega	16,951	50	38	12
Tallassee	5,144	22	16	6
Tarrant City	6,505	31	25	6
Taylor	1,980	2	2	0
Thomasville	4,474	21	16	5
Thorsby	2,068	6	6	0
Town Creek	1,206	2	2	0
Triana	493	2	2	0
Trinity	1,914	6	6	0
Troy	14,538	68	48	20
Trussville	19,199	57	45	12
Tuscaloosa	90,157	337	262	75
Tuscumbia	8,275	28	21	7
Tuskegee	11,287	38	26	12
Union Springs	4,566	16	10	6
Uniontown	1,413	8	8	0
Valley	8,774	37	27	10
Valley Head	649	3	2	1
Vance	839	3	3	0
Vernon	1,886	7	7	0
Vestavia Hills	31,055	67	65	2
Warrior	3,003	20	14	6
Weaver	2,686	10	7	3
Webb	1,361	2	2	0
Wedowee	815	9	9	0
West Blocton	1,425	2	2	0
Wetumpka	7,840	38	28	10
Wilton	630	1	1	0
Winfield	4,651	11	10	1
Woodstock	1,023	4	4	0
ALASKA				
Anchorage	280,068	553	383	170
Bethel	6,557	20	12	8
Bristol Bay Borough	963	10	4	6
Cordova	2,227	12	5	7
Craig	1,153	11	5	6
Dillingham	2,506	16	4	12
Emmonak	839	5	5	0
Fairbanks	35,131	50	46	4
Haines	2,255	7	3	4
Homer	5,808	20	12	8
Hoonah	716	10	3	7
Houston	2,153	1	1	0
Juneau	30,692	84	49	35
Kake	636	5	2	3
Kenai	7,784	26	17	9
Ketchikan	7,305	36	24	12
Klawock	730	2	2	0
Kodiak	6,159	34	18	16
Kotzebue	3,160	19	9	10
Nome	3,589	13	7	6
North Pole	2,276	13	12	1
North Slope Borough	6,419	64	47	17
Palmer	8,292	29	14	15
Petersburg	2,839	15	9	6
Sand Point	887	4	3	1
Seldovia	309	1	1	0
Seward	3,092	17	10	7

Table 78. Full-Time Law Enforcement Employees, by State and City, 2008—*Continued*

(Number.)

State/City	Population	Total law enforcement employees	Total officers	Total civilians
Sitka	8,879	34	19	15
Skagway	818	8	4	4
Soldotna	4,360	16	14	2
St. Paul	432	5	3	2
Togiak	823	5	5	0
Unalaska	3,789	28	13	15
Valdez	3,817	20	11	9
Wasilla	10,497	48	22	26
Whittier	161	3	3	0
Wrangell	1,998	13	7	6
ARIZONA				
Apache Junction	31,521	89	53	36
Avondale	85,376	151	96	55
Benson	4,995	25	16	9
Bisbee	5,958	21	15	6
Buckeye	32,070	88	66	22
Bullhead City	41,976	133	80	53
Camp Verde	11,011	34	22	12
Casa Grande	39,928	109	78	31
Chandler	253,076	502	336	166
Chino Valley	11,326	34	24	10
Clarkdale	4,328	12	10	2
Clifton	2,354	7	3	4
Colorado City	4,999	11	6	5
Coolidge	9,904	41	31	10
Cottonwood	11,520	44	28	16
Douglas	17,007	48	33	15
Eagar	4,536	11	8	3
El Mirage	27,543	52	44	8
Eloy	12,214	45	33	12
Flagstaff	60,400	170	116	54
Florence	17,880	43	28	15
Fredonia	1,108	4	4	0
Gilbert	220,373	334	224	110
Glendale	256,659	530	372	158
Globe	7,080	30	22	8
Goodyear	58,732	128	92	36
Hayden	1,249	8	7	1
Holbrook	5,094	23	15	8
Huachuca City	1,989	9	4	5
Jerome	357	5	5	0
Kearny	3,243	8	5	3
Kingman	28,725	86	57	29
Lake Havasu City	57,616	121	91	30
Mammoth	2,534	7	4	3
Marana	34,549	103	74	29
Mesa	456,821	1,328	831	497
Miami	1,786	11	7	4
Nogales	19,757	79	62	17
Oro Valley	40,785	133	102	31
Page	6,917	30	19	11
Paradise Valley	15,134	43	33	10
Parker	3,193	13	11	2
Patagonia	772	4	4	0
Peoria	151,493	280	186	94
Phoenix	1,585,838	4,420	3,351	1,069
Pima	2,077	3	3	0
Pinetop-Lakeside	4,665	23	15	8
Prescott	43,190	88	71	17
Prescott Valley	39,856	82	65	17
Quartzsite	3,544	14	13	1
Safford	9,329	25	21	4
Sahuarita	22,389	49	42	7
Scottsdale	238,905	697	421	276
Sedona	11,580	40	29	11
Show Low	12,394	43	30	13
Sierra Vista	43,642	89	62	27
Snowflake-Taylor	9,683	22	14	8
Somerton	11,837	34	24	10
South Tucson	5,606	23	16	7
Springerville	1,995	10	7	3
St. Johns	3,624	12	9	3
Superior	3,049	13	10	3
Surprise	101,141	187	134	53
Tempe	176,388	539	358	181
Thatcher	4,874	12	11	1
Tolleson	7,232	41	31	10
Tucson	528,917	1,406	1,037	369
Wellton	1,909	5	5	0
Wickenburg	6,716	23	15	8
Willcox	3,799	20	11	9
Williams	3,346	21	13	8
Winslow	9,842	33	24	9
Youngtown	5,301	12	11	1
Yuma	90,245	253	167	86
ARKANSAS				
Alma	5,054	18	11	7
Altheimer	1,116	2	1	1
Arkadelphia	10,826	27	22	5
Ashdown	4,407	12	11	1
Atkins	2,963	7	6	1
Augusta	2,278	7	7	0
Austin	1,719	3	3	0
Bald Knob	3,389	9	5	4
Barling	4,475	9	9	0
Bay	2,038	3	3	0
Bearden	992	2	2	0
Beebe	6,883	20	13	7
Bella Vista	16,120	27	20	7
Benton	29,121	63	52	11
Bentonville	35,970	82	56	26
Berryville	5,284	12	10	2
Blytheville	15,829	58	40	18
Bono	1,592	3	3	0
Booneville	4,070	12	8	4
Bradford	846	2	2	0
Brinkley	3,215	15	11	4
Bryant	15,218	41	29	12
Bull Shoals	2,109	3	3	0
Cabot	24,387	48	35	13
Caddo Valley	638	4	4	0
Camden	11,489	38	23	15
Cammack Village	775	6	4	2
Caraway	1,388	2	2	0
Carlisle	2,369	9	6	3
Cave City	2,057	3	3	0
Cave Springs	1,620	3	3	0
Centerton	9,522	11	10	1
Charleston	3,013	4	4	0
Cherokee Village	4,799	7	6	1
Clarendon	1,680	4	4	0
Clarksville	8,621	22	18	4
Clinton	2,388	9	8	1
Conway	58,945	152	107	45
Corning	3,330	11	7	4
Cotter	1,083	4	3	1
Crossett	5,474	24	14	10
Danville	2,472	6	5	1
Dardanelle	4,422	14	10	4
Decatur	1,948	6	6	0
De Queen	5,899	16	13	3
Dermott	3,247	11	6	5
Des Arc	1,720	4	4	0
De Witt	3,249	14	9	5
Diamond City	807	2	2	0
Diaz	1,164	2	2	0
Dierks	1,202	3	3	0
Dover	1,405	4	4	0
Dumas	4,592	24	12	12
Earle	2,763	8	6	2
El Dorado	19,706	68	51	17
Elkins	2,624	7	7	0
England	2,942	14	7	7
Etowah	338	1	1	0
Eudora	2,354	11	6	5
Eureka Springs	2,356	15	10	5
Fairfield Bay	2,491	15	8	7
Farmington	4,802	11	10	1

Table 78. Full-Time Law Enforcement Employees, by State and City, 2008—*Continued*

(Number.)

State/City	Population	Total law enforcement employees	Total officers	Total civilians
Fayetteville	73,999	177	118	59
Flippin	1,374	7	7	0
Fordyce	4,226	12	8	4
Forrest City	13,391	41	33	8
Fort Smith	84,847	204	162	42
Gassville	2,178	4	4	0
Gentry	2,885	10	8	2
Glenwood	2,017	3	3	0
Gosnell	3,609	9	9	0
Gravette	2,657	10	9	1
Greenbrier	4,414	14	10	4
Green Forest	3,027	8	6	2
Greenland	1,292	4	4	0
Greenwood	8,661	20	19	1
Greers Ferry	970	4	3	1
Gurdon	2,296	4	3	1
Guy	565	2	1	1
Hamburg	2,696	6	5	1
Hampton	1,489	4	4	0
Hardy	816	3	3	0
Harrisburg	2,108	5	4	1
Harrison	13,221	38	28	10
Hazen	1,471	5	4	1
Heber Springs	7,262	23	14	9
Helena-West Helena	12,147	45	30	15
Hermitage	750	3	3	0
Highfill	763	2	2	0
Highland	1,084	3	3	0
Hope	10,463	34	23	11
Horseshoe Bend	2,208	6	6	0
Hot Springs	39,451	131	98	33
Hoxie	2,627	6	4	2
Huntsville	2,411	8	7	1
Jacksonville	31,316	76	64	12
Jonesboro	64,187	154	133	21
Judsonia	2,169	3	2	1
Keiser	801	1	1	0
Kensett	1,820	4	4	0
Lake City	2,085	4	4	0
Lakeview	857	2	2	0
Lake Village	2,413	13	7	6
Leachville	1,781	3	3	0
Lepanto	2,020	7	4	3
Lewisville	1,145	2	2	0
Lincoln	2,077	5	5	0
Little Flock	3,132	8	8	0
Little Rock	187,978	639	522	117
Lonoke	4,536	16	11	5
Lowell	7,274	22	15	7
Luxora	1,202	2	2	0
Magnolia	11,083	28	21	7
Malvern	8,946	26	23	3
Mammoth Spring	1,117	3	2	1
Mansfield	1,128	3	3	0
Marianna	4,341	17	12	5
Marion	11,349	25	23	2
Marked Tree	2,632	12	8	4
Marmaduke	1,176	4	4	0
Marvell	1,124	5	2	3
Maumelle	16,657	35	25	10
Mayflower	2,207	5	5	0
McCrory	1,560	5	5	0
McGehee	3,980	23	8	15
McRae	701	1	1	0
Mena	5,581	14	13	1
Mineral Springs	1,255	3	3	0
Monette	1,223	3	3	0
Monticello	9,379	26	21	5
Morrilton	6,582	31	20	11
Mountain Home	12,637	52	33	19
Mountain View	3,081	9	8	1
Mulberry	1,732	3	3	0
Murfreesboro	1,656	3	3	0
Nashville	4,746	16	15	1
Newport	7,493	22	15	7
North Little Rock	59,369	220	187	33
Ola	1,230	3	3	0
Osceola	7,760	34	23	11
Ozark	3,562	10	8	2
Paragould	24,816	51	42	9
Paris	3,612	14	9	5
Pea Ridge	4,686	9	9	0
Perryville	1,450	5	5	0
Piggott	3,515	8	8	0
Pine Bluff	50,144	161	134	27
Plummerville	867	3	3	0
Pocahontas	6,728	14	13	1
Pottsville	2,838	5	5	0
Prairie Grove	3,754	10	10	0
Prescott	4,571	10	9	1
Quitman	739	4	4	0
Ravenden	490	1	1	0
Redfield	1,175	5	4	1
Rison	1,306	3	3	0
Rockport	805	6	5	1
Rogers	57,205	132	95	37
Rose Bud	453	3	2	1
Russellville	27,059	58	50	8
Salem	1,553	3	3	0
Searcy	22,062	56	40	16
Sheridan	4,668	27	14	13
Sherwood	24,486	84	60	24
Siloam Springs	14,988	51	32	19
Smackover	1,868	5	4	1
Springdale	69,759	158	117	41
Stamps	1,893	3	3	0
Star City	2,213	6	5	1
Stuttgart	8,969	27	19	8
Swifton	790	2	1	1
Texarkana	29,855	123	83	40
Trumann	6,792	22	15	7
Tuckerman	1,645	3	2	1
Van Buren	22,396	51	37	14
Vilonia	3,515	8	8	0
Waldron	3,597	9	8	1
Walnut Ridge	4,640	9	8	1
Ward	3,806	8	5	3
Warren	6,115	21	12	9
Weiner	729	1	1	0
West Fork	2,358	7	6	1
West Memphis	27,446	91	71	20
White Hall	5,152	15	13	2
Wynne	8,334	19	17	2
CALIFORNIA				
Alameda	69,998	138	94	44
Albany	15,909	35	25	10
Alhambra	86,404	130	84	46
Alturas	2,784	7	6	1
Anaheim	333,746	606	424	182
Anderson	10,739	29	18	11
Antioch	100,702	167	118	49
Arcadia	56,605	102	66	36
Arcata	17,073	32	22	10
Arroyo Grande	17,051	31	23	8
Arvin	15,219	22	15	7
Atascadero	28,200	40	28	12
Atherton	7,352	24	19	5
Atwater	27,450	43	33	10
Auburn	13,084	33	22	11
Azusa	46,840	89	62	27
Bakersfield	326,046	486	351	135
Baldwin Park	78,031	103	73	30
Banning	29,816	55	38	17
Barstow	24,942	51	34	17
Bear Valley	4,592	16	8	8
Beaumont	34,208	76	56	20
Bell	36,877	55	38	17
Bell Gardens	44,939	73	54	19

Table 78. Full-Time Law Enforcement Employees, by State and City, 2008—*Continued*

(Number.)

State/City	Population	Total law enforcement employees	Total officers	Total civilians
Belmont	24,588	45	32	13
Belvedere	2,050	9	8	1
Benicia	26,255	51	36	15
Berkeley	101,170	289	187	102
Beverly Hills	34,684	195	137	58
Bishop	3,444	19	13	6
Blythe	23,042	37	25	12
Brawley	22,611	44	32	12
Brea	38,762	144	103	41
Brentwood	52,741	73	57	16
Brisbane	3,641	18	15	3
Broadmoor	4,369	12	11	1
Buena Park	79,431	139	93	46
Burbank	103,640	251	155	96
Burlingame	27,474	63	44	19
Calexico	39,134	76	46	30
California City	14,652	23	17	6
Calipatria	7,676	5	5	0
Calistoga	5,165	15	11	4
Campbell	37,649	66	45	21
Capitola	9,457	33	22	11
Carlsbad	97,670	160	116	44
Carmel	3,870	22	14	8
Cathedral City	53,601	94	57	37
Ceres	43,819	73	51	22
Chico	84,086	139	90	49
Chino	84,595	146	97	49
Chowchilla	19,268	26	19	7
Chula Vista	223,408	333	245	88
Citrus Heights	84,361	128	83	45
City of Angels	3,825	10	9	1
Claremont	35,121	65	42	23
Clayton	11,217	13	11	2
Clearlake	15,117	29	20	9
Cloverdale	8,333	23	14	9
Clovis	93,848	154	104	50
Coalinga	18,691	28	18	10
Colma	1,440	26	19	7
Colton	51,177	106	72	34
Colusa	5,829	9	8	1
Concord	120,679	233	165	68
Corcoran	25,235	29	19	10
Corning	7,178	24	14	10
Corona	153,193	252	178	74
Coronado	22,694	61	40	21
Costa Mesa	108,898	238	162	76
Cotati	7,267	19	12	7
Covina	47,291	91	59	32
Crescent City	7,980	14	13	1
Culver City	38,850	153	114	39
Cypress	47,212	77	58	19
Daly City	100,542	154	113	41
Davis	63,179	94	59	35
Delano	54,273	68	44	24
Del Rey Oaks	1,523	6	6	0
Desert Hot Springs	25,471	28	23	5
Dinuba	20,366	50	38	12
Dixon	17,716	30	24	6
Dos Palos	4,992	9	7	2
Downey	108,184	164	107	57
East Palo Alto	33,513	39	29	10
El Cajon	92,225	189	121	68
El Centro	39,865	87	58	29
El Cerrito	22,116	51	42	9
Elk Grove	139,395	195	128	67
El Monte	123,049	214	146	68
El Segundo	16,310	101	67	34
Emeryville	9,704	57	40	17
Escalon	7,447	15	11	4
Escondido	136,508	223	159	64
Etna	766	3	2	1
Eureka	25,313	71	45	26
Exeter	10,108	17	16	1
Fairfax	7,039	16	11	5
Fairfield	104,927	189	123	66
Farmersville	10,170	18	16	2
Ferndale	1,391	4	4	0
Firebaugh	6,950	16	12	4
Folsom	69,523	117	88	29
Fontana	189,253	288	199	89
Fort Bragg	6,599	22	16	6
Fortuna	11,388	23	14	9
Foster City	28,927	54	39	15
Fountain Valley	55,524	83	61	22
Fowler	5,467	13	12	1
Fremont	200,964	281	179	102
Fresno	475,723	1,267	824	443
Fullerton	132,776	232	158	74
Galt	24,503	43	31	12
Gardena	58,814	115	90	25
Garden Grove	165,629	244	171	73
Gilroy	50,136	96	60	36
Glendale	197,182	401	258	143
Glendora	49,738	103	59	44
Gonzales	8,681	15	13	2
Grass Valley	12,345	38	28	10
Greenfield	15,145	21	17	4
Gridley	6,350	22	17	5
Grover Beach	13,030	29	19	10
Guadalupe	6,745	15	12	3
Gustine	5,120	11	9	2
Half Moon Bay	12,394	21	16	5
Hanford	50,602	73	54	19
Hawthorne	84,445	129	95	34
Hayward	140,984	295	191	104
Healdsburg	10,913	30	19	11
Hemet	71,789	108	78	30
Hercules	25,214	30	27	3
Hermosa Beach	19,513	59	34	25
Hillsborough	10,725	36	26	10
Hollister	34,917	34	30	4
Holtville	5,376	7	6	1
Huntington Beach	193,241	364	224	140
Huntington Park	61,307	105	62	43
Huron	7,288	17	13	4
Imperial	13,669	19	17	2
Indio	89,486	130	76	54
Inglewood	113,454	275	192	83
Ione	7,906	7	6	1
Irvine	209,278	271	182	89
Irwindale	1,451	39	30	9
Isleton	800	5	5	0
Jackson	4,398	12	11	1
Kensington	5,357	10	10	0
Kerman	13,092	22	19	3
King City	11,571	22	19	3
Kingsburg	11,336	22	16	6
Laguna Beach	24,035	82	47	35
La Habra	59,202	105	68	37
Lakeport	5,167	14	12	2
Lake Shastina	2,377	5	4	1
La Mesa	53,893	94	65	29
La Palma	15,652	31	24	7
La Verne	33,298	70	46	24
Lemoore	24,207	37	31	6
Lincoln	49,608	50	37	13
Lindsay	10,680	20	16	4
Livermore	80,258	148	93	55
Livingston	13,548	28	19	9
Lodi	62,251	114	76	38
Lompoc	40,344	73	50	23
Long Beach	467,055	1,361	963	398
Los Alamitos	11,687	25	21	4
Los Altos	27,989	45	29	16
Los Angeles	3,850,920	13,008	9,743	3,265
Los Banos	36,101	65	45	20
Los Gatos	29,233	63	42	21
Madera	57,636	78	58	20

Table 78. Full-Time Law Enforcement Employees, by State and City, 2008—*Continued*

(Number.)

State/City	Population	Total law enforcement employees	Total officers	Total civilians
Mammoth Lakes	7,469	26	22	4
Manhattan Beach	36,866	98	64	34
Manteca	65,989	106	78	28
Marina	17,865	39	30	9
Martinez	34,985	50	37	13
Marysville	11,766	31	19	12
Maywood	28,411	56	37	19
Menlo Park	29,862	69	47	22
Merced	78,598	146	104	42
Millbrae	20,681	24	19	5
Mill Valley	13,205	27	22	5
Milpitas	67,282	110	86	24
Modesto	205,750	362	261	101
Monrovia	37,679	81	53	28
Montclair	36,643	82	57	25
Montebello	62,318	118	79	39
Monterey	28,326	71	54	17
Monterey Park	61,664	111	78	33
Moraga	16,956	12	11	1
Morgan Hill	38,051	56	37	19
Morro Bay	10,257	23	17	6
Mountain View	70,401	146	97	49
Mount Shasta	3,509	14	9	5
Murrieta	105,666	131	89	42
Napa	74,420	115	74	41
National City	59,390	132	90	42
Nevada City	2,933	12	11	1
Newark	41,558	78	54	24
Newman	10,416	16	12	4
Newport Beach	79,821	231	142	89
Novato	52,662	78	55	23
Oakdale	20,611	36	26	10
Oakland	401,587	1,056	766	290
Oceanside	169,502	302	206	96
Ontario	172,543	333	228	105
Orange	134,852	233	159	74
Orland	7,215	12	10	2
Oroville	14,563	37	23	14
Oxnard	186,434	356	234	122
Pacifica	37,145	52	39	13
Pacific Grove	14,567	26	19	7
Palm Springs	48,558	155	94	61
Palo Alto	58,203	157	91	66
Palos Verdes Estates	13,665	34	24	10
Paradise	26,466	45	26	19
Parlier	13,443	20	17	3
Pasadena	144,545	379	246	133
Paso Robles	29,183	52	40	12
Petaluma	54,454	94	70	24
Piedmont	10,417	28	20	8
Pinole	18,643	51	35	16
Pismo Beach	8,506	33	23	10
Pittsburg	63,227	103	75	28
Placentia	50,043	64	48	16
Placerville	9,929	27	18	9
Pleasant Hill	32,664	64	45	19
Pleasanton	66,829	112	80	32
Pomona	153,201	325	187	138
Porterville	52,308	77	55	22
Port Hueneme	21,497	31	23	8
Red Bluff	14,033	39	24	15
Redding	90,881	172	118	54
Redlands	70,730	144	85	59
Redondo Beach	67,469	147	97	50
Redwood City	73,369	133	94	39
Reedley	23,277	43	30	13
Rialto	99,485	153	107	46
Richmond	101,680	243	167	76
Ridgecrest	25,539	48	34	14
Rio Dell	3,194	8	6	2
Rio Vista	7,980	11	10	1
Ripon	14,770	39	27	12
Riverside	299,384	554	385	169
Rocklin	53,803	82	53	29
Rohnert Park	40,431	109	81	28
Roseville	112,817	200	128	72
Ross	2,277	8	8	0
Sacramento	467,065	1,078	713	365
Salinas	143,520	247	177	70
San Anselmo	11,916	25	18	7
San Bernardino	200,617	488	343	145
San Bruno	39,999	64	46	18
San Carlos	26,922	37	30	7
Sand City	379	11	10	1
San Diego	1,271,655	2,775	1,987	788
San Fernando	23,842	53	37	16
San Francisco	798,144	2,773	2,391	382
San Gabriel	40,691	70	55	15
Sanger	26,255	40	31	9
San Jose	945,197	1,754	1,383	371
San Leandro	77,474	141	94	47
San Luis Obispo	43,421	87	62	25
San Marino	12,902	35	28	7
San Mateo	91,650	150	114	36
San Pablo	30,736	76	55	21
San Rafael	55,589	97	73	24
San Ramon	49,457	75	56	19
Santa Ana	339,674	677	365	312
Santa Barbara	85,791	202	137	65
Santa Clara	110,712	219	148	71
Santa Cruz	55,255	121	95	26
Santa Maria	86,744	159	110	49
Santa Monica	87,572	386	202	184
Santa Paula	28,617	45	34	11
Santa Rosa	154,874	261	178	83
Sausalito	7,139	23	18	5
Scotts Valley	11,129	27	19	8
Seal Beach	24,139	50	38	12
Seaside	33,659	67	49	18
Sebastopol	7,445	21	14	7
Selma	23,221	49	35	14
Shafter	15,892	29	20	9
Sierra Madre	10,908	20	16	4
Signal Hill	11,134	50	36	14
Simi Valley	121,572	189	127	62
Soledad	28,685	28	22	6
Sonora	4,617	18	14	4
South Gate	97,179	138	95	43
South Lake Tahoe	23,341	62	40	22
South Pasadena	24,608	50	35	15
South San Francisco	62,027	109	80	29
Stallion Springs	1,652	3	3	0
St. Helena	5,808	16	12	4
Stockton	293,073	652	413	239
Suisun City	27,093	36	25	11
Sunnyvale	131,052	289	223	66
Susanville	17,791	18	16	2
Sutter Creek	2,791	7	7	0
Taft	9,108	22	13	9
Tiburon	8,682	19	15	4
Torrance	141,819	318	230	88
Tracy	82,960	135	87	48
Trinidad	312	1	1	0
Truckee	16,317	30	26	4
Tulare	56,624	108	72	36
Tulelake	954	3	3	0
Turlock	69,738	120	79	41
Tustin	71,272	149	96	53
Twin Cities	20,924	45	34	11
Ukiah	14,971	39	28	11
Union City	70,409	104	77	27
Upland	72,929	116	78	38
Vacaville	92,424	176	112	64
Vallejo	115,330	144	117	27
Ventura	103,483	182	140	42
Vernon	90	73	52	21
Visalia	121,850	193	135	58
Walnut Creek	63,122	110	75	35

Table 78. Full-Time Law Enforcement Employees, by State and City, 2008—*Continued*

(Number.)

State/City	Population	Total law enforcement employees	Total officers	Total civilians
Watsonville	50,211	87	64	23
Weed	2,977	16	10	6
West Covina	106,524	174	122	52
Westminster	88,730	146	102	44
Westmorland	2,199	4	4	0
West Sacramento	48,715	109	72	37
Wheatland	3,784	8	8	0
Whittier	82,727	183	128	55
Williams	4,985	12	10	2
Willits	4,915	19	12	7
Willows	6,298	13	11	2
Winters	7,101	13	11	2
Woodlake	7,316	16	14	2
Woodland	54,210	90	65	25
Yreka	7,358	20	14	6
Yuba City	62,595	104	68	36
COLORADO				
Alamosa	8,599	28	24	4
Arvada	106,847	220	156	64
Aspen	5,767	34	24	10
Ault	1,400	7	5	2
Aurora	316,323	748	623	125
Avon	6,685	20	18	2
Basalt	3,224	13	10	3
Bayfield	2,015	5	5	0
Berthoud	5,339	9	8	1
Black Hawk	103	35	24	11
Boulder	93,410	248	162	86
Breckenridge	3,439	30	24	6
Brighton	32,171	68	53	15
Broomfield	55,820	185	105	80
Brush	5,390	11	9	2
Buena Vista	2,122	9	7	2
Burlington	3,945	10	9	1
Calhan	863	3	3	0
Campo	127	1	1	0
Canon City	15,885	49	35	14
Carbondale	6,221	17	14	3
Castle Rock	46,423	72	53	19
Cedaredge	2,250	8	6	2
Centennial	98,749	152	114	38
Center	2,373	5	4	1
Central City	548	4	4	0
Cherry Hills Village	6,329	25	21	4
Collbran	422	2	2	0
Colorado Springs	378,403	977	671	306
Columbine Valley	1,315	6	6	0
Commerce City	44,451	103	80	23
Cortez	8,599	50	28	22
Craig	9,160	29	23	6
Crested Butte	1,648	9	7	2
Cripple Creek	1,024	11	7	4
Dacono	4,079	11	10	1
De Beque	496	2	2	0
Del Norte	1,587	6	5	1
Delta	8,728	20	15	5
Denver	592,881	1,791	1,541	250
Dillon	806	10	9	1
Durango	16,205	60	49	11
Eagle	5,963	12	10	2
Eaton	4,379	9	8	1
Edgewater	5,088	18	15	3
Elizabeth	1,449	6	5	1
Empire	324	1	1	0
Englewood	32,605	100	69	31
Erie	17,519	21	19	2
Estes Park	6,367	29	19	10
Evans	19,244	34	30	4
Federal Heights	11,620	34	24	10
Firestone	8,997	26	21	5
Florence	3,612	22	8	14
Fort Collins	135,785	237	162	75
Fort Lupton	7,527	22	17	5
Fort Morgan	10,582	34	28	6

State/City	Population	Total law enforcement employees	Total officers	Total civilians
Fountain	20,136	53	40	13
Fowler	1,094	4	3	1
Fraser/Winter Park	1,770	10	9	1
Frederick	8,908	17	15	2
Frisco	2,681	16	13	3
Fruita	7,346	17	15	2
Georgetown	1,022	3	3	0
Glendale	4,822	38	24	14
Glenwood Springs	9,089	31	25	6
Golden	17,175	55	40	15
Grand Junction	48,870	193	111	82
Greeley	91,900	358	189	169
Green Mountain Falls	800	2	2	0
Greenwood Village	14,285	86	60	26
Gunnison	5,407	28	14	14
Haxtun	971	3	3	0
Hayden	1,559	6	6	0
Holyoke	2,231	4	4	0
Hotchkiss	1,081	3	3	0
Hugo	734	3	3	0
Idaho Springs	1,734	9	7	2
Ignacio	627	7	7	0
Johnstown	9,608	16	14	2
Kersey	1,450	4	4	0
Kiowa	576	2	2	0
Kremmling	1,533	4	4	0
Lafayette	25,091	52	41	11
La Junta	6,974	20	14	6
Lakeside	19	4	4	0
Lakewood	139,803	423	285	138
Lamar	7,905	25	21	4
La Salle	1,966	6	6	0
Las Animas	2,289	5	4	1
La Veta	849	3	3	0
Leadville	2,719	11	9	2
Limon	1,731	6	5	1
Littleton	40,676	98	72	26
Lochbuie	4,919	7	6	1
Log Lane Village	981	1	1	0
Lone Tree	9,488	45	40	5
Longmont	86,754	193	136	57
Louisville	18,794	38	33	5
Loveland	66,204	129	89	40
Mancos	1,255	4	3	1
Manitou Springs	5,130	20	15	5
Manzanola	472	2	1	1
Milliken	6,584	10	9	1
Minturn	1,187	3	2	1
Monte Vista	3,954	15	10	5
Montrose	17,895	58	38	20
Monument	2,651	16	13	3
Morrison	411	3	2	1
Mountain View	514	3	2	1
Mount Crested Butte	849	8	7	1
Nederland	1,357	4	3	1
New Castle	3,809	8	7	1
Northglenn	33,668	84	69	15
Olathe	1,750	5	4	1
Ouray	913	5	5	0
Pagosa Springs	1,735	10	9	1
Palisade	2,820	7	6	1
Palmer Lake	2,316	6	5	1
Paonia	1,622	5	5	0
Parachute	1,295	10	8	2
Parker	45,825	82	57	25
Platteville	2,641	7	7	0
Pueblo	104,017	249	192	57
Ridgway	755	3	3	0
Rifle	9,085	24	19	5
Rocky Ford	3,948	10	9	1
Salida	5,320	18	15	3
Sheridan	5,395	39	27	12
Silt	2,663	9	8	1
Silverthorne	4,024	18	15	3

Table 78. Full-Time Law Enforcement Employees, by State and City, 2008—*Continued*

(Number.)

State/City	Population	Total law enforcement employees	Total officers	Total civilians
Simla	695	2	2	0
Snowmass Village	1,832	14	10	4
South Fork	528	3	3	0
Steamboat Springs	9,470	39	24	15
Sterling	12,932	25	22	3
Stratton	606	1	1	0
Telluride	2,378	15	10	5
Thornton	114,923	199	158	41
Trinidad	9,101	33	23	10
Vail	4,760	62	28	34
Victor	407	4	3	1
Westminster	106,810	261	179	82
Wheat Ridge	30,582	100	72	28
Wiggins	956	2	2	0
Windsor	18,476	21	18	3
Woodland Park	6,568	29	20	9
Wray	2,098	8	7	1
Yuma	3,258	7	6	1
CONNECTICUT				
Ansonia	18,547	51	44	7
Avon	17,522	41	34	7
Berlin	20,515	49	37	12
Bethel	18,566	48	36	12
Bloomfield	20,833	60	48	12
Branford	29,020	62	49	13
Bridgeport	136,327	525	423	102
Bristol	60,994	149	125	24
Brookfield	16,504	41	31	10
Canton	10,251	19	14	5
Cheshire	28,864	60	49	11
Clinton	13,636	33	25	8
Coventry	12,278	19	14	5
Cromwell	13,631	34	25	9
Danbury	79,753	157	151	6
Darien	20,322	56	50	6
Derby	12,438	30	28	2
East Hampton	12,756	17	15	2
East Hartford	48,586	166	132	34
East Haven	28,686	55	52	3
Easton	7,374	18	15	3
East Windsor	10,717	30	23	7
Enfield	44,982	115	90	25
Fairfield	57,568	112	106	6
Farmington	25,262	57	41	16
Glastonbury	33,323	70	54	16
Granby	11,323	19	14	5
Greenwich	61,953	179	151	28
Groton	9,345	40	31	9
Groton Long Point	680	9	8	1
Groton Town	32,617	72	68	4
Guilford	22,491	43	36	7
Hamden	57,803	130	105	25
Hartford	124,610	521	422	99
Madison	18,901	28	19	9
Manchester	55,993	157	116	41
Meriden	59,345	130	117	13
Middlebury	7,356	17	11	6
Middletown	48,048	111	98	13
Milford	55,837	129	111	18
Monroe	19,415	50	39	11
Naugatuck	32,046	66	54	12
New Britain	70,553	153	143	10
New Canaan	19,946	51	45	6
New Haven	123,953	488	388	100
Newington	29,653	65	52	13
New London	25,891	106	90	16
New Milford	28,601	64	49	15
Newtown	27,007	52	47	5
North Branford	14,468	24	23	1
North Haven	24,119	57	48	9
Norwalk	83,503	184	167	17
Norwich	36,471	103	85	18
Old Saybrook	10,559	28	20	8
Orange	13,887	47	36	11
Plainfield	15,552	21	17	4
Plainville	17,190	42	35	7
Plymouth	12,055	22	22	0
Portland	9,638	11	10	1
Putnam	9,329	16	13	3
Redding	8,909	21	15	6
Ridgefield	23,893	47	42	5
Rocky Hill	18,910	44	34	10
Seymour	16,338	43	41	2
Shelton	40,243	66	57	9
Simsbury	23,709	45	35	10
Southington	42,434	85	66	19
South Windsor	26,131	52	39	13
Stamford	118,597	349	285	64
Stonington	18,394	46	34	12
Stratford	48,891	114	109	5
Suffield	15,303	25	20	5
Thomaston	7,854	15	12	3
Torrington	35,478	98	83	15
Trumbull	34,807	84	73	11
Vernon	29,815	63	50	13
Wallingford	44,880	91	68	23
Waterbury	107,157	348	278	70
Waterford	18,788	50	43	7
Watertown	22,182	49	38	11
West Hartford	60,411	138	119	19
West Haven	52,714	136	123	13
Weston	10,217	16	15	1
Westport	26,596	88	66	22
Wethersfield	25,718	58	47	11
Willimantic	16,267	45	40	5
Wilton	17,720	48	44	4
Winchester	10,758	26	21	5
Windsor	28,813	63	51	12
Windsor Locks	12,544	30	24	6
Wolcott	16,557	33	24	9
Woodbridge	9,227	33	25	8
DELAWARE				
Bethany Beach	958	10	9	1
Blades	1,017	3	3	0
Bridgeville	1,620	4	4	0
Camden	2,574	15	13	2
Cheswold	472	5	5	0
Clayton	1,480	9	8	1
Dagsboro	574	2	2	0
Delaware City	1,523	5	5	0
Delmar	1,517	12	11	1
Dewey Beach	316	7	7	0
Dover	36,291	117	90	27
Elsmere	5,701	12	11	1
Felton	876	4	4	0
Fenwick Island	363	6	5	1
Georgetown	5,196	20	18	2
Harrington	3,326	11	10	1
Laurel	3,891	16	15	1
Lewes	3,101	14	13	1
Middletown	12,006	26	24	2
Milford	8,472	39	30	9
Millsboro	2,560	15	14	1
Milton	1,823	11	10	1
Newark	30,115	79	63	16
New Castle	4,972	19	17	2
Newport	1,108	9	8	1
Ocean View	1,124	9	8	1
Rehoboth Beach	1,577	30	19	11
Seaford	7,231	38	27	11
Selbyville	1,783	8	7	1
Smyrna	8,581	29	22	7
South Bethany	522	6	6	0
Wilmington	72,888	388	302	86
Wyoming	1,392	3	3	0
DISTRICT OF COLUMBIA				
Washington	591,833	4,637	4,030	607

Table 78. Full-Time Law Enforcement Employees, by State and City, 2008—*Continued*

(Number.)

State/City	Population	Total law enforcement employees	Total officers	Total civilians
FLORIDA				
Alachua	9,398	27	20	7
Altamonte Springs	39,672	123	104	19
Altha	516	1	1	0
Apalachicola	2,197	8	7	1
Apopka	38,368	94	85	9
Arcadia	6,875	23	19	4
Astatula	1,815	5	5	0
Atlantic Beach	13,106	35	25	10
Atlantis	2,062	18	13	5
Auburndale	14,179	43	33	10
Aventura	29,683	114	78	36
Avon Park	8,980	27	23	4
Bal Harbour Village	3,083	37	29	8
Bartow	16,762	66	40	26
Bay Harbor Islands	4,893	29	22	7
Belleair	4,055	13	12	1
Belleair Beach	1,575	2	2	0
Belleair Bluffs	2,147	4	4	0
Belle Glade	16,494	42	38	4
Belleview	4,446	17	15	2
Biscayne Park	2,922	12	11	1
Blountstown	2,429	13	9	4
Boca Raton	84,630	261	176	85
Bonifay	2,749	6	5	1
Bowling Green	2,930	7	7	0
Boynton Beach	68,033	237	160	77
Bradenton	53,244	147	118	29
Bradenton Beach	1,534	10	10	0
Brooksville	7,898	25	22	3
Bunnell	1,879	15	12	3
Bushnell	2,223	10	9	1
Cape Coral	163,403	340	243	97
Carrabelle	1,233	6	6	0
Casselberry	24,527	73	52	21
Center Hill	1,025	3	3	0
Chattahoochee	4,077	10	9	1
Chiefland	2,081	13	11	2
Chipley	3,697	12	11	1
Clearwater	104,986	365	255	110
Clermont	13,220	64	49	15
Clewiston	7,167	26	16	10
Cocoa	16,327	91	66	25
Cocoa Beach	11,817	50	34	16
Coconut Creek	50,511	126	88	38
Coleman	727	2	2	0
Cooper City	29,060	75	56	19
Coral Gables	41,502	259	185	74
Coral Springs	126,222	291	197	94
Cottondale	872	3	3	0
Crescent City	1,800	7	5	2
Crestview	19,865	61	46	15
Cross City	1,812	5	5	0
Cutler Bay	28,760	48	44	4
Dade City	7,102	32	24	8
Dania	28,052	73	66	7
Davenport	2,188	11	10	1
Davie	90,268	233	161	72
Daytona Beach	63,642	288	238	50
Daytona Beach Shores	5,130	38	28	10
Deerfield Beach	73,665	152	127	25
De Funiak Springs	4,905	25	19	6
Deland	27,343	75	57	18
Delray Beach	63,795	220	152	68
Doral	22,898	123	92	31
Dunedin	35,844	35	35	0
Dunnellon	1,986	8	6	2
Eatonville	2,343	16	14	2
Edgewater	21,743	32	29	3
Edgewood	2,077	9	8	1
El Portal	2,290	8	8	0
Eustis	19,139	54	41	13
Fellsmere	4,710	10	9	1
Fernandina Beach	11,505	45	34	11
Flagler Beach	3,276	16	14	2
Florida City	9,730	41	31	10
Fort Lauderdale	182,932	679	484	195
Fort Myers	65,107	287	193	94
Fort Pierce	39,861	152	118	34
Fort Walton Beach	18,831	61	49	12
Fruitland Park	4,293	14	13	1
Gainesville	113,286	326	251	75
Golden Beach	862	18	17	1
Graceville	2,404	9	7	2
Greenacres City	32,448	113	52	61
Green Cove Springs	6,461	24	19	5
Greensboro	593	1	1	0
Gretna	1,576	5	5	0
Groveland	6,484	30	23	7
Gulf Breeze	6,559	27	19	8
Gulfport	12,245	39	29	10
Gulf Stream	732	11	11	0
Haines City	18,921	64	41	23
Hallandale	38,722	129	90	39
Hampton	452	2	2	0
Havana	1,666	14	10	4
Hialeah	207,908	453	336	117
Hialeah Gardens	19,441	49	35	14
Highland Beach	3,966	13	13	0
High Springs	4,479	17	13	4
Hillsboro Beach	2,260	18	15	3
Holly Hill	13,299	32	28	4
Hollywood	141,048	479	314	165
Holmes Beach	4,973	21	14	7
Homestead	60,184	149	106	43
Howey-in-the-Hills	1,273	7	6	1
Hypoluxo	2,582	4	4	0
Indialantic	2,909	17	11	6
Indian Creek Village	38	15	11	4
Indian Harbour Beach	8,292	26	19	7
Indian River Shores	3,377	22	20	2
Indian Rocks Beach	5,106	6	6	0
Indian Shores	4,222	13	11	2
Inglis	1,622	5	4	1
Interlachen	1,501	4	4	0
Jacksonville	806,080	3,000	1,693	1,307
Jacksonville Beach	21,686	82	61	21
Jasper	1,775	8	7	1
Jennings	833	1	1	0
Juno Beach	3,312	19	14	5
Jupiter	49,429	138	105	33
Jupiter Inlet Colony	383	5	5	0
Jupiter Island	653	20	15	5
Kenneth City	4,273	16	14	2
Key Biscayne	9,592	40	28	12
Key Colony Beach	760	5	5	0
Key West	22,084	117	84	33
Kissimmee	62,815	196	130	66
Lady Lake	13,687	41	29	12
Lake Alfred	4,471	15	10	5
Lake City	12,416	49	35	14
Lake Clarke Shores	3,291	11	11	0
Lake Hamilton	1,415	7	6	1
Lake Helen	2,762	8	7	1
Lakeland	92,669	335	221	114
Lake Mary	15,426	53	38	15
Lake Park	8,618	24	23	1
Lake Placid	1,875	9	7	2
Lake Wales	14,675	46	40	6
Lake Worth	35,119	94	87	7
Lantana	10,111	34	26	8
Largo	72,298	201	140	61
Lauderdale-by-the-Sea	5,795	26	24	2
Lauderdale Lakes	30,910	72	59	13
Lauderhill	66,802	137	112	25
Lawtey	691	1	1	0
Leesburg	21,766	91	68	23
Lighthouse Point	11,113	42	32	10

Table 78. Full-Time Law Enforcement Employees, by State and City, 2008—*Continued*

(Number.)

State/City	Population	Total law enforcement employees	Total officers	Total civilians
Live Oak	7,184	21	17	4
Longboat Key	7,216	26	19	7
Longwood	13,374	49	42	7
Lynn Haven	15,369	35	25	10
Madeira Beach	4,306	6	6	0
Madison	3,010	15	14	1
Maitland	14,406	48	39	9
Manalapan	335	15	10	5
Mangonia Park	1,218	14	13	1
Marco Island	15,703	34	32	2
Margate	54,002	169	109	60
Marianna	6,219	24	16	8
Mascotte	5,777	13	12	1
Medley	1,016	37	32	5
Melbourne	77,286	237	170	67
Melbourne Beach	3,117	9	8	1
Melbourne Village	667	5	5	0
Mexico Beach	1,288	8	7	1
Miami	427,740	1,489	1,073	416
Miami Beach	83,609	523	368	155
Miami Gardens	108,657	240	185	55
Miami Lakes	21,405	51	48	3
Miami Shores	9,424	44	34	10
Miami Springs	12,349	49	37	12
Milton	8,611	25	18	7
Miramar	112,055	242	179	63
Monticello	2,487	13	9	4
Mount Dora	12,284	50	35	15
Mulberry	3,147	22	16	6
Naples	21,460	105	70	35
Neptune Beach	6,732	27	19	8
New Port Richey	17,352	45	35	10
New Smyrna Beach	23,218	63	54	9
Niceville	12,290	25	20	5
North Bay Village	8,015	36	27	9
North Lauderdale	41,734	66	57	9
North Miami	55,057	161	123	38
North Miami Beach	37,424	151	109	42
North Palm Beach	12,088	40	30	10
North Port	59,721	123	97	26
Oak Hill	1,591	7	7	0
Oakland	1,149	8	7	1
Oakland Park	41,630	94	84	10
Ocala	53,799	236	155	81
Ocean Ridge	1,627	18	13	5
Ocoee	32,482	75	64	11
Okeechobee	5,937	26	20	6
Oldsmar	13,478	4	4	0
Opa Locka	15,243	48	36	12
Orange City	9,567	25	22	3
Orange Park	8,878	29	22	7
Orlando	229,808	1,029	740	289
Ormond Beach	38,173	90	66	24
Oviedo	31,022	77	59	18
Pahokee	6,595	17	15	2
Palatka	10,769	43	36	7
Palm Bay	101,759	254	163	91
Palm Beach	9,445	124	74	50
Palm Beach Gardens	50,154	144	111	33
Palm Beach Shores	1,558	15	10	5
Palmetto	14,277	51	37	14
Palmetto Bay	22,415	43	39	4
Palm Springs	16,144	51	39	12
Panama City	36,339	126	89	37
Panama City Beach	15,453	65	51	14
Parker	4,503	10	9	1
Parkland	25,375	33	29	4
Pembroke Pines	146,108	299	233	66
Pensacola	53,385	220	153	67
Perry	6,713	23	21	2
Pinellas Park	46,913	124	99	25
Plantation	83,480	284	182	102
Plant City	32,228	82	64	18
Pompano Beach	101,769	308	229	79
Ponce Inlet	3,217	18	12	6
Port Orange	55,358	97	81	16
Port Richey	3,393	17	11	6
Port St. Joe	3,522	13	11	2
Port St. Lucie	159,735	321	245	76
Punta Gorda	16,699	50	34	16
Quincy	6,780	31	24	7
Redington Beaches	1,471	3	3	0
Riviera Beach	37,039	156	112	44
Rockledge	24,929	65	49	16
Royal Palm Beach	31,339	60	56	4
Safety Harbor	16,991	3	3	0
Sanford	51,464	152	131	21
Sanibel	5,586	42	26	16
Sarasota	51,818	230	182	48
Satellite Beach	11,636	31	22	9
Sea Ranch Lakes	733	11	7	4
Sebastian	20,667	53	38	15
Sebring	10,746	40	33	7
Seminole	19,031	15	15	0
Sewall's Point	1,989	9	9	0
Shalimar	699	4	4	0
Sneads	1,928	8	5	3
South Bay	4,541	9	8	1
South Daytona	13,690	33	25	8
South Miami	10,644	51	43	8
South Palm Beach	1,453	9	9	0
South Pasadena	5,507	6	6	0
Southwest Ranches	7,191	15	15	0
Springfield	8,742	21	15	6
Starke	5,892	25	20	5
St. Augustine	12,191	61	50	11
St. Augustine Beach	6,099	18	16	2
St. Cloud	27,810	107	70	37
St. Pete Beach	9,870	38	28	10
St. Petersburg	243,111	738	509	229
Stuart	15,938	62	45	17
Sunny Isles Beach	16,185	57	44	13
Sunrise	89,139	286	174	112
Surfside	4,439	45	32	13
Sweetwater	12,897	26	20	6
Tallahassee	168,984	481	356	125
Tamarac	59,423	87	71	16
Tampa	336,911	1,293	979	314
Tarpon Springs	23,564	63	47	16
Tavares	14,037	41	30	11
Temple Terrace	22,304	73	52	21
Tequesta	5,855	24	17	7
Titusville	43,769	123	85	38
Treasure Island	7,412	28	19	9
Trenton	1,848	4	3	1
Umatilla	2,943	9	8	1
Valparaiso	6,224	13	9	4
Venice	21,086	67	48	19
Vero Beach	16,689	84	58	26
Village of Pinecrest	18,416	68	50	18
Virginia Gardens	2,143	7	6	1
Waldo	808	6	5	1
Wauchula	4,509	16	13	3
Webster	889	3	3	0
Welaka	809	1	1	0
Wellington	56,081	63	59	4
West Melbourne	15,745	49	36	13
West Miami	5,484	20	16	4
Weston	65,288	97	69	28
West Palm Beach	100,434	403	303	100
West Park	14,371	48	44	4
White Springs	818	3	3	0
Wildwood	3,760	25	18	7
Williston	2,783	20	12	8
Wilton Manors	12,567	40	30	10
Windermere	2,032	13	12	1
Winter Garden	30,577	79	63	16
Winter Haven	32,886	103	78	25

Table 78. Full-Time Law Enforcement Employees, by State and City, 2008—*Continued*

(Number.)

State/City	Population	Total law enforcement employees	Total officers	Total civilians
Winter Park	27,613	94	85	9
Winter Springs	32,789	90	70	20
Zephyrhills	13,092	47	31	16
Zolfo Springs	1,740	1	1	0
GEORGIA				
Abbeville	2,596	4	3	1
Acworth	19,929	50	38	12
Adairsville	3,256	14	11	3
Adel	5,410	22	20	2
Alapaha	685	2	1	1
Albany	75,715	207	177	30
Alma	3,526	12	10	2
Alpharetta	50,051	148	115	33
Alto	910	2	1	1
Americus	16,483	43	35	8
Aragon	1,076	5	4	1
Arlington	1,505	4	3	1
Athens-Clarke County	113,950	276	216	60
Atlanta	533,016	1,963	1,619	344
Auburn	7,516	22	17	5
Austell	7,202	37	23	14
Avondale Estates	2,855	12	12	0
Bainbridge	12,133	50	39	11
Baldwin	2,999	13	9	4
Ball Ground	949	4	4	0
Barnesville	5,956	20	18	2
Bartow	278	3	2	1
Baxley	4,515	16	14	2
Bloomingdale	2,666	14	11	3
Blythe	818	1	1	0
Bowdon	2,056	12	8	4
Braselton	3,300	14	13	1
Bremen	5,696	22	20	2
Brooklet	1,337	4	4	0
Brunswick	16,319	83	72	11
Buchanan	1,150	10	9	1
Buena Vista	1,656	5	5	0
Byron	4,295	22	19	3
Cairo	9,752	26	23	3
Calhoun	15,024	44	37	7
Camilla	5,706	18	15	3
Canton	24,138	52	46	6
Carrollton	23,259	74	62	12
Cartersville	18,839	62	50	12
Cave Spring	1,020	4	4	0
Cedartown	9,915	34	32	2
Centerville	7,380	20	17	3
Chamblee	11,250	48	34	14
Chatsworth	4,232	17	14	3
Chickamauga	2,503	5	5	0
Clarkesville	1,691	7	6	1
Clarkston	7,635	20	16	4
Claxton	2,417	9	8	1
Clayton	2,189	11	10	1
Cleveland	2,664	11	11	0
Cochran	4,904	17	16	1
College Park	20,094	119	89	30
Collins	547	1	1	0
Colquitt	1,897	10	9	1
Columbus	186,217	495	403	92
Commerce	6,443	33	24	9
Conyers	13,598	61	47	14
Cordele	11,436	37	31	6
Cornelia	3,893	22	19	3
Covington	15,126	63	54	9
Cumming	6,076	20	14	6
Dallas	10,833	23	17	6
Dalton	34,095	102	87	15
Danielsville	451	2	2	0
Darien	1,797	7	7	0
Davisboro	1,901	1	1	0
Dawson	4,546	16	10	6
Decatur	19,287	46	34	12
Dillard	247	3	3	0
Donalsonville	2,711	11	9	2
Doraville	10,408	72	48	24
Douglasville	31,673	104	85	19
Dublin	17,628	60	52	8
Duluth	26,345	70	54	16
Eastman	5,654	13	12	1
East Point	43,253	181	132	49
Edison	1,242	2	2	0
Elberton	4,546	21	18	3
Ellijay	1,579	10	9	1
Emerson	1,413	8	8	0
Eton	490	3	3	0
Euharlee	4,215	12	11	1
Fairburn	11,555	37	32	5
Fairmount	812	3	3	0
Fayetteville	15,675	50	45	5
Fitzgerald	9,166	36	28	8
Flowery Branch	4,329	13	13	0
Folkston	3,225	8	7	1
Forest Park	21,855	81	62	19
Forsyth	4,714	24	18	6
Fort Gaines	1,034	7	7	0
Fort Oglethorpe	9,921	32	30	2
Fort Valley	8,133	37	33	4
Franklin Springs	797	3	3	0
Gainesville	36,032	119	98	21
Garden City	9,428	49	40	9
Glennville	5,210	16	11	5
Gordon	2,114	12	7	5
Grantville	2,842	11	10	1
Gray	2,239	14	13	1
Greensboro	3,337	22	19	3
Griffin	23,561	106	91	15
Grovetown	9,143	41	40	1
Guyton	1,993	4	3	1
Hahira	2,353	7	6	1
Hampton	5,381	18	16	2
Hapeville	5,955	38	26	12
Harlem	1,910	14	8	6
Helen	850	13	10	3
Helena	2,444	3	3	0
Hephzibah	4,506	5	5	0
Hinesville	30,523	93	81	12
Hiram	2,058	15	13	2
Hogansville	2,933	18	12	6
Holly Springs	8,806	18	18	0
Hoschton	1,635	7	7	0
Ivey	1,075	2	2	0
Jackson	4,466	19	14	5
Jefferson	8,126	26	22	4
Jesup	10,301	32	30	2
Johns Creek	59,454	65	56	9
Jonesboro	3,923	27	24	3
Keysville	251	1	1	0
Kingsland	13,645	43	40	3
LaGrange	28,190	101	83	18
Lake Park	600	3	3	0
Lavonia	2,086	15	14	1
Lawrenceville	29,813	89	69	20
Lilburn	11,546	37	27	10
Lithonia	2,391	12	8	4
Loganville	10,997	28	26	2
Lookout Mountain	1,542	7	7	0
Ludowici	1,615	10	6	4
Macon	92,576	377	279	98
Manchester	3,765	19	14	5
Marietta	67,492	169	136	33
McDonough	20,236	43	39	4
McIntyre	716	5	5	0
McRae	4,682	8	7	1
Metter	4,324	13	12	1
Midville	457	1	1	0
Midway	1,065	5	4	1
Milledgeville	20,194	62	42	20

Table 78. Full-Time Law Enforcement Employees, by State and City, 2008—*Continued*

(Number.)

State/City	Population	Total law enforcement employees	Total officers	Total civilians
Millen	3,468	9	9	0
Milton	15,054	27	25	2
Monroe	13,707	42	37	5
Monticello	2,615	14	12	2
Morrow	5,534	35	31	4
Morven	617	2	2	0
Moultrie	15,294	44	39	5
Mount Airy	1,018	3	2	1
Nahunta	985	3	2	1
Nashville	4,840	20	16	4
Nelson	935	1	1	0
Newnan	30,967	83	72	11
Newton	788	1	1	0
Norcross	10,782	47	37	10
Oakwood	4,208	15	14	1
Oglethorpe	1,094	6	5	1
Omega	1,382	5	5	0
Oxford	2,586	3	3	0
Palmetto	5,245	21	19	2
Patterson	686	2	2	0
Peachtree City	34,882	64	60	4
Pearson	1,974	6	5	1
Pelham	3,869	16	14	2
Pembroke	2,499	10	7	3
Perry	13,010	45	39	6
Pine Lake	719	4	3	1
Pooler	14,813	32	27	5
Port Wentworth	4,307	23	19	4
Powder Springs	15,719	36	31	5
Quitman	4,581	21	15	6
Reidsville	2,448	9	8	1
Reynolds	1,000	5	5	0
Richland	1,566	4	4	0
Richmond Hill	10,644	37	30	7
Rincon	7,948	11	9	2
Ringgold	2,788	7	7	0
Roberta	743	3	3	0
Rockmart	4,566	20	18	2
Rome	36,527	108	94	14
Roswell	88,069	195	128	67
Royston	2,742	25	20	5
Sandersville	6,172	22	19	3
Sandy Springs	82,953	127	115	12
Sardis	1,189	4	4	0
Savannah-Chatham Metropolitan	211,475	821	587	234
Screven	788	3	2	1
Senoia	3,495	10	9	1
Shiloh	425	2	1	1
Smyrna	50,196	121	93	28
Snellville	20,467	59	49	10
Social Circle	4,681	21	17	4
Sparta	1,289	6	6	0
Springfield	2,115	8	7	1
Statesboro	27,119	69	57	12
St. Marys	16,916	37	34	3
Stone Mountain	7,714	21	20	1
Suwanee	15,848	45	36	9
Sylvania	2,489	12	9	3
Sylvester	5,694	22	18	4
Tallapoosa	3,110	16	15	1
Temple	4,710	12	10	2
Thomaston	9,134	29	26	3
Thomasville	19,108	66	58	8
Thunderbolt	2,666	10	8	2
Tifton	16,611	54	45	9
Tignall	625	2	1	1
Toccoa	9,110	31	30	1
Toomsboro	619	1	1	0
Trenton	2,426	7	7	0
Trion	2,068	8	7	1
Tybee Island	3,981	27	18	9
Tyrone	6,811	18	18	0
Union City	17,487	78	57	21
Union Point	1,542	8	7	1
Valdosta	47,989	152	131	21
Vidalia	11,312	40	32	8
Vienna	2,855	9	8	1
Villa Rica	14,072	39	32	7
Wadley	1,927	11	7	4
Warm Springs	471	1	1	0
Warner Robins	61,859	149	110	39
Washington	4,006	15	14	1
Watkinsville	2,933	7	7	0
Waverly Hall	809	4	4	0
Waycross	14,695	64	54	10
Waynesboro	5,770	23	17	6
Whitesburg	587	5	5	0
Winder	14,068	46	37	9
Winterville	1,163	2	2	0
Woodstock	25,125	43	34	9
Wrens	2,209	13	8	5
Zebulon	1,239	6	6	0
HAWAII				
Honolulu	906,349	2,620	2,125	495
IDAHO				
Aberdeen	1,750	7	4	3
American Falls	4,080	9	8	1
Bellevue	2,207	6	5	1
Blackfoot	10,917	27	24	3
Boise	203,770	375	302	73
Bonners Ferry	2,636	8	8	0
Buhl	4,044	10	8	2
Caldwell	41,766	77	60	17
Cascade	1,003	6	5	1
Chubbuck	11,800	31	19	12
Coeur d'Alene	43,278	84	68	16
Cottonwood	1,034	1	1	0
Emmett	6,428	14	13	1
Fruitland	4,709	11	9	2
Garden City	11,676	32	26	6
Gooding	3,186	9	7	2
Grangeville	3,076	6	6	0
Hagerman	770	2	2	0
Hailey	8,058	15	14	1
Heyburn	2,665	7	6	1
Homedale	2,485	6	6	0
Idaho City	480	1	1	0
Idaho Falls	53,566	134	91	43
Jerome	8,923	19	17	2
Kamiah	1,085	3	3	0
Kellogg	2,205	8	7	1
Ketchum	3,263	15	9	6
Kimberly	3,065	8	7	1
Lewiston	31,911	66	45	21
McCall	2,663	14	12	2
Meridian	69,466	92	71	21
Montpelier	2,323	6	6	0
Moscow	23,470	43	35	8
Mountain Home	12,328	35	27	8
Nampa	83,007	183	129	54
Orofino	3,052	7	6	1
Osburn	1,376	2	2	0
Parma	1,838	4	4	0
Payette	7,679	14	12	2
Pinehurst	1,544	1	1	0
Pocatello	54,946	122	87	35
Ponderay	704	6	5	1
Post Falls	26,473	63	36	27
Preston	4,980	7	6	1
Priest River	1,928	6	4	2
Rathdrum	6,876	13	10	3
Rexburg	29,177	37	30	7
Rigby	3,351	10	8	2
Rupert	5,010	15	13	2
Salmon	2,945	9	7	2
Sandpoint	8,402	26	21	5
Shelley	4,187	8	8	0
Soda Springs	3,065	8	7	1

Table 78. Full-Time Law Enforcement Employees, by State and City, 2008—*Continued*

(Number.)

State/City	Population	Total law enforcement employees	Total officers	Total civilians
Spirit Lake	1,744	5	4	1
St. Anthony	3,410	7	6	1
St. Maries	2,619	5	5	0
Sun Valley	1,450	11	10	1
Twin Falls	42,417	94	63	31
Weiser	5,318	15	13	2
Wendell	2,425	6	5	1
Wilder	1,431	3	3	0
ILLINOIS				
Abingdon	3,243	4	4	0
Addison	37,041	101	72	29
Albany	912	1	1	0
Albion	1,821	3	3	0
Aledo	3,561	8	7	1
Algonquin	31,279	60	50	10
Alorton	2,525	14	12	2
Alsip	18,693	57	42	15
Altamont	2,239	6	6	0
Alton	29,284	88	65	23
Amboy	2,573	4	4	0
Anna	5,058	8	8	0
Annawan	912	1	1	0
Antioch	14,465	41	28	13
Arcola	2,608	6	5	1
Arlington Heights	73,346	150	115	35
Arthur	2,128	5	5	0
Ashland	1,335	1	1	0
Assumption	1,196	1	1	0
Athens	1,791	3	3	0
Atkinson	951	2	2	0
Atlanta	1,634	2	2	0
Atwood	1,208	3	3	0
Auburn	4,303	10	6	4
Aurora	174,488	371	297	74
Aviston	1,740	1	1	0
Bannockburn	1,641	7	7	0
Barrington Hills	4,395	29	19	10
Barrington-Inverness	18,019	38	31	7
Bartlett	41,925	70	52	18
Bartonville	6,134	17	12	5
Batavia	27,679	53	45	8
Beardstown	5,932	12	8	4
Beckemeyer	1,084	1	1	0
Bedford Park	532	43	35	8
Beecher	3,104	10	9	1
Belleville	40,891	101	82	19
Bellwood	18,965	44	41	3
Belvidere	26,859	49	44	5
Benld	1,460	4	4	0
Bensenville	20,192	40	31	9
Benton	6,937	11	10	1
Berkeley	4,902	20	16	4
Berwyn	49,897	131	99	32
Bethalto	9,935	22	16	6
Bloomingdale	21,917	64	47	17
Bloomington	73,309	166	124	42
Blue Island	22,265	65	41	24
Blue Mound	1,016	1	1	0
Bolingbrook	72,385	170	119	51
Bourbonnais	18,289	29	22	7
Bradley	14,855	47	33	14
Braidwood	6,805	11	10	1
Breese	4,337	8	7	1
Bridgeport	2,090	2	2	0
Bridgeview	14,928	42	40	2
Brighton	2,392	6	4	2
Broadview	7,620	32	25	7
Brookfield	18,079	40	33	7
Brooklyn	620	8	6	2
Buda	570	1	1	0
Buffalo Grove	43,131	86	71	15
Bull Valley	841	3	3	0
Bunker Hill	1,743	4	3	1
Burbank	27,592	72	53	19
Burnham	3,982	12	8	4
Burr Ridge	11,412	33	29	4
Byron	3,894	8	7	1
Cahokia	15,088	40	28	12
Cairo	3,097	12	7	5
Calumet City	36,824	122	91	31
Calumet Park	7,969	31	24	7
Cambridge	2,084	1	1	0
Camp Point	1,189	2	2	0
Canton	14,495	33	24	9
Carbondale	26,376	80	62	18
Carlinville	5,938	17	12	5
Carlyle	3,365	8	7	1
Carmi	5,170	10	9	1
Carol Stream	39,699	93	64	29
Carpentersville	38,420	81	67	14
Carrier Mills	1,839	2	2	0
Carrollton	2,430	6	6	0
Carterville	5,464	7	7	0
Carthage	2,486	3	3	0
Cary	20,164	31	27	4
Casey	2,920	7	6	1
Caseyville	4,301	15	11	4
Central City	1,311	4	4	0
Centralia	13,488	36	27	9
Centreville	5,646	16	13	3
Chadwick	472	1	1	0
Champaign	76,187	153	121	32
Channahon	14,799	29	25	4
Charleston	20,191	35	33	2
Chatham	10,590	20	14	6
Chenoa	3,260	4	4	0
Cherry Valley	2,267	13	12	1
Chester	7,725	12	9	3
Chicago	2,829,304	14,307	13,359	948
Chicago Heights	30,579	103	74	29
Chicago Ridge	13,353	35	31	4
Chillicothe	5,839	14	9	5
Christopher	2,820	5	5	0
Cicero	80,428	177	152	25
Clarendon Hills	8,661	16	15	1
Clinton	7,153	15	13	2
Coal City	5,685	13	12	1
Coal Valley	4,053	8	7	1
Cobden	1,107	3	3	0
Colfax	1,003	1	1	0
Collinsville	26,019	65	46	19
Colona	5,196	11	10	1
Columbia	9,402	21	14	7
Cordova	694	2	2	0
Cortland	4,242	4	4	0
Coulterville	1,151	2	2	0
Country Club Hills	16,837	62	46	16
Countryside	5,788	34	27	7
Crest Hill	21,539	27	25	2
Crestwood	11,102	4	3	1
Crete	9,164	23	21	2
Creve Coeur	5,191	8	6	2
Crystal Lake	42,058	75	62	13
Cuba	1,332	2	2	0
Dallas City	977	1	1	0
Danvers	1,146	1	1	0
Danville	32,310	79	64	15
Darien	22,372	54	38	16
Decatur	76,044	199	166	33
Deerfield	19,731	52	38	14
De Kalb	44,309	74	61	13
De Pue	1,756	1	1	0
De Soto	1,574	4	3	1
Des Plaines	56,999	128	103	25
Divernon	1,120	2	2	0
Dixmoor	3,780	10	8	2
Dixon	15,183	31	27	4
Dolton	23,844	63	48	15

Table 78. Full-Time Law Enforcement Employees, by State and City, 2008—*Continued*

(Number.)

State/City	Population	Total law enforcement employees	Total officers	Total civilians
Downers Grove	48,908	107	77	30
Dupo	4,054	7	7	0
Du Quoin	6,333	15	11	4
Durand	1,089	1	1	0
Dwight	4,275	9	8	1
Earlville	1,840	3	3	0
East Alton	6,543	18	12	6
East Carondelet	624	1	1	0
East Dubuque	1,940	7	7	0
East Dundee	3,128	15	14	1
East Hazel Crest	1,538	10	9	1
East Moline	21,022	50	40	10
East Peoria	22,703	55	41	14
East St. Louis	28,691	98	69	29
Edwardsville	24,724	54	40	14
Effingham	12,457	34	21	13
Elburn	5,556	10	9	1
Eldorado	4,408	11	7	4
Elgin	105,535	246	183	63
Elizabeth	653	1	1	0
Elk Grove Village	33,399	108	94	14
Elmhurst	45,664	92	70	22
Elmwood	1,869	1	1	0
Elmwood Park	23,988	41	34	7
El Paso	2,775	5	5	0
Elwood	2,438	13	11	2
Energy	1,211	4	4	0
Erie	1,543	3	3	0
Eureka	5,263	6	6	0
Evanston	76,129	209	156	53
Evergreen Park	19,344	72	60	12
Fairbury	3,785	9	8	1
Fairfield	5,164	17	13	4
Fairmont City	2,242	10	8	2
Fairview	482	1	1	0
Fairview Heights	16,694	57	40	17
Farmer City	1,956	6	3	3
Farmington	2,426	5	5	0
Fisher	1,766	2	2	0
Flora	4,726	16	11	5
Flossmoor	9,353	24	19	5
Forest Park	15,278	52	37	15
Forest View	717	11	8	3
Fox Lake	11,335	30	25	5
Fox River Grove	5,202	13	13	0
Frankfort	18,589	33	29	4
Franklin Park	17,937	55	51	4
Freeburg	4,317	11	10	1
Freeport	24,572	73	55	18
Fulton	3,826	9	8	1
Galena	3,341	13	10	3
Galesburg	30,783	83	53	30
Galva	2,644	3	3	0
Geneseo	6,429	21	14	7
Geneva	24,794	47	36	11
Genoa	5,109	11	10	1
Georgetown	3,444	4	4	0
Germantown	1,219	1	1	0
Gibson City	3,306	9	7	2
Gifford	1,021	1	1	0
Gilberts	7,074	9	8	1
Gillespie	3,165	9	6	3
Gilman	1,709	3	3	0
Girard	2,170	5	5	0
Glasford	1,032	1	1	0
Glen Carbon	12,783	25	19	6
Glencoe	9,059	43	33	10
Glendale Heights	31,968	82	56	26
Glen Ellyn	27,159	50	42	8
Glenview	46,740	89	77	12
Glenwood	8,495	24	22	2
Golf	449	4	4	0
Grafton	729	5	5	0
Granite City	30,528	70	57	13
Grant Park	1,667	5	5	0
Granville	1,345	2	2	0
Grayslake	22,018	39	33	6
Grayville	1,577	5	1	4
Greenfield	1,073	2	2	0
Greenup	1,469	4	4	0
Greenville	7,174	14	10	4
Gurnee	30,799	91	63	28
Hainesville	3,990	6	5	1
Hamilton	2,774	4	4	0
Hampshire	4,964	13	13	0
Hampton	1,796	4	4	0
Hanover Park	36,766	77	54	23
Harrisburg	9,614	15	14	1
Hartford	1,475	5	4	1
Harvard	10,082	26	20	6
Harvey	28,030	114	72	42
Harwood Heights	8,051	35	26	9
Havana	3,316	10	6	4
Hawthorn Woods	8,175	11	10	1
Hazel Crest	14,084	34	28	6
Hebron	1,295	4	4	0
Henry	2,443	4	4	0
Herrin	12,261	23	16	7
Herscher	1,610	2	2	0
Hickory Hills	13,316	36	29	7
Highland	9,717	27	19	8
Highland Park	31,601	81	59	22
Highwood	5,406	14	13	1
Hillsboro	6,157	8	8	0
Hillside	8,442	36	29	7
Hinckley	2,090	3	3	0
Hinsdale	18,476	38	28	10
Hodgkins	2,023	23	22	1
Hoffman Estates	53,594	121	102	19
Homer	1,136	1	1	0
Hometown	4,109	5	1	4
Homewood	18,494	43	38	5
Hoopeston	5,638	17	12	5
Hopedale	918	2	2	0
Huntley	25,752	36	30	6
Indian Head Park	3,631	11	10	1
Irving	479	1	1	0
Island Lake	8,554	21	15	6
Itasca	8,636	34	26	8
Jacksonville	19,237	51	40	11
Jerome	1,280	7	7	0
Jerseyville	8,303	20	14	6
Johnsburg	6,814	11	10	1
Johnston City	3,498	4	4	0
Joliet	149,617	391	302	89
Jonesboro	1,830	3	3	0
Justice	12,567	30	24	6
Kankakee	26,489	87	72	15
Kenilworth	2,388	13	10	3
Kewanee	12,277	32	24	8
Kildeer	4,206	23	21	2
Kincaid	1,446	1	1	0
Kirkland	1,785	3	3	0
Knoxville	2,906	5	5	0
Lacon	1,847	3	3	0
La Grange	15,268	38	29	9
La Grange Park	12,399	29	23	6
Lake Bluff	6,247	23	17	6
Lake Forest	21,249	62	43	19
Lake in the Hills	30,372	57	41	16
Lakemoor	6,003	12	12	0
Lake Villa	9,046	18	17	1
Lakewood	3,873	9	8	1
Lake Zurich	20,874	54	35	19
La Moille	746	1	1	0
Lanark	1,452	1	1	0
Lansing	26,676	76	57	19
La Salle	9,488	30	24	6

Table 78. Full-Time Law Enforcement Employees, by State and City, 2008—*Continued*

(Number.)

State/City	Population	Total law enforcement employees	Total officers	Total civilians
Lebanon	4,173	11	11	0
Leland	959	1	1	0
Leland Grove	1,427	6	6	0
Lemont	16,308	33	27	6
Lenzburg	530	1	1	0
Le Roy	3,520	6	6	0
Lewistown	2,364	4	4	0
Lexington	1,892	3	3	0
Libertyville	21,954	59	42	17
Lincoln	14,549	26	25	1
Lincolnshire	7,827	36	25	11
Lincolnwood	11,812	44	33	11
Lindenhurst	14,887	18	16	2
Lisle	23,210	58	44	14
Litchfield	6,621	23	16	7
Lockport	25,802	46	39	7
Lombard	42,851	90	73	17
Loves Park	24,766	38	34	4
Ludlow	368	1	1	0
Lynwood	8,046	23	17	6
Lyons	10,347	35	28	7
Machesney Park	23,075	26	25	1
Macomb	18,735	32	29	3
Madison	4,569	14	10	4
Mahomet	6,436	8	7	1
Manhattan	7,308	10	9	1
Manito	1,626	3	3	0
Manteno	8,774	18	17	1
Marengo	7,693	22	16	6
Marion	17,421	40	29	11
Marissa	1,980	4	4	0
Markham	12,138	49	41	8
Maroa	1,527	4	4	0
Marquette Heights	2,829	5	5	0
Marseilles	4,922	14	9	5
Marshall	3,732	10	9	1
Martinsville	1,215	2	2	0
Maryville	7,514	17	12	5
Mascoutah	6,581	14	13	1
Mason City	2,359	5	5	0
Matteson	17,669	46	36	10
Mattoon	17,214	51	40	11
Maywood	25,044	76	59	17
McCook	237	23	18	5
McCullom Lake	1,095	1	1	0
McHenry	27,111	62	45	17
McLean	790	1	1	0
McLeansboro	2,737	5	5	0
Melrose Park	21,886	85	75	10
Mendota	6,998	23	15	8
Meredosia	967	1	1	0
Metamora	3,407	5	5	0
Metropolis	6,462	22	17	5
Midlothian	13,670	33	28	5
Milan	5,185	19	14	5
Milledgeville	929	2	2	0
Millstadt	3,366	8	8	0
Minier	1,245	2	2	0
Minonk	2,144	3	3	0
Minooka	11,629	24	21	3
Mokena	19,522	37	34	3
Moline	42,903	111	86	25
Monee	5,273	15	14	1
Monmouth	9,020	30	20	10
Montgomery	16,592	32	22	10
Monticello	5,336	7	6	1
Morris	13,769	34	25	9
Morrison	4,287	7	7	0
Morton	16,077	30	22	8
Morton Grove	22,518	59	45	14
Mound City	592	1	1	0
Mount Carmel	7,417	17	12	5
Mount Carroll	1,652	3	3	0
Mount Morris	3,069	5	4	1
Mount Olive	2,050	5	3	2
Mount Prospect	53,405	110	86	24
Mount Pulaski	1,578	2	2	0
Mount Sterling	1,883	10	5	5
Mount Vernon	16,315	58	45	13
Mount Zion	5,126	13	10	3
Moweaqua	1,802	2	2	0
Mundelein	32,935	73	54	19
Murphysboro	8,242	22	15	7
Naperville	144,205	300	186	114
Nashville	3,027	8	7	1
Nauvoo	1,169	3	3	0
Neoga	1,741	3	3	0
New Athens	2,007	4	4	0
New Baden	3,194	5	5	0
New Lenox	25,595	44	40	4
Newman	916	1	1	0
Newton	2,932	7	6	1
Niles	28,702	77	62	15
Nokomis	2,251	5	4	1
Normal	52,536	94	80	14
Norridge	13,965	53	37	16
North Aurora	16,283	32	30	2
Northbrook	34,099	94	66	28
North Chicago	32,551	77	58	19
Northfield	5,462	27	20	7
Northlake	11,481	55	38	17
North Pekin	1,684	2	2	0
North Riverside	6,236	35	26	9
Oak Brook	8,815	57	42	15
Oakbrook Terrace	2,423	25	22	3
Oak Forest	27,870	53	41	12
Oak Lawn	53,182	127	105	22
Oak Park	49,551	145	116	29
Oakwood	1,433	1	1	0
Oblong	1,522	1	1	0
O'Fallon	27,725	59	46	13
Oglesby	3,651	12	9	3
Okawville	1,331	3	3	0
Olney	8,308	19	13	6
Olympia Fields	4,690	21	19	2
Oregon	4,148	10	9	1
Orion	1,689	3	3	0
Orland Hills	7,299	14	13	1
Orland Park	56,224	125	96	29
Oswego	31,784	62	51	11
Ottawa	19,243	47	36	11
Palatine	67,440	141	112	29
Palestine	1,324	2	2	0
Palmyra	707	2	1	1
Palos Heights	12,644	29	27	2
Palos Hills	16,951	36	33	3
Palos Park	4,883	12	11	1
Pana	5,401	13	9	4
Paris	8,738	23	17	6
Park City	6,660	13	11	2
Park Forest	22,586	50	41	9
Park Ridge	36,729	68	55	13
Pawnee	2,520	10	6	4
Paxton	4,540	7	7	0
Pecatonica	2,231	4	4	0
Pekin	33,346	64	55	9
Peoria	113,616	290	250	40
Peoria Heights	6,209	16	11	5
Peotone	4,364	11	10	1
Peru	9,797	33	26	7
Petersburg	2,196	5	5	0
Pinckneyville	5,398	7	6	1
Piper City	741	1	1	0
Pittsfield	4,506	6	6	0
Plainfield	39,856	79	55	24
Plano	11,932	21	19	2
Polo	2,483	3	3	0
Pontiac	11,250	26	24	2

Table 78. Full-Time Law Enforcement Employees, by State and City, 2008—*Continued*

(Number.)

State/City	Population	Total law enforcement employees	Total officers	Total civilians
Pontoon Beach	6,109	18	13	5
Port Barrington	1,537	1	1	0
Posen	4,955	17	15	2
Potomac	654	1	1	0
Princeton	7,527	17	16	1
Prophetstown	1,919	4	3	1
Prospect Heights	16,031	29	26	3
Quincy	39,993	91	76	15
Rankin	586	1	1	0
Rantoul	12,338	39	31	8
Raymond	899	2	2	0
Red Bud	3,644	7	7	0
Richmond	2,516	4	4	0
Richton Park	12,926	31	26	5
Ridge Farm	857	1	1	0
Ridgway	859	3	3	0
Riverdale	14,185	46	38	8
River Forest	11,031	34	31	3
River Grove	9,992	30	24	6
Riverside	8,270	24	18	6
Robbins	6,274	12	4	8
Robinson	6,343	15	14	1
Rochelle	9,877	28	21	7
Rochester	3,208	8	8	0
Rockdale	2,008	4	4	0
Rock Falls	9,293	25	18	7
Rockford	157,262	335	302	33
Rock Island	38,072	110	84	26
Rockton	5,512	16	15	1
Rolling Meadows	23,501	81	56	25
Romeoville	39,701	92	69	23
Roodhouse	2,095	8	4	4
Roscoe	9,151	14	13	1
Roselle	23,256	53	37	16
Rosemont	3,926	95	75	20
Rossville	1,159	2	2	0
Round Lake	19,028	29	23	6
Round Lake Beach	28,196	53	43	10
Round Lake Heights	3,087	4	4	0
Round Lake Park	6,210	15	12	3
Roxana	1,491	6	5	1
Royalton	1,164	3	3	0
Rushville	3,117	4	4	0
Salem	7,416	21	14	7
Sandwich	7,423	22	16	6
Sauget	238	15	14	1
Sauk Village	10,326	34	25	9
Savanna	3,193	8	8	0
Schaumburg	71,753	176	129	47
Schiller Park	11,455	40	33	7
Seneca	2,115	7	3	4
Sesser	2,124	5	4	1
Shawneetown	1,307	3	3	0
Shelbyville	4,574	8	7	1
Sheridan	2,203	3	3	0
Sherman	3,834	6	6	0
Shiloh	11,146	18	17	1
Shorewood	15,994	31	27	4
Silvis	7,895	21	14	7
Skokie	67,087	146	112	34
Sleepy Hollow	3,687	8	7	1
Smithton	3,506	5	5	0
Somonauk	1,653	4	4	0
South Barrington	4,347	18	15	3
South Beloit	5,542	18	16	2
South Chicago Heights	3,783	11	7	4
South Elgin	21,626	42	32	10
Southern View	1,625	4	4	0
South Holland	21,124	45	43	2
South Jacksonville	3,254	6	5	1
South Pekin	1,210	2	2	0
South Roxana	1,804	5	5	0
Sparta	4,273	18	12	6
Springfield	117,762	318	269	49
Spring Grove	5,948	12	10	2
Spring Valley	5,363	14	11	3
St. Anne	1,241	3	3	0
Staunton	5,143	10	7	3
St. Charles	33,379	69	55	14
Steger	10,556	25	17	8
Sterling	15,074	43	30	13
St. Francisville	730	1	1	0
Stickney	5,765	23	16	7
Stockton	1,774	4	3	1
Stone Park	4,862	17	15	2
Stonington	895	2	2	0
Streamwood	37,389	73	61	12
Streator	13,748	31	24	7
Sugar Grove	10,506	18	17	1
Sullivan	4,340	10	8	2
Summit	10,240	35	29	6
Sumner	1,974	2	2	0
Swansea	13,022	28	22	6
Sycamore	17,898	31	28	3
Taylorville	12,169	28	22	6
Thomson	525	1	1	0
Thornton	2,384	13	12	1
Tilton	2,778	3	3	0
Tinley Park	60,293	107	79	28
Tolono	2,867	4	4	0
Tremont	2,078	3	3	0
Trenton	2,646	5	5	0
Troy	9,878	24	18	6
Tuscola	4,555	8	7	1
University Park	8,347	20	16	4
Urbana	39,685	66	53	13
Valmeyer	1,235	2	2	0
Vandalia	6,730	18	13	5
Venice	2,418	6	4	2
Vernon Hills	24,640	73	47	26
Vienna	1,294	4	4	0
Villa Grove	2,457	5	4	1
Villa Park	22,301	56	41	15
Virden	3,368	10	6	4
Virginia	1,679	1	1	0
Wamac	1,263	3	3	0
Warren	1,370	4	3	1
Warrensburg	1,166	2	2	0
Warrenville	13,025	39	32	7
Warsaw	1,599	3	3	0
Washburn	1,091	1	1	0
Washington	14,046	30	21	9
Waterloo	9,837	15	13	2
Waterman	1,467	2	2	0
Watseka	5,471	11	10	1
Wauconda	12,329	37	25	12
Waukegan	91,487	212	157	55
Wayne	2,382	5	5	0
Westchester	15,717	47	35	12
West Chicago	26,897	63	48	15
West City	754	9	5	4
West Dundee	8,307	24	21	3
Western Springs	12,638	29	21	8
West Frankfort	8,198	19	14	5
Westmont	25,032	55	40	15
West Salem	941	1	1	0
Westville	3,004	3	3	0
Wheaton	54,428	92	70	22
Wheeling	36,102	94	67	27
White Hall	2,459	8	5	3
Williamsfield	571	2	2	0
Willowbrook	8,843	29	25	4
Willow Springs	6,043	24	18	6
Wilmette	26,437	62	45	17
Wilmington	6,220	22	15	7
Winchester	1,546	2	2	0
Winfield	10,117	22	20	2
Winnebago	3,207	6	6	0

Table 78. Full-Time Law Enforcement Employees, by State and City, 2008—*Continued*

(Number.)

State/City	Population	Total law enforcement employees	Total officers	Total civilians
Winnetka	12,414	37	28	9
Winthrop Harbor	7,271	17	11	6
Witt	958	1	1	0
Wonder Lake	3,677	4	2	2
Wood Dale	13,866	51	34	17
Woodhull	792	1	1	0
Woodridge	34,560	79	53	26
Wood River	10,937	25	19	6
Woodstock	23,605	53	41	12
Worden	1,035	1	1	0
Worth	10,433	26	24	2
Yates City	664	1	1	0
Yorkville	16,906	35	30	5
Zeigler	1,667	4	4	0
Zion	25,409	64	48	16
INDIANA				
Albion	2,328	7	6	1
Alexandria	5,839	16	12	4
Anderson	57,019	136	117	19
Angola	7,951	21	17	4
Attica	3,291	6	6	0
Auburn	12,926	30	23	7
Aurora	4,072	13	10	3
Austin	4,621	6	6	0
Avon	11,847	23	21	2
Bargersville	2,730	6	5	1
Batesville	6,420	17	11	6
Bedford	13,458	42	32	10
Beech Grove	14,191	43	31	12
Berne	4,243	8	7	1
Bloomington	72,337	124	87	37
Bluffton	9,333	33	20	13
Boonville	6,713	17	14	3
Brazil	8,212	15	11	4
Bremen	4,659	16	12	4
Brownsburg	20,122	48	40	8
Burns Harbor	1,122	6	5	1
Carmel	65,982	124	104	20
Cedar Lake	10,817	21	16	5
Charlestown	7,252	20	15	5
Clinton	4,817	8	7	1
Columbia City	8,307	20	18	2
Columbus	39,889	83	74	9
Connersville	13,827	31	30	1
Corydon	2,755	7	7	0
Covington	2,425	6	6	0
Crawfordsville	15,061	46	31	15
Crown Point	24,479	53	40	13
Culver	1,494	4	4	0
Danville	8,229	17	15	2
Decatur	9,484	21	17	4
Delphi	2,872	9	6	3
Dyer	15,924	34	26	8
East Chicago	29,890	126	111	15
Elkhart	52,654	141	119	22
Elwood	8,968	19	14	5
Evansville	115,639	310	277	33
Fairmount	2,711	7	4	3
Fishers	70,594	96	89	7
Fort Wayne	251,194	485	447	38
Fowler	2,188	4	4	0
Franklin	23,088	57	41	16
Gas City	5,662	14	10	4
Georgetown	3,034	3	3	0
Goshen	32,152	69	59	10
Greencastle	10,028	18	16	2
Greendale	4,370	15	11	4
Greenwood	47,770	71	49	22
Griffith	16,216	39	31	8
Hagerstown	1,628	5	5	0
Hammond	76,498	259	210	49
Hartford City	6,281	15	13	2
Hebron	3,653	8	7	1
Highland	22,608	49	41	8
Hobart	28,139	68	53	15
Huntingburg	6,139	11	10	1
Huntington	16,537	46	35	11
Indianapolis	808,329	1,848	1,590	258
Jasonville	2,442	5	5	0
Jeffersonville	29,853	72	61	11
Kendallville	10,348	27	18	9
Knox	3,805	7	7	0
Kokomo	45,779	136	103	33
Lafayette	63,990	162	127	35
La Porte	21,031	50	42	8
Lawrence	43,216	66	58	8
Lawrenceburg	4,847	26	21	5
Lebanon	15,378	30	29	1
Ligonier	4,517	10	9	1
Linton	5,659	14	10	4
Logansport	18,626	49	41	8
Long Beach	1,536	6	5	1
Loogootee	2,590	5	4	1
Lowell	8,386	19	14	5
Lynn	1,044	2	2	0
Madison	12,651	35	27	8
Marion	30,127	85	69	16
Martinsville	11,717	29	20	9
Merrillville	32,353	64	51	13
Michigan City	31,726	95	86	9
Mishawaka	49,756	133	102	31
Monticello	5,245	17	13	4
Mooresville	11,788	28	22	6
Mount Vernon	6,993	15	14	1
Muncie	65,084	109	102	7
Munster	22,217	50	39	11
Nappanee	7,164	21	15	6
New Albany	36,934	67	62	5
New Castle	18,229	36	33	3
New Chicago	1,993	6	2	4
New Haven	13,735	29	20	9
New Whiteland	5,851	12	7	5
Noblesville	43,333	85	74	11
North Liberty	1,339	4	4	0
North Manchester	5,836	16	11	5
North Vernon	6,294	21	18	3
Oakland City	2,521	4	4	0
Peru	12,420	31	29	2
Plainfield	26,769	47	42	5
Plymouth	11,126	29	24	5
Portage	36,887	77	60	17
Portland	6,163	17	13	4
Princeton	8,500	18	16	2
Richmond	36,738	83	74	9
Rochester	6,448	19	14	5
Roseland	620	2	2	0
Rushville	6,090	18	13	5
Salem	6,535	15	10	5
Schererville	29,320	62	49	13
Scottsburg	5,939	14	13	1
Seymour	19,269	50	36	14
Shelbyville	18,461	53	41	12
South Bend	103,561	326	257	69
South Whitley	1,859	4	4	0
Speedway	12,527	47	34	13
St. John	12,871	25	19	6
Sullivan	4,464	9	7	2
Tell City	7,518	19	12	7
Terre Haute	58,860	147	128	19
Tipton	5,026	15	12	3
Union City	3,418	14	9	5
Valparaiso	30,169	55	49	6
Vincennes	17,863	40	36	4
Wabash	10,764	33	27	6
Walkerton	2,170	10	6	4
Warsaw	13,484	42	35	7
Washington	11,367	25	18	7
Waterloo	2,176	7	6	1

Table 78. Full-Time Law Enforcement Employees, by State and City, 2008—*Continued*

(Number.)

State/City	Population	Total law enforcement employees	Total officers	Total civilians
Westfield	21,121	42	38	4
West Lafayette	31,384	64	48	16
Westville	4,971	3	3	0
Whitestown	710	5	5	0
Whiting	4,726	26	19	7
Winchester	4,573	16	11	5
Winona Lake	4,255	5	5	0
IOWA				
Adel	4,188	9	8	1
Albia	3,539	7	6	1
Algona	5,316	14	10	4
Altoona	14,355	26	23	3
Ames	55,249	73	51	22
Anamosa	5,749	8	7	1
Ankeny	42,632	52	44	8
Atlantic	6,725	14	12	2
Audubon	2,094	3	3	0
Belle Plaine	2,823	4	4	0
Belmond	2,315	5	5	0
Bettendorf	32,592	58	45	13
Bloomfield	2,573	4	4	0
Boone	12,611	16	15	1
Burlington	25,214	57	41	16
Camanche	4,266	7	7	0
Carlisle	3,670	6	5	1
Carroll	9,992	16	15	1
Carter Lake	3,227	10	9	1
Cedar Falls	37,759	44	42	2
Cedar Rapids	126,984	218	197	21
Centerville	5,466	15	10	5
Chariton	4,454	7	6	1
Charles City	7,516	21	14	7
Cherokee	4,720	9	8	1
Clarinda	5,501	10	9	1
Clarion	2,723	8	7	1
Clear Lake	7,792	21	15	6
Clinton	26,483	55	46	9
Clive	14,717	25	22	3
Coralville	18,672	36	32	4
Council Bluffs	60,531	124	106	18
Cresco	3,732	7	7	0
Creston	7,483	16	12	4
Davenport	99,070	209	163	46
Decorah	7,916	19	12	7
Denison	7,265	18	13	5
Des Moines	196,680	500	383	117
De Witt	5,276	10	10	0
Dubuque	57,262	105	99	6
Dyersville	4,178	10	6	4
Eagle Grove	3,319	7	7	0
Eldora	2,734	4	4	0
Eldridge	4,900	7	7	0
Emmetsburg	3,621	7	6	1
Estherville	6,247	12	12	0
Evansdale	5,065	8	7	1
Fairfield	9,113	18	12	6
Forest City	4,094	8	8	0
Fort Dodge	25,100	40	37	3
Fort Madison	10,808	22	17	5
Garner	2,937	5	5	0
Glenwood	5,687	10	9	1
Grinnell	9,216	17	15	2
Grundy Center	2,515	4	4	0
Hampton	4,159	12	7	5
Harlan	5,041	9	8	1
Hawarden	2,373	4	4	0
Hiawatha	6,715	13	12	1
Humboldt	4,213	7	7	0
Independence	6,106	11	11	0
Indianola	14,572	23	21	2
Iowa City	67,600	100	72	28
Iowa Falls	5,007	15	11	4
Jefferson	4,184	7	7	0
Johnston	16,354	22	21	1
Keokuk	10,381	31	22	9
Knoxville	7,277	14	12	2
Le Claire	3,312	8	7	1
Le Mars	9,178	15	14	1
Leon	1,861	3	3	0
Manchester	4,854	13	9	4
Maquoketa	5,891	17	11	6
Marion	32,954	50	41	9
Marshalltown	25,792	59	43	16
Mason City	27,305	51	47	4
Missouri Valley	2,769	6	6	0
Monticello	3,719	7	6	1
Mount Pleasant	8,783	16	14	2
Mount Vernon	4,258	5	5	0
Muscatine	22,383	43	39	4
Nevada	6,639	10	9	1
New Hampton	3,439	7	7	0
Newton	15,111	29	23	6
North Liberty	11,990	10	10	0
Norwalk	8,709	14	12	2
Oelwein	6,064	17	11	6
Ogden	1,981	3	3	0
Orange City	5,906	7	7	0
Osage	3,425	7	6	1
Osceola	4,697	10	9	1
Oskaloosa	11,040	19	17	2
Ottumwa	24,479	43	36	7
Pella	10,470	19	14	5
Perry	9,049	20	13	7
Pleasant Hill	8,292	13	11	2
Pleasantville	1,581	3	3	0
Polk City	3,202	6	6	0
Prairie City	1,436	3	3	0
Red Oak	5,699	14	12	2
Rock Rapids	2,478	1	1	0
Rock Valley	3,023	4	4	0
Sac City	2,127	4	4	0
Sergeant Bluff	4,017	9	8	1
Sheldon	4,740	7	7	0
Shenandoah	4,995	11	8	3
Sioux Center	6,831	6	6	0
Sioux City	82,404	152	127	25
Spencer	10,952	27	19	8
Spirit Lake	4,695	11	10	1
St. Ansgar	959	1	1	0
State Center	1,351	1	1	0
Storm Lake	9,664	21	17	4
Story City	3,347	5	5	0
Tama	2,571	5	5	0
Tipton	3,006	6	6	0
Urbandale	39,345	50	46	4
Vinton	5,106	8	8	0
Washington	7,252	11	10	1
Waterloo	66,098	132	120	12
Waukee	13,279	13	12	1
Waukon	3,933	7	7	0
Waverly	9,307	17	16	1
Webster City	7,736	16	12	4
West Burlington	3,317	11	10	1
West Des Moines	55,765	78	65	13
West Liberty	3,695	7	6	1
West Union	2,436	4	4	0
Williamsburg	2,815	6	6	0
Wilton	2,820	4	4	0
Windsor Heights	4,536	15	13	2
Winterset	4,856	8	8	0
KANSAS				
Abilene	6,274	16	14	2
Alma	747	1	1	0
Altamont	1,052	3	3	0
Americus	932	1	1	0
Andover	10,308	29	21	8
Anthony	2,169	6	5	1
Arkansas City	11,073	35	25	10

Table 78. Full-Time Law Enforcement Employees, by State and City, 2008—*Continued*

(Number.)

State/City	Population	Total law enforcement employees	Total officers	Total civilians
Arma	1,520	5	5	0
Atchison	10,059	23	22	1
Attica	574	1	1	0
Atwood	1,071	2	2	0
Augusta	8,707	32	24	8
Baldwin City	4,307	9	8	1
Basehor	3,966	12	10	2
Baxter Springs	4,157	13	9	4
Bel Aire	6,787	13	12	1
Belle Plaine	1,531	5	5	0
Belleville	1,823	5	5	0
Beloit	3,603	9	8	1
Benton	807	2	2	0
Blue Rapids	1,014	1	1	0
Bonner Springs	7,106	27	24	3
Buhler	1,321	3	3	0
Burden	529	1	1	0
Burlingame	964	2	2	0
Burlington	2,622	9	7	2
Burrton	885	2	1	1
Caldwell	1,147	2	2	0
Caney	1,973	9	5	4
Canton	793	1	1	0
Cawker City	456	1	1	0
Chanute	8,788	23	20	3
Chapman	1,290	4	4	0
Cheney	2,011	4	4	0
Cherokee	722	1	1	0
Cherryvale	2,248	4	4	0
Chetopa	1,218	4	4	0
Claflin	654	1	1	0
Clay Center	4,342	7	6	1
Clearwater	2,354	7	6	1
Coffeyville	10,266	31	25	6
Colby	4,754	18	12	6
Coldwater	752	1	1	0
Columbus	3,202	11	9	2
Colwich	1,400	3	3	0
Concordia	5,110	17	11	6
Conway Springs	1,192	3	3	0
Council Grove	2,244	7	6	1
Derby	22,578	50	37	13
Dodge City	25,797	61	46	15
Eastborough	795	7	7	0
Edwardsville	4,498	15	14	1
El Dorado	12,569	26	24	2
Elkhart	1,907	3	3	0
Ellinwood	2,036	4	4	0
Ellis	1,919	5	5	0
Ellsworth	2,871	7	6	1
Elwood	1,122	4	4	0
Erie	1,143	3	2	1
Eudora	6,339	10	9	1
Fairway	3,818	10	9	1
Florence	597	2	1	1
Fort Scott	7,869	30	20	10
Frankfort	770	1	1	0
Frontenac	3,219	9	6	3
Galena	3,149	11	7	4
Garden City	28,636	84	53	31
Garden Plain	841	2	2	0
Gardner	17,598	39	37	2
Garnett	3,188	12	8	4
Girard	2,745	7	6	1
Goddard	3,967	9	9	0
Goessel	510	1	1	0
Goodland	4,281	11	10	1
Grandview Plaza	973	6	6	0
Great Bend	15,583	35	31	4
Halstead	1,888	6	5	1
Harper	1,395	3	3	0
Haven	1,158	3	3	0
Hays	20,115	51	30	21
Haysville	10,390	34	26	8
Herington	2,404	8	7	1
Hesston	3,715	7	6	1
Hiawatha	3,161	8	7	1
Hill City	1,378	3	3	0
Hillsboro	2,643	5	5	0
Hoisington	2,881	9	7	2
Holcomb	1,841	4	3	1
Holton	3,307	6	6	0
Howard	750	1	1	0
Hugoton	3,378	7	5	2
Humboldt	1,837	5	5	0
Hutchinson	40,526	102	66	36
Independence	9,210	32	23	9
Inman	1,187	2	2	0
Iola	5,788	22	15	7
Junction City	20,265	71	50	21
Kechi	1,740	5	4	1
Kingman	3,014	7	7	0
La Crosse	1,218	3	3	0
La Cygne	1,131	2	2	0
La Harpe	641	1	1	0
Lake Quivira	935	2	2	0
Lansing	10,815	18	17	1
Larned	3,612	12	9	3
Lawrence	91,089	173	141	32
Leavenworth	34,702	86	61	25
Leawood	31,442	82	60	22
Lebo	924	1	1	0
Lenexa	46,392	129	86	43
Liberal	20,183	47	33	14
Lindsborg	3,254	7	6	1
Linn Valley	586	2	2	0
Little River	514	1	1	0
Louisburg	3,959	8	8	0
Lyndon	994	2	2	0
Lyons	3,435	8	7	1
Macksville	480	1	1	0
Maize	2,950	8	7	1
Maple Hill	502	1	1	0
Marion	1,872	5	5	0
Marysville	3,073	9	8	1
McPherson	13,450	35	29	6
Meade	1,539	3	3	0
Medicine Lodge	1,936	7	6	1
Merriam	10,764	33	28	5
Minneapolis	1,976	5	5	0
Mission	9,709	31	29	2
Moran	522	1	1	0
Mound City	802	1	1	0
Moundridge	1,625	3	3	0
Mount Hope	854	2	2	0
Mulberry	573	2	2	0
Mulvane	5,921	18	12	6
Neodesha	2,628	8	7	1
Newton	18,052	36	32	4
Nickerson	1,140	3	3	0
North Newton	1,579	2	2	0
Norton	2,642	6	6	0
Norwich	495	1	1	0
Oakley	1,835	11	6	5
Oberlin	1,645	4	4	0
Olathe	121,472	204	164	40
Osage City	2,825	6	6	0
Osawatomie	4,516	14	9	5
Osborne	1,352	4	4	0
Oswego	1,977	5	5	0
Ottawa	12,937	31	26	5
Overbrook	932	1	1	0
Overland Park	171,909	308	257	51
Oxford	1,068	1	1	0
Paola	5,409	23	16	7
Park City	7,781	21	19	2
Parsons	11,078	33	26	7
Peabody	1,200	3	3	0

Table 78. Full-Time Law Enforcement Employees, by State and City, 2008—*Continued*

(Number.)

State/City	Population	Total law enforcement employees	Total officers	Total civilians
Perry	846	1	1	0
Pittsburg	19,571	57	40	17
Plainville	1,799	5	5	0
Pleasanton	1,330	3	3	0
Prairie Village	21,344	60	47	13
Pratt	6,387	20	14	6
Protection	526	1	1	0
Roeland Park	6,920	18	16	2
Rolla	414	1	1	0
Rose Hill	4,026	10	9	1
Rossville	1,069	3	3	0
Russell	4,233	18	8	10
Sabetha	2,482	6	6	0
Salina	46,542	108	78	30
Scott City	3,448	13	7	6
Sedgwick	1,644	1	1	0
Seneca	2,017	6	6	0
Shawnee	61,553	108	88	20
Silver Lake	1,372	2	2	0
South Hutchinson	2,542	9	7	2
Spring Hill	5,427	15	13	2
Stafford	1,030	4	4	0
Sterling	2,523	5	5	0
St. George	537	1	1	0
St. John	1,174	4	4	0
St. Marys	2,254	5	5	0
Stockton	1,391	5	5	0
Tonganoxie	4,371	11	10	1
Topeka	122,554	356	283	73
Towanda	1,356	2	2	0
Udall	740	1	1	0
Ulysses	5,590	11	10	1
Valley Center	6,394	15	11	4
Valley Falls	1,147	2	2	0
Victoria	1,189	2	2	0
Wa Keeney	1,676	4	4	0
Wakefield	856	1	1	0
Walton	287	1	1	0
Wamego	4,276	12	8	4
Waterville	609	1	1	0
Wathena	1,286	2	2	0
Weir	736	1	1	0
Wellington	7,712	20	17	3
Wellsville	1,746	4	4	0
Westwood	1,832	8	7	1
Wichita	362,602	815	629	186
Wilson	761	1	1	0
Winfield	11,458	32	23	9
Yates Center	1,367	3	3	0
KENTUCKY				
Adairville	925	2	1	1
Albany	2,316	9	8	1
Alexandria	8,452	15	13	2
Allen	148	1	1	0
Anchorage	3,092	15	10	5
Ashland	21,274	51	46	5
Auburn	1,499	2	2	0
Audubon Park	1,622	8	7	1
Augusta	1,277	3	3	0
Barbourville	3,575	18	14	4
Bardstown	11,194	24	23	1
Beattyville	1,104	7	5	2
Beaver Dam	3,121	5	5	0
Bellefonte	844	4	4	0
Bellevue	5,818	10	9	1
Benham	531	2	2	0
Benton	4,385	9	7	2
Berea	14,558	32	29	3
Bloomfield	890	2	1	1
Booneville	146	2	2	0
Bowling Green	54,865	146	111	35
Brandenburg	2,168	5	5	0
Brooksville	570	1	1	0
Brownsville	1,038	1	1	0
Burgin	913	1	1	0
Burkesville	1,685	10	5	5
Burnside	689	5	5	0
Butler	633	1	1	0
Cadiz	2,626	10	9	1
Calhoun	790	1	1	0
Calvert City	2,779	7	6	1
Campbellsville	11,009	24	22	2
Campton	407	1	1	0
Caneyville	661	1	1	0
Carlisle	2,101	9	5	4
Carrollton	3,893	9	8	1
Catlettsburg	1,954	8	8	0
Cave City	2,006	7	7	0
Central City	5,715	12	12	0
Clarkson	836	1	1	0
Clay City	1,362	2	2	0
Clinton	1,321	4	4	0
Cloverport	1,234	2	2	0
Cold Spring	6,003	12	12	0
Columbia	4,247	10	10	0
Corbin	8,394	26	19	7
Covington	43,018	133	111	22
Crab Orchard	864	1	1	0
Crofton	1,015	1	1	0
Cumberland	2,265	4	4	0
Cynthiana	6,264	12	11	1
Danville	15,437	35	33	2
Dawson Springs	2,900	7	4	3
Dayton	5,420	9	8	1
Earlington	1,566	1	1	0
Eddyville	2,412	6	6	0
Edgewood	8,831	14	14	0
Edmonton	1,642	7	7	0
Elizabethtown	23,926	58	43	15
Elkhorn City	1,003	2	2	0
Elkton	1,959	7	7	0
Elsmere	7,860	12	11	1
Eminence	2,216	6	6	0
Erlanger	17,164	56	45	11
Eubank	375	1	1	0
Evarts	1,034	4	4	0
Falmouth	2,077	8	7	1
Ferguson	931	1	1	0
Flatwoods	7,621	11	10	1
Fleming-Neon	787	2	2	0
Flemingsburg	2,683	7	7	0
Florence	27,761	64	60	4
Fort Mitchell	7,493	13	13	0
Fort Thomas	15,157	24	23	1
Fort Wright	5,411	13	12	1
Frankfort	27,014	70	65	5
Franklin	8,007	22	21	1
Fulton	2,374	13	9	4
Gamaliel	430	1	1	0
Georgetown	21,419	48	44	4
Glasgow	14,343	46	35	11
Glencoe	376	1	1	0
Graymoor-Devondale	3,110	2	2	0
Grayson	4,004	11	11	0
Greensburg	2,394	7	7	0
Greenville	4,235	9	9	0
Guthrie	1,435	4	4	0
Hardinsburg	2,442	4	4	0
Harlan	1,858	11	9	2
Harrodsburg	8,169	20	14	6
Hartford	2,650	6	6	0
Hawesville	979	1	1	0
Hazard	4,781	20	15	5
Henderson	27,805	67	58	9
Heritage Creek	1,676	10	10	0
Hickman	2,191	3	3	0
Highland Heights	5,697	18	18	0
Hillview	7,558	13	13	0

Table 78. Full-Time Law Enforcement Employees, by State and City, 2008—*Continued*

(Number.)

State/City	Population	Total law enforcement employees	Total officers	Total civilians
Hindman	756	2	2	0
Hodgenville	2,765	5	5	0
Hollow Creek	880	2	2	0
Hopkinsville	31,823	75	68	7
Horse Cave	2,319	4	4	0
Hustonville	355	1	1	0
Hyden	192	2	2	0
Independence	22,106	31	29	2
Indian Hills	3,343	8	8	0
Inez	431	1	1	0
Irvine	2,659	6	6	0
Irvington	1,415	4	4	0
Jackson	2,354	12	10	2
Jamestown	1,741	5	5	0
Jeffersontown	26,112	58	49	9
Jenkins	2,239	5	5	0
Junction City	2,197	3	3	0
La Center	1,037	1	1	0
La Grange	6,355	13	13	0
Lakeside Park-Crestview Hills	6,355	12	11	1
Lancaster	4,473	10	10	0
Lawrenceburg	10,024	22	14	8
Lebanon	5,949	20	15	5
Lebanon Junction	2,014	5	5	0
Leitchfield	6,539	14	13	1
Lewisburg	917	1	1	0
Lexington	281,473	630	548	82
Liberty	1,884	6	6	0
London	7,993	37	34	3
Louisa	2,078	7	7	0
Louisville Metro	629,679	1,453	1,207	246
Ludlow	4,888	11	10	1
Lynch	820	2	2	0
Lynnview	1,011	1	1	0
Madisonville	19,046	51	41	10
Marion	3,053	6	6	0
Martin	632	4	4	0
Mayfield	10,208	30	23	7
Maysville	9,183	30	24	6
Middlesboro	9,862	28	24	4
Monticello	6,191	11	10	1
Morehead	7,649	29	20	9
Morganfield	3,289	12	7	5
Morgantown	2,571	6	6	0
Mortons Gap	936	1	1	0
Mount Olivet	275	1	1	0
Mount Sterling	6,886	24	22	2
Mount Vernon	2,595	8	8	0
Mount Washington	12,354	15	14	1
Muldraugh	1,247	3	3	0
Munfordville	1,605	4	4	0
Murray	16,482	37	31	6
New Castle	909	1	1	0
Newport	15,409	48	44	4
Nicholasville	26,558	66	59	7
Nortonville	1,229	1	1	0
Oak Grove	9,806	19	14	5
Olive Hill	1,817	5	5	0
Owensboro	55,534	129	100	29
Owenton	1,487	6	4	2
Owingsville	1,580	5	5	0
Paducah	25,450	90	76	14
Paintsville	4,120	11	10	1
Paris	9,268	30	27	3
Park Hills	2,758	6	6	0
Perryville	755	1	1	0
Pikeville	6,277	28	21	7
Pineville	1,967	5	5	0
Pippa Passes	446	1	1	0
Powderly	889	1	1	0
Prestonsburg	3,843	17	17	0
Princeton	6,328	16	15	1
Prospect	5,541	10	9	1
Providence	3,456	6	6	0
Raceland	2,588	6	6	0
Radcliff	21,918	48	37	11
Ravenna	668	2	2	0
Richmond	32,982	94	64	30
Russell	3,566	12	12	0
Russell Springs	2,574	9	8	1
Russellville	7,290	21	19	2
Sadieville	316	1	1	0
Salyersville	1,568	2	2	0
Science Hill	669	3	2	1
Scottsville	4,573	20	13	7
Sebree	1,532	1	1	0
Shelbyville	11,300	24	23	1
Shepherdsville	9,199	27	25	2
Shively	16,210	30	25	5
Silver Grove	1,153	1	1	0
Smiths Grove	761	1	1	0
Somerset	12,438	39	36	3
Springfield	2,880	13	8	5
Stamping Ground	673	1	1	0
Stanton	3,150	6	6	0
St. Matthews	18,279	37	31	6
Sturgis	1,921	4	4	0
Taylor Mill	6,723	11	10	1
Taylorsville	1,234	5	5	0
Tompkinsville	2,631	12	9	3
Uniontown	1,022	2	2	0
Vanceburg	1,703	6	6	0
Versailles	7,804	39	38	1
Villa Hills	7,702	9	8	1
Vine Grove	4,192	7	7	0
Warsaw	1,796	5	5	0
Wayland	289	1	1	0
West Liberty	3,345	15	7	8
West Point	975	3	3	0
Whitesburg	1,476	6	6	0
Wilder	2,995	6	6	0
Williamsburg	5,206	11	11	0
Williamstown	3,516	8	7	1
Wilmore	5,917	10	9	1
Winchester	16,555	50	34	16
Wingo	595	1	1	0
Wurtland	1,048	1	1	0
LOUISIANA				
Abbeville	11,636	38	36	2
Addis	3,590	9	8	1
Alexandria	48,393	201	166	35
Amite	4,322	28	28	0
Baker	13,550	34	32	2
Baldwin	2,607	7	6	1
Ball	3,763	8	6	2
Basile	2,390	13	8	5
Bastrop	11,776	39	27	12
Baton Rouge	226,920	902	628	274
Bernice	1,635	5	5	0
Berwick	4,286	11	11	0
Blanchard	2,590	6	5	1
Bogalusa	12,607	61	39	22
Bossier City	62,500	237	198	39
Breaux Bridge	8,059	20	20	0
Broussard	7,854	26	22	4
Brusly	2,151	8	7	1
Church Point	4,666	17	17	0
Clarence	500	1	1	0
Clinton	1,878	9	8	1
Coushatta	2,095	6	6	0
Covington	9,553	50	38	12
Crowley	13,958	44	38	6
Cullen	1,379	3	3	0
Delhi	2,977	9	5	4
Denham Springs	10,269	39	31	8
De Quincy	3,214	14	14	0
De Ridder	10,134	30	24	6
Dixie Inn	345	2	2	0

Table 78. Full-Time Law Enforcement Employees, by State and City, 2008—*Continued*

(Number.)

State/City	Population	Total law enforcement employees	Total officers	Total civilians
Elton	1,232	11	7	4
Eunice	11,473	38	27	11
Farmerville	3,637	13	13	0
Ferriday	3,544	17	12	5
Franklin	7,694	24	23	1
Franklinton	3,719	22	16	6
French Settlement	1,071	2	2	0
Golden Meadow	2,122	4	3	1
Gonzales	9,252	35	35	0
Grambling	4,501	15	10	5
Gramercy	6,798	7	7	0
Gretna	15,821	109	89	20
Hammond	19,825	103	77	26
Harahan	8,976	28	25	3
Haughton	2,994	9	7	2
Homer	3,387	12	11	1
Houma	32,592	89	75	14
Iowa	2,599	13	10	3
Jackson	3,905	5	5	0
Jeanerette	5,895	12	7	5
Jena	2,852	7	6	1
Jennings	10,496	35	23	12
Jonesboro	3,703	12	8	4
Kaplan	5,089	16	12	4
Kenner	64,597	223	163	60
Kentwood	2,259	10	9	1
Kinder	2,394	17	17	0
Krotz Springs	1,263	6	4	2
Lafayette	113,770	305	246	59
Lake Arthur	2,860	9	5	4
Lake Charles	70,075	185	178	7
Lake Providence	4,469	8	7	1
Lecompte	1,321	5	4	1
Leesville	5,867	30	28	2
Mamou	3,438	18	12	6
Mandeville	12,047	52	37	15
Mansfield	5,395	20	15	5
Many	2,741	12	11	1
Marksville	5,676	23	19	4
McNary	199	2	1	1
Minden	13,019	29	28	1
Monroe	50,988	219	171	48
Moreauville	927	2	2	0
Morgan City	11,626	44	42	2
Napoleonville	664	3	2	1
Natchitoches	18,188	57	45	12
Newellton	1,268	3	3	0
Newllano	2,072	14	8	6
New Orleans	281,440	1,725	1,448	277
New Roads	4,739	20	19	1
Oakdale	8,115	20	20	0
Olla	1,345	4	4	0
Opelousas	23,090	76	62	14
Patterson	5,202	21	21	0
Pearl River	2,220	14	10	4
Pineville	14,725	62	55	7
Plaquemine	6,688	30	26	4
Pollock	381	3	2	1
Ponchatoula	6,482	26	21	5
Port Barre	2,337	16	10	6
Port Vincent	535	2	2	0
Rayne	8,523	25	25	0
Rayville	4,017	10	9	1
Ruston	21,056	44	36	8
Scott	8,713	23	22	1
Shreveport	199,434	681	589	92
Sicily Island	441	2	1	1
Simmesport	2,195	8	8	0
Slidell	27,379	107	71	36
Sorrento	1,437	6	5	1
Springhill	5,083	15	13	2
Sterlington	1,341	7	7	0
St. Gabriel	5,552	16	10	6
St. Martinville	7,024	20	15	5
Stonewall	1,913	3	3	0
Sulphur	19,400	60	42	18
Sunset	2,647	13	13	0
Tallulah	7,539	17	12	5
Thibodaux	14,126	59	49	10
Tickfaw	694	7	7	0
Vidalia	4,096	28	18	10
Ville Platte	8,247	24	22	2
Vinton	3,140	13	11	2
Washington	1,049	8	7	1
Westlake	4,565	22	22	0
West Monroe	12,916	83	79	4
Westwego	9,711	40	38	2
Winnfield	5,073	22	14	8
Woodworth	1,137	7	5	2
Youngsville	6,818	12	11	1
MAINE				
Ashland	1,446	3	3	0
Auburn	23,205	54	49	5
Augusta	18,344	55	40	15
Baileyville	1,560	4	4	0
Bangor	31,902	97	79	18
Bar Harbor	5,166	13	9	4
Bath	8,925	20	18	2
Belfast	6,795	14	13	1
Berwick	7,654	12	11	1
Bethel	2,669	4	4	0
Biddeford	21,663	67	46	21
Boothbay Harbor	2,272	7	6	1
Brewer	9,091	23	21	2
Bridgton	5,460	12	8	4
Brownville	1,296	2	2	0
Brunswick	21,885	50	35	15
Bucksport	4,913	11	7	4
Buxton	8,179	5	4	1
Calais	3,188	9	5	4
Camden	5,232	14	12	2
Cape Elizabeth	8,802	17	13	4
Caribou	8,135	16	15	1
Carrabassett Valley	478	1	1	0
Clinton	3,338	3	3	0
Cumberland	7,770	11	10	1
Damariscotta	1,923	6	5	1
Dexter	3,697	6	5	1
Dixfield	2,541	4	4	0
Dover-Foxcroft	4,276	5	5	0
East Millinocket	3,181	4	4	0
Eastport	1,546	4	4	0
Eliot	6,371	10	9	1
Ellsworth	7,149	19	15	4
Fairfield	6,755	13	12	1
Falmouth	10,693	23	17	6
Farmington	7,576	12	11	1
Fort Fairfield	3,455	4	4	0
Fort Kent	4,187	8	4	4
Freeport	8,241	17	12	5
Fryeburg	3,358	5	5	0
Gardiner	6,115	13	11	2
Gorham	15,665	25	23	2
Gouldsboro	2,009	2	2	0
Greenville	1,730	3	2	1
Hallowell	2,451	5	5	0
Hampden	6,919	13	12	1
Holden	3,001	3	3	0
Houlton	6,133	17	12	5
Jay	4,795	8	7	1
Kennebunk	11,489	28	21	7
Kennebunkport	4,024	17	12	5
Kittery	10,307	28	21	7
Lewiston	35,183	95	80	15
Limestone	2,267	3	3	0
Lincoln	5,263	7	6	1
Lincolnville	2,195	2	1	1
Lisbon	9,360	20	15	5

Table 78. Full-Time Law Enforcement Employees, by State and City, 2008—*Continued*

(Number.)

State/City	Population	Total law enforcement employees	Total officers	Total civilians
Livermore Falls	3,140	10	6	4
Machias	2,133	4	4	0
Madawaska	4,342	7	6	1
Madison	4,601	8	7	1
Mechanic Falls	3,220	5	5	0
Mexico	2,872	5	5	0
Milbridge	1,313	2	2	0
Millinocket	4,913	9	9	0
Milo	2,351	3	3	0
Monmouth	3,846	4	4	0
Mount Desert	2,181	11	7	4
Newport	3,120	6	6	0
North Berwick	4,888	9	8	1
Norway	4,784	8	7	1
Oakland	6,204	10	9	1
Ogunquit	1,273	12	10	2
Old Orchard Beach	9,400	27	19	8
Old Town	7,723	16	15	1
Orono	9,751	14	13	1
Oxford	3,917	5	4	1
Paris	4,990	8	7	1
Phippsburg	2,170	1	1	0
Pittsfield	4,246	6	6	0
Portland	62,656	205	154	51
Presque Isle	9,056	22	19	3
Rangeley	1,181	3	3	0
Richmond	3,421	5	5	0
Rockland	7,464	22	19	3
Rockport	3,551	6	5	1
Rumford	6,336	14	13	1
Sabattus	4,645	8	7	1
Saco	18,323	45	33	12
Sanford	21,294	57	39	18
Scarborough	19,228	48	33	15
Searsport	2,605	3	3	0
Skowhegan	8,751	14	13	1
South Berwick	7,253	12	8	4
South Portland	23,796	68	52	16
Southwest Harbor	1,953	5	5	0
Swan's Island	303	1	1	0
Thomaston	3,666	5	5	0
Topsham	9,972	13	12	1
Van Buren	2,482	3	3	0
Veazie	1,862	5	5	0
Waldoboro	5,049	8	7	1
Washburn	1,586	1	1	0
Waterville	15,964	41	31	10
Wells	10,012	29	21	8
Westbrook	16,310	39	38	1
Wilton	4,188	7	6	1
Windham	16,838	36	25	11
Winslow	7,895	10	9	1
Winthrop	6,467	14	9	5
Wiscasset	3,815	4	3	1
Yarmouth	8,095	18	12	6
York	13,840	38	27	11
MARYLAND				
Aberdeen	13,995	54	45	9
Annapolis	36,683	151	108	43
Baltimore	634,549	3,678	2,998	680
Baltimore City Sheriff		165	113	52
Bel Air	9,892	41	29	12
Berlin	4,023	19	14	5
Berwyn Heights	2,975	9	8	1
Bladensburg	7,677	22	16	6
Boonsboro	3,448	4	4	0
Bowie	53,311	42	35	7
Brunswick	5,270	11	9	2
Cambridge	11,901	60	46	14
Capitol Heights	4,156	13	9	4
Centreville	3,546	10	9	1
Chestertown	4,916	13	12	1
Cheverly	6,466	15	13	2
Chevy Chase Village	2,761	18	11	7
Colmar Manor	1,275	5	4	1
Cottage City	1,139	7	6	1
Crisfield	2,800	16	12	4
Cumberland	20,558	53	50	3
Delmar	3,407	12	11	1
Denton	3,951	14	13	1
District Heights	6,122	10	7	3
Easton	14,730	63	47	16
Edmonston	1,349	6	5	1
Elkton	15,228	46	39	7
Fairmount Heights	1,517	4	3	1
Federalsburg	2,611	12	12	0
Forest Heights	2,591	6	5	1
Frederick	60,034	174	133	41
Frostburg	7,758	19	15	4
Fruitland	4,412	18	17	1
Glenarden	6,399	10	9	1
Greenbelt	21,582	66	54	12
Greensboro	2,013	4	4	0
Hagerstown	40,002	129	103	26
Hampstead	5,506	10	9	1
Hancock	1,741	4	4	0
Havre de Grace	13,055	44	35	9
Hurlock	1,989	8	7	1
Hyattsville	15,591	56	43	13
Landover Hills	1,537	4	3	1
La Plata	9,101	15	14	1
Laurel	21,676	77	59	18
Luke	73	1	1	0
Manchester	3,572	7	6	1
Morningside	1,325	8	7	1
Mount Rainier	8,442	22	18	4
New Carrollton	12,640	13	11	2
North East	2,840	10	9	1
Oakland	1,843	5	4	1
Ocean City	7,090	135	107	28
Ocean Pines	11,164	21	15	6
Oxford	716	3	3	0
Perryville	3,817	11	9	2
Pocomoke City	3,869	23	16	7
Port Deposit	703	3	3	0
Preston	686	1	1	0
Princess Anne	3,003	14	12	2
Ridgely	1,535	6	6	0
Rising Sun	1,817	7	6	1
Riverdale Park	6,513	25	19	6
Rock Hall	1,425	4	4	0
Salisbury	28,455	115	84	31
Seat Pleasant	4,899	17	15	2
Smithsburg	3,009	5	4	1
Snow Hill	2,315	9	8	1
St. Michaels	1,079	9	8	1
Sykesville	4,444	8	7	1
Takoma Park	17,493	57	42	15
Taneytown	5,461	13	12	1
Thurmont	6,085	10	9	1
Trappe	1,151	1	1	0
University Park	2,316	8	8	0
Upper Marlboro	667	3	3	0
Westernport	1,950	3	3	0
Westminster	17,829	57	43	14
MASSACHUSETTS				
Abington	16,590	30	28	2
Acton	20,795	42	33	9
Acushnet	10,474	19	17	2
Adams	8,145	20	16	4
Agawam	28,353	56	48	8
Amesbury	16,421	37	31	6
Amherst	36,106	65	48	17
Andover	33,442	71	52	19
Aquinnah	355	4	4	0
Arlington	40,989	77	61	16
Ashburnham	6,009	15	10	5
Ashby	2,955	6	6	0

Table 78. Full-Time Law Enforcement Employees, by State and City, 2008—*Continued*

(Number.)

State/City	Population	Total law enforcement employees	Total officers	Total civilians
Ashfield	1,817	2	2	0
Ashland	15,927	31	27	4
Athol	11,637	24	17	7
Attleboro	43,228	95	82	13
Avon	4,285	20	15	5
Ayer	7,378	22	17	5
Barnstable	47,828	134	114	20
Barre	5,455	12	8	4
Becket	1,803	2	2	0
Bedford	13,215	36	28	8
Belchertown	14,094	29	24	5
Bellingham	15,979	37	30	7
Belmont	23,252	61	47	14
Berkley	6,519	6	6	0
Berlin	2,740	11	7	4
Bernardston	2,234	3	3	0
Beverly	39,435	74	69	5
Billerica	42,428	84	63	21
Blackstone	9,058	19	16	3
Bolton	4,522	15	10	5
Boston	604,465	2,862	2,213	649
Bourne	19,048	39	36	3
Boxford	8,088	13	13	0
Boylston	4,298	13	10	3
Braintree	34,495	81	74	7
Brewster	10,009	23	19	4
Bridgewater	25,546	35	34	1
Brockton	95,650	213	184	29
Brookfield	3,026	4	4	0
Brookline	54,527	155	132	23
Buckland	1,990	2	2	0
Burlington	25,319	71	63	8
Cambridge	101,362	305	275	30
Canton	22,054	42	41	1
Carlisle	4,900	15	10	5
Carver	11,592	21	17	4
Charlton	12,740	23	19	4
Chatham	6,735	24	18	6
Chelmsford	34,187	63	50	13
Chelsea	38,621	97	91	6
Chicopee	53,777	139	135	4
Chilmark	978	4	4	0
Clinton	14,101	32	27	5
Concord	17,543	42	35	7
Dalton	6,546	12	11	1
Danvers	26,958	60	47	13
Dartmouth	34,446	79	65	14
Dedham	24,217	72	60	12
Deerfield	4,729	9	8	1
Dennis	15,406	48	40	8
Dighton	6,819	13	10	3
Douglas	8,033	20	15	5
Dover	5,634	16	16	0
Dracut	29,608	48	43	5
Dudley	11,181	15	11	4
Dunstable	3,349	7	7	0
East Bridgewater	13,988	26	23	3
East Brookfield	2,065	3	3	0
Eastham	5,440	21	15	6
Easthampton	16,072	33	27	6
East Longmeadow	15,363	25	24	1
Easton	23,047	34	33	1
Edgartown	3,935	16	15	1
Egremont	1,351	3	3	0
Erving	1,546	3	3	0
Essex	3,328	12	7	5
Everett	37,172	106	99	7
Fairhaven	16,115	39	32	7
Fall River	90,760	304	240	64
Falmouth	33,302	67	61	6
Fitchburg	40,377	88	80	8
Foxborough	16,301	40	31	9
Framingham	64,519	128	118	10
Franklin	31,608	57	46	11
Freetown	8,990	17	17	0
Gardner	20,587	40	31	9
Georgetown	8,241	14	12	2
Gill	1,381	3	3	0
Gloucester	30,303	66	61	5
Goshen	960	2	2	0
Grafton	17,872	23	18	5
Granby	6,303	12	10	2
Granville	1,695	1	1	0
Great Barrington	7,353	15	14	1
Greenfield	17,651	50	34	16
Groton	10,776	21	16	5
Groveland	7,041	13	9	4
Hadley	4,786	15	11	4
Halifax	7,722	11	10	1
Hamilton	8,170	15	15	0
Hampden	5,321	15	10	5
Hanover	14,064	32	29	3
Hanson	10,010	27	22	5
Hardwick	2,653	3	3	0
Harwich	12,381	40	33	7
Hatfield	3,259	2	2	0
Haverhill	60,001	102	93	9
Hingham	22,724	57	48	9
Hinsdale	1,945	2	2	0
Holbrook	10,647	22	21	1
Holden	16,695	26	24	2
Holliston	13,953	23	22	1
Holyoke	39,722	145	126	19
Hopedale	6,195	16	12	4
Hopkinton	14,419	31	20	11
Hubbardston	4,531	9	5	4
Hudson	19,766	37	31	6
Hull	11,064	37	24	13
Ipswich	13,272	29	25	4
Kingston	12,405	30	23	7
Lakeville	10,678	21	17	4
Lancaster	7,130	12	11	1
Lawrence	69,812	180	151	29
Lee	5,782	12	11	1
Leicester	11,042	23	18	5
Lenox	5,106	10	9	1
Leominster	41,095	93	74	19
Leverett	1,753	2	2	0
Lexington	30,321	61	47	14
Lincoln	7,984	19	13	6
Littleton	8,776	21	16	5
Longmeadow	15,275	32	26	6
Lowell	110,136	319	239	80
Ludlow	22,530	40	34	6
Lunenburg	10,012	13	13	0
Lynn	90,042	197	178	19
Lynnfield	11,360	23	18	5
Malden	55,629	117	107	10
Manchester-by-the-Sea	5,268	18	14	4
Mansfield	23,057	48	36	12
Marblehead	19,994	39	32	7
Marion	5,226	14	14	0
Marlborough	38,253	76	64	12
Marshfield	24,600	48	45	3
Mashpee	14,417	45	37	8
Mattapoisett	6,468	18	18	0
Medfield	12,261	20	15	5
Medford	55,555	115	111	4
Medway	12,782	23	19	4
Mendon	5,823	17	13	4
Merrimac	6,459	11	7	4
Methuen	43,987	102	88	14
Middleboro	21,402	44	40	4
Middleton	9,545	14	13	1
Milford	27,322	56	45	11
Millbury	13,551	25	20	5
Millis	7,928	19	15	4
Millville	2,857	7	4	3

Table 78. Full-Time Law Enforcement Employees, by State and City, 2008—*Continued*

(Number.)

State/City	Population	Total law enforcement employees	Total officers	Total civilians
Milton	26,298	65	52	13
Monson	8,841	17	11	6
Montague	8,318	19	15	4
Monterey	963	1	1	0
Nahant	3,505	13	12	1
Nantucket	11,327	38	34	4
Natick	31,943	64	54	10
Needham	28,231	54	46	8
New Bedford	91,473	339	288	51
New Braintree	1,136	1	1	0
Newbury	6,950	13	12	1
Newburyport	17,133	25	24	1
Newton	83,191	181	139	42
Norfolk	10,666	19	17	2
North Adams	13,781	30	25	5
Northampton	28,341	70	58	12
North Andover	27,775	51	39	12
North Attleboro	27,994	60	47	13
Northborough	14,683	26	20	6
Northbridge	14,526	23	18	5
North Brookfield	4,834	6	6	0
Northfield	2,990	2	2	0
North Reading	14,040	30	29	1
Norton	19,366	27	26	1
Norwell	10,329	30	23	7
Norwood	28,119	70	59	11
Oak Bluffs	3,731	18	15	3
Oakham	1,936	3	3	0
Orange	7,831	14	13	1
Orleans	6,309	28	22	6
Oxford	13,671	24	20	4
Palmer	12,891	26	20	6
Paxton	4,546	13	9	4
Peabody	51,846	113	97	16
Pelham	1,404	2	2	0
Pembroke	18,806	28	26	2
Pepperell	11,438	19	18	1
Petersham	1,296	2	2	0
Phillipston	1,808	2	2	0
Pittsfield	42,597	111	88	23
Plainville	8,388	19	15	4
Plymouth	55,608	119	101	18
Plympton	2,788	7	7	0
Princeton	3,510	8	5	3
Provincetown	3,383	21	17	4
Quincy	95,061	228	198	30
Raynham	13,893	35	26	9
Reading	23,055	49	37	12
Rehoboth	11,649	28	23	5
Revere	56,445	100	92	8
Rochester	5,301	10	10	0
Rockland	17,789	40	32	8
Rockport	7,615	17	16	1
Rowley	5,881	16	13	3
Royalston	1,396	1	1	0
Rutland	8,049	9	8	1
Salem	41,531	85	79	6
Salisbury	8,609	21	20	1
Sandwich	20,258	35	34	1
Saugus	27,327	70	54	16
Scituate	17,879	35	30	5
Seekonk	13,610	35	33	2
Sharon	16,984	34	30	4
Sheffield	3,334	6	6	0
Shelburne	2,034	2	2	0
Shirley	7,738	15	10	5
Shrewsbury	33,706	58	45	13
Somerset	18,265	38	32	6
Somerville	74,012	153	128	25
Southampton	6,036	8	8	0
Southborough	9,569	21	16	5
Southbridge	16,886	39	36	3
South Hadley	16,921	33	28	5
Southwick	9,507	21	16	5
Spencer	12,041	21	17	4
Springfield	151,249	568	467	101
Sterling	7,950	17	13	4
Stockbridge	2,227	6	6	0
Stoneham	21,419	41	32	9
Stoughton	26,924	59	52	7
Stow	6,378	15	10	5
Sturbridge	9,266	22	18	4
Sudbury	17,190	35	29	6
Sunderland	3,714	5	5	0
Sutton	9,107	20	15	5
Swampscott	13,940	34	33	1
Swansea	16,274	37	31	6
Taunton	55,745	118	113	5
Templeton	7,911	15	10	5
Tewksbury	29,692	67	54	13
Tisbury	3,809	13	13	0
Topsfield	6,056	12	10	2
Townsend	9,394	17	15	2
Truro	2,139	15	10	5
Tyngsboro	11,955	28	22	6
Upton	6,629	13	12	1
Uxbridge	12,820	23	18	5
Wakefield	24,690	42	41	1
Walpole	23,113	43	38	5
Waltham	60,459	176	146	30
Ware	9,961	18	18	0
Wareham	21,250	58	50	8
Watertown	32,462	83	70	13
Wayland	13,002	29	22	7
Webster	16,736	32	28	4
Wellesley	26,975	52	39	13
Wellfleet	2,746	18	13	5
Wenham	4,608	11	10	1
Westborough	18,509	36	29	7
West Boylston	8,302	18	13	5
West Bridgewater	6,682	21	20	1
West Brookfield	3,827	7	6	1
Westfield	40,857	89	79	10
Westford	21,913	51	40	11
Westminster	7,446	18	13	5
West Newbury	4,283	11	7	4
Weston	11,723	33	27	6
Westport	15,253	33	29	4
West Springfield	27,565	93	82	11
West Tisbury	2,646	10	9	1
Westwood	13,995	37	28	9
Weymouth	53,180	108	93	15
Whately	1,554	2	2	0
Whitman	14,440	27	26	1
Wilbraham	14,098	29	28	1
Williamsburg	2,442	1	1	0
Williamstown	8,071	16	12	4
Wilmington	21,712	50	48	2
Winchendon	10,192	17	12	5
Winchester	21,171	46	38	8
Winthrop	20,404	35	33	2
Worcester	177,151	502	449	53
Wrentham	11,181	17	15	2
Yarmouth	23,903	64	54	10
MICHIGAN				
Adrian	21,241	36	33	3
Adrian Township	7,342	2	2	0
Albion	9,172	27	24	3
Algonac	4,571	9	8	1
Allegan	4,849	11	10	1
Allen Park	26,269	48	44	4
Alma	9,144	14	13	1
Almont	2,785	8	8	0
Alpena	10,395	19	17	2
Ann Arbor	115,148	203	149	54
Argentine Township	7,205	6	5	1
Armada	1,662	2	2	0
Auburn	2,036	3	2	1

Table 78. Full-Time Law Enforcement Employees, by State and City, 2008—*Continued*

(Number.)

State/City	Population	Total law enforcement employees	Total officers	Total civilians
Auburn Hills	20,952	71	56	15
Augusta	851	8	5	3
Bad Axe	3,076	9	9	0
Bancroft	593	1	1	0
Bangor	1,839	5	5	0
Baraga	1,176	3	3	0
Barry Township	3,561	2	2	0
Bath Township	11,846	12	11	1
Battle Creek	61,405	134	115	19
Bay City	33,703	64	59	5
Beaverton	1,073	1	1	0
Belding	5,727	9	8	1
Bellaire	1,130	3	3	0
Belleville	3,593	11	9	2
Bellevue	1,354	2	2	0
Benton Harbor	10,677	35	27	8
Benton Township	15,136	36	25	11
Berkley	14,770	34	28	6
Berrien Springs-Oronoko Township	9,436	9	8	1
Beverly Hills	9,856	29	25	4
Big Rapids	10,565	19	18	1
Birch Run	1,648	6	5	1
Birmingham	19,010	44	33	11
Blackman Township	25,926	29	28	1
Blissfield	3,202	6	6	0
Bloomfield Hills	3,770	29	26	3
Bloomfield Township	40,866	98	75	23
Boyne City	3,145	8	7	1
Breckenridge	1,284	2	2	0
Bridgeport Township	10,855	10	9	1
Bridgman	2,396	4	4	0
Brighton	7,237	19	17	2
Bronson	2,290	9	5	4
Brown City	1,265	2	2	0
Brownstown Township	29,523	49	38	11
Buchanan	4,343	10	9	1
Buena Vista Township	9,374	19	17	2
Burr Oak	750	1	1	0
Burton	30,303	46	42	4
Cadillac	10,351	18	15	3
Calumet	792	1	1	0
Cambridge Township	5,928	4	3	1
Canton Township	84,506	121	84	37
Capac	2,179	2	2	0
Carleton	2,569	4	3	1
Caro	4,044	9	8	1
Carrollton Township	5,973	8	7	1
Carson City	1,181	2	2	0
Caseville	842	2	2	0
Caspian	2,033	1	1	0
Cass City	2,510	4	4	0
Cassopolis	1,856	5	5	0
Cedar Springs	3,280	7	7	0
Center Line	8,127	26	22	4
Central Lake	974	1	1	0
Charlevoix	2,654	7	7	0
Charlotte	9,045	19	18	1
Cheboygan	4,994	10	9	1
Chelsea	5,095	12	8	4
Chesterfield Township	45,492	64	49	15
Chikaming Township	3,643	6	5	1
Chocolay Township	6,017	5	4	1
Clare	3,125	10	9	1
Clarkston	913	2	2	0
Clawson	12,213	19	18	1
Clayton Township	7,830	7	6	1
Clay Township	9,564	16	12	4
Clinton	2,428	4	4	0
Clinton Township	96,315	142	110	32
Clio	2,534	3	3	0
Coldwater	10,640	19	18	1
Coleman	1,127	1	1	0
Coloma Township	6,533	10	8	2
Colon	1,164	3	3	0
Columbia Township	7,656	6	6	0
Concord	1,089	2	2	0
Constantine	2,119	7	6	1
Corunna	3,314	3	2	1
Covert Township	3,064	6	6	0
Croswell	2,500	6	6	0
Crystal Falls	1,596	3	3	0
Davison	5,176	12	10	2
Davison Township	18,745	20	18	2
Dearborn	87,482	230	198	32
Dearborn Heights	52,538	110	85	25
Decatur	1,835	5	5	0
Deckerville	898	1	1	0
Denmark Township	1,799	1	1	0
Denton Township	5,499	5	5	0
Detroit	905,783	3,401	3,032	369
Dewitt	4,394	7	6	1
Dewitt Township	13,222	16	15	1
Douglas	2,166	8	7	1
Dowagiac	5,759	16	15	1
Dryden Township	4,655	4	4	0
Durand	3,773	5	5	0
East Grand Rapids	10,406	32	29	3
East Jordan	2,236	6	5	1
East Lansing	46,215	93	62	31
Eastpointe	32,464	59	54	5
East Tawas	2,738	7	6	1
Eaton Rapids	5,295	11	10	1
Ecorse	9,923	31	26	5
Elk Rapids	1,688	5	5	0
Elkton	759	2	2	0
Elsie	976	2	2	0
Emmett Township	11,887	18	16	2
Erie Township	4,707	6	5	1
Escanaba	12,198	45	32	13
Essexville	3,478	8	8	0
Evart	1,678	5	4	1
Farmington	9,826	30	23	7
Farmington Hills	78,602	166	118	48
Fenton	11,938	20	15	5
Ferndale	21,056	53	45	8
Flat Rock	9,016	27	24	3
Flint	113,462	233	201	32
Flint Township	31,920	50	42	8
Flushing	7,879	14	13	1
Flushing Township	10,240	11	10	1
Forsyth Township	4,880	5	4	1
Fowlerville	3,092	6	6	0
Frankenmuth	4,687	7	7	0
Frankfort	1,460	3	3	0
Franklin	2,935	10	10	0
Fraser	14,919	52	39	13
Fremont	4,216	9	8	1
Frost Township	1,125	1	1	0
Fruitport	1,075	10	9	1
Gagetown	369	1	1	0
Galesburg	1,926	4	2	2
Garden City	27,036	46	38	8
Gaylord	3,658	13	11	2
Genesee Township	23,362	27	25	2
Gerrish Township	3,125	7	7	0
Gibraltar	5,028	11	10	1
Gladstone	5,109	11	10	1
Gladwin	2,923	5	5	0
Grand Beach	241	4	4	0
Grand Blanc	7,595	20	18	2
Grand Blanc Township	35,853	53	46	7
Grand Haven	10,486	36	31	5
Grand Ledge	7,735	16	15	1
Grand Rapids	193,096	395	323	72
Grandville	16,828	28	26	2
Grant	861	1	1	0
Grayling	1,837	4	4	0
Green Oak Township	17,964	16	14	2

Table 78. Full-Time Law Enforcement Employees, by State and City, 2008—*Continued*

(Number.)

State/City	Population	Total law enforcement employees	Total officers	Total civilians
Greenville	8,183	20	17	3
Grosse Ile Township	10,010	24	17	7
Grosse Pointe	5,057	27	25	2
Grosse Pointe Farms	8,699	48	35	13
Grosse Pointe Park	11,099	49	43	6
Grosse Pointe Shores	2,532	21	18	3
Grosse Pointe Woods	15,313	46	40	6
Hamburg Township	21,893	16	15	1
Hampton Township	9,704	11	10	1
Hamtramck	20,722	44	44	0
Hancock	4,129	7	7	0
Harbor Beach	1,621	4	4	0
Harbor Springs	1,543	6	5	1
Harper Woods	12,708	38	35	3
Hart	1,923	4	4	0
Hartford	2,472	5	5	0
Hastings	6,915	16	14	2
Hazel Park	18,016	41	36	5
Hesperia	955	2	2	0
Hillsdale	7,841	17	15	2
Holland	33,874	72	60	12
Holly	6,342	18	13	5
Homer	1,756	2	2	0
Home Township	1,524	1	1	0
Houghton	6,910	8	7	1
Howard City	1,580	2	2	0
Howell	9,830	20	18	2
Hudson	2,328	3	3	0
Huntington Woods	5,806	18	17	1
Huron Township	15,731	25	20	5
Imlay City	3,725	10	9	1
Inkster	26,899	68	58	10
Ionia	12,689	19	17	2
Iron Mountain	7,776	14	14	0
Iron River	3,007	8	7	1
Ironwood	5,377	13	13	0
Ishpeming	6,449	11	10	1
Ishpeming Township	3,606	1	1	0
Ithaca	3,024	4	4	0
Jackson	33,755	85	66	19
Jonesville	2,248	5	5	0
Kalamazoo	72,110	303	249	54
Kalamazoo Township	21,941	40	32	8
Kalkaska	2,182	5	4	1
Keego Harbor	2,852	6	5	1
Kentwood	47,573	85	69	16
Kingsford	5,304	20	20	0
Kingston	425	1	1	0
Kinross Township	8,778	3	3	0
Laingsburg	1,263	2	2	0
Lake Angelus	310	5	5	0
Lake Linden	1,041	1	1	0
Lake Odessa	2,228	4	4	0
Lake Orion	2,723	8	4	4
Lakeview	1,091	2	2	0
L'anse	1,867	4	4	0
Lansing	114,415	322	240	82
Lansing Township	7,910	16	15	1
Lapeer	9,145	24	21	3
Lapeer Township	5,084	1	1	0
Lathrup Village	4,064	7	7	0
Laurium	1,985	4	4	0
Lawton	1,801	6	6	0
Leoni Township	13,701	10	9	1
Leslie	2,330	3	3	0
Lexington	1,059	3	3	0
Lincoln Park	35,673	61	51	10
Lincoln Township	14,312	13	11	2
Linden	3,474	5	5	0
Litchfield	1,403	3	3	0
Livonia	92,329	183	148	35
Lowell	4,181	8	6	2
Ludington	8,329	16	15	1
Luna Pier	1,541	4	4	0
Mackinac Island	467	6	5	1
Mackinaw City	841	6	6	0
Madison Heights	29,516	71	57	14
Madison Township	8,090	2	2	0
Mancelona	1,364	2	2	0
Manistee	6,508	14	13	1
Manistique	3,342	8	8	0
Manton	1,173	1	1	0
Marenisco Township	1,828	1	1	0
Marine City	4,396	5	5	0
Marion	808	1	1	0
Marlette	2,003	4	4	0
Marquette	20,793	37	31	6
Marshall	7,149	16	12	4
Marysville	10,067	17	14	3
Mason	8,269	14	13	1
Mattawan	2,862	5	5	0
Mayville	994	2	2	0
Melvindale	10,050	26	23	3
Memphis	1,111	1	1	0
Mendon	913	2	2	0
Menominee	8,310	14	13	1
Meridian Township	38,465	51	44	7
Metamora Township	4,691	5	5	0
Michiana	192	3	3	0
Midland	40,962	50	47	3
Milan	5,780	12	9	3
Milford	16,697	27	20	7
Millington	1,078	1	1	0
Monroe	21,461	45	40	5
Montague	2,286	5	5	0
Montrose Township	7,775	9	8	1
Morenci	2,276	3	3	0
Morrice	878	2	2	0
Mount Morris	3,223	8	7	1
Mount Morris Township	22,432	35	32	3
Mount Pleasant	26,565	39	32	7
Mundy Township	14,340	21	18	3
Munising	2,330	5	5	0
Muskegon	39,319	92	82	10
Muskegon Heights	11,596	25	22	3
Muskegon Township	18,424	16	15	1
Napoleon Township	7,057	2	2	0
Nashville	1,663	2	2	0
Negaunee	4,436	9	8	1
Newaygo	1,635	6	5	1
New Baltimore	11,949	21	17	4
New Buffalo	2,435	8	7	1
New Haven	5,402	10	9	1
Niles	11,229	28	19	9
North Branch	987	2	2	0
Northfield Township	8,578	13	12	1
North Muskegon	3,916	7	7	0
Northville	6,028	17	16	1
Northville Township	25,742	46	34	12
Norton Shores	23,408	30	28	2
Norvell Township	3,039	2	2	0
Norway	2,827	4	4	0
Novi	54,980	99	70	29
Oak Park	30,509	78	66	12
Olivet	1,832	3	3	0
Onaway	909	1	1	0
Ontwa Township-Edwardsburg	5,912	9	8	1
Orchard Lake	2,201	9	8	1
Oscoda Township	6,857	12	11	1
Otsego	3,824	7	6	1
Ovid	1,395	3	3	0
Owosso	15,094	23	21	2
Oxford	3,545	19	10	9
Parchment	1,801	3	3	0
Parma-Sandstone	6,850	2	2	0
Paw Paw	3,223	11	9	2
Pentwater	947	3	3	0
Perry	2,044	7	7	0

Table 78. Full-Time Law Enforcement Employees, by State and City, 2008—*Continued*

(Number.)

State/City	Population	Total law enforcement employees	Total officers	Total civilians
Petoskey	6,009	22	19	3
Pigeon	1,068	1	1	0
Pinckney	2,460	5	5	0
Pinconning	1,310	3	3	0
Pittsfield Township	35,064	51	39	12
Plainwell	3,856	9	8	1
Pleasant Ridge	2,469	6	6	0
Plymouth	8,622	16	15	1
Plymouth Township	25,676	46	31	15
Pontiac	66,366	95	72	23
Portage	46,210	73	56	17
Port Austin	653	1	1	0
Port Huron	30,937	59	50	9
Portland	3,697	6	6	0
Port Sanilac	625	1	1	0
Potterville	2,169	5	4	1
Prairieville Township	3,540	3	3	0
Raisin Township	7,364	5	4	1
Redford Township	46,399	81	64	17
Reed City	2,344	4	4	0
Reese	1,350	2	2	0
Richfield Township, Genesee County	8,708	10	8	2
Richfield Township, Roscommon County	4,158	7	6	1
Richland	765	2	2	0
Richland Township, Saginaw County	4,242	4	4	0
Richmond	5,754	12	9	3
River Rouge	8,532	20	19	1
Riverview	11,916	32	29	3
Rochester	11,098	26	20	6
Rockford	5,422	12	10	2
Rockwood	3,196	9	8	1
Rogers City	3,054	7	7	0
Romeo	3,762	12	8	4
Romulus	23,549	73	55	18
Rose City	692	1	1	0
Roseville	46,834	95	86	9
Royal Oak	57,098	101	85	16
Saginaw	55,634	108	97	11
Saginaw Township	38,815	52	47	5
Saline	9,068	20	14	6
Sandusky	2,631	6	5	1
Sault Ste. Marie	13,970	27	25	2
Schoolcraft	1,506	3	3	0
Scottville	1,247	3	3	0
Sebewaing	1,754	3	3	0
Shelby	1,896	4	4	0
Shelby Township	72,030	88	68	20
Shepherd	1,365	1	1	0
Somerset Township	4,745	4	3	1
Southfield	75,024	188	149	39
Southgate	28,055	47	38	9
South Haven	5,128	24	17	7
South Lyon	11,106	20	18	2
South Rockwood	1,632	4	4	0
Sparta	4,057	5	5	0
Spaulding Township	2,194	1	1	0
Spring Arbor Township	8,487	2	2	0
Springfield	5,058	14	13	1
Spring Lake-Ferrysburg	5,462	10	9	1
Springport Township	2,229	2	2	0
Standish	1,940	1	1	0
Stanton	1,485	1	1	0
St. Charles	2,058	3	3	0
St. Clair	5,815	9	9	0
St. Clair Shores	60,335	100	84	16
Sterling Heights	127,697	221	166	55
St. Ignace	2,351	7	6	1
St. Johns	7,257	12	10	2
St. Joseph	8,453	25	18	7
St. Joseph Township	9,621	12	11	1
St. Louis	6,854	7	6	1
Stockbridge	1,286	2	2	0
Sturgis	10,914	24	19	5
Sumpter Township	11,383	22	15	7
Suttons Bay	582	2	2	0
Swartz Creek	5,308	9	8	1
Sylvan Lake	1,642	5	5	0
Taylor	61,411	107	92	15
Tecumseh	8,724	16	14	2
Thetford Township	7,899	2	2	0
Thomas Township	12,379	8	7	1
Three Oaks	1,692	2	2	0
Three Rivers	7,175	20	16	4
Tittabawassee Township	8,884	6	5	1
Traverse City	14,318	35	32	3
Trenton	18,222	38	37	1
Troy	80,491	187	135	52
Tuscarora Township	3,069	8	7	1
Ubly	774	2	2	0
Unadilla Township	3,452	2	2	0
Union City	1,731	4	4	0
Utica	4,987	20	16	4
Van Buren Township	27,264	60	44	16
Vassar	2,679	5	5	0
Vernon	796	1	1	0
Vicksburg	2,184	8	8	0
Walker	23,928	47	37	10
Walled Lake	6,956	17	13	4
Warren	133,721	271	230	41
Waterford Township	70,676	106	77	29
Waterloo Township	3,000	3	3	0
Watertown Township	2,171	1	1	0
Watervliet	1,733	2	2	0
Wayland	3,817	6	5	1
Wayne	17,395	49	39	10
West Bloomfield Township	63,993	103	81	22
West Branch	1,835	6	5	1
Westland	79,944	125	100	25
White Cloud	1,396	2	2	0
Whitehall	2,801	8	8	0
White Lake Township	30,318	37	27	10
White Pigeon	1,561	4	4	0
Williamston	3,846	11	10	1
Wixom	13,485	23	19	4
Wolverine Lake	4,314	6	6	0
Woodhaven	12,932	34	31	3
Wyandotte	25,120	48	38	10
Wyoming	70,552	118	88	30
Yale	1,955	4	4	0
Ypsilanti	21,766	43	34	9
Zeeland	5,405	10	9	1
Zilwaukee	1,654	2	2	0
MINNESOTA				
Albany	2,132	5	5	0
Albert Lea	17,447	40	29	11
Alexandria	11,373	25	20	5
Annandale	3,126	5	5	0
Anoka	17,161	34	27	7
Appleton	3,121	4	4	0
Apple Valley	50,619	64	50	14
Aurora	1,733	4	4	0
Austin	22,875	34	31	3
Avon	1,320	3	3	0
Babbitt	1,579	4	4	0
Baxter	8,464	16	15	1
Bayport	3,254	5	5	0
Becker	4,308	6	5	1
Belgrade	710	2	2	0
Belle Plaine	5,146	9	7	2
Bemidji	13,574	34	31	3
Benson	3,045	8	7	1
Big Lake	10,135	15	12	3
Biwabik	959	3	3	0
Blackduck	766	2	2	0
Blaine	56,808	70	58	12
Blooming Prairie	1,971	3	3	0
Bloomington	80,996	144	114	30
Blue Earth	3,263	6	6	0

Table 78. Full-Time Law Enforcement Employees, by State and City, 2008—*Continued*

(Number.)

State/City	Population	Total law enforcement employees	Total officers	Total civilians
Brainerd	13,733	34	27	7
Breckenridge	3,225	7	7	0
Brooklyn Center	27,289	58	46	12
Brooklyn Park	71,891	124	99	25
Browns Valley	604	3	3	0
Brownton	785	2	2	0
Buffalo	14,614	22	18	4
Burnsville	58,974	85	75	10
Caledonia	2,848	5	4	1
Cambridge	7,907	15	13	2
Cannon Falls	4,053	10	9	1
Centennial Lakes	11,261	18	16	2
Champlin	23,785	31	26	5
Chaska	24,847	27	24	3
Chisholm	4,571	12	11	1
Cloquet	11,369	21	19	2
Cold Spring	3,788	9	8	1
Columbia Heights	17,894	32	26	6
Coon Rapids	61,776	74	65	9
Corcoran	5,762	8	7	1
Cottage Grove	33,396	43	36	7
Crookston	7,668	18	16	2
Crosby	2,218	9	8	1
Crystal	21,503	37	29	8
Dawson	1,355	3	3	0
Dayton	4,675	6	5	1
Deephaven-Woodland	4,204	8	7	1
Detroit Lakes	8,094	17	15	2
Dilworth	3,674	7	6	1
Duluth	84,171	169	140	29
Eagan	63,754	80	69	11
Eagle Lake	2,202	2	2	0
East Grand Forks	7,768	24	22	2
Eden Prairie	62,516	90	66	24
Edina	45,730	68	51	17
Elk River	23,659	40	31	9
Elmore	657	1	1	0
Ely	3,487	8	7	1
Eveleth	3,561	11	10	1
Fairmont	10,173	20	17	3
Faribault	22,082	41	33	8
Farmington	19,634	26	23	3
Fergus Falls	13,699	29	23	6
Floodwood	490	2	2	0
Forest Lake	17,965	28	25	3
Fridley	25,746	45	39	6
Gilbert	1,743	5	5	0
Glencoe	5,602	11	10	1
Glenwood	2,525	4	4	0
Golden Valley	19,969	36	29	7
Goodview	3,460	4	4	0
Grand Rapids	8,715	24	20	4
Granite Falls	2,869	5	5	0
Hallock	1,007	1	1	0
Hastings	22,125	35	30	5
Hermantown	9,435	16	14	2
Hibbing	16,155	36	32	4
Hokah	567	1	1	0
Hopkins	16,756	39	26	13
Houston	969	2	2	0
Hoyt Lakes	1,947	5	5	0
Hutchinson	14,023	34	23	11
International Falls	5,964	14	13	1
Inver Grove Heights	34,007	41	34	7
Jackson	3,333	7	7	0
Janesville	2,227	3	3	0
Jordan	5,647	11	8	3
Kasson	5,649	9	8	1
Kimball	713	4	4	0
La Crescent	5,013	8	7	1
Lake City	5,327	11	10	1
Lake Crystal	2,629	4	4	0
Lakefield	1,631	3	3	0
Lakes Area	8,349	15	13	2

State/City	Population	Total law enforcement employees	Total officers	Total civilians
Lakeville	55,600	61	52	9
Lester Prairie	1,796	3	3	0
Le Sueur	4,302	8	7	1
Lewiston	1,495	1	1	0
Lino Lakes	20,282	28	26	2
Litchfield	6,595	10	9	1
Little Falls	8,116	15	13	2
Long Prairie	2,817	6	6	0
Madison	1,562	3	3	0
Mankato	36,316	65	51	14
Maple Grove	63,335	78	65	13
Mapleton	1,660	3	3	0
Maplewood	36,249	59	54	5
Marshall	12,468	24	21	3
Medina	5,181	11	10	1
Melrose	3,156	6	5	1
Mendota Heights	11,616	18	17	1
Milaca	3,073	6	5	1
Minneapolis	376,753	1,122	891	231
Minnetonka	50,231	76	57	19
Minnetrista	8,541	16	12	4
Montevideo	5,181	11	10	1
Montgomery	3,338	7	6	1
Moorhead	35,704	64	52	12
Moose Lake	2,575	5	5	0
Mora	3,455	8	7	1
Morris	4,946	10	8	2
Mound	9,568	16	13	3
Mounds View	12,081	21	19	2
Mountain Iron	2,910	5	5	0
Mountain Lake	1,923	4	4	0
New Brighton	20,897	33	28	5
New Hope	20,540	37	30	7
Newport	3,558	8	8	0
New Prague	7,374	11	9	2
New Richland	1,165	2	2	0
New Ulm	13,105	28	23	5
North Branch	10,713	14	12	2
Northfield	19,610	26	21	5
North Mankato	12,467	12	11	1
North St. Paul	11,356	21	18	3
Oakdale	27,108	40	31	9
Oak Park Heights	4,078	10	9	1
Olivia	2,381	5	5	0
Orono	12,415	22	19	3
Ortonville	1,960	3	3	0
Osakis	1,575	3	3	0
Osseo	2,602	6	5	1
Owatonna	24,999	38	35	3
Park Rapids	3,600	11	10	1
Paynesville	2,271	5	4	1
Plainview	3,211	7	7	0
Plymouth	71,713	82	70	12
Princeton	4,885	13	11	2
Prior Lake	24,219	26	23	3
Proctor	2,815	8	7	1
Ramsey	23,791	27	23	4
Red Wing	15,655	35	29	6
Redwood Falls	5,050	13	11	2
Richfield	33,260	56	43	13
Robbinsdale	13,430	26	21	5
Rochester	100,589	181	124	57
Rogers	7,269	13	11	2
Roseau	2,776	6	5	1
Rosemount	21,944	25	22	3
Roseville	32,324	56	49	7
Sartell	14,319	18	17	1
Sauk Centre	3,945	7	6	1
Sauk Rapids	12,069	14	13	1
Savage	28,504	37	31	6
Shakopee	35,464	54	45	9
Silver Bay	1,849	5	5	0
Silver Lake	804	2	2	0
Slayton	1,840	4	4	0

Table 78. Full-Time Law Enforcement Employees, by State and City, 2008—*Continued*

(Number.)

State/City	Population	Total law enforcement employees	Total officers	Total civilians
Sleepy Eye	3,415	6	6	0
South Lake Minnetonka	12,264	16	14	2
South St. Paul	19,156	28	26	2
Springfield	2,149	5	5	0
Spring Grove	1,251	2	2	0
Spring Lake Park	6,539	13	11	2
St. Anthony	7,794	26	23	3
Staples	3,030	6	5	1
St. Charles	3,617	4	4	0
St. Cloud	67,404	131	102	29
St. Francis	7,676	12	10	2
Stillwater	18,053	26	23	3
St. James	4,306	8	7	1
St. Joseph	6,242	9	8	1
St. Louis Park	44,011	70	51	19
St. Paul	276,083	799	598	201
St. Paul Park	5,290	9	9	0
St. Peter	10,969	19	14	5
Thief River Falls	8,488	16	14	2
Tracy	2,048	4	4	0
Two Harbors	3,325	9	8	1
Virginia	8,433	20	19	1
Wabasha	2,518	7	6	1
Wadena	3,946	9	8	1
Waite Park	6,815	15	12	3
Warroad	1,647	6	5	1
Waseca	9,488	16	14	2
Wayzata	3,937	13	11	2
Wells	2,367	4	4	0
West Hennepin	5,716	11	9	2
West St. Paul	18,756	32	29	3
Wheaton	1,428	4	3	1
White Bear Lake	23,771	36	29	7
Willmar	17,786	38	34	4
Windom	4,191	9	8	1
Winnebago	1,342	3	3	0
Winona	26,682	44	39	5
Winsted	2,470	4	4	0
Woodbury	56,619	75	64	11
Worthington	10,878	32	24	8
Wyoming	3,898	7	7	0
Zumbrota	3,103	5	5	0
MISSISSIPPI				
Aberdeen	6,025	23	18	5
Amory	7,219	25	18	7
Batesville	7,815	46	36	10
Bay Springs	2,192	7	6	1
Bay St. Louis	8,200	33	29	4
Belzoni	2,388	16	10	6
Biloxi	43,589	190	134	56
Booneville	8,532	30	24	6
Brandon	21,151	55	42	13
Brookhaven	9,997	37	31	6
Bruce	2,010	6	5	1
Byhalia	1,300	14	9	5
Calhoun City	1,788	5	5	0
Canton	12,469	38	29	9
Charleston	1,884	11	10	1
Clarksdale	18,029	39	30	9
Cleveland	12,292	56	44	12
Clinton	26,564	62	43	19
Collins	2,746	13	9	4
Columbia	6,491	23	19	4
Columbus	23,802	75	64	11
Corinth	14,316	52	40	12
De Kalb	882	5	4	1
Durant	2,690	8	7	1
Edwards	1,302	1	1	0
Eupora	2,180	7	6	1
Florence	3,520	17	11	6
Flowood	7,156	56	44	12
Fulton	4,067	11	11	0
Gloster	1,035	4	2	2
Greenville	35,573	135	94	41
Greenwood	15,886	72	56	16
Grenada	14,664	48	45	3
Gulfport	65,704	266	194	72
Hattiesburg	50,799	236	134	102
Hazlehurst	4,383	20	16	4
Heidelberg	802	6	5	1
Hernando	11,694	43	33	10
Hollandale	2,942	10	6	4
Holly Springs	8,037	26	20	6
Horn Lake	24,692	64	50	14
Houston	3,879	9	6	3
Indianola	10,796	37	29	8
Itta Bena	1,856	15	7	8
Iuka	2,933	10	8	2
Jackson	174,734	657	441	216
Laurel	18,415	84	61	23
Leakesville	1,023	2	2	0
Leland	4,783	23	17	6
Lexington	1,856	10	9	1
Long Beach	17,528	48	32	16
Louisville	6,633	30	23	7
Lucedale	3,065	19	13	6
Macon	2,736	10	9	1
Madison	17,858	78	61	17
Magee	4,307	17	13	4
Magnolia	2,091	6	6	0
McComb	13,587	63	29	34
Meridian	38,123	116	99	17
Moorhead	2,375	6	5	1
Morton	3,436	10	10	0
Moss Point	14,008	36	21	15
Natchez	16,433	74	48	26
New Albany	8,106	26	24	2
Newton	3,680	13	8	5
Ocean Springs	17,247	59	43	16
Okolona	2,892	9	9	0
Olive Branch	32,060	64	60	4
Oxford	15,334	69	60	9
Pascagoula	23,139	96	63	33
Pass Christian	7,008	24	20	4
Pelahatchie	1,483	7	5	2
Petal	10,717	35	28	7
Philadelphia	7,992	37	27	10
Picayune	11,733	54	35	19
Pickens	1,189	3	3	0
Poplarville	2,993	13	12	1
Port Gibson	1,647	10	6	4
Purvis	2,653	11	8	3
Raymond	1,675	6	5	1
Ridgeland	21,645	94	64	30
Ripley	5,682	13	12	1
Sandersville	809	2	2	0
Senatobia	7,197	24	19	5
Shaw	2,142	8	3	5
Shelby	2,593	10	6	4
Southaven	44,570	118	96	22
Starkville	24,099	56	48	8
Summit	1,633	4	4	0
Tchula	2,162	5	4	1
Tupelo	36,283	129	115	14
Tylertown	1,921	7	6	1
Vicksburg	25,345	93	65	28
Water Valley	3,958	12	12	0
Waveland	7,212	28	26	2
Waynesboro	5,649	17	10	7
West Point	11,281	33	27	6
Winona	4,579	11	9	2
Yazoo City	11,443	36	22	14
MISSOURI				
Adrian	1,894	3	3	0
Advance	1,219	3	3	0
Alton	638	2	2	0
Anderson	1,930	4	4	0
Appleton City	1,279	2	2	0

Table 78. Full-Time Law Enforcement Employees, by State and City, 2008—*Continued*

(Number.)

State/City	Population	Total law enforcement employees	Total officers	Total civilians
Arbyrd	489	1	1	0
Archie	994	3	3	0
Arnold	20,669	61	49	12
Ash Grove	1,549	3	3	0
Ashland	2,200	10	5	5
Aurora	7,493	22	15	7
Ava	3,110	13	8	5
Ballwin	29,978	59	48	11
Bates City	268	1	1	0
Battlefield	4,496	5	5	0
Bella Villa	636	6	4	2
Belle	1,385	3	3	0
Bellefontaine Neighbors	10,163	31	30	1
Bellerive	254	7	7	0
Bellflower	392	1	1	0
Bel-Nor	1,481	7	7	0
Bel-Ridge	2,895	22	16	6
Belton	24,771	62	43	19
Berkeley	9,367	47	36	11
Bernie	1,800	9	5	4
Bethany	3,072	6	6	0
Beverly Hills	558	5	3	2
Billings	1,113	4	4	0
Birch Tree	623	1	1	0
Birmingham	219	1	1	0
Bismarck	1,543	3	3	0
Bland	563	2	1	1
Bloomfield	1,879	3	3	0
Blue Springs	55,913	111	82	29
Bolivar	11,129	24	19	5
Bonne Terre	7,369	10	10	0
Boonville	8,830	28	21	7
Bourbon	1,415	6	5	1
Bowling Green	5,260	14	9	5
Branson	7,572	54	40	14
Branson West	547	7	6	1
Braymer	955	4	2	2
Breckenridge Hills	4,478	14	14	0
Brentwood	7,170	35	27	8
Bridgeton	15,030	66	53	13
Brookfield	4,311	18	11	7
Bucklin	474	1	1	0
Buckner	2,792	8	6	2
Buffalo	3,338	7	6	1
Butler	4,276	15	10	5
Butterfield Village	422	2	1	1
Byrnes Mill	2,953	5	5	0
Cabool	2,134	10	6	4
California	4,172	7	6	1
Calverton Park	1,274	6	6	0
Camdenton	3,450	18	14	4
Cameron	9,064	23	17	6
Campbell	1,806	6	3	3
Canton	2,471	5	4	1
Cape Girardeau	37,374	93	77	16
Cardwell	722	2	2	0
Carl Junction	7,440	16	11	5
Carrollton	3,870	6	6	0
Carterville	1,969	6	6	0
Carthage	13,824	33	28	5
Caruthersville	6,177	23	22	1
Cassville	3,275	9	9	0
Center	642	1	1	0
Centralia	3,664	12	7	5
Chaffee	2,942	10	5	5
Charlack	1,344	11	9	2
Charleston	5,256	17	12	5
Chesterfield	46,200	97	87	10
Chillicothe	8,654	23	17	6
Clarkton	1,232	4	3	1
Claycomo	1,303	16	12	4
Clayton	16,094	59	52	7
Cleveland	690	2	2	0
Clever	1,470	3	3	0
Clinton	9,445	23	22	1
Cole Camp	1,149	3	3	0
Columbia	101,033	185	153	32
Concordia	2,367	5	5	0
Cool Valley	1,004	10	9	1
Cooter	419	2	1	1
Cottleville	2,919	13	12	1
Country Club Hills	1,279	9	9	0
Country Club Village	1,936	1	1	0
Crane	1,427	3	3	0
Crestwood	11,426	34	27	7
Creve Coeur	16,956	61	50	11
Crocker	992	2	2	0
Crystal City	4,585	21	16	5
Cuba	3,600	11	10	1
Deepwater	496	1	1	0
Dellwood	4,891	18	17	1
Desloge	5,190	10	10	0
De Soto	6,509	20	15	5
Des Peres	8,616	46	39	7
Dexter	7,723	24	18	6
Diamond	899	7	7	0
Dixon	1,528	6	5	1
Doniphan	1,890	11	7	4
Doolittle	665	1	1	0
Drexel	1,095	2	2	0
Duenweg	1,249	4	4	0
Duquesne	1,741	6	6	0
East Prairie	3,112	10	7	3
Edina	1,123	3	2	1
Edmundson	781	10	9	1
Eldon	4,976	11	10	1
El Dorado Springs	3,724	10	6	4
Ellington	991	3	3	0
Ellisville	9,249	22	21	1
Ellsinore	364	1	1	0
Elsberry	2,661	5	5	0
Eureka	9,319	27	23	4
Everton	307	1	1	0
Excelsior Springs	11,965	32	22	10
Exeter	753	1	1	0
Fair Grove	1,436	4	4	0
Fair Play	457	2	2	0
Farber	392	2	1	1
Farmington	16,125	35	27	8
Fayette	2,674	8	8	0
Ferguson	20,967	58	52	6
Ferrelview	577	1	1	0
Festus	11,411	39	28	11
Flordell Hills	861	42	38	4
Florissant	50,560	111	89	22
Foley	212	1	1	0
Foristell	332	8	7	1
Forsyth	1,701	8	7	1
Fredericktown	4,119	7	7	0
Freeman	602	1	1	0
Frontenac	3,548	27	21	6
Fulton	12,904	34	27	7
Gallatin	1,736	2	2	0
Garden City	1,674	4	4	0
Gideon	957	2	2	0
Gladstone	28,151	56	39	17
Glasgow	1,188	3	3	0
Glendale	5,494	15	12	3
Glen Echo Park	158	5	3	2
Goodman	1,268	3	3	0
Gower	1,440	3	3	0
Grain Valley	10,603	22	19	3
Granby	2,246	4	4	0
Grandin	237	1	1	0
Grandview	24,020	62	49	13
Greendale	691	7	7	0
Greenfield	1,236	3	3	0
Greenwood	4,725	10	10	0

Table 78. Full-Time Law Enforcement Employees, by State and City, 2008—*Continued*

(Number.)

State/City	Population	Total law enforcement employees	Total officers	Total civilians
Hallsville	958	3	3	0
Hamilton	1,792	4	4	0
Hannibal	17,418	42	33	9
Harrisonville	9,849	29	21	8
Hartville	599	2	2	0
Hayti	2,946	8	7	1
Hayti Heights	753	2	2	0
Hazelwood	25,398	85	66	19
Herculaneum	3,467	13	12	1
Hermann	2,736	12	7	5
Higginsville	4,533	15	9	6
Highlandville	912	2	2	0
Hillsboro	2,033	7	7	0
Hillsdale	1,382	15	13	2
Holcomb	672	2	2	0
Holden	2,573	7	6	1
Hollister	3,897	16	11	5
Holt	474	2	2	0
Holts Summit	3,736	10	8	2
Houston	2,018	6	6	0
Humansville	1,023	1	1	0
Huntsville	1,646	3	3	0
Iberia	680	2	2	0
Independence	110,376	285	207	78
Indian Point	748	2	2	0
Iron Mountain Lake	699	1	1	0
Ironton	1,319	5	4	1
Jackson	13,715	29	22	7
Jasper	1,064	2	2	0
Jefferson City	40,599	115	85	30
Jennings	14,603	42	38	4
Jonesburg	731	1	1	0
Joplin	49,551	96	86	10
Kahoka	2,169	3	3	0
Kansas City	451,454	1,979	1,325	654
Kearney	8,614	15	14	1
Kennett	10,689	27	21	6
Kimberling City	2,558	8	7	1
King City	887	1	1	0
Kinloch	424	7	4	3
Kirksville	17,120	29	26	3
Kirkwood	26,755	65	56	9
Knob Noster	3,357	12	6	6
Ladue	8,191	35	28	7
La Grange	923	9	8	1
Lake Lotawana	1,957	7	5	2
Lake Ozark	1,996	17	11	6
Lakeshire	1,284	5	5	0
Lake St. Louis	14,451	39	30	9
Lake Tapawingo	783	2	2	0
Lake Waukomis	896	1	1	0
Lake Winnebago	1,143	5	5	0
Lamar	4,541	13	11	2
La Monte	1,096	2	2	0
Lanagan	437	1	1	0
La Plata	1,430	3	3	0
Lathrop	2,353	3	3	0
Laurie	723	6	6	0
Lawson	2,354	6	5	1
Leadington	217	6	5	1
Leadwood	1,156	6	6	0
Lebanon	14,379	37	28	9
Lee's Summit	84,399	175	120	55
Lexington	4,508	10	9	1
Liberal	787	1	1	0
Liberty	30,479	55	39	16
Licking	1,505	4	4	0
Lilbourn	1,162	3	3	0
Linn	1,422	4	4	0
Linn Creek	301	2	2	0
Lockwood	915	2	2	0
Lone Jack	954	6	6	0
Lowry City	738	1	1	0
Macon	5,452	16	14	2
Malden	4,471	14	10	4
Manchester	18,595	40	38	2
Mansfield	1,349	4	4	0
Maplewood	8,625	31	28	3
Marble Hill	1,489	4	4	0
Marceline	2,298	9	6	3
Marionville	2,181	5	5	0
Marquand	265	1	1	0
Marshall	12,153	34	21	13
Marshfield	7,306	10	10	0
Marston	529	1	1	0
Marthasville	862	1	1	0
Maryland Heights	25,977	97	78	19
Maryville	10,850	21	21	0
Matthews	528	2	2	0
Maysville	1,128	1	1	0
Mayview	284	1	1	0
Memphis	1,953	4	4	0
Merriam Woods	1,356	2	2	0
Mexico	10,939	37	35	2
Milan	1,764	7	6	1
Miller	800	2	1	1
Miner	1,332	13	8	5
Moberly	14,138	45	31	14
Moline Acres	2,517	13	12	1
Monett	8,980	29	20	9
Montgomery City	2,503	6	6	0
Montrose	425	1	1	0
Morehouse	922	1	1	0
Morley	801	1	1	0
Mosby	248	1	1	0
Moscow Mills	2,506	7	7	0
Mound City	1,073	2	2	0
Mountain Grove	4,629	15	10	5
Mountain View	2,619	8	8	0
Mount Vernon	4,640	10	10	0
Napoleon	194	1	1	0
Naylor	599	1	1	0
Neosho	11,371	30	26	4
Nevada	8,286	27	19	8
Newburg	473	1	1	0
New Florence	749	2	2	0
New Franklin	1,102	2	2	0
New Haven	2,042	6	6	0
New London	1,005	2	2	0
New Madrid	2,999	7	6	1
New Melle	283	3	3	0
Niangua	494	1	1	0
Nixa	19,162	32	22	10
Noel	1,602	3	3	0
Norborne	757	1	1	0
Normandy	4,899	22	21	1
Northmoor	400	1	1	0
Northwoods	4,309	19	17	2
Oak Grove	7,013	16	15	1
Oakview Village	394	4	4	0
Odessa	4,706	11	10	1
O'Fallon	78,837	133	107	26
Old Monroe	311	1	1	0
Olivette	7,472	24	23	1
Oran	1,244	1	1	0
Oregon	875	1	1	0
Orrick	822	1	1	0
Osage Beach	4,748	39	26	13
Osceola	792	3	3	0
Overland	15,622	59	46	13
Owensville	2,474	9	7	2
Ozark	18,332	35	29	6
Pacific	7,288	24	17	7
Pagedale	3,402	17	16	1
Palmyra	3,410	10	7	3
Park Hills	8,965	14	13	1
Parkville	5,398	17	16	1
Parma	756	3	2	1

Table 78. Full-Time Law Enforcement Employees, by State and City, 2008—*Continued*

(Number.)

State/City	Population	Total law enforcement employees	Total officers	Total civilians
Pasadena Park	458	22	21	1
Peculiar	4,757	13	11	2
Perry	663	1	1	0
Perryville	8,195	28	26	2
Pevely	4,676	19	14	5
Piedmont	1,902	6	6	0
Pierce City	1,466	4	4	0
Pilot Grove	749	1	1	0
Pilot Knob	671	1	1	0
Pine Lawn	3,997	25	22	3
Pineville	872	6	6	0
Platte City	4,933	11	10	1
Platte Woods	455	2	2	0
Plattsburg	2,424	6	6	0
Pleasant Hill	7,223	18	12	6
Pleasant Hope	601	1	1	0
Pleasant Valley	3,517	13	8	5
Polo	607	1	1	0
Poplar Bluff	17,035	54	43	11
Portageville	2,902	13	9	4
Purdy	1,164	2	2	0
Puxico	1,145	2	2	0
Randolph	50	2	2	0
Raymore	18,181	39	27	12
Raytown	28,086	74	53	21
Reeds Spring	777	1	1	0
Republic	13,643	36	23	13
Rich Hill	1,496	4	2	2
Richland	1,769	6	5	1
Richmond	5,864	17	13	4
Richmond Heights	9,105	43	42	1
Riverside	2,986	33	25	8
Riverview	2,918	12	11	1
Rockaway Beach	591	2	2	0
Rock Hill	4,591	10	9	1
Rock Port	1,303	3	3	0
Rogersville	3,127	7	7	0
Rolla	18,703	53	32	21
Salem	4,816	18	13	5
Salisbury	1,559	4	3	1
Sarcoxie	1,370	3	3	0
Savannah	5,073	6	6	0
Scott City	4,542	22	17	5
Sedalia	20,930	56	44	12
Seligman	924	2	1	1
Senath	1,588	3	3	0
Seneca	2,276	6	6	0
Seymour	2,046	6	6	0
Shrewsbury	6,234	20	18	2
Sikeston	17,053	80	68	12
Silex	247	1	1	0
Slater	1,901	7	4	3
Smithville	8,192	15	15	0
Southwest City	925	4	4	0
Sparta	1,199	3	3	0
Springfield	155,106	383	306	77
St. Ann	12,772	53	38	15
St. Charles	64,012	151	111	40
St. Clair	4,427	16	14	2
Steele	2,108	6	6	0
Steelville	1,484	6	6	0
Ste. Genevieve	4,435	11	10	1
St. George	1,211	3	3	0
St. James	4,124	8	7	1
St. John	6,381	26	24	2
St. Joseph	76,377	158	114	44
St. Louis	356,204	1,997	1,405	592
St. Marys	383	1	1	0
Stover	1,050	3	3	0
St. Peters	55,545	102	86	16
Strafford	2,175	8	8	0
St. Robert	3,493	28	20	8
Sturgeon	914	2	2	0
Sugar Creek	3,504	21	15	6

State/City	Population	Total law enforcement employees	Total officers	Total civilians
Sullivan	6,738	26	18	8
Summersville	555	1	1	0
Sunset Hills	8,226	33	25	8
Sweet Springs	1,518	3	3	0
Tarkio	1,815	3	3	0
Thayer	2,152	10	6	4
Tipton	3,314	3	3	0
Town and Country	10,720	41	33	8
Tracy	209	1	1	0
Trenton	5,996	19	12	7
Troy	12,541	30	27	3
Truesdale	669	3	2	1
Union	9,715	23	21	2
Unionville	1,863	2	2	0
University City	36,402	78	62	16
Uplands Park	438	9	8	1
Urbana	436	1	1	0
Van Buren	817	3	3	0
Vandalia	4,420	6	4	2
Velda City	1,496	10	9	1
Velda Village Hills	1,036	5	3	2
Verona	726	1	1	0
Versailles	2,729	10	10	0
Viburnum	785	1	1	0
Vienna	645	1	1	0
Vinita Park	1,783	13	12	1
Walnut Grove	676	2	2	0
Warrensburg	18,928	37	33	4
Warrenton	7,415	22	18	4
Warsaw	2,246	7	7	0
Warson Woods	1,859	8	7	1
Washburn	475	2	2	0
Washington	14,394	31	28	3
Waverly	782	1	1	0
Waynesville	3,829	10	9	1
Weatherby Lake	1,849	4	4	0
Webb City	11,496	26	21	5
Webster Groves	22,402	48	46	2
Wellsville	1,333	3	3	0
Wentzville	25,842	72	55	17
Weston	1,652	5	5	0
West Plains	11,763	29	24	5
Wheaton	742	1	1	0
Willard	3,373	9	8	1
Willow Springs	2,144	7	6	1
Winfield	913	4	4	0
Winona	1,332	4	4	0
Woodson Terrace	4,013	20	17	3
Wright City	2,989	9	8	1
MONTANA				
Baker	1,609	3	3	0
Belgrade	8,361	18	15	3
Billings	103,196	162	137	25
Boulder	1,443	1	1	0
Bozeman	39,408	59	50	9
Bridger	728	2	2	0
Chinook	1,274	4	4	0
Colstrip	2,321	12	6	6
Columbia Falls	5,296	12	9	3
Columbus	1,957	5	4	1
Conrad	2,517	5	5	0
Cut Bank	3,129	9	8	1
Dillon	4,091	9	8	1
East Helena	2,149	4	4	0
Ennis	1,036	1	1	0
Eureka	1,009	3	3	0
Fort Benton	1,443	4	4	0
Glasgow	2,885	8	7	1
Glendive	4,585	11	7	4
Great Falls	59,093	119	80	39
Hamilton	4,824	11	10	1
Havre	9,621	26	19	7
Helena	29,054	75	53	22
Hot Springs	568	1	1	0

Table 78. Full-Time Law Enforcement Employees, by State and City, 2008—*Continued*

(Number.)

State/City	Population	Total law enforcement employees	Total officers	Total civilians
Joliet	620	1	1	0
Kalispell	21,056	45	34	11
Laurel	6,525	12	12	0
Lewistown	5,899	19	14	5
Libby	2,886	5	5	0
Livingston	7,457	14	13	1
Manhattan	1,559	3	3	0
Miles City	8,077	15	15	0
Missoula	68,445	120	100	20
Plains	1,254	3	3	0
Polson	5,170	11	10	1
Poplar	866	1	1	0
Red Lodge	2,484	7	7	0
Ronan City	2,028	4	4	0
Sidney	4,716	11	10	1
Stevensville	2,023	4	3	1
St. Ignatius	814	1	1	0
Thompson Falls	1,436	3	3	0
Three Forks	1,941	3	3	0
Troy	985	3	3	0
West Yellowstone	1,471	10	4	6
Whitefish	8,433	21	16	5
Wolf Point	2,508	6	5	1
NEBRASKA				
Albion	1,601	3	3	0
Alliance	7,963	22	17	5
Auburn	3,241	6	6	0
Aurora	4,180	8	7	1
Bayard	1,119	4	4	0
Beatrice	12,913	32	22	10
Bellevue	48,894	110	91	19
Blair	7,914	20	17	3
Bridgeport	1,443	3	3	0
Broken Bow	3,115	7	6	1
Central City	2,729	6	5	1
Chadron	5,473	19	13	6
Columbus	21,438	49	33	16
Cozad	4,264	7	7	0
Crete	6,292	18	11	7
David City	2,470	6	5	1
Emerson	821	2	2	0
Fairbury	3,764	7	6	1
Falls City	3,976	12	8	4
Fremont	25,362	49	40	9
Gering	7,633	18	15	3
Gordon	1,504	5	4	1
Gothenburg	3,710	7	6	1
Grand Island	45,022	86	75	11
Hastings	25,428	50	36	14
Holdrege	5,116	16	10	6
Imperial	1,774	4	4	0
Kearney	30,472	66	51	15
Kimball	2,198	6	5	1
La Vista	17,103	35	31	4
Lexington	10,172	18	16	2
Lincoln	251,550	414	314	100
Lyons	850	2	2	0
Madison	2,183	4	4	0
McCook	7,401	20	16	4
Milford	2,014	5	5	0
Minden	2,840	5	5	0
Mitchell	1,767	3	3	0
Nebraska City	7,049	16	15	1
Neligh	1,462	3	3	0
Norfolk	23,096	53	37	16
North Platte	24,098	67	42	25
Ogallala	4,474	12	11	1
Omaha	437,238	893	748	145
O'Neill	3,293	8	7	1
Ord	2,041	4	4	0
Papillion	22,833	42	38	4
Pierce	1,638	3	3	0
Plainview	1,197	4	2	2
Plattsmouth	6,932	17	15	2

State/City	Population	Total law enforcement employees	Total officers	Total civilians
Ralston	6,087	15	13	2
Schuyler	5,111	9	7	2
Scottsbluff	14,667	34	29	5
Scribner	958	1	1	0
Seward	6,759	13	11	2
Sidney	6,492	16	14	2
South Sioux City	12,005	29	28	1
St. Paul	2,205	4	4	0
Superior	1,793	4	4	0
Sutton	1,312	2	2	0
Tecumseh	1,577	4	3	1
Tekamah	1,706	3	3	0
Valentine	2,619	6	5	1
Valley	1,864	4	4	0
Wahoo	4,000	6	6	0
Waterloo	838	2	2	0
Wayne	5,257	14	9	5
West Point	3,340	7	6	1
Wilber	1,734	4	4	0
Wymore	1,597	3	3	0
York	7,884	20	14	6
NEVADA				
Boulder City	14,810	47	35	12
Carlin	2,119	6	5	1
Elko	17,449	43	38	5
Fallon	8,599	37	23	14
Henderson	256,091	562	371	191
Las Vegas Metropolitan Police Department	1,353,175	4,050	2,530	1,520
Lovelock	1,893	7	6	1
Mesquite	16,470	49	34	15
North Las Vegas	228,363	460	305	155
Reno	218,556	455	364	91
Sparks	88,913	163	111	52
West Wendover	5,090	20	12	8
Winnemucca	8,097	20	17	3
Yerington	3,992	7	6	1
NEW HAMPSHIRE				
Alexandria	1,546	1	1	0
Alstead	2,114	2	2	0
Alton	5,142	13	11	2
Amherst	11,829	19	18	1
Antrim	2,640	4	4	0
Ashland	2,033	3	3	0
Auburn	5,217	9	7	2
Barnstead	4,656	6	6	0
Barrington	8,521	11	10	1
Bartlett	2,947	5	4	1
Bedford	21,505	49	36	13
Belmont	7,215	17	14	3
Bennington	1,484	2	2	0
Berlin	10,082	30	22	8
Bethlehem	2,468	4	3	1
Boscawen	3,994	8	7	1
Bow	8,170	17	10	7
Bradford	1,532	3	3	0
Brentwood	3,999	6	6	0
Bristol	3,123	11	9	2
Campton	3,019	6	5	1
Candia	4,213	8	7	1
Canterbury	2,356	2	2	0
Carroll	748	4	4	0
Charlestown	4,882	8	5	3
Chester	4,832	4	3	1
Claremont	13,090	29	24	5
Colebrook	2,366	5	5	0
Concord	42,603	99	78	21
Conway	9,247	31	22	9
Danville	4,375	5	4	1
Deerfield	4,246	9	8	1
Deering	2,069	2	2	0
Derry	33,981	74	59	15
Dover	29,005	72	49	23
Dublin	1,589	4	3	1
Dunbarton	2,659	3	3	0

Table 78. Full-Time Law Enforcement Employees, by State and City, 2008—*Continued*

(Number.)

State/City	Population	Total law enforcement employees	Total officers	Total civilians
Durham	13,815	18	16	2
Enfield	4,858	8	7	1
Epping	6,252	14	13	1
Epsom	4,636	5	4	1
Exeter	14,817	33	24	9
Farmington	6,777	16	14	2
Fitzwilliam	2,311	3	3	0
Franconia	1,055	3	3	0
Freedom	1,447	3	3	0
Fremont	4,148	5	4	1
Gilford	7,475	23	17	6
Gilmanton	3,572	5	4	1
Goffstown	17,716	42	29	13
Gorham	2,818	10	7	3
Grantham	2,567	5	4	1
Greenland	3,417	7	7	0
Hampstead	8,998	7	7	0
Hampton	15,443	43	34	9
Hancock	1,813	3	3	0
Hanover	11,092	36	21	15
Haverhill	4,636	8	7	1
Henniker	5,147	10	8	2
Hillsborough	5,599	17	11	6
Hinsdale	4,206	8	7	1
Hooksett	13,934	40	29	11
Hopkinton	5,642	7	7	0
Hudson	25,009	63	47	16
Jaffrey	5,703	12	11	1
Keene	22,931	61	46	15
Kingston	6,269	9	8	1
Laconia	17,008	48	38	10
Lancaster	3,292	7	6	1
Lebanon	12,749	48	35	13
Lee	4,483	8	7	1
Lincoln	1,339	14	9	5
Lisbon	1,669	4	4	0
Litchfield	8,798	12	10	2
Littleton	6,215	9	8	1
Londonderry	25,182	83	68	15
Loudon	5,221	7	6	1
Madison	2,332	5	4	1
Manchester	109,083	278	219	59
Marlborough	2,094	3	3	0
Meredith	6,701	18	14	4
Merrimack	26,725	51	39	12
Middleton	1,829	4	4	0
Milford	15,197	30	25	5
Milton	4,604	9	8	1
Mont Vernon	2,414	2	2	0
Moultonborough	5,010	15	12	3
Nashua	86,845	230	172	58
New Boston	5,160	6	5	1
Newbury	2,127	3	3	0
New Durham	2,568	6	5	1
Newfields	1,620	4	4	0
New Hampton	2,263	6	6	0
Newington	806	11	10	1
New Ipswich	5,307	6	5	1
New London	4,524	13	8	5
Newmarket	9,679	19	12	7
Newport	6,498	17	13	4
Newton	4,546	7	4	3
Northfield	5,222	11	10	1
North Hampton	4,558	13	12	1
Northumberland	2,337	3	3	0
Northwood	4,136	8	7	1
Nottingham	4,595	7	6	1
Ossipee	4,727	10	9	1
Pelham	12,706	26	19	7
Pembroke	7,410	14	12	2
Peterborough	6,171	13	11	2
Pittsfield	4,431	9	8	1
Plaistow	7,644	25	17	8
Plymouth	6,425	16	10	6
Portsmouth	20,455	84	64	20
Raymond	10,259	26	17	9
Rindge	6,688	9	8	1
Rochester	30,781	73	54	19
Rollinsford	2,641	4	4	0
Rye	5,171	10	9	1
Sandown	5,900	7	7	0
Sandwich	1,329	2	2	0
Seabrook	8,578	32	27	5
Somersworth	11,905	30	24	6
South Hampton	885	1	1	0
Strafford	4,101	4	4	0
Stratham	7,315	11	10	1
Sugar Hill	611	2	2	0
Sunapee	3,392	5	5	0
Thornton	2,129	5	4	1
Tilton	3,586	21	19	2
Troy	2,080	4	4	0
Wakefield	5,487	10	9	1
Walpole	3,705	4	3	1
Warner	2,987	5	4	1
Washington	1,082	1	1	0
Waterville Valley	272	7	6	1
Weare	9,251	12	11	1
Webster	1,892	3	3	0
Wilton	3,970	7	6	1
Winchester	4,309	8	7	1
Windham	13,457	26	19	7
Wolfeboro	6,581	16	12	4
Woodstock	1,173	5	5	0
NEW JERSEY				
Aberdeen Township	18,527	42	35	7
Absecon	8,096	33	26	7
Allendale	6,579	19	14	5
Allenhurst	698	13	9	4
Allentown	1,848	5	4	1
Alpine	2,475	13	13	0
Andover Township	6,552	19	13	6
Asbury Park	16,459	102	89	13
Atlantic City	39,425	468	374	94
Atlantic Highlands	4,601	20	15	5
Audubon	8,809	22	20	2
Avalon	2,089	29	21	8
Avon-by-the-Sea	2,168	15	12	3
Barnegat Township	22,762	57	47	10
Barrington	6,877	15	14	1
Bay Head	1,263	9	8	1
Bayonne	57,170	249	212	37
Beach Haven	1,386	11	10	1
Beachwood	10,795	21	19	2
Bedminster Township	8,343	18	16	2
Belleville	33,679	120	111	9
Bellmawr	11,055	25	23	2
Belmar	5,885	27	21	6
Belvidere	2,620	6	5	1
Bergenfield	25,666	51	43	8
Berkeley Heights Township	13,337	33	27	6
Berkeley Township	42,799	97	72	25
Berlin	8,075	21	20	1
Berlin Township	5,370	21	19	2
Bernards Township	26,641	54	38	16
Bernardsville	7,767	20	16	4
Beverly	2,568	8	8	0
Blairstown Township	5,924	8	6	2
Bloomfield	43,827	146	133	13
Bloomingdale	7,449	19	17	2
Bogota	7,927	20	15	5
Boonton	8,446	26	21	5
Boonton Township	4,396	12	12	0
Bordentown	3,825	14	12	2
Bordentown Township	10,385	29	23	6
Bound Brook	10,165	25	22	3
Bradley Beach	4,797	22	18	4
Branchburg Township	15,005	28	26	2

Table 78. Full-Time Law Enforcement Employees, by State and City, 2008—*Continued*

(Number.)

State/City	Population	Total law enforcement employees	Total officers	Total civilians
Brick Township	78,218	177	129	48
Bridgeton	24,714	77	64	13
Bridgewater Township	44,434	95	77	18
Brielle	4,856	15	15	0
Brigantine	12,705	47	36	11
Brooklawn	2,246	7	7	0
Buena	3,717	16	10	6
Burlington	9,416	41	36	5
Burlington Township	21,388	56	46	10
Butler	8,130	18	17	1
Byram Township	8,491	17	16	1
Caldwell	7,145	21	21	0
Camden	76,182	486	396	90
Cape May	3,677	31	24	7
Carlstadt	6,011	33	31	2
Carney's Point Township	7,923	27	22	5
Carteret	22,878	71	60	11
Cedar Grove Township	12,697	34	32	2
Chatham	8,209	28	22	6
Chatham Township	10,118	28	23	5
Cherry Hill Township	70,946	168	145	23
Chesilhurst	1,917	11	10	1
Chester	1,634	7	6	1
Chesterfield Township	7,023	11	10	1
Chester Township	7,822	17	16	1
Cinnaminson Township	15,259	34	32	2
Clark Township	14,326	52	41	11
Clayton	7,528	20	18	2
Clementon	4,849	18	16	2
Cliffside Park	22,713	56	46	10
Clifton	78,180	188	158	30
Clinton	2,544	10	10	0
Clinton Township	13,957	29	27	2
Closter	8,682	27	22	5
Collingswood	13,694	42	37	5
Colts Neck Township	10,116	23	22	1
Cranbury Township	4,027	19	18	1
Cranford Township	21,839	68	51	17
Cresskill	8,622	27	21	6
Deal	1,040	20	16	4
Delanco Township	4,529	10	9	1
Delaware Township	4,692	8	7	1
Delran Township	17,038	36	31	5
Demarest	5,135	15	15	0
Denville Township	16,549	45	35	10
Deptford Township	30,899	74	69	5
Dover	17,900	38	33	5
Dumont	16,984	44	36	8
Dunellen	6,950	22	18	4
Eastampton Township	6,544	18	17	1
East Brunswick Township	47,299	119	93	26
East Greenwich Township	7,491	22	20	2
East Hanover Township	11,382	42	34	8
East Newark	2,141	10	7	3
East Orange	65,218	342	280	62
East Rutherford	8,771	37	33	4
East Windsor Township	26,786	61	47	14
Eatontown	14,058	47	37	10
Edgewater	9,770	35	34	1
Edgewater Park Township	7,719	15	14	1
Edison Township	99,562	235	189	46
Egg Harbor City	4,363	16	15	1
Egg Harbor Township	40,550	124	95	29
Elizabeth	124,823	466	348	118
Elk Township	3,945	11	11	0
Elmer	1,332	2	2	0
Elmwood Park	18,667	44	42	2
Emerson	7,330	22	19	3
Englewood	28,132	105	81	24
Englewood Cliffs	5,807	27	26	1
Englishtown	1,901	8	8	0
Essex Fells	2,001	13	13	0
Evesham Township	45,837	84	76	8
Ewing Township	36,483	95	81	14

State/City	Population	Total law enforcement employees	Total officers	Total civilians
Fairfield Township, Essex County	7,585	48	42	6
Fair Haven	5,891	17	13	4
Fair Lawn	30,550	74	63	11
Fairview	13,517	37	33	4
Fanwood	7,108	20	20	0
Far Hills	904	6	6	0
Flemington	4,223	16	15	1
Florence Township	11,478	31	25	6
Florham Park	12,596	38	33	5
Fort Lee	36,474	128	109	19
Franklin	5,100	15	15	0
Franklin Lakes	11,677	27	22	5
Franklin Township, Gloucester County	17,288	33	30	3
Franklin Township, Hunterdon County	3,121	7	7	0
Franklin Township, Somerset County	59,965	145	125	20
Freehold	11,478	40	33	7
Freehold Township	35,161	86	70	16
Frenchtown	1,456	2	2	0
Galloway Township	36,577	85	72	13
Garfield	29,012	72	64	8
Garwood	4,311	20	16	4
Gibbsboro	2,416	6	6	0
Glassboro	19,573	51	45	6
Glen Ridge	6,662	34	27	7
Glen Rock	11,147	24	22	2
Gloucester City	11,318	33	30	3
Gloucester Township	64,946	133	111	22
Green Brook Township	7,055	29	23	6
Greenwich Township, Gloucester County	4,983	21	18	3
Greenwich Township, Warren County	5,201	12	11	1
Guttenberg	10,526	27	22	5
Hackensack	42,775	138	114	24
Hackettstown	9,431	19	18	1
Haddonfield	11,335	24	22	2
Haddon Heights	7,222	16	15	1
Haddon Township	14,260	32	30	2
Haledon	8,370	18	16	2
Hamburg	3,512	9	8	1
Hamilton Township, Atlantic County	24,995	90	69	21
Hamilton Township, Mercer County	90,282	209	178	31
Hammonton	13,558	43	34	9
Hanover Township	13,695	39	32	7
Harding Township	3,323	15	14	1
Hardyston Township	8,614	26	20	6
Harrington Park	4,879	12	12	0
Harrison	14,059	62	49	13
Harrison Township	12,695	19	18	1
Harvey Cedars	394	9	9	0
Hasbrouck Heights	11,423	32	30	2
Haworth	3,398	14	13	1
Hawthorne	18,015	37	32	5
Hazlet Township	20,910	51	44	7
Helmetta	2,026	5	5	0
High Bridge	3,676	7	7	0
Highland Park	14,166	34	27	7
Highlands	5,315	18	14	4
Hightstown	5,255	19	14	5
Hillsborough Township	38,718	69	55	14
Hillsdale	9,845	21	20	1
Hillside Township	21,177	91	76	15
Hi-Nella	989	5	5	0
Hoboken	40,618	171	156	15
Ho-Ho-Kus	4,017	19	16	3
Holland Township	5,236	7	6	1
Holmdel Township	16,991	53	43	10
Hopatcong	15,490	38	28	10
Hopewell Township	17,968	39	31	8
Howell Township	51,433	115	98	17
Independence Township	5,665	9	8	1
Interlaken	878	5	5	0
Irvington	56,237	219	191	28
Island Heights	1,883	4	4	0
Jackson Township	53,641	109	89	20
Jamesburg	6,404	18	13	5

Table 78. Full-Time Law Enforcement Employees, by State and City, 2008—*Continued*

(Number.)

State/City	Population	Total law enforcement employees	Total officers	Total civilians
Jefferson Township	21,904	46	39	7
Jersey City	241,588	1,045	885	160
Keansburg	10,516	44	34	10
Kearny	36,759	122	115	7
Kenilworth	7,611	31	30	1
Keyport	7,460	25	19	6
Kinnelon	9,583	17	16	1
Lacey Township	26,327	60	46	14
Lake Como	1,771	11	11	0
Lakehurst	2,705	12	10	2
Lakewood Township	70,864	159	131	28
Lambertville	3,712	12	10	2
Laurel Springs	1,886	7	7	0
Lavallette	2,757	16	12	4
Lawnside	2,818	10	8	2
Lawrence Township, Mercer County	32,059	81	68	13
Lebanon Township	6,229	10	9	1
Leonia	8,609	25	19	6
Lincoln Park	10,631	33	27	6
Linden	39,197	166	134	32
Lindenwold	17,077	46	43	3
Linwood	7,229	24	20	4
Little Egg Harbor Township	21,067	57	47	10
Little Falls Township	11,631	27	22	5
Little Ferry	10,495	30	27	3
Little Silver	6,096	21	16	5
Livingston Township	27,945	85	71	14
Lodi	23,871	52	42	10
Logan Township	6,191	21	20	1
Long Beach Township	3,538	49	38	11
Long Branch	32,331	122	100	22
Long Hill Township	8,601	28	25	3
Longport	1,080	20	15	5
Lopatcong Township	8,713	14	13	1
Lower Alloways Creek Township	1,879	18	13	5
Lower Township	19,963	61	46	15
Lumberton Township	12,258	27	24	3
Lyndhurst Township	19,397	56	50	6
Madison	16,056	38	34	4
Magnolia	4,307	12	12	0
Mahwah Township	24,225	60	52	8
Manalapan Township	39,115	81	66	15
Manasquan	6,208	24	18	6
Manchester Township	41,877	85	68	17
Mansfield Township, Burlington County	8,359	17	14	3
Mansfield Township, Warren County	8,098	16	15	1
Mantoloking	453	8	7	1
Mantua Township	15,262	28	26	2
Manville	10,869	28	22	6
Maple Shade Township	19,132	44	35	9
Maplewood Township	21,970	77	63	14
Margate City	8,545	44	34	10
Marlboro Township	41,011	91	72	19
Matawan	8,753	25	23	2
Maywood	9,156	27	23	4
Medford Lakes	4,074	9	8	1
Medford Township	22,809	63	48	15
Mendham	5,049	13	12	1
Mendham Township	5,531	18	15	3
Merchantville	3,743	16	14	2
Metuchen	13,121	32	28	4
Middlesex	13,632	33	31	2
Middle Township	16,077	63	50	13
Middletown Township	66,105	131	103	28
Midland Park	6,776	14	13	1
Millburn Township	18,557	63	54	9
Milltown	6,968	19	16	3
Millville	28,551	97	83	14
Monmouth Beach	3,564	11	10	1
Monroe Township, Gloucester County	32,951	81	67	14
Monroe Township, Middlesex County	37,412	66	49	17
Montclair	36,707	133	109	24
Montgomery Township	23,570	39	30	9
Montvale	7,344	22	20	2
Montville Township	21,097	47	40	7
Moonachie	2,742	21	18	3
Moorestown Township	19,613	48	38	10
Morris Plains	5,550	21	16	5
Morristown	19,117	67	59	8
Morris Township	20,966	56	44	12
Mountain Lakes	4,260	14	14	0
Mountainside	6,526	26	21	5
Mount Arlington	5,813	15	14	1
Mount Ephraim	4,359	14	13	1
Mount Holly Township	10,246	25	23	2
Mount Laurel Township	39,148	82	67	15
Mount Olive Township	26,042	63	54	9
Mullica Township	6,024	15	14	1
Neptune City	5,120	20	16	4
Neptune Township	28,356	92	74	18
Netcong	3,228	12	9	3
Newark	279,788	1,707	1,317	390
New Brunswick	50,605	163	138	25
Newfield	1,670	6	6	0
New Hanover Township	9,364	3	3	0
New Milford	15,942	36	33	3
New Providence	11,790	32	26	6
Newton	8,122	37	25	12
North Arlington	14,732	39	31	8
North Bergen Township	55,652	139	121	18
North Brunswick Township	39,878	101	83	18
North Caldwell	7,028	22	17	5
Northfield	7,901	25	24	1
North Haledon	9,039	23	18	5
North Hanover Township	7,393	10	9	1
North Plainfield	21,087	54	48	6
Northvale	4,539	15	15	0
North Wildwood	4,819	35	27	8
Norwood	6,246	15	14	1
Nutley Township	26,178	83	69	14
Oakland	13,454	31	26	5
Oaklyn	3,994	13	12	1
Ocean City	14,802	72	59	13
Ocean Gate	2,128	6	6	0
Oceanport	5,737	20	15	5
Ocean Township, Monmouth County	28,298	76	63	13
Ocean Township, Ocean County	8,926	27	17	10
Ogdensburg	2,548	6	6	0
Old Bridge Township	66,463	140	105	35
Old Tappan	6,071	13	12	1
Oradell	7,789	23	21	2
Orange	30,979	136	114	22
Oxford Township	2,596	5	4	1
Palisades Park	19,563	41	31	10
Palmyra	7,424	18	16	2
Paramus	26,232	114	93	21
Park Ridge	8,932	19	18	1
Parsippany-Troy Hills Township	50,990	130	108	22
Passaic	66,723	225	194	31
Paterson	145,542	563	477	86
Paulsboro	6,046	20	19	1
Peapack and Gladstone	2,558	9	8	1
Pemberton	1,503	6	5	1
Pemberton Township	27,995	60	55	5
Pennington	2,653	6	6	0
Pennsauken Township	34,897	120	93	27
Penns Grove	4,663	21	16	5
Pennsville Township	13,332	25	23	2
Pequannock Township	17,102	36	31	5
Perth Amboy	48,853	143	119	24
Phillipsburg	14,406	38	36	2
Pine Beach	2,067	6	5	1
Pine Hill	11,231	24	22	2
Pine Valley	23	4	4	0
Piscataway Township	52,585	112	92	20
Pitman	9,169	16	15	1
Plainfield	46,124	181	149	32
Plainsboro Township	21,219	46	34	12

Table 78. Full-Time Law Enforcement Employees, by State and City, 2008—*Continued*

(Number.)

State/City	Population	Total law enforcement employees	Total officers	Total civilians
Pleasantville	18,713	71	58	13
Plumsted Township	8,253	12	11	1
Pohatcong Township	3,320	16	15	1
Point Pleasant	19,959	43	35	8
Point Pleasant Beach	5,401	31	24	7
Pompton Lakes	11,106	25	21	4
Princeton	13,456	45	34	11
Princeton Township	17,512	40	31	9
Prospect Park	5,592	16	15	1
Rahway	28,286	89	82	7
Ramsey	14,620	34	30	4
Randolph Township	25,293	50	41	9
Raritan	7,033	23	18	5
Raritan Township	22,712	37	34	3
Readington Township	16,010	25	23	2
Red Bank	11,843	48	42	6
Ridgefield	10,854	30	28	2
Ridgefield Park	12,383	40	31	9
Ridgewood	24,165	47	42	5
Ringwood	12,688	28	22	6
Riverdale	2,909	22	18	4
River Edge	10,648	25	21	4
Riverside Township	7,717	16	16	0
Riverton	2,629	7	6	1
River Vale Township	9,648	24	21	3
Robbinsville Township	12,157	35	26	9
Rochelle Park Township	6,166	25	20	5
Rockaway	6,268	16	15	1
Rockaway Township	25,606	68	56	12
Roseland	5,343	33	28	5
Roselle	20,593	65	55	10
Roselle Park	12,775	41	34	7
Roxbury Township	23,278	54	47	7
Rumson	7,205	22	17	5
Runnemede	8,338	22	20	2
Rutherford	17,487	44	39	5
Saddle Brook Township	13,593	34	31	3
Saddle River	3,839	23	18	5
Salem	5,634	30	24	6
Sayreville	42,408	108	92	16
Scotch Plains Township	22,911	53	46	7
Sea Bright	1,804	12	11	1
Sea Girt	2,030	14	11	3
Sea Isle City	2,927	34	23	11
Seaside Heights	3,326	30	22	8
Seaside Park	2,301	20	15	5
Secaucus	15,254	67	59	8
Ship Bottom	1,440	11	10	1
Shrewsbury	3,763	21	16	5
Somerdale	5,045	14	13	1
Somers Point	11,351	29	24	5
Somerville	12,675	38	31	7
South Amboy	7,773	35	30	5
South Bound Brook	4,884	14	13	1
South Brunswick Township	40,941	104	82	22
South Hackensack Township	2,274	18	17	1
South Harrison Township	3,141	6	6	0
South Orange	15,885	63	57	6
South Plainfield	22,708	71	56	15
South River	15,716	37	30	7
South Toms River	3,707	13	12	1
Sparta Township	19,262	50	39	11
Spotswood	8,151	23	19	4
Springfield	14,710	48	42	6
Springfield Township	3,509	9	8	1
Spring Lake	3,486	18	14	4
Spring Lake Heights	5,102	13	13	0
Stafford Township	26,659	82	58	24
Stanhope	3,577	10	9	1
Stillwater Township	4,299	5	5	0
Stone Harbor	1,004	22	16	6
Stratford	6,988	16	15	1
Summit	20,560	57	48	9
Surf City	1,556	10	10	0
Swedesboro	2,066	8	8	0
Teaneck Township	38,828	120	100	20
Tenafly	14,303	44	37	7
Tewksbury Township	6,085	13	12	1
Tinton Falls	19,409	41	40	1
Toms River Township	95,410	213	158	55
Totowa	10,649	31	28	3
Trenton	82,140	460	358	102
Tuckerton	3,874	10	10	0
Union Beach	6,638	18	15	3
Union City	61,931	212	165	47
Union Township	53,777	189	137	52
Upper Saddle River	8,545	24	18	6
Ventnor City	12,195	53	41	12
Vernon Township	24,943	42	32	10
Verona	12,494	33	29	4
Vineland	58,606	182	155	27
Voorhees Township	31,210	66	52	14
Waldwick	9,452	22	17	5
Wallington	11,273	23	21	2
Wall Township	26,287	89	73	16
Wanaque	11,787	27	23	4
Warren Township	16,052	38	30	8
Washington	6,665	14	13	1
Washington Township, Bergen County	9,621	22	22	0
Washington Township, Gloucester County	51,670	91	84	7
Washington Township, Morris County	18,493	44	31	13
Washington Township, Warren County	6,905	14	13	1
Watchung	6,727	37	30	7
Waterford Township	10,609	26	24	2
Wayne Township	53,956	145	117	28
Weehawken Township	12,265	62	56	6
Wenonah	2,334	7	7	0
Westampton Township	8,775	26	24	2
West Amwell Township	2,992	7	6	1
West Caldwell Township	10,442	35	29	6
West Deptford Township	22,266	46	41	5
Westfield	29,419	73	59	14
West Long Branch	8,361	26	21	5
West Milford Township	27,892	55	48	7
West New York	46,286	131	119	12
West Orange	42,470	133	118	15
Westville	4,453	16	15	1
West Wildwood	399	5	5	0
West Windsor Township	26,949	60	47	13
Westwood	10,707	30	26	4
Wharton	6,081	22	21	1
Wildwood	5,253	53	41	12
Wildwood Crest	4,046	28	21	7
Willingboro Township	37,258	86	74	12
Winfield Township	1,443	9	9	0
Winslow Township	39,622	103	86	17
Woodbine	2,448	2	2	0
Woodbridge Township	98,154	252	203	49
Woodbury	10,433	30	27	3
Woodbury Heights	3,036	8	7	1
Woodcliff Lake	5,937	19	18	1
Woodland Park	11,592	33	28	5
Wood-Ridge	7,457	25	22	3
Woodstown	3,330	10	9	1
Woolwich Township	10,144	19	18	1
Wyckoff Township	16,964	33	25	8
NEW MEXICO				
Alamogordo	35,660	118	73	45
Albuquerque	527,464	1,488	1,029	459
Angel Fire	1,127	5	4	1
Artesia	10,460	46	29	17
Aztec	6,851	18	15	3
Bayard	2,358	6	6	0
Belen	7,159	23	17	6
Bernalillo	7,179	24	20	4
Bloomfield	7,181	26	20	6
Bosque Farms	4,010	13	12	1
Carlsbad	24,966	74	48	26

Table 78. Full-Time Law Enforcement Employees, by State and City, 2008—*Continued*

(Number.)

State/City	Population	Total law enforcement employees	Total officers	Total civilians
Carrizozo	1,028	4	3	1
Cimarron	822	2	2	0
Clayton	2,054	14	7	7
Clovis	33,263	75	53	22
Corrales	7,930	21	18	3
Cuba	637	6	5	1
Deming	15,430	40	34	6
Dexter	1,245	4	4	0
Espanola	9,530	28	21	7
Estancia	1,522	6	5	1
Eunice	2,668	13	7	6
Farmington	42,956	159	125	34
Gallup	18,642	93	62	31
Grants	8,883	19	13	6
Hatch	1,642	9	7	2
Hobbs	29,751	112	70	42
Hurley	1,355	4	3	1
Jal	2,072	9	5	4
Las Cruces	91,982	244	163	81
Las Vegas	13,419	52	35	17
Lordsburg	2,598	11	10	1
Los Alamos	18,541	70	29	41
Los Lunas	12,395	37	33	4
Lovington	9,843	30	23	7
Magdalena	853	4	4	0
Melrose	708	1	1	0
Milan	2,586	14	6	8
Moriarty	1,758	11	10	1
Portales	12,107	36	23	13
Questa	1,871	3	1	2
Red River	485	10	4	6
Rio Rancho	79,647	199	124	75
Roswell	45,619	109	77	32
Ruidoso	9,031	39	24	15
Ruidoso Downs	2,656	18	8	10
Santa Clara	1,813	8	7	1
Santa Fe	74,496	192	147	45
Santa Rosa	2,508	14	8	6
Silver City	9,915	35	30	5
Socorro	8,478	27	19	8
Sunland Park	14,341	19	16	3
Taos	5,332	28	21	7
Taos Ski Valley	56	3	3	0
Tatum	726	5	2	3
Texico	1,032	3	2	1
Truth or Consequences	6,617	13	11	2
Tucumcari	5,030	28	15	13
Tularosa	2,850	10	5	5
NEW YORK				
Addison Town and Village	2,511	1	1	0
Akron Village	2,973	2	2	0
Albany	94,152	456	332	124
Albion Village	5,553	11	11	0
Alexandria Bay Village	1,109	2	2	0
Alfred Village	4,970	6	6	0
Allegany Village	1,764	3	2	1
Altamont Village	1,708	1	1	0
Amherst Town	110,351	189	153	36
Amity Town and Belmont Village	2,128	1	1	0
Amityville Village	9,247	27	25	2
Amsterdam	17,481	38	37	1
Arcade Village	1,890	6	6	0
Ardsley Village	4,933	20	20	0
Asharoken Village	637	3	3	0
Auburn	27,173	78	70	8
Baldwinsville Village	7,165	18	15	3
Batavia	15,156	33	29	4
Bath Village	5,428	14	12	2
Beacon	14,522	37	35	2
Bedford Town	18,626	48	43	5
Bethlehem Town	33,349	60	42	18
Binghamton	44,746	153	139	14
Blooming Grove Town	12,348	18	16	2
Bolivar Village	1,108	1	1	0
Boonville Village	2,054	3	3	0
Brighton Town	34,226	46	40	6
Brockport Village	8,108	12	11	1
Bronxville Village	6,561	22	22	0
Buchanan Village	2,259	5	5	0
Buffalo	270,289	943	800	143
Cairo Town	6,582	2	2	0
Caledonia Village	2,136	5	5	0
Cambridge Village	1,813	4	4	0
Camden Village	2,257	3	3	0
Camillus Town and Village	23,231	26	24	2
Canajoharie Village	2,161	5	5	0
Canandaigua	11,159	29	25	4
Canton Village	6,075	10	8	2
Catskill Village	4,241	16	15	1
Cayuga Heights Village	3,667	7	6	1
Cazenovia Village	2,861	3	3	0
Centre Island Village	428	5	5	0
Chatham Village	1,694	3	2	1
Cheektowaga Town	78,303	165	129	36
Chester Town	9,973	13	13	0
Chester Village	3,585	12	11	1
Chittenango Village	4,890	5	4	1
Cicero Town	28,331	15	14	1
Clarkstown Town	78,869	198	170	28
Clifton Springs Village	2,141	2	2	0
Cohoes	15,032	47	35	12
Colchester Town	2,036	2	2	0
Colonie Town	78,272	152	108	44
Cooperstown Village	1,898	6	5	1
Cornwall Town	9,825	16	12	4
Cortland	18,342	46	43	3
Dansville Village	4,464	5	5	0
Depew Village	15,275	34	28	6
Deposit Village	1,592	3	3	0
Dewitt Town	21,397	40	37	3
East Aurora-Aurora Town	13,491	22	17	5
Eastchester Town	18,793	53	46	7
East Fishkill Town	29,314	39	32	7
East Hampton Town	18,998	95	68	27
East Syracuse Village	2,974	12	10	2
Ellenville Village	3,877	11	10	1
Ellicott Town	5,229	13	12	1
Elmira	29,255	89	79	10
Elmira Town	5,855	4	4	0
Elmsford Village	4,779	18	18	0
Endicott Village	12,428	39	35	4
Evans Town	16,827	30	24	6
Fairport Village	5,442	11	10	1
Fort Plain Village	2,179	2	2	0
Franklinville Village	1,699	2	2	0
Freeport Village	42,249	103	86	17
Fulton City	11,209	37	35	2
Garden City Village	21,741	63	50	13
Gates Town	28,383	35	28	7
Geddes Town	10,482	17	15	2
Geneseo Village	7,669	8	8	0
Geneva	13,156	42	37	5
Glen Cove	25,982	56	52	4
Glens Falls	13,923	35	29	6
Glenville Town	21,444	35	22	13
Gloversville	14,989	35	33	2
Goshen Town	8,534	12	11	1
Goshen Village	5,531	20	17	3
Granville Village	2,541	6	6	0
Great Neck Estates Village	2,668	16	13	3
Greece Town	92,932	98	90	8
Greene Village	1,654	1	1	0
Greenwich Village	1,825	4	4	0
Greenwood Lake Village	3,428	8	6	2
Groton Village	2,401	2	1	1
Guilderland Town	33,215	51	34	17
Hamburg Town	43,980	80	62	18
Hamburg Village	9,349	16	14	2

Table 78. Full-Time Law Enforcement Employees, by State and City, 2008—*Continued*

(Number.)

State/City	Population	Total law enforcement employees	Total officers	Total civilians
Harriman Village	2,253	7	7	0
Harrison Town	26,809	82	73	9
Hastings-on-Hudson Village	7,981	21	21	0
Haverstraw Town	36,019	77	72	5
Herkimer Village	6,973	22	21	1
Highland Falls Village	3,708	14	10	4
Holley Village	1,688	2	2	0
Hornell	8,498	20	19	1
Horseheads Village	6,208	15	13	2
Hudson	6,788	31	25	6
Hunter Town	2,707	1	1	0
Huntington Bay Village	1,446	6	6	0
Hyde Park Town	20,355	19	16	3
Ilion Village	8,033	20	18	2
Irondequoit Town	49,767	70	57	13
Irvington Village	6,688	22	21	1
Jamestown	29,279	73	62	11
Johnson City Village	14,745	45	40	5
Johnstown	8,428	26	25	1
Kenmore Village	14,973	25	25	0
Kent Town	14,247	26	21	5
Kings Point Village	5,126	24	22	2
Kingston	22,520	86	80	6
Kirkland Town	8,376	6	6	0
Lackawanna	17,549	67	47	20
Lake Placid Village	2,777	18	14	4
Lake Success Village	2,792	27	24	3
Lancaster Town	23,329	65	50	15
Larchmont Village	6,598	28	27	1
Le Roy Village	4,147	12	9	3
Lewisboro Town	12,607	2	2	0
Liberty Village	3,881	18	15	3
Little Falls	4,878	12	11	1
Liverpool Village	2,348	6	5	1
Lloyd Harbor Village	3,597	14	13	1
Lloyd Town	10,853	13	10	3
Lockport	20,597	55	51	4
Long Beach	34,478	91	73	18
Lowville Village	3,184	6	6	0
Lloyd Harbor Village	3,597	14	13	1
Lloyd Town	10,853	13	10	3
Lynbrook Village	19,132	56	48	8
Lyons Village	3,395	10	8	2
Macedon Town and Village	8,785	3	3	0
Malone Village	5,782	15	15	0
Mamaroneck Village	18,450	58	52	6
Manlius Town	24,954	46	38	8
Marlborough Town	8,335	12	9	3
Massena Village	10,530	26	21	5
Maybrook Village	4,133	3	3	0
Medina Village	6,011	11	10	1
Menands Village	3,798	13	10	3
Middleport Village	1,778	3	3	0
Middletown	25,928	88	75	13
Mohawk Village	2,473	4	4	0
Montgomery Town	8,749	15	14	1
Monticello Village	6,551	27	24	3
Moriah Town	3,468	2	2	0
Mount Kisco Village	10,484	37	33	4
Mount Morris Village	2,867	6	6	0
Mount Vernon	67,810	231	203	28
Newburgh	28,180	106	91	15
Newburgh Town	31,111	72	59	13
New Hartford Town and Village	19,231	32	21	11
New Rochelle	73,376	247	185	62
New Windsor Town	25,279	57	45	12
New York	8,345,075	49,664	35,761	13,903
New York Mills Village	3,326	5	5	0
Niagara Falls	51,192	166	146	20
Niagara Town	8,401	7	6	1
Niskayuna Town	21,925	29	29	0
Nissequogue Village	1,534	3	3	0
North Castle Town	12,237	41	38	3
North Greenbush Town	11,888	19	17	2

State/City	Population	Total law enforcement employees	Total officers	Total civilians
Northport Village	7,376	19	15	4
North Syracuse Village	6,596	13	12	1
Norwich	7,021	20	19	1
Ocean Beach Village	143	4	4	0
Old Brookville Village	2,222	50	39	11
Old Westbury Village	5,362	31	26	5
Olean	14,165	38	32	6
Oneida	10,768	28	24	4
Oneonta City	13,224	29	25	4
Orangetown Town	36,759	99	90	9
Orchard Park Town	28,599	38	33	5
Ossining Village	23,907	69	60	9
Oswego City	17,303	52	44	8
Owego Village	3,676	9	8	1
Oxford Village	1,542	1	1	0
Oyster Bay Cove Village	2,212	11	11	0
Painted Post Village	1,751	4	4	0
Peekskill	24,820	74	60	14
Penn Yan Village	5,153	13	12	1
Perry Village	3,667	5	5	0
Plattsburgh City	19,521	55	48	7
Port Chester Village	28,237	65	62	3
Port Dickinson Village	1,597	5	4	1
Port Jervis	9,152	33	32	1
Port Washington	18,237	72	65	7
Poughkeepsie	29,606	141	106	35
Poughkeepsie Town	43,453	96	84	12
Pulaski Village	2,280	1	1	0
Quogue Village	1,114	14	13	1
Riverhead Town	34,618	105	85	20
Rochester	205,341	923	759	164
Rockville Centre Village	23,513	61	51	10
Rome	33,746	80	76	4
Rouses Point Village	2,344	1	1	0
Rye	15,275	44	39	5
Rye Brook Village	9,720	29	28	1
Sag Harbor Village	2,333	14	13	1
Sands Point Village	2,795	21	21	0
Saranac Lake Village	4,801	11	11	0
Schenectady	61,506	216	166	50
Shelter Island Town	2,453	10	9	1
Sidney Village	3,692	9	9	0
Silver Creek Village	2,798	6	5	1
Sodus Village	1,598	1	1	0
Solvay Village	6,429	15	13	2
Southampton Town	50,089	155	108	47
South Nyack Village	3,374	6	6	0
Spring Valley Village	26,337	65	57	8
Stony Point Town	15,226	31	30	1
Syracuse	138,211	563	494	69
Tonawanda	14,792	34	29	5
Tonawanda Town	56,605	157	106	51
Troy	47,567	138	122	16
Tuckahoe Village	6,253	29	26	3
Tupper Lake Village	3,824	10	10	0
Tuxedo Park Village	720	6	3	3
Tuxedo Town	3,003	15	12	3
Ulster Town	12,733	33	29	4
Utica	58,234	189	171	18
Vestal Town	27,412	42	38	4
Wallkill Town	27,643	48	42	6
Walton Village	2,824	7	6	1
Wappingers Falls Village	5,386	7	4	3
Warwick Town	19,998	42	35	7
Washingtonville Village	6,185	18	16	2
Waterford Town and Village	8,579	12	9	3
Waterloo Village	5,020	9	8	1
Watertown	27,546	72	68	4
Watervliet	9,788	29	26	3
Watkins Glen Village	2,032	6	6	0
Waverly Village	4,338	11	10	1
Webb Town	1,934	5	5	0
Webster Town and Village	41,735	34	30	4
Wellsville Village	4,874	15	11	4

Table 78. Full-Time Law Enforcement Employees, by State and City, 2008—*Continued*

(Number.)

State/City	Population	Total law enforcement employees	Total officers	Total civilians
Westfield Village	3,361	5	5	0
Westhampton Beach Village	1,937	19	16	3
West Seneca Town	43,837	80	66	14
White Plains	57,932	235	218	17
Whitesboro Village	3,772	8	8	0
Whitestown Town	9,310	6	6	0
Windham Town	1,928	3	3	0
Woodbury Town	10,309	26	22	4
Yonkers	199,615	726	649	77
Yorktown Town	37,928	65	57	8
Yorkville Village	2,565	3	3	0
NORTH CAROLINA				
Aberdeen	5,662	26	24	2
Ahoskie	4,196	20	16	4
Albemarle	15,423	55	49	6
Andrews	1,707	6	5	1
Angier	4,414	11	10	1
Apex	33,244	68	54	14
Archdale	9,291	31	25	6
Asheboro	24,458	85	78	7
Asheville	74,215	266	195	71
Atlantic Beach	1,811	22	18	4
Aurora	593	2	2	0
Ayden	5,020	22	18	4
Badin	1,336	5	5	0
Bailey	681	2	2	0
Bakersville	350	2	1	1
Bald Head Island	305	12	11	1
Banner Elk	921	10	9	1
Beaufort	4,245	18	17	1
Beech Mountain	330	14	10	4
Belhaven	2,009	8	4	4
Belmont	9,263	43	34	9
Benson	3,471	15	14	1
Bethel	1,739	7	7	0
Beulaville	1,121	5	5	0
Biltmore Forest	1,561	14	13	1
Biscoe	1,680	9	8	1
Black Creek	696	2	2	0
Black Mountain	7,892	22	18	4
Bladenboro	1,667	6	6	0
Blowing Rock	1,482	13	10	3
Boiling Spring Lakes	4,773	10	9	1
Boiling Springs	3,796	8	8	0
Boone	13,885	43	35	8
Boonville	1,115	4	4	0
Brevard	6,674	29	23	6
Broadway	1,151	4	4	0
Brookford	425	1	1	0
Bryson City	1,388	8	7	1
Bunn	407	3	3	0
Burgaw	4,160	11	10	1
Burlington	50,058	146	102	44
Burnsville	1,647	8	8	0
Butner	6,636	46	41	5
Cameron	322	1	1	0
Candor	834	5	5	0
Canton	3,882	20	14	6
Cape Carteret	1,433	7	7	0
Carolina Beach	5,989	29	26	3
Carrboro	17,958	39	37	2
Carthage	2,027	11	10	1
Cary	125,277	189	159	30
Caswell Beach	483	4	4	0
Catawba	806	3	3	0
Chadbourn	2,063	10	9	1
Chapel Hill	52,034	136	112	24
Charlotte-Mecklenburg[1]	758,769	2,122	1,637	485
Cherryville	5,554	23	18	5
China Grove	3,722	12	12	0
Chocowinity	716	3	3	0
Claremont	1,143	9	8	1
Clayton	16,013	46	42	4
Cleveland	833	5	5	0
Clinton	8,876	36	33	3
Clyde	1,255	4	4	0
Columbus	977	6	6	0
Concord	65,725	176	151	25
Conover	7,302	25	24	1
Conway	668	2	2	0
Cooleemee	982	4	4	0
Cornelius	24,983	56	41	15
Cramerton	3,109	12	12	0
Creedmoor	3,606	17	13	4
Dallas	3,734	17	13	4
Davidson	9,933	17	16	1
Denton	1,479	6	6	0
Dobson	1,454	4	4	0
Drexel	1,869	5	5	0
Dunn	10,004	46	37	9
Durham	221,785	584	450	134
East Bend	664	2	2	0
Eden	15,393	53	44	9
Edenton	4,992	14	12	2
Elizabeth City	19,813	68	56	12
Elizabethtown	3,762	15	14	1
Elkin	4,079	21	17	4
Elon	6,986	16	15	1
Emerald Isle	3,672	18	13	5
Enfield	2,331	11	10	1
Erwin	4,807	10	9	1
Fair Bluff	1,139	3	3	0
Fairmont	2,717	14	11	3
Farmville	4,630	24	19	5
Fayetteville	171,457	489	334	155
Fletcher	4,725	13	12	1
Forest City	7,086	34	32	2
Four Oaks	1,912	5	5	0
Foxfire Village	491	2	2	0
Franklin	3,953	19	18	1
Franklinton	1,972	10	9	1
Fremont	1,429	7	4	3
Fuquay-Varina	16,674	33	28	5
Garner	26,378	67	61	6
Garysburg	1,140	2	2	0
Gaston	886	2	2	0
Gastonia	71,486	195	168	27
Gibsonville	4,732	15	14	1
Glen Alpine	1,076	3	3	0
Goldsboro	37,445	107	93	14
Graham	14,543	38	35	3
Granite Falls	4,570	16	14	2
Granite Quarry	2,234	7	7	0
Greensboro	249,561	700	593	107
Greenville	77,960	212	172	40
Grifton	2,234	8	8	0
Hamlet	5,749	22	18	4
Havelock	22,135	33	27	6
Henderson	15,841	59	50	9
Hendersonville	12,027	50	38	12
Hertford	2,149	8	7	1
Hickory	41,414	144	115	29
Highlands	950	12	12	0
High Point	102,298	260	209	51
Hillsborough	5,559	31	28	3
Holden Beach	858	9	9	0
Holly Ridge	830	9	8	1
Holly Springs	21,432	45	36	9
Hope Mills	13,004	36	28	8
Hot Springs	636	1	1	0
Hudson	3,023	12	11	1
Huntersville	45,273	85	75	10
Indian Beach	93	4	4	0
Jackson	646	2	1	1
Jacksonville	75,770	136	108	28
Jefferson	1,361	3	3	0
Jonesville	2,269	11	10	1
Kannapolis	42,065	98	71	27

[1] The employee data presented in this table for Charlotte-Mecklenburg represent only Charlotte-Mecklenburg Police Department employees and exclude Mecklenburg County Sheriff's Office employees.

Table 78. Full-Time Law Enforcement Employees, by State and City, 2008—*Continued*

(Number.)

State/City	Population	Total law enforcement employees	Total officers	Total civilians
Kenansville	904	5	5	0
Kenly	1,930	8	7	1
Kernersville	22,782	84	64	20
Kill Devil Hills	6,670	29	22	7
King	6,863	21	18	3
Kings Mountain	11,136	37	31	6
Kingstown	844	1	1	0
Kinston	22,168	80	71	9
Kitty Hawk	3,344	17	15	2
Knightdale	7,571	23	22	1
Kure Beach	2,647	10	9	1
La Grange	2,745	6	6	0
Lake Lure	1,005	11	10	1
Lake Royale		4	4	0
Lake Waccamaw	1,448	4	4	0
Landis	3,111	9	8	1
Laurel Park	2,151	7	7	0
Laurinburg	15,442	45	39	6
Leland	4,992	32	29	3
Lenoir	17,843	65	49	16
Lexington	20,375	73	64	9
Liberty	2,726	11	10	1
Lilesville	422	1	1	0
Lillington	3,257	13	12	1
Lincolnton	10,779	33	28	5
Littleton	642	4	4	0
Locust	2,624	10	9	1
Long View	4,940	15	15	0
Louisburg	3,764	13	12	1
Lowell	2,746	9	9	0
Lumberton	21,849	76	67	9
Madison	2,256	11	10	1
Maggie Valley	817	9	8	1
Magnolia	989	2	2	0
Maiden	3,461	14	13	1
Manteo	1,330	8	7	1
Marion	5,112	30	25	5
Marshall	830	3	3	0
Mars Hill	1,770	5	5	0
Marshville	3,198	5	5	0
Matthews	27,140	67	55	12
Maxton	2,696	13	8	5
Mayodan	2,600	16	14	2
Maysville	963	2	2	0
McAdenville	660	2	2	0
Mebane	10,534	24	18	6
Middlesex	857	4	4	0
Mint Hill	20,096	29	27	2
Mocksville	4,634	22	21	1
Monroe	32,216	91	76	15
Montreat	715	5	5	0
Mooresville	22,003	73	54	19
Morehead City	9,683	48	38	10
Morganton	17,069	98	62	36
Morrisville	14,976	32	30	2
Mount Airy	8,729	52	39	13
Mount Gilead	1,405	4	4	0
Mount Holly	9,982	34	27	7
Mount Olive	4,380	17	16	1
Murfreesboro	2,333	15	10	5
Murphy	1,565	10	7	3
Nags Head	3,064	23	21	2
Nashville	4,594	15	14	1
Navassa	1,801	2	2	0
New Bern	28,855	134	89	45
Newland	649	5	5	0
Newport	4,318	10	10	0
Newton	13,359	42	33	9
Newton Grove	631	3	3	0
Norlina	1,008	5	5	0
North Topsail Beach	976	12	11	1
Northwest	936	3	3	0
North Wilkesboro	4,139	25	22	3
Norwood	2,131	8	7	1
Oakboro	1,166	5	5	0
Oak Island	8,397	28	21	7
Ocean Isle Beach	533	13	13	0
Old Fort	961	6	5	1
Oxford	8,628	38	31	7
Parkton	431	1	1	0
Pembroke	2,760	18	14	4
Pikeville	703	2	2	0
Pilot Mountain	1,269	9	8	1
Pinebluff	1,419	4	4	0
Pinehurst	12,422	29	24	5
Pine Knoll Shores	1,553	10	9	1
Pine Level	1,551	5	5	0
Pinetops	1,252	8	6	2
Pineville	6,642	43	32	11
Pink Hill	525	2	2	0
Pittsboro	2,582	11	11	0
Plymouth	3,826	12	12	0
Princeton	1,275	3	3	0
Raeford	3,466	17	15	2
Raleigh	388,661	803	689	114
Ramseur	1,715	8	8	0
Randleman	3,678	14	14	0
Ranlo	2,310	7	7	0
Red Springs	3,502	21	17	4
Reidsville	15,027	53	45	8
Richlands	913	5	5	0
Rich Square	845	2	2	0
River Bend	3,123	5	5	0
Roanoke Rapids	16,347	40	37	3
Robersonville	1,548	7	7	0
Rockingham	8,802	40	35	5
Rockwell	1,998	4	4	0
Rocky Mount	56,950	170	128	42
Rolesville	2,519	11	10	1
Roseboro	1,462	4	4	0
Rose Hill	1,409	4	4	0
Rowland	1,148	7	6	1
Roxboro	8,681	38	33	5
Rutherfordton	4,019	15	15	0
Salisbury	28,747	106	87	19
Saluda	566	4	4	0
Sanford	29,414	102	81	21
Scotland Neck	2,163	8	7	1
Seagrove	258	1	1	0
Selma	6,921	24	22	2
Seven Devils	168	5	5	0
Shallotte	1,759	14	13	1
Sharpsburg	2,400	7	7	0
Shelby	21,415	88	70	18
Siler City	8,725	26	21	5
Smithfield	12,759	44	40	4
Southern Pines	12,604	38	30	8
Southern Shores	2,670	10	10	0
Southport	3,108	12	11	1
Sparta	1,778	6	6	0
Spencer	3,370	14	13	1
Spindale	3,838	13	13	0
Spring Lake	8,122	25	21	4
Spruce Pine	1,984	9	9	0
Stallings	8,960	24	22	2
Stanfield	1,106	4	4	0
Stanley	3,299	13	9	4
Stantonsburg	703	4	4	0
Star	797	4	4	0
Statesville	26,474	91	68	23
St. Pauls	2,035	16	11	5
Sugar Mountain	209	5	5	0
Sunset Beach	2,348	12	12	0
Surf City	1,986	19	17	2
Swansboro	1,915	9	9	0
Sylva	2,427	14	13	1
Tabor City	2,636	10	9	1
Tarboro	10,187	33	27	6

Table 78. Full-Time Law Enforcement Employees, by State and City, 2008—*Continued*

(Number.)

State/City	Population	Total law enforcement employees	Total officers	Total civilians
Taylortown	876	2	2	0
Thomasville	26,528	73	65	8
Topsail Beach	587	8	7	1
Trent Woods	3,962	5	5	0
Troutman	1,819	12	12	0
Troy	3,373	11	10	1
Tryon	1,714	10	8	2
Valdese	4,523	13	12	1
Vanceboro	845	1	1	0
Vass	780	3	3	0
Wadesboro	5,061	27	21	6
Wagram	785	2	2	0
Wake Forest	27,532	60	51	9
Wallace	3,611	17	14	3
Walnut Cove	1,602	8	7	1
Walnut Creek	854	2	2	0
Warrenton	732	6	5	1
Warsaw	3,164	16	12	4
Washington	10,097	41	32	9
Waxhaw	3,665	18	15	3
Waynesville	9,921	40	32	8
Weaverville	2,591	14	13	1
Weldon	1,279	9	9	0
Wendell	5,260	17	15	2
West Jefferson	1,120	7	7	0
Whispering Pines	2,139	10	9	1
Whitakers	767	3	3	0
White Lake	565	6	6	0
Whiteville	5,226	28	24	4
Wilkesboro	3,168	22	20	2
Williamston	5,362	21	20	1
Wilmington	100,944	321	266	55
Wilson	48,140	134	113	21
Wilson's Mills	1,587	2	2	0
Windsor	2,110	9	9	0
Wingate	3,954	6	6	0
Winston-Salem	226,460	649	493	156
Winterville	4,803	21	20	1
Woodfin	4,841	15	14	1
Woodland	757	1	1	0
Wrightsville Beach	2,680	25	23	2
Yadkinville	2,862	13	12	1
Youngsville	748	9	8	1
Zebulon	4,566	22	21	1
NORTH DAKOTA				
Beulah	2,877	6	5	1
Bismarck	59,988	113	85	28
Bowman	1,451	3	3	0
Burlington	993	2	2	0
Cando	1,030	2	2	0
Carrington	2,080	4	4	0
Cavalier	1,333	4	4	0
Crosby	939	2	2	0
Devils Lake	6,610	18	16	2
Dickinson	15,910	43	29	14
Elgin	546	1	1	0
Ellendale	1,486	1	1	0
Emerado	472	2	2	0
Fargo	92,883	149	131	18
Fessenden	499	1	1	0
Grafton	3,991	10	9	1
Grand Forks	52,064	94	78	16
Harvey	1,610	3	3	0
Hazen	2,219	4	4	0
Hillsboro	1,470	2	2	0
Jamestown	14,578	32	28	4
Lamoure	819	1	1	0
Larimore	1,289	2	2	0
Lincoln	2,660	2	2	0
Linton	1,015	1	1	0
Lisbon	2,182	3	3	0
Mandan	17,860	40	29	11
Mayville	1,986	1	1	0
Minot	35,124	82	60	22
Napoleon	698	1	1	0
Northwood	871	2	2	0
Oakes	1,778	4	3	1
Powers Lake	244	1	1	0
Rolla	1,423	3	3	0
Rugby	2,538	4	4	0
Steele	649	1	1	0
Thompson	949	1	1	0
Valley City	6,242	18	13	5
Wahpeton	7,603	16	14	2
Watford City	1,367	5	5	0
West Fargo	24,266	42	32	10
Williston	12,387	31	23	8
Wishek	896	2	2	0
OHIO				
Aberdeen	1,540	3	2	1
Ada	5,793	11	8	3
Addyston	973	1	1	0
Akron	206,845	519	472	47
Alliance	22,285	53	40	13
Amelia	3,626	12	11	1
Amherst	11,683	25	20	5
Ansonia	1,078	2	2	0
Arcanum	1,969	4	4	0
Archbold	4,468	8	8	0
Arlington Heights	818	3	3	0
Ashland	21,900	38	28	10
Ashtabula	19,691	37	32	5
Ashville	3,291	9	9	0
Athens	21,981	33	26	7
Aurora	14,659	35	27	8
Austintown	35,185	48	39	9
Avon	17,501	38	30	8
Avon Lake	24,434	34	29	5
Bainbridge Township	11,225	27	19	8
Baltimore	2,909	3	3	0
Barberton	26,637	54	41	13
Barnesville	4,054	6	5	1
Batavia	1,698	4	4	0
Bath Township, Summit County	10,257	27	20	7
Bay Village	14,598	26	22	4
Bazetta Township	6,011	6	6	0
Beach City	1,094	2	2	0
Beavercreek	39,965	63	46	17
Beaver Township	6,087	16	12	4
Bedford	12,975	44	33	11
Bedford Heights	10,513	68	35	33
Bellaire	4,560	10	10	0
Bellbrook	6,969	17	12	5
Bellevue	7,840	15	12	3
Bellville	1,710	4	4	0
Belpre	6,498	14	9	5
Bentleyville Village	900	3	3	0
Berea	17,679	37	32	5
Berlin Heights	635	1	1	0
Bethel	2,622	6	5	1
Bethesda	1,358	1	1	0
Beverly	1,338	3	3	0
Bexley	12,261	35	28	7
Blanchester	4,326	7	7	0
Blendon Township	7,775	12	11	1
Bloomdale	708	1	1	0
Bluffton	3,973	6	6	0
Boardman	39,244	61	50	11
Boston Heights	1,232	5	5	0
Bowling Green	29,919	58	43	15
Bratenahl	1,267	13	10	3
Brecksville	12,903	37	31	6
Bridgeport	2,049	7	5	2
Broadview Heights	17,577	43	30	13
Brookfield Township	9,474	10	9	1
Brooklyn	10,408	39	34	5
Brooklyn Heights	1,452	17	17	0
Brook Park	19,177	53	44	9

Table 78. Full-Time Law Enforcement Employees, by State and City, 2008—*Continued*

(Number.)

State/City	Population	Total law enforcement employees	Total officers	Total civilians
Brookville	5,381	12	11	1
Brunswick	35,050	53	40	13
Bryan	8,263	25	18	7
Buchtel	603	1	1	0
Buckeye Lake	3,046	3	3	0
Bucyrus	12,222	25	19	6
Burton	1,431	2	2	0
Butler Township	8,147	16	15	1
Byesville	2,531	4	4	0
Cadiz	3,308	5	5	0
Caldwell	1,995	2	2	0
Cambridge	11,251	27	23	4
Camden	2,186	3	3	0
Canal Fulton	5,015	10	9	1
Canfield	6,876	20	15	5
Canton	78,006	213	173	40
Carey	3,786	11	7	4
Carrollton	3,209	7	7	0
Celina	10,243	22	16	6
Centerville	22,926	53	41	12
Chagrin Falls	3,638	18	10	8
Champion Township	9,236	8	8	0
Cheshire	79	1	1	0
Chester Township	10,956	14	13	1
Cheviot	8,200	10	10	0
Chillicothe	22,192	54	48	6
Cincinnati	332,608	1,310	1,083	227
Circleville	13,667	33	24	9
Clay Center	306	3	3	0
Clayton	12,934	15	15	0
Clay Township, Ottawa County	2,728	5	5	0
Clearcreek Township	12,710	14	13	1
Cleveland	433,452	1,885	1,613	272
Cleves	2,605	4	4	0
Clinton Township	4,012	9	9	0
Clyde	6,165	18	14	4
Coal Grove	2,072	8	7	1
Coitsville Township	1,630	2	2	0
Coldwater	4,409	6	6	0
Columbiana	6,018	12	12	0
Conneaut	12,343	27	20	7
Copley Township	14,089	35	26	9
Crestline	4,943	13	9	4
Creston	2,115	4	3	1
Crooksville	2,416	6	5	1
Cuyahoga Falls	51,211	105	86	19
Dalton	1,563	2	2	0
Danville	1,071	2	2	0
Dayton	154,218	507	419	88
Deer Park	5,615	12	8	4
Defiance	15,926	31	28	3
Delaware	34,028	64	49	15
Delhi Township	31,362	30	28	2
Delphos	6,709	18	14	4
Dennison	2,874	4	4	0
Dover	12,494	22	21	1
Dublin	38,825	84	63	21
East Cleveland	24,510	72	53	19
Eastlake	19,503	46	33	13
East Liverpool	11,984	25	19	6
Eaton	8,022	20	14	6
Edgerton	1,967	3	3	0
Elida	1,902	2	2	0
Elmwood Place	2,425	4	4	0
Empire	283	1	1	0
Englewood	12,767	25	20	5
Enon	2,550	4	4	0
Evendale	2,892	22	20	2
Fairborn	32,463	60	43	17
Fairfax	1,815	8	7	1
Fairfield	42,315	91	71	20
Fairfield Township	17,374	18	17	1
Fairlawn	7,050	35	24	11
Fairport Harbor	3,219	8	7	1
Fairview Park	15,752	28	27	1
Fayette	1,288	2	2	0
Findlay	37,291	91	73	18
Forest	1,431	2	2	0
Forest Park	18,117	48	40	8
Fort Loramie	1,473	3	3	0
Fort Recovery	1,342	2	2	0
Fort Shawnee	3,699	6	5	1
Franklin	12,996	31	24	7
Frazeysburg	1,296	1	1	0
Fredericktown	2,473	4	4	0
Fremont	16,682	39	33	6
Gahanna	33,828	73	59	14
Galion	10,843	19	15	4
Garfield Heights	27,746	80	62	18
Gates Mills	2,276	15	11	4
Geneva	6,299	16	12	4
Geneva-on-the-Lake	1,491	5	5	0
Genoa	2,294	4	4	0
Genoa Township	15,423	28	25	3
Germantown	5,072	11	10	1
German Township, Clark County	7,247	3	3	0
German Township, Montgomery County	3,277	6	6	0
Gibsonburg	2,449	5	5	0
Girard	10,097	19	15	4
Glendale	2,175	7	7	0
Glenwillow	632	4	4	0
Gnadenhutten	1,294	2	2	0
Goshen Township, Clermont County	16,462	14	13	1
Goshen Township, Mahoning County	3,450	12	11	1
Grandview Heights	6,251	23	19	4
Granville	5,399	12	9	3
Greenfield	5,120	11	9	2
Greenhills	3,753	8	7	1
Green Springs	1,205	2	2	0
Greenville	12,772	30	23	7
Greenwich	1,510	4	4	0
Grove City	33,869	76	59	17
Groveport	5,352	20	19	1
Hamilton	62,498	168	143	25
Hanging Rock	291	6	4	2
Harrison	9,117	24	22	2
Harveysburg	632	1	1	0
Heath	8,926	25	18	7
Hebron	2,160	8	7	1
Hicksville	3,398	9	8	1
Highland Heights	8,636	29	22	7
Hilliard	27,936	66	51	15
Hinckley Township	7,943	12	9	3
Holgate	1,112	1	1	0
Holland	1,330	9	9	0
Howland Township	16,435	19	18	1
Hubbard Township	5,712	7	6	1
Huber Heights	37,284	65	50	15
Hudson	23,144	35	28	7
Huron	7,311	18	13	5
Independence	6,785	48	34	14
Indian Hill	5,895	24	19	5
Ironton	11,321	22	17	5
Jackson	6,168	23	17	6
Jackson Township, Mahoning County	2,266	6	6	0
Jackson Township, Montgomery County	3,835	5	5	0
Jackson Township, Starke County	40,942	50	41	9
Jefferson	3,420	7	6	1
Jewett	772	1	1	0
Johnstown	4,062	15	10	5
Junction City	838	1	1	0
Kalida	1,161	4	4	0
Kent	28,265	56	42	14
Kenton	8,015	21	16	5
Kettering	53,714	110	81	29
Kirtland	7,428	14	9	5
Kirtland Hills	805	10	9	1
Lagrange	2,022	6	6	0

Table 78. Full-Time Law Enforcement Employees, by State and City, 2008—*Continued*

(Number.)

State/City	Population	Total law enforcement employees	Total officers	Total civilians
Lake Township	7,438	16	15	1
Lakewood	50,690	121	94	27
Lancaster	37,134	86	66	20
Lawrence Township	8,469	6	6	0
Lebanon	20,850	38	29	9
Leipsic	2,178	4	4	0
Lexington	4,121	13	9	4
Liberty Township	11,884	24	19	5
Lima	37,507	97	76	21
Lisbon	2,996	10	6	4
Lithopolis	1,057	3	3	0
Liverpool Township	4,165	5	5	0
Lockland	3,394	15	13	2
Logan	7,474	18	13	5
London	9,645	23	18	5
Lorain	70,302	127	99	28
Lordstown	3,546	13	9	4
Loudonville	2,999	10	6	4
Louisville	9,501	12	9	3
Lowellville	1,139	3	3	0
Luckey	988	1	1	0
Lynchburg	1,414	4	3	1
Lyndhurst	13,842	41	31	10
Madeira	9,090	14	13	1
Madison Township, Franklin County	18,111	17	15	2
Madison Township, Lake County	17,001	18	16	2
Magnolia	924	2	2	0
Mansfield	49,428	124	97	27
Maple Heights	23,639	60	42	18
Marblehead	839	3	3	0
Mariemont	3,116	11	10	1
Marietta	14,095	38	31	7
Marion	35,489	83	64	19
Marlboro Township	4,728	4	3	1
Marysville	17,804	35	30	5
Mason	30,582	50	43	7
Maumee	13,848	60	45	15
Mayfield Heights	17,715	47	37	10
Mayfield Village	3,115	23	15	8
McArthur	2,052	4	4	0
McClure	712	3	3	0
McComb	1,624	3	3	0
McConnelsville	1,695	4	4	0
Mechanicsburg	1,692	3	3	0
Mentor	51,917	116	82	34
Mentor-on-the-Lake	8,308	16	11	5
Miamisburg	19,874	44	40	4
Miami Township, Clermont County	39,711	40	37	3
Miami Township, Montgomery County	25,208	43	36	7
Middlefield	2,406	13	10	3
Middletown	51,266	116	80	36
Midvale	590	1	1	0
Mifflin Township	3,047	5	5	0
Milford	6,315	17	15	2
Millersburg	3,614	10	7	3
Minerva	3,908	14	9	5
Minerva Park	1,194	5	5	0
Mingo Junction	3,301	11	10	1
Minster	2,773	6	5	1
Monroe	15,025	28	22	6
Monroeville	1,348	4	4	0
Montgomery	10,221	24	21	3
Montpelier	4,016	9	8	1
Montville Township	6,424	11	11	0
Moreland Hills	3,069	14	13	1
Mount Eaton	240	4	4	0
Mount Orab	2,793	8	8	0
Mount Sterling	1,818	11	6	5
Munroe Falls	5,185	8	8	0
Napoleon	8,837	22	16	6
Navarre	1,421	5	5	0
Nelsonville	5,420	8	8	0
New Albany	7,034	23	17	6
Newark	47,283	102	81	21
New Boston	2,143	13	9	4
New Bremen	3,046	6	6	0
Newburgh Heights	2,131	6	4	2
Newcomerstown	3,888	13	8	5
New Concord	2,644	4	4	0
New Franklin	15,021	18	13	5
New Lexington	4,525	12	8	4
New London	2,606	4	4	0
New Madison	752	10	10	0
New Middletown	1,558	3	3	0
New Richmond	2,531	4	4	0
Newton Falls	4,657	9	6	3
Newtown	4,112	8	7	1
New Washington	914	2	2	0
Niles	19,307	41	35	6
North Baltimore	3,342	11	11	0
North Canton	16,886	32	24	8
North College Hill	9,355	15	14	1
Northfield	3,659	8	8	0
North Kingsville	2,571	5	5	0
North Olmsted	31,347	71	55	16
North Ridgeville	28,301	48	39	9
North Royalton	29,458	60	38	22
Northwood	5,525	28	21	7
Norton	11,477	21	15	6
Norwalk	16,607	32	25	7
Norwood	19,923	54	52	2
Oak Harbor	2,795	6	4	2
Oak Hill	1,618	3	3	0
Oakwood, Montgomery County	8,437	39	33	6
Oakwood, Paulding County	554	1	1	0
Oakwood Village	3,677	14	12	2
Oberlin	8,350	23	17	6
Olmsted Falls	8,258	16	10	6
Ontario	5,234	27	21	6
Orange Village	3,280	15	14	1
Oregon	18,948	60	46	14
Orrville	8,378	19	14	5
Orwell	1,471	6	5	1
Owensville	842	2	1	1
Oxford	22,243	39	25	14
Oxford Township	2,630	3	3	0
Painesville	18,168	44	40	4
Parma	77,980	152	95	57
Parma Heights	19,778	40	33	7
Pataskala	12,964	17	16	1
Payne	1,103	1	1	0
Peebles	1,836	2	2	0
Pemberville	1,352	2	2	0
Pepper Pike	5,697	27	20	7
Perkins Township	12,882	25	18	7
Perrysburg	17,043	43	32	11
Perry Township, Allen County	3,602	1	1	0
Perry Township, Columbiana County	4,609	5	5	0
Perry Township, Franklin County	3,615	11	10	1
Perry Township, Montgomery County	3,816	3	3	0
Perry Township, Starke County	28,063	29	23	6
Pickerington	18,435	35	26	9
Pierce Township	11,075	17	17	0
Piqua	20,609	38	32	6
Plain City	3,633	9	9	0
Poland Township	11,123	13	11	2
Port Clinton	6,175	18	13	5
Portsmouth	20,043	44	41	3
Powell	13,205	18	16	2
Powhatan Point	1,659	3	3	0
Ravenna	11,375	34	25	9
Reading	10,288	24	20	4
Reminderville	2,604	8	8	0
Reynoldsburg	33,727	68	54	14
Richfield	3,601	24	17	7
Richmond Heights	10,148	30	22	8
Rio Grande	866	2	2	0
Rittman	6,267	12	9	3

Table 78. Full-Time Law Enforcement Employees, by State and City, 2008—*Continued*

(Number.)

State/City	Population	Total law enforcement employees	Total officers	Total civilians
Riverside	25,357	33	32	1
Roaming Shores Village	1,196	2	2	0
Rockford	1,094	2	2	0
Roseville	1,885	3	3	0
Rossford	6,401	14	13	1
Ross Township	7,944	2	2	0
Russell Township	5,597	8	7	1
Russia	618	1	1	0
Sabina	2,802	5	5	0
Sagamore Hills	9,548	12	10	2
Salem	11,763	16	15	1
Saline Township	1,336	4	4	0
Salineville	1,323	3	3	0
Sandusky	25,625	62	52	10
Seaman	1,075	2	2	0
Sebring	4,534	10	7	3
Seven Hills	11,646	18	17	1
Seville	2,437	8	7	1
Shadyside	3,531	5	4	1
Shaker Heights	26,473	93	68	25
Sharon Township	2,359	10	10	0
Sharonville	13,158	48	38	10
Shawnee Hills	585	2	2	0
Shawnee Township	8,626	16	10	6
Sheffield Lake	8,889	16	12	4
Shelby	9,330	19	15	4
Sidney	19,978	52	40	12
Silverton	5,167	16	13	3
Smith Township	4,835	5	5	0
Smithville	1,296	3	3	0
Solon	22,057	78	46	32
Somerset	1,543	2	2	0
South Bloomfield	1,707	3	3	0
South Charleston	1,779	1	1	0
South Euclid	21,196	55	41	14
South Russell	3,929	9	9	0
South Solon	385	3	3	0
South Zanesville	1,988	3	3	0
Spencerville	2,158	4	4	0
Springboro	17,936	30	25	5
Springdale	10,144	46	39	7
Springfield	61,999	147	127	20
Springfield Township, Hamilton County	40,018	55	49	6
Springfield Township, Mahoning County	6,009	8	8	0
Springfield Township, Summit County	15,339	19	17	2
St. Bernard	4,521	15	14	1
St. Clairsville	5,055	14	10	4
Steubenville	18,745	56	46	10
St. Henry	2,379	2	2	0
St. Marys	8,083	20	15	5
Stow	34,260	53	43	10
St. Paris	1,957	4	4	0
Strasburg	2,721	4	4	0
Streetsboro	14,532	34	26	8
Strongsville	42,749	97	77	20
Struthers	10,755	20	16	4
Sugarcreek Township	6,991	22	15	7
Sunbury	3,399	12	11	1
Sycamore	868	1	1	0
Sylvania Township	26,135	58	43	15
Tallmadge	17,405	30	27	3
Terrace Park	2,163	7	6	1
Thornville	1,188	1	1	0
Tiffin	17,263	43	30	13
Tipp City	9,267	22	19	3
Toledo	317,401	773	639	134
Toronto	5,202	10	10	0
Tremont City	343	1	1	0
Trenton	11,057	19	14	5
Trotwood	26,140	44	41	3
Troy	22,002	47	42	5
Twinsburg	17,520	46	33	13
Uhrichsville	5,505	9	8	1
Union City	1,647	5	5	0
Uniontown	2,835	10	8	2
Union Township, Clermont County	44,087	75	58	17
University Heights	12,592	36	30	6
Upper Arlington	31,514	61	48	13
Urbana	11,383	21	21	0
Utica	2,099	10	4	6
Valley View, Cuyahoga County	2,017	20	18	2
Valleyview, Franklin County	564	1	1	0
Vandalia	14,106	39	30	9
Van Wert	10,195	30	22	8
Vermilion	10,756	23	18	5
Wadsworth	20,657	37	29	8
Waite Hill	563	5	5	0
Wakeman	937	2	2	0
Walbridge	3,095	4	4	0
Walton Hills	2,284	22	15	7
Wapakoneta	9,418	19	14	5
Warren	43,809	100	82	18
Warrensville Heights	13,594	49	35	14
Warren Township	6,045	8	8	0
Washington Court House	13,666	28	22	6
Waterville	5,228	13	12	1
Waterville Township	5,694	4	4	0
Wauseon	7,299	18	14	4
Waverly	4,393	17	13	4
Waynesville	3,094	3	2	1
Wellington	4,690	8	6	2
Wellston	5,932	16	12	4
Wells Township	2,831	4	4	0
West Alexandria	1,296	3	3	0
West Carrollton	12,762	32	25	7
West Chester Township	55,672	118	89	29
Westerville	35,773	87	73	14
West Jefferson	4,270	13	10	3
West Lafayette	2,491	5	5	0
Westlake	30,580	74	54	20
West Liberty	1,729	2	2	0
West Union	3,100	6	5	1
Whitehall	17,995	56	45	11
Wickliffe	12,953	41	31	10
Willard	6,690	19	15	4
Williamsburg	2,365	13	13	0
Willoughby	22,384	59	44	15
Willoughby Hills	8,545	27	19	8
Willowick	13,692	35	25	10
Wilmington	12,571	27	25	2
Windham	2,716	6	4	2
Wintersville	3,786	10	9	1
Woodlawn	2,586	14	14	0
Woodville	1,971	5	5	0
Wooster	26,105	43	38	5
Worthington	13,183	47	34	13
Wyoming	8,374	21	19	2
Xenia	27,740	70	46	24
Yellow Springs	3,589	10	8	2
Youngstown	72,887	216	176	40
Zanesville	25,060	88	50	38
OKLAHOMA				
Achille	531	5	3	2
Ada	16,599	44	35	9
Altus	19,097	61	43	18
Alva	4,677	11	9	2
Anadarko	6,301	19	13	6
Antlers	2,477	11	6	5
Apache	1,538	3	3	0
Ardmore	24,738	62	44	18
Arkoma	2,181	6	3	3
Atoka	3,081	16	15	1
Bartlesville	35,497	78	51	27
Beaver	1,389	3	3	0
Beggs	1,364	8	4	4
Bethany	19,522	39	30	9
Bixby	21,114	34	25	9
Blackwell	7,117	22	15	7

Table 78. Full-Time Law Enforcement Employees, by State and City, 2008—*Continued*

(Number.)

State/City	Population	Total law enforcement employees	Total officers	Total civilians
Blanchard	6,616	16	12	4
Boise City	1,211	3	3	0
Boley	1,087	1	1	0
Bristow	4,388	13	9	4
Broken Arrow	92,075	171	125	46
Broken Bow	4,137	18	14	4
Caddo	983	5	4	1
Calera	1,820	9	7	2
Calumet	532	2	2	0
Carnegie	1,544	7	4	3
Catoosa	6,724	15	14	1
Chandler	2,835	10	6	4
Checotah	3,474	15	13	2
Chelsea	2,237	7	4	3
Cherokee	1,415	9	3	6
Chickasha	17,218	36	25	11
Choctaw	11,337	13	11	2
Chouteau	2,008	8	7	1
Claremore	17,491	54	38	16
Clayton	725	7	3	4
Cleveland	3,151	5	5	0
Clinton	8,638	24	16	8
Coalgate	1,858	7	6	1
Colbert	1,117	6	5	1
Collinsville	4,821	16	10	6
Comanche	1,517	4	4	0
Cordell	2,930	11	7	4
Coweta	9,043	14	8	6
Crescent	1,372	5	4	1
Cushing	9,631	19	12	7
Davenport	877	2	2	0
Davis	2,616	12	8	4
Del City	22,052	44	31	13
Dewar	899	2	2	0
Dewey	3,321	11	9	2
Dibble	287	4	3	1
Drumright	2,878	4	4	0
Duncan	22,535	51	44	7
Durant	16,432	33	30	3
Edmond	79,529	140	116	24
Elk City	11,180	38	26	12
El Reno	16,295	43	31	12
Enid	47,017	108	92	16
Eufaula	2,771	15	12	3
Fairfax	1,464	6	3	3
Fairview	2,534	7	4	3
Fort Gibson	4,367	16	11	5
Frederick	3,929	13	11	2
Geary	1,216	10	5	5
Glenpool	9,697	24	17	7
Goodwell	1,134	5	4	1
Grandfield	956	2	2	0
Grove	6,374	30	20	10
Guthrie	11,195	28	21	7
Guymon	10,580	18	13	5
Harrah	5,200	10	9	1
Hartshorne	2,055	5	5	0
Haskell	1,781	5	4	1
Healdton	2,761	6	3	3
Heavener	3,231	13	8	5
Henryetta	6,043	17	12	5
Hinton	2,134	4	4	0
Hobart	3,613	11	5	6
Holdenville	5,453	14	10	4
Hollis	1,922	10	6	4
Hominy	3,651	10	6	4
Hooker	1,698	7	3	4
Howe	717	4	2	2
Hugo	5,431	17	15	2
Hulbert	535	4	3	1
Hydro	1,008	2	2	0
Idabel	6,841	25	19	6
Jay	3,084	12	8	4
Jenks	15,703	21	16	5
Jones	2,712	5	5	0
Kaw City	359	1	1	0
Kiefer	1,545	5	4	1
Kingfisher	4,516	12	10	2
Kingston	1,591	6	6	0
Kiowa	700	7	6	1
Konawa	1,387	5	4	1
Krebs	2,118	7	7	0
Lawton	91,459	230	165	65
Lexington	2,102	8	5	3
Lindsay	2,899	12	8	4
Locust Grove	1,584	8	6	2
Lone Grove	5,281	11	8	3
Luther	1,116	6	5	1
Madill	3,790	13	12	1
Mangum	2,689	9	5	4
Mannford	2,845	10	7	3
Marietta	2,540	7	6	1
Marlow	4,580	10	10	0
Maysville	1,293	3	2	1
McAlester	18,291	59	45	14
McLoud	4,178	11	6	5
Meeker	981	4	4	0
Miami	13,321	42	30	12
Midwest City	56,168	116	89	27
Minco	1,795	4	4	0
Moore	52,494	83	77	6
Mooreland	1,242	2	2	0
Morris	1,310	3	3	0
Mountain View	785	2	2	0
Muldrow	3,176	9	6	3
Muskogee	40,115	111	90	21
Mustang	17,763	27	20	7
Newcastle	7,228	25	17	8
Newkirk	2,117	7	6	1
Nichols Hills	4,015	19	15	4
Nicoma Park	2,383	6	6	0
Noble	5,764	16	11	5
Norman	108,016	176	127	49
Nowata	3,984	8	6	2
Oilton	1,119	3	3	0
Okemah	2,921	11	7	4
Oklahoma City	552,452	1,301	1,043	258
Okmulgee	12,585	34	28	6
Oologah	1,159	4	4	0
Owasso	27,460	61	45	16
Pauls Valley	6,097	19	14	5
Pawhuska	3,452	10	6	4
Pawnee	2,169	5	5	0
Perkins	2,615	6	6	0
Perry	5,018	22	14	8
Piedmont	5,505	13	10	3
Pocola	4,491	9	5	4
Ponca City	24,435	66	55	11
Porum	735	2	2	0
Poteau	8,277	34	27	7
Prague	2,130	11	5	6
Pryor	9,291	31	22	9
Purcell	6,143	19	18	1
Ringling	1,043	1	1	0
Roland	3,299	7	5	2
Rush Springs	1,349	4	4	0
Sallisaw	8,831	31	22	9
Sand Springs	18,572	41	31	10
Sapulpa	20,991	59	46	13
Sayre	3,113	12	7	5
Seminole	6,801	19	13	6
Shawnee	30,398	72	53	19
Skiatook	6,707	24	17	7
Snyder	1,375	5	4	1
Spencer	4,027	9	8	1
Spiro	2,328	4	4	0
Stigler	2,836	13	9	4
Stillwater	48,045	108	74	34

Table 78. Full-Time Law Enforcement Employees, by State and City, 2008—*Continued*

(Number.)

State/City	Population	Total law enforcement employees	Total officers	Total civilians
Stilwell	3,472	18	13	5
Stratford	1,484	2	2	0
Stringtown	419	2	2	0
Stroud	2,739	11	8	3
Sulphur	4,810	12	10	2
Tahlequah	16,663	39	31	8
Talihina	1,237	10	6	4
Tecumseh	6,746	12	11	1
Texhoma	926	2	2	0
The Village	9,759	26	21	5
Tishomingo	3,216	7	6	1
Tonkawa	3,014	13	7	6
Tulsa	382,954	931	823	108
Tushka	369	3	3	0
Tuttle	6,067	14	10	4
Valliant	741	5	3	2
Vian	1,456	6	4	2
Vinita	6,028	21	15	6
Wagoner	8,016	19	13	6
Walters	2,461	4	4	0
Warner	1,447	4	4	0
Warr Acres	9,422	25	20	5
Washington	542	1	1	0
Watonga	5,635	10	7	3
Waukomis	1,200	3	3	0
Waurika	1,774	2	2	0
Waynoka	896	3	3	0
Weatherford	10,129	31	20	11
Weleetka	922	6	2	4
Westville	1,651	10	6	4
Wetumka	1,399	5	5	0
Wewoka	3,298	12	8	4
Wilburton	2,864	8	7	1
Wilson	1,627	5	4	1
Woodward	12,257	41	26	15
Wright City	789	3	3	0
Wynnewood	2,279	5	4	1
Yale	1,480	5	2	3
Yukon	22,686	53	37	16
OREGON				
Albany	48,075	91	62	29
Amity	1,482	2	2	0
Ashland	21,535	38	30	8
Astoria	9,891	26	16	10
Athena	1,193	2	2	0
Aumsville	3,440	7	6	1
Aurora	1,042	2	2	0
Baker City	9,355	18	16	2
Bandon	2,837	8	7	1
Beaverton	92,198	158	128	30
Bend	77,898	105	81	24
Black Butte		7	6	1
Boardman	2,947	7	6	1
Brookings	6,368	20	13	7
Burns	2,639	4	3	1
Canby	15,985	30	25	5
Cannon Beach	1,742	8	7	1
Carlton	1,591	3	3	0
Central Point	16,966	31	26	5
Clatskanie	1,635	6	5	1
Coburg	1,028	4	4	0
Columbia City	1,997	1	1	0
Condon	643	2	1	1
Coos Bay	15,818	36	23	13
Coquille	4,159	8	7	1
Cornelius	11,589	15	14	1
Corvallis	51,343	80	53	27
Cottage Grove	9,118	24	17	7
Culver	1,228	1	1	0
Dallas	15,892	29	18	11
Eagle Point	8,714	10	8	2
Elgin	1,651	3	3	0
Enterprise	1,698	4	4	0
Eugene	150,297	292	178	114
Fairview	10,046	14	13	1
Florence	8,469	23	14	9
Forest Grove	20,743	30	27	3
Gearhart	1,134	3	3	0
Gervais	2,470	5	5	0
Gladstone	12,080	16	14	2
Gold Beach	1,841	5	4	1
Grants Pass	33,673	69	42	27
Gresham	100,935	159	120	39
Hermiston	15,186	34	23	11
Hillsboro	94,373	151	115	36
Hines	1,392	3	3	0
Hood River	6,822	17	14	3
Hubbard	2,789	7	6	1
Independence	9,579	16	13	3
Jacksonville	2,178	7	5	2
John Day	1,486	9	4	5
Junction City	5,434	14	8	6
Keizer	35,698	49	41	8
King City	2,418	5	5	0
Klamath Falls	19,676	45	39	6
La Grande	12,524	33	18	15
Lake Oswego	36,864	73	43	30
Lakeview	2,330	6	6	0
Lebanon	15,068	34	22	12
Lincoln City	8,018	34	25	9
Madras	5,433	12	10	2
Malin	630	2	1	1
Manzanita	630	3	3	0
McMinnville	31,470	43	33	10
Medford	73,019	146	96	50
Milton-Freewater	6,318	17	11	6
Milwaukie	20,684	42	38	4
Molalla	7,304	15	12	3
Monmouth	9,709	15	13	2
Mount Angel	3,468	8	6	2
Myrtle Creek	3,528	9	7	2
Myrtle Point	2,439	5	5	0
Newberg-Dundee	25,878	35	22	13
Newport	9,896	23	19	4
North Bend	9,690	25	17	8
North Plains	1,838	2	2	0
Nyssa	3,011	7	7	0
Oakridge	3,165	11	6	5
Ontario	11,092	29	22	7
Oregon City	31,683	43	35	8
Pendleton	16,490	24	21	3
Philomath	4,504	10	9	1
Phoenix	4,319	11	9	2
Pilot Rock	1,491	2	2	0
Portland	553,023	1,259	989	270
Prairie City	883	1	1	0
Prineville	10,307	28	18	10
Rainier	1,820	7	6	1
Redmond	25,092	46	34	12
Reedsport	4,274	18	11	7
Rockaway Beach	1,394	3	3	0
Rogue River	1,946	12	6	6
Roseburg	21,009	39	35	4
Salem	153,831	308	196	112
Sandy	9,127	15	12	3
Scappoose	6,377	12	11	1
Seaside	6,262	29	21	8
Shady Cove	2,296	6	4	2
Sherwood	18,023	24	21	3
Silverton	9,682	18	16	2
Springfield	57,081	110	70	40
Stanfield	1,939	4	4	0
Stayton	7,377	18	15	3
St. Helens	12,655	22	20	2
Sunriver		12	11	1
Sutherlin	7,266	17	15	2
Sweet Home	8,869	23	17	6
Talent	6,222	17	8	9

Table 78. Full-Time Law Enforcement Employees, by State and City, 2008—*Continued*

(Number.)

State/City	Population	Total law enforcement employees	Total officers	Total civilians
The Dalles	11,913	22	20	2
Tigard	50,536	80	64	16
Tillamook	4,502	13	10	3
Toledo	3,318	13	8	5
Troutdale	15,571	26	22	4
Tualatin	26,758	44	36	8
Turner	1,741	3	3	0
Umatilla	6,504	10	8	2
Vernonia	2,281	4	4	0
Warrenton	4,503	9	8	1
West Linn	25,299	37	31	6
Winston	4,776	8	7	1
Woodburn	22,365	41	32	9
Yamhill	868	3	3	0
PENNSYLVANIA				
Abington Township	53,937	120	93	27
Adams Township, Butler County	9,296	5	5	0
Adams Township, Cambria County	6,065	3	3	0
Akron	4,020	4	4	0
Albion	1,503	2	2	0
Alburtis	2,448	4	4	0
Aldan	4,245	5	5	0
Aliquippa	10,659	18	18	0
Allegheny Township, Blair County	6,903	5	4	1
Allegheny Township, Westmoreland County	8,182	9	8	1
Allentown	107,335	286	199	87
Altoona	46,236	59	51	8
Ambler	6,192	15	13	2
Ambridge	7,006	13	13	0
Amity Township	11,874	13	12	1
Annville Township	4,745	8	5	3
Apollo	1,628	1	1	0
Archbald	6,488	3	3	0
Arnold	5,210	12	11	1
Ashland	3,103	4	4	0
Ashley	2,672	2	2	0
Aspinwall	2,699	7	6	1
Aston Township	16,864	18	16	2
Athens	3,217	7	6	1
Athens Township	5,018	10	9	1
Auburn	800	1	1	0
Avalon	4,804	6	6	0
Avoca	2,666	2	2	0
Avonmore Boro	761	2	2	0
Baden	4,008	5	5	0
Baldwin Borough	18,430	26	24	2
Baldwin Township	2,034	5	5	0
Bally	1,100	2	2	0
Bangor	5,257	10	9	1
Barrett Township	4,293	7	7	0
Beaver	4,364	9	8	1
Beaver Falls	9,024	19	18	1
Bedminster Township	6,228	7	6	1
Bell Acres	1,372	4	4	0
Bellefonte	6,166	12	10	2
Bellevue	7,968	15	12	3
Bellwood	1,872	2	2	0
Ben Avon	1,744	13	11	2
Bensalem Township	58,400	205	102	103
Berks-Lehigh Regional	28,644	30	29	1
Berlin	2,085	1	1	0
Bern Township	7,180	13	13	0
Berwick	10,199	16	15	1
Bethel Park	31,477	44	38	6
Bethel Township, Berks County	4,539	2	2	0
Bethlehem	72,537	174	151	23
Bethlehem Township	23,807	34	32	2
Biglerville	1,150	2	2	0
Birdsboro	5,193	8	7	1
Birmingham Township	4,256	4	4	0
Blairsville	3,383	4	2	2
Blair Township	4,734	4	4	0
Blakely	6,765	3	3	0
Blawnox	1,436	4	4	0
Bloomsburg Town	12,601	21	15	6
Blossburg	1,447	2	2	0
Boyertown	3,941	8	7	1
Brackenridge	3,222	4	4	0
Braddock Hills	1,826	2	2	0
Bradford	8,368	22	22	0
Bradford Township	4,768	5	5	0
Brandywine Regional	10,069	15	14	1
Brecknock Township, Berks County	4,926	6	6	0
Brentwood	9,512	17	15	2
Briar Creek Township	3,069	8	8	0
Bridgeport	4,371	10	9	1
Bridgeville	4,868	10	9	1
Bridgewater	877	3	3	0
Brighton Township	7,903	6	6	0
Bristol	9,633	17	15	2
Bristol Township	53,748	89	77	12
Brockway	2,052	2	2	0
Brookhaven	7,832	9	8	1
Brookville	3,984	7	6	1
Brownsville	2,631	2	2	0
Buckingham Township	19,437	23	21	2
Buffalo Township	7,261	5	5	0
Burgettstown	1,474	1	1	0
Bushkill Township	8,179	13	11	2
Butler	13,921	24	23	1
Butler Township, Butler County	16,554	23	21	2
Butler Township, Luzerne County	9,278	10	9	1
Butler Township, Schuylkill County	6,142	4	4	0
Caernarvon Township	3,461	10	9	1
California	6,597	8	7	1
Caln Township	12,148	22	20	2
Cambria Township	6,327	4	4	0
Cambridge Springs	2,240	3	3	0
Camp Hill	7,384	6	5	1
Canonsburg	8,711	16	15	1
Canton	1,700	3	3	0
Carbondale	9,228	14	14	0
Carlisle	18,427	37	32	5
Carnegie	7,926	14	12	2
Carrolltown	959	1	1	0
Carroll Township, Washington County	5,455	2	2	0
Carroll Township, York County	5,811	11	11	0
Carroll Valley	3,542	5	4	1
Castle Shannon	8,016	13	12	1
Catasauqua	6,567	8	7	1
Catawissa	1,535	3	3	0
Cecil Township	10,367	17	16	1
Center Township	11,680	26	26	0
Centerville	3,200	2	2	0
Central Berks Regional	7,468	13	12	1
Chalfont	4,186	7	6	1
Chambersburg	17,947	35	32	3
Charleroi	5,694	8	6	2
Chartiers Township	7,381	11	11	0
Cheltenham Township	36,027	95	83	12
Chester	36,638	113	103	10
Chester Township	4,454	12	11	1
Cheswick	1,739	3	3	0
Chippewa Township	9,688	8	7	1
Churchill	3,246	10	10	0
Clairton	7,830	13	13	0
Clarion	5,226	9	8	1
Clarks Summit	6,530	6	5	1
Clay Township	5,849	4	4	0
Clearfield	6,170	7	7	0
Cleona	2,116	4	4	0
Clifford Township	2,462	1	1	0
Clifton Heights	6,551	10	9	1
Coaldale	2,122	4	4	0
Coal Township	10,259	13	12	1
Coatesville	11,689	36	29	7
Cochranton	1,066	1	1	0
Colebrookdale District	6,434	11	10	1

Table 78. Full-Time Law Enforcement Employees, by State and City, 2008—*Continued*

(Number.)

State/City	Population	Total law enforcement employees	Total officers	Total civilians
Collegeville	4,968	9	8	1
Collier Township	6,477	16	15	1
Collingdale	8,378	9	8	1
Colonial Regional	20,091	25	23	2
Columbia	10,023	22	19	3
Conemaugh Township, Cambria County	2,462	2	2	0
Conewago Township, Adams County	6,108	9	8	1
Conewango Township	3,550	4	4	0
Conneaut Lake Regional	3,510	4	3	1
Connellsville	8,475	16	15	1
Conoy Township	3,336	15	14	1
Conshohocken	8,639	21	19	2
Conyngham	1,839	2	2	0
Coopersburg	2,562	7	7	0
Coplay	3,371	4	4	0
Coraopolis	5,604	12	9	3
Cornwall	3,490	9	8	1
Corry	6,305	16	12	4
Coudersport	2,380	4	4	0
Covington Township	2,188	1	1	0
Cranberry Township	27,315	32	28	4
Crescent Township	2,823	3	3	0
Cresson	1,481	2	2	0
Cresson Township	4,264	3	2	1
Croyle Township	2,216	1	1	0
Cumberland Township, Adams County	6,318	9	9	0
Cumberland Township, Greene County	6,390	4	4	0
Cumru Township	17,542	28	25	3
Curwensville	2,460	2	2	0
Dale	1,359	2	2	0
Dallas	2,481	4	4	0
Dallas Township	8,691	7	7	0
Dalton	1,218	2	2	0
Danville	4,475	10	9	1
Darby Township	9,534	13	13	0
Decatur Township	3,043	1	1	0
Delmont	2,419	4	4	0
Derry	2,778	3	3	0
Derry Township, Dauphin County	22,050	46	39	7
Dickson City	5,907	5	5	0
Donegal Township	2,625	2	2	0
Donora	5,245	6	6	0
Dormont	8,406	16	15	1
Douglass Township, Berks County	3,526	3	3	0
Downingtown	7,889	19	16	3
Doylestown	8,142	21	16	5
Doylestown Township	18,752	24	22	2
Dublin Borough	2,142	2	2	0
Du Bois	7,653	13	13	0
Duboistown	1,188	1	1	0
Duncannon	1,502	2	2	0
Duncansville	1,169	2	2	0
Dunmore	13,909	21	21	0
Dupont	2,582	8	8	0
Duquesne	6,663	17	16	1
Duryea	4,344	1	1	0
East Bangor	1,090	1	1	0
East Berlin	1,430	1	1	0
East Buffalo Township	5,945	8	8	0
East Cocalico Township	10,484	23	21	2
East Conemaugh	1,163	2	2	0
East Coventry Township	6,795	8	7	1
East Deer Township	1,321	1	1	0
East Earl Township	6,543	7	7	0
Eastern Adams Regional	9,915	12	10	2
Eastern Pike Regional	5,495	9	8	1
East Fallowfield Township	7,458	8	7	1
East Franklin Township	3,944	4	2	2
East Hempfield Township	23,515	36	32	4
East Lampeter Township	14,968	44	40	4
East Lansdowne	2,476	5	3	2
East McKeesport	2,796	2	2	0
East Norriton Township	13,575	31	28	3
Easton	26,072	64	58	6

State/City	Population	Total law enforcement employees	Total officers	Total civilians
East Pennsboro Township	19,890	20	19	1
East Pikeland Township	6,804	8	7	1
East Pittsburgh	1,835	1	1	0
Easttown Township	10,536	15	14	1
East Vincent Township	6,454	8	8	0
East Washington	1,855	1	1	0
East Whiteland Township	10,684	21	19	2
Ebensburg	2,950	3	3	0
Economy	9,084	12	11	1
Eddystone	2,344	10	9	1
Edgewood	3,011	12	10	2
Edgeworth	1,589	6	4	2
Edinboro	6,562	8	8	0
Edwardsville	4,669	4	4	0
Elizabeth	1,457	2	2	0
Elizabethtown	12,110	18	16	2
Elizabeth Township	12,820	14	13	1
Elkland	1,659	2	2	0
Ellwood City	7,972	12	11	1
Emlenton Borough	734	2	2	0
Emmaus	11,359	21	19	2
Emporium	2,216	2	2	0
Emsworth	2,373	13	11	2
Ephrata	13,059	33	29	4
Erie	103,881	182	161	21
Etna	3,556	8	7	1
Everett	1,846	4	4	0
Exeter	5,930	5	4	1
Exeter Township, Berks County	26,988	34	32	2
Exeter Township, Luzerne County	2,532	1	1	0
Fairview Township, Luzerne County	4,298	5	5	0
Fairview Township, York County	16,897	18	16	2
Fallowfield Township	4,188	1	1	0
Falls Township, Bucks County	33,696	59	52	7
Fawn Township	2,305	7	3	4
Ferguson Township	16,590	23	20	3
Ferndale	1,653	1	1	0
Findlay Township	5,034	23	16	7
Fleetwood	4,014	6	6	0
Folcroft	6,837	10	10	0
Ford City	3,157	3	3	0
Forest City	1,732	2	2	0
Forest Hills	6,231	12	11	1
Forks Township	14,603	24	23	1
Forty Fort	4,250	2	2	0
Forward Township	3,482	5	5	0
Foster Township	4,223	4	4	0
Fountain Hill	4,578	10	9	1
Fox Chapel	5,130	12	12	0
Frackville	4,127	5	5	0
Franconia Township	12,624	17	15	2
Franklin Park	12,109	13	12	1
Franklin Township, Beaver County	4,290	1	1	0
Franklin Township, Carbon County	4,914	4	4	0
Frazer Township	1,198	3	3	0
Freedom	1,592	1	1	0
Freedom Township	3,168	2	2	0
Freeland	3,390	2	2	0
Freemansburg	2,056	3	3	0
Freeport	1,805	2	2	0
Galeton	1,214	2	2	0
Gallitzin	1,874	4	4	0
Geistown	2,354	1	1	0
Gettysburg	8,097	15	11	4
Gilberton	824	2	1	1
Gilpin Township	2,514	1	1	0
Girard	2,924	4	4	0
Glassport	4,542	6	6	0
Glenolden	7,213	10	9	1
Granville Township	4,925	9	7	2
Greencastle	4,100	6	5	1
Greenfield Township, Blair County	3,742	3	3	0
Greensburg	15,283	38	28	10
Green Tree	4,326	12	11	1

Table 78. Full-Time Law Enforcement Employees, by State and City, 2008—*Continued*

(Number.)

State/City	Population	Total law enforcement employees	Total officers	Total civilians
Greenville	6,094	10	9	1
Greenwood Township	2,068	1	1	0
Grove City	7,742	11	10	1
Hamburg	4,178	6	5	1
Hampden Township	27,012	25	24	1
Hampton Township	17,210	20	17	3
Hanover	14,972	22	20	2
Hanover Township, Luzerne County	11,008	15	15	0
Hanover Township, Washington County	2,708	9	3	6
Harmar Township	3,017	7	7	0
Harmony Township	3,050	5	5	0
Harrisburg	47,118	230	179	51
Harrison Township	9,963	21	18	3
Harveys Lake	2,936	8	4	4
Hastings	1,289	1	1	0
Hatboro	7,123	17	14	3
Hatfield Township	19,990	31	26	5
Haverford Township	48,044	81	69	12
Hazleton	21,788	34	31	3
Hegins Township	3,371	2	2	0
Heidelberg	1,145	3	3	0
Heidelberg Township, Berks County	1,764	1	1	0
Heidelberg Township, Lebanon County	4,148	2	2	0
Hellam Township	9,082	8	8	0
Hellertown	5,658	11	10	1
Hemlock Township	2,242	6	6	0
Hempfield Township	3,855	7	6	1
Hermitage	16,315	32	29	3
Highspire	2,604	7	6	1
Hilltown Township	13,494	20	17	3
Hollidaysburg	5,530	11	8	3
Homer City	1,714	2	2	0
Homestead	3,501	13	12	1
Honesdale	4,706	9	9	0
Honey Brook	1,516	1	1	0
Hooversville	711	1	1	0
Hopewell Township	12,303	16	15	1
Horsham Township	24,734	49	40	9
Hughesville	2,041	1	1	0
Hummelstown	4,431	7	7	0
Huntingdon	6,799	13	12	1
Independence Township, Beaver County	2,681	3	3	0
Indiana	14,823	29	22	7
Indiana Township	7,026	9	9	0
Industry	1,790	2	2	0
Ingram	3,366	4	4	0
Irwin	4,046	4	4	0
Ivyland	842	2	2	0
Jackson Township, Butler County	3,724	10	8	2
Jackson Township, Cambria County	4,713	2	2	0
Jackson Township, Luzerne County	4,765	4	4	0
Jamestown	576	1	1	0
Jeannette	9,863	17	14	3
Jefferson Hills Borough	9,644	17	16	1
Jefferson Township, Mercer County	2,308	1	1	0
Jenkins Township	4,903	2	2	0
Jenkintown	4,296	13	11	2
Jermyn	2,222	1	1	0
Jersey Shore	4,290	7	6	1
Jessup	4,568	2	2	0
Jim Thorpe	4,889	7	6	1
Johnsonburg	2,687	2	2	0
Johnstown	23,172	51	45	6
Kane	3,762	5	5	0
Kennedy Township	9,765	15	11	4
Kennett Square	5,276	15	12	3
Kidder Township	1,424	10	10	0
Kilbuck Township	658	14	11	3
Kingston	12,968	25	19	6
Kingston Township	7,087	11	11	0
Kiskiminetas Township	4,755	1	1	0
Kittanning	4,342	9	8	1
Knox	1,097	2	2	0
Koppel	772	1	1	0
Kulpmont	2,744	1	1	0
Kutztown	5,091	12	10	2
Laceyville	368	1	1	0
Laflin Borough	1,493	3	3	0
Lake City	2,883	3	3	0
Lancaster	54,595	192	161	31
Lancaster Township, Butler County	2,568	2	2	0
Lansdale	15,515	26	20	6
Lansdowne	10,660	19	16	3
Lansford	4,161	42	40	2
Larksville	4,446	4	4	0
Latimore Township	2,841	3	3	0
Laureldale	3,770	5	5	0
Lawrence Township, Clearfield County	7,476	10	9	1
Lebanon	24,212	54	47	7
Leechburg	2,203	2	2	0
Leetsdale	1,114	4	4	0
Leet Township	1,496	5	5	0
Lehighton	5,463	10	9	1
Lehigh Township, Northampton County	10,847	13	12	1
Lehman Township	3,322	2	2	0
Lewisburg	5,515	10	8	2
Liberty	2,432	1	1	0
Liberty Township, Adams County	1,284	1	1	0
Ligonier	1,608	3	3	0
Ligonier Township	6,754	3	3	0
Limerick Township	16,941	17	16	1
Lincoln	1,120	1	1	0
Linesville	1,093	1	1	0
Lititz	9,054	16	13	3
Littlestown	4,128	7	7	0
Locust Township	2,524	3	3	0
Logan Township	11,859	18	16	2
Lower Allen Township	17,862	23	21	2
Lower Burrell	12,098	16	16	0
Lower Frederick Township	4,817	3	3	0
Lower Gwynedd Township	11,375	19	18	1
Lower Heidelberg Township	5,369	8	8	0
Lower Makefield Township	32,212	42	38	4
Lower Merion Township	57,367	155	136	19
Lower Milford Township	3,901	1	1	0
Lower Moreland Township	12,609	26	21	5
Lower Paxton Township	45,354	67	60	7
Lower Pottsgrove Township	12,210	18	16	2
Lower Providence Township	26,430	38	33	5
Lower Salford Township	14,520	21	19	2
Lower Saucon Township	11,343	16	14	2
Lower Southampton Township	19,084	33	30	3
Lower Swatara Township	8,514	11	10	1
Lower Windsor Township	7,836	11	10	1
Luzerne Township	6,637	1	1	0
Lykens	1,850	2	2	0
Macungie	3,123	5	5	0
Mahanoy City	4,380	4	4	0
Mahanoy Township	3,727	1	1	0
Mahoning Township, Carbon County	4,405	5	5	0
Mahoning Township, Montour County	4,283	7	6	1
Malvern	3,104	5	4	1
Manheim	4,635	9	8	1
Manheim Township	36,306	69	54	15
Manor	2,901	3	3	0
Manor Township, Lancaster County	19,128	22	20	2
Mansfield	3,192	5	5	0
Marietta	2,591	15	14	1
Marion Township, Beaver County	880	1	1	0
Marion Township, Berks County	1,745	2	2	0
Marlborough Township	3,263	4	4	0
Marple Township	23,452	38	33	5
Martinsburg	2,120	2	2	0
Marysville	2,436	1	1	0
Masontown	3,395	5	5	0
Mayfield	1,699	1	1	0
McAdoo	2,090	2	2	0
McCandless	27,235	29	27	2

Table 78. Full-Time Law Enforcement Employees, by State and City, 2008—*Continued*

(Number.)

State/City	Population	Total law enforcement employees	Total officers	Total civilians
McDonald Borough	2,110	2	2	0
McKeesport	22,076	54	51	3
McKees Rocks	6,011	10	9	1
McSherrystown	2,800	5	5	0
Meadville	13,208	25	22	3
Mechanicsburg	8,772	17	16	1
Media	5,407	24	16	8
Mercer	2,211	4	4	0
Mercersburg	1,604	2	2	0
Meshoppen	427	1	1	0
Meyersdale	2,281	3	2	1
Middleburg	1,333	3	2	1
Middlesex Township, Butler County	5,469	3	3	0
Middlesex Township, Cumberland County	6,832	10	9	1
Middletown	8,823	16	15	1
Middletown Township	46,788	61	54	7
Midland	2,841	5	4	1
Mifflin	607	1	1	0
Mifflinburg	3,520	10	9	1
Mifflin County Regional	26,321	27	25	2
Milford	2,861	2	2	0
Millcreek Township, Erie County	51,622	75	59	16
Millcreek Township, Lebanon County	3,174	3	3	0
Millersburg	2,462	5	4	1
Millersville	7,196	14	12	2
Millvale	3,650	4	4	0
Millville	943	1	1	0
Milton	6,331	10	9	1
Minersville	4,223	5	5	0
Mohnton	3,093	5	5	0
Monaca	5,737	8	8	0
Monessen	8,015	12	12	0
Monongahela	4,405	10	8	2
Monroeville	27,531	56	52	4
Montgomery	5,067	3	3	0
Montgomery Township	24,166	45	36	9
Montrose	1,536	1	1	0
Moon Township	22,677	36	30	6
Moore Township	9,458	8	7	1
Moosic	5,777	10	10	0
Morris-Cooper Regional	5,631	1	1	0
Morrisville	9,604	12	11	1
Morton	2,631	5	4	1
Moscow	1,958	3	3	0
Mount Carmel	5,859	9	9	0
Mount Carmel Township	2,566	5	5	0
Mount Holly Springs	1,914	2	2	0
Mount Joy	7,306	15	13	2
Mount Lebanon	30,326	55	44	11
Mount Oliver	3,647	9	9	0
Mount Pleasant	4,382	3	3	0
Mount Pleasant Township	3,632	1	1	0
Mount Union	2,339	4	4	0
Muhlenberg Township	18,589	30	28	2
Muncy	2,461	3	3	0
Munhall	11,185	26	22	4
Murrysville	19,511	26	21	5
Myerstown	3,114	3	3	0
Nanticoke	10,205	14	13	1
Narberth	4,039	5	5	0
Neshannock Township	9,341	8	7	1
Nether Providence Township	13,160	16	15	1
Neville Township	1,121	13	11	2
Newberry Township	15,531	18	16	2
New Bethlehem	980	2	2	0
New Brighton	9,320	9	9	0
New Britain	2,270	6	5	1
New Britain Township	11,003	14	12	2
New Castle	24,232	37	35	2
New Castle Township	395	1	1	0
New Cumberland	7,073	9	8	1
New Garden Township	11,857	12	10	2
New Hanover Township	9,285	11	10	1
New Holland	5,152	13	12	1
New Hope	2,272	11	9	2
New Kensington	13,594	28	23	5
Newport	1,469	2	2	0
Newport Township	4,770	1	1	0
New Sewickley Township	7,586	9	8	1
Newton Township	2,787	1	1	0
Newtown	2,371	5	5	0
Newtown Township, Bucks County	18,966	32	28	4
Newtown Township, Delaware County	11,817	18	16	2
Newville	1,311	2	2	0
New Wilmington	2,378	4	4	0
Norristown	31,195	79	69	10
Northampton	9,890	13	11	2
Northampton Township	40,879	49	43	6
North Belle Vernon	1,951	3	2	1
North Braddock	5,811	4	4	0
North Catasauqua	2,839	5	5	0
North Charleroi	1,307	1	1	0
North Cornwall Township	6,558	10	9	1
North Coventry Township	7,702	13	12	1
North East, Erie County	4,186	7	6	1
Northeastern Regional	11,118	12	10	2
Northern Berks Regional	12,425	15	14	1
Northern Cambria Borough	3,922	5	5	0
Northern Regional	27,783	30	28	2
Northern York Regional	65,214	50	46	4
North Fayette Township	13,054	24	20	4
North Franklin Township	4,639	6	6	0
North Huntingdon Township	29,381	36	29	7
North Lebanon Township	10,939	12	10	2
North Londonderry Township	6,976	9	8	1
North Middleton Township	11,252	10	9	1
North Sewickley Township	5,620	1	1	0
North Strabane Township	12,288	20	19	1
Northumberland	3,495	5	5	0
North Versailles Township	12,200	22	18	4
North Wales	3,229	5	4	1
Northwest Lancaster County Regional	17,962	16	15	1
Northwest Lawrence County Regional	6,687	2	2	0
Norwood	5,782	7	7	0
Oakmont	6,413	7	7	0
O'Hara Township	9,536	16	15	1
Ohio Township	4,116	5	5	0
Ohioville	3,611	2	2	0
Oil City	10,608	23	18	5
Old Forge	8,521	4	4	0
Old Lycoming Township	5,273	9	8	1
Oley Township	3,655	6	6	0
Olyphant	4,944	5	5	0
Orangeville Area	1,635	1	1	0
Orwigsburg	2,972	4	4	0
Oxford	4,662	12	11	1
Paint Township	3,153	5	4	1
Palmerton	5,244	9	8	1
Palmer Township	20,311	34	31	3
Palmyra	6,981	10	9	1
Parkesburg	3,439	11	10	1
Patterson Area	3,566	4	4	0
Patton	1,845	2	2	0
Patton Township	13,258	19	17	2
Paxtang	1,486	3	3	0
Pen Argyl	3,643	5	5	0
Penbrook	2,915	6	6	0
Penn Hills	43,835	58	53	5
Pennridge Regional	10,479	15	13	2
Penn Township, Butler County	5,150	4	3	1
Penn Township, Lancaster County	8,495	12	11	1
Penn Township, Westmoreland County	20,221	21	19	2
Penn Township, York County	15,931	22	20	2
Pequea Township	4,533	8	8	0
Perkasie	8,633	22	18	4
Perryopolis	1,718	2	2	0
Peters Township	20,244	23	21	2
Philadelphia	1,441,117	7,623	6,764	859

Table 78. Full-Time Law Enforcement Employees, by State and City, 2008—*Continued*

(Number.)

State/City	Population	Total law enforcement employees	Total officers	Total civilians
Phoenixville	16,410	28	27	1
Pine Grove	2,045	1	1	0
Pitcairn	3,338	2	2	0
Pittsburgh	309,757	912	850	62
Pittston	7,556	10	10	0
Plainfield Township	6,152	13	12	1
Plains Township	10,452	17	16	1
Pleasant Hills	7,734	19	17	2
Plum	26,108	30	24	6
Plumstead Township	11,825	16	14	2
Plymouth	6,055	4	4	0
Plymouth Township, Montgomery County	16,323	52	45	7
Pocono Mountain Regional	35,481	42	37	5
Pocono Township	11,214	18	18	0
Point Marion	1,247	1	1	0
Point Township	3,828	5	5	0
Polk	995	2	2	0
Portage	2,582	2	2	0
Port Allegany	2,188	3	3	0
Port Carbon	1,749	2	2	0
Port Vue	3,838	4	4	0
Pottstown	21,285	60	46	14
Pottsville	14,416	28	28	0
Prospect Park	6,386	9	9	0
Punxsutawney	5,937	11	8	3
Pymatuning Township	3,559	4	4	0
Quakertown	8,656	23	15	8
Quarryville	2,166	4	4	0
Raccoon Township	3,211	4	4	0
Radnor Township	31,231	57	47	10
Ralpho Township	3,884	6	6	0
Rankin	2,105	1	1	0
Reading	80,860	227	199	28
Redstone Township	6,051	1	1	0
Reserve Township	3,525	6	6	0
Reynoldsville	2,546	2	2	0
Rice Township	2,919	5	5	0
Richland Township, Bucks County	12,700	13	11	2
Richland Township, Cambria County	12,342	20	19	1
Ridgway	4,104	4	4	0
Ridley Park	6,993	10	10	0
Ridley Township	29,895	37	32	5
Riverside	1,821	3	3	0
Roaring Brook Township	1,809	2	2	0
Roaring Spring	2,257	2	2	0
Robesonia	2,058	2	2	0
Robeson Township	7,640	7	6	1
Robinson Township, Allegheny County	13,373	26	21	5
Robinson Township, Washington County	2,117	2	2	0
Rochester	3,644	11	9	2
Rochester Township	2,862	4	4	0
Rockledge	2,478	5	5	0
Roseto	1,643	2	2	0
Rosslyn Farms	424	2	2	0
Ross Township	30,448	43	43	0
Rostraver Township	11,625	15	14	1
Royalton	943	1	1	0
Royersford	4,356	8	7	1
Rush Township	3,724	3	3	0
Rye Township	2,534	1	1	0
Sadsbury Township, Chester County	3,385	2	2	0
Salem Township, Luzerne County	4,114	3	3	0
Salisbury Township	14,057	18	16	2
Sandy Lake	692	1	1	0
Sandy Township	11,550	10	9	1
Saxton	755	1	1	0
Sayre	5,457	14	14	0
Schuylkill Haven	5,164	8	8	0
Schuylkill Township, Chester County	7,733	13	11	2
Scottdale	4,410	7	7	0
Scott Township, Allegheny County	15,850	20	19	1
Scott Township, Columbia County	5,033	11	11	0
Scott Township, Lackawanna County	4,928	5	5	0
Scranton	72,247	170	150	20

State/City	Population	Total law enforcement employees	Total officers	Total civilians
Selinsgrove	5,283	7	6	1
Seven Springs	117	7	6	1
Seward	453	1	1	0
Sewickley	4,077	13	12	1
Sewickley Heights	916	5	3	2
Shaler Township	27,911	28	27	1
Shamokin	7,326	14	14	0
Shamokin Dam	1,438	3	3	0
Sharon	14,853	29	27	2
Sharon Hill	5,317	8	7	1
Sharpsburg	3,258	6	6	0
Sharpsville	4,095	6	5	1
Sheffield Township	2,203	2	2	0
Shenandoah	5,157	8	7	1
Shenango Township, Lawrence County	7,640	6	6	0
Shillington	5,022	8	8	0
Shippensburg	5,611	12	10	2
Shippingport	219	2	2	0
Shiremanstown	1,469	2	2	0
Shohola Township	2,426	1	1	0
Silver Lake Township	1,732	2	2	0
Silver Spring Township	13,110	15	14	1
Sinking Spring	3,603	6	6	0
Slatington	4,405	7	7	0
Slippery Rock	3,320	4	4	0
Smethport	1,561	2	2	0
Smith Township	4,467	1	1	0
Solebury Township	8,795	15	13	2
Somerset	6,366	7	6	1
Souderton	6,553	6	6	0
South Abington Township	9,528	12	10	2
South Annville Township	3,193	2	2	0
South Beaver Township	2,819	4	4	0
South Buffalo Township	2,794	2	2	0
South Centre Township	1,909	4	4	0
South Coatesville	1,078	1	1	0
South Connellsville Borough	2,153	2	2	0
Southern Regional York County	10,007	12	11	1
South Fayette Township	13,213	18	17	1
South Fork	1,025	2	2	0
South Greensburg	2,219	2	2	0
South Heidelberg Township	7,264	7	7	0
South Lebanon Township	8,637	8	7	1
South Londonderry Township	7,336	6	6	0
South Park Township	13,811	18	17	1
South Pymatuning Township	2,801	2	2	0
South Strabane Township	8,767	15	14	1
South Waverly	963	3	3	0
Southwestern Regional	18,269	14	13	1
Southwest Greensburg	2,200	2	2	0
Southwest Mercer County Regional	11,149	21	20	1
Southwest Regional	2,159	3	2	1
South Whitehall Township	19,679	40	37	3
South Williamsport	6,008	9	8	1
Spring City	3,407	4	3	1
Springdale	3,482	2	2	0
Springdale Township	1,647	3	3	0
Springettsbury Township	24,957	35	32	3
Springfield Township, Bucks County	5,084	2	2	0
Springfield Township, Delaware County	22,809	40	34	6
Springfield Township, Montgomery County	18,843	30	29	1
Spring Garden Township	12,146	20	18	2
Spring Township, Berks County	26,765	30	28	2
Spring Township, Centre County	6,866	7	6	1
State College	54,065	78	65	13
St. Clair Boro	2,989	6	6	0
Steelton	5,590	9	8	1
Stewartstown	2,004	6	5	1
St. Marys City	13,432	16	15	1
Stoneboro	1,013	1	1	0
Stonycreek Township	2,903	2	2	0
Stowe Township	6,090	8	7	1
Strasburg	2,747	4	4	0
Stroud Area Regional	34,393	59	54	5

Table 78. Full-Time Law Enforcement Employees, by State and City, 2008—*Continued*

(Number.)

State/City	Population	Total law enforcement employees	Total officers	Total civilians
Sugarcreek	4,968	5	5	0
Sugarloaf Township, Luzerne County	4,053	6	6	0
Summerhill Township	2,576	2	2	0
Summit Hill	2,978	6	4	2
Summit Township	2,251	2	2	0
Sunbury	9,768	14	12	2
Susquehanna Regional	6,711	15	14	1
Susquehanna Township, Dauphin County	22,920	42	40	2
Swarthmore	6,074	9	9	0
Swatara Township	22,413	42	40	2
Sweden Township	710	2	2	0
Swissvale	8,751	14	14	0
Swoyersville	7,605	7	7	0
Sykesville	1,167	2	2	0
Tamaqua	6,583	10	9	1
Tarentum	4,526	8	7	1
Tatamy	1,101	1	1	0
Taylor	6,167	7	7	0
Telford	4,617	7	6	1
Throop	4,056	4	4	0
Tidioute	717	1	1	0
Tilden Township	3,831	2	2	0
Tinicum Township, Bucks County	4,224	5	5	0
Tinicum Township, Delaware County	4,201	17	15	2
Titusville	5,751	13	13	0
Towamencin Township	17,601	36	24	12
Towanda	2,833	6	6	0
Trafford	3,008	2	2	0
Trainer	1,833	6	6	0
Tredyffrin Township	28,963	50	50	0
Troy	1,464	3	3	0
Tullytown	1,961	7	6	1
Tulpehocken Township	3,564	3	2	1
Tunkhannock	1,772	4	4	0
Tunkhannock Township, Wyoming County	4,285	4	4	0
Turtle Creek	5,544	6	6	0
Union City	3,294	3	3	0
Uniontown	11,670	18	18	0
Union Township, Lawrence County	5,025	3	3	0
Upland	2,868	2	2	0
Upper Burrell Township	2,128	2	2	0
Upper Chichester Township	17,705	25	23	2
Upper Darby Township	78,550	145	126	19
Upper Dublin Township	25,860	47	40	7
Upper Gwynedd Township	15,978	25	22	3
Upper Makefield Township	8,509	19	18	1
Upper Merion Township	26,457	85	64	21
Upper Moreland Township	24,166	50	39	11
Upper Nazareth Township	5,877	4	3	1
Upper Perkiomen	6,350	10	9	1
Upper Pottsgrove Township	5,201	9	8	1
Upper Providence Township, Delaware County	11,078	14	13	1
Upper Providence Township, Montgomery County	19,516	24	22	2
Upper Saucon Township	14,888	21	20	1
Upper Southampton Township	15,249	25	22	3
Upper St. Clair Township	18,812	35	28	7
Upper Uwchlan Township	11,351	10	10	0
Upper Yoder Township	5,494	13	13	0
Uwchlan Township	18,715	24	22	2
Valley Township	6,609	4	4	0
Vandergrift	4,998	8	8	0
Vernon Township	5,415	5	4	1
Verona	2,837	5	4	1
Walker Township	980	1	1	0
Walnutport	2,214	4	4	0
Warminster Township	33,702	58	52	6
Warren	9,378	20	16	4
Warrington Township	23,162	34	31	3
Warwick Township, Bucks County	14,715	22	20	2
Warwick Township, Lancaster County	17,221	18	16	2
Washington, Washington County	14,586	33	31	2
Washington Township, Fayette County	4,158	3	3	0
Washington Township, Northampton County	4,897	4	4	0

State/City	Population	Total law enforcement employees	Total officers	Total civilians
Washington Township, Westmoreland County	7,360	7	7	0
Watsontown	2,090	5	5	0
Waynesboro	9,934	21	19	2
Waynesburg	4,169	9	8	1
Weatherly	2,604	3	3	0
Weissport	428	1	1	0
Wellsboro	3,228	6	6	0
Wernersville	2,501	2	2	0
Wesleyville	3,301	11	10	1
West Brandywine Township	7,756	8	7	1
West Caln Township	8,430	2	2	0
West Chester	18,273	60	47	13
West Conshohocken	1,515	10	9	1
West Deer Township	11,949	12	11	1
West Earl Township	7,724	6	6	0
West Fallowfield Township	2,596	1	1	0
Westfield	1,115	2	2	0
West Goshen Township	21,168	31	27	4
West Grove Borough	2,771	2	2	0
West Hazleton	3,313	2	1	1
West Hempfield Township	16,059	21	19	2
West Hills Regional	10,667	12	11	1
West Homestead	1,994	8	7	1
West Lampeter Township	15,609	16	15	1
West Manchester Township	18,433	29	26	3
West Manheim Township	7,477	7	7	0
West Mead Township	5,075	2	2	0
West Mifflin	20,648	44	38	6
West Norriton Township	14,533	32	28	4
West Penn Township	4,350	3	3	0
West Pikeland Township	4,069	4	4	0
West Pike Run	1,834	1	1	0
West Pittston	4,913	4	4	0
West Pottsgrove Township	3,777	10	9	1
West Reading	4,050	17	15	2
West Sadsbury Township	2,501	4	3	1
West Salem Township	3,334	10	9	1
West Shore Regional	6,621	11	9	2
Westtown-East Goshen Regional	31,632	34	32	2
West View	6,669	12	8	4
West Vincent Township	4,251	4	4	0
West Whiteland Township	18,190	30	28	2
West Wyoming	2,689	2	2	0
West York	4,210	9	9	0
Whitehall	13,379	25	20	5
Whitehall Township	27,037	59	52	7
White Haven Borough	1,144	2	2	0
Whitemarsh Township	17,634	40	33	7
White Oak	7,995	12	11	1
White Township	1,309	4	4	0
Whitpain Township	18,800	40	32	8
Wiconisco Township	1,106	1	1	0
Wilkes-Barre	40,976	96	87	9
Wilkinsburg	17,504	27	24	3
Wilkins Township	6,298	12	12	0
Williamsburg	1,251	2	2	0
Williamsport	29,380	57	53	4
Willistown Township	10,755	19	17	2
Wilson	7,647	9	8	1
Windber	4,025	3	2	1
Wrightsville	2,260	4	3	1
Wyoming	3,003	5	5	0
Wyomissing	10,448	29	23	6
Yeadon	11,385	16	14	2
York	40,221	116	101	15
York Area Regional	58,148	55	50	5
Youngsville	1,666	2	2	0
Zelienople	3,926	10	9	1
RHODE ISLAND				
Barrington	16,272	30	23	7
Bristol	22,387	47	37	10
Burrillville	16,465	34	26	8
Central Falls	18,667	53	43	10
Charlestown	8,087	25	20	5

Table 78. Full-Time Law Enforcement Employees, by State and City, 2008—*Continued*

(Number.)

State/City	Population	Total law enforcement employees	Total officers	Total civilians
Coventry	34,342	74	60	14
Cranston	79,987	177	144	33
Cumberland	34,359	59	48	11
East Greenwich	13,294	42	34	8
East Providence	48,413	117	98	19
Foster	4,505	12	8	4
Glocester	10,528	19	14	5
Hopkinton	7,961	20	15	5
Jamestown	5,458	21	15	6
Johnston	28,515	92	75	17
Lincoln	22,075	42	35	7
Little Compton	3,500	15	11	4
Middletown	16,004	35	31	4
Narragansett	16,399	55	41	14
Newport	25,030	107	85	22
New Shoreham	1,014	9	5	4
North Kingstown	26,547	60	49	11
North Providence	32,689	91	71	20
North Smithfield	11,292	24	21	3
Pawtucket	71,712	195	154	41
Portsmouth	16,879	36	34	2
Providence	170,965	581	484	97
Richmond	7,652	18	13	5
Scituate	10,853	21	14	7
Smithfield	21,198	53	40	13
South Kingstown	29,218	74	55	19
Tiverton	14,935	38	27	11
Warren	10,965	28	22	6
Warwick	84,326	227	176	51
Westerly	23,276	64	51	13
West Greenwich	6,527	18	11	7
West Warwick	29,029	70	57	13
Woonsocket	43,301	116	99	17
SOUTH CAROLINA				
Abbeville	5,529	24	20	4
Aiken	29,630	110	86	24
Allendale	3,664	13	11	2
Anderson	26,498	121	93	28
Andrews	2,940	9	8	1
Atlantic Beach	395	5	5	0
Aynor	588	9	7	2
Bamberg	3,432	12	10	2
Barnwell	4,785	18	16	2
Batesburg-Leesville	5,545	25	20	5
Beaufort	11,772	51	46	5
Belton	4,639	14	13	1
Bennettsville	8,854	37	34	3
Bethune	369	1	1	0
Bishopville	3,918	17	15	2
Blacksburg	1,900	12	11	1
Blackville	2,841	9	7	2
Bluffton	4,386	38	35	3
Bonneau	348	3	3	0
Bowman	1,144	1	1	0
Branchville	1,034	3	2	1
Brunson	573	3	3	0
Burnettown	2,658	2	2	0
Calhoun Falls	2,178	8	8	0
Camden	7,073	30	26	4
Cameron	411	1	1	0
Campobello	596	11	10	1
Cayce	12,605	74	61	13
Central	4,147	11	10	1
Chapin	704	8	6	2
Charleston	111,645	514	381	133
Cheraw	5,397	29	23	6
Chesnee	1,069	5	5	0
Chester	5,988	27	27	0
Chesterfield	1,308	5	4	1
Clemson	12,941	34	25	9
Clinton	8,930	35	30	5
Clio	727	3	3	0
Clover	4,772	20	16	4
Columbia	125,485	364	327	37

State/City	Population	Total law enforcement employees	Total officers	Total civilians
Conway	15,306	61	46	15
Cottageville	680	6	4	2
Coward	676	2	2	0
Cowpens	2,391	6	6	0
Darlington	6,598	29	26	3
Denmark	3,002	12	10	2
Dillon	6,333	28	24	4
Due West	1,269	6	6	0
Duncan	3,058	14	14	0
Easley	20,286	55	43	12
Edgefield	4,412	8	8	0
Edisto Beach	722	7	7	0
Ehrhardt	552	7	6	1
Elgin	1,114	8	8	0
Elloree	696	3	3	0
Estill	2,332	9	4	5
Eutawville	328	4	3	1
Fairfax	3,094	8	7	1
Florence	31,508	122	96	26
Folly Beach	2,359	18	11	7
Forest Acres	9,889	35	28	7
Fort Lawn	803	4	4	0
Fort Mill	9,612	38	31	7
Fountain Inn	7,560	32	25	7
Gaffney	12,942	42	38	4
Georgetown	8,470	44	33	11
Goose Creek	37,227	82	60	22
Great Falls	2,023	5	4	1
Greeleyville	397	2	2	0
Greenville	59,038	225	178	47
Greenwood	22,399	57	49	8
Greer	24,220	73	56	17
Hampton	2,766	11	11	0
Hanahan	15,950	39	31	8
Hardeeville	1,947	19	17	2
Harleyville	687	7	7	0
Hartsville	7,419	35	32	3
Hemingway	499	5	5	0
Holly Hill	1,344	7	7	0
Honea Path	3,649	13	13	0
Inman	1,963	8	8	0
Irmo	11,584	23	21	2
Isle of Palms	4,686	28	18	10
Iva	1,193	7	5	2
Jackson	1,642	4	4	0
Jamestown	100	3	2	1
Johnsonville	1,452	5	4	1
Johnston	2,331	8	8	0
Jonesville	893	4	4	0
Kingstree	3,243	22	20	2
Lake City	6,689	27	19	8
Lake View	784	4	4	0
Lamar	987	4	4	0
Lancaster	9,913	46	35	11
Landrum	2,583	10	9	1
Lane	517	2	2	0
Latta	1,483	11	10	1
Laurens	9,706	34	29	5
Lexington	15,673	45	41	4
Liberty	3,057	17	11	6
Lincolnville	837	1	1	0
Loris	2,330	14	10	4
Lyman	2,842	8	7	1
Lynchburg	555	3	3	0
Manning	3,937	20	19	1
Marion	6,782	27	24	3
Mauldin	20,891	53	43	10
Mayesville	1,009	2	2	0
McBee	704	2	1	1
McColl	2,327	6	6	0
McCormick	2,677	7	7	0
Moncks Corner	6,996	29	26	3
Mount Pleasant	67,027	170	133	37
Mullins	4,689	22	21	1

Table 78. Full-Time Law Enforcement Employees, by State and City, 2008—*Continued*

(Number.)

State/City	Population	Total law enforcement employees	Total officers	Total civilians
Myrtle Beach	30,850	243	184	59
Newberry	10,942	33	30	3
New Ellenton	2,231	7	7	0
Nichols	394	3	3	0
Ninety Six	1,916	5	5	0
North	775	3	3	0
North Augusta	20,616	68	51	17
North Charleston	92,749	404	310	94
North Myrtle Beach	16,073	110	78	32
Orangeburg	12,755	95	68	27
Pacolet	2,790	6	6	0
Pageland	2,509	15	11	4
Pamplico	1,153	4	4	0
Pawleys Island	141	6	5	1
Pelion	597	3	3	0
Pickens	3,006	14	13	1
Pine Ridge	1,775	3	2	1
Port Royal	10,331	21	20	1
Prosperity	1,060	4	4	0
Ridgeland	2,632	16	15	1
Ridgeville	2,076	2	2	0
Rock Hill	66,906	162	122	40
Salem	132	1	1	0
Salley	412	1	1	0
Saluda	2,920	12	10	2
Santee	712	10	6	4
Scranton	996	2	2	0
Seneca	8,154	42	32	10
Simpsonville	17,033	48	38	10
Society Hill	683	5	5	0
South Congaree	2,385	7	6	1
Spartanburg	38,726	150	131	19
Springdale	2,916	9	9	0
Springfield	481	2	2	0
St. George	2,108	10	10	0
St. Matthews	1,965	6	6	0
St. Stephen	1,756	7	7	0
Sullivans Island	1,874	9	8	1
Summerton	1,023	7	6	1
Summerville	46,405	100	80	20
Sumter	38,547	159	109	50
Surfside Beach	4,782	28	21	7
Swansea	790	5	4	1
Tega Cay	4,799	25	19	6
Timmonsville	2,381	8	7	1
Travelers Rest	4,523	21	15	6
Turbeville	704	4	3	1
Union	7,999	36	34	2
Varnville	2,051	7	7	0
Wagener	874	3	3	0
Walhalla	3,626	16	14	2
Walterboro	5,777	30	23	7
Ware Shoals	2,343	8	7	1
Wellford	2,330	13	11	2
West Columbia	13,983	63	51	12
Westminster	2,658	9	9	0
West Pelzer	909	3	3	0
West Union	302	1	1	0
Whitmire	1,528	5	4	1
Williamston	3,936	20	16	4
Williston	3,194	9	8	1
Winnsboro	3,545	26	25	1
Woodruff	4,065	15	12	3
Yemassee	866	7	7	0
York	7,834	35	28	7
SOUTH DAKOTA				
Aberdeen	24,382	49	41	8
Alcester	893	2	2	0
Armour	659	1	1	0
Avon	518	1	1	0
Belle Fourche	4,926	10	9	1
Beresford	2,224	8	4	4
Box Elder	3,312	11	9	2
Brandon	7,445	12	11	1
Brookings	19,546	37	28	9
Burke	565	1	1	0
Canton	4,275	5	5	0
Centerville	843	1	1	0
Chamberlain	2,249	5	5	0
Colman	542	1	1	0
Corsica	575	1	1	0
Deadwood	1,283	14	11	3
Eagle Butte	953	2	2	0
Elk Point	1,911	2	2	0
Estelline	662	1	1	0
Eureka	927	2	2	0
Faith	441	3	2	1
Flandreau	2,250	6	5	1
Freeman	1,182	2	2	0
Gettysburg	1,061	2	2	0
Gregory	1,171	3	3	0
Groton	1,404	3	3	0
Highmore	723	1	1	0
Hot Springs	4,040	8	7	1
Huron	10,788	31	24	7
Jefferson	596	2	2	0
Kadoka	647	1	1	0
Kimball	682	1	1	0
Lead	2,874	6	5	1
Lemmon	1,167	3	3	0
Lennox	2,846	3	3	0
Leola	382	1	1	0
Madison	6,294	12	11	1
Martin	1,002	2	2	0
McIntosh	208	1	1	0
McLaughlin	739	2	1	1
Menno	664	1	1	0
Milbank	3,191	6	6	0
Miller	1,319	4	4	0
Mitchell	14,861	32	30	2
Mobridge	3,086	13	7	6
New Effington	224	1	1	0
North Sioux City	2,549	8	6	2
Parkston	1,489	3	3	0
Philip	726	2	2	0
Pierre	14,051	37	25	12
Platte	1,278	2	2	0
Rapid City	64,556	130	106	24
Rosholt	428	1	1	0
Scotland	792	1	1	0
Selby	652	1	1	0
Sioux Falls	155,110	255	217	38
Sisseton	2,447	7	7	0
Spearfish	10,144	27	19	8
Springfield	1,490	2	2	0
Sturgis	5,937	19	16	3
Summerset	451	1	1	0
Tea	4,373	5	5	0
Timber Lake	424	1	1	0
Tripp	633	1	1	0
Tyndall	1,103	2	2	0
Vermillion	10,251	17	16	1
Viborg	771	1	1	0
Wagner	1,545	3	3	0
Watertown	20,565	50	36	14
Webster	1,692	5	5	0
Whitewood	845	3	3	0
Winner	2,768	9	7	2
Worthing	1,184	1	1	0
Yankton	13,660	37	26	11
TENNESSEE				
Adamsville	2,118	9	6	3
Alamo	2,317	3	3	0
Alcoa	8,625	48	41	7
Alexandria	872	3	3	0
Algood	3,366	11	11	0
Ardmore	1,151	11	7	4
Ashland City	4,658	15	14	1

Table 78. Full-Time Law Enforcement Employees, by State and City, 2008—*Continued*

(Number.)

State/City	Population	Total law enforcement employees	Total officers	Total civilians
Athens	14,237	31	29	2
Atoka	7,500	17	16	1
Baileyton	494	2	2	0
Bartlett	48,044	140	107	33
Baxter	1,379	4	4	0
Bean Station	3,047	7	7	0
Belle Meade	3,454	20	15	5
Bells	2,252	5	5	0
Benton	1,119	8	7	1
Berry Hill	745	17	13	4
Bethel Springs	775	1	1	0
Big Sandy	511	2	2	0
Blaine	1,757	2	2	0
Bluff City	1,618	8	8	0
Bolivar	5,586	26	21	5
Brentwood	36,341	72	58	14
Brighton	2,672	6	6	0
Bristol	25,485	90	67	23
Brownsville	10,337	36	25	11
Bruceton	1,453	4	4	0
Burns	1,409	2	2	0
Calhoun	522	3	3	0
Camden	3,662	20	15	5
Carthage	2,224	11	7	4
Caryville	2,395	6	6	0
Celina	1,345	6	4	2
Centerville	3,998	20	12	8
Chapel Hill	1,317	5	5	0
Charleston	666	6	3	3
Chattanooga	171,611	605	431	174
Church Hill	6,771	11	10	1
Clarksville	121,386	284	241	43
Cleveland	39,420	99	88	11
Clifton	2,693	6	6	0
Clinton	9,554	27	25	2
Collegedale	7,599	23	22	1
Collierville	40,001	128	91	37
Collinwood	1,017	3	3	0
Columbia	34,080	91	80	11
Cookeville	29,276	85	64	21
Coopertown	3,356	13	12	1
Copperhill	447	4	4	0
Cornersville	953	4	4	0
Covington	9,175	31	30	1
Cowan	1,736	6	6	0
Cross Plains	1,647	3	3	0
Crossville	11,563	44	41	3
Crump	1,453	3	2	1
Cumberland City	327	3	3	0
Dandridge	2,619	12	11	1
Dayton	6,676	19	17	2
Decatur	1,463	4	4	0
Decaturville	822	1	1	0
Decherd	2,135	13	12	1
Dickson	13,861	49	44	5
Dover	1,592	6	6	0
Dresden	2,605	10	9	1
Dunlap	5,046	14	12	2
Dyer	2,397	6	6	0
Dyersburg	17,222	68	58	10
East Ridge	19,630	41	33	8
Elizabethton	13,909	38	34	4
Elkton	605	3	2	1
Englewood	1,741	5	5	0
Erin	1,449	6	5	1
Erwin	5,805	13	12	1
Estill Springs	2,265	6	6	0
Ethridge	555	1	1	0
Etowah	3,768	17	13	4
Fairview	7,917	19	18	1
Fayetteville	7,102	25	23	2
Franklin	58,997	147	124	23
Friendship	594	1	1	0
Gainesboro	836	4	4	0
Gallatin	29,507	88	65	23
Gallaway	707	4	4	0
Gates	847	1	1	0
Gatlinburg	5,755	55	45	10
Germantown	41,160	108	87	21
Gibson	399	2	1	1
Gleason	1,387	6	5	1
Goodlettsville	16,781	53	40	13
Gordonsville	1,316	5	5	0
Grand Junction	307	1	1	0
Graysville	1,427	5	5	0
Greenbrier	6,575	14	12	2
Greeneville	15,453	46	44	2
Greenfield	2,019	8	7	1
Halls	2,181	8	8	0
Harriman	6,659	21	20	1
Henderson	6,374	17	16	1
Hendersonville	47,819	112	81	31
Henning	1,276	4	4	0
Henry	548	2	2	0
Hohenwald	3,822	13	12	1
Hollow Rock	938	2	2	0
Hornbeak	418	1	1	0
Humboldt	9,072	31	25	6
Huntingdon	4,132	16	12	4
Huntland	870	4	4	0
Jacksboro	2,054	6	6	0
Jackson	63,620	246	207	39
Jamestown	1,899	9	9	0
Jasper	3,107	8	8	0
Jefferson City	8,127	21	19	2
Jellico	2,528	9	6	3
Johnson City	61,690	179	150	29
Jonesborough	5,165	21	16	5
Kenton	1,294	5	5	0
Kimball	1,399	9	9	0
Kingsport	44,350	154	111	43
Kingston	5,557	13	12	1
Kingston Springs	2,941	5	5	0
Knoxville	184,559	471	375	96
Lafayette	4,383	30	15	15
La Follette	8,195	28	21	7
Lake City	1,837	10	7	3
Lakewood	2,594	4	4	0
La Vergne	30,638	61	45	16
Lawrenceburg	10,784	38	32	6
Lebanon	24,599	87	71	16
Lenoir City	7,978	24	23	1
Lewisburg	10,888	42	32	10
Lexington	7,851	31	26	5
Livingston	3,553	20	14	6
Lookout Mountain	1,863	22	16	6
Loretto	1,706	3	3	0
Loudon	4,850	16	15	1
Madisonville	4,638	18	15	3
Manchester	9,972	38	32	6
Martin	10,080	36	29	7
Maryville	27,259	59	52	7
Mason	1,216	6	6	0
Maynardville	1,899	3	3	0
McEwen	1,658	5	4	1
McKenzie	5,405	20	15	5
McMinnville	13,251	34	31	3
Medina	2,022	10	10	0
Memphis	672,046	2,523	2,098	425
Middleton	614	3	3	0
Milan	7,854	31	25	6
Millersville	6,361	16	12	4
Millington	10,282	51	39	12
Minor Hill	447	2	2	0
Monteagle	1,200	13	6	7
Monterey	2,922	7	7	0
Morristown	27,579	93	87	6
Moscow	569	5	5	0

Table 78. Full-Time Law Enforcement Employees, by State and City, 2008—*Continued*

(Number.)

State/City	Population	Total law enforcement employees	Total officers	Total civilians
Mountain City	2,397	10	10	0
Mount Carmel	5,478	8	7	1
Mount Juliet	21,177	51	40	11
Mount Pleasant	4,401	17	12	5
Munford	6,538	15	14	1
Murfreesboro	102,536	269	221	48
Nashville	602,181	1,555	1,230	325
Newbern	3,140	19	13	6
New Hope	1,036	1	1	0
New Johnsonville	1,964	4	4	0
New Market	1,335	5	4	1
Newport	7,466	31	28	3
New Tazewell	2,874	11	11	0
Niota	800	3	3	0
Nolensville	2,662	6	6	0
Norris	1,469	7	7	0
Oakland	4,825	17	15	2
Oak Ridge	27,540	73	57	16
Obion	1,073	3	3	0
Oliver Springs	3,314	14	10	4
Oneida	3,854	19	14	5
Paris	9,941	37	26	11
Parsons	2,353	6	6	0
Petersburg	598	3	2	1
Pigeon Forge	6,237	65	53	12
Pikeville	1,899	3	3	0
Piperton	1,207	11	9	2
Pittman Center	666	2	2	0
Pleasant View	4,074	5	5	0
Portland	11,321	37	28	9
Powells Crossroads	1,221	1	1	0
Pulaski	7,797	28	25	3
Puryear	673	2	2	0
Red Bank	11,512	24	22	2
Red Boiling Springs	1,060	5	5	0
Ridgely	1,521	6	5	1
Ridgetop	1,711	6	6	0
Ripley	7,661	34	25	9
Rockwood	5,575	17	16	1
Rogersville	4,331	19	14	5
Rossville	522	5	5	0
Rutherford	1,243	4	4	0
Rutledge	1,286	4	4	0
Savannah	7,293	29	18	11
Scotts Hill	911	3	3	0
Selmer	4,684	19	17	2
Sevierville	16,652	70	55	15
Sewanee	2,579	12	8	4
Shelbyville	19,902	50	41	9
Signal Mountain	7,089	16	15	1
Smithville	4,345	12	11	1
Smyrna	37,935	108	79	29
Sneedville	1,320	1	1	0
Soddy-Daisy	12,407	30	24	6
Somerville	2,966	12	12	0
South Carthage	1,315	4	4	0
South Fulton	2,403	7	6	1
South Pittsburg	3,128	12	8	4
Sparta	4,928	17	15	2
Spencer	1,682	3	3	0
Spring City	1,999	7	7	0
Springfield	17,210	53	38	15
Spring Hill	27,290	47	37	10
St. Joseph	857	1	1	0
Surgoinsville	1,774	3	2	1
Sweetwater	6,638	20	18	2
Tazewell	2,143	6	6	0
Tellico Plains	963	7	6	1
Tiptonville	4,009	6	6	0
Townsend	263	4	4	0
Tracy City	1,656	5	5	0
Trenton	4,477	22	16	6
Trezevant	885	1	1	0
Trimble	720	2	2	0
Troy	1,213	4	4	0
Tullahoma	18,776	42	36	6
Tusculum	2,296	2	2	0
Union City	10,612	43	36	7
Vonore	1,517	11	10	1
Wartburg	920	4	4	0
Wartrace	580	1	1	0
Watertown	1,410	7	4	3
Waverly	4,172	14	13	1
Waynesboro	2,117	8	7	1
Westmoreland	2,189	10	6	4
White Bluff	2,528	3	3	0
White House	9,973	27	18	9
White Pine	2,101	9	8	1
Whiteville	4,459	10	10	0
Whitwell	1,595	8	5	3
Winchester	7,898	25	23	2
Winfield	1,000	3	3	0
Woodbury	2,555	9	8	1
TEXAS				
Abernathy	2,746	4	4	0
Abilene	116,267	242	178	64
Addison	13,837	83	63	20
Alamo	16,686	38	28	10
Alamo Heights	7,454	29	20	9
Alice	19,855	44	35	9
Allen	83,242	150	103	47
Alpine	6,227	15	9	6
Alto	1,187	4	4	0
Alton	10,876	16	12	4
Alvarado	4,198	21	15	6
Alvin	22,847	72	49	23
Amarillo	187,674	420	308	112
Andrews	9,708	25	16	9
Angleton	18,703	48	36	12
Anna	1,905	9	9	0
Anson	2,285	4	4	0
Anthony	4,149	11	10	1
Anton	1,128	1	1	0
Aransas Pass	8,957	31	22	9
Arcola	1,256	7	6	1
Argyle	3,548	9	8	1
Arlington	375,836	790	614	176
Arp	958	4	4	0
Athens	12,348	32	24	8
Atlanta	5,482	19	15	4
Austin	753,535	2,034	1,466	568
Azle	11,371	31	24	7
Baird	1,668	2	2	0
Balch Springs	20,011	52	35	17
Balcones Heights	2,971	22	18	4
Ballinger	3,720	8	6	2
Bangs	1,591	2	2	0
Bastrop	8,190	24	20	4
Bay City	17,705	48	31	17
Bayou Vista	1,697	5	5	0
Baytown	70,596	185	137	48
Beaumont	109,103	285	244	41
Bedford	49,210	128	76	52
Bee Cave	2,852	17	15	2
Beeville	12,697	23	18	5
Bellaire	18,316	57	42	15
Bellmead	9,593	22	16	6
Bellville	4,448	12	11	1
Belton	17,536	37	28	9
Benbrook	23,017	49	38	11
Bertram	1,405	3	3	0
Beverly Hills	2,049	12	8	4
Big Sandy	1,353	6	6	0
Big Spring	23,952	55	37	18
Bishop	3,132	10	5	5
Blanco	1,604	5	4	1
Bloomburg	360	1	1	0
Blue Mound	2,357	13	8	5

Table 78. Full-Time Law Enforcement Employees, by State and City, 2008—*Continued*

(Number.)

State/City	Population	Total law enforcement employees	Total officers	Total civilians
Boerne	9,875	45	29	16
Bogata	1,254	3	3	0
Bonham	10,669	26	18	8
Borger	12,744	36	23	13
Bovina	1,721	2	2	0
Bowie	5,565	20	14	6
Brady	5,252	16	9	7
Brazoria	2,988	11	7	4
Breckenridge	5,578	17	12	5
Bremond	861	2	2	0
Brenham	15,237	34	30	4
Bridge City	8,550	17	12	5
Bridgeport	6,146	26	16	10
Brookshire	3,955	15	10	5
Brookside Village	2,004	5	5	0
Brownfield	8,947	23	14	9
Brownsville	176,893	306	234	72
Brownwood	19,597	58	37	21
Bruceville-Eddy	1,543	3	3	0
Bryan	72,815	161	124	37
Bullard	1,839	7	6	1
Bulverde	4,624	14	13	1
Burkburnett	10,506	25	19	6
Burleson	35,166	74	53	21
Burnet	5,835	14	13	1
Cactus	2,602	5	4	1
Caddo Mills	1,212	3	3	0
Caldwell	3,734	13	12	1
Calvert	1,361	4	4	0
Cameron	5,771	11	7	4
Canton	3,666	18	14	4
Canyon	14,202	23	20	3
Carrollton	125,607	218	158	60
Carthage	6,600	22	15	7
Castle Hills	4,175	27	20	7
Castroville	3,074	10	8	2
Cedar Hill	46,153	82	66	16
Cedar Park	64,020	96	70	26
Celina	5,716	7	7	0
Center	5,775	24	16	8
Childress	6,497	10	6	4
Chillicothe	702	2	2	0
Cibolo	14,734	23	21	2
Cisco	3,759	9	7	2
Clarksville	3,464	9	9	0
Cleburne	29,954	73	54	19
Cleveland	8,021	32	20	12
Clifton	3,617	8	7	1
Clint	974	1	1	0
Clute	10,777	36	27	9
Clyde	3,754	9	8	1
Cockrell Hill	4,275	19	12	7
Coffee City	209	2	2	0
Coleman	4,626	15	10	5
College Station	81,925	155	109	46
Colleyville	24,472	50	38	12
Collinsville	1,523	3	3	0
Colorado City	3,883	12	7	5
Columbus	3,905	11	10	1
Comanche	4,194	9	7	2
Combes	2,837	4	4	0
Commerce	9,497	22	18	4
Conroe	54,554	138	102	36
Converse	16,057	45	32	13
Coppell	39,541	72	57	15
Copperas Cove	30,052	66	50	16
Corinth	21,890	31	28	3
Corpus Christi	286,558	627	448	179
Corrigan	1,906	14	6	8
Corsicana	26,711	48	36	12
Cottonwood Shores	1,202	4	4	0
Crandall	3,796	10	10	0
Crane	3,050	11	6	5
Crockett	6,880	18	16	2
Crowell	980	1	1	0
Crowley	12,680	33	25	8
Crystal City	7,127	16	11	5
Cuero	6,453	12	11	1
Cuney	148	2	1	1
Daingerfield	2,476	9	8	1
Dalhart	6,882	17	14	3
Dallas	1,276,214	4,196	3,393	803
Dalworthington Gardens	2,429	17	13	4
Danbury	1,682	3	3	0
Dayton	7,399	21	16	5
Decatur	6,413	26	21	5
Deer Park	30,900	72	50	22
De Kalb	1,802	7	6	1
De Leon	2,347	5	5	0
Del Rio	36,922	98	73	25
Denison	24,276	59	46	13
Denton	120,295	207	154	53
Denver City	4,017	13	8	5
DeSoto	48,131	104	69	35
Devine	4,508	12	8	4
Diboll	5,550	20	14	6
Dickinson	17,884	42	32	10
Dilley	3,592	6	5	1
Dimmitt	3,676	7	5	2
Donna	16,984	33	24	9
Double Oak	3,331	6	6	0
Driscoll	803	2	1	1
Dublin	3,823	13	9	4
Dumas	13,698	28	24	4
Duncanville	36,221	65	53	12
Eagle Lake	3,684	9	8	1
Eagle Pass	26,766	75	61	14
Early	2,769	8	7	1
Eastland	3,907	11	9	2
East Mountain	627	1	1	0
Edcouch	4,506	7	6	1
Eden	2,356	3	3	0
Edgewood	1,446	4	4	0
Edinburg	71,734	156	115	41
Edna	5,780	11	9	2
El Campo	10,612	37	29	8
Electra	2,921	11	6	5
Elgin	10,486	23	18	5
El Paso	612,374	1,455	1,129	326
Elsa	6,771	18	13	5
Ennis	19,646	41	34	7
Euless	53,157	123	84	39
Everman	5,750	18	13	5
Fairfield	3,648	17	13	4
Fair Oaks Ranch	6,341	15	15	0
Falfurrias	4,932	10	8	2
Farmers Branch	26,362	111	73	38
Farmersville	3,472	8	7	1
Farwell	1,264	2	2	0
Ferris	2,539	12	8	4
Flatonia	1,432	4	4	0
Florence	1,127	2	2	0
Floresville	7,594	16	15	1
Flower Mound	70,761	105	73	32
Floydada	3,094	6	6	0
Forest Hill	13,926	38	27	11
Forney	15,855	31	20	11
Fort Stockton	7,293	26	18	8
Fort Worth	701,345	1,899	1,486	413
Frankston	1,234	4	4	0
Fredericksburg	11,110	33	29	4
Freeport	12,539	42	30	12
Freer	2,950	13	5	8
Friendswood	34,066	74	56	18
Friona	3,574	10	6	4
Frisco	99,472	189	133	56
Gainesville	16,650	49	36	13
Galena Park	10,243	21	15	6

Table 78. Full-Time Law Enforcement Employees, by State and City, 2008—*Continued*

(Number.)

State/City	Population	Total law enforcement employees	Total officers	Total civilians
Galveston	56,870	203	158	45
Ganado	1,824	3	3	0
Garland	219,135	447	319	128
Gatesville	15,139	23	16	7
Georgetown	49,644	97	66	31
Giddings	5,470	17	12	5
Gilmer	5,260	21	18	3
Gladewater	6,317	20	15	5
Glenn Heights	11,339	26	18	8
Godley	1,024	5	5	0
Gonzales	7,374	24	17	7
Gorman	1,243	3	3	0
Graham	8,496	22	21	1
Granbury	8,315	39	33	6
Grand Prairie	162,706	317	217	100
Grand Saline	3,224	7	7	0
Granger	1,357	4	4	0
Granite Shoals	2,829	8	7	1
Grapeland	1,376	3	2	1
Grapevine	51,136	126	91	35
Greenville	25,886	69	49	20
Gregory	2,211	4	4	0
Groesbeck	4,297	8	7	1
Groves	14,321	23	21	2
Gun Barrel City	6,083	20	15	5
Hale Center	2,138	3	3	0
Hallettsville	2,498	7	6	1
Hallsville	2,998	7	5	2
Haltom City	40,239	97	70	27
Hamlin	1,887	8	4	4
Harker Heights	25,579	54	44	10
Harlingen	64,922	153	122	31
Haskell	2,591	3	3	0
Hawk Cove	620	2	2	0
Hawkins	1,531	8	8	0
Hawley	572	1	1	0
Hearne	4,601	18	12	6
Heath	7,863	20	19	1
Hedwig Village	2,354	24	17	7
Helotes	7,033	20	18	2
Hemphill	1,029	4	4	0
Hempstead	7,599	17	15	2
Henderson	11,644	38	30	8
Hereford	14,444	28	22	6
Hewitt	13,788	30	22	8
Hickory Creek	3,864	10	10	0
Hidalgo	12,238	52	38	14
Highland Park	9,105	69	54	15
Highland Village	17,004	37	29	8
Hill Country Village	1,109	12	12	0
Hillsboro	8,972	33	23	10
Hitchcock	7,254	16	12	4
Holland	1,132	1	1	0
Holliday	1,785	3	3	0
Hollywood Park	3,306	12	11	1
Hondo	9,035	21	19	2
Hooks	2,935	6	6	0
Horizon City	13,488	19	17	2
Horseshoe Bay	2,473	16	15	1
Houston	2,238,895	6,750	5,048	1,702
Howe	2,730	7	7	0
Hubbard	1,769	5	5	0
Hudson	4,277	5	5	0
Hudson Oaks	1,988	14	13	1
Humble	15,026	75	56	19
Huntsville	38,097	54	48	6
Hurst	38,702	116	71	45
Hutchins	3,104	21	15	6
Hutto	15,488	27	22	5
Idalou	2,101	3	3	0
Ingleside	9,023	24	17	7
Ingram	1,910	7	6	1
Iowa Park	6,292	18	12	6
Irving	200,470	496	342	154
Italy	2,137	4	4	0
Itasca	1,673	5	5	0
Jacinto City	9,949	25	20	5
Jacksboro	4,513	11	9	2
Jacksonville	14,302	38	28	10
Jamaica Beach	1,107	5	5	0
Jarrell	1,439	3	2	1
Jasper	7,228	31	23	8
Jefferson	1,946	8	7	1
Jersey Village	7,299	32	23	9
Johnson City	1,565	4	4	0
Jones Creek	2,107	4	3	1
Jonestown	2,472	15	14	1
Joshua	5,788	13	12	1
Jourdanton	4,367	8	8	0
Junction	2,569	5	5	0
Karnes City	3,345	7	6	1
Katy	14,106	59	43	16
Kaufman	8,775	22	16	6
Keene	6,408	16	10	6
Keller	39,598	82	51	31
Kemah	2,482	23	19	4
Kemp	1,300	4	4	0
Kempner	1,186	1	1	0
Kenedy	3,311	8	7	1
Kennedale	7,108	26	19	7
Kerens	1,840	3	3	0
Kermit	5,078	17	10	7
Kerrville	22,942	66	49	17
Kilgore	12,120	47	38	9
Killeen	115,906	259	189	70
Kingsville	24,253	59	43	16
Kirby	8,568	18	13	5
Kirbyville	1,949	6	4	2
Kountze	2,167	9	7	2
Kress	766	1	1	0
Kyle	28,543	33	21	12
Lacy-Lakeview	5,864	23	15	8
La Feria	6,972	17	13	4
Lago Vista	6,305	23	16	7
La Grange	4,690	9	9	0
Laguna Vista	3,534	7	7	0
La Joya	4,923	17	11	6
Lake Dallas	7,724	21	13	8
Lake Jackson	27,603	59	44	15
Lakeside	1,328	4	4	0
Lakeview	6,518	15	11	4
Lakeway	10,976	34	26	8
Lake Worth	4,792	30	22	8
La Marque	14,072	37	27	10
Lamesa	8,890	22	16	6
Lampasas	8,000	27	19	8
Lancaster	36,584	68	56	12
La Porte	34,552	99	73	26
Laredo	222,870	500	421	79
La Vernia	1,214	6	6	0
Lavon	421	9	8	1
League City	71,651	128	91	37
Leander	26,680	45	33	12
Leon Valley	10,152	30	23	7
Levelland	12,399	31	21	10
Lewisville	100,947	199	139	60
Lexington	1,238	3	3	0
Liberty	8,403	26	18	8
Lindale	4,811	20	14	6
Linden	2,129	6	5	1
Little Elm	29,616	34	31	3
Littlefield	6,027	21	13	8
Live Oak	12,958	43	29	14
Livingston	6,345	23	16	7
Llano	3,254	9	7	2
Lockhart	13,869	32	23	9
Lockney	1,692	3	3	0
Lone Star	1,606	6	6	0

Table 78. Full-Time Law Enforcement Employees, by State and City, 2008—*Continued*

(Number.)

State/City	Population	Total law enforcement employees	Total officers	Total civilians
Longview	77,272	227	162	65
Lorena	1,702	4	4	0
Lorenzo	1,189	1	1	0
Los Fresnos	5,469	21	14	7
Lubbock	219,594	499	359	140
Lufkin	34,214	98	75	23
Luling	5,483	24	15	9
Lumberton	10,243	18	15	3
Lytle	2,786	6	6	0
Madisonville	4,392	12	10	2
Magnolia	1,267	10	9	1
Malakoff	2,331	4	4	0
Manor	3,711	15	13	2
Mansfield	46,560	206	81	125
Manvel	5,353	13	8	5
Marble Falls	7,638	39	27	12
Marfa	1,860	8	4	4
Marion	1,147	5	3	2
Marlin	5,950	21	15	6
Marshall	23,874	65	47	18
Mart	2,591	3	3	0
Martindale	1,150	5	5	0
Mathis	5,331	16	8	8
McAllen	130,039	400	262	138
McGregor	4,890	18	11	7
McKinney	126,659	198	155	43
Meadows Place	6,688	15	14	1
Melissa	4,362	8	7	1
Memorial Villages	11,907	40	33	7
Memphis	2,230	2	2	0
Mercedes	15,066	39	31	8
Meridian	1,514	3	2	1
Merkel	2,625	4	4	0
Mesquite	132,600	303	228	75
Mexia	6,610	27	17	10
Midland	105,049	197	152	45
Midlothian	16,847	40	29	11
Milford	744	5	5	0
Mineola	5,195	18	12	6
Mineral Wells	16,804	36	28	8
Mission	68,236	176	125	51
Missouri City	77,075	99	76	23
Monahans	6,282	14	10	4
Mont Belvieu	2,677	14	9	5
Montgomery	588	9	9	0
Morgans Point Resort	4,529	8	7	1
Mount Pleasant	14,853	35	26	9
Muleshoe	4,297	14	8	6
Munday	1,222	2	2	0
Murphy	16,612	32	22	10
Mustang Ridge	941	3	3	0
Nacogdoches	32,265	71	57	14
Nash	2,423	8	8	0
Nassau Bay	4,059	14	13	1
Navasota	7,522	22	17	5
Nederland	16,033	35	22	13
Needville	3,550	5	5	0
New Boston	4,641	12	9	3
New Braunfels	53,803	127	103	24
New Deal	744	2	1	1
Nocona	3,250	10	5	5
Nolanville	2,829	9	8	1
Northlake	1,205	8	8	0
North Richland Hills	65,552	165	114	51
Oak Ridge	249	1	1	0
Oak Ridge North	3,420	17	17	0
Odessa	97,644	189	143	46
O'Donnell	915	1	1	0
Olmos Park	2,304	12	12	0
Olney	3,250	9	5	4
Olton	2,187	5	4	1
Onalaska	1,507	6	6	0
Orange	17,287	51	38	13
Orange Grove	1,423	4	4	0
Ore City	1,184	4	4	0
Overton	2,360	9	6	3
Ovilla	3,966	10	9	1
Oyster Creek	1,251	8	5	3
Paducah	1,229	7	1	6
Palacios	5,038	17	13	4
Palestine	18,197	42	33	9
Pampa	17,140	36	24	12
Panhandle	2,515	4	4	0
Pantego	2,368	14	11	3
Paris	26,121	79	59	20
Parker	2,896	7	7	0
Pasadena	147,114	337	257	80
Pearland	83,185	133	116	17
Pearsall	7,663	14	12	2
Pecos	7,726	40	18	22
Pelican Bay	1,616	5	5	0
Penitas	1,181	11	5	6
Perryton	8,331	14	7	7
Pflugerville	37,454	85	65	20
Pharr	66,084	152	106	46
Pilot Point	4,454	10	8	2
Pinehurst	2,153	10	6	4
Pineland	873	2	2	0
Pittsburg	4,684	11	10	1
Plainview	21,574	39	31	8
Plano	265,739	501	342	159
Pleasanton	9,762	24	18	6
Point Comfort	707	1	1	0
Ponder	1,396	1	1	0
Port Aransas	3,826	20	12	8
Port Arthur	55,032	151	119	32
Port Isabel	5,301	20	16	4
Portland	16,604	35	24	11
Port Lavaca	11,379	25	19	6
Port Neches	12,574	20	17	3
Poteet	3,663	5	5	0
Pottsboro	2,157	7	7	0
Premont	2,815	4	4	0
Presidio	4,841	4	3	1
Primera	3,491	6	5	1
Princeton	6,072	11	10	1
Progreso	5,449	10	9	1
Prosper	7,007	10	9	1
Queen City	1,542	6	6	0
Quinlan	1,447	3	3	0
Quitman	2,260	7	6	1
Ralls	1,994	3	3	0
Ranger	2,578	5	5	0
Ransom Canyon	1,120	3	3	0
Raymondville	9,475	23	12	11
Red Oak	9,323	28	21	7
Refugio	2,701	8	7	1
Reno	3,077	4	3	1
Richardson	100,597	232	140	92
Richland Hills	8,099	25	17	8
Richmond	13,637	40	30	10
Richwood	3,446	10	8	2
Riesel	1,017	4	3	1
Rio Grande City	14,080	36	26	10
Rising Star	837	1	1	0
River Oaks	6,932	24	18	6
Roanoke	3,852	36	28	8
Robinson	10,358	29	20	9
Robstown	12,132	32	24	8
Rockdale	5,920	15	9	6
Rockport	9,622	24	22	2
Rockwall	36,467	80	62	18
Rollingwood	1,414	6	6	0
Roma	11,377	33	24	9
Roman Forest	4,045	7	7	0
Roscoe	1,240	1	1	0
Rosebud	1,332	3	3	0
Rose City	501	1	1	0

Table 78. Full-Time Law Enforcement Employees, by State and City, 2008—*Continued*

(Number.)

State/City	Population	Total law enforcement employees	Total officers	Total civilians
Rosenberg	34,273	80	63	17
Round Rock	102,411	196	141	55
Rowlett	57,010	104	75	29
Royse City	9,597	16	15	1
Runaway Bay	1,404	4	4	0
Rusk	5,216	13	11	2
Sabinal	1,635	5	5	0
Sachse	19,651	39	28	11
Saginaw	20,765	45	38	7
Salado	2,055	2	2	0
San Angelo	90,739	177	144	33
San Antonio	1,351,244	2,819	2,155	664
San Augustine	2,352	7	6	1
San Benito	24,807	54	46	8
San Diego	4,445	7	6	1
Sanger	8,013	15	13	2
San Juan	34,103	47	36	11
San Marcos	52,473	123	97	26
San Saba	2,535	4	4	0
Sansom Park Village	4,167	16	11	5
Santa Anna	1,006	2	2	0
Santa Fe	10,603	22	16	6
Santa Rosa	3,164	4	4	0
Schertz	30,609	63	46	17
Seabrook	11,760	38	32	6
Seadrift	1,436	2	2	0
Seagoville	11,867	28	20	8
Seagraves	2,332	4	3	1
Sealy	6,320	17	15	2
Seguin	26,348	59	44	15
Selma	4,881	28	25	3
Seminole	6,078	12	11	1
Seven Points	1,238	10	5	5
Seymour	2,663	11	7	4
Shallowater	2,292	5	5	0
Shamrock	1,809	7	3	4
Shavano Park	3,255	16	15	1
Shenandoah	2,022	27	23	4
Sherman	38,039	88	61	27
Silsbee	6,834	21	16	5
Sinton	5,360	9	8	1
Slaton	5,739	18	13	5
Smithville	4,501	16	10	6
Snyder	10,418	23	18	5
Socorro	32,444	37	27	10
Somerset	1,862	4	4	0
Somerville	1,683	4	4	0
Sonora	3,082	4	3	1
Sour Lake	1,738	6	5	1
South Houston	16,496	38	29	9
Southlake	26,837	57	52	5
South Padre Island	2,797	36	25	11
Southside Place	1,669	11	7	4
Spearman	2,909	4	4	0
Springtown	3,167	15	11	4
Spring Valley	3,803	23	18	5
Spur	954	1	1	0
Stafford	20,051	57	44	13
Stamford	3,080	9	7	2
Stanton	2,205	4	4	0
Stephenville	16,945	49	35	14
Stratford	1,872	1	1	0
Sudan	994	1	1	0
Sugar Land	81,763	182	135	47
Sullivan City	4,440	13	9	4
Sulphur Springs	15,493	38	29	9
Sunrise Beach Village	755	3	3	0
Sunset Valley	870	13	13	0
Surfside Beach	891	7	6	1
Sweeny	3,591	7	7	0
Sweetwater	10,365	26	21	5
Taft	3,348	7	7	0
Tahoka	2,528	4	4	0
Tatum	1,205	3	3	0
Taylor	16,048	39	27	12
Teague	4,765	10	8	2
Temple	58,812	156	130	26
Terrell	19,722	49	35	14
Terrell Hills	5,197	13	12	1
Texarkana	36,300	100	90	10
Texas City	44,768	112	88	24
The Colony	43,724	75	52	23
Thorndale	1,321	2	2	0
Thrall	897	3	3	0
Three Rivers	1,677	5	4	1
Tioga	931	2	2	0
Tolar	680	1	1	0
Tomball	10,412	51	37	14
Tool	2,459	12	8	4
Trinity	2,736	10	6	4
Trophy Club	8,141	16	15	1
Troup	2,116	9	8	1
Troy	1,410	4	4	0
Tulia	4,575	13	7	6
Tye	1,141	4	4	0
Tyler	98,042	233	185	48
Universal City	18,430	35	25	10
University Park	24,561	52	39	13
Uvalde	16,263	48	35	13
Valley View	799	1	1	0
Van	2,592	14	14	0
Van Alstyne	2,987	13	9	4
Vernon	10,998	30	19	11
Victoria	62,464	137	108	29
Vidor	10,901	30	22	8
Waco	123,208	315	236	79
Waelder	996	3	3	0
Wake Village	5,562	7	6	1
Waller	2,073	9	8	1
Wallis	1,306	3	3	0
Watauga	24,114	54	36	18
Waxahachie	28,110	67	51	16
Weatherford	26,696	68	53	15
Webster	10,196	60	45	15
Weimar	2,004	7	6	1
Wells	793	2	1	1
Weslaco	33,096	95	68	27
West	2,701	7	7	0
West Columbia	4,191	18	11	7
West Lake Hills	3,145	19	13	6
West Orange	3,827	9	8	1
Westover Hills	697	14	11	3
West Tawakoni	1,754	4	4	0
West University Place	15,578	27	19	8
Wharton	9,221	32	23	9
Whitehouse	7,791	20	13	7
White Oak	6,326	18	14	4
Whitesboro	4,043	12	7	5
White Settlement	16,330	50	36	14
Whitney	2,051	9	7	2
Wichita Falls	101,279	279	182	97
Willis	4,320	16	14	2
Willow Park	4,431	16	11	5
Wills Point	3,884	11	10	1
Wilmer	3,599	18	12	6
Windcrest	5,259	25	18	7
Wink	882	1	1	0
Winnsboro	3,950	14	9	5
Winters	2,545	5	5	0
Wolfe City	1,648	3	3	0
Wolfforth	3,538	10	9	1
Woodville	2,261	10	9	1
Woodway	8,776	37	26	11
Wortham	1,079	3	2	1
Wylie	38,693	49	42	7
Yoakum	5,477	16	9	7
Yorktown	2,155	4	4	0

Table 78. Full-Time Law Enforcement Employees, by State and City, 2008—*Continued*

(Number.)

State/City	Population	Total law enforcement employees	Total officers	Total civilians
UTAH				
Alpine/Highland	25,593	22	20	2
Alta	371	8	4	4
American Fork/Cedar Hills	37,173	39	34	5
Blanding	3,181	6	5	1
Bountiful	44,098	53	38	15
Brian Head	126	5	5	0
Brigham City	18,682	30	25	5
Cedar City	28,883	41	34	7
Centerville	15,488	20	17	3
Clearfield	27,649	43	31	12
Clinton	20,646	18	17	1
Draper	40,607	40	33	7
East Carbon	1,257	4	4	0
Enoch	5,130	5	4	1
Ephraim	5,245	5	5	0
Fairview	1,182	1	1	0
Farmington	17,185	16	13	3
Garland	1,990	4	4	0
Grantsville	8,815	11	9	2
Gunnison	2,781	3	3	0
Harrisville	5,748	10	9	1
Heber	10,024	20	16	4
Helper	1,863	6	6	0
Hildale	1,993	11	6	5
Hurricane	13,622	19	17	2
Ivins	8,148	15	11	4
Kamas	1,521	2	2	0
Kanab	3,794	9	7	2
Kaysville	25,672	21	19	2
La Verkin	4,583	3	3	0
Layton	65,029	100	73	27
Lehi	48,465	41	37	4
Lindon	10,247	15	14	1
Logan	48,670	86	57	29
Mantua	752	1	1	0
Mapleton	7,775	9	7	2
Midvale	27,875	56	46	10
Minersville	815	1	1	0
Moab	4,877	20	15	5
Monticello	1,957	4	4	0
Moroni	1,296	1	1	0
Mount Pleasant	2,749	3	3	0
Murray	45,760	94	74	20
Naples	1,597	6	6	0
Nephi	5,295	11	9	2
North Ogden	17,441	19	16	3
North Park	12,272	10	9	1
North Salt Lake	13,217	18	16	2
Ogden	83,353	166	135	31
Orem	94,228	125	88	37
Park City	8,104	39	29	10
Parowan	2,638	3	3	0
Payson	17,703	19	17	2
Perry	3,962	5	4	1
Pleasant Grove/Lindon	32,755	32	24	8
Pleasant View	6,906	9	8	1
Price	8,146	19	17	2
Provo	119,189	150	101	49
Richfield	7,152	15	13	2
Riverdale	8,015	23	19	4
Roosevelt	4,928	12	11	1
Roy	35,279	46	39	7
Salem	6,082	10	9	1
Salina	2,391	6	5	1
Salt Lake City	180,514	580	427	153
Sandy	96,998	139	113	26
Santaquin/Genola	8,861	10	10	0
Saratoga Springs	19,624	18	15	3
Smithfield	9,448	9	8	1
South Jordan	51,044	59	50	9
South Ogden	15,783	31	26	5
South Salt Lake	21,490	73	58	15
Spanish Fork	29,880	31	28	3
Springville	27,753	35	27	8
St. George	74,356	140	102	38
Stockton	583	1	1	0
Sunset	4,887	9	8	1
Syracuse	23,333	21	19	2
Taylorsville City	58,600	60	56	4
Tooele	30,364	37	32	5
Tremonton	6,579	12	10	2
Vernal	8,496	25	22	3
Washington	18,184	21	18	3
Wellington	1,556	4	4	0
West Bountiful	5,350	11	10	1
West Jordan	105,772	133	97	36
West Valley	124,128	235	188	47
Willard	1,702	2	2	0
Woods Cross	8,671	13	11	2
VERMONT				
Bennington	15,087	32	25	7
Brattleboro	11,542	25	22	3
Burlington	38,370	121	89	32
Chester	3,029	5	4	1
Colchester	17,245	35	28	7
Dover	1,440	6	5	1
Essex	19,564	37	29	8
Hartford	10,739	29	19	10
Lyndonville	1,228	2	2	0
Manchester	4,293	12	8	4
Middlebury	8,208	16	14	2
Milton	10,671	13	12	1
Montpelier	7,779	24	16	8
Morristown	5,570	11	11	0
Newport	5,206	12	10	2
Northfield	5,743	7	6	1
Randolph	5,068	5	5	0
Richmond	4,180	4	4	0
Rutland	16,775	52	41	11
South Burlington	17,785	47	39	8
Springfield	8,616	20	15	5
St. Albans	7,263	30	19	11
Swanton	6,458	5	4	1
Williston	8,458	18	15	3
Wilmington	2,370	7	6	1
Windsor	3,618	7	6	1
Winhall	787	6	5	1
Winooski	6,434	24	17	7
VIRGINIA				
Abingdon	7,991	25	23	2
Alexandria	140,891	449	321	128
Altavista	3,371	12	12	0
Amherst	2,203	5	5	0
Appalachia	1,735	6	6	0
Ashland	7,125	27	24	3
Bedford	6,260	26	22	4
Berryville	3,177	9	8	1
Big Stone Gap	5,661	18	16	2
Blacksburg	41,509	79	62	17
Blackstone	3,511	16	11	5
Bluefield	5,163	23	17	6
Boykins	602	1	1	0
Bridgewater	5,404	9	9	0
Bristol	17,563	75	54	21
Broadway	3,031	4	4	0
Brookneal	1,250	3	3	0
Buena Vista	6,475	16	14	2
Burkeville	467	1	1	0
Cape Charles	1,518	5	5	0
Cedar Bluff	1,042	3	3	0
Charlottesville	41,216	143	115	28
Chase City	2,310	10	9	1
Chatham	1,259	4	4	0
Chesapeake	220,812	512	381	131
Chilhowie	1,746	6	6	0
Chincoteague	4,306	14	10	4
Christiansburg	19,466	70	53	17

Table 78. Full-Time Law Enforcement Employees, by State and City, 2008—*Continued*

(Number.)

State/City	Population	Total law enforcement employees	Total officers	Total civilians
Clarksville	1,252	9	8	1
Clifton Forge	3,946	15	10	5
Clintwood	1,498	4	4	0
Coeburn	1,982	8	7	1
Colonial Beach	3,784	17	12	5
Colonial Heights	17,843	54	50	4
Courtland	1,246	3	1	2
Covington	6,130	27	17	10
Crewe	2,255	6	6	0
Culpeper	14,072	51	42	9
Damascus	1,084	7	5	2
Danville	44,383	137	128	9
Dayton	1,354	10	9	1
Dublin	2,199	10	9	1
Dumfries	4,805	16	14	2
Edinburg	874	2	2	0
Elkton	2,619	7	6	1
Emporia	5,593	34	24	10
Exmore	1,346	8	8	0
Fairfax City	23,486	80	64	16
Falls Church	10,979	42	32	10
Farmville	7,216	28	27	1
Franklin	8,955	38	26	12
Fredericksburg	22,740	97	73	24
Fries	552	1	1	0
Front Royal	14,688	45	35	10
Galax	6,796	38	24	14
Gate City	2,040	5	5	0
Glade Spring	1,543	2	2	0
Glasgow	1,009	1	1	0
Glen Lyn	164	1	1	0
Gordonsville	1,700	6	6	0
Gretna	1,187	4	4	0
Grottoes	2,182	6	5	1
Grundy	961	5	5	0
Halifax	1,259	5	5	0
Hampton	145,897	408	276	132
Harrisonburg	44,346	103	87	16
Haymarket	1,265	4	3	1
Haysi	177	2	2	0
Herndon	21,900	71	56	15
Hillsville	2,644	12	11	1
Honaker	1,444	5	4	1
Hopewell	23,035	65	53	12
Hurt	1,208	1	1	0
Independence	895	2	2	0
Jonesville	966	3	3	0
Kenbridge	1,290	6	6	0
Kilmarnock	1,188	5	5	0
La Crosse	587	4	4	0
Lawrenceville	1,353	5	5	0
Lebanon	3,163	12	11	1
Leesburg	39,899	94	76	18
Lexington	7,026	19	17	2
Louisa	1,568	6	6	0
Luray	4,856	13	11	2
Lynchburg	71,805	227	164	63
Manassas	35,290	125	94	31
Manassas Park	11,528	46	32	14
Marion	6,013	20	18	2
Martinsville	14,430	59	53	6
Middleburg	959	4	4	0
Middletown	1,148	1	1	0
Mount Jackson	1,791	4	4	0
Narrows	2,155	4	4	0
New Market	1,859	5	5	0
Newport News	178,308	563	415	148
Norfolk	235,067	879	757	122
Norton	3,691	24	17	7
Occoquan	830	2	2	0
Onancock	1,392	4	4	0
Onley	475	4	4	0
Orange	4,639	18	15	3
Parksley	797	3	3	0
Pearisburg	2,770	8	7	1
Pembroke	1,167	1	1	0
Pennington Gap	1,726	6	6	0
Petersburg	32,677	150	106	44
Pocahontas	419	1	1	0
Poquoson	11,850	23	21	2
Portsmouth	101,782	323	233	90
Pound	1,073	4	4	0
Pulaski	8,997	36	28	8
Purcellville	5,175	14	13	1
Quantico	613	2	2	0
Radford	16,109	47	34	13
Remington	678	1	1	0
Rich Creek	683	1	1	0
Richlands	3,997	23	18	5
Richmond	199,674	1,012	733	279
Roanoke	91,983	316	262	54
Rocky Mount	4,546	21	19	2
Salem	25,193	90	63	27
Saltville	2,220	8	7	1
Shenandoah	1,862	5	5	0
Smithfield	7,071	26	22	4
South Boston	7,856	28	26	2
South Hill	4,556	22	20	2
Stanley	1,328	3	3	0
Staunton	23,746	69	53	16
Stephens City	1,479	3	3	0
St. Paul	966	4	4	0
Strasburg	4,334	21	19	2
Suffolk	83,470	224	176	48
Tappahannock	2,177	11	10	1
Tazewell	4,268	14	12	2
Timberville	1,714	4	4	0
Victoria	1,747	6	5	1
Vienna	14,889	50	41	9
Vinton	7,876	34	24	10
Virginia Beach	434,163	968	812	156
Warrenton	9,190	21	19	2
Warsaw	1,360	3	3	0
Waverly	2,160	11	6	5
Waynesboro	21,846	62	51	11
Weber City	1,310	5	5	0
West Point	3,145	9	8	1
White Stone	340	1	1	0
Williamsburg	12,445	52	36	16
Winchester	25,904	84	70	14
Wise	3,232	14	13	1
Woodstock	4,297	18	17	1
Wytheville	8,148	43	28	15
WASHINGTON				
Aberdeen	16,116	49	37	12
Airway Heights	5,239	13	12	1
Algona	2,764	9	7	2
Anacortes	17,020	31	23	8
Arlington	17,187	29	24	5
Asotin	1,118	3	3	0
Auburn	50,660	135	102	33
Bainbridge Island	22,041	28	22	6
Battle Ground	14,099	32	26	6
Bellevue	122,459	272	182	90
Bellingham	78,804	162	111	51
Black Diamond	3,979	11	10	1
Blaine	4,948	14	11	3
Bonney Lake	16,482	33	28	5
Bothell	32,464	80	55	25
Bremerton	33,735	82	66	16
Brewster	2,075	8	6	2
Brier	6,362	9	7	2
Buckley	5,488	9	9	0
Burien	31,342	33	32	1
Burlington	8,869	30	24	6
Camas	18,527	29	24	5
Castle Rock	2,118	6	5	1
Centralia	15,772	38	31	7

Table 78. Full-Time Law Enforcement Employees, by State and City, 2008—*Continued*

(Number.)

State/City	Population	Total law enforcement employees	Total officers	Total civilians
Chehalis	7,243	22	17	5
Cheney	10,653	20	14	6
Chewelah	2,291	7	6	1
Clarkston	7,123	14	13	1
Cle Elum	3,480	10	8	2
Clyde Hill	3,049	10	9	1
Colfax	2,741	6	6	0
College Place	9,159	14	11	3
Colton	383	1	1	0
Colville	4,939	14	12	2
Connell	3,018	7	7	0
Cosmopolis	1,687	6	5	1
Coulee City	641	1	1	0
Coulee Dam	1,057	7	7	0
Coupeville	1,860	4	4	0
Covington	18,158	13	13	0
Des Moines	29,013	57	44	13
Dupont	7,407	11	10	1
Duvall	6,171	17	15	2
East Wenatchee	12,328	24	21	3
Eatonville	2,495	7	6	1
Edgewood	9,833	11	10	1
Edmonds	40,214	66	56	10
Ellensburg	17,540	36	27	9
Elma	3,146	8	7	1
Enumclaw	11,066	29	16	13
Ephrata	7,298	18	15	3
Everett	98,552	242	198	44
Everson	2,159	6	6	0
Federal Way	84,775	160	129	31
Ferndale	11,325	22	18	4
Fife	8,322	53	30	23
Fircrest	6,299	10	9	1
Forks	3,221	10	6	4
Gig Harbor	6,631	20	17	3
Goldendale	3,720	10	9	1
Grand Coulee	1,920	7	7	0
Grandview	9,418	24	18	6
Granger	2,968	7	5	2
Granite Falls	3,055	9	8	1
Hoquiam	8,902	19	17	2
Issaquah	24,326	58	32	26
Kalama	2,182	5	5	0
Kelso	12,063	32	28	4
Kenmore	20,688	12	12	0
Kennewick	62,930	109	90	19
Kent	84,966	185	130	55
Kettle Falls	1,577	5	4	1
Kirkland	47,619	104	67	37
Kittitas	1,225	2	2	0
La Center	1,953	11	9	2
Lacey	39,037	68	50	18
Lake Forest Park	12,562	25	20	5
Lake Stevens	13,698	28	23	5
Lakewood	57,081	121	102	19
Langley	1,035	4	4	0
Liberty Lake	6,947	9	9	0
Long Beach	1,380	7	6	1
Longview	36,887	69	54	15
Lynden	11,812	18	14	4
Lynnwood	33,602	112	79	33
Mabton	2,084	4	4	0
Maple Valley	17,626	10	10	0
Marysville	34,192	79	52	27
Mattawa	3,379	3	3	0
McCleary	1,593	3	3	0
Medical Lake	4,709	7	6	1
Medina	3,626	10	8	2
Mercer Island	24,134	32	30	2
Mill Creek	15,776	32	24	8
Milton	6,927	13	12	1
Monroe	16,764	48	37	11
Montesano	3,613	10	8	2
Morton	1,091	4	3	1
Moses Lake	18,283	39	31	8
Mossyrock	506	1	1	0
Mountlake Terrace	20,015	42	31	11
Mount Vernon	31,237	54	43	11
Moxee	2,251	4	4	0
Mukilteo	20,870	31	27	4
Napavine	1,618	5	4	1
Newcastle	10,080	7	7	0
Normandy Park	6,222	15	13	2
North Bend	4,622	1	1	0
North Bonneville	807	1	1	0
Oakesdale	389	1	1	0
Oak Harbor	23,068	39	26	13
Ocean Shores	4,964	16	14	2
Odessa	911	2	2	0
Olympia	45,189	94	66	28
Omak	4,685	15	12	3
Oroville	1,564	5	4	1
Orting	6,262	9	9	0
Othello	6,429	22	16	6
Pacific	6,076	14	12	2
Palouse	930	3	3	0
Pasco	55,612	78	67	11
Port Angeles	18,835	54	32	22
Port Orchard	7,960	22	20	2
Port Townsend	9,161	19	15	4
Poulsbo	7,991	22	18	4
Prosser	5,097	19	11	8
Pullman	26,587	40	28	12
Puyallup	36,860	75	56	19
Quincy	5,553	13	11	2
Raymond	2,917	7	6	1
Reardan	597	1	1	0
Redmond	49,921	120	81	39
Renton	61,536	166	121	45
Republic	951	3	3	0
Richland	45,522	67	57	10
Ridgefield	4,547	8	7	1
Ritzville	1,720	4	4	0
Rosalia	586	2	2	0
Roy	810	4	3	1
Royal City	1,966	3	3	0
Ruston	880	4	4	0
Sammamish	35,395	22	22	0
SeaTac	25,743	42	39	3
Seattle	598,077	1,825	1,318	507
Sedro Woolley	10,902	20	14	6
Selah	7,136	14	13	1
Sequim	6,161	22	19	3
Shelton	9,322	32	18	14
Shoreline	52,571	48	48	0
Snohomish	8,822	26	21	5
Snoqualmie	9,103	15	12	3
Soap Lake	1,861	4	4	0
South Bend	1,807	4	3	1
Spokane	201,491	413	296	117
Spokane Valley	85,551	102	101	1
Springdale	278	1	1	0
Stanwood	6,130	13	11	2
Steilacoom	6,124	12	11	1
Sultan	4,295	5	5	0
Sumas	1,237	6	6	0
Sumner	9,723	31	18	13
Sunnyside	14,985	41	24	17
Tacoma	196,851	428	382	46
Tenino	2,229	6	5	1
Tieton	1,171	2	2	0
Toledo	680	1	1	0
Tonasket	941	5	4	1
Toppenish	9,236	20	15	5
Tukwila	17,237	82	66	16
Tumwater	13,564	31	25	6
Twisp	892	2	2	0
Union Gap	5,644	23	18	5
University Place	30,529	25	24	1
Vader	616	1	1	0

Table 78. Full-Time Law Enforcement Employees, by State and City, 2008—*Continued*

(Number.)

State/City	Population	Total law enforcement employees	Total officers	Total civilians
Vancouver	163,574	233	201	32
Walla Walla	30,830	73	44	29
Wapato	4,569	19	11	8
Warden	2,592	5	4	1
Washougal	12,256	21	19	2
Wenatchee	29,976	54	43	11
Westport	2,575	9	7	2
West Richland	10,689	17	14	3
White Salmon	2,348	6	6	0
Wilbur	873	2	2	0
Winlock	1,256	2	2	0
Winthrop	376	3	3	0
Woodinville	10,280	10	10	0
Woodland	4,894	12	10	2
Yakima	83,027	185	135	50
Yelm	5,716	16	14	2
Zillah	2,669	8	7	1
WEST VIRGINIA[2]				
WISCONSIN				
Adams	1,791	5	5	0
Albany	1,104	3	3	0
Algoma	3,166	6	6	0
Altoona	6,573	13	12	1
Amery	2,774	8	7	1
Antigo	8,031	19	16	3
Appleton	69,975	140	113	27
Arcadia	2,308	5	5	0
Ashland	7,999	20	19	1
Ashwaubenon	17,299	56	45	11
Avoca	587	1	1	0
Bangor	1,368	3	3	0
Baraboo	11,089	33	27	6
Barron	3,143	5	5	0
Bayfield	574	3	3	0
Bayside	4,288	21	14	7
Beaver Dam	15,260	34	29	5
Belleville	2,336	5	5	0
Beloit	36,737	89	76	13
Beloit Town	7,468	15	13	2
Berlin	5,086	13	12	1
Big Bend	1,285	3	3	0
Black River Falls	3,435	8	7	1
Blair	1,253	2	2	0
Bloomer	3,342	8	7	1
Bloomfield	5,976	7	7	0
Boscobel	3,128	6	6	0
Brillion	2,815	8	7	1
Brodhead	3,068	12	8	4
Brookfield	39,267	83	65	18
Brookfield Township	6,149	14	13	1
Brown Deer	11,732	36	30	6
Burlington	10,473	27	21	6
Burlington Town	6,465	10	9	1
Butler	1,784	9	8	1
Caledonia	25,608	44	34	10
Campbellsport	1,967	2	2	0
Campbell Township	4,470	5	5	0
Cedarburg	11,043	29	20	9
Chenequa	586	9	8	1
Chetek	2,162	6	5	1
Chilton	3,598	6	6	0
Chippewa Falls	13,330	30	24	6
Cleveland	1,380	2	1	1
Clinton	2,271	6	6	0
Clintonville	4,330	15	11	4
Colby-Abbotsford	3,563	7	6	1
Columbus	5,032	12	10	2
Combined Locks	3,156	5	5	0
Coon Valley	697	1	1	0
Cornell	1,408	3	3	0
Cottage Grove	5,958	13	12	1
Crandon	1,852	4	3	1
Cross Plains	3,618	6	5	1
Cuba City	2,006	5	4	1
Cudahy	18,596	40	30	10
Cumberland	2,252	5	5	0
Darien	1,650	7	6	1
Darlington	2,238	5	5	0
DeForest	9,074	19	16	3
Delafield	6,901	17	15	2
Delavan	8,417	24	19	5
Delavan Town	4,839	12	11	1
Denmark	2,154	3	3	0
De Pere	23,015	35	31	4
Dodgeville	4,534	10	9	1
Durand	1,867	3	3	0
Eagle River	1,555	6	6	0
Eagle Village	1,846	2	2	0
East Troy	4,212	7	7	0
Eau Claire	65,344	131	99	32
Edgar	1,471	1	1	0
Edgerton	5,281	10	9	1
Eleva	642	1	1	0
Elkhart Lake	1,175	3	3	0
Elkhorn	9,317	19	16	3
Elk Mound	801	4	4	0
Ellsworth	3,141	7	6	1
Elm Grove	5,980	23	16	7
Elroy	1,447	3	3	0
Evansville	5,027	9	8	1
Everest	16,032	27	24	3
Fennimore	2,224	5	5	0
Fitchburg	23,599	52	40	12
Fond du Lac	42,037	76	70	6
Fontana	1,866	7	6	1
Fort Atkinson	12,004	26	20	6
Fox Lake	1,466	2	2	0
Fox Point	6,780	18	17	1
Fox Valley	17,562	28	25	3
Franklin	35,751	72	56	16
Frederic	1,192	2	2	0
Geneva Town	4,756	8	6	2
Genoa City	2,939	6	5	1
Germantown	19,508	42	31	11
Glendale	13,190	50	46	4
Grafton	11,533	29	22	7
Grand Chute	20,836	33	29	4
Grand Rapids	7,647	6	4	2
Grantsburg	1,423	3	3	0
Green Bay	100,531	214	175	39
Greendale	13,979	36	29	7
Greenfield	36,217	79	57	22
Green Lake	1,140	4	4	0
Hales Corners	7,715	21	17	4
Hartford	13,995	29	25	4
Hartland	8,717	18	16	2
Hayward	2,304	8	8	0
Hazel Green	1,108	2	2	0
Highland	819	1	1	0
Hillsboro	1,265	2	2	0
Hobart-Lawrence	10,388	5	4	1
Holmen	7,910	10	9	1
Horicon	3,553	10	8	2
Hortonville	2,788	6	5	1
Hudson	12,504	26	23	3
Hurley	1,560	6	6	0
Independence	1,213	2	2	0
Iron Ridge	987	1	1	0
Jackson	6,350	13	12	1
Janesville	63,353	113	101	12
Jefferson	7,845	17	14	3
Juneau	2,611	7	6	1
Kaukauna	15,519	26	24	2
Kenosha	96,977	204	194	10
Kewaskum	4,197	7	7	0
Kewaunee	2,814	6	6	0
Kiel	3,509	8	7	1
Kohler	1,968	8	7	1

[2] No 2008 police employee data were received for the state of West Virginia.

Table 78. Full-Time Law Enforcement Employees, by State and City, 2008—*Continued*

(Number.)

State/City	Population	Total law enforcement employees	Total officers	Total civilians
La Crosse	50,569	113	92	21
Ladysmith	3,476	11	10	1
Lake Delton	2,938	17	16	1
Lake Geneva	8,203	31	22	9
Lake Hallie	6,065	7	6	1
Lake Mills	5,504	11	11	0
Lancaster	3,846	8	7	1
Lodi	2,937	10	5	5
Luxemburg	2,261	2	2	0
Madison	231,231	534	436	98
Manitowoc	32,891	73	64	9
Maple Bluff	1,306	5	5	0
Marathon City	1,546	2	2	0
Marinette	10,641	28	24	4
Marion	1,192	3	3	0
Markesan	1,289	3	3	0
Marshall Village	3,696	10	8	2
Marshfield	18,847	45	38	7
Mauston	4,332	9	8	1
Mayville	5,322	12	10	2
McFarland	7,827	16	14	2
Medford	4,012	10	9	1
Menasha	16,829	36	29	7
Menomonee Falls	34,590	83	59	24
Menomonie	15,477	33	27	6
Mequon	23,483	46	38	8
Merrill	9,587	25	22	3
Middleton	17,059	43	33	10
Milton	5,832	11	9	2
Milwaukee	602,131	2,710	2,016	694
Mineral Point	2,529	6	6	0
Minocqua	4,947	14	9	5
Mishicot	1,368	1	1	0
Mondovi	2,604	4	4	0
Monona	8,047	26	20	6
Monroe	10,470	35	26	9
Mosinee	4,039	8	7	1
Mount Horeb	6,884	11	10	1
Mount Pleasant	26,193	53	40	13
Mukwonago	7,046	21	14	7
Muskego	23,025	48	37	11
Neenah	25,005	50	40	10
Neillsville	2,555	7	6	1
New Berlin	39,091	91	71	20
New Glarus	2,051	5	5	0
New Holstein	3,122	8	7	1
New Lisbon	2,542	4	4	0
New London	6,897	19	17	2
New Richmond	8,273	17	16	1
Niagara	1,726	4	4	0
North Fond du Lac	5,118	14	12	2
North Hudson	3,790	4	3	1
Oak Creek	33,833	80	58	22
Oconomowoc	14,612	28	22	6
Oconomowoc Town	8,178	13	12	1
Oconto	4,595	8	8	0
Oconto Falls	2,782	5	5	0
Omro	3,379	7	6	1
Onalaska	16,873	30	27	3
Oregon	9,445	18	16	2
Osceola	2,723	7	6	1
Oshkosh	64,747	113	95	18
Osseo	1,608	4	4	0
Palmyra	1,749	4	4	0
Park Falls	2,323	8	7	1
Pepin	928	1	1	0
Peshtigo	3,208	7	6	1
Pewaukee	13,229	28	25	3
Pewaukee Village	8,997	18	16	2
Phillips	1,461	5	5	0
Platteville	9,600	26	20	6
Pleasant Prairie	20,126	30	28	2
Plover	11,796	21	18	3
Plymouth	8,304	16	16	0
Portage	9,811	30	22	8
Port Washington	11,086	23	18	5
Poynette	2,548	5	4	1
Prairie du Chien	5,739	15	14	1
Prescott	4,029	9	8	1
Princeton	1,411	5	5	0
Pulaski	3,556	6	6	0
Racine	82,226	258	195	63
Readstown	375	1	1	0
Reedsburg	8,687	28	20	8
Rhinelander	7,641	20	17	3
Rice Lake	8,284	20	18	2
Richland Center	5,068	13	11	2
Ripon	7,204	19	14	5
River Falls	14,093	24	22	2
River Hills	1,649	12	12	0
Rome Town	3,045	8	7	1
Rothschild	5,370	12	10	2
Sauk Prairie	4,189	15	13	2
Saukville	4,327	13	11	2
Seymour	3,446	7	6	1
Shawano	8,670	21	19	2
Sheboygan	47,813	111	85	26
Sheboygan Falls	7,815	16	14	2
Shorewood	13,426	30	25	5
Shorewood Hills	1,653	7	6	1
Silver Lake	2,518	5	4	1
Siren	814	3	3	0
Slinger	4,566	10	9	1
Somerset	2,397	6	5	1
South Milwaukee	21,114	39	33	6
Sparta	9,007	20	18	2
Spencer	1,822	3	3	0
Spooner	2,557	7	6	1
Spring Green	1,429	4	3	1
Stanley	3,615	4	4	0
St. Croix Falls	2,148	6	5	1
Stevens Point	24,848	58	45	13
St. Francis	9,173	26	21	5
Stoughton	12,934	26	20	6
Strum	1,024	9	9	0
Sturgeon Bay	8,915	22	21	1
Sturtevant	6,780	10	9	1
Summit	5,128	8	8	0
Sun Prairie	28,793	71	47	24
Superior	26,530	62	56	6
Theresa	1,299	6	2	4
Thiensville	3,196	8	7	1
Three Lakes	2,238	4	4	0
Tomah	8,812	22	20	2
Tomahawk	3,647	8	7	1
Town of East Troy	3,893	6	6	0
Town of Madison	5,941	20	18	2
Town of Menasha	17,392	33	26	7
Trempealeau	1,508	2	2	0
Twin Lakes	5,660	18	13	5
Two Rivers	11,680	30	27	3
Valders	969	1	1	0
Verona	11,262	19	17	2
Viroqua	4,316	10	8	2
Walworth	2,667	7	6	1
Washburn	2,084	5	5	0
Waterloo	3,235	9	8	1
Watertown	23,130	52	38	14
Waukesha	66,984	151	113	38
Waunakee	11,341	19	17	2
Waupaca	5,865	15	14	1
Waupun	10,642	20	18	2
Wausau	37,981	78	71	7
Wautoma	2,076	7	6	1
Wauwatosa	45,298	122	93	29
West Allis	59,602	154	132	22
West Bend	29,958	74	55	19
Westby	2,134	3	3	0

Table 78. Full-Time Law Enforcement Employees, by State and City, 2008—*Continued*

(Number.)

State/City	Population	Total law enforcement employees	Total officers	Total civilians
West Milwaukee	4,051	19	16	3
West Salem	4,825	7	6	1
Whitefish Bay	13,702	27	24	3
Whitehall	1,601	4	4	0
Whitewater	14,122	35	24	11
Williams Bay	2,676	8	7	1
Winneconne	2,508	6	5	1
Wisconsin Dells	2,484	19	13	6
Wisconsin Rapids	17,372	43	38	5
Woodruff	2,005	6	5	1
WYOMING				
Afton	1,774	5	5	0
Baggs	391	2	2	0
Basin	1,234	4	4	0
Buffalo	4,690	21	13	8
Casper	53,430	124	94	30
Cheyenne	55,931	129	104	25
Cody	9,225	22	20	2
Diamondville	649	3	2	1
Douglas	5,722	23	17	6
Evanston	11,492	39	27	12
Evansville	2,338	11	9	2
Gillette	25,678	73	46	27
Glenrock	2,387	10	7	3
Green River	12,113	41	31	10
Greybull	1,728	7	6	1
Guernsey	1,082	3	3	0
Hanna	861	5	4	1
Hulett	464	2	2	0
Jackson	9,753	34	23	11
Kemmerer	2,401	7	6	1
Lander	7,158	16	15	1
Laramie	27,260	68	49	19
Lovell	2,246	9	6	3
Lusk	1,327	4	4	0
Mills	3,169	13	11	2
Moorcroft	858	5	4	1
Newcastle	3,334	14	7	7
Pine Bluffs	1,140	6	2	4
Powell	5,370	24	17	7
Rawlins	8,651	29	17	12
Riverton	9,907	38	25	13
Rock Springs	19,800	61	43	18
Saratoga	1,739	5	5	0
Sheridan	16,827	54	30	24
Sundance	1,211	4	4	0
Thermopolis	2,897	14	8	6
Torrington	5,396	20	14	6
Wheatland	3,327	10	9	1
Worland	4,901	10	10	0

Table 79. Full-Time Law Enforcement Employees, by State and University and College, 2008

(Number.)

State, university/college, campus	Student enrollment[1]	Total law enforcement employees	Total officers	Total civilians
ALABAMA				
Alabama State University	5,608	31	21	10
Auburn University				
Montgomery	5,138	24	14	10
Calhoun Community College[2]		6	5	1
Jacksonville State University	9,077	18	14	4
Troy University	28,955	13	9	4
University of Alabama:				
Birmingham	16,246	150	79	71
Huntsville	7,264	15	11	4
Tuscaloosa	25,544	71	61	10
University of Montevallo	2,949	16	9	7
University of North Alabama	7,097	17	15	2
University of South Alabama	13,779	44	25	19
University of West Alabama	4,011	9	6	3
ALASKA				
University of Alaska:				
Anchorage	16,463	19	12	7
Fairbanks	8,618	16	11	5
ARIZONA				
Arizona State University				
Main Campus	51,481	140	71	69
Arizona Western College	6,953	9	6	3
Central Arizona College	4,951	10	7	3
Northern Arizona University	21,347	26	16	10
Pima Community College	32,982	33	26	7
Yavapai College	9,060	9	8	1
ARKANSAS				
Arkansas State University:				
Beebe	4,311	4	3	1
Jonesboro	11,130	22	18	4
Arkansas Tech University	7,476	11	9	2
Henderson State University	3,603	8	7	1
Northwest Arkansas Community College	6,470	14	8	6
Southern Arkansas University	3,147	7	6	1
University of Arkansas:				
Fayetteville	18,648	38	30	8
Little Rock	12,135	36	25	11
Medical Sciences	2,538	47	39	8
Monticello	3,187	7	6	1
Pine Bluff	3,200	19	14	5
University of Central Arkansas	12,619	34	25	9
CALIFORNIA				
Allan Hancock College	13,176	6	4	2
California State Polytechnic University:				
Pomona	21,477	32	20	12
San Luis Obispo	19,777	38	18	20
California State University:				
Bakersfield	7,700	14	10	4
Channel Islands	3,599	27	13	14
Chico	17,034	27	17	10
Dominguez Hills	12,082	23	17	6
East Bay	13,124	22	12	10
Fresno	22,383	28	19	9
Fullerton	37,130	28	20	8
Long Beach	36,868	54	27	27
Los Angeles	21,051	38	22	16
Monterey Bay	4,080	16	14	2
Northridge	35,446	38	24	14
Sacramento	28,829	30	21	9
San Bernardino	17,066	22	13	9
San Jose[2]		53	29	24
San Marcos	9,159	36	16	20
Stanislaus	8,836	22	11	11
College of the Sequoias	11,697	6	5	1
Contra Costa Community College	7,147	37	25	12
Cuesta College	10,920	7	6	1
El Camino College	24,895	32	25	7
Foothill-De Anza College	42,247	20	10	10
Fresno Community College	21,624	18	15	3
Humboldt State University	7,773	22	14	8
Marin Community College	6,476	8	7	1
Pasadena Community College	26,672	13	8	5
Reedley Community College	12,158	4	3	1
Riverside Community College	30,961	29	20	9
San Bernardino Community College	12,839	15	10	5

[1] The student enrollment figures provided by the United States Department of Education are for the 2007 school year, the most recent available. The enrollment figures include full-time and part-time students.
[2] Student enrollment figures were not available.

Table 79. Full-Time Law Enforcement Employees, by State and University and College, 2008—*Continued*

(Number.)

State, university/college, campus	Student enrollment[1]	Total law enforcement employees	Total officers	Total civilians
San Diego State University	35,695	51	28	23
San Francisco State University	30,125	46	24	22
San Jose/Evergreen Community College	18,512	12	6	6
Santa Rosa Junior College	25,626	24	12	12
Solano Community College	11,163	6	4	2
Sonoma State University	8,770	17	12	5
University of California:				
Berkeley	34,940	121	71	50
Davis	29,796	77	43	34
Hastings College of Law	1,262	14	14	0
Irvine	26,483	40	30	10
Los Angeles	37,476	95	57	38
Merced	1,871	18	10	8
Riverside	17,187	41	29	12
San Diego	27,020	66	35	31
San Francisco	2,999	121	39	82
Santa Barbara	21,410	46	32	14
Santa Cruz	15,825	47	21	26
Ventura County Community College District	12,603	16	15	1
West Valley-Mission College	20,042	11	7	4
COLORADO				
Adams State College	2,830	6	5	1
Arapahoe Community College	6,538	10	7	3
Auraria Higher Education Center[2]		39	25	14
Colorado State University				
Fort Collins	27,569	65	41	24
Fort Lewis College	3,928	8	7	1
Pikes Peak Community College	11,407	18	16	2
Red Rocks Community College	7,223	2	2	0
University of Colorado:				
Boulder	31,796	54	35	19
Colorado Springs	8,660	21	14	7
Denver	21,658	58	22	36
Health Sciences Center[2]		5	5	0
University of Northern Colorado	12,702	19	14	5
CONNECTICUT				
Central Connecticut State University	12,106	26	20	6
Eastern Connecticut State University	5,137	26	20	6
Southern Connecticut State University	11,930	34	27	7
University of Connecticut:				
Health Center[2]		27	14	13
Storrs, Avery Point, and Hartford[2]		82	70	12
Western Connecticut State University	6,211	24	16	8
Yale University	11,454	94	79	15
DELAWARE				
Delaware State University	3,756	38	18	20
University of Delaware	20,342	78	46	32
FLORIDA				
Florida A&M University	11,562	64	37	27
Florida Atlantic University	26,193	53	42	11
Florida Gulf Coast University	9,339	20	13	7
Florida International University	38,182	57	40	17
Florida State University:				
Panama City[2]		6	5	1
Tallahassee	40,555	72	57	15
New College of Florida	767	17	11	6
Pensacola Junior College	10,728	15	12	3
Santa Fe College	14,824	21	17	4
Tallahassee Community College	13,776	25	8	17
University of Central Florida	48,398	94	57	37
University of Florida	51,725	157	87	70
University of North Florida	16,406	35	27	8
University of South Florida:				
St. Petersburg[2]		16	12	4
Tampa	44,870	59	43	16
University of West Florida	10,358	29	20	9
GEORGIA				
Abraham Baldwin Agricultural College	3,665	12	12	0
Albany State University	4,033	28	17	11
Armstrong Atlantic State University	6,848	14	8	6
Augusta State University	6,588	24	17	7
Berry College	1,858	17	13	4
Clark Atlanta University	4,271	37	14	23
Coastal Georgia Community College	2,942	8	8	0
Columbus State University	7,593	30	23	7
Dalton State College	4,532	10	9	1

[1] The student enrollment figures provided by the United States Department of Education are for the 2007 school year, the most recent available. The enrollment figures include full-time and part-time students.
[2] Student enrollment figures were not available.

Table 79. Full-Time Law Enforcement Employees, by State and University and College, 2008—*Continued*

(Number.)

State, university/college, campus	Student enrollment[1]	Total law enforcement employees	Total officers	Total civilians
Emory University	12,570	68	49	19
Georgia College and State University	6,249	23	16	7
Georgia Institute of Technology	18,742	82	61	21
Georgia Military College[2]		4	3	1
Georgia Perimeter College	21,473	72	32	40
Georgia Southern University	16,841	35	30	5
Georgia State University	27,134	102	67	35
Gordon College	3,703	10	9	1
Kennesaw State University	20,607	49	23	26
Medical College of Georgia	2,392	43	32	11
Mercer University	7,308	35	26	9
Middle Georgia College	3,444	16	10	6
Morehouse College	2,810	38	12	26
Morris-Brown College[2]		8	3	5
North Georgia College and State University	5,227	14	10	4
Savannah State University	3,169	35	15	20
Southern Polytechnic State University	4,460	17	14	3
South Georgia College	1,754	6	6	0
University of Georgia	33,831	91	71	20
Valdosta State University	11,280	30	21	9
Young Harris College	639	3	3	0
ILLINOIS				
Black Hawk College	6,311	10	9	1
Chicago State University	6,810	34	25	9
College of DuPage	25,768	20	15	5
College of Lake County	16,010	19	12	7
Eastern Illinois University	12,179	20	17	3
Governors State University	5,692	11	7	4
Illinois State University	20,274	25	22	3
John A. Logan College	7,559	8	7	1
Joliet Junior College	13,149	18	10	8
Loyola University	15,545	57	32	25
Moraine Valley Community College	15,859	15	11	4
Morton College	5,057	4	2	2
Northeastern Illinois University	12,814	23	19	4
Northern Illinois University	25,254	94	59	35
Northwestern University:				
Chicago[2]		12	11	1
Evanston[2]		75	34	41
Oakton Community College	10,805	12	11	1
Parkland College	9,407	18	13	5
Rock Valley College	7,923	16	12	4
Southern Illinois University:				
Carbondale	20,983	44	34	10
Edwardsville	13,398	43	34	9
School of Medicine[2]		14	2	12
South Suburban College	6,260	15	11	4
Triton College	15,658	17	11	6
University of Illinois:				
Chicago	25,747	124	74	50
Springfield	4,855	22	15	7
Urbana	42,326	67	52	15
Waubonsee College	8,731	4	4	0
Western Illinois University	13,331	31	26	5
William Rainey Harper College[2]		15	9	6
INDIANA				
Ball State University	19,849	34	27	7
Indiana State University	10,543	34	25	9
Indiana University:				
Bloomington	38,990	53	43	10
Gary	4,790	15	11	4
Indianapolis[2]		40	32	8
New Albany	6,241	12	10	2
Marian College	2,043	8	5	3
Purdue University	40,534	50	40	10
IOWA				
Iowa State University	26,160	37	30	7
University of Iowa	29,117	57	32	25
University of Northern Iowa	12,692	26	18	8
KANSAS				
Emporia State University	6,354	9	9	0
Fort Hays State University	9,588	9	8	1
Kansas City Community College	5,801	10	9	1
Kansas State University	23,332	34	18	16
Pittsburg State University	7,087	17	13	4

[1] The student enrollment figures provided by the United States Department of Education are for the 2007 school year, the most recent available. The enrollment figures include full-time and part-time students.

[2] Student enrollment figures were not available.

Table 79. Full-Time Law Enforcement Employees, by State and University and College, 2008—*Continued*

(Number.)

State, university/college, campus	Student enrollment[1]	Total law enforcement employees	Total officers	Total civilians
University of Kansas:				
Main Campus	28,569	52	28	24
Medical Center[2]		63	31	32
Washburn University	6,901	18	13	5
Wichita State University	14,226	37	25	12
KENTUCKY				
Eastern Kentucky University	15,839	40	26	14
Kentucky State University	2,696	10	9	1
Morehead State University	8,897	27	16	11
Murray State University	10,778	23	16	7
Northern Kentucky University	14,785	27	19	8
University of Kentucky	25,856	101	49	52
University of Louisville	20,592	64	30	34
Western Kentucky University	19,258	31	20	11
LOUISIANA				
Delgado Community College	13,210	33	25	8
Grambling State University	5,161	19	10	9
Louisiana State University:				
Baton Rouge[2]		61	59	2
Health Sciences Center, New Orleans	2,234	33	33	0
Health Sciences Center, Shreveport	800	63	45	18
Shreveport	3,948	10	10	0
McNeese State University	8,095	22	16	6
Nicholls State University	6,864	16	11	5
Northwestern State University	9,037	26	20	6
Southeastern Louisiana University	14,744	32	25	7
Southern University and A&M College:				
Baton Rouge	8,288	30	23	7
New Orleans	2,648	11	10	1
Shreveport	2,337	12	11	1
Tulane University	10,125	49	34	15
University of Louisiana:				
Lafayette	16,345	27	21	6
Monroe	8,541	27	20	7
University of New Orleans	11,363	28	28	0
MAINE				
University of Maine:				
Farmington	2,351	6	5	1
Orono	11,912	32	19	13
University of Southern Maine	10,453	26	16	10
MARYLAND				
Bowie State University	5,464	29	15	14
Coppin State University	3,932	33	17	16
Frostburg State University	4,993	20	16	4
Morgan State University	7,208	55	35	20
Salisbury University	7,581	25	17	8
St. Mary's College	2,002	13	1	12
Towson University	19,758	62	39	23
University of Baltimore	5,421	38	14	24
University of Maryland:				
Baltimore City	5,884	150	61	89
Baltimore County	12,041	31	22	9
College Park	36,014	128	87	41
Eastern Shore	4,086	9	6	3
MASSACHUSETTS				
Amherst College	1,683	18	12	6
Assumption College	2,872	27	16	11
Bentley College	5,636	37	25	12
Boston College	14,621	61	47	14
Boston University	32,053	64	52	12
Brandeis University	5,333	25	21	4
Bridgewater State College	9,934	36	21	15
Bristol Community College	7,388	9	4	5
Clark University	3,210	13	11	2
Dean College	1,302	12	8	4
Emerson College	4,380	21	17	4
Fitchburg State College	6,692	20	17	3
Framingham State College	5,903	15	12	3
Harvard University	25,690	112	87	25
Lasell College	1,403	15	14	1
Massachusetts College of Art	2,312	23	9	14
Massachusetts College of Liberal Arts	1,841	12	8	4
Massachusetts Institute of Technology	10,220	59	56	3
Massasoit Community College	7,064	16	13	3
Merrimack College	2,098	19	14	5
Mount Holyoke College	2,204	19	15	4

[1] The student enrollment figures provided by the United States Department of Education are for the 2007 school year, the most recent available. The enrollment figures include full-time and part-time students.

[2] Student enrollment figures were not available.

Table 79. Full-Time Law Enforcement Employees, by State and University and College, 2008—*Continued*

(Number.)

State, university/college, campus	Student enrollment[1]	Total law enforcement employees	Total officers	Total civilians
Northeastern University	24,434	78	55	23
North Shore Community College	7,107	20	19	1
Quinsigamond Community College	6,654	13	11	2
Salem State College	10,085	25	21	4
Smith College	3,065	16	15	1
Springfield College	4,755	43	16	27
Tufts University				
Medford	9,758	61	43	18
University of Massachusetts:				
Amherst	25,873	83	63	20
Dartmouth	9,080	42	26	16
Harbor Campus, Boston	13,433	36	29	7
Wentworth Institute of Technology	3,728	18	12	6
Western New England College	3,657	26	17	9
Westfield State College	5,392	18	16	2
Worcester Polytechnic Institute	4,158	20	16	4
MICHIGAN				
Central Michigan University	26,611	29	19	10
Delta College	10,406	11	8	3
Eastern Michigan University	22,837	33	26	7
Ferris State University	13,087	19	14	5
Grand Rapids Community College	15,212	14	11	3
Grand Valley State University	23,464	20	16	4
Lansing Community College	19,465	19	16	3
Macomb Community College	22,081	37	30	7
Michigan State University	46,045	105	70	35
Michigan Technological University	6,744	12	9	3
Mott Community College	10,455	8	4	4
Northern Michigan University	9,358	25	21	4
Oakland Community College	24,532	27	25	2
Oakland University	18,081	27	21	6
Saginaw Valley State University	9,662	12	10	2
University of Michigan:				
Ann Arbor	41,042	91	55	36
Dearborn	8,336	17	6	11
Flint	6,883	23	9	14
Western Michigan University	24,433	64	29	35
MINNESOTA				
University of Minnesota:				
Duluth	11,184	11	10	1
Morris	1,686	6	3	3
Twin Cities	50,883	64	45	19
MISSISSIPPI				
Coahoma Community College	2,216	6	5	1
Itawamba Community College	5,871	10	9	1
Jackson State University	8,698	64	35	29
Mississippi State University	17,039	35	27	8
University of Mississippi:				
Medical Center	1,702	84	60	24
Oxford	15,129	48	30	18
MISSOURI				
Lincoln University	3,156	18	8	10
Mineral Area College	3,061	9	8	1
Missouri Southern State University	5,593	8	1	7
Missouri University of Science and Technology	6,166	20	10	10
Missouri Western State University	5,342	13	10	3
Northwest Missouri State University	6,511	13	11	2
Southeast Missouri State University	10,624	26	19	7
St. Louis Community College:				
Florissant Valley	6,250	12	9	3
Meramec	10,168	12	9	3
Truman State University	5,920	10	8	2
University of Central Missouri	10,918	22	18	4
University of Missouri:				
Columbia	28,405	45	30	15
Kansas City	14,442	43	28	15
St. Louis	15,527	24	19	5
Washington University	13,382	44	27	17
MONTANA				
Montana State University	11,932	33	17	16
University of Montana	13,628	25	13	12
NEBRASKA				
University of Nebraska:				
Kearney	6,478	10	7	3
Lincoln	22,973	48	30	18

[1] The student enrollment figures provided by the United States Department of Education are for the 2007 school year, the most recent available. The enrollment figures include full-time and part-time students.

Table 79. Full-Time Law Enforcement Employees, by State by University and College, 2008—*Continued*

(Number.)

State, university/college, campus	Student enrollment[1]	Total law enforcement employees	Total officers	Total civilians
NEVADA				
Truckee Meadows Community College	12,166	11	6	5
University of Nevada:				
Las Vegas	27,960	54	36	18
Reno	16,681	29	23	6
NEW JERSEY				
Brookdale Community College	14,025	26	13	13
Essex County College	10,995	50	13	37
Kean University	13,394	53	27	26
Middlesex County College	12,097	16	11	5
Monmouth University	6,494	36	21	15
Montclair State University	16,736	43	31	12
New Jersey Institute of Technology	8,288	59	28	31
Richard Stockton College of New Jersey	7,355	32	24	8
Rowan University	10,091	56	22	34
Rutgers University:				
Camden	5,159	37	17	20
Newark	10,553	64	33	31
New Brunswick	34,804	90	55	35
Stevens Institute of Technology	5,241	21	16	5
The College of New Jersey	6,964	27	16	11
University of Medicine and Dentistry:				
Camden[2]		19	19	0
Newark	5,617	120	33	87
New Brunswick[2]		39	30	9
William Paterson University	10,443	43	25	18
NEW MEXICO				
Eastern New Mexico University	4,173	9	8	1
New Mexico Highlands University	3,457	13	2	11
New Mexico State University	16,722	30	16	14
University of New Mexico	25,672	51	31	20
Western New Mexico University	2,697	3	2	1
NEW YORK				
Ithaca College	6,660	24	16	8
State University of New York:				
Binghamton	14,435	43	32	11
Buffalo	28,054	66	60	6
Maritime College	1,487	11	6	5
Stony Brook[2]		147	70	77
Upstate Medical Center[2]		13	13	0
State University of New York Agricultural and Technical College:				
Alfred	3,184	17	12	5
Canton	2,737	13	12	1
Cobleskill	2,592	10	9	1
Farmingdale[2]		21	17	4
Morrisville[2]		11	10	1
State University of New York College:				
Brockport	8,303	19	17	2
Buffalo	10,993	30	28	2
Cortland	7,056	25	19	6
Environmental Science and Forestry	2,299	13	11	2
Fredonia[2]		16	15	1
Geneseo[2]		21	16	5
Oneonta	5,893	27	17	10
Oswego	8,660	28	21	7
Plattsburgh	6,259	20	14	6
Utica-Rome[2]		14	10	4
NORTH CAROLINA				
Appalachian State University	15,871	39	24	15
Beaufort County Community College	1,476	1	1	0
Belmont Abbey College	1,337	8	7	1
Davidson College	1,674	9	8	1
Duke University	13,598	157	48	109
Elizabeth City State University	3,061	15	9	6
Elon University	5,456	14	13	1
Fayetteville State University	6,692	34	18	16
Methodist College	2,118	23	5	18
North Carolina Agricultural and Technical State University	10,498	55	24	31
North Carolina Central University	8,383	47	26	21
North Carolina School of the Arts	867	15	14	1
North Carolina State University				
Raleigh	31,802	69	47	22
Queens University	2,243	7	6	1
Saint Augustine's College	1,284	41	7	34

[1] The student enrollment figures provided by the United States Department of Education are for the 2007 school year, the most recent available. The enrollment figures include full-time and part-time students.

[2] Student enrollment figures were not available.

Table 79. Full-Time Law Enforcement Employees, by State by University and College, 2008—*Continued*

(Number.)

State, university/college, campus	Student enrollment[1]	Total law enforcement employees	Total officers	Total civilians
University of North Carolina:				
Asheville	3,701	21	13	8
Chapel Hill	28,136	81	43	38
Charlotte	22,388	40	32	8
Greensboro	18,627	54	31	23
Pembroke	5,937	16	12	4
Wilmington	12,180	40	26	14
Wake Forest University	6,788	43	17	26
Western Carolina University	9,056	22	16	6
Winston-Salem State University	5,870	34	14	20
NORTH DAKOTA				
North Dakota State College of Science	2,417	3	3	0
North Dakota State University	12,527	15	12	3
University of North Dakota	12,559	14	12	2
OHIO				
Bowling Green State University	18,619	28	23	5
Capital University	3,713	11	7	4
Central State University	2,022	14	13	1
Cleveland State University	15,038	43	23	20
College of Mount St. Joseph	2,282	21	9	12
Columbus State Community College	23,057	34	16	18
Cuyahoga Community College	24,563	34	29	5
Kent State University	22,819	36	28	8
Lakeland Community College	8,934	14	10	4
Marietta College	1,605	7	4	3
Miami University	15,968	36	26	10
Muskingum College	2,099	6	5	1
Notre Dame College	1,490	4	4	0
Ohio State University:				
Columbus	52,568	57	52	5
Wooster[2]		5	5	0
Ohio University	21,089	27	22	5
Sinclair Community College	18,691	26	22	4
University of Akron	23,007	45	40	5
University of Cincinnati	29,319	106	60	46
University of Rio Grande	2,243	6	5	1
Wilberforce University	834	5	5	0
Wright State University	16,151	28	19	9
Youngstown State University	13,595	22	17	5
OKLAHOMA				
Cameron University	5,469	12	12	0
East Central University	4,463	5	5	0
Murray State College	2,281	1	1	0
Northeastern Oklahoma A&M College	1,913	10	8	2
Northeastern State University:				
Broken Arrow[2]		2	2	0
Tahlequah[2]		17	13	4
Oklahoma State University:				
Main Campus	23,213	43	31	12
Okmulgee	3,301	7	6	1
Tulsa[2]		7	5	2
Rogers State University	3,903	4	4	0
Seminole State College	2,068	4	3	1
Southeastern Oklahoma State University	3,893	8	7	1
Southwestern Oklahoma State University	4,989	7	6	1
Tulsa Community College	16,881	16	10	6
University of Central Oklahoma	15,495	22	16	6
University of Oklahoma:				
Health Sciences Center	3,754	60	45	15
Norman	26,068	70	38	32
PENNSYLVANIA				
California University	8,206	16	13	3
Cheyney University	1,438	14	13	1
Clarion University	6,795	13	10	3
Dickinson College	2,381	20	12	8
East Stroudsburg University	7,053	17	14	3
Edinboro University	7,686	15	14	1
Elizabethtown College	2,360	17	5	12
Indiana University	14,018	31	22	9
Kutztown University	10,295	23	17	6
Lehigh University	6,845	30	20	10
Lock Haven University	5,241	12	10	2
Millersville University	8,306	15	12	3
Moravian College	1,989	12	8	4

[1] The student enrollment figures provided by the United States Department of Education are for the 2007 school year, the most recent available. The enrollment figures include full-time and part-time students.

[2] Student enrollment figures were not available.

Table 79. Full-Time Law Enforcement Employees, by State and University and College, 2008—*Continued*

(Number.)

State, university/college, campus	Student enrollment[1]	Total law enforcement employees	Total officers	Total civilians
Pennsylvania State University:				
Altoona	4,034	11	9	2
Beaver	793	5	5	0
Behrend	4,171	10	6	4
Berks	2,824	9	8	1
Harrisburg	3,907	9	7	2
Hazelton	1,232	5	5	0
McKeesport[2]		6	4	2
Mont Alto	1,204	4	4	0
University Park	43,252	55	46	9
Shippensburg University	7,765	19	16	3
Slippery Rock University	8,325	21	15	6
University of Pittsburgh:				
Bradford	1,407	6	5	1
Pittsburgh	27,020	142	74	68
West Chester University	13,219	20	20	0
RHODE ISLAND				
Brown University	8,167	73	38	35
University of Rhode Island	15,650	29	23	6
SOUTH CAROLINA				
Benedict College	2,641	26	22	4
Bob Jones University[2]		4	4	0
Clemson University	17,585	41	32	9
Coastal Carolina University	7,872	72	20	52
College of Charleston	11,316	63	31	32
Columbia College	1,510	14	11	3
Erskine College	892	2	2	0
Francis Marion University	3,864	13	12	1
Greenville Technical College	14,300	8	8	0
Lander University	2,408	12	10	2
Medical University of South Carolina	2,537	76	56	20
Midlands Technical College	10,706	6	6	0
Presbyterian College	1,180	8	7	1
South Carolina State University	4,933	28	19	9
Spartanburg Methodist College	797	3	3	0
The Citadel	3,300	14	13	1
Trident Technical College	12,076	22	20	2
University of South Carolina:				
Aiken	3,267	8	8	0
Columbia	27,272	85	57	28
Upstate	4,916	14	13	1
Winthrop University	6,382	21	14	7
SOUTH DAKOTA				
South Dakota State University	11,645	20	15	5
TENNESSEE				
Austin Peay State University	9,094	25	14	11
Christian Brothers University	1,874	15	8	7
East Tennessee State University	13,119	26	21	5
Middle Tennessee State University	23,246	35	27	8
Northeast State Technical Community College	5,237	5	5	0
Southwest Tennessee Community College	10,617	31	24	7
Tennessee State University	9,065	59	25	34
Tennessee Technological University	10,321	23	15	8
University of Memphis	20,379	36	31	5
University of Tennessee:				
Chattanooga	9,558	28	17	11
Knoxville	29,937	89	50	39
Martin	7,171	16	12	4
Memphis[2]		53	24	29
Vanderbilt University	11,847	134	103	31
Volunteer State Community College	7,065	7	6	1
Walters State Community College	5,825	9	8	1
TEXAS				
Abilene Christian University	4,675	14	13	1
Alamo Community College District[2]		75	53	22
Alvin Community College	4,169	11	9	2
Amarillo College	10,387	16	14	2
Angelo State University	6,239	17	13	4
Austin College	1,339	8	7	1
Baylor Health Care System[2]		167	55	112
Baylor University				
Waco	14,174	31	24	7
Blinn College	14,589	10	9	1
Central Texas College	21,532	10	9	1

[1] The student enrollment figures provided by the United States Department of Education are for the 2007 school year, the most recent available. The enrollment figures include full-time and part-time students.
[2] Student enrollment figures were not available.

Table 79. Full-Time Law Enforcement Employees, by State and University and College, 2008—*Continued*

(Number.)

State, university/college, campus	Student enrollment[1]	Total law enforcement employees	Total officers	Total civilians
College of the Mainland	3,521	7	6	1
Eastfield College	10,653	10	9	1
El Paso Community College	25,023	41	34	7
Grayson County College	3,811	4	4	0
Hardin-Simmons University	2,435	8	7	1
Houston Baptist University	2,339	21	13	8
Lamar University				
Beaumont	10,213	30	16	14
Laredo Community College	7,831	23	21	2
McLennan Community College	8,079	14	5	9
Midwestern State University	6,027	14	9	5
Mountain View College	7,009	11	11	0
North Lake College	9,835	20	19	1
Paris Junior College	4,343	3	3	0
Rice University	5,161	44	27	17
Richland College	15,311	20	19	1
Southern Methodist University	10,829	32	26	6
South Plains College	6,602	6	6	0
Southwestern University	1,294	7	6	1
Stephen F. Austin State University	11,607	41	23	18
St. Mary's University	3,920	18	15	3
Sul Ross State University	2,717	9	7	2
Tarleton State University	9,460	16	12	4
Texas A&M International University	5,179	21	16	5
Texas A&M University:				
College Station	46,542	123	58	65
Commerce	8,813	26	16	10
Corpus Christi	8,563	24	14	10
Galveston	1,614	7	6	1
Kingsville	6,567	21	15	6
Texas Christian University	8,668	37	22	15
Texas Southern University	9,540	46	31	15
Texas State Technical College:				
Harlingen	4,957	12	8	4
Marshall	705	4	4	0
Waco	4,210	18	16	2
Texas State University				
San Marcos	28,121	37	31	6
Texas Technological University				
Lubbock	28,260	88	51	37
Texas Woman's University	12,168	36	16	20
Trinity University	2,686	25	14	11
Tyler Junior College	8,217	14	5	9
University of Houston:				
Central Campus	34,663	105	45	60
Clearlake	7,522	25	15	10
Downtown Campus	11,793	34	18	16
University of Mary Hardin-Baylor	2,651	19	19	0
University of North Texas:				
Denton	34,710	76	36	40
Health Science Center	1,153	20	11	9
University of Texas:				
Arlington	24,889	102	34	68
Austin	50,170	145	59	86
Brownsville	17,215	37	16	21
Dallas	14,556	40	21	19
El Paso	20,154	52	23	29
Health Science Center, San Antonio	2,868	115	32	83
Health Science Center, Tyler[2]		20	5	15
Houston[2]		360	96	264
Medical Branch	2,422	95	51	44
Pan American	17,435	36	14	22
Permian Basin	3,559	13	5	8
San Antonio	28,533	95	44	51
Southwestern Medical School	2,253	137	43	94
Tyler	6,137	18	9	9
Western Texas College	1,844	3	3	0
West Texas A&M University	7,502	14	10	4
UTAH				
Brigham Young University	34,174	38	27	11
College of Eastern Utah	2,085	1	1	0
Southern Utah University	7,057	5	4	1
University of Utah	28,025	101	32	69
Utah State University	14,893	18	12	6
Utah Valley University	23,840	10	8	2
Weber State University	18,081	11	10	1

[1] The student enrollment figures provided by the United States Department of Education are for the 2007 school year, the most recent available. The enrollment figures include full-time and part-time students.

[2] Student enrollment figures were not available.

Table 79. Full-Time Law Enforcement Employees, by State and University and College, 2008—*Continued*

(Number.)

State, university/college, campus	Student enrollment[1]	Total law enforcement employees	Total officers	Total civilians
VERMONT				
University of Vermont	12,239	35	23	12
VIRGINIA				
Christopher Newport University	4,884	22	17	5
College of William and Mary	7,795	24	19	5
Emory and Henry College	1,026	4	2	2
Ferrum College	1,233	7	7	0
George Mason University	30,276	62	45	17
Hampton University	5,658	41	21	20
James Madison University	17,918	34	27	7
J. Sargeant Reynolds Community College	12,557	19	11	8
Longwood University	4,727	23	15	8
Norfolk State University	6,155	40	25	15
Northern Virginia Community College	41,266	40	39	1
Old Dominion University	22,287	56	46	10
Radford University	9,122	27	21	6
Thomas Nelson Community College	9,368	15	13	2
University of Mary Washington	5,001	20	11	9
University of Richmond	4,324	33	19	14
University of Virginia	24,257	121	55	66
University of Virginia's College at Wise	1,803	9	8	1
Virginia Commonwealth University	31,700	171	73	98
Virginia Military Institute	1,378	6	6	0
Virginia Polytechnic Institute and State University	29,898	65	46	19
Virginia State University	4,720	32	16	16
Virginia Western Community College	8,653	8	8	0
WASHINGTON				
Central Washington University	10,505	17	14	3
Eastern Washington University	10,686	11	10	1
Evergreen State College	4,586	16	10	6
University of Washington	40,218	74	47	27
Washington State University:				
Pullman	24,396	21	17	4
Vancouver[2]		4	3	1
Western Washington University	14,276	20	14	6
WEST VIRGINIA[3]				
WISCONSIN				
University of Wisconsin:				
Eau Claire	10,854	12	11	1
Green Bay	6,110	12	5	7
La Crosse	9,994	12	7	5
Madison	41,563	112	63	49
Milwaukee	29,338	44	32	12
Oshkosh	12,772	13	11	2
Parkside	5,010	14	9	5
Platteville	7,189	8	7	1
Stevens Point	9,115	8	4	4
Stout	8,477	10	9	1
Superior	2,753	6	1	5
Whitewater	10,737	13	12	1
WYOMING				
Sheridan College	3,277	2	2	0
University of Wyoming	12,875	24	13	11

[1] The student enrollment figures provided by the United States Department of Education are for the 2007 school year, the most recent available. The enrollment figures include full-time and part-time students.
[2] Student enrollment figures were not available.
[3] No 2008 police employee data were received for the state of West Virginia.

Table 80. Full-Time Law Enforcement Employees, by State and Metropolitan and Nonmetropolitan Counties, 2008

(Number.)

State/County	Total law enforcement employees	Total officers	Total civilians
ALABAMA–Metropolitan Counties			
Autauga	62	23	39
Bibb	12	11	1
Blount	78	43	35
Calhoun	83	40	43
Colbert	50	30	20
Elmore	82	33	49
Etowah	152	57	95
Geneva	18	10	8
Greene	27	10	17
Hale	9	7	2
Henry	24	11	13
Houston	83	52	31
Jefferson	705	547	158
Lawrence	41	22	19
Lee	147	58	89
Limestone	107	42	65
Lowndes	41	12	29
Madison	301	106	195
Montgomery	175	131	44
Morgan	170	51	119
Russell	90	32	58
Shelby	208	145	63
St. Clair	46	40	6
Tuscaloosa	202	100	102
Walker	65	32	33
ALABAMA–Nonmetropolitan Counties			
Baldwin	261	92	169
Barbour	32	14	18
Bullock	12	6	6
Butler	12	10	2
Chambers	54	49	5
Cherokee	38	18	20
Choctaw	13	5	8
Clarke	33	14	19
Cleburne	24	9	15
Coffee	47	21	26
Conecuh	37	11	26
Coosa	20	8	12
Covington	24	22	2
Crenshaw	10	9	1
Cullman	135	78	57
Dale	23	19	4
Dallas	48	24	24
De Kalb	88	38	50
Escambia	63	23	40
Fayette	16	11	5
Franklin	43	15	28
Jackson	74	29	45
Lamar	20	8	12
Macon	38	20	18
Marengo	32	12	20
Marion	27	13	14
Marshall	91	36	55
Monroe	55	19	36
Perry	16	7	9
Pickens	27	8	19
Pike	29	16	13
Randolph	35	13	22
Talladega	103	40	63
Tallapoosa	54	25	29
Washington	13	5	8
Wilcox	23	8	15
Winston	23	10	13
ARIZONA–Metropolitan Counties			
Maricopa	3,552	767	2,785
Mohave	254	94	160
Pima	1,466	554	912
Pinal	468	210	258
Yavapai	422	137	285
Yuma	303	66	237
ARIZONA–Nonmetropolitan Counties			
Apache	75	28	47
Cochise	200	88	112
Gila	140	49	91
Graham	66	21	45
Greenlee	35	13	22
La Paz	97	35	62
Navajo	161	52	109
ARKANSAS–Metropolitan Counties			
Benton	191	111	80
Cleveland	12	8	4
Craighead	41	30	11
Crawford	60	27	33
Crittenden	133	35	98
Faulkner	160	45	115
Franklin	19	9	10
Garland	117	39	78
Grant	15	13	2
Jefferson	156	51	105
Lincoln	23	10	13
Lonoke	39	22	17
Madison	17	9	8
Miller	28	23	5
Perry	16	8	8
Poinsett	40	11	29
Pulaski	444	122	322
Saline	79	39	40
Sebastian	139	46	93
Washington	283	148	135
ARKANSAS–Nonmetropolitan Counties			
Arkansas	50	12	38
Ashley	44	19	25
Baxter	49	44	5
Boone	39	23	16
Bradley	6	5	1
Calhoun	11	6	5
Carroll	20	17	3
Chicot	7	6	1
Clark	27	15	12
Clay	21	7	14
Cleburne	36	22	14
Columbia	32	14	18
Conway	34	15	19
Cross	31	15	16
Dallas	26	5	21
Desha	8	7	1
Drew	25	10	15
Fulton	14	7	7
Greene	44	11	33
Hempstead	43	16	27
Hot Spring	23	21	2
Howard	21	10	11
Independence	76	47	29
Izard	28	13	15
Jackson	21	12	9
Johnson	36	13	23
Lafayette	24	19	5
Lawrence	22	12	10
Lee	7	5	2
Little River	19	8	11
Logan	25	12	13
Marion	20	10	10
Mississippi	88	30	58
Monroe	13	4	9
Montgomery	17	9	8
Nevada	16	5	11
Newton	10	6	4
Ouachita	30	16	14
Phillips	16	13	3
Pike	15	7	8
Polk	25	11	14

Table 80. Full-Time Law Enforcement Employees, by State and Metropolitan and Nonmetropolitan Counties, 2008—*Continued*

(Number.)

State/County	Total law enforcement employees	Total officers	Total civilians
Pope	84	31	53
Prairie	17	7	10
Randolph	12	10	2
Scott	15	8	7
Searcy	13	7	6
Sevier	28	11	17
Sharp	20	10	10
St. Francis	41	18	23
Stone	20	8	12
Union	58	30	28
Van Buren	29	17	12
White	89	44	45
Woodruff	17	6	11
Yell	26	14	12
CALIFORNIA–Metropolitan Counties			
Alameda	1,682	1,037	645
Butte	281	113	168
Contra Costa	1,004	681	323
El Dorado	406	206	200
Fresno	1,091	899	192
Imperial	270	180	90
Kern	1,209	908	301
Kings	228	83	145
Los Angeles	16,393	9,513	6,880
Madera	114	79	35
Marin	321	210	111
Merced	257	201	56
Monterey	430	314	116
Napa	129	98	31
Orange	3,645	1,854	1,791
Placer	434	231	203
Riverside	4,109	2,166	1,943
Sacramento	2,402	1,510	892
San Benito	69	59	10
San Bernardino	3,399	1,764	1,635
San Diego	3,953	2,328	1,625
San Francisco	1,066	883	183
San Joaquin	869	354	515
San Luis Obispo	382	157	225
San Mateo	601	435	166
Santa Barbara	654	479	175
Santa Clara	683	522	161
Santa Cruz	341	138	203
Shasta	240	163	77
Solano	477	115	362
Sonoma	706	507	199
Stanislaus	661	470	191
Sutter	134	102	32
Tulare	686	499	187
Ventura	1,223	723	500
Yolo	256	84	172
Yuba	177	136	41
CALIFORNIA–Nonmetropolitan Counties			
Alpine	18	15	3
Amador	90	48	42
Calaveras	110	60	50
Colusa	64	31	33
Del Norte	65	33	32
Glenn	68	28	40
Humboldt	238	184	54
Inyo	57	38	19
Lake	156	58	98
Lassen	94	72	22
Mariposa	69	55	14
Mendocino	172	130	42
Modoc	29	23	6
Mono	44	27	17
Nevada	185	69	116
Plumas	68	34	34
Sierra	15	11	4
Siskiyou	121	91	30
Tehama	117	85	32
Trinity	36	17	19
Tuolumne	131	65	66
COLORADO–Metropolitan Counties			
Adams	532	364	168
Arapahoe	501	322	179
Boulder	361	216	145
Clear Creek	64	24	40
Douglas	429	284	145
Elbert	35	28	7
El Paso	636	454	182
Gilpin	39	26	13
Jefferson	773	535	238
Larimer	414	191	223
Mesa	235	117	118
Park	66	33	33
Teller	87	55	32
Weld	338	121	217
COLORADO–Nonmetropolitan Counties			
Alamosa	40	23	17
Archuleta	49	15	34
Baca	11	4	7
Bent	8	8	0
Chaffee	56	17	39
Cheyenne	9	5	4
Conejos	21	8	13
Costilla	13	7	6
Crowley	11	7	4
Custer	20	8	12
Delta	61	27	34
Dolores	5	3	2
Eagle	94	51	43
Fremont	88	36	52
Garfield	130	107	23
Grand	44	19	25
Gunnison	30	13	17
Hinsdale	5	4	1
Huerfano	26	12	14
Jackson	7	4	3
Kiowa	5	4	1
Kit Carson	28	20	8
Lake	18	9	9
La Plata	123	90	33
Las Animas	38	14	24
Lincoln	19	7	12
Logan	46	23	23
Mineral	4	3	1
Moffat	41	17	24
Montezuma	64	28	36
Montrose	96	50	46
Morgan	50	25	25
Otero	21	19	2
Ouray	7	7	0
Phillips	4	3	1
Pitkin	38	22	16
Prowers	30	9	21
Rio Blanco	29	14	15
Routt	45	22	23
Saguache	18	8	10
San Juan	4	3	1
San Miguel	39	35	4
Sedgwick	9	6	3
Summit	71	55	16
Washington	42	32	10
Yuma	20	8	12
DELAWARE–Metropolitan Counties			
New Castle County Police Department	464	356	108
FLORIDA–Metropolitan Counties			
Alachua	836	294	542
Baker	55	47	8
Bay	514	213	301
Brevard	1,158	496	662
Broward	1,134	451	683
Charlotte	633	294	339
Clay	562	267	295
Collier	1,008	626	382
Escambia	1,040	386	654

Table 80. Full-Time Law Enforcement Employees, by State and Metropolitan and Nonmetropolitan Counties, 2008—*Continued*

(Number.)

State/County	Total law enforcement employees	Total officers	Total civilians
Flagler	171	118	53
Gadsden	66	44	22
Gilchrist	56	28	28
Hernando	424	244	180
Hillsborough	3,340	1,213	2,127
Indian River	489	202	287
Jefferson	47	20	27
Lake	724	482	242
Lee	1,512	642	870
Leon	351	235	116
Manatee	1,035	661	374
Marion	841	393	448
Martin	526	266	260
Miami-Dade	4,483	3,091	1,392
Nassau	241	147	94
Okaloosa	354	255	99
Orange	1,851	1,243	608
Osceola	587	379	208
Palm Beach	3,014	1,251	1,763
Pasco	1,063	470	593
Pinellas	1,251	670	581
Polk	1,541	645	896
Santa Rosa	262	189	73
Sarasota	921	408	513
Seminole	1,044	392	652
St. Johns	571	274	297
St. Lucie	673	509	164
Volusia	64	60	4
Wakulla	97	58	39
FLORIDA–Nonmetropolitan Counties			
Bradford	69	25	44
Calhoun	21	14	7
Citrus	359	222	137
Columbia	197	91	106
DeSoto	82	53	29
Dixie	61	26	35
Franklin	66	48	18
Glades	40	26	14
Gulf	40	27	13
Hamilton	58	21	37
Hardee	92	43	49
Hendry	131	64	67
Highlands	335	132	203
Holmes	24	18	6
Jackson	78	58	20
Lafayette	10	9	1
Levy	155	78	77
Liberty	27	15	12
Madison	69	55	14
Monroe	505	207	298
Okeechobee	208	90	118
Putnam	188	115	73
Sumter	228	152	76
Suwannee	99	57	42
Taylor	47	32	15
Union	20	12	8
Walton	204	161	43
Washington	83	58	25
GEORGIA–Metropolitan Counties			
Augusta-Richmond	708	636	72
Baker	10	4	6
Barrow	196	95	101
Bartow	223	180	43
Bibb	314	274	40
Brantley	24	17	7
Brooks	42	21	21
Bryan	43	38	5
Butts	78	37	41
Carroll	180	98	82
Catoosa	137	71	66
Chatham	416	341	75
Chattahoochee	11	6	5
Cherokee	402	346	56
Clarke	149	124	25
Clayton County Police Department	389	331	58
Cobb	674	454	220
Cobb County Police Department	740	600	140
Coweta	214	136	78
Crawford	34	16	18
Dade	28	25	3
Dawson	116	62	54
DeKalb	829	633	196
DeKalb County Police Department	1,568	1,067	501
Dougherty County Police Department	53	45	8
Douglas	316	219	97
Echols	9	8	1
Fayette	223	142	81
Floyd	150	77	73
Forsyth	378	324	54
Fulton	1,007	856	151
Fulton County Police Department	201	137	64
Glynn	93	40	53
Glynn County Police Department	127	114	13
Gwinnett County Police Department	962	676	286
Hall	487	284	203
Haralson	62	54	8
Harris	62	44	18
Heard	39	20	19
Henry County Police Department	277	238	39
Houston	300	112	188
Jasper	38	22	16
Jones	74	42	32
Lamar	59	28	31
Lanier	17	13	4
Lee	77	40	37
Liberty	108	65	43
Long	17	15	2
Lowndes	228	149	79
Madison	69	35	34
McDuffie	34	15	19
McIntosh	55	30	25
Meriwether	50	30	20
Monroe	93	53	40
Murray	67	39	28
Newton	233	132	101
Oconee	76	52	24
Oglethorpe	42	18	24
Paulding	179	148	31
Pickens	56	47	9
Rockdale	241	226	15
Spalding	181	150	31
Terrell	22	9	13
Twiggs	41	21	20
Walker	116	78	38
Walton	180	156	24
Whitfield	194	165	29
GEORGIA–Nonmetropolitan Counties			
Appling	45	13	32
Bacon	12	12	0
Baldwin	99	59	40
Banks	56	33	23
Ben Hill	48	43	5
Berrien	41	18	23
Calhoun	15	6	9
Camden	119	72	47
Candler	17	7	10
Charlton	30	18	12
Chattooga	44	44	0
Clay	11	5	6
Clinch	21	11	10
Coffee	107	66	41
Cook	45	18	27
Crisp	63	58	5
Dodge	38	21	17
Dooly	65	20	45
Early	48	25	23
Elbert	26	24	2
Emanuel	35	17	18

Table 80. Full-Time Law Enforcement Employees, by State and Metropolitan and Nonmetropolitan Counties, 2008—*Continued*

(Number.)

State/County	Total law enforcement employees	Total officers	Total civilians
Gilmer	109	60	49
Glascock	7	6	1
Gordon	95	63	32
Grady	39	17	22
Greene	52	30	22
Habersham	40	33	7
Hancock	41	28	13
Hart	40	23	17
Jackson	133	81	52
Jeff Davis	33	15	18
Jefferson	45	43	2
Jenkins	16	15	1
Laurens	102	69	33
Lumpkin	67	45	22
Macon	23	10	13
Miller	25	13	12
Mitchell	52	24	28
Peach	61	40	21
Pierce	30	13	17
Polk	25	25	0
Polk County Police Department	38	35	3
Pulaski	22	10	12
Putnam	61	30	31
Quitman	8	7	1
Rabun	50	50	0
Randolph	28	14	14
Schley	8	4	4
Seminole	19	10	9
Stephens	71	31	40
Stewart	8	4	4
Sumter	92	43	49
Talbot	17	7	10
Taliaferro	16	9	7
Tattnall	45	17	28
Taylor	22	21	1
Thomas	81	77	4
Tift	109	57	52
Toombs	59	27	32
Towns	20	17	3
Treutlen	14	9	5
Troup	128	78	50
Turner	33	14	19
Upson	64	35	29
Ware	122	37	85
Warren	6	6	0
Washington	37	20	17
Webster	6	5	1
Wheeler	8	4	4
White	65	42	23
Wilcox	18	10	8
Wilkes	31	13	18
Wilkinson	24	16	8
HAWAII–Nonmetropolitan Counties			
Hawaii Police Department	552	419	133
Kauai Police Department	176	125	51
Maui Police Department	447	328	119
IDAHO–Metropolitan Counties			
Ada	562	139	423
Bannock	66	40	26
Boise	14	11	3
Bonneville	94	64	30
Canyon	301	79	222
Franklin	13	10	3
Gem	25	13	12
Jefferson	31	18	13
Kootenai	148	76	72
Nez Perce	37	19	18
Owyhee	21	12	9
Power	17	9	8
IDAHO–Nonmetropolitan Counties			
Adams	17	10	7
Bear Lake	13	6	7
Benewah	18	9	9

State/County	Total law enforcement employees	Total officers	Total civilians
Bingham	51	30	21
Blaine	26	22	4
Bonner	60	38	22
Boundary	21	11	10
Butte	13	7	6
Camas	6	4	2
Caribou	15	9	6
Cassia	50	32	18
Clark	7	3	4
Clearwater	24	16	8
Custer	15	8	7
Elmore	41	23	18
Fremont	24	16	8
Gooding	18	11	7
Idaho	31	22	9
Jerome	20	15	5
Latah	38	25	13
Lemhi	7	6	1
Lewis	12	6	6
Lincoln	7	5	2
Madison	34	22	12
Minidoka	25	16	9
Oneida	12	6	6
Payette	31	16	15
Shoshone	29	18	11
Teton	15	8	7
Twin Falls	71	44	27
Valley	28	15	13
Washington	17	12	5
ILLINOIS–Metropolitan Counties			
Alexander	10	8	2
Bond	19	11	8
Boone	97	40	57
Calhoun	11	6	5
Champaign	158	132	26
Clinton	37	16	21
Cook	6,837	2,342	4,495
De Kalb	96	42	54
Du Page	511	386	125
Ford	25	8	17
Grundy	57	28	29
Henry	73	23	50
Jersey	30	14	16
Kane	286	93	193
Kankakee	204	60	144
Kendall	119	56	63
Lake	506	188	318
Macon	156	50	106
Macoupin	48	44	4
Madison	171	84	87
Marshall	17	8	9
McHenry	388	106	282
McLean	135	55	80
Menard	15	8	7
Mercer	29	12	17
Monroe	27	14	13
Peoria	203	73	130
Piatt	32	11	21
Rock Island	158	63	95
Sangamon	226	78	148
Stark	13	5	8
St. Clair	172	159	13
Tazewell	106	41	65
Vermilion	84	34	50
Will	592	279	313
Winnebago	401	117	284
Woodford	40	37	3
ILLINOIS–Nonmetropolitan Counties			
Adams	70	28	42
Brown	6	5	1
Bureau	37	20	17
Carroll	25	9	16
Cass	8	7	1

Table 80. Full-Time Law Enforcement Employees, by State and Metropolitan and Nonmetropolitan Counties, 2008—*Continued*

(Number.)

State/County	Total law enforcement employees	Total officers	Total civilians
Christian	35	17	18
Clark	18	9	9
Clay	17	11	6
Coles	47	23	24
Crawford	21	9	12
Cumberland	12	8	4
De Witt	41	16	25
Douglas	32	14	18
Edgar	19	8	11
Edwards	12	4	8
Effingham	44	20	24
Fayette	32	11	21
Franklin	46	17	29
Fulton	45	22	23
Gallatin	4	4	0
Greene	14	6	8
Hamilton	7	3	4
Hancock	22	9	13
Hardin	2	2	0
Henderson	14	8	6
Iroquois	30	19	11
Jackson	74	26	48
Jasper	19	9	10
Jefferson	61	22	39
Jo Daviess	38	20	18
Johnson	13	8	5
Knox	57	19	38
La Salle	108	46	62
Lawrence	17	7	10
Lee	40	22	18
Livingston	59	30	29
Logan	37	20	17
Marion	34	13	21
Mason	23	9	14
Massac	31	13	18
McDonough	25	13	12
Montgomery	30	14	16
Morgan	35	15	20
Moultrie	24	10	14
Ogle	73	30	43
Perry	32	12	20
Pike	26	11	15
Pope	5	2	3
Pulaski	16	11	5
Putnam	12	7	5
Randolph	26	13	13
Richland	24	8	16
Saline	42	31	11
Schuyler	9	3	6
Scott	6	2	4
Shelby	25	12	13
Stephenson	81	29	52
Union	18	10	8
Wabash	9	4	5
Warren	22	12	10
Washington	21	10	11
Wayne	23	10	13
White	26	7	19
Whiteside	55	24	31
Williamson	69	35	34
INDIANA–Metropolitan Counties			
Allen	338	124	214
Bartholomew	83	38	45
Benton	14	6	8
Boone	69	28	41
Brown	38	13	25
Carroll	20	10	10
Clark	137	36	101
Dearborn	81	31	50
Delaware	110	48	62
Elkhart	207	67	140
Floyd	93	31	62
Gibson	41	17	24
Greene	41	14	27

State/County	Total law enforcement employees	Total officers	Total civilians
Hamilton	246	65	181
Hancock	70	39	31
Howard	106	35	71
Johnson	127	100	27
Lake	478	173	305
La Porte	156	58	98
Madison	106	51	55
Morgan	73	26	47
Newton	40	17	23
Ohio	9	9	0
Owen	32	12	20
Porter	145	59	86
Posey	13	12	1
Putnam	32	15	17
Shelby	81	26	55
St. Joseph	270	118	152
Sullivan	36	11	25
Tippecanoe	151	48	103
Tipton	27	12	15
Vanderburgh	247	103	144
Vermillion	24	18	6
Warrick	79	37	42
Washington	35	12	23
Wells	39	15	24
Whitley	43	14	29
INDIANA–Nonmetropolitan Counties			
Blackford	30	9	21
Crawford	17	8	9
Daviess	62	18	44
Decatur	40	13	27
Fayette	33	11	22
Grant	131	45	86
Henry	71	29	42
Huntington	40	14	26
Jackson	54	15	39
Jay	28	11	17
Jefferson	36	14	22
Knox	37	12	25
Kosciusko	75	37	38
LaGrange	67	18	49
Marshall	61	21	40
Martin	20	8	12
Miami	35	15	20
Noble	73	20	53
Orange	29	10	19
Parke	35	11	24
Perry	17	7	10
Pike	26	10	16
Pulaski	44	14	30
Randolph	41	15	26
Ripley	29	10	19
Scott	27	11	16
Spencer	15	14	1
Starke	28	15	13
Steuben	62	21	41
Wabash	37	15	22
Warren	19	7	12
Wayne	106	61	45
White	34	13	21
IOWA–Metropolitan Counties			
Benton	26	12	14
Black Hawk	132	100	32
Bremer	30	12	18
Dallas	45	21	24
Dubuque	83	71	12
Grundy	16	12	4
Guthrie	12	5	7
Harrison	25	9	16
Johnson	97	63	34
Jones	24	10	14
Linn	163	108	55
Madison	16	7	9
Mills	19	10	9
Polk	450	140	310

Table 80. Full-Time Law Enforcement Employees, by State and Metropolitan and Nonmetropolitan Counties, 2008—*Continued*

(Number.)

State/County	Total law enforcement employees	Total officers	Total civilians
Pottawattamie	179	49	130
Scott	165	43	122
Story	81	30	51
Warren	29	19	10
Washington	43	18	25
Woodbury	117	33	84
IOWA–Nonmetropolitan Counties			
Adair	9	6	3
Adams	10	6	4
Allamakee	15	8	7
Appanoose	9	8	1
Audubon	8	5	3
Boone	32	11	21
Buchanan	28	12	16
Buena Vista	26	9	17
Butler	20	11	9
Calhoun	11	6	5
Carroll	10	9	1
Cass	16	8	8
Cedar	35	10	25
Cerro Gordo	72	19	53
Cherokee	17	6	11
Chickasaw	14	8	6
Clarke	18	6	12
Clay	18	10	8
Clayton	26	11	15
Clinton	42	24	18
Crawford	14	12	2
Davis	13	5	8
Decatur	11	6	5
Des Moines	49	22	27
Emmet	18	8	10
Fayette	32	10	22
Floyd	16	9	7
Franklin	11	8	3
Fremont	18	7	11
Greene	15	7	8
Hamilton	30	9	21
Hancock	15	8	7
Hardin	29	10	19
Henry	29	12	17
Howard	8	7	1
Humboldt	15	9	6
Ida	16	9	7
Iowa	24	11	13
Jackson	14	8	6
Jasper	46	14	32
Jefferson	28	10	18
Keokuk	8	4	4
Kossuth	24	9	15
Lee	30	15	15
Louisa	22	11	11
Lucas	13	5	8
Lyon	25	10	15
Mahaska	24	8	16
Marion	34	12	22
Marshall	55	18	37
Mitchell	18	6	12
Monroe	12	5	7
Montgomery	19	8	11
Muscatine	65	22	43
O'Brien	30	11	19
Osceola	13	8	5
Page	15	8	7
Palo Alto	16	8	8
Plymouth	27	10	17
Pocahontas	14	7	7
Poweshiek	21	11	10
Ringgold	10	6	4
Sac	18	7	11
Shelby	14	8	6
Sioux	35	13	22
Tama	22	12	10
Taylor	9	5	4
Union	11	5	6
Van Buren	11	5	6
Wapello	38	9	29
Wayne	11	6	5
Webster	36	18	18
Winnebago	9	6	3
Winneshiek	23	10	13
Worth	19	8	11
Wright	20	8	12
KANSAS–Metropolitan Counties			
Butler	53	49	4
Douglas	131	81	50
Franklin	58	27	31
Geary	71	26	45
Jackson	25	16	9
Jefferson	40	23	17
Johnson	616	498	118
Leavenworth	98	47	51
Linn	20	9	11
Miami	42	22	20
Osage	41	23	18
Pottawatomie	45	26	19
Riley County Police Department	178	102	76
Sedgwick	523	177	346
Shawnee	195	112	83
Wabaunsee	17	6	11
Wyandotte	155	58	97
KANSAS–Nonmetropolitan Counties			
Allen	28	9	19
Anderson	16	15	1
Atchison	37	11	26
Barber	11	5	6
Barton	39	20	19
Bourbon	9	7	2
Brown	20	7	13
Chase	5	5	0
Chautauqua	14	4	10
Cheyenne	4	4	0
Clark	9	4	5
Clay	20	8	12
Cloud	13	13	0
Coffey	31	12	19
Cowley	46	24	22
Crawford	71	33	38
Decatur	3	3	0
Dickinson	27	15	12
Edwards	8	4	4
Elk	10	4	6
Ellis	29	18	11
Ellsworth	15	7	8
Finney	101	40	61
Ford	55	26	29
Gove	5	4	1
Graham	7	3	4
Grant	16	6	10
Gray	16	10	6
Greeley	7	3	4
Greenwood	23	12	11
Hamilton	12	6	6
Harper	7	5	2
Haskell	17	11	6
Hodgeman	8	4	4
Jewell	8	4	4
Kearny	21	11	10
Kingman	17	7	10
Kiowa	11	6	5
Labette	38	19	19
Lane	10	5	5
Lincoln	12	8	4
Logan	4	3	1
Lyon	83	28	55
Marshall	18	7	11
McPherson	33	16	17
Meade	19	5	14

Table 80. Full-Time Law Enforcement Employees, by State and Metropolitan and Nonmetropolitan Counties, 2008—*Continued*

(Number.)

State/County	Total law enforcement employees	Total officers	Total civilians
Montgomery	40	22	18
Morris	12	7	5
Morton	10	6	4
Nemaha	18	8	10
Neosho	29	14	15
Ness	13	7	6
Norton	10	10	0
Osborne	15	8	7
Ottawa	14	8	6
Pawnee	14	8	6
Phillips	14	9	5
Pratt	9	8	1
Rawlins	4	3	1
Reno	77	44	33
Republic	13	7	6
Rice	6	5	1
Rooks	10	5	5
Rush	8	3	5
Russell	18	9	9
Saline	102	44	58
Scott	4	3	1
Seward	43	13	30
Sheridan	8	3	5
Sherman	13	6	7
Smith	5	5	0
Stafford	9	4	5
Stanton	13	5	8
Thomas	13	12	1
Trego	4	4	0
Wallace	2	2	0
Washington	6	6	0
Wichita	9	4	5
Wilson	26	11	15
Woodson	10	6	4
KENTUCKY–Metropolitan Counties			
Boone	141	131	10
Bourbon	6	5	1
Boyd	28	25	3
Bracken	4	3	1
Bullitt	45	40	5
Campbell	12	9	3
Campbell County Police Department	33	32	1
Christian	32	28	4
Clark	16	12	4
Daviess	55	41	14
Edmonson	8	5	3
Gallatin	10	9	1
Gallatin County Police Department	1	1	0
Grant	15	13	2
Greenup	15	14	1
Hancock	7	6	1
Hardin	41	37	4
Henderson	24	20	4
Henry	8	6	2
Jefferson	289	237	52
Jessamine	31	23	8
Kenton	37	32	5
Kenton County Police Department	58	36	22
Larue	4	3	1
McLean	10	8	2
Meade	16	13	3
Nelson	29	22	7
Oldham	17	15	2
Oldham County Police Department	34	31	3
Pendleton	7	6	1
Scott	33	31	2
Shelby	24	23	1
Spencer	7	6	1
Trigg	7	7	0
Trimble	4	2	2
Warren	58	34	24
Webster	8	6	2
Woodford	9	9	0

State/County	Total law enforcement employees	Total officers	Total civilians
KENTUCKY–Nonmetropolitan Counties			
Adair	8	6	2
Anderson	15	15	0
Ballard	12	11	1
Barren	19	17	2
Bath	2	1	1
Bell	22	9	13
Breathitt	5	2	3
Breckinridge	8	6	2
Butler	8	6	2
Caldwell	9	7	2
Calloway	27	20	7
Carroll	2	1	1
Carter	10	8	2
Casey	8	7	1
Clay	18	16	2
Clinton	7	6	1
Crittenden	4	3	1
Cumberland	6	5	1
Elliott	3	2	1
Estill	6	4	2
Fleming	9	9	0
Franklin	20	19	1
Fulton	5	4	1
Garrard	9	7	2
Graves	14	10	4
Grayson	11	8	3
Green	4	4	0
Harrison	10	10	0
Hart	8	7	1
Hopkins	23	16	7
Jackson	4	4	0
Johnson	15	11	4
Knott	13	5	8
Knox	9	8	1
Laurel	37	24	13
Lawrence	7	5	2
Lee	1	1	0
Leslie	9	7	2
Letcher	14	11	3
Lewis	6	4	2
Lincoln	11	9	2
Livingston	7	7	0
Logan	22	21	1
Lyon	5	5	0
Madison	34	22	12
Magoffin	4	3	1
Marion	8	6	2
Marshall	19	18	1
Martin	5	3	2
Mason	13	11	2
McCracken	41	37	4
McCreary	6	5	1
Menifee	4	4	0
Mercer	9	9	0
Metcalfe	5	3	2
Monroe	7	5	2
Montgomery	16	14	2
Morgan	5	3	2
Muhlenberg	14	13	1
Nicholas	4	2	2
Ohio	21	17	4
Owen	7	5	2
Owsley	3	2	1
Perry	24	12	12
Pike	32	13	19
Powell	6	4	2
Pulaski	38	30	8
Robertson	1	1	0
Rockcastle	5	4	1
Rowan	13	10	3
Russell	11	10	1
Simpson	14	11	3

Table 80. Full-Time Law Enforcement Employees, by State and Metropolitan and Nonmetropolitan Counties, 2008—*Continued*

(Number.)

State/County	Total law enforcement employees	Total officers	Total civilians
Taylor	13	11	2
Todd	3	2	1
Union	9	8	1
Washington	6	6	0
Wayne	12	11	1
Whitley	19	16	3
Wolfe	3	2	1
LOUISIANA–Metropolitan Counties			
Ascension	260	226	34
Bossier	369	300	69
Caddo	642	437	205
Calcasieu	797	697	100
Cameron	72	47	25
De Soto	99	83	16
East Baton Rouge	821	821	0
East Feliciana	63	63	0
Grant	64	51	13
Iberville	130	77	53
Jefferson	1,449	1,005	444
Lafayette	645	425	220
Lafourche	336	233	103
Livingston	302	302	0
Ouachita	393	393	0
Plaquemines	188	185	3
Pointe Coupee	94	94	0
Rapides	498	389	109
St. Bernard	246	216	30
St. Charles	374	279	95
St. Helena	46	19	27
St. Martin	164	117	47
St. Tammany	700	297	403
Terrebonne	282	223	59
Union	48	31	17
West Baton Rouge	174	119	55
West Feliciana	80	58	22
LOUISIANA–Nonmetropolitan Counties			
Acadia	108	108	0
Allen	54	29	25
Assumption	78	52	26
Avoyelles	377	377	0
Beauregard	72	54	18
Bienville	44	26	18
Caldwell	29	29	0
Catahoula	110	13	97
Claiborne	103	41	62
Concordia	258	258	0
Evangeline	53	18	35
Iberia	310	134	176
Jackson	102	102	0
Jefferson Davis	56	43	13
La Salle	43	43	0
Lincoln	61	45	16
Madison	68	68	0
Morehouse	158	40	118
Natchitoches	83	52	31
Red River	36	19	17
Richland	149	129	20
Sabine	71	71	0
St. James	95	52	43
St. Landry	197	96	101
St. Mary	184	165	19
Tangipahoa	245	105	140
Tensas	37	32	5
Vermilion	134	66	68
Vernon	148	106	42
Washington	110	61	49
Webster	135	44	91
West Carroll	17	17	0
Winn	32	32	0
MAINE–Metropolitan Counties			
Androscoggin	27	18	9
Cumberland	59	52	7
Penobscot	28	24	4
Sagadahoc	27	24	3
York	29	26	3

State/County	Total law enforcement employees	Total officers	Total civilians
MAINE–Nonmetropolitan Counties			
Aroostook	22	16	6
Franklin	26	15	11
Hancock	17	15	2
Kennebec	25	22	3
Knox	19	18	1
Lincoln	31	29	2
Oxford	18	17	1
Piscataquis	19	8	11
Somerset	16	15	1
Waldo	18	16	2
Washington	13	12	1
MARYLAND–Metropolitan Counties			
Allegany	11	9	2
Allegany County Bureau of Police	16	16	0
Anne Arundel	98	72	26
Anne Arundel County Police Department	859	638	221
Baltimore County	98	83	15
Baltimore County Police Department	2,211	1,896	315
Calvert	133	112	21
Carroll	99	66	33
Cecil	88	77	11
Charles	420	290	130
Frederick	238	176	62
Harford	366	281	85
Howard	73	46	27
Howard County Police Department	587	419	168
Montgomery	170	145	25
Montgomery County Police Department	1,738	1,277	461
Prince George's	333	236	97
Prince George's County Police Department	1,772	1,504	268
Queen Anne's	54	49	5
Somerset	25	22	3
Washington	234	94	140
Wicomico	110	87	23
MARYLAND–Nonmetropolitan Counties			
Caroline	34	30	4
Dorchester	47	38	9
Garrett	55	30	25
Kent	28	23	5
St. Mary's	244	128	116
Talbot	28	26	2
Worcester	51	44	7
MICHIGAN–Metropolitan Counties			
Barry	53	30	23
Bay	80	35	45
Berrien	163	72	91
Calhoun	180	76	104
Cass	72	35	37
Clinton	59	25	34
Eaton	140	72	68
Genesee	254	144	110
Ingham	202	114	88
Ionia	53	21	32
Jackson	132	52	80
Kalamazoo	205	161	44
Kent	545	207	338
Lapeer	81	49	32
Livingston	124	71	53
Macomb	502	250	252
Monroe	202	96	106
Muskegon	120	51	69
Newaygo	58	30	28
Oakland	1,025	841	184
Ottawa	223	128	95
Saginaw	122	62	60
St. Clair	177	66	111
Van Buren	87	44	43
Washtenaw	286	134	152
Wayne	1,230	1,064	166
MICHIGAN–Nonmetropolitan Counties			
Alcona	25	14	11
Alger	14	11	3
Allegan	109	61	48
Alpena	26	13	13

Table 80. Full-Time Law Enforcement Employees, by State and Metropolitan and Nonmetropolitan Counties, 2008—*Continued*

(Number.)

State/County	Total law enforcement employees	Total officers	Total civilians
Antrim	48	19	29
Arenac	22	9	13
Baraga	13	6	7
Benzie	40	13	27
Branch	49	25	24
Charlevoix	31	18	13
Cheboygan	34	16	18
Chippewa	21	17	4
Clare	23	20	3
Crawford	27	15	12
Delta	34	18	16
Dickinson	30	14	16
Emmet	46	24	22
Gladwin	40	16	24
Gogebic	21	14	7
Grand Traverse	127	66	61
Gratiot	36	19	17
Hillsdale	45	29	16
Houghton	20	20	0
Huron	37	22	15
Iosco	21	4	17
Iron	21	8	13
Isabella	49	24	25
Kalkaska	35	18	17
Keweenaw	7	6	1
Lake	73	16	57
Leelanau	21	19	2
Lenawee	103	46	57
Luce	5	4	1
Mackinac	21	9	12
Manistee	28	13	15
Marquette	52	22	30
Mason	39	20	19
Mecosta	48	23	25
Menominee	14	13	1
Midland	58	36	22
Missaukee	27	12	15
Montcalm	60	28	32
Montmorency	26	11	15
Oceana	36	20	16
Ogemaw	26	16	10
Ontonagon	12	9	3
Osceola	36	18	18
Oscoda	16	10	6
Otsego	23	11	12
Presque Isle	26	14	12
Roscommon	38	24	14
Sanilac	30	26	4
Schoolcraft	10	2	8
Shiawassee	69	34	35
St. Joseph	49	24	25
Tuscola	49	30	19
Wexford	51	25	26
MINNESOTA–Metropolitan Counties			
Anoka	241	128	113
Benton	72	27	45
Blue Earth	73	25	48
Carlton	48	19	29
Carver	149	88	61
Chisago	85	41	44
Clay	64	33	31
Dakota	168	78	90
Dodge	33	23	10
Hennepin	790	327	463
Houston	24	13	11
Isanti	57	20	37
Nicollet	29	11	18
Olmsted	150	57	93
Polk	30	24	6
Ramsey	400	236	164
Scott	125	38	87
Sherburne	275	66	209
Stearns	182	64	118
St. Louis	235	96	139
Wabasha	36	19	17
Washington	231	91	140
Wright	219	139	80
MINNESOTA–Nonmetropolitan Counties			
Aitkin	46	19	27
Becker	57	21	36
Beltrami	78	33	45
Big Stone	8	5	3
Brown	36	10	26
Cass	58	35	23
Chippewa	18	8	10
Clearwater	18	8	10
Cook	18	11	7
Cottonwood	20	9	11
Crow Wing	127	43	84
Douglas	73	24	49
Faribault	22	9	13
Fillmore	31	18	13
Freeborn	54	21	33
Goodhue	102	39	63
Grant	11	7	4
Hubbard	43	15	28
Itasca	72	63	9
Jackson	19	8	11
Kanabec	34	15	19
Kandiyohi	112	35	77
Kittson	10	5	5
Koochiching	18	10	8
Lac Qui Parle	9	5	4
Lake	26	15	11
Lake of the Woods	9	5	4
Le Sueur	31	17	14
Lincoln	10	4	6
Lyon	39	12	27
Mahnomen	21	13	8
Marshall	18	12	6
Martin	30	11	19
McLeod	59	25	34
Meeker	42	18	24
Mille Lacs	67	25	42
Morrison	61	19	42
Mower	51	22	29
Murray	13	9	4
Nobles	35	12	23
Norman	8	5	3
Otter Tail	80	33	47
Pennington	31	8	23
Pine	78	29	49
Pipestone	22	12	10
Pope	15	7	8
Red Lake	10	6	4
Redwood	24	11	13
Renville	26	11	15
Rice	47	23	24
Rock	16	11	5
Roseau	22	12	10
Sibley	22	10	12
Steele	26	19	7
Stevens	12	6	6
Swift	12	6	6
Todd	33	14	19
Traverse	11	5	6
Wadena	19	8	11
Waseca	28	12	16
Watonwan	21	8	13
Wilkin	16	6	10
Winona	57	19	38
Yellow Medicine	21	8	13
MISSISSIPPI–Metropolitan Counties			
DeSoto	229	115	114
Forrest	118	92	26
George	29	16	13
Hancock	53	47	6
Harrison	353	110	243

Table 80. Full-Time Law Enforcement Employees, by State and Metropolitan and Nonmetropolitan Counties, 2008—*Continued*

(Number.)

State/County	Total law enforcement employees	Total officers	Total civilians
Hinds	466	111	355
Madison	133	54	79
Marshall	56	29	27
Perry	21	10	11
Rankin	165	81	84
Simpson	45	16	29
Stone	22	20	2
Tate	44	22	22
Tunica	136	69	67
MISSISSIPPI–Nonmetropolitan Counties			
Adams	56	28	28
Alcorn	32	15	17
Amite	7	6	1
Attala	12	7	5
Benton	17	5	12
Bolivar	113	18	95
Carroll	10	9	1
Chickasaw	32	13	19
Choctaw	11	6	5
Claiborne	29	13	16
Coahoma	12	11	1
Covington	15	12	3
Greene	15	8	7
Grenada	14	11	3
Holmes	12	12	0
Jasper	26	12	14
Jones	35	31	4
Kemper	15	9	6
Lauderdale	119	51	68
Leake	17	15	2
Lee	125	44	81
Leflore	32	20	12
Lincoln	45	20	25
Lowndes	49	41	8
Marion	19	13	6
Monroe	53	22	31
Neshoba	18	18	0
Newton	14	8	6
Noxubee	10	4	6
Oktibbeha	28	25	3
Panola	69	29	40
Pearl River	123	37	86
Pike	53	27	26
Prentiss	32	13	19
Smith	17	11	6
Sunflower	26	10	16
Tallahatchie	26	10	16
Tippah	24	9	15
Tishomingo	24	13	11
Union	38	17	21
Walthall	18	8	10
Warren	69	42	27
Washington	66	37	29
Wayne	20	9	11
Webster	4	4	0
Wilkinson	15	7	8
Winston	10	9	1
Yazoo	13	11	2
MISSOURI–Metropolitan Counties			
Andrew	14	10	4
Bates	32	12	20
Bollinger	14	8	6
Boone	74	58	16
Buchanan	111	70	41
Caldwell	48	7	41
Callaway	25	23	2
Cape Girardeau	71	45	26
Cass	90	72	18
Christian	75	47	28
Clay	183	111	72
Clinton	22	15	7
Cole	62	48	14
Dallas	15	12	3
De Kalb	12	6	6
Franklin	129	105	24
Greene	287	147	140
Howard	7	6	1
Jackson	117	84	33
Jasper	140	90	50
Jefferson	213	140	73
Lafayette	46	33	13
Lincoln	98	59	39
McDonald	32	16	16
Moniteau	9	5	4
Newton	66	37	29
Osage	12	9	3
Platte	115	79	36
Polk	37	22	15
Ray	34	14	20
St. Charles	221	152	69
St. Louis County Police Department	1,023	781	242
Warren	61	56	5
Washington	36	21	15
Webster	26	13	13
MISSOURI–Nonmetropolitan Counties			
Adair	31	11	20
Atchison	9	4	5
Audrain	39	30	9
Barry	35	21	14
Barton	17	7	10
Benton	24	17	7
Butler	41	24	17
Camden	56	50	6
Carroll	13	7	6
Carter	7	2	5
Cedar	18	12	6
Clark	11	5	6
Cooper	9	8	1
Crawford	39	29	10
Dade	9	4	5
Daviess	6	5	1
Dent	18	12	6
Douglas	10	5	5
Dunklin	23	9	14
Gasconade	12	12	0
Gentry	5	5	0
Grundy	6	4	2
Harrison	11	5	6
Henry	24	19	5
Hickory	14	9	5
Holt	8	3	5
Howell	39	26	13
Iron	15	7	8
Johnson	46	36	10
Knox	4	2	2
Laclede	20	19	1
Lawrence	28	25	3
Lewis	11	5	6
Linn	6	5	1
Livingston	22	11	11
Macon	15	13	2
Madison	12	10	2
Maries	10	6	4
Marion	37	16	21
Mercer	8	3	5
Miller	17	15	2
Mississippi	46	10	36
Monroe	9	8	1
Montgomery	16	15	1
Morgan	48	28	20
New Madrid	26	12	14
Nodaway	11	10	1
Oregon	9	6	3
Ozark	18	9	9
Pemiscot	44	16	28
Perry	30	20	10
Pettis	55	23	32
Phelps	64	29	35

Table 80. Full-Time Law Enforcement Employees, by State and Metropolitan and Nonmetropolitan Counties, 2008—*Continued*

(Number.)

State/County	Total law enforcement employees	Total officers	Total civilians
Pike	29	11	18
Pulaski	26	16	10
Putnam	4	3	1
Ralls	8	7	1
Randolph	34	17	17
Reynolds	11	7	4
Ripley	9	8	1
Saline	32	19	13
Schuyler	8	3	5
Scotland	5	2	3
Scott	37	20	17
Shannon	9	5	4
Shelby	10	5	5
St. Clair	66	20	46
Ste. Genevieve	51	39	12
St. Francois	73	60	13
Stoddard	24	13	11
Stone	56	45	11
Sullivan	5	4	1
Taney	57	42	15
Texas	17	8	9
Vernon	29	14	15
Wayne	12	6	6
Worth	3	2	1
Wright	13	8	5
MONTANA–Metropolitan Counties			
Carbon	9	8	1
Cascade	130	36	94
Missoula	156	50	106
Yellowstone	158	52	106
MONTANA–Nonmetropolitan Counties			
Beaverhead	17	7	10
Big Horn	30	14	16
Blaine	10	9	1
Broadwater	23	9	14
Carter	3	3	0
Chouteau	15	8	7
Custer	16	6	10
Daniels	3	3	0
Dawson	15	6	9
Deer Lodge	35	20	15
Fallon	3	3	0
Fergus	19	9	10
Flathead	122	52	70
Gallatin	88	51	37
Garfield	3	2	1
Glacier	13	12	1
Golden Valley	2	2	0
Granite	9	5	4
Hill	29	12	17
Jefferson	21	12	9
Judith Basin	4	4	0
Lake	49	20	29
Liberty	4	4	0
Lincoln	37	20	17
Madison	14	9	5
McCone	4	4	0
Meagher	4	4	0
Musselshell	6	6	0
Park	21	14	7
Petroleum	1	1	0
Phillips	11	7	4
Pondera	10	9	1
Powder River	3	3	0
Powell	17	10	7
Prairie	3	3	0
Ravalli	52	29	23
Richland	17	8	9
Roosevelt	18	14	4
Rosebud	25	14	11
Sanders	23	8	15
Sheridan	8	7	1
Silver Bow	90	44	46
Stillwater	9	7	2
Sweet Grass	12	6	6
Teton	13	9	4
Toole	20	12	8
Treasure	2	2	0
Valley	18	8	10
Wibaux	2	2	0
NEBRASKA–Metropolitan Counties			
Cass	39	24	15
Dakota	15	14	1
Dixon	14	7	7
Douglas	199	130	69
Lancaster	95	73	22
Sarpy	190	129	61
Saunders	37	13	24
Seward	14	12	2
Washington	48	25	23
NEBRASKA–Nonmetropolitan Counties			
Adams	18	16	2
Antelope	11	6	5
Arthur	1	1	0
Banner	1	1	0
Blaine	1	1	0
Boone	6	5	1
Box Butte	20	5	15
Boyd	3	3	0
Brown	9	5	4
Buffalo	44	25	19
Burt	8	4	4
Butler	13	9	4
Cedar	8	4	4
Chase	8	4	4
Cherry	12	5	7
Cheyenne	7	6	1
Clay	10	5	5
Colfax	9	7	2
Cuming	6	5	1
Custer	7	6	1
Dawes	9	3	6
Dawson	55	28	27
Deuel	5	4	1
Dodge	23	16	7
Dundy	8	4	4
Fillmore	11	7	4
Franklin	7	3	4
Frontier	8	5	3
Furnas	13	8	5
Gage	14	11	3
Garden	8	3	5
Garfield	2	2	0
Gosper	5	4	1
Grant	1	1	0
Greeley	2	1	1
Hall	35	29	6
Hamilton	9	9	0
Harlan	8	4	4
Hayes	2	2	0
Hitchcock	7	4	3
Holt	6	5	1
Hooker	1	1	0
Howard	10	5	5
Jefferson	14	7	7
Kearney	12	7	5
Keith	13	6	7
Keya Paha	3	2	1
Kimball	6	2	4
Knox	11	6	5
Lincoln	49	23	26
Logan	2	2	0
Loup	1	1	0
Madison	19	15	4
McPherson	1	1	0
Merrick	11	6	5

Table 80. Full-Time Law Enforcement Employees, by State and Metropolitan and Nonmetropolitan Counties, 2008—*Continued*

(Number.)

State/County	Total law enforcement employees	Total officers	Total civilians
Morrill	9	4	5
Nance	10	6	4
Nemaha	6	6	0
Nuckolls	7	4	3
Otoe	27	16	11
Pawnee	4	3	1
Perkins	10	5	5
Phelps	25	6	19
Pierce	6	3	3
Platte	63	18	45
Polk	10	6	4
Red Willow	7	5	2
Richardson	10	6	4
Rock	8	3	5
Saline	10	10	0
Scotts Bluff	25	17	8
Sheridan	7	6	1
Sherman	6	5	1
Sioux	1	1	0
Stanton	8	7	1
Thayer	10	6	4
Thomas	1	1	0
Valley	7	3	4
Wayne	4	3	1
Webster	10	5	5
Wheeler	2	2	0
York	23	9	14
NEVADA–Metropolitan Counties			
Carson City	139	96	43
Storey	27	24	3
Washoe	723	421	302
NEVADA–Nonmetropolitan Counties			
Churchill	49	40	9
Douglas	115	99	16
Elko	65	51	14
Esmeralda	14	10	4
Eureka	20	13	7
Humboldt	49	34	15
Lander	27	16	11
Lincoln	31	26	5
Lyon	107	68	39
Mineral	24	18	6
Nye	149	106	43
Pershing	19	12	7
White Pine	30	24	6
NEW HAMPSHIRE–Metropolitan Counties			
Rockingham	48	25	23
NEW HAMPSHIRE–Nonmetropolitan Counties			
Carroll	27	14	13
Cheshire	21	10	11
Merrimack	32	17	15
NEW JERSEY–Metropolitan Counties			
Atlantic	133	103	30
Bergen	526	441	85
Bergen County Police Department	164	93	71
Burlington	92	71	21
Camden	175	147	28
Cape May	152	131	21
Cumberland	62	56	6
Essex	347	288	59
Gloucester	104	88	16
Hudson	300	209	91
Hunterdon	24	19	5
Mercer	179	141	38
Middlesex	222	181	41
Monmouth	696	501	195
Morris	341	262	79
Ocean	233	137	96
Passaic	695	531	164
Salem	181	157	24
Somerset	227	183	44
Sussex	148	124	24
Union	213	169	44
Warren	23	19	4
NEW MEXICO–Metropolitan Counties			
Bernalillo	327	252	75
Sandoval	58	51	7
San Juan	121	91	30
Torrance	17	11	6
Valencia	52	40	12
NEW MEXICO–Nonmetropolitan Counties			
Catron	13	7	6
Chaves	50	40	10
Cibola	17	12	5
Colfax	13	11	2
Curry	25	15	10
De Baca	3	3	0
Eddy	54	45	9
Grant	39	36	3
Hidalgo	17	9	8
Lea	61	41	20
Lincoln	26	17	9
Luna	34	31	3
McKinley	46	36	10
Otero	49	35	14
Quay	8	8	0
Rio Arriba	26	22	4
Roosevelt	17	14	3
San Miguel	11	8	3
Sierra	14	12	2
Socorro	11	8	3
Taos	25	19	6
Union	5	4	1
NEW YORK–Metropolitan Counties			
Albany	176	129	47
Broome	74	55	19
Chemung	50	43	7
Dutchess	131	110	21
Erie	177	143	34
Herkimer	11	6	5
Livingston	71	48	23
Madison	39	30	9
Monroe	345	285	60
Nassau	3,544	2,721	823
Niagara	139	106	33
Oneida	106	89	17
Onondaga	297	249	48
Ontario	114	66	48
Orange	111	99	12
Orleans	26	26	0
Oswego	74	56	18
Rensselaer	39	33	6
Saratoga	148	112	36
Schenectady	20	14	6
Schoharie	29	15	14
Suffolk	408	268	140
Suffolk County Police Department	3,205	2,620	585
Tioga	56	37	19
Ulster	87	68	19
Warren	106	72	34
Washington	37	31	6
Wayne	66	54	12
Westchester Public Safety	340	267	73
NEW YORK–Nonmetropolitan Counties			
Allegany	46	36	10
Cayuga	41	37	4
Chautauqua	117	73	44
Chenango	49	24	25
Clinton	23	23	0
Columbia	55	45	10
Cortland	52	33	19
Delaware	27	13	14
Essex	7	5	2
Franklin	12	3	9
Fulton	47	30	17
Genesee	68	41	27
Greene	32	29	3
Jefferson	54	45	9

Table 80. Full-Time Law Enforcement Employees, by State and Metropolitan and Nonmetropolitan Counties, 2008—*Continued*

(Number.)

State/County	Total law enforcement employees	Total officers	Total civilians
Lewis	26	16	10
Montgomery	40	24	16
Otsego	19	19	0
Schuyler	22	20	2
Seneca	42	31	11
St. Lawrence	35	34	1
Sullivan	47	46	1
Wyoming	40	30	10
NORTH CAROLINA–Metropolitan Counties			
Alamance	264	129	135
Alexander	47	28	19
Anson	59	30	29
Brunswick	200	123	77
Buncombe	376	239	137
Burke	115	86	29
Cabarrus	224	188	36
Caldwell	113	63	50
Catawba	176	125	51
Chatham	96	75	21
Cumberland	537	280	257
Currituck	94	62	32
Davie	74	46	28
Durham	419	166	253
Edgecombe	126	52	74
Forsyth	546	235	311
Franklin	93	57	36
Gaston County Police Department	217	131	86
Greene	40	24	16
Guilford	528	246	282
Haywood	93	48	45
Henderson	186	131	55
Hoke	107	51	56
Johnston	168	98	70
Madison	34	20	14
Mecklenburg	1,302	316	986
Nash	122	75	47
New Hanover	382	290	92
Onslow	120	100	20
Orange	140	115	25
Pender	91	55	36
Person	78	41	37
Pitt	276	125	151
Randolph	217	153	64
Rockingham	128	88	40
Stokes	63	40	23
Union	238	166	72
Wake	812	351	461
Wayne	149	85	64
Yadkin	66	36	30
NORTH CAROLINA–Nonmetropolitan Counties			
Alleghany	30	13	17
Ashe	44	23	21
Avery	32	24	8
Beaufort	79	50	29
Bertie	30	21	9
Bladen	82	56	26
Camden	18	17	1
Carteret	91	47	44
Caswell	51	29	22
Cherokee	58	25	33
Chowan	38	19	19
Clay	42	16	26
Cleveland	126	83	43
Columbus	105	60	45
Craven	106	64	42
Dare	140	63	77
Davidson	194	130	64
Duplin	95	70	25
Gates	14	12	2
Graham	14	12	2
Granville	60	43	17
Halifax	85	58	27
Harnett	174	107	67
Hertford	56	23	33

State/County	Total law enforcement employees	Total officers	Total civilians
Iredell	198	153	45
Jackson	72	47	25
Jones	20	11	9
Lee	77	46	31
Lenoir	93	56	37
Lincoln	169	100	69
Macon	66	44	22
Martin	35	33	2
McDowell	62	40	22
Mitchell	16	14	2
Montgomery	45	31	14
Moore	114	74	40
Northampton	51	25	26
Pamlico	35	13	22
Pasquotank	50	41	9
Perquimans	14	12	2
Polk	36	25	11
Richmond	69	51	18
Robeson	231	128	103
Rowan	173	121	52
Rutherford	127	73	54
Sampson	127	73	54
Scotland	66	40	26
Stanly	91	47	44
Surry	103	68	35
Swain	39	16	23
Transylvania	67	52	15
Tyrrell	16	10	6
Vance	97	48	49
Warren	50	31	19
Washington	41	21	20
Watauga	82	43	39
Wilkes	118	69	49
Wilson	135	86	49
Yancey	29	14	15
NORTH DAKOTA–Metropolitan Counties			
Burleigh	80	47	33
Cass	133	69	64
Grand Forks	33	27	6
Morton	32	20	12
NORTH DAKOTA–Nonmetropolitan Counties			
Adams	4	4	0
Barnes	16	6	10
Benson	4	4	0
Billings	4	4	0
Bottineau	14	10	4
Bowman	3	3	0
Burke	5	4	1
Cavalier	11	5	6
Dickey	5	4	1
Divide	3	3	0
Dunn	5	4	1
Eddy	4	4	0
Emmons	4	3	1
Foster	4	3	1
Golden Valley	5	4	1
Grant	3	3	0
Griggs	3	3	0
Hettinger	4	4	0
Kidder	3	2	1
Lamoure	5	4	1
Logan	4	2	2
McHenry	7	7	0
McIntosh	3	3	0
McKenzie	13	6	7
McLean	28	20	8
Mercer	23	13	10
Mountrail	14	9	5
Nelson	5	4	1
Oliver	5	4	1
Pembina	12	8	4
Pierce	8	4	4
Ramsey	7	6	1
Ransom	5	4	1

Table 80. Full-Time Law Enforcement Employees, by State and Metropolitan and Nonmetropolitan Counties, 2008—*Continued*

(Number.)

State/County	Total law enforcement employees	Total officers	Total civilians
Renville	5	5	0
Richland	15	13	2
Rolette	14	5	9
Sargent	5	4	1
Sheridan	2	2	0
Sioux	1	1	0
Slope	1	1	0
Stark	15	12	3
Steele	3	3	0
Stutsman	11	9	2
Towner	3	2	1
Traill	9	5	4
Walsh	17	10	7
Ward	42	18	24
Wells	3	3	0
Williams	28	16	12
OHIO–Metropolitan Counties			
Allen	161	77	84
Belmont	66	54	12
Brown	32	27	5
Butler	359	173	186
Carroll	27	20	7
Clark	152	125	27
Clermont	201	87	114
Cuyahoga	1,043	178	865
Delaware	187	86	101
Erie	74	36	38
Fairfield	133	103	30
Franklin	868	642	226
Fulton	30	20	10
Geauga	149	67	82
Greene	163	101	62
Hamilton	1,006	300	706
Jefferson	76	34	42
Lake	202	57	145
Lawrence	46	34	12
Licking	190	134	56
Lorain	241	77	164
Lucas	518	289	229
Madison	36	33	3
Mahoning	321	304	17
Medina	86	62	24
Miami	139	54	85
Montgomery	485	222	263
Morrow	37	18	19
Ottawa	62	61	1
Portage	132	55	77
Preble	61	18	43
Richland	142	48	94
Stark	240	138	102
Summit	490	394	96
Trumbull	133	44	89
Warren	183	97	86
Washington	88	48	40
OHIO–Nonmetropolitan Counties			
Adams	33	23	10
Ashland	77	43	34
Ashtabula	80	38	42
Athens	27	22	5
Auglaize	56	22	34
Champaign	25	23	2
Clinton	68	37	31
Coshocton	59	50	9
Darke	68	41	27
Defiance	36	22	14
Fayette	37	23	14
Gallia	33	22	11
Guernsey	41	19	22
Hancock	82	32	50
Hardin	28	24	4
Henry	22	20	2
Highland	57	57	0
Hocking	24	20	4
Huron	69	30	39
Logan	88	41	47
Marion	39	30	9
Meigs	13	11	2
Mercer	47	32	15
Monroe	20	17	3
Morgan	15	10	5
Muskingum	119	81	38
Noble	16	5	11
Paulding	34	14	20
Perry	16	11	5
Putnam	53	32	21
Ross	91	52	39
Sandusky	59	34	25
Scioto	81	45	36
Seneca	82	34	48
Shelby	65	37	28
Tuscarawas	103	32	71
Van Wert	36	19	17
Vinton	15	10	5
Williams	27	22	5
Wyandot	24	13	11
OKLAHOMA–Metropolitan Counties			
Canadian	56	29	27
Cleveland	99	46	53
Comanche	38	28	10
Creek	69	36	33
Grady	12	10	2
Le Flore	20	14	6
Lincoln	30	12	18
Logan	45	13	32
McClain	27	14	13
Oklahoma	744	194	550
Okmulgee	13	12	1
Osage	70	39	31
Pawnee	19	13	6
Rogers	60	27	33
Sequoyah	17	14	3
Tulsa	557	510	47
Wagoner	52	14	38
OKLAHOMA–Nonmetropolitan Counties			
Adair	30	11	19
Alfalfa	9	4	5
Atoka	20	8	12
Beaver	13	7	6
Beckham	30	9	21
Blaine	16	7	9
Bryan	18	15	3
Caddo	31	15	16
Carter	56	18	38
Cherokee	29	20	9
Choctaw	19	7	12
Cimarron	8	4	4
Coal	13	8	5
Cotton	11	6	5
Craig	27	10	17
Custer	29	9	20
Delaware	44	17	27
Dewey	10	3	7
Ellis	17	5	12
Garfield	27	20	7
Garvin	28	12	16
Grant	10	5	5
Greer	5	2	3
Harmon	3	3	0
Harper	11	5	6
Haskell	7	6	1
Hughes	13	7	6
Jackson	38	13	25
Jefferson	14	6	8
Johnston	25	7	18
Kay	37	13	24
Kingfisher	15	7	8
Kiowa	11	10	1
Latimer	19	8	11
Love	14	6	8
Major	10	4	6

Table 80. Full-Time Law Enforcement Employees, by State and Metropolitan and Nonmetropolitan Counties, 2008—*Continued*

(Number.)

State/County	Total law enforcement employees	Total officers	Total civilians
Marshall	22	5	17
Mayes	41	17	24
McCurtain	22	18	4
McIntosh	24	17	7
Murray	9	5	4
Muskogee	94	36	58
Noble	17	5	12
Nowata	22	10	12
Okfuskee	19	8	11
Ottawa	38	17	21
Payne	57	26	31
Pittsburg	44	12	32
Pontotoc	12	10	2
Pottawatomie	20	17	3
Pushmataha	24	9	15
Roger Mills	13	8	5
Seminole	23	13	10
Stephens	16	13	3
Texas	37	11	26
Tillman	17	5	12
Washington	41	17	24
Washita	15	5	10
Woods	6	5	1
Woodward	18	9	9
OREGON–Metropolitan Counties			
Benton	96	90	6
Clackamas	315	214	101
Columbia	38	15	23
Deschutes	210	82	128
Jackson	75	54	21
Lane	320	66	254
Marion	349	93	256
Multnomah	821	97	724
Polk	66	49	17
Washington	520	220	300
Yamhill	96	45	51
OREGON–Nonmetropolitan Counties			
Baker	26	12	14
Clatsop	52	25	27
Coos	86	25	61
Crook	31	17	14
Curry	33	13	20
Douglas	156	120	36
Gilliam	6	5	1
Grant	16	4	12
Harney	20	5	15
Hood River	35	18	17
Jefferson	51	17	34
Josephine	78	28	50
Klamath	75	29	46
Lake	8	7	1
Lincoln	94	30	64
Linn	146	69	77
Malheur	50	20	30
Morrow	27	27	0
Sherman	6	5	1
Tillamook	60	56	4
Umatilla	74	49	25
Union	11	9	2
Wallowa	13	7	6
Wasco	30	15	15
Wheeler	14	3	11
PENNSYLVANIA–Metropolitan Counties			
Allegheny	190	156	34
Allegheny County Police Department	283	211	72
Beaver	32	26	6
Cumberland	31	26	5
Luzerne	10	10	0
Lycoming	16	11	5
Montgomery	123	103	20
Pike	10	6	4
Washington	30	26	4
Westmoreland	61	53	8
York	112	101	11
PENNSYLVANIA–Nonmetropolitan Counties			
Clarion	9	6	3
Elk	6	5	1
Franklin	16	13	3
Greene	7	6	1
Jefferson	5	4	1
Snyder	4	4	0
Tioga	7	5	2
SOUTH CAROLINA–Metropolitan Counties			
Aiken	233	125	108
Anderson	199	178	21
Berkeley	195	127	68
Calhoun	24	22	2
Charleston	725	254	471
Darlington	69	61	8
Dorchester	149	112	37
Edgefield	63	31	32
Fairfield	51	45	6
Florence	233	119	114
Greenville	477	385	92
Horry	255	194	61
Horry County Police Department	292	269	23
Kershaw	73	64	9
Laurens	109	64	45
Lexington	384	241	143
Pickens	136	99	37
Richland	532	491	41
Saluda	53	21	32
Spartanburg	325	296	29
Sumter	136	125	11
York	305	150	155
SOUTH CAROLINA–Nonmetropolitan Counties			
Abbeville	56	30	26
Allendale	14	11	3
Bamberg	16	13	3
Barnwell	44	26	18
Beaufort	249	223	26
Cherokee	94	47	47
Chester	84	44	40
Chesterfield	79	44	35
Clarendon	47	44	3
Colleton	136	65	71
Dillon	81	30	51
Georgetown	156	74	82
Greenwood	114	70	44
Hampton	33	27	6
Jasper	31	26	5
Lancaster	121	76	45
Lee	32	28	4
Marion	36	31	5
Marlboro	29	24	5
McCormick	37	14	23
Newberry	91	47	44
Oconee	139	82	57
Orangeburg	112	78	34
Union	51	27	24
Williamsburg	73	36	37
SOUTH DAKOTA–Metropolitan Counties			
Lincoln	19	17	2
McCook	7	6	1
Meade	55	17	38
Minnehaha	189	70	119
Pennington	98	68	30
Turner	10	8	2
Union	27	7	20
SOUTH DAKOTA–Nonmetropolitan Counties			
Aurora	4	3	1
Beadle	29	7	22
Bennett	3	2	1
Bon Homme	8	3	5
Brookings	20	12	8
Brown	45	13	32
Brule	9	4	5
Buffalo	1	1	0

Table 80. Full-Time Law Enforcement Employees, by State and Metropolitan and Nonmetropolitan Counties, 2008—*Continued*

(Number.)

State/County	Total law enforcement employees	Total officers	Total civilians
Butte	13	5	8
Campbell	2	2	0
Charles Mix	13	5	8
Clark	4	4	0
Clay	10	7	3
Codington	23	7	16
Corson	3	2	1
Custer	13	12	1
Davison	8	6	2
Day	7	4	3
Deuel	8	4	4
Dewey	3	2	1
Douglas	2	2	0
Edmunds	7	4	3
Fall River	16	6	10
Faulk	9	3	6
Grant	8	3	5
Gregory	3	2	1
Haakon	2	2	0
Hamlin	4	4	0
Hand	3	2	1
Hanson	2	2	0
Harding	3	2	1
Hughes	20	5	15
Hutchinson	3	3	0
Jackson	2	2	0
Jerauld	4	3	1
Jones	2	2	0
Kingsbury	6	5	1
Lake	10	5	5
Lawrence	46	18	28
Lyman	5	4	1
Marshall	11	6	5
McPherson	1	1	0
Mellette	4	3	1
Miner	4	3	1
Moody	8	4	4
Perkins	4	3	1
Potter	3	2	1
Roberts	26	4	22
Sanborn	3	2	1
Shannon	1	1	0
Spink	13	8	5
Stanley	6	5	1
Sully	3	3	0
Todd	1	1	0
Tripp	6	5	1
Walworth	10	2	8
Yankton	10	9	1
Ziebach	2	2	0
TENNESSEE–Metropolitan Counties			
Anderson	149	57	92
Blount	176	141	35
Bradley	200	101	99
Cannon	33	13	20
Carter	78	42	36
Cheatham	65	31	34
Chester	32	13	19
Dickson	124	54	70
Fayette	93	34	59
Grainger	35	15	20
Hamblen	68	32	36
Hamilton	375	149	226
Hartsville-Trousdale	41	18	23
Hawkins	59	38	21
Hickman	47	24	23
Jefferson	77	36	41
Knox	961	307	654
Loudon	61	40	21
Macon	58	24	34
Madison	229	69	160
Marion	42	18	24
Montgomery	327	77	250
Polk	50	18	32
Robertson	109	43	66
Rutherford	393	189	204
Sequatchie	37	17	20
Shelby	1,898	528	1,370
Smith	38	19	19
Stewart	41	18	23
Sullivan	255	104	151
Sumner	241	69	172
Tipton	72	40	32
Unicoi	45	25	20
Union	34	18	16
Washington	180	79	101
Williamson	204	112	92
Wilson	220	84	136
TENNESSEE–Nonmetropolitan Counties			
Bedford	79	30	49
Benton	45	21	24
Bledsoe	22	12	10
Campbell	59	32	27
Carroll	36	19	17
Claiborne	81	26	55
Clay	20	8	12
Cocke	59	33	26
Coffee	79	43	36
Crockett	30	12	18
Cumberland	93	45	48
Decatur	20	14	6
DeKalb	36	15	21
Dyer	66	26	40
Fentress	28	16	12
Franklin	56	32	24
Gibson	70	31	39
Giles	56	23	33
Greene	159	62	97
Grundy	26	16	10
Hancock	32	14	18
Hardeman	42	22	20
Hardin	54	18	36
Haywood	46	21	25
Henderson	31	20	11
Henry	62	34	28
Houston	23	10	13
Humphreys	33	17	16
Jackson	40	14	26
Johnson	38	15	23
Lake	21	10	11
Lauderdale	65	21	44
Lawrence	75	44	31
Lewis	26	12	14
Lincoln	56	23	33
Marshall	47	23	24
Maury	142	77	65
McMinn	73	34	39
McNairy	30	11	19
Meigs	28	10	18
Monroe	65	36	29
Moore	25	13	12
Morgan	42	16	26
Obion	61	24	37
Overton	53	23	30
Perry	29	12	17
Pickett	14	9	5
Putnam	122	56	66
Rhea	54	54	0
Roane	65	44	21
Scott	64	27	37
Sevier	174	89	85
Van Buren	27	17	10
Warren	78	40	38
Wayne	30	13	17
Weakley	42	21	21
White	63	31	32
TEXAS–Metropolitan Counties			
Aransas	63	24	39
Archer	11	7	4
Armstrong	7	3	4

Table 80. Full-Time Law Enforcement Employees, by State and Metropolitan and Nonmetropolitan Counties, 2008—*Continued*

(Number.)

State/County	Total law enforcement employees	Total officers	Total civilians
Atascosa	73	29	44
Austin	58	38	20
Bandera	48	28	20
Bastrop	195	78	117
Bell	260	88	172
Bexar	1,788	529	1,259
Bowie	45	39	6
Brazoria	341	162	179
Brazos	190	79	111
Burleson	35	13	22
Caldwell	84	24	60
Calhoun	64	25	39
Callahan	11	5	6
Cameron	415	103	312
Carson	13	6	7
Chambers	81	41	40
Clay	19	11	8
Collin	480	155	325
Comal	234	116	118
Coryell	64	23	41
Crosby	15	5	10
Dallas	2,230	452	1,778
Delta	19	10	9
Denton	561	202	359
Ector	202	94	108
Ellis	224	82	142
El Paso	1,034	237	797
Fort Bend	641	421	220
Goliad	25	13	12
Grayson	136	59	77
Gregg	252	95	157
Guadalupe	208	76	132
Hardin	63	31	32
Harris	3,807	2,370	1,437
Hays	261	122	139
Hidalgo	688	252	436
Hunt	138	44	94
Irion	9	4	5
Jefferson	391	138	253
Johnson	132	86	46
Jones	27	9	18
Kaufman	252	86	166
Kendall	69	48	21
Lampasas	33	17	16
Liberty	64	46	18
Lubbock	345	145	200
McLennan	300	104	196
Medina	56	23	33
Midland	156	73	83
Montgomery	625	353	272
Nueces	303	64	239
Orange	134	65	69
Parker	112	82	30
Potter	203	94	109
Randall	161	68	93
Robertson	28	11	17
Rockwall	113	39	74
Rusk	69	42	27
San Jacinto	43	21	22
San Patricio	90	42	48
Smith	327	153	174
Tarrant	1,322	496	826
Taylor	178	75	103
Tom Green	172	58	114
Travis	1,453	754	699
Upshur	74	42	32
Victoria	184	89	95
Waller	68	36	32
Wichita	185	38	147
Williamson	456	189	267
Wilson	70	26	44
Wise	127	55	72
TEXAS–Nonmetropolitan Counties			
Anderson	80	40	40
Andrews	33	12	21
Angelina	100	45	55
Bailey	23	6	17
Baylor	8	3	5
Bee	42	19	23
Blanco	18	10	8
Borden	3	2	1
Bosque	35	17	18
Brewster	20	12	8
Briscoe	3	2	1
Brown	65	25	40
Burnet	80	51	29
Camp	17	7	10
Cass	45	19	26
Castro	19	9	10
Cherokee	74	31	43
Childress	15	5	10
Cochran	13	7	6
Coke	6	5	1
Coleman	12	6	6
Collingsworth	8	3	5
Colorado	44	20	24
Comanche	25	9	16
Concho	11	5	6
Cooke	73	21	52
Cottle	2	2	0
Crane	10	5	5
Crockett	13	8	5
Culberson	14	7	7
Dallam	24	4	20
Dawson	17	6	11
Deaf Smith	35	12	23
Dewitt	30	11	19
Dickens	6	2	4
Dimmit	25	21	4
Donley	10	6	4
Duval	38	17	21
Eastland	28	10	18
Edwards	10	4	6
Erath	51	21	30
Falls	11	6	5
Fannin	36	16	20
Fayette	38	18	20
Fisher	9	5	4
Floyd	7	3	4
Foard	4	3	1
Franklin	24	10	14
Freestone	43	16	27
Frio	20	11	9
Gaines	25	13	12
Garza	13	7	6
Gillespie	35	22	13
Glasscock	3	3	0
Gonzales	45	16	29
Gray	37	12	25
Grimes	54	25	29
Hale	68	16	52
Hall	9	3	6
Hamilton	26	14	12
Hansford	10	5	5
Hardeman	12	7	5
Harrison	84	43	41
Hartley	5	5	0
Haskell	8	3	5
Hemphill	16	8	8
Henderson	154	81	73
Hill	68	27	41
Hockley	28	11	17
Hood	123	42	81
Hopkins	53	25	28
Houston	39	22	17
Howard	33	13	20
Hudspeth	35	16	19
Hutchinson	31	12	19
Jack	35	12	23
Jackson	33	15	18

Table 80. Full-Time Law Enforcement Employees, by State and Metropolitan and Nonmetropolitan Counties, 2008—*Continued*

(Number.)

State/County	Total law enforcement employees	Total officers	Total civilians
Jasper	44	17	27
Jeff Davis	2	2	0
Jim Hogg	36	20	16
Jim Wells	62	26	36
Karnes	18	9	9
Kenedy	17	11	6
Kent	4	1	3
Kerr	95	45	50
Kimble	16	12	4
King	2	2	0
Kinney	15	6	9
Kleberg	70	21	49
Knox	8	3	5
Lamar	78	27	51
Lamb	30	13	17
La Salle	31	13	18
Lavaca	29	12	17
Lee	28	9	19
Leon	40	22	18
Limestone	54	18	36
Lipscomb	12	6	6
Live Oak	29	12	17
Llano	49	25	24
Loving	3	2	1
Lynn	21	7	14
Madison	25	10	15
Marion	15	14	1
Martin	8	4	4
Mason	7	4	3
Matagorda	75	36	39
McCulloch	12	6	6
McMullen	4	3	1
Menard	9	5	4
Milam	51	14	37
Mills	9	6	3
Mitchell	11	5	6
Montague	24	8	16
Moore	48	16	32
Morris	22	9	13
Motley	2	2	0
Nacogdoches	90	47	43
Navarro	126	56	70
Newton	20	11	9
Nolan	30	11	19
Ochiltree	18	8	10
Oldham	11	6	5
Palo Pinto	50	19	31
Panola	45	26	19
Parmer	19	6	13
Pecos	33	18	15
Polk	88	49	39
Presidio	20	5	15
Rains	23	10	13
Reagan	21	8	13
Real	7	3	4
Red River	31	16	15
Reeves	382	15	367
Refugio	40	19	21
Roberts	6	5	1
Runnels	25	6	19
Sabine	18	8	10
San Augustine	15	5	10
San Saba	9	4	5
Schleicher	11	5	6
Scurry	23	9	14
Shackelford	14	5	9
Shelby	26	15	11
Sherman	10	5	5
Somervell	41	20	21
Starr	94	29	65
Stephens	10	5	5
Sterling	3	3	0
Stonewall	7	2	5
Sutton	13	4	9
Swisher	12	6	6
Terrell	12	6	6
Terry	39	9	30
Throckmorton	6	2	4
Titus	58	21	37
Trinity	16	10	6
Tyler	31	20	11
Upton	23	11	12
Uvalde	34	16	18
Val Verde	50	34	16
Van Zandt	68	27	41
Walker	70	35	35
Ward	29	12	17
Washington	58	34	24
Wharton	70	39	31
Wheeler	10	5	5
Wilbarger	18	7	11
Willacy	38	11	27
Winkler	29	10	19
Wood	60	23	37
Yoakum	19	8	11
Young	33	14	19
Zapata	105	41	64
Zavala	30	11	19
UTAH–Metropolitan Counties			
Cache	148	114	34
Davis	398	99	299
Juab	24	9	15
Morgan	13	11	2
Salt Lake	1,260	343	917
Summit	104	53	51
Tooele	89	34	55
Utah	382	131	251
Washington	156	41	115
Weber	95	94	1
UTAH–Nonmetropolitan Counties			
Beaver	29	16	13
Box Elder	82	29	53
Carbon	31	21	10
Daggett	4	3	1
Duchesne	55	20	35
Emery	43	25	18
Garfield	27	6	21
Grand	32	17	15
Iron	78	35	43
Kane	26	12	14
Millard	50	25	25
Piute	3	3	0
Rich	10	4	6
San Juan	37	16	21
Sanpete	28	23	5
Sevier	72	31	41
Uintah	50	39	11
Wasatch	44	35	9
Wayne	5	5	0
VERMONT–Metropolitan Counties			
Chittenden	17	15	2
Franklin	26	17	9
VERMONT–Nonmetropolitan Counties			
Addison	16	9	7
Bennington	18	15	3
Caledonia	6	4	2
Essex	2	1	1
Lamoille	17	10	7
Orange	3	3	0
Orleans	5	3	2
Rutland	22	19	3
Washington	12	10	2
Windsor	14	11	3
VIRGINIA–Metropolitan Counties			
Albemarle County Police Department	155	123	32
Amelia	24	16	8
Amherst	70	64	6
Appomattox	33	30	3

Table 80. Full-Time Law Enforcement Employees, by State and Metropolitan and Nonmetropolitan Counties, 2008—*Continued*

(Number.)

State/County	Total law enforcement employees	Total officers	Total civilians
Arlington County Police Department	442	360	82
Bedford	80	78	2
Botetourt	119	98	21
Campbell	66	58	8
Caroline	66	48	18
Charles City	17	10	7
Chesterfield County Police Department	582	478	104
Clarke	29	18	11
Craig	14	9	5
Cumberland	23	16	7
Dinwiddie	47	43	4
Fairfax County Police Department	1,716	1,454	262
Fauquier	130	114	16
Fluvanna	41	27	14
Franklin	97	77	20
Frederick	132	115	17
Giles	35	25	10
Gloucester	117	96	21
Goochland	39	30	9
Greene	33	26	7
Hanover	233	214	19
Henrico County Police Department	763	582	181
Isle of Wight	50	43	7
James City County Police Department	99	94	5
King and Queen	20	12	8
King William	34	21	13
Loudoun	556	460	96
Louisa	58	48	10
Mathews	20	13	7
Montgomery	130	114	16
Nelson	15	14	1
New Kent	39	28	11
Pittsylvania	132	114	18
Powhatan	50	35	15
Prince George County Police Department	75	57	18
Prince William County Police Department	684	553	131
Pulaski	52	42	10
Roanoke County Police Department	150	138	12
Rockingham	164	52	112
Scott	35	26	9
Spotsylvania	192	156	36
Stafford	211	155	56
Surry	20	11	9
Sussex	42	37	5
Warren	92	43	49
Washington	70	52	18
York	109	103	6
VIRGINIA–Nonmetropolitan Counties			
Accomack	62	52	10
Alleghany	58	42	16
Augusta	78	69	9
Bath	18	12	6
Bland	18	11	7
Brunswick	52	39	13
Buchanan	43	32	11
Buckingham	23	17	6
Carroll	36	30	6
Charlotte	37	34	3
Culpeper	93	77	16
Dickenson	28	21	7
Essex	20	20	0
Floyd	27	18	9
Grayson	29	22	7
Greensville	34	22	12
Halifax	42	34	8
Henry	124	110	14
Highland	11	6	5
King George	45	31	14
Lancaster	34	29	5
Lee	36	36	0
Lunenburg	21	14	7
Madison	31	19	12
Mecklenburg	51	48	3

State/County	Total law enforcement employees	Total officers	Total civilians
Middlesex	23	17	6
Northampton	85	67	18
Northumberland	28	17	11
Nottoway	24	14	10
Orange	47	36	11
Page	66	52	14
Patrick	53	39	14
Prince Edward	29	29	0
Rappahannock	24	24	0
Richmond	20	12	8
Rockbridge	38	29	9
Russell	52	34	18
Shenandoah	76	68	8
Smyth	46	46	0
Southampton	69	58	11
Tazewell	52	44	8
Westmoreland	32	22	10
Wise	59	57	2
Wythe	47	40	7
WASHINGTON–Metropolitan Counties			
Asotin	14	12	2
Benton	64	52	12
Chelan	72	60	12
Clark	231	147	84
Cowlitz	62	47	15
Douglas	37	30	7
Franklin	29	27	2
King	832	520	312
Kitsap	159	123	36
Pierce	383	325	58
Skagit	116	59	57
Skamania	27	23	4
Snohomish	351	277	74
Spokane	198	142	56
Thurston	113	89	24
Whatcom	99	81	18
Yakima	104	68	36
WASHINGTON–Nonmetropolitan Counties			
Adams	20	17	3
Clallam	45	35	10
Columbia	14	9	5
Ferry	26	9	17
Garfield	16	8	8
Grant	64	49	15
Grays Harbor	77	38	39
Island	51	43	8
Jefferson	48	22	26
Kittitas	43	36	7
Klickitat	44	18	26
Lewis	60	41	19
Lincoln	30	17	13
Mason	67	52	15
Okanogan	35	30	5
Pacific	24	20	4
Pend Oreille	35	16	19
San Juan	32	19	13
Stevens	33	28	5
Wahkiakum	11	9	2
Walla Walla	32	27	5
Whitman	21	19	2
WEST VIRGINIA[1]			
WISCONSIN–Metropolitan Counties			
Brown	307	146	161
Calumet	51	24	27
Chippewa	68	54	14
Columbia	95	40	55
Dane	551	452	99
Douglas	85	29	56
Eau Claire	51	44	7
Fond du Lac	119	56	63
Iowa	39	25	14
Kenosha	340	127	213
Kewaunee	37	35	2

[1] No 2008 police employee data were received for the state of West Virginia.

Table 80. Full-Time Law Enforcement Employees, by State and Metropolitan and Nonmetropolitan Counties, 2008—*Continued*

(Number.)

State/County	Total law enforcement employees	Total officers	Total civilians
La Crosse	108	41	67
Marathon	176	66	110
Milwaukee	914	489	425
Oconto	57	26	31
Outagamie	195	75	120
Ozaukee	102	79	23
Pierce	47	43	4
Racine	252	144	108
Rock	194	91	103
Sheboygan	181	77	104
St. Croix	82	74	8
Washington	164	69	95
Waukesha	331	151	180
Winnebago	188	127	61
WISCONSIN–Nonmetropolitan Counties			
Ashland	38	17	21
Barron	73	30	43
Bayfield	41	21	20
Buffalo	23	12	11
Burnett	31	17	14
Clark	50	47	3
Crawford	30	24	6
Dodge	170	74	96
Door	60	45	15
Dunn	53	25	28
Florence	18	11	7
Forest	38	18	20
Grant	47	25	22
Green	56	34	22
Green Lake	41	17	24
Iron	19	10	9
Jackson	48	21	27
Jefferson	125	101	24
Juneau	47	47	0
Lafayette	27	15	12
Langlade	41	22	19
Lincoln	59	29	30
Manitowoc	71	57	14
Marinette	54	29	25
Marquette	37	18	19
Menominee	15	10	5
Monroe	40	24	16
Oneida	87	38	49
Pepin	18	7	11
Polk	76	29	47
Portage	89	45	44
Price	32	20	12
Richland	32	18	14
Rusk	33	17	16
Sauk	161	120	41
Sawyer	45	29	16
Shawano	109	39	70
Taylor	40	17	23
Trempealeau	50	24	26
Vernon	46	28	18
Vilas	69	34	35
Walworth	207	81	126
Washburn	30	20	10
Waupaca	99	38	61
Waushara	67	26	41
Wood	74	43	31
WYOMING–Metropolitan Counties			
Laramie	86	47	39
Natrona	58	46	12
WYOMING–Nonmetropolitan Counties			
Albany	22	21	1
Big Horn	11	9	2
Campbell	62	46	16
Carbon	27	17	10
Converse	20	11	9
Crook	14	7	7
Fremont	38	34	4
Goshen	13	11	2
Hot Springs	9	7	2
Johnson	12	11	1
Lincoln	30	18	12
Niobrara	17	5	12
Park	30	20	10
Platte	12	9	3
Sheridan	27	21	6
Sublette	40	34	6
Sweetwater	39	35	4
Teton	42	24	18
Uinta	38	24	14
Washakie	9	8	1
Weston	8	7	1

Table 81. Full-Time Law Enforcement Employees, by State and Agency, 2008

(Number.)

State, agency, unit/office	Total law enforcement employees	Total officers	Total civilians
ALABAMA—State Agencies			
Alabama Alcoholic Beverage Control Board	131	109	22
Alabama Conservation Department Marine Police	74	60	14
Alabama Department of Mental Health	5	4	1
Alabama Public Service Commission Enforcement Division	8	7	1
State Capitol Police	33	25	8
ALABAMA—Other Agencies			
2nd Judicial Circuit Drug Task Force	3	2	1
24th Judicial Circuit Drug and Violent Crime Task Force	5	4	1
Madison-Morgan County Strategic Counterdrug Team	17	14	3
ALASKA—State Agencies			
Alcohol Beverage Control Board	9	5	4
ALASKA—Other Agencies			
Anchorage International Airport	65	62	3
Fairbanks International Airport	30	23	7
ARIZONA—State Agencies			
Arizona State Capitol	68	31	37
ARKANSAS—State Agencies			
Camp Robinson	29	19	10
State Capitol Police	23	20	3
CALIFORNIA—State Agencies			
Atascadero State Hospital	128	116	12
California State Fair	10	5	5
Coalinga State Hospital	227	219	8
Department of Parks and Recreation			
Capital	601	601	0
Napa State Hospital	107	97	10
Patton State Hospital	50	39	11
CALIFORNIA—Other Agencies			
East Bay Regional Parks			
Alameda County	75	54	21
Fontana Unified School District	74	15	59
Monterey Peninsula Airport	6	6	0
Port of San Diego Harbor	170	143	27
San Bernardino Unified School District	83	26	57
San Francisco Bay Area Rapid Transit			
Contra Costa County	284	202	82
Stockton Unified School District	24	18	6
Twin Rivers Unified School District	27	21	6
COLORADO—State Agencies			
Colorado Mental Health Institute	78	18	60
COLORADO—Other Agencies			
Two Rivers Drug Enforcement Team	6	5	1
CONNECTICUT—State Agencies			
State Capitol Police	38	28	10
CONNECTICUT—Other Agencies			
Metropolitan Transportation Authority	752	694	58
DELAWARE—State Agencies			
Attorney General:			
Kent County	53	26	27
New Castle County	273	144	129
Sussex County	51	22	29
Division of Alcohol and Tobacco Enforcement	18	15	3
Environmental Control	13	11	2
Fish and Wildlife	29	24	5
Park Rangers	21	21	0
River and Bay Authority	66	50	16
State Capitol Police	63	39	24
State Fire Marshal	55	19	36
DELAWARE—Other Agencies			
Amtrak Police	12	12	0
Drug Enforcement Administration			
Wilmington Resident Office	13	9	4
Wilmington Fire Department	12	12	0
DISTRICT OF COLUMBIA—Other Agencies			
Metro Transit Police	553	425	128
FLORIDA—State Agencies			
Capitol Police	85	63	22
Department of Environmental Protection, Division of Law Enforcement			
Leon County	177	132	45
Department of Law Enforcement			
Leon County, Tallahassee	1,919	481	1,438
Florida Game Commission			
Leon County	817	642	175
State Treasurer's Office			
Division of Insurance Fraud	167	129	38

Table 81. Full-Time Law Enforcement Employees, by State and Agency, 2008—*Continued*

(Number.)

State, agency, unit/office	Total law enforcement employees	Total officers	Total civilians
FLORIDA—Other Agencies			
Duval County Schools	30	15	15
Florida School for the Deaf and Blind	16	9	7
Fort Lauderdale Airport	144	93	51
Jacksonville Airport Authority	41	35	6
Lee County Port Authority	69	41	28
Melbourne International Airport	11	10	1
Miami-Dade County Public Schools	219	181	38
Miccosukee Tribal	64	40	24
Palm Beach County School District	248	160	88
Port Everglades	163	63	100
Sarasota-Bradenton International Airport	14	13	1
Seminole Tribal	204	144	60
St. Petersburg-Clearwater International Airport	7	7	0
Tampa International Airport	147	65	82
Volusia County Beach Management	64	60	4
GEORGIA—State Agencies			
Atlanta State Farmers Market	17	17	0
Department of Natural Resources			
Social Circle	243	223	20
Georgia Bureau of Investigation			
Headquarters	872	135	737
Georgia Department of Transportation			
Office of Investigations	3	3	0
Georgia World Congress	43	33	10
Ports Authority			
Savannah	125	83	42
GEORGIA—Other Agencies			
Atlanta Public Schools	12	7	5
Augusta Board of Education	42	34	8
Bibb County Board of Education	33	28	5
Chatham County Board of Education	45	37	8
Cherokee County Marshal	14	7	7
Cobb County Board of Education	41	38	3
DeKalb County School System	91	85	6
Forsyth County Fire Investigation Unit	3	3	0
Fulton County School System	59	58	1
Gwinnett County Public Schools	24	20	4
Habersham County Public Schools	2	2	0
Hartsfield-Jackson Atlanta International Airport	161	130	31
Metropolitan Atlanta Rapid Transit Authority	342	295	47
Pickens County Board of Education	4	4	0
Stone Mountain Park	25	21	4
ILLINOIS—State Agencies			
Illinois Commerce Commission	21	14	7
Illinois Department of Natural Resources	164	150	14
Secretary of State Police			
District 3	263	143	120
ILLINOIS—Other Agencies			
Burlington Northern Santa Fe Railroad	23	20	3
Capitol Airport Authority	4	4	0
Cook County Forest Preserve	103	97	6
Crystal Lake Park District	3	3	0
CSX Transportation	21	21	0
Decatur Park District	5	5	0
Du Page County Forest Preserve	29	25	4
Elgin, Joliet and Eastern Railway	6	6	0
John H. Stroger Hospital	51	46	5
Lake County Forest Preserve	20	17	3
Norfolk Southern Railway	39	39	0
Pekin Park District	1	1	0
Rockford Park District	20	19	1
Springfield Park District	6	6	0
Will County Forest Preserve	13	12	1
INDIANA—State Agencies			
Indiana State Excise Police	94	88	6
Northern Indiana Commuter Transportation District	9	8	1
INDIANA—Other Agencies			
St. Joseph County Airport Authority	17	17	0
KANSAS—State Agencies			
Kansas Alcoholic Beverage Control	36	21	15
Kansas Bureau of Investigation	285	82	203
Kansas Department of Wildlife and Parks	179	177	2
Kansas Lottery Security Division	7	5	2
Kansas Racing Commission			
Security Division	41	10	31
Securities Office			
Investigation Section	30	7	23

Table 81. Full-Time Law Enforcement Employees, by State and Agency, 2008—*Continued*

(Number.)

State, agency, unit/office	Total law enforcement employees	Total officers	Total civilians
KANSAS—Other Agencies			
Blue Valley School District	6	6	0
Iowa Tribal	10	10	0
Johnson County Park	19	18	1
Metropolitan Topeka Airport Authority	24	20	4
Potawatomi Tribal	15	8	7
Sac and Fox Tribal	7	6	1
Shawnee Mission Public Schools	10	10	0
Topeka Fire Department			
Arson Investigation	4	4	0
Unified School District:			
Auburn-Washburn	5	1	4
Bluestem	1	1	0
Goddard	4	4	0
Maize	4	4	0
Topeka	14	13	1
Wyandotte County Parks and Recreation	13	13	0
KENTUCKY—State Agencies			
Alcohol Beverage Control	34	30	4
Fish and Wildlife Enforcement	150	142	8
Kentucky Horse Park	8	8	0
Park Security	58	58	0
Unlawful Narcotics Investigation			
Treatment and Education	24	21	3
KENTUCKY—Other Agencies			
Barren County Drug Task Force	2	1	1
Buffalo Trace-Gateway Narcotics Task Force	3	3	0
Cincinnati-Northern Kentucky International Airport	67	52	15
Clark County School System	1	1	0
Daniel Boone National Forest	10	9	1
Fayette County Schools	31	27	4
Graves County Schools	1	1	0
Greater Hardin County Narcotics Task Force	7	6	1
Jefferson County Board of Education	27	21	6
Lake Cumberland Area Drug Enforcement Task Force	8	7	1
Lexington Bluegrass Airport	28	20	8
Louisville Regional Airport Authority	45	37	8
McCracken County Public Schools	4	4	0
Montgomery County School District	2	2	0
Nicholas County Schools	1	1	0
Northern Kentucky Narcotics Enforcement Unit	3	2	1
Pennyrile Narcotics Task Force	19	16	3
South Central Kentucky Drug Task Force	6	6	0
Warren County Drug Task Force	2	1	1
LOUISIANA—State Agencies			
Department of Public Safety			
State Capitol Detail	51	43	8
Tensas Basin Levee District	4	3	1
MARYLAND—State Agencies			
Comptroller of the Treasury			
Field Enforcement Division	50	23	27
Department of Public Safety and Correctional Services			
Internal Investigations Unit	25	20	5
General Services:			
Annapolis, Anne Arundel County	69	31	38
Baltimore City	106	37	69
Natural Resources Police	512	261	251
Rosewood	23	5	18
Springfield Hospital	13	4	9
State Fire Marshal	74	41	33
Transit Administration	195	142	53
Transportation Authority	597	435	162
MARYLAND—Other Agencies			
Maryland-National Capital Park Police:			
Montgomery County	110	87	23
Prince George's County	129	103	26
MASSACHUSETTS-Other Agencies			
Beth Israel Deaconess Medical Center	56	10	46
MICHIGAN—Other Agencies			
Bishop International Airport	7	7	0
Capitol Region Airport Authority	21	16	5
Huron-Clinton Metropolitan Authority:			
Hudson Mills Metropark	3	3	0
Kensington Metropark	10	10	0
Lower Huron Metropark	9	9	0
Stony Creek Metropark	10	10	0
Wayne County Airport	136	124	12

Table 81. Full-Time Law Enforcement Employees, by State and Agency, 2008—*Continued*

(Number.)

State, agency, unit/office	Total law enforcement employees	Total officers	Total civilians
MINNESOTA—State Agencies			
Capitol Security			
St. Paul	55	11	44
MINNESOTA—Other Agencies			
Minneapolis-St. Paul International Airport	117	82	35
Three Rivers Park District	43	26	17
MISSOURI—State Agencies			
Capitol Police	38	31	7
Department of Conservation	195	185	10
Division of Alcohol and Tobacco Control	45	40	5
Gaming Commission			
Enforcement Division	109	107	2
State Fire Marshal	25	23	2
State Park Rangers	48	47	1
State Water Patrol	122	96	26
MISSOURI—Other Agencies			
Bootheel Drug Task Force	6	6	0
Clay County Drug Task Force	5	5	0
Clay County Park Authority	7	7	0
Jackson County Drug Task Force	21	19	2
Jackson County Park Rangers	17	15	2
Lambert-St. Louis International Airport	103	90	13
Southeast Missouri Drug Task Force	5	4	1
Springfield-Branson Airport	10	10	0
St. Charles County Park Rangers	12	12	0
St. Peters Ranger Division	5	5	0
MONTANA—State Agencies			
Gambling Investigations Bureau	23	20	3
NEVADA—State Agencies			
Taxicab Authority	63	37	26
NEVADA—Other Agencies			
Clark County School District	201	161	40
Washoe County School District	44	39	5
NEW HAMPSHIRE—State Agencies			
Liquor Commission	35	23	12
NEW JERSEY—State Agencies			
Department of Human Services	139	131	8
Human Services			
Woodland Township	4	4	0
Hunterdon Developmental Center	8	8	0
New Jersey Transit Police	265	198	67
Palisades Interstate Parkway	28	25	3
NEW JERSEY—Other Agencies			
Park Police:			
Camden County	21	20	1
Morris County	32	31	1
Union County	86	74	12
Prosecutor:			
Atlantic County	173	76	97
Bergen County	263	169	94
Burlington County	149	88	61
Camden County	240	163	77
Cape May County	78	36	42
Cumberland County	108	36	72
Essex County	459	162	297
Gloucester County	95	35	60
Hudson County	230	102	128
Hunterdon County	58	24	34
Mercer County	178	106	72
Middlesex County	205	80	125
Monmouth County	284	80	204
Morris County	149	67	82
Ocean County	173	79	94
Passaic County	189	82	107
Salem County	54	20	34
Somerset County	123	53	70
Sussex County	53	33	20
Union County	259	78	181
Warren County	60	22	38
NEW MEXICO—Other Agencies			
Acoma Tribal	19	13	6
Laguna Tribal	39	20	19
Santa Clara Tribal	15	8	7
Taos Pueblo Tribal	10	5	5
Zuni Tribal	30	19	11

Table 81. Full-Time Law Enforcement Employees, by State and Agency, 2008—*Continued*

(Number.)

State, agency, unit/office	Total law enforcement employees	Total officers	Total civilians
NEW YORK—State Agencies			
State Park:			
Allegany Region	17	14	3
Central Region	16	14	2
Finger Lakes Region	17	15	2
Genesee Region	15	14	1
Long Island Region	77	76	1
New York City Region	30	26	4
Niagara Region	35	34	1
Palisades Region	46	45	1
Saratoga/Capital Region	20	19	1
Taconic Region	16	15	1
NEW YORK—Other Agencies			
New York City Metropolitan Transportation Authority	750	693	57
Onondaga County Parks	1	1	0
Suffolk County Parks	48	46	2
NORTH CAROLINA—State Agencies			
Caswell Center Hospital	4	4	0
Department of Human Resources	9	9	0
Division of Alcohol Law Enforcement	135	114	21
North Carolina Arboretum	3	3	0
North Carolina State Bureau of Investigation	594	362	232
State Capitol Police	77	56	21
State Fairgrounds	6	1	5
State Park Rangers:			
Carolina Beach	6	4	2
Cliffs of the Neuse	4	2	2
Crowders Mountain	7	5	2
Dismal Swamp	6	3	3
Elk Knob	3	3	0
Eno River	10	7	3
Falls Lake Recreation Area	20	18	2
Fort Fisher	5	3	2
Fort Macon	6	5	1
Goose Creek	5	3	2
Gorges	2	2	0
Hammocks Beach	5	4	1
Hanging Rock	12	5	7
Jockey's Ridge	9	5	4
Jones Lake	8	5	3
Jordan Lake State Recreation Area	30	17	13
Kerr Lake	11	9	2
Lake James	5	4	1
Lake Norman	4	3	1
Lake Waccamaw	7	4	3
Lumber River	4	3	1
Medoc Mountain	3	3	0
Merchants Millpond	7	4	3
Morrow Mountain	8	6	2
Mt. Mitchell	5	4	1
New River-Mount Jefferson	11	8	3
Pettigrew	1	1	0
Pilot Mountain	4	4	0
Raven Rock	4	2	2
Singletary Lake	5	2	3
South Mountains	10	8	2
Stone Mountain	9	7	2
Weymouth Woods/Sandhills Nature Preserve	4	3	1
William B. Umstead	12	5	7
NORTH CAROLINA—Other Agencies			
Asheville Regional Airport	19	14	5
Durham County Alcohol Beverage Control Law Enforcement Office	3	3	0
Nash County Alcohol Beverage Control Enforcement	2	2	0
Piedmont Triad International Airport	19	17	2
Raleigh-Durham International Airport	32	30	2
Triad Alcohol Beverage Control Law Enforcement	6	5	1
Wilmington International Airport	13	9	4
OHIO—State Agencies			
Cleveland Lakefront State Parks	25	15	10
Ohio Department of Natural Resources	518	418	100
OHIO—Other Agencies			
Cedar Point	11	11	0
Cleveland Metropolitan Park District	77	67	10
Columbus and Franklin County Metropolitan Park District	36	36	0
Delaware County Preservation Parks	6	6	0
Erie MetroParks	6	6	0
Greater Cleveland Regional Transit Authority	111	98	13
Hamilton County Park District	37	34	3

Table 81. Full-Time Law Enforcement Employees, by State and Agency, 2008—*Continued*

(Number.)

State, agency, unit/office	Total law enforcement employees	Total officers	Total civilians
Johnny Appleseed Metropolitan Park District	8	8	0
Lake Metroparks	14	12	2
Lima Park Services			
Ranger Division	4	4	0
Lorain County Metropolitan Park District	14	14	0
Port Columbus International Airport	62	41	21
Robinson Memorial Hospital	9	9	0
Sandusky County Park District	5	5	0
Toledo-Lucas County Port Authority	11	11	0
Toledo Metropolitan Park District	25	25	0
Wood County Park District	6	6	0
OKLAHOMA—State Agencies			
Capitol Park Police	69	28	41
OKLAHOMA—Other Agencies			
Jenks Public Schools	6	6	0
Madill Public Schools	1	1	0
McAlester Public Schools	3	3	0
Norman Public Schools	4	4	0
Putnam City Campus	12	8	4
OREGON—State Agencies			
Liquor Commission:			
Benton County	1	1	0
Clatsop County	2	1	1
Coos County	2	1	1
Douglas County	2	1	1
Jackson County	7	6	1
Klamath County	1	1	0
Lane County	5	4	1
Lincoln County	2	1	1
Malheur County	1	1	0
Marion County	5	4	1
Multnomah County	22	19	3
Umatilla County	2	2	0
Washington County	2	2	0
OREGON—Other Agencies			
Port of Portland	66	53	13
PENNSYLVANIA—State Agencies			
Department of Environmental Resources	10	5	5
State Capitol Police	141	132	9
State Park Police			
Pymatuning	6	6	0
PENNSYLVANIA—Other Agencies			
Allegheny County District Attorney			
Criminal Investigation Division	31	25	6
Allegheny County Port Authority	61	44	17
Bangor Area School District	3	3	0
Canadian Pacific Railway	2	2	0
County Detective:			
Berks County	34	34	0
Bucks County	19	16	3
Butler County	4	4	0
Chester County	23	20	3
Dauphin County	13	10	3
Lebanon County	7	6	1
Lehigh County	14	13	1
Schuylkill County	7	7	0
Westmoreland County	59	15	44
York County	12	11	1
Delaware County District Attorney			
Criminal Investigation Division	38	33	5
Delaware County Park	59	58	1
Easton Area School District	7	6	1
Harrisburg International Airport	25	14	11
Tyrone Area School District	1	1	0
Washington County Alternative Education	1	1	0
Westmoreland County Park	22	22	0
Wilkes-Barre Area School District	5	5	0
RHODE ISLAND—State Agencies			
Department of Environmental Management	40	31	9
Rhode Island State Airport	52	43	9
SOUTH CAROLINA—State Agencies			
Bureau of Protective Services	77	72	5
Department of Mental Health	122	71	51
Department of Natural Resources:			
Abbeville County	3	3	0
Aiken County	5	5	0
Allendale County	3	3	0
Anderson County	4	4	0

Table 81. Full-Time Law Enforcement Employees, by State and Agency, 2008—*Continued*

(Number.)

State, agency, unit/office	Total law enforcement employees	Total officers	Total civilians
Bamberg County	3	3	0
Barnwell County	4	4	0
Beaufort County	8	8	0
Berkeley County	6	6	0
Calhoun County	2	2	0
Charleston County	32	29	3
Cherokee County	4	4	0
Chester County	3	3	0
Chesterfield County	3	3	0
Clarendon County	5	5	0
Colleton County	4	4	0
Darlington County	4	4	0
Dillon County	2	2	0
Dorchester County	8	8	0
Edgefield County	3	3	0
Fairfield County	2	2	0
Florence County	8	7	1
Georgetown County	8	8	0
Greenville County	4	4	0
Greenwood County	5	5	0
Hampton County	4	4	0
Horry County	7	7	0
Jasper County	3	3	0
Kershaw County	5	5	0
Lancaster County	3	3	0
Laurens County	3	3	0
Lee County	2	2	0
Lexington County	5	5	0
Marion County	3	3	0
Marlboro County	3	3	0
McCormick County	4	4	0
Newberry County	5	5	0
Oconee County	5	5	0
Orangeburg County	5	5	0
Pickens County	11	8	3
Richland County	65	38	27
Saluda County	4	4	0
Spartanburg County	6	5	1
Sumter County	3	3	0
Union County	3	3	0
Williamsburg County	5	5	0
York County	5	4	1
Employment Security Commission	3	3	0
Forestry Commission:			
Aiken County	1	1	0
Anderson County	1	1	0
Barnwell County	1	1	0
Beaufort County	1	1	0
Berkeley County	1	1	0
Calhoun County	1	1	0
Charleston County	1	1	0
Chesterfield County	3	3	0
Colleton County	2	2	0
Darlington County	2	2	0
Fairfield County	1	1	0
Florence County	1	1	0
Georgetown County	1	1	0
Greenville County	1	1	0
Hampton County	1	1	0
Horry County	1	1	0
Kershaw County	2	2	0
Lee County	1	1	0
Lexington County	2	2	0
Oconee County	1	1	0
Orangeburg County	1	1	0
Pickens County	1	1	0
Richland County	2	2	0
Sumter County	4	4	0
Williamsburg County	2	2	0
York County	1	1	0
South Carolina School for the Deaf and Blind	1	1	0
State Museum	4	3	1
State Ports Authority	73	39	34
State Transport Police:			
Abbeville County	13	13	0
Aiken County	48	26	22
Allendale County	7	7	0
Anderson County	16	13	3

Table 81. Full-Time Law Enforcement Employees, by State and Agency, 2008—*Continued*

(Number.)

State, agency, unit/office	Total law enforcement employees	Total officers	Total civilians
Berkeley County	19	16	3
Cherokee County	11	11	0
Darlington County	12	12	0
United States Department of Energy Savannah River Plant	64	57	7
SOUTH CAROLINA—Other Agencies			
Charleston County Aviation Authority	40	29	11
Greenville-Spartanburg International Airport	22	16	6
SOUTH DAKOTA—State Agencies			
Division of Criminal Investigation	149	43	106
TENNESSEE—State Agencies			
Alcoholic Beverage Commission	54	32	22
Department of Correction Internal Affairs	13	9	4
State Fire Marshal	34	30	4
State Park Rangers:			
Bicentennial Capitol Mall	5	5	0
Big Hill Pond	3	3	0
Big Ridge	4	4	0
Bledsoe Creek	2	2	0
Booker T. Washington	3	3	0
Burgess Falls Natural Area	2	2	0
Cedars of Lebanon	4	4	0
Chickasaw	3	3	0
Cove Lake	3	3	0
Cumberland Mountain	4	4	0
Cumberland Trail	6	6	0
David Crockett	4	4	0
Davy Crockett Birthplace	3	3	0
Dunbar Cave Natural Area	3	3	0
Edgar Evins	3	3	0
Fall Creek Falls	8	8	0
Fort Loudon State Historic Park	4	4	0
Fort Pillow State Historic Park	2	2	0
Frozen Head Natural Area	4	4	0
Harpeth Scenic Rivers	3	3	0
Harrison Bay	4	4	0
Henry Horton	4	4	0
Hiwassee/Ocoee State Scenic Rivers	6	6	0
Indian Mountain	2	2	0
Johnsonville State Historic Park	1	1	0
Long Hunter	3	3	0
Meeman-Shelby Forest	4	4	0
Montgomery Bell	7	7	0
Mousetail Landing	3	3	0
Natchez Trace	4	4	0
Nathan Bedford Forrest	4	4	0
Norris Dam	4	4	0
Old Stone Fort State Archaeological Park	3	3	0
Panther Creek	3	3	0
Paris Landing	5	5	0
Pickett	4	4	0
Pickwick Landing	5	5	0
Pinson Mounds State Archaeological Park	2	2	0
Radnor Lake Natural Area	5	5	0
Red Clay State Historic Park	2	2	0
Reelfoot Lake	4	4	0
Roan Mountain	4	4	0
Rock Island	4	4	0
Sgt. Alvin C. York	2	2	0
South Cumberland Recreation Area	5	5	0
Standing Stone	4	4	0
Sycamore Shoals State Historic Park	2	2	0
Tim's Ford	5	5	0
T.O. Fuller	4	4	0
Warrior's Path	3	3	0
TennCare Office of Inspector General	56	16	40
Tennessee Bureau of Investigation	462	182	280
Tennessee Department of Revenue Special Investigations Unit	55	32	23
Wildlife Resources Agency:			
Region 1	41	40	1
Region 2	61	57	4
Region 3	44	43	1
Region 4	46	45	1
TENNESSEE—Other Agencies			
Chattanooga Housing Authority	6	5	1
Chattanooga Metropolitan Airport	10	10	0
Dickson Parks and Recreation	12	3	9

Table 81. Full-Time Law Enforcement Employees, by State and Agency, 2008—*Continued*

(Number.)

State, agency, unit/office	Total law enforcement employees	Total officers	Total civilians
Drug Task Force:			
1st Judicial District	7	6	1
2nd Judicial District	6	5	1
3rd Judicial District	5	4	1
4th Judicial District	2	1	1
5th Judicial District	6	5	1
8th Judicial District	2	1	1
9th Judicial District	1	1	0
10th Judicial District	13	10	3
12th Judicial District	2	2	0
13th Judicial District	3	3	0
14th Judicial District	2	2	0
15th Judicial District	2	1	1
17th Judicial District	2	1	1
18th Judicial District	9	8	1
19th Judicial District	8	7	1
21st Judicial District	12	10	2
22nd Judicial District	2	2	0
23rd Judicial District	6	4	2
24th Judicial District	2	1	1
25th Judicial District	1	1	0
Knoxville Metropolitan Airport	47	28	19
Memphis International Airport	64	50	14
Metropolitan Board of Parks and Recreation Nashville-Davidson	25	24	1
Nashville International Airport	78	62	16
Smyrna/Rutherford County Airport Authority	4	4	0
Tri-Cities Regional Airport	16	15	1
West Tennessee Violent Crime Task Force	7	6	1
TEXAS—Other Agencies			
Amarillo International Airport	13	13	0
Cameron County Park Rangers	10	10	0
Dallas-Fort Worth International Airport	373	257	116
Hospital District:			
Dallas County	84	55	29
Tarrant County	65	44	21
Houston Metropolitan Transit Authority	260	182	78
Independent School District:			
Aldine	49	43	6
Alvin	21	16	5
Angleton	4	3	1
Athens	3	2	1
Austin	98	69	29
Bay City	7	6	1
Brownsville	131	30	101
Cedar Hill	24	5	19
Conroe	63	46	17
Corpus Christi	56	32	24
East Central	10	8	2
Ector County	30	28	2
El Paso	44	35	9
Fort Bend	49	42	7
Humble	28	21	7
Judson	21	20	1
Katy	42	35	7
Kaufman	5	4	1
Killeen	14	14	0
Klein	39	28	11
Laredo	95	26	69
Mexia	3	3	0
Midland	16	10	6
North East	61	55	6
Pasadena	40	33	7
Pflugerville	13	13	0
Raymondville	4	4	0
Socorro	34	28	6
Spring	40	38	2
Spring Branch	39	33	6
Taft	1	1	0
United	163	54	109
UTAH—State Agencies			
Parks and Recreation	82	81	1
Wildlife Resources	75	66	9
UTAH—Other Agencies			
Granite School District	40	17	23
Utah County Attorney Investigations Division	7	5	2
Utah Transit Authority	48	36	12

Table 81. Full-Time Law Enforcement Employees, by State and Agency, 2008—*Continued*

(Number.)

State, agency, unit/office	Total law enforcement employees	Total officers	Total civilians
VERMONT—State Agencies			
Department of Motor Vehicles	47	32	15
VIRGINIA—State Agencies			
Alcoholic Beverage Control Commission	154	116	38
Department of Conservation and Recreation	265	110	155
Southside Virginia Training Center	18	16	2
Virginia State Capitol	78	67	11
VIRGINIA—Other Agencies			
Chesapeake Bay Bridge-Tunnel	100	36	64
Norfolk Airport Authority	44	37	7
Port Authority			
Norfolk	96	89	7
Reagan National Airport	259	182	77
Richmond International Airport	38	29	9
WASHINGTON—Other Agencies			
Colville Tribal	35	24	11
Lummi Tribal	21	19	2
Nisqually Tribal	17	13	4
Nooksack Tribal	9	7	2
Port of Seattle	122	94	28
Skokomish Tribal	5	4	1
Swinomish Tribal	13	11	2
WEST VIRGINIA[1]			
WISCONSIN—State Agencies			
Capitol Police	46	37	9
Department of Natural Resources	356	331	25
WISCONSIN—Other Agencies			
Lac du Flambeau Tribal	9	7	2
Menominee Tribal	28	22	6
Oneida Tribal	25	19	6
OTHER OUTLYING AREAS			
Guam	375	313	62
FEDERAL AGENCY			
National Institutes of Health	117	94	23

[1] No 2008 police employee data were received for the state of West Virginia.

APPENDIXES

APPENDIX I. METHODOLOGY

Submitting Uniform Crime Reporting (UCR) Program data to the Federal Bureau of Investigation (FBI) is a collective effort on the part of city, county, state, tribal, and federal law enforcement agencies to present a nationwide view of crime. Law enforcement agencies in 46 states and the District of Columbia voluntarily contribute crime data to the UCR Program through their respective state UCR programs. For those states that do not have a state program, local agencies submit crime statistics directly to the FBI. The state UCR Programs function as liaisons between local agencies and the FBI. Many states have mandatory reporting requirements, and many state programs collect data beyond the scope of the UCR Program to address crime problems specific to their particular jurisdictions. In most cases, state programs also provide direct and frequent service to participating law enforcement agencies, make information readily available for statewide use, and help streamline the national program's operations.

Criteria for State UCR Programs

The criteria established for state Programs ensure consistency and comparability in the data submitted to the national Program, as well as regular and timely reporting. These criteria are:

1. The state Program must conform to the national UCR Program standards, definitions, and information required.
2. The state criminal justice agency must have a proven, effective, statewide program and have instituted acceptable quality control procedures.
3. The state crime reporting must cover a percentage of the population at least equal to that covered by the national UCR Program through direct reporting.
4. The state Program must have adequate field staff assigned to conduct audits and to assist contributing agencies in record-keeping practices and crime-reporting procedures.
5. The state Program must furnish the FBI with all of the detailed data regularly collected by the FBI from individual agencies that report to the state Program in the form of duplicate returns, computer printouts, and/or appropriate electronic media.
6. The state Program must have the proven capability (tested over a period of time) to supply all the statistical data required in time to meet publication deadlines of the national UCR Program.

Data Completeness and Quality

The FBI, in order to fulfill its responsibilities in connection with the UCR Program, continues to edit and review individual agency reports for completeness and quality. National program staff members directly contact individual contributors within the state, when necessary, in connection with crime-reporting matters; staff members also coordinate such contact with the UCR Program. Upon request, they conduct training programs within the state on law enforcement record-keeping and crime-reporting procedures. The FBI conducts an audit of each state's UCR data collection procedures once every three years, in accordance with audit standards established by the federal government. Should circumstances develop in which the state program does not comply with the aforementioned requirements, the national program may institute a direct collection of Uniform Crime Reports from law enforcement agencies within the state.

Reporting Procedures

Law enforcement agencies tabulate the number of Part I offenses (murder and nonnegligent manslaughter, forcible rape, robbery, aggravated assault, burglary, larceny-theft, motor vehicle theft, and arson) brought to their attention based on records of all reports of crime received from victims, officers who discover infractions, or other sources, and submit them each month to the FBI either directly or through their state UCR Programs.

Unfounded offenses, clearances, and value of property—When, through investigation, an agency determines that complaints of crimes are unfounded or false, the agency eliminates that offense from its crime tally through an entry on the monthly report. The report also provides the total number of actual Part I offenses, the number of offenses cleared, and the number of clearances that involve only offenders under the age of 18. (Law enforcement can clear crimes in one of two ways: by the arrest of at least one person who is charged and turned over to the court for prosecution or by exceptional means—when some element beyond law enforcement's control precludes the arrest of a known offender.) Law enforcement agencies also submit monthly to the FBI the value of property stolen and recovered in connection with the offenses and detailed information pertaining to criminal homicide.

Persons arrested—In addition to reporting Part I offenses, law enforcement agencies provide monthly to the UCR Program data on the age, sex, and race of persons arrested for Part I and Part II offenses. Part II offenses encompass all crimes, except traffic violations, that are not classified as Part I offenses.

Officers killed or assaulted—Law enforcement agencies also report monthly to the UCR Program information regarding law enforcement officers killed or assaulted, and yearly, the number of full-time sworn and civilian law enforcement personnel employed as of October 31.

Editing Procedures

The UCR Program thoroughly examines each report it receives for arithmetical accuracy and for deviations in crime data from month to month and from present to past years that may indicate errors. UCR staff members compare an agency's monthly reports with its previous submissions and with reports from similar agencies to identify any unusual fluctuations in the agency's crime count. Large variations in crime levels may indicate modified records procedures, incomplete reporting, or changes in the jurisdiction's geopolitical structure.

Evaluation of trends—Data reliability is a high priority of the FBI, which brings any deviations or arithmetical adjustments to the attention of state UCR Programs or the submitting agencies. Typically, FBI staff members study the monthly reports to evaluate periodic trends prepared for individual reporting units. Any significant increase or decrease becomes the subject of a special inquiry. Changes in crime reporting procedures or annexations that affect an agency's jurisdiction can influence the level of reported crime. When this occurs, the FBI excludes the figures for specific crime categories or totals, if necessary, from the trend tabulations.

Training for contributors—In addition to the evaluation of trends, the FBI provides training seminars and instructional materials on crime reporting procedures to assist contributors in complying with UCR standards. Throughout the country, the national Program maintains liaison with state Programs and law enforcement personnel and holds training sessions to explain the purpose of the Program, the rules of uniform classification and scoring, and the methods of assembling the information for reporting. When an individual agency has specific problems in compiling its crime statistics and its remedial efforts are unsuccessful, personnel from the FBI's Criminal Justice Information Services Division may visit the contributor to aid in resolving the difficulties.

UCR Handbook—The national UCR Program publishes a Uniform Crime Reporting Handbook (revised 2004), which details procedures for classifying and scoring offenses and serves as the contributing agencies' basic resource for preparing reports. The national staff also produces letters to UCR contributors, State Program Bulletins, and UCR Newsletters as needed. These provide policy updates and new information, as well as clarification of reporting issues.

The final responsibility for data submissions rests with the individual contributing law enforcement agency. Although the FBI makes every effort through its editing procedures, training practices, and correspondence to ensure the validity of the data it receives, the accuracy of the statistics depends primarily on the adherence of each contributor to the established standards of reporting. Deviations from these established standards that cannot be resolved by the national UCR Program may be brought to the attention of the Criminal Justice Information Systems Committees of the International Association of Chiefs of Police and the National Sheriffs' Association.

Population Estimation

For the 2008 population estimates used in this report, the FBI computed individual rates of growth from one year to the next for every city/town and county using 2000 decennial population counts and 2001 through 2007 population estimates from the U.S. Census Bureau. Each agency's rates of growth were averaged; that average was then applied and added to its 2007 Census population estimate to derive the agency's 2008 population estimate.

Population estimates for 2007 are based on the percent change in the state population from the U.S. Census Bureau's 2006 revised estimates and 2007 provisional estimates. Population estimates for 2004 are based on the percent change in the state population from the U.S. Census Bureau's 2003 revised estimates and 2004 provisional estimates. Population estimates for 1999 are based on the percent change in the state population from the U.S. Census Bureau's 1998 revised estimates and 1999 provisional estimates.

NIBRS Conversion

Thirty-one state Programs are certified to provide their UCR data in the expanded National Incident-Based Reporting System (NIBRS) format. For presentation in this book, the NIBRS data were converted to the historical Summary Reporting System data. The UCR Program staff constructed the NIBRS database to allow for such conversion so that UCR's long-running time series could continue.

Crime Trends

Trend statistics offer the data user an additional perspective from which to study crime by showing fluctuations from year to year. Percent change tabulations in this publication are computed only for the reporting agencies that provided comparable data for the periods under consideration. The program excludes all figures from the trend calculations, except those received for common months from common agencies. Also excluded are unusual fluctuations that the program determines are the result of variables such as improved records procedures, annexations, etc.

Caution to Users

Data users should exercise care in making any direct comparison between data in this publication and those in prior issues of *Crime in the United States*. Because of differing levels of participation from year to year and reporting problems that require the UCR Program to estimate crime counts for certain contributors, the data are not comparable from year to year. In addition, this publication may contain updates to data provided in prior years' publications. Therefore, for example, the 2007 supplemental homicide data in last year's publication may not match the 2007 data in this publication.

2008 Arrest Data

Limited arrest data were received from Illinois; i.e., only Chicago and Rockford provided statistics in accordance with UCR guidelines.

- Except for the cities of Minneapolis and St. Paul, the Minnesota State UCR Program's guidelines for reporting forcible rape arrest counts do not comply with the national UCR Program's guidelines; i.e., Minnesota data include arrests made for forcible rapes of male victims. Therefore, the state forcible rape counts that are published include only the totals received from Minneapolis and St. Paul.
- For 2008, only arrest totals (with no age or gender breakdowns) are available for Florida. Therefore, Florida arrest totals are included only in Table 69, "Arrests by State, 2008."
- No 2008 arrest data were received from the District of Columbia's Metropolitan Police Department. The two agencies in the District of Columbia for which 12 months of arrest data were received, Metro Transit Police and the National Zoological Park, have no attributable population.
- No 2008 arrest data were received from the New York City Police Department. However, arrest totals for this agency were estimated by the national UCR Program and were included in Table 29 "Estimated Number of Arrests, 2008."

Offense Estimation

Tables 1 through 5 and Table 7 of this publication contain statistics for the entire United States. Because not all law enforcement agencies provide data for complete reporting periods, the FBI includes estimated crime numbers in these presentations. The FBI estimates data for three areas: metropolitan statistical areas (MSAs), cities outside MSAs, and nonmetropolitan counties. The FBI computes estimates for participating agencies not providing 12 months of complete data. For agencies supplying 3 to 11 months of data, the national UCR Program estimates for the missing data by following a standard estimation procedure using the data provided by the agency. If an agency has supplied less than 3 months of data, the FBI computes estimates by using the known crime figures of similar areas within a state and assigning the same proportion of crime volumes to nonreporting agencies. The estimation process considers the following: population size covered by the agency; type of jurisdiction, e.g., police department versus sheriff's office; and geographic location.

Estimation of State-Level Data

In response to various circumstances, the FBI calculates estimated offense totals for certain states. For example, some states do not provide forcible rape figures in accordance with UCR guidelines. In addition, problems at the state level have, at times, resulted in no useable data. Also, the conversion of the National Incident-Based Reporting System (NIBRS) data to Summary data has contributed to the need for unique estimation procedures. A summary of state-specific and offense-specific estimation procedures can be found online at <http://www.fbi.gov/ucr/cius2008/about/table_methodology.htmls>.

APPENDIX II. DEFINITIONS

The Uniform Crime Reporting (UCR) Program divides offense into two groups. Contributing agencies submit information on the number of Part I offenses known to law enforcement; those offenses cleared by arrest or exceptional means; and the age, sex, and race of persons arrested for each of thse offenses. Contributors provide only arrest data for Part II offenses.

Part I offenses include murder, and nonnegligent manslaughter, forcible rape, robbery, aggravated assault, burglary, larceny-theft, motor vehicle theft, and arson.

Violent crime is composed of four offenses: murder and nonnegligent manslaughter, forcible rape, robbery, and aggravated assault. According to the UCR Program's definition, violent crimes involve force or threat of force.

Criminal homicide—a.) Murder and nonnegligent manslaughter: the willful (nonnegligent) killing of one human being by another. Deaths caused by negligence, attempts to kill, assaults to kill, suicides, and accidental deaths are excluded. The program classifies justifiable homicides separately and limits the definition to (1) the killing of a felon by a law enforcement officer in the line of duty; or (2) the killing of a felon, during the commission of a felony, by a private citizen. b.) Manslaughter by negligence: the killing of another person through gross negligence. Traffic fatalities are excluded.

Forcible rape—The carnal knowledge of a female forcibly and against her will. Assaults and attempts to commit rape by force or threat of force are also included. Statutory rape (no force used—female victim is under the age of consent) and other sex offenses are excluded. Sexual attacks on males are counted as aggravated assaults or sex offenses, depending on the circumstances and the extent of any injuries.

Robbery—The taking or attempted taking of anything of value from the care, custody, or control of a person or persons by force or threat of force or violence and/or by putting the victim in fear.

Aggravated assault—An unlawful attack by one person upon another for the purpose of inflicting severe or aggravated bodily injury. This type of assault usually is accompanied by the use of a weapon or by means likely to produce death or great bodily harm. Attempted aggravated assaults that involve the display of—or threat to use—a gun, knife, or other weapon is included in this crime category because serious personal injury would likely result if the assault were completed. When aggravated assault and larceny-theft occur together, the offense falls under the category of robbery. Simple assaults are excluded.

Property crime includes the offenses of burglary, larceny-theft, motor vehicle theft, and arson. The object of the theft-type offenses is the taking of money or property, but there is no force or threat of force against the victims. The property crime category includes arson because the offense involves the destruction of property; however, arson victims may be subjected to force.

Burglary (breaking or entering)—The unlawful entry of a structure to commit a felony or a theft. The use of force to gain entry need not have occurred. The UCR Program has three subclassifications for burglary: forcible entry, unlawful entry where no force is used, and attempted forcible entry. The UCR definition of "structure" includes, for example, apartment, barn, house trailer or houseboat when used as a permanent dwelling, office, railroad car (but not automobile), stable, and vessel (i.e., ship).

Larceny-theft (except motor vehicle theft)—The unlawful taking, carrying, leading, or riding away of property from the possession or constructive possession of another. Examples are thefts of bicycles or automobile accessories, shoplifting, pocket-picking, or the stealing of any property or article that is not taken by force and violence or by fraud. Attempted larcenies are included. Embezzlement, confidence games, forgery, worthless checks, and the like, are excluded.

Motor vehicle theft—The theft or attempted theft of a motor vehicle. It includes the stealing of automobiles, trucks, buses, motorcycles, snowmobiles, and the like. The taking of a motor vehicle for temporary use by persons having lawful access is excluded from this definition. A motor vehicle is self-propelled and runs on land surface and not on rails. Motorboats, construction equipment, airplanes, and farming equipment are specifically excluded from this category.

Arson—Any willful or malicious burning or attempt to burn, with or without intent to defraud, a dwelling house, public building, motor vehicle, aircraft, personal property of another, and the like. Limited data are available for arson because of limited participation and varying collection procedures by local law enforcement agencies. Arson statistics are included in trend, clearance, and arrest tables throughout *Crime in the United States*, but they are not included in any estimated volume data.

In addition to reporting Part I offenses, law enforcement agencies provide the UCR Program with monthly data on persons arrested for all crimes except traffic violations. These arrest data include the age, sex, and race of arrestees for both Part I and Part II offenses. **Part II** offenses encompass all crimes, except traffic violations, that are not classified as Part I offenses, including:

Other assaults (simple)—Assaults and attempted assaults which are not of an aggravated nature and do not result in serious injury to the victim.

Forgery and counterfeiting—The altering, copying, or imitating of something, without authority or right, with the intent to deceive or defraud by passing the copy or thing altered or imitated as that which is original or genuine; or the selling, buying, or possession of an altered, copied, or imitated thing with the intent to deceive or defraud. Attempts are included.

Fraud—The intentional perversion of the truth for the purpose of inducing another person or other entity in reliance upon it to part with something of value or to surrender a legal right. Fraudulent conversion and obtaining of money or property by false pretenses. Confidence games and bad checks, except forgeries and counterfeiting, are included.

Embezzlement—The unlawful misappropriation or misapplication by an offender to his/her own use or purpose of money, property, or some other thing of value entrusted to his/her care, custody, or control.

Stolen property; buying, receiving, possessing—Buying, receiving, possessing, selling, concealing, or transporting any property with the knowledge that it has been unlawfully taken, as by burglary, embezzlement, fraud, larceny, robbery, etc. Attempts are included.

Vandalism—To willfully or maliciously destroy, injure, disfigure, or deface any public or private property, real or personal, without the consent of the owner or person having custody or control by cutting, tearing, breaking, marking, painting, drawing, covering with filth, or any other such means as may be specified by local law. Attempts are included.

Weapons; carrying, possessing, etc.—The violation of laws or ordinances prohibiting the manufacture, sale, purchase, transportation, possession, concealment, or use of firearms, cutting instruments, explosives, incendiary devices, or other deadly weapons. Attempts are included.

Prostitution and commercialized vice—The unlawful promotion of or participation in sexual activities for profit, including attempts.

Sex offenses (except forcible rape, prostitution, and commercialized vice)—Statutory rape, offenses against chastity, common decency, morals, and the like. Attempts are included.

Drug abuse violations—The violation of laws prohibiting the production, distribution, and/or use of certain controlled substances. The unlawful cultivation, manufacture, distribution, sale, purchase, use, possession, transportation, or importation of any controlled drug or narcotic substance. Arrests for violations of state and local laws, specifically those relating to the unlawful possession, sale, use, growing, manufacturing, and making of narcotic drugs. The following drug categories are specified: opium or cocaine and their derivatives (morphine, heroin, codeine); marijuana; synthetic narcotics/manufactured narcotics that can cause true addiction (demerol, methadone); and dangerous nonnarcotic drugs (barbiturates, benzedrine).

Gambling—To unlawfully bet or wager money or something else of value; assist, promote, or operate a game of chance for money or some other stake; possess or transmit wagering information; manufacture, sell, purchase, possess, or transport gambling equipment, devices, or goods; or tamper with the outcome of a sporting event or contest to gain a gambling advantage.

Offenses against the family and children—Unlawful nonviolent acts by a family member (or legal guardian) that threaten the physical, mental, or economic well-being or morals of another family member and that are not classifiable as other offenses, such as assault or sex offenses. Attempts are included.

Driving under the influence—Driving or operating a motor vehicle or common carrier while mentally or physically impaired as the result of consuming an alcoholic beverage or using a drug or narcotic.

Liquor laws—The violation of state or local laws or ordinances prohibiting the manufacture, sale, purchase, transportation, possession, or use of alcoholic beverages, not including driving under the influence and drunkenness. Federal violations are excluded.

Drunkenness—To drink alcoholic beverages to the extent that one's mental faculties and physical coordination are substantially impaired. Excludes driving under the influence.

Disorderly conduct—Any behavior that tends to disturb the public peace or decorum, scandalize the community, or shock the public sense of morality.

Vagrancy—The violation of a court order, regulation, ordinance, or law requiring the withdrawal of persons from the streets or other specified areas; prohibiting persons from remaining in an area or place in an idle or aimless manner; or prohibiting persons from going from place to place without visible means of support.

All other offenses—All violations of state or local laws not specifically identified as Part I or Part II offenses, except traffic violations.

Suspicion—Arrested for no specific offense and released without formal charges being placed.

Curfew and loitering laws (persons under 18 years of age)—Violations by juveniles of local curfew or loitering ordinances.

Runaways (persons under 18 years of age)—Limited to juveniles taken into protective custody under the provisions of local statutes.

APPENDIX III. GEOGRAPHIC AREA DEFINITIONS

The UCR Program collects crime data and supplemental information that make it possible to generate a variety of statistical compilations, including data presented by reporting areas. These statistics allow data users to analyze local crime data in conjunction with those for areas of similar geographic location or population size. The reporting areas that the UCR Program uses in its data breakdowns include community types, population groups, and regions and divisions. For community types, the UCR Program considers proximity to metropolitan areas using the designations created by the U.S. Office of Management and Budget (OMB). (Generally, sheriffs, county police, and state police report crimes within counties but outside of cities; local police report crimes within city limits.) The number of inhabitants living in a locale (based on the U.S. Census Bureau's figures) determines the population group into which the program places it. For its geographic breakdowns, the UCR Program divides the United States into regions, divisions, and states.

Regions and Divisions

The map above illustrates the nine divisions that make up the four regions of the United States. The UCR Program uses this widely recognized geographic organization when compiling the nation's crime data. The regions and divisions are as follows:

Northeast

New England—Connecticut, Maine, Massachusetts, New Hampshire, Rhode Island, and Vermont

Middle Atlantic—New York, New Jersey, and Pennsylvania

Midwest

East North Central—Illinois, Indiana, Michigan, Ohio, and Wisconsin

West North Central—Iowa, Kansas, Minnesota, Missouri, Nebraska, North Dakota, and South Dakota

South

South Atlantic—Delaware, District of Columbia, Florida, Georgia, Maryland, North Carolina, South Carolina, Virginia, and West Virginia

East South Central—Alabama, Kentucky, Mississippi, and Tennessee

West South Central—Arkansas, Louisiana, Oklahoma, and Texas

West

Mountain—Arizona, Colorado, Idaho, Montana, Nevada, New Mexico, Utah, and Wyoming

Pacific—Alaska, California, Hawaii, Oregon, and Washington

Community Types

To assist data users who wish to analyze and present uniform statistical data about metropolitan areas, the UCR Program uses reporting units that represent major population centers. The program compiles data for the following three types of communities:

United States Divisions

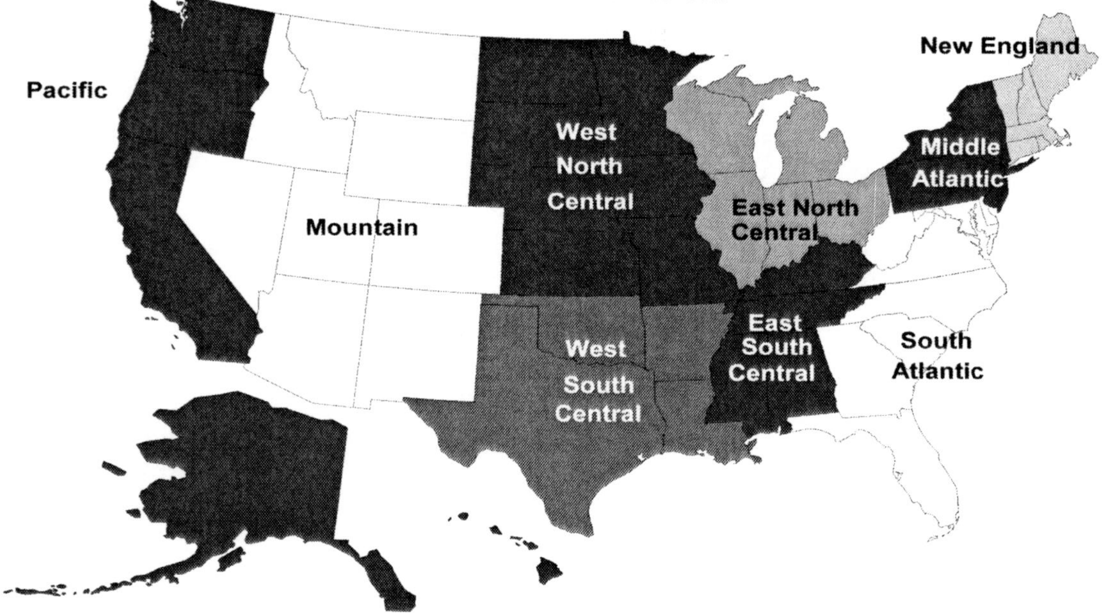

Metropolitan statistical areas (MSAs)—Each MSA contains a principal city or urbanized area with a population of at least 50,000 inhabitants. MSAs include the principal city, the county in which the city is located, and other adjacent counties that have a high degree of economic and social integration with the principal city and county (as defined by the OMB), which is measured through commuting. In the UCR Program, counties within an MSA are considered metropolitan counties. In addition, MSAs may cross state boundaries.

In 2008, approximately 83.5 percent of the nation's population lived in MSAs. Some presentations in this publication refer to Metropolitan Divisions, which are subdivisions of an MSA that consists of a core with "a population of at least 2.5 million persons. A Metropolitan Division consists of one or more main/secondary counties that represent an employment center or centers, plus adjacent counties associated with the main county or counties through commuting ties," (Federal Register 65 [249]). Also, some tables reference suburban areas, which are subdivisions of MSAs that exclude the principal cities but include all the remaining cities (those having fewer than 50,000 inhabitants) and the unincorporated areas of the MSAs.

Because the elements that comprise MSAs, particularly the geographic compositions, are subject to change, the UCR Program discourages data users from making year-to-year comparisons of MSA data.

Cities outside MSAs—Ordinarily, cities outside MSAs are incorporated areas. In 2008, cities outside MSAs made up 6.6 percent of the nation's population.

Nonmetropolitan counties outside MSAs—Most nonmetropolitan counties are composed of unincorporated areas. In 2008, 9.9 percent of the nation's population resided in nonmetropolitan counties.

Metropolitan and nonmetropolitan community types are further illustrated in the following table:

Metropolitan	Nonmetropolitan
Principal cities (50,000+ inhabitants) Suburban cities	Cities outside metropolitan areas
Metropolitan counties	Nonmetropolitan counties

Population Groups

The UCR Program uses the following population group designations:

Individual law enforcement agencies are the source of UCR data. The number of agencies included in each population group may vary from year to year because of population growth, geopolitical consolidation, municipal incorporation, etc. In noncensus years, the UCR Program estimates population figures for individual jurisdictions. (A more comprehensive explanation of population estimations can be found in Appendix I.)

Population Group	Political Label	Population Range
I	City	250,000 or more
II	City	100,000 to 249,999
III	City	50,000 to 99,999
IV	City	25,000 to 49,999
V	City	10,000 to 24,999
VI	City[1]	Fewer than 10,000
VIII (Nonmetropolitan county)	County[2]	N/A
IX (Metropolitan county)	County[2]	N/A

[1]Includes universities and colleges to which no population is attributed.
[2]Includes state police agencies to which no population is attributed.

The categories below show the number of agencies contributing to the UCR Program within each population group for 2008:

Population Group	Number of Agencies	Population Covered
I	76	56,533,626
II	198	29,258,709
III	473	32,254,198
IV	857	29,339,789
V	1,902	30,126,399
VI[1]	9,115	26,460,633
VIII (Nonmetropolitan county)[2]	3,028	30,099,179
IX (Metropolitan county)[2]	2,150	69,987,191
Total	17,799	304,059,724

[1]Includes universities and colleges to which no population is attributed.
[2]Includes state police to which no population is attributed.

APPENDIX IV. THE NATION'S TWO CRIME MEASURES

The Department of Justice administers two statistical programs to measure the magnitude, nature, and impact of crime in the nation: the Uniform Crime Reporting (UCR) Program and the National Crime Victimization Survey (NCVS). Each of these programs produces valuable information about aspects of the nation's crime problem. Because the UCR and NCVS programs are conducted for different purposes, use different methods, and focus on somewhat different aspects of crime, the information they produce together provides a more comprehensive panorama of the nation's crime problem than either could produce alone.

Uniform Crime Reporting (UCR) Program

The UCR Program, administered by the Federal Bureau of Investigation (FBI), was created in 1929 and collects information on the following crimes reported to law enforcement authorities: murder and nonnegligent manslaughter, forcible rape, robbery, aggravated assault, burglary, larceny-theft, motor vehicle theft, and arson. Law enforcement agencies also report arrest data for 21 additional crime categories.

The UCR Program compiles data from monthly law enforcement reports and from individual crime incident records transmitted directly to the FBI or to centralized state agencies that report to the FBI. The program thoroughly examines each report it receives for reasonableness, accuracy, and deviations that may indicate errors. Large variations in crime levels may indicate modified records procedures, incomplete reporting, or changes in a jurisdiction's boundaries. To identify any unusual fluctuations in an agency's crime counts, the program compares monthly reports to previous submissions of the agency and to those for similar agencies.

The FBI annually publishes its findings in a preliminary release in the spring of the following calendar year, followed by a detailed annual report, *Crime in the United States*, issued in the fall. (The printed copy of *Crime in the United States* is now published by Bernan Press.) In addition to crime counts and trends, this report includes data on crimes cleared, persons arrested (age, sex, and race), law enforcement personnel (including the number of sworn officers killed or assaulted), and the characteristics of homicides (including age, sex, and race of victims and offenders; victim-offender relationships; weapons used; and circumstances surrounding the homicides). Other periodic reports are also available from the UCR Program.

The state and local law enforcement agencies participating in the UCR Program are continually converting to the more comprehensive and detailed National Incident-Based Reporting System (NIBRS). The NIBRS provides detailed information about each criminal incident in 22 broad categories of offenses.

The UCR Program presents crime counts for the nation as a whole, as well as for regions, states, counties, cities, towns, tribal law enforcement areas, and colleges and universities. This allows for studies among neighboring jurisdictions and among those with similar populations and other common characteristics.

National Crime Victimization Survey

The NCVS, conducted by the Bureau of Justice Statistics (BJS), began in 1973. It provides a detailed picture of crime incidents, victims, and trends. After a substantial period of research, the BJS completed an intensive methodological redesign of the survey in 1993. It conducted this redesign to improve the questions used to uncover crime, update the survey methods, and broaden the scope of crimes measured. The redesigned survey collects detailed information on the frequency and nature of the crimes of rape, sexual assault, personal robbery, aggravated and simple assault, household burglary, theft, and motor vehicle theft. It does not measure homicide or commercial crimes (such as burglaries of stores).

Twice a year, Census Bureau personnel interview household members in a nationally representative sample of approximately 43,000 households (about 76,000 people). Approximately 150,000 interviews of individuals 12 years of age and over are conducted annually. Households stay in the sample for 3 years, and new households rotate into the sample on an ongoing basis.

The NCVS collects information on crimes suffered by individuals and households, whether or not those crimes were reported to law enforcement. It estimates the proportion of each crime type reported to law enforcement, and it summarizes the reasons that victims give for reporting or not reporting.

The survey provides information about victims (age, sex, race, ethnicity, marital status, income, and educational level); offenders (sex, race, approximate age, and victim-offender relationship); and crimes (time and place of occurrence, use of weapons, nature of injury, and economic consequences). Questions also cover victims' experiences with the criminal justice system, self-protective measures used by victims, and possible substance abuse by offenders. Supplements are added to the survey periodically to obtain detailed information on specific topics, such as school crime.

The BJS published the first data from the redesigned NCVS in a June 1995 bulletin. The publication of NCVS data includes *Criminal Victimization in the United States*, an annual report that covers the broad range of detailed information collected by the NCVS. The bureau also publishes detailed reports on topics such as crime against women, urban crime, and gun use in crime. The National Archive of Criminal Justice Data at the University of

Michigan archives the NCVS data files to help researchers perform independent analyses.

Comparing the UCR Program and the NCVS

Because the BJS designed the NCVS to complement the UCR Program, the two programs share many similarities. As much as their different collection methods permit, the two measure the same subset of serious crimes with the same definitions. Both programs cover rape, robbery, aggravated assault, burglary, theft, and motor vehicle theft; both define rape, robbery, theft, and motor vehicle theft virtually identically. (Although rape is defined analogously, the UCR Program measures the crime against women only, and the NCVS measures it against both sexes.)

There are also significant differences between the two programs. First, the two programs were created to serve different purposes. The UCR Program's primary objective is to provide a reliable set of criminal justice statistics for law enforcement administration, operation, and management. The BJS established the NCVS to provide previously unavailable information about crime (including crime not reported to police), victims, and offenders.

Second, the two programs measure an overlapping but nonidentical set of crimes. The NCVS includes crimes both reported and not reported to law enforcement. The NCVS excludes—but the UCR Program includes—homicide, arson, commercial crimes, and crimes committed against children under 12 years of age. The UCR Program captures crimes reported to law enforcement but collects only arrest data for simple assaults and sexual assaults other than forcible rape.

Third, because of methodology, the NCVS and UCR have different definitions of some crimes. For example, the UCR defines burglary as the unlawful entry or attempted entry of a structure to commit a felony or theft. The NCVS, not wanting to ask victims to ascertain offender motives, defines burglary as the entry or attempted entry of a residence by a person who had no right to be there.

Fourth, for property crimes (burglary, theft, and motor vehicle theft), the two programs calculate crime rates using different bases. The UCR Program rates for these crimes are per capita (number of crimes per 100,000 persons), whereas the NCVS rates for these crimes are per household (number of crimes per 1,000 households).

Because the number of households may not grow at the same annual rate as the total population, trend data for rates of property crimes measured by the two programs may not be comparable. In addition, some differences in the data from the two programs may result from sampling variation in the NCVS and from estimating for nonresponsiveness in the UCR Program.

The BJS derives the NCVS estimates from interviewing a sample and are, therefore, subject to a margin of error. The bureau uses rigorous statistical methods to calculate confidence intervals around all survey estimates, and describes trend data in the NCVS reports as genuine only if there is at least a 90-percent certainty that the measured changes are not the result of sampling variation. The UCR Program bases its data on the actual counts of offenses reported by law enforcement agencies. In some circumstances, the UCR Program estimates its data for nonparticipating agencies or those reporting partial data. Apparent discrepancies between statistics from the two programs can usually be accounted for by their definitional and procedural differences, or resolved by comparing NCVS sampling variations (confidence intervals) of crimes said to have been reported to police with UCR Program statistics.

For most types of crimes measured by both the UCR Program and the NCVS, analysts familiar with the programs can exclude those aspects of crime not common to both from analysis. Resulting long-term trend lines can be brought into close concordance. The impact of such adjustments is most striking for robbery, burglary, and motor vehicle theft, whose definitions most closely coincide.

With robbery, the BJS bases the NCVS victimization rates on only those robberies reported to the police. It is also possible to remove UCR Program robberies of commercial establishments, such as gas stations, convenience stores, and banks, from analysis. When users compare the resulting NCVS police-reported robbery rates and the UCR Program noncommercial robbery rates, the results reveal closely corresponding long-term trends.

Conclusion

Each program has unique strengths. The UCR Program provides a measure of the number of crimes reported to law enforcement agencies throughout the country. The program's Supplementary Homicide Reports provide the most reliable, timely data on the extent and nature of homicides in the nation. The NCVS is the primary source of information on the characteristics of criminal victimization and on the number and types of crimes not reported to law enforcement authorities.

By understanding the strengths and limitations of each program, it is possible to use the UCR Program and NCVS to achieve a greater understanding of crime trends and the nature of crime in the United States. For example, changes in police procedures, shifting attitudes towards crime and police, and other societal changes can affect the extent to which people report and law enforcement agencies record crime. NCVS and UCR Program data can be used in concert to explore why trends in reported and police-recorded crime may differ.

INDEX

INDEX